WILEY

GAAP 2005

Interpretation and Application of
GENERALLY ACCEPTED
ACCOUNTING PRINCIPLES

Subscriber
Update
Service

BECOME A SUBSCRIBER!

Did you purchase this product from a bookstore?

If you did, it's important for you to become a subscriber. John Wiley & Sons, Inc. may publish, on a periodic basis, supplements and new editions to reflect the latest changes in the subject matter that you ***need to know*** in order stay competitive in this ever-changing industry. By contacting the Wiley office nearest you, you'll receive any current update at no additional charge. In addition, you'll receive future updates and revised or related volumes on a 30-day examination review.

If you purchased this product directly from John Wiley & Sons, Inc., we have already recorded your subscription for this update service.

To become a subscriber, please call **1-877-762-2974** or send your name, company name (if applicable), address, and the title of the product to:

mailing address: **Supplement Department**
John Wiley & Sons, Inc.
One Wiley Drive
Somerset, NJ 08875

e-mail: **subscriber@wiley.com**
fax: **1-732-302-2300**
online: **www.wiley.com**

For customers outside the United States, please contact the Wiley office nearest you:

Professional & Reference Division
John Wiley & Sons Canada, Ltd.
22 Worcester Road
Etobicoke, Ontario M9W 1L1
CANADA
416- 236-4433
Phone: 1-800-567-4797
Fax: 416-236-4447
canada@jwiley.com

John Wiley & Sons, Ltd.
The Atrium
Southern Gate, Chichester
West Sussex, PO19 8SQ
ENGLAND
Phone: 44-1243 779777
Fax: 44-1243 775878
Email: customer@wiley.co.uk

John Wiley & Sons Australia, Ltd.
33 Park Road
P.O. Box 1226
Milton, Queensland 4064
AUSTRALIA
Phone: 61-7-3859-9755
Fax: 61-7-3859-9715
Email: brisbane@johnwiley.com.au

John Wiley & Sons (Asia) Pte. Ltd.
2 Clementi Loop #02-01
SINGAPORE 129809
Phone: 65-64632400
Fax: 65-64634604/5/6
Customer Service: 65-64604280
Email: enquiry@wiley.com.sg

WILEY GAAP 2005

Interpretation and Application of
GENERALLY ACCEPTED
ACCOUNTING PRINCIPLES

Barry J. Epstein
Ralph Nach
Ervin L. Black
Patrick R. Delaney

WILEY
JOHN WILEY & SONS, INC.

Published by John Wiley & Sons, Inc., Hoboken, New Jersey
Published simultaneously in Canada

For general information on our other products and services, please contact our Customer Care Department within the US at 800-762-2974, outside the US at 317-572-3993 or fax 317-572-4002.

Wiley also publishes its books in a variety of electronic formats. Some content that appears in print may not be available in electronic books.

ISBN 0-471-66834-6

Printed in the United States of America
10 9 8 7 6 5 4 3 2 1

CONTENTS

PREFACE

GAAP: Interpretation and Application provides analytical explanations and copious illustrations of all current generally accepted accounting principles. The book integrates principles promulgated by all the relevant standard-setting bodies—the FASB, including its Emerging Issues Task Force's consensus summaries and discussion issues, and the AICPA's Accounting Standards Executive Committee (AcSEC) These materials are synthesized into a user-oriented topical format, eliminating the need for readers to first be knowledgeable about the names or numbers of the salient professional standards.

The focus of the book is the practitioner and the myriad practical problems faced in applying GAAP. Accordingly, meaningful, "real world"- type examples abound, guiding users in the application of GAAP to complex fact situations that must be dealt with in the actual practice of accounting In addition to this emphasis, a major strength of the book is that it does explain the theory of GAAP in sufficient detail to serve as a valuable adjunct to accounting textbooks. Not merely a reiteration of currently promulgated GAAP, it provides the user with the underlying conceptual basis for the rules, to enable the reasoning by analogy that is so necessary in dealing with a complex, fast-changing world of commercial arrangements and transaction structures. It is based on the authors' belief that proper application of GAAP demands an understanding of the logical underpinnings of its technical requirements.

Each chapter of this book, or major section thereof, provides an overview discussion of the perspective and key issues associated with the topics covered; a listing of the professional pronouncements which guide practice; and a detailed discussion of the concepts and the accompanying examples. A comprehensive checklist, following the main text, offers practical guidance to preparing financial statements in accordance with GAAP, with supplemental insights into SEC-mandated disclosures as needed. Usability is enhanced by the comprehensive index, and by the exhaustive listing of professional pronouncements which are keyed to both the text in this book and to the codification of accounting standards prepared by the FASB (i.e., the Current Text).

The authors' wish is that this book will serve practitioners, faculty, and students, as a reliable reference tool, to facilitate their understanding of, and ability to apply, the complexities of the authoritative literature. Comments from readers, both as to errors and omissions and as to proposed improvements for future editions, should be addressed to Barry J. Epstein, c/o John Wiley & Sons, Inc., 155 N. 3rd Street, Suite 502, DeKalb, Illinois 60115, prior to May 15, 2005, for consideration for the 2006 edition.

Barry J. Epstein
Ralph Nach
Ervin L. Black
August 1, 2004

ABOUT THE AUTHORS

Barry J. Epstein, PhD, CPA, is a partner with Russell Novak & Company, LLP, a Chicago-based firm, where he specializes in technical consultation on accounting and auditing matters and corporate governance, and serves as a consulting and testifying expert for various litigation matters including accountants' malpractice, contractual dispute resolution, and commercial damages modeling. He has previously served in senior technical and litigation consulting positions with several regional and national CPA firms, as a corporate finance executive, and as a college professor. Dr. Epstein has authored or coauthored six books (including *Wiley IAS Interpretation and Application*) and several articles, and has previously coauthored a weekly business column for an international newspaper. He has served on several state and national technical committees, including the AICPA's Board of Examiners, and served as chair of the Illinois CPA Society's senior accounting technical committee. He has also lectured widely on technical accounting and auditing topics over most of his thirty-five-year career, which has been primarily in public accounting. Dr. Epstein received his doctorate from the University of Pittsburgh, and holds degrees from DePaul University and the University of Chicago. He is a member of the Illinois CPA Society, the AICPA, and the American Accounting Association.

Ralph Nach, CPA, is managing director in charge of technical training in the national office of American Express Tax & Business Services, Inc. Mr. Nach has been a practitioner for over twenty-five years, during which he has specialized in accounting, auditing, and financial reporting issues. Mr. Nach holds a BSBA with honors from the Walter E. Heller School of Business Administration of Roosevelt University in Chicago, and is a CPA in Illinois. Previously Mr. Nach served in capacities including accountant, auditor, technical reviewer, educator, and consultant for several public accounting firms including Arthur Andersen LLP, and taught graduate accounting and finance at Northwestern University. Mr. Nach has coauthored several other books and speaks nationally on accounting, auditing, and financial reporting topics. He is a member of the American Institute of Certified Public Accountants and chairs its Educational Management Exchange Subcommittee (EDMAX). He is also a member of the Illinois CPA Society, where he has served as a chairman and/or member of numerous committees.

Ervin L. Black, PhD., is an associate professor in the School of Accountancy and Information Systems, Marriott School of Management, at Brigham Young University, where he specializes in financial and international accounting. Dr. Black has authored or coauthored thirteen articles in accounting research journals, including *The Journal of Accounting and Economics, Accounting Horizons, The Journal of Business Finance and Accounting,* and *The Journal of the American Taxation Association*. In addition, he has coauthored chapters on international accounting, and is a coauthor of two textbooks (including *International Accounting and Multinational Enterprises*, 6th Edition forthcoming, Wiley). Dr. Black received his doctorate from the University of Washington, and holds an MBA and Bachelor of Arts degrees from Brigham Young University. He is a member of the American Accounting Association, European and British Accounting Association, and the International Association for Accounting Education and Research.

Patrick R. Delaney, PhD, CPA, was the Arthur Andersen LLP Alumni Professor of Accountancy and Chair of the Department of Accountancy at Northern Illinois University. He received his PhD in Accountancy from the University of Illinois. Professor Delaney served as a Faculty Resident with Arthur Andersen LLP. He was the author of *CPA Examination Review*, 2-volume and 4-part sets, including the related components of the Wiley CPA preparation system. He was past president of the Rockford Chapter, Institute of Management Accountants; served on Illinois CPA Society Committees (previously as Vice-President and member, Board of Directors; Chairman of Accounting Principles Committee; chair of the Relations with Accounting Educators and Students Committee; and chair of Educator CPA Issues Committee); and had served on numerous other professional committees. He was a member of the American Accounting Association, American Institute of Certified Public Accountants, and the Institute of Management Accountants. Professor Delaney had published in *The Accounting Review* and was the recipient of NIU's Excellence in Teaching Award and the Illinois CPA Society's Outstanding Educator Award.

ACKNOWLEDGEMENT

We gratefully acknowledge the assistance of Dr. Angela L.J. Hwang, Assistant Professor of Accounting, Eastern Michigan University, for suggesting materials incorporated into Chapter 22 of this edition.

AUTHORITATIVE ACCOUNTING PRONOUNCEMENTS

Listed below are all of the authoritative accounting pronouncements **currently in effect** as we go to press. The current text refers to the FASB's *Accounting Standards—Current Text,* which is divided into two volumes: General Standards and Industry Standards. These volumes as well as two volumes of Original Pronouncements may be ordered from the AICPA (800-862-4272) or FASB (203-847-0700). The Emerging Issues Task Force Abstracts, which are in a separate book, may be ordered from the FASB. AICPA Statements of Position by the Accounting Standards Executive Committee may be ordered from the AICPA. These are available individually or in the publication entitled *AICPA Technical Practice Aids*. Places in this text where the pronouncements are discussed may be found by referencing the last column in the listings below.

Pronouncement Abbreviations

The following is a key to the abbreviations used throughout the book to refer to authoritative pronouncements:

Pronouncement	*Abbreviation*
Accounting Principles Board Opinion	APB
Accounting Research Bulletin	ARB
Statements of Financial Accounting Concepts	CON
Statements of Financial Accounting Standards	FAS
Financial Accounting Standards Board Interpretation	FIN
FASB Technical Bulletin	FTB
EITF Discussion of Technical Matters	D
Emerging Issues Task Force Issue	EITF
AICPA Accounting Interpretation	AIN
AICPA Audit and Accounting Guide	AAG
AICPA Practice Bulletin of Accounting Standards Executive Committee (AcSEC)	PB
AICPA Statements of Position	SOP
SEC Staff Accounting Bulletin	SAB
AICPA Auditing Standards Board Statement of Auditing Standards	SAS
FASB Staff Position	FSP

Accounting Research Bulletins (ARB), Accounting Procedures Committee, AICPA (1953-1959)

Number[*]	*Title*	*Current text reference*	*GAAP Interp. & Applic. page reference*
43	Restatement and Revision of Accounting Research Bulletins Nos. 1-42 (originally issued 1939-1953)		
	Ch. 1 Prior Bulletins	A31, B51, C08, C23, R36, R70, R75	790
	Ch. 2 Form of Statements	F43	52
	Ch. 3 Working Capital	B05, I78	43, 45, 163, 166, 559, 561
	Ch. 4 Inventory Pricing	I78	219, 220, 226, 237, 244, 604
	Ch. 7 Capital Accounts	C20, Q15	835

[*] *Missing numbers throughout this listing represent pronouncements that have been completely superseded.*

(FASB cont.)

(FASB cont.)

Number	Title	Current text reference	GAAP Interp. & Applic. page reference
109	Accounting for Income Taxes (continued)	Q15, R36, Re6	701, 702, 703, 704,705, 706, 707, 709, 710, 711, 712, 713, 714, 715, 716, 720, 721, 722, 724, 727, 728, 729, 730, 736 759, 821, 835, 881, 953, 983, 1018, 1068
110	Reporting by Defined Benefit Pension Plans of Investment Contracts	Pe5	1001, 1002
111	Rescission of FASB Statement 32 and Technical Corrections	A06, A35, B51, C38, L35, R75	906
112	Employers' Accounting for Postemployment Benefits	C44, C59, F25, P32, P40	564, 771
113	Accounting and Reporting for Reinsurance of Short-Duration and Long-Duration Contracts	C59, I50, In6	159, 177, 1018
114	Accounting by Creditors for Impairment of a Loan	C59, D22, I08, In6	162, 310, 406, 433, 434, 436, 437, 438, 439, 448, 449, 579, 591, 593, 594, 966, 971, 972, 973, 1011, 1012
115	Accounting for Certain Investments in Debt and Equity Securities	B05, Bt7, C25, I08, I27, I80, I82, In6, L20, Mo4	38, 41, 43, 44, 50, 68, 100, 131, 135, 140, 146, 149, 159, 162, 163, 168, 171, 187, 210, 211, 214, 217, 288, 310, 395, 396, 398, 399, 400, 401, 402, 403, 405, 406, 407, 410, 411, 412, 420, 433, 434, 435, 436, 437, 444, 448, 450, 550, 594, 615, 716, 793, 841, 973, 975, 1017, 1028, 1032, 1035, 1056
116	Accounting for Contributions Received and Contributions Made	C67, No5	787, 1048, 1053, 1058
117	Financial Statements of Not-for-Profit Organizations	C25, No5	105, 1048, 1052, 1055

(FASB cont.)

(FASB cont.)

(*FASB cont.*)

(FASB cont.)

Number	Title	Current text reference	GAAP Interp. & Applic. page reference
150	Accounting for Certain Financial Instruments with Characteristics of Both Liabilities and Equity	E11, F41	579, 603, 604, 605, 779, 823, 824, 828, 829, 830, 831, 832, 833, 867, 872, 878, 881

Financial Accounting Standards Board (FASB) Interpretations (1974-2004)

Number	Title	Current text reference	GAAP Interp. & Applic. page reference
1	Accounting Changes Related to the Cost of Inventory (APB 20)	A06	909
4	Applicability of FASB Statement 2 to Purchase Business Combinations	B51	464, 472, 549
6	Applicability of FASB Statement 2 to Computer Software	R50	
7	Applying FASB Statement 7 in Statements of Established Enterprises	De4	90
8	Classification of a Short-Term Obligation Repaid Prior to Being Replaced by a Long-Term Security (FAS 6)	B05	563
9	Applying APB Opinions 16 and 17 When a Savings and Loan or Similar Institution Is Acquired in a Purchase Business Combination (APB 16 and 17)	B51, Bt7, I60	
14	Reasonable Estimation of the Amount of a Loss (FAS 5)	C59	131, 139, 566
18	Accounting for Income Taxes in Interim Periods (APB 28)	I73	730, 733, 736, 740, 887
19	Lessee Guarantee of the Residual Value of Leased Property (FAS 13)	L10	627
20	Reporting Accounting Changes under AICPA Statements of Position (APB 20)	A06	914
21	Accounting for Leases in a Business Combination (FAS 13)	L10	
23	Leases of Certain Property Owned by a Governmental Unit or Authority (FAS 13)	L10	
24	Leases Involving Only Part of a Building (FAS 13)	L10	
26	Accounting for Purchase of a Leased Asset by the Lessee during the Term of the Lease (FAS 13)	L10	
27	Accounting for Loss on a Sublease (FAS 13 and APB 30)	L10	
28	Accounting for Stock Appreciation Rights and Other Variable Stock Option or Award Plans (APB 15 and 25)	C47	795, 797, 798, 803, 804, 811, 839
30	Accounting for Involuntary Conversions of Nonmonetary Assets to Monetary Assets (APB 29)	N35	
33	Applying FASB Statement 34 to Oil and Gas Producing Operations (FAS 34)	I67	
35	Criteria for Applying the Equity Method of Accounting for Investments in Common Stock (APB 18)	I82	423, 716
36	Accounting for Exploratory Wells in Progress at the End of a Period (FAS 19)	Oi5	

(FIN cont.)

Number	Title	Current text reference	GAAP Interp. & Applic. page reference
37	Accounting for Translation Adjustment upon Sale of Part of an Investment in a Foreign Entity (FAS 52)	F60	932
38	Determining the Measurement Date for Stock Option, Purchase, and Award Plans Involving Junior Stock (APB 25)	C47	795, 825
39	Offsetting of Amounts Related to Certain Contracts (APB 10 and FAS 105)	B10	48, 572
40	Applicability of Generally Accepted Accounting Principles to Mutual Life Insurance and Other Enterprises (FAS 12, 60, 97, and 113)	A10, In6, Re6	1018
41	Offsetting of Amounts Related to Certain Repurchase and Reverse Repurchase Agreements	B10	48, 572
42	Accounting for Transfers of Assets in Which a Not-for-Profit Organization Is Granted Variance Power (FAS 116)		
43	Real Estate Sales (FAS 66)	R10, Re1	287, 288, 301, 671, 680, 681
44	Accounting for Certain Transactions Involving Stock Compensation (APB 25)	C47	573, 799, 800, 801, 802, 825, 836, 838, 844, 846
45	Guarantor's Accounting and Disclosure Requirements for Guarantees, Including Indirect Guarantees of Indebtedness of Others (FAS 5, 57, and 107 and Rescission of FIN 34)	C59, G80, R36	565, 568, 570, 571, 572, 573, 575
46(R)	Consolidation of Variable Interest Entities—An Interpretation of ARB No. 51 (Revised 2003)	C53, C54, F39	141, 144, 456, 522, 523, 524, 525, 526, 527, 529, 530, 531, 532, 533, 535, 623, 628, 629, 630, 632, 633, 635, 636, 638, 642, 659, 676, 678, 679

Financial Accounting Standards Board
FASB Technical Bulletins (1979-2004)

Number	Title	Current text reference	GAAP Interp. & Applic. page reference
79-1	(Revised) Purpose and Scope of FASB Technical Bulletins and Procedures for Issuance		
79-3	Subjective Acceleration Clauses in Long-Term Debt Agreements	B05	562
79-4	Segment Reporting of Puerto Rican Operations	S30	902
79-5	Meaning of the Term "Customer" as It Applies to Health Care Facilities under FASB Statement 14	S30	
79-9	Accounting in Interim Periods for Changes in Income Tax Rates	I73	
79-10	Fiscal Funding Clauses in Lease Agreements	L10	683
79-12	Interest Rate Used in Calculating the Present Value of Minimum Lease Payments	L10	683

(FTB cont.)

Number	Title	Current text reference	GAAP Interp. & Applic. page reference
79-13	Applicability of FASB Statement 13 to Current Value Financial Statements	L10	683
79-14	Upward Adjustment of Guaranteed Residual Values	L10	683
79-15	Accounting for Loss on a Sublease Not Involving the Disposal of a Segment	L10	684
79-16	(Revised) Effect on a Change in Income Tax Rate on the Accounting for Leveraged Leases	L10	684
79-17	Reporting Cumulative Effect Adjustment from Retroactive Application of FASB 13	--	
79-18	Transition Requirements of Certain FASB Amendments and Interpretations of FASB Statement 13	--	
79-19	Investor's Accounting for Unrealized Losses on Marketable Securities Owned by an Equity Method Investee	I80, I82	159
80-1	Early Extinguishments of Debt through Exchange for Common or Preferred Stock	L35	
80-2	Classification of Debt Restructurings by Debtors and Creditors	D22	591
81-6	Applicability of Statement 15 to Debtors in Bankruptcy Situations	D22	590
82-1	Disclosure of the Sale or Purchase of Tax Benefits through Tax Leases	I27	684
84-1	Accounting for Stock Issued to Acquire the Results of a Research and Development Arrangement	R55	
85-1	Accounting for the Receipt of Federal Home Loan Mortgage Corporation Participating Preferred Stock	Bt7	980
85-3	Accounting for Operating Leases with Scheduled Rent Increases	L10	646
85-4	Accounting for Purchases of Life Insurance	I50	
85-5	Issues Relating to Accounting for Business Combinations	B51	548
85-6	Accounting for a Purchase of Treasury Shares at a Price Significantly in Excess of the Current Market Price of the Shares and the Income Statement Classification of Costs Incurred in Defending against a Takeover Attempt	C23, G40, I17, I60	79, 470, 846
86-2	Accounting for an Interest in the Residual Value of a Leased Asset: • Acquired by a Third Party or • Retained by a Lessor That Sells the Related Minimum Rental Payments	L10	662, 684
87-2	Computation of a Loss on an Abandonment	Re6	
87-3	Accounting for Mortgage Servicing Fees and Rights	Mo4	981, 985
88-1	Issues Relating to Accounting for Leases	L10	650, 662, 685
90-1	Accounting for Separately Priced Extended Warranty and Product Maintenance Contracts	R75	276
94-1	Application of Statement 115 to Debt Securities in a Troubled Debt Restructuring	I80	162, 406
97-1	Accounting under Statement 123 for Certain Employee Stock Purchase Plans with a Look-Back Option	C36	815, 846
01-1	Effective Date for Certain Financial Institutions of Certain Provisions of Statement 140 Related to the Isolation of Transferred Financial Assets	F39	129, 985

Financial Accounting Standards Board
Staff Positions (FSP)

(FSP cont.)

Number	Title	GAAP Interp. & Applic. page reference
FIN 46(R)-2	Calculation of Expected Losses under FASB Interpretation No. 46 (Revised December 2003), *Consolidation of Variable Interest Entities*	558
FIN 46(R)-3	Evaluating Whether As a Group the Holders of the Equity Investment at Risk Lack the Direct or Indirect Ability to Make Decisions about an Entity's Activities through Voting Rights or Similar Rights under FASB Interpretation No. 46 (Revised December 2003), *Consolidation of Variable Interest Entities*	558
FAS 129-1	Disclosure Requirements under FASB Statement No. 129, *Disclosure of Information about Capital Structures*, Relating to Contingently Convertible Securities	600, 621
FAS 141-1 and FAS 142-1	Interaction of FASB Statements No. 141, *Business Combinations*, and No. 142, *Goodwill and Other Intangible Assets*, and EITF Issue No. 04-2, *Whether Mineral Rights are Tangible or Intangible Assets*	387
FIN 46(R)-4	Technical Correction of FASB Interpretation No. 46 (Revised December 2003), *Consolidation of Variable Interest Entities*, Relating to Its Effects on Question No. 12 EITF Issue No. 96-21, *Implementation Issues in Accounting for Leasing Transactions Involving Special-Purpose Entities*	558
FAS 106-2	Accounting and Disclosure Requirements Related to the Medicare Prescription Drug, Improvement and Modernization Act of 2003	
FAS 97-1	Situations in Which Paragraphs 17(b) and 20 or FASB Statement No. 97, *Accounting and Reporting by Insurance Enterprises for Certain Long-Duration Contracts and for Realized Gains and Losses from the Sale of Investments*, Permit or Require Accrual of an Unearned Revenue Liability	

Financial Accounting Standards Board
Statements of Financial Accounting Concepts (CON)(1978-2002)

Number	Title	GAAP Interp. & Applic. page reference
1	Objectives of Financial Reporting by Business Enterprises	21, 26, 99
2	Qualitative Characteristics of Accounting Information	21, 22, 27
4	Objectives of Financial Reporting by Nonbusiness Organizations	
5	Recognition and Measurement in Financial Statements of Business Enterprises	21, 22, 29, 96, 99, 253, 466, 476, 995
6	Elements of Financial Statements	20, 21, 22, 23, 30, 39, 40, 64, 160, 251, 588, 694, 779, 827, 831
7	Using Cash Flow Information and Present Value in Accounting Measurements	21, 22, 32, 33, 337, 347, 350, 351, 458, 692, 1047

Emerging Issues Task Force Issues (1984-2003)

Number	*Title*	*Status*	*GAAP Interp. & Applic. page reference*
84-1	Tax Reform Act of 1984; Deferred Income Taxes of Stock Life Insurance Companies	Resolved by FAS 109.	
84-2	Tax Reform Act of 1984; Deferred Income Taxes Relating to Domestic International Sales Corporations	Resolved by FAS 109.	
84-3	Convertible Debt "Sweeteners"	Nullified by FAS 84.	
84-4	Acquisition, Development, and Construction Loans	Resolved by Practice Bulletin 1.	310, 979
84-5	Sale of Marketable Securities with a Put Option	Partially nullified by FAS 140; see also FAS 133.	447
84-6	Termination of Defined Benefit Pension Plans	Consensus nullified by FAS 88.	
84-7	Termination of Interest Rate Swaps	Partially nullified and partially resolved by FAS 133.	212
84-8	Variable Stock Purchase Warrants Given by Suppliers to Customers	Affected by FAS 123. See Issue 96-18.	
84-9	Deposit Float of Banks	Superseded by AICPA Audit and Accounting Guide	980
84-10	LIFO Conformity of Companies Relying on Insilco Tax Court Decision	Guidance provided by AICPA Issues Paper on LIFO Accounting, issued 11/30/84. See also Issue 84-24.	
84-11	Offsetting Installment Note Receivables and Bank Debt ("Note Monetization")	Resolved by FIN 39.	
84-12	Operating Leases with Scheduled Rent Increases	Resolved by FAS 109.	
84-13	Purchase of Stock Options and Stock Appreciation Rights in a Leveraged Buyout	Consensus reached; clarified by FIN 44.	470, 545
84-14	Deferred Interest Rate Setting	Nullified by FAS 133.	213
84-15	Grantor Trusts Consolidation	No consensus, see FAS 140.	
84-16	Earnings Per Share Cash-Yield Test for Zero Coupon Bonds	Resolved by FAS 85; superseded by FAS 128.	
84-17	Profit Recognition on Sales of Real Estate with Graduated Payment Mortgages and Insured Mortgages	Consensus reached. See Issue 87-9.	307
84-18	Stock Option Pyramiding	Consensus reached; clarified by FIN 44.	836, 838
84-19	Mortgage Loan Payment Modifications	Consensus reached. See D-52.	980
84-20	GNMA Dollar Rolls	Partial consensus reached. Remaining issues resolved by SOP 85-2, which has been incorporated in the AICPA *Guide on Savings Institutions*. Issue partially resolved by FAS 125; see D-52.	980

(EITF cont.)

Number	Title	Status	GAAP Interp. & Applic. page reference
84-21	Sale of a Loan with a Partial Participation Retained	Resolved by FAS 140.	980
84-22	Prior Years' Earnings Per Share Following a Savings and Loan Association Conversion and Pooling	Resolved by FAS 141.	980
84-23	Leveraged Buyout Holding Company Debt	Guidance provided by SEC *Staff Accounting Bulletin 73*. Disclosure guidance provided by FAS 133.	
84-24	LIFO Accounting Issues	Resolved by SEC *Staff Accounting Bulletin 58*.	
84-25	Offsetting Nonrecourse Debt with Sales-Type or Direct Financing Lease Receivables	Resolved by FTB 86-2	
84-26	Defeasance of Special-Purpose Borrowings	Resolved by FAS 140.	
84-27	Deferred Taxes on Subsidiary Stock Sales	Resolved by FAS 109.	
84-28	Impairment of Long-Lived Assets	Resolved by FAS 144.	
84-29	Gain and Loss Recognition on Exchanges of Productive Assets and the Effect of Boot	Codified in Issue 01-2.	
84-30	Sales of Loans to Special-Purpose Entities	Resolved by FIN 46(R).	
84-31	Equity Certificates of Deposit	Resolved by FAS 133.	980
84-33	Acquisition of a Tax Loss Carryforward—Temporary Parent-Subsidiary Relationship	Resolved by FAS 144.	545
84-34	Permanent Discount Restricted Stock Purchase Plans	Not resolved, but guidance provided by SEC; see also FAS 123 and FIN 44.	
84-35	Business Combinations: Sale of Duplicate Facilities and Accrual of Liabilities	Partially resolved by FAS 87, FAS 106, FTB 85-5, and SEC *Staff Accounting Bulletin 61*. See also Issues 95-3, 95-14, and 96-5.	
84-36	Interest Rate Swap Transactions	Nullified by FAS 133.	
84-37	Sale-Leaseback Transaction with Repurchase Option	Partially resolved by FAS 98; see also Issues 90-15 and 97-10.	
84-38	Identical Common Shares for a Pooling of Interests	Resolved by FAS 109.	
84-39	Transfers of Monetary and Nonmonetary Assets among Individuals and Entities under Common Control	No consensus reached.	
84-40	Long-Term Debt Repayable by a Capital Stock Transaction	Issue 1 nullified by FIN 46(R); Issue 2 resolved by FAS 150.	837
84-41	Consolidation of Subsidiary after Instantaneous In-Substance Defeasance	Resolved by FAS 94.	
84-42	Push-Down of Parent Company Debt to a Subsidiary	Guidance provided by SEC *Staff Accounting Bulletin 73*.	

(EITF cont.)

Number	Title	Status	GAAP Interp. & Applic. page reference
84-43	Income Tax Effects of Asset Revaluations in Certain Foreign Countries	Consensus nullified by FAS 109.	
84-44	Partial Termination of a Defined Benefit Pension Plan	Resolved by FAS 88.	
85-1	Classifying Notes Received for Capital Stock	Consensus reached.	837
85-2	Classification of Costs Incurred in a Take-over Defense	Consensus nullified by FTB 85-6; no consensus on part 2.	
85-3	Tax Benefits Relating to Asset Dispositions Following an Acquisition of a Financial Institution	Consensus nullified by FAS 109.	
85-4	Downstream Mergers and Other Stock Transactions between Companies under Common Control	Resolved by FTB 85-5.	
85-5	Restoration of Deferred Taxes Previously Eliminated by Net Operating Loss Recognition	Resolved by FAS 109.	
85-6	Futures Implementation Questions	Resolved by FAS 80 (superseded by FAS 133).	
85-7	Federal Home Loan Mortgage Corporation Stock	Resolved by FTB 85-1.	980
85-8	Amortization of Thrift Intangibles	Consensus reached, partially nullified by FAS 142. Additional guidance provided by SEC. See also FAS 147.	980
85-9	Revenue Recognition on Options to Purchase Stock of Another Entity	Partial consensus reached; partially nullified by FAS 133.	211
85-10	Employee Stock Ownership Plan Contribution Funded by a Pension Plan Termination	Consensus nullified by FAS 88.	
85-11	Use of an Employee Stock Ownership Plan in a Leveraged Buyout	No consensus, but SOP 93-6 rendered this moot.	
85-12	Retention of Specialized Accounting for Investments in Consolidation	Consensus reached; see also FAS 115.	545
85-13	Sale of Mortgage Service Rights on Mortgages Owned by Others	Consensus reached; see also Issue 95-5.	981
85-14	Securities That Can Be Acquired for Cash in a Pooling of Interests	Nullified by FAS 141.	
85-15	Recognizing Benefits of Purchased Net Operating Loss Carryforwards	Consensus nullified by FAS 109.	
85-16	Leveraged Leases	Consensus reached. Partially resolved by FAS 98.	672
85-17	Accrued Interest upon Conversion of Convertible Debt	Consensus reached.	613
85-18	Earnings Per Share Effect of Equity Commitment Notes	Consensus reached. Partially nullified by FAS 128.	981
85-20	Recognition of Fees for Guaranteeing a Loan	Partial consensus nullified by FAS 133; additional guidance provided by SEC SAB 60 and by FAS 91.	572, 981

(EITF cont.)

(EITF cont.)

Number	Title	Status	GAAP Interp. & Applic. page reference
85-42	Amortization of Goodwill Resulting from Recording Time Savings Deposits at Fair Values	Consensus reached, partially nullified by FAS 142.	982
85-43	Sale of Subsidiary for Equity Interest in Buyer	Resolved by Issue 86-29.	
85-44	Differences between Loan Loss Allowances for GAAP and RAP	Consensus reached.	982
85-45	Business Combinations: Settlement of Stock Options and Awards	Partial consensus reached.	470, 545
85-46	Partnership's Purchase of Withdrawing Partner's Equity	No resolution.	
86-1	Recognizing Net Operating Loss Carryforwards	Consensus nullified by FAS 109.	
86-2	Retroactive Wage Adjustments Affecting Medicare Payments	Deemed no longer technically helpful.	
86-3	Retroactive Regulations Regarding IRC Section 338 Purchase Price Allocations	Deemed no longer technically helpful.	
86-4	Income Statement Treatment of Income Tax Benefit for Employee Stock Ownership Plan Dividends	Consensus nullified by FAS 109.	
86-5	Classifying Demand Notes with Repayment Terms	Consensus reached.	572
86-6	Antispeculation Clauses in Real Estate Sales Contracts	Consensus reached.	307
86-7	Recognition by Homebuilders of Profit from Sales of Land and Related Construction Contracts	Consensus reached; see guidance in FAS 66.	308
86-8	Sale of Bad Debt Recovery Rights	Partial consensus reached.	151
86-9	IRC Section 338 and Push-Down Accounting	Consensus reached. Additional guidance provided by FAS 109 and Issue 94-10.	725
86-10	Pooling with 10 Percent Cash Payout Determined by Lottery	Nullified by FAS 141.	
86-11	Recognition of Possible 1986 Tax Law Changes	Resolved by FAS 109.	
86-12	Accounting by Insureds for Claims-Made Insurance Policies	Codified in Issue 03-8.	
86-13	Recognition of Inventory Market Declines at Interim Reporting Dates	Consensus reached.	890, 894
86-14	Purchased Research and Development Projects in a Business Combination	See guidance in FIN 4 and FAS 2.	
86-15	Increasing-Rate Debt	Consensus partially nullified by FAS 133; see also SEC SAB 77.	572
86-16	Carryover of Predecessor Cost in Leveraged Buyout Transactions	Consensus superseded by Issue 88-16.	509, 546
86-17	Deferred Profit on Sale-Leaseback Transaction with Lessee Guarantee of Residual Value	Consensus reached. Affected by FAS 98.	674
86-18	Debtor's Accounting for a Modification of Debt Terms	Superseded by Issue 96-19 and later resolved by FIN 39.	

(EITF cont.)

Number	Title	Status	GAAP Interp. & Applic. page reference
86-19	Change in Accounting for Other Postemployment Benefits	Resolved by FAS 106.	
86-20	Accounting for Other Postemployment Benefits of an Acquired Company	Consensus nullified by FAS 106.	
86-21	Application of the AICPA Notice to Practitioners Regarding Acquisition, Development, and Construction Arrangements to Acquisition of an Operating Property	Consensus partially nullified by FAS 133.	982
86-22	Display of Business Restructuring Provisions in the Income Statement	Resolved by SEC SAB 67. See Issues 87-4 and 94-3.	
86-24	Third-Party Establishment of Collateralized Mortgage Obligations	Deemed no longer useful; see FAS 140.	213
86-25	Offsetting Foreign Currency Swaps	Consensus reached; affected by FIN 39. Also see FAS 133.	212
86-26	Using Forward Commitments as a Surrogate for Deferred Rate Setting	Resolved by FAS 133.	
86-27	Measurement of Excess Contributions to a Defined Contribution Plan or Employee Stock Ownership Plan	Consensus partially nullified by SOP 93-6. See SOP 93-6 for transition provisions.	
86-28	Accounting Implications of Indexed Debt Instruments	Partial consensus reached; partially nullified by FAS 133.	213
86-29	Nonmonetary Transactions: Magnitude of Boot and the Exceptions to the Use of Fair Value	Consensus reached. Codified by Issue 01-2.	448, 545
86-30	Classification of Obligations When a Violation Is Waived by the Creditor	Consensus reached.	572
86-31	Reporting the Tax Implications of a Pooling of a Bank and a Savings and Loan Association	Consensus reached. Nullified by FAS 141.	982
86-32	Early Extinguishment of a Subsidiary's Mandatorily Redeemable Preferred Stock	Consensus reached.	546, 837
86-33	Tax Indemnifications in Lease Agreements	Consensus reached.	674
86-34	Futures Contracts Used as Hedges of Anticipated Reverse Repurchase Transactions	Consensus reached; nullified by FAS 133.	213
86-35	Debentures with Detachable Stock Purchase Warrants	Codified in Issue 00-19.	
86-36	Invasion of a Defeasance Trust	Partial consensus superseded by FAS 140.	613
86-37	Recognition of Tax Benefit of Discounting Loss Reserves of Insurance Companies	Consensus nullified by FAS 109.	
86-38	Implications of Mortgage Prepayments on Amortization of Servicing Rights	Nullified by FAS 125 and FAS 140; section C superseded by Issue 99-20.	982
86-39	Gains from the Sale of Mortgage Loans with Servicing Rights Retained	Consensus nullified by FAS 125 and FAS 140.	
86-40	Investments in Open-End Mutual Funds That Invest in US Government Securities	Consensus reached. Affected by FAS 115.	211
86-41	Carryforward of the Corporate Alternative Minimum Tax Credit	Consensus nullified by FAS 109. See also Issue 87-8.	

(EITF cont.)

Number	Title	Status	GAAP Interp. & Applic. page reference
86-42	Effect of a Change in Tax Rates on Assets and Liabilities Recorded Net-of-Tax in a Purchase Business Combination	Consensus nullified by FAS 109.	
86-43	Effect of a Change in Tax Law or Rates on Leveraged Leases	Consensus reached. See also Issue 87-8 and FAS 109.	726
86-44	Effect of a Change in Tax Law on Investments in Safe Harbor Leases	Consensus reached.	726
86-45	Imputation of Dividends on Preferred Stock Redeemable at the Issuer's Option with Initial Below-Market Dividend Rate	Resolved by SEC SAB 68. May be addressed in FASB project on financial instruments.	
86-46	Uniform Capitalization Rules for Inventory under the Tax Reform Act of 1986	Consensus reached.	225, 244
87-1	Deferral Accounting for Cash Securities That Are Used to Hedge Rate or Price Risk	Resolved by FAS 133.	
87-2	Net Present Value Method of Valuing Speculative Foreign Exchange Contracts	Consensus nullified by FAS 133.	212
87-4	Restructuring of Operations: Implications of SEC *Staff Accounting Bulletin 67*	Consensus reached. See FAS 144 and Issue 94-3.	91
87-5	Troubled Debt Restructurings: Interrelationship between FASB Statement 15 and the AICPA Savings and Loan Guide	Consensus nullified by FAS 114.	
87-6	Adjustments Relating to Stock Compensation Plans	Nullified by FIN 44.	
87-7	Sale of an Asset Subject to a Lease and Nonrecourse Financing: "Wrap-Lease Transactions"	Consensus reached. Partially resolved by FTB 88-1.	674
87-8	Tax Reform Act of 1986: Issues Related to the Alternative Minimum Tax	Partial consensus nullified by FAS 109.	726
87-9	Profit Recognition on Sales of Real Estate with Insured Mortgages or Surety Bonds	Consensus reached. See Issue 88-12.	308
87-10	Revenue Recognition by Television "Barter" Syndicators	Consensus reached.	1047
87-11	Allocation of Purchase Price to Assets to Be Sold	Nullified by FAS 144.	469, 546, 549
87-12	Foreign Debt-for-Equity Swaps	Consensus reached.	214
87-13	Amortization of Prior Service Cost for a Defined Benefit Plan When There Is a History of Plan Amendments	Resolved by FAS 87 Q&A.	
87-15	Effect of a Standstill Agreement on Pooling-of-Interests Accounting	Consensus nullified by FAS 141.	
87-16	Whether the 90 Percent Test for a Pooling of Interests Is Applied Separately to Each Company or on a Combined Basis	Consensus nullified by FAS 141.	
87-17	Spin-Offs or Other Distributions of Loans Receivable to Shareholders	Codified by Issue 01-2.	546
87-18	Use of Zero Coupon Bonds in a Troubled Debt Restructuring	Partial consensus; affected by FAS 114 and FAS 144. Partially resolved by FAS 140.	151

(EITF cont.)

Number	Title	Status	GAAP Interp. & Applic. page reference
87-19	Substituted Debtors in a Troubled Debt Restructuring	Consensus reached.	613
87-20	Offsetting Certificates of Deposit against High Coupon Debt	Partially resolved by FAS 140; see also Issue 96-19.	
87-21	Change of Accounting Basis in Master Limited Partnership Transactions	Consensus reached; SEC set restrictive conditions for recognition of new basis. See also FAS 141.	546
87-22	Prepayments to the Secondary Reserve of the FSLIC	Consensus reached.	982
87-23	Book Value Stock Purchase Plans	Consensus partially nullified by SOP 93-6; see also Issue 88-6. Partially clarified by FIN 44.	824, 837
87-24	Allocation of Interest to Discontinued Operations	Consensus reached.	95
87-25	Sale of Convertible, Adjustable-Rate Mortgages with Contingent Repayment Agreement	Resolved by FAS 140.	
87-26	Hedging of Foreign Currency Exposure with a Tandem Currency	Consensus nullified by FAS 133.	212
87-27	Poolings of Companies That Do Not Have a Controlling Class of Common Stock	Nullified by FAS 141.	
87-28	Provision for Deferred Taxes on Increases in Cash Surrender Value of Key-Person Life Insurance	Resolved by FAS 109.	
87-29	Exchange of Real Estate Involving Boot	Codified by Issue 01-2.	
87-30	Sale of a Short-Term Loan Made under a Long-Term Credit Commitment	Consensus reached; affected by FAS 140.	214
87-31	Sale of Put Options on Issuer's Stock	Issue codified in Issue 00-19.	
87-33	Stock Compensation Issues Related to Market Decline	Nullified by FIN 44.	
87-34	Sale of Mortgage Servicing Rights with a Subservicing Agreement	Consensus reached. See Issues 89-5, 90-21, and 95-5.	982
88-1	Determination of Vested Benefit Obligation for a Defined Benefit Pension Plan	Consensus reached.	772
88-3	Rental Concessions Provided by Landlord	Resolved by FTB 88-1 and Issues 88-10 and 94-3.	
88-4	Classification of Payment Made to IRS to Retain Fiscal Year	Consensus reached.	726
88-5	Recognition of Insurance Death Benefits	Partial consensus reached. Partially resolved by FAS 109.	773
88-6	Book Value Stock Plans in an Initial Public Offering	Consensus reached; partially clarified by FIN 44.	824, 837
88-8	Mortgage Swaps	Consensus nullified by FAS 133.	213
88-9	Put Warrants	Consensus nullified by FAS 128, 133, and 150, or superseded by Issue 96-13.	825, 837

(EITF cont.)

(EITF cont.)

Number	Title	Status	GAAP Interp. & Applic. page reference
89-1	Accounting by a Pension Plan for Bank Investment Contracts and Guaranteed Investment Contracts	Resolved by FAS 110 and SOP 94-4.	
89-2	Maximum Maturity Guarantees on Transfers of Receivables with Recourse	Consensus nullified by FAS 140.	
89-3	Balance Sheet Presentation of Savings Accounts in Financial Statements of Credit Unions	Consensus reached.	984
89-4	Accounting for a Purchased Investment in a Collateralized Mortgage Obligation Instrument or in a Mortgage-Backed Interest-Only Certificate	Superseded by Issue 99-20.	
89-5	Sale of Mortgage Loan Servicing Rights	Consensus superseded by Issue 95-5.	
89-7	Exchange of Assets or Interest in a Subsidiary for a Noncontrolling Equity Interest in a New Entity	Codified by Issue 01-2.	546
89-8	Expense Recognition for Employee Stock Ownership Plans	Consensus nullified by SOP 93-6. See SOP 93-6 for transition provisions.	
89-9	Accounting for In-Substance Foreclosures	Consensus nullified by FAS 114.	
89-10	Sponsor's Recognition of Employee Stock Ownership Plan Debt	Consensus nullified by SOP 93-6. See SOP 93-6 for transition provisions.	
89-11	Sponsor's Balance Sheet Classification of Capital Stock with a Put Option Held by an Employee Stock Ownership Plan	Consensus reached; partially nullified by FAS 133. Also see Interpretation 45.	838
89-12	Earnings-Per-Share Issues Related to Convertible Preferred Stock Held by an Employee Stock Ownership Plan	Consensus nullified by SOP 93-6. See SOP 93-6 for transition provisions.	
89-13	Accounting for the Cost of Asbestos Removal	Consensus reached. See Issue 90-8. Affected by FAS 143 and 144.	375
89-14	Valuation of Repossessed Real Estate	Consensus reached. Additional guidance provided by SOP 92-3.	309
89-15	Accounting for a Modification of Debt Terms When the Debtor Is Experiencing Financial Difficulties	Superseded by Issue 02-4.	
89-16	Consideration of Executory Costs in Sale-Leaseback Transactions	Consensus reached.	675
89-17	Accounting for the Retail Sale of an Extended Warranty Contract in Connection with the Sale of a Product	Consensus nullified by FTB 90-1.	
89-18	Divestitures of Certain Investment Securities to an Unregulated Commonly Controlled Entity under FIRREA	Consensus affected by FAS 115.	214
89-19	Accounting for a Change in Goodwill Amortization for Business Combinations Initiated prior to the Effective Date of FASB Statement 72.	Consensus reached.	984

(EITF cont.)

Number	Title	Status	GAAP Interp. & Applic. page reference
89-20	Accounting for Cross-Border Tax Benefit Leases	Consensus reached.	675
90-2	Exchange of Interest-Only and Principal-Only Securities for a Mortgage-Backed Security	Consensus nullified by FAS 140.	
90-3	Accounting for Employers' Obligations for Future Contributions to a Multiemployer Pension Plan	Consensus reached.	773
90-4	Earnings-Per-Share Treatment of Tax Benefits for Dividends on Stock Held by an Employee Stock Ownership Plan	Nullified by FAS 128. Additional guidance in Issue 92-3.	
90-5	Exchanges of Ownership Interests between Entities under Common Control	Consensus reached.	547
90-6	Accounting for Certain Events Not Addressed in Issue 87-11 Relating to an Acquired Operating Unit to Be Sold	Nullified by FAS 144.	469, 547
90-7	Accounting for a Reload Stock Option	Consensus reached; see also Issue 84-18 and FIN 44.	838
90-8	Capitalization of Costs to Treat Environmental Contamination	Consensus reached, partially nullified by FAS 143.	375
90-9	Changes to Fixed Employee Stock Option Plans as a Result of Restructuring	Consensus nullified by FIN 44.	
90-10	Accounting for a Business Combination Involving a Majority-Owned Investee of a Venture Capital Company	Nullified by FAS 141.	
90-11	Accounting for Exit and Entrance Fees Incurred in a Conversion from the Savings Association Insurance Fund to the Bank Insurance Fund	Deemed no longer technically helpful.	
90-12	Allocating Basis to Individual Assets and Liabilities for Transactions within the Scope of Issue 88-16	Consensus reached.	509, 547
90-13	Accounting for Simultaneous Common Control Mergers	Consensus reached. See Issue 86-29. Guidance provided by FAS 141.	547
90-14	Unsecured Guarantee by Parent of Subsidiary's Lease Payment in a Sale-Leaseback Transaction	Consensus reached.	675
90-15	Impact of Nonsubstantive Lessors, Residual Value Guarantees, and Other Provisions in Leasing Transactions	Superseded by FIN 46.	676, 678
90-16	Accounting for Discontinued Operations Subsequently Retained	Consensus affected by FAS 144.	
90-17	Hedging Foreign Currency Risks with Purchased Options	Superseded by FAS 133.	212
90-18	Effect of a "Removal of Accounts" Provision on the Accounting for a Credit Card Securitization	Consensus reached. See Issue 88-22 and FAS 140.	984
90-19	Convertible Bonds with Issuer Option to Settle for Cash upon Conversion	Consensus reached; affected by FAS 128 and partially affirmed by FAS 133. Also see FAS 145.	614

(EITF cont.)

Number	Title	Status	GAAP Interp. & Applic. page reference
90-20	Impact of an Uncollateralized Irrevocable Letter of Credit on a Real Estate Sale-Leaseback Transaction	Consensus reached.	309, 676
90-21	Balance Sheet Treatment of a Sale of Mortgage Servicing Rights with a Subservicing Agreement	Consensus reached. See Issues 88-18, 95-5, and D-52.	984
90-22	Accounting for Gas-Balancing Arrangements	No resolution; see FAS 133.	
91-1	Hedging Intercompany Foreign Currency Risks	Consensus nullified by FAS 133.	205
91-2	Debtor's Accounting for Forfeiture of Real Estate Subject to a Nonrecourse Mortgage	No consensus reached.	309
91-3	Accounting for Income Tax Benefits from Bad Debts of a Savings and Loan Association	Resolved by FAS 109.	
91-4	Hedging Foreign Currency Risks with Complex Options and Similar Transactions	Resolved by FAS 133.	
91-5	Nonmonetary Exchange of Cost-Method Investments	Consensus reached. Affected by FAS 115, 130, and 141.	547
91-6	Revenue Recognition of Long-Term Power Sales Contracts	Consensus partially nullified by FAS 133. See Issue 96-17.	1070
91-7	Accounting for Pension Benefits Paid by Employers after Insurance Companies Fail to Provide Annuity Benefits	Consensus reached.	773
91-8	Application of FASB Statement 96 to a State Tax Based on the Greater of a Franchise Tax or an Income Tax	Consensus modified by FAS 109.	
91-9	Revenue and Expense Recognition for Freight Services in Process	Consensus reached.	275
91-10	Accounting for Tax Increment Financing Entities and Special Assessments	Consensus reached.	376
92-1	Allocation of Residual Value or First-Loss Guarantee to Minimum Lease Payments in Leases Involving Land and Building(s)	Consensus reached.	676
92-2	Measuring Loss Accruals by Transferors for Transfers of Receivables with Recourse	Consensus reached. Additional guidance provided by SEC. See also Issue 88-11. Issue affected by FAS 140.	152
92-3	Earnings-Per-Share Treatment of Tax Benefits for Dividends on Unallocated Stock Held by an Employee Stock Ownership Plan (Consideration of the Implications of FASB Statement 109 on Issue 2 of EITF Issue 90-4)	Consensus affected by SOP 93-6.	881
92-4	Accounting for a Change in Functional Currency When an Economy Ceases to Be Considered Highly Inflationary	Consensus reached. See Issue 92-8.	953
92-5	Amortization Period for Net Deferred Credit Card Origination Costs	Consensus reached. See Issue 93-1.	984

(EITF cont.)

Number	*Title*	*Status*	*GAAP Interp. & Applic. page reference*
92-7	Accounting by Rate-Regulated Utilities for the Effects of Certain Alternative Revenue Programs	Consensus reached.	1070
92-8	Accounting for the Income Tax Effects under FASB Statement 109 of a Change in Functional Currency When an Economy Ceases to Be Considered Highly Inflationary	Consensus reached.	953
92-9	Accounting for the Present Value of Future Profits Resulting from the Acquisition of a Life Insurance Company	Consensus reached.	1024
92-10	Loan Acquisitions Involving Table Funding Arrangements	Consensus nullified by FAS 125.	
92-12	Accounting for OPEB Costs by Rate-Regulated Enterprises	Consensus reached. Additional guidance provided by FAS 144.	1070
92-13	Accounting for Estimated Payments in Connection with the Coal Industry Retiree Health Benefit Act of 1992	Consensus reached.	95, 773
93-1	Accounting for Individual Credit Card Acquisitions	Consensus reached.	984
93-2	Effect of Acquisition of Employer Shares for/by an Employee Benefit Trust on Accounting for Business Combinations	Nullified by FAS 141.	
93-3	Plan Assets under FASB Statement 106	Consensus reached.	773
93-4	Accounting for Regulatory Assets	Consensus partially nullified by FAS 144. See Issue 92-12.	1070
93-5	Accounting for Environmental Liabilities	Consensus incorporated in and nullified by SOP 96-1.	577
93-6	Accounting for Multiple-Year Retrospectively-Rated Contracts by Ceding and Assuming Enterprises	Consensus reached. See Issue 93-14.	1025
93-7	Uncertainties Related to Income Taxes in a Purchase Business Combination	Consensus reached.	548
93-8	Accounting for the Sale and Leaseback of an Asset That Is Leased to Another Party	Consensus reached.	677
93-9	Application of FASB Statement 109 on Foreign Financial Statements Restated for General Price-Level Changes	Consensus reached.	953
93-10	Accounting for Dual Currency Bonds	Resolved by FAS 133.	
93-11	Accounting for Barter Transactions Involving Barter Credits	Consensus affected by FAS 144.	376, 1042
93-12	Recognition and Measurement of the Tax Benefit of Excess Tax-Deductible Goodwill Resulting from a Retroactive Change in Tax Law	Consensus reached.	726
93-13	Effect of a Retroactive Change in Enacted Tax Rates That Is Included in Income from Continuing Operations	Consensus reached.	727

(EITF cont.)

Number	Title	Status	GAAP Interp. & Applic. page reference
93-14	Accounting for Multiple-Year Retrospectively-Rated Insurance Contracts by Insurance Enterprises and Other Enterprises	Consensus reached. See Issue 93-6, D-35, and Interpretation 45.	572, 1025
93-16	Application of FASB Statement 109 to Basis Differences within Foreign Subsidiaries That Meet the Indefinite Reversal Criterion of APB Opinion 23	Consensus reached.	727
93-17	Recognition of Deferred Tax Assets for a Parent Company's Excess Tax Basis in the Stock of a Subsidiary That Is Accounted for as a Discontinued Operation	Consensus reached.	727
93-18	Recognition of Impairment for an Investment in a Collateralized Mortgage Obligation Instrument or in a Mortgage-Backed Interest-Only Certificate	Superseded by Issue 99-20.	
94-1	Accounting for Tax Benefits Resulting from Investments in Affordable Housing Projects	Consensus reached.	
94-2	Treatment of Minority Interests in Certain Real Estate Investment Trusts	Consensus reached. See Issue 95-7 for consensus reached on implementation issues.	309
94-3	Liability Recognition for Certain Employee Termination Benefits and Other Costs to Exit an Activity (Including Certain Costs Incurred in a Restructuring)	Nullified by FAS 146.	
94-4	Classification of an Investment in a Mortgage-Backed Interest-Only Certificate as Held-to-Maturity	Resolved by FAS 125.	
94-5	Determination of What Constitutes All Risks and Rewards and No Significant Unresolved Contingencies in a Sale of Mortgage Loan Servicing Rights under Issue 89-5	Superseded by Issue 95-5.	
94-6	Accounting for the Buyout of Compensatory Stock Options	Consensus nullified by FIN 44.	
94-7	Accounting for Financial Instruments Indexed to, and Potentially Settled in, a Company's Own Stock	Codified by Issue 96-13.	
94-8	Accounting for Conversion of a Loan into a Debt Security in a Debt Restructuring	Consensus reached.	615
94-9	Determining a Normal Servicing Fee Rate for the Sale of an SBA Loan	Consensus nullified by FAS 125.	
94-10	Accounting by a Company for the Income Tax Effects of Transactions among or with Its Shareholders under FASB Statement 109	Consensus reached.	727
95-1	Revenue Recognition on Sales with a Guaranteed Minimum Resale Value	Consensus reached; see also FAS 133.	677

(EITF cont.)

(EITF cont.)

Number	Title	Status	GAAP Interp. & Applic. page reference
95-18	Accounting and Reporting for a Discontinued Business Segment When the Measurement Date Occurs After the Balance Sheet Date but Before the Issuance of Financial Statements	Nullified by FAS 144.	
95-19	Determination of the Measurement Date for the Market Price of Securities Issued in a Purchase Business Combination	Codified by Issue 99-12.	549, 551
95-20	Measurement in the Consolidated Financial Statements of a Parent of the Tax Effects Related to the Operations of a Foreign Subsidiary That Receives Tax Credits Related to Dividend Payments	Consensus reached.	728
95-21	Accounting for Assets to Be Disposed of Acquired in a Purchase Business Combination	Resolved by FAS 144.	549
95-22	Balance Sheet Classification of Borrowings Outstanding under Revolving Credit Agreements That Include Both a Subjective Acceleration Clause and a Lockbox Arrangement	Consensus reached.	573
95-23	The Treatment of Certain Site Restoration/Environmental Exit Costs When Testing a Long-Lived Asset for Impairment	Consensus reached; partially nullified by FAS 143. Also see FAS 144.	376
96-1	Sale of Put Options on Issuer's Stock That Require or Permit Cash Settlement	Issue codified in Issue 96-13.	
96-2	Impairment Recognition When a Nonmonetary Asset Is Exchanged or Is Distributed to Owners and Is Accounted for at the Asset's Recorded Amount	Codified by Issue 01-2.	
96-3	Accounting for Equity Instruments That Are Issued for Consideration other than Employee Services under FASB Statement 123	Superseded by Issue 96-18.	838
96-4	Accounting for Reorganizations Involving a Non-Pro Rata Split-off of Certain Nonmonetary Assets to Owners	Codified by Issue 01-2.	549
96-5	Recognition of Liabilities for Contractual Termination Benefits or Changing Benefit Plan Assumptions in Anticipation of a Business Combination	Consensus reached.	549
96-6	Accounting for the Film and Software Costs Associated with Developing Entertainment and Educational Software Products	Guidance provided by SEC.	999
96-7	Accounting for Deferred Taxes on In-Process Research and Development Activities Acquired in a Purchase Business Combination	Consensus reached.	549, 728
96-8	Accounting for a Business Combination When the Issuing Company Has Targeted Stock	Nullified by FAS 141.	

(EITF cont.)

Number	Title	Status	GAAP Interp. & Applic. page reference
96-9	Classification of Inventory Markdowns and Other Costs Associated with a Restructuring	Guidance provided by SEC.	
96-10	Impact of Certain Transactions on the Held-to-Maturity Classification under FASB Statement 115	Consensus partially nullified by FAS 125. See D-51.	447
96-11	Accounting for Forward Contracts and Purchased Options to Acquire Securities Covered by FASB Statement 115	Consensus reached.	211
96-12	Recognition of Interest Income and Balance Sheet Classification of Structured Notes	Consensus partially nullified by FAS 133.	211
96-13	Accounting for Derivative Financial Instruments Indexed to, and Potentially Settled in, a Company's Own Stock	Codified by Issue 00-19.	214, 451, 820, 837, 840, 842
96-14	Accounting for the Costs Associated with Modifying Computer Software for the Year 2000	Deemed no longer technically helpful.	
96-15	Accounting for the Effects of Changes in Foreign Currency Exchange Rates on Foreign-Currency-Denominated Available-for-Sale Debt Securities	Consensus reached; partially nullified by FAS 133.	211
96-16	Investor's Accounting for an Investee When the Investor Owns a Majority of the Voting Stock but the Minority Shareholder or Shareholders Have Certain Approval or Veto Rights	Consensus reached. See also Issue 98-6 and FIN 46(R).	447
96-17	Revenue Recognition under Long-Term Power Sales Contracts That Contain Both Fixed and Variable Pricing Terms	Consensus reached; partially nullified by FAS 133.	1070
96-18	Accounting for Equity Instruments with Variable Terms That Are Issued for Consideration other than Employee Services under FASB Statement 123	Consensus reached; further guidance provided by Issue 00-8.	619, 818, 839, 842, 845
96-19	Debtor's Accounting for a Modification or Exchange of Debt Instruments	Consensus reached.	615
96-20	Impact of FASB Statement 125 on Consolidation of Special-Purpose Entities	Nullified by FAS 140.	
96-21	Implementation Issues in Accounting for Leasing Transactions Involving Special-Purpose Entities	Consensus reached. See Issues 97-1 and 97-10, FIN 45 and FIN 46(R).	678
96-22	Applicability of the Disclosures Required by FASB Statement 114 When a Loan Is Restructured in a Troubled Debt Restructuring into Two (or More) Loans	Consensus reached.	616
96-23	The Effects of Financial Instruments Indexed to, and Settled in, a Company's Own Stock on Pooling-of-Interests Accounting for a Subsequent Business Combination	Resolved by FAS 141.	

(EITF cont.)

Number	Title	Status	GAAP Interp. & Applic. page reference
97-1	Implementation Issues in Accounting for Lease Transactions, Including Those Involving Special-Purpose Entities	Consensus reached. See Issue 99-10 and FIN 45. Partially nullified by FIN 46(R).	679
97-2	Application of APB Opinion 16 and FASB Statement 94 to Medical Entities	Consensus reached; clarification provided by FIN 44 and 46(R).	549
97-3	Accounting for Fees and Costs Associated with Loan Syndications and Loan Participations After the Issuance of FASB Statement 125, *Accounting for Transfers and Servicing of Financial Assets and Extinguishment of Liabilities*	Consensus reached.	153
97-4	Deregulation of the Pricing of Electricity—Issues Related to the Application of FASB Statement 71, *Accounting for the Effects of Certain Types of Regulation*, and 101, *Regulated Enterprises—Accounting for the Discontinuation of the Application of FASB Statement 71*	Consensus reached.	1069
97-5	Accounting for Delayed Receipt of Option Shares upon Exercise under APB Opinion 25, *Accounting for Stock Issued to Employees*	Resolved by FASB staff; clarification provided by FIN 44. See also Issues 84-18 and 87-6.	
97-6	Application of EITF Issue 96-20, *Impact of FASB Statement 125, Accounting for Transfers and Servicing of Financial Assets and Extinguishment of Liabilities, on Consolidation of Special-Purpose Entities*, to Qualifying SPEs Receiving Transferred Financial Assets prior to the Effective Date of Statement 125	Consensus nullified by FAS 140; see also Issue 96-20.	
97-7	Accounting for Hedges of Foreign Currency Risk Inherent in an Available-for-Sale Marketable Equity Security	Consensus reached; partially nullified by FAS 133.	448
97-8	Accounting for Contingent Consideration Issued in a Purchase Business Combination	Consensus reached; see also FAS 133.	550
97-9	Effect on Pooling-of-Interests Accounting of Certain Contingently Exercisable Options or Other Equity Instruments	Consensus nullified by FAS 141.	
97-10	The Effect of Lessee Involvement in Asset Construction	Consensus reached.	679, 680
97-11	Accounting for Internal Costs Relating to Real Estate Property Acquisitions	Consensus reached.	310
97-12	Accounting for Increased Share Authorizations in an IRS Section 423 Employee Purchase Plan under APB Opinion 25, *Accounting for Stock Issued to Employees*	Consensus reached; clarification provided by FIN 44.	

(EITF cont.)

Number	Title	Status	GAAP Interp. & Applic. page reference
97-13	Accounting for Costs Incurred in Connection with a Consulting Contract or an Internal Project That Combines Business Process Reengineering and Information Technology Transformation	Consensus reached. See SOP 98-1.	999
97-14	Accounting for Deferred Compensation Arrangements Where Amounts Earned Are Held in a Rabbi Trust and Invested	Consensus reached; clarification provided by FIN 44.	840
97-15	Accounting for Contingency Arrangements Based on Security Prices in a Purchase Business Combination	Consensus reached; see also FAS 133.	550
98-1	Valuation of Debt Assumed in a Purchase Business Combination	Consensus reached.	550
98-2	Accounting by a Subsidiary for an Investment in Its Parent Company's Stock	Issue will not be further deliberated; no consensus.	550, 841
98-3	Determining Whether a Transaction Is an Exchange of Similar Productive Assets or a Business Combination	Consensus reached; see also Issue 00-5 and FAS 141.	60, 550
98-4	Accounting by a Joint Venture for Business Received at Its Formation	See discussion at Issue 98-3.	551
98-5	Accounting for Convertible Securities with Beneficial Conversion Features or Contingently Adjustable Conversion Ratios	Consensus reached; see also Issue 00-27, FAS 133, and D-60.	597, 602, 616, 617
98-6	Investor's Accounting for an Investment in a Limited Partnership When the Investor Is the Sole General Partner and the Limited Partners Have Certain Approved or Veto Rights	No consensus reached; no further discussion planned.	
98-7	Accounting for Exchanges of Similar Equity Method Investments	Codified by Issue 01-2.	448
98-8	Accounting for Transfers of Investments That Are in Substance Real Estate	Consensus reached and affirmed by FAS 140; see also Issue 84-4.	127, 310
98-9	Accounting for Contingent Rent in Interim Financial Periods	Partial consensus reached; further guidance in SEC SAB 101.	680, 894
98-10	Accounting for Energy Trading and Risk Management Activities	Superseded by Issue 02-3.	
98-11	Accounting for Acquired Temporary Differences in Certain Purchase Transactions That Are Not Accounted for as Business Combinations	Consensus reached; see also FAS 109.	728
98-12	Application of EITF Issue 96-13, *Accounting for Derivative Financial Instruments Indexed to, and Potentially Settled in, a Company's Own Stock*, to Certain Derivative Financial Instruments Issued with Other Instruments	Consensus nullified by FAS 150.	
98-13	Accounting by an Equity Method Investor for Investee Losses When the Investor Has Loans to and Investments in Other Securities of the Investee	Consensus reached	433, 434, 448

(EITF cont.)

(EITF cont.)

Number	*Title*	*Status*	*GAAP Interp. & Applic. page reference*
99-18	Effect on Pooling-of-Interests Accounting of Financial Instruments Indexed to, and Potentially Settled in a Company's Own Stock	Resolved by FAS 141.	
99-19	Reporting Revenue Gross as a Principal Versus Net as an Agent	Consensus reached.	315
99-20	Recognition of Interest Income and Impairment on Certain Investments	Consensus reached; see also Issue 99-20. Additional guidance at D-44 and D-75, at SEC SAB 59, and in SAB 92.	131, 450
00-1	Investor Balance Sheet and Income Statement Display under the Equity Method for Investments in Certain Partnerships and Other Unincorporated Noncontrolled Ventures	Consensus reached.	450
00-2	Accounting for Web Site Development Costs	Consensus reached.	379
00-3	Application of AICPA Statement of Position 97-2, Software Revenue Recognition, to Arrangements That Include the Right to Use Software Stored on Another Entity's Hardware	Consensus reached.	1000
00-4	Majority Owner's Accounting for the Minority Interest in a Subsidiary and a Derivative	Partial consensus reached; see also Issue 00-6 and FAS 150.	552
00-5	Determining Whether a Nonmonetary Transaction Is an Exchange of Similar Productive Assets	Codified by Issue 01-2.	379
00-6	Accounting for Freestanding Derivative Financial Instruments Indexed to, and Potentially Settled in, the Stock of a Consolidated Subsidiary	See FAS 144.	451, 842
00-7	Application of EITF Issued 96-13, *Accounting for Derivative Financial Instruments Indexed to, and Potentially Settled in, a Company's Own Stock*, to Equity Derivative Transactions That Contain Provisions That Require Net Cash Settlement If Certain Events Occur	Codified in Issue 00-19.	
00-8	Accounting by a Grantee for an Equity Instrument to Be Received in Conjunction with Providing Goods or Services	Consensus reached.	316, 842
00-9	Classification of a Gain or Loss from a Hedge on Debt That Is Extinguished.	Consensus reached.	95
00-10	Accounting for Shipping and Handling Revenues and Costs	Consensus reached.	95
00-11	Meeting the Ownership Transfer Requirements of FASB Statement 13, *Accounting for Leases*, for Leases of Real Estate	Consensus reached.	681
00-12	Accounting by an Investor for Costs Incurred on Behalf of an Equity Method Investee	Consensus reached.	

(EITF cont.)

Number	Title	Status	GAAP Interp. & Applic. page reference
00-13	Determining When Equipment Is "Integral Equipment" Subject to FASB Statements 66, *Accounting for Sales of Real Estate*, and 98, *Accounting for Leases*	Consensus reached.	301, 681
00-14	Accounting for Certain Sales Incentives	Consensus reached.	322
00-15	Classification in the Statement of Cash Flows of the Income Tax Benefit Received by a Company upon Exercise of a Nonqualified Employee Stock Option	Consensus reached.	114, 729
00-16	Recognition and Measurement of Employer Payroll Taxes on Stock-Based Compensation	Consensus reached.	842
00-17	Measuring the Fair Value of Energy-Related Contracts in Applying Issue 98-10.	Superseded by Issue 02-3.	216
00-18	Accounting Recognition for Certain Transactions Involving Equity Instruments Granted to other than Employees	Partial consensus reached; further discussion planned.	842, 845
00-19	Accounting for Derivative Financial Instruments Indexed to, and Potentially Settled in, a Company's Own Stock	Consensus reached. Consensus later revised by Issue 03-7.	843, 881
00-20	Accounting for Costs Incurred to Acquire or Originate Information for Database Content and Other Collections of Information	Agreed to discontinue further discussion.	
00-21	Accounting for Revenue Arrangements with Multiple Deliverables	No further discussion planned.	316
00-22	Accounting for "Points" and Certain Other Time-Based or Volume-Based Sales Incentive Offers, and Offers for Free Products or Services to Be Delivered in the Future	No further discussion planned.	322, 565
00-23	Issues Related to the Accounting for Stock Compensation under APB Opinion No. 25 and FASB Interpretation No. 44	Consensus reached.	573, 799, 801, 802, 844
00-24	Revenue Recognition: Sales Arrangements That Include Specified-Price Trade-In Rights	Partially nullified by FIN 45. No further discussion planned.	
00-25	Vendor Income Statement Characterization of Consideration from a Vendor to a Retailer	Codified in Issue 01-9.	322
00-26	Recognition by a Seller of Losses on Firmly Committed Executory Contracts	Agreed to discontinue discussion.	
00-27	Application of Issue No. 98-5 to Certain Convertible Securities	Consensus reached; further discussion planned.	597, 602, 617
01-1	Accounting for a Convertible Instrument Granted or Issued to a Nonemployee for Goods or Services or a Combination of Goods or Services and Cash	Consensus reached.	619
01-2	Interpretations of APB Opinion No. 29	Partial consensus reached, no further discussion planned.	344, 346, 379
01-3	Accounting in a Purchase Business Combination for Deferred Revenue of an Acquiree	Agreed to discontinue further discussion.	552

(EITF cont.)

Number	Title	Status	GAAP Interp. & Applic. page reference
01-4	Accounting for Sales of Fractional Interests in Equipment	Agreed to discontinue further discussion.	
01-5	Application of FASB Statement No. 52 to an Investment Being Evaluated for Impairment That Will Be Disposed Of	Consensus reached.	953
01-6	The Meaning of "Indexed to a Company's Own Stock"	Consensus reached.	
01-7	Creditor's Accounting for a Modification or Exchange of Debt Instruments	Consensus reached.	153
01-8	Determining Whether an Arrangement Is a Lease	Consensus reached.	681
01-9	Accounting for Consideration Given by a Vendor to a Customer (Including a Reseller of the Vendor's Products)	Consensus reached.	322
01-10	Accounting for the Impact of the Terrorist Attacks of September 11, 2001	Consensus reached; guidance from FAS 144.	79, 96
01-11	Application of ETIF Issue No. 00-19 to a Contemporaneous Forward Purchase Contract and Written Put Option	Resolved by FAS 150.	
01-12	The Impact of the Requirements of FASB Statement No. 133 on Residual Value Guarantees in Connection with a Lease	Consensus reached.	
01-13	Income Statement Display of Business Interruption Insurance Recoveries	Consensus reached.	96
01-14	Income Statement Characterization of Reimbursements Received for "Out-of-Pocket" Expenses Incurred	Consensus reached; guidance from Issue 99-19.	96, 276
02-1	Balance Sheet Classification of Assets Received in Exchange for Equity Instruments	Consensus reached.	59
02-2	When Separate Contracts That Meet the Definition of Financial Instruments Should Be Combined for Accounting Purposes	No consensus reached; no further discussion planned.	216
02-3	Accounting for Contracts Involved in Energy Trading and Risk Management Activities	Partial consensus reached.	217
02-4	Determining Whether a Debtor's Modification or Exchange of Debt Instruments Is within the Scope of FASB Statement No. 15	Consensus reached.	589, 619
02-5	Definition of "Common Control" in Relation to FASB Statement No. 141	No consensus reached; no further discussion planned.	553
02-6	Classification in the Statement of Cash Flows of Payment Made to Settle an Asset Retirement Obligation within the Scope of FASB Statement No. 143	Consensus reached.	114
02-7	Unit of Accounting for Testing Impairment of Indefinite-Lived Intangible Assets	Consensus reached.	381
02-8	Accounting for Options Granted to Employees in Unrestricted, Publicly Traded Shares of an Unrelated Entity	Consensus reached.	

(EITF cont.)

Number	Title	Status	GAAP Interp. & Applic. page reference
02-9	Accounting for Changes That Result in a Transferor Regaining Control of Financial Assets Sold	Consensus ratified; no further discussion planned.	153
02-10	Determining Whether a Debtor is Legally Released as Primary Obligor When the Debtor Guarantees the Obligation of the Entity Undertaking Related Payments	Not asked to reach a consensus; further discussion discontinued.	
02-11	Accounting for Reverse Spinoffs	Consensus reached.	553
02-12	Permitted Activities of a Qualifying Special-Purpose Entity in Issuing Beneficial Interests under FASB No. 140	Further discussion discontinued.	
02-13	Deferred Income Tax Considerations in Applying the Goodwill Impairment Test in FASB Statement No. 142	Consensus reached.	383
02-14	Whether the Equity Method of Accounting Applies When an Investor Does Not Have an Investment in Voting Stock of an Investee but Exercises Significant Influence through Other Means	No consensus; further discussion is expected.	451
02-15	Determining Whether Certain Conversions of Convertible Debt to Equity Securities are within the Scope of FASB Statement No. 84	Consensus reached.	619
02-16	Accounting by a Customer (Including a Reseller) for Certain Consideration Received from a Vendor	Consensus reached.	97, 324
02-17	Recognition of Customer Relationship Intangible Assets Acquired in a Business Combination	Consensus reached.	383, 553
02-18	Accounting for Subsequent Investments in an Investee after Suspension of Equity Method Less Recognition	Consensus ratified.	452
03-01	The Meaning of Other Than Temporary Impairment and Its Application to Certain Investments	Further discussion is expected at a future meeting.	217, 452
03-02	Accounting for the Transfer to the Japanese Government of the Substitutional Portion of Employee Pension Fund Liabilities	Consensus reached.	773
03-03	Applicability of Topic No. D-79 to Claims-Made Insurance Policies	Codified in Issue 03-8.	574
03-04	Accounting for "Cash Balance" Pension Plans	Consensus reached.	774
03-05	Applicability of AICPA Statement of Position 97-2 to Non-Software Deliverables in an Arrangement Containing More-Than-Incidental Software	Consensus reached.	1000
03-06	Participating Securities and the Two-Class Method under FASB Statement No. 128	No consensus reached; further discussion planned.	881
03-07	Accounting for the Settlement of the Equity-Settled Portion of a Convertible Debt Instrument That Permits or Requires the Conversion Spread to Be Settled in Stock (Instrument C of Issue 90-19)	Consensus reached on some Issues; revisions made to prior consensuses on Issues 1 and 2 of Issue 00-19.	620

(EITF cont.)

Number	Title	Status	GAAP Interp. & Applic. page reference
03-08	Accounting for Claims-Made Insurance and Retroactive Insurance Contracts by the Insured Entity	Consensus reached.	574
03-09	Interaction of Paragraphs 11 and 12 of FASB Statement No. 142 Regarding Determination of the Useful Life and Amortization of an Intangible Asset	Further discussion expected.	
03-10	Application of Issue No. 02-16 by Resellers to Sales Incentives Offered to Consumers by Manufacturers	Consensus reached.	98, 325
03-11	Reporting Realized Gains and Losses on Derivative Instruments That Are Subject to FASB Statement No. 133 and Not "Held for Trading Purposes" as Defined in EITF Issue No. 02-3	Consensus reached.	218
03-12	Impact of FASB Interpretation No. 45 on Issue No. 95-1	Consensus reached.	574, 682
03-13	Applying the Conditions in Paragraph 42 of FASB Statement No. 144 in Determining Whether to Report Discontinued Operations	Tentative conclusion reached; further discussion expected.	
03-14	Participants' Accounting for Emissions Allowances under a "Cap and Trade" Program	Decision made to remove this Issue from agenda.	
03-15	Interpretation of Constraining Conditions of a Transferee in a CBO Structure	Placed on hold pending further developments in QSPE deliberations.	
03-16	Accounting for Investments in Limited Liability Companies	Tentative conclusion reached; further discussion expected.	452
03-17	Subsequent Accounting for Executory Contracts That Have Been Recognized on an Entity's Balance Sheet	Further discussion expected.	
04-01	Accounting for Preexisting Contractual Relationships between the Parties to a Purchase Business Combination	Further discussion expected.	
04-02	Whether Mineral Rights Are Tangible or Intangible Assets and Related Issues	Consensus reached on Issue 1; Issue 2 dropped.	384
04-03	Mining Assets—Impairment and Business Combinations	Consensus reached on all Issues.	384
04-04	Allocation of Goodwill to Reporting Units for a Mining Enterprise	Discussion discontinued.	

EITF DISCUSSION OF TECHNICAL MATTERS

Listed below are EITF documents that contain discussion by the Emerging Issues Task Force of technical matters that have long-term relevance and do not relate specifically to a numbered EITF Issue. The more important of these are briefly annotated.

Number	Title
D-1	Implications and Implementation of an EITF Consensus This established the status in the GAAP hierarchy of EITF consensuses, how changes to conform thereto should be accounted for, and related matters.

Number	Title
D-2	Applicability of FASB Statement 65 to Savings and Loan Associations
D-4	Argentine Government Guarantee of US Dollar-Denominated Loans to the Argentine Private Sector
D-8	Accruing Bad-Debt Expense at Inception of a Lease This establishes that the former practice of accruing a bad debt provision at least inception, which would then be offset by unearned income consistent with other initial direct costs, is inappropriate.
D-10	Required Use of Interest Method in Recognizing Interest Income This clarified that other interest recognition methods (Rule of 78s, etc.) would not be acceptable alternatives to the (effective rate) interest method.
D-11	Impact of Stock Market Decline This addressed the need for disclosure of post-balance-sheet date events in the specific context of the sharp stock market decline which occurred in late 1987.
D-12	Foreign Currency Translation—Selection of Exchange Rate When Trading Is Temporarily Suspended
D-18	Accounting for Compensation Expense If Stock Appreciation Rights Are Canceled Establishes that compensation cost accrued pursuant to FASB Interpretation 28 should not later be reversed if rights were canceled as a result of a proposed SEC rule change.
D-21	Phase-in Plans When Two Plants Are Completed at Different Times but Share Common Facilities
D-23	Subjective Acceleration Clauses and Debt Classification This clarified the distinctions between FAS 6, dealing with classification of short-term debt as noncurrent under defined circumstances, and FTB 79-3, which addresses the potential need to classify long-term debt having a subjective acceleration clause as current.
D-24	Sale-Leaseback Transactions with Continuing Involvement This responded to several specific circumstances illustrating application of the FAS 98 requirement that precludes sale-leaseback accounting (with attendant gain or loss recognition) when there is any continuing involvement by the seller other than that of a normal lessee.
D-27	Accounting for the Transfer of Excess Pension Assets to a Retiree Health Care Benefits Account This states that the transfer of excess pension assets, whether or not made pursuant to the Revenue Reconciliation (Tax) Act of 1990, should be recognized as a negative contribution to the pension fund and a positive contribution to the health care plan; no gain or loss arises from this transaction.
D-30	Adjustment Due to Effect of a Change in Tax Laws or Rates This simply reinforced the FAS 109 requirement that the effect of changes in laws or rates is to be recognized when enacted.
D-31	Temporary Differences Related to LIFO Inventory and Tax-to-Tax Differences This clarified that differences between tax and book LIFO inventory valuations must be tax effected. It also reinforced the rule that only book tax differences are temporary differences under FAS 109; thus differences between "outside basis" and "inside basis" would not give rise to deferred taxes to be recognized in the financial statements.
D-32	Intraperiod Tax Allocation of the Tax Effect of Pretax Income from Continuing Operations This item states that while the tax effect of pretax income from continuing operations would not be affected by other items (e.g., extraordinary items) on the income statement, the tax effect of a loss from continuing operations would consider the tax effects of other items, per paragraph 140 of FAS 109.
D-33	Timing of Recognition of Tax Benefits for Prereorganization Temporary Differences and Carryforwards This expands the requirements under FAS 109, relevant to pre- and postacquisition carryforwards, to also apply to pre- and postreorganization carryforwards.
D-34	Accounting for Reinsurance: Questions and Answers about FASB Statement 113

Number	Title
D-35	FASB Staff Views on Issue 93-6, *Accounting for Multiple-Year Retrospectively-Rated Contracts by Ceding and Assuming Enterprises*
D-36	Selection of Discount Rates Used for Measuring Defined Benefit Pension Obligations and Obligations of Postretirement Benefit Plans other than Pensions This sets forth the SEC's position that discount rates be reflective of current rates as of the balance sheet date.
D-39	Questions Related to the Implementation of FASB Statement 115 This responded to a number of specific factual situations later subsumed by subsequent professional pronouncements.
D-42	The Effect on the Calculation of Earnings Per Share for the Redemption or Induced Conversion of Preferred Stock This sets forth the SEC staff position that any excess of fair value of consideration transferred over the carrying value of the preferred stock would be accounted for similar to dividends paid to the preferred stockholders for purposes of computing EPS, including when there is a negative excess amount.
D-43	Assurance That a Right of Setoff Is Enforceable in a Bankruptcy under FASB Interpretation 39 This clarifies the "enforceable at law" as used to define a right of setoff encompasses that the right would be upheld in bankruptcy.
D-44	Recognition of Other-Than-Temporary Impairment upon the Planned Sale of a Security Whose Cost Exceeds Fair Value When there is no expectation of price recovery before a planned sale after the balance sheet date, the decline in fair value should be deemed other than temporary for purposes of loss recognition.
D-46	Accounting for Limited Partnership Investments The SEC's position is that the equity method should be used for investments in limited partnerships unless "minor," meaning under about a 3 to 5% interest.
D-47	Accounting for the Refund of Bank Insurance Fund and Savings Association Insurance Fund Premiums
D-49	Classifying Net Appreciation on Investments of a Donor-Restricted Endowment Fund
D-50	Classification of Gains and Losses from the Termination of an Interest Rate Swap Designated to Commercial Paper
D-51	The Applicability of FASB Statement 115 to Desecuritizations of Financial Assets The matter of descuritizations was not addressed by either FAS 115 or 125, but this topic states that, analogizing from the guidance in FAS 125 on securitizations, no gain or loss would be recognized if a transferor of a securitized pool of assets receives only the underlying loans in exchange. Also, if the assets received are held to maturity, the mere fact of the descuritization transaction would not contradict the intent to hold to maturity.
D-53	Computation of Earnings Per Share for a Period That Includes a Redemption on an Induced Conversion of a Portion of a Class of Preferred Stock This is a further consideration of the matter addressed at D-42; this topic states that any excess in the context of a partial redemption would be attributed fully to the shares redeemed.
D-54	Accounting by the Purchaser for a Seller's Guarantee of the Adequacy of Liabilities for Losses and Loss Adjustment Expenses of an Insurance Enterprise Acquired in a Purchase Business Combination
D-55	Determining a Highly Inflationary Economy under FASB Statement 52
D-56	Accounting for a Change in Functional Currency and Deferred Taxes When an Economy Becomes Highly Inflationary
D-57	Accounting Issues Relating to the Deposit Insurance Funds Act of 1996

Number	Title
D-61	Classification by the Issuer of Redeemable Instruments That Are Subject to Remarketing Agreements Long-term debt which the holder has the ability to put back to the issuer, even if the issuer has a "best efforts" remarketing agreement which likely would result in any redeemed debt being immediately resold, must be reported by the issuer as a current obligation.
D-62	Computation of Diluted Earnings Per Share for an Entity with a Year-to-Date Loss from Continuing Operations Including One or More Quarters with Income from Continuing Operations This addresses the possible conflict between the "no antidilution" provision of FAS 128 and other provisions of that statement directing how year-to-date EPS is to be computed by the treasury stock method when cumulative results are negative but some of the interim periods had been profitable. The conclusion is that the year-to-date results (profit or loss) will determine whether dilutive securities will be included or excluded, which means that dilutive securities included in income of the interim periods would be excluded from year-to-date diluted EPS if there is a loss for the year-to-date. Weighted-average shares outstanding for the year-to-date would be based not on the average of shares deemed outstanding in each of the interim period to date (some of which may have been profitable, others having losses, and thus some including dilutive securities which were ignored in the others), but rather based on the net results for the year-to-date.
D-63	Call Options "Embedded" in Beneficial Interests Issued by a Qualifying Special-Purpose Entity This expressed the SEC's position that when the transferor of financial assets is indirectly given, via call options embedded in the beneficial interests issued by the SPE, a right to reacquire the assets from the SPE transferee, the transaction must be accounted for as a secured borrowing, not a sale. The same result would be obtained if the call option were attached to the transferred assets rather than the beneficial interests.
D-65	Maintaining Collateral in Repurchase Agreements and Similar Transactions under FASB Statement 125 This holds that to demonstrate that a transfer involves an agreement which obligates and entitles the transferor to repurchase or redeem assets before maturity, the transferor must be able to execute the repurchase or redemption; at all times, the transferor must have cash or collateral sufficient to purchase replacement assets from others, if necessary.
D-66	Effect of a Special-Purpose Entity's Powers to Sell, Exchange, Repledge, or Distribute Transferred Financial Assets under FASB Statement 125 This discusses the impact of SPE status of limited powers to sell, pledge, or exchange transferred financial assets. It holds that limited powers to sell, pledge, or exchange do not prevent the SPE from being qualifying, if certain other conditions are met, as described in FAS 125. This item also explores the meaning of "proceeds" in the context of the SPE's permitted activity of collecting cash proceeds and reinvesting them. A number of illustrative examples are provided.
D-67	Isolation of Assets Transferred by Financial Institutions under FASB Statement 125
D-68	Accounting by an Equity Method Investor for Investee Losses When the Investor Has Loans to and Investments in Other Securities of an Investee This topic relates to the recognition of losses of an investee by the equity method investor in excess of the carrying value of the investment, when the investor also holds other debt or equity issued by the investee. The conclusion, based on a reading of APB 18, is that losses should be recognized up to the total carrying value of voting stock plus all other advances or investments in the investee entity.

Number	Title
D-69	Gain Recognition on Transfers of Financial Assets under FASB Statement 125 This topic expressed the SEC's concern that gain recognition in situations in which financial assets are sold or securitized with some assets being retained or liabilities incurred was being computed on a discretionary basis; it stresses that the provisions of FAS 125 are not elective in nature. The fair value allocation methodology to be used is set forth in FAS 125, and any assumptions made are to be consistently applied over time and adequately disclosed.
D-70	Questions Related to the Implementation of FASB Statement 131 This addresses certain questions arising from the requirement to disclose results of operations on a segment basis. It underscores the requirement that disclosures be consistent with how the chief operating decision maker of the reporting entity evaluates the performance of the segments. It also clarifies that the threshold for segment disclosure, by evaluating the contribution of the segment versus that of the total enterprise, is not altered by the fact that segment results may internally be evaluated by inconsistent criteria by management.
D-71	Accounting Issues Relating to the Introduction of the European Economic and Monetary Union (EMU) This holds that costs incurred to adapt recordkeeping systems to the new euro currency are to be expensed as incurred. This conclusion was reached by analogizing from the position taken with regard to Y2K software repairs and upgrades in EITF 96-14. Also, this topic reports the SEC position that comparative financial reports including periods before the euro was adopted may incorporate restatements of prior periods' results using the euro exchange rates as of January 1, 1999, with full disclosure being made. Finally, it reports the FASB's belief that cumulative translation adjustments (pertaining to consolidated subsidiaries or equity investees) would not be affected by the euro adoption.
D-72	Effect of Contracts That May Be Settled in Stock or Cash on the Computation of Diluted Earnings Per Share This addresses an inconsistency between FAS 128 (which gives credence to past experience in deciding whether contracts that may be settled in cash or common stock should be deemed potential common stock for diluted EPS computation purposes) and EITF 96-13 (which gives no weight to past experience regarding treatment of freestanding contracts which would be optionally settled in the entity's stock). It concludes that adjustments similar to those specified by FAS 128 should be made, when warranted by past experience, for those set forth in EITF 96-13 as well. However, since this matter is to be further deliberated, this guidance is said to be nonauthoritative.
D-73	Reclassification and Subsequent Sales of Securities in Connection with the Adoption of FASB Statement 133 Pertaining to the FAS 133 transition provision that permits transfers from held-to-maturity to other classifications without "tainting" other held-to-maturity securities, this states that if financial assets transferred are later sold in the same reporting quarter, the transfer must be to the trading category. Any gain or loss as of the date of the reclassification must be taken into income as part of the cumulative effect of adopting FAS 133, and not included as realized gain or loss from trading for the quarter.
D-74	Issues Concerning the Scope of the AICPA Guide on Investment Companies
D-76	Accounting by Advisors for Offering Costs Paid on Behalf of Funds When the Advisor Does Not Receive Both 12b-1 Fees and Contingent Deferred Sales Charges When advisors of closed-end funds choose to bear offering costs on behalf of the fund and are not reimbursed through both 12b-1 fees and CDSC fees, the benefits expected from the expenditures paid by an advisor in connection with the distribution of shares do not meet the definition of an asset of the advisor as provided in CON 6. Accordingly, such offering costs paid by the investment advisor should be expensed as incurred.

Number	Title
D-77	Accounting for Legal Costs Expected to Be Incurred in Connection with a Loss Contingency While practice in this area seems to be mixed, the SEC expects a registrant's accounting policy to be applied consistently and APB 22 requires disclosure of material accounting policies and the methods of applying those policies.
D-78	Accounting for Supervisory Goodwill Litigation Awards or Settlements "Supervisory goodwill" is not a form of **financial assistance** contemplated by FAS 72. If, as an outcome of litigation resulting from the savings and loan crisis of the late 1980s/early 1990s, thrifts obtain settlements from the government, the settlement meets the definition of a gain as discussed in CON 6. Accordingly, the entire amount of the settlement should be recognized as a gain in the statement of operations.
D-79	Accounting for Retroactive Insurance Contracts Purchased by Entities other than Insurance Enterprises This addresses how a noninsurance entity should account for a purchased retroactive insurance policy and whether the transaction results in gain recognition. Notwithstanding that FAS 113 applies only to insurance enterprises, it was concluded that purchased retroactive insurance contracts that indemnify the insured should be accounted for in a manner similar to the manner in which reinsurance contracts are accounted for under Statement 113.
D-80	Application of FASB Statements No. 5 and No. 114 to a Loan Portfolio This addresses the implications of positions set forth in a FASB *Viewpoints* article entitled, "Application of FASB Statements 5 and 114 to a Loan Portfolio." The SEC stated that if a registrant were to change its accounting to conform to the views expressed in that article, it should report and disclose the adjustment like a cumulative effect of a change in accounting principles as set forth in APB 20.
D-82	Effect of Preferred Stock Dividends Payable in Common Shares on Computation of Income Available to Common Stockholders This addresses preferred stock dividends to be paid in the payor's common shares. These are to be deducted from net income (added to net loss) in computing income available for common shareholders, in the same manner as are cash dividends on preferred stock.
D-83	Accounting for Payroll Taxes Associated with Stock Option Exercises This states the staff position, with regard to the tax implications of exercises of employee stock options, that payroll taxes, even though directly related to the appreciation on stock options, are operating expenses and should be reflected as such in the statement of operations.
D-84	Accounting for Subsequent Investments in an Investee After Suspension of Equity Method Loss Recognition When an Investor Increases Its Ownership Interest from Significant Influence to Control through a Market Purchase of Voting Securities The SEC staff addressed a fact pattern in which a subsequent investment was made in an equity method investee after there had been a suspension of equity method loss recognition in accordance with APB 18. In such a circumstance, the excess over fair value of underlying net assets is to be allocated to all identifiable tangible and intangible assets of the investee in accordance with the FAS 141 (which superseded APB 16, but did not change the purchase method accounting to be applied).
D-85	Application of Certain Transition Provisions in SEC Staff Accounting Bulletin No. 101 This provides interpretive guidance regarding the need for retroactive application of certain elements of SAB 101 (dealing with revenue recognition, and more particularly with regard to two issues: The factors to be considered in determining whether revenue should be presented on a gross or net basis in an income statement; and retailers' presentation of revenue from sales of leased or licensed departments.) Retroactive application was not required, but in the alternative a cumulative effect presentation under the provisions of APB 20 was necessary. (Subsequently, a deferred implementation date was granted for the provisions of SAB 101.)

Number	Title
D-86	Issuance of Financial Statements This addresses the matter of when financial statements are considered to be "issued," which is important in the context of responsibility for false or misleading information filed with the SEC. According to SEC staff, financial statements are "issued" as of the date they are distributed for general use and reliance in a form and format that complies with generally accepted accounting principles (GAAP) and, in the case of annual financial statements, that contain an audit report that indicates that the auditors have complied with generally accepted auditing standards (GAAS) in completing their audit. Issuance of financial statements then would generally be the earlier of when the annual or quarterly financial statements are widely distributed to all shareholders and other financial statement users or filed with the SEC. The issuance of an earnings release does not constitute issuance of financial statements because the earnings release would not be in a form and format that complies with GAAP and GAAS.
D-87	Determination of the Measurement Date for Consideration Given by the Acquirer in a Business Combination When That Consideration Is Securities other than Those Issued by the Acquirer Regarding the date that should be used to measure the consideration given by the acquirer to shareholders of an acquired company in a purchase business combination when that consideration is securities other than those issued by the acquirer, these should be measured on the date the business combination is consummated. Measurement at the consummation date also avoids issues associated with fixing the value of investment securities when FAS 115 or APB 18 requires the carrying value of the investment to be adjusted for changes in fair value or operating results of the investee, respectively.
D-88	Planned Major Maintenance Activities Pending the outcome of the AcSEC project dealing with capitalization of property costs, this provides guidance for the disclosure of a reporting entity's policy regarding repair and maintenance costs incurred in connection with planned major maintenance activities. It also requires that any liability balance that has been reported otherwise, such as a component of accumulated depreciation, be reclassified to the liability section of the balance sheet. It also effectively encouraged entities to cease use of the "accrue-in-advance" method of anticipating major repair expenditures, since these probably fail to meet the definition of liabilities under GAAP.
D-89	Accounting for Costs of Future Medicare Compliance Audits Commitments by health care providers for the future performance of compliance audits, made in settlement agreements arising from Medicare fraud allegations, do not create liabilities under the definition set forth in FASB Concepts Statement 6. Accordingly, accrual of the present value of these future costs at the time of such agreements would not be appropriate under GAAP.
D-90	Grantor Balance Sheet Presentation of Unvested, Forfeitable Equity Instruments Granted to a Nonemployee When forfeitable, unvested equity instruments are issued to a nonemployee (e.g., vendor), notwithstanding the existence of substantial penalties for nonperformance, the shares should not be considered to have been issued until performance later occurs. Measurement date is not to be recognized, therefore, at the date of issuance.
D-91	Application of APB Opinion No. 25 and FASB Interpretation No. 44 to an Indirect Repricing of a Stock Option This concerns a FASB response to a very specific set of assumed facts whereby the accounting for previously issued fixed options must be changed to variable, due to the issuance of new options clearly linked to the now out-of-the-money earlier awards. In general, whether variable accounting under APB 25 and FIN 44 becomes required is highly dependent upon specific facts and circumstances.

Number	Title
D-93	Accounting for the Rescission of the Exercise of Employee Stock Options For a given fact-specific scenario in which exercised options are "rescinded" during the same tax year, variable accounting would be required for any replacement options granted, since it would be presumed that the new options contained the same rescission rights, the existence of which makes variable accounting mandatory. Depending on the circumstances, there might be expanded disclosures required as well. For purposes of EPS calculations, the weighted average number of shares outstanding must include shares issued under option arrangements that were subsequently rescinded, until the effective date of such rescission.
D-95	Effect of Participating Convertible Securities on the Computation of Basic Earnings Per Share Convertible securities that are participating must be considered in the computation of basic EPS under FAS 128, if the effect is dilutive, with the computation performed using either the "if converted" or "two class" method. The dilutive effect cannot be less than would result from application of the "two class" method if the same participating securities were not convertible into common stock.
D-96	Accounting for Management Fees Based on a Formula Certain performance fees are earned if defined benchmarks are exceeded (e.g., S&P 500 index for investment managers) which are generally measured on an annual basis, thus raising a concern over interim reporting. The SEC prefers that revenues not be accrued on an interim basis when later changes could result in this revenue being reduced or eliminated for the year as a whole. However, it is acceptable to accrue revenue on an interim basis to the extent that the formula provides for compensation in the event of termination on those dates. The accounting policy disclosures must set forth the manner in which revenues are being recognized. In no case can revenues be recognized based upon a projection of future performance; under SAB 101 the fee revenue must be fixed or determinable prior to recognition for financial reporting purposes.
D-97	Push-Down Accounting Push-down (or "new basis") accounting is required by the SEC if an entity becomes substantially wholly owned by another entity as a result of a single or a related series of transactions whereby at least 95% of the common stock is acquired. Such accounting is permitted, not required, if from 80% to 95% of the shares are acquired. Push-down accounting is prohibited if less than 80% of the shares are obtained in the transaction(s). This would be true even if the wholly owned status was intended to be temporary (e.g., when minority shares are to be sold to new investors). In making a determination of whether an entity has become "substantially wholly owned," it is appropriate to aggregate holdings of investors which "mutually promoted" the acquisition and which "collaborate" on control of the investee. To overcome the rebuttable presumption that investors are acting in concert in such situations, a number of criteria (relating to independence, risk of ownership, absence of subsequent collaboration, etc.) are set forth.
D-98	Classification and Measurement of Redeemable Securities Per SEC rules, equity that is not "permanent" (i.e., that can be redeemed by the holder's demand or by conditions not under the issuer's control) must be displayed outside of the equity section of the balance sheet. (There are no similar requirements under general GAAP, however.) The potential effects of normal liquidation events, however, do not necessitate such presentation. Determining whether securities are subject to redemption at the holder's option is fact-specific and my not be obvious in some instances. If securities must be redeemed if, for example, a registration statement is not filed by a defined date, or if there is noncompliance with debt covenants, inclusion as equity would be prohibited. Similarly, if the preferred stock is subject to a change-in-control provision and the preferred holders control a majority of votes on the board of directors, the preferred stock would be excludable from equity. Where redemption values vary over time, the stock should be presented at its redemption amount at the balance sheet date, which may or may not involve accretion over time (by the interest method, generally), depending on its terms.

Number	Title
D-99	Questions and Answers Related to Servicing Activities in a Qualifying Special-Purpose Entity under FASB Statement No. 140 A number of specific issues pertaining to the definition of a "qualified special-purpose entity" under FAS 140 are addressed, principally relating to the actions that may be taken by the SPE (foreclosing on loans, etc.) that would not jeopardize its being deemed a qualified SPE for purposes of sale accounting under the standard.
D-100	Clarification of Paragraph 61(b) of FASB Statement No. 141 and Paragraph 49(b) of FASB Statement No. 142 Under FAS 141, intangible assets other than goodwill resulting from business combinations are to be separately accounted for, but under prior GAAP (APB 17) it was not uncommon for intangibles thus obtained to be aggregated as goodwill, since the accounting was identical. The transition provisions for FAS 142 permit disaggregating intangibles, but only to the extent that separate accounting records (even if aggregated for financial reporting purposes) had been maintained. The amount of purchase cost allocated to goodwill and other intangible assets cannot be redetermined as part of this process, however. A failure to properly separate formerly aggregated intangibles would potentially distort subsequent determinations of goodwill impairment, since under FAS 141 this determination is based on the value of goodwill after fully assigning purchase cost to all intangibles, including those not formally recognized.
D-101	Clarification of Reporting Unit Guidance in Paragraph 30 of FASB Statement No. 142 Whether a component of an operating segment is a reporting unit for purposes of applying FAS 142, for purposes of applying the requirement to determine goodwill impairment, depends on whether the component functions as a business, whether discrete financial information is available about that component, whether it is accountable to and in regular contact with segment managers, and whether it is qualitatively distinct from other components of the operating segment. It is possible that components aggregated for purposes of reporting under FAS 131 could be separate for purposes of applying FAS 142.
D-102	Documentation of the Method Used to Measure Hedge Ineffectiveness under FASB Statement No. 133 This underscores the importance of documenting, at inception, the methodology of assessing hedge ineffectiveness, even as a variety of methods are acceptable for use. Absent proper documentation, hedge accounting under FAS 133 cannot be used.
D-104	Clarification of Transition Guidance in Paragraph 51 of FASB Statement No. 144 FAS 144 provides that prior accounting (FAS 121 or APB 30) may be continued for up to one year for segments being treated as assets subject to disposal as of the date of implementation of the new standard. This clarifies that the one-year limitation would not apply to segments that are operating in a "runoff" mode (which are not accepting new business, etc.), even if those remaining activities will not be completed by the end of that period.
D-106	Clarification of Q&A No. 37 of FASB Special Report, *A Guide to Implementation of Statement 87 on Employers' Accounting for Pensions* When accounting for pensions, a minimum liability must be determined as of the measurement date, which must not be more than three months prior to the balance sheet date. Appendix D-106 addresses and revises the Q&A No. 37 guidance for determining the additional minimum liability for entities with a December 31 financial report date that uses a September 30 valuation date for pension plan assets and liabilities.
D-107	Lessor Consideration of Third-Party Residual Value Guarantees This provides the SEC's views on FASB Statement No. 13, *Accounting for Leases*. Certain lease arrangements, especially within the equipment leasing industry, may involve a guarantee of the expected residual value of leased property by an unrelated party. Therefore, the SEC considered whether the minimum lease payments at inception should include the residual value guarantees for a portfolio of leased assets. Since the guaranteed residual value for a particular individual leased asset would not be known to the lessor who has a portfolio of leased assets, the SEC staff believes the residual values should not be included within the minimum lease payments.

AICPA STATEMENTS OF POSITION (1974-2003)

Number	Title	GAAP Interp. & Applic. page reference
75-2	Accounting Practices of Real Estate Investment Trusts	310
76-3	Accounting Practices for Certain Employees' Stock Ownership Plans	825
78-9	Accounting for Investments in Real Estate Ventures	310
81-1	Accounting for Performance of Construction-Type and Certain Production-Type Contracts	91, 257, 258, 259, 260, 261, 262, 267, 269, 270, 995, 996
82-1	Accounting and Reporting for Personal Financial Statements	956, 958
85-3	Accounting by Agricultural Producers and Agricultural Cooperatives	
88-1	Accounting for Developmental and Preoperating Costs, Purchases and Exchanges of Takeoff and Landing Slots, and Airframe Modifications	385
90-3	Definition of the Term *Substantially the Same* for Holders of Debt Instruments, as Used in Certain Audit Guides and a Statement of Position	980
90-7	Financial Reporting by Entities in Reorganization under the Bankruptcy Code	834, 835
92-1	Accounting for Real Estate Syndication Income	310
92-3	Accounting for Foreclosed Assets	385
92-5	Accounting for Foreign Property and Liability Reinsurance	1020, 1025
92-6	Accounting and Reporting by Health and Welfare Benefit Plans	1001, 1008
93-1	Financial Accounting and Reporting for High-Yield Debt Securities by Investment Companies	1030
93-2	Determination, Disclosure, and Financial Statement Presentation of Income, Capital Gain, and Return of Capital Distributions by Investment Companies	1030
93-3	Rescission of Accounting Principles Board Statements	
93-4	Foreign Currency Accounting and Financial Statement Presentation for Investment Companies	1031
93-6	Employers' Accounting for Employee Stock Ownership Plans	710, 780, 825, 826, 830, 881
93-7	Reporting on Advertising Costs	386, 891, 999
94-3	Reporting of Related Entities by Not-for-Profit Organizations	548, 1050, 1060
94-4	Reporting of Investment Contracts Held by Health and Welfare Benefit Plans and Defined Contribution Pension Plans	1002, 1009
94-5	Disclosures of Certain Matters in the Financial Statements of Insurance Enterprises	1026
94-6	Disclosure of Certain Significant Risks and Uncertainties	54, 55, 56, 96, 258, 567
95-1	Accounting for Certain Insurance Activities of Mutual Life Insurance Enterprises	1021, 1026
95-2	Financial Reporting by Nonpublic Investment Partnerships	1031
95-3	Accounting for Certain Distribution Costs of Investment Companies	1031
96-1	Environmental Remediation Liabilities	96, 335, 376, 576
97-1	Accounting by Participating Mortgage Loan Borrowers	620

(SOP cont.)

(SOP cont.)

Number	Title	GAAP Interp. & Applic. page reference
03-5	Financial Highlights of Separate Accounts—An Amendment to the Audit and Accounting Guide *Audits of Investment Companies*	

Audit and Accounting Guides

Agricultural Producers and Cooperatives
Airlines
Analytical Procedures
Audit Sampling
Auditing Derivative Instruments, Hedging Activities, and Investments in Securities
Auditing Revenue in Certain Industries
Brokers and Dealers in Securities
Casinos
Common Interest Realty Associations
Consideration of Internal Control in a Financial Statement Audit
Construction Contractors
Depository and Lending Institutions
Employee Benefit Plans
Entities with Oil and Gas Producing Activities
Federal Government Contractors
Health Care Organizations
Investment Companies
Life and Health Insurance Entities
Not-for-Profit Organizations
Personal Financial Statements
Property and Liability Insurance Companies
Prospective Financial Information
Real Estate Appraisal Information
Service Organizations: Applying SAS No. 70
State and Local Governmental Units

OTHER GAAP SOURCES

Issues Papers of the Accounting Standards Division

Issues Papers of the AICPA's Accounting Standards Division primarily identify financial accounting and reporting issues that the Division believed needed addressing by the Financial Accounting Standards Board. These pronouncements constitute generally accepted accounting principles but are not mandatory.

Title	Date Issued
Accounting for Changes in Estimates	12/15/78
Joint Venture Accounting	7/17/79
"Push Down" Accounting	10/30/79
Accounting in Consolidation for Issuances of a Subsidiary Stock	6/30/80
Certain Issues That Affect Accounting for Minority Interest in Consolidated Financial Statements	3/17/81
Depreciation of Income-Producing Real Estate	11/16/81
The Acceptability of "Simplified LIFO" for Financial Reporting Purposes	10/14/82
Accounting for Employee Capital Accumulation Plans	11/4/82
Computation of Premium Deficiencies in Insurance Enterprises	3/26/84
Identification and Discussion of Certain Financial Accounting and Reporting Issues Concerning LIFO Inventories	11/30/84
Accounting for Options	3/6/86

Title	*Date Issued*
The Use of Discounting in Financial Reporting for Monetary Items with Uncertain Terms other than Those Covered by Existing Authoritative Literature	9/9/87
Quasi Reorganizations	10/28/88

Practice Bulletins

1. Purpose and Scope of AcSEC Practice Bulletins and Procedures for Their Issuance

Title	*Date Issued*
ACRS Lives and GAAP	11/23/81
Accounting by Colleges and Universities for Compensated Absences	9/13/82
ADC Arrangements	2/10/86

No.	Title	Date
2.	Elimination of Profits Resulting from Intercompany Transfers of LIFO Inventories	11/87
4.	Accounting for Foreign Debt/Equity Swaps	5/88
5.	Income Recognition on Loans to Financially Troubled Countries	7/88
6.	Amortization of Discounts on Certain Acquired Loans	8/89
8.	Application of FASB Statement 97 to Insurance Enterprises	11/90
11.	Accounting for Preconfirmation Contingencies in Fresh Start Reporting	3/94
13.	Direct Response Advertising and Probable Future Benefits	12/94
14.	Accounting and Reporting by Limited Liability Companies and Limited Liability Partnerships	4/95
15.	Accounting by the Issuer of Surplus Notes	1/95

Web sites

See page 23.

1 RESEARCHING GAAP PROBLEMS

DEVELOPMENT OF GAAP

What Is GAAP?

> *The phrase "generally accepted accounting principles" is a technical accounting term that encompasses the conventions, rules, and procedures necessary to define accepted accounting practice at a particular time. It includes not only broad guidelines of general application, but also detailed practices and procedures. Those conventions, rules, and procedures provide a standard by which to measure financial presentations.* Auditing Standards Board (ASB), AU 411

Generally accepted accounting principles (GAAP) are concerned with the measurement of economic activity, the time when such measurements are made and recorded, the disclosures surrounding these activities, and the preparation and presentation of summarized economic information in the form of financial statements. GAAP develops when questions arise about how to best accomplish those activities—measurement, timing of recognition, disclosure, or presentation. In response to those questions, either GAAP is promulgated via official pronouncements of authoritative bodies empowered to create it, or it evolves over time when authoritative bodies fail to respond. Thus, GAAP is a reaction to and a product of the economic environment in which it is developed. As such, the development of accounting and financial reporting standards has somewhat lagged the progression of increasingly intricate economic structures and transactions.

There are two broad categories of accounting principles—recognition and disclosure. Recognition principles determine the timing and measurement of items that enter the accounting cycle and impact the financial statements. These are quantitative standards that require economic information to be reflected numerically.

Disclosure principles deal with factors that are not always numerical. Disclosures involve qualitative information that is an essential ingredient of a full set of financial statements. Their absence would make the financial statements created by recognition principles misleading by themselves. Disclosure principles complement recognition principles by explaining assumptions underlying the numerical information and giving other information on accounting policies, contingencies, uncertainties, etc., which are essential ingredients in the analytical process of accounting.

The Hierarchy of GAAP

The determination of which accounting principle is applicable under a particular set of conditions might be difficult or even impossible without a determination of the hierarchy of GAAP by an authoritative body. In AU 411 (SAS 69), the ASB identified the following as the sources of established generally accepted accounting principles:

A. Accounting principles promulgated by a body designated by the AICPA Council to establish such principles, pursuant to rule 203 [ET section 203.01] of the AICPA Code of Professional Conduct.
B. Pronouncements of bodies, composed of expert accountants, that deliberate accounting issues in public forums for the purpose of establishing accounting principles or describing existing accounting practices that are generally accepted, provided those pronouncements have been exposed for public comment and have been cleared by a body referred to in category A.
C. Pronouncements of bodies, organized by a body referred to in category A and composed of expert accountants, that deliberate accounting issues in public forums for the purpose of interpreting or establishing accounting principles or describing existing accounting practices that are generally accepted, or pronouncements referred to in category B that have been cleared by a body referred to in category A but have not been exposed for public comment.
D. Practices or pronouncements that are widely recognized as being generally accepted because they represent prevalent practice in a particular industry, or the knowledgeable application to specific circumstances of pronouncements that are generally accepted.

Compliance with accounting pronouncements included in category A is mandatory. An auditor should not express an unqualified opinion if the financial statements contain a material departure from category A pronouncements unless, due to unusual circumstances, adherence to the pronouncements would make the statements misleading. Rule 203 implies that application of officially established accounting principles almost always results in fair presentation in conformity with generally accepted accounting principles.

If an accounting treatment is not specified by a pronouncement covered by Rule 203, the accountant/auditor should progress through the hierarchy to categories B, C, or D and use the treatment specified by the source in the highest category. If an accounting pronouncement in category B, C, or D is relevant to the circumstances, an auditor must follow that pronouncement or be able to justify the conclusion that another treatment is generally accepted.

For financial statements of entities other than governmental entities[1]

a. Category A, officially established accounting principles, consists of Financial Accounting Standards Board (FASB) Statements of Financial Accounting Standards (denoted as FAS in this book) and Interpretations (denoted as FIN), Accounting Principles Board (APB) Opinions, and AICPA Accounting Research Bulletins (ARB).
b. Category B consists of FASB Technical Bulletins (FTB) and, if cleared by the FASB, AICPA Industry Audit and Accounting Guides and AICPA Statements of Position (SOP).
c. Category C consists of AICPA Accounting Standards Executive Committee (AcSEC) Practice Bulletins (PB) that have been cleared by the FASB and consensus positions of the FASB Emerging Issues Task Force (EITF).
d. Category D includes AICPA accounting interpretations (AIN), implementation guides (Qs and As) published by the FASB staff, FASB staff positions (FSP), and practices that are widely recognized and prevalent either generally or in the industry.

If unable to locate guidance using one of the above sources of established accounting principles, other accounting literature may be considered. These would include FASB Statements of Financial Accounting Concepts, AICPA Issues Papers, International Financial Reporting Standards of the International Accounting Standards Board and of its predecessor, the International Accounting Standards Committee, Governmental Accounting Standards Board (GASB) Statements, Interpretations and Technical Bulletins, Federal Accounting Standards Advisory Board (FASAB) Statements, Interpretations, and Technical Bulletins, pronouncements of other professional associations or regulatory agencies, Technical Information Service Inquiries and Replies included in AICPA Technical Practice Aids, and accounting textbooks, handbooks and articles. The use of those other sources depends upon their relevance to particular circumstances, the specificity of the guidance, and the general recognition of the author or issuing organization as an authority. This would mean that

---

[1] *The description of a governmental entity, which was agreed to in a joint meeting of the FASB and GASB Boards in 1996, states*

> *Public corporations and bodies corporate and politic are governmental organizations. Other organizations are governmental organizations if they have one or more of the following characteristics:*
>
> *a. Popular election of officers or appointment (or approval) of a controlling majority of the members of the organization's governing body by officials of one or more state or local governments;*
> *b. The potential for unilateral dissolution by a government with the net assets reverting to a government; or*
> *c. The power to enact and enforce a tax levy.*
>
> *Furthermore, organizations are presumed to be governmental if they have the ability to issue directly (rather than through a state or municipal authority) debt that pays interest exempt from federal taxation. However, organizations possessing only that ability (to issue tax-exempt debt) and none of the other governmental characteristics may rebut the presumption that they are governmental if their determination is supported by compelling relevant evidence.*

This publication does not describe GAAP for governmental entities. Readers who are interested in learning more should consult the publication ***Wiley GAAP for Governments****.*

FASB publications in this category would be more influential in establishing an acceptable accounting practice than would an accounting textbook. Guidance in this category would require more judgment and a broader search of literature than would be true in the other four categories.

Who Created GAAP?

Committee on Accounting Procedure. The first serious attempt to create generally accepted accounting principles began in 1930, primarily as a consequence of the stock market crash of the 1920s and the widespread perception that an absence of uniform and stringent financial reporting requirements had contributed to that crash. The American Institute of Accountants, later to become the American Institute of Certified Public Accountants (AICPA), created a special committee to work with the New York Stock Exchange toward the goal of establishing standards for accounting procedures. The special committee recommended five rules to the Exchange that later (in 1938) were published as Accounting Research Bulletin (ARB) 1 of the Committee on Accounting Procedure. The Committee subsequently published 51 such bulletins, including Accounting Research Bulletin 43, which consolidated and superseded Bulletins 1-42. (A listing of the Accounting Research Bulletins and other standards that have not been completely superseded appears at the front of this publication, together with references to the pages of *Wiley GAAP* that discuss those pronouncements.) The Committee was also instrumental in attempting to achieve uniformity in accounting terminology. However, the Committee's limited resources and lack of serious research efforts in support of its pronouncements were questioned in the late 1950s, particularly as a number of very complex controversial topics loomed on the horizon.

Accounting Principles Board. The profession's response was to substitute the Accounting Principles Board (APB) for the Committee on Accounting Procedure, in order to facilitate the development of principles based primarily on the research of the Accounting Research Division. Under this new strategy, the Division was to undertake extensive and exhaustive research, publish its findings, and then permit the Accounting Principles Board to take the lead in the discussions that would ensue concerning accounting principles and practices. The Board's authority was enforced primarily through prestige and Rule 203 of the Code of Professional Ethics. Furthermore, formal approval of Board issuances by the Securities and Exchange Commission (SEC) gave additional support to its activities.

During the fourteen years of the Board, 31 opinions and 4 statements were issued. They dealt with amendments of Accounting Research Bulletins, opinions on the form and content of financial statements, and issuances requiring changes in both the recognition and disclosure principles of the profession. However, the Board did not utilize the Accounting Research Division, which published fifteen research studies during its lifetime. Both the Board and the Division acted independently in selecting topics for their respective agendas. The Board issued pronouncements in areas where little research had been done, and the Division performed research studies without seeking to be all-inclusive or exhaustive in analysis. The Accounting Principles Board did not operate differently than the Committee on Accounting Procedure.

Financial Accounting Standards Board. As a result of these operational problems and based on the recommendations of the Wheat Study Group, the Financial Accounting Standards Board (FASB) was formed in 1972. The Board consists of seven full-time members; they have diverse backgrounds with three coming from public accounting, two from private industry and one each from academia and from an oversight body. The Board is assisted by a staff of professionals who conduct research and work directly with the Board.

FASB is recognized as authoritative through Financial Reporting Release 1 by the Securities and Exchange Commission and through Rule 203, Rules of Conduct by the AICPA.

FASB is an independent body relying on the Financial Accounting Foundation for selection of its members and receipt of its budgets. FASB is supported by the sale of its publications and by fees assessed on all public companies based on their market capitalizations. (The imposition of this fee was established by the Sarbanes-Oxley Act and replaces the voluntary private-sector contributions that previously supported the Foundation. The change was made to allay any past public concerns about the FASB's perceived independence from contributors.) The Board of Trustees of the Foundation is made up from members of the

American Accounting Association
American Institute of Certified Public Accountants
Association for Investment Management and Research
Financial Executives Institute
Government Finance Officers Association
Institute of Management Accountants
National Association of State Auditors, Comptrollers, and Treasurers
Securities Industry Association

The Board issues several types of pronouncements.[2] The most important of these are Statements of Financial Accounting Standards and Interpretations, which are used to clarify or elaborate on existing Statements or pronouncements of predecessor bodies. Standards and Interpretations constitute category A GAAP. Technical Bulletins, which are category B GAAP, usually address issues not covered directly by existing standards and are primarily used to provide guidance where it is not expected to be costly or create a major change. Bulletins are discussed at Board meetings and subject to Board veto. Both Bulletins and Interpretations are designed to be responsive to implementation and practice problems on relatively narrow subjects.

The FASB staff can issue implementation guides and staff positions, which are category D GAAP. In a question-and-answer format, implementation guides address specific questions that arise when a standard is initially issued. Staff positions are responses to questions on appropriate application of FASB literature that are expected to have widespread relevance. The questions addressed in implementation guides and staff positions are submitted by phone, letter, or through the FASB Web site's technical inquiry service. Implementation guides and staff positions are drafted by the staff and issued provided that a majority of the FASB Board members do not object. In addition, staff positions must be exposed on the FASB Web site for a 30-day comment period before issuance.

American Institute of Certified Public Accountants (AICPA). The Accounting Standards Executive Committee (AcSEC) is the senior technical committee at the AICPA. It is composed of fifteen volunteer members, representative of industry, academia, analysts, and

---

[2] *To date, the FASB has issued 150 Statements on Financial Accounting Standards, 46 Interpretations, and 53 Technical Bulletins, and has devoted substantial time and resources towards developing a Conceptual Framework for Financial Accounting, which has resulted in the issuance of 7 Concepts Statements, of which 6 are extant. (Since a number of standards have been superseded and a few more have been withdrawn, the number of standards, interpretations, etc., which remain in force are somewhat fewer than the total promulgated. However, the preponderance of GAAP extant is the product of the FASB, and not of its predecessors.)*

both national and regional public accounting firms. All AcSEC members are CPAs and members of the AICPA.

AcSEC is authorized to set accounting standards and to speak for the AICPA on accounting matters. The accounting standards that AcSEC issues are prepared largely through the work of AICPA committees and task forces. AcSEC issues Statements of Position (SOPs) and industry audit and accounting guides, which are reviewed and cleared by the FASB and thus constitute category B GAAP. SOPs provide guidance on financial accounting and reporting issues. Industry audit and accounting guides provide guidance to auditors in examining and reporting on financial statements of entities in specific industries and provide standards on accounting problems unique to a particular industry. AcSEC Practice Bulletins (category C GAAP) usually provide guidance on very narrowly defined accounting issues. Until recently, the standards issued by AcSEC addressed topics broadly applicable to all industries in addition to industry-specific topics. Effective November 2002, FASB effectively reclaimed the sole authority to promulgate general-purpose GAAP. AcSEC therefore agreed that in the interest of streamlining standard setting and moving towards principles-based accounting standards, it would confine its standard-setting role to the issuance of industry-specific accounting and auditing standards.

Emerging Issues Task Force (EITF). The Emerging Issues Task Force (EITF) was formed in 1984 by the FASB in order to assist the Board in identifying current or emerging issues and implementation problems before divergent practices become entrenched. The guidance provided is often on narrow issues that are of immediate interest and importance. Task Force members are drawn primarily from public accounting firms but also include individuals who would be aware of issues and practices that should be considered by the group. The Task Force meets every other month with persons representing the SEC and the FASB for discussion, but not for voting purposes.

For each agenda item, an issues paper is developed by members, their firms, or the FASB staff. After discussion by the Task Force, a consensus may be reached on the issue, in which case further action by the FASB is not needed. If no consensus is reached, the problem may end up on the Board agenda or be resolved by the SEC or the AICPA. It is also possible that no consensus is reached and the issue remains unresolved with no organization currently working on the problem. These issues may be in especially narrow areas having little broad-based interest. Occasionally, FASB may include a narrow issue in the scope of a broader project and reaffirm or supersede the work of the Task Force.

FASB publishes a volume of EITF Abstracts, which are summaries of each issue paper and the results of Task Force discussion. This listing of Issues in the front section of *Wiley GAAP* identifies that status of all matters considered by EITF to the date of this publication.

Although EITF pronouncements are technically category C GAAP, they are so specialized that generally there is no category A or B GAAP on their respective topics. The SEC believes that a Task Force consensus is GAAP for public companies, and they will question any accounting that differs from it. In addition, the SEC believes that the EITF works to supply a public forum to discuss accounting concerns and to assist in providing advice. Thus, they are supportive of the Task Force work. In the authors' opinion, EITF consensuses should be adhered to in all financial reporting purporting to comply with GAAP.

The EITF also publishes **Discussion Issues,** which are FASB staff announcements and SEC staff announcements of technical matters that are deemed important by the FASB or SEC staff, but that do not relate specifically to a numbered EITF issue. These announcements are designed to help provide guidance on the application of relevant accounting pronouncements. A listing of the EITF Discussion Issues, with a short summary of each, appears at the front of *Wiley GAAP*, following the listing of the EITF Issues.

Other sources. Not all GAAP has resulted from a deliberation process and the issuance of pronouncements by authoritative bodies. Certain principles and practices evolved into current acceptability without adopted standards. For example, depreciation methods such as straight-line and declining balance are both acceptable, as are inventory costing methods such as LIFO and FIFO. There are, however, no definitive pronouncements that can be found to state this. Furthermore, there are many disclosure principles that evolved into general accounting practice because they were required by the SEC in documents submitted to them. Among these are reconciling the actual rate with the statutory rate used in determining income tax expense, when not otherwise obvious from the financial statements themselves. Even much of the content of balance sheets and income statements has evolved over the years without adopted standards.

How Is GAAP Created?

The FASB and AICPA adhere to rigorous "due process" when creating new guidance in category A and in category B GAAP. The goal is to involve experts who would be affected by the newly issued guidance so that the standards created will result in information that reports economic activity as objectively as possible without attempting to influence behavior in any particular direction. Ultimately, however, the guidance is the judgment of the FASB or the AICPA, based on research, public input, and deliberation. The process described below is the FASB's procedures; the AICPA follows similar procedures in its projects.

The FASB receives requests for new standards from all parts of its diverse constituency, including auditors, industry groups, the EITF, and the SEC. Requests for action include both suggestions for new topics and suggestions for reconsideration of existing pronouncements. For each major project it adds to its technical agenda, the FASB begins by appointing an advisory task force of approximately fifteen outside experts. Care is taken to ensure that various points of view are represented on the task force. The task force meets with and advises the Board and staff on the definition and scope of the project and the nature and extent of any additional research that may be needed. The FASB and its staff then meet to debate the significant issues in the project and to arrive at tentative conclusions. As it does so, the FASB and its staff study existing literature on the subject and conduct or commission any additional research as may be necessary. The task force meetings and the Board meetings are open to public observation and a public record is maintained.

If the accounting problem being considered by the Board is especially complex, the FASB will begin by publishing a Discussion Memorandum or an other discussion document. The discussion document generally sets forth the definition of the problem, the scope of the project, and the financial accounting and reporting issues; discusses research findings and relevant literature; and presents alternative solutions to the issues under consideration and the arguments and implications relative to each. It is distributed to interested parties by request and available on the FASB Web site. The document is prepared by the FASB staff with the advice and assistance of the task force. It specifies a deadline for written comments and often contains an invitation to present viewpoints at a public hearing.

Any individual or organization may request to speak at the public hearing, which is conducted by the FASB and the staff assigned to the project. Public observers are welcome. After each individual speaks, the FASB and staff ask questions. Questions are based on written material submitted by the speakers prior to the hearing as well as on the speaker's oral comments. In addition to the hearing, the staff analyzes all the written comments submitted. The FASB members study this analysis and read the comment letters to help them in reaching conclusions. The hearing transcript and written comments become part of the public record.

After the comment letters and oral presentations responding to the discussion document are considered, formal deliberations begin. (If the accounting problem is not as complex and no discussion document was issued, the due process begins at this point.) The FASB deliberates at meetings that are open to public observation, although observers do not participate in the discussions. The agenda for each meeting is announced in advance. Prior to each Board meeting, the staff presents a written analysis and recommendations of the issues to be discussed. During the meeting, the staff presents orally a summary of the written materials and the Board discusses each issue presented. The Board meets as many times as is necessary to resolve the issues.

When the Board has reached tentative conclusions on all the issues in the project, the staff prepares an Exposure Draft. The Exposure Draft sets forth the Board's conclusions about the proposed standards of financial accounting and reporting, the proposed effective date and method of transition, background information, and an explanation of the basis for the Board's conclusions. The Board reviews, and if necessary, revises, the Exposure Draft. Then, a vote is taken about whether the Exposure Draft can be published for public comment. A majority of the Board members must vote to approve an Exposure Draft for issuance for comment. If four votes are not obtained, the FASB holds additional meetings and redrafts the Exposure Draft.[3]

Any individual or organization can provide comments about the conclusions in the Exposure Draft during the exposure period, which is generally sixty days or more. The Board may also decide to have a public hearing to hear constituents' views. At the conclusion of the comment period, all comment letters and oral presentations are analyzed by the staff, and the Board members read the letters and the staff analysis. Then, the Board is ready to redeliberate the issues, with the goal of issuing final accounting standards.

As in the earlier process, all Board meetings are open to the public. During these meetings, the Board considers the comments received and may revise their earlier conclusions. If substantial modifications are made, the Board will issue a revised Exposure Draft for additional public comment. If so, the Board also may decide that another public hearing is necessary. When the Board is satisfied that all reasonable alternatives have been adequately considered, the staff drafts a final pronouncement for the Board's vote. Four votes are required for adoption of a pronouncement. Once issued, the standards become GAAP after the effective date stated in the pronouncement.

Materiality

Materiality as a concept has great significance in understanding, researching, and implementing GAAP. Each Statement of Financial Accounting Standards (FAS) issued by the FASB concludes by stating that the provisions of the statement are not applicable to immaterial items.

Materiality is defined by the FASB as the magnitude of an omission or misstatement in the financial statements that makes it probable that a reasonable person relying on those statements would have been influenced by the information or made a different judgment if the correct information had been known. However, that definition does not sufficiently explain the concept to provide guidance in distinguishing material information from

---

[3] *Prior to April 24, 2002, five of the seven Board members, rather than a simple majority, had to approve a document for issuance. The requirement was changed to a simple majority in response to criticisms that the FASB's due process was inefficient and that it was taking too long to respond to identified accounting problems. Originally, FASB's procedures permitted simple majority rule but this was changed to a "supermajority" when several controversial standards were enacted by 4-3 votes. Thus, voting requirements have changed several times and could change again.*

immaterial information. The individual accountant must exercise professional judgment in evaluating information and concluding on its materiality. Materiality as a criterion has both quantitative and qualitative aspects.

Quantitatively, materiality has been defined in a few pronouncements. For example, in FAS 131, *Disclosures about Segments of an Enterprise and Related Information*, a material segment or customer is defined as 10% or more of revenues. The Securities and Exchange Commission has in several of its pronouncements defined materiality as 1% of total assets for receivables from officers and stockholders, 5% of total assets for separate balance sheet disclosure of items, and 10% of total revenue for disclosure of oil and gas producing activities.

Although materiality judgments are primarily quantitative, the nature of a transaction or event can affect a determination of whether that transaction or event is material. For example, a transaction that, if recorded, changes a profit to a loss or changes compliance with ratios in a debt covenant to noncompliance would be material even if it involved an otherwise immaterial amount. Also, a transaction that might be judged immaterial if it occurred as part of routine operations may be material if its occurrence helps meet certain objectives. For example, a transaction that allows management to achieve a target or obtain a bonus would be considered material, regardless of the actual amount involved.

Another factor in judging materiality is the degree of precision that is possible to attain when making an estimate. For example, accounts payable can usually be estimated more accurately than a possible loss from the incurrence of a disposal obligation. An error that would be material in estimating accounts payable might be acceptable in estimating the contingency.

Certain events or transactions may be deemed material because of the nature of the item, regardless of the dollar amounts involved, and thus require disclosure under any circumstance. Offers to buy or sell assets for more or less than book value, litigation proceedings against the company pursuant to price-fixing or antitrust allegations, and active negotiations involving future profitability are all examples of items that would not be capable of being evaluated for materiality based solely upon numerical calculations.

It is clear that materiality, as traditionally defined by the accounting and auditing establishment, may no longer comport with the definition implicitly applied by financial statement users, including the SEC and other regulatory authorities. Given the eruption of financial reporting frauds in the late 1990s and early 2000s, a more nuanced and complex definition is probably required. In general, a decision regarding the application of GAAP (e.g., the choice of a nonstandard costing or revenue recognition method for a particular transaction) should be viewed as being immaterial only if all conceivable effects, such as the impact on common financial statement ratios or trends, are expected to be truly immaterial. A strict application of a quantitative threshold—say, 5% of net income-should be avoided. The SEC, in Staff Accounting Bulletin 99, provides a useful discussion of this issue.

The Crisis of Confidence Regarding GAAP

In recent years, GAAP as a body of standards, and the standard-setting process itself, have increasingly come under attack. However, the year 2002 initiated a period of swift reforms in the generally slow-to-evolve realm of financial reporting. A string of accounting scandals unfolded and the entire US financial reporting system was put under the microscope by the nation's leaders, the international financial community, the media, and the general public. What resulted was not only landmark legislation in the form of the Sarbanes-Oxley Act, but also a thorough and ongoing self-examination undertaken by all accountants—from CEOs to auditors to regulators to standard setters.

In November 2001, Enron publicly acknowledged that it had failed to comply with existing accounting requirements in at least two areas—sales of stock to special-purpose entities (SPE) and nonconsolidation of certain SPE. This noncompliance caused material overstatements of assets, shareholders' equity, and net income, and the concealment of substantial debt obligations for several years. Within days of this announcement, Enron's stock price fell, eventually to under twenty-five cents. As the ensuing events unfolded, public policy discussions and media criticisms of GAAP, of standard setting in the private sector, and of the accounting industry reached unprecedented levels. The criticisms centered primarily on the failure of financial statements to warn investors of the impending collapse of Enron, and on the lack of independence of a self-regulating profession that offers both consulting and auditing services to its clients.

In July 2002, an announcement by WorldCom of its accounting irregularities led to a similar drop in stock price and additional criticism of the profession. Numerous other high-profile business failures and accounting scandals also occurred or came to light during this period. By mid-2002, more than a dozen bills had been introduced in Congress, with the stated goal of bringing reform to the accounting industry.

The Sarbanes-Oxley Act of 2002. After countless congressional hearings involving prominent leaders of the accounting profession and members of the SEC, one bill emerged to be signed into law—the Sarbanes-Oxley Act of 2002. Among its sweeping changes were the following provisions:

1. Establishes the Public Company Accounting Oversight Board (PCAOB), to oversee the audits of public companies that are subject to the securities laws of the United States and to establish auditing, quality control, ethics, independence, and other standards relating to the preparation of audit reports. Three of the five PCAOB members cannot be and must not have been certified public accountants.
2. Severely limits an audit firm's ability to provide nonaudit services to an issuer that is an audit client.
3. Requires the CEO and the CFO of each issuer to certify in each periodic report to the SEC
   a. The appropriateness of the financial statements and disclosures and
   b. That those financial statements and disclosures fairly present, in all material respects, the operational and financial condition of the issuer.
4. Requires the SEC to conduct a study of off-balance-sheet transactions and the use of special-purpose entities, and to report to Congress its recommendations.
5. Requires the GAO to conduct a study regarding the consolidation of public accounting firms since 1989, including the present and future impact of the consolidation, and the solutions to any problems it discovers.

Another important provision of the Sarbanes-Oxley Act, set forth in Section 404, increases corporate management's responsibility for assessing the effectiveness of internal control over financial reporting. Operational management, as well as financial management, must be more cognizant of their joint responsibility for quality financial reporting. Management's methods for assessing internal controls will, and should, vary from company to company. Corporate management must assess the risk of material misstatement along two dimensions: (1) Inherent risk—the susceptibility of one or more financial statement assertions to a material misstatement, and (2) Fraud risk—the risk of material misstatement due to fraudulent financial reporting or misappropriation of assets.

The principal regulatory focus of the Sarbanes-Oxley Act is on auditors and corporate management, which is appropriate because the Enron, WorldCom, and other scandals were primarily the result of management fraud and audit failures, rather than faulty accounting standards. However, there are several requirements of the Act that have the possibility of affecting GAAP and its standards setters.

First, the Act defines the required characteristics of an accounting standards-setting body. For the time being, standards will continue to be set by FASB, as the SEC reaffirmed in April 2003 that it will continue to acknowledge FASB's pronouncements as being generally accepted. However, FASB is expected to announce some changes to demonstrate that it "has adopted procedures to ensure prompt consideration, by majority vote of its members, of changes to accounting principles necessary to reflect emerging accounting issues and changing business practices" and "considers, in adopting accounting principles. . . the extent to which international convergence on high quality accounting standards is necessary or appropriate."

Second, the Act requires that the SEC conduct a study on the adoption by the United States financial reporting system of a principles-based accounting system. The study

> *shall include an examination of—(i) the extent to which principles-based accounting and financial reporting exists in the United States; (ii) the length of time required for change from a rules-based to a principles-based financial reporting system; (iii) the feasibility of and proposed methods by which a principles-based system may be implemented; and (iv) a thorough economic analysis of the implementation of a principles-based system.*

That study was released on July 25, 2003, to the House and Senate and can be found on the SEC's Web site (www.sec.gov). Briefly, it finds that the distinction between rules-based and principles-based standards is largely artificial, inasmuch as good standards must be (and have generally been) based on sound principles, and that a pure, principles-only set of standards, without practical guidance, would not serve the public interest.

Principles-based standards. Some have suggested that rules-based accounting standards contributed to the Enron and WorldCom collapses. It is true that detailed rules (e.g., capital lease requirements such as the 90% test) encourage carefully constructed evasions (e.g., 89% leases), which often provoke even more detailed rules. Some suggest that the answer to the problem of "gaming the rules" and the ever-increasing complexity of resulting standards might lie in embracing a principles-based, as opposed to rules-based, approach to standards setting. To some extent, the standards published by the International Accounting Standards Board have that characteristic (although perhaps to lesser extent than is believed), and a movement toward principles-based standards might also facilitate convergence of US GAAP and international standards.

The idea of a principles-based approach to US standard setting is not new. FASB's conceptual framework contains the body of principles that underlies US accounting and reporting. The FASB has used the conceptual framework in developing its accounting standards for more than twenty years. However, FASB has sometimes bowed to pressure to provide exceptions to its principles in order to achieve "desired" accounting results (e.g., to limit volatility of reported earnings).

Under a principles-based approach as implemented by FASB, accounting standards would continue to be developed from the conceptual framework, but the principles would apply more broadly than under existing standards. That is, there would be fewer exceptions to the principles in the standards. In addition, FASB, EITF, and AICPA would provide less interpretive and implementation guidance for applying the standards because the overall principle should provide the necessary foundation for the answer. Exceptions are extremely limited in a principles-based approach. In addition, a principles-based approach requires accountants to exercise good professional judgment and to resist the urge to seek specific answers and rulings on every implementation issue. It also requires the SEC and users of financial information to accept the consequences of applying professional judgment, which means there will be some divergence in practice and will result in some loss of comparability.

FASB issued for public comment a proposal for a principles-based approach to US standard setting in October 2002 and held a public roundtable meeting with respondents to the proposal in December 2002. Many respondents agreed on the need for standards that emphasize principles over detailed rules and report the economic substance of transactions or events. However, many concluded that complex rules are primarily driven by increasingly complex economic transactions (e.g., the explosive growth in the use of hedging and financial derivatives), and that there is no way to return to a simpler time or to simpler GAAP. Also, many respondents expressed concern about using principles-based standards in the current legal and regulatory environment. The well-known penchant for litigation means that, as former Federal Reserve Board Chairman Paul Volcker observed, "(T)he American tradition is to have clear and definite rules, so firms can defend themselves from the hoards of lawyers who stand ready to sue auditors for making a bad judgment."

Standards overload. The recent criticisms of rule-based standards join earlier criticisms about the complexity of accounting standards. Some accountants complain about "standards overload," saying that there are too many accounting standards, which are individually too complex to be understood and implemented, and that too many organizations (SEC, FASB, AICPA, etc.) are empowered to issue these pronouncements. Complaints regarding standards overload are not new, and with 150 FASB Statements and myriad other standards (including hundreds of EITF Issues), these complaints must be given some credence. However, the solution, if there is one, is not obvious. Nor is it clear that financial reporting frauds, audit failures, or other such phenomena have been the result of this overload.

Some say that a solution would be to reduce and simplify GAAP, especially for entities having characteristics suggesting that the risk of misleading the users of the financial statements might be low. For example, some recommend a size test, with smaller entities following a subset of the standards that would be mandated for larger entities (a system actually in place in the UK). Even this superficially simple suggestion has complications, however; size could arguably be determined by assets, revenues, net worth, or number of owners. Others recommend that public entities, regardless of size, follow a more comprehensive set of standards than privately owned businesses.

Those who disagree say that differing standards would reduce the quality of financial reporting. For example, if decisions about which entities should follow which standards were made using a single criterion for all standards (such as size or ownership), some entities that engage heavily in a certain type of transaction (e.g., derivative financial instruments) might not be subject to the standards for that transaction—even though the recognition, measurement, and disclosure of those transactions was critical to understanding the financial condition and results of operations of the entity. To solve that problem, criteria would need to be based in some way on the underlying subject matter of the standard, which would result in an accountant having to examine each standard to determine if it would apply to a particular entity. That could compound the standards overload problem rather than solve it.

This "big GAAP vs. little GAAP" debate has raged off and on for decades. When advocates of differential standards are challenged, however, they typically have been unable to identify alternative recognition or measurement principles for large (or public) entities vs. those for smaller (or privately held) entities. Generally, at best certain disclosures are cited as candidates for slimming down in financial statements of the smaller or private companies. In short, there may be less than meets the eye to this entire controversy.

In fact, the FASB has experimented in recent years with differential standards for disclosures. FAS 126 exempts nonpublic companies from certain financial instrument disclosures if the entity's total assets are less than $100 million and the entity has not held or issued any derivative financial instruments. Nonpublic companies also are not required to disclose earnings per share (FAS 128), segment information (FAS 131), or certain pension and postretirement information (FAS 132). These exemptions have not, however, been widely cited as representing progress on this presumed problem of standards overload.

To address the perceived problem that there are too many complex standards and too many organizations issuing standards, FASB has begun a simplification and codification project. A major part of this project is the examination of principles-based standards discussed in the previous section of this chapter. Another part is the codification of existing standards. FASB indicated that it would begin to include references to all applicable US accounting literature in its future standards and in the *Current Text*. In addition, the FASB is seeking to partner with others in developing an online database that will include all of the US accounting literature in a single, more easily accessed form.

In another part of the project, FASB will attempt to reduce the complexity of accounting standards by controlling whether other standard-setting bodies issue pronouncements. FASB is changing the processes of the EITF to give FASB more direct involvement with the agenda, deliberations, and conclusions of the EITF. FASB has added two board members to the EITF Agenda Committee and now requires that FASB ratify each consensus at a public board meeting before it becomes GAAP. Also, FASB and the AICPA have agreed that AcSEC will cease issuing SOP that create broadly applicable GAAP. (The AICPA may continue to issue industry accounting and auditing standards.) FASB also intends to work with representatives from the EITF, AICPA, and SEC to develop a model for deciding if additional authoritative standards are necessary on a given topic and then how to most effectively segregate duties among those bodies with respect to issuing those standards.

FASB also wants to more thoroughly assess the cost-benefit relationships of proposed standards; presumably, complex standards are more costly to implement, and thus the costs are more likely to outweigh the expected benefits to users. If so, enactment is less probable. To understand the costs of a proposed standard, FASB intends to actively engage its constituents in a discussion of the costs as a formal step in the Board's due process. To understand more fully the benefits of a proposed standard, FASB has created a User Advisory Council, a group of forty professionals representing a variety of investment and analytical disciplines, which will be consulted on specific projects as well as helping the Board formulate its overall agenda.

Although these FASB initiatives are a step in the right direction, it remains to be seen whether they successfully answer criticisms of standards overload. The financial environment is increasingly complex and increasingly litigious, which makes a lessening of the burden of GAAP unlikely.

Potential harmful effects of standards. In general, reporting entities have not welcomed proposals for new standards, since these inevitably involve change, costs of implementation, and perhaps, a period of confusion while the marketplace assimilates the new information. The business community often claims that FASB does not understand the economic impact of new standards on their businesses. They complain that the implementation of certain accounting standards will harm their ability to be competitive in the global marketplace and impede their ability to raise debt or equity capital on favorable terms. Two early examples were the issuance of FAS 43 (compensated absences) and FAS 106 (postretirement benefits). In both cases, the business community said that the new standard would force them to reduce benefits to employees—and in some cases they did just that. The counterargument was perhaps more impressive: as a consequence of formerly failing to fully account for promises made or benefits granted, companies were misled regarding their true financial condition, which, once exposed, resulted in changes in behavior that were long overdue. Managers were harmed by their former ignorance; they were not hurt by the truth.

In two recent cases, dissatisfaction with proposed standards escalated to the point where the business community asked the federal government to intervene. When FASB proposed that the value of stock options granted to employees should be reflected as an expense in the financial statements, the business community, and particularly technology firms, loudly claimed that the proposed recognition would have a dramatic and negative economic effect. First, the argument went, it would force them to discontinue issuing stock options, which would prevent the companies from compensating valuable employees. Second, to the extent options were granted and reflected in expense, it would cause the firms' costs of capital to increase significantly because of lower levels of reported profitability. Finally, it would put US firms at a competitive disadvantage to foreign companies that did not have to expense the value of stock options (or were not offering this benefit to employees).

Before the battle was over, "sense of the House" and "sense of the Senate" resolutions had been introduced, objecting to FASB's tentative conclusions, and a bill had been introduced that would have, if enacted, precluded the recognition of the value of stock options as an expense as a matter of law. This debate threatened not only the stock-based compensation standard, but also the future of accounting standard setting in the private sector itself. That concern contributed to FASB's decision to issue FAS 123 with only a requirement for disclosure of the value of stock options, with recognition and measurement optionally continuing under prior (APB 25) rules. Not surprisingly, virtually all publicly held companies continued to utilize the "implicit value" approach of APB 25, even though FAS 123 clearly states that the "fair value" approach is preferable GAAP. (Interestingly, after the Enron and WorldCom scandals, and the resulting Sarbanes-Oxley legislation, some companies began to voluntarily expense options, and FASB responded by issuing an Exposure Draft in March 2004 that would require companies to expense equity-based compensation, which is now considered highly likely to be accepted.

Later, when FASB was pursuing its derivative financial instruments project, the business community again approached the Congress with a request for it to intercede in the debate. Although the federal government was not as quick to intervene in this instance, FASB was again criticized by several members of Congress and by their staff. To have been thus criticized and, in part, thwarted by influential government officials twice in a span of five years might have proved to be detrimental as the Congress considered legislation in response to the collapse of Enron Corp. However, standard setting in the private sector, and the supremacy of FASB in the standard-setting role, appear to have survived those challenges, at least for the near future.

The Business Reporting Research Project

In answering Congressional and other challenges to continued private sector standard setting and to GAAP as it currently exists, the AICPA's chair cited the fact that economic change has been much more swift than has been the response of those setting standards, and that the existing financial reporting model may have become obsolete. Annual and quarterly reporting has become insufficient to meet investor needs and, ultimately, there must be a move towards a real-time disclosure system. As reported in the AICPA study, *Improving Business Reporting—A Customer Focus* (1994), investors and creditors have many unmet needs for information. Those needs extend far beyond what is provided by the current financial reporting model. To capture the sense of reporting nonfinancial information in addition to financial information, the study adopted the broader term "business reporting."

In early 1996, FASB issued an Invitation to Comment on the study's conclusions and those of another group. One of the issues raised was whether FASB should broaden its attention beyond financial statements and related disclosures to also address the types of nonfinancial information that would be included in a comprehensive business-reporting model. Overall, respondents had mixed views on FASB involvement with nonfinancial information. FASB has not added any projects to its agenda to require disclosure of nonfinancial information as of this date. Nonetheless, in 1998 the Board decided to undertake research on business reporting, with the goal of identifying the types of information businesses were already voluntarily providing, and the means used to deliver it.

FASB has produced four reports setting forth results of this project as follows:

1. *Update of Electronic Distribution of Business Reporting Information—Survey of Business Reporting Research Information on Companies' Internet Sites (May 2002),* an update of the report issued in 2000, which describes the reporting of business information over the Internet and identifies notable practices.
2. *Improving Business Reporting: Insights into Voluntary Disclosures* (January 2001), which identifies the kinds of business information that corporations in eight selected industries are reporting outside of their financial statements.
3. *GAAP-SEC Disclosure Requirements* (March 2001), which identifies redundancies between GAAP and SEC disclosure requirements and ways to eliminate them.
4. *Business and Financial Reporting: Challenges from the New Economy* (April 2001), which examines the perceived "disconnect" between information provided in financial statements ("old economy" financial reporting) and the information needs of investors and creditors ("new economy" financial reporting).

RESEARCHING GAAP PROBLEMS

The research procedures presented are intended to serve as a general model for approaching research on accounting issues or questions you may have. These procedures are only intended as an illustration of the process, not as a "cookbook" approach. These procedures should be refined and adapted to each individual fact situation.

Research Procedures

Step 1: Identify the Problem

- The first objective is to gain an understanding of the problem or question.
- Problems and research questions can arise from new authoritative pronouncements, changes in a firm's economic operating environment, or new transactions.
- It is important to remember that research can be performed before or after the critical event has occurred.
- If little is known about the subject area, it may be useful to consult general reference sources (e.g., Journal of Accountancy, CPA Journal, Business Week) to become more familiar with the topic and build up some "economic horse sense" in the area (i.e., the basic what, why, how, when, who, where).

Step 2: Analyze the Problem

- In this step, the objective is to identify critical factors, issues, and questions that relate to the research problem.
    - What are the options? Brainstorm possible alternative accounting treatments.

- What are the goals of the transaction? Are these goals compatible with full and transparent disclosure and recognition?
- What limitations or factors can impact the accounting treatment?

Step 3: Refine the Problem Statement

- In this step, the objective is to clearly articulate the critical issues in a way that will facilitate research and analysis.

Step 4: Identify Plausible Alternatives

- Plausible alternative solutions are based upon prior knowledge or theory.
- Additional alternatives may be identified as steps 5-7 are completed.
- The purpose of identifying and discussing different alternatives is to be able to respond to key accounting issues that arise out of a specific situation.
- The alternatives are the potential methods of accounting for the situation from which only one will ultimately be chosen.
- Exploring alternatives is important because many times there is no one cut-and-dry solution to the situation.
- Ambiguity often surrounds many transactions and related accounting issues and, accordingly, the accountant and business advisor must explore the alternatives and use professional judgment in deciding on the proper course of action.
- Remember that other accountants may reasonably disagree with the judgment used or conclusions made, but this does not necessarily mean they are right.

Step 5: Generate a Research Strategy

- Determine which authorities or literature need to be searched. Often it will be necessary to search all authoritative literature (FASB, EITF, SEC, AICPA, etc.) as well as current reporting practices (e.g., annual reports).
- Generate keywords or phrases that will form the basis of an electronic research.
- Consider trying a broad search to

  1. Assist in developing an understanding of the area,
  2. Identify appropriate search terms, and
  3. Identify related issues and terminology.

- Consider trying very precise searches to identify if there is authoritative literature directly on point.

Step 6: Search Authoritative Literature (described in additional detail below)

- This step involves implementation of the research strategy through searching, identifying, and locating applicable information.
  - Research using *Wiley GAAP*.
  - Research published GAAP.
  - Research other literature.
  - Research practice.
  - Use theory.
  - Find analogous events and/or concepts.

Step 7: Evaluation

- Analyze and evaluate all of the information obtained.
- This evaluation should lead to the development of a solution or recommendation. Again it is important to remember that steps 3-7 describe activities that will interact

with each other and lead to a more refined process in total, and a more complete solution. These steps may involve several iterations.

Search Authoritative Literature (Step 6)—Further Explanation

The following sections discuss in more detail how to search authoritative literature as outlined in Step 6.

Researching using *Wiley GAAP*. This publication can assist in researching generally accepted accounting principles for the purpose of identifying technical answers to specific inquiries. You can begin your search in one of two ways: by using the contents page at the front of *Wiley GAAP* to determine the chapter in which the answer to your question is likely to be discussed, or by using the index at the back of this publication to identify specific pages of the publication that discuss the subject matter relating to your question. The path chosen depends in part on how specific the question is; an initial reading of the chapter or relevant section thereof will provide a broader perspective on the subject. For example, if one wanted to know how to account for pledging receivables as collateral, it would be best to start with Chapter 5. However, if one's interest was limited to securitizations of credit card portfolios, it might be better to search the index, because securitizations are a very specialized type of transaction involving receivables, addressed in only a few pages of the text.

Each chapter in this publication is organized in the following manner:

- A chapter table of contents on the first page of the chapter
- Perspective and Issues, providing an overview of the chapter contents and noting any current controversy or proposed GAAP changes affecting the chapter's topics
- A box listing the Sources of GAAP
- Definition of Terms, defining any specialized terms unique to the chapter's subject matter
- Concepts, Rules, and Examples, setting forth the detailed guidance and examples
- Emerging Issues Task Force Issues Summaries, describing the issues addressed by the EITF, which are generally narrowly defined questions about how to apply GAAP in a particular circumstance
- When relevant, there will also be other GAAP summaries, such as FASB Technical Bulletins, AICPA Statements of Position, and so forth. Key provisions of these, as well as the EITF issues, are also incorporated into the body of the text, as appropriate.

If more information is desired after reading the chapter, or the verbatim requirements set forth in the underlying standards are needed, the Sources of GAAP box can be used to find the authoritative pronouncements related to the topic. Upon locating these pronouncements, look them up in the Authoritative Accounting Pronouncements section preceding this chapter, which lists all authoritative pronouncements **currently in effect** in numerical order. The listed pronouncements are referenced both to the *Current Text* published by FASB and to pages in this publication. Using this list, one can trace to or from this publication to both the original pronouncements and/or the *Current Text*. Likewise, the reader familiar with the professional literature can use the listing of authoritative accounting pronouncements to quickly locate the pages in this publication relevant to each specific pronouncement. The reader can therefore locate more detail on each and every topic covered in this publication, and also be aware of which few, specialized topics and pronouncements are not covered within this publication.

The current status of each EITF Issue is indicated—that is, whether superseded, resolved, or consensus reached by the EITF, or whether further discussion is pending. EITF Issues are summarized at the ends of the chapters to which they relate. For those consensuses having more pervasive impact, discussion is also integrated within the chapters themselves. Because EITF issues are generally on narrowly defined issues (often for which no category A or B GAAP exists) the EITF consensus will represent the highest level of GAAP available on the topic. EITF summaries are included in this publication in recognition of their importance.

Researching authoritative sources of GAAP. To extend one's research on GAAP issues beyond the materials presented in this book, one would begin with the publications that set forth the accounting standards in the GAAP hierarchy—the FASB, the AICPA, and the EITF.

FASB publishes both looseleaf and bound sets of books, as well as CD-ROMs, of the *Current Text* and the *Original Pronouncements*. The former integrates all of the currently recognized category A GAAP alphabetically in topic order (e.g., Accounting Changes, Business Combinations, etc.). The AICPA Research Bulletins, APB Opinions, and FASB Statements and Interpretations have been combined in this integrated document. Supplemental guidance from the AICPA Accounting Interpretations and FASB Technical Bulletins is also incorporated. All these materials have been edited down from the original pronouncements and thus may lack the clarity that can be obtained only from the unedited version. Each paragraph in the *Current Text* is referenced to the pronouncement from which it is drawn, which is useful for research or follow-up. The first volume of the *Current Text* deals with general standards, while the second contains standards for specialized industries. Descriptive materials, including reasons for conclusions, is absent from the *Current Text*.

The *Original Pronouncements* contains all of the AICPA Accounting Research Bulletins, Interpretations and Terminology Bulletins, the APB Opinions, Statements and Interpretations, the FASB Standards, Interpretations, Concepts, Technical Bulletins, and Exposure Drafts. Paragraphs containing accounting principles that have been superseded or dropped are shaded to alert the user. All changes are identified in detail on a status page placed at the beginning of each pronouncement, which can also assist the user in finding other relevant materials.

Generally, if a quick answer to a specific question is needed, the *Current Text* can be accessed readily. If a fuller understanding of the answer and the reasons underlying it are required, the *Original Pronouncements* may be preferable. In many cases, both sources should be consulted.

FASB also publishes the *EITF Abstracts* (category C GAAP). Each EITF issue discussed by the Task Force is included in the book, regardless of whether a consensus was reached, in the order in which they were added to the EITF agenda. A status section at the end of each issue indicates whether the consensus has been superseded or remains relevant and whether any additional EITF discussion is planned. Many issues are discussed a number of times, and in some cases consensuses are withdrawn or modified in subsequent considerations of a given issue. Accordingly, care must be exercised because, unlike FASB Statements, for example, issues addressed in EITF consensuses can evolve without adequate notice that they are affected by later-developed standards.

EITF Abstracts also includes EITF Discussion Issues, which are FASB or SEC staff announcements of positions taken on issues that have yet to be resolved, or even addressed, by the EITF or other standard-setting bodies. While not within the GAAP hierarchy, these do represent current thinking on the particular topic and should be given due consideration in resolving practice problems. The more important of these are covered in this book.

In February 2003, FASB staff began issuing application guidance (like that found in FASB Staff Implementation Guides and EITF Discussion Issues) through FASB Staff Positions (which belong to category D GAAP). The staff positions will be initially communicated through the FASB Web site and will remain there until incorporated into printed FASB literature. FASB staff positions are answers to questions about appropriate application of FASB literature expected to be of widespread relevance to constituents and for which the FASB staff believes that there is only one acceptable answer. The more important of these are covered in this book.

The AICPA publishes all its outstanding Statements of Position and Practice Bulletins in *AICPA Technical Practice Aids.* That book is set up similarly to FASB's *Original Pronouncements*, with the SOP and Practice Bulletins included in the order in which they were issued. There are 26 audit and accounting guides, which are listed at the front of this publication following the AICPA Statements of Position. These publications are available in soft-cover and on CD-ROM.

Researching nonpromulgated GAAP. Researching nonpromulgated GAAP consists of reviewing pronouncements in areas similar to those being researched, reading accounting literature mentioned in the GAAP hierarchy as "other sources" to be used when sources at levels A to D do not exist, and careful reading of the relevant portions of the FASB Conceptual Framework (Appendix). Understanding concepts and intentions espoused by accounting experts can give the essential clues to a logical formulation of alternatives and conclusions regarding problems that have not yet been addressed by the standard-setting bodies.

Both the AICPA and FASB publish a myriad of nonauthoritative literature. FASB publishes the documents it uses in its due process: Discussion Memorandums, Invitations to Comment, Exposure Drafts, and Preliminary Views. It also publishes research reports, *Status Report,* and implementation guidance. The AICPA publishes its Exposure Drafts, as well as Technical Practice Aids, Issues Papers, comment letters on proposals of other standard-setting bodies, and the *Journal of Accountancy.* Technical Practice Aids are answers published by the AICPA Technical Information Service to questions about accounting and auditing standards. AICPA Issues Papers are research documents about accounting and reporting problems that the AICPA believes should be resolved by FASB. They provide information about alternative accounting treatments used in practice. These two AICPA publications, which are not approved by FASB, have no authoritative status, but those who depart from their guidance should be prepared to justify that departure based upon the facts and circumstances of the particular situation. Listings of FASB and AICPA publications are available at their Web sites. (A list of Web site addresses is located at the end of this chapter, immediately before the Appendix.)

The Securities and Exchange Commission issues Staff Accounting Bulletins and makes rulings on individual cases that come before it, which create and impose accounting standards on those whose financial statements are to be submitted to the Commission. The SEC, through acts passed by Congress, has been given broad powers to prescribe accounting practices and methods for all statements filed with it.

The International Accounting Standards Board publishes its standards, interpretations, the *Framework for the Preparation and Presentation of Financial Statements*, and project archives. Summaries of the standards and interpretations and the project archives are available at the Board's Web site, along with instructions for purchasing the complete standards, interpretations, and other materials.

The American Accounting Association is an organization consisting primarily of accounting educators. It is devoted to encouraging research into accounting theory and practice. The issuances of the AAA tend to be normative, that is, prescribing what GAAP ought to be like, rather than explaining current standards. However, the monographs, committee reports, and *The Accounting Review* published by the AAA may be useful sources for research into applicable accounting standards.

Governmental agencies such as the Government Accounting Office and the Cost Accounting Standards Board have certain publications that may assist in researching written standards. Also, industry organizations and associations may be other helpful sources.

Certain publications are helpful in identifying practices used by entities that may not be promulgated as standards. The AICPA publishes an annual survey of the accounting and disclosure policies of many public companies in *Accounting Trends and Techniques* and maintains a library of financial statements that can be accessed through a computerized search process (NAARS). EDGAR (Electronic Data Gathering, Analysis, and Retrieval) publishes the SEC filings of public companies, which includes the companies' financial statements. Through selection of keywords and/or topics, these services can provide information on how other entities resolved similar problems.

The conceptual framework. FASB has issued seven pronouncements called Statements of Financial Accounting Concepts (CON) in a series designed to constitute a foundation of financial accounting standards. The framework is designed to prescribe the nature, function, and limits of financial accounting and to be used as a guideline that will lead to consistent standards. These conceptual statements do not establish accounting standards or disclosure practices for particular items. They are not enforceable under the Rules of Conduct of the Code of Professional Ethics.

FASB's conceptual framework is intended to serve as the foundation upon which the Board can construct standards that are both sound and internally consistent. The fact that the framework was intended to guide FASB in establishing standards is embodied in the preface to each of the Concepts Statements. The preface to CON 6 states

> *The Board itself is likely to be the most direct beneficiary of the guidance provided by the Statements in this series. They will guide the Board in developing accounting and reporting standards by providing the Board with a common foundation and basic reasoning on which to consider merits of alternatives.*

The conceptual framework is also intended for use by the business community to help understand and apply standards and to assist in their development. This goal is also mentioned in the preface to each of the Concepts Statements, as this excerpt from CON 6 shows.

> *However, knowledge of the objectives and concepts the Board will use in developing standards also should enable those who are affected by or interested in financial accounting standards to understand better the purposes, content, and characteristics of information provided by financial accounting and reporting. That knowledge is expected to enhance the usefulness of, and confidence in, financial accounting and reporting. The concepts also may provide some guidance in analyzing new or emerging problems of financial accounting and reporting in the absence of applicable authoritative pronouncements.*

The FASB Special Report, *The Framework of Financial Accounting Concepts and Standards* (1998), states that the conceptual framework should help solve complex financial accounting or reporting problems by

- *Providing a set of common premises as a basis for discussion;*
- *Providing precise terminology;*
- *Helping to ask the right questions;*
- *Limiting areas of judgment and discretion and excluding from consideration potential solutions that are in conflict with it; and*
- *Imposing intellectual discipline on what traditionally has been a subjective and ad hoc reasoning process.*

Of the seven CON, the fourth, *Objectives of Financial Reporting by Nonbusiness Organizations*, is not covered here due to its specialized nature.

CON 1, *Objectives of Financial Reporting by Business Enterprises*, identified three objectives of financial reporting. The objectives are to provide useful information for economic decisions, to provide understandable information capable of predicting cash flows, and to provide relevant information about economic resources and the transactions, events, and circumstances that change them.

CON 2, *Qualitative Characteristics of Accounting Information*, identifies the qualities that make information useful. Under a cost-benefit constraint, the primary qualities of useful information are that it be relevant and reliable. Relevant information is timely and either aids in predicting the future or in providing knowledge of the past (feedback value). Reliable information is verifiable and neutral and it faithfully represents events. In addition, such information must be comparable, consistent, and understandable.

CON 3, *Elements of Financial Statements of Business Enterprises*, has been replaced by CON 6. CON 6 carried forward essentially all of the concepts in CON 3, then added the elements unique to the financial statements of not-for-profit organizations.

CON 5, *Recognition and Measurement in Financial Statements of Enterprises*, sets forth recognition criteria that determine what information should be in financial statements and the timing of when that information will appear. A full set of such statements would show financial position at the end of a period, earnings, comprehensive income and cash flows for the period, and investments by and distributions to owners during the period.

CON 6, *Elements of Financial Statements*, defines ten elements as the basic components of financial statements. Three of these elements (assets, liabilities, and equity) relate to the balance sheet and are discussed in depth in Chapter 2. Five elements (revenues, expenses, gains, losses, and comprehensive income) relate to the performance of an entity over time and are discussed in Chapter 3. The remaining two elements (investments by owners and distributions to owners) relate to the transfer between a business enterprise and its owners and are discussed in Chapter 17.

CON 7, *Using Cash Flow Information and Present Value in Accounting Measurements*, provides a framework for using future cash flows as the basis for accounting measurements either at initial recognition or when assets are remeasured at fair value (fresh-start measurements). It also provides a framework for using the interest method of amortization. It provides the principles that govern measurement using present value, especially when the amount of future cash flows, their timing, or both are uncertain. However, it does not address recognition questions, such as which transactions and events should be valued using present value measures or when fresh-start measurements are appropriate.

The appendix to this chapter discusses CON 1, 2, 5, 6, and 7 in greater detail.

Example of how to solve a GAAP problem. As an example of how to solve a GAAP problem, let us examine how the FASB and its staff approached a question raised by the Edison Electric Institute (EEI) in the project that eventually led to FAS 143, *Asset Retirement Obligations*.

The EEI requested that the FASB add a project to its agenda to determine the appropriate accounting for removal costs, such as the costs of nuclear decommissioning and similar costs affecting other industries. At the time this was raised, the existing accounting practices for removal costs were inconsistent as to the criteria used for recognition, measurement, and the presentation of the obligation in the financial statements. Some entities did not recognize any obligations for removal costs until actually incurred. Other entities estimated the cost of retiring the asset and accrued a portion of that amount each period as an expense, with an offsetting liability, so that when the asset was retired a liability for full amount of the removal costs would already be on the ledger. Still others recognized the expense but displayed the credit side of the entry as a contra asset rather than a liability.

FASB looked for an analogous situation and found one in FAS 19, *Financial Accounting and Reporting by Oil and Gas Producing Companies*. Paragraph 37 of that standard states that "estimated dismantlement, restoration, and abandonment cost shall be taken into account in determining amortization and depreciation rates." The effect of that paragraph was that the credit side of the entry was to accumulated depreciation, which could result in an accumulated depreciation amount that exceeded the cost of the asset. There was no recognition of an obligation to dismantle and restore the property (a liability). Instead the focus was on achieving a particular pattern of expense recognition. Because the amount of the obligation that the entity had incurred was not a central concern under FAS 19, the FASB (which embraced a balance sheet orientation in its conceptual framework, which was issued after FAS 19 was promulgated) rejected it and sought another solution.

FASB considered the definition of a liability in paragraphs 36-40 of CON 6 to determine whether nuclear decommissioning and similar asset retirements could be considered liabilities of the entities owning the assets. Since the first characteristic of a liability—that an entity has "a present duty or responsibility to one or more other entities that entails settlement by probable future transfer or use of assets at a specified or determinable date, on occurrence of a specified event, or on demand"—would be met when an entity is required by current laws, regulations, or contracts to settle an asset retirement obligation upon retirement of the asset, FASB concluded that accounting for this liability would be the central goal of the new standard.

In some situations, the duty or responsibility to remove the asset is created by an entity's own promise. In other situations, the duty or responsibility is created by circumstances in which an entity finds itself bound to perform, and others are justified in relying on the entity to perform. Thus, in its initial deliberations, the FASB decided that entities should report both legal and constructive obligations in their financial statements. Paragraph 36 of CON 6, which defines the essential characteristics of a liability, recognizes both types of obligations. It states

> *...although most liabilities rest generally on a foundation of legal rights and duties, existence of a legally enforceable claim is not a prerequisite for an obligation to qualify as a liability if for other reasons the entity has the duty or responsibility to pay cash, to transfer other assets, or to provide services to another entity.*

Paragraph 40 of CON 6 provides further insight. It states

> *Liabilities stemming from equitable or constructive obligations are commonly paid in the same way as legally binding contracts, but they lack the legal sanction that characterizes most liabilities and may be binding primarily because of social or moral sanctions or custom. An equitable obligation stems from ethical or moral constraints rather than from rules of common or statute law....*

During its due process, FASB heard from constituents that without improved guidance for determining whether a constructive obligation exists, inconsistent application of the final standard would result. After further consideration of the qualitative characteristics of reliability and comparability found in CON 2, and the recognition characteristic of reliability in CON 5, the FASB decided to confine recognition only to legal obligations, including legal obligations created under the doctrine of promissory estoppel.

FASB also considered the second characteristic of a liability, that "the duty or responsibility obligates a particular entity, leaving it little or no discretion to avoid the future sacrifice." It concluded that an asset retirement obligation had that characteristic.

FASB considered the third and final characteristic of a liability, that "the transaction or other event obligating the entity has already happened." It concluded that an entity must look to the nature of the duty or responsibility to assess whether the obligating event has occurred. FASB provides the example of a nuclear power facility: although the operator assumes responsibility for decontamination upon receipt of a license, it is not until the facility is operated and contamination occurs that there is an obligating event.

When contemplating the manner in which the asset retirement obligation could be measured, FASB was guided by CON 7. In that concepts statement, FASB concluded that "the only objective of present value, when used in accounting measurements at initial recognition and fresh-start measurements, is to estimate fair value." Based on this, FASB determined that an asset retirement obligation should be measured at fair value, but in the (typical) absence of quoted market prices or prices for similar liabilities, entities should use present value techniques to measure the liability.

In deciding upon the appropriate designation of the debit offsetting the entry recording the obligation, FASB first made reference to the definition of an asset under CON 6. FASB concluded that capitalized asset retirement costs would not qualify for presentation as a separate asset because no separate future economic benefit flows from these costs. Thus, asset retirement costs do not meet the definition of an asset in paragraph 25 of CON 6. However, FASB observed that current accounting practice includes in the historical-cost basis of an asset all the costs that are necessary to prepare the asset for its intended use. FASB concluded that the requirement for capitalization of the asset retirement cost as part of the historical cost of the asset and then depreciating that asset both (1) obtains a measure of cost that more closely reflects the entity's total investment in the asset, and (2) permits the allocation of that cost to expense in the periods over which the related asset would be expected to provide benefits.

Thus, in this actual situation, by reasoning from analogous situations and applying established accounting concepts, FASB was able to develop an important new standard. In a like manner, solutions to GAAP practice problems can be reached. Those solutions will serve the reporting entity in achieving GAAP-compliant financial reporting until a standards-setting body resolves the problem by issuing authoritative guidance.

Accounting Web sites

AICPA Online	http://www.aicpa.org	Includes accounting news section; CPE information; section on professional ethics; information on relevant Congressional/Executive actions; online publications, such as the *Journal of Accountancy*; Accounting Standards Executive Committee; also has links to other organizations
American Accounting Association	http://www.aaahq.org/index.cfm	Accounting news; publications; faculty information; searchable; links to other sites
Electronic Accountant	http://www.electronicaccountant.com	Includes Internet Tax Research; Career Center; discussions on accounting, auditing, financial planning, and other topics; searchable
FASB	http://www.fasb.org	Information on FASB; includes list of new Pronouncements/Statements; summaries of selected projects; summaries/status of all FASB Statements
GASB	http://www.gasb.org	Information on GASB; new GASB documents; summaries/status of all GASB statements; proposed Statements; Technical Bulletins; Interpretations

International Accounting Standards Board (IASB)	http://www.iasb.org.uk	Information on the IASB; lists of Pronouncements, Exposure Drafts, project summaries, and conceptual framework
NASBA	http://www.nasba.org	National State Boards of Accountancy; includes listings for all state organizations and publications
Rutgers Accounting Web	http://www.accounting.rutgers.edu	Includes links to journals and publications, software, publishers, educational institutions, government agencies, more
SEC	http://www.sec.gov	SEC digest and statements; EDGAR searchable database; information on current SEC rulemaking; links to other sites

APPENDIX

CONCEPTUAL FRAMEWORK

Components of the Conceptual Framework

The components of the conceptual framework for financial accounting and reporting include objectives, qualitative characteristics, elements, recognition, measurement, financial statements, earnings, funds flow, and liquidity. The relationship between these components is illustrated in the following diagram taken from a FASB Invitation to Comment, *Financial Statements and Other Means of Financial Reporting.*

In the diagram, components to the left are more basic and those to the right depend on components to their left. Components are closely related to those above or below them.

The most basic component of the conceptual framework is the objectives. The objectives underlie the other phases and are derived from the needs of those for whom financial information is intended. The qualitative characteristics are the criteria to be used in choosing and evaluating accounting and reporting policies.

Elements of financial statements are the components from which financial statements are created. They include assets, liabilities, equity, investments by owners, distributions to owners, comprehensive income, revenues, expenses, gains, and losses. In order to be included in financial statements, an element must meet criteria for recognition and possess a characteristic that can be reliably measured.

Conceptual Framework
for Financial Accounting and Reporting

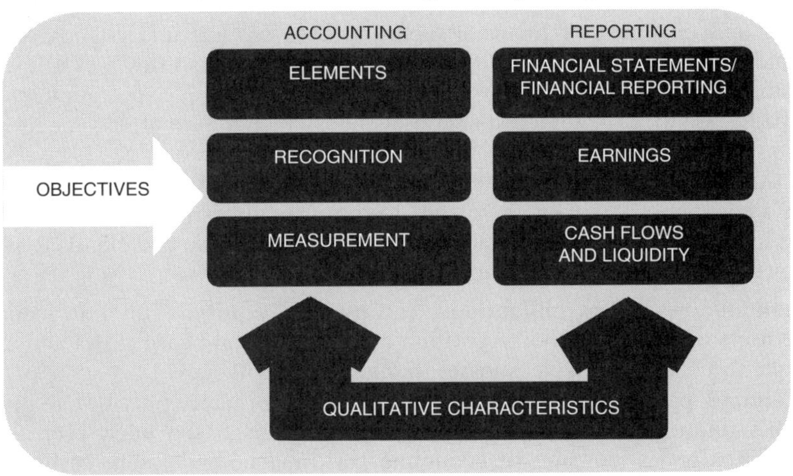

Reporting or display considerations is concerned with what information should be provided, who should provide it, and where it should be displayed. How the financial statements (financial position, earnings, and cash flow) are presented is the focal point of this part of the conceptual framework project.

Unlike a Statement of Financial Accounting Standards (FAS), a Statement of Financial Accounting Concepts (CON) does not establish GAAP. Since GAAP may be inconsistent with the principles set forth in the conceptual framework, the FASB expects to reexamine existing accounting standards. Until that time, a CON does not require a change in existing GAAP. CON do not amend, modify, or interpret existing GAAP, nor do they justify a departing from GAAP based upon interpretations derived from them.

CON 1: Objectives of Financial Reporting by Business Enterprises

CON 1 identifies the objectives (purposes) of financial reporting and indicates that these objectives apply to all financial reporting; they are not limited to financial statements. Financial reporting includes the financial statements and other forms of communication that provide accounting information (corporate annual reports, prospectuses, annual reports filed with the Securities and Exchange Commission, news releases, and management forecasts).

CON 1 identifies three objectives of financial reporting. The **first objective** of financial reporting is to provide information that is useful in making business and economic decisions. Users of financial information are divided into internal and external groups. Internal users include management and directors of the business enterprise. Internal reports tend to provide information that is more detailed than the information available to or used by external users. External users include both individuals who have or intend to have a direct economic interest in a business and those who have an indirect interest because they advise or represent those individuals with a direct interest. These users include owners, lenders, suppliers, potential investors and creditors, employees, customers, financial analysts and advisors, brokers, underwriters, stock exchanges, lawyers, economists, taxing authorities, regulatory authorities, legislators, financial press and reporting agencies, labor unions, trade associations, business researchers, teachers, students, and the public. CON 1 is directed at general-purpose external financial reporting by a business enterprise as it relates to the ability of that enterprise to generate favorable cash flows. External users' needs are emphasized because these users lack the authority to obtain the financial information they want and need from an enterprise. Thus, external users must rely on the information provided to them by management.

The **second objective** of financial reporting is to provide understandable information that will aid investors and creditors in predicting the future cash flows of a firm. Investors and creditors want information about cash flows because the expectation of cash flows affects a firm's ability to pay interest and dividends, which in turn affects the market price of that firm's stocks and bonds.

The **third objective** of financial reporting is to provide information relative to an enterprise's economic resources, the claims to those resources (obligations), and the effects of transactions, events, and circumstances that change resources and claims to resources. A description of these informational needs follows:

- **Economic resources, obligations, and owners' equity.** This information provides the users of financial reporting with a measure of future cash flows and an indication of the firm's strengths, weaknesses, liquidity, and solvency.
- **Economic performance and earnings.** Past performance provides an indication of a firm's future performance. Furthermore, earnings based upon accrual accounting provide a better indicator of economic performance and future cash flows than do current cash receipts and disbursements. Accrual basis earnings are a better indicator because a charge for recovery of capital (depreciation/amortization) is made in determining these earnings. The relationship between earnings and economic performance results from matching the costs and benefits (revenues) of economic activity during a given period by means of accrual accounting. Over the life of an enterprise, economic performance can be determined by net cash flows or by total earnings since the two measures would be equal.
- **Liquidity, solvency, and funds flows.** Information about cash and other funds flows from borrowings, repayments of borrowings, expenditures, capital transactions, economic resources, obligations, owners' equity, and earnings may aid the user of financial reporting information in assessing a firm's liquidity or solvency.

- **Management stewardship and performance.** The assessment of a firm's management with respect to the efficient and profitable use of the firm's resources is usually made on the basis of economic performance as reported by periodic earnings. Because earnings are affected by factors other than current management performance, earnings may not be a reliable indicator of management performance.
- **Management explanations and interpretations.** Management is responsible for the efficient use of a firm's resources. Thus, it acquires knowledge about the enterprise and its performance that is unknown to the external user. Explanations by management concerning the financial impact of transactions, events, circumstances, uncertainties, estimates, judgments, and any effects of the separation of the results of operations into periodic measures of performance enhance the usefulness of financial information.

CON 2: Qualitative Characteristics of Accounting Information

The purpose of financial reporting is to provide decision makers with useful information. When accounting choices are to be made by individuals or by standard-setting bodies, those choices should be based upon the usefulness of that information to the decision-making process. This CON identifies the qualities or characteristics that make information useful in the decision-making process. It also establishes a terminology and set of definitions to provide a greater understanding of the characteristics. The following diagram from CON 2 summarizes the qualitative characteristics of accounting information:

A Hierarchy of Accounting Qualities

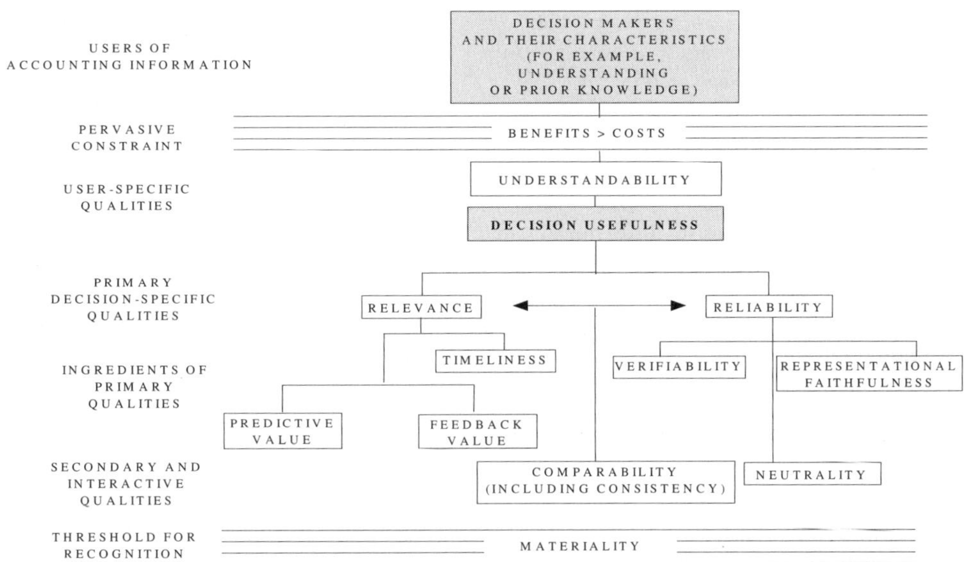

Usefulness for decision making. This is the most important characteristic of information. Information must be useful to be beneficial to the user. To be useful, accounting information must be both relevant and reliable. Both of these characteristics are affected by the completeness of the information provided.

Relevance. Information is relevant to a decision if it makes a difference to the decision maker in his/her ability to predict events or to confirm or correct expectations. Relevant information will reduce the decision maker's assessment of the uncertainty of the outcome of a decision even though it may not change the decision itself. Information is relevant if it provides knowledge concerning past events (feedback value) or future events (predictive value) and if it is timely. Disclosure requirement information is relevant because it provides information about past events and it improves the predictability of future events. The predictive value of accounting information does not imply that such information is a prediction. The predictive value refers to the utility that a piece of information has as an input into a predictive model. Although timeliness alone will not make information relevant, information must be timely to be relevant. It must be available before it loses its ability to influence the decision maker.

Reliability. Financial statements are an abstraction of the activities of a business enterprise. They simplify the activities of the actual firm. To be reliable, financial statements must portray the important financial relationships of the firm itself. Information is reliable if it is verifiable and neutral and if users can depend on it to represent that which it is intended to represent (representational faithfulness).

Information may not be representationally faithful if it is biased. Bias is the tendency for an accounting measure to be consistently too high or too low. Bias may arise because the measurer does not use the measurement method properly or because the measurement method does not represent what it purports to represent.

Verifiability means that several independent measures will obtain the same accounting measure. An accounting measure that can be repeated with the same result (consensus) is desirable because it serves to detect and reduce measurer bias. Cash is highly verifiable. Inventories and depreciable assets tend to be less verifiable because alternative valuation methods exist. The direct verification of an accounting measure would serve to minimize measurer bias and measurement bias. The verification of the procedures used to obtain the measure would minimize measurer bias only. Finally, verifiability does not guarantee representational faithfulness or relevance.

The characteristic of **neutrality** means that accounting information should serve to communicate without attempting to influence behavior in a particular direction. This does not mean that accounting should not influence behavior or that it should affect everyone in the same way. It means that information should not favor certain interest groups.

To be useful, accounting information should be **comparable**. The characteristic of comparability allows the users of accounting information to assess the similarities and differences either among different entities for the same time period or for the same entity over different time periods. Comparisons are usually made on the basis of quantifiable measurements of a common characteristic. Therefore, to be comparable, the measurements used must be reliable with respect to the common characteristic. Noncomparability can result from the use of different inputs, procedures, or systems of classification. Noncomparability can also arise when the data measurements lack representational faithfulness.

The characteristic of **consistency** also contributes to information usefulness. Consistency is an interperiod comparison that requires the use of the same accounting principles from one period to another. Although a change of an accounting principle to a more preferred method results in inconsistency, the change is acceptable if the effect of the change is disclosed. Consistency does not insure comparability. If the measurements used are not representationally faithful, comparability will not be achieved.

Trade-offs. Although it is desirable that accounting information contain the characteristics that have been identified above, not all of these characteristics are compatible. Often, one characteristic may be obtained only by sacrificing another. The trade-offs that must be made are determined on the basis of the relative importance of the characteristics.

This relative importance, in turn, is dependent upon the nature of the users and their particular needs.

Constraints. The qualitative characteristics of useful accounting information are subject to two constraints: the **materiality** and the **relative cost benefit** of that information. An item of information is material and should be reported if it is significant enough to have an effect on the decision maker. Materiality requires judgment. It is dependent upon the relative size of an item, the precision with which the item can be estimated, and the nature of the item. No general standards of materiality are provided (although an appendix to CON 2 lists several guidelines that have been applied).

Accounting information provides the user with certain benefits. Associated with this benefit, however, is the cost of using that information and of providing it to the user. Information should be provided only if its benefits exceed its cost. Unfortunately, it is difficult to value the benefit of accounting information. It is also difficult to determine whether the burden of the cost of disclosure and the benefits of such disclosure are distributed fairly.

Role of conservatism. Any discussion of the qualitative characteristics of accounting information would be incomplete without some reference to the doctrine of conservatism. Conservatism is a reaction to uncertainty. For many years, accountants have been influenced by conservatism. Conservatism in accounting may mislead users if it results in a deliberate understatement of net assets and net income. Such understatement is undertaken to minimize the risk of uncertainty to outside lenders. Unfortunately, such understatements often lead to overstatements in subsequent years, produce biased financial statements, and conflict with the characteristics of representational faithfulness, neutrality, and comparability.

CON 5: Recognition and Measurement in Financial Statements of Business Enterprises

CON 5 indicates that financial statements are the principal means of communicating useful financial information. A full set of such statements contains

- Financial position at end of the period
- Earnings for the period
- Comprehensive income for the period
- Cash flows during the period
- Investments by and distributions to owners during the period

Financial statements result from simplifying, condensing, and aggregating transactions. Therefore, no one financial statement provides sufficient information by itself and no one item or part of each statement can summarize the information.

A statement of financial position provides information about an entity's assets, liabilities, and equity. Earnings is a measure of entity performance during a period. It is similar to net income but excludes accounting adjustments from earlier periods such as cumulative effect changes in accounting principles. Comprehensive income comprises all recognized changes in equity other than those arising from investments by and distributions to owners. A statement of cash flows reflects receipts and payments of cash by major sources and uses including operating, financing, and investing activities. The investments by and distributions to owners reflect the capital transactions of an entity during a period.

Income is determined by the concept of financial capital maintenance which means that only if the money amount of net assets increases during a period (excluding capital transactions) is there a profit. For recognition in financial statements, subject to both cost benefit and materiality constraints, an item must meet the following criteria:

1. **Definition**—Meet the definition of an element in financial statements
2. **Measurability**—Have a relevant attribute measurable with sufficient reliability

3. **Relevance**
4. **Reliability**

Items reported in the financial statements are based on historical cost, replacement cost, market value, net realizable value, and present value of cash flows. Price level changes are not recognized in these statements and conservatism guides the application of recognition criteria.

CON 6: Elements of Financial Statements

CON 6 defines ten interrelated elements that are used in the financial statements of business enterprises.

1. **Assets**—Probable future economic benefits obtained or controlled by a particular entity as a result of past transactions or events
2. **Liabilities**—Probable future sacrifices of economic benefits arising from present obligations of a particular entity to transfer assets or provide services to other entities in the future as a result of past transactions or events
3. **Equity (net assets)**—The residual interest in the assets that remains after deducting its liabilities. In a business enterprise, equity is the ownership interest.
4. **Revenues**—Inflows or other enhancements of assets of an entity or settlement of its liabilities (or a combination of both) from delivering or producing goods, rendering services, or other activities that constitute the entity's ongoing major and central operations
5. **Expenses**—Outflows or other using up of assets or incurrences of liabilities (or a combination of both) from delivering or producing goods, rendering services, or carrying out other activities that constitute the entity's ongoing major and central operations
6. **Gains**—Increases in equity (net assets) from peripheral or incidental transactions of an entity and from all other transactions and other events and circumstances affecting the entity except those that result from revenues or investments by owners
7. **Losses**—Decreases in equity (net assets) from peripheral or incidental transactions of an entity and from all other transactions and other events and circumstances affecting the entity except those that result from expenses or distributions to owners
8. **Comprehensive income**—The change in equity of a business enterprise during a period from transactions and other events and circumstances from sources other than investments by owners or distributions to owners
9. **Investments by owners**—Increases in equity of a particular business enterprise resulting from transfers to it for the purpose of increasing ownership interests
10. **Distributions to owners**—Decreases in the equity of a particular business enterprise resulting from transferring assets, rendering services, or incurring liabilities to owners

The various elements articulate; that is, a change in one element causes an offsetting change in another item of the same type or causes another element to change by the same amount. For example, a purchase of a building for cash and a mortgage note increases an asset (building), decreases another asset (cash), and increases a liability (mortgage note). A diagram from CON 6 that illustrates the articulation of the elements is included below.

In this publication, assets, liabilities, and equity are described more fully in Chapter 2. Revenues, expenses, gains, losses, and comprehensive income are described in Chapter 3. Investments by owners and distributions to owners are described in Chapter 17.

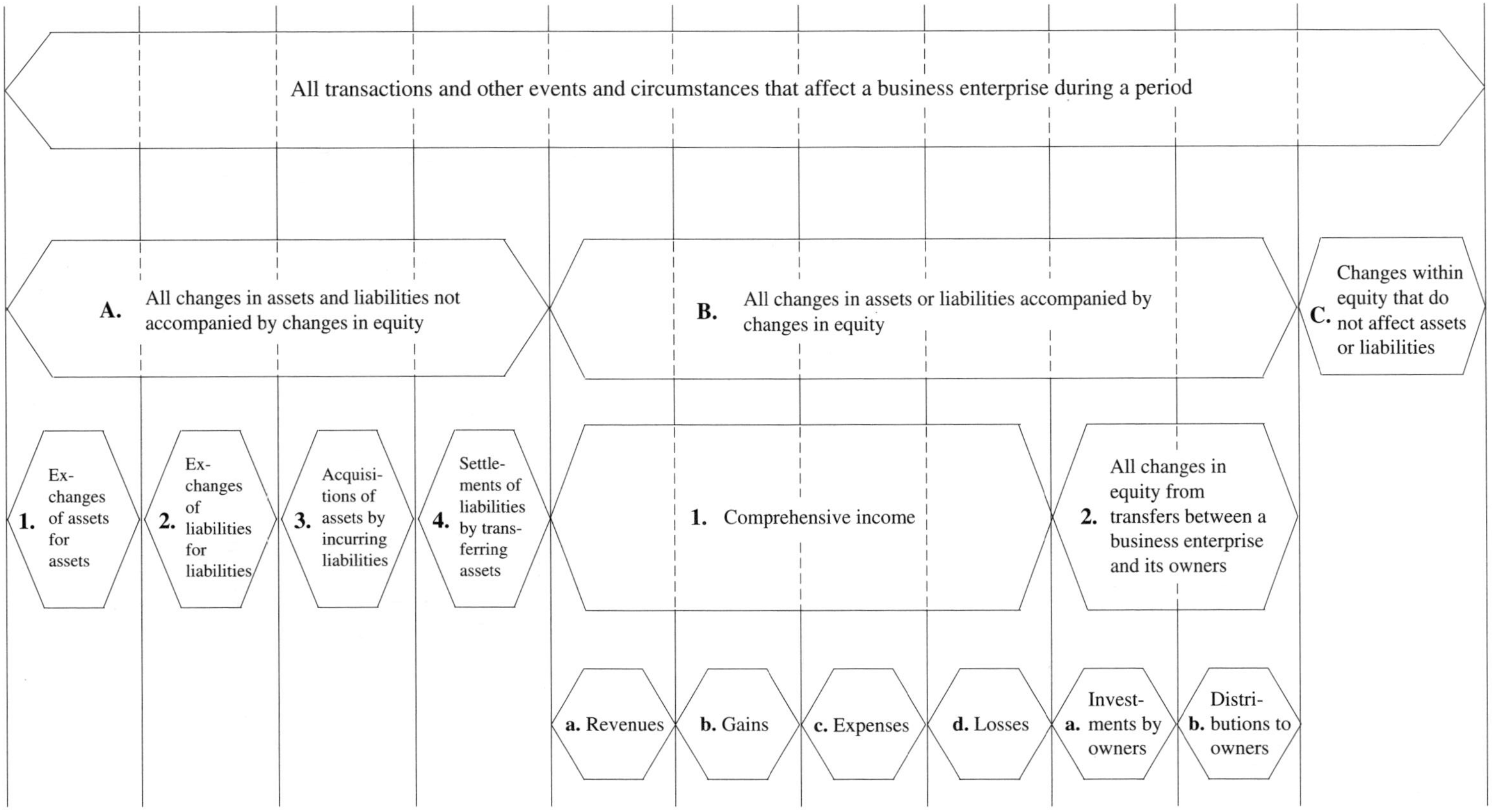
All transactions and other events and circumstances that affect a business enterprise during a period
A. All changes in assets and liabilities not accompanied by changes in equity
B. All changes in assets or liabilities accompanied by changes in equity
C. Changes within equity that do not affect assets or liabilities
1. Ex-changes of assets for assets
2. Ex-changes of liabilities for liabilities
3. Acquisi-tions of assets by incurring liabilities
4. Settle-ments of liabilities by trans-ferring assets
1. Comprehensive income
2. All changes in equity from transfers between a business enterprise and its owners
a. Revenues
b. Gains
c. Expenses
d. Losses
a. Invest-ments by owners
b. Distri-butions to owners

CON 6 also defines several significant financial accounting and reporting terms that are used in the Concepts Statements (and FASB pronouncements issued after the Concepts Statements). An **event** is a happening of consequence to an entity. It can be an internal event (the use of raw materials) or an external event with another entity (the purchase of labor) or with the environment in which the business operates (a technological advance by a competitor). A **transaction** is a particular kind of event. It is an external event that involves transferring something of value to another entity. **Circumstances** are a condition, or set of conditions, that create situations that might otherwise have not occurred and might not have been anticipated. **Accrual accounting** attempts to record the financial effects on a entity of transactions and of other events and circumstances that have consequences for the entity in the periods in which those transactions, events, and circumstances occur rather than in the periods in which cash is received or paid by the entity. Thus, accrual accounting is based not only on cash transactions but also on credit transactions, bartering, changes in prices, changes in the form of assets or liabilities, and other transactions, events and circumstances that involve no current cash transfers but will have cash consequences in the future. **Accrual** is the accounting process of recognizing the effects of future cash receipts and payments in the current period. **Deferral** is the accounting process of recognizing a liability resulting from a current cash receipt or an asset resulting from a current cash payment. **Realization** is the process of converting noncash assets into cash. **Recognition** is the process of formally incorporating a transaction or other event into the financial statements. **Matching** is the simultaneous recognition of the revenues and expenses that result directly and jointly from the same transaction or other event. **Allocation** is the process of assigning expenses to periods when the transactions or events that cause the using up of the benefits cannot be identified or when the cause can be identified but the actual amount of benefit used up cannot be reliably measured.

CON 6 also discusses the elements used in the financial statements of not-for-profit organizations. Of the ten elements, seven are used by not-for-profit organizations. The three elements omitted are investments by owners, distributions to owners, and comprehensive income. They are omitted because not-for-profit organizations do not have owners. The seven remaining elements are defined for not-for-profit organizations the same as they are for business enterprises. The net assets (equity) of not-for-profit organizations is divided into three classes—unrestricted, temporarily restricted, and permanently restricted—based on the existence or absence of donor-imposed restrictions. A portion of Chapter 24 describes the accounting and reporting of not-for-profit organizations.

CON 7: Using Cash Flow Information and Present Value in Accounting Measurements

CON 7 provides a framework for using future cash flows as the basis for accounting measurements either at initial recognition or when assets are remeasured at fair value (fresh-start measurements). It also provides a framework for using the interest method of amortization. It provides the principles that govern measurement using present value, especially when the amount of future cash flows, their timing, or both are uncertain. However, it does not address recognition questions, such as which transactions and events should be valued using present value measures or when fresh-start measurements are appropriate.

Fair value is the objective for most measurements at initial recognition and for fresh-start measurements in subsequent periods. At initial recognition, the cash paid or received (historical cost or proceeds) is usually assumed to be fair value, absent evidence to the contrary. For fresh-start measurements, a price that is observed in the marketplace for an essentially similar asset or liability is fair value. If purchase prices and market prices are available, there is no need to use alternative measurement techniques to approximate fair value. However, if alternative measurement techniques must be used for initial recognition and for fresh-start measurements, those techniques should attempt to capture the elements that when taken together would comprise a market price if one existed. The objective is to estimate the price likely to exist in the marketplace if there were a marketplace—fair value.

CON 7 states that the only objective of using present value in accounting measurements is fair value. It is necessary to capture, to the extent possible, the economic differences in the marketplace between sets of estimated future cash flows. A present value measurement that fully captures those differences must include the following elements:

1. An estimate of the future cash flow, or in more complex cases, series of future cash flows at different times
2. Expectations about possible variations in the amount or timing of those cash flows
3. The time value of money, represented by the risk-free rate of interest
4. The risk premium—the price for bearing the uncertainty inherent in the asset or liability
5. Other factors, including illiquidity and market imperfections

How CON 7 measures differ from currently utilized present value techniques. Current present value techniques typically use a single set of estimated cash flows and a single discount (interest) rate. In current present value techniques, adjustments for factors 2. through 5. described in the previous paragraph are incorporated in the selection of the discount rate. In the CON 7 approach, only the third factor listed (the time value of money) is included in the discount rate; the other factors cause adjustments in arriving at risk-adjusted expected cash flows. CON 7 introduces the expected cash flow approach, which focuses on the range of possible estimated cash flows and their respective probabilities.

When computing present value, current techniques use the cash flows most likely to occur. CON 7 uses expected cash flow. The difference is the value that should be assigned to the cash flows other than the most likely one. To illustrate, a cash flow might be $100, $200, or $300 with probabilities of 10%, 50%, and 40%, respectively. The most likely cash flow is the one with 50% probability, or $200. The expected cash flow is $230 (=$100 x .1 + $200 x .5 + $300 x .4).

The CON 7 method can also accommodate uncertainty in the timing of cash flows. Current techniques cannot; choosing one of the possible receipt dates is required. For example, a cash flow of $10,000 may be received in one year, two years, or three years with probabilities of 15%, 60%, and 25%, respectively. Current present value techniques would compute the present value using the most likely time for the payment—two years. The example below shows the computation of present value using the CON 7 method. Again, the expected present value of $8,973 differs from the traditional notion of a best estimate of $9,027 (the 60% probability) in this example.

Present value of $10,000 in 1 year at 5%	$9,523	
Adjusted for 15% probability		$1,428
Present value of $10,000 in 2 years at 5.25%	$9,027	
Adjusted for 60% probability		5,416
Present value of $10,000 in 3 years at 5.5%	$8,516	
Adjusted for 25% probability		2,129
Expected present value		$8,973

Measuring liabilities. The measurement of liabilities involves different problems from the measurement of assets; however, the underlying objective is the same. When using present value techniques to estimate the fair value of a liability, the objective is to estimate the value of the assets required currently to (1) settle the liability with the holder or (2) transfer the liability to an entity of comparable credit standing. To estimate the fair value of an entity's notes or bonds payable, accountants look to the price at which other entities are willing to hold the entity's liabilities as assets. For example, the proceeds of a loan are the price that a lender paid to hold the borrower's promise of future cash flows as an asset.

The most relevant measurement of an entity's liabilities should always reflect the credit standing of the entity. An entity with a good credit standing will receive more cash for its promise to pay than an entity with a poor credit standing. For example, if two entities both promise to pay $750 in three years with no stated interest payable in the interim, Entity A, with a good credit standing, might receive about $630 (a 6% interest rate). Entity B, with a poor credit standing, might receive about $533 (a 12% interest rate). Each entity initially records its respective liability at fair value, which is the amount of proceeds received—an amount that incorporates that entity's credit standing.

Present value techniques can also be used to value a guarantee of a liability. Assume that Entity B in the above example owes Entity C. If Entity A were to assume the debt, it would want to be compensated $630—the amount that it could get in the marketplace for its promise to pay $750 in three years. The difference between what Entity A would want to take the place of Entity B ($630) and the amount that Entity B receives ($533) is the value of the guarantee ($97).

Interest method of allocation. CON 7 describes the factors that suggest that an interest method of allocation should be used. It states that the interest method of allocation is more relevant than other methods of cost allocation when it is applied to assets and liabilities that exhibit one or more of the following characteristics:

a. The transaction is, in substance, a borrowing and lending transaction.
b. Period-to-period allocation of similar assets or liabilities employs an interest method.
c. A particular set of estimated future cash flows is closely associated with the asset or liability.
d. The measurement at initial recognition was based on present value.

Accounting for changes in expected cash flows. If the timing or amount of estimated cash flows changes and the asset or liability is not remeasured at a fresh-start measure, the interest method of allocation should be altered by a catch-up approach. That approach adjusts the carrying amount to the present value of the revised estimated future cash flows, discounted at the original effective interest rate.

Application of present value tables and formulas.

Present value of a single future amount. To take the present value of a single amount that will be paid in the future, apply the following formula; where *PV* is the present value of $1 paid in the future, *r* is the interest rate per period, and *n* is the number of periods between the current date and the future date when the amount will be realized.

$$PV = \frac{1}{(1+r)^n}$$

In many cases the results of this formula are summarized in a present value factor table.

(n) Periods	2%	3%	4%	5%	6%	7%	8%	9%	10%
1	0.9804	0.9709	0.9615	0.9524	0.9434	0.9346	0.9259	0.9174	0.9091
2	0.9612	0.9426	0.9246	0.9070	0.8900	0.8734	0.8573	0.8417	0.8265
3	0.9423	0.9151	0.8890	0.8638	0.8396	0.8163	0.7938	0.7722	0.7513
4	0.9239	0.8885	0.8548	0.8227	0.7921	0.7629	0.7350	0.7084	0.6830
5	0.9057	0.8626	0.8219	0.7835	0.7473	0.7130	0.6806	0.6499	0.6209

Example

Suppose one wishes to determine how much would need to be invested today to have $10,000 in 5 years if the sum invested would earn 8%. Looking across the row with n=5 and finding the present value factor for the r=8% column, the factor of 0.6806 would be identified. Multiplying $10,000 by 0.6806 results in $6,806, the amount that would need to be invested today to have $10,000 at the end of 5 years. Alternatively, using a calculator and applying the present value of a single sum formula, one could multiply $10,000 by $1/(1+.08)^5$, which would also give the same answer—$6,806.

Present value of a series of equal payments (an annuity). Many times in business situations a series of equal payments paid at equal time intervals is required. Examples of these include payments of semiannual bond interest and principal or lease payments. The present value of each of these payments could be added up to find the present value of this annuity, or alternatively a much simpler approach is available. The formula for calculating the present value of an annuity of $1 payments over *n* periodic payments, at a periodic interest rate of *r* is

$$\text{PV}_{\text{Annuity}} = \frac{\left(1 - \frac{1}{(1+r)^n}\right)}{r}$$

The results of this formula are summarized in an annuity present value factor table.

(n) Periods	2%	3%	4%	5%	6%	7%	8%	9%	10%
1	0.9804	0.9709	0.9615	0.9524	0.9434	0.9346	0.9259	0.9174	0.9091
2	1.9416	1.9135	1.8861	1.8594	1.8334	1.8080	1.7833	1.7591	1.7355
3	2.8839	2.8286	2.7751	2.7233	2.6730	2.6243	2.5771	2.5313	2.4869
4	3.8077	3.7171	3.6299	3.5460	3.4651	3.3872	3.3121	3.2397	3.1699
5	4.7135	4.5797	4.4518	4.3295	4.2124	4.1002	3.9927	3.8897	3.7908

Example

Suppose 4 annual payment of $1,000 will be needed to satisfy an agreement with a supplier. What would be the amount of the liability today if the interest rate the supplier is charging is 6% per year? Using the table to get the present value factor, the n=4 periods row, and the 6% column, gives you a factor of 3.4651. Multiply this by $1,000 and you get a liability of $3,465.10 that should be recorded. Using the formula would also give you the same answer with r=6% and n=4.

Caution must be exercised when payments are not to be made on an annual basis. If payments are on a semiannual basis n=8, but *r* is now 3%. This is because *r* is the periodic interest rate, and the semiannual rate would not be 6%, but half of the 6% annual rate. Note that this is somewhat simplified, since due to the effect of compound interest 3% semi-annually is slightly more than a 6% annual rate.

Example of the relevance of present values. A measurement based on the present value of estimated future cash flows provides more relevant information than a measurement based on the undiscounted sum of those cash flows. For example, consider the following four future cash flows, all of which have an undiscounted value of $100,000:

1. Asset A has a fixed contractual cash flow of $100,000 due tomorrow. The cash flow is certain of receipt.
2. Asset B has a fixed contractual cash flow of $100,000 due in twenty years. The cash flow is certain of receipt.
3. Asset C has a fixed contractual cash flow of $100,000 due in twenty years. The amount that ultimately will be received is uncertain. There is an 80% probability that the entire $100,000 will be received. There is a 20% probability that $80,000 will be received.
4. Asset D has an *expected* cash flow of $100,000 due in twenty years. The amount that ultimately will be received is uncertain. There is a 25% probability that $120,000 will be received. There is a 50% probability that $100,000 will be received. There is a 25% probability that $80,000 will be received.

Assuming a 5% risk-free rate of return, the present values of the assets are

1. Asset A has a present value of $99,986. The time value of money assigned to the one-day period is $14 [$100,000 x .05/365 days]
2. Asset B has a present value of $37,689 [$100,000/$(1 + .05)^{20}$]
3. Asset C has a present value of $36,181 [(100,000 x .8 + 80,000 x .2)/$(1 + .05)^{20}$]
4. Asset D has a present value of $37,689 [($120,000 x .25 + 100,000 x .5 + 80,000 x .25)/$(1 + .05)^{20}$]

Although each of these assets has the same undiscounted cash flows, few would argue that they are economically the same or that a rational investor would pay the same price for each. Investors require compensation for the time value of money. They also require a risk premium. That is, given a choice between Asset B with expected cash flows that are certain and Asset D with cash flows of the same expected amount that are uncertain, investors will place a higher value on Asset B, even though they have the same expected present value. CON 7 says that the risk premium should be subtracted from the expected cash flows before applying the discount rate. Thus, if the risk premium for Asset D was $500, the risk-adjusted present values would be $37,500 {[($120,000 x .25 + 100,000 x .5 + 80,000 x .25) – 500]/$(1 + .05)^{20}$}.

Practical matters. Like any accounting measurement, the application of an expected cash flow approach is subject to a cost-benefit constraint. The cost of obtaining additional information must be weighed against the additional reliability that information will bring to the measurement. As a practical matter, an entity that uses present value measurements often has little or no information about some or all of the assumptions that investors would use in assessing the fair value of an asset or a liability. Instead, the entity must use the information that is available to it without undue cost and effort when it develops cash flow estimates. The entity's own assumptions about future cash flows can be used to estimate fair value using present value techniques, as long as there are no contrary data indicating that investors would use different assumptions. However, if contrary data exist, the entity must adjust its assumptions to incorporate that market information.

2 BALANCE SHEET

PERSPECTIVE AND ISSUES

Balance sheets (also known as statements of financial position) present information about assets, liabilities, and shareholders' equity (also known as net assets, net worth, or, if appropriate, partner's capital) and their relationships to each other. They reflect an entity's resources (assets) and its financing structure (liabilities and equity) in conformity with generally accepted accounting principles. The balance sheet reports the aggregate effect of transactions at a **point in time,** whereas the income statement, statement of retained earnings, and statement of cash flows report the effect of transactions over a **period of time**.

For years, users of financial statements put more emphasis on the income statement than on the balance sheet. Investors' main concern was the short-run maximization of earnings per share. During the late 1960s and early 1970s company growth and desirability was measured by earnings growth. But the combination of inflation and recession during the 1970s and the emphasis in FASB's Conceptual Framework Project on the asset-liability approach to theory brought about a rediscovery of the balance sheet. This shift toward the balance sheet has marked a departure from the traditional transaction-based concept of income toward a capital maintenance concept proposed by economists. Under this approach to income measurement, the amount of beginning net assets would be compared to the amount of ending net assets, and the difference would be adjusted for dividends and capital transactions. Only to the extent that an entity maintained its net assets (after adjusting for capital transactions) would income be earned. By using a capital maintenance concept, investors can better predict the overall profit potential of the firm.

The balance sheet is studied in order to measure a firm's liquidity, financial flexibility and ability to generate profits, pay debts when due, and pay dividends. A firm's liquidity refers to the timing of cash flows in the normal course of business. Liquidity indicates the firm's ability to meet its obligations as they fall due. The concept of financial flexibility is broader than the concept of liquidity. Financial flexibility is a company's ability to take effective actions to alter the amounts and timing of cash flows so it can respond to unexpected needs and opportunities. Financial flexibility includes the ability to issue new capital or unused lines of credit.

The rights of the shareholders of a firm and the rights of other capital-supplying parties (bondholders and creditors) of a firm are many and varied. The disclosure of these rights is an important objective in the presentation of financial statements. The rights of shareholders and creditors are mutually exclusive claims against the entity's assets, and the rights of creditors (liabilities) take precedence over the rights of shareholders (equity). Both sources of capital are concerned with two basic rights: the right to share in the cash or property disbursements (interest and dividends) and the right to share in the assets in the event of liquidation.

Although a balance sheet shows an entity's financial position, it does not purport to report the entity's value. It cannot for reasons that include

- The values of certain assets, such as human resources, secret processes, and competitive advantages are not included in a balance sheet despite the fact that they have value and will generate future cash flows.
- The values of other assets are measured at historical cost, rather than market value or specific value to the entity. For example, property and equipment are measured at original cost reduced by depreciation, but the underlying asset's value can significantly exceed that adjusted cost and the asset may continue to be productive even though fully depreciated.
- The values of most liabilities are measured at the present value of cash flows at the date the liability was incurred rather than at the current market rate. When market rates increase, the value of a below-market interest rate is not recognized in the balance sheet, nor is the loss from paying a rate in excess of market rate if interest rates fall.

In recent years, FASB standards have increasingly employed fair value as the relevant measure for items presented in the balance sheet. For example, FAS 115, *Accounting for Certain Investments in Debt and Equity Securities,* changed the relevant measure for most investments in securities to fair value from the lower of cost or market. FAS 133, *Accounting for Derivative Instruments and Hedging Activities,* requires derivative financial instruments to be reported at fair value which, prior to that pronouncement, were not reported on the balance sheet at all. A project currently on the FASB agenda proposes that certain liabilities be reported at fair value as well. Measuring more assets and liabilities at fair value enhances the ability of a balance sheet to report the entity's value.

In many industries, it is common for the balance sheet to be divided into categories. Assets are classified as "current" if they are reasonably expected to be converted into cash, sold, or consumed either within one year or within one operating cycle, whichever is longer. Liabilities are classified as "current" if they are expected to be liquidated through the use of current assets or the creation of other current liabilities. The excess or deficiency of current assets over or under current liabilities, which is referred to as net working capital, identifies, if positive, the relatively liquid portion of total entity capital that serves as a buffer for meeting unexpected obligations arising within the ordinary operating cycle of the business.

In some industries, the concept of working capital has little importance and the balance sheet is not classified. Such industries are broker-dealer, investment companies, real estate companies, and utilities. Personal financial statements are unclassified for the same reason.

Sources of GAAP						
ARB	*APB*	*FAS*	*FIN*	*FTB*	*EITF*	*CON*
43, Ch. 2, 3A	6, 10, 12, 21, 22	5, 6, 12, 57, 78, 95, 115, 130	8, 39, 45	793	02-1	6

DEFINITIONS OF TERMS

Assets. Probable future economic benefits obtained or controlled by a particular entity as a result of past transactions or events (CON 6).

The following three characteristics must be present for an item to qualify as an asset:

1. The asset must provide probable future economic benefit that enables it to provide future net cash inflows.
2. The entity must be able to receive the benefit and restrict other entities' access to that benefit.
3. The event that provides the entity with the right to the benefit has occurred.

Those three characteristics must be present if an item is to meet the definition of an asset. Assets have other characteristics, but those characteristics are not essential to the definition. For example, most assets are exchangeable, legally enforceable, or tangible. But an item can still be an asset even if it cannot be exchanged, provided that the entity that owns it can use it in a manner that generates future cash flows or other benefits. Similarly, rights to an item need not be legally enforceable if the rights can be enforced in other ways, such as by using social or moral persuasion. Finally, items need not be tangible. Securities, patents, and similar ownership rights are assets despite the fact that they cannot be touched or seen.

The characteristic possessed by all assets is service potential (also called future economic benefit); the ability to provide directly or indirectly services or benefits to the owner of the asset, usually in the form of future cash inflows. Once recognized, an asset remains on a balance sheet until the asset is exchanged for another or used to settle a liability, its future economic benefits are used up, or the asset can no longer provide future benefits (obsolescence).

Liabilities. Probable future sacrifices of economic benefits arising from present obligations of a particular entity to transfer assets or provide services to other entities in the future as a result of past transactions or events (CON 6).

The following three characteristics must be present for an item to qualify as a liability:

1. A liability requires that the entity settle a present obligation by the probable future transfer of an asset on demand, when a specified event occurs, or at a particular date.
2. The obligation cannot be avoided.
3. The event that obligates the entity has occurred.

Liabilities usually result from transactions in which entities obtain economic resources. For example, trade payables result from purchasing raw materials; salaries and wages payable result from using employees' time, and notes payable result from obtaining cash from a lender. Other liabilities may arise from nonreciprocal transfers such as the declaration of dividends to the owners of the entity or the pledge of assets to charitable organizations. An entity may involuntarily incur a liability. A liability may be imposed on the entity by government or by the court system in the form of taxes, fines, or levies. A liability may arise from price changes or interest rate changes.

Liabilities are imposed by agreement, by law, by court, by equitable or constructive obligation, and by business ethics and custom. Liabilities may be legally enforceable or they may be equitable obligations that arise from social, ethical, or moral requirements.

Liabilities continue in existence until the entity is no longer responsible for discharging them. Most liabilities are discharged either by transferring an asset or incurring another liability. However, some liabilities simply expire. For example, warranty liabilities are estimates of goods that will be returned for repair or replacement or cash that will have to be paid to a dissatisfied customer. At the end of the warranty period, any remaining liability simply is written off.

FASB is considering amending the definition of liabilities to include certain financial instruments (or components of compound financial instruments) that require or permit settlement by issuance of equity shares. This has been necessitated by the renewed attention being directed at FASB's longstanding project dealing with certain instruments that have traditionally been reported as equity although having certain characteristics of liabilities, such as puttable shares; with other instruments having characteristics of both debt and equity, such as convertible bonds and dual-indexed financial instruments; and with the general issue of distinguishing liabilities from equity. (See discussions in Chapters 13 and 17.)

Equity. Equity is the residual interest in the assets that remains after deducting its liabilities. In a business enterprise, the equity is the ownership interest (CON 6).

Equity is increased by owners' investments and by comprehensive income, and it is reduced by distributions to the owners. Equity of a business enterprise is the source of its distributions to the owners; all such distributions of enterprise assets to owners are voluntary. Because equity is a residual (the net amount of assets less liabilities), equity is affected by all transactions and events that increase or decrease assets without increasing or decreasing liabilities by the same amount.

A diagram taken from CON 6 that appears in the Appendix of Chapter 1 illustrates this relationship. For example, issuing a bond does not change equity because the increase in the asset (cash) is the same as the increase in the liability (bonds payable). Paying the interest on the bond does change equity. The decrease in the asset (cash) is not offset by a corresponding decrease in the liability (bonds payable).

In practice, the distinction between equity and liabilities may be difficult to ascertain. Securities such as convertible debt and preferred stock may have characteristics of both equity (residual ownership interest) and liabilities (nondiscretionary future sacrifices). For these items, accounting standards are used to ensure that similar transactions are reported in a similar manner by different entities.

Valuation account. The valuation account is a separate item on a balance sheet that reduces or increases the carrying amount of an asset or a liability. It is neither an asset nor a liability in its own right; it is merely part of the related asset or liability. For example, an estimate of uncollectible amounts reduces the carrying amount of a receivable, and a bond premium increases the carrying amount of a payable.

CONCEPTS, RULES, AND EXAMPLES

Limitations of a Balance Sheet

Although a balance sheet shows an entity's **financial position** at a point in time, it does not purport to report the entity's **value** at that point in time. There are several reasons why this is so. One limitation of the balance sheet is that many assets and liabilities are reported at historical exchange prices, which are used because they are objective and capable of being independently verified. However, historical exchange prices will equal values only at the time of the actual transaction; thereafter, the two will almost always diverge.

Many accountants believe that the balance sheet would be more useful if the assets were restated to reflect current values. These current values might or might not be market related, and may simply be historical cost adjusted for the changing value of the dollar. However, for some assets and liabilities, cost is a close approximation of current value. The cost of monetary assets such as cash, short-term investments, and receivables closely approximates their current values. The cost of current liabilities, which are liabilities that require either a current asset or another current liability to liquidate, is payable in a short period and closely approximates current values. If they were to be discounted, any discount amount would likely be immaterial because of the short time period before making payment.

For other assets and liabilities, cost can be significantly different from current value. Productive assets such as property, plant, equipment, and intangibles are reported at cost net of accumulated depreciation, depletion, or amortization. Those amounts may differ from their current values to the entity (value in use) or to others (exit or net realizable values). Long-term liabilities are recorded as the discounted value of future payments to be made under contract. On the date of debt issuance, the discount rate equals the market rate and current value equals balance sheet cost. However, as time passes and the market rate fluctuates, the recorded cost will not necessarily approximate the current value.

Although assets are often stated at historical cost, if market information indicates a permanent and material decline in value, generally accepted accounting principles usually require immediate recognition of the economic loss. In contrast, recognition of an appreciation in value is normally recorded only when realized through an arm's-length transaction (e.g., a sale). However, financial reporting standards have been changing to more often reflect changes in market values, increases as well as decreases, in the financial statements. FAS 115 (1993) and FAS 133 (1998) require that debt securities, most equity securities, and derivative financial instruments be reported at fair value. Reporting liabilities at fair value is less common under current GAAP, but there are certain exceptions, including mandatorily redeemable preferred stock, which is classified as debt per FAS 150 and measured initially and subsequently at fair value.

Another limitation of the balance sheet is that it ignores the effects of the time value of money on the items presented. Although certain receivables and payables may be discounted (APB 21), most items are stated at face value regardless of the timing of the cash flows that will ultimately be generated.

In the historical cost balance sheet, estimates are frequently used to determine the carrying/book values of many of the assets. Estimates are used in determining the collectibility of receivables, salability of inventory, and useful life of long-term assets. All of these estimates impact the amount to be presented in the balance sheet; for example, estimated uncollectible accounts are deducted from accounts receivable to derive the net realizable value displayed in the balance sheet. While estimates are necessary in order to divide and separate economic events occurring between two distinct accounting periods, these require informed judgments for which there is little guidance in accounting literature.

A final limitation of the balance sheet is that it ignores items that are of financial value to the firm but that cannot be objectively determined. For example, internally generated goodwill, a skilled and trained workforce, and secret processes are of financial value, but since these values are not measurable under current accounting principles and practices, they are not presented on the balance sheet. Only assets obtained in a market transaction are recorded on the books and records of an entity.

Form of Balance Sheet

The format of a balance sheet is not specified by any authoritative pronouncement. Instead, formats and titles have developed as a matter of tradition and, in some cases, through industry practice.

Two basic formats are used.

1. The balanced format, in which the sum of the amounts for liabilities and equity are added together on the face of the statement to illustrate that assets equal liabilities plus equity
2. The equity format, which shows totals for assets, liabilities, and equity but no sums, illustrating that assets less liabilities equals equity

Those two formats can take one of two forms.

1. The account form, which shows assets on the left-hand side of the page and liabilities and equity on the right-hand side
2. The report form, which is a top-to-bottom or running presentation

The three elements that are displayed in the heading of a balance sheet are

1. The name of the entity whose financial position is being presented
2. The title of the statement
3. The date of the statement

The entity's name should appear as written in the legal document that created it (e.g., the certificate of incorporation, partnership agreement, etc.). The title may also reflect the legal status of the enterprise as a corporation, partnership, sole proprietorship, or divisions of some other entity. Where the entity's name does not disclose its legal status, supplemental information could be added to the title in order to clarify that status. A few examples are as follows:

ABC Company
(a partnership)

ABC Company
(a sole proprietorship)

ABC Company
(a division of DEF, Inc.)

The use of the titles "balance sheet," "statement of financial position," or "statement of financial condition" denotes the use of generally accepted accounting principles. If some other comprehensive basis of accounting, such as income tax or cash, is used, the title of the financial statement must be adjusted to reflect this variation. Titles such as "Statements of Assets and Liabilities—Tax Basis" would be necessary to differentiate the financial statement being presented from a balance sheet.

The last day of the fiscal period should be used as the statement date. Usually, that is a month-end date unless the entity uses a fiscal reporting period always ending on a particular day of the week such as Friday or Sunday. In these cases, the balance sheet would be dated accordingly (i.e., December 26, October 1, etc.).

Balance sheets generally should be uniform in appearance from one period to the next. The form, terminology, captions, and pattern of combining insignificant items should be consistent. If comparative statements are presented, the prior year's information should be restated to conform with the current year's presentation if changes in presentation are made.

Classification of Assets

Assets, liabilities, and stockholders' equity are separated in the balance sheet so that important relationships can be shown and attention can be focused on significant subtotals.

Current assets. Per ARB 43, Chapter 3, current assets are cash and other assets that are reasonably expected to be realized in cash or sold or consumed during the normal operating cycle of the business. When the normal operating cycle is less than one year, a one-year period is used to distinguish current assets from noncurrent assets. When the operating cycle exceeds one year, the operating cycle will serve as the proper period for purposes of current asset classification. When the operating cycle is very long, the usefulness of the concept of current assets diminishes. The following items would be classified as current assets:

1. **Cash and cash equivalents** include cash on hand consisting of coins, currency, undeposited checks; money orders and drafts; deposits in banks; and certain short-term, highly liquid investments. Anything accepted by a bank for deposit would be considered as cash. Cash must be available for a demand withdrawal. Cash that is restricted as to withdrawal, such as certificates of deposit, would not be included with cash because of the time restrictions. Also, cash must be available for current use in order to be classified as a current asset. Cash that is restricted in use would not be included in cash unless its restrictions will expire within the operating cycle. Cash restricted for a noncurrent use, such as cash designated for the purchase of property or equipment, would not be included in current assets. Per FAS 95, cash equivalents include short-term, highly liquid investments that (1) are readily convertible to known amounts of cash and (2) are so near their maturity (maturities of three months or less from the date of purchase by the enterprise) that they present negligible risk of changes in value because of changes in interest rates. Treasury bills, commercial paper, and money market funds are all examples of cash equivalents. Chapter 5 discusses cash in more detail.
2. **Short-term investments** are readily marketable securities acquired through the use of temporarily idle cash. To be classified as current assets, management must be willing and able to sell the security to meet current cash needs or the investment must mature within one year (or the operating cycle, if longer). These securities are accounted for under FAS 115. Securities classified as trading securities under FAS 115 must be reported as current assets. Securities classified as held-to-maturity or available-for-sale are reported as either current or noncurrent dependent upon management's intended holding period, the security's maturity date (if any), or both. It is not necessary to show the FAS 115 classification on the face of the balance sheet. Short-term investments can be combined into a single line if the classification details appear in the notes to the financial statements. The balance sheet presentation might be as follows:

Marketable securities	$xxx

   Chapter 6 discusses short-term investments in more detail.
3. **Receivables** include accounts and notes receivable, receivables from affiliate companies, and officer and employee receivables. The term "accounts receivable" represents amounts due from customers arising from transactions in the ordinary course of business. Valuation allowances, if any, should be clearly stated. Allowances for uncollectibility may be based on a percentage of sales or based on direct analysis of the receivables. Valuation allowances to reflect the time value of money (discounts) should be reported with the related receivable. If material, the receivables should be broken down into their component parts. Receivables pledged as

collateral should be reported as a separate line on the balance sheet or should be disclosed in the notes to financial statements. A receivables section might be presented as follows:

Receivables:	
Accounts	$xxx
Notes	xxx
	xxx
Less allowance for doubtful accounts	(xxx)
	xxx
Affiliate companies	xxx
Officers and employees	xxx
	$xxx

Chapter 5 discusses receivables in more detail.

4. **Inventories** are goods on hand and available for sale. The basis of valuation and the method of pricing should be disclosed.

Inventories—at the lower of cost or market (specific identification)	$xxx

In the case of a manufacturing concern, raw materials, work in process, and finished goods should be disclosed separately on the balance sheet or in the notes to financial statements.

Inventories:	
Finished goods	$xxx
Work in process	xxx
Raw materials	xxx
	$xxx

Chapter 7 discusses inventories in more detail.

5. **Prepaid expenses** are prepayments made to secure the use of assets or the receipt of services at a future date. Prepaid expenses will not be converted to cash, but they are classified as current assets because, if not prepaid, they would have required the use of current assets during the coming year (or operating cycle, if longer). Prepaid rent, prepaid insurance, prepaid interest, and prepaid advertising are examples of prepaid expenses. Chapter 5 discusses prepaid expenses in more detail.

Noncurrent assets. Excluded from the classification of current assets are assets that will not be realized in cash during the next year (or operating cycle, if longer). The following assets would be classified as noncurrent assets:

1. **Long-term investments** are investments that are intended to be held for an extended period of time (longer than one operating cycle). The following are the three major types of long-term investments:

   a. **Debt and equity securities** are stocks, bonds, and long-term notes. Securities that are classified as available-for-sale or held-to-maturity investments under FAS 115 would be included here if management intended to hold them for more than one year. Under FAS 115, the classifications of these securities need not be reported on the face of the balance sheet if they are reported in the notes.

Long-term investments:		
Investments in A company stock		$xxx
Notes receivable	$ xxx	
Less discount on notes receivable	(xxx)	xxx
Investment in B company bonds		xxx
		$xxx

   b. **Tangible assets** not currently used in operations (e.g., land held for sale).

c. **Investments held in special funds** (e.g., sinking funds, pension funds, amounts held for plant expansion, and cash surrender values of life insurance policies).

Chapter 10 describes investments in more detail.

2. **Property, plant, and equipment** are assets of a durable nature that are to be used in the production or sale of goods, sale of other assets, or rendering of services rather than being held for sale (e.g., machinery and equipment, buildings, furniture and fixtures, natural resources, and land). These should be disclosed with related accumulated depreciation/depletion as follows:

Property, plant, and equipment	$xxx
Less accumulated depreciation	(xxx)
or	$xxx
Property, plant, and equipment (net of $xxx accumulated depreciation)	$xxx

Accumulated depreciation may be shown in total or by major classes of depreciable assets. In addition to showing this amount on the balance sheet, the notes to the financial statements should contain balances of major classes of depreciable assets, by nature or function, at the balance sheet date. Assets under capital leases should be separately disclosed. A general description of the method or methods used in computing depreciation with respect to major classes of depreciable assets (APB 12) should also be included in the notes to financial statements. Chapter 9 discusses property, plant, and equipment in more detail.

3. **Intangible assets** include rights that are expected to have future economic benefits and purchased goodwill. Goodwill is the reputation of an entity with its customers. Goodwill that is purchased in a business combination is recognized, internally generated goodwill is not. Patents, copyrights, logos, and trademarks are examples of rights that are recognized as intangible assets. Intangible assets whose value diminishes through use or the passage of time are amortized to expense. Generally, the amortization of an intangible asset is credited directly to the asset account, although it is acceptable to use an accumulated amortization account. Intangible assets with an indefinite economic useful life are tested for impairment at periodic intervals. Chapter 11 discusses goodwill in more detail. Chapter 9 discusses other intangible assets.
4. **Other assets.** Other assets is an all-inclusive heading which incorporates accounts that do not fit neatly into any of the other asset categories (e.g., long-term prepaid expenses, deferred taxes, bond issue costs, noncurrent receivables, and restricted cash).

Classification of Liabilities

Liabilities are displayed on the balance sheet in the order of payment. The distinction between current and noncurrent assets and liabilities generally rests upon both the ability of the entity and the intent of the entity to liquidate or not to liquidate within the traditional one-year time frame.

Current liabilities. Per ARB 43, Chapter 3, obligations are classified as current if their liquidation is reasonably expected to require the use of existing resources properly classifiable as current assets or to create other current obligations. Obligations that are due on demand or that are callable at any time by the lender are classified as current regardless of the intent of the entity or lender. The following items would be classified as current liabilities:

1. **Accounts payable** are obligations that arise primarily from the acquisition of goods and services entering the operating cycle. Accounts payable includes amounts for trade payables, salaries and wages payable, commissions and bonuses payable.
2. **Notes payable** also are obligations that generally arise from the acquisition of goods and services. They differ from accounts payable because the supplier or vendor finances the purchase on terms longer than the customary period for trade payables. The supplier or vendor generally charges interest for the privilege. If interest is not charged, it is imputed in accordance with APB 21. (Imputation of interest is discussed further in Chapter 13.) Valuation accounts for the resulting discount are shown with the note, as follows:

Notes payable, net of discounts of $xx		$ xxx
or		
Notes payable	$ xxx	
Less discounts	(xxx)	$ xxx

3. **Dividends payable** are obligations to distribute cash or other assets to stockholders that arise from the declaration of dividends by the entity's board of directors.
4. **Advances and deposits** are collections of cash or other assets in advance to ensure the future delivery of goods or services. Advances and deposits are classified as current **liabilities** if the goods and services are to be delivered within the next year (or the operating cycle, if longer). Advances and deposits include such items as subscriptions payable, advance rentals, and customer deposits. Certain advances and deposits are sometimes titled unearned revenues.
5. **Agency collections and withholdings** are liabilities that arise because the entity acts as an agent for another. Employee tax withholdings, sales taxes, and wage garnishments are examples of agency collections.
6. **Current portion of long-term debt** is the portion of a long-term obligation that will be settled during the next year (or operating cycle, if longer) by using current assets. Generally, this amount includes only the payments due within the next year under the terms of the underlying agreement. However, if a covenant in a long-term debt agreement has been violated and, as a result, the investor can demand payment, the entire debt amount is classified as current unless the lender waives the right to call the debt for a period in excess of one year (or one operating cycle, if longer). In two cases, obligations to be paid in the next period should not be classified as current liabilities. Debt expected to be refinanced through another long-term issue and debt that will be retired through the use of noncurrent assets, such as a bond sinking fund, are treated as noncurrent liabilities because the liquidation does not require the use of current assets or the creation of other current liabilities.

Chapter 12 discusses current liabilities in more detail.

Noncurrent liabilities. Obligations that are not expected to be liquidated within one year (or the current operating cycle, if longer) are classified as noncurrent. The following items would be classified as noncurrent:

1. **Notes and bonds payable** are obligations that will be paid in more than one year (or one operating cycle, if longer). Most notes and bonds require periodic payments of interests, and some require periodic payments of principal. If the stated rate of interest on a note or bond is different than the market rate on the day the note or bond is issued, the proceeds from issuance will differ from the face amount of the note or bond. If the market rate is higher than the stated rate, the bonds will be issued at a discount, which means that the proceeds were less than the face amount. If the market rate is lower than the stated rate, the bonds will be issued at a premium

which means that the proceeds exceed the face amount. Valuation accounts for the resulting discount or premiums are shown with the note, as follows:

Notes payable, including premium of $xx		$xxx
or		
Notes payable	$xxx	
Plus premium	$xxx	$xxx

Discounts and premiums are amortized using the effective-interest-rate method, which results in a steady interest rate over the life of the debt. Chapter 13 discusses notes and bonds payable in more detail.

2. **Lease obligations** are debts that arise from obtaining the use of property or equipment via a capital lease contract. Chapter 14 discusses lease obligations.
3. **Accrued expenses** are long-term obligations that arise out of the normal course of business. Pension obligations, postemployment obligations, and postretirement obligations are long-term obligations to provide future retirement, insurance, or other benefits to employees as a result of their past service. Those obligations are described in more detail in Chapter 16. Deferred income taxes are liabilities to pay taxes in the future that result from differences between net income, which is reported in compliance with GAAP, and taxable income, which is reported in compliance with tax law. Chapter 15 discusses deferred income taxes.
4. **Written put options on the option writer's (issuer's) equity shares and forward contracts to purchase an issuer's equity shares that require physical or net cash settlement** are classified as liabilities on the issuer's balance sheet. The obligation is classified as noncurrent unless the date at which the contract will be settled is within the next year (or operating cycle, if longer). These contracts are discussed further in Chapter 13.
5. **Certain financial instruments that embody an unconditional obligation to issue a variable number of equity shares and financial instruments other than outstanding shares that embody a conditional obligation to issue a variable number of equity shares** are classified as a liability in the issuer's balance sheet. The obligation is classified as noncurrent unless the date at which the financial instrument will be settled is within the next year (or operating cycle, if longer). Chapter 13 discusses these financial instruments.
6. **Contingent obligations** are recorded when it is probable that an obligation will occur as the result of a past event. In most cases, a future event will eventually confirm the amount payable, the payee, or the date payable. Examples of contingent obligations are lawsuits that have not been settled, product warranty obligations, guarantees of indebtedness (other than the obligation to stand ready to perform, which is a noncontingent liability), and agreements to repurchase an asset or make future payments. The classification of a contingent liability as current or noncurrent depends on when the confirming even will occur and how soon afterwards payment must be made. Contingencies are discussed further in Chapter 12.
7. **Mandatorily redeemable shares** are recorded as liabilities per FAS 150. A mandatory redemption clause requires common or preferred stock to be redeemed (retired) at a specific date(s) or upon occurrence of an event which is uncertain as to timing although ultimately certain to occur. This feature is in contrast to callable preferred stock, which may be redeemed at the issuing corporation's option and which is appropriately categorized as equity. The obligation is classified as noncurrent unless the date at which the shares must be redeemed is within the next year (or

operating cycle, if longer). For additional discussion on these securities see Chapters 13 and 17.

Offsetting Assets and Liabilities

In general, assets and liabilities are not offset against each other. Offsetting in the financial statements is a proper presentation only where the right of setoff exists. FIN 39 states that right of setoff exists only when all the following conditions are met:

1. Each of the two parties owes the other determinable amounts (although they may be in different currencies and bear different rates of interest).
2. The entity has the right to set off against the amount owed by the other party.
3. The entity intends to set off.
4. The right of setoff is legally enforceable.

In particular cases, state laws or bankruptcy laws may impose restrictions or prohibitions against the right of setoff. Furthermore, when maturities differ, only the party with the nearest maturity can offset because the party with the later maturity must settle in the manner determined by the party with the earlier maturity.

The offsetting of cash or other assets against a tax liability or other amounts due to governmental bodies is acceptable only under limited circumstances. When it is clear that a purchase of securities is in substance an advance payment of taxes payable in the near future and the securities are acceptable for the payment of taxes, amounts may be offset. Primarily this occurs as an accommodation to governmental bodies that issue tax anticipation notes in order to accelerate the receipt of cash for future taxes.

For forwards, interest rate swaps, currency swaps, options, and other conditional or exchange contracts, the conditions for the right of offset must exist or the fair value of contracts in a loss position cannot be offset against the fair value of contracts in a gain position. Nor can accrued receivable amounts be offset against accrued payable amounts. If, however, there is a master netting arrangement, then fair value amounts recognized for forwards, interest or currency swaps, options, or other such contracts may be offset without respect to the conditions previously specified.

FIN 41 permits the offset of amounts recognized as payables in repurchase agreements against amounts recognized as receivables in reverse repurchase agreements with the same counterparty. If certain conditions are met, an entity may, but is not required to, offset the amounts recognized. The additional conditions are

1. The repurchase agreements and the reverse repurchase agreements must have the same explicit settlement date.
2. The repurchase agreements and the reverse repurchase agreements must be executed in accordance within a master netting agreement.
3. The securities underlying the repurchase agreements and the reverse repurchase agreements exist in "book entry" form.
4. The repurchase agreements and the reverse repurchase agreements will be settled on a securities transfer system that transfers ownership of "book entry" securities, and banking arrangements are in place so that the entity must only keep cash on deposit sufficient to cover the net payable.
5. The same account at the clearing bank is used for the cash inflows of the settlement of the reverse repurchase agreements and the cash outflows in the settlement of repurchase agreement.

Classification of Stockholders' Equity

Stockholders' equity is the ownership interest of the stockholders in the assets of the corporation. It is the residual amount after liabilities are subtracted from assets. Stockholders' equity arises from three sources: contributed capital, retained earnings, and accumulated other comprehensive income. Stockholders' equity is discussed further in Chapter 17.

Contributed capital. Contributed capital is the amount of equity invested in the corporation by its owners. It consists of capital stock and additional paid-in capital. Contributed capital arises from issuance of common and preferred stock to investors, from transactions by the corporation in its own stock (for example, treasury stock, stock dividends, conversion of convertible bonds) and from donation of assets or services.

Capital stock. Capital stock is the par or stated value of preferred and common shares. In the past, capital stock was the legal capital of the corporation—the amount that could not be distributed to stockholders so that the interest of creditors would be protected. In recent years, some states have changed laws so that legal capital includes additional paid-in capital (i.e., in those states the distinction between the capital stock and additional paid-in capital is gone). The face of the balance sheet often provides information about the type of issues, the par or stated value per share, and the number of shares authorized, issued, and outstanding. For preferred stock, the liquidation preferences and features (e.g., whether participating, cumulative, convertible, or callable) are also shown, as follows:

6% cumulative preferred stock, $100 par value, callable at $115, 10,000 shares authorized and outstanding	$xxx
Common stock, $10 par value per share, 2,000,000 shares authorized, 1,500,000 shares issued and outstanding	$xxx

Additional paid-in capital. There are two major categories of additional paid-in capital.

1. Paid-in capital in excess of par/stated value, which is the difference between the actual issue price and par/stated value. Amounts in excess should be disclosed separately for common stock and each issue of preferred stock as follows:

Additional paid-in capital—6% preferred stock	$xxx
Additional paid-in capital—common stock	$xxx

2. Paid-in capital from other transactions which includes treasury stock, retirement of stock, stock dividends recorded at market, lapse of stock purchase warrants, conversion of convertible bonds in excess of the par value of the stock, and any other additional capital from the company's own stock transactions.

Donated capital. Donated capital results from gifts of assets or services to the corporation. Transactions that create donated capital are uncommon. If those transaction occur, the amount of donated capital, which is measured at the fair value of the asset or services received, is displayed on the face of the balance sheet, as follows:

Donated capital	$xxx

Retained earnings. Retained earnings is the cumulative earnings of the corporation from the date of inception (or reorganization) to the date of the financial statements less the cumulative distribution to stockholders either directly (dividends or reacquisition of shares) or indirectly (treasury stock).

In the past, some corporations would appropriate (set aside) a portion of retained earnings for a special purpose and indicate on the face of the balance sheet or in the notes to the financial statements that the appropriated amount was unavailable for dividends. That practice is uncommon today.

Accumulated other comprehensive income. Other comprehensive income is the change in equity of a business enterprise during a period that arises from sources other than net income and transactions with owners. Under current accounting standards, its accumulated components include net unrealized holding gains and losses on investments classified as available-for-sale securities (FAS 115), the effective portion of the gain or loss on derivative instruments designated and qualified as either cash-flow hedges or hedges of forecasted foreign-currency-denominated transactions (FAS 133), the excess of minimum pension liability over unrecognized prior service cost (FAS 87), and unrealized gains (losses) on foreign currency translations (FAS 52). The components of accumulated other comprehensive income are shown either in the statement of changes in stockholders' equity or in the stockholders' equity section, as follows:

Accumulated other comprehensive income		
Foreign currency translation adjustments	$xx	
Pension liability adjustment	xx	
Unrealized gains on securities	xx	xx

Treasury stock. Treasury stock is shares of the corporation that have been issued, repurchased by the corporation, and that have not been retired or canceled. These shares have no voting rights and they receive no dividends. Treasury stock is traditionally shown as the last item (a deduction) within the stockholders' equity section. (In very limited circumstances involving employee compensation plans, treasury stock can be shown as an asset.) The number of shares and the method of valuation are generally shown, as follows:

Treasury stock, 1,000 shares at cost	$ xxx

Classification of Partners' Capital

In partnership entities, the balance sheet is the same as all other entities except for the net worth section. In a partnership, this section is usually referred to as partners' capital. In partnership accounting, the net worth section of the balance sheet includes the equity interests of the partners. Although each individual partner's capital need not be displayed, the totals for each class of partner, general or limited, should be shown. Loans to or from partners should be displayed as assets and liabilities of the partnership and not as reductions or additions to partners' capital. Payments to partners of interest on loans are properly classified as expenses on the income statement. Payments to partners of interest on capital or of salaries are considered an allocation of profits and are usually not expensed on the income statement. However, in an attempt to emulate corporate financial reporting, some partnerships, with adequate disclosure, do display such payments as expenses.

Relation to the Other Financial Statements

Financial statements interrelate because they reflect different aspects of the same transactions. For example, an increase in trade receivables (balance sheet) does not occur without an increase in revenue (income statement). A purchase of equipment increases an asset (balance sheet) and decreases cash (statement of cash flows). Likewise, policy decisions generally impact more than one financial statement. A decision to value inventory using the first-in, first-out method (balance sheet) determines the amount of cost of goods sold (income statement). No single financial statement provides all the information that is necessary when making decisions about investing in or lending money to an entity. Instead, most financial analysis examines relationships between the statements (for example, return on equity, turnover ratios, and cash flow per share).

Disclosures

In addition to the measurement accounting principles that guide the values placed on the elements included in the balance sheet, there are disclosure accounting principles which specify the disclosures that are necessary because the financial statements would be misleading because of their omission.

The following are five techniques of disclosure:

1. Parenthetical explanations
2. Notes to the financial statements
3. Cross-references
4. Valuation accounts
5. Supporting schedules

Parenthetical explanations. Supplemental information is disclosed by means of parenthetical explanations following the appropriate balance sheet items. For example

Common stock ($10 par value, 200,000 shares authorized, 150,000 issued)	$1,500,000

Parenthetical explanations have an advantage over both notes to the financial statements and supporting schedules. Parenthetical explanations place the disclosure in the body of the statement. The supplemental information could be overlooked if it is placed in a note or schedule.

Notes to financial statements. If the additional information cannot be disclosed in a relatively short and concise parenthetical explanation, a note should be used. For example

Inventories (see note 1)	$2,550,000

The notes to the financial statements would contain the following:

> **Note 1:** Inventories are stated at the lower of cost or market. Cost is determined on the first-in, first-out method and market is determined on the basis of estimated net realizable value. The market value of the inventory is $2,720,000.

Cross-references. Cross-referencing is used when there is a direct relationship between two accounts on the balance sheet. For example, among the current assets, the following might be shown if $1,500,000 of accounts receivable were pledged as collateral for a $1,200,000 bank loan:

Accounts receivable pledged to bank	$1,500,000

Included in the current liabilities would be the following:

Bank loan payable—secured by accounts receivable	$1,200,000

Valuation accounts. Valuation accounts are used to reduce or increase the carrying amount of some assets and liabilities found in financial statements. Accumulated depreciation reduces the book value for property, plant, and equipment, and a bond premium (discount) increases (decreases) the face value of a bond payable as shown in the following illustrations:

Equipment	$18,000,000	
Less accumulated depreciation	(1,625,000)	$16,375,000
Bonds payable	$20,000,000	
Less discount on bonds payable	(1,300,000)	$18,700,000
Bonds payable	$20,000,000	
Add premium on bonds payable	1,300,000	$21,300,000

Supporting schedules. A supporting schedule might be used to provide additional detail about an item in the financial statements. For example, consolidating schedules might be included in addition to the basic financial statement or a five-year summary of selected financial data might be included. In general, supporting schedules are not used to provide information required by GAAP because those schedules are not part of the financial statements and are subjected to only limited procedures by auditors.

Accounting policies. There are many different methods of valuing assets, recognizing revenues, and assigning costs. Financial statement users must be aware of the accounting policies used by enterprises so that sound economic decisions can be made. Per APB 22, the disclosures should identify and describe the accounting principles followed by the entity and methods of applying those principles that materially affect the determination of financial position, changes in cash flows, or results of operations. The accounting policies should encompass those accounting principles and methods that involve the following:

1. Selection from acceptable alternatives
2. Principles and methods peculiar to the industry
3. Unique applications of GAAP

The accounting policies disclosure should not duplicate information disclosed elsewhere as part of the financial statements. The accounting policies usually appear in a separate section called "Summary of Significant Accounting Policies" or as the first note of the notes to the financial statements.

Related parties. According to FAS 57, *Related-Party Disclosures*, financial statements should include disclosure of material related-party transactions other than compensation arrangements, expense allowances, or other similar items that occur in the ordinary course of business.

A related party is essentially any party that controls or can significantly influence the management or operating policies of the company to the extent that the company may be prevented from fully pursuing its own interests. Related parties include affiliates, investees accounted for by the equity method, trusts for the benefit of employees, principal owners, management, and immediate family members of owners or management.

Entities should disclose transactions with related parties even if there is no accounting recognition made for such transactions (e.g., a service is performed without payment). Disclosures should not imply that related-party transactions were on terms essentially equivalent to arm's-length dealings unless those claims can be substantiated. If financial position or the results of operations of the reporting entity could change significantly because of common control or common management, the nature of the ownership or management control should be disclosed, even if there were no transactions between the entities.

The disclosures generally should include

1. Nature of relationship.
2. Description of transactions and effects of such transactions on the financial statements for each period for which an income statement is presented.
3. Dollar amount of transactions for each period for which an income statement is presented and effects of any change in the terms of such transactions as compared to the terms used in prior periods.
4. Amounts due to and from related parties as of the date of each balance sheet presented together with the terms and manner of settlement.

Comparative statements. In order to increase the usefulness of financial statements, many companies include financial statements for the prior year in their annual reports. Some also include five or ten-year summaries of condensed financial information. These comparative statements allow investment analysts and other interested readers to perform comparative analysis of pertinent information. ARB 43, Chapter 2 states the presentation of comparative financial statements in annual reports enhances the usefulness of such reports and brings out more clearly the nature and trends of current changes affecting the enterprise.

That presentation emphasizes the fact that the statements for a series of periods are far more significant than those for a single period and that the accounts for one period are but an installment of what is essentially a continuous history.

Subsequent events. The balance sheet is dated as of the last day of the fiscal period, but a period of time usually elapses before the financial statements are issued. During this period, significant events or transactions may have occurred that materially affect the company's financial position. These events and transactions are called subsequent events. Significant events occurring between the balance sheet date and issue date of the financial statements could make those financial statements misleading if not disclosed.

There are two types of subsequent events (which are defined at SAS 1, *Subsequent Events*). The first type consists of events that provide additional evidence about conditions that existed at the date of the balance sheet and which affect the estimates inherent in the process of preparing financial statements. The second type consists of events that provide evidence with respect to conditions that did not exist at the date of the balance sheet but arose subsequent to that date. The first type results in adjustments of the financial statements. The second type does not require adjustment of the financial statements but may require disclosure in order to keep the financial statements from being misleading. Disclosure can be made in the form of notes, supporting schedules, and pro forma statements.

Examples of subsequent events

1. A loss on an uncollectible trade account receivable that results from a customer's deteriorating financial condition, which led to bankruptcy subsequent to the balance sheet date, would be indicative of conditions existing at the balance sheet date, thereby calling for adjustment of the financial statements before their issuance. On the other hand, a loss on an uncollectible trade account receivable resulting from a customer's major casualty, such as a fire or flood subsequent to the balance sheet date, would not be indicative of conditions existing at the balance sheet date, and the adjustment of the financial statements would not be appropriate. However, if the amount is material, disclosure would be required.
2. A loss arising from the recognition after the balance sheet date that plant and equipment had been impaired because of reduced marketability for the product or service it can produce would be an economic event in process at the balance sheet date and would require adjustment and recognition of the loss.
3. A settlement of a lawsuit would require adjustment of the financial statements if the event that gave rise to the claim occurred prior to the balance sheet date. However, only disclosure is required if the event that gave rise to the claim occurred after the balance sheet date, and then only if the amount involved were material.
4. The second type of events (those not existing at the balance sheet date) that require disclosure but not adjustment include the following:

   a. Sale of a bond or capital stock issue
   b. Purchase of a business
   c. Loss of plant or inventories as a result of fire or flood
   d. Gains or losses on certain marketable securities

Contingencies. A contingency is defined in FAS 5 as an existing condition, situation, or set of circumstances involving uncertainty as to possible gain or loss. The uncertainty will ultimately be resolved when one or more future events occur or fail to occur. Resolution of the uncertainty may confirm the acquisition of an asset, the reduction of a liability, the loss or impairment of an asset, or the incurrence of a liability.

If it is probable that an asset has been impaired or that a liability has been incurred at the date of the financial statements and the amount of that loss can be reasonably estimated, the loss is accrued by a charge to earnings and the recognition of a liability. Contingencies requiring accrual are discussed more fully in Chapter 12.

However, if it is only reasonably possible that a future event will confirm that an asset was impaired or a liability has been incurred at the balance sheet date, an entity should disclose the contingency if the amount involved could have a material effect on the financial statements. The disclosure should include the nature of the contingency and either an estimate of the amount of the loss or the range of possible losses. If an estimate of loss cannot be made, that fact must be disclosed.

If the likelihood is remote that a loss has been incurred, no disclosure is necessary in most circumstances. However, guarantees of the indebtedness of others, guarantees to repurchase receivables or other assets, and obligations of commercial banks under standby letters of credit are always disclosed. The required disclosure should include the nature and amount of the guarantee. Discussion of the recognition and disclosure of guarantees is included in Chapter 12.

An estimated gain from a **gain contingency** usually is not reflected in the balance sheet or income statement because doing so might recognize revenue prior to its realization. Adequate disclosure of the gain contingency must be made, but care must be taken to avoid misleading implications as to the likelihood of realization. For example, if the entity may be able to recover some portion of an incurred loss by proceeding against a third party, that fact might be disclosed.

Contracts and negotiations. All significant contractual agreements and negotiations should be disclosed in the notes to the financial statements. For example, lease contract provisions, pension obligations, requirements contracts, bond indenture covenants, and stock option plans should be clearly disclosed in the notes.

Risks and Uncertainties

AICPA Statement of Position 94-6, *Disclosure of Certain Significant Risks and Uncertainties*, requires disclosure in financial statements about risks and uncertainties existing as of the date of those statements that could significantly affect the amounts reported in the near term. **Near term** is defined as a period of time not to exceed one year from the date of the financial statements. The four areas of disclosure required by SOP 94-6 are risks and uncertainties relating to the entity's nature of operations, use of estimates in the preparation of financial statements, certain significant estimates, and current vulnerability due to certain concentrations.

Nature of operations. SOP 94-6 requires that entities disclose the major products or services that they sell or provide. In addition, entities must disclose the principal markets that they serve as well as the location of such markets.

If an entity operates in more than one industry, it must disclose all industries it is operating within as well as the relative importance of each industry. The basis for determining the relative importance of each industry (assets, revenue, or earnings) should also be disclosed. Quantification is not required in disclosures about the nature of operations. Comparisons of relative importance for entities operating in more than one business can be conveyed by the use of words such as predominantly, equally, or major and other.

Use of estimates in the preparation of financial statements. Financial statements should disclose as an explanation that the preparation of financial statements in accordance with GAAP requires the use of estimates by management. The purpose of this disclosure is to clearly alert users to the pervasiveness of estimates.

Certain significant estimates. SOP 94-6 requires disclosures regarding estimates used in valuing assets, liabilities, or gain or loss contingencies if **both** of the following conditions are met (SOP 94-6):

1. It is at least **reasonably possible** that the estimate of the effect on the financial statements of a condition, situation, or set of circumstances that existed at the date of the financial statements will change in the **near term** due to one or more future confirming events.
2. The effect of the change would be **material** to the financial statements.

For the purposes of determining materiality, it is not the amount of an estimate that determines whether an item is material and must be disclosed, but rather the effect of using a different estimate that determines materiality.

The disclosure should indicate the nature of the uncertainty and that it is reasonably possible that the estimate will change in the near term. SOP 94-6 is separate from and does not change FAS 5, *Accounting for Contingencies*. If an estimate is covered under FAS 5 as a loss contingency, the disclosure should include an estimate of the possible range of loss, or state that an estimate cannot be made. Disclosure of any factors that would make an estimate sensitive to change is encouraged but not required.

Many entities use risk-reduction techniques to mitigate losses. If the effect of a change in the estimate is unlikely to be material because of risk-reduction techniques, the entity is encouraged, but not required, to disclose the uncertainty as well as the relevant risk-reduction techniques.

Examples of items that may be based on estimates that are particularly sensitive to change in the near term (SOP 94-6)

1. Inventory subject to rapid technological obsolescence
2. Specialized equipment subject to technological obsolescence
3. Valuation allowances for deferred tax assets based on future taxable income
4. Capitalized motion picture film production costs
5. Capitalized computer software costs
6. Deferred policy acquisition costs of insurance enterprises
7. Valuation allowances for commercial and real estate loans
8. Environmental remediation-related obligations
9. Litigation-related obligations
10. Contingent liabilities for obligations of other entities
11. Amounts reported for long-term obligations, such as amounts reported for pensions and postemployment benefits
12. Net proceeds recoverable, the provisions for expected loss to be incurred, or both, on disposition of a business or assets
13. Amounts reported for long-term contracts

Current vulnerability due to concentrations. Vulnerability from concentrations occurs when entities fail to diversify in order to mitigate risk. Financial statements must disclose such concentrations if management knows prior to issuance of the financial statements that all of the following conditions are met (SOP 94-6):

1. The concentration exists at the date of the financial statements.
2. The concentration makes the enterprise vulnerable to the risk of a near-term severe impact.
3. It is at least **reasonably possible** that the events that could cause the severe impact will occur in the near term.

Examples of concentrations that require disclosure (SOP 94-6)

1. Concentrations in the volume of business transacted with a particular customer, supplier, lender, grantor, or contributor
2. Concentrations in revenue from particular products, services, or fundraising events

3. Concentrations in the available sources of supply of materials, labor, services, or of licenses or other rights used in the entity's operations
4. Concentrations in the market or geographic area in which an entity conducts its operations

The potential for severe impact can occur as the result of the total or partial loss of a business relationship, price or demand changes, loss of patent protection, changes in the availability of a resource or right, or the disruption of operations in a market or geographic area. For purposes of SOP 94-6, it is always considered reasonably possible in the near term that any customer, grantor, or contributor will be lost and that operations located outside an entity's home country will be disrupted.

For concentrations of labor subject to collective bargaining agreements and concentrations of operations outside an entity's home country, the following additional disclosures are required (SOP 94-6):

1. For labor subject to collective bargaining agreements, disclosure should include both the percentage of the labor force covered by a collective bargaining agreement and the percentage of the labor force covered by a collectible bargaining agreement that will expire within one year.
2. For operations located outside the entity's home country, disclosure should include the carrying amounts of net assets and the geographic areas in which they are located.

Example of Balance Sheet Classification and Presentation

The classification and presentation of information in a balance sheet may be highly aggregated, highly detailed, or anywhere in between. In general, highly aggregated balance sheets are used in annual reports and other presentations provided to the public. Highly detailed balance sheets are used internally by management. The following highly aggregated balance sheet includes only a few lines items. The additional details required by generally accepted accounting principles are found in the notes to the financial statements.

ABC Corporation
Balance Sheet
December 31, 2005

Assets	
Current assets	xxx
Long-term investments	xxx
Plant, property, and equipment, net	xxx
Deferred tax assets	xxx
Intangible and other assets	xxx
Total assets	xxx
Liabilities and Shareholders' Equity	
Current liabilities	xxx
Accrued expenses	xxx
Deferred tax liabilities	xxx
Long-term debt	xxx
Total liabilities	xxx
Capital stock	xxx
Additional paid-in capital	xxx
Retained earnings	xxx
Accumulated other comprehensive income	xxx
Total shareholders' equity	xxx
Total liabilities and shareholders' equity	xxx

The following comprehensive balance sheet includes more line items (for details about specific assets and liabilities) than are found in many balance sheets.

ABC Corporation
Balance Sheet
December 31, 2005

Assets			
Current assets:			
Cash and bank deposits:			
Restricted to current bond maturity	$xxx		
Unrestricted	xxx	$xxx	
Short-term investments:			
Marketable equity securities (trading)		xxx	
Marketable debt securities (available-for-sale)		xxx	
Refundable income taxes		xxx	
Receivables from affiliates		xxx	
Accounts receivable	xxx		
Less allowance for doubtful accounts	(xxx)	xxx	
Notes receivable due in 2005	xxx		
Less discounts on notes receivable	(xxx)	xxx	
Dishonored notes receivable		xxx	
Installment notes due in 2006		xxx	
Interest receivable		xxx	
Creditors' accounts with debit balances		xxx	
Advances to employees		xxx	
Inventories (carried at lower of cost or market by FIFO):			
Finished goods	xxx		
Work in process	xxx		
Raw materials	xxx	xxx	
Prepaid expenses:			
Prepaid rent	xxx		
Prepaid insurance	xxx	xxx	
Total current assets			$xxx
Long-term investments:			
Investments in equity securities (available-for-sale)		xxx	
Investments in bonds (held-to-maturity)		xxx	
Investments in equity securities (at cost, plus equity in undistributed net earnings since acquisition)		xxx	
Investments in unused land and facilities		xxx	
Cash surrender value of officers' life insurance policies		xxx	
Sinking fund for bond retirement		xxx	
Plant expansion fund		xxx	
Total long-term investments			$xxx
Property, plant, and equipment:			
Land		$xxx	
Buildings		xxx	
Machinery and equipment		xxx	
Furniture and fixtures		xxx	
Leased assets		xxx	
Leasehold improvements		xxx	
Less accumulated depreciation and amortization		(xxx)	
Total property, plant, and equipment			xxx
Intangible assets net of amortization:			
Goodwill of acquired businesses		$xxx	
Patents		xxx	
Trademarks		xxx	
Total intangible assets, net			xxx
Other assets:			
Installment notes due after 2006		$xxx	
Unamortized bond issue costs		xxx	
Total other noncurrent assets			xxx
Total assets			$xxx

Liabilities and Stockholders' Equity			
Current liabilities:			
Accounts payable		$xxx	
Commercial paper and other short-term notes		xxx	
Salaries, wages, and commissions payable		xxx	
Taxes withheld from employees		xxx	
Income taxes payable		xxx	
Dividends payable		xxx	
Rent revenue collected in advance		xxx	
Other advances from customers		xxx	
Current portion of long-term debt		xxx	
Current obligations under capital leases		xxx	
Deferred tax liability		xxx	
Short-term portion of accrued warranty		xxx	
Other accrued liabilities		xxx	
Total current liabilities			$xxx
Noncurrent liabilities:			
Notes payable due after 2006	$xxx		
Plus unamortized note premium	xxx	$xxx	
Long-term bonds:			
10% debentures due 2015	xxx		
9 1/2% collateralized obligations maturing serially to 2008	xxx		
8% convertible subordinated debentures due 2020	xxx		
Less unamortized discounts net of premiums	(xxx)	xxx	
Accrued pension cost		xxx	
Obligations under capital leases		xxx	
Deferred tax liability		xxx	
Long-term portion of accrued warranty		xxx	
Total noncurrent liabilities			xxx
Total liabilities			$xxx
Capital stock:			
$12.50 convertible preferred stock, $100 stated value, 200,000 shares authorized, 175,000 outstanding	$xxx		
12% cumulative preferred stock, $100 stated value, callable at $115, 100,000 shares authorized and outstanding	xxx		
Common stock, $10 stated value, 500,000 shares authorized, 450,000 issued, 15,000 held in treasury	xxx		
Common stock subscribed 10,000 shares	xxx		
Less: Subscriptions receivable	(xxx)	$xxx	
Additional paid-in capital:			
From 12% cumulative preferred	xxx		
From common stock	xxx		
From treasury stock transactions	xxx		
From stock dividends	xxx		
From expiration of stock options	xxx		
Warrants outstanding	xxx	xxx	
Retained earnings		xxx	
Accumulated other comprehensive income:			
Net unrealized loss on available-for-sale securities	(xxx)		
Unrealized loss from foreign currency translation	(xxx)		
Excess of minimum pension liability over unrecognized prior service cost	(xxx)	(xxx)	
Less: Treasury stock at cost		(xxx)	
Total stockholders' equity			$xxx
Total liabilities and stockholders' equity			$xxx

EMERGING ISSUES TASK FORCE ISSUES SUMMARIES

02-1 Balance Sheet Classification of Assets Received in Exchange for Equity Instruments

This issue discusses the classification in the balance sheet of assets acquired in exchange for the issuance of fully vested, nonforfeitable equity instruments. If the asset acquired is other than a **nonrecourse** note or receivable or **any** note, receivable, or prepaid right to receive goods or services in the future obtained from a related party, it should be displayed in the grantor's balance sheet as an asset. If the asset acquired is a nonrecourse note or receivable or a note, receivable or prepaid right to receive goods or services in the future obtained from a related party, the transaction is in substance the issuance of an option and therefore, the nonrecourse note or other receivable should be classified in the grantor's balance sheet as contra equity. The Task Force considered whether transferability (or lack thereof) of the equity instruments should affect the balance sheet display of the asset, but decided that it should not.

Unvested, forfeitable equity instruments granted to other than an employee should be accounted for as unissued until the equity instruments vest. Consequently, there would be no recognition at the measurement date.

APPENDIX

ALTERNATIVE BALANCE SHEET SEGMENTATIONS UNDER GAAP

Classification of the balance sheet into current and noncurrent assets and liabilities was discussed in the body of this chapter. However, there are other segmentation schemes that are required under GAAP for various supplementary reporting purposes, depending upon the circumstances. Since these requirements do not utilize a common taxonomy, the following explanation will be referenced throughout *Wiley GAAP*.

Classification of assets (and sometimes liabilities also) may be required for the presentation of segment information under FAS 131. This requirement only applies to publicly held entities, although nonpublic companies may also elect to make such disclosures. Under FAS 131, it will be necessary to identify **operating segments** and **reportable segments** of the business. (Terms are defined below.)

A different classification strategy is required for purposes of testing for impairment of goodwill, under FAS 142. This standard created the concept of the **reporting unit** as a basis for making such an evaluation.

Yet another term, **business,** is defined in EITF 98-3 and is often used as a threshold criterion of what could not be considered a special-purpose entity (as addressed in various standards, including FAS 140).

Finally, another classification system is invoked under FAS 144 in testing for asset impairments. This standard established the concepts of **asset groups** and **disposal groups**.

The graphic below has been developed to illustrate how these different classification schemes overlap. It is possible that a given entity, if reporting segment data and if it has goodwill from a business combination on its balance sheet, may be required to apply most or all of these taxonomies in meeting its financial reporting obligations—to disclose segment information, to test for goodwill impairment, and to test for impairment of long-lived assets other than goodwill.

Definitions (with references to professional standards and the chapter of *Wiley GAAP* that covers the topic)

Operating segment (FAS 131, Chapter 20)—A component of an enterprise engaged in business activity for which it may earn revenues and incur expenses, about which separate financial information is available that is evaluated regularly by the chief operating decision makers in deciding how to allocate resources and in assessing performance.

Reportable segment (FAS 131, Chapter 20)—A segment is considered to be reportable if it is significant to the enterprise as a whole. A segment is regarded as significant if it satisfies any one of the three quantitative tests prescribed by FAS 131.

Reporting unit (FAS 142, Chapter 9)—A reporting unit is an operating segment or one level below an operating segment (referred to as a component). A component of an operating segment is a reporting unit if the component constitutes a business for which discrete financial information is available and segment management regularly reviews the operating results of that component. However, two or more components of an operating segment shall be aggregated and deemed a single reporting unit if the components have similar economic characteristics. An operating segment shall be deemed to be a reporting unit if all of its components are similar, if none of its components is a reporting unit, or if it comprises only a single component.

Business ((EITF 98-3, Chapter 11)—A business is a self-sustaining integrated set of activities and assets conducted and managed for the purpose of providing a return to investors.

Asset group (FAS 144, Chapter 9)—For a long-lived asset or assets to be held and used, the lowest level for which identifiable cash flows are largely independent of the cash flows of other groups of assets and liabilities.

Disposal group (FAS 144, Chapters 3 and 9)—For a long-lived asset or assets to be disposed of by sale or otherwise, assets to be disposed of together as a group in a single transaction and liabilities directly associated with those assets that will be transferred in the transaction.

Illustrative Organizational Groupings

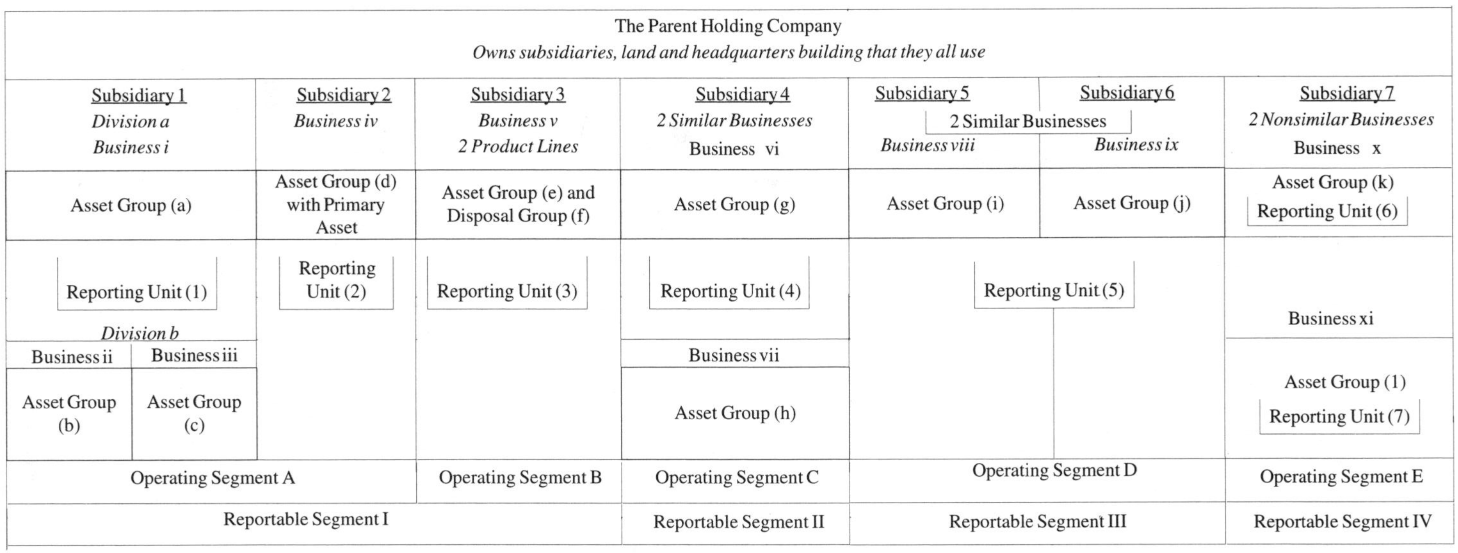

3 STATEMENTS OF INCOME AND COMPREHENSIVE INCOME

PERSPECTIVE AND ISSUES

The primary focus of financial reporting is to provide information about an entity's performance that is useful to present and potential investors, creditors, and others when they are making financial decisions. In financial reporting, performance is primarily measured by net income and its components, which are provided in the income statement. Although information in the income statement is information about past performance, investors, creditors, and others use that information to predict future performance.

In contrast to the balance sheet, which provides information about an entity at a point in time, an income statement provides information about a period of time. It reflects information about the transactions and other events occurring within the period. Most of the weaknesses of an income statement are a result of its periodic nature. Entities are continually creating and selling goods and services, and at any single point in time some of those processes will be incomplete. Thus, measurement of net income for a period involves estimates. The degree of completion of inventories, the amounts of inventories that have been manufactured or purchased but ultimately will not be sold, and the amounts of goods and services that have been sold but ultimately will not result in cash receipts are just of few of the many estimates that must be made in order to present an income statement. The entity's ability (or inability) to make these estimates is reflected in the performance measure for the period.

Historically, performance was measured only by the income statement. During the 1990s, a second performance measure was required—comprehensive income. Comprehensive income is a more inclusive notion of performance than net income. It includes all recognized changes in equity that occur during a period except those resulting from investments by owners and distributions to owners. Thus, included in comprehensive income but excluded from net income are foreign currency adjustments, unrealized changes in the fair value of available-for-sale securities, the effective portion of the gain or loss on derivative instruments designated and qualified as either a cash-flow hedging item or a hedge of a forecasted foreign-currency-denominated transaction, and minimum pension liability adjustments. Because comprehensive income includes the effects on an entity of economic events largely outside of its management's control, some have said that net income is a measure of management's performance and comprehensive income is a measure of entity performance.

The requirement to report comprehensive income in addition to net income is another step in the movement toward the capital maintenance concept of income mentioned in Chapter 2. Under that concept of income, income is earned only if the entity's net assets at the end of the period exceed its net assets at the beginning of the period after excluding the effects of transactions with owners. A capital maintenance concept of income is more consistent with investors' expectations that an investment should generate more financial resources than were invested.

Instead of, or in addition to, net income or comprehensive income, some companies are using "pro forma earnings" and other measures to report corporate performance. The practice has generated debate and confusion because companies calculate and report those "earnings" using definitions that vary from company to company (and sometimes even within the same company from quarter to quarter). In response to growing concerns about this practice, and as a result of the Sarbanes-Oxley Act of 2002, in January 2003, the SEC adopted a new disclosure regulation, Regulation G. This regulation requires public companies that disclose or release non-GAAP financial measures (such as pro forma earnings) to include in that same disclosure or release a presentation of the most directly comparable GAAP financial measure, along with a reconciliation of the disclosed non-GAAP measure to the most directly comparable GAAP financial measure. FASB has also indicated an interest in this matter, and it has begun a project on financial performance reporting. These matters are discussed later in this chapter.

Sources of GAAP

ARB	APB	FAS	FTB	EITF	SOP	FSP
43, Ch. 2	9, 16, 18, 20, 30	7, 15, 16, 101, 128, 130, 133, 141, 142, 144, 145	85-6	87-4, 87-24, 92-13, 95-3, 00-9, 00-10, 01-10, 01-13, 01-14, 02-16, 3-10	98-5	146-1

DEFINITIONS OF TERMS

Component of an entity. The operations and cash flows that can be clearly distinguished, operationally and for financial reporting purposes, from the rest of the entity. All of the following are components of an entity:

1. A reportable segment, which is a segment considered to be significant to an enterprise's operations; a segment that has passed one of three 10% tests (assets, revenues, or operating profit or loss) or has been identified as being reportable through other criteria (FAS 131)
2. An operating segment, which is a component of an enterprise that may earn revenues and incur expenses, and about which separate financial information is available that is evaluated regularly by the chief operating decision maker in deciding how to allocate resources and in assessing performance (FAS 131)

3. A reporting unit, which is an operating segment or one level below an operating segment (FAS 142)
4. A subsidiary
5. An asset group, which is the lowest level for which identifiable cash flows are largely independent of the cash flows of other groups of assets and liabilities (FAS 144)

Comprehensive income. The change in equity of a business enterprise during a period from transactions and other events and circumstances from nonowner sources. It includes all changes in equity during a period, except those resulting from investments by owners and distributions to owners (CON 6).

Development stage enterprise. An entity that is devoting substantially all its efforts to establishing itself as a new business and either its principal operations have not commenced or its principal operations have commenced but have not generated a significant amount of revenue.

Distribution to owners. Decreases in net assets of a particular enterprise resulting from the entity transferring assets, rendering services, or incurring liabilities to owners.

Distributions to owners reduce the ownership interest of the receiving owners in the entity and reduce the net assets of the entity by the amount of the distribution. Such transactions are displayed in the statement of changes in equity.

Expenses. Decreases in assets or increases in liabilities during a period resulting from delivery of goods, rendering of services, or other activities constituting the enterprise's central operations (CON 6).

Extraordinary item. Events and transactions that are distinguished by their unusual nature and by the infrequency of their occurrence (APB 30).

Gains. Increases in equity (net assets) from peripheral or incidental transactions of an entity and from all other transactions and other events and circumstances affecting the entity during a period except those that result from revenues or investments by owners (CON 6).

Investments by owners. Increases in net assets of a particular enterprise resulting from transfers to it of something valuable to obtain or increase ownership interests (or equity) in it.

Investments by owners may be in the form of assets, services, or the payment of entity liabilities. These investments are displayed in the statement of changes in equity. The purchase of an ownership interest from another owner is not a net investment because such a transfer does not increase the net assets of the entity.

Losses. Decreases in equity (net assets) from peripheral or incidental transactions of an entity from all other transactions and other events and circumstances affecting the entity during a period except those that result from expenses or distributions to owners (CON 6).

Realization. The process of converting noncash resources and rights into money or, more precisely, the sale of an asset for cash or claims to cash (CON 6).

Recognition. The process of formally recording or incorporating an item in the financial statements of an entity (CON 6).

Revenues. Increases in assets or decreases in liabilities during a period from delivering goods, rendering services, or other activities constituting the enterprise's central operations (CON 6).

CONCEPTS, RULES, AND EXAMPLES

Limitations of the Income Statement

Economists have generally adopted a wealth maintenance concept of income. Under this concept, income is the maximum amount that can be consumed during a period and still leave the enterprise with the same amount of wealth at the end of the period as existed at the beginning. Wealth is determined with reference to the current market values of the net productive assets at the beginning and end of the period. Therefore, the economists' definition of income would fully incorporate market value changes (both increases and decreases in wealth) in the determination of periodic income.

Accountants, on the other hand, have generally defined income by reference to specific events that give rise to recognizable elements of revenue and expense during a reporting period. The events that produce reportable items of revenue and expense are a subset of economic events that determine economic income. Many changes in the market values of wealth components are deliberately excluded from the measurement of accounting income, but are included in the measurement of economic income.

The discrepancy between accounting and economic measures of income is primarily the result of accountants' concerns for reliability and measurability. Those concerns prevent revenue and gains from being recognized until an acceptable level of assurance is obtained about the existence and amount of those revenues and gains. In general, accountants do not recognize revenues or gains until they are realizable—convertible into known amounts of cash or claims to cash.

However, some gains are realizable but are still not reported in net income. Holding gains on certain debt and equity investments are readily convertible into known amounts of cash. Those gains are currently excluded from net income for two reasons. First, many consider net income to be a measure of management's performance, and holding gains and losses result from market fluctuations that are outside the control of management. To report holding gains and losses in net income decreases the ability to use that measure to judge management performance. Second, many entities that purchase large amounts of investments finance those investments with liabilities, making money off the spread (the difference between the investment return and the interest expense). Including in net income unrealized holding gains and losses on only the investments, and not the related liabilities, could cause volatility in earnings that is not representative of how those entities are impacted by economic events. However, FASB is currently working on a project that could lead to reporting certain liabilities at fair value; thus, future changes in accounting standards may eliminate this as a difference between accounting and economic measures of income.

Another reason for the discrepancy between accounting and economic measures of income is the periodic nature of the income statement. Both accountants and economists realize that the earnings process occurs throughout the various stages of production, sales, and final delivery of the product. However, the difficulty in measuring the precise rate at which this earnings process is taking place has led accountants to conclude that income should normally be recognized only when it is fully realized. **Realization** generally implies that the enterprise producing the item has completed all of its obligations relating to the product and that collection of the resulting receivable is assured beyond reasonable doubt. A system of revenue recognition based on realization provides a way of dealing with the periodic nature of the income statement.

The economic measure of income would be relatively simple to apply on a life-cycle basis. Economic income would be measured by the difference between its wealth at the termination point versus its wealth at the origination date, plus withdrawals or other distributions and minus additional investments over the course of its life. However, applying the same measurement strategy to discrete fiscal periods, as accountants do, is substantially more difficult. Allocating earnings to individual years, quarters, or months requires both estimates and judgment. Consequently, accountants have concluded that there must be unambiguous guidelines for revenue recognition. These have required recognition only at the completion of the earnings cycle.

Accountants have moved closer to an economic measure of income by introducing the measure "comprehensive income" into the financial statements. Comprehensive income is the change in equity resulting from all sources other than distributions to owners and investments by owners. Thus, definitionally, it is similar to economic income. However, because of the realization and recognition concerns discussed earlier, comprehensive income remains a subset of economic income.

Whether economic income, comprehensive income, net income, or some other measure is the appropriate measure of income is partially dependent upon the perspective of the party doing the measuring. From the perspective of the outside investors taken as a whole, income might be defined as earnings before any payments to those investors, including bondholders and preferred stockholders as well as common shareholders. On the other hand, from the perspective of the common shareholders, income might better be defined as earnings after payments to other investors, including creditors and preferred shareholders. Analysts regularly use earnings before income taxes, depreciation, and amortization. Perhaps the best accounting can do is provide the broadest possible measure (comprehensive income) and include in the financial statements information that allows each reader to compute the measure that is most meaningful to him or her.

Recognition and Measurement

Revenues. Revenues represent actual or expected cash inflows that result from an entity's central operations. Revenues are generally recognized at the culmination of the earnings process—when the entity has substantially completed all it must do to be entitled to future cash inflows (or to retain cash already transferred). Most often, an exchange transaction indicates that revenues have been earned. Merchandise is delivered or services are rendered to a customer, resulting in the receipt of cash or the right to receive cash in the future. Revenues are generally measured by the values of the assets exchanged (or liabilities incurred). Chapter 8 discusses revenue recognition in more detail.

Revenues are different from gains for three reasons. Revenues result from an entity's central operations; gains result from incidental or peripheral activities of the entity. Revenues are usually earned; gains result from nonreciprocal transactions (such as winning a lawsuit or receiving a gift) or other economic events for which there is no earnings process. Revenues are reported gross; gains are reported net.

The existence of an exchange transaction generally is critical to the accounting recognition of revenue. However, an exchange transaction is viewed in a broader sense than the legal concept of a sale. Whenever an exchange of rights and privileges takes place, an exchange transaction is deemed to have occurred. For example, interest revenue and interest expense are earned or incurred ratably over a period without a discrete transaction taking place. Accruals are recorded periodically in order to reflect the interest realized by the passage of time. In a like manner, the percentage-of-completion method recognizes revenue based upon the measure of progress on a long-term construction project. The earnings process is considered to occur simultaneously with the measure of progress (e.g., the incurrence of costs).

The timing of revenue recognition also varies based on the realizability of the future cash flows. For example, the production of certain commodities takes place in an environment in which the ultimate realization of revenue is so assured that revenue can be recognized upon the completion of the production process. At the opposite extreme is the situation in which an exchange transaction has taken place, but significant uncertainty exists as to the ultimate collectibility of the amount. For example, in certain sales of real estate, where the down payment percentage is extremely small and the security for the buyer's notes is minimal, revenue is often not recognized until the time collections are actually received.

The revenue recognition system that is based on realization has worked reasonably well over the years. However, new types of transactions, products, and services have challenged that system. Revenue recognition issues top the list of reasons for financial reporting restatements. In May 2002, FASB announced that it was adding a major revenue recognition project to its agenda. That project may lead to a new accounting standard on revenue recognition generally and also might involve amending the related guidance on revenues and liabilities in certain of the Board's Concepts Statements.

Chapter 8 provides more information about FASB's project and about revenue recognition under special circumstances.

Expenses. Expenses represent actual or expected cash outflows that result from an entity's central operations. Expenses are generally recognized when an asset either is consumed in an entity's central operations or is no longer expected to provide the level of future benefits expected when that asset was recognized.

Expenses are different from losses for three reasons. Expenses result from an entity's central operations; losses result from incidental or peripheral activities of the entity. Expenses are often incurred during the earnings process; losses often result from nonreciprocal transactions (such as thefts or fines) or other economic events unrelated to an earnings process. Expenses are reported gross; losses are reported net.

Although many cash outflows are recognized directly as expenses, that is done for expediency; most expenses are first assets, if only for a moment. Measuring the consumption of assets is done by one of three pervasive measurement principles: associating cause and effect, systematic and rational allocation, or immediate recognition.

Some costs, such as materials and direct labor consumed in the manufacturing process, are relatively easy to identify with the related revenue elements. The matching principle requires that all expenses incurred in the generation of revenue should be recognized in the same accounting period as the related revenues are recognized. Thus, those cost elements are included in inventory and expensed as cost of sales when a product is sold and revenue from the sale is recognized. That process is associating cause and effect.

Other costs are more closely associated with specific accounting periods. In the absence of a cause and effect relationship, the asset's cost should be allocated to the accounting periods benefited in a systematic and rational manner. This form of expense recognition involves assumptions about the expected length of benefit and the relationship between benefit and cost of each period. Depreciation of fixed assets, amortization of intangibles, and allocation of rent and insurance are examples of costs that are recognized by the use of a systematic and rational method.

All other costs are normally expensed in the period in which they are incurred. This includes costs for which no clear-cut future benefits can be identified, costs that were recorded as assets in prior periods but for which no remaining future benefits can be identified, and costs for which no rational allocation scheme can be devised.

The general approach for recognizing expenses is first to attempt to match costs with the related revenues. Next, a method of systematic and rational allocation should be attempted. If both of those measurement principles are inappropriate, the cost should be immediately expensed.

Expenses do not include distributions to owners. Expenses of a corporation are easily identified and separated from distributions to stockholders. In both the sole proprietorship and partnership form of entity, the identification process can be more difficult. Items such as interest or salaries paid to partners or owners may be thought of as distributions of profits rather than expenses. However, many entities adopt the philosophy that financial reporting should be the same regardless of legal form (economic substance takes precedence over legal form). Under the corporate form of business, interest on stockholder loans and salaries paid to stockholders are clearly classified as expenses and not as distributions. Accordingly, these items may be treated as expenses for both partnerships and sole proprietorships. However, full disclosure and consistency of financial reporting treatment would be required. Circumstances may involve treating certain payments, such as guaranteed salaries, as expenses while classifying other "salaries" as profit distributions.

Gains and losses. Gains are increases in equity resulting from transactions and economic events other than those that generate revenues or are investments from owners. Losses are decreases in equity resulting from transactions and economic events other than those that generate expenses or are distributions to owners. Gains and losses result from an entity's peripheral transactions (e.g., sale of used equipment), from economic events outside of the control of management (e.g., holding gains on securities), or from nonreciprocal transactions (e.g., lawsuit settlements, fines, and thefts).

Gains and losses are often described in financial statements by their sources, for example, realized gains (losses) on sale of securities or earthquake loss. They are usually measured at net amounts. For example, gains (losses) from sales of assets are measured by subtracting the unexpired cost of the asset from the proceeds, and holding gains (losses) are measured by subtracting the value at the beginning of the period from the value at the end of the period.

Gains often result from transactions and other events that involve no earnings process; therefore, in terms of recognition, it is more significant that the gain be realized or realizable than earned. Losses are recognized when it becomes evident that future economic benefits of a previously recognized asset have been reduced or eliminated, or that a liability has been incurred without associated economic benefits.

Other comprehensive income. Comprehensive income is the change in equity that results from revenue, expenses, gains, and losses during a period, as well as any other recognized changes in equity that occur for reasons other than investments by owners and distributions to owners.

Other comprehensive income (comprehensive income less net income) is defined to include, under current standards, the effects of foreign currency translation, minimum pension liability adjustments, the effective portion of the gain or loss on derivative instruments designated and qualified as either a cash-flow hedging item or a hedge of a forecasted foreign-currency-denominated transaction, and unrealized gains and losses on certain investments in debt and equity securities. Other comprehensive income is recognized and measured in accordance with the accounting pronouncement that deems it part of other comprehensive income. Thus, foreign currency adjustments are recognized and measured in accordance with FAS 52 (Chapter 22); additional pension liabilities are recognized and measured in accordance with FAS 87 (Chapter 16); hedges are recognized and measured in accordance with FAS 133 (Chapter 6) and unrealized gains and losses are recognized and measured in accordance with FAS 115 (Chapter 10). In general, those items are recognized and measured whenever a complete set of financial statements is prepared.

Format of Statements of Income and Comprehensive Income

The basic order of presentation of information in an income statement (or statement of income and comprehensive income) is defined by a series of accounting pronouncements, as shown by the diagram below. Other than in the section "income from continuing operations," the display of revenues, expenses, gains, losses, and other comprehensive income is predetermined by authoritative pronouncement. Only within income from continuing operations does tradition and industry practice determine the presentation.

The sections containing information about other comprehensive income and comprehensive income, shown in the shaded area on the diagram, can be presented in a combined statement of income and comprehensive income. Alternatively, that information can be reported in a stand-alone statement of comprehensive income or in an expanded statement of changes in stockholder's equity. In FAS 130, FASB encourages the use of either a combined statement in which other comprehensive income appears below net income or a stand-alone statement that begins with net income. Regardless of the reporting location chosen, totals for net income, other comprehensive income, and comprehensive income must appear in the statement, and the statement must be of the same prominence as other financial statements. Information about other comprehensive income cannot be presented only in the notes to financial statements. For ease of reading, this publication uses the term "income statement" to include a combined statement of income and comprehensive income.

Statement of Income and Comprehensive Income	*Report net of tax?*	*Reference*
Income from continuing operations Sales or service revenues Costs of goods sold Operating expenses Gains and losses Other revenues and expenses Items that are unusual or infrequent, but not both Income tax expense related to continuing operations	No	APB 30
Results from discontinued operations Income (loss) from operations of a discontinued component Gain (loss) from disposal of a discontinued component	Yes	FAS 144, FAS 16
Extraordinary items Items that are both unusual and infrequent Remaining excess of fair value over cost of acquired net assets in a business combination Investor's share of an equity method investee's extraordinary item	Yes	APB 9, APB 30, FAS 101, FAS 141, FTB 85-6
Cumulative effect of a change in accounting principle	Yes	APB 20
Net income		
Other comprehensive income Foreign currency adjustments Unrealized gains (losses) on securities Minimum pension liability Gains/losses on cash-flow hedging items Gains/losses on hedges of forecasted foreign-currency-denominated transactions Income tax related to other comprehensive income (if components are not shown net of tax)	Choice	FAS 130, FAS 133
Comprehensive income		
Earnings per share information		FAS 128

NOTE: Alternatively, information in the shaded area can be presented as a separate statement or in a statement of changes in stockholders' equity.

The three items that are shown in the heading of an income statement are

1. The name of the entity whose results of operations is being presented
2. The title of the statement
3. The period of time covered by the statement

The entity's legal name should be used and supplemental information could be added to disclose the entity's legal form as a corporation, partnership, sole proprietorship, or other form if that information is not apparent from the entity's name. The use of the titles "Income Statement," "Statement of Income and Comprehensive Income," "Statement of Operations," or "Statement of Earnings" denotes preparation in accordance with generally accepted accounting principles. If another comprehensive basis of accounting were used, such as the cash or income tax basis, the title of the statement would be modified accordingly. "Statement of Revenue and Expenses—Income Tax Basis" or "Statement of Revenue and Expenses—Modified Cash Basis" are examples of such titles.

The date of an income statement must clearly identify the time period involved, such as "Year Ending March 31, 2005." That dating informs the reader of the length of the period covered by the statement and both the starting and ending dates. Dating such as "The Period Ending March 31, 2005" or "Through March 31, 2005" is not useful because of the lack of precision in those titles. Income statements are rarely presented for periods in excess of one year but are frequently seen for shorter periods such as a month or a quarter. Entities whose operations form a natural cycle may have a reporting period end on a specific day (e.g., the last Friday of the month). These entities should head the income statement "For the 52 Weeks Ended March 28, 2005" (each week containing seven days, beginning on a Saturday and ending on a Friday). Although that fiscal period includes only 364 days, it is still considered an annual reporting period.

Income statements generally should be uniform in appearance from one period to the next. The form, terminology, captions, and pattern of combining insignificant items should be consistent. If comparative statements are presented, the prior year's information should be restated to conform to the current year's presentation if changes in presentation are made.

Aggregation of items should not serve to conceal significant information, such as netting revenues against expenses or combining dissimilar types of resources, expenses, gains, or losses. The category "other or miscellaneous expense" should contain, at maximum, an immaterial total amount of aggregated insignificant items. Once this total approaches 10% of total expenses, some other aggregations with explanatory titles should be selected.

Income from Continuing Operations

The section "income from continuing operations" includes all revenues, expenses, gains, and losses that are not required to be reported in other sections of an income statement.

There are two generally accepted formats for the presentation of income from continuing operations: the single-step and the multiple-step formats.

In the single-step format, items are classified into two groups: revenues and expenses. The operating revenues and other revenues are itemized and summed to determine total revenues. The cost of goods sold, operating expenses, and other expenses are itemized and summed to determine total expenses. The total expenses (including income taxes) are deducted from the total revenues to arrive at income from continuing operations.

Example of single-step format for income from continuing operations

Revenues:		
Sales (net of discounts and returns and allowances)	$xxx	
Gain on sale of equipment	xxx	
Interest income	xxx	
Dividend income	xxx	$xxx
Expenses:		
Cost of goods sold	$xxx	
Selling expenses	xxx	
General and administrative expenses	xxx	
Interest expense	xxx	xxx
Income from continuing operations		xxx

Some believe that a multiple-step format enhances the usefulness of information about an entity's performance by reporting the interrelationships of revenues and expenses, using subtotals to report significant amounts. In a multiple-step format, operating revenues and expenses are separated from nonoperating revenues and expenses to provide more information concerning the firm's primary activities. This format breaks the revenue and expense items into various intermediate income components so that important relationships can be shown and attention can be focused on significant subtotals. Some examples of common intermediate income components are as follows:

1. **Gross profit (margin)**—The difference between net sales and cost of goods sold.
2. **Operating income**—Gross profit less operating expenses.
3. **Income before income taxes**—Operating income plus any other revenue items and less any other expense items.

Example of a multiple-step format for income from continuing operations

Sales:			
Sales			$xxx
Less: Sales discounts		$xxx	
Sales returns and allowances		xxx	(xxx)
Net sales			$xxx
Cost of goods sold			xxx
Gross profit			$xxx
Operating expenses:			
Selling expenses			
Sales salaries	$xxx		
Commissions	xxx		
Advertising expense	xxx		
Delivery expense	xxx		
Selling supplies expense	xxx		
Depreciation of store furniture and equipment	xxx	$xxx	
General and administrative expenses			
Officers' salaries	$xxx		
Office salaries	xxx		
Bad debts expense	xxx		
Office supplies expense	xxx		
Depreciation of office furniture and fixtures	xxx		
Depreciation of building	xxx		
Insurance expense	xxx		
Utilities expense	xxx	xxx	
Total operating expense			(xxx)
Operating income			$xxx
Other revenues:			
Dividend income		$xxx	
Interest income		xxx	xxx
Other expenses:			
Interest expense			(xxx)
Income from continuing operations			$xxx

The following items of revenue, expense, gains, and losses are included within income from continuing operations:

1. **Sales or service revenues** are charges to customers for the goods and/or services provided during the period. This section should include information about discounts, allowances, and returns in order to determine net sales or net revenues.
2. **Cost of goods sold** is the cost of the inventory items sold during the period. In the case of a merchandising firm, net purchases (purchases less discounts, returns, and allowances plus freight-in) are added to beginning inventory to get cost of goods

available for sale. From the cost of goods available for sale amount, the ending inventory is deducted to get cost of goods sold.

Example of calculation of cost of goods sold of a merchandising company

Beginning inventory			$xxx
Add: Purchases		$xxx	
Freight-in		xxx	
Cost of purchases		xxx	
Less: Purchase discounts	$xx		
Purchase returns and allowances	xx	(xxx)	
Net purchases			xxx
Cost of goods available for sale			xxx
Less: Ending inventory			(xxx)
Cost of goods sold			$xxx

A manufacturing company computes the cost of goods sold in a slightly different way. This requires that the company first computes the costs of goods manufactured. Cost of goods manufactured can be computed as follows:

Example of computation of cost of goods manufactured

Direct materials inventory, beginning of period	$xxx	
Purchases of materials (including freight-in and deducting purchase discounts)	xxx	
Total direct materials available	$xxx	
Direct materials inventory, end of period	(xxx)	
Direct materials used		$xxx
Direct labor		xxx
Factory overhead:		
Depreciation of factory equipment	$xxx	
Utilities	xxx	
Indirect factory labor	xxx	
Indirect materials	xxx	
Other overhead items	xxx	xxx
Manufacturing cost incurred during the period		$xxx
Add: Work in process, beginning of period		xxx
Less: Work in process, end of period		(xxx)
Cost of goods manufactured during the period		$xxx

Once the cost of goods manufactured has been calculated, the cost of goods sold can be computed. The cost of goods manufactured is added to the beginning inventory to arrive at cost of goods available for sale. The ending inventory is then deducted from the cost of goods available for sale to determine the cost of goods sold.

Example of computation of cost of goods sold of a manufacturing company

Finished goods inventory, beginning of period	$xxx
Add: Cost of goods manufactured during the period	xxx
Cost of goods available for sale	$xxx
Less: Finished goods inventory, end of period	(xxx)
Cost of goods sold during the period	$xxx

3. **Operating expenses** are primary recurring costs associated with central operations (other than cost of goods sold) that are incurred in order to generate sales. Operating expenses are normally reported in the following two categories:

   a. Selling expenses
   b. General and administrative expenses

   Selling expenses are those expenses directly related to the company's efforts to generate sales (e.g., sales salaries, commissions, advertising, delivery expenses, depreciation of store furniture and equipment, and store supplies). General and administrative expenses are expenses related to the general administration of the company's operations (e.g., officers and office salaries, office supplies, depreciation of office furniture and fixtures, telephone, postage, accounting and legal services, and business licenses and fees).

4. **Gains and losses** result from the peripheral transactions of the entity. If immaterial, they are usually combined and shown with the normal, recurring revenues and expenses. If they are individually material, they should be disclosed on a separate line. Examples are write-downs of inventories and receivables, effects of a strike, gains and losses on the disposal of equipment, and gains and losses from exchange or translation of foreign currencies. Holding gains on available-for-sale securities are included in other comprehensive income rather than income from continuing operations.
5. **Other revenues and expenses** are revenues and expenses not related to the central operations of the company (e.g., interest revenues and expenses, and dividend revenues).
6. **Unusual or infrequent** items are items that are either unusual or infrequent, but not both. They should be reported as a separate component of income from continuing operations.
7. **Goodwill impairment losses** are presented as a separate line item in the income from continuing operations section of the income statement. FAS 142 prohibits the amortization of goodwill and instead requires that goodwill be tested for impairment at least annually. If goodwill is found to be impaired, it is to be written down to fair value. The resultant loss is included in the operations section of the income statement. However, if a goodwill impairment loss is associated with a discontinued operation, the loss is included (on a net-of-tax basis) within the results of discontinued operations.
8. **Exit or disposal activity costs** are included in income from continuing operations before income taxes. Exit or disposal activities are restructurings and other activities that materially change the scope of business undertaken by an entity or the manner in which a business is conducted. If a subtotal such as "income from operations" is presented, the costs of exit or disposal activities will normally be included in that subtotal. However, if the costs are associated with exit or disposal activities that involve a discontinued operation, they are to be included in the results of discontinued operations (see below). If an entity's responsibility to settle the liability associated with an exit or disposal activity is removed or discharged, the related costs are reversed through the same line item(s) in the income statement that were used when those costs were initially recognized. (Exit or disposal activities are discussed in more detail later in this chapter.)
9. **Income tax expense** related to continuing operations is that portion of the total income tax expense applicable to continuing operations.

The section ends in a subtotal that varies depending upon the existence of discontinued operations, extraordinary items, and accounting changes. For example, the subtotal is usually titled "income from continuing operations" only when there is a section for discontinued operations in one of the years presented. If there is only a section for extraordinary items, the subtotal is usually titled "income before extraordinary items." If there is only an accounting change, the subtotal is usually titled "income before the cumulative effects of a change in accounting principle." The titles are adjusted accordingly if more than one of the sections are necessary. If there are no discontinued operations, extraordinary items, or accounting changes, the subtotal is titled "net income."

Examples of the format for presentation of various income statement items

Discontinued operations and an extraordinary item

Income (loss) from continuing operations		$ xxx
Discontinued operations		
Income (loss) from operations of Division Z, less applicable income taxes of $xxx	$xxx	
Income (loss) on disposal of Division Z, less applicable income taxes of $xxx	xxx	xxx
Income (loss) before extraordinary item		$ xxx
Extraordinary item, less applicable income taxes of $xxx (Note _)		xxx
Net income		$ xxx
Per share of common stock*		
Income (loss) from continuing operations		$x.xx
Net income		$x.xx

Discontinued operations and a change in accounting principle

Income (loss) from continuing operations		$ xxx
Discontinued operations		
Income (loss) from operations of Division Z, less applicable income taxes of $xxx	$xxx	
Income (loss) on disposal of Division Z, less applicable income taxes of $xxx	xxx	xxx
Income (loss) before cumulative effect		$ xxx
Cumulative effect on prior years (to **date of last year's income statement**) of changing to (change described), less applicable income taxes of $xxx (Note _)		xxx
Net income		$ xxx
Per share of common stock*		
Income (loss) from continuing operations		$x.xx
Net income		$x.xx

Extraordinary item and a change in accounting principle

Income (loss) before extraordinary item and cumulative effect of a change in accounting principle	$ xxx
Extraordinary item, less applicable income taxes of $xxx (Note _)	xxx
Cumulative effect on prior years (to **date of last year's income statement**) of changing to (change described), less applicable income taxes of $xxx (Note _)	xxx
Net income	$ xxx
Per share of common stock*	
Income (loss) before extraordinary item and a change in accounting principle	$x.xx
Net income	$x.xx

* *These examples assume that per share amounts of discontinued operations, extraordinary items, and cumulative effect of a change in accounting principles are shown in the notes.*

Results from Discontinued Operations

In August 2001, FASB issued FAS 144, which, in addition to changing the standards on reporting for long-lived assets to be disposed of, also changed the requirements for reporting discontinued operations. Reporting of discontinued operations was originally set forth by APB 30; FASB concluded that an expansion of those provisions was warranted, so that more disposal situations would trigger the display of discontinued operations.

Under APB 30's provisions, there was requirement that a discontinued operation be a segment of the business. By contrast, under FAS 144 the reporting requirements apply to a "component of an entity." A component of an entity is distinguishable from the rest of the entity because it has its own operations and cash flows.

If a component of an entity is either classified as held-for-sale or has been disposed of during the period, the results of its operations are to be reported in discontinued operations, provided that **both** of the following conditions are met:

- The operations and cash flows of the component have been or will be removed from the ongoing operations of the entity as a result of the disposal transaction, **and**
- The entity will have no significant continuing involvement in the operations of the component after the disposal transaction.

The conditions that must be met for a component to be classified as held-for-sale are set forth in Chapter 9.

Examples of determination of whether to report discontinued operations

Software Solutions Plus develops and sells software for several markets. It has a children's educational line, a children's game line, a business office line, and a desktop publishing line. The product line is the lowest level at which the operations and cash flows can be clearly distinguished by management. Thus, each product line is an operating segment and a component of the entity.

Case 1

Software Solutions Plus decides to exit the game business and commits to a plan to sell the children's game line. The assets and liabilities of the product line are classified as held-for-sale at that date. Software Solutions Plus will have no continuing involvement with the children's game software after the sale is closed. In addition, Software Solutions Plus has decided that it will not develop any new computer games for the children's market. In this case, the conditions are met to report the children's game line as a discontinued operation.

Case 2

Instead of exiting the children's game business entirely as in Case 1, Software Solutions Plus decides to keep its game programmers on its staff and have them develop new children's games. However, instead of selling the games to the home market via distributors as it had been doing, each existing and newly developed game will be marketed and sold to other software game companies. Software Solutions Plus will not provide technical support for any particular game software after it is sold. In this case, although Software Solutions Plus will not have any continuing involvement with the games after they are sold, it will continue to have revenues and expenses related to the children's game product line. Thus, the first of the two conditions required for discontinued operations treatments is not met. The change in the manner of marketing the line cannot be reported in discontinued operations.

Case 3

Software Solutions Plus decides to discontinue developing and selling its graphics drawing program product, which is part of the desktop publishing product line. In this case, because the graphics drawing program product is not a component of the entity on its own, but instead is part of the component desktop publishing product line, the sale of the graphics drawing program cannot be reported in discontinued operations.

Case 4

Software Solutions Plus commits to a plan to sell the desktop publishing line to another software company. The assets and liabilities of the product line are classified as held-for-sale at that date. As part of the sales agreement, Software Solutions Plus will receive a sizable royalty for each program sold and will provide technical support to the buyer's programming staff and to customers for the next three years. In this case, because Software Solutions Plus will continue to receive cash flows from the product line and will continue to have significant involvement with the product line after the product line is sold, the sale of the desktop publishing product line cannot be reported in discontinued operations. In the third year after the sale, Software Solutions Plus should reassess whether the conditions necessary to report the activity in discontinued operations have been met.

In the period in which a component of an entity is either classified as held-for-sale or has been disposed of, the results of operations of that component and any gain or loss recognized on disposal is reported as a separate component of income, before extraordinary items and the cumulative effect of accounting changes (if any). The income statements of any prior periods being presented should be restated to also reflect the results of operations of the component as discontinued operations. All amounts should be reported less applicable income taxes (benefits), as shown in the example below.

Example of income statement presentation for discontinued operations

	2005	2004
Income from continuing operations before income taxes	598	583
Income taxes	239	233
Income from continuing operations	359	350
Discontinued operations (Note ___)		
Loss from operations of discontinued component	1,165	1,045
Loss on disposal of discontinued component	167	
Income tax benefit	(532)	(418)
Loss on discontinued operations	800	627
Net income	(441)	(282)

This example shows the loss on disposal on the face of the income statement. Alternatively, the amount can be shown in the notes to the financial statements, as long as the disclosure identifies the caption in the income statement in which the loss in included.

Computing the gain or loss on disposal. To compute the loss (or gain) on disposal, the entity must first compute the fair value of the component; less the cost to sell it. **Costs to sell** are the incremental direct costs to transact the sale. In other words, costs to sell result directly from the decision to sell the component, are essential to the sales transaction, and would not have been incurred by the entity absent the decision to sell the component. Examples of costs to sell are broker commissions, legal fees, title transfer fees, and closing costs. In the limited situations in which the sale will occur more than one year after the component is classified as held-for-sale, the costs to sell should be discounted to present value. (For more information about long-lived assets held for sale, see Chapter 9.)

Next, the entity must compute the carrying value of the component. The carrying amounts of assets (other than long-lived assets) and liabilities are first adjusted in accordance with GAAP, and any adjustments are excluded from the gain or loss from disposal. For example, if trade accounts receivable are being sold as part of a component, the adequacy of the valuation allowance would be assessed as of the date the component is classified as held-for-sale, and any adjustment needed to bring the allowance to the proper balance would be included in bad debt expense. Similarly, if the sale of the component includes assumption of bonds payable, the accumulated amortization of any premium or discount on those bonds would be brought up to date, and this adjustment would be included in interest expense.

The gain or loss on disposal is computed by comparing the total carrying amount to the fair value net of costs to sell. A loss is recognized in the period in which the component is classified as held-for-sale if the total carrying amount exceeds the fair value less costs to sell. If the fair value less costs to sell exceeds the carrying amount (that is, there is a gain on disposal), the gain is not recognized until the actual sale occurs.

The treatment of operating losses of a component designated as held-for-sale has changed markedly from prior practice. Under FAS 144, losses from operations of the component subsequent to the date the component is classified as held-for-sale are to be recognized in the period in which they are incurred. Previously (under APB 30), those losses were to be anticipated, accrued, and included in the loss or gain on disposal as of the date of classification as held-for-sale. (This change was made because the accrual of estimated future losses under APB 30 resulted in the recognition of obligations that did not conform to the definition of liabilities under FASB's Conceptual Framework.)

Example of computing the gain or loss on disposal

Today's Telecommunications has decided to close its pager division, which is a component of the entity. It has committed to a plan to sell the assets and liabilities of the division and has properly reclassified the division as held-for-sale at that date.

- The division has incurred $1,750 losses from operations from the beginning of the year to the date it was reclassified as held-for-sale.
- The fair value of the assets and liabilities of the division are $10,775.
- Brokers' commissions and other costs to sell are estimated to be $1,650.
- The carrying value of the assets and liabilities of the division is $12,525 before the GAAP adjustments (depreciation, amortization, adjustment of valuation accounts, and similar periodic adjustments) are made.
- The GAAP adjustments reduce the carrying value of the assets and liabilities by $125.
- Losses from operations of the division from the date it is classified as held-for-sale to the end of the fiscal year are $580. (This loss does not include the GAAP adjustments noted above.)
- Anticipated future losses from operations of the division from the end of this fiscal year to the expected sales date are $1,999.
- The tax rate is 40%.

The income statement presentation of discontinued operations would be

Discontinued operations (Note ___)	
Loss from operations of discontinued division, net of tax of $982	1,473
Loss on disposal of discontinued division, net of tax of $1,310	1,965
Loss on discontinued operations	3,438

The loss from operations of the discontinued pager division is the sum of the $1,750 loss incurred prior to the date the assets and liabilities were classified as held-for-sale, plus the $125 GAAP adjustments that were recorded, plus the $580 loss incurred from the date the division was classified as held-for-sale to the end of the fiscal year. The sum ($2,455) less the tax effects of $982 ($2,455 x 40%) is the loss from operations of $1,473. Note that the former practice, under APB 30, of distinguishing between operating results before and after the date of classification (called the measurement date under the former standard), has been abandoned.

The loss on disposal is the difference between the carrying value of the division and its fair value less costs to sell. The carrying value of the division is $12,400 ($12,525 less the GAAP adjustments of $125). The fair value of the division less costs to sell is $9,125 ($10,775 fair value less costs to sell of $1,650). The difference of $3,275 less the tax effects of $1,310 ($3,275 x 40%) is the loss on disposal of $1,965. The anticipated future losses from operations of the division will be reported in discontinued operations in the future period in which they occur. They are not included in the loss on disposal in the current fiscal year.

Future periods. Subsequent to the fiscal year in which the assets and liabilities of a component are classified as held-for-sale, the discontinued operations section of an income statement includes

1. Results of operations of the discontinued component
2. Certain adjustments that are directly related to the disposal of a component of an entity, such as

a. Resolution of contingencies associated with the terms of the disposal transaction, such as purchase price adjustments and indemnification issues with the purchaser
b. Resolution of contingencies associated with the operations of the component prior to its disposal, such as environmental or product warranty obligations retained by the seller
c. Settlement of employee benefit plan obligations directly associated with the disposal transaction that occur no later than one year after the disposal transaction. (See the discussion of settlements and curtailments of plan liabilities in Chapter 16.)

When adjustments of this nature occur, they should be classified separately in discontinued operations of the current period and the notes to the financial statements should disclose the nature and amount of these adjustments.

Example of discontinued operations in a future period

Continuing the previous example, the sale of Today's Telecommunications' pager division, which is a component of the entity, closed in the year subsequent to the fiscal year in which the assets and liabilities were classified as held-for-sale.

- The actual sales price less costs to sell was $9,725.
- The net carrying value of the assets and liabilities on the date of sale was $12,225.
- The loss from operations from the end of the fiscal year to the date of sale was $2,045.
- The tax rate is 40%.

The income statement presentation of discontinued operations would be

Discontinued operations (Note ___)	
Loss from operations of discontinued division, net of tax of $818	1,227
Gain on disposal of discontinued division, net of tax of $310	465
Loss on discontinued operations	762

The loss from operations of the discontinued pager division is the $2,045 less the tax effects of $818 ($2,045 x 40%).

The loss on disposal is the difference between the carrying value of the division and its sales price less the loss recognized in the prior period. The carrying value of the division was $12,225; the sales price less costs to sell was $9,725, for an actual loss of $2,500. The loss recognized in the prior period was $3,275, so an adjustment of $775 ($2,500 less $3,275) is necessary. The tax effects on the adjustment are $310 ($775 x 40%), so the net adjustment is a gain of $465 ($775 – $310).

Extraordinary Items

An event or transaction should be presumed to be an ordinary and usual activity (and thus, included in income from continuing operations) unless the event or transaction is both of an unusual nature and infrequent in its occurrence.

Unusual nature. The underlying event or transaction should possess a high degree of abnormality and be of a type clearly unrelated to, or only incidentally related to, the ordinary and typical activities of the entity, taking into account the environment in which the entity operates.

In determining whether an event or transaction is of an unusual nature, the following special characteristics of the entity should be considered:

1. Type and scope of operations
2. Lines of business
3. Operating policies
4. Industry in which the entity operates

5. Geographic location of its operations
6. Nature and extent of government regulation

An event that is of an unusual nature for one entity can be an ordinary and usual activity of another because of the above characteristics. Whether an event or transaction is beyond the control of management is irrelevant in the determination of whether it is of an unusual nature.

Infrequency of occurrence. The underlying event or transaction should be of a type that would not reasonably be expected to recur in the foreseeable future, taking into account the environment in which the entity operates.

Items specifically included or excluded from extraordinary items. Accounting pronouncements have specifically required the following items to be disclosed as extraordinary, even though they may not meet the criteria stated above:

1. The investor's share of an investee's extraordinary item when the investor uses the equity method of accounting for the investee (APB 18).
2. Net effect of adjustments relating to the discontinuation of the application of FAS 71 (FAS 101).
3. The remaining excess of fair value of acquired net assets over cost pursuant to FAS 141. Chapter 11 provides additional information about the excess over cost in a business combination transaction.

Material gains and losses from the extinguishment of debt and gains from troubled debt restructurings previously were items specifically required to be classified as extraordinary. FAS 145 rescinded that requirement, so those gains and losses will now be evaluated using the unusual and infrequent criteria described above.

The following items are, by definition, **not** extraordinary items:

1. Write-down or write-off of receivables, inventories, equipment leased to others, or intangible assets
2. Foreign currency gains and losses
3. Gains and losses on the disposal of a segment of a business
4. Gains and losses from sale or abandonment of property, plant, or equipment used in operations
5. Effects of a strike
6. Adjustments of accruals on long-term contracts
7. Losses and costs incurred as a result of the September 11, 2001 events (EITF 01-10)

Per FTB 85-6, neither the cost incurred by a company to defend itself from a takeover attempt nor the cost incurred as part of a "standstill" agreement meet the criteria for extraordinary classifications as discussed in APB 30.

Presentation. Extraordinary items should be segregated from the results of ordinary operations and be shown net of taxes in a separate section of the income statement, following "discontinued operations" and preceding "cumulative effect of a change in accounting principle," if any. If more than one extraordinary item occurs during a period, they should be reported separately or details should be included in the notes to financial statements.

Example of the income statement presentation for extraordinary items

An extraordinary item would be presented as follows:

Income before extraordinary items	$xxx
Extraordinary items (less applicable income taxes of $__) (Note __)	xxx
Net income	$xxx

Accounting Changes

A change in accounting principle results from adoption of a generally accepted accounting principle different from the one previously used for reporting purposes. The term **accounting principle** includes not only accounting principles and practices, but also the methods of applying them. Changes in accounting principles (or the method of applying them) must be justified by those who make the change (the entity's management), unless they are made in order to comply with a FASB position. (See Chapter 21 for a detailed discussion of accounting changes.)

Example of disclosure for a change in accounting principle

ABC Company
Income Statement
For the Year Ended December 31, 2005

	2005	*2004*
Sales	$xxx	$xxx
(Details omitted)		
Income before cumulative effect of a change in accounting principle	$xxx	$xxx
Cumulative effect on prior years (to 12/31/04) of changing to (change described) (net of $__ tax)	xxx	___
Net income	$xxx	$xxx
Per share amounts (simple capital structure)		
Income before cumulative effect of a change in accounting principle	$xxx	$xxx
Cumulative effect on prior years (to12/31/04) of changing to (change described)	xxx	___
Earnings per common share	$xxx	$xxx
Pro forma* amounts assuming the new (change principle) is applied retroactively:		
Net income	$xxx	$xxx
Earnings per share	$xxx	$xxx

* *The pro forma amount above is not to be confused with the pro forma income numbers that the SEC has expressed concern about, and which is addressed,* ***inter alia****, by the Sarbanes-Oxley Act of 2002 and by SEC Regulation G.*

Other Comprehensive Income

Under current accounting standards, other comprehensive income includes foreign currency adjustments, unrealized changes in the fair value of available-for-sale securities, the effective portion of the gain or loss on derivative instruments designated and qualified as either a cash-flow hedge or a hedge of a forecasted foreign-currency-denominated transaction, and minimum pension liability adjustments. FAS 130 requires that the components of other comprehensive income along with totals for net income, other comprehensive income, and comprehensive income must appear in a statement of the same prominence as other financial statements. (However, an entity that has no items of other comprehensive income in any period presented is required to report only net income.) Presenting those required amounts in a combined statement of income and comprehensive income is only one of three permissible methods. The other two are discussed later in this chapter.

Some items impact other comprehensive income in one period and then affect net income in the same or a later period. For example, an unrealized holding gain on an available-for-sale security is included in other comprehensive income in the period in which the market fluctuation occurs. Later, perhaps years later, the security is sold and the realized gains are included in net income. An adjustment to the unrealized holding gain component of other comprehensive income is necessary to avoid double counting the gain—once in net income in the current year and also in other comprehensive income in the earlier period. Adjustments of that type are called reclassification adjustments.

Usually, a sale triggers the need for a reclassification adjustment. The sale of an available-for-sale security in the current period triggers the need for an adjustment for the gains (losses) included in other comprehensive income in a prior period. Likewise, the sale of an investment in a foreign entity triggers an adjustment for foreign currency items included in other comprehensive income that are related to that entity. Amounts accumulated in other comprehensive income from cash flow hedges are reclassified into earnings in the same period(s) in which the hedged forecasted transactions (such as a forecasted sale) affects earnings. If it becomes probable that the forecasted transaction will not occur, the net gain or loss in accumulated other comprehensive income must be immediately reclassified. An adjustment is also necessary upon the complete (or substantially complete) liquidation of an investment in a foreign entity. Only minimum pension liabilities will not require reclassification adjustments (because they will not be reported in net income in a future period).

Reclassification adjustments can be presented on the face of the statement with the components of other comprehensive income or can be netted against the related component and the details of the reclassification provided in the notes to financial statements.

The tax effects of items reported in other comprehensive income must also be included in other comprehensive income. The items of other comprehensive income can be reported either net of related tax effects on the face of the statement or gross with the tax effects related to all components reported on a single, separate line. If gross reporting is used, the notes to the financial statements must disclose the tax effects related to each component (if there is more than one component). The following examples illustrate the two presentations.

Example of the "net of tax" presentation

Hypothetical Corporation
Statement of Income and Comprehensive Income
For the Year Ended December 31, 2005
($000 omitted)

Sales		$395,400
(details omitted)		
Net earnings		83,250
Other comprehensive income		
Foreign currency translation adjustment, net of $5,100 tax		11,900
Unrealized gain on securities:		
Unrealized holding gains arising during period, net of $7,500 tax	17,500	
Less: Reclassification adjustment, net of $1,500 tax, for gain included currently in net income	(3,500)	14,000
Cash flow hedges		
Net derivative losses arising during the period, net of $4,800 tax	(11,200)	
Less: Reclassification adjustment for losses included currently in net income, net of $7,762 tax	18,113	6,913
Minimum pension liability adjustment, net of $1,950 tax		(4,550)
Other comprehensive income		28,263
Comprehensive income		$111,513

Example of the "gross of tax" presentation

Hypothetical Corporation
Statement of Income and Comprehensive Income
For the Year Ended December 31, 2005
($000 omitted)

Sales		$395,400
(details omitted)		
Net earnings		83,250
Other comprehensive income		
Foreign currency translation adjustment		17,000
Unrealized gains on securities:		
Unrealized holding gains arising during period	25,000	
Less: Reclassification adjustment for gain included currently in net income	(5,000)	20,000

Cash flow hedges		
Net derivative losses arising during the period	(16,000)	
Less: Reclassification adjustment for losses included currently in net income	25,875	9,875
Minimum pension liability adjustment		(6,500)
Tax effects of items included in other comprehensive income		(12,112)
Other comprehensive income		28,263
Comprehensive income		$111,513

If the "gross" approach illustrated above were utilized, it would also be necessary to present in the notes to the financial statements details regarding the allocation of the tax effects to the several items included in other comprehensive income. An example of that note disclosure follows.

Note X: Income Taxes

The tax effects of items included in other comprehensive income for the year ended December 31, 2005, are as follows:

	Before-tax amount	*Tax expense (benefit)*	*Net-of-tax amount*
Foreign currency translation adjustments	$17,000	$ 5,100	$11,900
Unrealized gains on securities:			
Unrealized holding gains arising during period	25,000	7,500	17,500
Reclassification adjustment	(5,000)	(1,500)	(3,500)
Net unrealized holding gains	20,000	6,000	14,000
Cash flow hedges:			
Net derivative losses arising during the period	(16,000)	4,800	(11,200)
Reclassification adjustment	25,875	(6,913)	18,113
Net effects of cash flow hedges	9,875	(2,113)	6,913
Minimum pension liability adjustment	(6,500)	(1,950)	(4,550)
Other comprehensive income	$40,375	$12,112	$28,263

Earnings Per Share

Earnings per share is often used in evaluating a firm's stock price and in assessing the firm's future earnings and ability to pay dividends. Because of the importance of earnings per share, the profession has concluded that it should be disclosed on the face of the income statement.

Earnings per share is a very compact indicator of a company's performance. In order to assess quality of earnings, FAS 128 requires presentation of **basic earnings per share** on the face of the income statement for public-market issued common stock or potential common stock (such as options, warrants, convertible securities or contingent stock agreements). Shares outstanding are determined by the weighted-average method. Earnings is defined as both income from continuing operations and net income available to common stockholders. Thus, dividends declared on preferred stock and dividends for the period on cumulative preferred stock, whether or not earned or paid, are deducted from both income from continuing operations and net income before computing per share amounts.

Diluted earnings per share is computed similarly to basic earnings per share but the number of shares outstanding is adjusted to include the number of additional common shares that would be issued if the potentially dilutive shares had been issued.

Entities with simple capital structures, that is, only common stock, should display basic earnings per share for both continuing operations and net income on the face of the income statement. All other entities are required to display both basic and diluted per share amounts for both continuing operations and net income. For discontinued operations, extraordinary items, or cumulative effect of an accounting change, basic and diluted per share amounts may be either reported on the face of the income statement or disclosed in the notes. More details on the per share calculations can be found in Chapter 18.

Example of the presentation and computation of earnings per share

Assume that 100,000 shares were outstanding throughout the year.

ABC Company
Income Statement
For the Year Ended December 31, 2005

Sales		$2,000,000
Cost of goods sold		750,000
Gross profit		$1,250,000
Selling and administrative expenses		500,000
Income from operations		$ 750,000
Other revenues and expense		
Interest income	$40,000	
Interest expense	(30,000)	10,000
Income before unusual or infrequent items and income taxes		$ 760,000
Unusual or infrequent items:		
Loss from permanent impairment of value of manufacturing facilities		(10,000)
Income from continuing operations before income taxes		$ 750,000
Income taxes		300,000
Income from continuing operations		$ 450,000
Discontinued operations:		
Loss from operations of Division X, including loss on disposal of $100,000 and income tax benefit of $20,000		$30,000
Income before extraordinary item and cumulative effect of accounting change		$ 420,000
Extraordinary item—loss from earthquake less applicable income taxes of $8,000		(12,000)
Cumulative effect on prior years of retroactive application of new depreciation method, less applicable income taxes of $40,000		(60,000)
Net income		$ 348,000
Basic EPS computation		
Income from continuing operations ($450,000/100,000)		$ 4.50
Extraordinary items* ($12,000/100,000)		(0.12)
Accounting change* ($60,000/100,000)		(0.60)
Discontinued operations* ($30,000/100,000)		(0.30)
Net income available for common stockholders		$ 3.48

* *May be shown in the notes to the financial statements.*

Prior Period Adjustments

FAS 16 defines a prior period adjustment and clearly states that only the following items shall be excluded from the determination of net income for the current period:

1. The correction of an error in the financial statements of a prior period
2. Adjustments that result from realization of income tax benefits of preacquisition operating loss carryforwards of purchased subsidiaries

APB 9 specifies the recording and presentation of a prior period adjustment. When prior period adjustments are recorded, the resulting effects on the net income of prior periods shall be disclosed in the year in which the adjustments are made. The adjustments are reported at both their gross amount and net of applicable income taxes. If the statements are presented for only a single period, then the beginning balance of retained earnings is restated to reflect the effects of the correction or change. When comparative statements are presented, adjustments should be made of the amounts of net income (and the components thereof) and retained earnings balance (as well as other affected balances) for all of the periods included in the financial statements.

An example of the accounting presentation for a prior period adjustment appears in Chapter 21.

Statement of Income and Retained Earnings

An acceptable practice is to combine the income statement and the statement of retained earnings into a single statement called the Statement of Income and Retained Earnings. The income statement is prepared in the normal manner. The beginning balance in retained earnings is added to the net income (loss) figure. Declared dividends are deducted to obtain the retained earnings ending balance.

Example of a statement of income and retained earnings

Baker, Inc.
Statement of Income and Retained Earnings
For the Year Ended December 31, 2005

Sales		$2,482
Cost of goods sold		1,489
Gross margin on sales		$ 993
Operating expenses		
Selling expenses	$ 220	
Administrative expenses	255	475
Income from operations		$ 518
Other revenues/gains (expenses/losses)		
Interest revenue (expense)—net	$ (40)	
Gain on sale of investment in ABC Company	100	
Gain on translation of foreign currencies	20	80
Income before unusual or infrequent items		$ 598
Unusual or infrequent items:		
Write-down of property and equipment	$ (20)	
Loss from permanent impairment of value of distributing facility	(50)	(70)
Income from continuing operations before provision for income taxes		$ 528
Provision for income taxes		211
Income from continuing operations		$ 317
Discontinued operations:		
Loss from operations of discontinued Division Z (less applicable taxes of $466)	$ (699)	
Loss on disposal of Division Z (less applicable taxes of $67)	(100)	(799)
Loss before extraordinary items and cumulative effect of a change in accounting principle		$ (482)
Extraordinary loss from earthquake (less applicable income taxes of $30)		(45)
Cumulative effect on prior years of retroactive application of new depreciation method (less applicable income taxes of $80)		(120)
Net loss		$ (647)
Retained earnings, January 1, 2005	$1,900	
Prior period adjustment:		
Correction of depreciation error (less applicable income taxes of $28)	(42)	
Adjusted retained earnings, January 1, 2005		1,858
Deduct dividends:		
Preferred stock	$ (40)	
Common stock	(30)	(70)
Retained earnings, December 31, 2005		$1,141
Per share amounts (100 shares)*		
Income from continuing operations		$ 3.17
Net loss		$ (6.47)

* *Assumes other per share amounts are included in notes to financial statements.*

Reporting Comprehensive Income in a Statement other than a Combined Statement of Income and Comprehensive Income

Entities are not required to present information about comprehensive income in a combined statement of income and comprehensive income. Instead, they need only to present the components of other comprehensive income along with totals for net income, other comprehensive income, and comprehensive income in a statement of the same prominence as other financial statements. Thus, two other alternatives are available.

1. In an expanded statement of changes in stockholder's equity, or
2. In a stand-alone statement of comprehensive income

In FAS 130, FASB encourages the use of either a combined statement of income and comprehensive income or a stand-alone statement that begins with net income. In practice, the expanded statement of changes in stockholder's equity is also widely used.

Example of presentation of comprehensive income in the statement of changes in stockholders' equity

If comprehensive income is reported in the statement of changes in stockholders' equity, there are several formats that can be employed to accomplish this goal. Each of these modes of presentation is somewhat cumbersome, primarily because one element of comprehensive income (earnings) must be added to retained earnings while another (comprehensive income) is not.

Consider the case of Leisuretime Industries, which has preferred and common shares outstanding, and also has two classes of other comprehensive income. If Leisuretime Industries chooses to report comprehensive income in the statement of changes in stockholders' equity (rather than in either a freestanding statement of comprehensive income or combined statement of earnings and comprehensive income), one of two formats might be selected. These are illustrated below.

Leisuretime Industries
Statement of Changes in Stockholders' Equity
For the Year Ended December 31, 2005
($000 omitted)

	Preferred stock	*Common stock*	*Comprehensive income*	*Retained earnings*	*Accumulated other comprehensive income*	*Total*
Balances, January 1, 2005	$500,000	$4,500,000		$715,600	$ (5,950)	$5,709,650
Comprehensive income						
Net income			$66,760	66,760		
Other comprehensive income:						
Foreign currency translation adjustments, net of tax			3,000			
Unrealized gains on securities:						
Unrealized holding gains arising during period, net of tax			23,000			
Less: reclassification adjustment, net of tax, for gain included in net income			(5,500)			
Other comprehensive income			20,500		20,500	
Comprehensive income			$87,260			87,260
Proceeds from issuance of shares	50,000	200,000				250,000
Dividends paid				(24,825)		(24,825)
Balances, December 31, 2005	$550,000	$4,700,000		$757,535	$14,550	$6,022,085

Leisuretime Industries
Statement of Changes in Stockholders' Equity
For the Year Ended December 31, 2005
($000 omitted)

	Preferred stock	*Common stock*	*Retained earnings*	*Foreign currency translation*	*Unrealized gains on securities*	*Total*
Balances, January 1, 2005	$500,000	$4,500,000	$715,600	$(9,275)	$ 3,325	$5,709,650
Comprehensive income						
Net income			66,760			66,760
Other comprehensive income:						
Foreign currency translation adjustments, net of tax				3,000		3,000
Unrealized gains on securities:						
Unrealized holding gains arising during period, net of tax					23,000	23,000
Less: reclassification adjustment, net of tax, for gain included in net income					(5,500)	(5,500)
Other comprehensive income						20,500
Comprehensive income						87,260
Proceeds from issuance of shares	50,000	200,000				250,000
Dividends paid			(24,825)			(24,825)
Balances, December 31, 2005	$550,000	$4,700,000	$757,535	$(6,275)	$20,825	$6,022,085

Financial Performance Reporting

In 2002, FASB began a project on financial performance reporting, which probably would prohibit the two alternative displays of comprehensive income that are discussed in the previous section of this chapter. A principle objective of the project is the development of standards of reporting that enhance the predictive and feedback value of the information that is presented in the statement of comprehensive income. FASB's initial conclusion is that a business entity should report **all** items of revenue, expense, gains, and losses in a single statement of comprehensive income. (FASB has not decided on the title for that statement.) That statement would be separated into at least three major functional categories: business activities, financing activities, and other gains and losses.

Certain current display conventions could change as a result of this project. For example, FASB has decided that extraordinary items should be included, to the extent relevant in a given period, within each of the functional categories, rather than being reported separately near the bottom of the income statement. Additionally, extraordinary items would not be reported net of taxes. All income taxes, except those related to discontinued operations, would be reported together as a separate category following the functional categories. Other display conventions would remain similar to current practice. For example, FASB has decided that discontinued operations would be presented as a separate classification, net of tax, below the other functional classifications and after income taxes.

FASB is also considering adding a second dimension to the statement. It is currently considering separating items of revenue, expense, gains, and losses into initial recognition and remeasurement-type items. Remeasurement-type items would be accounting adjustments that are a result of subsequent changes to the value of a recognized asset or liability, rather than the initial recognition of a transaction. That additional dimension might be accomplished by columns, which would be similar to the IASB's tentative decision to present a statement of comprehensive income with a columnar distinction that separates revenues, expenses, gains, and losses into income flows and remeasurements.

FASB is coordinating its activities on performance reporting with the IASB. As of April 2004, it has reached the following conclusions on the reporting and classification of items of revenue, expense, gains, and losses:

1. A principal objective of the project is to develop standards of reporting that enhance the predictive and feedback value of the information that is presented in the statement of comprehensive income, which is consistent with the IASB's objective.
2. Although the title for this statement has not been arrived at, a business entity will report all items of revenue, expense, gains, and losses in a single statement of comprehensive income.
3. The three major categories in the statement of comprehensive income would be: business activities, financing, and other gains and losses.
4. Income taxes would be presented as a separate classification after the categories.
5. Discontinued operations effects (as defined by FASB Statement 144, *Accounting for the Impairment or Disposal of Long-Lived Assets*) would be presented as a separate classification, net of tax effects, below other categories and after income taxes.
6. The effects of extraordinary events and transactions, before the effects of income taxes, should be included within each of the categories to which they relate.
7. Remeasurement-type events are being explored to determine whether information on the statement of comprehensive income should be separated based on *remeasurement-type* events consistent with the IASB's proposed model.
8. The category and display criteria for items of *other comprehensive income*, as defined in FASB Statement 130, *Reporting Comprehensive Income*, would be retained.
9. A subtotal labeled *net income (loss) from continuing operations* would be required to be displayed before discontinued operations and other comprehensive income.
10. A subtotal within the statement of comprehensive income labeled *earnings* would not be required.

FASB and IASB Boards agreed to form a joint working group to research and form recommendations to reduce areas of divergence and develop a timetable for the issuance of public documents for this project. This public document is expected sometime during 2004.

Pro Forma Earnings

In addition to net income and comprehensive income, companies have increasingly been making reference in press releases and published materials to an alternative, purportedly meaningful measure of performance, "pro forma earnings." This practice has generated controversy and confusion because there is no standard definition for "pro forma earnings." Different reporting entities can, and do, define pro forma earnings on ad hoc bases, and sometimes a given entity fails even to consistently define this amount from period to period. (The term "pro forma" suggests that numbers that are not actual historical results are being cast in the form of a report on historical performance—e.g., when after a midyear business acquisition the full year's results are presented as if the merger had occurred on January 1.)

The reporting of pro forma earnings has proliferated within the past few years. Often, even when GAAP-basis earnings are stated in the same announcement as the pro forma measure, it is the latter which receives most of the attention. In a number of instances, pro forma earnings have been based on very aggressive exclusions of operating costs and, sometimes, inclusion of onetime gains.

Companies defend their pro forma calculations as merely responding to the marketplace's need for a measure that gives insight into the company's future performance. Pro forma earnings, they say, are necessary to compensate for deficiencies in GAAP. Because

GAAP-basis net income is affected by various noncash charges and credits, as well as by nonrecurring gains and losses, some believe that this standard measure may not provide investors with the most meaningful and accurate guide to the entity's future results of operations. They say that investors need access to a number that measures only the performance of the reporting entity's ongoing "normalized" operations.

Assuming for the moment that GAAP-basis net income is a flawed indicator of future performance, their argument would have greater validity if a standardized pro forma measure had been promulgated by the accounting profession or uniformly applied by the investment community. A standard definition does not exist, however. Despite the lack of standardization, there has been an increasing willingness on the part of investors to accept the pro forma numbers without understanding what they are or how they have been computed.

For reporting entities, part of the allure of pro forma earnings is that it can be defined to exclude some or all of a range of "unusual" items. Not surprisingly, most of the excluded items have been charges, such as those for worker layoffs, restructurings, assets impairments, and inventory obsolescence. Even if not expected to recur annually, many of these charges are quite normal and may be anticipated to recur at irregular intervals in the life of a given business.

A further practice, which is improper but unfortunately not uncommon, has been for reporting entities to opportunistically charge off an exaggerated loss in the current period, perhaps in connection with such randomly occurring events as discontinued operations. The loss is then excluded from pro forma earnings. The excess reserves (sometimes referred to as "cookie jar reserves") then become available to be drawn down in future periods. The drawdowns of the excess reserves increase net income in future periods, but those drawdowns will not be excluded from pro forma earnings the way the original loss had been. The result will be to boost both GAAP-basis net income and pro forma earnings in future years. (This is not to suggest that all companies that announce pro forma earnings use "cookie jar reserves" to commit financial fraud. However, investors' acceptance of undefined measures of earnings increases the temptation to engage in irregularities that misstate the results of operations.)

Not surprisingly, these practices began to receive attention from the SEC. Its chairman stated in early 2002 that enforcement actions would be taken against any company that uses pro forma earnings to mislead its investors. In January 2003, the SEC adopted a new disclosure regulation, Regulation G, that implements the chairman's warning.

Regulation G states that a public company, or a person acting on its behalf, is not to make public a non-GAAP financial measure that, taken together with the information accompanying that measure, either contains an untrue statement of a material fact or omits a material fact that would be necessary to make the presentation of the non-GAAP financial measure not misleading. Further, Regulation G requires a public company that discloses or releases a non-GAAP financial measure to include in that disclosure or release a presentation of the most directly comparable GAAP financial measure and a reconciliation of the disclosed non-GAAP measure to that directly comparable GAAP financial measure.

The regulations also prohibit certain non-GAAP measures from inclusion in SEC filings. Public companies must not

1. Exclude from non-GAAP liquidity measures charges or liabilities that required, or will require, cash settlement, or would have required cash settlement absent an ability to settle in another manner. However, earnings before interest and taxes (EBIT) and earnings before interest, taxes, depreciation, and amortization (EBITDA) are permissible.
2. Create a non-GAAP performance measure that eliminates items identified as nonrecurring, infrequent, or unusual if the nature of the excluded item is such that it is

(a) reasonably likely to recur within two years or (b) similar to a charge or gain that occurred within the prior two years.

3. Present non-GAAP financial measures on the face of the registrant's financial statements prepared in accordance with GAAP or in the accompanying notes.
4. Present non-GAAP financial measures on the face of any pro forma financial information required to be disclosed by Article 11 of Regulation S-X (e.g., business combinations or disposals).
5. Use titles or descriptions of non-GAAP financial measures that are the same as, or confusingly similar to, titles or descriptions used for GAAP measures.

The SEC's action is expected to curb the abuse of pro forma earnings measures, but it does little to standardize the measures in use. Others, however, have proposed approaches to standardize the computation of pro forma earnings. For example, the rating agency Standard & Poors (S&P) has introduced a measure that it will use in its COMPUSTAT database, in its US equity indices, and in its financial statement analysis. It has denoted this measure as "core earnings." S&P defines core earnings as net income, as defined by GAAP, specifically *including* these items.

- Employee stock option grant expenses
- Restructuring charges from ongoing operations
- Write-downs of depreciable or amortizable operating assets
- Pension costs
- Purchased research and development

And specifically *excluding* these items

- Discontinued operations
- Extraordinary items
- Impairment of goodwill charges
- Gains and losses from asset sales
- Pension gains
- Unrealized gains and losses from hedging activities
- Merger and acquisition fees
- Litigation settlements

S&P's definition may help investors and also serve to reverse, or at least constrain, the expanding use of subjectively defined, alternative income measures. Although there may be a demand for a performance measure other than net income or comprehensive income, such a measure will not be useful unless it is standardized so that comparisons can be confidently made among different entities or within the same entity over time. Auditors also need standardization guidelines in order to perform effective monitoring of a company's activities and management.

Development Stage Enterprises

FAS 7 indicates that **development stage enterprises** should prepare their financial statements in accordance with the same GAAP applicable to established operating entities. FAS 7 indicated that specialized accounting practices are unacceptable and that accounting treatment should be governed by the nature of the transaction rather than the age of the entity. FAS 7 also provided that a development stage enterprise should disclose certain additional information that would alert readers to the fact that the company is in the development stage. Disclosure requirements include

1. All disclosures applicable to operating entities

2. Identification of the statements as those of a development stage enterprise
3. Disclosure of the nature of development stage activities
4. A balance sheet that, in the equity section, includes the cumulative net losses since inception
5. An income statement showing current period revenue and expense as well as the cumulative amount from the inception of the entity
6. A statement of cash flows showing cash flows for the period as well as those from inception
7. A statement of stockholders' equity showing the following from the enterprise's inception:
    a. For each issuance, the date and number of equity securities issued for cash or other consideration
    b. For each issuance, the dollar amounts (per share and in total) assigned to the consideration received for equity securities
    c. For each issuance involving noncash consideration, the nature of the consideration and the basis used in assigning the valuation
8. For the first period in which an enterprise is no longer a development stage enterprise, it shall disclose that in prior periods the entity was a development stage enterprise. If comparative statements are presented, the foregoing disclosure presentations (2-7) need not be shown.

FIN 7 allows parent or equity method investor companies to capitalize or defer some development stage company costs that would have to be expensed by the development stage company. Costs may be deferred if recoverable within the entire entity.

Reporting on the Costs of Start-up Activities

SOP 98-5 provides guidance on financial reporting of start-up costs and organization costs and requires such costs to be expensed as incurred. Start-up costs are defined as one-time activities related to opening a new facility, introducing a new product or service, conducting activities in a new territory, pursuing a new class of customer, initiating a new process in an existing facility, or some new operation. Those costs are sometimes referred to as preopening costs, preoperating costs, organization costs, and start-up costs. Routine ongoing efforts to improve existing quality of products, services, or facilities are not start-up costs. Other costs, related to specific activities listed below, are excluded from the SOP and should be accounted for in accordance with other existing authoritative literature. These include

1. Costs of acquiring or constructing long-lived assets and getting them ready for their intended uses. (However, the costs of using long-lived assets that are allocated to start-up activities [for example, depreciation of equipment] are within the scope of the SOP.)
2. Costs of acquiring or producing inventory
3. Costs of acquiring intangible assets. (However, the costs of using intangible assets that are allocated to start-up activities [for example, amortization of a purchased patent] are within the scope of the SOP.)
4. Costs related to internally developed assets (for example, internal-use computer software costs). (However, the costs of using those assets that are allocated to start-up activities are within the scope of the SOP.)
5. Costs that are within the scope of FAS 2, *Accounting for Research and Development*, and FAS 71, *Accounting for the Effects of Certain Types of Regulation*
6. Costs of fund-raising incurred by not-for-profit organizations

7. Costs of raising capital
8. Costs of advertising
9. Costs incurred in connection with existing contracts as stated in SOP 81-1, *Accounting for Performance of Construction-Type and Certain Production-Type Contracts.*
10. Costs of merger or acquisition activities
11. Costs of ongoing customer acquisition, such as policy acquisition costs and loan origination costs

Exit and Disposal (Restructuring) Costs

Restructuring costs have received a good deal of attention in recent years because of revelations of abuses that have used charges as "big bath" write-offs and to create "cookie jar" reserves later employed to smooth future earnings.

Restructuring charges are costs that are incurred or will be incurred in connection with a plan of action that will materially change the scope of business undertaken by an entity or the manner in which a business is conducted. They typically include costs such as employee benefits, costs associated with product line elimination or relocation, costs for new systems development or acquisitions, retraining costs, and losses on asset impairment and dispositions. A series of FASB and EITF pronouncements address the costs commonly recognized in restructurings. They are

1. FAS 13, which discusses the accounting for a termination of a capital lease (Chapter 14).
2. FAS 87 and 88, which discuss an employer's accounting for pension plans (Chapter 16).
3. FAS 106, which discusses an employer's accounting for postretirement benefits other than pensions (Chapter 16).
4. FAS 112, which discusses an employer's accounting for postemployment benefits (Chapter 16).
5. FAS 144, which discusses the accounting for long-lived assets that will be disposed of, including discontinued operations (Chapter 9).
6. EITF 95-3, which discusses costs associated with exiting a company newly acquired in a business combination (Chapter 11).
7. EITF 95-14 and 96-5, which discuss costs in anticipation of a business combination (Chapter 11).
8. FAS 146, which discusses the accounting for certain onetime termination benefits, costs to terminate contracts other than capital leases, and costs to consolidate facilities or relocate employees (this chapter).
9. EITF 87-4, which discusses the application of SEC Staff Accounting Bulletin 67 (this chapter).

Employee termination benefits. In June 2002, FASB issued FAS 146, *Accounting for Costs Associated with Exit or Disposal Activities*, which supersedes the guidance provided in EITF 94-3, *Liability Recognition for Certain Employee Termination Benefits and Other Costs to Exit an Activity (Including Certain Costs Incurred in a Restructuring).* In general, the liability for employee termination benefits is recognized under FAS 146 in a manner similar, but not exactly the same, as it was under EITF 94-3.

FAS 146 applies to termination benefits provided to current employees that are involuntarily terminated under the terms of a benefit arrangement that applies for a specified termination event or for a specified future period. Those benefits are referred to as onetime termination benefits. If an entity has a history of providing similar benefits to employees involuntarily terminated in earlier events, the benefits are presumed to be part of an ongoing benefit arrangement (rather than a onetime benefit arrangement) unless there is evidence to the contrary.

Specifically excluded from consideration were employee termination benefits

1. Paid pursuant to the terms of an ongoing employee benefit plan, regardless of whether the plan was preexisting or is newly created
2. Paid under the terms of an individual deferred compensation agreement

A onetime benefit arrangement exists at the date the plan of termination meets all of the following criteria:

1. Management approves and commits to the termination plan.
2. The termination plan specifies the number of employees to be terminated, their job classifications or functions, and their locations, as well as the expected completion date.
3. The termination plan establishes the terms of the benefit arrangement in sufficient detail that employees are able to determine the type and amount of benefits that they will receive if they are involuntarily terminated.
4. Actions required to complete the plan indicate that significant changes to the plan are unlikely.
5. The terms of the plan have been communicated to employees (the communication date).

The timing of recognition of the liability for onetime termination benefits depends on whether the employees are required to render service beyond a minimum retention period. The minimum retention period is the notification period that an entity is required to provide to employees in advance of a termination event as a result of law, statute, or contract, or in the absence of a legal notification period, the minimum retention period cannot exceed sixty days.

If employees are entitled to receive the termination benefits regardless of when they leave or if employees will not be retained to render service beyond the minimum retention period, the liability for the termination benefits is recognized and measured at its fair value at the communication date.

If employees are required to render service until they are terminated in order to receive the termination benefit and will be retained beyond the minimum retention period, the liability for the termination benefits is measured at its fair value at the communication date and recognized ratably over the service period.

Examples of the determination of the minimum retention period and recognition

Master Mobile Communications announces that it will close its Donnybrook plant and terminate all 120 employees there. The terms of the plan meet the criteria above. There are three major groups of employees: management, union workers, and nonunion workers. Management is required to stay and render service until the plant's closing, which is four months from now, and each of the twelve management employees will receive $10,000. The union workers' contract states that they must be notified ninety days in advance before they can be terminated. The union workers will be terminated in ninety days. The termination benefit for each of the fifty union employees is one week per every six months of employment. The nonunion workers can leave at any time within the next three months and still collect the termination benefit. Each of the fifty-eight nonunion employees will receive a termination benefit of $1,000 for each year of service. There is no state statute specifying a notification period.

Case 1: Management

Management is required to work until termination, so it is necessary to determine whether the service period is beyond the minimum retention period. There is no state statute specifying a notification period, but the Worker Adjustment and Retraining Act, which applies to entities with over 100 employees, requires a sixty-day notification period for this plant's closing. Thus, the minimum retention period is sixty days. Management must work beyond the minimum retention period, so the $120,000 liability (12 x $10,000) is recognized at $30,000 per month for the next four months. Present value techniques are not necessary to measure the liability because the discount period is so short that the face amount would not differ materially from the fair value.

Case 2: Union employees

The union employees' contract requires a ninety-day notification period, so the minimum retention period for these employees is ninety days. The union workers will be terminated at the end of the ninety-day period, so they will not be required to work beyond the minimum retention period. If the total of the termination benefits for the fifty union employees is $142,500, a liability of $142,500 is recognized at the communication date. Present value techniques are not necessary to measure the liability because the discount period is so short that the face amount would not differ materially from the fair value.

Case 3: Nonunion workers

Nonunion workers are not required to work until the termination date to collect the termination benefit. Therefore, it is not necessary to determine the minimum retention period for these employees. If the 58 nonunion employees have 230 years of service among them, a liability of $230,000 is recognized at the communication date. Present value techniques are not necessary to measure the liability because the discount period is so short that the face amount would not differ materially from the fair value.

If subsequent to the communication date there are changes in either the timing or amount of the expected termination benefit cash flows, the cumulative effect of the change should be computed and reported in the same line item(s) in the income statement in which the costs were initially reported. If present value techniques were used to measure the initial liability, the same credit-adjusted risk-free rate should be used to remeasure the liability.

Changes in the liability due to the passage of time (accretion) are recognized as accretion expense in the income statement. If employees are not required to provide services or are required to provide services only during the minimum retention period, accretion expense is charged for the passage of time after the communication date. If employees are required to provide services beyond the minimum retention period, accretion expense is charged for the passage of time after the termination date. Accretion expense should not be titled interest expense or be considered interest costs subject to capitalization.

According to FSP 146-1, if newly offered benefits represent a revision to an ongoing arrangement that is not limited to a specified termination event or to a specified future period, the benefits represent an enhancement to an ongoing benefit arrangement. Therefore, these benefits are to be accounted for under the provisions of one or more of the following pronouncements:

- FAS 87—Pensions
- FAS 88—Settlements and Curtailments
- FAS 106—Postretirement Benefits other than Pensions
- FAS 112—Postemployment Benefits

If a plan of termination changes, and employees that were expected to be terminated within the minimum retention period are retained to render service beyond that period, the liability amount should be recomputed as though it had been known at the initial communication date that those employees would be required to render services beyond the minimum retention period. The cumulative effect of the change is recognized as a change in the liability and reported in the same line item(s) in the income statement in which the costs were initially reported. The remainder of the liability is recognized ratably from the date of change to the termination date.

If a plan of termination includes both voluntary and involuntary termination benefits, a liability for the involuntary benefits are recognized as described above. A liability for the incremental voluntary benefits (the excess of the voluntary benefit amount over the involuntary benefit amount) is recognized in accordance with FAS 88 (Chapter 16). That is, if the benefits are special termination benefits offered only for a short period of time, the liability is recognized when the employees accept the offer and the amount can be reasonably estimated. If, instead, the voluntary termination benefits are contractual termination benefits (for example, required by a union contract or a pension contract) the liability is recognized when it is probable that employees will be entitled to benefits and the amount can be reasonably estimated.

Contract termination and other costs to exit an activity. In addition to employee termination costs, an entity may incur contract termination costs, relocation costs, plant consolidation costs, and other costs associated with the exit or disposal activity. FASB rejected the EITF 94-3 consensus that an entity's commitment to a plan, by itself, creates a present obligation to others that meets the definition of a liability. Instead, FAS 146 sets forth the following standards for recognition.

A liability for the costs to terminate a contract before the end of its term is recognized and measured at its fair value when the entity actually terminates the contract in accordance with the contractual term (e.g., by written notice).

A liability for the costs that will continue to be incurred under a contract for its remaining term without economic benefit to the entity is recognized and measured at its fair value when the entity ceases using the right conveyed by the contract (the cease-use date). If the contract is an operating lease, the fair value of the liability should be determined based on the remaining lease rentals, reduced by estimated sublease rentals, even if the entity does not intend to find a sublease. However, remaining operating lease payments should not be reduced to an amount less than zero by the estimated sublease payments.

A liability for other costs associated with the exit or disposal activity should be recognized when the liability is incurred, which is generally when the goods or services associated with the activity are received. The liability should not be recognized before it is incurred even if the costs are incremental and a direct result of the exit or disposal plan.

Reporting and disclosure. The costs of exit or disposal activities must be included in income from continuing operations before income taxes. If the subtotal "income from operations" is presented, the costs must be included in that subtotal. If the costs are associated with exit or disposal activities that involve a discontinued operation, they are included in the results of discontinued operations. If an entity's responsibility to settle the liability associated with an exit or disposal activity is removed or discharged, the related costs are reversed through the same line item(s) in the income statement that were used when those costs were initially recognized.

The following information should be disclosed in the period in which an exit or disposal plan is initiated, and in each period until the activity is completed:

1. A description of the activity and the expected completion date.
2. For each of the major categories of costs (e.g., onetime termination benefits, contract termination costs, and other costs), the amount expected to be incurred, the

amount incurred during the period, and the cumulative amount incurred to date, in total for the entity and for each reportable segment (Chapter 20).

3. For each of the major categories of costs, a reconciliation of the beginning and ending liability balances, showing separately the costs incurred during the period, the costs paid or otherwise settled during the period, and any adjustments.
4. The reasons for any adjustments to the liability amounts.
5. The line items(s) in the income statement in which the exit or disposal costs are aggregated.
6. If a liability for a cost associated with the exit or disposal activity is not recognized because the amount cannot be reasonably estimated, that fact and the reasons therefor.

EMERGING ISSUES TASK FORCE ISSUES SUMMARIES

87-24 Allocation of Interest to Discontinued Operations

A consensus was reached that the allocation of interest expense to discontinued operations is required on debt that will be assumed by the buyer and debt that is required to be repaid as a result of the disposal transaction. Allocation to discontinued operations of other consolidated interest is permitted but not required. If the corporation decides to allocate, the EITF provides guidance regarding the maximum amount and methods of allocation. Additionally, the Task Force reached a consensus that general corporate overhead may not be allocated to discontinued operations.

92-13 Accounting for Estimated Payments in Connection with the Coal Industry Retiree Health Benefit Act of 1992

Enterprises that have ongoing operations in the coal industry should account for their obligation under the Act as either participation in a multiemployer plan or as a liability. Enterprises that choose to report a liability and enterprises that do not have ongoing operations in the coal industry should account for the loss under FAS 5 and report the estimated loss as an extraordinary item.

95-3 Recognition of Liabilities in Connection with a Purchase Business Combination

If costs to exit an activity of an acquiree and involuntary termination or relocation costs relative to employees of an acquiree are anticipated at or very shortly after the acquisition, they should be reflected in the allocation of the purchase price, unless the costs are incurred to generate revenue of the combined entity after the acquisition, in which case these would be period costs.

00-9 Classification of a Gain or Loss from a Hedge of Debt That Is Extinguished (Modified by FAS 145)

The issue is whether a gain or loss from debt extinguishment should be classified as an extraordinary item if the gain or loss results from an adjustment to the carrying amount of the debt as required by the hedge accounting requirements of FAS 133. If the hedge was a fair value hedge, the component of gain or loss that results from the prior adjustment of the debt's carrying amount (because of the hedge) should be classified with the extinguishment gain or loss. If the hedge was a cash flow hedge of debt, the reclassification to earnings of the amount in accumulated comprehensive income required by FAS 133 should be excluded from extinguishment gain or loss. A determination of whether a gain or loss on extinguishment of debt should be reported as an extraordinary item should be made in accordance with the criteria in APB 30.

00-10 Accounting for Shipping and Handling Fees and Costs

Shipping and handling costs are a major expense for product sellers. The amounts charged to customers for shipping and handling often differ from the amounts the seller pays for delivery. Any and all amounts related to shipping and handling billed to a customer in a sale transaction should be classified as revenue.

01-10 Accounting for the Impact of the Terrorist Attacks of September 11, 2001

After the terrorist attacks the immediate reaction was to deem the resulting losses as extraordinary. However, after further deliberations, the practical difficulties in making the determination of which costs were associated directly with the events caused a reversal of position. Losses associated with the attacks were not, therefore, classifiable as extraordinary.

The consensus was that losses and costs incurred as a result of the September 11, 2001 events were to be classified as part of income from continuing operations in the statement of operations. If those losses and costs met the criteria for disclosure of unusual or infrequently occurring items of APB 30, they were to have been reported as a separate component of income from continuing operations, either on the face of the statement of operations or in the notes to the financial statements. Any insurance recoveries of losses and costs incurred were also to be classified within income from continuing operations. A recovery of a loss not yet recognized in the financial statements or an amount recovered in excess of a loss recognized in the financial statements (that is, a contingent gain) would not be recognized until any contingencies relating to the insurance claim have been resolved.

Liabilities for losses and costs incurred as a result of the September 11 events were to be recognized when the criteria in CON 5 were met; that is, when the obligation met the definition of a liability, was measurable with sufficient reliability, was relevant to decision making, and the information is representationally faithful, verifiable, and neutral. The guidance in FAS 5 was also to be used to determine when to recognize liability. Mere intent to incur costs (or even a compulsion to incur those costs in order to remain in business) would not meet the definition of a liability. For example, the costs of restoring a facility (whether capitalizable or not) to a condition suitable for occupancy would be recognized as the restoration efforts occur.

Expanded disclosure in the notes to the financial statements was required for all periods affected by the September 11 events, as follows:

- A description of the nature and amounts of losses and costs recognized as a result of the September 11 events and the amount of related insurance recoveries (if any) recognized
- A description of contingencies resulting from the September 11 events that had not yet been recognized in the financial statements but that were reasonably expected to impact the entity's financial statements in the near term
- Applicable disclosures pursuant to SOP 94-6
- Applicable disclosures about environmental obligations (and recoveries) pursuant to SOP 96-1

The EITF also decided that

- FAS 144 and the literature identified in Appendix D thereof was to be used to determine when to recognize asset impairments related to the tragedy.
- A liability was to be recognized as of September 11 for operating lease rentals on temporarily unusable equipment or facilities provided that the period of time that the equipment or facilities will be unusable can be reasonably estimated.

- Operating lease payments for equipment or facilities temporarily idled that were not unusable were to be charged to expense as those payments become payable.
- Operating lease expenses on temporarily unusable and temporarily idled equipment or facilities were subject to further consideration in EITF 99-14 (discussed in Chapter 14).
- Entities were to continue to recognize depreciation expense on capitalized equipment or facilities that were temporarily unusable or temporarily idled.
- Federal assistance provided to air carriers in the form of direct compensation was to be classified as part of income from continuing operations in the statement of operations, reported as a separate line item or in other nonoperating income.

01-13 Income Statement Display of Business Interruption Insurance Recoveries

An entity may choose how to classify business interruption insurance recoveries in the statement of operations if the chosen classification is not contrary to existing generally accepted accounting principles. For example, the requirements of APB 30 must be met to classify business interruption insurance recoveries as an extraordinary item. The following information should be disclosed in the notes to the financial statements in the period(s) in which insurance recoveries are recognized:

1. The nature of the event resulting in business interruption losses
2. The aggregate amount of business interruption insurance recoveries recognized during the period and the line item(s) in the statement of operations in which those recoveries are reported (including amounts reported as an extraordinary item pursuant to APB 30)

01-14 Income Statement Characterization of Reimbursements Received for "Out-of-Pocket" Expenses Incurred

Entities that provide services as part of their central ongoing operations (for example, consultants, lawyers, and accountants) generally incur incidental expenses for travel, photocopies, telecommunications, facsimile transmissions, and similar items that are reimbursed by the client. In some cases, the customer pays actual expenses incurred; in other cases, the parties negotiate a flat fee to compensate the service provider. Reimbursements received for out-of-pocket expenses incurred should be classified as revenue in the income statement.

02-16 Accounting by a Customer (Including a Reseller) for Certain Consideration Received from a Vendor

Cash consideration received by a customer from a vendor is presumed to be a reduction of the prices of the vendor's products or services and should, therefore, reduce cost of sales when recognized in the customer's income statement. However, that presumption is overcome when the consideration is either (1) a payment for assets or services delivered to the vendor, in which case the cash consideration is reported as revenue when recognized in the customer's income statement, or (2) a reimbursement of costs incurred by the customer to sell the vendor's products, in which case the cash consideration reduces that cost when recognized in the customer's income statement.

Cash consideration meets condition (1)—a payment for assets or services delivered to the vendor—if the vendor receives, or will receive, an identifiable benefit (goods or services) in exchange for the consideration. The benefit must be sufficiently separable from the customer's purchase of the vendor's products that the customer would have entered into an exchange transaction with an entity other than the vendor to provide that benefit. If the amount of cash consideration paid by the vendor exceeds the estimated fair value of the benefit received, the excess amount should reduce cost of sales when recognized in the customer's income statement.

Cash consideration meets condition (2)—reimbursement of costs incurred by the customer to sell the vendor's products—if it is a reimbursement of a specific incremental, identifiable cost incurred by the customer in selling the vendor's products or services. If the amount of cash consideration paid by the vendor exceeds the cost being reimbursed, the excess should reduce cost of sales when recognized in the customer's income statement. (See Chapter 8 for further discussion of this EITF issue.)

03-10 Application of EITF 02-16, *Accounting by a Customer (Including a Reseller) for Certain Consideration Received from a Vendor*, by Resellers to Sales Incentives Offered to Consumers by Manufacturers

Vendor's sales incentives offered directly to consumers are not subject to the guidance in EITF 02-16; thus, the vendor recognizes revenue rather than a reduction in cost of sales. Vendor's sales incentives offered directly to consumers are those that meet all of the following criteria:

- The reseller accepts manufacturers' incentives from the consumer in partial (or full) payment of the price charged by the reseller for the vendor's product.
- The reseller receives a direct reimbursement from the vendor (or a clearinghouse authorized by the vendor) based on the face amount of the incentive.
- The terms of reimbursement to the reseller for the incentive must not be influenced by or negotiated in conjunction with any other incentive arrangements between the vendor and the reseller, but rather are determined only by the terms of the incentive offered to the consumer, and
- The reseller is subject to an agency relationship with the vendor, whether expressed or implied, in the sales incentive transaction between the vendor and the consumer.

4 STATEMENT OF CASH FLOWS

PERSPECTIVE AND ISSUES

FAS 95, as amended, establishes standards for cash flow reporting. A statement of cash flows is a required part of a complete set of financial statements for business enterprises and not-for-profit organizations. Only defined benefit plans, certain other employee benefit plans, and highly liquid investment companies that meet specified conditions are not required to present the statement.

The primary purpose of the statement of cash flows is to provide information about cash receipts and cash payments of an entity during a period. A secondary purpose is to provide information about the investing and financing activities during the period.

Specifically, the statement of cash flows helps investors and creditors assess

1. Ability to generate future positive cash flows
2. Ability to meet obligations and pay dividends
3. Reasons for differences between net income and net cash receipts and payments
4. The cash and noncash aspects of investing and financing transactions on an entity's financial position

CON 1 states that "financial reporting should provide information that is useful to present and potential investors, creditors, and other users for making rational investment and credit decisions." Since the ultimate objective of investment and credit decisions is the maximization of net cash inflows, information for assessing the amounts, timing, and uncertainty of prospective cash flows is needed. CON 5 concludes that financial statements must show cash flows during the period in order to be complete.

Sources of GAAP		
CON	*EITF*	*FAS*
1, 5	95-13, 00-15, 02-6	95, 102, 104, 115, 117, 133, 149

DEFINITIONS OF TERMS

Cash equivalents. Short-term, highly liquid investments that (1) are readily convertible to known amounts of cash and (2) are so near their maturity (maturity of three months or less from the date of purchase by the enterprise) that they present negligible risk of changes in value because of changes in interest rates. Treasury bills, commercial paper, and money market funds are all examples of cash equivalents.

Direct method. A method which derives the net cash provided by operating activities from the components of operating cash receipts and payments as opposed to adjusting net income for items not affecting cash.

Financing activities. The transactions a firm engages in to acquire and repay capital (e.g., borrowings, sale of capital stock, repayments, etc.).

Indirect (reconciliation) method. A method which derives the net cash provided by operating activities by adjusting net income for revenue and expense items not resulting from cash transactions.

Investing activities. The transactions the firm engages in which affect its investments in noncurrent assets (e.g., purchase or sale of plant, property, and equipment).

Operating activities. The transactions not classified as financing or investing activities, generally involving producing and delivering goods or providing services.

CONCEPTS, RULES, AND EXAMPLES

Cash Focus

The statement of cash flows includes only inflows and outflows of cash and cash equivalents. Cash equivalents include any short-term highly liquid investments (see definition for criteria) used as a temporary investment of idle cash. The effects of investing and financing activities that do not result in receipts or payments of cash are to be reported in a separate schedule immediately following the statement or in the notes to the financial statements. The reasoning for not including noncash items in the statement of cash flows and placing them in a separate schedule is that it preserves the statement's primary focus on cash flows from operating, investing, and financing activities. Thus, if a transaction is part cash and part noncash, only the cash portion is reported in the statement of cash flows.

Classification

The statement of cash flows requires classification of cash receipts and cash disbursements into three categories.

Investing activities include the acquisition and disposition of (1) long-term productive assets or (2) securities held in available-for-sale or held-to-maturity portfolios that are not considered cash equivalents. Investing activities also include the lending of money and the collection on loans.

However, per FAS 102, as amended by FAS 115, cash flows are classified as operating cash flows if they originate from the purchase or sale of loans, debt, or equity instruments acquired specifically for resale and are carried at market value in a trading account.

Financing activities include obtaining resources from and returning resources to the owners. Also included is obtaining resources from creditors on long-term credit and repaying the amount borrowed. The financing activities of not-for-profit organizations also include receiving contributions from donors that require the resources to be used for long-term purposes, such as endowment or the purchase of long-lived assets.

Operating activities include all transactions that are not classified as investing or financing activities. Operating activities include delivering or producing goods for sale and providing services. All tax-related cash flows are classified as operating activities. Note, however, that an Exposure Draft currently under consideration would amend FAS 95 to require that certain cash flows relating to the portion of tax expense associated with share-based compensation would be classified as financing activities. See discussion of this ED, which if adopted would become effective December 15, 2004, at the end of this chapter.

The following are examples of the statement of cash flows classification:

	Operating	*Investing*	*Financing*
Cash Inflows	• Receipts from sale of goods or services	• Principal collections from loans and sales of other entities' debt instruments*	• Proceeds from issuing stock
	• Sale of loans, debt, or equity instruments carried in trading portfolio	• Sale of equity instruments* of other enterprises and from returns of investment in those instruments	• Proceeds from issuing debt (short-term or long-term)
	• Returns on loans (interest) • Returns on equity securities (dividends)	• Sale of plant & equipment	• Not-for-profits' donor-restricted cash gifts that are limited to long-term purposes
Cash Outflows	• Payments for inventory	• Loans made and acquisitions of other entities' debt instruments*	• Payment of dividends
	• Payments to employees and other suppliers	• Purchase of equity instruments* of other enterprises	• Repurchase of entity's stock
	• Payments of taxes • Payments of interest • Purchase of loans, debt, or equity instruments carried in trading portfolio • Payments of asset retirement obligations	• Purchase of plant & equipment	• Repayment of debt principal, including capital lease obligations

* *Held in available-for-sale or held-to-maturity portfolios*

Noncash Investing and Financing Activities

(May be disclosed following statement or in the notes)

- Acquiring an asset through a capital lease or by assuming long-term debt
- Conversion of debt to equity
- Exchange of noncash assets or liabilities for other noncash assets or liabilities
- Issuance of stock to acquire assets
- Obtaining an investment asset or a building by receiving a contribution

Example of a statement of cash flows (without detail of the required operating activities section)

Liquid Corporation
Statement of Cash Flows
For the Year Ended December 31, 2005

Net cash flows from operating activities		$ xxx
Cash flows from investing activities:		
Purchase of property, plant, and equipment	$(xxx)	
Sale of equipment	xx	
Collection of notes receivable	xx	
Net cash **used** in investing activities		(xx)

Cash flows from financing activities:		
Sale of common stock	xxx	
Repayment of long-term debt	(xx)	
Reduction of notes payable	(xx)	
Net cash **provided** by financing activities		xx
Effect of exchange rate changes on cash		xx
Net increase (decrease) in cash		$ xxx
Cash and cash equivalents at beginning of year		xxx
Cash and cash equivalents at end of year		$xxxx
Schedule of noncash financing and investing activities:		
Conversion of bonds into common stock		$ xxx
Property acquired under capital leases		xxx
		$ xxx

Operating Activities Presentation

Direct vs. indirect. The operating activities section of the statement of cash flows can be presented under the direct or indirect method. However, the FASB has expressed a preference for the direct method of presenting net cash from operating activities. Additionally, during interviews that were conducted recently as part of the FASB's project on financial performance reporting by business enterprises many, if not most, investors, creditors, and advisors (for example, equity and credit analysts) preferred a statement of cash flows that reports operating cash flows under the direct method.

The **direct method** shows the items that affected cash flow. Cash received and cash paid are presented, as opposed to converting accrual-basis income to cash flow information. At a minimum, entities using the direct method are required to report the following classes of operating cash receipts and payments:

1. Cash collected from customers
2. Interest and dividends received
3. Other operating cash receipts
4. Cash paid to employees and other suppliers
5. Interest and income taxes paid
6. Other operating cash payments

The direct method allows the user to clarify the relationship between the company's net income and its cash flows. For example, payments of expenses are shown as cash disbursements and are deducted from cash receipts. In this way, the user is able to recognize the cash receipts and cash payments for the period. The information needed to prepare the operating activities section using the direct method can often be obtained by converting information already appearing in the balance sheet and income statement. Formulas for conversion of various income statement amounts for the direct method presentation from the accrual basis to the cash basis are summarized below.

Accrual basis		*Additions*		*Deductions*		*Cash basis*
Net sales	+	Beginning AR	–	Ending AR AR written off	=	Cash received from customers
Cost of goods sold	+	Ending inventory Beginning AP	–	Manufacturing depreciation and amortization Beginning inventory Ending AP	=	Cash paid to suppliers
Operating expenses	+	Ending prepaid expenses Beginning accrued expenses	–	Sales and administrative depreciation and amortization Beginning prepaid expenses Ending accrued expenses payable Bad debts expense	=	Cash paid for operating expenses

When the direct method is used, a separate schedule reconciling net income to net cash flows from operating activities must also be provided. That schedule reports the same information as the operating activities section prepared using the indirect method. Therefore, a firm must prepare and present both the direct and indirect methods when using the direct method for reporting cash from operating activities.

The **indirect method** is the most widely used presentation of cash from operating activities, primarily because it is easier to prepare. It focuses on the differences between net income and cash flows. The indirect format begins with net income, which is obtained directly from the income statement. Revenue and expense items not affecting cash are added or deducted to arrive at net cash provided by operating activities. For example, depreciation and amortization would be added back because they reduce net income without affecting cash.

The statement of cash flows prepared using the indirect method emphasizes changes in the components of most current asset and current liability accounts. Changes in inventory, accounts receivable, and other current accounts are used to determine the cash flow from operating activities. It is important to note that the change in accounts receivable should be calculated using the balances net of the allowance account in order to assure write-offs of uncollectible accounts are treated properly. Other adjustments under the indirect method include changes in the account balances of deferred income taxes and the income (loss) from investments reported using the equity method. However, short-term borrowing used to purchase equipment would be classified as a financing activity.

The following diagram may facilitate understanding of the adjustments to net income necessary for converting accrual-based net income to cash-basis net income when using the indirect method. The diagram is simply an expanded balance sheet equation.

	*Current assets**	–	*Noncurrent assets*	=	*Current liabilities*	+	*Long-term liabilities*	+	*Income*	*Accrual income adjustment to convert to cash flow*
1.	Increase			=					Increase	Decrease
2.	Decrease			=					Decrease	Increase
3.				=	Increase				Decrease	Increase
4.				=	Decrease				Increase	Decrease

* *Other than cash and cash equivalents*

For example, using Row 1, a credit sale would increase accounts receivable and accrual-basis income but would not affect cash. Therefore, its effect must be removed from the accrual income in order to convert to cash income. The last column indicates that the increase in a current asset balance must be deducted from income to obtain cash flow. Using Row 2, a decrease in a current asset, such as prepaid rent, indicates that net income was decreased, by rent expense, without a cash outflow in the current period. Thus, the decrease in prepaid rent would be added back to convert to cash income.

Similarly, an increase in a current liability, Row 3, must be added to income to obtain cash flows (e.g., accrued wages are on the income statement as an expense, but they do not require cash; the increase in wages payable must be added back to remove this noncash expense from accrual-basis income). Using Row 4, a decrease in a current liability, such as accounts payable, indicates that cash was used but the expense was incurred in an earlier period. Thus, the decrease in accounts payable would be subtracted to include this disbursement in cash income.

If the indirect method is chosen, then the amount of interest and income tax paid must be included in the related disclosures.

The major drawback to the indirect method involves the user's difficulty in comprehending the information presented. This method does not show where the cash came from or where the cash went to. Only adjustments to accrual-basis net income are shown. In some cases the adjustments can be confusing. For instance, the sale of equipment resulting in an accrual-basis loss would require that the loss be added to net income to arrive at net cash from operating activities. (The loss was deducted in the computation of net income, but because the sale will be shown as an investing activity, the loss must be added back to net income.)

Although the indirect method is more commonly used in practice, the authors believe that the direct method is preferable. It portrays both the amounts of funds provided by and used in the firm's operations, instead of presenting net income and reconciling items. The direct method reports only the items that affect cash flow (inflows/outflows of cash) and ignores items that do not affect cash flow (depreciation, gains, etc.). Both the direct method and the indirect method are shown below.

Direct method

Cash flows from operating activities:		
Cash received from sale of goods	$xxx	
Cash interest received	xxx	
Cash dividends received	xxx	
Cash provided by operating activities		$xxx
Cash paid to suppliers	(xxx)	
Cash paid for operating expenses	(xxx)	
Cash interest paid	(xxx)	
Cash paid for taxes	(xxx)	
Cash disbursed for operating activities		(xxx)
Net cash flows from operating activities		$xxx

Indirect method

Cash flows from operating activities:	
Net income	$ xx
Add/deduct items not affecting cash:	
Decrease (increase) in accounts receivable	(xx)
Depreciation expense	xx
Increase (decrease) in accounts payable	xx
Decrease (increase) in inventories	xx
Loss on sale of equipment	xx
Net cash flows from operating activities	$xxx

Other Requirements

Gross vs. net basis. The emphasis in the statement of cash flows is on gross cash receipts and payments. For instance, reporting the net change in bonds payable would obscure the financing activities of the entity by not disclosing separately cash inflows from issuing bonds and cash outflows from retiring bonds. In a few circumstances, netting of cash flows is allowed. Items having quick turnovers, large amounts, and short maturities may be presented as net cash flows if the cash receipts and payments pertain to (1) investments (other than cash equivalents), (2) loans receivable, and (3) debts (original maturity of three months or less).

Extraordinary items and discontinued operations. FAS 95 permits, but does not require, separate disclosure of cash flows related to extraordinary items and to discontinued operations. If an entity chooses to disclose this information, disclosure must be consistent for all periods affected.

Cash flow per share. This information shall **not** be reported in the financial statements of an enterprise. The reason for this is that the FASB does not want the cash flow statement to have equal status with the income statement.

Entities Exempt from Providing a Statement of Cash Flows

Per FAS 102, a statement of cash flows is not required for a defined benefit pension plan that presents the financial information under the guidelines of FAS 35. Other employee benefit plans are exempted provided that the financial information presented is similar to the requirements of FAS 35. Investment enterprises or a common trust fund held for the collective investment and reinvestment of moneys are not required to provide a statement of cash flows if the following conditions are met:

1. Substantially all of the entity's investments are highly liquid.
2. The entity's investments are carried at market value.
3. The entity has little or no debt, based on average debt outstanding during the period, in relation to average total assets.
4. The entity provides a statement of changes in net assets.

Net Reporting by Financial Institutions

Per FAS 104, banks, savings institutions, and credit unions are allowed to report net cash receipts and payments for the following:

1. Deposits placed with other financial institutions
2. Withdrawals of those deposits
3. Time deposits accepted
4. Repayments of time deposits
5. Loans made to customers
6. Principal collections of loans made to customers

Not-for-Profit Organizations

FAS 117 requires not-for-profit organizations to include a statement of cash flows in a complete set of financial statements. The statement of cash flows is prepared as it is for business enterprises with the following differences:

1. The indirect method of reporting cash flows from operations (or reconciliation of net income to net cash flows from operations required when the direct method is used) is prepared beginning with the change in net assets.
2. Investing activities also include receiving contributions that are restricted by the donor to the purchase or improvement of long-lived assets or for long-term investment such as permanent or term endowment.
3. Noncash activities include gifts of long-lived assets and gifts of securities held for long-term investment.

Reporting Hedging Transactions

Per FAS 104, as amended by FAS 133, the cash flows resulting from derivative instruments that are accounted for as fair value hedges or cash flow hedges may be classified as the same type of cash flows as the hedged items provided that that accounting policy is disclosed. However, if the derivative instrument used to hedge includes at inception an other-than-insignificant financing element, all cash inflows and outflows of the derivative instrument are reported by the borrower as cash flows from financing activities. A derivative that at inception includes off-market terms, or requires up-front cash payment, or both, often contains a financing element. A derivative instrument is viewed as including a financing element if its contractual terms have been structured to ensure that net payments will be made by one party in the earlier periods of the derivative's term and subsequently returned by the counterparty in the later periods (other than elements that are inherent in at-the-money derivative instruments with no prepayments). If for any reason hedge accounting is discontinued, then any cash flows subsequent to the date of discontinuance are classified consistent with the nature of the instrument.

Reporting Foreign Currency Cash Flows

If an entity has foreign currency transactions or foreign operations, it should translate the foreign currency cash flows using exchange rates in effect at the time of the cash flows. A weighted-average exchange rate for the period can be used for the translation if the result is substantially the same. The effect of changes in exchange rates on any cash balances held in foreign currencies should be shown as a separate part of the reconciliation of the change in cash and cash equivalents during the period. An example of reporting the effect of exchange rate changes is shown in the statement of cash flows in the "Classification" section of this chapter.

Noncash exchange gains and losses recognized in net income should be reported as a separate item when reconciling net income and operating activities.

For a more detailed discussion of the exchange rate effects on the statement of cash flows, see Chapter 21.

Preparation of the Statement

Under a cash and cash equivalents basis, the changes in the cash account and any cash equivalent account is the "bottom line" figure of the statement of cash flows. Using the 2004 and 2005 balance sheet shown below, an increase of $25,000 can be computed. This is the difference between the totals for cash and treasury bills between 2004 and 2005 ($41,000 – $16,000).

When preparing the statement of cash flows using the direct method, gross cash inflows from revenues and gross cash outflows to suppliers and for expenses are presented in the operating activities section.

In preparing the reconciliation of net income to net cash flow from operating activities (indirect method), changes in all accounts (other than cash and cash equivalents) that are related to operations are additions to or deductions from net income to arrive at net cash provided by operating activities.

A T-account analysis may be helpful when preparing the statement of cash flows. A T-account is set up for each account, and beginning (2004) and ending (2005) balances are taken from the appropriate balance sheet. Additionally, a T-account for cash and cash equivalents from operating activities and a master or summary T-account of cash and cash equivalents should be used.

Example of preparing a statement of cash flows

The financial statements below will be used to prepare the statement of cash flows.

Johnson Company
Balance Sheets
December 31, 2005 and 2004

	2005	*2004*
Assets		
Current assets:		
Cash	$ 37,000	$ 10,000
Treasury bills	4,000	6,000
Accounts receivable—net	9,000	11,000
Inventory	14,000	9,000
Prepaid expenses	10,000	13,000
Total current assets	$ 74,000	$ 49,000

	2005	2004
Noncurrent assets:		
Investment in available-for-sale securities	7,500	15,000
Add (less) adjustment for changes in fair value	1,000	(3,000)
Investment in XYZ (35%)	16,000	14,000
Patent	5,000	6,000
Leased asset	5,000	--
Property, plant, and equipment	39,000	37,000
Less accumulated depreciation	(7,000)	(3,000)
Total assets	$140,500	$115,000
Liabilities		
Current liabilities:		
Accounts payable	$ 2,000	$ 12,000
Notes payable—current	9,000	--
Interest payable	3,000	2,000
Dividends payable	5,000	2,000
Income taxes payable	2,180	1,000
Lease obligation	700	--
Total current liabilities	21,880	17,000
Noncurrent liabilities:		
Deferred tax liability	9,360*	4,920*
Bonds payable	10,000	25,000
Lease obligation	4,300	--
Total liabilities	$ 45,540	$ 46,920
Stockholders' equity		
Common stock, $10 par value	$ 33,000	$ 26,000
Additional paid-in capital	16,000	3,000
Retained earnings	45,320	41,000
Accumulated other comprehensive income		
Net unrealized loss on available-for-sale securities	640	(1,920)
Total stockholders' equity	$ 94,960	$ 68,080
Total liabilities and stockholders' equity	$140,500	$115,000

* *Net of deferred tax asset ($540) and ($1,080) respectively.*

Johnson Company
Statement of Earnings and Comprehensive Income
For the Year Ended December 31, 2005

Sales		$100,000
Other income		8,500
		$108,500
Cost of goods sold, excluding depreciation		60,000
Selling, general, and administrative expenses		12,000
Depreciation		8,000
Amortization of patents		1,000
Interest expense		2,000
		$ 83,000
Income before taxes		$ 25,500
Income taxes:		
Current	$6,180	
Deferred	3,000	9,180
Net income		$ 16,320
Other comprehensive income, net of tax		
Unrealized gains on securities:		
Unrealized holding gains (less applicable income taxes of $900)		1,600
Add reclassification adjustment (less applicable income taxes of $540)		960
Total other comprehensive income		$ 2,560
Comprehensive income		$ 18,880

Additional information (all relating to 2005)

1. Equipment costing $6,000 with a book value of $2,000 was sold for $5,000.
2. The company received a $3,000 dividend from its investment in XYZ, accounted for under the equity method and recorded income from the investment of $5,000 that is included in other income.
3. The company issued 200 shares of common stock for $5,000.
4. The company signed a note payable for $9,000.
5. Equipment was purchased for $8,000.
6. The company converted $15,000 bonds payable into 500 shares of common stock. The book value method was used to record the transaction.
7. A dividend of $12,000 was declared.
8. Equipment was leased on December 31, 2005. The principal portion of the first payment due December 31, 2006, is $700.
9. The company sold half of their available-for-sale investments during the year for $8,000. The fair value of the remaining available-for-sale investments was $8,500 on December 31, 2005.
10. The income tax rate is 36%.

Summary of Cash and Cash Equivalents

Inflows	Outflows	
(d) 5,000		
	8,000 (g)	
(h) 5,000	9,000 (i)	
(n) 9,000		
(s) 8,000		
(t) 15,000		
42,000	17,000	
	25,000	Net increase in cash
42,000	42,000	

Cash and Cash Equivalents—Oper. Act.

Debit	Credit
(a) 16,320	
(b) 8,000	
(c) 1,000	3,000 (d)
(e) 3,000	5,000 (f)
(f) 3,000	
(j) 2,000	5,000 (k)
(l) 3,000	10,000 (m)
(o) 1,000	
(p) 1,180	500 (s)
38,500	23,500
	15,000 (t)
38,500	38,500

Accounts Receivable (net)

Debit	Credit
11,000	
	2,000 (j)
9,000	

Inventory

Debit	Credit
9,000	
(k) 5,000	
14,000	

Prepaid Expenses

Debit	Credit
13,000	
	3,000 (l)
10,000	

Investment in AFS Securities

Debit	Credit
15,000	
	7,500 (s)
7,500	

Adjustment for Changes in FV of AFS Securities

Debit	Credit
	3,000
(s) 1,500	
(s) 2,500	
1,000	

Investment in XYZ

Debit	Credit
14,000	
(f) 5,000	3,000 (f)
16,000	

Patent

Debit	Credit
6,000	
	1,000 (c)
5,000	

Leased Equipment

Debit	Credit
(r) 5,000	
5,000	

Prop., Plant, & Equip.

Debit	Credit
37,000	
	6,000 (d)
(g) 8,000	
39,000	

Accumulated Depr.

Debit	Credit
	3,000
	8,000 (b)
(d) 4,000	
	7,000

Accounts Payable

Debit	Credit
	12,000
(m) 10,000	
	2,000

Notes Payable	
	9,000 (n)
	9,000

Interest Payable	
	2,000
(o) 1,000	2,000 (o)
	3,000

Dividends Payable	
	2,000
(i) 9,000	12,000 (i)
	5,000

Income Taxes Payable	
	1,000
(p) 5,000	6,180 (p)
	2,180

Deferred Tax Liability (Net)	
	4,920
	3,000 (e)
	540 (s)
	900 (s)
	9,360

Bonds Payable	
	25,000
(q) 15,000	
	10,000

Lease Obligation	
	5,000 (r)
	5,000

Common Stock	
	26,000
	2,000 (h)
	5,000 (q)
	33,000

Addl. Paid-in Capital	
	3,000
	3,000 (h)
	10,000 (q)
	16,000

Retained Earnings	
	41,000
	16,320 (a)
(i) 12,000	
	45,320

Unrealized Gain (Loss) on AFS Securities	
1,920	
	960 (s)
	1,600 (s)
	640

Explanation of entries

a. Cash and Cash Equivalents—Operating activities is debited for $16,320 (net income) and the credit is to Retained Earnings.

b. Depreciation is not a cash flow; however, depreciation expense was deducted to arrive at net income. Therefore, Accumulated Depreciation is credited and Cash and Cash Equivalents—Operating activities is debited.

c. Amortization of patents is another expense not requiring cash; therefore, Cash and Cash Equivalents—Operating activities is debited and Patent is credited.

d. The sale of equipment (additional information, item 1.) resulted in a $3,000 gain. The gain is computed by comparing the book value of $2,000 with the sales price of $5,000. Cash proceeds of $5,000 are an inflow of cash. Since the gain was included in net income, it must be deducted from net income to determine cash provided by operating activities. This is necessary to avoid counting the $3,000 gain both in cash provided by operating activities and in investing activities. The following entry would have been made on the date of sale:

Cash	5,000	
Accumulated depreciation ($6,000 – $2,000)	4,000	
Property, plant, and equipment		6,000
Gain on sale of equipment ($5,000 – $2,000)		3,000

Adjust the T-accounts as follows: debit Summary of Cash and Cash Equivalents for $5,000, debit Accumulated Depreciation for $4,000, credit Property, Plant, and Equipment for $6,000, and credit Cash and Cash Equivalents—Operating activities for $3,000. Note that per FAS 95, the gross gain, not the net of tax gain, is removed from operating activities. The tax effect on this gain is left in operating activities.

e. The deferred income tax liability account shows an increase of $4,440. The $3,000 increase that pertains to amounts reported in the income statement must be added to income from operations. Although the $3,000 was deducted as part of income tax expense in determining net income, it did not require an outflow of cash. Therefore, debit Cash and Cash Equivalents—Operating activities and credit Deferred Taxes. The other two amounts in the deferred tax liability account are covered below, under paragraph "s."

f. Item 2. under the additional information indicates that the investment in XYZ is accounted for under the equity method. The investment in XYZ had a net increase of $2,000, which is the result of the equity in the earnings of XYZ of $5,000 and the receipt of a $3,000 dividend.

Dividends received (an inflow of cash) would reduce the investment in XYZ, while the equity in the income of XYZ would increase the investment without affecting cash. The journal entries would have been

Cash (dividend received)	3,000	
Investment in XYZ		3,000
Investment in XYZ	5,000	
Equity in earnings of XYZ		5,000

The dividend received ($3,000) is an inflow of cash, and the equity earnings are not. Debit Investment in XYZ for $5,000, credit Cash and Cash Equivalents—Operating activities for $5,000, debit Cash and Cash Equivalents—Operating activities for $3,000, and credit Investment in XYZ for $3,000.

g. The Property, Plant, and Equipment account increased because of the purchase of $8,000 (additional information, item 5.). The purchase of assets is an outflow of cash. Debit Property, Plant, and Equipment for $8,000 and credit Summary of Cash and Cash Equivalents.

h. The company sold 200 shares of common stock during the year (additional information, item 3.). The entry for the sale of stock was

Cash	5,000	
Common stock (200 shares x $10)		2,000
Additional paid-in capital		3,000

This transaction resulted in an inflow of cash. Debit Summary of Cash and Cash Equivalents $5,000, credit Common Stock $2,000, and credit Additional Paid-in Capital $3,000.

i. Dividends of $12,000 were declared (additional information, item 7.). Only $9,000 was actually paid in cash resulting in an ending balance of $5,000 in the Dividends Payable account. Therefore, the following entries were made during the year:

Retained earnings	12,000	
Dividends payable		12,000
Dividends payable	9,000	
Cash		9,000

These transactions result in an outflow of cash. Debit Retained Earnings $12,000 and credit Dividends Payable $12,000. Additionally, debit Dividends Payable $9,000 and credit Summary of Cash and Cash Equivalents $9,000 to indicate the cash dividends paid during the year.

j. Accounts Receivable (net) decreased by $2,000. This is added as an adjustment to net income in the computation of cash provided by operating activities. The decrease of $2,000 means that an additional $2,000 cash was collected on account above and beyond the sales reported in the income statement. Debit Cash and Cash Equivalents—Operating activities and credit Accounts Receivable for $2,000.

k. Inventories increased by $5,000. This is subtracted as an adjustment to net income in the computation of cash provided by operating activities. Although $5,000 additional cash was spent to increase inventories, this expenditure is not reflected in accrual-basis cost of goods sold. Debit Inventory and credit Cash and Cash Equivalents—Operating activities for $5,000.

l. Prepaid Expenses decreased by $3,000. This is added back to net income in the computation of cash provided by operating activities. The decrease means that no cash was spent when incurring the related expense. The cash was spent when the prepaid assets were purchased, not when they were expensed on the income statement. Debit Cash and Cash Equivalents—Operating activities and credit Prepaid Expenses for $3,000.

m. Accounts Payable decreased by $10,000. This is subtracted as an adjustment to net income. The decrease of $10,000 means that an additional $10,000 of purchases were paid for in cash; therefore, income was not affected but cash was decreased. Debit Accounts Payable and credit Cash and Cash Equivalents—Operating activities for $10,000.

n. Notes Payable increased by $9,000 (additional information, item 4.). This is an inflow of cash and would be included in the financing activities. Debit Summary of Cash and Cash Equivalents and credit Notes Payable for $9,000.

o. Interest Payable increased by $1,000, but interest expense reported on the income statement was $2,000. Therefore, although $2,000 was expensed, only $1,000 cash was paid ($2,000 expense – $1,000 increase in interest payable). Debit Cash and Cash Equivalents—Operating activities for $1,000 for the noncash portion, debit Interest Payable for $1,000 for the cash portion, and credit Interest Payable for $2,000 for the expense.

p. The following entry was made to record the incurrence of the tax liability:

Income tax expense	9,180	
Income taxes payable		6,180
Deferred tax liability		3,000

Therefore, $9,180 was deducted in arriving at net income. The $3,000 credit to Deferred Income Taxes was accounted for in entry e. above. The $6,180 credit to Taxes Payable does not, however, indicate that $6,180 cash was paid for taxes. Since Taxes Payable increased $1,180, only $5,000 must have been paid and $1,180 remains unpaid. Debit Cash and Cash Equivalents—Operating activities for $1,180, debit Income Taxes Payable for $5,000, and credit Income Taxes Payable for $6,180.

q. Item 6. under the additional information indicates that $15,000 of bonds payable were converted to common stock. This is a **noncash** financing activity and should be reported in a separate schedule. The following entry was made to record the transaction:

Bonds payable	15,000	
Common stock (500 shares x $10 par)		5,000
Additional paid-in capital		10,000

Adjust the T-accounts with a debit to Bonds Payable, $15,000; a credit to Common Stock, $5,000; and a credit to Additional Paid-in Capital, $10,000.

r. Item 8. under the additional information indicates that leased equipment was acquired on the last day of 2005. This is also a noncash financing activity and should be reported in a separate schedule. The following entry was made to record the lease transaction:

Leased asset	5,000	
Lease obligation		5,000

s. The company sold half of its available-for-sale investments during the year for $8,000 (additional information, item 9.). The entry for the sale of the investments was

Cash	8,000	
Investment in available-for-sale securities		7,500
Gain on sale of investments		500

This transaction resulted in an inflow of cash. Debit Summary of Cash and Cash Equivalents $8,000, credit Investment in Available-for-Sale Securities $7,500, and credit Cash and Cash Equivalents—Operating activities $500. The following additional journal entries were made:

Adjustment for changes in FV	1,500	
Other comprehensive income ($1,500 x 64%)		960
Deferred tax liability ($1,500 x 36%)		540

To adjust the allowance account for the sale, one-half of the amounts provided at the end of 2004 must be taken off the books when the related securities are sold.

Adjustment for changes in FV	2,500	
Unrealized gain on available-for-sale securities ($2,500 x 64%)		1,600
Deferred tax liability ($2,500 x 36%)		900

To adjust for the change in FV of the remaining securities at year-end (additional information, item 9.). The book value of the securities before the adjustment above is $6,000 ($7,500 – $1,500). The fair value of the securities is $8,500. An adjustment of $2,500 is necessary.

t. The cash and cash equivalents from operations ($15,000) is transferred to the Summary of Cash and Cash Equivalents.

All of the changes in the noncash accounts have been accounted for and the balance in the Summary of Cash and Cash Equivalents account of $25,000 is the amount of the year-to-year increase in cash and cash equivalents. The formal statement may now be prepared using the T-account, Summary of Cash and Cash Equivalents. The alphabetic characters in the statement below refer to the entries in that T-account. The following statement of cash flows is prepared under the direct method. The calculations for gross receipts and gross payments needed for the direct method are shown below the statement.

Johnson Company
Statement of Cash Flows
For the Year Ended December 31, 2005

Cash flow from operating activities			
Cash received from customers	$102,000		
Dividends received	3,000		
Cash provided by operating activities			$105,000
Cash paid to suppliers	$ 75,000		
Cash paid for expenses	9,000		
Interest paid	1,000		
Income taxes paid	5,000		
Cash paid for operating activities			(90,000)
Net cash flow provided by operating activities		(t)	$ 15,000
Cash flow from investing activities			
Sale of equipment	5,000	(d)	
Sale of investments	8,000	(s)	
Purchase of property, plant, and equipment	(8,000)	(g)	
Net cash provided by investing activities			5,000
Cash flow from financing activities			
Sale of common stock	$ 5,000	(h)	
Increase in notes payable	9,000	(n)	
Dividends paid	(9,000)	(i)	
Net cash provided by financing activities			5,000
Net increase in cash and cash equivalents			$ 25,000
Cash and cash equivalents at beginning of year			16,000
Cash and cash equivalents at end of year			$ 41,000

Calculation of amounts for operating activities section

Cash received from customers = Net sales + Beginning AR – Ending AR

$100,000 + $11,000 – $9,000 = $102,000

Cash paid to suppliers = Cost of goods sold + Beginning AP – Ending AP + Ending inventory – Beginning inventory

$60,000 + $12,000 – $2,000 + $14,000 – $9,000 = $75,000

Cash paid for operating expenses = Operating expenses + Ending prepaid expenses – Beginning prepaid expenses – Depreciation expense (and other noncash operating expenses)

$12,000 + $8,000 + $1,000 + $10,000 – $13,000 – $8,000 – $1,000 = $9,000

Interest paid = Interest expense + Beginning interest payable – Ending interest payable

$2,000 + $2,000 – $3,000 = $1,000

Taxes paid = Income taxes + Beginning income taxes payable – Ending income taxes payable – Change in deferred income taxes—operating portion

$9,180 + $1,000 – $2,180 – $3,000 = $5,000

When a statement of cash flows is prepared using the direct method of reporting operating cash flows, the reconciliation of net income to operating cash flows must also be provided. The T-account, Cash and Cash Equivalents—Operating Activities is used to prepare the reconciliation. The alphabetic characters in the reconciliation below refer to the entries in the T-account.

Reconciliation of net income to net cash provided by operating activities			
Net income		(a)	$16,320
Add (deduct) items not using (providing) cash:			
Depreciation	8,000	(b)	
Amortization	1,000	(c)	
Gain on sale of equipment	(3,000)	(d)	
Increase in deferred taxes	3,000	(e)	
Equity in XYZ	(2,000)	(f)	
Decrease in accounts receivable	2,000	(j)	
Increase in inventory	(5,000)	(k)	
Decrease in prepaid expenses	3,000	(l)	
Decrease in accounts payable	(10,000)	(m)	
Increase in interest payable	1,000	(o)	
Increase in income taxes payable	1,180	(p)	
Gain on sale of AFS securities	(500)	(s)	(1,320)
Net cash flow provided by operating activities		(t)	$15,000
Schedule of noncash transactions			
Conversion of bonds into common stock		(q)	$15,000
Acquisition of leased equipment		(r)	$ 5,000

Disclosure of accounting policy

For purposes of the statement of cash flows, the Company considers all highly liquid debt instruments purchased with original maturities of three months or less to be cash equivalents.

Statement of Cash Flows for Consolidated Entities

A consolidated statement of cash flows must be presented when a complete set of consolidated financial statements is issued. The consolidated statement of cash flows would be the last statement to be prepared as the information to prepare it will come from the other consolidated statements (consolidated balance sheet, income statement, and statement of retained earnings). The preparation of these other consolidated statements is discussed in Chapter 11.

The preparation of a consolidated statement of cash flows involves the same analysis and procedures as the statement for an individual entity with a few additional items. When the indirect method is used, the additional noncash transactions relating to the business combination such as the differential amortization must also be reversed and all transfers to affiliates must be eliminated, as they do not represent cash inflows or outflows of the consolidated entity.

All unrealized intercompany profits should have been eliminated in preparation of the other statements. Any income or loss allocated to noncontrolling parties would need to be added back, as it would have been eliminated in computing consolidated net income but does not represent a true cash outflow or inflow. Finally, only dividend payments that are not intercompany should be recorded as cash outflows in the financing activities section.

In preparing the operating activities section of the statement by the indirect method following a purchase business combination, the changes in assets and liabilities related to operations since acquisition should be derived by comparing the consolidated balance sheet as of the date of acquisition with the year-end consolidated balance sheet. These changes will be combined with those for the acquiring company up to the date of acquisition as adjustments to net income. The effects due to the acquisition of these assets and liabilities are reported under investing activities.

EMERGING ISSUES TASK FORCE ISSUES SUMMARIES

95-13 Classification of Debt Issue Costs in the Statement of Cash Flows

Cash paid for debt issue costs should be shown as a financing activity in the statement of cash flows.

00-15 Classification in the Statement of Cash Flows of the Income Tax Benefit Received by a Company upon Exercise of a Nonqualified Employee Stock Option

This issue discusses how a company should classify in the statement of cash flows the income tax benefit (reduction of a cash flow) from an employee's exercise of a nonqualified stock option and whether disclosure of the benefit is necessary. The reduction of income taxes paid should be classified as an operating cash flow. Disclosure of a material tax benefit is required if that benefit is not presented as a separate line in the statement of cash flows or the statement of changes in stockholders' equity.

02-6 Classification in the Statement of Cash Flows of Payments Made to Settle an Asset Retirement Obligation within the Scope of FASB Statement No. 143

FAS 143, *Asset Retirement Obligations*, requires recognition of a liability for a legal obligation associated with the retirement of a long-lived asset if that obligation results from the acquisition, construction, development, and/or the normal operation of the long-lived asset. Cash payments made to settle an asset retirement obligation should be classified in the statement of cash flows as an operating activity.

EXPOSURE DRAFT OUTSTANDING

Proposed FAS: Share-Based Payment—an amendment of Statements No. 123 and 95

Although this Exposure Draft is primarily concerned with share-based payments and eliminating the use of APB 25, it also amends FAS 95. The proposed requirements of this Standard would be effective for public and nonpublic companies that did not use the minimum-value method as of the beginning of the first fiscal year beginning after December 15, 2004. Nonpublic companies that used the minimum-value method would have an additional year to adopt the new statement.

As pertains to FAS 95, this ED amends FAS 95 to require that excess tax benefits be reported as a financing cash inflow rather than as a reduction of taxes paid, which would affect cash from operating activities. Specifically the ED amends FAS 95 as follows:

1. Cash inflows from financing activities would include cash retained as a result of the tax deductibility of increases in the value of equity instruments issued to parties under share-based payment arrangements that are not included in compensation cost recognizable for financial reporting purposes.
2. Cash outflows for operating activities would include cash that would have been paid for income taxes under item 1. above.
3. If a company uses the direct method of reporting net cash flow from operating activities, the company should separately report the cash that would have been paid for income taxes if increases in the value of equity instruments issued to parties under share-based payment arrangements that are not recognizable as compensation cost for financial reporting purposes also had not been deductible in determining taxable income, per items 1. and 2. above.

5 CASH, RECEIVABLES, AND PREPAID EXPENSES

PERSPECTIVE AND ISSUES

The asset side of a balance sheet displays the resources available to the entity to support its current and future operations. To provide information about liquidity, the assets are often divided into current and noncurrent assets. Current assets consist of cash and other assets that are reasonably expected to be realized in cash or sold or consumed during the normal operating cycle of the business. When the normal operating cycle is less than one year, a one-year period is used to distinguish current assets from noncurrent assets. If the operating cycle exceeds one year, the operating cycle is the proper period to use for current asset identification. When information about current assets is accompanied by information about current liabilities, readers of the financial statements can assess the working capital of the entity (current assets less current liabilities) and its current ratio (current assets divided by current liabilities). Both of those measures provide useful information about the liquidity of the entity.

Current assets usually include cash, short-term investments, receivables, inventory, and prepaid expenses. This chapter discusses cash, receivables, and prepaids. Chapter 6 discusses short-term investments, and Chapter 7 discusses inventory. This chapter also discusses the standards in FAS 140, *Accounting for Transfers and Servicing of Financial Assets and Extinguishments of Liabilities.* FAS 140 is included in this chapter because it describes the proper accounting for sales of receivables to third parties and the use of receivables as collateral in secured borrowings. This chapter also includes FAS 140's standards for repurchase agreements and securities lending. Although those two types of transfers usually involve investments, they are discussed in this chapter because the same underlying theory—the financial components approach—is used for those transactions as is used for transfers involving receivables. FAS 140's standards for extinguishment of debt are set forth in Chapter 13.

Recognition and measurement of cash is generally straightforward. However, it is necessary to inform readers of the financial statements about any limitations on the ability to use cash in current operations.

Trade receivables and other customary trade term receivables that are due in no longer than one year are measured at outstanding face value (principal) adjusted for any chargeoffs and the allowance for doubtful accounts, provided that management has the intent and ability to hold those receivables for the foreseeable future or until maturity or payoff. Loans receivable that management will hold until maturity or payoff are valued at outstanding principal adjusted for any chargeoffs, the allowance for loan losses, any deferred fees or costs on originated loans, and any unamortized premiums of discounts on purchased loans.

If a receivable is due on terms exceeding one year, the proper valuation is the present value of future payments to be received, computed by using an interest rate commensurate with the risks involved at the date of the receivable's creation. In many situations the interest rate commensurate with the risks involved is the rate stated in the agreement between the payee and the obligor. However, if the receivable is noninterest-bearing or if the rate stated in the agreement is not indicative of the market rate for a debtor of similar creditworthiness under similar terms (the market rate), interest is imputed at the market rate. The resulting discount is amortized as additional interest income over the life of the agreement (APB 21).

Receivables that are pledged or assigned to a lender as collateral for a lending agreement remain under the control of the entity and therefore remain on its balance sheet. It is necessary, however, to inform readers of the financial statements about the pledge or assignment.

Receivables are sometimes sold in order to generate cash before the receivables are due. If the transferor has no continuing involvement with the transferred assets or with the transferee, it is clear that a sale has taken place, and a gain or loss on sale is measured and recognized. However, in many cases, the transferor of the receivables has continuing involvement with the transferred assets because it sells the receivables with recourse for uncollectible amounts, retains an interest in the receivables, or agrees to service the receivables after the sale. The greater the control that the transferor retains over the receivables, the more likely that the transfer will be accounted for as a secured borrowing rather than a sale.

Under the financial components approach used in FAS 140, a sale is recognized only if control over the transferred assets is surrendered. A determination that control has been surrendered is made if three criteria are met. If control has been surrendered, an entity recognizes the financial and servicing assets it controls, removes from its books the carrying value of any assets surrendered, recognizes any liabilities assumed, and removes from its books any liabilities that are extinguished. The same accounting and the same three criteria are applied to all transfers of financial assets, regardless of their types. Thus, the standards apply to sales of receivables with recourse, sales of receivables with retained interests or servicing, securitizations (the transformation of the receivables into securities that are sold to other investors), repurchase agreements (a "sale" of a security accompanied by an agreement to "repurchase" it at a future date), and securities lending agreements.

If control has not been surrendered, the transfer of financial assets is accounted for as a secured borrowing. The accounting for the collateral by the debtor and the secured party depends on whether the debtor has defaulted and the nature of the rights and obligations that result from the collateral agreement. If the secured party (the lender) has the right to sell or repledge the collateral, then the debtor reports that asset in its balance sheet separately from other assets not so encumbered. If the secured party does in fact sell the collateral, it recognizes the proceeds from the sale and its obligation to return the collateral. Accounting for the sale of the collateral is also subject to the standards set forth by FAS 140. If the original debtor defaults on the secured borrowing agreement, thereby forfeiting the right to redeem the collateral, the lender will recognize the collateral as its asset, measured at fair value, or, if it has already sold the collateral, derecognize its obligation to return the collateral; concurrently, the debtor will derecognize the collateral, as it no longer has an equitable claim to it.

Sources of GAAP

ARB	APB	FAS	FTB	SOP	EITF
43, Ch. 1A 43, Ch 3A	6, 21	6, 114, 140	01-1	01-6 03-3	86-8, 87-18, 88-11, 88-22, 88-23, 90-18, 92-2, 97-3, 01-7, 02-9, D-51, D-52, D-63, D-64, D-65,D-66, D-69, D-75, D-94, D-99
FSP					
140-1					

DEFINITIONS OF TERMS

Accounts receivable. Amounts due from customers for goods or services provided in the normal course of business operations.

Aging the accounts. Computation of the adjustment for uncollectibility of accounts receivable outstanding at the end of the period based upon the length of time the accounts have been unpaid.

Assignment. The formal procedure for collateralization of borrowings through the use of accounts receivable. It normally does not involve debtor notification.

Beneficial interests. Rights to receive all or portions of specified cash inflows to a trust or other entity.

Cash. Coins and currency on hand and balances in checking accounts available for immediate withdrawal.

Cash equivalents. Short-term, highly liquid investments that are readily convertible to known amounts of cash and are so near their maturity that they present negligible risk of changes in value due to changes in interest rates. Examples include treasury bills, commercial paper, and money market funds.

Collateral. Personal or real property used to secure the performance of a loan or other obligation. Upon default of the obligation the collateral may be sold by the lender in order to satisfy the obligation.

Current assets. Those assets that are reasonably expected to be realized in cash or sold or consumed within a year or within the normal operating cycle of the entity, if longer than a year.

Factoring. The outright sale of accounts receivable to a third-party financing entity. The sale may be with or without recourse.

Financial asset. Cash, evidence of an ownership interest in an entity, or a contract that conveys to another entity a right to (1) receive cash or a financial instrument from a first entity, or (2) exchange other financial instruments on potentially favorable terms with the first entity.

Financial liability. A contract that imposes on one entity a contractual obligation to (1) deliver cash or a financial instrument to another entity, or (2) exchange other financial instruments on potentially unfavorable terms with another entity.

Interest-only strip. The contractual right to receive some or all of the interest due on a financial instrument without the rights to receive the principal.

Net realizable value. The amount of cash anticipated to be produced in the normal course of business from an asset, net of any direct costs of the conversion into cash.

Operating cycle. The average time between the acquisition of materials or services and the cash realization from the sale of products or services produced using the acquired materials or services.

Percentage-of-sales method. Computing the adjustment for uncollectible accounts receivable based on the historical relationship between bad debts and gross credit sales.

Pledging. Using an asset as collateral for borrowings. It generally refers to borrowings secured by accounts receivable.

Recourse. The right of a transferee (factor) to receive payment from the transferor of receivables for uncollectible accounts, prepayments by the debtors, merchandise returns, or other defects in the eligibility of the receivables.

Securitization. The transformation of receivables into securities that are sold to other investors.

Servicing asset. A contract to service financial assets that provides the servicer with estimated future revenues (e.g., fees, late charges) that more than adequately compensate the servicer for performing the service.

Servicing liability. A contract to service financial assets that provides the servicer with estimated future revenues (e.g., fees, late charges) that are not expected to adequately compensate the servicer for performing the service.

Transfer. Conveyance of a noncash financial asset by or to someone other than issuer of financial asset.

CONCEPTS, RULES, AND EXAMPLES

Cash

To be included as cash in the balance sheet, funds must be represented by coins, currency, undeposited checks, money orders, drafts, and demand deposits available without restriction. Cash that is restricted as to use would not be included with cash unless the restrictions on it expire within the year (or the operating cycle, if longer). Thus, cash legally required to be held in a sinking fund should be shown as a current asset if it will be used to retire the current portion of long-term debt. However, if material, it would be reported on a separate line rather than included with cash. Cash in a demand deposit account that is being held for the retirement of long-term debts that do not mature currently should be excluded from current assets and shown as a noncurrent investment. FAS 6 identifies the intent of management as a key criterion in the classification of cash. To be included in cash, it must be management's intention that the cash be available for current purposes. Thus, cash that is designated for the purchase of property or equipment would be included in noncurrent assets.

It is more common to see the caption "Cash and Cash Equivalents" in the balance sheet. That caption includes other forms of near-cash as well as demand deposits and liquid, short-term securities. **Cash equivalents** must be available upon demand in order to justify inclusion.

Compensating balances. An entity will often be required to maintain a minimum amount of cash on deposit (compensating balance). The purpose of this balance is to substitute for service fees foregone by the bank (or fees at a rate less than market) or to increase the yield on a loan to the lender. Since most organizations must maintain a certain working balance in their cash accounts simply to handle routine transactions and to cushion against unforeseen variations in the demand for cash, borrowers often will not find compensating balance arrangements objectionable. Nevertheless, the compensating balance is not available for unrestricted use and penalties will result if it is used. If material, the portion of an entity's cash account that is a compensating balance must be segregated and shown as a separate line item on the balance sheet. The line should be shown as a noncurrent asset if related borrowings are noncurrent liabilities. If the borrowings are current liabilities or if the compensating balance reduces fees that would have been incurred in the next year, it is acceptable to show the compensating balance as a **separately captioned** current asset.

Cash in savings accounts subject to a statutory notification requirement and cash in certificates of deposit maturing during the current **operating cycle** or within one year may be included as current assets but, if material, should be separately captioned in the balance sheet to avoid the misleading implication that these funds are available immediately upon demand. Typically, such items will be included in the **short-term investments** caption, but these could be labeled as time deposits or restricted cash deposits.

Petty cash and other imprest cash accounts are usually combined in financial statements with other cash accounts.

Prepaid Expenses

Prepaid expenses are prepayments made to secure the use of assets or the receipt of services at a future date. Prepaid expenses will not be converted to cash, but they are classified as current assets because, if not prepaid, they would have required the use of current assets during the coming year (or operating cycle, if longer). Prepaid rent, prepaid insurance, prepaid interest, and prepaid advertising are examples of prepaid expenses. The balance in the prepaid expense account is amortized to expense on a ratable basis over the period in which the benefits (services) are received. For example, if rent is prepaid for the quarter at the beginning of the quarter, two months of the rent will be included in the prepaid rent account. At the beginning of the second month, the equivalent of one month's rent (half the account balance) would be expensed. At the beginning of the third month, the remaining account balance would be expensed.

Receivables

Accounts receivable, open accounts, or trade accounts are agreements by customers to pay for services received or merchandise obtained. **Notes receivable** are formalized obligations evidenced by written promissory notes. Other categories of receivables include trade acceptances, third-party instruments, and amounts due from officers, stockholders, employees, or affiliated companies. The latter categories of receivables generally arise from cash advances but could result from sales of merchandise or the provision of services. The nature of amounts due from trade customers is often different from that of balances receivable from related parties, such as employees or stockholders. Thus, generally accepted accounting principles require that the different classes of receivables be separately identified either on the face of the balance sheet or in the notes.

Receivables due within one year (or one operating cycle, if longer) generally should be presented at outstanding face value (principal) adjusted for any chargeoffs and valuation allowances. Valuation allowances adjust the carrying amount of receivables downward because not all of those receivables will ultimately be realized as cash. For example, valuation allowances are reported for amounts estimated to be uncollectible and also for the estimated returns, allowances, and other discounts to be taken by customers prior to or at the time of payment. In practice, the deductions that would be made for estimated returns, allowances, and trade discounts are usually deemed to be immaterial and such adjustments are rarely made. However, if it is known that sales are recorded for merchandise that is shipped "on approval" and available data suggests that a sizable proportion of such sales are returned by the customers, then the estimated future returns must be accrued. Similarly, material amounts of anticipated discounts and allowances should be recorded in the period of sale.

Valuation allowance for bad debts. The recording of a valuation allowance for anticipated uncollectible amounts is almost always necessary. The direct write-off method, in which a receivable is charged off only when it is clear that it cannot be collected, is unsatisfactory since it overstates assets and results in a mismatching of revenues and expenses. Proper matching can only be achieved if bad debts are recorded in the same fiscal period as the revenues to which they are related. Since the amount of uncollectible accounts is not known with certainty, an estimate must be made.

There are two popular estimation techniques. The **percentage-of-sales** method is principally oriented towards achieving the best possible matching of revenues and expenses. **Aging the accounts** is more oriented toward the presentation of the correct net realizable value of the trade receivables in the balance sheet. Both methods are acceptable and widely employed.

For the percentage-of-sales method, historical data are analyzed to ascertain the relationship between bad debts and credit sales. The derived percentage is then applied to the current period's sales revenues in order to arrive at the appropriate debit to bad debts expense for the year. The offsetting credit is made to Allowance for Uncollectibles. When specific customer accounts are subsequently identified as uncollectible, they are written off against this allowance.

Example of percentage-of-sales method

Total credit sales for year:	$7,500,000
Bad debt ratio from prior years or other data source:	1.75% of credit sales
Computed year-end adjustment for bad debts expense:	$131,250 ($7,500,000 x .0175)

The entry required is

Bad debts expense	131,250	
Allowance for uncollectibles		131,250

Care must be taken to ensure that the bad debt ratio computed will be representative of uncollectibility of the current period's credit sales. A ratio based on historical experience may require an adjustment to reflect the current economic climate. For example, if a large percentage of customers are concentrated in a geographic area that is experiencing an economic downturn, rates of default may increase.

When aging the accounts, an analysis is prepared of the customer receivables at the balance sheet date. Each customer's balance is categorized by the number of days or months the underlying invoices have remained outstanding. Based on the entity's past experience or on other available statistics, historical bad debts percentages are applied to each of these aggregate amounts, with larger percentages being applied to the older accounts. The end result of this process is a computed total dollar amount that is the proper balance in the allowance for uncollectibles at the balance sheet date. The computed amount is compared to the balance in the valuation account, and an adjustment is made for the differences. Thus, the adjustment needed will be an amount other than the amount computed by the aging.

Example of the aging method

		Age of accounts		
	Under 30 days	*30-90 days*	*Over 90 days*	*Total*
Gross receivables	$1,100,000	$425,000	$360,000	
Bad debt percentage	0.5%	2.5%	15%	
Provision required	$5,500	$10,625	$54,000	$70,125

The credit balance required in the allowance account is $70,125. Assuming that a **debit** balance of $58,250 already exists in the allowance account (from charge-offs during the year that exceeded the credit balance in the allowance account at the previous year-end), the necessary entry is

Bad debts expense	128,375	
Allowance for uncollectibles		128,375

Both of the estimation techniques will produce approximately the same result over the course of a number of years. Nonetheless, these adjustments are based upon estimates and will never be totally accurate. When facts subsequently become available to indicate that the amount provided as an allowance for uncollectible accounts was incorrect, an adjustment classified as a change in estimate is made. For information about impairment of loans receivable and troubled debt restructurings, see Chapter 13.

Valuation allowance for unearned interest. If a receivable is due on terms exceeding one year, the proper valuation is the present value of future payments to be received, determined by using an interest rate commensurate with the risks involved at the date of the receivable's creation. In many situations the interest rate commensurate with the risks involved is the rate stated in the agreement between the payee and the debtor. However, if the receivable is noninterest-bearing or if the rate stated in the agreement is not indicative of the market rate for a debtor of similar creditworthiness under similar terms (the market rate), interest is imputed at the market rate. A valuation allowance is used to adjust the face amount of the receivable to the present value at the market rate. The balance in the valuation allowance is amortized as additional interest income over the life of the agreement.

APB 21 specifies when and how interest is to be imputed when the receivable is noninterest-bearing or the stated rate on the receivable is not reasonable. APB 21 applies to transactions at arm's length between unrelated parties, as well as to transactions in which captive finance companies offer favorable financing to increase sales of related companies. APB 21 divides receivables into three categories for discussion: notes issued solely for cash, notes issued for cash and a right or privilege, and notes issued in exchange for property, goods, or services.

When a note is issued solely for cash, its present value is necessarily assumed to be equal to the cash proceeds. The interest rate is that rate which equates the cash proceeds received by the borrower to the amounts to be paid in the future. For example, if a borrower agrees to pay $1,060 in one year in exchange for cash today of $1,000, the interest rate implicit in that agreement is 6%. A valuation allowance of $60 is applied to the face amount ($1,060) so that the receivable in included in the balance sheet at its present value ($1,000).

When a note receivable that bears an unrealistic rate of interest is issued in exchange for cash, an additional right or privilege is usually granted. The difference between the present value of the receivable and the cash advanced is the value assigned to the right or privilege. It is an addition to the cost of the products purchased for the purchaser/lender and an additional revenue to the debtor.

Example of accounting for a note issued for both cash and a contractual right

1. Schwartz borrows $10,000 from Weiss via an unsecured five-year note. Simple interest at 2% is due at maturity.
2. Schwartz agrees to sell Weiss a car for $15,000, which is less than its market price.
3. The market rate of interest on a note with similar terms and a borrower of similar creditworthiness is 10%.

The present value factor for an amount due in five years at 10% is .62092. Therefore, the present value of the note is $6,830 [($10,000 principal + $1,000 interest at the stated rate) x .62092]. According to APB 21, the $3,170 ($10,000 – $6,830) difference between the present value of the note and the face value of the note is regarded as part of the cost/purchase price of the car. The following entry would be made by Weiss to record the transaction:

Note receivable	10,000	
Car	18,170	
Cash		25,000
Discount on note receivable		3,170

The discount on note receivable is amortized using the effective interest method, as follows:

	Effective interest (10%)	*Stated interest (2%)*	*Amortization*	*Note and interest receivable*
01/01/01				6,830
01/01/02	683	200	(483)	7,513
01/01/03	751	200	(551)	8,264
01/01/04	826	200	(626)	9,091
01/01/05	909	200	(709)	10,000
01/01/06	1,000	200	(800)	11,000

The entry for the first year would be

Discount on note receivable	483	
Interest receivable	200	
Interest revenue		683

When a note is issued in exchange for property, goods, or services and the transaction is entered into at arm's length, the stated interest rate is presumed to be fair unless (1) no interest rate is stated, (2) the stated rate is unreasonable, (3) the face value of the note receivable is materially different from fair value of the property, goods, or services received, or (4) the face value of the note receivable is materially different from the current market value of the note at the date of the transaction. According to APB 21, when the rate on the note is not fair, the note is to be recorded at the fair market value of the property, goods, or services sold or the market value of the note, whichever is the more clearly determinable. The difference is recorded as a discount or premium and amortized to interest income.

Example of accounting for a note exchanged for goods

1. Green sells Brown inventory that has a fair market value of $8,573.
2. Green receives a two-year noninterest-bearing note having a face value of $10,000.

In this situation, the fair market value of the consideration is readily determinable and, thus, represents the amount at which the note is to be recorded. The following entry would be made by Green:

Notes receivable	10,000	
Discount on notes receivable		1,427
Sales revenue		8,573

The discount will be amortized to interest expense over the two-year period using the interest rate implied in the transaction, which is 8%. The present value factor is .8573 ($8,573/$10,000). Using a present value table for amount due in two years, .8573 is located under the 8% rate.

If neither the fair value of the property, goods, or services sold nor the fair value of the note receivable is determinable, then the present value of the note must be determined using an imputed market interest rate. This rate will then be used to establish the present value of the note by discounting all future payments on the note at that rate. General guidelines for determining the appropriate interest rate, which are provided by APB 21, include the prevailing rates of similar instruments with debtors having similar credit ratings and the rate the debtor could obtain for similar financing from other sources. Other factors to be considered include any collateral or restrictive covenants involved, the current and expected prime rate, and other terms pertaining to the instrument. The objective is to approximate the rate of interest that would have resulted if an independent borrower and lender had negotiated a similar transaction under comparable terms and conditions. This determination is as of the issuance date, and any subsequent changes in market interest rates are irrelevant.

Additional discussion about present value techniques, including additional examples, is found in Chapter 13.

Financing activities, including trade receivables. Receivables generally arise from extending credit to others. Banks, savings institutions, finance companies, credit unions, and mortgage companies are generally thought of as the types of entities that extend credit. However, all entities that sell on credit to customers (that is, trade receivables) also extend credit, however briefly. SOP 01-6, *Accounting by Certain Entities (Including Entities with Trade Receivables) That Lend to or Finance the Activities of Others,* sets standards for the recognition, measurement, presentation, and disclosure of financing and lending transactions of all types.

The scope of the SOP is very broad. The only financing and lending transactions exempt from the standards established by this SOP are those (1) of entities that report receivables at fair value with gains and losses included in earnings or (2) that are subject to a category (a) standard that conflicts with the guidance in the SOP. It is not clear at this time how many changes the SOP will cause to the financial statements of entities that are not financing companies. The provisions of the SOP are discussed below, at the end of this chapter, and further in Chapter 23.

If an entity has the intent and ability to hold trade receivables or loans for the foreseeable future or until maturity or payoff, those receivables should be reported in the balance sheet at outstanding principal (face) amount less any chargeoffs and allowance for uncollectibles. In addition, loans originated by the entity should be reported net of deferred fees or costs of originating them, and purchased loans should be reported net of any unamortized premium or discount. Once a decision has been made to sell loans, those loans should be transferred to a held-for-sale category on the balance sheet and reported at the lower of cost or fair value. Any amount by which cost exceeds fair value should be accounted for as a valuation allowance.

When a trade receivable or loan is deemed uncollectible, the balance should be charged off against the allowance for uncollectible receivables. Recoveries of loans and trade receivables that were previously charged off should be recorded when received—either by a credit directly to earnings or by a credit to the allowance for uncollectible receivables. A credit loss on a financial instrument with off-balance-sheet risk should be recorded as a liability rather than being included in a valuation account of a recognized financial instrument. When settled, the credit loss should be deducted from the liability account.

SOP 01-6 also includes standards for recognizing **fees related to receivables**. Delinquency fees should be recognized when chargeable, provided that collectibility is reasonably assured. Prepayment fees should not be recognized until prepayments have occurred. Rebates of finance charges due because payments are made earlier than required should be recognized when the receivables are prepaid and should be accounted for as adjustments to interest income.

Pledging, assigning, and factoring receivables. An organization can alter the timing of cash flows resulting from sales to its customers by using its accounts receivable as collateral for borrowings or by selling the receivables outright. A wide variety of arrangements can be structured by the borrower and lender, but the most common are pledging, assignment, and factoring.

Pledging is an agreement in which accounts receivable are used as collateral for loans. The customers whose accounts have been pledged are not aware of this event, and their payments are still remitted to the original entity to which the debt was owed. The pledged accounts merely serve as security to the lender, giving comfort that sufficient assets exist to generate cash flows adequate in amount and timing to repay the debt. However, the debt is paid by the borrower whether or not the pledged receivables are collected and whether or not the pattern of their collection matches the payments due on the debt.

The only accounting issue relating to pledging is that of adequate disclosure. The accounts receivable, which remain assets of the borrowing entity, continue to be shown as current assets in its financial statements but must be identified as having been pledged. This identification can be accomplished either parenthetically or by note disclosures. Similarly, the related debt should be identified as having been collateralized by the receivables.

Example of disclosure for pledged receivables

Current assets:	
Accounts receivable, net of allowance for doubtful accounts of $600,000 ($3,500,000 of which has been pledged as collateral for bank loans)	8,450,000
Current liabilities:	
Bank loans payable (collateralized by pledged accounts receivable)	2,700,000

A more common practice is to include the disclosure in the notes to the financial statements. Since the borrower has not surrendered control of the pledged receivables, it continues to carry the pledged receivables as its assets (FAS 140). (More complex collateral arrangements are described in the section "Accounting for collateral" later in this chapter.)

The assignment of accounts receivable is a more formalized transfer of the receivables to the lending institution. The lender will make an investigation of the specific receivables that are being proposed for assignment and will approve those that it deems worthy as collateral. Usually customers are not aware that their accounts have been assigned and they continue to forward their payments to the original obligee (the borrowing entity). In some cases, the assignment agreement requires that collection proceeds be immediately delivered to the lender. The borrower is, however, the primary obligor of the debt and is required to make timely payment on the debt whether or not the receivables are collected as anticipated. The borrowing is with recourse, and the general credit of the borrower is pledged to the payment of the debt.

Since the lender knows that not all the receivables will be collected on a timely basis by the borrower, only a fraction of the face value of the receivables will be advanced as a loan to the borrower. Typically, this amount ranges from 70 to 90%, depending upon the credit history and collection experience of the borrower.

Assigned accounts receivable remain the assets of the borrower and continue to be presented in its financial statements, with appropriate disclosure of the assignment similar to that illustrated for pledging. Prepaid finance charges would be debited to a prepaid expense account and amortized to expense over the period to which the charges apply.

In the typical case involving the assignment of receivables, the borrower retains control of the receivables, and it is clear that the transaction is a secured borrowing rather than a sale. If it is unclear whether the borrower has retained control of the receivables, a determination must be made as to whether to account for the transfer as a sale or as a secured borrowing. Making that determination is discussed later in this chapter in the section titled "Transfers of Financial Assets under FAS 140."

Factoring involves the outright sale of receivables to a finance company known as a factor. These arrangements involve (1) notification to the customer to forward future payments to the factor and (2) the transfer of receivables without recourse. The factor assumes the risk of an inability to collect. Thus, once a factoring arrangement is completed, the transferor has no further involvement with the accounts, except for a return of merchandise.

In its simplest form, the receivables are sold and the difference between the cash received and the carrying value is recognized as a gain or loss.

Example of accounting for the factoring of receivables without recourse

Thirsty Corp. enters into an agreement with Rich Company to sell a group of its receivables without recourse for $180,055. A total face value of $200,000 accounts receivable (against which a 5% allowance had been recorded) are involved. The entries required are as follows:

Cash	180,055	
Allowance for bad debts (200,000 x .05)	10,000	
Loss on sale of receivables	19,945	
Bad debts expense		10,000
Accounts receivable		200,000

The classic variety of factoring provides two financial services to the business: it permits the entity to obtain cash earlier than waiting for customers to pay, and it transfers to the factor the risk of bad debts. The factor is compensated for each of the services. Interest is charged based on the anticipated length of time between the date the factoring is consummated and the expected collection date of the receivables sold. A fee is charged based upon the factor's anticipated bad debt losses.

Example of accounting for the factoring of receivables without recourse

Thirsty Corp. enters into an agreement with Rich Company to sell a group of its receivables without recourse. The receivables have a total face value of $200,000 (against which a 5% allowance had been recorded). The factor will charge 20% interest computed on the weighted-average time to maturity of the receivables of thirty-six days plus a 3% fee.

The entries required are as follows:

Cash	180,055	
Allowance for bad debts (200,000 x .05)	10,000	
Interest expense (or prepaid) (200,000 x .20 x 36/365)	3,945	
Factoring fee (200,000 x .03)	6,000	
Loss on sale of receivables	10,000	
Bad debts expense		10,000
Accounts receivable		200,000

The interest expense, factor's fee and loss can be combined into a $19,945 loss on the sale of receivables.

Some companies factor receivables as a means of transferring the risk of bad debts, but leave the cash on deposit with the factor until the weighted-average due date of the receivables, thereby avoiding interest charges. This arrangement is still referred to as factoring, since the customer receivables have been sold. However, the borrowing entity does not receive cash but creates a new receivable, usually captioned "Due from Factor." This receivable, in contrast to the original customer receivables, is essentially riskless and will be presented in the balance sheet without a deduction for estimated uncollectibles.

Merchandise returns will normally be the responsibility of the transferor, who must then make the appropriate settlement with the factor. To protect against the possibility that merchandise returns will diminish the total of receivables to be collected, a factor will frequently advance only a portion of the face amount of the factored receivables (less any interest and factoring fee deductions). The factor will retain a certain fraction of the total proceeds relating to the portion of sales that are anticipated to be returned by customers. This sum is known as the factor's holdback. When merchandise is returned to the transferor, an entry is made offsetting the receivable from the factor. At the end of the return privilege period, any remaining holdback will become due and payable to the transferor.

Example of accounting for the factoring of receivables without recourse

1. Thirsty Corp. enters into an agreement with Rich Company to sell a group of its receivables without recourse. The receivables have a total face value of $200,000 (against which a 5% allowance had been recorded). The factor will charge 20% interest computed on the weighted-average time to maturity of the receivables of thirty-six days plus a 3% fee. A 5% holdback will also be retained.
2. Thirsty's customers return for credit $4,800 of merchandise.
3. The customer return privilege period expires and the remaining holdback is paid to the transferor.

The entries required are as follows:

		Debit	Credit
1.	Cash	180,055	
	Allowance for bad debts (200,000 x .05)	10,000	
	Interest expense (or prepaid) (200,000 x .20 x 36/365)	3,945	
	Factoring fee (200,000 x .03)	6,000	
	Factor's holdback receivable [$10,000/($10,000 + $190,000) x $190,000]	9,500	
	Loss on sale of receivables	500	
	Bad debts expense		10,000
	Accounts receivable		200,000

The interest expense, factor's fee and loss can be combined into a $10,445 charge to loss on the sale of receivables.

		Debit	Credit
2.	Sales returns and allowances	4,800	
	Factor's holdback receivable		4,800
3.	Cash	5,200	
	Factor's holdback receivable		4,700
	Loss on sale of receivables		500

The factor's holdback receivable on the seller's books is required by FAS 140 to be an allocation of the carrying value of the receivables ($190,000) between the assets sold (the receivables) and the assets retained (the holdback) based on their relative fair values at the date of the factoring agreement. The factor holds back 5% of the face value ($200,000) for a total of $10,000. Upon settlement the loss or gain recorded at the origination of the factoring arrangement needs to be adjusted because the factor pays the remaining holdback of $5,200 ($10,000 holdback – $4,800 returns) in settlement of an asset with a carrying value of $4,700 ($9,500 – $4,800).

Factoring transfers title. Where there is a no recourse provision or other continuing involvement with the receivables, the removal of the receivables from the borrower's balance sheet is clearly warranted.

Another variation is known as factoring with recourse. Accounting for factoring with recourse requires a determination of whether the transfer is a sale or a secured borrowing. That determination is made using the standards in FAS 140.

Transfers of Financial Assets under FAS 140

If receivables or other financial assets are transferred to another entity and the transferor has no continuing involvement with the transferred assets or with the transferee, it is clear that a sale has taken place, and a gain or loss on sale is measured and recognized. However, in many cases, the transferor of the receivables has continuing involvement with the transferred assets, either because it sells the receivables with recourse for uncollectible amounts, retains an interest in the receivables, or agrees to service the receivables after the sale. The more control that the transferor retains over the receivables, the more the transfer appears to be in substance a secured borrowing rather than a sale.

FAS 140 provides standards to determine whether a transfer of financial assets is a sale or a secured borrowing. The standards use a financial components approach in which a single financial asset is viewed as a mix of component assets (controlled economic benefits) and component liabilities (obligations for probable future sacrifices of economic benefits). The focus is on who controls the components and whether that control has changed as a result of a given transfer. If the transferor has surrendered control of the transferred assets, the transfer is a sale. If the transferor retains control of the transferred assets, the transfer is a secured borrowing.

Scope. FAS 140 covers transfers of noncash financial assets by and to an entity other than the issuer of the financial asset. Thus, a transfer includes selling a receivable, transferring a receivable to a trust, or using a receivable as security for a loan. A transfer does not include the origination of a receivable, the settlement of a receivable, or the restructuring of a receivable in a troubled debt restructuring because those transactions are transfers involving the issuer of the receivable.

Among the types of transfers of financial assets for which FAS 140 establishes standards are

- Transfers of receivables with recourse (factoring)
- Transfers of undivided partial interests in receivables (retained interests)
- Transfers of receivables with servicing retained
- Transfers of minimum lease payments under sales-type and direct financing leases and any related guaranteed residual
- Securitizations
- Repurchase agreements
- Securities lending
- Transfers of receivables as collateral

The foregoing types of transactions are discussed in this chapter. In addition, FAS 140 sets standards for extinguishments of liabilities, which matters are discussed in Chapter 13.

Examples of items **included** in the scope of FAS 140

1. Beneficial interests in a securitization trust that holds nonfinancial assets such as securitized stranded costs or similar imposed rights (unless a third party must consolidate the trust).
2. A litigation judgment that is enforceable and contractually reduced to a fixed payment schedule.
3. Transfer of an equity method investment unless subject to EITF 01-2 (similar productive assets) or EITF 98-8 (sale of real estate).
4. A forward contract on a financial instrument that may be net settled or physically settled by exchange for cash or some other financial asset.
5. Recognized financial instruments that may be either financial assets or financial liabilities at some point (forward or swap contracts), which must meet the criteria of both paragraphs 9 and 16 to be derecognized.
6. Dollar rolls in connection with the transfer of existing securities.
7. Transfers of investments in subsidiaries that have not been consolidated because the parent carries the investment at fair value (e.g., an investment company).

The following items are **excluded** from the scope of FAS 140:

1. The right to receive the minimum lease payments under an **operating** lease since it is an unrecognized financial asset.
2. Transfers of servicing rights that are contractually separated from the serviced assets because they are nonfinancial assets.

3. Payment of cash or conveyances of noncash financial assets in partial or full settlement of a debt. An origination, settlement, or restructuring of a receivable is not a transfer since it does not involve a conveyance of a noncash financial asset by or to someone other than the issuer.
4. Acquisition of treasury stock by exchanging noncash financial assets, because it is an investment by or a distribution to owners.
5. Desecuritization of securities into loans or other financial assets.
6. Securitized stranded costs of electric utilities (although enforceable rights) are not considered financial assets since they arise from an imposition of tax rather than a contractual agreement.
7. Contingent receivables from litigation before terms are reduced to a contract.
8. Transfer of ownership interest in a consolidated subsidiary if the subsidiary's assets are not all financial assets.
9. Recognized derivatives that are nonfinancial assets (an option to purchase commodities) at the date of transfer.
10. Dollar rolls when the underlying securities do not yet exist or are to be announced (TBA GNMA rolls).
11. Transfers of **unguaranteed** residual values on transfers of sales-type or direct financing lease receivables.

Surrender of control. A transfer of financial assets (or a portion of a financial asset) is a sale if the transferor surrenders control over those assets in exchange for consideration. However, control is not surrendered to the extent that the consideration received is a beneficial interest in the transferred assets. For example, a transferor's exchange of one form of beneficial interests in a trust for an equivalent, but different, form in the same transferred financial assets cannot be accounted for as a sale. If the trust initially issued the beneficial interests, the exchange is not even a transfer under FAS 140.

Paragraph 9 specifies that control is deemed to have been surrendered by the transferor only if **all** of the following conditions are met:

1. The assets transferred are beyond the reach of the transferor and its affiliates, its creditors, potential bankruptcy trustees or other receivers, except for an affiliate that is a qualifying special-purpose entity (SPE).

   NOTE: FIN 46(R) introduces the concept of variable interest entities, or VIE, which largely superseded the concept of SPE, but entities that met the criteria for qualifying special-purpose entities, or QSPE, under FAS 140 will continue to be so classified.
2. The transferee (or if the transferee is a qualifying SPE, each holder of its beneficial interests) has the right to pledge or exchange the assets (or beneficial interests) it received, and no condition both (1) constrains the transferee (or holder) from taking advantage of its right to pledge or exchange and (2) provides more than a trivial benefit to the transferor.
3. The transferor does not maintain effective control over the transferred assets. A transferor maintains effective control if (1) an agreement both entitles and obligates the transferor to repurchase or redeem the assets before their maturity or (2) the transferor has the ability to unilaterally cause the holder to return specific assets. If the transferor can cause the holder to return assets only through a cleanup call, that ability does not indicate effective control. (A cleanup call is an option to purchase the remaining transferred financial assets, or the remaining beneficial interests in a qualifying SPE if the amount of outstanding assets or beneficial interests falls to a prespecified level at which the cost of servicing those assets or beneficial interests becomes burdensome in relation to the benefits of servicing.)

All available evidence should be assessed to determine if transferred assets would be beyond the reach of the powers of a bankruptcy trustee (or equivalent). It is irrelevant to this determination that the possibility of bankruptcy is remote at the date of the transfer. Instead, the transferor must endeavor to isolate the assets in the event of bankruptcy. In many cases, companies use two transfers to isolate the transferred assets. First, a company transfers the assets to a wholly owned corporation that is designed in a way that prevents the transferor or its creditors from reclaiming the assets (or makes the possibility that they can remote). Next, the wholly owned corporation transfers the assets to a trust. The trust is prevented from undertaking any business other than management of the assets and from incurring any liabilities. (Thus, there are no creditors to force bankruptcy of the trust.) A determination that the transferred assets are beyond the reach of a bankruptcy trustee may require a legal opinion regarding the application of the laws of the relevant jurisdiction.

Assets transferred by a bank or other financial institution that is subject to possible receivership by the FDIC can be considered isolated from the transferor even if the FDIC or another creditor can require their return, provided that the return can only occur in receivership, after a default, and in exchange for a payment of, at a minimum, principal and interest earned at the contractual yield to the date the investors are paid. (That rule does not apply to situations in which the transferor can require return of the assets in exchange for payment of principal and interest earned at the contractual yield to the date the investors are paid. In those cases the assets are not isolated from the transferor.) FTB 01-1, *Effective Date for Certain Financial Institutions of Certain Provisions of Statement 140 Related to the Isolation of Transferred Financial Assets*, deferred application of the isolation criterion for banks and certain other financial institutions until periods beginning after December 31, 2001. FTB 01-1 also gave those institutions up to five years of additional transition time to comply with this criterion regarding transfers of assets to certain securitization master trusts. That additional transition time applies only if all beneficial interests issued to investors after July 23, 2001, permit the changes in structure that are necessary to comply.

A transferee has control of transferred assets if there is the unconstrained right to both pledge and exchange the assets. It is more difficult to tell if the transferee has control if the transferee can pledge the transferred assets but cannot sell them. The key to a determination of control by a transferee with the right to pledge **or** exchange the assets rests on whether the transferee obtains all or most of the cash inflows that are the primary economic benefits of the pledged or exchanged assets. Generally, the right of first refusal, prohibition of a sale to competitors, and the requirement to obtain transferor permission that won't be unreasonably withheld (judgment is necessary in this case) to sell or pledge won't preclude accounting as a sale. Agreements that constrain the transferee from pledge or exchange are accounted for as secured borrowings.

Maintaining effective control. The criteria in paragraph 9 must be met in order for a transfer to be accounted for as a sale, and the criteria in paragraphs 27-34 and 47-54 (implementation guidance) are an integral part of paragraph 9. If the transferor maintains effective control, the transfer is accounted for as a secured borrowing and not as a sale.

The transferor must not be able to unilaterally take back the transferred assets. Therefore, a call option, a forward purchase contract, or a removal of accounts provision will in most cases defeat the determination that a sale has taken place. The transferor cannot take back the transferred assets even through the liquidation of the SPE. For example, a transferor that holds a residual interest in an SPE must be precluded from participating in any auction that SPE may hold at the termination of its existence because presumably it would be willing to pay a price above any other bidder because it would receive any excess over fair value back via its residual interest.

A transferor maintains effective control over the transferred assets if a repurchase or redemption agreement meets all of the following conditions:

1. The assets covered by the agreement must be the same or substantially the same as the transferred assets. In order to meet this condition, the assets transferred and those to be repurchased or redeemed must meet all of the following conditions:
   a. The same primary obligor or, in the case of government-guaranteed instruments, the same guarantor and terms of the guarantee. (If the asset is debt guaranteed by a sovereign government, central bank, government-sponsored enterprise or agency thereof, the guarantor and the terms of the guarantee must be the same.)
   b. Identical form and type providing the same risks and rights
   c. The same maturity, or, in the case of mortgage-backed pass-through or pay-through securities, have similar remaining weighted-average maturities that provide approximately the same market yield
   d. Identical contractual interest rates
   e. Similar collateral
   f. The same aggregate unpaid principal amount or principal amounts that are within accepted "good delivery" standards for the type of security being transferred
2. The transferor is able to repurchase or redeem the assets on substantially the agreed terms even if the transferee were to default. In order to meet this condition, the transferor must, during the entire term of the contract, have obtained cash or other collateral sufficient to fund substantially the entire cost of purchasing replacement assets from others. For example, a contractual provision that terminates a repurchase agreement immediately if the value of the collateral become insufficient to fund substantially all of the cost of purchasing replacement assets would satisfy the requirement, as would a margining provision.
3. The redemption or repurchase agreement is executed concurrently with the transfer of the assets and requires repurchase or redemption prior to maturity at a fixed or determinable price.

Accounting for transfers. Upon any transfer (whether accounted for as a sale or as a secured borrowing), the transferor will allocate, based on relative fair values at the date of transfer, the previous carrying amount between the retained interests, if any, and the assets transferred. Retained interests are interests in the transferred assets over which control has not been given up by the transferor. They include **servicing assets and liabilities,** undivided interests in the transferred assets, and beneficial interests in assets transferred to a qualifying special-purpose entity in a securitization.

If a sale, the transferor (seller) should

1. Derecognize all assets sold
2. Recognize all assets obtained (including cash, options, swaps, etc.) and liabilities incurred (including forward commitments and servicing liabilities) in consideration as proceeds
3. Measure assets controlled and liabilities incurred at fair value initially if they are part of the proceeds of the sale (new assets and liabilities). If it is not practical to estimate the fair value of the assets, the transferor will record those assets at zero. If it is not practical to estimate the fair value of the liabilities, the transferor will not recognize any gain on the transaction and will record liabilities at the greater of

a. Excess fair value of the assets obtained minus the fair value of the liabilities incurred, over the carrying value of the assets transferred or
b. The amount to be recorded in conjunction with FAS 5 and FIN 14 that represents the minimum amount in an estimated range of a probable liability.

4. Recognize gains or losses in earnings.

All financial asset transfers not meeting the sale criteria are required to be accounted for as secured borrowings with collateral (or other security interest) pledged.

Measuring assets and liabilities after completion of a transfer. FAS 140 addresses initial recognition and measurement but, except for servicing, does not address subsequent measurement. Existing GAAP must be used for that purpose. For example

1. Interest-only strips, retained interests in securitizations, loans, other receivables, or other financial assets that can contractually be prepaid or otherwise settled in such a way that the holder would not recover substantially all of its recorded investment (except for derivative instruments that are within the scope of FAS 133) should be subsequently measured like investments in debt securities classified as available-for-sale or trading under FAS 115.
2. Equity securities that have readily determinable fair values should be subsequently measured in accordance with FAS 115.
3. Debt securities should be subsequently measured in accordance with FAS 115, FAS 65 (mortgage-backed securities) or EITF 99-20 (purchased and retained beneficial interests in securitized financial assets).
4. Derivative financial instruments should be subsequently measured in accordance with FAS 133.

If it was initially impracticable to measure the fair value of an asset or liability but it later becomes practicable, the transferor does not remeasure the asset or liability (or the gain or loss) under FAS 140 unless it is a servicing asset or liability. However, adjustment of the carrying value may be required by other standards, such as FAS 115.

The provisions of FAS 140 apply to a wide range of transfers of financial instruments. Some of those are discussed in the following paragraphs.

Transfers of receivables with recourse. Some entities have such a poor history of uncollectible accounts that factors are only willing to purchase their accounts if a substantial fee is collected to compensate for the risk. If the company believes that the receivables are of a better quality, a way to avoid excessive factoring fees is to sell these receivables with recourse. This variation of factoring is really an assignment of receivables with notification to the customers.

In a transfer of receivables with recourse, the transferor is obligated to make payments to the transferee or to repurchase receivables sold upon the happening of an uncertain future event. Typically, recourse provisions compensate the transferee for uncollectible accounts, but they can also be written to compensate the transferee for such uncertain future events as prepayments of the receivables, merchandise returns, or other events that change the anticipated cash flows from the receivables. The effect of a recourse provision on the application of FAS 140's surrender of control provisions (paragraph 9) may vary by jurisdiction and by the level of recourse provided. For example, in some jurisdictions, full recourse will not place the receivables beyond the reach of the transferor and its creditors but a limited recourse provision may. Thus, some transfers of receivables with recourse will meet the criteria of paragraph 9 and be accounted for as a sale. Others will fail the criteria and be accounted for as a secured borrowing.

In computing the gain or loss to be recognized at the date of a transfer of receivables that meets the criteria of paragraph 9, the borrower (transferor) must take into account the anticipated chargebacks from the transferee. This action requires an estimate by the transferor, based on past experience. Adjustments should be made at the time of sale for the estimated effects of any bad debts, prepayments by customers (where the receivables are interest-bearing or where cash discounts are available), and any defects in the eligibility of the transferred receivables.

Example of accounting for the transfer of receivables with recourse

1. Thirsty Corp. enters into an agreement with Rich Company to sell a group of its receivables with a face value of $200,000 on which a 5% allowance had been recorded. Rich Company (the factor) will charge 20% interest computed on the weighted-average time to maturity of the receivables of thirty-six days and a 3% fee. A 5% holdback will also be retained.
2. Generally, 40% of Thirsty's customers take advantage of a 2% cash discount.
3. The factor accepts the receivables subject to recourse for nonpayment.
4. In this jurisdiction, the transfer qualifies as a sale.

Under FAS 140, Thirsty must record the recourse liability. It has accepted the obligation for all credit losses and has, in effect, guaranteed the receivables. The recourse obligation is measured as the estimate of uncollectibles (5% of face value).

The entry required to record the sale is

Cash	180,055	
Allowance for bad debts	10,000	
Interest expense (200,000 x .20 x 36/365)	3,945	
Factoring fee (200,000 x .03)	6,000	
Factor's holdback receivable [$10,000/($10,000 + $190,000) x $190,000]	9,500	
Loss on sale of receivables	2,100	
Due to factor for discounts (200,000 x .40 x .02)		1,600
Accounts receivable		200,000
Recourse obligation		10,000

Simplified, the entry is

Cash	180,055	
Allowance for bad debts	10,000	
Factor's holdback receivable (9,500 – 1,600)	7,900	
Loss on sale of receivables (3,945 + 6,000 + 2,100)	12,045	
Accounts receivable		200,000
Recourse obligation		10,000

The accounts receivable net of the allowance for bad debts (a valuation account) is removed from the transferor's books as it has been sold. Previously accrued bad debts expense is not reversed, however, as the transferor still expects to incur that expense through the recourse provision of the factoring agreement. (Alternatively, the bad debts expense could have been reversed and the charge to loss on sale increased by $10,000.) The loss on sale of receivables is the sum of the interest charged by the factor ($3,945), the factor's fee ($6,000), the expected chargeback for cash discounts to be taken ($1,600), and the difference between the holdback receivable at face value and at carrying value ($500). The factor's holdback receivable is a retained interest in the receivables transferred, and it is measured by allocating the original carrying amount ($190,000) between the assets sold ($190,000) and the assets retained ($10,000).

If, subsequent to the sale of the receivables, the actual experience relative to the recourse terms differs from the provision made at the time of the sale, a change in an accounting estimate results. It is reflected as an additional gain or loss in the subsequent period. These changes are not corrections of errors or retroactive adjustments.

If the above facts apply, but the transfer does not qualify as a sale, the borrower's entry will be

Cash	180,055	
Interest expense (or prepaid)	3,945	
Factoring fee	6,000	
Factor borrowing payable		190,000

In a secured borrowing, the accounts receivable remain on the borrower's books. Both the accounts receivable and the factor borrowings payable should be cross-referenced on the face of the balance sheet or in the notes to the financial statements. The accounting for the collateral under FAS 140 depends upon the terms of the collateral agreement. Accounting for collateral is discussed later in this chapter.

Retained interests. Interests in transferred assets that are not a part of the proceeds of a sale are considered retained interests that are still under the control of the transferor. Retained interests include undivided interests for which control has not been given up by the transferor, servicing assets and liabilities, and beneficial interests in assets transferred to a qualifying special-purpose entity in a securitization. In general, the more extensive an interest that the transferor of assets retains, the less likely the transaction will be classified as a sale and the more likely the transaction will be classified as a secured borrowing. The primary reason for this result is that in a true sale, the transferor should no longer bear the risks or reap the rewards associated with the transferred assets. If a determination cannot be made between classification as proceeds of a sale or as retained interests, the asset should be classified as proceeds and should be measured at fair value.

Retained interests are to be measured by allocating the carrying value of the transferred assets before the transfer between the assets sold (if any) and the assets retained based on their fair values on the date of transfer. This allocation is similar to that recommended in EITF 88-11 and must be applied to all transfers that have retained interests, regardless of whether or not they qualify as sales. It should be noted that this fair value allocation may result in a relative change in basis unless the fair values are proportionate to their carrying values. Thus, the gain or loss from any sale component could also be affected.

The retained interests continue to be the transferor's assets since control of these assets has not been transferred. Thus, the retained interest is considered continuing control over a previously owned asset (although the form may have changed). It should not be remeasured at fair value, nor should a gain or loss be recognized on it.

Example: Sale of partial interest in receivables

Facts Given

Receivables' fair value	$16,500
Receivables' book value	15,000

Seller sells 80% of receivables and agrees to service them. The benefits of servicing are just adequate to compensate for the servicing, thus there is no servicing asset or liability.

	FV	*80% FV*	*20% FV*	*Allocated 80% BV**	*Allocated 20% BV**
Receivables sold	$16,500	$13,200		$12,000	
Retained amount (20%)			$3,300		$3,000

* *Allocated based on the relative fair values.*

Seller's Journal Entry

Cash	13,200	
Receivables		12,000
Gain		1,200

Seller reports retained amount at $3,000.

Example: Sale of loans with various types of retained interests

Facts Given

Loans' fair value and amount of cash proceeds	$16,500
Loans' book value	15,000
Fair value of recourse obligation	(900)
Fair value of call option* on portfolio of $16,500	800
Fair value of interest rate swap on portfolio of $16,500	700

* *An option that permits the seller/transferor to repurchase the same or similar loans.*

Seller's Journal Entries

1. Sale only

Cash	16,500	
Loans		15,000
Gain		1,500

2. Sale with recourse obligation

Cash	16,500	
Loans		15,000
Recourse obligation		900
Gain		600

3. Sale with recourse obligation and call option to purchase the loans sold or similar loans

Cash	16,500	
Call	800	
Loans		15,000
Recourse obligation		900
Gain		1,400

4. Sale with recourse obligation, call and swap (seller provides floating interest rate return although the underlying loans are at fixed interest rate terms)

Cash	16,500	
Call	800	
Swap	700	
Loans		15,000
Recourse obligation		900
Gain		2,100

5. Partial sale with recourse obligation, call and swap. Seller sells 80% of loans.

	FV	*80% FV*	*20% FV*	*Allocated 80% BV**	*Allocated 20% BV**
Loans	$16,500	$13,200		$11,579	
Call	800	640		561	
Swap	700	560		491	
Recourse obligation	(900)	(720)		(631)	
Retained amount (20%)			$ 3,420		$3,000
	$17,100	$13,680	$ 3,420	$12,000	$3,000

Cash	13,200	
Call	640	
Swap	560	
Loans		12,000
Recourse obligation		720
Gain		1,680

Seller reports retained amount at $3,000.

* *Allocated based on the relative fair values.*

In some transfers of receivables, the transferor provides **credit enhancement** (similar to a recourse provision) by retaining a beneficial interest that absorbs the credit risk. If there is no liability beyond the transferor's retained subordinated interests, the retained interest is initially measured at allocated carrying value based on relative fair value, and no recourse liability is necessary. The retained interest would be subsequently measured like other retained interests held in the same form.

Cash reserve accounts and subordinated beneficial interests created as credit enhancements are retained interests and are accounted for as such even if the seller collects the proceeds and deposits a portion in the cash reserve account. (New asset credit enhancements such as financial guarantees and credit derivatives are measured at the fair value of the amount to benefit the transferor.) Paragraphs 68-70 provide guidance on estimating fair values and should be used in the case of credit enhancements. One possible method of estimating fair value of a credit enhancement is the cash-out method. Using that method, cash flows are discounted from the date the credit enhancement asset becomes available to the transferor (i.e., when the cash in the credit enhancement account is expected to be paid out to the transferor). The present value can be computed using an expected present value technique with a risk-free rate or a "best estimate" technique with an appropriate discount rate. Among other transferor assumptions, time period of restrictions, reinvestment income, and potential losses due to uncertainties must be included. FAS 140 does not provide guidance concerning subsequent measurement of credit enhancements.

FSP 140-1, *Accounting for Accrued Interest Receivable Related to Securitized and Sold Receivables under Statement 140*, holds that if the right to collect accrued interest and fees receivable (AIR) is transferred with receivables to a qualifying special-purpose entity (QSPE), those rights are one of the components of the sale transaction and should be accounted for as a retained beneficial interest (presumably to the extent that cash flows from the AIR will return to the transferor). Because the AIR cannot be contractually prepaid or settled in such a way that the transferor would not recover substantially all of its recorded investment, the beneficial interest is not required to be subsequently measured like an investment in debt securities classified as available for sale or trading under FAS 115.

Servicing. Servicing of financial assets can include such activities as

1. Collecting payments (principal, interest, and escrows)
2. Paying taxes and insurance from escrows
3. Monitoring delinquencies
4. Foreclosing
5. Investing funds temporarily prior to their distribution
6. Remitting fees to guarantors, trustees, and service providers
7. Accounting for and remitting distributions to holders of beneficial interests

Although inherent in holding most financial assets, servicing is a distinct asset or liability only when separated contractually from the underlying financial asset. The servicing asset usually results either from separate purchase or assumption of rights or from securitization with retained servicing. The servicer's obligations are specified in the contract.

Every time a transferor undertakes a duty to service financial assets, it should recognize either a servicing asset or a servicing liability. There are two exceptions. An entity does not recognize a servicing asset or liability if

1. The benefits of servicing neither exceed nor are less than adequate compensation, that is, there is no asset or liability to record.
2. The transfer is to a qualifying SPE in a guaranteed mortgage securitization and the transferor retains all of the resulting securities and classifies them as held-to-

maturity debt securities. In this case, the servicing asset or liability may either be reported together with the asset being serviced or be reported separately. The choice is the election of an accounting policy.

If a transferor receives merely adequate compensation for servicing the transferred assets, there is no asset or liability to be recognized because a new or outside servicer would not receive or pay to obtain the right to service if the compensation was just equal to adequate compensation.

Adequate compensation for servicing is determined by the marketplace. The concept of adequate compensation is judged by requirements that would be imposed by a new or outside servicer. It includes profit demanded by the marketplace and does not vary with the specific servicing costs of the servicer. Thus, it would not be acceptable to use the servicer's cost plus a profit margin to estimate the fair value of a servicing asset or liability.

Typically, the benefits are more than adequate compensation for the servicing and the servicing contract results in an asset. The benefits include

1. Fees
2. Late charges
3. Float
4. Other income

If the above benefits are not expected to provide adequate compensation, the contract results in a liability. With regard to the sale of assets, a servicing liability would reduce the net proceeds and would affect the gain or loss calculation.

If servicing is retained, any resulting servicing assets are measured at book value allocated based on relative fair value at the date of sale, if practical. Servicing liabilities undertaken, servicing assets purchased, and servicing liabilities assumed are measured at fair value.

Example: Sale of receivables with servicing liability

Facts Given

Receivables' fair value	$16,500
Receivables' book value	15,000
Servicing liability of $16,500 portfolio	(500)

Partial sale of receivables with servicing liability retained. Seller sells 80% of receivables.

	FV	*80% FV*	*20% FV*	*Receivables allocated 80% BV**	*Receivables allocated 20% BV**
Receivables sold	$16,500	$13,200		$12,000	
Servicing liability**	(500)	(400)			
Retained amount (20%)			$3,200		$3,000
	$16,000	$12,800	$3,200	$12,000	$3,000

* *Allocated based on the relative fair values.*
** *Liabilities are initially measured at fair value, if practicable.*

Journal Entry

Cash	13,200	
Servicing liability		400
Receivables		12,000
Gain		800

Seller reports retained receivables at $3,000 and the servicing liability at its fair value of $400.

FAS 140 imposes standards for both initial measurement and subsequent measurement of servicing assets and liabilities. Specifically, servicing assets or servicing liabilities from each contract are to be accounted for separately as follows:

1. Assets are to be reported separately from liabilities. They are not netted.
2. Initially measure retained servicing assets at allocated carrying value based on relative fair values at date of sale or securitization.
3. Initially measure at fair value all purchased servicing assets, assumed servicing liabilities, and servicing liabilities undertaken in a sale or securitization.
4. Account separately for interest-only strips (future interest income from serviced assets that exceeds servicing fees).
5. Amortize servicing assets in proportion to and over the period of estimated net servicing income (the excess of servicing revenues over servicing costs).
6. Evaluate and measure impairment of servicing assets as follows:
   a. Stratify recognized servicing assets based on predominant risk (asset size, type, interest rate, term, location, date of organization, etc.)
   b. Individual stratum should have impairment recognized through a valuation allowance in the amount of the excess of carrying value over fair value.
   c. Adjust the valuation allowances to reflect subsequently needed changes. Excess fair value for a stratum should not be recognized.
7. Amortize servicing liabilities in proportion to and over the period of net servicing loss (excess of servicing costs over servicing revenues). In cases where subsequent changes have increased the fair value of the servicing liability above the carrying value, an increased liability and a loss should be recognized.

A servicing asset is remeasured for impairment based on the fair value of the contract and not on the gain or loss from carrying out the terms of the contract. FAS 140 (paragraph 63) requires that entities separately evaluate and measure impairment of designated strata of servicing assets. Stratification requires that judgment be used when selecting the most important characteristic. FAS 140 does not require that either the most predominant risk characteristic or more than one predominant risk characteristic be used to stratify the servicing assets for purposes of evaluating and measuring impairment. Different stratification criteria may be used for FAS 140 impairment testing and for FAS 133 grouping of similar assets to be designated as a hedged portfolio in a fair value hedge. The stratum selected should be used consistently and a change is accounted for as a change in estimate under APB 20. The change and reasons for the change should be included in the disclosures made in accordance with paragraph 17 of FAS 140.

A servicing liability is remeasured for increases in fair value, which would be recognized as a loss. Similar to the accounting for changes in a valuation allowance for an impaired asset, increases in the servicing obligation may be recovered, but the obligation cannot be adjusted to less than the amortized measurement of its initially recognized amounts.

The fair value of a servicing asset or liability at date of transfer is best measured by quoted market prices for similar servicing responsibilities. There is the potential for significantly different estimates of fair value when a quoted market price is not available. The transferor should analyze all available information to obtain the best estimate of the fair value of the servicing contract. These include

1. The amount that would result in a current transaction between willing parties other than in a forced or liquidation sale
2. The legitimacy of the offer
3. The third party's specific knowledge about relevant factors
4. The experience of the broker with similar contracts
5. The price of other parties that have demonstrated an interest

6. The right to benefit from cash flows of potential future transactions (late charges, ancillary revenue, etc.)
7. The nature of the assets being serviced

In cases where there are few servicing contracts purchased or sold, present value methods may be used for estimating the fair value of servicing. Disclosure is required of the methods and significant assumptions followed to determine the estimate of fair value (unless not practicable) of recognized servicing assets and liabilities.

Example: Sale of receivables with servicing asset retained

Facts Given

Receivables' fair value	$16,500
Receivables' book value	15,000
Servicing asset fair value on portfolio of $16,500	700
Recourse obligation on portfolio of $16,500	(900)

1. Servicing asset retained, no recourse obligation

	FV	*%*	*BV allocated*
Receivables sold	$16,500	96	$14,400
Servicing asset	700	4	600
	$17,200	100	$15,000

Journal Entry

Cash	16,500	
Servicing asset	600	
Receivables		15,000
Gain		2,100

2. Partial sale of receivables with servicing asset retained and recourse obligation. Seller sells 80% of receivables.

	FV	*80% FV*	*20% FV*	*Allocated 80% BV**	*Allocated 20% BV**
Receivables sold	$16,500	$13,200		$11,512	
Servicing asset	700	560		488	
Recourse obligation	(900)	(720)			
Retained amount (20%)			$3,260		$3,000
	$16,300	$13,040	$3,260	$12,000	$3,000

* *Allocated based on the relative fair values of the assets.*

Journal Entry

Cash	13,200	
Servicing asset	488	
Receivables		12,000
Recourse obligation		720
Gain		968

Seller reports retained receivables at $3,000.

If it is not practicable to measure the fair value of servicing at the date of transfer, the transferor must evaluate whether a liability has been incurred and should not automatically assume that an asset exists. If it is determined that a liability does not exist, then a value of zero should be assigned to the servicing asset that cannot be measured. If it is determined that a liability does exist, a valuation technique using discounted cash flows should be used to estimate its fair value.

Example: Estimate of fair values is not practical

Entity A sells loans with a recourse obligation to repurchase any delinquent loans and retains the servicing, which is expected to provide more than adequate compensation for performance.

	Case I Asset fair value cannot be determined	Case II Liability fair value cannot be determined
Loans' fair value	$16,500	$16,500
Loans' book value	15,000	15,000
Fair value of servicing asset	?	700
Fair value of recourse obligation	(900)	?

Proceeds

	Case I	Case II
Cash	$16,500	$16,500
Less: Recourse obligation	(900)	?
Net proceeds	$15,600	$16,500

Allocation of book value based on fair value of assets

	FV	%	BV allocated	FV	%	BV allocated
Loans sold	$15,600	100	$15,000	$16,500	96	$14,400
Servicing assets	0	0	0	700	4	600
	$15,600	100	$15,000	$17,200	100	$15,000

Journal Entries

	Case I Dr	Case I Cr	Case II Dr	Case II Cr
Cash	16,500		16,500	
Servicing asset	0		600	
Loans		15,000		15,000
Recourse obligation		900		2,100
Gain		600		0

In Case I, it is not practicable to measure the fair value of servicing, but it is known that the servicing is expected to provide at least adequate compensation. Thus, servicing is an asset and not a liability. If it is not practicable to measure the fair value of an asset, that asset is measured at zero. In Case II, it is not practicable to measure the fair value of the recourse obligation. If it is not practicable to measure the fair value of a liability, no gain is recorded on the sale. The liability is recorded at the greater of (1) the excess fair value of the assets obtained minus the fair value of the liabilities incurred over the carrying value of the assets transferred or (2) the amount to be recorded in conjunction with FAS 5 and FIN 14. In Case II, the liability is recognized at the excess fair value.

SOP 03-3 addresses the accounting for the differences between contractual and expected future cash flows of acquired (i.e., nonoriginated) loans when these differences are attributable, at least in part, to a decline in the debtor's credit quality subsequent to loan inception. This standard is effective for loans acquired after December 15, 2004, with early adoption encouraged.

Under the provisions of this standard, purchased loans are to be displayed at the initial investment amount on the balance sheet. The amount of any discount will not be displayed in the balance sheet nor should the acquirer carry over an allowance for loan losses established by the seller. This prohibition applies equally to stand-alone purchases of loans and to those that occur as part of purchase business combinations. Expanded disclosure requirements have also been established.

When loans are acquired with evidence of deterioration in credit quality since origination, the acquirer is required to estimate the cash flows expected to be collected on the loan. This exercise is to be done both at the purchase date and again periodically over the lives of the loans. Cash flows in excess of the initial investment (purchase price) expected to be collected should be recognized as yield; this is referred to as "accretable yield." On the other hand, contractual cash flows in excess of expected cash flows (the nonaccretable difference) are **not** to be recognized as yield.

The accounting for changing expectations regarding future cash flows depends on whether these are decreases or increases. If, subsequent to acquisition, there are decreases in the probable cash flows, impairments are to be recognized in the current period's statement of income. In other words, such a development cannot be handled prospectively, as a yield adjustment, over the remaining lives of the loans.

By contrast, probable increases in subsequent cash flows expected to be collected should be recognized prospectively as a yield adjustment. In cases where a new, higher yield on a loan is established (due to a probable increase in cash flows to be collected), that yield should be used as the effective interest rate in any later test for impairment.

Subcontracting the servicing to another entity is not accounted for under FAS 140 because it does not involve a transfer. It should be accounted for under other existing guidance.

In the unusual case that servicing assets are assumed without a cash payment, the facts and circumstances will determine how the transaction is recorded. For example, the servicing asset may represent consideration for goods or services provided by the transferee to the transferor of the servicing. The servicing assets also might be received in full or partial satisfaction of a receivable from the transferor of the servicing. Another possibility is that the transferor (the party providing servicing) is in substance making a capital contribution to the transferee (the party receiving the servicing) in exchange for an increased ownership interest. Additionally, the possibility that there is an overstatement of the value of the servicing by the transferee must be carefully considered.

The amount to be paid to a replacement servicer under the terms of the servicing contract is not relevant to the determination of adequate compensation. This amount could, however, be relevant for determining the contractually specified servicing fees.

Rights to future income from serviced assets that exceed contractually specified servicing fees should be accounted for as a servicing asset, an interest-only strip, or both, depending on whether the servicer would continue to receive the value of the right to future income if a replacement servicer started servicing the assets. Generally, the value of the right to receive future cash flows from ancillary sources such as late fees is included with the servicing asset if retention of the right depends on servicing being performed satisfactorily. An interest-only strip doesn't depend on satisfactory performance of servicing, and any portion that would continue to be received if servicing were shifted to a replacement servicer would be accounted for separately as a financial asset and subsequently measured as an investment in debt securities classified as available-for-sale or trading under FAS 115.

Sales-type and direct financing lease receivables. Lease receivables are composed of two components: minimum lease payments and residual values. Minimum lease payments are requirements for lessees to pay cash, and thus are financial assets subject to FAS 140 if transferred. Residual values are the rights to the leased equipment at the end of the lease. If the residual value is guaranteed at the inception of the lease, the right is a financial asset subject to FAS 140 if transferred. If the residual value is not guaranteed (or if it is guaranteed after the inception of the lease), transfers of that residual value are not subject to FAS 140. When entities sell lease receivables, the gross investment of the lease is allocated between minimum lease payments, residual values guaranteed at inception, and residual values not guaranteed at inception. If the entity retains servicing rights, it should also record a servicing asset or liability if appropriate. FAS 140 does not apply to sales of operating lease payments.

Example of sale of interest in lease payments

Lucky Leasing sells a senior interest in the guaranteed cash flows of a financing lease for \$12,200. It retains a subordinated interest in the guaranteed cash flows and the residual value that is not guaranteed. The lease has the following components:

	Face value	*Present value*
Minimum lease payments	$ 8,350	$ 7,000
Guaranteed residual value	7,000	5,875
Residual value not guaranteed	1,400	1,175
Total investment in lease	$16,750	$14,050

The present values are computed using the implicit lease rate. The fair value of the subordinated interest retained is $1,200. Lucky Leasing receives no explicit compensation for servicing the lease, but it estimates that the benefits of servicing are just adequate to compensate it for its servicing responsibilities (that is, there is no servicing asset or liability). The allocation of the carrying amount for the interest sold is as follows:

	Fair value	*Allocated cost*
Senior interest sold	$12,200	$11,722
Subordinated interest retained	1,200	1,153
Totals	$13,400	$12,875

The entry to record the sale would be as follows:

Cash	12,200	
Subordinated interest	1,153	
Residual value	1,175	
Net investment in lease		14,050
Gain on sale		478

Securitizations. Entities that generate a large number of similar receivables, such as mortgages, credit card receivables, or car loans, sometimes securitize those receivables. Securitization is the transformation of the receivables into securities that are sold to other investors. For example, mortgages can be converted into mortgage-backed securities, which entitle the investors to receive specific cash flows generated by the mortgages. With an established market, issuance of the securities can cost less than using the receivables as collateral for a borrowing. Because SPE assets are isolated from a possible transferor's bankruptcy, the SPE's credit quality is enhanced and the financing costs on the debt are reduced. For even lower financing costs, the SPE can obtain credit enhancements in the form of recourse debt, subordinate assignments, or guarantees. Additionally, the resulting securities are more liquid than the underlying receivables. Securitizations are accounted for as sales only if (1) a qualified special-purpose entity is used to buy the assets, (2) each holder of its beneficial interests has the right to pledge or exchange the beneficial interest and there is no condition that both constrains the holder from taking advantage of that right and provides more than a trivial benefit to the transferor, and (3) the transferor does not maintain effective control over the assets.

The transferor (also called issuer or sponsor) forms a securitization mechanism (separate corporation or a trust, referred to as a special-purpose entity [SPE]) to buy the assets and to issue the securities. The securitization mechanism then generates beneficial interests in the assets or resulting cash flows that are sold. The form of the securities chosen depends on such things as the nature of the assets, income tax considerations, and returns to be received. A properly structured (that is, qualifying) SPE should not be consolidated in the financial statements of the transferor or its affiliates. (Note that, although FIN 46(R) creates the concept of *variable interest entities*, or VIE, which largely replaces the earlier concept of special-purpose entities, the concept of *qualifying special-purpose entities*, or QSPE, as established by FAS 140, continues unchanged.)

For example, a transferor originates long-term loans and accumulates them on its balance sheet (referred to as warehousing). When the group of loans reaches a sufficient size, the loans are sold to an SPE. During the accumulation phase, the transferor finances the cost of holding the loans with prearranged lines of credit, known as warehouse lines. Often the transferor hedges the price risk of the loans as they await sale. This is referred to as an on-balance-sheet warehousing.

Alternatively, a transferor may use a properly structured off-balance-sheet warehousing to securitize assets. In an off-balance-sheet warehouse, the transferor creates a temporary securitization vehicle. A bank typically extends credit to the securitization vehicle in the form of a variable-funding note. Using the proceeds of the note, the vehicle acquires loans from the transferor as they are originated. The principal of the note increases, up to a ceiling, as the transferor transfers additional loans to the securitization vehicle. When the loans have reached the ceiling amount of the note, the bank puts the note back to the securitization vehicle, forcing the vehicle to sell the loans to a permanent SPE to raise the cash to pay the note.

Payments by the securitization mechanism are usually classified as **pay-through, pass-through** or **revolving-period**. In a **pay-through,** cash flows from the assets pay off the debt securities. The assets are essentially collateral. In a **pass-through,** undivided interests are issued and the investors share in the net cash flows. In a **revolving-period,** undivided interests are issued, but until liquidation, the net cash flows are split between buying additional assets and paying off investors.

An SPE is considered qualified if it meets the criteria set forth by FAS 140. In general, those criteria require that the SPE remain on "autopilot" after its creation. The SPE is required to be a passive custodian for the benefit of the holders of its beneficial interests. All of the SPE's responses to changes in business conditions must be predetermined and spelled out in the agreements that create the SPE. The SPE cannot make business decisions, nor can it direct an agent to make business decisions on its behalf. The four criteria are

1. The SPE is demonstrably distinct from the transferor. To be demonstrably distinct, the transferor, its affiliates, or its agents cannot unilaterally dissolve the SPE and either
    a. At least 10% of the fair value of its beneficial interests is held by parties other than the transferor, its affiliates, or its agents or
    b. The transfer is a guaranteed mortgage securitization. A guaranteed mortgage securitization is a securitization of mortgage loans that is within the scope of FAS 65 and includes a substantive guarantee by a third party.
2. The permitted activities of the SPE
    a. Must be significantly limited
    b. Must have been entirely specified in the legal documents that established the SPE or created the beneficial interests in the transferred assets it holds
    c. May be significantly changed only with the approval of a majority of the holders of the beneficial interests not including the transferor, its affiliates, or its agents
3. The SPE may hold only
    a. Financial assets that are passive in nature. A financial asset is passive only if holding the asset requires no decisions of the holder other than decisions inherent in servicing. For example, an equity instrument is not passive if the SPE is permitted to choose how to vote the shares, and an investment accounted for by the equity method is not passive since that method is used when the investor has the ability to exercise significant influence over that investment.
    b. Passive derivative instruments related to beneficial interests issued or sold to parties other than the transferor, its affiliates, or its agents. Options to call or

put are not passive investments, since they require a decision as to whether to exercise the rights. Interest rate swaps, caps, and floors are passive derivative instruments.

c. Financial assets that would reimburse the SPE if the servicer failed to adequately perform or if others failed to pay timely. The financial assets must have been entered into when the SPE was created, when assets were transferred to it, or when it issued beneficial interests.
d. Servicing rights related to the financial assets it holds
e. Nonfinancial assets obtained in connection with the collection of financial assets it holds (but the SPE may hold them only temporarily).
f. Cash collected from financial assets it holds
g. Investments purchased pending distribution to holders of beneficial interests, provided that those investments are appropriate for that purpose. For example, the investments must be relatively risk-free and have a maturity date no later than the expected distribution date.

4. The SPE can sell or dispose of noncash financial assets only in automatic response to one of the following conditions:

   a. Occurrence of an event that causes the fair value of those financial assets to decline by a specified degree below the fair value of those assets when the SPE obtained them. The occurrence of the event must be outside the control of the transferor, its affiliates, or its agents. The nature of the event must be specified in the legal documents that established the SPE or created the beneficial interests in the transferred assets it holds.
   b. Exercise of a right to put a beneficial interest back to the SPE by a beneficial interest holder other than the transferor, its affiliates, or its agents
   c. Exercise by the transferor of a call or a removal-of-accounts provision (ROAP), provided that the exercise is specified in the legal documents that established the SPE, transferred assets to the SPE, or created the beneficial interests in the transferred assets it holds. Care must be exercised in designing a call or a ROAP because it can be construed as giving the transferor the ability to unilaterally cause the holder to return specific assets (and thus the transfer will not be a sale). In general, any call or ROAP that allows the transferor to specify the assets to be removed or that are conditioned upon an event within the transferor's control (such as a transferor's decision to exit a product line) will cause the transfer to fail the FAS 140 criteria. Calls or ROAPs that allow the transferor to remove defaulted receivables are permitted, as are those that allow limited access for random removal of excess assets.
   d. Termination of the SPE or maturity of the beneficial interests in those financial assets on a fixed or determinable date that was specified at the inception

5. The SPE can make decisions inherent in servicing the transferred assets. For example

   a. An SPE that performs servicing can restructure or "work out" a loan, as long as its discretion is significantly limited and the parameters of that discretion are fully described in the legal documents that established the SPE or that created the beneficial interests in the transferred assets. However, the SPE cannot initiate a new lending to the borrower as a result of the workout. Nor can the SPE have the ability to determine whether to restructure (or work out) the loan versus disposing of the loan, since that decision is generally not automatic because it requires use of judgment and estimates.

b. An SPE can pay certain expenses (e.g. property taxes or insurance) that are the responsibility of the debtor if the debtor fails to pay them.
c. An SPE can advance funds to make timely payments to the holders of the beneficial interests and later reimburse itself for those advances.
d. An SPE can decide whether to initiate foreclosure proceedings, as long as its discretion is significantly limited and the parameters of that discretion are fully described in the legal documents that established the SPE or that created the beneficial interests in the transferred assets.
e. An SPE can decide how to dispose of foreclosed assets that it temporarily holds, as long as its discretion is significantly limited and the parameters of that discretion are fully described in the legal documents that established the SPE or that created the beneficial interests in the transferred assets.
f. An SPE can decide how to dispose of defaulted loans only if a servicing agreement that was in effect when the SPE was established describes specific conditions in which the servicer is required to dispose of a loan. In other words, the SPE must have no choice but to dispose of the defaulted loan when the described conditions occur.

FIN 46(R), which was intended to curb the use of unconsolidated SPE structures, excludes QSPE from the definition of VIE. Subsequent to its issuance, there has been an incentive to convert former SPE to QSPE, thereby avoiding consolidation under FIN 46(R). In response to this emerging problem, FASB issued an Exposure Draft, *Qualifying Special-Purpose Entities and Isolation of Transferred Assets: an amendment of FASB Statement No. 140*, in mid-2003. If enacted, it will prohibit an entity from being a qualifying special-purpose entity (QSPE) if it enters into an agreement that obligates a transferor, its affiliates, or its agents to deliver additional cash or other assets to fulfill the QSPE's obligations to beneficial interest holders (except certain servicing advances and forward contracts to transfer additional financial assets.) The conditions that would be amended under this ED for QSPE are to

1. Limit the relationship of a transferor with QSPE.
2. Prohibit any party from being in a position to enhance or protect the value of its interest in a QSPE by providing financial support for or making decisions about reissuing beneficial interests.
3. Prohibit QSPE from holding equity instruments.
4. Clarify the requirements related to instruments with maturity dates after the termination date of the entity.

In addition, the ED provides that if the result of a transfer is issuance of beneficial interests, a transferor has not surrendered control of transferred assets in a two-step transfer unless the second step involves a QSPE. The ED also clarifies that to qualify for derecognition, transferred assets must be isolated from all entities in the consolidated group that includes the transferor, except for certain bankruptcy-remote entities.

The proposed effective date of the amendment to FAS 140 would be, for publicly held companies, the first interim period after the issuance of the final statement. The effective date for private entities would be the beginning of the first annual period after the statement is issued. Existing QSPE would be offered "grandfathering" terms: If a formerly qualifying SPE is found to not be a QSPE under the condition of this proposed statement, it could continue to be considered a QSPE if it maintains its qualifying status under the previous accounting standards. (For information about consolidating nonqualifying SPE, see the discussion in Chapter 11.)

Various financial components arise from securitizations. Examples include servicing contracts, interest-only strips, retained interests, recourse obligations, options, swaps, and forward contracts. All controlled assets and liabilities must be recognized under FAS 140.

Example of a securitization deal involving four classes of securities

Principal of loans held by the securitizer/transferor	$10,000,000
Accrued interest on loans held by the securitizer/transferor	230,000
Deferred origination costs of loans held by the securitizer/transferor	100,000
Deferred origination fees of loans held by the securitizer/transferor	(200,000)
Loss allowance on loans held by the securitizer/transferor	(250,000)
Net carrying amount of loans	$ 9,880,000

Classes of securities issued and prices:

	Principal	*Price*	*Fair value*
Class A	$9,000,000	100	$ 9,000,000
Class B	1,000,000	90	900,000
Interest-only strip (retained)			150,000
Residual class (retained)			100,000
Total fair value			$10,150,000

Servicing is retained by the transferor and has a fair value of $75,000
Transaction costs are $100,000
Proceeds are $9,800,000 ($9,000,000 Class A + $900,000 Class B – $100,000 costs)

Allocation of carrying value:

	Fair value	*Percent*	*Allocation*	*Sold*	*Retained*
Class A	$ 9,000,000	88.0	$8,696,332	$8,696,332	
Class B	900,000	8.8	869,633	869,633	
Interest-only strip	150,000	1.5	144,939		$144,939
Residual class	100,000	1.0	96,626		96,626
Servicing	75,000	.7	72,470		72,470
Total	$10,225,000	100.0	$9,880,000	$9,565,965	$314,035

The entry to record the sale would be as follows:

Cash	9,800,000	
Interest-only strip	144,939	
Residual class	96,626	
Servicing asset	72,470	
Loan loss allowance	250,000	
Deferred origination fees	200,000	
Loans receivable		$10,000,000
Interest receivable		230,000
Deferred origination costs		100,000
Gain on sale of loans		234,035

The entry to mark the securities retained to fair value under FAS 115 would be

Interest-only strip	5,061	
Residual class	3,374	
Comprehensive income (unless trading)		8,435

Just as it is necessary to distinguish new assets, which are recorded at fair value, from retained interests, which are recorded at allocated carrying value, when accounting for a transfer to another enterprise, it is necessary to do so when accounting for a transfer to an SPE. In certain securitization transactions, more than one transferor contributes assets to a single qualifying SPE. A transferor should treat the beneficial interests it receives in a securitization that commingles assets from more than one transferor as

1. New assets to the extent that the sources of the cash flows to be received by the transferor are assets transferred by another entity
2. Retained interests to the extent that the sources of the cash flows are assets transferred by the transferor
3. New assets to the extent that any derivatives, guarantees, or other contracts were entered into by the qualifying SPE to "transform" the transferred assets. (They are new because they were entered into by the qualifying SPE rather than transferred into the qualifying SPE by another entity.)

After a securitization, the beneficial interests held by the transferor either are in the form of securities that are accounted for under FAS 115 or are required to be accounted for as available-for-sale securities or trading securities in accordance with FAS 140. Thus, the transferor must classify the beneficial interests into one of the FAS 115 categories. If beneficial interests held by the transferor after the transfer convey rights to the same cash flows as the transferor was entitled to receive from securities that it transferred to the SPE, the FAS 115 classification of the beneficial interests should be the same as the securities held before the transfer. For example, if prior to the transfer the debt securities were accounted for as available-for-sale securities in accordance with FAS 115, the beneficial interests should be classified as available-for-sale securities if the transferor receives the cash flows from those securities via its beneficial interest. In contrast, if the transferred assets were not Statement 115 securities prior to the transfer but the beneficial interests were issued in the form of debt securities or in the form of equity securities that have readily determinable fair values, then the transferor has the opportunity to decide the appropriate FAS 115 classification at the date of the transfer.

Revolving-period securitizations present some unique issues because they contain an implicit forward contract to sell new receivables during the revolving period. The forward contract may become valuable to the transferor or burdensome depending upon how interest rates and market conditions change. The value of the implicit forward contract arises from the difference between the rate promised to the holders of the beneficial interests and the market rate of return on similar investments. For example, if the agreed-upon rate to holders is 5% and the market rate is 7%, the forward contract's value to the transferor is 2% of the amount of the investment for each year remaining in the revolving period after the initially transferred receivables are collected. When receivables are sold to a revolving-period securitization trust, gain or loss recognition is limited to receivables that exist and have been sold. Similarly, servicing assets or liabilities are limited to servicing receivables that exist and have already been transferred. As proceeds from collection of the receivables are used to purchase new receivables for the trusts, each additional transfer is treated as a separate sale, with its own gain or loss calculation. Those additional transfers also can result in recognition of additional servicing assets and liabilities.

FAS 140 does not address the accounting for desecuritization of securities into loans or other financial assets. EITF Topic D-51, *The Applicability of FASB Statement No. 115 to Desecuritizations of Financial Assets*, addresses that issue. That staff announcement states that the guidance in FAS 140 should be extended by analogy to desecuritizations. Thus, the transfer of securities or beneficial interests in a securitized pool of financial assets in which the transferor receives in exchange only the financial assets underlying those securities or beneficial interests would not be accounted for as a sale.

Repurchase agreements. Repurchase agreements are used to obtain short-term use of funds. Under the terms of a repurchase agreement the transferor transfers a security to a transferee in exchange for cash. Concurrently, the transferor agrees to reacquire the security at a future date for an amount equal to the cash exchanged and an interest factor. Many repurchase agreements are for short terms, often overnight.

It is necessary to determine if the repurchase agreement meets the requirements described in the section, "Surrender of control." Usually the critical determination is whether the repurchase agreements gives the transferor effective control over the transferred assets. That determination is made by applying the criteria described in the section, "Maintaining effective control." In most cases, if the repurchase is required prior to the maturity of the security transferred and the cash transferred is sufficient to repurchase the assets if the transferee defaults, the transferor retains effective control and the agreement is accounted for as a secured borrowing. For example, fixed-coupon and dollar-roll repurchase agreements, and other contracts under which the securities to be repurchased need not be the same as the securities sold, qualify as borrowings if the return of substantially the same securities as those transferred is assured. However, if a transferor does not maintain control over the transferred assets and other criteria in FAS 140 are met, the transfer is accounted for as a sale and a forward commitment.

Example of a repurchase agreement

Mighty Manufacturing has $1,995,000 excess cash that it desires to invest for a 7-day period. It transfers the cash to Lion Bank in exchange for $2,000,000 of commercial paper. At the end of the 7-day period, Lion Bank agrees to repurchase the commercial paper for $1,996,500. Mighty Manufacturing does not have the right to sell or pledge the commercial paper during the 7-day period.

The entries to record the origination of the agreement:

Mighty Manufacturing			*Lion Bank*		
Investment	1,995,000		Cash	1,995,000	
Cash		1,995,000	Short-term payable		1,995,000

The entries to record the termination of the agreement seven days later:

Mighty Manufacturing			*Lion Bank*		
Cash	1,996,500		Short-term payable	1,995,000	
Investment		1,995,000	Interest expense	1,500	
Interest income		1,500	Cash		1,996,500

Securities lending transactions. Broker-dealers and other financial services companies initiate securities lending transactions when they need to obtain specific securities to cover a short sale or a customer's failure to deliver securities sold. The transferor/lender provides the securities to the transferee/borrower in exchange for "collateral," usually in an amount greater than the fair value of the borrowed securities. This collateral is commonly cash but could alternatively be other securities or standby letters of credit.

When the collateral is cash, the transferor/lender invests the cash during the period that the security is loaned. The investment return on the cash collateral is larger than the fees paid by the lender under the agreement (the rebate). Because the cash collateral is usually valued daily and adjusted frequently for changes in the market value of the underlying securities, the transaction has very low credit risk.

In determining whether to account for a securities lending transaction as a sale or a secured borrowing, the same criteria used for other asset transfers are applied. Many securities lending transactions are accompanied by an agreement that entitles and obligates the transferor/lender to repurchase or redeem the transferred assets before their maturity. Thus, the transferor maintains effective control over the securities lent. If that is the case, the transaction is accounted for as a secured borrowing. The following is an example of a securities lending transaction accounted for as a secured borrowing:

Example: Securities lending transaction (30 days)

Fair value of loaned security	$16,500
Book value of loaned security	16,500
Collateral (cash)	16,995
Transferor/lender's return from investing cash	5%
Transferor/lender's rebate to transferee/borrower	4%

Transferor/lender's journal entries

At date of loan:

	Debit	Credit
Securities pledged	16,500	
Securities		16,500
To record transfer of securities as a loan		
Cash	16,995	
Loan agreement payable		16,995
To record receipt of cash collateral		
Money market instrument	16,995	
Cash		16,995
To invest cash collateral		

At end of 30 days:

	Debit	Credit
Cash	17,065	
Interest income		70
Money market instrument		16,995
To transfer cash from money market and record interest earned		
Securities	16,500	
Securities pledged		16,500
To record securities returned by transferee/borrower		
Loan agreement payable	16,995	
Interest rebate	56	
Cash		17,051
To return cash collateral and pay rebate		

Accounting for collateral. Accounting for collateral depends both on whether the secured party has the right to sell or repledge the collateral and on whether the debtor has defaulted. Ordinarily, the transferor should carry the collateral as an asset and the transferee should not record the pledged asset.

The collateral provisions of FAS 140 apply to all transfers (repurchase agreements, dollar-roll, securities lending, etc.) of financial assets pledged as collateral and accounted for as a secured borrowing. The provisions do not apply to the accounting for cash in secured borrowing transactions.

If the secured party (transferee) has the right to sell or repledge the collateral, then the debtor (transferor) reclassifies the asset used as collateral and reports it in the balance sheet separately from other assets not similarly encumbered. That is, the debtor (transferor) continues to hold the collateral assets as its own, and the secured party (transferee) does not recognize the collateral asset. If the secured party (transferee) sells the collateral, it recognizes the proceeds from the sale and the obligation to return the collateral to the debtor (transferor).

Although collateral is required to be reclassified and reported separately by the transferor if the transferee has the right to sell or repledge the collateral, that requirement does not change the transferor's measurement of the collateral. The same measurement principles should be used as before the transfer and the collateral should not be derecognized. The subsequent measurement of transferee's obligation to return the collateral in securities borrowing and resale agreement transactions is not addressed by FAS 140.

If the transferor defaults and is not entitled to the return of the collateral, it should be derecognized by the transferor. If not already recognized, the transferee should record its asset at fair value.

Financial assets subject to prepayment. FAS 140 requires interest-only strips, loans, other receivables, or retained interests in securitizations to be measured like investments in debt securities. If they can be contractually prepaid or settled in a way that precludes recovery of substantially all of the recorded investment, they should be classified as available-for-sale or trading under FAS 115. Only assets meeting all of the FAS 115 requirements and acquired late enough in life that, even if prepaid, the holder would recover substantially all of its recorded investment may be initially classified as held-to-maturity. The probability of prepayment or settlement is not relevant to the classification under FAS 115.

Although financial assets that do not meet the securities definition of FAS 115 must be measured in the same manner as investments under FAS 115, other provisions of that Statement (disclosures, etc.) are not required to be applied.

Disclosures

FAS 140. FAS 140 disclosures include

1. For collateral
   a. If the entity has entered into repurchase agreements or securities lending transactions, its policy for requiring collateral or other security
   b. If the entity has pledged any of its assets as collateral that are not reclassified and separately reported on the balance sheet, the carrying amount and classification of those assets on the date on the most recent balance sheet
   c. If the entity has accepted collateral that it is permitted by contract or custom to sell or repledge, the fair value of that collateral as of the date of each balance sheet, the portion of that collateral that it has sold or repledged, and the sources and uses of that collateral
2. Description of items for which it is not practicable to estimate fair value and reasons why it is not practicable
3. For servicing assets and liabilities
   a. Amounts recognized and amortized during the period
   b. Fair value recognized, method and assumptions used to estimate fair value
   c. Risk characteristics used to stratify recognized servicing assets in order to measure impairments
   d. Valuation allowance and all related activity for each period for which results of operations are reported
4. If the entity has securitized any financial assets during any period presented and accounted for that securitization as a sale, it must disclose the following information for each major asset type (e.g., mortgage loans, auto loans, credit card receivables)
   a. Accounting policies for initially measuring the retained interests
   b. The method used in measuring the fair value of the retained interests and the key assumptions used in that measurement (at a minimum, assumptions about discount rates, expected prepayments, expected weighted-average life of prepayable assets, anticipated credit losses)
   c. A description of the entity's continuing involvement with the assets securitized
   d. The amount of the gain or loss from sale of the assets in the securitization
   e. Cash flows between the SPE and the entity

5. If the entity has retained interests in securitized financial assets at the most recent balance sheet presented, it must disclose the following information for each major asset type (e.g., mortgage loans, auto loans, credit card receivables)
   a. Accounting policy for subsequently measuring the retained interests
   b. The method used in measuring the fair value of the retained interests and the key assumptions used in that measurement (at a minimum, assumptions about discount rates, expected prepayments, expected weighted-average life of prepayable assets, anticipated credit losses, expected static pool losses, if applicable)
   c. A sensitivity analysis or stress test showing the hypothetical effect on the fair value of the retained interests of two or more unfavorable variations from the expected level for each key assumption (computed independently of any other change in the key assumptions) and a description of the objectives, methodology, and limitations of the sensitivity analysis or stress test
   d. For the securitized assets and any other financial assets managed with them, the total principal amount, the portion derecognized, the portion remaining, and delinquencies as of the end of the period, and the credit losses, net of recoveries, during the period. This disclosure should exclude securitized assets that the entity manages but with which the entity does not have any other continuing involvement.
   e. Average balances during the period for the securitized assets and any other financial assets managed with them. (This disclosure is not required but merely encouraged.)

SOP 01-6. SOP 01-6 includes disclosure requirements for all entities involved in financing activities (including trade receivables).

1. The following amounts must be reported separately on the face of the balance sheet:
   a. The amount of receivables held for sale
   b. The amount of foreclosed or repossessed assets, which can be included in the other assets category if the notes to the financial statements disclose the amount
2. The balance sheet or notes should report
   a. Separately, each major category of loans and trade receivables
   b. The allowance for doubtful accounts or loan losses
   c. Any unearned income, unamortized premiums or discounts, and any net unamortized deferred fees and costs related to loans or trade receivables
   d. The recorded investment in loans (and trade receivables, if applicable) on nonaccrual status, as of each balance sheet presented
   e. The recorded investment in loans (and trade receivables, if applicable) on accrual status that are past due ninety days or more, as of each balance sheet presented
   f. The carrying amount of financial instruments that serve as collateral for borrowings
3. The "summary of significant accounting principles" note should include the following:
   a. The basis for accounting for trade receivables, loans receivable, and lease financings, including those held for sale
   b. Whether aggregate or individual asset basis is used in determining the lower of cost or fair value of nonmortgage loans held for sale

   c. The classification and method of accounting for receivables that can be contractually prepaid or otherwise settled in a way that the entity would not recover substantially all of its recorded investment
   d. The method for recognizing interest income on loan and trade receivables, including related fees and costs, and the method of amortizing net deferred fees or costs
   e. The accounting policies and methodology used to estimate the allowance for doubtful accounts and/or loan losses, including the factors that influenced management's judgment (such as existing economic conditions and historical losses)
   f. The accounting policies and methodology used to estimate any liability for off-balance-sheet credit losses, including the factors that influenced management's judgment
   g. The policy for placing loans (and trade receivables, if applicable) on nonaccrual status
   h. The policy for recording payments received on loans (and trade receivables, if applicable) that are in nonaccrual status
   i. The policy for resuming interest accruals on loans that are in nonaccrual status
   j. The policy for charging off uncollectible trade receivables and loans
   k. Whether past due or delinquency status is based on how recently payments have been made or on contractual terms

4. The aggregate amount of gains or losses on sales of loans or trade receivables (including the amounts of adjustments to record receivables held for sale at the lower of cost or fair value) should be presented separately in the financial statements or disclosed in the notes.

EMERGING ISSUES TASK FORCE ISSUES SUMMARIES

86-8 Sale of Bad Debt Recovery Rights

A financial institution sells to a third party the right to an amount of future recoveries from loans previously written off by the financial institution. The buyer is entitled to the purchase price plus a market rate of interest on the unrecovered purchased price. The transaction is a secured borrowing from the seller's perspective. There was no consensus on whether the proceeds should reduce the loan-loss allowance.

87-18 Use of Zero Coupon Bonds in a Troubled Debt Restructuring (affected by FASB Statement No. 140 and 144)

In connection with a troubled debt restructuring, a debtor, with the creditor's approval, sells the collateral and invests the proceeds in zero coupon bonds that are held as collateral for the restructured loan by the creditor. The bonds mature on a schedule that meets the debt service requirements under the new terms. The fair value of the zero coupon bonds is less than the creditor's net investment in the loan. The creditor should recognize a loss for the difference between the net investment and the fair value less cost to sell (as that term is used in FAS 144) of assets received. To the extent that those losses are not offset against allowances for uncollectible accounts or other valuation accounts, they should be included in measuring net income for the period.

The debtor is required by FAS 140 to reclassify the zero coupon bonds to another asset account (such as bonds pledged as collateral) if the creditor can sell or repledge them.

88-11 Allocation of Recorded Investment When a Loan or Part of a Loan Is Sold (affected by FASB Statement No. 140)

Relative fair values at the date of transfer should be used to allocate the recorded investment between the portion of the loan retained and the portion sold. Amounts in the allowance for loan losses should be excluded when considering the recorded investment to be allocated. Any gain recognized when selling a portion of the loan should not exceed that which would be recognized if the entire loan was sold. A portion of the recorded investment should be allocated to excess servicing if it is retained.

88-22 Securitization of Credit Card Portfolios (affected by FASB Statement No. 140)

Amounts received from transferring to investors a participating interest in credit card receivables in a trust should be accounted for as a sale if the conditions in paragraph 9 of FAS 140 are met.

The type of liquidation method specified in the securitization agreement does not affect the determination of whether the transferor would get sale treatment.

Gain on the sale of receivables should be limited to amounts related to receivables that exist at the sale date. The gain generally will not be material. Terms of the agreement should be examined to determine whether a loss should be recognized for expected costs to be incurred for future servicing obligations. Transaction costs relating to the sale may be recognized over the initial and reinvestment period in a rational and systematic manner unless a loss is indicated.

88-23 Lump-Sum Payments under Union Contracts

This EITF consensus relates solely to union contracts and not to individual employment contracts. In negotiating union contracts, lump-sum cash payments made to employees in lieu of all or a portion of a base-wage rate increase may be deferred and amortized. The Task Force's consensus requires that (1) there is no evidence that the payment is related to past services, (2) the payment will benefit a future period in the form of a lower base-wage rate, and (3) the amortization period not extend beyond the contract period. Facts surrounding the contract and negotiations must be reviewed to determine how to account for the payment.

92-2 Measuring Loss Accruals by Transferors for Transfers of Receivables with Recourse (affected by FASB Statement No. 140)

All probable credit losses (not only those recognized in accordance with FAS 5) over the life of the receivables transferred should be included in the recourse obligation recorded at the date of sale. The recourse obligation can be recognized on a present value (PV) basis if the cash flows can be reasonably estimated. If PV is used, the interest rate used in subsequent accruals should be the same rate used in determining the initial obligation.

The recourse obligation is a liability and should not be offset unless a right of setoff exists (see FIN 39).

If the seller's recourse obligation is contractually limited to and paid from an escrow account (consisting of excess cash from the coupon interest on the receivables over the interest passed through to the buyer), the escrow is a retained interest that is initially measured at previous carrying value allocated in proportion to relative fair values.

97-3 Accounting for Fees and Costs Associated with Loan Syndications and Loan Participation after the Issuance of FASB Statement No. 140

A consensus was reached that the accounting for financial asset transfers as described in FAS 140 is applicable to loan participation, including those which are "in-substance loan syndications."

A consensus was also reached that all transactions legally structured as loan syndications including "in-substance loan participation," should be accounted for as loan syndications per FAS 91.

01-7 Creditor's Accounting for a Modification or Exchange of Debt Instruments

A creditor should not account for a loan refinancing or restructuring (other than a troubled debt restructuring) as a minor modification of a debt instrument if the present value of the cash flows under the terms of the new debt instrument are at least ten percent different from the present value of the remaining cash flows under the terms of the original debt instrument. If the difference in the cash flows is less than ten percent, a creditor should consider the specific facts and circumstances surrounding the modification to determine whether that modification is minor. FAS 91 describes the accounting for minor modifications of debt instruments.

02-9 Accounting for Changes That Result in a Transferor Regaining Control of Financial Assets Sold

If a transferor is required to rerecognize financial assets in which it holds a beneficial interest because the transferor's contingent right (for example, a "ROAP" or other contingent call option on the transferred financial assets) becomes **exercisable,** no gain or loss should be recognized. The transferor should continue to account for its beneficial interest in those assets apart from the rerecognized assets. That is, the beneficial interest should not be combined with and accounted for with the rerecognized assets. A gain or loss may be recognized upon the **exercise** of a ROAP or similar contingent right with respect to the "repurchased" portion of the transferred assets that were sold if the ROAP or similar contingent right held by the transferor is not accounted for as a derivative under Statement 133 and is not at-the-money. The exercise would result in a recombination of the beneficial interest with the repurchased assets.

If a transferor is required to rerecognize financial assets because the SPE becomes nonqualifying, no gain or loss should be recognized with respect to the "repurchase" by the transferor of the financial assets originally sold that remain outstanding in the SPE (or the portion thereof if the transferor retained a partial interest in those assets). The fair value of the rerecognized assets will equal the fair value of the liability assumed by the transferor because the transferor is contractually required to pass on all of the cash flows from the rerecognized assets to the SPE for distribution in accordance with the contractual documents governing the SPE. The transferor should continue to account for its beneficial interest in those assets, if any, apart from the rerecognized assets.

Under no circumstances should an allowance be **initially** recorded for assets (loans) that are rerecognized at their fair value.

The accounting for the servicing asset related to the previously sold financial assets does not change because the transferor, as servicer, is still contractually required to collect the asset's cash flows for the benefit of the SPE and otherwise service the assets. The transferor should continue to recognize the servicing asset and assess the asset for impairment as required by FAS 140.

STATEMENTS OF POSITION

01-6 Accounting by Certain Entities (Including Entities with Trade Receivables) That Lend to or Finance the Activities of Others

Some of the standards included in this SOP are described within the chapter under the headings "Financing activities, including trade receivables" and "Disclosures." The provisions that apply primarily to banks, savings institutions, finance companies, credit unions, and mortgage companies are not included in this chapter. Those entities should refer to Chapter 23 and the SOP for more guidance. The remainder of the standard is discussed below.

Some organizations transfer the servicing rights on loans. The SOP includes standards to determine whether those transfers are sales. Those criteria are

- The guidance in EITF 95-5, which is discussed in Chapter 6
- Whether the seller has received written approval from the investor (if required)
- Whether the buyer is a currently approved seller/servicer and is not at risk of losing approved status
- Whether the buyer has made a nonrefundable deposit large enough to demonstrate a commitment to pay the remaining sales price (if the sale is seller-financed)
- Whether the seller is adequately compensated for any temporary servicing provided

Sales of servicing rights should be recognized in income subject to the considerations above. If the servicing rights sold are on loans that are retained, the carrying amount should be allocated between servicing rights and loans retained using the relative fair value method used in FAS 140.

Some entities agree to purchase loans at a stated price in return for a standby commitment fee. If the settlement date of a standby commitment to purchase loans is reasonable (i.e., within a normal loan commitment period), then the commitment fee should be recognized in accordance with FAS 91. If the settlement date is not within a reasonable period, or if the entity does not have the intent and ability to accept delivery without selling assets, the standby commitment should be accounted for as a written put option. That is, the standby commitment fee should be recorded as a liability. Thereafter, the liability is reported at the greater of the initial standby commitment fee or the fair value of the written put option, with the offsetting entry reported in current operations.

A factor should recognize purchase discounts such as factoring commissions in accordance with FAS 91 or AICPA PB 6 if the transfer of receivables is a sale under FAS 140. Otherwise, the transfer should be accounted for as a secured loan and the factoring commissions should be recognized over the period of the loan in accordance with FAS 91.

03-3 Accounting for Certain Loans or Debt Securities Acquired in a Transfer

This SOP is discussed in this chapter and also in Chapter 23, Banking and Thrift. It is applicable to all nongovernmental entities, including not-for-profit organizations. SOP 03-3 addresses the accounting for the differences between contractual and expected future cash flows of acquired loans when these differences are attributable, at least in part, to credit quality. It should be applied prospectively for loans acquired in fiscal years beginning after December 15, 2004.

Additional disclosures that should be made as a result of this SOP are

1. How prepayments on loans receivable are accounted for.

2. For loans acquired through purchase, including in a business combination, separately for loans accounted for as debt securities, and for those not accounted for as debt securities

   a. The outstanding balance (undiscounted cash flows owed).
   b. The carrying amount at the beginning of the period.
   c. The carrying amount at the end of the period.
   d. A reconciliation of the amount accretable yield at the beginning of the period to the amount of accretable yield at the end of the period.
   e. For loans acquired in the current period

      (1) The contractually required payments receivable.
      (2) The cash flows expected to be collected.
      (3) The fair value at acquisition.
      (4) The carrying amount of any acquired loans in nonaccrual status.

   f. The carrying amount of all loans in nonaccrual status.
   g. For loans not accounted for as debt securities

      (1) The amount of any expense recognized for impairment.
      (2) The amount of any reduction in a valuation allowance for losses that results from an increase in cash flows previously expected to be collected.
      (3) The amount of the allowance for uncollectible loans at the beginning of the period.
      (4) The amount of the allowance for uncollectible loans at the end of the period.

When loans are acquired with evidence of deterioration in credit quality since origination, the acquirer is required to estimate the cash flows expected to be collected on the loan. This exercise is to be done both at the purchase date and again periodically over the lives of the loans. Cash flows in excess of the initial investment (purchase price) expected to be collected should be recognized as yield; this is referred to as "accretable yield." On the other hand, contractual cash flows in excess of expected cash flows (the nonaccretable difference) are **not** to be recognized as yield.

Changing expectations of future cash flows are to be handled differently, depending on whether these are decreases or increases. If, subsequent to acquisition, there are decreases in the probable cash flows, impairments are to be recognized. In other words, such a development cannot be handled prospectively as a yield adjustment over the remaining lives of the loans.

By contrast, probable increases in subsequent cash flows expected to be collected should be recognized prospectively as a yield adjustment. In cases where a new, higher yield on a loan is established (due to a probable increase in cash flows to be collected), that yield should be used as the effective interest rate in any later test for impairment.

If loans are refinanced or restructured after acquisition, these cannot be accounted for as new loans, unless these are troubled debt restructurings, addressed by FAS 15, FAS 114, and FAS 115.

Under the provisions of SOP 03-3, acquired loans are not to be aggregated for purposes of determining evidence of postorigination credit deterioration. Rather, each loan, even if purchased in a pool, must be individually evaluated. However, subsequent pooling or aggregation of smaller-balance homogeneous loans is allowed for purpose of recognition, measurement, and disclosure. To be accounted for in the aggregate, loans must have a common credit risk (such as past due status or credit score) and have a common predominant risk characteristic (such as type of loan or date of origination). Furthermore, aggregation is limited to loans purchased in the same fiscal quarter.

SOP 03-3 does not provide general guidance as to the recognition of income, because that guidance does not exist for originated loans. However, income recognition will still be prohibited on loans for which an investor expects to substantially improve the collateral for resale or expects to use the collateral in operations.

Variable loans with index rate decreases, contractual cash flow decreases, and expected cash flow decreases should be evaluated based on the change in expected cash flows attributable to the decrease in index rates. Those changes should be recognized prospectively, rather than as impairments. The decrease in expected cash flows due to index rate decreases must be ascertained, and those changes are to be evaluated against the loan's contractual payments receivable, which must be calculated based on the index rate as it changes over the life of the loan.

6 SHORT-TERM INVESTMENTS AND FINANCIAL INSTRUMENTS

PERSPECTIVE AND ISSUES

FAS 133, *Accounting for Derivative Instruments and Hedging Activities,* after some delay, became effective for fiscal years beginning after June 15, 2000. Several of its provisions were slightly altered by FAS 138. Scores of informal interpretations have since been reported by a special implementation guidance group established by FASB, and as of mid-2002 a minor amendment to FAS 133 has been formally proposed. Given the enormous complexity of this area, coupled with the fact that "special accounting" for hedging continues to exist under GAAP (which would be eliminated if a pure "fair value" model for all financial assets and liabilities were adopted), it is inevitable that further interpretive guidance will be forthcoming. Practitioners therefore must be particularly alert to these evolving requirements, to an extent virtually unequaled for any other GAAP practice area.

FAS 133 applies to all entities and requires that all derivative instruments (DI) be recognized as either assets or liabilities on the balance sheet, at their respective fair values. Gains and losses on DI which are not designated as hedges are always to be recognized currently in earnings (or, in the case of a not-for-profit entity, in the change in net assets). Special accounting (effectively, the deferral of gains or losses) for derivatives is permissible only when the instrument has been designated as a hedge, and then only to the extent that the hedge is effective.

Depending upon which of the conditions specified in the standard are met, a derivative may be specifically designated as a hedge of fair value changes, of cash flows, or of certain foreign currency exposures.

Hedges of the changes in fair value can be associated with a recognized asset or liability or of an unrecognized firm commitment. In a fair value hedge, gains and losses of both the DI and the hedged item are recognized currently in earnings. For a perfectly effective hedge, these will fully offset each period, but in most cases this will not be achieved. Thus a residual charge or credit to earnings will often occur each period that the hedge position is in place.

Cash flows hedges pertain to forecasted transactions. The effective portions of these hedges are initially reported in other comprehensive income and are reclassified into earnings when the forecasted transactions affect earnings. Any ineffective portions of the hedges are reported currently in earnings.

Hedges of the foreign currency exposure of a net investment in a foreign operation also qualify for special accounting treatment. In a foreign currency net investment hedge, the gain or loss is reported in other comprehensive income as part of the cumulative translation adjustment. In the case of foreign currency hedges of unrecognized firm commitments, the gain or loss is reported the same way as a fair value hedge. A gain or loss on a foreign currency hedge that is associated with an available-for-sale security will also be reported the same way as a fair value hedge. Finally, a gain or loss arising from a hedge relating to a foreign currency denominated forecasted transaction is reported in the same way as a cash flow hedge. (These hedges are discussed in this chapter and in Chapter 22.)

Not-for-profits (NFP) cannot use hedge accounting for forecasted transactions. This is because NFP do not report other comprehensive income—all such items are included in the statement of activity, which provides an all-inclusive measure of changes in net assets for the period. In other regards, FAS 133 requirements are equally applicable to NFP entities.

A nonderivative financial instrument cannot generally be designated as a hedge. One exception, however, occurs when that instrument is denominated in a foreign currency and is designated as a hedge of a net investment in a foreign operation or an unrecognized firm commitment.

Hedge effectiveness is necessary if the accounting set forth in FAS 133 is to be employed. This does not require perfect effectiveness (which is almost never encountered), but the standard is not explicit regarding the degree of effectiveness which must be attained. The method used for assessing the effective and ineffective portions of a hedge must be established at the inception of the hedge and must be consistent with the approach used by the reporting entity for managing risk. Once a hedge fails to meet a minimum threshold of effectiveness, it is dedesignated and hedge accounting ceases.

FAS 133, as amended, superseded FAS 80, 105, and 119; amended ARB 43 and FAS 52, 60, 65, 95, 107, 113, 115, 124, 125, and 126, and TB 79-19; and nullified or modified numerous EITF consensuses.

Rules pertaining to the recognition of transfers of financial assets and to the extinguishments of financial liabilities have gone through several changes in recent years. The prior reliance on the "risks and rewards" approach was replaced in 1996 by the "control over financial assets" approach of FAS 125. Most of the guidance found in this standard was carried forward by its replacement, FAS 140, issued in late 2000. Under the provisions of FAS 140, subsequent to a transfer of financial assets an entity recognizes the financial and servicing assets it controls and the liabilities it has incurred, derecognizes financial assets when control has been surrendered, and derecognizes liabilities when extinguished. Multiple criteria pertaining to surrender of control must all be met for sale treatment to apply. Derivatives and liabilities resulting from a transfer of financial assets are measured at fair value. In-substance defeasance of debt (under which both the debt and the related segregated assets were removed from the obligor's balance sheet) has been banned. New requirements were also established for "qualified special-purpose entities."

FAS 115 is GAAP regarding investments in all debt securities and in those equity securities that have a readily determinable fair value. It classifies these securities into one of three categories: held-to-maturity, trading, or available-for-sale. The first of these can only be applied to debt securities, which are then to be reported at amortized cost. The trading category can include both debt and equity securities, which are to be reported at fair value. The available-for-sale category is used for those investments that do not fit in either of the other two classifications; these are also reported at fair value in the balance sheet.

FAS 115 does not change the accounting for financial liabilities and does not apply to DI. In the case of an investment subject to this standard with an embedded derivative, the host instrument is accounted for under FAS 115 and the embedded derivative is accounted for under FAS 133.

FAS 107 requires entities to disclose the fair value of **all** (recognized and unrecognized) financial instruments that it is practicable to estimate, including liabilities. Pertinent descriptive information regarding the instrument is to be disclosed if an estimate of fair value cannot be made without incurring excessive costs. Certain types of financial instruments—including pensions, postretirement benefits, deferred compensation, insurance contracts, lease contracts, and warranty obligations—are excluded from the requirements of this standard. FAS 107 was amended by FAS 133 to include the disclosure requirements from now-superseded FAS 105 concerning concentrations of credit risk for **all** financial instruments.

FAS 126 made FAS 107 disclosures optional for entities meeting all the following criteria:

1. Enterprise is nonpublic.
2. Total enterprise assets are less than $100 million on financial statement date.
3. During the reporting period, enterprise has not held or issued any derivative financial instruments.

FAS 149, effective in 2003, amended certain provisions of FAS 133, largely to incorporate positions previously enunciated by the FASB's Derivatives Implementation Group. It also conforms accounting for derivatives to positions incorporated in other professional standards issued since FAS 133 was promulgated.

As a general principle, the offsetting of assets and liabilities is not permitted. However, when a right of setoff exists—defined as a debtor's legal right to discharge debt owed to another party by applying against the debt an amount the other party owes to the debtor—offsetting is allowed. FIN 39 makes another exception in the case of multiple forward, swap, and similar contracts executed with the same party under master netting arrangements. The conditions to be met are

1. Each of the two parties owes the other determinable amounts.
2. The reporting party has the right to set off.
3. The reporting party intends to set off.
4. The right of setoff is enforceable at law.

Sources of GAAP

ARB	*APB*	*FAS*	*FIN*	*EITF*
43, Ch. 3A	22	52, 65, 80, 95, 102, 107, 109, 111, 112, 115, 123, 126, 127, 130, 133, 137, 138, 140, 145, 149	39 *FTB* 94-1	84-7, 84-14, 85-9, 85-29, 86-24, 86-25, 86-28, 86-34, 86-40, 87-2, 87-12, 87-26, 87-30, 88-8, 89-18, 90-17, 95-5, 96-11, 96-12, 96-13, 96-15, 99-1, 00-17, 00-19, 01-6, 02-2, 02-3, 03-1, 03-11, D-11, D-39, D-50, D-73, D-75, D-102

DEFINITIONS OF TERMS

Accounting loss. Accounting loss refers to the loss that may have to be recognized due to credit and market risk as a direct result of the rights and obligations of a financial instrument.

Bifurcation. Separation of embedded derivative instrument from the host contract so that separate accounting can be applied to the embedded derivative instrument.

Carrying amount (value). The amount at which securities are being carried, net of allowances.

Contractual obligations. All contractual obligations that are financial instruments meet the definition of a liability set forth in CON 6, *Elements of Financial Statements*. Some may not be recognized as liabilities in financial statements—may be "off-balance-sheet"—because they fail to meet some other criterion for recognition. For some financial instruments, the obligation is owed to or by a group of entities rather than a single entity.

Contractual rights. All contractual rights that are financial instruments meet the definition of asset set forth in CON 6. Some may not be recognized as assets in financial statements—may be "off-balance-sheet"—because they fail to meet some other criterion for recognition. For some financial instruments, the obligation is held by or due from a group of entities rather than a single entity.

Cost (of a security). The original purchase price plus all costs incidental to the acquisition (e.g., brokerage fees and taxes) unless a new cost basis is assigned as a result of a decline in market value which is other than temporary.

Credit risk. Credit risk is the possibility that a loss may occur from the failure of another party to perform according to the terms of a contract.

Derivative. A financial instrument or contract (options, swaps, futures, etc.) whose value is derived from some other financial measure (underlyings, that is, commodity prices, interest rates, exchange rates, indexes of financial items, etc.) and includes payment provisions (notional amounts, that is, cash, commodities, shares of stock, etc.).

Equity instrument. Any evidence of an ownership interest in an entity.

Financial asset. Any asset that is (1) cash, (2) a contractual right to receive cash or another financial asset from another entity, (3) a contractual right to exchange other financial instruments on potentially favorable terms with another entity, or (4) an equity instrument of another entity.

Financial instrument. A financial instrument is cash, evidence of an ownership interest in an entity, or a contract that both

a. Imposes on one entity a contractual obligation (1) to deliver cash or another financial instrument to a second entity or (2) to exchange financial instruments on potentially unfavorable terms with the second entity.
b. Conveys to that second entity a contractual right (1) to receive cash or another financial instrument from the first entity or (2) to exchange other financial instruments on potentially favorable terms with the first entity.

Financial instrument with off-balance-sheet risk. A financial instrument has off-balance-sheet risk of accounting loss if the risk of accounting loss to the entity may exceed the amount recognized as an asset, if any, or if the ultimate obligation may exceed the amount that is recognized as a liability in the statement of financial position.

Financial liability. Any liability that is a contractual obligation (1) to deliver cash or another financial asset to another entity or (2) to exchange financial instruments on potentially unfavorable terms with another entity.

Firm commitment. An agreement with an unrelated party, binding on both parties and usually legally enforceable. The agreement usually specifies all significant terms (including quantity to be exchanged, fixed price, timing of the transaction) and includes a disincentive for nonperformance that is sufficiently large enough to make performance probable.

Forecasted transaction. A transaction that is expected to occur for which there is no firm commitment. Because no transaction or event has yet occurred, when the transaction or event does occur, it will be at the prevailing market price.

Market risk. Market risk is the possibility that future changes in market prices may make a financial instrument less valuable.

Marketable equity securities. Instruments representing actual ownership interest, or the rights to buy or sell such interests, and which are actively traded or listed on a national securities exchange.

Net realizable value. The amount of cash anticipated to be produced in the normal course of business from an asset, net of any direct costs of the conversion into cash.

Normal purchases and sales. Contracts without a settlement provision and without a market mechanism to facilitate net settlement; or which require delivery of nonfinancial assets that constitute normal purchases or normal sales of the reporting entity.

Notional amount. A number of currency units, shares, bushels, pounds, or other units specified in a derivative instrument.

Other-than-temporary decline. A downward movement in the value of a marketable equity security for which there are known causes. The decline indicates a remote likelihood of a price recovery.

Realized gain (loss). The difference between the cost or adjusted cost of a marketable security and the net selling price realized by the seller which is to be included in the determination of net income in the period of the sale.

Risk of accounting loss. The risk of accounting loss from a financial instrument includes the (1) possibility that a loss may occur from the failure of another party to perform according to the terms of a contract (credit risk), (2) the possibility that future changes in market prices may make a financial instrument less valuable (market risk), and (3) the risk of theft or physical loss. FAS 105 addresses credit and market risk only.

Short-term investments. Securities or other assets acquired with excess cash, having ready marketability and intended by management to be liquidated, if necessary, within the current operating cycle.

Temporary decline. A downward fluctuation in the value of a marketable equity security that has no known causes that suggest the decline is of a permanent nature.

Unrealized gain (loss). The unrealized difference between the market value of short-term investments and their carrying value which is deemed not to be of a permanent nature.

Valuation allowance. An account used to value marketable equity securities at fair value. The offset is either a gain or loss account (for trading securities) or a contra equity account (for available-for-sale securities).

CONCEPTS, RULES, AND EXAMPLES

Short-Term Investments

Short-term (or temporary) investments usually consist of marketable debt and equity securities. Accordingly, investments that are held for purposes of control of another entity or pursuant to an ongoing business relationship, for example, stock held in a supplier, would be excluded from current assets and would instead be listed as **other assets** or **long-term investments** (see Chapter 10).

Debt securities and marketable equity securities. FAS 115 is GAAP governing the accounting for all debt securities and for equity securities that have a readily determinable fair value. FTB 94-1 includes restructured loans involving a modification of terms (even if a restructuring took place before the effective date of FAS 114) under FAS 115 if such loans meet the definition of a security. Equity securities include not only stock, but also the rights to purchase stock, such as warrants or call options, and the right to sell stock, such as put options. FAS 115 does not apply to securities accounted for by the equity method. These securities are accounted for in accordance with APB 18 and are discussed in Chapter 10. This statement also does not apply to specialized industries that account for substantially all debt and equity securities at market or fair value with changes recognized in earnings or in the change in net assets. Not-for-profit organizations are excluded from the provisions of FAS 115, but the statement does apply to cooperatives and mutual enterprises (including credit unions and mutual insurance companies). In addition, unsecuritized loans are not covered, but mortgage-backed securities are covered. Accounting for financial liabilities is not changed.

The standard requires all debt securities and equity securities with readily determinable fair values to be classified into one of three categories.

Classification of Debt and Equity Securities

Categories	*Type*	*Characteristics*	*Reported on balance sheet*	*Reported in income*
1. Held-to-maturity	Debt	Positive intent and ability to hold until maturity	Amortized cost	Interest Realized gains and losses
2. Trading	Debt & equity	Bought and held principally to sell short-term	Fair value	Interest and dividends Realized gains and losses Unrealized gains and losses
3. Available-for-sale	Debt & equity	Neither held-to-maturity nor trading securities	Fair value Unrealized gains and losses to accumulated other comprehensive income (component of owners' equity)	Interest and dividends Realized gains and losses

If a classified balance sheet is presented, the debt and equity securities owned by an entity should be grouped into current and noncurrent portfolios. All trading securities are classified as current assets. The determination of current or noncurrent status for individual held-to-maturity and individual available-for-sale securities is made on the basis of whether or not the securities are considered working capital available for current operations (ARB 43, chapter 3A).

Fair value. FAS 115 applies to equity securities if

1. Prices or bid-and-ask quotations are available on SEC registered exchanges or from the NASDAQ or the National Quotation Bureau. Unless qualified for sale within one year, restricted stock does not meet this definition.
2. Traded on a foreign market of comparable breadth and scope as the US markets identified above.
3. Fair value per unit (share) of a mutual fund is determined and published and is the basis for current transactions.

Classification. Classification is to be made at acquisition. The appropriateness of classification should be reassessed at each reporting date.

Held-to-maturity debt securities. If an entity has the **positive intent** and the **ability** to hold debt securities to maturity, they are measured at amortized cost. All **transfers** or **sales** of securities in this category must disclose the following in the notes for each period for which the results of operations are presented:

1. Amortized cost
2. Realized or unrealized gain or loss
3. Circumstances leading to the decision to sell or transfer

Isolated, nonrecurring, and unusual events that could not have been reasonably anticipated may cause a sale or transfer without calling intent or ability to hold into question. Other changes in circumstances that are not considered inconsistent include

1. Material deterioration in creditworthiness of the issuer
2. Elimination or reduction of tax-exempt status of interest through a change in tax law
3. Major business disposition or combination
4. Statutory or regulatory changes that materially modify what a permissable investment is or the maximum level of the security to be held
5. Downsizing in response to a regulatory increase in the industry's capital requirements
6. A material increase in risk weights for regulatory risk-based capital purposes

This category does not include securities available for sale in response to a need for liquidity or changes in

1. Market interest rates
2. Foreign currency risk
3. Funding sources and terms
4. Yield and availability of alternative investments
5. Prepayment risk

For asset-liability management purposes, similar or identical securities may be classified differently depending upon intent and ability to hold.

Under FAS 140, securities such as interest-only strips, which can be settled in a manner where recorded amounts might not be substantially recovered, cannot be classified as held-to-maturity. Dependent upon the circumstances these are to be categorized as either trading or available-for-sale.

FAS 133 specifies that a held-to-maturity debt security denominated in a foreign currency should be accounted for under FAS 52.

Maturity date. The sale of a security within three months of its maturity meets the requirement to hold to maturity since the interest rate risk is substantially diminished. Likewise, if a call is considered probable, a sale within three months of that date meets the requirement. The sale of a security after collection of at least 85% of the principal outstanding at acquisition (due to prepayments or to scheduled payments of principal and interest in equal installments) also qualifies since the "tail" portion no longer represents an efficient investment due to the economic costs of accounting for the remnants. Scheduled payments are not required to be equal for variable-rate debt.

Example of held-to-maturity debt securities

The 12/31/04 debt security portfolio categorized as held-to-maturity is as follows:

Security	*Maturity value*	*Amortized cost*	*Assumed fair value*
DEF 12% bond, due 12/31/05	$ 10,000	$10,320	$10,200
PQR mortgage-backed debt, due 12/31/07	$100,000	$92,000	$90,000
JKL 8% bond, due 12/31/11	$ 10,000	$ 8,929	$ 9,100

The balance sheet would report all the securities in this category at amortized cost and would classify them as follows:

Security	*Maturity date*	*Balance sheet*	*Classification*
DEF	12/31/05	$10,320	Current
PQR	12/31/07	$92,000	Noncurrent
JKL	12/31/11	$ 8,929	Noncurrent

Interest income, including premium and discount amortization, is included in income. Any realized gains or losses are also included in income.

Trading securities. If an entity has debt and/or equity securities (with readily determinable fair value) that it intends to actively and frequently buy and sell for short-term profits, those securities are classified as trading securities. Unless classified as held-to-maturity securities, FAS 65 mortgage-backed securities held for sale require classification as trading securities. The securities in this category are required to be carried at fair value on the balance sheet as current assets. All applicable interest and dividends, realized gains and losses, and unrealized gains and losses on changes in fair value are included in income from continuing operations.

Example of accounting for trading securities

The year one current trading securities portfolio is as follows:

Security	*Cost*	*Market*	*Difference (market minus cost)*
ABC	$1,000	$ 900	$(100)
MNO calls	1,500	1,700	200
STU	2,000	1,400	(600)
XYZ 7% bond	2,500	2,600	100
	$7,000	$6,600	$(400)

A $400 adjustment is required in order to recognize the decline in market value. The entry required is

Unrealized loss on trading securities	400	
Trading securities—MNO calls	200	
Trading securities—XYZ 7% bond	100	
Trading securities—ABC		100
Trading securities—STU		600

The unrealized loss would appear on the income statement as part of other expenses and losses. Dividend income and interest income (including premium and discount amortization) is included in income. Any realized gains or losses from the sale of securities are also included in income.

An alternative to direct write-up and write-down of securities is the use of an asset valuation allowance account to adjust the portfolio totals. In the above example, the entry would be

Unrealized loss on trading securities	400	
Valuation allowance (contra asset)		400

The valuation allowance of $400 would be deducted from historical cost to obtain a fair value of $6,600 for the trading securities on the balance sheet.

All trading securities are classified as current assets and the balance sheet would appear as follows:

Current assets:	
Trading securities at fair value (cost = $7,000)	$6,600

The year two current trading portfolio is as follows:

Security	New securities cost	Old securities X1 market	X2 market	Difference*
ABC		$ 900	$1,000	$100
DEF Puts	$1,500		1,500	0
STU		1,400	1,800	400
VWX	2,700		2,800	100
	$4,200	$2,300	$7,100	$600

* *Difference = X2 market – (Cost or X1 market)*

A $600 adjustment is required in order to recognize the increase in market value. The entry required is

Trading securities—ABC	100	
Trading securities—STU	400	
Trading securities—VWX	100	
Unrealized gain on trading securities		600

The unrealized gain would appear on the income statement as part of other income.

Example of accounting for a realized gain

1. The same information as given in the above example for year one
2. In year two, the MNO calls are sold for $1,600 and the XYZ 7% bonds are sold for $2,700.

The entry required to record the sale is

Cash	4,300	
Realized loss on sale of trading securities	100	
Realized gain on sale of trading securities		100
Trading securities—MNO calls (X1 market)		1,700
Trading securities—XYZ 7% bonds (X1 market)		2,600

Under the valuation allowance method, the current trading portfolio would appear as follows:

Security	Cost	X2 market
ABC	$1,000	$1,000
DEF Puts	1,500	1,500
STU	2,000	1,800
VWX	2,700	2,800
	$7,200	$7,100

The required entries to recognize the increase in market value and the realized gain are

Valuation allowance	300	
Unrealized gain on trading securities		300

To adjust the valuation allowance to reflect the unrealized loss of $100 at the end of year two on the remaining trading portfolio

Cash	4,300	
Trading securities—MNO calls (Cost)		1,500
Trading securities—XYZ 7% bonds (Cost)		2,500
Realized gain on sale of trading securities		300

The balance sheet under both methods would appear as follows:

Current assets:	
Trading securities at fair value (cost = $7,200)	$7,100

Available-for-sale. Investments in debt securities and in equity securities with a readily determinable fair value that are **not** classified as either trading securities or held-to-maturity are classified as available-for-sale. The securities in this category are required to be carried at fair value on the balance sheet. The determination of current or noncurrent status for individual securities depends on whether the securities are considered working capital (ARB 43, chapter 3A).

Other than the possibility of having some noncurrent securities on the balance sheet, the major difference between trading securities and available-for-sale securities is the handling of unrealized gains and losses. Unlike trading securities, the **unrealized** gains and losses are excluded from net income. Instead, they are reported in other comprehensive income per FAS 130. All applicable interest (including premium and discount amortization) and any realized gains or losses from the sale of securities are included in income from continuing operations.

Deferred tax effects. The recognition of unrealized gains and losses for financial statement purposes is likely to have deferred tax effects. See the discussion in Chapter 10, page 404.

Transfers. Fair value is used for transfers between categories. When the security is transferred, any unrealized holding gains and losses are accounted for in the following manner:

1. **From trading**—Already recognized and should not be reversed
2. **Into trading**—Recognize immediately in income
3. **Available-for-sale debt security into held-to-maturity**—Continue to report the unrealized holding gain or loss at the transfer date as other comprehensive income and amortize the gain or loss over the investment's remaining life as an adjustment of yield in the same manner as a premium or discount. The transferred-in security will probably record a premium or discount since fair value is used. Thus, the two amortizations will tend to cancel each other on the income statement.
4. **Held-to-maturity debt security into available-for-sale**—Recognize in other comprehensive income per FAS 130. Few transfers are expected from the held-to-maturity category.

See examples in Chapter 10.

Impairment. Other-than-temporary impairment (probable that all contractual amounts due won't be collected) of either the held-to-maturity or available-for-sale securities should be recognized as a realized loss. The cost basis should be written down to fair value and the write-down should be included in net income. The accounting should then proceed as required for the category. Subsequent recoveries will not change the new cost basis.

Cash flow statement. Cash flows resulting from sales, purchases or maturity of securities should be accounted for as follows:

1. Trading – Operating activity
2. Held-to-maturity – Investing activity
3. Available-for-sale – Investing activity

Cash flows from 2. and 3. above are required to be reported gross (cash inflows from gross proceeds separately from outflows for purchase of investments) for each security classification.

Options

Call and put options can be effectively used as valuable hedging instruments or as highly leveraged speculative ventures. One call contract gives the **buyer** the right to **buy** 100 shares of the underlying security at a specific exercise price, regardless of the market price. The **seller** of the call, on the other hand, must **sell** the security to the buyer at that exercise price, regardless of the market price. For example, assume a Disney July 35 call has a quoted market price of $6 (per share or $600 per contract). These facts indicate that a buyer that pays $600 to a seller for a call has the right to purchase 100 shares of Disney at any time until July (typically the end of trading on the third Friday of the month quoted) for $35 per share. The buyer can exercise this right at any time until it expires. The seller of the call must stand ready to deliver 100 shares to the buyer for $35 per share until expiration. Typically, the buyer expects the market price to rise and the seller expects the market price to stay the same or to fall.

A put is the opposite of a call. A put gives the **buyer** the right to **sell** the underlying security at the exercise price regardless of the market price. It gives the **seller** the obligation to **buy** at the exercise price. Typically, the buyer expects the market price to fall and the seller expects the market price to stay the same or to rise. Strips, straps, straddles, and spreads are combinations and/or variations of the basic call and the basic put. These and other compound instruments should be analyzed in terms of their constituent elements, and accounted for accordingly.

Example

Seller D owns 100 shares of Disney at a cost of $75 per share and sells 1 Disney July 35 call to Buyer E at $6. The following positions result if the market price:

		Position	
		Seller (D)	Buyer (E)
1.	Stays at 35 and there is no exercise	+$600	–$600

D receives the $600 premium and E pays for the right to call the stock. If the market price doesn't move, the option expires; E is out $600 and D collects it.

2.	Rises to 55 and there is an exercise and immediate sale	+$600 (0 + $600)	+$1,400 ($2,000 – $600)

If the price rises to $55 per share and the security is called, D sells the security to E at $35 ($0 profit on the shares) and is effectively $600 (the amount of the premium) better off. E, however, buys the security at $35 per share and immediately sells it for $55 per share. E gains $2,000 from the security sale less the $600 premium and is $1,400 better off.

3.	Falls to 15 and there is no exercise	–$1,400 (– $2,000 + $600)	–$600 (0 – $600)

If the market price falls to $15 per share, D incurs an effective $2,000 decrease in value of the shares held, less the $600 premium received. E does not exercise the option and loses the premium paid.

The issue in accounting for options is whether cost or market values—or some combination—should be used in accounting for the option itself and for the associated underlying security. For instance, assume M buys 100 shares of XYZ at $15 per share and the security price immediately moves to $25 per share. At this point, M buys a November 25 put contract at $100 for the contract. M has effectively hedged and guaranteed a minimum profit of $900 [(100 shares x $10) – ($1 x 100 shares)] regardless of market price movement, since

XYZ can be sold for $25 per share until the third Friday in November. If the price continues upward, the put will expire unexercised and M will continue to benefit point for point. If the price stays the same, M locks in a profit of $900. If the price falls, M has locked in a profit of $900. The question is whether these facts can be accounted for by applying the cost principle to both option and security, by applying the market principle to both option and security, or by applying some combination of both principles.

Before FAS 133, FAS 115 was the only relevant guidance, and it was not really definitive. FAS 115 contains the requirements for accounting investments. Theoretically, therefore, FAS 115 only applied to *purchased* puts and calls, since *written* options are liabilities, not investments. Likewise, cash settled options and equity indexed options do not represent ownership interests and debt securities options are not covered by FAS 115. In the absence of formal standards, however, numerous aspects of the issue had been addressed by the EITF. The result was that options were usually carried at market value.

Financial Instruments

FAS 133, as amended by FAS 138, specifies recognition of all derivative instruments (not just derivative **financial** instruments) in the balance sheet as assets or liabilities measured at fair value. Derivatives can be specifically designated as hedges. The standard superseded FAS 80, 105, and 119, and it also amended numerous other FAS and nullified or modified numerous EITF consensuses. FAS 133 carried forward the financial components approach first set forth in FAS 125 and continued by FAS 140.

Derivative financial instruments. Derivatives are financial instruments that derive their value from changes in a benchmark based on stock prices, interest rates, mortgage rates, currency rates, commodity prices or some other agreed-upon reference. Option contracts and forward contracts are the two basic forms of derivatives, and they can be either publicly or privately traded. Forward contracts have symmetrical gain and loss characteristics—that is, they provide exposure to both losses and gains from market movements, although generally there is no initial premium to be paid. Forward contracts are usually settled on or near the delivery date by paying or receiving cash, rather than by physical delivery. On the other hand, option contracts have asymmetrical loss functions: they provide little or no exposure to losses (beyond the premium paid) from unfavorable market movements, but can provide large benefits from favorable market movements. Both futures and options have legitimate roles to play in hedging programs, if properly understood and managed.

Typical derivative financial instruments include

1. Option contracts
2. Interest rate caps
3. Interest rate floors
4. Fixed-rate loan commitments
5. Note issuance facilities
6. Letters of credit
7. Forward contracts
8. Forward interest rate agreements
9. Interest rate collars
10. Futures
11. Swaps
12. Instruments with similar characteristics

It should be noted that DFI exclude all on-balance-sheet **receivables** and **payables** including

1. Mortgage-backed securities
2. Interest-only obligations
3. Principal-only obligations
4. Indexed debt
5. Other optional characteristics incorporated within those receivables and payables (such as convertible bond conversion or call terms)

In addition, DFI exclude contracts that either

1. Require exchange for a nonfinancial commodity or
2. Permit settlement by delivering a nonfinancial commodity

Thus, most product (petroleum, grain, etc.) futures contracts would be excluded, while swaps (if settled in cash) would be included.

As with other financial instruments, derivatives can be acquired for investment purposes or for speculation. For enterprises which are not in the business of speculation, however, the typical purpose of DFI is to manage risk, such as that associated with stock price movements, interest rate variations, currency fluctuations, and commodity price volatility. The parties involved tend to be brokerage firms, financial institutions, insurance companies, and large corporations, although any two or more entities of any size can hold or issue derivatives.

The DFI are contracts that are supposed to protect or hedge one or more of the parties from adverse movement in the underlying base, which can be a financial instrument position held by the entity or a commitment to acquire same at some future date, among others. Unfortunately, these protections or hedges are rarely perfect and sometimes the hedge, once established, is later modified, even indirectly—such as by disposing of the underlying position while retaining the former hedge—so that the DFI becomes in effect a speculative position. The DFI themselves can become risky and, if leveraged, small adverse price or interest rate variations can produce significant losses. Thus, instead of providing protection, many DFI have actually generated losses and the failure to manage these instruments properly has contributed to a popular perception that hedging itself is a suspect activity.

Over recent decades, financial engineering resulted in the creation of a wide range of derivative instruments, from interest rate swaps (exchanging variable- or floating-rate debt for fixed-rate debt) and interest rate caps (limiting exposure to rising interest rates) to such "exotics" as structured notes, inverse floaters, and interest-only strips. Accounting concerns about these losses arose from what formerly had been the off-balance-sheet nature of many DFI, the amount of capital that should be required for trading DFI, and the suitability of DFI for holders, given the risks of loss that could result. Over the past several decades, many users and issuers reassessed their policies regarding DFI and examined and strengthened their internal controls to limit their risk exposure. In hindsight it is clear that the failure to explicitly account for many of these derivative instruments contributed to the failure to effectively manage investments in derivatives, and a central reason for the development of what became FAS 133 was to explicitly account for, and raise the visibility of, these instruments.

Prior to the promulgation of FAS 133, a preferred method of accounting for DFI had not been established. In many cases, the individual positions were accounted for separately at fair value with the gains or losses reported in operating income or in net income; in other cases, hedge accounting was used with its associated deferral of gains and losses. As its initial step, the FASB mandated disclosures in an attempt to require relevant information to be given to interested parties, as an indication of the DFI's risk. FAS 133 subsequently specified the formal recognition and measurement principles to be applied to derivatives holdings.

A number of anomalies existed under prior GAAP. For example, options held and certain other DFI were originally not disclosed because they did not represent off-balance-sheet risk of accounting loss. Later, under enhanced disclosure requirements, the requirements included information about the transaction being hedged and about the time period until occurrence, a description of the classes of DFI used to hedge, amounts of explicitly deferred hedging gains or losses, and events that would result in recognition in earnings of deferred items. Disclosures about interest rate, commodity price, foreign exchange, or other market risks, which would be useful for comparing strategic results with the objectives of derivatives usage and would be consistent with the entity's management of risk, were encouraged but not required. Different entities reported this information in different ways, and the development and evolution of effective ways of reporting this data was being actively encouraged.

Fair value information was also relegated to footnotes under prior GAAP, either spread among several notes, or set forth in a summary table. In addition, the relationship between the carrying amounts and what was reported in the balance sheet was to be disclosed. "Traded" (including dealing and other activities measured at fair value with gains or losses recognized in earnings) financial instruments were to be distinguished from those that were categorized as "other than traded." In disclosing fair value of a DFI, that fair value was not to be aggregated, netted or combined (even if considered related) with either the fair value of a nonderivative financial instrument or other DFI, except as permitted by FASBI 39 (addressing the right of offset).

All of the various former disclosure requirements have been superseded by FAS 133. This standard has incorporated most of the earlier disclosure requirements, modified for the new accounting rules regarding the use of fair value accounting and for the hedge accounting provisions of FAS 133.

Off-balance-sheet and credit risk. Under an earlier standard, various disclosures were required of information (1) about financial instruments with off-balance-sheet risks of accounting loss that exceeded the amounts recorded, if any, in the statement of financial position and (2) about all financial instruments with concentrations of credit risk. It addressed credit and market risks only.

The earlier definitional limitations were overcome when a universally agreed-upon definition of financial instruments was adopted, to include cash, any ownership interest in an entity, or a contract that both imposes a contractual obligation on one entity (1) to surrender cash or another financial instrument to a second entity or (2) to exchange financial instruments on potentially unfavorable terms with the second entity, and simultaneously conveys a contractual right to the second entity (1) to receive from the first entity cash or another financial instrument or (2) to exchange with the first entity other financial instruments on potentially favorable terms.

A **contractual obligation** whose economic benefit or sacrifice is receipt or delivery of a financial instrument other than cash was to be considered a financial instrument. For example, a note that is payable in US Treasury bonds gives an issuer the contractual obligation to deliver and gives a holder the contractual right to receive bonds, not cash. But because the bonds represent obligations of the US Treasury to pay cash, they are considered financial instruments. Therefore, the note is also a financial instrument to both the holder of the note and the issuer of the note.

Another type of financial instrument is one that gives an entity the **contractual right** or obligation to exchange other financial instruments on potentially favorable or unfavorable terms. An example of this type of financial instrument would be a call option to purchase a US Treasury note for $100,000 in six months. The option holder has a contractual right to exchange the financial instrument on potentially favorable terms. Six months later, if the market value of the note exceeds $100,000, the holder will exercise the option because the terms are favorable. The writer of the call option has a contractual obligation to exchange financial instruments on potentially unfavorable terms if the holder exercises the option. The writer is normally compensated for accepting this obligation by being paid a premium.

A put option to sell a Treasury note has similar effects, although the change in market values making it worthwhile to exercise the option will be a decline in prices, rather than an increase. The holder of the put option, as with the call option, effectively has an unlimited profit potential and little or no risk of loss, whereas the writer of the option has unlimited risk of loss and only a fixed income to be received. Options, such as those discussed here, are financial instruments which are derivatives. A bank's commitment to lend $100,000 to a customer at a fixed rate of 10% any time during the next six months at the customer's option is also a financial instrument.

An interest rate swap can be explained as a series of forward contracts to exchange, for example, fixed cash payments for variable cash receipts. The cash receipts would be computed by multiplying a floating-rate market index by a notional amount. An interest rate swap is both a contractual right and a contractual obligation to both parties.

Excluded from financial instrument classification under the now-superseded FAS 105, however, were options and contracts that contain the right or obligation to exchange a financial instrument for a **physical** asset, such as bushels of wheat. For example, two entities enter a sale-purchase contract in which the purchaser agrees to take delivery of wheat or gold six months later and pay the seller $100,000 at the time of delivery. The contract is not considered a financial instrument because it requires the delivery of wheat or gold that are not considered financial instruments.

Also excluded from financial instrument classification are contingent items that may ultimately require the payment of cash but do not as yet arise from contracts. An example would be a contingent liability for tort judgments payable. However, when such an obligation becomes enforceable and is reduced to a fixed payment schedule, it would then be considered a financial instrument.

Prior GAAP had required entities to disclose in the body of the financial statements, or in footnotes, information about financial instruments with off-balance-sheet risk. Disclosures were to be by category of financial instrument; and were to include the face, contract, or notional principal amount; and the nature and terms of the instruments including a discussion of (1) the credit and market risks; (2) the cash requirements; and (3) the related accounting policies (pursuant to APB 22).

For financial instruments with off-balance-sheet credit risk, disclosure was required, in the body of the financial statements or in notes thereto, of information about the amount of accounting loss the entity would have incurred if any party to the financial instrument failed completely to perform according to the terms of the contract. Disclosure was also necessary if any collateral proved worthless. Finally, the entity's policy for requiring collateral on financial instruments subject to credit risks, information about access to that collateral, and the nature and brief description of collateral supporting financial instruments was required to be disclosed.

A financial instrument had off-balance-sheet risk of **accounting loss** if there was a risk that an accounting loss to the entity could exceed the amount recognized as an asset or if the ultimate obligation could exceed the amount that was recognized as a liability in the statement of financial position. The risk of accounting loss includes the possibility that the loss may occur from credit risk or from market risk. The issue of off-balance-sheet risk of loss has been effectively made moot by the requirement under FAS 133 that all derivative instruments be reported at fair value. Also, the requirements of FAS 115, mandating the fair value reporting (or at least disclosure) of most financial instruments held as investments, reduces the opportunities for off-balance-sheet risk to occur.

Fair value disclosures. Disclosure is required under FAS 107, which has been amended by FAS 133, of the reporting entity's credit risk arising from all its holdings of financial instruments. It also requires that entities disclose the fair values of all (recognized and unrecognized) financial instruments that it is practicable to estimate, including liabilities. Pertinent descriptive information as to the fair value of the instrument is to be presented if an estimate to fair value cannot be made without incurring excessive costs.

Fair value has been defined as the exchange price in a current transaction (other than in a forced or liquidation sale) between willing parties. If a quoted market price is available, it should be used. If there is more than one market price, the one used should be the one from the most active market. The possible effect on market price from the sale of large holdings and/or from thinly traded issues can be disregarded for purposes of this statement.

If quoted market prices are unavailable, management's best estimate of fair value can be used. Some bases from which an estimate may be made include

1. Matrix pricing models
2. Option pricing models
3. Financial instruments with similar characteristics adjusted for risks involved
4. Financial instruments with similar valuation techniques (i.e., present value) adjusted for risks involved

FAS 107 contains examples of procedures for estimating fair value.

If the **carrying amount** for trade receivables and payables approximates fair value (which is usually the case), no disclosure is required.

If an estimate of fair value cannot be made without incurring excessive costs, disclose the following:

1. Information pertinent to estimating fair value such as carrying amount, effective interest rate, and maturity
2. Reasons why estimating fair values is not practicable

FAS 107 did not change any other requirements of GAAP in regard to financial instruments. It applies to all entities and to all financial instruments except pensions, postretirement benefits, deferred compensation, defeased debt, insurance contracts, lease contracts, warranty obligations and a limited number of other instruments. Despite possible variations in definitions, amounts computed under other GAAP requirements satisfy the requirements of FAS 107.

Disclosures are required for each year included for comparative purposes and may be in the body of the financial statements or in the notes. Methods and significant assumptions used should be disclosed.

Example

Note 1: Summary of Accounting Policies

The Corporation does not deal or trade financial instruments. Derivatives are limited in use and leveraged swaps and items with embedded terms are not used.

Derivative products and other financial instruments are used for nontrading purposes including the management of foreign currency exposure and interest rate positions. Asset amounts are reported as other assets. Liability amounts are reported as other liabilities. Gains or losses are recognized as other income or expense currently or deferred if qualified as a hedge.

Note X: Financial Instruments Disclosures of Fair Value

The estimates of fair value of financial instruments are summarized as follows (in 000s):

Carrying amounts approximate fair values:

	Carrying amount
Cash	$987
Cash equivalents	876
Trade receivables	765
Trade payables	654

Fair values approximate carrying values because of the short time until realization.

Assets with fair values exceeding carrying amounts:

	Carrying amount	Fair value
Short-term securities	$876	$987
Long-term investments	765	876
Forward foreign exchange contracts	154	165

Estimated fair values are based on available quoted market prices, present value calculations and option pricing models.

Liabilities with carrying amounts exceeding fair values:

	Carrying amount	Fair value
Long-term debt	$(543)	$(432)

Estimated fair values are based on quoted market prices, present value calculations, and the prices of the same or similar instruments after considering risk, current interest rates, and remaining maturities.

Unrecognized financial instruments:

	Carrying amount	Fair value
Interest rate swap agreements		
Net receivable	$1,012	$1,865
Net payable	(1,753)	(1,543)
Commitments to extend credit	(5,432)	(4,321)
Financial guarantees	(6,543)	(7,654)

Estimated fair values after considering risk, current interest rates, and remaining maturities were based on the following:

Interest rate swaps—Amounts to be received or paid to terminate swap agreements at reporting date.

Credit commitments—Value of the same or similar instruments after considering credit ratings of counterparties.

Financial guarantees—Cost to settle or terminate obligations with counterparties at reporting date.

Fair value not estimated:

	Carrying amount	Fair value
Long-term investment	$1,234	Unavailable

Fair value could not be estimated without incurring excessive costs. Investment is carried at original cost and represents an 8% investment in the common stock of a privately held **untraded** company that supplies the corporation. Management considers the risk of loss to be negligible.

Accounting for Derivatives and Hedging Transactions Per FAS 133: An Overview

Following a lengthy period of development, during which a number of possible sets of rules were debated, FAS 133 was implemented beginning in 2000. This standard, while far more comprehensive than any of the predecessors discussed above, is still not an all-inclusive standard on the accounting for all financial instruments. FAS 133 addresses the accounting for derivatives (which formerly presented the most intractable financial reporting problems) and continues, in much modified form, the practice of "special accounting" for hedges, which would not be necessary if a universal fair value financial reporting rule were imposed.

Fair values are defined in FAS 133 as they were in FAS 107, discussed above. The new standard will resolve a number of previous inconsistencies and other inadequacies found in previous standards, including

- The effects of derivative instruments were not easily understood, were often not properly displayed in the financial statements, and, sometimes, were not even recognized in the financial statements.
- The available accounting guidance was incomplete. Many derivative instruments were carried off balance sheet.
- The accounting guidance was inconsistent. There was different measurement of various derivative instruments, and different qualifications for alternative types of hedging.
- The guidance that did exist was difficult to apply. There was a variety of sources and no single comprehensive approach.

FAS 133 requires standardized accounting and reporting for all derivative instruments (including derivatives which are embedded in other instruments) and for hedging activities.

Underlying principles. There are four key principles underlying the new standard.

1. Derivative instruments are assets and liabilities.
2. The fair value of derivative instruments is the only relevant measure to be reported.
3. Only true assets and liabilities should be reported as such. Gains and losses from derivative instruments are not separate liabilities or assets and should not be reported as such.
4. Only designated qualifying items that are effectively offset by changes in fair value or cash flows during the term of the hedge should use the special accounting for hedging.

Derivative instruments represent rights and obligations, and these must be reported as assets and liabilities at fair value (which reflects the current cash equivalent). Gains and losses on derivative instruments not designated as hedges are recognized in earnings (or as a change in net assets, in the case of not-for-profit enterprises). The ability to apply hedge accounting requires that specified criteria be met, because of its elective nature and because of its reliance on management intent. Strategic risk hedges do not meet the qualifying criteria. Thus, hedge accounting is limited to relationships involving derivative instruments and certain foreign currency denominated instruments that are designated as hedges and meet the qualifying criteria.

Terminology

FAS 133 defines a number of important terms that are used to describe various derivative instruments and hedging relationships. These include the following:

Derivative instruments. In FAS 133, derivative instruments are defined by their three distinguishing characteristics. Specifically, derivative instruments are financial instruments or other contracts that have

1. One or more underlyings and one or more notional amounts (or payment provisions or both);
2. No initial net investment or a smaller net investment than required for contracts expected to have a similar response to market changes; and
3. Terms that require or permit
   a. Net settlement
   b. Net settlement by means outside the contract
   c. Delivery of an asset that results in a position substantially the same as net settlement

In contrast to prior GAAP, FAS 133 defines derivative instruments by reference to specific characteristics, rather than in terms of classes or categories of financial instruments. These distinctive features are believed to distinguish the fundamental nature of derivative instruments such as options and futures.

Fair value. Defined as in FAS 107 as the amount at which the asset or liability could be bought or settled in an arm's-length transaction; measured by reference to market prices or estimated by net present value of future cash flows, options pricing models, or by other techniques.

Financial instrument. Defined as cash, evidence of an ownership interest in an entity, or a contract that both imposes on one entity a contractual obligation to deliver cash or another financial instrument to a second entity, or to exchange other financial instruments on potentially unfavorable terms with the second entity, **and** conveys to that second entity a contractual right to receive cash or another financial instrument from the first entity or to exchange other financial instruments on potentially favorable terms with the first entity. For purposes of this definition, contractual obligations include those that are conditioned upon the occurrence of a specified event as well as those that are unconditional.

Firm commitment. An agreement with an unrelated party, binding on both, usually legally enforceable, specifying all significant terms and including a disincentive for nonperformance sufficient to make performance likely.

Forecasted transaction. A transaction expected to occur for which there is no firm commitment, and thus, which gives the entity no present rights or obligations. Under FAS 133, forecasted transactions can be hedged and special hedge accounting can be applied.

Initial net investment. A derivative instrument is one where the initial net investment is zero or is less than the notional amount (possibly plus a premium or minus a discount). This characteristic refers to the relative amount of investment. Derivative instruments allow the holder an opportunity to take part in the rate or price change without owning the underlying asset or owing the actual liability. If an amount approximating the notional amount must be invested or received, it is not a derivative instrument. The two basic forms of derivative instruments are futures contracts and options. The futures contract involves little or no initial net investment. Settlement is usually near the delivery date. Call options, when purchased, require a premium payment that is less than the cost of purchasing the equivalent number of shares. Even though this distinguishing characteristic is the result of only one of the parties, it determines the application for both.

FAS 149 has amended FAS 133 to specify that if the initial net investment in the contract, after adjusting for the time value of money, is less by more than a nominal amount, then an initial net investment that would be commensurate with the amount that would be exchanged either to acquire the asset related to the underlying or to incur the obligation related to the underlying, the threshold condition for classification as a derivative is met. The amount of the asset acquired or liability incurred, for purpose of this determination, should be comparable to the *effective* notional amount of the contract. The effective notional amount is the stated notional amount adjusted for any leverage factor.

Net settlements. To qualify as a derivative instrument, one of the following settlement criteria must be met:

1. No delivery of an asset equal to the notional amount is required. For example, an interest rate swap does not involve delivery of the instrument in which the notional amount is expressed.
2. Delivery of an asset equal to the notional amount is required of one of the parties, but an exchange (or other market mechanism, institutional arrangement or side agreement) facilitates net settlement. For example, a call option has this attribute.

3. Delivery by one of the parties of an asset equal to the notional amount is required but the asset is either readily convertible to cash (as with a contract for the delivery of a marketable equity security), or is required but that asset is itself a derivative instrument (as is the case for a swaption [an option on a swap]).

This characteristic means that the derivative instrument can be settled by a net delivery of assets (the medium of exchange does not have to be cash). Contract terms based on changes in the price or rate of the notional that implicitly or explicitly require or permit net settlement qualify. Situations where one of the parties can liquidate their net investment or be relieved of the contract rights or obligations without significant transaction costs because of a market arrangement (broadly interpreted) or where the delivered asset can be readily converted to cash also meet the requirements for net settlement. It is assumed that an exchange-traded security is readily converted to cash. Thus, commodity-based contracts for gold, oil, wheat, etc. are now included under this standard. The convertible to cash condition requires an active market and consideration of interchangeability and transaction volume. Determining if delivery of a financial asset or liability equal to the notional amount is a derivative instrument may depend upon whether it is readily convertible into cash. Different accounting will result if the notional is not readily converted to cash. Using the notional as collateral does not necessarily mean it is readily convertible to cash.

Notional amount. The notional amount (or payment provision) is the referenced units of measure associated with the underlying asset or liability, such as shares of stock, principal amount, face value, stated value, basis points, barrels of oil, etc. It may be that amount plus a premium or minus a discount. The interaction of the price or rate (underlying) with the referenced associated asset or liability (notional amount) determines whether settlement is required and, if so, the amount.

Underlyings. An underlying is commonly a specified price or rate such as a stock price, interest rate, currency rate, commodity price, or a related index. However, any variable (financial or physical) with (1) observable changes or (2) objectively verifiable changes such as a credit rating, insurance index, climatic or geological condition (temperature, rainfall) qualifies. Unless it is specifically excluded, a contract based on any qualifying variable is accounted for under FAS 133 if it has distinguishing characteristics 2. and 3. above.

Contracts Not Subject to FAS 133

The following contracts are considered exceptions and are not subject to the requirements of FAS 133:

1. **Regular-way security trades**—Delivery of a security readily convertible to cash within the time period generally established by marketplace regulations or conventions where the trade takes place rather than by the usual procedure of an individual enterprise. Contracts for the delivery of securities that are not readily convertible to cash are not subject to FAS 133's provisions because net settlement would not be possible.

   For example, most trades of equity securities in the US require settlement in three business days. If an individual contract requires settlement in more than three business days (even if this is normal for a particular entity), this exception would not apply, unless (per FAS 149, which amended FAS 133) the reporting entity is required to account for such transactions on a trade-date basis. This exception also applies to when-issued and to-be-announced securities, if there is no other way to purchase or sell them and if the trade will settle within the shortest period permitted.

Based on the foregoing, the following may be excluded: forward purchases or sales of to-be-announced securities, and when-issued, as-issued, or if-issued securities.

2. **Normal purchases and normal sales**—Contracts for future delivery of assets (other than derivative instruments or financial instruments) that are readily convertible to cash and for which there is no net settlement provision and no market mechanism to ease net settlement. Terms must be consistent with normal transactions and quantities must be reasonable in relation to needs. All relevant factors are to be considered. An example would include contracts similar to binding purchase orders. However, take or pay contracts that require little or no initial net investment, and that have products readily convertible to cash that do not qualify as normal purchases, would be a derivative instrument, and not an exception.

   The purpose of the "normal purchases and normal sales" definition was to exclude certain routine types of transactions from the required accounting as derivative instruments. FAS 138 expanded this exemption to include certain contracts which do contain net settlement or market mechanisms if it is judged probable, at the inception and throughout the duration of such contracts, that they will not in fact settle net and will instead result in physical delivery. Notwithstanding, this more broadly based exemption from the accounting requirements of FAS 133, certain contracts will not qualify for exemption in any case; these include contracts the price of which are based on an underlying that is not clearly and closely related to the assets being sold or purchased, and those requiring cash settlement for any gains or losses or otherwise settled net on a periodic basis. Documentary evidence is required to support the use of the expanded exemption from the FAS 133 provisions.

   FAS 149 has further addressed the "normal purchases and sales" provisions of FAS 133. Under the amendment, power purchase or sales agreements (whether forwards, options, or some combination thereof) pertaining to delivery of electricity qualify for this exception only if a series of conditions are all met. The contracts cannot permit net settlement, but must require physical delivery, and must be capacity contracts, as differentiated from ordinary option contracts. For the seller, the quantities deliverable under the contracts must be quantities normally to be sold; for the buyer, quantities must be those normally to be used or sold, and the buyer must be an entity which is contractually obligated to maintain sufficient capacity to meet the needs of its customers. Certain additional requirements, and further exceptions, are set forth by FAS 149.

   Counterparties may reach different conclusions as to whether the contracts are a derivative instrument. Asymmetrical results are acceptable (i.e., the exception may apply to one party but not the other).

3. **Certain insurance contracts**—Contracts where the holder is only compensated when an insurable event (other than price or rate change) takes place and

   a. The value of the holder's asset or liability is adversely changed or
   b. The holder incurs a liability.

   For example, contracts generally not considered to be derivative instruments include those within the scope of FAS 60, 97, and 113, traditional life insurance, and traditional property and casualty insurance policies.

   Most traditional insurance contracts will not be derivative instruments. Some, however, can include embedded derivatives that must be accounted for separately. For example, embedded derivatives may be found in indexed annuity contracts, variable life and annuity contracts, and property and casualty contracts involving changes in currency rates.

4. **Certain financial guarantee contracts**—Contracts that call for payments only to reimburse for a loss from debtor failure to pay when due. However, a credit-indexed contract requiring payment for changes in credit ratings (an underlying) would not be an exception.
5. **Certain contracts that are not exchange traded**—Contracts with underlyings based on one of the following:

   a. Climatic, geological or other physical variable: for example, inches of rain or heating-degree days;
   b. Value or price involving a nonfinancial asset not readily converted to cash or a nonfinancial liability that does not require delivery of an asset that is readily converted to cash; or
   c. Specified volumes of revenue of one of the parties: examples are royalty agreements or contingent rentals based on related sales.

   In the case of a mixture of underlyings, some of which are exceptions, the predominant characteristic of the combined variable of the contract is the determinant. If there is a high correlation with the behavior of the excepted variables above, it is an exception and if there is a high correlation with the nonexcepted variables, it is a derivative instrument.
6. **Derivatives that serve as impediments to sales accounting**—A derivative instrument that affects the accounting for the transfer of an asset. For example, a call option on transferred assets under FAS 140 would prevent accounting for the transfer as a sale. This is necessary, since recognizing the call as a derivative instrument would result in double counting. For instance, a lessor guarantee of the residual value may prevent the accounting for a sales-type lease.

In addition to the foregoing, the following are not considered derivative instruments:

1. Contracts issued or held that are both

   a. Indexed to the enterprise's own stock, and
   b. Classified in shareholders' equity.

   Derivative instruments are assets or liabilities. Items properly accounted for in shareholders' equity are thus excluded from the definition of derivatives. Contracts that can or must be settled through issuance of an equity instrument but that are indexed in part or in full to something other than the enterprise's own stock are considered derivative instruments if they qualify and they are to be classified as assets or liabilities. Some of these kinds of items will be revisited later by the FASB.
2. Contracts issued in connection with stock-based compensation arrangements as addressed in FAS 123.

   Many instruments under FAS 123 are classified in shareholder equity. The FASB felt that those properly classified as liabilities have been adequately addressed.
3. Contracts issued as contingent consideration in a business combination under FAS 141.

   Contracts in a business combination that are similar to, but are not accounted for as contingent consideration under FAS 141, are subject to this standard as derivative instruments or embedded derivative instruments.

The exceptions for the above three issued contracts are not applicable to the counterparties.

Embedded Derivative Instruments

An enterprise is not allowed to circumvent the requirements of FAS 133 recognition and measurement by embedding a derivative instrument in another contract. If these embedded derivative instruments would otherwise be subject to this standard, they are included in its scope. However, some common compound instruments that generally have been in existence for some time and that bear a close economic relationship to the host contract are excluded from FAS 133 for practical reasons.

Embedded derivative instruments are defined as explicit or implicit terms affecting (1) the cash flows or (2) the value of other exchanges required by contract in a way similar to a derivative instrument (one or more underlying can modify the cash flows or exchanges). An embedded derivative instrument is to be separated from the host contract and accounted for separately as a derivative instrument by both parties **if and only if** all of the following three criteria are met:

1. Risks and economic characteristics are not **clearly and closely related** to those of the host contract;
2. The hybrid instrument is not required to be measured at fair value under GAAP with changes reported in earnings; and
3. A separate instrument with the same terms as the embedded derivative instrument would be accounted for as a derivative instrument. For this condition, the initial net investment of the hybrid instrument is not the same as that for the embedded derivative instrument.

These three conditions for the separate accounting for embedded derivatives are explained in the following paragraphs.

Risks and economic characteristics are not clearly and closely related to those of the host contract. If the underlying is an interest rate or interest rate index that changes the net interest payments of an interest-bearing contract, it is considered clearly and closely related **unless** one of the following conditions exist:

1. The hybrid instrument can be settled contractually in a manner that permits any possibility whatsoever that the investor would not recover **substantially all** of the initial recorded investment.
2. The embedded derivative instrument could under any possibility whatsoever
   a. At least double the investor's initial rate of return (ROR) on the host contract and
   b. Could also result in a ROR at least twice the market return for a similar contract (same host contract terms and same debtor credit quality).

The date acquired (or incurred) is the assessment date for the existence of the above conditions. Thus, the issuer and an acquirer in a secondary market could account for the instrument differently because of different points in time.

Example of embedded instruments which are separately accounted for

Assuming that the host contract is a debt instrument, the following are considered not to be clearly and closely related and would normally have to be separated out as embedded derivatives:

1. Interest rate indexes, floors, caps and collars not meeting the criteria for exclusion (see below);
2. Leveraged inflation-indexed interest payments or rentals;

3. Calls and puts that do not accelerate repayment of the principal but require a cash settlement equal to the option price at date of exercise. Subsequently added options that cause one party to be exposed to performance or default risk by different parties for the embedded option than for the host contract;
4. Term extending options where there is no reset of interest rates;
5. Equity-indexed interest payments;
6. Commodity-indexed interest or principal payments;
7. A convertible debt conversion option for the investor if it qualifies as a derivative instrument (readily convertible to cash, etc.); and
8. A convertible preferred stock conversion option if the terms of the preferred stock (not the conversion option) are more similar to debt (a cumulative fixed rate with a mandatory redemption feature) than to equity (cumulative, participating, perpetual).

Example of embedded instruments which are not separately accounted for

Assuming that the host contract is a debt instrument, the following are considered to be clearly and closely related and would not normally have to be separated out as embedded derivative instruments:

1. Interest rate indexes (see below);
2. Interest rate floors, caps and collars, if **at issuance**
   a. The cap is at or above the current market price (or rate) and/or
   b. The floor is at or below the current market price (or rate).
3. Nonleveraged inflation-indexed interest payments or rentals.
4. Credit-sensitive payments (interest rate resets for debtor creditworthiness).
5. "Plain-vanilla" servicing rights not containing a separate embedded derivative instrument.
6. Calls and puts that can accelerate repayment of principal unless
   a. The debt involves substantial premium or discount (zero coupon) and
   b. The call or put is only contingently exercisable (not exercisable unless default occurs) and is indexed only to credit risk or interest rates.
7. Term-extending options if the interest rate is concurrently reset to approximately the current market rate for the extended term and the host contract had no initial significant discount.
8. Contingent rentals based on a variable interest rate.

Based on the foregoing, calls and puts embedded in equity instruments are normally accounted for as follows:

1. **Investor**—Both the call and the put are embedded derivative instruments.
2. **Issuer**—Only the put could be an embedded derivative instrument. The put and the call would not be embedded derivative instruments if they are both
   a. Indexed to their own stock and
   b. Classified in shareholders' equity.

The hybrid instrument is not required to be measured at fair value under GAAP with changes reported in earnings. For example, most unsettled foreign currency transactions are subject to FAS 52. Gains or losses are recognized in earnings and thus instruments of this nature are not considered embedded derivative instruments. Trading and available-for-sale securities that have cash flows denominated in a foreign currency also are not considered embedded derivative instruments.

A separate instrument with the same terms as the embedded derivative instrument would be accounted for as a derivative instrument. For this condition, the initial net investment of the hybrid instrument is not the same as that for the embedded derivative instrument.

To illustrate, a convertible debt conversion option for the **issuer** would not be an embedded derivative instrument since a separate option with the same terms would not be a derivative instrument because it is indexed to the issuer's own stock and would be classified in shareholders' equity.

Another example would involve convertible preferred stock. A convertible preferred stock conversion option would not be an embedded derivative instrument if the terms of the preferred stock (not the conversion option) are more similar to equity (cumulative, participating, perpetual) than to debt (a cumulative fixed rate with a mandatory redemption feature).

Interest-only strips and principal-only strips are specifically not subject to this standard assuming (1) the original financial instrument did not contain an embedded derivative instrument and (2) they don't incorporate any new terms from the original. In addition, foreign currency derivative instruments are specifically not separated from the host contract if (1) the currency of the primary economic environment is the functional currency of one of the parties or (2) the good or service price is routinely denominated in that currency in international commerce.

If an embedded derivative instrument is separated from the host, the accounting is as follows:

1. The embedded derivative instrument is accounted for based on FAS 133; and
2. The host contract is accounted for based on GAAP for that instrument, without the embedded derivative instrument.

If the embedded derivative instrument cannot be reliably identified and measured separately, the entire contract must be measured at fair value with the gain or loss recognized in income. In this case, the contract cannot be designated as a hedging instrument.

Gains and losses of derivative instruments not designated as hedges are recognized in earnings or, for a not-for-profit organization, in the change in net assets.

Hedging Activities—General Requirements

Overview. Matters relating to hedging activities constitute the core of the new standard and represent the most difficult accounting issues. While the standard requires that all derivatives be reported at fair value in the balance sheet, the changes in fair value will be reported in different ways depending on the nature and effectiveness of the hedging activities to which they are related, if held for hedging purposes. FAS 133 identifies changes in the fair values of derivatives as being the result of (1) effective hedging, (2) ineffective hedging, or (3) unrelated to hedging. Furthermore, the hedging itself can be related to the fair value of an existing asset or liability or of a firm commitment, the cash flow associated with forecasted transactions, or foreign currency exposures.

After meeting specified conditions, a qualified derivative may be specifically designated as a total or partial (expressed as a percentage where the risk exposure profile is the same as that in the whole derivative) hedge of

1. Changes in the fair value of
    a. A recognized asset or liability, or
    b. An unrecognized firm commitment.

    In a fair value hedge, all gains and losses (of both the derivative instrument and the hedged item) are recognized in earnings in the period of change.
2. Variable cash flows of a forecasted transaction.

In a cash flow hedge, the effective portion of the hedge is reported in other comprehensive income and is reclassified into earnings when the forecasted transaction affects earnings.

3. Foreign currency exposure of

   a. A net investment in a foreign operation

      In a foreign currency net investment hedge, the gain or loss is reported in other comprehensive income as part of the cumulative translation adjustment to the extent that it is effective.

   b. An unrecognized firm commitment

      In a foreign currency unrecognized firm commitment hedge, the gain or loss is reported the same way as a fair value hedge (see category 1., above).

   c. An available-for-sale security

      In a foreign currency available-for-sale security hedge, the gain or loss is reported the same way as a fair value hedge (see category 1., above).

   d. A foreign currency denominated forecasted transaction.

      In a foreign currency denominated forecasted transaction hedge, the gain or loss is reported in the same way as a cash flow hedge (see category 2., above).

Hedge portions that are not effective are reported in earnings immediately.

A nonderivative financial instrument cannot generally be designated as a hedge. One exception, however, occurs when that instrument is denominated in a foreign currency and is designated as a hedge under 3a. or 3b. above. Not-for-profit enterprises cannot use hedge accounting for forecasted transactions.

Effectiveness—General observations. The method used for assessing the effective and ineffective portions of a hedge must be defined at the time of designation, must be used throughout the hedge period and must be consistent with the approach used for managing risk. Similar hedges should usually be assessed for effectiveness in a similar manner unless a different method can be justified. If an improved method is identified and is to be applied prospectively to an existing hedge, that hedge must be discontinued. The new method can then be designated and a new hedge relationship can be established.

Factors to be included in the effectiveness assessment must be specified at inception. The effect of all excluded factors and ineffective amounts are to be included in earnings. For example, if an option contract hedge is assessed for effectiveness based on changes in the option's intrinsic value, the change due to the time value of the contract would be excluded from the effectiveness assessment and that amount would be included in earnings. As another example, differences in key terms between the hedged item and the hedging instrument such as notional amounts, maturities, quantities, location or delivery dates would cause ineffectiveness and that amount would be included in earnings.

Fair Value Hedges

The change in the fair value of an entire financial asset or liability for a period is computed as the fair value at the end of the period, adjusted to exclude changes in fair value (1) from payments received or made (partial recoveries or settlements) and (2) from the passage of time, minus the fair value at the beginning of the period.

To qualify as a fair value hedge, both the hedged items and the designated hedging instruments must meet **all** of the following criteria:

1. At the hedge's origin, formal documentation exists of the

   a. Hedging relationship;
   b. Risk management objectives;
   c. Strategy for undertaking the hedge;
   d. Identification of the hedged item, the hedging instrument, the nature of the risk being hedged, the method of assessing effectiveness and the components (if any) that are excluded (such as time value) from the effectiveness assessment; and the
   e. Reasonable method to be used in recognizing in earnings the asset or liability representing the gain or loss in the case of a hedged firm commitment.

2. The hedging relationship is expected to be highly effective in producing offsetting fair value changes throughout the hedge period. This relationship must be assessed at least every three months and each time financial statements or earnings are reported.
3. If hedging with a **written** option, the combination must provide as much potential for gains from positive fair value changes as potential for losses from negative fair value changes. If a net premium is received, a combination of options is considered a written option. The combination of a written option and some other nonoption derivative is also considered a written option.

Unless foreign currency is involved, a nonderivative instrument cannot be designated as a hedging instrument.

According to FAS 133, an asset or liability will be eligible for designation as a hedged item in a fair value hedge (to which a hedging position will be related, for purposes of reporting gain or loss) if the hedged item is specifically identified as all or a specific portion of a recognized asset or liability, or an unrecognized firm commitment; is exposed to fair value changes that are attributable to the hedged risk such that earnings would be affected; and is not either remeasured at fair value for financial reporting purposes, or an equity method investment, or an equity method or minority interest in a consolidated subsidiary, a firm commitment related to the foregoing, or an equity instrument issued by the entity. Other limitations also apply, affecting held-to-maturity debt securities and nonfinancial assets.

More specifically, to be eligible for designation as a hedged item, an asset or liability must meet **all** of the following criteria:

1. The single item (or portfolio of similar items) must be specifically identified as hedging all or a specific portion.
   a. If similar items are aggregated and hedged, each item has to share the risk exposure that is being hedged (i.e. each individual item must respond in a generally proportionate manner to the change in fair value).
   b. A specific portion must be one of the following:
      (1) A percentage of the total asset, liability, or portfolio;
      (2) One or more selected contractual cash flows: for instance, the present value of the interest payments due in the first two years of a four-year debt instrument;
      (3) An embedded put, call, cap, or floor that does not qualify as an embedded derivative in an existing asset or liability; or
      (4) Residual value in a lessor's net investment in a sales-type or direct financing lease.
2. The item has an exposure to fair value changes that could affect earnings (this does not apply to not-for-profit enterprises).

3. The item is **not**

   a. Remeasured with changes reported currently in earnings; for example, a foreign currency denominated item;
   b. An APB 18 equity method investment or an equity investment in a consolidated subsidiary;
   c. A minority interest;
   d. A firm commitment to enter into a business combination or to acquire or dispose of

      (1) A subsidiary;
      (2) A minority interest; or
      (3) An equity method investee; or

   e. An entity-issued equity interest classified in stockholder's equity.

4. The item is not a held-to-maturity debt security (or similar portfolio) unless the hedged risk is for something other than for fair value changes in market interest rates or foreign exchange rates; examples include hedges of fair value due to changes in the obligor's creditworthiness, and hedges of fair value due to changes in a prepayment option component.
5. If the item is a nonfinancial asset or liability (other than a recognized loan servicing right or a nonfinancial firm commitment with financial components), the designated hedged risk is the fair value change of the total hedged item (at its actual location, if applicable); FAS 133 stipulates that the price of a major ingredient cannot be used, and the price of a similar item at a different location cannot be used without adjustment.
6. If the item is a financial asset or liability, a recognized loan servicing right or a nonfinancial firm commitment with financial components, the designated hedge risk is the risk of changes in fair value from fair value changes in

   a. The total hedged item;
   b. Market interest rates;
   c. Related foreign currency rates;
   d. The obligor's creditworthiness; or
   e. Two or more of the above, other than a.

Prepayment risk for a financial asset cannot be hedged, but an option component of a prepayable instrument can be designated as the hedged item in a fair value hedge. Embedded derivatives have to be considered also in designating hedges. For instance, in a hedge of interest rates, the effect of an embedded prepayment option must be considered in the designation of the hedge.

Reporting gains and losses from fair value hedges. The accounting for qualifying fair value hedges' gains and losses is as follows:

- On the hedging instrument, gains and losses are recognized in earnings.
- On the hedged item, gains and losses are recognized in earnings, even if they would normally be included in other comprehensive income if not hedged. For example, gains and losses on an available-for-sale security would be taken into income, if this is being hedged. The carrying amount of the hedged item is adjusted by the gains and losses resulting from the hedged risk.

Differences between the gains and losses on the hedged item and the hedging instrument are either due to amounts excluded from the assessment of hedging effectiveness, or are due to ineffectiveness. These gains and losses are to be recognized currently in earnings.

Example

An available-for-sale security carrying amount is adjusted by the amount resulting from the hedged risk, a fair value hedge.

Hedged item:	Available-for-sale security
Hedging instrument:	Put option
Underlying:	Price of the security
Notional amount:	100 shares of the security

On July 1, X1, Company XYZ purchased 100 shares of Disney at a cost of $15 per share and classified it as an available-for-sale security. On October 1, Company XYZ purchased for $350 an at-the-money put on Disney with an exercise price of $25 and an expiration date of April X2. This put purchase locks in a profit of $650 ($1,000 spread in market price less $350 cost of the put), if the price stays at $25 or goes lower, but allows continued profitability if the price of the Disney stock continues to go up. Company XYZ specifies that only the intrinsic value of the option is to be used to measure effectiveness. Thus, the time value decreases in the fair value of the put will be charged against the income of the period. Company XYZ then documents the hedge's strategy, objectives, hedging relationships, and method of measuring effectiveness. The following table shows the fair value of the hedged item and the hedging instrument.

Case 1

	10/1/X1	*12/31/X1*	*3/31/X2*	*4/17/X2*
Hedged Item				
Disney share price	$ 25	$ 22	$ 20	$ 20
Number of shares	100	100	100	100
Total	$2,500	$2,200	$2,000	$2,000
Hedging Instrument				
Put option (100 shares)				
Intrinsic value	$ 0	$ 300	$ 500	$ 500
Time value	350	215	53	0
Total	$ 350	$ 515	$ 553	$ 500
Intrinsic Value Gain (Loss) on Put	$ 0	$ 300	$ 200	$ 0

Entries: Tax Effects and Transaction Costs Are Ignored

Date	Event	Account	Debit	Credit
7/1/X1	Purchase:	Available-for-sale security	1,500	
		Cash		1,500
9/30/X1	End of Quarter:	Valuation allowance—available-for-sale security	1,000	
		Other comprehensive income		1,000
10/1/X1	Put Purchase:	Put option	350	
		Cash		350
12/31/X1	End of Year:	Put option	300	
		Hedge gain (intrinsic value gain)		300
		Hedge loss	135	
		Put option (time value loss)		135
		Hedge loss	300	
		Valuation allowance—available-for-sale security (market value loss)		300

Partial Balance Sheet
Effect of Hedging Relationships
December 31, X1
Dr (Cr)

Cash	$(1,850)
Available-for-sale securities	1,200
Plus: Valuation allowance	1,000
Put option	515
Other comprehensive income	(1,000)
Retained earnings	135

Entries

3/31/X2	End of Quarter:	Put option	200	
		Hedge gain (intrinsic value changes)		200
		Hedge loss	162	
		Put option (time value loss)		162
		Hedge loss	200	
		Available-for-sale security (market value loss)		200
4/17/X2	Put Expires:	Put option	0	
		Hedge gain (intrinsic value changes)		0
		Hedge loss	53	
		Put option (time value changes)		53
		Hedge loss	0	
		Available-for-sale security (market value changes)		0

Partial Balance Sheet
Effect of Hedging Relationships
April 17, X2 (Expiration of put)
Dr (Cr)

Cash	$(1,850)
Available-for-sale securities	1,500
Plus: Valuation allowance	500
Put option	500
Other comprehensive income	(1,000)
Retained earnings	350

At or before expiration, an in-the-money put must be sold or exercised. Assuming that it is sold, the entry would be

Cash	500	
Put option		500

On the other hand, if the put is exercised, the entry would be

Cash (exercise price)	2,500	
Other comprehensive income	1,000	
Available-for-sale security		1,500
Valuation allowance		500
Put option		500
Gain on sale		1,000

The net effect on retained earnings of the hedge and sale is a net gain of $650 ($1,000 – $350)

Case 2

Hedged Item	*10/1/X1*	*12/31/X1*	*3/31/X2*	*4/17/X2*
Disney share price	$ 25	$ 28	$ 30	$ 31
Number of shares	100	100	100	100
Total	$2,500	$2,800	$3,000	$3,100
Hedging Instrument				
Put option (100 shares)				
Intrinsic value	$ 0	$ 0	$ 0	$ 0
Time value	350	100	25	0
Total	$ 350	$ 100	$ 25	$ 0
Intrinsic Value Gain (Loss) on Put	$ 0	$ 0	$ 0	$ 0

Entries: Tax Effects and Transaction Costs Are Ignored

7/1/X1	Purchase:	Available-for-sale security	1,500	
		Cash		1,500
9/30/X1	End of Quarter:	Valuation allowance—available-for-sale security	1,000	
		Other comprehensive income		1,000
10/1/X1	Put Purchase:	Put option	350	
		Cash		350
12/31/X1	End of Year:	Put option	0	
		Hedge gain (intrinsic value gain)		0
		Hedge loss	250	
		Put option (time value loss)		250
		Valuation allowance—available-for-sale security	300	
		Hedge gain (market value gain)		300

Partial Balance Sheet
Effect of Hedging Relationships
December 31, X1
Dr (Cr)

Cash	$(1,850)
Available-for-sale securities	1,500
Plus: Valuation allowance	1,300
Put option	100
Other comprehensive income	(1,000)
Retained earnings	(50)

Entries

3/31/X2	End of Quarter:	Put option	0	
		Hedge gain (intrinsic value change)		0
		Hedge loss	75	
		Put option (time value loss)		75
		Valuation allowance—available-for-sale security	200	
		Hedge gain (market value gain)		200
4/17/X2	Put Expires:	Put option	0	
		Hedge gain (intrinsic value change)		0
		Hedge loss	25	
		Put option (time value change)		25
		Valuation allowance—available-for-sale security	100	
		Hedge gain (market value change)		100

Effect of Hedging Relationships
April 17, X2 (Expiration of put)
Dr (Cr)

Cash	$(1,850)
Available-for-sale securities	1,500
Plus: Valuation allowance	1,600
Put option	0
Other comprehensive income	(1,000)
Retained earnings	(250)

The put expired unexercised and Company XYZ must decide whether to sell the security. If it continues to hold, normal FAS 115 accounting would apply. If it continues to hold and a new put is purchased, the above example would be applicable again with the present position as a starting point. If the security is sold, the entry would be

Cash (market value)	3,100	
Other comprehensive income	1,000	
Available-for-sale security		1,500
Valuation allowance		1,600
Gain on sale		1,000

Measuring the effectiveness of fair value hedges. Although there are specific conditions applicable to the hedge type (fair value or cash flow), in general, the assumption of no ineffectiveness in a hedging relationship between an interest-bearing financial instrument and an interest rate swap (or a compound hedging instrument composed of an interest rate swap and a mirror-image call or put option) can be made if **all** of the following conditions are met:

1. The principal amount of the interest-bearing asset or liability being hedged and the notional amount of the swap match;
2. The fair value of the swap is zero at inception, if the hedging instrument is solely an interest rate swap. If the hedging instrument is a compound derivative containing the swap and a mirror-image call or put, the premium for the option must be paid or received in the same manner as the premium on the option embedded in the hedged item, and further conditions must be met depending on whether the premium on the option element of the hedged item was paid upon inception or over the life of the instrument.
3. The net settlements under the swap are computed the same way on each settlement date;
4. The financial instrument is not prepayable, but this criterion does not apply to an interest-bearing asset or liability that is prepayable only due to an embedded call option when the hedging instrument is a compound derivative composed of a swap and a mirror-image call option; and
5. The terms are typical for those instruments and don't invalidate the assumption of effectiveness.
6. The maturity date of the instrument and the expiration date of the swap match;
7. No floor or ceiling on the variable interest rate of the swap exists; and
8. The interval (three to six months or less) between repricings is frequent enough to assume the variable rate is a market rate.

The fixed rate on the hedged item is not required to exactly match the fixed rate on the swap. The fixed and variable rates on the swap can be changed by the same amount. As an example, a swap payment based on LIBOR and a swap receipt based on a fixed rate of 5% can be changed to a payment based on LIBOR plus 1% and a receipt based on 6%.

Under FAS 133, a "shortcut method" is permitted to be used to compute fair value adjustments, which produces the same reporting results as when the method illustrated above has been applied. This shortcut is only appropriate for a fair value hedge of a fixed-rate asset or liability using an interest rate swap and only with the assumption of no ineffectiveness is appropriate (i.e., if the criteria above have been met.[1] The FASB's decision to redefine inter-

---

[1] *The steps in the shortcut method are as follows:*

a. *Determine the difference between the fixed rate to be received on the swap and the fixed rate to be paid on the bonds.*
b. *Combine that difference with the variable rate to be paid on the swap.*
c. *Compute and recognize interest expense using that combined rate and the fixed-rate liability's principal amount. (Amortization of any purchase premium or discount on the liability also must be considered, although that complication is not incorporated in this example.)*
d. *Determine the fair value of the interest rate swap.*
e. *Adjust the carrying amount of the swap to its fair value and adjust the carrying amount of the liability by an offsetting amount.*

est rate risk (by permitting "benchmark rate" hedging in FAS 138) necessitated that is also address the effect on the shortcut method for fair value hedges and cash flow hedges.

For fair value hedges, an assumption of no ineffectiveness is invalidated when the interest rate index embodied in the variable leg of the interest rate swap is different from the benchmark interest rate being hedged. In situations in which the interest rate index embodied in the variable leg of the swap has greater credit risk than that embodied in the benchmark interest rate, the effect of the change in the swap's credit sector spread over that in the benchmark interest rate would represent hedge ineffectiveness because it relates to an unhedged risk (credit risk) rather than to the hedged risk (interest rate risk).

In situations in which the interest rate index embodied in the variable leg of the swap has less credit risk than that embodied in the benchmark interest rate, the effect of the change in a certain portion of the hedged item's spread over the swap interest rate would also represent hedge ineffectiveness. In order for an entity to comply with an assumption of no ineffectiveness, the index on which the variable leg of the swap is based should match the benchmark interest rate designated as the interest rate risk being hedged for the hedging relationship.

Discontinuance of a fair value hedge. The accounting for a fair value hedge should not continue if any of the events below occur.

1. The criteria are no longer met;
2. The derivative instruments expire or are sold, terminated or exercised; or
3. The designation is removed.

If the fair value hedge is discontinued, a new hedging relationship may be designated with a different hedging instrument and/or a different hedged item, as long as the criteria established in FAS 133 are met.

Ineffectiveness of a fair value hedge. Unless the shortcut method is applicable, the reporting entity must assess the hedge's effectiveness at the inception of the hedge and at least every three months thereafter. In addition, FAS 133 requires that at the inception of the hedge the method to be used to assess hedge effectiveness must be identified. To comply, the reporting entity should decide which changes in the derivative's fair value will be considered in assessing the effectiveness of the hedge, and the method to be used to assess hedge effectiveness. Regarding the former, some derivative instruments (options) have two components: intrinsic value and time value. The intrinsic value of a call option is the excess, if any, of the market price over the strike or exercise price; the intrinsic value of an option recognizes that the price of the underlying item may move above the strike price (for a call) or below the strike price (for a put) during the exercise period. The enterprise elects to measure effectiveness either including or excluding time value; it must do so consistently once the designation is made.

Hedge effectiveness must be assessed in two different ways—in **prospective** considerations and in **retrospective** evaluations. FAS 133 provides flexibility in selecting the method the entity will use in assessing hedge effectiveness, but an entity should assess effectiveness for similar hedges in a similar manner and that the use of different methods for similar hedges should be justified.

Prospectively, the entity must, at both inception and on an ongoing basis, be able to justify an expectation that the relationship will he **highly effective** in achieving offsetting changes in fair value over future periods. That expectation can be based upon regression or other statistical analysis of past changes in fair values or on other relevant information. **Retrospectively,** the entity must, at least quarterly, determine whether the hedging relationship has been **highly effective** in having achieved offsetting changes in fair value through the date of periodic assessment. That assessment can also be based upon regression or other statistical analysis of past changes in fair values, as well as on other relevant information. If at inception the entity elects to use the same regression analysis approach for both prospective and retrospective effectiveness evaluations, then during the term of that hedging relationship those regression analysis calculations should generally incorporate the same number of data points. As an alternative to using regression or other statistical analysis, an entity could use the dollar-offset method to perform the retrospective evaluations of assessing hedge effectiveness.

FAS 133 does not define **hedging effectiveness** quantitatively. However, it is useful in this regard to contemplate the similar international accounting standard, IAS 39. That standard specifies that a hedge is normally regarded as highly effective if, at inception and throughout the life of the hedge, the enterprise can expect that the change in fair values of the hedging instrument and the hedged item will "almost fully offset." In addition, the standard requires that actual results be within a range of 80 - 125%. Interpretive guidance to that standard suggests that the appropriateness of any method of assessing hedge effectiveness depends on the nature of the risk being hedged and the type of hedging instrument used. Any method of assessing effectiveness must be reasonable and consistent with other similar hedges unless different methods are explicitly justified.

Logic suggests that the approach used under IAS 39 could also be applied under FAS 133, with a range of 80-125% being defined as effectiveness for hedge accounting purposes.

Impairment. All assets or liabilities designated as fair value hedges are subject to the normal GAAP requirements for impairment. Those requirements are to be applied, however, only after the carrying amounts have been adjusted for the period's hedge accounting. Since the hedging instrument is a separate asset or liability, its fair value is not considered in applying the impairment criteria to the hedged item.

Cash Flow Hedges

The second major subset of hedging arrangements relate to uncertain future cash flows, as contrasted with hedged items engendering uncertain fair values. A derivative instrument may be designated as a hedge to the exposure of fluctuating expected future cash flows produced by a particular risk. The exposure may be connected with an existing asset or liability or with a forecasted transaction. To qualify as a cash flow hedge, both the hedged items and the designated hedging instruments must meet **all** of the following criteria:

1. At the hedge's origin, formal documentation exists of the
   a. Hedging relationship;
   b. Risk management objectives;
   c. Strategy for undertaking the hedge; and
   d. Identification of the hedged transaction, the hedging instrument, the nature of the hedged risk, the method of assessing effectiveness and the components (if any) that are excluded (such as time value) from the effectiveness assessment.
2. Documentation must include
   a. All relevant details;
   b. The specific nature of any asset or liability involved;
   c. When (date on or period within) a forecasted transaction is expected to occur; and
   d. The expected currency amount (exact amount of foreign currency being hedged) or expected quantity (specific physical quantities such as number of

items, weight, etc.) of a forecasted transaction. If a price risk is being hedged in a forecasted sale or purchase, the hedged transaction **cannot**

(1) Be specified solely in terms of expected currency amounts; or
(2) Be specified as a percentage of sales or purchases.

The current price of the transaction should be identified and the transaction should be described so that it is evident that a given transaction is or is not the hedged transaction. For instance, a forecasted sale of the first 2,000 units in January is proper, but the forecasted sale of the last 2,000 units is not because they cannot be identified when they occur—the month has to end before the last units sold can be identified.

3. The hedging relationship is expected to be highly effective in producing offsetting cash flows throughout the hedge period. This relationship must be assessed at least every three months and each time financial statements or earnings are reported.
4. If hedging with a **written** option, the combination must provide at least as much potential for positive cash flow changes as exposure to negative cash flow changes. A derivative that results from the combination of a written option and another nonoption derivative is also considered a written option.
5. A link must be used to modify interest receipts or payments of a recognized financial asset or liability from one variable rate to another variable rate. It has to be between a designated asset (or group of similar assets) and a designated liability (or group of similar liabilities) and it has to be highly effective. A link occurs when the basis of one leg of an interest rate swap is the same as the basis of the interest rate receipt of a designated asset and the basis of the other leg of the swap is the same as the basis of the interest payments for a designated liability.

A nonderivative instrument cannot be designated as a hedging instrument for a cash flow hedge.

In addition to the above, to be eligible for designation as a cash flow hedge, a forecasted transaction must meet **all** of the following criteria:

1. The single transaction (or group of individual transactions) must be specifically identified. If individual transactions are grouped and hedged, each has to share the same risk exposure that is being hedged (i.e. each individual transaction must respond in a proportionate manner to the change in cash flow). Thus, a forecasted sale and a forecasted purchase cannot both be included in the same group of transactions.
2. The occurrence is probable.
3. It is a transaction with an external party (unless a foreign currency cash flow hedge) and it has an exposure to cash flow changes that could affect earnings.
4. The transaction is **not** to be remeasured under GAAP with changes reported in earnings; for example, foreign currency denominated items would be excluded for this reason. Forecasted sales on credit and forecasted accrual of royalties on probable future sales are not considered the forecasted acquisition of a receivable. Also, if related to a recognized asset or liability, the asset or liability is not remeasured under GAAP with changes in fair value resulting from the hedged risk reported in earnings.
5. The item is not a held-to-maturity debt security (or similar portfolio) unless the hedged risk is for something other than for cash flow changes in market interest rates, as for example, in a hedge of cash flow changes due to an obligor's creditworthiness or default.

6. It does **not** involve
   a. A business combination;
   b. A parent company's interest in consolidated subsidiaries;
   c. A minority interest;
   d. An equity method investment; or
   e. An entity-issued equity interest classified in stockholder's equity.
7. If it involves a purchase or sale of a **nonfinancial** asset, the hedged risk is
   a. The change in the functional-currency-equivalent cash flows resulting from changes in the related foreign currency rates; or
   b. The change in cash flows relating to the total hedged purchase or sales price (at its actual location, if applicable); for example, the price of a similar item at a different location cannot be used.
8. If it involves a purchase or sale of a **financial** asset or liability or the variable cash flow of an existing financial asset or liability, the hedged risk is the risk of changes in cash flow of
   a. The total hedged item;
   b. Market interest rates;
   c. Related foreign currency rates;
   d. Obligor's creditworthiness or default; or
   e. Two or more of the above, other than a.

Prepayment risk for a financial asset cannot be hedged.

Gains and losses from cash flow hedges. The accounting for qualifying cash flow hedges' gains and losses is as follows:

1. The effective portion of the gain or loss on the derivative instrument is reported in other comprehensive income.
2. The ineffective portion of the gain or loss on the derivative instrument is reported in earnings.
3. Any component excluded from the computation of the effectiveness of the derivative instrument is reported in earnings.
4. Accumulated other comprehensive income from the hedged transaction should be adjusted to the lesser (in absolute amounts) of the following:
   a. The cumulative gain or loss on the derivative from the creation of the hedge minus any component excluded from the determination of hedge effectiveness and minus any amounts reclassified from accumulated other comprehensive income into earnings;
   b. The portion of the cumulative gain or loss on the derivative needed to offset the cumulative change in expected future cash flow on the transaction from the creation of the hedge minus any amounts reclassified from accumulated other comprehensive income into earnings.

   The adjustment of accumulated other comprehensive income should recognize in other comprehensive income either a part or all of the gain or loss on the adjustment of the derivative instrument to fair value.
5. Any remaining gain or loss is reported in earnings.

Reclassifications to earnings. In the period that the hedged forecasted transaction affects earnings, amounts in accumulated other comprehensive income should be reclassified into earnings. If the transaction results in an asset or liability, amounts in accumulated other comprehensive income should be reclassified into earnings when the asset or liability affects earnings through cost of sales, depreciation, interest expense, etc. Any time that a net loss on the combined derivative instrument and the hedged transaction is expected, the amount that isn't expected to be recovered should immediately be reclassified into earnings.

Example of a "plain vanilla" interest rate swap

On July 1, 2005, Abbott Corp. borrows $5 million with a fixed maturity (no prepayment option) of June 30, 2009, carrying interest at prime + 1/2%. Interest only is due semiannually. At the same date, it enters into a "plain vanilla" type swap arrangement, calling for fixed payments at 8% and receipt of prime + 1/2%, on a notional amount of $5 million. At that date prime is 7.5%, and there is no premium due on the swap arrangement.

This swap qualifies as a cash flow hedge under FAS 133, and it is appropriate to assume no ineffectiveness, since the criteria set forth in that standard are all met.

NOTE: These criteria are that: the notional amount of the swap and the principal amount of the debt are equal; the fair value of the swap at inception is zero; the formula for computing net settlements under the swap is constant during its term; the debt is not prepayable; all interest payments on the debt are designated as being hedged and no payments beyond the term of the swap are so designated; there is no floor or cap on the variable rate of the debt that is not likewise designated for the swap; the repricing dates of the swap match those of the variable rate debt; and the same index is designated for the hedging instrument and the underlying obligation.

Accordingly, as rates change over the term of the debt and of the swap arrangement, changes in the value of the swap are reflected in other comprehensive income, and the swap will appear on the balance sheet as an asset or liability at fair value. As the maturity of the debt approaches, the value of the swap will converge on zero. Periodic interest expense in the income statement will be at the effective rate of 8%.

Assume that the prime rate over the four-year term of the loan, as of each interest payment date, is as follows, along with the fair value of the remaining term of the interest rate swap at those dates:

Date	Prime rate (%)	Fair value of swap*
December 31, 2005	6.5	$ - 150,051
June 30, 2006	6.0	- 196,580
December 31, 2006	6.5	- 111,296
June 30, 2007	7.0	- 45,374
December 31, 2007	7.5	0
June 30, 2008	8.0	23,576
December 31, 2008	8.5	24,038
June 30, 2009	8.0	0

* *Fair values are determined as the present values of future cash flows resulting from expected interest rate differentials, based on current prime rate, discounted at 8%.*

Regarding the fair values presented in the foregoing table, it should be assumed that the market (fair) values are precisely equal to the present value, at each valuation date (assumed to be the interest payment dates), of the differential future cash flows resulting from utilization of the swap. Future variable interest rates (prime + 1/2%) are assumed to be the same as the existing rates at each valuation date (i.e., there is no basis for any expectation of rate changes, and therefore the best estimate is that the current rate will persist over time). The discount rate, 8%, is assumed to be constant over time.

Thus, for example, the fair value of the swap at December 31, 2005, would be the present value of an annuity of seven payments (the number of remaining semiannual interest payments due) of $25,000 each (pay 8%, receive 7%, based on then-existing prime rate of 6.5%) to be made to the swap counterparty, discounted at an annual rate of 8% (using 4% for the semiannual discounting, which is a slight simplification). This computation yields a present value of a stream of seven $25,000 payments to the swap counterparty amounting to $150,051 at December 31, 2005, which is a liability to be reported by the entity at that date. The offset is a debit to other comprehensive income, since the hedge is (presumably) judged to be 100% effective in this case. Semiannual accounting entries will be as follows:

December 31, 2005

Interest expense	175,000	
Accrued interest (or cash)		175,000

To accrue or pay semiannual interest on the debt at the variable rate of prime + 1/2% (7.0%)

Interest expense	25,000	
Accrued interest (or cash)		25,000

To record net settlement on swap arrangement [8.0 - 7.0%]

Other comprehensive income	150,051	
Swap contract		150,051

To record the fair value of the swap contract as of this date (a net liability because fixed rate payable to counterparty of 8% exceeds floating rate receivable from counterparty of 7%)

June 30, 2006

Interest expense	162,500	
Accrued interest (or cash)		162,500

To accrue or pay semiannual interest on the debt at the variable rate of prime + 1/2% (6.5%)

Interest expense	37,500	
Accrued interest (or cash)		37,500

To record net settlement on swap arrangement [8.0 - 6.5%]

Other comprehensive income	46,529	
Swap contract		46,529

To record the fair value of the swap contract as of this date (increase in obligation because of further decline in prime rate)

December 31, 2006

Interest expense	175,000	
Accrued interest (or cash)		175,000

To accrue or pay semiannual interest on the debt at the variable rate of prime + 1/2% (7.0%)

Interest expense	25,000	
Accrued interest (or cash)		25,000

To record net settlement on swap arrangement [8.0 - 7.0%]

Swap contract	85,284	
Other comprehensive income		85,284

To record the fair value of the swap contract as of this date (decrease in obligation due to increase in prime rate)

June 30, 2007

Interest expense	187,500	
Accrued interest (or cash)		187,500

To accrue or pay semiannual interest on the debt at the variable rate of prime + 1/2% (7.5%)

Interest expense	12,500	
Accrued interest (or cash)		12,500

To record net settlement on swap arrangement [8.0 - 7.5%]

Swap contract	65,922	
Other comprehensive income		65,922

To record the fair value of the swap contract as of this date (decrease in obligation due to further increase in prime rate)

December 31, 2007

Interest expense	200,000	
Accrued interest (or cash)		200,000

To accrue or pay semiannual interest on the debt at the variable rate of prime + 1/2% (8.0%)

Interest expense	0	
Accrued interest (or cash)		0

To record net settlement on swap arrangement [8.0 - 8.0%]

Swap contract	45,374	
Other comprehensive income		45,374

To record the fair value of the swap contract as of this date (further increase in prime rate to the original rate of inception of the hedge eliminates fair value of the derivative)

June 30, 2008

Interest expense	212,500	
Accrued interest (or cash)		212,500

To accrue or pay semiannual interest on the debt at the variable rate of prime + 1/2% (8.5%)

Receivable from counterparty (or cash)	12,500	
Interest expense		12,500

To record net settlement on swap arrangement [8.0 - 8.5%], counterparty remits settlement

Swap contract	23,576	
Other comprehensive income		23,576

To record the fair value of the swap contract as of this date (increase in prime rate creates net asset position for derivative)

December 31, 2008

Interest expense	225,000	
Accrued interest (or cash)		225,000

To accrue or pay semiannual interest on the debt at the variable rate of prime + 1/2% (9.0%)

Receivable from counterparty (or cash)	25,000	
Interest expense		25,000

To record net settlement on swap arrangement [8.0 - 9.0%], counterparty remits settlement

Swap contract	462	
Other comprehensive income		462

To record the fair value of the swap contract as of this date (increase in asset value due to further rise in prime rate)

June 30, 2009 (Maturity)

Interest expense	212,500	
Accrued interest (or cash)		212,500

To accrue or pay semiannual interest on the debt at the variable rate of prime + 1/2% (8.5%)

Receivable from counterparty (or cash)	12,500	
Interest expense		12,500
Other comprehensive income	24,038	
Swap contract		24,038

To record the fair value of the swap contract as of this date (value declines to zero as expiration date approaches)

Example of an option on an interest rate swap

The facts of this example are a variation on the previous example. Abbott Corp. anticipates as of June 30, 2005, that as of June 30, 2007, it will become a borrower of $5 million with a fixed maturity four years hence (June 30, 2011). Based on its current credit rating, it expects to be able to borrow at prime + 1/2%. As of June 30, 2005, it is able to purchase, for a single payment of $25,000, a "swaption" (an option on an interest rate swap), calling for fixed pay at 8% and variable receipt at prime + 1/2%, on a notional amount of $5 million, for a term of four years. The option will expire in two years. At June 30, 2005, prime is 7.5%.

NOTE: The interest rate behavior in this example differs somewhat from the prior example, to better illustrate the "one-sidedness" of options, versus the obligation under a swap arrangement or other futures and forwards.

It will be assumed that the time value of the swaption expires ratably over the two years.

This swaption qualifies as a cash flow hedge under FAS 133. However, while the change in fair value of the contract is an effective hedge of the cash flow variability of the prospective debt issuance, the premium paid is a reflection of the time value of money and is thus to be expensed ratably over the period that the swaption is outstanding.

The table below gives the prime rate at semiannual intervals including the two-year period prior to the debt issuance, plus the four years during which the forecasted debt (and the swap, if the option is exercised) will be outstanding, as well as the fair value of the swaption (and later, the swap itself) at these points in time.

Date	Prime rate (%)	Fair value of swaption/swap*
December 31, 2005	7.5	$ 0
June 30, 2006	8.0	77,925
December 31, 2006	6.5	0
June 30, 2007	7.0	- 84,159
December 31, 2007	7.5	0
June 30, 2008	8.0	65,527
December 31, 2008	8.5	111,296
June 30, 2009	8.0	45,374
December 31, 2009	8.0	34,689
June 30, 2010	7.5	0
December 31, 2010	7.5	0
June 30, 2011	7.0	0

* *Fair value is determined as the present value of future expected interest rate differentials, based on current prime rate, discounted at 8%. An "out of the money" swaption is valued at zero, since the option does not have to be exercised. Since the option is exercised on June 30, 2007, the value at that date is recorded, although negative.*

The value of the swaption contract is only recorded (unless and until exercised, of course, at which point it becomes a contractually binding swap) if it is positive, since if "out of the money" the holder would forego exercise in most instances and thus there is no liability by the holder to be reported. (This example is an illustration of the opposite, however, as despite having a negative value the option holder determines that exercise is advisable.) At June 30, 2006, for example, the swaption is an asset, since the reference variable rate (prime + 1/2% or 8.5%) is greater than the fixed swap rate of 8%, and thus the expectation is that the option will be exercised at expiration. This would, if present rates hold steady, which is the naïve assumption, result in a series of eight semiannual payments from the swap counterparty in the amount of $12,500. Discounting this at a nominal 8%, the present value as of the debt origination date (to be June 30, 2007) would be $84,159, which, when further discounted to June 30, 2006, yields a fair value of $77,925.

Note that the following period (December 31, 2006) prime drops to such an extent that the value of the swaption evaporates entirely (actually goes negative, which will not be reported since the holder is under no obligation to exercise it), and the carrying value is therefore eliminated. At expiration, the holder does (for this example) exercise, notwithstanding a negative fair value, and from that point forward the fair value of the swap will be reported, whether positive (an asset) or negative (a liability).

As noted above, assume that, at the option expiration date, despite the fact that prime + 1/2% is below the fixed pay rate on the swap, the management of Abbott Corp. is convinced that rates will climb over the four-year term of the loan, and thus exercises the swaption at that date. Accounting journal entries over the six years are as follows:

June 30, 2005

Swaption contract	25,000	
Cash		25,000

To record purchase premium on swaption contract

December 31, 2005

Loss on hedging transaction	6,250	
Swaption contract		6,250

To record change in time value of swaption contract—charge premium to income since this represents payment for time value of money, which expires ratably over two-year term

June 30, 2006

Swaption contract	77,925	
Other comprehensive income		77,925
To record the fair value of the swaption contract as of this date		
Loss on hedging transaction	6,250	
Swaption contract		6,250
To record change in time value of swaption contract—charge premium to income since this represents payment for time value of money, which expires ratably over two-year term		

December 31, 2006

Other comprehensive income	77,925	
Swaption contract		77,925
To record the change in fair value of the swaption contract as of this date; since contract is "out of the money," it is not written down below zero (i.e., a net liability is not reported)		
Loss on hedging transaction	6,250	
Swaption contract		6,250
To record change in time value of swaption contract—charge premium to income since this represents payment for time value of money, which expires ratably over two-year term		

June 30, 2007

Other comprehensive income	84,159	
Swap contract		84,159
To record the fair value of the swap contract as of this date—a net liability is reported since swap option was exercised		
Loss on hedging transaction	6,250	
Swaption contract		6,250
To record change in time value of swaption contract—charge premium to income since this represents payment for time value of money, which expires ratably over two-year term		

December 31, 2007

Interest expense	200,000	
Accrued interest (or cash)		200,000
To accrue or pay interest on the debt at the variable rate of prime + 1/2% (8.0%)		
Interest expense	0	
Accrued interest (or cash)		0
To record net settlement on swap arrangement [8.0 - 8.0%]		
Swap contract	84,159	
Other comprehensive income		84,159
To record the change in the fair value of the swap contract as of this date		

June 30, 2008

Interest expense	212,500	
Accrued interest (or cash)		212,500
To accrue or pay interest on the debt at the variable rate of prime + 1/2% (8.5%)		
Receivable from counterparty (or cash)	12,500	
Interest expense		12,500
To record net settlement on swap arrangement [8.0 - 8.5%]		
Swap contract	65,527	
Other comprehensive income		65,527
To record the fair value of the swap contract as of this date		

December 31, 2008

Interest expense	225,000	
Accrued interest (or cash)		225,000
To accrue or pay interest on the debt at the variable rate of prime + 1/2% (9.0%)		
Receivable from counterparty (or cash)	25,000	
Interest expense		25,000
To record net settlement on swap arrangement [8.0 - 9.0%]		

Swap contract	45,769	
Other comprehensive income		45,769
To record the fair value of the swap contract as of this date		

June 30, 2009

Interest expense	212,500	
Accrued interest (or cash)		212,500
To accrue or pay interest on the debt at the variable rate of prime + 1/2% (8.5%)		
Receivable from counterparty (or cash)	12,500	
Interest expense		12,500
To record net settlement on swap arrangement [8.0 - 8.5%]		
Other comprehensive income	65,922	
Swap contract		65,922
To record the change in the fair value of the swap contract as of this date (declining prime rate causes swap to lose value)		

December 31, 2009

Interest expense	212,500	
Accrued interest (or cash)		212,500
To accrue or pay interest on the debt at the variable rate of prime + 1/2% (8.5%)		
Receivable from counterparty (or cash)	12,500	
Interest expense		12,500
To record net settlement on swap arrangement [8.0 - 8.5%]		
Other comprehensive income	10,685	
Swap contract		10,685
To record the fair value of the swap contract as of this date (decline is due to passage of time, as the prime rate expectations have not changed from the earlier period)		

June 30, 2010

Interest expense	200,000	
Accrued interest (or cash)		200,000
To accrue or pay interest on the debt at the variable rate of prime + 1/2% (8.0%)		
Receivable from counterparty (or cash)	0	
Interest expense		0
To record net settlement on swap arrangement [8.0 - 8.0%]		
Other comprehensive income	34,689	
Swap contract		34,689
To record the decline in the fair value of the swap contract to zero as of this date		

December 31, 2010

Interest expense	200,000	
Accrued interest (or cash)		200,000
To accrue or pay interest on the debt at the variable rate of prime + 1/2% (8.0%)		
Receivable from counterparty (or cash)	0	
Interest expense		0
To record net settlement on swap arrangement [8.0 - 8.0%]		
Swap contract	0	
Other comprehensive income		0
No change to the zero fair value of the swap contract as of this date		

June 30, 2011 (Maturity)

Interest expense	187,500	
Accrued interest (or cash)		187,500
To accrue or pay interest on the debt at the variable rate of prime + 1/2% (7.5%)		
Interest expense	12,500	
Accrued interest (or cash)		12,500
To record net settlement on swap arrangement [8.0 - 7.5%]		
Other comprehensive income	0	
Swap contract		0
No change to the zero fair value of the swap contract, which expires as of this date		

Effectiveness of cash flow hedges. The assumption of no ineffectiveness in a cash flow hedge between an interest-bearing financial instrument and an interest rate swap can be assumed if all of the following conditions are met:

1. The principal amount and the notional amount of the swap match;
2. The fair value of the swap is zero at origin;
3. The net settlements under the swap are computed the same way on each settlement date;
4. The financial instrument is not prepayable; and
5. The terms are typical for those instruments and don't invalidate the assumption of effectiveness.
6. All variable rate interest payments or receipts on the instrument during the swap term are designated as hedged and none beyond that term;
7. No floor or cap on the variable rate of the swap exists unless the variable rate instrument has one. If the instrument does, the swap must have a comparable (not necessarily equal) one;
8. Repricing dates match; and
9. The index base for the variable rates match.

The variable rate on the instrument is not required to exactly match the variable rate on the swap. The fixed and variable rates on the swap can be changed by the same amount.

Example of using options to hedge future purchase of inventory

Friendly Chemicals Corp. uses petroleum as a feedstock from which it produces a range of chemicals for sale to producers of synthetic fabrics and other consumer goods. It is concerned about the rising price of oil and decides to hedge a major purchase it plans to make in mid-2005. Oil futures and options are traded on the New York Mercantile exchange and other markets; Friendly decides to use options rather than futures because it is only interested in protecting itself from a price increase; if prices decline, it wishes to reap that benefit rather than suffer the loss which would result from holding a futures contract in a declining market environment.

At December 31, 2005, Friendly projects a need for ten million barrels of crude oil of a defined grade to be purchased by mid-2006; this will suffice for production through mid-2007. The current world price for this grade of crude is $14.50 per barrel, but prices have been rising recently. Management desires to limit its crude oil costs to no higher than $15.75 per barrel, and accordingly purchases, at a cost of $2 million, an option to purchase up to ten million barrels at a cost of $15.55 per barrel (which, when added to the option premium, would make the total cost $15.75 per barrel if the full ten million barrels are acquired), at any time through December 2006.

Management has studied the behavior of option prices and has concluded that changes in option prices which relate to time value are not correlated to price changes and hence are ineffective in hedging price changes. On the other hand, changes in option prices which pertain to pricing changes (intrinsic value changes) are highly effective as hedging vehicles. The table below reports the value of these options, analyzed in terms of time value and intrinsic value, over the period from December 2005 through December 2006.

Date	Price of oil/barrel	Fair value of option relating to Time value*	Intrinsic value
December 31, 2005	$14.50	$2,000,000	$ 0
January 31, 2006	14.90	1,900,000	0
February 28, 2006	15.30	1,800,000	0
March 31, 2006	15.80	1,700,000	2,500,000
April 30, 2006	16.00	1,600,000	4,500,000
May 31, 2006	15.85	1,500,000	3,000,000
June 30, 2006**	16.00	700,000	2,250,000
July 31, 2006	15.60	650,000	250,000
August 31, 2006	15.50	600,000	0
September 30, 2006	15.75	550,000	1,000,000
October 31, 2006	15.80	500,000	1,250,000
November 30, 2006	15.85	450,000	1,500,000
December 31, 2006***	15.90	400,000	1,750,000

* *This example does not address how the time value of options would be computed in practice.*
** *Options for five million barrels exercised; remainder held until end of December, then sold.*
*** *Values cited are immediately prior to sale of remaining options.*

At the end of June 2006, Friendly Chemicals exercises options for 5 million barrels, paying $15.55 per barrel for oil selling on the world markets for $16.00 each. It holds the remaining options until December, when it sells these for an aggregate price of $2.1 million, a slight discount to the nominal fair value at that date.

The inventory acquired in mid-2006 is processed and included in goods available for sale. Sales of these goods, in terms of the five million barrels of crude oil which were consumed in their production, are as follows:

Date	Equivalent barrels sold in month	Equivalent barrels on hand at month end
June 30, 2006	300,000	4,700,000
July 31, 2006	250,000	4,450,000
August 31, 2006	400,000	4,050,000
September 30, 2006	350,000	3,700,000
October 31, 2006	550,000	3,150,000
November 30, 2006	500,000	2,650,000
December 31, 2006	650,000	2,000,000

Based on the foregoing facts, the journal entries prepared on a **monthly** basis (for illustrative purposes) for the period December 2005 through December 2006 are as follows:

December 31, 2005

Option contract	2,000,000	
Cash		2,000,000

To record purchase premium on option contract for up to ten million barrels of oil at price of $15.55 per barrel

January 31, 2006

Loss on hedging transaction	100,000	
Option contract		100,000

To record change in time value of option contract—charge premium to income since this represents payment for time value of money, which expires ratably over two-year term and does not qualify for hedge accounting treatment

Option contract	0	
Other comprehensive income		0

To reflect change in intrinsic value of option contracts (no value at this date)

February 28, 2006

Loss on hedging transaction	100,000	
Option contract		100,000

To record change in time value of option contract—charge premium to income since this represents payment for time value of money, which expires ratably over two-year term and does not qualify for hedge accounting treatment

Option contract	0	
Other comprehensive income		0

To reflect change in intrinsic value of option contracts (no value at this date)

March 31, 2006

Loss on hedging transaction	100,000	
Option contract		100,000

To record change in time value of option contract—charge premium to income since this represents payment for time value of money, which expires ratably over two-year term and does not qualify for hedge accounting treatment

Option contract	2,500,000	
Other comprehensive income		2,500,000

To reflect change in intrinsic value of option contracts

April 30, 2006

Loss on hedging transaction	100,000	
Option contract		100,000

To record change in time value of option contract—charge premium to income since this represents payment for time value of money, which expires ratably over two-year term and does not qualify for hedge accounting treatment

Option contract	2,000,000	
Other comprehensive income		2,000,000

To reflect change in intrinsic value of option contracts (further increase in value)

May 31, 2006

Loss on hedging transaction	100,000	
Option contract		100,000

To record change in time value of option contract—charge premium to income since this represents payment for time value of money, which expires ratably over two-year term and does not qualify for hedge accounting treatment

Other comprehensive income	1,500,000	
Option contract		1,500,000

To reflect change in intrinsic value of option contracts (decline in value)

June 30, 2006

Loss on hedging transaction	800,000	
Option contract		800,000

To record change in time value of option contract—charge premium to income since this represents payment for time value of money, which expires ratably over two-year term and does not qualify for hedge accounting treatment; since one-half the options were exercised in June, the remaining unexpensed time value of that portion is also entirely written off at this time

Option contract	1,500,000	
Other comprehensive income		1,500,000

To reflect change in intrinsic value of option contracts (further increase in value) ***before*** *accounting for exercise of options on five million barrels*

June 30 intrinsic value of options before exercise	4,500,000
Allocation to oil purchased at $15.55	2,250,000
Remaining intrinsic value of option	2,250,000

The allocation to exercised options will be maintained in other comprehensive income until transferred to cost of goods sold as a contra cost, as the five million barrels are sold, at the rate of 45¢ per equivalent barrel ($16.00 – $15.55).

Inventory	77,750,000	
Cash (or accounts payable)		77,750,000

To record purchase of five million barrels of oil at option price of $15.55/barrel

Inventory	2,250,000	
Option contract		2,250,000

To increase the recorded value of the inventory to include the fair value of options given up (exercised) in acquiring the oil (taken together, the cash purchase price and the fair value of options surrendered add to $16 per barrel, the world market price at date of purchase)

Cost of goods sold	4,800,000	
Inventory		4,800,000

To record cost of goods sold (300,000 barrels at $16) before amortizing deferred hedging gain in other comprehensive income

Other comprehensive income	135,000	
Cost of goods sold		135,000

To amortize deferred hedging gain at rate of 45¢ per barrel sold

July 31, 2006

Loss on hedging transaction	50,000	
Option contract		50,000

To record change in time value of option contract—charge premium to income since this represents payment for time value of money, which expires ratably over two-year term, and does not qualify for hedge accounting treatment

Other comprehensive income	2,000,000	
Option contract		2,000,000

To reflect change in intrinsic value of remaining option contracts (decline in value)

Cost of goods sold	4,000,000	
Inventory		4,000,000

To record cost of goods sold (250,000 barrels at $16) before amortizing deferred hedging gain in other comprehensive income

Other comprehensive income	112,500	
Cost of goods sold		112,500

To amortize deferred hedging gain at rate of 45¢ per barrel sold

August 31, 2006

Loss on hedging transaction	50,000	
Option contract		50,000

To record change in time value of option contract—charge premium to income since this represents payment for time value of money, which expires ratably over two-year term, and does not qualify for hedge accounting treatment

Other comprehensive income	250,000	
Option contract		250,000

To reflect change in intrinsic value of remaining option contracts (decline in value to zero)

Cost of goods sold	6,400,000	
Inventory		6,400,000

To record cost of goods sold (400,000 barrels at $16) before amortizing deferred hedging gain in other comprehensive income

Other comprehensive income	180,000	
Cost of goods sold		180,000

To amortize deferred hedging gain at rate of 45¢ per barrel sold

September 30, 2006

Loss on hedging transaction	50,000	
Option contract		50,000

To record change in time value of option contract—charge premium to income since this represents payment for time value of money, which expires ratably over two-year term, and does not qualify for hedge accounting treatment

Option contract	1,000,000	
Other comprehensive income		1,000,000

To reflect change in intrinsic value of remaining option contracts (increase in value)

Cost of goods sold	5,600,000	
Inventory		5,600,000

To record cost of goods sold (350,000 barrels at $16) before amortizing deferred hedging gain in other comprehensive income

Other comprehensive income	157,500	
Cost of goods sold		157,500

To amortize deferred hedging gain at rate of 45¢ per barrel sold

October 31, 2006

Loss on hedging transaction	50,000	
Option contract		50,000

To record change in time value of option contract—charge premium to income since this represents payment for time value of money, which expires ratably over two-year term, and does not qualify for hedge accounting treatment

Option contract	250,000	
Other comprehensive income		250,000

To reflect change in intrinsic value of remaining option contracts (further increase in value)

Cost of goods sold	8,800,000	
Inventory		8,800,000

To record cost of goods sold (550,000 barrels at $16) before amortizing deferred hedging gain in other comprehensive income

Other comprehensive income	247,500	
Cost of goods sold		247,500

To amortize deferred hedging gain at rate of 45¢ per barrel sold

November 30, 2006

Loss on hedging transaction	50,000	
Option contract		50,000

To record change in time value of option contract—charge premium to income since this represents payment for time value of money, which expires ratably over two-year term, and does not qualify for hedge accounting treatment

Option contract	250,000	
Other comprehensive income		250,000

To reflect change in intrinsic value of remaining option contracts (further increase in value)

Cost of goods sold	8,000,000	
Inventory		8,000,000

To record cost of goods sold (500,000 barrels at $16) before amortizing deferred hedging gain in other comprehensive income

Other comprehensive income	225,000	
Cost of goods sold		225,000

To amortize deferred hedging gain at rate of 45¢ per barrel sold

December 31, 2006

Loss on hedging transaction	50,000	
Option contract		50,000

To record change in time value of option contract—charge premium to income since this represents payment for time value of money, which expires ratably over two-year term, and does not qualify for hedge accounting treatment

Option contract	250,000	
Other comprehensive income		250,000

To reflect change in intrinsic value of remaining option contracts (further increase in value) before sale of options

Cost of goods sold	10,400,000	
Inventory		10,400,000

To record cost of goods sold (650,000 barrels at $16) before amortizing deferred hedging gain in other comprehensive income

Other comprehensive income	292,500	
Cost of goods sold		292,500
To amortize deferred hedging gain at rate of 45¢ per barrel sold		
Cash	2,100,000	
Loss on sale of options	50,000	
Option contract		2,150,000
Other comprehensive income	1,750,000	
Gain on sale of options		1,750,000

To record sale of remaining option contracts; the cash price was $50,000 lower than carrying value of asset sold (options having unexpired time value of $400,000 plus intrinsic value of $1,750,000), but transfer of other comprehensive income to income recognizes formerly deferred gain; since no further inventory purchases are planned in connection with this hedging activity, the unrealized gain is taken into income

Note that at December 31, 2006, other comprehensive income has a remaining credit balance of $900,000, which represents the deferred gain pertaining to the two million equivalent barrels of oil in inventory. As this is sold, the other comprehensive income will be transferred to cost of goods sold as a reduction of cost of sales.

Discontinuance of a cash flow hedge. The accounting for a cash flow hedge should not continue if any of the events below occur.

1. The criteria are no longer met;
2. The derivative instrument expires or is sold, terminated or exercised; or
3. The designation is removed by management.

The net gain or loss in accumulated other comprehensive income should remain there until it is properly reclassified when the hedged transaction affects earnings. If it is probable that the original forecasted transactions won't occur, the net gain or loss in accumulated other comprehensive income should immediately be reclassified into earnings.

If the cash flow hedge is discontinued, a new hedging relationship may be designated with a different hedging instrument and/or a different hedged item as long as the criteria established in FAS 133 are met.

Ineffectiveness of a cash flow hedge. In assessing the effectiveness of a cash flow hedge, the time value of money generally will need to be considered, if significant in the circumstances. Doing so becomes especially important if the hedging instrument involves periodic cash settlements. For example, a **tailing strategy** with futures contracts is a situation in which an entity likely would reflect the time value of money. When employing such a strategy, the entity adjusts the size or contract amount of futures contracts used in a hedge so that earnings (or expense) from reinvestment (or funding) of daily settlement gains (or losses) on the futures do not distort the results of the hedge. To assess offset of expected cash flows when a tailing strategy has been used, an entity could reflect the time value of money, possibly comparing the present value of the hedged forecasted cash flow with the results of the hedging instrument.

As with fair value hedges, FAS 133 does not provide a quantitative definition of **hedging effectiveness** for cash flow hedges. Again, it is useful in this regard to contemplate the similar international accounting standard, IAS 39, which specifies that a hedge is regarded as highly effective if, at inception and throughout the life of the hedge, the enterprise can expect that the change in cash flows of the hedging instrument and the hedged item will "almost fully offset." Actual results within a range of 80-125% could reasonably be expected to qualify as effective.

Impairment. All assets or liabilities designated as cash flow hedges are subject to normal GAAP requirements for impairment. Those requirements are to be applied, however, after hedge accounting has been applied for the period. Since the hedging instrument is a separate asset or liability, its expected cash flow or fair value is not considered in applying the impairment criteria to the hedged item. If an impairment loss or recovery on a hedged forecasting asset or liability is recognized, any offsetting amount should be immediately reclassified from accumulated other comprehensive income into earnings.

Expanded application of interest rate hedging. FAS 138 amended FAS 133 to permit the use of hedge accounting where the interest rate being hedged is the "benchmark interest rate." As used in the standard, this rate will be either the risk-free rate (i.e., that applicable to direct Treasury borrowings) or the LIBOR swap rate. LIBOR-based swaps in fact are the most commonly employed interest rate hedging vehicles, and it was the persistence of requests made to the FASB's derivatives implementation group regarding the application of hedge accounting to such swaps that resulted in this amendment.

The FASB has thus concluded that, with respect to the separation of interest rate risk and credit risk, the risk of changes in credit sector spread and any credit spread attributable to a specific borrower should be encompassed in credit risk rather than interest rate risk. Under such an approach, an entity would be permitted to designate the risk of changes in the risk-free rate as the hedged risk, and any spread above that rate would be deemed to reflect credit risk. The Board concluded that considering all the effects of credit risk together was more understandable and more operational than this distinction between interest rate risk and credit risk that was at first set forth in the implementation guidance for FAS 133.

FAS 138 requires that all contractual cash flows be used in determining the changes in fair value of the hedged item when benchmark interest rates are being employed. In other words, cash flows pertaining to the portion of interest payments which is related to the entity's credit risk (the risk premium over the benchmark rate) cannot be excluded from the computation.

The accounting for an interest rate hedge using a benchmark rate is very similar to that illustrated beginning on page 190 of this chapter. However, the variable rate used, rather than reflecting the credit riskiness of the party doing the hedging (which was prime + ½% in that illustration), would instead be the benchmark rate (e.g., the rate on Treasury five-year notes). Since changes in the benchmark rate might not exactly track the changes in the underlying instrument (due to changes in the "credit spread" which are a reflection of changes in the underlying party's perceived credit risk), the hedge will likely be imperfect, such that a net gain or loss will be reflected in periodic earnings.

Foreign Currency Hedges

The FASB's basic objectives in hedge accounting for foreign currency exposure are

1. To continue to permit the hedge accounting required under FAS 52; and
2. To increase the consistency of accounting guidance by broadening the scope of hedges that are eligible for this treatment.

Unlike FAS 52, this standard allows hedges of forecasted foreign currency transactions, including some intercompany transactions. Hedging foreign currency intercompany cash flows with foreign currency options is a common practice that is allowed under certain conditions by EITF 91-1. FAS 133 modifies that accounting to permit using other derivative instruments (forward contracts, etc.) because the accounting for all derivative instruments should be the same.

FAS 133 precluded hedge accounting for an asset or liability that is remeasured for changes in price attributable to the risk being hedged when those changes are reported currently in earnings. It also precluded fair value or cash flow hedge accounting for foreign currency risk associated with any asset or liability that is denominated in a foreign currency and remeasured into the functional currency under FAS 52. Subsequently, the FASB considered removing the preclusion for any asset or the liability denominated in a foreign currency because, even though the transaction gain or loss on the undesignated asset or liability and the change in fair value of the undesignated derivative were reported currently in earnings, different measurement criteria were used for each instrument, which created volatility in earnings. It eventually decided to permit all recognized foreign-currency-denominated assets and liabilities for which a foreign currency transaction gain or loss is recognized in earnings to be hedged items.

Designated hedging instruments and hedged items qualify for fair value hedge accounting and cash flow hedge accounting under FAS 138 only if all of the criteria in FAS 133 for fair value hedge accounting and cash flow hedge accounting are met. The FASB concluded that fair value hedges could be used for all recognized foreign-currency-denominated asset or liability hedging situations and that cash flow hedges could be used for recognized foreign-currency-denominated asset or liability hedging situations in which all of the variability in the functional-currency-equivalent cash flows are eliminated by the effect of the hedge. Remeasurement of the foreign-currency-denominated assets and liabilities will continue to be based on the guidance in FAS 52, which requires remeasurement based on spot exchange rates, regardless of whether a fair value hedging relationship or a cash flow hedging relationship exists.

Foreign currency net investment hedge. Either a derivative instrument or a nonderivative financial instrument (that can result in a foreign currency transaction gain or loss under FAS 52) can be designated as a hedge of a foreign currency exposure of a net investment in a foreign operation. The gain or loss from the designated instrument to the extent that it is effective is reported as a translation adjustment. The hedged net investment is accounted for under FAS 52.

Foreign currency unrecognized firm commitment hedge. Either a derivative instrument or a nonderivative financial instrument (that can result in a foreign currency transaction gain or loss under FAS 52) can be designated as a fair value hedge of an unrecognized firm commitment (or a specific portion) attributable to foreign currency. If the criteria are met, this hedging relationship is accounted for as a fair value hedge. (An example appears in Chapter 21.)

Foreign currency available-for-sale security hedge. Only a derivative instrument can be designated as a fair value hedge of an available-for-sale **debt** security (or a specific portion) attributable to foreign currency. If the criteria are met, this hedging relationship is accounted for as a fair value hedge. For an available-for-sale **equity** security to be accounted for as a fair value hedge, it must meet all of the fair value hedge criteria **and** the following two requirements:

1. The security **cannot** be traded on an exchange (or similar marketplace) denominated in the investor's functional currency; and
2. Dividends (or other cash flows) to the holders must be denominated in the same foreign currency as that expected to be received upon the sale of the security.

If the available-for-sale equity security qualifies as a foreign currency hedge, the change in fair value from foreign exchange risk is reported in earnings and not in other comprehensive income.

Any gain or loss on a designated nonderivative hedging instrument from foreign currency risk is determined under FAS 52 (as the increase or decrease in functional currency cash flows produced by the change in spot exchange rates) and is reported in earnings along with the change in the carrying amount of the hedged firm commitment.

Foreign-currency-denominated forecasted transaction. Only a derivative instrument can be designated as a cash flow hedge of a foreign-currency-denominated forecasted transaction. The parties to this transaction can either be external or intercompany. To qualify for hedge accounting, **all** of the following criteria must be met:

1. An operating unit with foreign currency exposure is a party to the derivative instrument;
2. The transaction is denominated in a currency that is **not** the functional currency;
3. All of the criteria for a cash flow hedge are met (with the possible exception of allowing a qualifying intercompany transaction); and
4. If a group of individual transactions is involved, both an inflow and an outflow of foreign currency cannot be included in the same group.

If the foregoing criteria are met, this hedging relationship is accounted for as a cash flow hedge.

Using certain intercompany derivatives as hedging instruments in cash flow hedges of foreign currency risk in the consolidated financial statements. FAS 138 has amended FAS 133 to permit the use of intercompany derivatives as the hedging instruments in cash flow hedges of foreign currency risk in the consolidated financial statements, if those intercompany derivatives are offset by unrelated third-party contracts on a net basis. The new standard defines an "internal derivative" as a foreign currency derivative contract that has been entered into with another member of a consolidated group and which can be a hedging instrument in a foreign currency cash flow hedge of a forecasted borrowing, purchase, or sale or an unrecognized firm commitment in the consolidated financial statements only if the following two conditions are satisfied. First, from the perspective of the member of the consolidated group using the derivative as a hedging instrument, specific criteria for foreign currency cash flow hedge accounting are satisfied. Second, the members of the consolidated group who are not using the derivative as a hedging instrument must either (1) enter into a derivative contract with an unrelated third party to offset the exposure that results from that internal derivative or (2) if certain defined conditions are met, enter into derivative contracts with unrelated third parties that would offset, on a net basis for each foreign currency, the foreign exchange risk arising from multiple internal derivative contracts.

Organizations That Do Not Report Earnings

Not-for-profits or other organizations not reporting earnings should recognize gains or losses on nonhedging derivative instruments and hedging instruments as a change in net assets. Changes in the carrying amount of the hedged items are also recognized as a change in net assets.

Organizations that do not report earnings cannot use cash flow hedges. If the hedging instrument is a foreign currency net investment hedge, it is accounted for in the same manner as described above.

Summary of Accounting for Hedges

		Type of hedge—FAS 133	
Attribute	*Fair value*	*Cash flow*	*Foreign currency (FC)*
Types of hedging instruments permitted	Derivatives	Derivatives	Derivatives or nonderivatives depending on the type of hedge
Balance sheet valuation of hedging instrument	Fair value	Fair value	Fair value
Recognition of gain or loss on changes in value of hedging instrument	Currently in earnings	Effective portion currently as a component of other comprehensive income (OCI) and reclassified to earnings in future period(s) that forecasted transaction affects earnings Ineffective portion currently in earnings	**FC denominated firm commitment** Currently in earnings **Available-for-sale security (AFS)** Currently in earnings **Forecasted FC transaction** Same as cash flow hedge **Net investment in a foreign operation** OCI as part of the cumulative translation adjustment to the extent it is effective as a hedge
Recognition of gain or loss on changes in the fair value of the hedged item	Currently in earnings	Not applicable; these hedges are not associated with recognized assets or liabilities	**FC denominated firm commitment** Currently in earnings **Available-for-sale security (AFS)** Currently in earnings **Forecasted FC transaction** Not applicable; same as cash flow hedge

Disclosures

FAS 133 requires certain disclosures for derivative instruments and nonderivative instruments designated and qualifying as hedging instruments. Specifically required are the objectives for holding or issuing the instruments, the context needed to understand the objectives, the strategies for achieving them, the risk management policy and a description of items or transactions which are hedged for each of the following:

1. Fair value hedges;
2. Cash flow hedges;
3. Foreign currency net investment hedges; and
4. All other derivatives.

Derivative instruments not designated as hedges are to have the purpose of their activity disclosed. Qualitative disclosures concerning the use of derivative instruments are encouraged, particularly in a context of overall risk management strategies employed by the entity. The FASB also encourages disclosure of similar quantitative information about other nonderivative financial instruments or nonfinancial assets and liabilities related by activity to derivative instruments.

Hedge disclosures. In addition to the above, for every reporting period for which a complete set of financial statements is issued, there are required disclosures by hedge type.

Fair value hedges. For all designated and qualified instruments and the related hedged items that give rise to foreign currency transaction gains or losses under FAS 52, disclosure is required of the net gain or loss included in earnings, a description of where it is reported, and the amounts due to

1. Hedge ineffectiveness;
2. Components that were excluded from the assessment of effectiveness; and
3. Hedged firm commitments that no longer qualify as hedges.

Cash flow hedges. For all designated and qualified instruments and the related hedged items in cash flow hedges, the following are disclosed:

1. The net gain or loss in earnings, a description of where it is reported, and the amounts due to
    a. Hedge ineffectiveness; and
    b. Components that were excluded from the assessment of effectiveness;
2. A description of events that will result in reclassification of amounts in accumulated other comprehensive income to earnings and the net amount expected to be reclassified during the next twelve months;
3. The maximum length of time of any cash flow hedges of forecasted transactions (excluding those relating to payment of variable interest on existing financial instruments); and
4. The amount reclassified from accumulated other comprehensive income into earnings because a cash flow hedge was discontinued due to it being probable that the original forecasted transactions wouldn't occur.

Foreign currency net investment hedges. For all such designated and qualified instruments that give rise to foreign currency transaction gains or losses under FAS 52, the net gain or loss that is included in the cumulative translation adjustment.

Comprehensive income. The net gain or loss from cash flow hedges on derivative instruments reported in other comprehensive income must be shown as a separate classification. Accumulated other comprehensive income disclosures should show separately the following:

1. Beginning and ending accumulated derivative instrument gain or loss;
2. Net change from current period hedging transactions; and
3. Net amount of reclassifications to earnings.

Transition

When FAS 133 was initially applied, great efforts were often required to identify all freestanding derivative instruments to be recognized as assets or liabilities, and to measure these at their respective fair values. Certain elections were also possible, such as that permitting (but not requiring) the separation of compound derivative instruments composed of a foreign currency derivative and another derivative into two parts, with each accounted for at fair value not to exceed the aggregate the fair value of the compound derivative instrument. The then-existing differences between fair values and carrying amounts were to be reported as transition adjustments.

At transition, offsetting gains and losses on hedged assets, liabilities, and firm commitments were to be recognized by adjusting their respective carrying amounts. Deferred losses or gains on derivative instruments that were to be reported as assets or liabilities were derecognized and reported as transition adjustments. Gains or losses on derivative instruments reported in other comprehensive income as fair value hedges of available-for-sale securities were also to be reported as part of the transition adjustment. On the other hand, gains or losses on derivative instruments reported in accumulated other comprehensive income because of cash flow hedges of a forecasted transaction related to available-for-sale securities were to remain in accumulated other comprehensive income and were not to be reported in the transition adjustment.

Gains or losses on derivative instruments that adjusted the carrying amounts of recognized hedged assets or liabilities prior to initial application were not affected and were not reported in transition adjustments.

Regarding embedded derivatives, the reporting entity was allowed to elect to either (1) recognize as assets or liabilities all embedded derivatives required to be separated from their host contracts or (2) select from defined alternate transition dates for the embedded derivatives. If the entity chose option (2), it had to recognize as separate assets and/or liabilities only derivatives embedded in hybrid instruments issued, acquired, or substantively modified by the entity on or after the selected transition date. This election was to be applied on an "all-or-none" basis and was not to be applied selectively to hybrid instruments. Other detailed rules applied if the embedded derivatives were separated.

The transition adjustments were to be reported in net income or in other comprehensive income, as appropriate, and deemed to be a cumulative effect of a change in accounting principle under APB 20. How the derivative instrument had been accounted for under prior GAAP was the determining factor for reporting the transition adjustment in earnings, in other comprehensive income, or as allocated between both. All other transition adjustments were to be reported as cumulative effect adjustments of net income.

Transition adjustment amounts reported as cumulative effect adjustments of accumulated other comprehensive income were to be subsequently reclassified into earnings in the normal manner under FAS 133. When initially applied, the amounts of gains and losses from the transition adjustment being reclassified from accumulated other comprehensive income into earnings during the next twelve months needed to be disclosed.

At initial application, held-to-maturity securities (including financial assets received or retained in a previous desecuritization) could have been transferred to the available-for-sale or trading categories without calling into question the intent to hold other debt securities to maturity in the future. This movement was potentially desirable so that the security or some component (interest rates, fair value, etc.) of it could be designated as the hedged item. The unrealized holding gain or loss was to be reported as required by FAS 115 and included in the transition adjustment discussed above.

At initial application of FAS 133, available-for-sale securities could have been transferred to the trading category. After any related transition adjustment had been recognized, any remaining unrealized holding gain or loss was to be reclassified into earnings (not as a transition adjustment) as required by FAS 115. If a derivative instrument was being used as a hedge of cash flows associated with a forecasted transaction related to an available-for-sale security transferred into the trading category upon adoption, and the entity had reported a gain or loss in other comprehensive income, the gain or loss would have been reclassified into earnings (not as a transition adjustment) upon transfer.

With regard to servicing rights, for contracts in existence before January 1997, the previously recognized servicing rights and "excess servicing" receivables, to the extent these did not exceed the contractually specified servicing fees, were to be combined and reported net as a servicing asset or liability. Any excess over the contractually agreed fees was required to be reclassified as an "interest-only strip" and the subsequent remeasurement provisions of FAS 140 were to be separately applied to the servicing asset and the interest-only strip.

EMERGING ISSUES TASK FORCE ISSUES SUMMARIES

Short-Term Investments

85-9 Revenue Recognition of Options to Purchase Stock of Another Entity

If debt is issued with detachable warrants to acquire the stock of **another** entity, no income should be recognized until the warrant is exercised or expires and a liability should be recorded for the value of the warrant. No consensus was reached on the accounting for exchangeable debt. In practice, most accountants follow APB 14. The SEC observer, however, did not believe APB 14 was applicable and thought that separation was required.

86-40 Investments in Open-End Mutual Funds That Invest in US Government Securities

The investment in the mutual fund should be at fair value per FAS 115.

96-11 Accounting for Forward Contracts and Purchased Options to Acquire Securities Covered by FASB Statement 115

This issue addresses the accounting only when terms require physical settlement. Forward contracts and purchased options with no intrinsic value at acquisition should be designated and accounted for as prescribed in FAS 115.

96-12 Recognition of Interest Income and Balance Sheet Classification of Structured Notes

When recognizing interest income on structured note securities in an available-for-sale or held-to-maturity portfolio, the retrospective interest method should be used if three conditions are satisfied. These are

1. Either the original investment amount or the maturity amount of the contractual principal is at risk
2. Return of investment on note is subject to volatility arising from
   a. No stated rate or stated rate is not a constant percentage or in same direction as changes in market-based interest rates or interest rate index, or
   b. Fixed or variable coupon rate is lower than that for interest for traditional notes with similar maturity and a portion of potential yield is based on occurrence of future circumstances or events
3. Contractual maturity of bond is based on a specific index or on occurrence of specific events or situations outside the control of contractual parties

96-15 Accounting for the Effects of Changes in Foreign Currency Exchange Rates on Foreign-Currency-Denominated Available-for-Sale Debt Securities (AFS)

Total changes in fair value of foreign-currency-denominated AFS debt securities should be reported in stockholders' equity.

Foreign currency transaction losses and gains arising from a foreign-currency-denominated liability or forward exchange contract should be reported in the FAS 115 component of stockholders' equity. Then, it would offset the change in market value of a foreign-currency-denominated AFS debt security if the foreign-currency-denominated AFS debt security or forward exchange contract is either identified or does serve as a hedge of the foreign-currency-denominated AFS debt security.

Options

90-17 Hedging Foreign Currency Risks with Purchased Options

FAS 52 foreign currency risk is risk associated with transactions and commitments in currencies other than the transacting entity's functional currency. Hedge accounting is appropriate for purchased foreign currency options used to hedge an anticipated transaction if the conditions of FAS 80 are met. Specifically

1. The hedged item must expose the entity to foreign currency risks.
2. The option must be designated as a hedge and must reduce exposure to risk.
3. Expected terms and significant characteristics of the transaction must be identified.
4. It is probable that the transaction will occur.

Consensus was reached that purchased options having little or no intrinsic value at the time designated as a hedge and meeting the high correlation criteria **would** qualify for hedge accounting in the following situations:

1. Hedging foreign export sales
2. Hedging identifiable anticipated transactions with risk

The above options would **not** qualify for hedge accounting in the following situations:

1. Hedging foreign subsidiary sales
2. Hedging anticipated transactions with no enterprise risk
3. Hedging net income
4. Hedging competitive risk

The propriety of hedge accounting for "anticipated sales for several years" depends on the assessment of the transaction using FAS 80 criteria. The further into the future the transaction is expected, the less likely it will meet the criteria.

Foreign Currency Forwards

86-25 Offsetting Foreign Currency Swaps

The currency swap accrual cannot be netted against the foreign currency debt. They are separate transactions without the right of setoff.

87-2 Net Present Value Method of Valuing Speculative Foreign Exchange Contracts

Discounting is allowed but not required in applying para 19 of FAS 52.

87-26 Hedging of a Foreign Currency Exposure with a Tandem Currency

A tandem currency may not be used to hedge a net investment in a foreign subsidiary only because it is less expensive. FAS 52 phrases "practical" or "feasible" refer to the availability of a hedging investment.

Swaps

84-7 Termination of Interest Rate Swaps

If accounted for as a hedge, terminated interest rate swaps should not be recognized immediately in income. Instead, the accounting should follow FAS 80 and the gain or loss should be deferred until the offsetting gain or loss on the hedged transaction is recognized. No consensus was reached on nonhedge transactions.

88-8 Mortgage Swaps

The notional amount of mortgage-backed securities and the related debt in a mortgage swap are similar to an executory contract and should not be recognized at the inception of the transaction. Except for mortgage swaps that qualify for hedge accounting, it is appropriate to recognize subsequent changes in the market value (at market or the lower of cost or market) of the swap over its term in a manner consistent with the company's accounting for similar investments. Consensus was reached that hedge accounting is appropriate if hedge criteria under GAAP are met. The SEC observer noted that mortgage swap hedges should be accounted for by financial institutions in the trading account and would be recorded at market value.

Other Financial Instruments

84-14 Deferred Interest Rate Setting

If the deferred rate setting agreement is an integral part (i.e., must be with the underwriter of the debt) of the original issuance of debt, any cash receipt or cash payment should be accounted for over the term of the debt as a yield adjustment to interest expense.

86-24 Third-Party Establishment of Collateralized Mortgage Obligations (CMO)

The sale of mortgages to an unrelated third party which then uses them as collateral to issue CMO should be accounted for as a sale. The gain or loss from the sale should be recognized in the period of the transaction and should include the present value of the residual interest if it can be reliably estimated. The recognition phase of the FASB's project on financial instruments will address this issue.

86-28 Accounting Implications of Indexed Debt Instruments

The issuer is required to allocate the proceeds between the investor's right to receive contingent payments and the debt instrument if the right is separable. No consensus was reached regarding a nonseparable right. As the index increases, a liability or an additional liability is required if the issuer must pay a contingent payment at maturity. The balance sheet date index value should be used and future changes should not be anticipated. If there were no proceeds initially allocated, any additional liability is an adjustment of the debt's carrying amount. Settlement by delivering the actual commodity fixes the issuer's cost of settlement. This issue is to be addressed as a part of the FASB's financial instrument project.

86-34 Futures Contracts Used as Hedges of Anticipated Reverse Repurchase Transactions

Gains or losses on futures contracts could qualify for FAS 80 hedge accounting if they reduce the interest rate risk and if the criteria of para 9 of FAS 80 is met. All relevant facts and circumstances should be considered.

Upon the sale of fixed-rate assets, if deferral criteria continue to be met, gains should be recognized while futures losses continue to be deferred. The future contracts were designated as hedges of the reverse repurchase liabilities.

If the hedge is terminated prior to the future issuance of short-term debt, the FAS 80 high correlation requirement is not applicable after discontinuance.

87-12 Foreign Debt-for-Equity Swaps

If the foreign government requires the proceeds to be invested in that country, the difference between the US dollar values of the two transactions should be used, first, to reduce the basis of long-lived assets acquired in compliance with the arrangement and, second, to reduce the basis of existing long-lived assets (starting with the fixed asset with the longest remaining life and following that order to the shortest remaining life) other than goodwill. If all long-lived assets are reduced to zero, the remaining excess is reported as negative goodwill.

87-30 Sale of a Short-Term Loan Made under a Long-Term Credit Commitment

If the long-term credit commitment contains a substantive **subjective** covenant, the transaction should be recorded as a sale. If it contains only **objective** covenants, it is only a sale if those covenants are substantive.

Substantive means that they are specific to the borrower and are expected to be meaningful and relevant. There was also consensus that long-term commitment fees should be recognized in accordance with FAS 91.

89-18 Divestitures of Certain Investment Securities to an Unregulated Commonly Controlled Entity under FIRREA

The transfer of securities to an affiliate at book value does **not** obviate the need for the savings association to account for the securities at fair value per FAS 115. The SEC observer noted that gain recognition would not be appropriate when the securities are sold to the affiliate.

95-5 Determination of What Risks and Rewards, if Any, Can Be Retained and Whether Any Unresolved Contingencies May Exist in a Sale of Mortgage Loan Servicing Rights

This consensus supersedes the consensus reached in Issue 89-5. If substantially all risks and rewards of ownership have irrevocably passed to the buyer and any protection provisions retained by the seller are minor and can be reasonably estimated, then sales of rights to service mortgage loans should be recognized at the date title passes. If a sale is recognized and minor protection provisions exist, a liability should be accrued for the estimated obligation associated with those protection provisions. Protection provisions are considered to be minor if (1) the provisions are no more than 10% of the sales price and (2) the risk of prepayment is retained for no longer than 120 days. Additionally, temporary subservicing agreements in which the subservicing will be performed by the seller for a short period of time will not necessarily preclude recognizing a sale at the closing date.

96-13 Accounting for Derivative Financial Instruments Indexed to, and Potentially Settled in, a Company's Own Stock

The consensuses reached in this EITF involve detailed illustrations of models applied to freestanding contracts that are indexed to, and potentially settled in, a company's own stock. Refer to the original consensus for detailed guidance.

99-2 Accounting for Weather Derivatives

The consensus addresses a new but rapidly growing risk management tool, weather derivative contracts. At issue was whether such contracts should be reported under accrual accounting, under settlement accounting, under insurance accounting, marked to fair value through earnings at each reporting date, or under some other method. Also at issue was whether the accounting for these derivatives should vary based on the type of contract. Past practice had been diverse.

FAS 133 provides that contracts that are not exchange traded are not subject to the requirements of that Statement if settlement is based on a climatic or geological variable or on some other physical variable. Any derivative based on a physical variable that eventually becomes exchange-traded automatically becomes subject to the requirements of FAS 133.

The Task Force consensus is that an entity that enters into a non-exchange-traded forward-based weather derivative in connection with nontrading activities should account for the contract by applying an "intrinsic value method." The intrinsic value method computes an amount based on the difference between the expected results from an upfront allocation of the cumulative strike and the actual results during a period, multiplied by the contract price (for example, dollars per heating degree day). The use of external statistical sources, such as the National Weather Service, is necessary in applying this technique.

Furthermore, the Task Force concluded that an entity that purchases a non-exchange-traded option-based weather derivative in connection with nontrading activities should amortize to expense the premium paid (or due) and apply the intrinsic value method to measure the contract at each interim balance sheet date. The premium asset should be amortized in a rational and systematic manner.

Also, it was decided that all entities that sell or write a non-exchange-traded option-based weather derivative should initially recognize the premium as a liability and recognize any subsequent changes in fair value currently in earnings (the premium would not be amortized).

The Task Force observed that a purchased or written weather derivative may contain an "embedded" premium or discount when the contract terms are not consistent with current market terms. In those circumstances, the premium or discount should be quantified, removed from the calculated benchmark strike, and accounted for as noted above.

Finally, the Task Force reached a consensus that all weather derivative contracts entered into under trading or speculative activities should be accounted for at their fair value, with subsequent changes in fair value reported currently in earnings.

99-3 Application of Issue No. 96-13 to Derivative Instruments with Multiple Settlement Alternatives

EITF 96-13 established a framework for accounting for freestanding derivative contracts that are indexed to, and potentially settled in, a company's own stock. The initial balance sheet classification generally is based on the concept that contracts that require net cash settlement are assets or liabilities and contracts that require settlement in shares are equity instruments. If the contract provides the issuer with a choice of net cash settlement or settlement in shares, the 96-13 model assumes settlement in shares; if the contract provides the counterparty with a choice of net cash settlement or settlement in shares, net cash settlement is assumed. It is unclear, however, how the issuer should account for a contract, indexed to and potentially settled in the issuer's stock, with multiple settlement alternatives if the settlement alternatives differ depending on whether the contract is in a gain or a loss position.

Accordingly, this issue deals with the matter of how certain contracts indexed to, and potentially settled in, a company's own stock, that contain multiple settlement alternatives should be accounted for.

The consensus is that a contract indexed to, and potentially settled in, the issuer's stock, with multiple settlement alternatives that require the issuer to receive net cash when the contract is in a gain position, but pay (1) net stock or (2) either net cash or net stock at the issuer's option when the contract is in a loss position should be accounted for as an equity instrument. The consensus does not apply to a contract that is predominantly a purchased option in which the amount of cash that could be received when the contract is in a gain position is significantly larger than the amount that could be paid when the contract is in a loss position because, for example, there is a small contractual limit on the amount of the loss; rather, those contracts should be accounted for as assets or liabilities.

A consensus was also reached that a contract indexed to, and potentially settled in, the issuer's stock, with multiple settlement alternatives that require the issuer to pay net cash when the contract is in a loss position, but receive (1) net stock or (2) either net cash or net stock at the issuer's option when the contract is in a gain position should be accounted for as an asset or a liability.

00-17 Measuring the Fair Value of Energy-Related Contracts in Applying EITF Issue No. 98-10, *Accounting for Contracts Involved in Energy Trading and Risk Management Activities*

Issue 00-17 provides guidance on measuring the fair value of energy-related contracts (energy transportation, storage, and tolling contracts) and the related energy purchase and sales contracts. Energy contracts, including energy-related contracts, should be reported at fair value on a stand-alone (individual) contract basis, using the best information available in the circumstances. The price at which a contract is exchanged is its initial fair value, although market transactions may provide for recognition of a "dealer's profit." Subsequent changes in fair values should be estimated using current market transactions, if available. If market transactions are not available, valuation techniques, including option-pricing models, should be used.

02-2 When Separate Contracts That Meet the Definition of Financial Instruments Should Be Combined for Accounting Purposes

This issue, not yet finalized, addresses situations in which entities enter into multiple contracts that individually meet the definition of a financial instrument under FAS 133, but for which the financial reporting impact of recording those contracts separately may be different from the impact of recording those contracts on a combined basis. Preliminarily, the sense is that two or more financial instruments should be required to be combined for accounting purposes if all of the following four criteria are met:

1. The transactions or contracts are with the same counterparties (or are structured through an intermediary).
2. The transactions or contracts are entered into in contemplation of one another.
3. The separate transactions or contracts share at least one underlying, and changes in that underlying (holding the prices of all other underlyings constant) result in at least one substantially offsetting change in fair value for those transactions or contracts.
4. The structure of the arrangement (separate contracts) does not serve a substantive business purpose that is fundamentally unrelated to the accounting (that is, the business purpose is not directly or indirectly based on the accounting result) and that could not have been accomplished in a single contact or transaction.

Any final consensus would likely include exceptions (e.g., for treasury functions commonly having multiple transactions with the same counterparties on a daily basis). The outcome of this issue may also impact the FASB's liability and equity project.

02-3 Issues Involved in Accounting for Derivative Contracts Held for Trading Purposes and Contracts Involved in Energy Trading and Risk Management Activities

Partially as a consequence of the Enron financial reporting scandal, EITF revisited the wisdom of permitting mark to market accounting for energy trading contracts, particularly where such contracts had no quoted market prices or current similar transactions. In Issue 00-17, EITF had held that valuation models, including options-pricing models, could be used to determine fair value, albeit only in the absence of market transactions. Also at issue were the matters of (1) recognizing unrealized gains (or losses) at the inception of such contracts and (2) gross or net presentation of gains and losses (whether realized or unrealized) would be appropriate.

EITF concluded that Issue 98-10 should be rescinded, and that energy contracts should not be marked to market value. It concluded, as well, that the common practice of carrying energy physical inventories at fair value had no basis under GAAP, unless so provided under higher-level GAAP. Furthermore, net presentation of gains and losses derived from derivatives is required under FAS 133, even if physical settlement occurs, if the derivatives are held for trading purposes (as that term is defined in FAS 115). It was also decided that a derivative held for trading purposes may be designated as a hedging instrument, if the FAS 133 criteria are all met, on a prospective basis (i.e., from date of the consensus), notwithstanding the FAS 133 prohibition on designation of derivative instruments held for trading as "hedges."

03-01 The Meaning of Other-than-Temporary Impairment and Its Application to Certain Investments

This Issue addressed the meaning of the long-employed criterion, other than temporary. Essentially, it is to be the refutable presumption that impairments of investments are indeed other than temporary, and thus (in the case of available-for-sale and held-to-maturity investments) are to be reported currently in results of operations, unless there is positive evidence to support the alternative contention—that the impairment is instead only temporary, and thus (for held-to-maturity investments) not to be recognized at all. A similar approach is also applicable to evaluation of impairments to equity method investments.

While no consensus has yet been achieved, the proposed guidance would hold that an investment would be considered impaired if its fair value is less than its amortized cost basis (hereinafter referred to as its carrying amount). For an investment with no readily determinable fair value, the fair value of the investment would be measured when an impairment indicator is present. Certain underlying principles would be established for determining whether an impairment is other than temporary. Thus, unless positive evidence indicating that an investment's carrying amount is recoverable within a reasonable period of time outweighs negative evidence to the contrary, an impairment would be deemed other than temporary.

Under the proposed guidance, if an investment has been impaired for one year, it would be unlikely that sufficient objective and verifiable positive evidence would be available to support the recoverability of the investment's carrying value to overcome the extent of the negative evidence, except for certain investments with noncontingent contractual future cash flows. That one-year period would not be a "bright-line" for purposes of determining whether an impairment is other than temporary.

Other guidance is expected to be developed to address impairment of debt securities, and how impairment criteria intersect with the classification of investments (i.e., whether the presumption that impairment continuing for longer than one year is other than temporary may be inconsistent with the held-to-maturity classification when there is not substantial doubt that the investor will collect all contractual interest and principal payments).

03-11 Reporting Realized Gains and Losses on Derivative Instruments That Are Subject to FASB Statement No. 133, *Accounting for Derivative Instruments and Hedging Activities,* and Not "Held for Trading Purposes," as Defined in EITF Issue No. 02-3, *Issues Involved in Accounting for Derivative Contracts Held for Trading Purposes and Contracts Involved in Energy Trading and Risk Management Activities*

The issue addressed is whether realized gains or losses on derivative contracts that are *not* held for trading purposes should be presented gross or net in the income statement irrespective of whether the derivative is designated as a hedging instrument.

The Task Force reached a consensus that determining whether realized gains and losses on physically settled derivative contracts *not* held for trading purposes should be reported in the income statement on a gross or net basis is a matter of judgment that depends on the relevant facts and circumstances. Consideration of the facts and circumstances should be made in the context of the various activities of the entity, and not based solely on the terms of the individual contracts. For making an evaluation of the facts and circumstances in order to determine whether an arrangement should be reported on a gross or net basis, EITF noted that the economic substance of the transaction as well as the guidance set forth in APB 29 relative to nonmonetary exchanges and the gross versus net reporting indicators provided in Issue 99-19 may be considered. The economic substance of the transaction should be given precedence over its legal form. This consensus has been ratified by FASB.

D-102 Documentation of the Method Used to Measure Hedge Ineffectiveness under FASB Statement No. 133

FAS 133 implies that an entity must document, at inception of a hedge, the method that will be used to measure hedge ineffectiveness (in addition to the method to be used to assess effectiveness) in order to meet the documentation requirements of the standard. In a staff announcement addressing the documentation requirements for all types of hedges—fair value, cash flow, and net investment hedges, the FASB has stated that formal documentation is required, at the inception of a hedge, of the hedging relationship and the entity's risk management objective and strategy for undertaking the hedge, including identification of

1. The hedging instrument,
2. The hedged item or transaction,
3. The nature of the risk being hedged,
4. The method that will be used to retrospectively and prospectively assess the hedging instrument's effectiveness, and
5. The method that will be used to measure hedge ineffectiveness.

These requirements were effective prospectively (from November 15, 2001) and would not cause hedging relationships entered into previously to be questioned due to lack of this required documentation.

7 INVENTORY

PERSPECTIVE AND ISSUES

The accounting for inventories is a major consideration for many entities because of its significance to both the income statement (cost of goods sold) and the balance sheet (current assets). Inventories are defined in ARB 43, Chapter 4 as

> *...those items of tangible personal property which are held for sale in the ordinary course of business, are in the process of production for such sale, or are to be currently consumed in the production of goods or services to be available for sale.*

The complexity of accounting for inventories arises from factors that include

1. The high volume of activity (or turnover) and the associated challenges of keeping accurate, up-to-date records.
2. Choosing from among various cost flow alternatives that are permitted by GAAP.
3. Ensuring compliance with complex US income tax laws and regulations when electing to use the last-in, first-out (LIFO) method.
4. Monitoring and properly accounting for adjustments necessitated by applying the lower of cost or market method to the inventory.

There are two types of entities for which the accounting for inventories is relevant. The merchandising entity (generally a retailer or wholesaler/distributor) purchases inventory for resale to its customers. The manufacturer buys **raw materials,** and processes those raw materials using labor and equipment into **finished goods** that are then sold to its customers. While the production process is progressing, the costs of the raw materials, salaries and wages paid to the labor force (and related benefits), depreciation of the machinery, and an allocated portion of the manufacturer's overhead are accumulated by the accounting system as **work in process** (WIP). Finished goods inventory is the completed product which is on hand awaiting shipment or sale.

In the case of either type of entity we are concerned with answering the same basic questions.

1. At what point in time should the items be included in inventory (ownership)?
2. What costs incurred should be included in the valuation of inventories?
3. What cost flow assumption should be used?
4. At what value should inventories be reported (LCM)?

ARB 43, Chapter 4 discusses the definition, valuation, and classification of inventory. APB 28 addresses the measurement and classification of inventories during interim periods. Finally, FAS 48 concerns revenue recognition when the buyer has the right to return the product, and FAS 49 addresses product financing arrangements.

Sources of GAAP				
ARB	*APB*	*FAS*	*EITF*	*PB*
43, Ch. 4; 51	20, 28, 29	48, 49	86-46	2

DEFINITIONS OF TERMS

Base stock. Based on the theory that a minimal level of inventory is a permanent investment. This amount is maintained on the balance sheet at its historical cost.

Ceiling. In lower of cost or market computations, market (replacement cost) cannot be higher than the ceiling (net realizable value). Net realizable value is selling price less selling costs and costs to complete.

Consignments. A marketing method in which the consignor ships goods to the consignee, who acts as an agent for the consignor in selling the goods. The inventory remains the property of the consignor until sold by the consignee.

Direct (variable) costing. This method includes only variable manufacturing costs in the cost of ending finished goods inventory. This method is not acceptable for financial reporting purposes.

Dollar-value LIFO. A variation of conventional LIFO in which layers of inventory are priced in dollars adjusted by price indices, instead of layers of inventory priced at unit prices.

Double-extension. A method used to compute the conversion price index. The index indicates the relationship between the base-year and current prices in terms of a percentage.

Finished goods. The completed, but unsold, products produced by a manufacturer.

First-in, first-out (FIFO). A cost flow assumption; the first goods purchased or produced are assumed to be the first goods sold.

Floor. In lower of cost or market computations, market is limited to net realizable value less a normal profit, called the floor. Market (replacement cost) cannot be below the floor.

Full absorption (full costing). In accordance with GAAP, this method includes all manufacturing costs (fixed and variable) in the cost of finished goods inventory.

Goods in transit. Goods that are in the process of being shipped from seller to buyer and that are en route at period end.

Gross profit. The result of subtracting cost of sales from net sales. Also referred to as "gross margin."

Gross profit method. A method used to estimate the amount of ending inventory based on the cost of goods available for sale, sales, and the gross profit percentage.

Inventory. Those items of tangible property which are held for sale in the normal course of business, are in the process of being produced for such purpose, or are to be used in the production of such items.

Inventory layer. Under the LIFO method, an increase in inventory quantity during a period.

Last-in, first-out (LIFO). A cost flow assumption; the last goods purchased are assumed to be the first goods sold.

LIFO conformity rule. A statutory requirement that, in the US, if the LIFO method is used for income tax purposes, it must also be used for financial reporting purposes.

LIFO liquidation. Liquidation of the LIFO base or old inventory layers when inventory quantities decrease. This liquidation can distort income since old costs are being charged to cost of goods sold and matched against current revenues.

LIFO reserve. The difference, at a specified date, between inventory valued using LIFO and inventory valued using the method the company uses for internal management or reporting purposes.

LIFO retail. An inventory costing method which combines the LIFO cost flow assumption and the retail inventory method.

Link-chain. Method of applying dollar-value LIFO by developing a single cumulative index. This method may be used instead of double-extension only when there are substantial changes in product lines over the years.

Lower of cost or market. Inventories must be valued at lower of cost or market (replacement cost). Market cannot exceed the ceiling (net realizable value) or be less than the floor (net realizable value less a normal markup).

Markdown. A decrease below original retail price. A markdown cancellation is an increase (not above original retail price) in retail price after a markdown.

Markup. An increase above original retail price. A markup cancellation is a decrease (not below original retail price) in retail price after a markup.

Moving average. An inventory costing method used in conjunction with a perpetual inventory system. A weighted-average cost per unit is recomputed after every purchase. Cost of goods sold are recorded at the most recent moving average cost.

Parking transaction. An arrangement which attempts to remove inventory and a current liability from the balance sheet. See **Product financing arrangement**.

Periodic inventory system. An inventory system where actual quantities are determined and recorded inventories adjusted as a result of a physical count taken at set intervals.

Perpetual inventory system. An inventory system where records of inventory quantities are maintained and updated as transactions occur.

Product financing arrangement. An arrangement whereby a firm buys inventory for another firm which agrees to purchase the inventory over a certain period at specified prices which include handling and financing costs.

Purchase commitment. A noncancelable commitment to purchase goods. Losses on such commitments are recognized when the contract price exceeds fair value, even if this occurs prior to delivery.

Raw materials. For a manufacturing firm, materials on hand awaiting entry into the production process.

Replacement cost. The cost to reproduce an inventory item by purchase or manufacture. In lower of cost or market computations, the term market means replacement cost, subject to the ceiling and floor limitations.

Retail method. An inventory costing method which uses a cost ratio to reduce ending inventory (valued at retail) to cost.

Specific identification. An inventory system where the seller identifies which specific items are sold and which remain in ending inventory.

Standard costs. Predetermined unit costs, which are acceptable for financial reporting purposes if adjusted periodically to reflect current conditions and if their use approximates the results that would be obtained by applying one of the recognized cost assumptions.

Weighted-average. An inventory costing method where ending inventory and cost of goods sold are priced at the weighted-average cost of all items available for sale.

Work in process. For a manufacturing firm, the inventory of partially completed products.

CONCEPTS, RULES, AND EXAMPLES

Ownership of Goods

For accounting purposes, it is necessary to determine when title has legally passed in order to obtain an accurate measurement of inventory quantity. The most common error made in this area is to assume that the entity has title only to the goods it physically holds. This may be incorrect in two ways: (1) goods held may not be owned, and (2) goods that are not held may be owned. Four issues affect the determination of ownership: (1) goods in transit, (2) consignment sales, (3) product financing arrangements, and (4) sales made with the buyer having the right of return.

At year-end, any **goods in transit** from seller to buyer must be included in one of those parties' inventories based on the conditions of the sale. Such goods are included in the inventory of the firm financially responsible for transportation costs. This responsibility may be indicated by shipping terms such as FOB, which is used in overland shipping contracts, and by FAS, CIF, C&F, and ex-ship, which are used in maritime contracts.

The term FOB is an abbreviation of "free on board." If goods are shipped FOB destination, transportation costs are paid by the seller and title does not pass until the carrier delivers the goods to the buyer. These goods are part of the seller's inventory while in transit. If goods are shipped FOB shipping point, transportation costs are paid by the buyer and title passes when the carrier takes possession. These goods are part of the buyer's inventory while in transit. The terms FOB destination and FOB shipping point often indicate a specific location at which title to the goods is transferred, such as FOB Cleveland. This means that the seller retains title and risk of loss until the goods are delivered to a common carrier in Cleveland who will act as an agent for the buyer.

A seller who ships FAS (free alongside) must bear all expense and risk involved in delivering the goods to the dock next to (alongside) the vessel on which they are to be shipped. The buyer bears the cost of loading and of shipment. Title passes when the carrier takes possession of the goods.

In a CIF (cost, insurance, and freight) contract the buyer agrees to pay in a lump sum the cost of the goods, insurance costs, and freight charges. In a C&F contract, the buyer promises to pay a lump sum that includes the cost of the goods and all freight charges. In either case, the seller must deliver the goods to the carrier and pay the costs of loading. Both title and risk of loss pass to the buyer upon delivery of the goods to the carrier.

A seller who delivers goods ex-ship bears all expense and risk until the goods are unloaded, at which time both title and risk of loss pass to the buyer.

In **consignments,** the consignor ships goods to the consignee who acts as the agent of the consignor in trying to sell the goods. In some consignments, the consignee receives a commission. In other arrangements, the consignee "purchases" the goods simultaneously with the sale of the goods to the customer. Goods out on consignment are included in the inventory of the consignor and are excluded from the inventory of the consignee.

FAS 49 addresses the issues involved with **product financing arrangements**. A product financing arrangement is a transaction in which an entity sells and agrees to repurchase inventory with the repurchase price equal to the original sales price plus the carrying and financing costs. The purpose of this transaction is to allow the seller (sponsor) to arrange financing of his/her original purchase of the inventory. The substance of the transaction is illustrated by the diagram below.

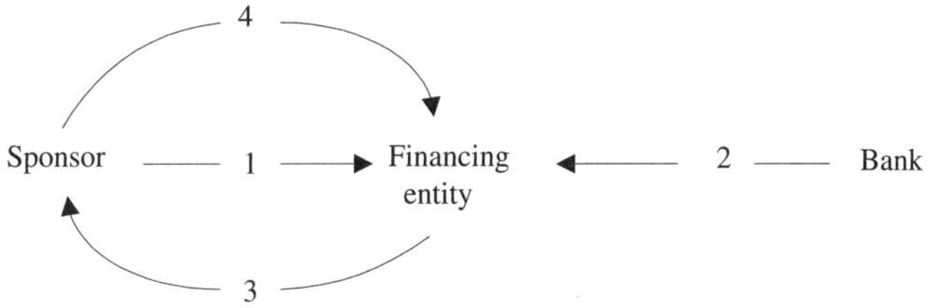

1. In the initial transaction the sponsor "sells" inventoriable items to the financing entity in return for the remittance of the sales price and at the same time agrees to repurchase the inventory at a specified price (usually the sales price plus carrying and financing costs) over a specified period of time.
2. The financing entity borrows from a bank (or other financial institution) using the newly purchased inventory as collateral.
3. The financing entity actually remits the funds to the sponsor and the sponsor presumably uses these funds to pay off the debt incurred as a result of the original purchase.
4. The sponsor then repurchases the inventory for the specified price plus costs from the financing entity at a later time when the funds are available.

FASB ruled that the substance of this transaction is that of a borrowing transaction. That is, the transaction is, in substance, no different from the sponsor obtaining third-party financing to purchase inventory. FASB, in FAS 49, ruled that the proper accounting is to record a liability when the funds are received for the initial transfer of the inventory in the amount of the selling price. The sponsor is then to accrue carrying and financing costs in accordance with his/her normal accounting policies. These accruals are eliminated and the liability satisfied when the sponsor repurchases the inventory. The inventory is **not** taken off the balance sheet of the sponsor and a sale is not recorded. This is logical because the goods do not physically move and this is merely a financing arrangement. Thus, although legal title has passed to the financing entity, for purposes of measuring and valuing inventory, the inventory is considered to be owned by the sponsor.

Another area which requires special consideration is the situation which exists when the buyer is granted a **right of return,** as defined by FAS 48. Consideration must be given to the propriety of recognizing revenue at the point of sale under such a situation (this topic is discussed in detail in Chapter 8). The sale is recorded if the future amount of the returns can be reasonably estimated. If a reasonable estimate cannot be made, then the sale is not recorded until the returns are unlikely. This, too, results in a situation where, although legal title has passed to the buyer, the seller must continue to include the goods in its measurement and valuation of inventory.

Accounting for Inventories

A major objective of accounting for inventories is the matching of appropriate costs against revenues in order to arrive at the proper determination of gross profit. Inventories are recorded in the accounting records using either a periodic or perpetual system.

In a **periodic** inventory system, inventory quantities are determined periodically by a physical count. The quantity of each item is then priced using the cost flow assumption that the enterprise had adopted as its accounting policy for that type of inventory. Cost of goods sold is computed by adding beginning inventory and net purchases (or cost of goods manufactured) and subtracting ending inventory.

Alternatively, a **perpetual** inventory system keeps a running total of the quantity (and possibly the cost) of inventory on hand by recording all sales and purchases as they occur. When inventory is purchased, the inventory account (rather than purchases) is debited. When inventory is sold, the cost of goods sold and reduction of inventory are recorded. Periodic physical counts are necessary only to verify the perpetual records and to satisfy the US income tax requirement [IRC§471(b)(1)] that a taxpayer perform "...a physical count of inventories at each location on a regular and consistent basis...."

Valuation of Inventories

The primary basis of accounting for inventories is cost. Cost is defined as the sum of the applicable expenditures and charges directly or indirectly incurred in bringing an article to its existing condition and location.

This definition allows for a wide interpretation of the costs to be included in inventory. For **raw materials** and merchandise inventory which are purchased outright, the identification of cost is relatively straightforward. The cost of these purchased inventories will include all expenditures incurred in bringing the goods to the point of sale and putting them in a salable condition. These costs include the purchase price, transportation costs, insurance while in transit, and handling costs.

It is important to note that purchases can be recorded at their gross amount or net of any allowable discount. If recorded at gross, the discounts taken represent a reduction in the purchase cost for purposes of determining cost of goods sold. On the other hand, if they are recorded at net, any lost discounts are treated as a financial expense, **not** part of cost of goods sold. The net method is considered to be theoretically preferable, but the gross method is simpler and, thus, more commonly used. Either method is acceptable under GAAP, provided that it is consistently applied.

Per APB 29, if similar items of inventory are exchanged with another entity, the earnings process is not culminated. Consequently, no profit or loss is recognized as a result of the exchange transaction. The acquired items are recorded at the book value of the items given up.

Generally interest costs incurred during the production of inventory are not capitalized under FAS 34. A complete discussion regarding the capitalization of interest costs is provided in Chapter 9.

One notable exception to recording inventories at cost is provided by the hedge accounting requirements of FAS 133. If inventory has been hedged in a fair value hedge, changes in the fair value of inventory are recognized on the balance sheet as they occur with the offsetting charge or credit recognized currently in earnings. Hedging is discussed in detail in Chapter 6.

Full absorption costing—GAAP. The basis for valuing any inventory is cost. The basis for establishing cost in a manufacturing enterprise is to include both acquisition and production costs. This concept is commonly referred to as full absorption or full costing. As a result, the **WIP** and **finished goods** inventory accounts are to include an appropriate portion of direct materials, direct labor, and indirect production costs (both fixed and variable). The difficulty in determining cost is in the allocation of indirect costs. Prior to the Tax Reform Act of 1986 (TRA 1986), production costing for GAAP and for income tax purposes were very similar. However, TRA 1986 included provisions referred to as Uniform Capitalization (UNICAP) which changed inventory costing for tax purposes by requiring certain additional indirect costs that are not capitalizable under GAAP to be capitalized rather than expensed for income tax purposes.

Under some circumstances expenses related to an idle facility, excessive spoilage, double freight, and rehandling costs may be abnormal and, therefore, require treatment as period costs. On the other hand, there may be instances in which certain general and administrative expenses are directly related to the production process and, therefore, are allocable to the WIP and finished goods inventory. Selling costs do not constitute inventory costs. Indirect production costs—costs that are incident to and necessary for production—are ordinarily included in inventory under full absorption costing. Indirect production costs include

- Repairs
- Maintenance
- Utilities
- Rent
- Indirect labor
- Production supervisory wages
- Indirect materials and supplies
- Quality control and inspection
- Small tools not capitalized

Full absorption costing—income tax. TRA 1986 requires that manufacturers capitalize rather than expense these additional items.

1. Depreciation and amortization in excess of that reported in financial statements.
2. Percentage depletion in excess of cost.
3. Rework labor, scrap, and spoilage costs.
4. Allocable general and administrative costs related to the production function.

For tax purposes, these costs, as well as the indirect production costs listed above for inventory costing under GAAP, are allocated to the WIP and finished goods inventory. Examples of general and administrative costs that must be allocated include payroll department costs, wages of security guards, and the president's salary. The difference between the GAAP and tax inventory carrying values is a temporary difference, which requires deferred income tax accounting (discussed in Chapter 15).

Uniform capitalization rules—income tax vs. GAAP. TRA 1986 established the UNICAP rules for inventory costs for tax purposes, which raised new accounting issues. These issues were considered by the Emerging Issues Task Force (Issue 86-46) and involve whether the costs capitalized for tax purposes should also be capitalized under GAAP and if so, whether the new costing method would be preferable for purposes of justifying a change in accounting principle.

The Task Force reached a consensus that capitalizing a cost for tax purposes does not indicate that it is preferable or appropriate to capitalize the cost for financial reporting purposes. Although a cost may be required to be capitalized for tax purposes, an enterprise must analyze its individual facts and circumstances to determine whether to capitalize the cost for financial reporting purposes based on the nature of its operations and industry practice.

Direct costing. The alternative to absorption costing is direct costing. Direct costing is also referred to as variable costing and requires classifying only direct materials, direct labor, and variable overhead related to production as inventory costs. All fixed costs are accounted for as period costs. The exclusion of all overhead from inventory costs does not constitute an accepted accounting procedure, consequently, direct costing is not allowable for GAAP. Treasury regulations also require the allocation of fixed overhead to inventory for tax purposes.

Inventory capitalization for retailers/wholesalers—income tax vs. GAAP. Prior to TRA 1986, retailers and wholesalers recorded their inventory as the invoice price plus the cost of applicable sales tax and freight-in under both GAAP and tax law. TRA 1986 applied UNICAP to certain retailers and wholesalers and introduced a requirement that additional costs be capitalized. Inventories of retailers/wholesalers whose average annual gross receipts for the preceding three years are $10 million or less are exempt from applying UNICAP.

The costs which must be capitalized have been divided into two categories. The first category is direct costs and includes the inventory invoice price plus transportation. Also included in direct costs is the cost of labor for purchasing, storing, and handling inventory items. The second category is indirect costs and consists of any costs that directly benefit or are incurred because of the performance of a resale activity. The following types of indirect costs must be capitalized under UNICAP:

1. Off-site storage or warehousing
2. Purchasing
3. Handling, processing, assembly, and repackaging
4. Allocable general and administrative costs related to the above three functions

The indirect costs are allocated between inventory and cost of goods sold by using traditional methods (specific identification, standard costing methods, etc.) or one of three simplified methods. Temporary differences require deferred income tax accounting.

Specific identification. The theoretical basis for valuing inventories and cost of goods sold requires assigning the production and/or acquisition costs to the specific goods to which they relate. This method of inventory valuation is usually referred to as specific identification. Specific identification is generally not practical as the product will generally lose its separate identity as it passes through the production and sales process. Exceptions to this would arise in situations involving small inventory quantities with high unit value and low turnover rate. Because of the limited applicability of specific identification, it is necessary to make certain assumptions regarding the cost flows associated with inventory. These cost flows may or may not reflect the physical flow of the inventory.

Cost flow assumptions. According to ARB 43, Chapter 4

> *...cost for inventory purposes shall be determined under any one of several assumptions as to the flow of cost factors; the major objective in selecting a method should be to choose the one which, under the circumstances, most clearly reflects periodic income.*

The most common cost flow assumptions used are (1) first-in, first-out (FIFO), (2) last-in, first-out (LIFO), and (3) weighted-average. Additionally, there are variations to each of these assumptions which are commonly used in practice.

In selecting which cost flow assumption to adopt as its accounting policy for a particular type of industry, management should consider a variety of factors. First, the industry norm should be examined as this will facilitate interfirm comparison by financial statement users. The appropriateness of using a particular cost flow assumption will vary depending on the nature of the industry and the expected economic climate. The appropriate method in a period of rising prices differs from the method that is appropriate for a period of declining prices. Each of the foregoing assumptions and their relative advantages or disadvantages are discussed below. Examples are provided to enhance understanding of the application.

First-in, first-out (FIFO). The **FIFO method** of inventory valuation assumes that the first goods purchased are the first goods used or sold, regardless of the actual physical flow. This method is thought to most closely parallel the physical flow of the units in most industries. The strength of this cost flow assumption lies in the inventory amount reported on the balance sheet. Because the earliest goods purchased are the first ones removed from the inventory account, the remaining balance is composed of items priced at more recent cost. This yields results similar to those obtained under current cost accounting on the balance sheet. However, the FIFO method does not necessarily reflect the most accurate income figure as historical costs are being matched against current revenues.

The following example illustrates the basic principles involved in the application of FIFO:

	Units available	*Units sold*	*Actual unit cost*	*Actual total cost*
Beginning inventory	100	--	$2.10	$210
Sale	--	75		--
Purchase	150	--	2.80	420
Sale	--	100		--
Purchase	50	--	3.00	150
Total	300	175		$780

Given this data, the cost of goods sold and ending inventory balance are determined as follows:

	Units	*Unit cost*	*Total cost*
Cost of goods sold	100	$2.10	$210
	75	2.80	210
	175		420
Ending inventory	50	3.00	150
	75	2.80	210
	125		360
Totals	300		$780

Notice that the total of the units in cost of goods sold and ending inventory, as well as the sum of their total costs, is equal to the goods available for sale and their respective total costs.

The FIFO method provides the same results under either the periodic or perpetual system.

Last-in, first-out (LIFO). The **LIFO method** of inventory valuation assumes that the last goods purchased are the first goods used or sold. This allows the matching of current costs with current revenue and provides the best measure of gross profit. However, unless costs remain relatively unchanged over time, the LIFO method will usually misstate the ending inventory balance for balance sheet purposes because inventory usually consists of costs from earlier periods. LIFO does not usually follow the physical flow of merchandise or materials. However, the matching of physical flow with cost flow is not an objective of accounting for inventories.

The LIFO method is not a promulgated accounting principle. Rather, the basis for LIFO is found in the US Internal Revenue Code (the Code) §472 and, as such, is a tax concept. US Treasury regulations indicate that any taxpayer who maintains inventories may select LIFO application for any or all inventoriable items. This election is made with the taxpayer's tax return on Form 970 after the close of any taxable year. Partial adoption of LIFO is allowed for both accounting and income tax purposes. (See Appendix B for a further discussion of partial adoption of LIFO for accounting purposes.)

Once elected, the LIFO method must continue to be used in future periods. In order to revert to another method, the taxpayer must apply for a change in accounting method on Form 3115 within the first 180 days of the taxable year during which the change is desired. A change to or from the LIFO method is an accounting change (see Chapter 21).

LIFO restrictions. In addition, for tax reporting purposes a taxpayer must adhere to the following two significant restrictions for the portions of its inventory valued under LIFO:

1. The inventory is to be valued at cost regardless of market value (i.e., application of the lower of cost or market rule is not allowed).
2. The taxpayer may not use a different inventory method in ascertaining profit or loss of the entity for external financial reports (i.e., if LIFO is elected for tax purposes, it

must also be used for accounting purposes). This is known as the **LIFO conformity rule**. (See Appendix A for exceptions to this rule.)

The quantity of ending inventory on hand at the beginning of the year of election is termed the "base layer." This inventory is valued at actual (full absorption) cost, and unit cost for each inventory item is determined by dividing total cost by the quantity on hand. At the end of the initial and subsequent years, increases in the quantity of inventory on hand are referred to as increments, or **LIFO layers**. These increments are valued individually by applying one of the following costing methods to the quantity of inventory representing a layer:

1. The actual cost of the goods most recently purchased or produced.
2. The actual cost of the goods purchased or produced in order of acquisition.
3. An average unit cost of all goods purchased or produced during the current year.
4. A hybrid method which will more clearly reflect income (for tax purposes, this method must meet with the approval of the IRS Commissioner).

Thus, after using the LIFO method for five years, it is possible that an enterprise could have ending inventory consisting of the base layer and five additional layers (or increments) provided that the quantity of ending inventory increased every year.

The single goods (unit) LIFO approach is illustrated in the following example:

Rose Co. is in its first year of operation and elects to use the periodic LIFO method of inventory valuation. The company sells only one product. Rose applies the LIFO method using the order of current year acquisition cost. The following data are given for years 1 through 3:

		Units			*Purchase cost*	
Year 1	*Beginning inventory*	*Purchased*	*Sold*	*Ending inventory*	*Unit cost*	*Total cost*
Purchase		200			$2.00	$400
Sale			100		--	--
Purchase		200			3.00	600
Sale			150		--	--
	--	400	250	150		
Year 2						
Purchase		300			$3.20	$960
Sale			200		--	--
Purchase		100			3.30	330
	150	400	200	350		
Year 3						
Purchase		100			$3.50	$350
Sale			200		--	--
Sale			100		--	--
	350	100	300	150		

In year 1 the following occurred:

1. The total goods available for sale were 400 units.
2. The total sales were 250 units.
3. Therefore, the ending inventory was 150 units.

The ending inventory is valued at the earliest current year acquisition cost of $2.00 per unit. Thus, ending inventory is valued at $300 (150 x $2.00).

Another way to look at this is to analyze both cost of goods sold and ending inventory.

	Units	*Unit cost*	*Total cost*
Cost of goods sold	200	$3.00	$600
	50	2.00	100
	250		$700
Ending inventory	150	2.00	$300

Note that the base-year cost is $2.00 and that the base-year level is 150 units. Therefore, if ending inventory in the subsequent period exceeds 150 units, a new layer (or increment) will be created.

Year 2	Units	Unit cost	Total cost	
Cost of goods sold	100	$3.30	$330	
	100	3.20	320	
	200		$650	
Ending inventory	150	2.00	$300	Base-year layer
	200	3.20	640	Year 2 increment
	350		$940	

If ending inventory exceeds 350 units in the next period, a third layer (increment) will be created.

Year 3	Units	Unit cost	Total cost	
Cost of goods sold	100	$3.50	$350	
	200	3.20	640	
	300		$990	
Ending inventory	150	2.00	$300	Base-year layer

Notice how the decrement of 200 units in year 3 eliminated the entire year 2 increment. Thus, any year 4 increase in the quantity of inventory would result in a **new** increment which would be valued at year 4 prices.

In situations where the ending inventory decreases from the level established at the close of the preceding year, the enterprise experiences a decrement or **LIFO liquidation**. Decrements reduce or eliminate previously established LIFO layers. Once any part of a layer has been eliminated, it **cannot** be reinstated after year-end. For example, if in its first year after the election of LIFO an enterprise establishes a layer (increment) of ten units, then in the next year inventory decreases by four units leaving the first layer at six units, the enterprise cannot reestablish the first layer (back up to ten units) in the year that inventory next increases. Rather, it will be forced to create a new layer for the increase. The effect of LIFO liquidations in periods of rising prices is to release from ending inventory into cost of goods sold costs which are below the current cost being paid. Thus, the resultant effect of a LIFO liquidation is to increase income for **both** accounting and tax purposes. Because of this, LIFO is most commonly used by companies in industries in which levels of inventories are maintained or increased.

LIFO liquidations can take two forms, voluntary or involuntary. A voluntary liquidation exists when an enterprise decides, for one reason or another, to let inventory levels drop. Such a liquidation occurs because current prices may be too high, less inventory is needed for efficient production, or maybe because of a transition in product lines. Involuntary LIFO liquidations stem from reasons beyond the control of management, such as a strike, material shortages, shipping delays, etc. Regardless of the reason, all liquidations result in a corresponding increase in income (assuming rising prices).

To compute the effect of the liquidation, the company must compute the difference between actual cost of sales and what cost of sales would have been had the inventory been reinstated. The Internal Revenue Service has ruled that this hypothetical reinstatement must be computed under the company's normal pricing procedures for valuing its LIFO increments. In the above example the effect of the year 3 LIFO liquidation would be computed as follows:

Hypothetical inventory reinstatement:

200 units @ $3.50 – $3.20 = $60

Hypothetically, if there had been an increment instead of a decrement in year 3 and the year 2 inventory layer had remained intact, 200 more units (out of the 300 total units sold in year

3) would have been charged to cost of goods sold at the year 3 price of $3.50 instead of the year 2 price of $3.20. Therefore, the difference between $3.50 and the actual amount charged to cost of sales for these 200 units liquidated ($3.20) measures the effect of the liquidation.

The following is considered acceptable GAAP disclosure in the event of a LIFO liquidation:

> During 2005, inventory quantities were reduced below their levels at December 31, 2004. As a result of this reduction, LIFO inventory costs computed based on lower prior years' acquisition costs were charged to cost of goods sold. If this LIFO liquidation had not occurred and cost of sales had been computed based on the cost of 2005 purchases, cost of goods sold would have increased by approximately $xxx and net income decreased by approximately $xx or $x per share.

An inordinate amount of recordkeeping is required in applying the unit LIFO method. The recordkeeping is much greater as the number of products increases. For this reason a "pooling" approach is generally applied to LIFO inventories.

Pooling is the process of grouping items which are naturally related and then treating this group as a single unit in determining LIFO cost. Because the quantity of ending inventory includes many items, decreases in one item can be offset by increases in others, whereas under the unit LIFO approach a decrease in any one item results in a liquidation of all or a portion of a LIFO layer.

The problem in applying the pooling method emanates from the tax regulations, not the practical application. The tax regulations state that each type of good in the opening inventory must be compared with a similar type in the closing inventory. These items must be similar as to character, quality, and price. This qualification has generally been interpreted to mean identical. The effect of this statement is to require a separate pool for each item under the unit LIFO method. The need for a simpler, more practical approach to using the LIFO concept and allowing for a greater use of the pooling technique was met by dollar-value LIFO.

Dollar-value LIFO. Use of dollar-value LIFO may be elected by any taxpayer. The dollar-value LIFO method of inventory valuation determines the cost of inventories by expressing base-year costs in terms of total dollars rather than specific prices of specific units. The dollar-value method also gives rise to an expanded interpretation of the use of pools. Increments and liquidations are treated the same as under the unit LIFO approach but are reflected only in terms of a **net** increment or liquidation for the entire pool.

Identifying pools. Three alternatives exist for determining pools under dollar-value LIFO: (1) the natural business unit, (2) multiple pools, and (3) pools for wholesalers, retailers, jobbers, etc.

The natural business unit is defined by the existence of separate and distinct processing facilities and operations and the maintenance of separate income (loss) records. The concept of the natural business unit is generally dependent upon the type of product being produced, not the various stages of production for that product. Thus, the pool can (and will) contain raw materials, WIP, and finished goods. The three examples below, taken from the treasury regulations, illustrate the application of the natural business unit concept.

Example 1

A corporation manufactures, in one division, automatic clothes washers and dryers of both commercial and domestic grade as well as electric ranges and dishwashers. The corporation manufactures, in another division, radios and television sets. The manufacturing facilities and processes used in manufacturing the radios and television sets are distinct from those used in manufacturing the automatic clothes washers, etc. Under these circumstances, the enterprise would consist of two business units and two pools would be appropriate: one consisting of all of the LIFO inventories involved with the manufacture of clothes washers and dryers, electric ranges and dishwashers and the other consisting of all of the LIFO inventories involved with the production of radios and television sets.

Example 2

A taxpayer produces plastics in one of its plants. Substantial amounts of the production are sold as plastics. The remainder of the production is shipped to a second plant of the taxpayer for the production of plastic toys which are sold to customers. The taxpayer operates its plastics plant and toy plant as separate divisions. Because of the different product lines and the separate divisions, the taxpayer has two natural business units.

Example 3

A taxpayer is engaged in the manufacture of paper. At one stage of processing, uncoated paper is produced. Substantial amounts of uncoated paper are sold at this stage of processing. The remainder of the uncoated paper is transferred to the taxpayer's finishing mill where coated paper is produced and sold. This taxpayer has only one natural business unit since coated and uncoated paper are within the same product line.

The treasury regulations require that a pool consist of all items entering into the entire inventory investment of a natural business unit, unless the taxpayer elects to use the multiple-pooling method.

The multiple-pooling method is the grouping of substantially similar items. In determining substantially similar items, consideration is given to the processing applied, the interchangeability, the similarity of use, and the customary practice of the industry. While the election of multiple pools will necessitate additional recordkeeping, it may result in a better estimation of gross profit and periodic net income.

According to Reg. §1.472-8(c), inventory items of wholesalers, retailers, jobbers, and distributors are to be assigned to pools by major lines, types, or classes of goods. The natural business unit method may be used with permission of the Commissioner.

All three methods of pooling allow for a change in the components of inventory. New items which properly fall within the pool may be added, and old items may disappear from the pool, but neither will necessarily effect a change in the total dollar value of the pool.

Computing dollar-value LIFO. The purpose of the dollar-value LIFO method of valuing inventory is to convert inventory which is priced at end-of-year prices to that same inventory priced at base-year (or applicable LIFO layer) prices. The dollar-value method achieves this result through the use of a conversion price index. The inventory at current year cost is divided by the appropriate index to arrive at the base-year cost. The main focus is on the determination of the conversion price index. There are four basic methods that can be used in the computation of the LIFO value of a dollar-value pool: (1) double-extension, (2) link-chain, (3) the index method, and (4) the alternative LIFO method for auto dealers.

Double-extension method. This method was originally developed to compute the conversion price index. It involves extending the entire quantity of ending inventory for the current year at both base-year prices and end-of-year prices to arrive at a total dollar value for each, hence the title of double-extension. The end-of-year dollar total is then divided by the base-year dollar total to arrive at the index, usually referred to as the conversion price index. This index indicates the relationship between the base-year and current prices in terms of a percentage. Each layer (or increment) is valued at its own percentage. Although a representative sample is allowed (meaning that not all of the items need to be double-extended; this is discussed in more detail under indexing), the recordkeeping under this method is very burdensome. The base-year price must be kept for each inventory item. Depending upon the number of different items included in the inventory of the company, the necessary records may be too detailed to keep past the first year.

The following example illustrates the double-extension method of computing the LIFO value of inventory. The example presented is relatively simple and does not attempt to incorporate all of the complexities of LIFO inventory accounting.

Example

Isaacson, Inc. uses the dollar-value method of LIFO inventory valuation and computes its price index using the double-extension method. Isaacson has a single pool which contains two inventory items, A and B. Year 1 is the company's initial year of operations. The following information is given for years 1 through 4:

		Ending quantity (units) and current unit price			
	Ending inventory	*A*		*B*	
Year	*current prices*				
1	$100,000	5,000	$6.00	7,000	$10.00
2	120,300	6,000	6.30	7,500	11.00
3	122,220	5,800	6.40	7,400	11.50
4	133,900	6,200	6.50	7,800	12.00

In year 1 there is no computation of an index; the index is 100%. The LIFO cost is the same as the actual current year cost. This is the base year.

In year 2 the first step is to double-extend the quantity of ending inventory at base-year and current year costs.

Item	*Quantity*	*Base-year cost/unit*	*Extended*	*Current year cost/unit*	*Extended*
A	6,000	$ 6.00	$ 36,000	$ 6.30	$ 37,800
B	7,500	10.00	75,000	11.00	82,500
			$111,000		$120,300*

* *When using the double-extension method and extending **all** of the inventory items to arrive at the index, this number must equal the ending inventory at current prices. If a sampling method is used (as discussed under indexing), this number **divided by** your ending inventory at current prices is the percentage sampled.*

Now we can compute the conversion price index which is

$$\frac{\text{Ending inventory at current year prices}}{\text{Ending inventory at base-year prices}}$$

In this case $\frac{120,300}{111,000} = 108.4\%$ (rounded)

Next, compute the year 2 layer at base-year cost by taking the current year-ending inventory at base-year prices (if you only extend a sample of the inventory, this number is arrived at by dividing the ending inventory at current year prices by the conversion price index) of $111,000 and subtracting the base-year cost of $100,000. In year 2 we have an increment (layer) of $11,000 valued at base-year costs.

The year 2 layer of $11,000 at base-year cost must be converted so that the layer is valued at the prices in effect when it came into existence (i.e., at year 2 prices). This is done by multiplying the increment at base-year cost ($11,000) by the rounded conversion price index (1.084). The result is the year 2 layer at LIFO prices.

Base-year layer	$100,000
Year 2 layer ($11,000 x 1.084)	11,924
	$111,924

In year 3 the same basic procedure is followed.

Item	*Quantity*	*Base-year cost/unit*	*Extended*	*Current year cost/unit*	*Extended*
A	5,800	$ 6.00	$ 34,800	$ 6.40	$ 37,120
B	7,400	10.00	74,000	11.50	85,100
			$108,800		$122,220

There has been a decrease in the base-year cost of the ending inventory ($111,000 –$108,800 = $2,200) which is referred to as a decrement. A decrement results in the decrease (or elimination) of previously provided layers. In this situation, the computation of the index is not necessary as there is no LIFO layer that requires a valuation. If a sampling approach has been used, the index is needed to arrive at the ending inventory at base-year cost and thus determine if there has been an increment or decrement.

Now the ending inventory at base-year cost is $108,800. The base-year cost layer is still intact at $100,000, so the cumulative increment is $8,800. Since this is less than the $11,000 increment of year 2, no additional increment is established in year 3. The LIFO cost of the inventory is shown below.

Base-year layer	$100,000
Year 2 layer ($8,800 x 1.084)	9,539
	$109,539

The fourth year then follows the same steps.

Items	Quantity	Base-year cost/unit	Extended	Current year cost/unit	Extended
A	6,200	$ 6.00	$ 37,200	$ 6.50	$ 40,300
B	7,800	10.00	78,000	12.00	93,600
			$115,200		$133,900

The conversion price index is 116.2% (133,900/115,200).

A current year increment exists because the ending inventory at base-year prices in year 4 of $115,200 exceeds the year 3 number of $108,800. The current year increment of $6,400 must be valued at year 4 prices. Thus, the LIFO cost of the year 4 inventory is

Base-year layer	$100,000
Year 2 layer ($8,800 x 1.084)	9,539
Year 4 layer ($6,400 x 1.162)	7,437
	$116,976

It is important to point out that once a layer is reduced or eliminated it is never reinstated (as with the year 2 increment) after year-end.

Link-chain method. Since the computations for application become arduous even if only a few items exist in the inventory, consider the problems that arise when there is a constant change in the inventory mix or in situations in which the breadth of the inventory is large. The link-chain method of applying dollar-value LIFO was developed to combat these problems.

Another purpose served by the link-chain method is to eliminate the problem created by a significant turnover in the components of inventory. Under the double-extension or indexing method, the regulations require that any new products added to the inventory be recorded at base-year prices. If these are not available, then the earliest cost available after the base year is used. If the item was not in existence in the base year, the taxpayer may reconstruct the base cost, using a reasonable method to determine what the cost would have been if the item had been in existence in the base year. Finally, as a last resort, the purchase price can be used. While this does not appear to be a problem on the surface, imagine a base period which is twenty-five to fifty years in the past. The difficulty involved with finding the base-year cost may require using a more current cost, thus eliminating some of the LIFO benefit. Imagine a situation faced by a company in a "hi-tech" industry where inventory is continually being replaced by newer, more advanced products. The effect of this rapid change under the double-extension method (because the new products did not exist in the base period) is to use current prices as base-year costs. When inventory has such a rapid turnover, the overall LIFO advantage becomes diluted as current and base-year costs are often synonymous. This situation is the major reason for the development of the link-chain method.

The link-chain method was originally developed for (and limited to) those companies that wanted to use LIFO but, because of a substantial change in product lines over time, were unable to recreate or keep the historical records necessary to make accurate use of the double extension method. It is important to note that the double-extension and link-chain methods are not selective alternatives for the same situation. For tax purposes, the link-chain election **requires** that substantial change in product line be evident over the years, and may not be elected solely because of its ease of application. The double-extension and index methods must be demonstrably impractical in order to elect the link-chain method. However, a company may use different computational techniques for financial reporting and tax purposes. Therefore, the link-chain method could be used for financial reporting purposes even if a different application is used for tax purposes.

The link-chain method is the process of developing a single cumulative index which is applied to the ending inventory amount priced at the beginning-of-the-year costs. Thus, the index computed at the end of each year is "linked" to the index from all previous years. A separate cumulative index is used for each pool regardless of the variations in the components of these pools over the years. Technological change is accommodated by the method used to calculate each current year index. The index is derived by double-extending a representative sample (generally thought to be between 50% and 75% of the dollar value of the pool) at both beginning-of-year prices and end-of-year prices. This annual index is then applied to (multiplied by) the previous period's cumulative index to arrive at the new current year cumulative index.

An example of the link-chain method is shown below. The end-of-year costs and inventory quantities used are the same as those used in the double-extension example.

Assume the following inventory data for years 1-4. Year 1 is assumed to be the initial year of operation for the company. The LIFO method is elected on the first income tax return. Assume that A and B constitute a single pool.

Product	*Ending inventory quantity*	*Cost per unit*		*Extension*	
		Beg. of yr.	*End of yr.*	*Beginning*	*End*
Year 1					
A	5,000	N/A	$ 6.00	N/A	$ 30,000
B	7,000	N/A	10.00	N/A	70,000
					$100,000
Year 2					
A	6,000	$ 6.00	6.30	$ 36,000	$ 37,800
B	7,500	10.00	11.00	75,000	82,500
				$111,000	$120,300
Year 3					
A	5,800	6.30	6.40	$ 36,540	$ 37,120
B	7,400	11.00	11.50	81,400	85,100
				$117,940	$122,220
Year 4					
A	6,200	6.40	6.50	$ 39,680	$ 40,300
B	7,800	11.50	12.00	89,700	93,600
				$129,380	$133,900

The initial year (base year) does not require the computation of an index under any LIFO method. The base-year index will always be 1.00.

Thus, the base-year inventory layer is $100,000 (the end-of-year inventory stated at base-year cost).

The second year requires the first index computation. Notice that in year 2 our extended totals are

Product	Beginning-of-year prices	End-of-year prices
A	$ 36,000	$ 37,800
B	75,000	82,500
	$111,000	$120,300

The year 2 index is 1.084 (120,300/111,000). This is the same as computed under the double-extension method because the beginning-of-the-year prices reflect the base-year price. This will not always be the case, as sometimes new items may be added to the pool, causing a change in the index.

Thus, the cumulative index is the 1.084 current year index multiplied by the preceding year index of 1.00 to arrive at a link-chain index of 1.084.

This index is then used to restate the inventory to base-year cost by dividing the inventory at end-of-year prices by the cumulative index: $120,300/1.084 = $111,000. The determination of the LIFO increment or decrement is then basically the same as the double-extension method. In year 2 the increment (layer) at base-year cost is $11,000 ($111,000 – 100,000). This layer must be valued at the prices effective when the layer was created, or extended at the cumulative index for that year. This results in an ending inventory at LIFO cost of

	Base-year cost	Index	LIFO cost
Base-year layer	$100,000	1.00	$100,000
Year 2 layer	11,000	1.084	11,924
	$111,000		$111,924

The index for year 3 is computed as follows:

	Beginning-of-year prices	End-of-year prices
A	$ 36,540	$ 37,120
B	81,400	85,100
	$117,940	$122,220

122,220/117,940 = 1.036

The next step is to determine the cumulative index which is the product of the preceding year's cumulative index and the current year index, or 1.123 (1.084 x 1.036). The new cumulative index is used to restate the inventory at end-of-year dollars to base-year cost. This is accomplished by dividing the end-of-year inventory by the new cumulative index. Thus, current inventory at base-year cost is $108,833 ($122,220 ÷ 1.123). In this instance we have experienced a decrement (a decrease from the prior year's $111,000). The determination of ending inventory is

	Base-year cost	Index	LIFO cost
Base-year layer	$100,000	1.00	$100,000
Year 2 layer	8,833	1.084	9,575
Year 3 layer	--	1.123	--
	$108,833		$109,575

Finally, the same steps are performed for the year 4 computation. The current year index is 1.035 (133,900/129,380). The new cumulative index is 1.162 (1.035 x 1.123). The base-year cost of the current inventory is $115,232 (133,900/1.162). Thus, LIFO inventory at the end of year 4 is

	Base-year cost	Index	LIFO cost
Base-year layer	$100,000	1.00	$100,000
Year 2 layer	8,833	1.084	9,575
Year 3 layer	--	1.123	--
Year 4 layer	6,399	1.162	7,435
	$115,232		$117,010

Notice how even though the numbers used were the same as those used in the double-extension example, the results were different (year 4 inventory under double-extension was $116,976), however, not by a significant amount. It is much easier to keep track of beginning-of-the-year prices than base-year prices, but perhaps more importantly, it is easier to establish beginning-of-the-year prices for **new items** than to establish their base-year price. This latter reason is why the link-chain method is so much more desirable than the double-extension method. However, before electing or applying this method, a company must be able to establish a sufficient need as defined in the treasury regulations.

Indexing. Indexing methods can basically be broken down into two types: (1) an internal index and (2) an external index.

The internal index is merely a variation of the double-extension method. The regulations allow for a representative sample (or some other statistical method) of the inventory to be double-extended. The representative index computed from the sample is then used to restate the inventory to base-year cost and to value the new layer.

The external index method referred to in treasury regulations as the Inventory Price Index Computation (IPIC) Method involves using indices published by the Bureau of Labor Statistics (BLS)[1] and applying them to specified categories of inventory included in the taxpayer's LIFO pools. Initially, the full benefit of electing to use IPIC was limited to small businesses (defined as three-year average sales of less than $5 million). Other businesses that did not meet the small business criteria were required to adjust the changes in the indices to 80% of the change, thus making election of the method less attractive. The undesirability of the election for large taxpayers was compounded by the fact that using the reduced indices did not constitute GAAP and the company would have been required to use different LIFO inventories for GAAP and income tax purposes and account for the temporary difference using deferred income tax accounting. Final regulations issued in 2001, however, have eliminated this large-taxpayer rule and, effective for taxable years ending on or after December 31, 2001, the 20% reduction requirement for large taxpayers has been eliminated.

Automobile dealers' alternative LIFO method. Beginning in September 1992 a simplified dollar-value method became available for use by retail automobile dealers for valuing inventory of new automobiles and light-duty trucks. The use of this method and its acceptance for tax purposes is conditioned on the application of several LIFO submethods, definitions and special rules. The reader is referred to Rev. Proc. 92-79 for a further discussion of this method.

LIFO issues paper. The GAAP for the application of LIFO has been based upon tax rules rather than on financial accounting pronouncements. LIFO is cited in GAAP as an acceptable inventory method but specific rules regarding its implementation are not provided. The tax regulations, on the other hand, do provide specific rules for the implementation of LIFO and require financial statement conformity. For this reason, tax rules have essentially defined the financial accounting treatment of LIFO inventories. In recognition of the lack of authoritative accounting guidelines in the implementation of LIFO, the AICPA's Accounting Standards Division prepared an Issues Paper on this topic. "Identification and Discussion of Certain Financial Accounting and Reporting Issues Concerning LIFO Inventories," prepared by the Task Force on LIFO Inventory Problems, identifies financial accounting issues resulting from the use of LIFO and includes advisory conclusions for these problems. Issues Papers, however, do not establish standards of financial accounting. This Issues Paper is summarized in an appendix to this chapter.

Interim treatment of LIFO. Interim reporting issues associated with LIFO are discussed in Chapter 19 which deals with Interim Reporting.

Weighted-average and moving-average. Another method of inventory valuation involves averaging and is commonly referred to as the weighted-average method. The cost of goods available for sale (beginning inventory and net purchases) is divided by the number of units available for sale to obtain a weighted-average cost per unit. Ending inventory and cost of goods sold are then priced at this average cost. Assume the following data:

---

[1] *For more information see http://www.bls.gov*

	Units available	*Units sold*	*Actual unit cost*	*Actual total cost*
Beginning inventory	100	--	$2.10	$210
Sale	--	75	--	--
Purchase	150	--	2.80	420
Sale	--	100	--	--
Purchase	50	--	3.00	150
Total	300	175		$780

The weighted-average cost per unit is $780/300, or $2.60. Ending inventory is 125 units (300 – 175) at $2.60, or $325; cost of goods sold is 175 units at $2.60, or $455.

When the weighted-average assumption is applied to a perpetual inventory system, the average cost is recomputed after each purchase. This process is referred to as a moving average. Cost of goods sold is recorded using the most recent average. This combination is called the moving-average method and is applied below to the same data used in the weighted-average example above.

	Units on hand	*Purchases in dollars*	*Cost of sales in dollars*	*Inventory total cost*	*Inventory moving-average unit cost*
Beginning inventory	100	$ --	$ --	$210.00	$2.10
Sale (75 units @ $2.10)	25	--	157.50	52.50	2.10
Purchase (150 units, $420)	175	420.00	--	472.50	2.70
Sale (100 units @ $2.70)	75	--	270.00	202.50	2.70
Purchase (50 units, $150)	125	150.00	--	352.50	2.82

Cost of goods sold is 75 units at $2.10 and 100 units at $2.70, or $427.50.

Comparison of cost assumptions. Of the three basic cost flow assumptions, LIFO and FIFO produce the most extreme results, while results from using the weighted-average method generally fall somewhere in between. The selection of one of these methods involves a detailed analysis of the organization's objectives, industry practices, and current and expected future economic conditions.

In periods of rising prices the LIFO method is generally thought to best fulfill the objective of providing the clearest measure of periodic net income. It does not, however, provide an accurate estimate of the inventory value in an inflationary environment. However, this can usually be overcome by the issuance of supplementary data. In periods of rising prices a prudent business should use the LIFO method because it will result in a decrease in the current income tax liability when compared to other alternatives. In a deflationary period, the opposite is true.

FIFO is a balance-sheet-oriented costing method. It gives the most accurate estimate of the current value of inventory during periods of changing prices. In periods of rising prices, the FIFO method will result in higher income taxes than the other alternatives, while in a deflationary period FIFO provides for a lesser income tax burden. However, a major advantage of the FIFO method is that it is not subject to all of the regulations and requirements of the tax code as is LIFO.

The average methods do not provide an estimate of current cost information on either the balance sheet or income statement. The average methods will not serve to minimize the income tax burden, nor will they result in the highest income taxes among the various alternatives.

Although price trends and underlying objectives are important in the selection of a cost flow assumption, other considerations are the risk of LIFO liquidations, cash flow, capital maintenance, restrictive covenants imposed by lenders, etc.

Lower of cost or market (LCM). As stated in ARB 43, Chapter 4

> *...a departure from the cost basis of pricing the inventory is required when the utility of the goods is no longer as great as its cost.... Where there is evidence that the utility of goods...will be less than cost...the difference should be recognized as a loss of the current period.*

Loss of utility can occur for a variety of reasons including damage, spoilage, obsolescence, changes in market prices, etc. The application of LCM is a means of attempting to measure loss of utility and recognize the effects in the period in which it occurs.

The term market means current **replacement cost** not to exceed a **ceiling** of net realizable value (selling price less reasonably estimable costs of completion and disposal) or be less than a **floor** of net realizable value adjusted for a normal profit margin.

LCM is not applied in conjunction with the LIFO method of inventory valuation for income tax purposes. However, it is important to note that LCM/LIFO is applied for financial reporting purposes. Such application gives rise to a temporary difference in the carrying value of inventory between financial statements and income tax returns. Appendix B provides additional guidance on LCM/LIFO for financial reporting.

LCM may be applied to either the entire inventory or to each individual inventory item. The primary objective for selecting between the alternative methods of applying the LCM rule is to select the one which most clearly reflects periodic income. The rule is most commonly applied to the inventory on an item-by-item basis. The reason for this application is twofold.

1. It is required by tax purposes unless it involves practical difficulties, and
2. It provides the most conservative valuation of inventories, because decreases in the value of one item are not offset by increases in the value of another.

The application of these principles is illustrated in the example below. Assume the following information for products A, B, C, D, and E:

Item	*Cost*	*Replacement cost*	*Est. selling price*	*Cost to complete*	*Normal profit percentage*	*Normal profit amount*
A	$2.00	$1.80	$ 2.50	$0.50	24%	$0.60
B	4.00	1.60	4.00	0.80	24%	0.96
C	6.00	6.60	10.00	1.00	18%	1.80
D	5.00	4.75	6.00	2.00	20%	1.20
E	1.00	1.05	1.20	0.25	12.5%	0.15

First, determine the market value and then compare this to historical cost. Market value is equal to the replacement cost, but cannot exceed the net realizable value (NRV) nor be below net realizable value less the normal profit percentage.

Market Determination

Item	*Cost*	*Replacement cost*	*NRV (ceiling)*	*NRV less profit (floor)*	*Market*	*LCM*
A	$2.00	$1.80	$2.00	$1.40	$1.80	$1.80
B	4.00	1.60	3.20	2.24	2.24	2.24
C	6.00	6.60	9.00	7.20	7.20	6.00
D	5.00	4.75	4.00	2.80	4.00	4.00
E	1.00	1.05	0.95	0.80	0.95	0.95

NRV (ceiling) equals selling price less costs of completion (e.g., item A: $2.50 – .50 = $2.00). NRV less profit (floor) is self-descriptive (e.g., item A: $2.50 – .50 –.60 = $1.40). Market is replacement cost unless lower than the floor or higher than the ceiling. Note that market must be designated before LCM is determined. Finally, LCM is the lower of cost or market value.

Replacement cost is a valid measure of the future utility of the inventory item since increases or decreases in the purchase price generally foreshadow related increases or decreases in the selling price. The ceiling and the floor provide safeguards against the recognition of either excessive profits or excessive losses in future periods in those instances where the selling price and replacement cost do not move in the same direction in a proportional manner. The ceiling avoids the recognition of additional losses in the future when the selling price is falling faster than replacement cost. Without the ceiling constraint, inventories would be carried at an amount in excess of their net realizable value. The floor avoids the recognition of abnormal profits in the future when replacement cost is falling faster than the selling price. Without the floor, inventories would be carried at a value less than their net realizable value minus a normal profit.

The loss from writing inventories down to LCM is generally reflected on the income statement in cost of goods sold. If material, the loss must be separately captioned in the income statement. While GAAP is not explicit as to presentation, it would appear that this adjustment could either be displayed as a separately identified charge within cost of goods sold, or as an administrative expense. The write-down is recorded as a debit to a loss account and a credit either to an inventory or a valuation allowance account.

Special valuation methods. There are instances in which an accountant must estimate the value of inventories without an actual physical count. Some of the methods used are the retail method, the LIFO retail method, and the gross profit method.

Retail method. The conventional retail method is used by retailers to estimate the cost of their ending inventory. The retailer can either take a physical inventory at retail prices or estimate ending retail inventory and then use the cost-to-retail ratio to convert the ending inventory at retail to its estimated cost. This eliminates the process of going back to original invoices or other documents in order to determine the original cost for each inventoriable item. The retail method can be used under any of the three cost flow assumptions discussed earlier: FIFO, LIFO, or average cost. As with ordinary FIFO or average cost, the LCM rule is also applied when either one of these two cost assumptions is used in conjunction with the retail method.

The key to applying the retail method is determining the cost-to-retail ratio. The calculation of this ratio varies depending upon the cost flow assumption selected. The cost-to-retail ratio provides a measure of the relationship between the **cost** of goods available for sale and the **retail** price of these same goods. This ratio is used to convert the ending retail inventory back to cost. The computation of the cost-to-retail ratio for each of the available methods is described below. The use of the LIFO cost flow assumption with this method is discussed in the next section.

1. **FIFO cost**—The concept of FIFO indicates that the ending inventory is made up of the latest purchases. Therefore, beginning inventory is excluded from the computation of the cost-to-retail ratio, and the computation uses the cost of current year net purchases divided by their retail value adjusted for both net markups and net markdowns.
2. **FIFO (LCM)**—The computation is basically the same as FIFO cost except that markdowns are excluded from the computation of the cost-to-retail ratio.
3. **Average cost**—Average cost assumes that ending inventory consists of all goods available for sale. Therefore, the cost-to-retail ratio is computed by dividing the cost of goods available for sale (Beginning inventory + Net purchases) by the retail value of these goods adjusted for both net markups and net markdowns.
4. **Average cost (LCM)**—Is computed in the same manner as average cost except that markdowns are excluded from the calculation of the cost-to-retail ratio.

A simple example illustrates the computation of the cost-to-retail ratio under both the FIFO cost and average cost methods in a situation where no markups or markdowns exist.

	FIFO cost			Average cost	
	Cost	Retail		Cost	Retail
Beginning inventory	$100,000	$ 200,000		$100,000	$ 200,000
Net purchases	500,000 (a)	800,000 (b)		500,000	800,000
Total goods available for sale	$600,000	1,000,000		$600,000 (c)	1,000,000 (d)
Sales at retail		(800,000)			(800,000)
Ending inventory—retail		$ 200,000			$ 200,000
Cost-to-retail ratio	(a) 500,000 / (b) 800,000	= 62.5%		(c) 600,000 / (d) 1,000,000	60%
Ending inventory—cost					
200,000 x 62.5%		$ 125,000			
200,000 x 60%					$ 120,000

Note that the only difference in the two examples is the numbers used to calculate the cost-to-retail ratio.

The lower of cost or market aspect of the retail method is a result of the treatment of net markups and net markdowns. **Net markups** (markups less markup cancellations) are net increases above the original retail price, which are generally caused by changes in supply and demand. **Net markdowns** (markdowns less markdown cancellations) are net decreases below the original retail price. An approximation of lower of cost or market is achieved by including net markups but excluding net markdowns from the cost-to-retail ratio.

To understand this approximation, assume a toy is purchased for $6, and the retail price is set at $10. It is later marked down to $8. A cost-to-retail ratio including markdowns would be $6 divided by $8 or 75%, and ending inventory would be valued at $8 times 75%, or $6 (original cost). The logic behind including markdowns in the cost-to-retail ratio is the assumption that these inventories would eventually be marked down and that markdowns are a normal part of business for this enterprise and/or these types of inventories. A cost-to-retail ratio excluding markdowns would be $6 divided by $10 or 60%, and ending inventory would be valued at $8 times 60%, or $4.80 (LCM). The logic behind excluding markdowns from the cost-to-retail ratio is that the enterprise did not expect to mark these inventory items down and that this is not a normal occurrence. The write-down to $4.80 reflects the loss in utility which is evidenced by the reduced retail price.

The application of the lower of cost or market rule is illustrated for both the FIFO and average cost methods in the example below. Remember, if the markups and markdowns below had been included in the previous example **both** would have been included in the cost-to-retail ratio.

	FIFO cost (LCM)			Average cost (LCM)	
	Cost	Retail		Cost	Retail
Beginning inventory	$100,000	$ 200,000		$100,000	$ 200,000
Net purchases	500,000 (a)	800,000 (b)		500,000	800,000
Net markups	--	250,000 (b)		--	250,000
Total goods available for sale	$600,000	1,250,000		$600,000 (c)	1,250,000 (d)
Net markdowns		(50,000)			(50,000)
Sales at retail		(800,000)			(800,000)
Ending inventory—retail		$ 400,000			$ 400,000
Cost-to-retail ratio	(a) 500,000 / (b) 1,050,000	= 47.6%		(c) 600,000 / (d) 1,250,000	= 48%
Ending inventory—LCM					
400,000 x 47.6%		$ 190,400			
400,000 x 48%					$ 192,000

Under the FIFO (LCM) method all of the markups are considered attributable to the current period purchases. While this is not necessarily accurate, it provides the most conservative estimate of the ending inventory.

There are a number of additional inventory topics and issues which affect the computation of the cost-to-retail ratio. Purchase discounts and freight affect only the cost column in this computation. The sales figure which is subtracted from the adjusted cost of goods available for sale in the retail column must be gross sales after adjustment for sales returns. Sales discounts are not included in the computation. If sales are recorded at gross, then deduct the gross sales figure. If sales are recorded at net, then both the recorded sales and sales discount must be deducted to give the same effect as deducting gross sales. Normal spoilage is generally allowed for in the firm's pricing policies, and for this reason it is deducted from the retail column **after** the calculation of the cost-to-retail ratio. Abnormal spoilage, on the other hand, is deducted from **both** the cost and retail columns **before** the cost-to-retail calculation as it could otherwise distort the ratio. It is then generally reported as a separate loss, either within cost of goods sold or administrative expenses. Abnormal spoilage generally arises from a major theft or casualty, while normal spoilage is usually due to shrinkage or breakage. These determinations and their treatments will vary depending upon the company's policies.

When applying the retail method, separate computations are made for any departments which experience significantly higher or lower profit margins. Distortions arise in applying the retail method when a department sells goods with margins that vary in a proportion different from the margins of goods purchased during the period. In this case, the cost-to-retail percentage would not be representative of the mix of goods in ending inventory. Also, manipulations of income are possible by planning the timing of markups and markdowns.

The retail method is an acceptable method of valuing inventories for income tax purposes. Income tax regulations require valuation at lower of cost or market (except for LIFO) and regular and consistent physical counts of inventory at each location.

LIFO retail method. As with other LIFO concepts, treasury regulations are the governing force behind the LIFO retail method. The regulations differentiate between a "variety" store which is required to use an internally computed index and a "department" store which can use a price index published by the Bureau of Labor Statistics. The computation of an internal index was previously discussed in the dollar-value LIFO section. It involves applying the double-extension method to a representative sample of the ending inventory. Selection of a published index is to be in accordance with the regulations set forth by the Treasury.

The steps used in computing the value of ending inventory under the LIFO retail method are listed below and then applied to an example for illustrative purposes.

1. Calculate (or select) the current year conversion price index. Recall that in the base year this index will be 1.00.
2. Calculate the value of the ending inventory at both cost and retail. Remember, as with other LIFO methods, tax regulations **do not** permit the use of LCM, so both markups and markdowns are included in the computation of the cost-to-retail ratio. However, the beginning inventory is excluded from goods available for sale at cost and at retail.
3. Restate the ending inventory at retail to base-year retail. Divide the current ending inventory at retail by the current year index determined in step 1.
4. Layers are then treated as they were for the dollar-value LIFO example presented earlier. If the ending inventory restated to base-year retail exceeds the previous year's amount at base-year retail, a new layer is established.
5. The computation of LIFO cost is the last step and requires multiplying each layer at base-year retail by the appropriate price index and multiplying this product by the cost-to-retail ratio in order to arrive at the LIFO cost for each layer.

The following example illustrates a two-year period to which the LIFO retail method is applied. The first period represents the first year of operations for the company and is its base year.

Year 1

Step 1 — Because this is the base year, there is no need to compute an index, as it will always be 1.00.

Step 2 —

	Cost	*Retail*
Beginning inventory	$ --	$ --
Purchases	582,400	988,600
Markups	--	164,400
Markdowns	--	(113,000)
Subtotal	582,400	1,040,000
Total goods available for sale	$582,400	1,040,000
Sales—at retail		840,000
Ending year 1 inventory—at retail		$ 200,000

Cost-to-retail ratio $\frac{\text{(a) } 582{,}400}{\text{(b) } 1{,}040{,}000}$ = 56%

Ending inventory at cost
$200,000 x 56% $112,000

Step 3 — Because this is the base year, the restatement to base-year cost is not necessary; however, the computation would be
$200,000/1.00 = $200,000.

Steps 4 and 5 — The determination of layers is again unnecessary in the base year; however, the computation would take the following format.

	Ending inventory at base-year retail	*Conversion price index*	*Cost-to-retail ratio*	*LIFO cost*
Base year ($200,000/1.00)	$200,000	1.00	0.56	$112,000

Year 2

Step 1 — We make the assumption that the computation of an internal index yields a result of 1.12 (obtained by double-extending a representative sample).

Step 2 —

	Cost	*Retail*
Beginning inventory	$112,000	$ 200,000
Purchases	716,300	1,168,500
Markups	--	87,500
Markdowns	--	(21,000)
Subtotal	$716,300	1,235,000
Total goods available for sale		1,435,000
Sales—at retail		1,171,800
Ending year 2 inventory—at retail		$ 263,200

Cost-to-retail ratio $\frac{716{,}300}{1{,}235{,}000}$ = 58%

Step 3 — The restatement of ending inventory at current year retail to base-year retail is done using the index computed in step 1. In this case it is $263,200/1.12 = $235,000.

Steps 4 and 5 — There is a LIFO layer in year 2 because the $235,000 inventory at base-year retail exceeds the year 1 amount of $200,000.

The computation of the LIFO cost for each layer is shown below.

	Ending inventory At base-year retail	*Conversion price index*	*Cost-to-retail ratio*	*LIFO cost*
Base year ($200,000/1.00)	$200,000	1.00	0.56	$112,000
Year 2 layer	35,000	1.12	0.58	22,736
	$235,000			
Ending year 2 inventory at LIFO cost				$134,736

The treatment of subsequent increments and decrements is the same for this method as it is for the regular dollar-value method.

Gross profit method. The gross profit method is used to estimate ending inventory when a physical count is not taken. It can also be used to evaluate the reasonableness of a given inventory amount. Assume the following data:

Beginning inventory	$125,000
Net purchases	450,000
Sales	600,000
Estimated gross profit percentage	32%

Ending inventory is estimated as follows:

Beginning inventory	$125,000
Net purchases	450,000
Cost of goods available for sale	575,000
Cost of goods sold [$600,000 – (32% x $600,000)] or (68% x $600,000)	408,000
Estimated ending inventory	$167,000

The gross profit method is used for interim reporting estimates, analyses by auditors, and estimates of inventory lost in fires or other catastrophes. The method is not acceptable for either income tax or annual financial reporting purposes. Thus, its major purposes are for internal and interim reporting.

Other valuation methods.

Base stock. The base stock method assumes that a certain level of inventory investment is necessary for normal business activities and is, therefore, permanent. The base stock inventory is carried at historical cost. Decreases in the base stock are considered temporary and are charged to cost of goods sold at replacement cost. Increases are carried at current year costs. The base stock approach is seldom used in practice since it is not allowed for income tax purposes, and the LIFO method yields similar results.

Standard costs. Standard costs are predetermined unit costs used by manufacturing firms for planning and control purposes. Standard costs are often used for accounting purposes, and raw materials, work in process, and finished goods inventories are all recorded at standard costs. The use of standard costs in financial reporting is acceptable if adjustments are made periodically to reflect current conditions and if their use approximates the same results that would be obtained by applying one of the recognized cost flow assumptions.

Relative sales value. Relative sales (or net realizable) values are used to assign costs to inventory items purchased or manufactured in groups. This method is applicable to joint products, subdivided assets such as real estate lots, and basket purchases.

For example, products A and B have the same processes performed on them up to the split-off point. The total cost incurred to this point is $80,000. This cost can be assigned to products A and B using their relative sales value at the split-off point. If A could be sold for $60,000 and B for $40,000, the total sales value is $100,000. The cost would be assigned on the basis of each product's relative sales value. Thus, A would be assigned a cost of $48,000 (60,000/100,000 x 80,000) and B a cost of $32,000 (40,000/100,000 x 80,000).

Other Inventory Topics

Purchase commitments. Purchase commitments generally are not recognized in the financial statements because they are executory in nature. However, footnote disclosure is required for firm purchase commitments which are material in amount.

If at a balance sheet date the contract price of these commitments exceeds the market value, the estimated loss is recognized and reported in the income statement. This results in recognition of loss before the inventory is actually purchased.

Inventories valued at selling price. In exceptional cases, inventories may be reported at sales price less disposal costs. Such treatment is justified when cost is difficult to determine, quoted market prices are available, marketability is assured, and units are interchangeable. Precious metals, certain agricultural products, and meat are examples of inventories valued in this manner. When inventory is valued above cost, revenue is recognized before the point of sale. Full disclosure in the financial statements is required.

Interim reporting (also see Chapter 19). The principles used to determine ending inventory and cost of goods sold in annual reports are also used in interim reports, although four exceptions are allowed (under APB 28). These are

1. The gross profit method may be used to estimate cost of goods sold and ending inventory.
2. When LIFO layers are liquidated during the interim period but are expected to be replaced by year-end, cost of goods sold should reflect current costs rather than old LIFO costs.
3. Temporary market declines need not be recognized if substantial evidence exists that market prices will recover. If LCM losses recorded in one interim period are recovered by year-end, the recovery is recognized as a gain.
4. Planned standard cost variances expected to be offset by year-end can be deferred.

EMERGING ISSUES TASK FORCE ISSUES SUMMARIES

86-46 Uniform Capitalization Rules for Inventory under the Tax Reform Act of 1986

The fact that a cost is capitalizable for income tax purposes does not, by itself, indicate that it is preferable, or even appropriate, to capitalize that cost for financial reporting purposes. Individual facts and circumstances are to be analyzed to determine if costs are to be capitalized for financial reporting purposes.

EXPOSURE DRAFT OUTSTANDING

Proposed FAS: Inventory Costs—an amendment of ARB 43, Chapter 4

This proposed standard would amend ARB 43, Chapter 4, regarding the treatment of certain defined inventory costs. The intent is to converge ARB 43 with the corresponding international accounting standard, IAS 2, to prevent inconsistent application of the principles of inventory costing. If approved, the proposed changes would go into effect for fiscal years beginning after December 15, 2004.

Paragraph 5 of ARB 43, Chapter 4, currently reads, "under some circumstances, items such as idle facility expense, excessive spoilage, double freight, and rehandling costs may be so abnormal as to require treatment as current period charges…" By adopting the language of IAS 2, double freight, rehandling costs, and abnormal amounts of spoilage are classified as current period charges, regardless of whether they appear to be abnormal. Convergence is not expected to substantially change practice under US GAAP.

APPENDIX A

LIFO CONFORMITY RULE

As stated earlier in this chapter, Treasury Regulations require that in order to take advantage of LIFO for income tax purposes, a company must also use LIFO for determining income, profit, or loss for financial statement purposes. The regulations also cite certain exceptions to this general rule. Among the exceptions allowable under the regulations are the following:

1. The use of an inventory method other than LIFO in presenting information reported as a supplement to or explanation of the taxpayer's primary presentation of income in financial reports to outside parties. [Reg. §1.472-2(e)(1)(i)]
2. The use of an inventory method other than LIFO to determine the value of the taxpayer's inventory for purposes of reporting the value of such inventory as an asset on the balance sheet. [Reg. §1.472-2(e)(1)(ii)]
3. The use of an inventory method other than LIFO for purposes of determining information reported in internal management reports. [Reg. §1.472-2(e)(1)(iii)]
4. The use of an inventory method other than LIFO for financial reports covering a period of less than one year. [Reg. §1.472- 2(e)(1)(iv)]
5. The use of lower of LIFO cost or market to value inventories for financial statements while using LIFO cost for tax purposes. [Reg. §1.472-2(e)(1)(v)]
6. For inventories acquired in a section 351 transaction, the use of the transferor's acquisition dates and costs for GAAP while using redetermined LIFO layers for tax purposes. [Reg. §1.472-2(e)(1)(vii)]
7. The inclusion of certain costs (under full absorption) in inventory for tax purposes, as required by regulations, while not including those same costs in inventory under GAAP (full absorption). [Reg. §1.472-2(e)(8)(i)]
8. The use of different methods of establishing pools for GAAP purposes and tax purposes. [Reg. §1.472-2(e)(8)(ii)]
9. The use of different determinations of the time sales or purchases are accrued for GAAP purposes and tax purposes. [Reg. §1.472-2(e)(8)(xii)]
10. In the case of a business combination, the use of different methods to allocate basis for GAAP purposes and tax purposes. [Reg. §1.472-2(e)(8)(xiii)]

Another important consideration in applying the LIFO conformity rule is the law concerning related corporations. In accordance with the Tax Reform Act of 1984, all members of the same group of financially related corporations are treated as a single taxpayer when applying the conformity rule. Previously, taxpayers were able to circumvent the conformity rule by having a subsidiary on LIFO, while the non-LIFO parent presented combined non-LIFO financial statements. This is a violation of the conformity requirement [Sec. 472(g)].

APPENDIX B

TASK FORCE ON LIFO INVENTORY PROBLEMS

Most of the prescribed rules concerning the implementation of LIFO have their origins in the Internal Revenue Code and Treasury Regulations. Because authoritative financial accounting pronouncements on implementing LIFO are virtually nonexistent, GAAP has followed income tax laws and regulations. In 1984, the AICPA Task Force on LIFO Inventory problems released an Issues Paper to discuss certain financial accounting issues related to LIFO. Issues Papers constitute generally accepted accounting principles but are not mandatory. The key conclusions from this Issues Paper (entitled "Identification and Discussion of Certain Financial Accounting and Reporting Issues Concerning LIFO Inventories") are described below.

1. **Specific goods vs. dollar-value.** Either the specific goods approach or dollar-value approach to LIFO is acceptable for financial reporting. Disclosure of whether the specific goods or dollar-value approach is used is not required.
2. **Pricing current year purchases.** Three approaches to pricing LIFO inventory increments are available under income tax regulations—earliest acquisition price, latest acquisition price, and average acquisition price. The earliest acquisition price approach is the most compatible with financial reporting objectives, but all three are acceptable for financial reporting.
3. **Quantity to use to determine price.** The price used to determine the inventory increment should be based on the cost of the quantity or dollars of the increment rather than on the cost of the quantity or dollars equal to the ending inventory. Disclosure of which approach is used is not required.
4. **Disclosure of LIFO reserve or replacement cost.** The LIFO reserve or replacement cost and its basis for determination should be disclosed for financial reporting.
5. **Partial adoption of LIFO.** If a company changes to LIFO, it should do so for all of its inventories. Partial adoption should only be allowed if there exists a valid business reason for not fully adopting LIFO. A planned gradual adoption of LIFO over several time periods is considered acceptable if valid business reasons exist (lessening the income statement effect of adoption in any one year is not a valid business reason). Where partial adoption of LIFO has been justified, the extent to which LIFO has been adopted should be disclosed. This can be disclosed by indicating either the portion of the ending inventory priced on LIFO or the portion of cost of sales resulting from LIFO inventories.
6. **Methods of pooling.** The Task Force addressed several issues related to establishing pools. An entity should have valid business reasons for establishing its LIFO pools. Additionally, the existence of a separate legal entity that has no economic substance is not reason enough to justify separate pools. Disclosure of details regarding an entity's pooling arrangements is not required.
7. **New items entering a pool.** New items should be added to a pool based on what the items would have cost had they been acquired in the base period (reconstructed cost) rather than based on their current cost. The reconstructed cost should be determined based on the most objective sources available including published vendor price lists, vendor quotes, and general industry indexes. Where necessary, the use of a substitute base year in making the LIFO computation is acceptable. Disclosure of the way that new items are priced is not required.
8. **Dollar-value index.** The required index can be developed using two possible approaches, the unit cost method or the cost component method. The unit cost method

measures changes in the index based on the weighted-average increase or decrease in the unit costs of raw materials, work in process, and finished goods inventory. The cost component method, on the other hand, measures changes in the index by the weighted-average increase or decrease in the component costs of material, labor, and overhead that make up ending inventory. Either of these methods is acceptable.

9. **LIFO liquidations.** The effects on income of LIFO inventory liquidations should be disclosed in the notes to the financial statements. A replacement reserve for the liquidation should not be provided. When an involuntary LIFO liquidation occurs, the effect on income of the liquidation should not be deferred.

   When a LIFO liquidation occurs, there are three possible ways to measure its effect on income.

   a. The difference between actual cost of sales and what cost of sales would have been had the inventory been reinstated under the entity's normal pricing procedure
   b. The difference between actual cost of sales and what cost of sales would have been had the inventory been reinstated at year-end replacement cost
   c. The amount of the LIFO reserve at the beginning of the year which was credited to income (excluding the increase in the reserve due to current year price changes)

   The first method is considered preferable. Disclosure of the effect of the liquidation should give effect only to pools with decrements (i.e., there should be no netting of pools with decrements against other pools with increments).

10. **Lower of cost or market.** The most reasonable approach to applying the lower of cost or market rules to LIFO inventory is to base the determination on groups of inventory rather than on an item-by-item approach. A pool constitutes a reasonable grouping for this purpose. An item-by-item approach is permitted by authoritative accounting literature, particularly for obsolete or discontinued items.

    For companies with more than one LIFO pool, it is permissible to aggregate the pools in applying the lower of cost or market test if the pools are similar. Where the pools are significantly dissimilar, aggregating the pools is not appropriate.

    Previous write-downs to market value of the cost of LIFO inventories should be reversed after a company disposes of the physical units of the inventory for which reserves were provided. The reserves at the end of the year should be based on a new computation of cost or market.

11. **LIFO conformity and supplemental disclosures.** A company may present supplemental non-LIFO disclosures within the historical cost framework. If nondiscretionary variable expenses (i.e., profit sharing based on earnings) would have been different based on the supplemental information, then the company should give effect to such changes. Additionally, the supplemental disclosure should reflect the same type of income tax effects as required by generally accepted accounting principles in the primary financial statements.

    A company may use different LIFO applications for financial reporting than it uses for income tax purposes. Any such differences should be accounted for as temporary differences with the exception of differences in the allocation of cost to inventory in a business combination. Any differences between LIFO applications used for financial reporting and those used for income tax purposes need not be disclosed beyond the requirements of FAS 109.

12. **Interim reporting and LIFO.** The Task Force's conclusions on interim reporting of LIFO inventory are discussed on pages 890-891.

13. **Different financial and income tax years.** A company which has a year-end for financial reporting different from that for income tax reporting should make a separate LIFO calculation for financial purposes using its financial reporting year as a discrete period for that calculation.
14. **Business combinations accounted for by the purchase method.** Inventory acquired in a business combination accounted for by the purchase method will be recorded at fair value at the date of the combination. The acquired company may be able to carry over its prior basis for that inventory for income tax purposes, causing a difference between GAAP and income tax basis. An adjustment should be made to the fair value of the inventory only if it is reasonably estimated to be liquidated in the future. The adjustment would be for the income tax effect of the difference between income tax and GAAP basis.

    Inventory acquired in such a combination should be considered the LIFO base inventory if the inventory is treated by the company as a separate business unit or a separate LIFO pool. If instead the acquired inventory is combined into an existing pool, then the acquired inventory should be considered as part of the current year's purchases.
15. **Changes in LIFO applications.** A change in a LIFO application is a change in accounting principle. LIFO applications refer to the approach (i.e., dollar value or specific goods), computational technique, or the numbers or contents of the pools.

    The AICPA Task Force did not discuss intercompany transfers in the 1984 Issues Paper; however, the AICPA issued Practice Bulletin 2 in 1987 to provide guidance for this complex area.

    The focus of this bulletin is the LIFO liquidation effect caused by transferring inventories which in turn create intercompany profits. This liquidation can occur when (1) two components of the same taxable entity transfer inventory, for example, when a LIFO method component transfers inventory to a non-LIFO component, or (2) when two separate taxable entities that consolidate transfer inventory, even though both use the LIFO method.

    This LIFO liquidation creates profit which must be eliminated along with other intercompany profits.

8 REVENUE RECOGNITION – EVOLVING PRINCIPLES AND SPECIALIZED APPLICATIONS

REVENUE RECOGNITION — GENERAL PRINCIPLES

The principles guiding recognition of revenues for financial reporting purposes are central to GAAP and in most instances are unambiguous and straightforward. In fact, the underlying principles have not changed in decades. However, some disturbing trends in recent years resulted in revenue recognition practices having been instrumental in the perpetration of numerous instances of financial reporting frauds.

First, business practices have continued to grow increasingly complex, involving, among other things, a marked shift from manufacturing to a services-based economy, where the proper timing for revenue recognition is often more difficult to ascertain. Second, there has been an undeniable increase in the willingness of managers, whose compensation packages are often directly linked to the company's stock price and reported earnings, to "stretch" accounting rules to facilitate earnings management. And third, it has been well documented that, too often, independent auditors have been willing to accommodate managements' wishes, particularly in the absence of specific rules under GAAP to support denying their requests. These actions have often had disastrous consequences, if not immediately, then at least in the longer run.

Errors or deliberate distortions involving revenue recognition fall into two categories: situations in which revenue legitimately earned is reported in the incorrect fiscal (financial reporting) period, often referred to as "cutoff" errors, and situations in which revenue is recognized although never actually earned. Given the emphasis on periodic reporting (e.g., quarterly earnings announcements in the case of publicly held entities), even simple "cutoff" errors can have enormous impact, notwithstanding the fact that these should tend to offset over several periods. As a practical matter, all instances of improper revenue recognition are very serious, and these constitute a challenge to all accountants attempting to properly interpret and apply GAAP, including independent auditors.

The various rules with respect to recognition of revenue for different types of transactions have evolved over a long period of time and have been written piecemeal by different standard setters in differing economic environments. There are, in fact, currently more than 140 pieces of authoritative literature dealing with various aspects of revenue recognition, contributing perhaps to the confusion that may have resulted in at least some of the misapplications of GAAP. One response has been the initiation of a joint project by the FASB and its international counterpart, IASB, the objective of which are to (1) eliminate inconsistencies in the existing literature, (2) provide additional, needed guidance for new types of transactions and arrangements that have arisen in the current economic environment, and (3) provide a framework for addressing future revenue recognition issues.

As of mid-2004, this project has resulted in a decision to pursue an approach based on changes in assets and liabilities and that is not overridden by tests based on notions of realization and completion of the earnings process. This new approach is deemed to be consistent with principles espoused by CON 6, and will have the beneficial effect of sidestepping the task of assessing completion of the earnings process, which, particularly for service transactions, is difficult and fraught with subjectivity. A final standard would likely supersede much existing literature, including venerable standards such as APB 29 and FAS 48, addressing, respectively, nonmonetary transactions and rights of return.

The underlying revenue recognition principle will be that "a reporting entity should recognize revenues in the accounting period in which they arise and measure them at their fair value on the date that they arise if it can determine both their occurrence and measurement with sufficient clarity." The corresponding underlying recognition principle will be "a reporting entity should measure revenues arising from an increase in its assets or a decrease in its liabilities (or a combination thereof) at the fair value of that increase or decrease."

A series of six recognition principles flowing from these overarching standards has been agreed to (a proposed seventh recognition principle has been withdrawn), as have six measurement principles. These are as follows:

Recognition Principle 1

Contractual revenues cannot arise before a contract with a customer exists.

Recognition Principle 2

A reporting entity should recognize contractual revenues when an increase in its claims against its customers can be determined to have occurred and the fair value of that increase can be measured with sufficient reliability.

Recognition Principle 3

A reporting entity should recognize contractual revenues when a decrease in claims against it by its customers can be determined to have occurred and the fair value of that decrease can be measured with sufficient reliability.

Recognition Principle 4

Increases in assets or decreases in liabilities that give rise to contractual revenues may stem from contractual promises that can be either express or implied.

Recognition Principle 5

Contractual revenues should be recognized at contract inception if the fair values of the contractual assets obtained on that date exceed the fair values of the contractual liabilities simultaneously incurred, and if those revenues can be measured with sufficient reliability.

Recognition Principle 6

Subsequent to contract inception, contractual revenues should be recognized upon the reporting entity's performance of its obligations under the contract, as evidenced by a decrease in its contractual liabilities or an increase in its contractual assets, the fair value of which can be determined with sufficient reliability.

Measurement Principle 1

The estimates of the fair value that the reporting entity uses to measure revenues arising from increases in its assets or decreases in its liabilities should be those that have the highest relative reliability.

Measurement Principle 2

The estimates of the fair value of revenues that are consistent with Level 3 of the fair value hierarchy should be developed by means of multiple valuation techniques that maximize market inputs, such as a market approach or an income approach, whenever information necessary to apply those techniques is available.

Measurement Principle 3

The fair value of revenues from increases in the reporting entity's contractual assets reflects the effects of credit risk, the time value of money, and dilution risk.

Measurement Principle 4

The measures that reflect the effects of credit risk on the fair value of a reporting entity's revenues also should reflect expectations of recoveries, if any, in case of breach of the contract by the customer.

Measurement Principle 5

Any express or implied rights of return and refund, allowance, rebates, discounts, credits, and other similar rights granted to customers that reduce revenues by reducing the reporting entity's contractual liabilities should be measured at fair value.

Measurement Principle 6

Revenues arising from increases in contractual assets that stem from the reporting entity's rights to the customer's stand ready performance in case of occurrence or non-occurrence of a specified event should be measured at fair value that reflects the assessment of the probability that the specified event will occur.

Notwithstanding this agreement on basic approach, the joint FASB-IASB project still has many fundamental decisions yet to be made. As of mid-2004, FASB's expectations are for proposed amendments to CON 6 and a broad-based statement of principles on revenue recognition to be issued in late 2004. The timings of final statements have not been announced.

In terms of currently enforceable guidance, under long-established GAAP, revenue, whether from the sale of product or provision of services, is to be recognized only when it has been earned. According to CON 5, *Recognition and Measurement in Financial Statements of Business Enterprises*,

> *...(a)n entity's revenue-earning activities involve delivering or producing goods, rendering services, or other activities that constitute its ongoing major or central operations, and revenues are considered to have been earned when the entity has substantially accomplished what it must do to be entitled to the benefits represented by the revenues.*

In other words, in order to be recognized revenue must be realized or realizable, and it must have been earned.

CON 5 notes that "the two conditions (being realized or realizable, and being earned) are usually met by the time product or merchandise is delivered or services are rendered to customers, and revenues from manufacturing and selling activities and gains and losses from sales of other assets are commonly recognized at time of sale (usually meaning delivery)." Moreover, "if services are rendered or rights to use assets extend continuously over time (for example, interest or rent), reliable measures based on contractual prices established in advance are commonly available, and revenues may be recognized as earned as time passes." In other words, for most traditional and familiar types of transactions, the point at which it is appropriate to recognize revenue will be quite clear.

The SEC, reflecting on the conceptual foundation for revenue recognition, has observed in Staff Accounting Bulletin 101 that

> *...revenue generally is realized or realizable and earned when* ***all*** *of the following criteria are met:*
>
> 1. *There is persuasive evidence that an arrangement exists*
> 2. *Delivery has occurred or services have been rendered*
> 3. *The seller's price to the buyer is fixed or determinable, and*
> 4. *Collectibility is reasonably assured*

Note that, while SEC rules and "unofficial" guidance are not necessarily to be deemed GAAP for nonpublic companies, to the extent that these provide insights into standards found in the GAAP hierarchy, they should always be viewed as relevant guidance and followed, absent other, contradictory rules established under GAAP. In the absence of any other source found in the GAAP hierarchy, SEC pronouncements may represent the best thinking on the subject and are considered authoritative for all reporting entities.

With regard to the four criteria set forth above, consideration should be directed at the following discussion, which is drawn partially from SAB 101.

First, regarding persuasive evidence of an arrangement, attention must be paid to the customary manner in which the reporting entity engages in revenue-producing transactions with its customers or clients. Since these transactions are negotiated between the buyer and seller and can have unique or unusual terms, there are (and can be) no absolute standards. Thus, for an enterprise that traditionally obtains appropriate documentation (purchase orders, etc.) from its customers before concluding sales to them, advance deliveries to customers, even if later ratified by receipt of the proper paperwork, would not be deemed a valid basis for revenue recognition at the time of delivery.

When evaluating purported revenue transactions, the substance of the transactions must always be considered, and not merely their form. It has become increasingly commonplace to "paper over" transactions in ways that can create the basis for inappropriate revenue recognition. For example, transactions that are actually consignment arrangements might be described as "sales" or as "conditional sales," but revenue recognition would not be appropriate until the consigned goods are later sold to a third-party purchaser.

Careful analysis of the rights and obligations of the parties and the risks borne by each at various stages of the transactions should reveal when and whether an actual sale has occurred and whether revenue recognition is warranted. In general, if the buyer has a right to return the product in question, coupled with a deferred or conditional payment obligation and/or significant remaining performance obligations by the seller, revenue will not be recognizable by the seller at the time of initial delivery. Similarly, if there is an implicit or explicit obligation by the seller to repurchase the item transferred, a real sales transaction has not occurred. The buyer must assume the risks of ownership in all cases if revenue is to be recognized.

With regard to whether delivery has occurred or services have been rendered, ownership and risk taking must have been transferred to the buyer if revenue is to be recognized by the seller. Thus, if the seller is holding goods for delivery to the buyer because the buyer's receiving dock workers are on strike and no deliveries are being accepted, revenue generally cannot be recognized in the reporting period, even if these delayed deliveries are made subsequent to period end. (There are limited exceptions to this general principle, typically involving a written request from the buyer for delayed delivery under a "bill and hold" arrangement, having a valid business purpose.)

Delivery, as used here, implies more than simply the physical relocation of the goods to the buyer's place of business. Rather, it means that the goods have actually been accepted by the customer, which, depending on the terms of the relevant contract, could be conditioned on whether inspection, testing, and/or installation have been completed, and the buyer has committed to pay for the items purchased. For revenue recognition to be justified, substantial performance of the terms of delivery must have occurred, and if any terms remain uncompleted, there should be a basis grounded on historical experience to assume that these matters will be satisfactorily attended to.

In some instances there are multiple "deliverables"; in such cases, revenue is not recognized for any given element if later deliverables are essential for the functionality of the already delivered element. In other situations, such as in various licensing arrangements, physical "delivery" may occur well before product usage by the buyer can take place (e.g., software for the future year's tax preparation delivered before the current year end), and revenue is not to be recognized prior to the initial date of expected use by the buyer.

In the case of many service transactions, large up-front fees are often charged, nominally in recognition of the selling of a membership, the signing of a contract, or for enrolling the customer in a program. (For example, initiation fees to join a health club where the terms of membership also obligate the member to pay ongoing fees.) Unless the services provided to the customer at inception are substantial, the rebuttable presumption is that the revenue received has not been earned, but rather must be deferred and recognized, usually ratably, over the period that substantive services are provided. Thus, initiation fees are amortized over the membership period.

The seller's price to the buyer is fixed or determinable when a customer does not have the unilateral right to terminate or cancel the contract and receive a cash refund. Depending on customary practice, extended return privileges might imply that this condition has not been met in given circumstances. Prices that are conditional on the occurrence of future events are not fixed or determinable from the perspective of revenue recognition.

In theory, until the refund rights have expired, or the specified future events have occurred, revenue should not be recognized. As a practical matter, however, assuming that the amount of refunds can be reliably estimated (based on past experience, industry data, etc.), revenues, net of expected refunds, can be recognized on a pro rata basis. Absent this ability to reliably estimate, however, revenue recognition is deferred.

The final factor, reasonable assurance of collectibility, implies that the accrual for bad debts (uncollectible accounts receivable) can be estimated with reasonable accuracy, both to accomplish proper periodic matching of revenue and expenses, and to enable the presentation of receivables at net realizable value, as required under GAAP. An inability to accomplish this objective necessitates deferral of revenue recognition—generally until collection occurs, or at least until it becomes feasible to estimate the uncollectible portion with sufficient accuracy.

Evolving Problems in Revenue Recognition

Certain of the more attention-getting problems in applying the general principles of revenue recognition are discussed in the following paragraphs.

Financial statement presentation: gross vs. net. In general, it is well established that reporting on a "gross" basis is appropriate when the entity takes ownership of the goods being sold to its customers, as a middleman, for example, with the risks and rewards of ownership accruing to it. For example, if the entity runs the risk of obsolescence or spoilage during the period it holds the merchandise, gross reporting would normally be appropriate. On the other hand, if the entity merely acts as an agent for the buyer or seller from whom it earns a commission, then "net" reporting would be more appropriate.

In recent years there have been increasing reports of enterprises that inflate revenues reported in their income statements by reporting transactions on a "gross" basis, notwithstanding that the entity's real economic role is as an agent for buyer and/or seller. This distortion became widespread in the case of Internet commerce-based "dot-com companies" and other start-up and innovative businesses typically not reporting earnings, for which market valuations were heavily influenced by absolute levels of and trends in gross revenues. Reporting revenues "gross" rather than "net" often had an enormous impact on the perceived value of those enterprises. (Whether valuations based on revenues are valid, even if revenues are properly reported, is beyond the scope of this discussion.)

Factors to consider in determining whether sales are properly reported "gross" or "net" include

1. Whether the entity acts as a principal or an agent in the transactions
2. Whether the entity takes title to the property
3. Whether the entity has the normal risks and rewards of ownership
4. Whether the entity acts as an agent or broker (including performing services, in substance, as an agent or broker) with compensation on a commission or fee basis

Barter transactions. Barter transactions (nonmonetary exchanges, as described in APB 29) are not a problem, assuming that they represent the culmination of an earnings process. However, in recent years there have been many reports of transactions that appear to have been concocted merely to create the illusion of revenue-generating activities. Examples include advertising swaps engaged in by some "dot-com" enterprises, and the excess capacity swaps of fiber optic communications concerns. Both of these and other situations involved immediate recognition of revenues coupled with deferred recognition of costs, and typically in aggregate were equal exchanges not providing profits to either party. Furthermore, these examples do not represent culminations of the normal earnings process (e.g., fiber optic networks were built in order to sell communications services to end users, not for the purpose of swapping capacity with other similar operations).

In hindsight, most observers can see why these and many other aggressive reporting practices deviated from established or implied GAAP; although there are still some who insist that because GAAP failed to explicitly address these precise scenarios, the accounting for the transactions was open to interpretation. Since GAAP (even the highly rules-based US GAAP) cannot possibly hope to overtly address all the various innovative transaction structures that exist and will be invented, it is necessary to apply basic principles and reason by analogy to newly emerging circumstances. Of great importance to financial statement preparers (and internal and external auditors) is obtaining a thorough understanding of the nature and normal operations of the business enterprise being reported upon, application of "substance over form" reasoning, and the goal of faithfully representing the economics of transactions.

Channel stuffing. Many difficult issues of revenue recognition involve practices that may or may not involve GAAP departures, depending on the facts and circumstances. Channel stuffing is a prime example of this type of matter. To the extent that late-in-the-period sales spurts are real events (e.g., stimulated by vendor sales contests, etc.), the revenues are properly recognized since they reflect the underlying economic events and are not mere accounting artifacts. At the opposite extreme, sales made after period end but recorded as having occurred earlier (e.g., because the accounting records had been "held open") are clearly improper even under the most generous interpretations of applicable GAAP. In between these extremes, however, might be sales made prior to the period-end cutoff but that were stimulated by "side agreements," such as a promise to customers of extended return privileges. In some such circumstances, it will be that a substantial portion of these sales will be subsequently nullified, as unrealistically large orders inevitably lead to later large returns made for full credit.

For purposes of financial reporting under GAAP, valuation allowances are established for expected sales returns and allowances. (In practice, this is rarely done because the amounts involved are so small, unlike the more familiar allowances for uncollectible accounts.) This is dictated by both the matching concept (recording returns and allowances in the same fiscal period in which the revenue is recognized) and the requirement to present accounts receivable at net realizable value. When the potential product returns are not subject to reasonable estimation (as when a sales promotion effort of the type just described is first being attempted by the reporting entity),it might not be permissible to recognize revenues at all, pending subsequent developments (FAS 48). Furthermore, from the SEC's perspective, factors such as the following could require deferral of revenues at the time goods are shipped to customers, pending resolution of material uncertainties.

1. Significant levels of product inventory in the distribution channel
2. Lack of "visibility" into, or the inability to determine or observe, the levels of inventory in a distribution channel and the current level of sales to end users
3. Expected introductions of new products that may result in the technological obsolescence of, and larger than expected returns of, current products
4. The significance of a particular distributor to the company's (or a reporting segment of the company's) business, sales and marketing
5. The newness of a product
6. The introduction of competitors' products with superior technology or greater expected market acceptance could affect market demand and changing trends in that demand for an entity's products

Mischaracterization of extraordinary or unusual transactions as components of gross revenue. Not all revenue recognition errors and frauds involve questions of when or if revenue should be recognized. In some instances, classification in the income statement is of greater concern. While matters in this group often do not result in a distortion of net results of operations, they can seriously distort important indicators of performance trends. When this occurs, it most often involves reporting unusual or infrequent gains on sales of segments or specific assets as revenue from product or service transactions. A variation on this involves reporting unusual gains as offsets to one or more categories of operating expenses, similarly distorting key financial ratios and other indicators, again without necessarily invalidating the net income measure.

Mischaracterizing transactions as involving "arm's-length" third parties, thus justifying unwarranted gain recognition. Transfers of inventory or other assets to a related entity typically defers gain or income recognition until subsequent transfer to an "arm's-length" party. In some cases, sales have been disguised as being to unrelated entities with gain being recognized, when in fact the "buyer" was a nominee of the seller, or the financing was provided or guaranteed by the seller, or the "buyer" was a "special-purpose entity" that failed to meet the complex and changing requirements under GAAP required for gain recognition. (Note that what were formerly described as "special-purpose entities" have now been denoted as "variable interest entities" under FIN 46, which is discussed elsewhere in this book.) Depending upon the facts of the situation, this can result in gains being improperly recognized, or the gross amount of the transaction being improperly recognized in the seller/transferor's financial statements.

Selling undervalued assets to generate reportable gains. This issue again ranges from deliberate but real economic transactions that have as a goal the inflation of reportable revenues or gains, to misrepresented events having no economic substance but the same objective. Among the former is the deliberate invasion of low-cost LIFO inventory "layers," which boosts gross margins and net profits for the period, albeit at the cost of having to later replenish inventories with higher-cost goods. To the extent that this depletion of lower-cost inventory really occurs, there is no GAAP alternative to reflecting these excess profits currently, although the threat of full disclosure may prove to be somewhat of a deterrent.

Regarding the latter category, in some instances the ability to generate gains could indicate that errors occurred in recording a previous transaction. Thus, large gains flowing from the sale of assets recently acquired in a purchase business combination transaction could well mean the purchase price allocation process had been flawed. If this is true, a reallocation of purchase price would be called for, and some or all of the apparent gains would be eliminated.

Related to the foregoing is the strategy of retiring outstanding debt in order to generate reportable gains. (Gains on debt extinguishment were previously required to be shown as extraordinary items under GAAP, until the issuance of FAS 145 in April 2002 effectively eliminated this practice.) In periods of higher-than-historical interest rates, lenders will agree to early extinguishment of outstanding obligations at a discount, hence creating gains for the borrower, albeit replacement debt at current yields will result in higher interest costs over future years. To the extent the debt is really retired, however, this is a real economic event, and the consequent gain is reported in current earnings under GAAP.

Deliberate misstatement of percentage of completion on long-term construction contracts. Under SOP 81-1 (detailed later in this chapter), profits on certain long-term construction-type contracts are recognized ratably over the period of construction. An obvious and often easy way to distort periodic results of operations is to deliberately over- or understate the degree to which one or more discrete projects has been completed as of period end. This, coupled with the difficulty and importance of estimating remaining costs to be incurred to complete each project, makes profit recognition under this required method of accounting challenging to verify.

Disclosures

APB 22 requires disclosures of "…important judgments as to appropriateness of principles relating to the recognition of revenue." SAB 101 expresses the opinion of the SEC staff that because revenue recognition generally involves the exercise of judgment, companies are always required to disclose their revenue recognition policies. SAB 101 also provides that, when applicable, the notes to the financial statements are to include disclosure of

1. The revenue recognition policy for each material type of transaction
2. If the company enters into multiple-element sales arrangements (e.g., bundling of related products and/or services), the method of accounting for each element and the method used to determine each element and value it
3. Material changes in estimates of returns in accordance with FAS 48 (e.g., changing the percentage of sales used to establish the allowance).

In addition, SEC Regulation S-X requires that each of the following categories of revenue (and the related costs), if applicable, be stated separately on the face of the income statement:

1. Sales of tangible products (net of discounts, returns, and allowances)
2. Income from rentals
3. Revenue from services
4. Other revenues

In addition to the foregoing, the financial statement preparer should consider the applicability of FAS 57, *Related Party Disclosures,* and SOP 94-6, *Disclosure of Certain Significant Risks and Uncertainties.* (See Chapter 2.)

Specialized Applications

The remainder of this chapter discusses specialized principles that have been established for accounting for the following types of transactions:

1. Long-term construction contracts
2. Service revenues
3. Sales when collection is uncertain
4. Revenue recognition when right of return exists
5. Profit recognition on real estate sales
6. Real estate operations
7. Franchising
8. Other special accounting and reporting issues

Each of these sections may be read as an individual unit.

LONG-TERM CONSTRUCTION CONTRACTS

PERSPECTIVE AND ISSUES

Accounting for long-term construction contracts involves questions as to when revenue is to be recognized and how to measure the revenue to be recorded. The basic GAAP governing the recognition of long-term contract revenue is contained in ARB 45, *Long-Term Construction-Type Contracts,* AcSEC Statement of Position 81-1, *Accounting for Performance of Construction-Type and Certain Production-Type Contracts,* and the AICPA *Audit and Accounting Guide for Construction Contractors.*[1] In accordance with SAS 69, Account-

[1] *The SOP is included as an appendix to the Audit and Accounting Guide.*

ing Research Bulletins (ARB) are "category A" (the highest level) GAAP, and SOP 81-1 and the Audit and Accounting Guide are "category B" GAAP.

The accounting for long-term construction contracts is complicated by the need to rely upon estimates of revenues, costs to be incurred, and progress toward completion.

Sources of GAAP				
CON	*ARB*	*APB*	*FAS*	*SOP*
5	45	20	109	81-1, 98-5

DEFINITIONS OF TERMS

Back charges. Billings for work performed or costs incurred by one party (the biller) that, in accordance with the agreement, should have been performed or incurred by the party billed.

Change order. A legal document executed by a contractor and customer (which can be initiated by either) that modifies selected terms of a contract (e.g., pricing, timing and scope of work) without the necessity of redrafting the entire contract.

Claims. Amounts in excess of the agreed contract price that a contractor seeks to collect from customers for customer-caused delays, errors in specifications and designs, unapproved change orders, or other causes of unanticipated costs. (SOP 81-1)

Combining contracts. Grouping two or more contracts into a single profit center for accounting purposes.

Completed-contract method. A method of accounting that recognizes revenue only after the contract is complete.

Cost-to-cost method. A percentage-of-completion method used to determine the extent of progress toward completion on a contract. The ratio of costs incurred from project inception through the end of the current period (numerator) to the total estimated costs of the project (denominator) is applied to the contract price (as adjusted for change orders) to determine total contract revenue earned to date.

Estimated cost to complete. The anticipated additional cost of materials, labor, subcontracting costs, and indirect costs (overhead) required to complete a project at a scheduled time.

Percentage-of-completion method. A method of accounting that recognizes revenue on a contract as work progresses.

Precontract costs. Costs incurred before a contract has been accepted (e.g., architectural designs, purchase of special equipment, engineering fees, and start-up costs).

Profit center. A unit for the accumulation of revenues and costs for the measurement of contract performance.

Progress billings on long-term contracts. Requests for partial payments sent to the customer in accordance with the terms of the contract at agreed-upon intervals as various project milestones are reached.

Segmenting contracts. Dividing a single contract or group of contracts into two or more profit centers for accounting purposes.

Subcontractor. A second-level contractor who enters into a contract with a prime (general) contractor to perform a specific part or phase of a construction project.

Substantial completion. The point at which the major work on a contract is completed and only insignificant costs and potential risks remain.

Work-in-progress (WIP). The accumulated construction costs of the project that have been incurred since project inception.

CONCEPTS, RULES, AND EXAMPLES

Long-term construction contract revenue is recognizable over time as construction progresses rather than at the completion of the contract. This "as earned" approach to revenue recognition is justified because under most long-term construction contracts both the buyer and the seller (contractor) obtain legally enforceable rights. The buyer has the legal right to require specific performance from the contractor and, in effect, has an ownership claim to the contractor's work in progress. The contractor, under most long-term contracts, has the right to require the buyer to make progress payments during the construction period. The substance of this business activity is that revenue is earned continuously as the work progresses.

Methods of Accounting

ARB 45 describes the two generally accepted methods of accounting for long-term construction contracts.

The percentage-of-completion method.

> *The* ***percentage-of-completion method*** *recognizes income as work on a contract (or group of closely related contracts) progresses. The recognition of revenues and profits is generally related to costs incurred in providing the services required under the contract.*

Under this method, **work-in-progress (WIP)** is accumulated in the accounting records. At any point in time if the cumulative billings to date under the contract exceed the amount of the WIP plus the portion of the contract's estimated gross profit attributable to that WIP, then the contractor recognizes a current liability captioned "billings in excess of costs and estimated earnings." This liability recognizes the remaining obligation of the contractor to complete additional work prior to recognizing the excess billing as revenue.

If the reverse is true, that is, the accumulated WIP and gross profit earned exceed billings to date, then the contractor recognizes a current asset captioned "costs and estimated earnings in excess of billings." This asset represents the portion of the contractor's revenues under the contract that have been earned but not yet billed under the contract provisions. Where more than one contract exists, these assets and liabilities are determined on a project-by-project basis, with the accumulated assets and liabilities being separately stated on the balance sheet. Assets and liabilities are not offset unless a right of offset exists. Thus, the net debit balances for certain contracts are not ordinarily offset against net credit balances for other contracts. An exception may exist if the balances relate to contracts that meet the criteria for combining described in SOP 81-1 and discussed later in this section.

Under the percentage-of-completion method, income is not based on cash collections or interim billings. Cash collections and interim billings are based upon contract terms that do not necessarily measure contract performance.

The completed-contract method. Per ARB 45

> *The* ***completed-contract method*** *recognizes income only when the contract is complete, or substantially complete.*

Under this method, contract costs and related billings are accumulated in the accounting records and reported as deferred items on the balance sheet until the project is complete or substantially complete. A contract is regarded as substantially complete if remaining costs of completion are immaterial. When the accumulated costs (WIP) exceed the related billings, the excess is presented as a current asset (inventory account). If billings exceed related costs, the difference is presented as a current liability. This determination is also made on a project-by-project basis with the accumulated assets and liabilities being separately stated on the balance sheet. An excess of accumulated costs over related billings is presented as a current asset, and an excess of accumulated billings over related costs is presented in most cases as a current liability.

Preferability assessment. SOP 81-1 deems the percentage-of-completion method to be preferable when estimates are reasonably dependable and the following conditions exist:

1. Contracts executed by the parties include provisions that clearly specify the enforceable rights regarding goods or services to be provided and received by the parties, the consideration to be exchanged, and the manner and terms of settlement.
2. The buyer can be expected to satisfy his or her obligations under the contract.
3. The contractor can be expected to perform his or her contractual obligations.

SOP 81-1 presumes that contractors generally have the ability to produce estimates that are sufficiently dependable to justify the use of the percentage-of-completion method of accounting. Persuasive evidence to the contrary is necessary to overcome this presumption.

The principal advantage of the completed-contract method is that it is based on final results, whereas the percentage-of-completion method is dependent upon estimates for unperformed work. The principal disadvantage of the completed-contract method is that when the period of a contract extends into more than one accounting period, there will be an irregular recognition of income.

These two methods are not be used as acceptable alternatives for the same set of circumstances. ARB 45 states that, in general, when estimates of costs to complete and extent of progress toward completion of long-term contracts are reasonably dependable, the percentage-of-completion method is preferable. When lack of dependable estimates or inherent hazards cause forecasts to be doubtful, the completed-contract method is preferable.

The completed-contract method may also be acceptable when a contractor has numerous relatively short-term contracts and when results of operations do not vary materially from those that would be reported under the percentage-of-completion method.

Based on the contractor's individual circumstances, a decision is made as to whether to apply completed-contract or percentage-of-completion accounting as the entity's basic accounting policy. If warranted by different facts and circumstances regarding a particular contract or group of contracts, that contract or group of contracts is to be accounted for under the other method with accompanying financial statement disclosures of this departure from the normal policy.

Costs Incurred

Precontract costs. Precontract costs are costs incurred **before** a contract has been entered into, with the expectation of the contract being accepted and thereby recoverable through future billings. Precontract costs include architectural designs, costs of learning a new process, and any other costs that are expected to be recovered if the contract is accepted. SOP 98-5, *Reporting on the Costs of Start-Up Activities,* requires that precontract costs be expensed as incurred, as they are the equivalent of start-up costs in other types of businesses. Consequently, precontract costs are not permitted to be included in WIP. Contract costs incurred after the acceptance of the contract are costs incurred towards the completion of the project and are accumulated in work-in-progress (WIP).

If precontract costs are incurred in connection with a current contract in anticipation of obtaining additional future contracts, those costs are nevertheless accounted for as costs of the current contract. If such costs are not incurred in connection with a current contract, then they must be expensed as incurred. There is no look-back provision in this standard. A contractor may not retroactively record precontract costs as WIP if a contract is subsequently executed.

Contract costs. Contract costs are costs identifiable with or allocable to specific contracts. Generally, contract costs include all direct costs such as direct materials, direct labor, and any indirect costs (overhead) allocable to the contracts. Contract costs can be broken down into two categories: costs incurred to date and estimated costs to complete.

The company may choose to defer costs related to producing excess goods in anticipation of future orders of the same item. Cost associated with excess production can be treated as inventory if the costs are considered recoverable.

Estimated costs to complete. These are the **anticipated costs** required to complete a project at a scheduled time. They are comprised of the same elements as the original total estimated contract costs and are based on prices expected to be in effect when the costs will be incurred.

The latest estimates are used to determine the progress towards completion. SOP 81-1 provides the practices to be followed when estimating costs to complete.

Systematic and consistent procedures are to be used. These procedures are to be correlated with the cost accounting system in order to facilitate a comparison between actual and estimated costs. Additionally, the determination of estimated total contract costs is to identify the significant cost elements.

Estimated costs are to reflect any expected price increases. These expected price increases are not "blanket provisions" for all contract costs, but rather specific provisions for each specific type of cost. Expected increases in each of the cost elements such as wages, materials, and overhead items are considered separately.

Finally, estimates of costs to complete are to be reviewed periodically to reflect new information. Estimates of costs are to be examined for price fluctuations and reviewed for possible future problems, such as labor strikes or direct material delivery delays.

Accounting for contract costs is similar to accounting for inventory. Costs necessary to ready the asset for sale (transfer of possession and occupancy by the customer) are recorded in WIP as incurred. WIP includes both direct and indirect costs but not general and administrative expenses or selling expenses since, by definition, they are not identifiable with a particular contract and are therefore treated as period costs. However, general and administrative expenses **may** be included in contract costs under the completed contract method since this could result in better matching of revenues and costs, especially in years when no contracts were completed.

Subcontractor costs. Since a contractor may not be able to perform all facets of a construction project, one or more subcontractors may be engaged. Amounts earned by the subcontractor are included in contract costs as the work is completed. These amounts are directly attributable to the project and included in WIP, similar to direct materials and direct labor.

Back charges. Contract costs may require adjustment for back charges. A back charge is a billing by the contractor to a subcontractor (or a reduction in the amount due to that subcontractor under the subcontract) for costs incurred by the contractor to complete or correct work that the contract stipulated was to have been performed by the subcontractor. These charges are often disputed by the parties involved.

Example of a back charge situation

The subcontract (the contract between the general contractor and the subcontractor) obligates the subcontractor to raze a building and prepare the land for construction of a replacement building. The general contractor had to clear away debris left by the subcontractor before construction could begin. The general contractor expects to be reimbursed for the work since it was required to be performed by the subcontractor. The contractor back charges the subcontractor for the costs of debris removal.

The contractor treats the back charge as a receivable from the subcontractor (or a reduction in the amount payable to the subcontractor) and reduces contract costs by the amount recoverable. If the subcontractor disputes the back charge, the cost becomes a claim. Claims are an amount in excess of the agreed contract price or amounts not included in the original contract price that the contractor seeks to collect. Claims are only recorded as additional contract revenue if the requirements set forth in SOP 81-1 are met.

The subcontractor records the back charge as a payable and as additional contract costs if it is probable the amount will be paid. If the amount or validity of the liability is disputed, the subcontractor considers the probable outcome in order to determine the proper accounting treatment.

Types of Contracts

Four types of contracts are distinguished based on their pricing arrangements: (1) fixed-price or lump-sum contracts, (2) time-and-materials contracts, (3) cost-type contracts, and (4) unit-price contracts.

Fixed-price contracts are contracts for which the price is not usually subject to adjustment because of costs incurred by the contractor. The contractor bears the risks of cost overruns.

Time-and-materials contracts are contracts that provide for payments to the contractor based on direct labor hours at fixed rates and the contractor's cost of materials.

Cost-type contracts provide for reimbursement of allowable or otherwise defined costs incurred plus a fee representing profits. Some variations of cost-plus contracts are (1) cost-without-fee: no provision for a fee, (2) cost-plus-fixed-fee: contractor reimbursed for costs plus provision for a fixed fee, and (3) cost-plus-award-fee: same as (2) plus provision for an award based on performance. The contract price on a cost-type contract is determined by the sum of the reimbursable expenditures and a fee. The fee is the profit margin (revenue less direct expenses) to be earned on the contract.

Unit-price contracts are contracts under which the contractor is paid a specified amount for every unit of work performed.

Contract costs (incurred and estimated to complete) are used to compute the gross profit or loss recognized. Under the percentage-of-completion method, gross profit or loss is recognized each period. The revenue recognized is matched against the contract costs incurred (similar to cost of goods sold) to determine gross profit or loss. Under the completed contract method, the gross profit or loss is determined at the **substantial completion** of the contract, and no revenue or contract costs are recognized until this point.

Additionally, inventoriable costs (accumulated in WIP) are never to exceed the net realizable value (NRV) of the contract. When contract costs exceed their NRV, they must be written down, requiring a contract loss to be recognized in the current period (this will be discussed in greater detail later). This is similar to accounting for inventory.

Revenue Measurement

In practice, various methods are used to measure the extent of progress toward completion. The most common methods are the cost-to-cost method, efforts-expended method, units-of-delivery method, and units-of-work-performed method. Each of these methods of measuring progress on a contract can be identified as either an input or output measure.

The input measures attempt to identify progress on a contract in terms of the efforts devoted to it. The cost-to-cost and efforts-expended methods are examples of input measures. Under the cost-to-cost method, the percentage of completion is estimated by comparing total costs incurred from the inception of the job to date (numerator) to total costs expected for the entire job (denominator).

Output measures are made in terms of results by attempting to identify progress toward completion by physical measures. The units-of-delivery and units-of-work-performed methods are examples of output measures. Under both of these methods, an estimate of completion is made in terms of achievements to date.

Both input and output measures have drawbacks in certain circumstances. A significant problem of input measures is that the relationship between input and productivity is only indirect; inefficiencies and other factors can cause this relationship to change. A particular drawback of the cost-to-cost method is that costs of uninstalled materials and other up-front costs may produce higher estimates of the percentage-of-completion because of their early incurrence. These costs are excluded from the cost-to-cost computation or allocated over the contract life when it appears that a better measure of contact progress will be obtained.

A significant problem of output measures is that the cost, time, and effort associated with one unit of output may not be comparable to that of another. For example, because of the cost of the foundation, the costs to complete the first story of a twenty-story office building can be expected to be greater than the costs of the remaining nineteen floors.

Because ARB 45 recommends that "recognized income [is to] be that percentage of estimated total income...that incurred costs to date bear to estimated total costs," the **cost-to-cost** method has become one of the most popular measures used to determine the extent of progress toward completion.

Under the cost-to-cost method, the percentage of **revenue** to recognize can be determined by the following formula:

$$\left(\frac{\text{Cost to date}}{\text{Cost to date} + \text{Estimated costs to complete}} \times \text{Contract price}\right) - \text{Revenue previously recognized} = \text{Current revenue recognized}$$

By slightly modifying this formula, current **gross profit** can also be determined.

$$\left(\frac{\text{Cost to date}}{\text{Cost to date} + \text{Estimated costs to complete}} \times \text{Expected total gross profit}\right) - \text{Gross profit previously recognized} = \text{Current gross profit earned}$$

Example of percentage-of-completion (cost-to-cost) and completed-contract methods with profitable contract

Assume a $500,000 contract that requires three years to complete and incurs a total cost of $405,000. The following data pertain to the construction period:

	Year 1	*Year 2*	*Year 3*
Costs incurred during the period	$150,000	$210,000	$ 45,000
Cumulative costs incurred to date	150,000	360,000	405,000
Estimated costs yet to be incurred at year-end	300,000	40,000	--
Estimated total costs	450,000	400,000	--
Progress billings made during the year	100,000	370,000	30,000
Cumulative billings to date	100,000	470,000	500,000
Collections of billings	75,000	300,000	125,000

Journal Entries Common to Completed-Contract and Percentage-of-Completion Methods

	Year 1		*Year 2*		*Year 3*	
Work-in-progress	150,000		210,000		45,000	
Cash, payables, etc.		150,000		210,000		45,000
Contract receivables	100,000		370,000		30,000	
Billings on contracts		100,000		370,000		30,000
Cash	75,000		300,000		125,000	
Contract receivables		75,000		300,000		125,000

Journal Entries for Completed-Contract Method Only

Billings on contracts	500,000	
Cost of revenues earned	405,000	
Contract revenues earned		500,000
Work-in-progress		405,000

Journal Entries for Percentage-of-Completion Method Only

Cost of revenues earned	150,000		210,000		45,000	
Work-in-progress		150,000		210,000		45,000
Billings on contracts	100,000		370,000		30,000	
Contract revenues earned		166,667		283,333		50,000
Costs and estimated earnings in excess of billings on uncompleted contracts	66,667			66,667		
Billings in excess of costs and estimated earnings on uncompleted contracts				20,000	20,000	

Income Statement Presentation

	Year 1	Year 2	Year 3	Total
Percentage-of-completion				
Contract revenues earned	$166,667*	$283,333**	$ 50,000***	$ 500,000
Cost of revenues earned	(150,000)	(210,000)	(45,000)	(405,000)
Gross profit	$ 16,667	$ 73,333	$ 5,000	$ 95,000
Completed-contract				
Contract revenues earned	--	--	$ 500,000	$ 500,000
Cost of revenues completed	--	--	(405,000)	(405,000)
Gross profit	--	--	$ 95,000	$ 95,000

$$* \quad \frac{\$150{,}000}{450{,}000} \times 500{,}000 = \$166{,}667$$

$$** \quad \left(\frac{\$360{,}000}{400{,}000} \times 500{,}000\right) - 166{,}667 = \$283{,}333$$

$$*** \quad \left(\frac{\$405{,}000}{405{,}000} \times 500{,}000\right) - 166{,}667 - 283{,}333 = \$50{,}000$$

Balance Sheet Presentation

		Year 1	Year 2	Year 3
Percentage-of-completion				
Current assets:				
Contract receivables		$25,000	$ 95,000	*
Costs and estimated earnings in excess of billings on uncompleted contracts		66,667		
Current liabilities:				
Billings in excess of costs and estimated earnings on uncompleted contracts, year 2			20,000	
Completed-contract				
Current assets:				
Contract receivables		$25,000	$ 95,000	*
Costs in excess of billings on uncompleted contracts				
Work-in-progress	150,000			
Less billings on long-term contracts	(100,000)	$50,000		
Current liabilities:				
Billings in excess of costs on uncompleted contracts, year 2 ($470,000 – 360,000)			$110,000	

* *Since the contract was completed, there are no balance sheet amounts at the end of year 3.*

Some contractors adopt an accounting policy of not recognizing any gross profit on a contract that is less than 10% complete. This election is usually made for two reasons.

1. The contractor is qualified to make and has made the election permitted by Internal Revenue Code §460(b)(5) to defer the recognition of such gross profit for US federal income tax purposes and wishes to avoid computational differences between applying the percentage-of-completion method for financial reporting and tax purposes, and
2. The contractor believes that this policy is prudent given the uncertainties associated with a contract that is so close to inception.

The GAAP effect of such a policy is usually immaterial and the accountant normally need not be concerned about it being a departure from GAAP.

Contract Losses

When the current estimate of total contract costs exceeds the current estimate of total contract revenues, a provision for the entire loss on the entire contract is made. Losses are recognized in the period in which they become evident under either the percentage-of-completion method or the completed-contract method. The loss is computed on the basis of the **total** estimated costs to complete the contract, including the contract costs incurred to date plus estimated costs (use the same elements as contract costs incurred) to complete. The loss is presented as a separately captioned current liability on the balance sheet.

In any year when a **percentage-of-completion** contract has an expected loss, the amount of the loss reported in that year is computed as follows:

Reported loss = Total expected loss + All profit previously recognized

Example of percentage-of-completion and completed-contract methods with loss contract

Using the previous information, if the estimated costs yet to be incurred at the end of year two were $148,000, the total expected loss is $8,000 [$500,000 – (360,000 + 148,000)], and the total loss reported in year two would be $24,667 ($8,000 + 16,667). Under the completed-contract method, the loss recognized is simply the total expected loss, $8,000.

Journal entry at end of year 2	*Percentage-of-completion*		*Completed-contract*	
Loss on uncompleted long-term contract (expense)	24,667		8,000	
Estimated loss on uncompleted contract (liability)		24,667		8,000

Profit or Loss Recognized on Contract (Percentage-of-Completion Method)

	Year 1	*Year 2*	*Year 3*
Contract price	$500,000	$500,000	$500,000
Estimated total costs:			
Costs incurred contract-to-date	$150,000	$360,000	$506,000*
Estimated costs yet to be incurred	300,000	148,000	--
Estimated total costs for the three-year period, actual for year 3	$450,000	$508,000	$506,000
Estimated gross profit (loss), actual for year 3	50,000	(8,000)	(6,000)
Summary of Effect on Results of Operations			
Current end-of-year estimate of gross profit (loss) actual for year 3	--	$ (8,000)	$ (6,000)
Accumulated effect of gross profit (loss) recognized in prior years	--	16,667	(8,000)
Effect on gross profit (loss) recognized in current year	--	$ (24,667)	$ 2,000

* *Assumed*

Profit or Loss Recognized on Contract
(Completed-Contract Method)

	Year 1	*Year 2*	*Year 3*
Contract price	$500,000	$500,000	$500,000
Estimated total costs:			
Costs incurred to date	$150,000	$360,000	$506,000*
Estimated cost yet to be incurred	300,000	148,000	--
Estimated total costs for the three-year period, actual for year 3	$450,000	$508,000	$506,000
Estimated profit (loss), inception-to-date, actual for year 3	$ 50,000	$ (8,000)	$ (6,000)
Loss previously recognized	--	--	$ (8,000)
Amount of estimated income (loss) recognized in the current period, actual for year 3	--	$ (8,000)	$ 2,000

* *Assumed*

Upon completion of the project during year 3, it can be seen that the actual loss was only $6,000 ($500,000 – $506,000); therefore, the estimated loss provision was overstated in previous years by $2,000. However, since this is a change of an estimate, the $2,000 difference must be handled prospectively; consequently, $2,000 of income is recognized in year 3 ($8,000 loss previously recognized – $6,000 actual loss).

Combining and Segmenting Contracts

The profit center for accounting purposes is usually a single contract, but under some circumstances the profit center may be a combination of two or more contracts, a segment of a contract or of a group of combined contracts. The contracts must meet requirements in SOP 81-1 in order to combine, or segment; otherwise, each individual contract is presumed to be the profit center.

For accounting purposes, a group of contracts may be combined if they are so closely related that they are, in substance, parts of a single project with an overall profit margin. Per SOP 81-1, a group of contracts may be combined if the contracts

1. Are negotiated as a package in the same economic environment with an overall profit margin objective.
2. Constitute an agreement to do a single project.
3. Require closely interrelated construction activities.
4. Are performed concurrently or in a continuous sequence under the same project management.
5. Constitute, in substance, an agreement with a single customer.

Segmenting a contract is a process of breaking up a larger unit into smaller units for accounting purposes. If the project is segmented, revenues are assigned to the different elements or phases to achieve different rates of profitability based on the relative value of each element or phase to the estimated total contract revenue. According to SOP 81-1, a project may be segmented if all of the following steps were taken and are documented and verifiable:

1. The contractor submitted bona fide proposals on the separate components of the project and on the entire project.
2. The customer had the right to accept the proposals on either basis.
3. The aggregate amount of the proposals on the separate components approximated the amount of the proposal on the entire project.

A project that does not meet the above criteria may still be segmented if all of the following are applicable:

1. The terms and scope of the contract or project clearly call for the separable phases or elements.
2. The separable phases or elements of the project are often bid or negotiated separately in the marketplace.
3. The market assigns different gross profit rates to the segments because of factors such as different levels of risk or differences in the relationship of the supply and demand for the services provided in different segments.
4. The contractor has a significant history of providing similar services to other customers under separate contracts for each significant segment to which a profit margin higher than the overall profit margin on the project is ascribed.
5. The significant history with customers who have contracted for services separately is one that is relatively stable in terms of pricing policy rather than one unduly weighted by erratic pricing decisions (responding, for example, to extraordinary economic circumstances or to unique customer-contractor relationships).
6. The excess of the sum of the prices of the separate elements over the price of the total project is clearly attributable to cost savings incident to combined performance of the contract obligations (for example, cost savings in supervision, overhead, or equipment mobilization). Unless this condition is met, segmenting a contract with a price substantially less than the sum of the prices of the separate phases or elements is inappropriate even if the other conditions are met. Acceptable price variations are allocated to the separate phases or elements in proportion to the prices ascribed to each. In all other situations a substantial difference in price (whether more or less) between the separate elements and the price of the total project is evidence that the contractor has accepted different profit margins. Accordingly, segmenting is not appropriate, and the contracts are the profit centers.
7. The similarity of services and prices in the contract segments and services and the prices of such services to other customers contracted separately are documented and verifiable.

Note that the criteria for combining and segmenting are to be applied consistently to contracts with similar characteristics and in similar circumstances.

Joint Ventures and Shared Contracts

Especially large or risky contracts are sometimes shared by more than one contractor. When the owner of the contract requests competitive bids, many contractors will form syndicates or joint ventures in order to bid on and successfully obtain a contract that each contractor individually could not perform.

When this occurs, a separate set of accounting records is maintained for the joint venture. If the percentages of interest for each of the venturers are identical in more than one contract, the joint venture might keep its records almost like another construction company. Usually, the joint venture is for a single contract and ends upon completion of that contract.

A joint venture is a type of partnership, organized for a limited purpose. An agreement of the parties and the terms of the contract successfully bid upon will determine the nature of the accounting records. Income statements are usually cumulative statements showing totals from date of contract inception until reporting date. Each venturer records its share of the amount from the venture's income statement less its previously recorded portion of the venture's income as a single line item similar to the equity method for investments. Similarly, balance sheets of each venturer present a single line asset balance, "investment in and advances to joint ventures." In most cases, footnote disclosure is similar to the equity method and presents condensed financial statements of material joint ventures.

Accounting for Change Orders

Change orders are modifications of specifications or provisions of an original contract. Contract revenue and costs are adjusted to reflect change orders that are approved by the contractor and customer. According to SOP 81-1, accounting for a change order depends on the scope and price of the change.

If the scope and price have both been agreed to by the customer and contractor, contract revenue and cost are both adjusted to reflect the change order.

According to SOP 81-1, accounting for unpriced change orders depends on their characteristics and the circumstances in which they occur. Under the completed-contract method, costs attributable to unpriced change orders are deferred as contract costs if it is probable that total contract costs, including costs attributable to the change orders, will be recovered from contract revenues. Recovery is deemed probable if the future event or events are likely to occur.

Per SOP 81-1, the following guidelines apply when accounting for unpriced change orders under the percentage-of-completion method:

1. If it is **not** probable that the costs will be recovered through a change in the contract price, costs attributable to unpriced change orders are treated as costs of contract performance in the period in which the costs are incurred.
2. If it is probable that the costs will be recovered through a change in the contract price, the costs are deferred (excluded from the costs of contract performance) until the parties have agreed on the change in contract price, or alternatively, treated as costs of contract performance in the period in which they are incurred with a corresponding increase to contract revenue in the amount of the costs incurred.
3. If it is probable that the contract price will be adjusted by an amount that **exceeds** the costs attributable to the change order and both of the following apply:
   a. The amount of the excess can be reliably estimated, and
   b. Realization of the full contract price adjustment is probably **beyond a reasonable doubt,**

   the original contract price is adjusted for the full amount of the adjustment as the costs are recognized.

However, since the substantiation of the amount of future revenue is difficult, satisfaction of the condition of "realization beyond a reasonable doubt" should only be considered satisfied in circumstances in which an entity's historical experience provides such assurance or in which an entity has received a bona fide pricing offer from a customer and records only the amount of the offer as revenue.

Accounting for Contract Options

Per SOP 81-1, an addition or option to an existing contract is treated as a separate contract if any of the following circumstances exist:

1. The product or service to be provided differs significantly from the product or service provided under the original contract.
2. The price of the new product or service is negotiated without regard to the original contract and involves different economic judgments.
3. The products or services to be provided under the exercised option or amendment are similar to those under the original contract, but the contract price and anticipated contract cost relationship are significantly different.

If the addition or option does not meet the above circumstances, the contracts are combined unless the addition or option does not meet the criteria for combining, in which case it is treated as a change order.

Accounting for Claims

Claims represent amounts in excess of the agreed-upon contract price that a contractor seeks to collect from customers for unanticipated additional costs. The recognition of additional contract revenue relating to claims is appropriate if it is probable that the claim will result in additional revenue and if the amount can be reliably estimated. SOP 81-1 specifies that all of the following conditions must exist in order for the probable and estimable requirements to be satisfied:

1. The contract or other evidence provides a legal basis for the claim; or a legal opinion has been obtained, stating that under the circumstances there is a reasonable basis to support the claim.
2. Additional costs are caused by circumstances that were unforeseen at the contract date and are not the result of deficiencies in the contractor's performance.
3. Costs associated with the claim are identifiable or otherwise determinable and are reasonable in view of the work performed.
4. The evidence supporting the claim is objective and verifiable, not based on management's "feel" for the situation or on unsupported representations.

When the above requirements are met, revenue from a claim is recorded only to the extent that contract costs relating to the claim have been incurred.

When the above requirements are not met, SOP 81-1 states that a contingent asset is disclosed in accordance with FAS 5.

Accounting Changes

According to APB 20, a change in method of accounting for long-term construction contracts is a special change in principle requiring retroactive treatment and restatement of previous financial statements. (See Chapter 21 for further discussion.)

Revisions in revenue, cost, and profit estimates or in measurements of the extent of progress toward completion are changes in accounting estimates. These changes are accounted for prospectively in order for the financial statements to fully reflect the effects of the latest available estimates.

Deferred Income Taxes

Deferred income taxes resulting from temporary differences are classified in accordance with FAS 109, *Accounting for Income Taxes*. Contract-related deferred income taxes result from the use of a method of income recognition for income tax purposes different from the method used for financial reporting purposes. (Refer to Chapter 15 for further discussion of deferred income taxes.)

SERVICE REVENUES

PERSPECTIVE AND ISSUES

Services represent over half of the transactions completed in the US economy, but there are no official pronouncements that provide specific accounting standards for them. Accounting for service transactions has evolved primarily through industry practice, and as a result, different accounting methods have developed to apply the fundamental principles of revenue and cost recognition. In fact, different accounting methods are used by similar entities for practically identical transactions. Because of these wide variations, at one point in time the FASB and the AICPA combined efforts in an attempt to establish accounting standards for service transactions through their issuance of *Accounting for Certain Service Transactions, FASB Invitation to Comment* (the Invitation). The Invitation contained an AICPA draft Statement of Position that set forth conclusions on the following:

1. The guidelines to apply to transactions in which both services and products are provided
2. The appropriate manner of revenue recognition
3. The classification of costs as initial direct costs, direct costs, and indirect costs and the accounting for each
4. The accounting for initiation and installation fees

This project did not lead to the establishment of GAAP, either as a FASB standard or a SOP. However, FASB is currently pursuing, in joint effort with the IASB, a major project addressing revenue recognition, which would resolve the accounting for service transactions. That project is not expected to yield final standards before 2005. The following discussion reflects the conclusions in the AICPA draft SOP, as well as other promulgated guidance. In the interim, until definitive standards regarding revenue recognition are promulgated, this section can still provide relevant guidance on service industry issues. In addition, the guidance provided by the SEC in Staff Accounting Bulletin 101, discussed in the introductory materials to this chapter, is relevant to accounting for service transactions and should be deemed relevant to accounting by even nonpublic reporting entities.

Sources of GAAP

Other	*FTB*	*EITF*	*SOP*
*	90-1	91-9, 01-14	98-5

* *SEC Staff Accounting Bulletin 101*

DEFINITIONS OF TERMS

Collection method. A method that recognizes revenue when cash is collected.

Completed performance method. A method that recognizes revenue after the last significant act has been completed.

Direct costs. Costs that are related specifically to the performance of services under a contract or other arrangement.

Indirect costs. Costs that are incurred as a result of service activities that are not directly allocable to specific contracts or customer arrangements.

Initiation fee. A one-time, up-front charge that gives the purchaser the privilege of using a service or facilities.

Installation fee. A one-time, up-front charge for making equipment operational so that it functions as intended.

Out-of-pocket costs. Costs incurred incidental to the performance of services that are often reimbursable to the service firm by the customer either at actual cost or at an agreed-upon rate (e.g., meals, lodging, airfare, taxi fares, etc.).

Precontract or preengagement costs. Costs incurred prior to execution of a service contract or engagement letter.

Product transaction. A transaction between a seller and a purchaser in which the seller supplies tangible merchandise to the purchaser.

Proportional performance method. A method that recognizes revenue on the basis of the number of acts performed in relation to the total number of acts to be performed.

Service transaction. A transaction between a seller and a purchaser in which the seller performs work, or agrees to maintain a readiness to perform work, for the purchaser.

Specific performance method. A method that recognizes revenue after one specific act has been performed.

CONCEPTS, RULES, AND EXAMPLES

The AICPA has defined service transactions as follows:

> *...transactions between a seller and a purchaser in which, for a mutually agreed price, the seller performs, agrees to perform, agrees to perform at a later date, or agrees to maintain readiness to perform an act or acts, including permitting others to use enterprise resources that do not alone produce a tangible commodity or product as the principal intended result (the Invitation).*

Generally accepted accounting principles require that revenue generally be recognized when (1) it is **realized or realizable** and (2) it has been **earned**. With respect to service transactions, the AICPA concluded

> *...revenue from service transactions [is to] be based on performance, because performance determines the extent to which the earnings process is complete or virtually complete.*

In practice, performance may involve the execution of a defined act, a set of similar or identical acts, or a set of related but not similar or identical acts. Performance may also occur with the passage of time. Accordingly, one of the following four methods can serve as a guideline for the recognition of revenue from service transactions:

1. The specific performance method
2. The proportional performance method
3. The completed performance method
4. The collection method

Service vs. Product Transactions

Many transactions involve the sale of a tangible product and a service; therefore, for proper accounting treatment, it must be determined whether the transaction is primarily a service transaction accompanied by an incidental product, primarily a product transaction accompanied by an incidental service, or a sale in which both a service transaction and a product transaction occur. The following criteria apply:

1. If the seller offers both a service and a product in a single transaction and if the terms of the agreement for the sale of the service are worded in such a manner that the inclusion or exclusion of the product would not change the total transaction price, the product is incidental to the rendering of the service; the transaction is a **service transaction** that is accounted for in accordance with one of the four methods presented. For example, fixed-price equipment maintenance contracts that include parts at no additional charge are service transactions.
2. If the seller offers both a service and a product in a single transaction and if the terms of the agreement for the sale of the product are worded in such a manner that the inclusion or exclusion of the service would not change the total transaction price, the rendering of the service is incidental to the sale of the product; the transaction is a **product transaction** that is accounted for as such. For example, the sale of a product accompanied by a guarantee or warranty for repair is considered a product transaction.
3. If the seller offers both a product and a service and the agreement states the product and service are separate elements such that the inclusion or exclusion of the service

would vary the total transaction price, the transaction consists of two components: a product transaction that is accounted for separately as such, and a service transaction that is accounted for in accordance with one of the four accepted methods.

Revenue Recognition Methods

Once a transaction is determined to be a service transaction, one of the following four methods is used to recognize revenue. The method chosen is to be based on the nature and extent of the service(s) to be performed.

1. **Specific performance method.** The specific performance method is used when performance consists of the execution of a single act. Revenue is recognized at the time the act takes place. For example, a stockbroker records sales commissions as revenue upon the sale of a client's investment.
2. **Proportional performance method.** The proportional performance method is used when performance consists of a number of identical or similar acts.
   a. If the service transaction involves a **specified number** of **identical** or **similar** acts, an equal amount of revenue is recorded for each act performed. For example, a refuse disposal company recognizes an equal amount of revenue for each weekly removal of a customer's garbage.
   b. If the service transaction involves a specified number of defined but **not** identical or similar acts, the revenue recognized for each act is based on the following formula:

   $$\frac{\text{Direct cost of individual act}}{\text{Total estimated direct costs of the transaction}} \times \text{Total revenues from complete transaction}$$

   For example, a correspondence school that provides lessons, examinations, and grading would use this method. If the measurements suggested in the preceding equation are impractical or not objectively determinable, revenue is recognized on a systematic and rational basis that reasonably relates revenue recognition to service performance.
   c. If the service transaction involves an **unspecified** number of acts over a fixed time period for performance, revenue is recognized over the period during which the acts will be performed by using the straight-line method unless a better method of relating revenue and performance is appropriate. For example, a health club might recognize revenue on a straight-line basis over the term of a member's membership. Many professional service firms record revenues on their engagements on an "as-performed basis" by valuing labor time, as expended, at a standard hourly billing rate and accumulating these amounts as an asset, work-in-progress (WIP). For periodic reporting, ending balances of WIP (and the related revenue recognized) must be adjusted by recording valuation allowances for unbillable or unrealizable WIP.
3. **Completed performance method.** The completed performance method is used when more than one act must be performed and when the final act is so significant to the entire transaction taken as a whole that performance cannot be considered to have taken place until the performance of that final act occurs. For example, a moving company packs, loads, and transports merchandise; however, the final act of delivering the merchandise is so significant that revenue is not recognized until the goods reach their intended destination. If the services are to be performed in an **indeterminable** number of acts over an **indeterminable** period of time and if an ob-

jective measure for estimating the degree to which performance has taken place can't be found, revenue is recognized under the completed performance method.

4. **Collection method.** The collection method is used in circumstances when there is a significant degree of uncertainty surrounding the collection of service revenue. Under this method, revenue is not recognized until the cash is collected. For example, personal services may be provided to a customer whose ability to pay is uncertain.

Expense Recognition

GAAP, in general, requires that costs be recognized as expense in the period that the revenue with which they are associated is recognized (the matching principle). Costs are deferred only when they are expected to be recoverable from future revenues. When applying these principles to service transactions, special consideration must be given to the different types of costs that might arise. The major classifications of costs arising from service transactions are as follows:

1. **Precontract or preengagement costs.** These are costs that are incurred **before** the service contract (or engagement letter in many professional services firms) has been executed between the parties. They can include legal fees for negotiating contract terms, costs of credit investigations, and the salaries and benefits of individuals involved in negotiating contracts with prospective clients. (See the related discussion in the long-term construction contracts section of this chapter.)
2. **Direct costs.** Costs that are specifically attributable to providing service under a specific contract or contracts. For example, service labor and repair parts on a fixed-price maintenance contract.
3. **Indirect costs.** Costs that are incurred as a result of all service activity but that are not directly allocable to any specific contracts or engagements.
4. **Out-of-pocket costs.** Costs incurred incidental to the performance of services that are often reimbursable to the service firm by the customer either at actual cost or at an agreed-upon rate (e.g., meals, lodging, airfare, taxi fare, etc.).
5. **Overhead.** General costs of running the business that do not fall into any of the above categories, often referred to as selling, general, and administrative expenses. These include uncollectible receivables, advertising, sales commissions, and facilities costs (depreciation, rent, maintenance, etc.).

Accounting treatment. The costs listed above are accounted for as follows:

1. **Precontract or preengagement costs.** Expense as incurred as start-up costs under SOP 98-5 under all of the service revenue recognition methods.
2. **Direct costs.** Expense as incurred under all of the service revenue recognition methods because of the close correlation between the amount of direct costs incurred and the extent of performance achieved. Direct costs incurred prior to performance, referred to as **initial direct costs** (e.g., expendable materials purchased for use on the job/engagement that are purchased and held by the service enterprise as a form of inventory), are deferred and recorded as prepayments (or supplies inventory, depending on the nature of the item). Under the specific performance or completed performance methods, these costs are recognized as expenses at the time of service performance at the point that revenue is recognized. Under the proportional performance method, initial direct costs are charged to expense in proportion to the recognition of service revenue (i.e., by applying the ratio of revenues recognized in the period to total expected revenues over the life of the contract).

3. **Indirect costs.** Under all of the revenue recognition methods, indirect costs are expensed as incurred.
4. **Out-of-pocket costs.** Under all of the revenue recognition methods, out-of-pocket costs are expensed as incurred with the related client billings presented as revenue in the statement of income.
5. **Overhead.** Under all of the revenue recognition methods, overhead is expensed as incurred.

Losses on service transactions are recognized when direct costs incurred to date plus estimated remaining direct costs of performance exceed the current estimated net realizable revenue from the contract. The loss (Direct costs incurred to date + Estimated remaining direct costs – Estimated realizable revenue) is first applied to reduce any recorded deferred costs to zero, with any remaining loss recognized on the income statement and credited to an estimated liability.

Initiation and Installation Fees

Many service transactions also involve the charging of a nonrefundable initiation or activation fee with subsequent periodic payments for future services and/or a nonrefundable fee for installation of equipment essential to providing future services with subsequent periodic payments for the services. These nonrefundable fees may, in substance, be partly or wholly advance charges for future services.

Initiation or activation fees. If there is an objectively determinable value for the right or privilege granted by the fee, that value is recognized as revenue on the initiation date. Any related direct costs are recognized as expense on the initiation date. If the value of the right or privilege cannot be objectively determined, the fee is recorded as a liability for future services and recognized as revenue in accordance with one of the revenue recognition methods.

Installation fees. If the equipment and its installation costs are essential for the service to be provided and if customers cannot normally purchase the equipment in a separate transaction, the installation fee is considered an advance charge for future services. The fee is recognized as revenue over the estimated service period. The costs of installation and the installed equipment are amortized over the period the equipment is expected to generate revenue. If customers can normally purchase the equipment in a separate transaction, the installation fee is part of a product transaction that is accounted for separately as such.

Recommended Disclosures—Not Required by GAAP

1. The revenue recognition method used and its justification
2. Information concerning unearned revenues
3. Information concerning deferred costs
4. Periods over which services are to be performed

EMERGING ISSUES TASK FORCE ISSUES SUMMARIES

91-9 Revenue and Expense Recognition for Freight Services in Process

The Task Force discussed the appropriate accounting methods which could be used for recognizing revenue and expense related to a freight service company's freight-in-transit at the end of a reporting period. A consensus was reached that recognition of revenue when freight is received from the shipper or when freight leaves the carrier's terminal with expenses recognized as incurred is not acceptable.

01-14 Income Statement Characterization of Reimbursements Received for "Out-of-Pocket" Expenses Incurred

Incidental to the performance of their services, enterprises such as law, accounting, architectural, engineering, and consulting firms often incur expenses referred to as "out-of-pocket" expenses. Examples of out-of-pocket expenses include meals, lodging, airfare, taxi fares, etc. These expenses are billed to clients (1) as a pass-through, (i.e., at actual cost to the service firm without a markup), (2) at a marked-up amount, or (3) included in the billing rate or negotiated price for the services. The EITF concluded that any such billings for out-of-pocket costs are to be classified as revenue in the statement of income and not as a reduction in expenses.

FASB TECHNICAL BULLETINS

90-1 Accounting for Separately Priced Extended Warranty and Product Maintenance Contracts

Background: Extended warranties provide additional protection to that of the manufacturer's original warranty or lengthen the period of coverage specified in the manufacturer's original warranty. A product maintenance contract is an agreement for services to maintain a product for a certain length of time.

Question: How should revenue and costs from a separately priced extended warranty or product maintenance contract be recognized?

Response: Revenue from these contracts is deferred and recognized on a straight-line basis unless evidence exists that costs are incurred on some other basis. If so, revenue is allocated to each period using the ratio of the period's cost to estimated total cost. Direct costs of obtaining a contract are capitalized and recognized as expense in the ratio that revenue recognized each period bears to total anticipated revenue on that contract. Any other costs are charged to expense as incurred. Losses on these contracts are recognized immediately if the sum of the future costs and remaining unamortized direct acquisition costs exceed the related unearned revenue.

SALES WHEN COLLECTION IS UNCERTAIN

PERSPECTIVE AND ISSUES

Under GAAP, revenue recognition customarily does not depend upon the collection of cash. Accrual accounting techniques normally record revenue at the point of a credit sale by establishing a receivable. When uncertainty arises surrounding the collectibility of this amount, the receivable is appropriately adjusted by establishing a valuation allowance. In some cases, however, the collection of the sales price may be so uncertain that an objective measure of ultimate collectibility cannot be established. When such circumstances exist, the seller either uses the installment method or the cost recovery method to recognize the transaction (APB 10). Both of these methods allow for a deferral of gross profit until cash has been collected.

An installment transaction occurs when a seller delivers a product or performs a service and the buyer makes periodic payments over an extended period of time. Under the installment method, revenue recognition is deferred until the period(s) of cash collection. The seller recognizes both revenues and cost of sales at the time of the sale; however, the related gross profit is deferred to those periods in which cash is collected. Under the cost recovery method, both revenues and cost of sales are recognized at the time of the sale, but none of the related gross profit is recognized until the entire cost of sales has been recovered. Once the seller has recovered all cost of sales, any additional cash receipts are recognized as revenue.

APB 10 does not specify when one method is preferred over the other. However, the cost recovery method is more conservative than the installment method because gross profit is deferred until all costs have been recovered; therefore, it is appropriate for situations of extreme uncertainty.

Sources of GAAP	
APB	*CON*
10	3

DEFINITIONS OF TERMS

Cost recovery method. The method of accounting for an installment basis sale whereby the gross profit is deferred until all cost of sales has been recovered.

Deferred gross profit. The gross profit from an installment basis sale that will be recognized in future periods.

Gross profit rate. The percentage computed by dividing gross profit by revenue from an installment sale.

Installment method. The method of accounting for a sale whereby gross profit is recognized in each period in which cash from the sale is collected.

Installment sale. A sales transaction for which the sales price is collected through the receipt of periodic payments over an extended period of time.

Net realizable value. The portion of the recorded amount of an asset expected to be realized in cash upon its liquidation in the ordinary course of business.

Realized gross profit. The gross profit recognized in the current period.

Repossessions. Merchandise sold by a seller under an installment arrangement that the seller physically takes back after the buyer defaults on the payments.

CONCEPTS, RULES, AND EXAMPLES

The Installment Method

The **installment method** was developed in response to the increasing incidence of sales contracts that allowed buyers to make payments over several years. As the payment period becomes longer, the risk of loss resulting from uncollectible accounts increases; consequently, circumstances surrounding a receivable may lead to considerable uncertainty as to whether payments will actually be received. Under these circumstances, the uncertainty of cash collection dictates that revenue recognition be deferred until the actual receipt of cash.

The installment method can be used in most sales transactions for which payment is to be made through periodic installments over an extended period of time and the collectibility of the sales price cannot be reasonably estimated. This method is applicable to the sales of real estate (covered in the last section of this chapter), heavy equipment, home furnishings, and other merchandise sold on an installment basis. Installment method revenue recognition is not in accordance with accrual accounting because revenue recognition is not normally based upon cash collection; however, its use is justified in certain circumstances on the grounds that accrual accounting may result in "front-end loading" (i.e., all of the revenue from a transaction being recognized at the point of sale with an improper matching of related costs). For example, the application of accrual accounting to transactions that provide for installment payments over periods of ten, twenty, or thirty years may underestimate losses from contract defaults and other future contract costs.

Applying the installment method. When a seller uses the installment method, both revenue and cost of sales are recognized at the point of sale, but the related gross profit is deferred to those periods during which cash will be collected. As receivables are collected, a portion of the **deferred gross profit** equal to the gross profit rate times the cash collected is recognized as income. When this method is used, the seller must compute each year's **gross profit rate** and also must maintain records of installment accounts receivable and deferred revenue that are separately identified by the year of sale. All general and administrative expenses are normally expensed in the period incurred.

The steps to use in accounting for sales under the installment method are as follows:

1. During the current year, record sales and cost of sales in the regular manner. Record **installment sales** transactions separately from other sales. Set up installment accounts receivable identified by the year of sale (e.g., Installment Accounts Receivable—2005).
2. Record cash collections from installment accounts receivable. Care must be taken so that the cash receipts are properly identified as to the year in which the receivable arose.
3. At the end of the current year, transfer installment sales revenue and installment cost of sales to deferred gross profit properly identified by the year of sale. Compute the current year's gross profit rate on installment sales as follows:

$$\text{Gross profit rate} = 1 - \left(\frac{\text{Cost of installment sales}}{\text{Installment sales revenue}}\right)$$

Alternatively, the gross profit rate can be computed as follows:

$$\text{Gross profit rate} = \frac{\text{Installment sales revenue} - \text{Cost of installment sales}}{\text{Installment sales revenue}}$$

4. Apply the current year's gross profit rate to the cash collections from the current year's installment sales to compute the realized gross profit from the current year's installment sales.

$$\text{Realized gross profit} = \text{Cash collections from the current year's installment sales} \times \text{Current year's gross profit rate}$$

5. Separately apply each of the previous years' gross profit rates to cash collections from those years' installment sales to compute the realized gross profit from each of the previous years' installment sales.

$$\text{Realized gross profit} = \text{Cash collections from the previous years' installment sales} \times \text{Previous years' gross profit rate}$$

6. Defer the current year's unrealized gross profit to future years. The deferred gross profit to carry forward to future years is computed as follows:

$$\text{Deferred gross profit (2005)} = \text{Ending balance installment account receivable (2005)} \times \text{Gross profit rate (2005)}$$

Example of the installment method of accounting

	2005	*2006*	*2007*
Sales on installment	$400,000	$450,000	$600,000
Cost of installment sales	(280,000)	(337,500)	(400,000)
Gross profit on sales	$120,000	$112,500	$200,000
Cash collections:			
2005 sales	$150,000	$175,000	$ 75,000
2006 sales		$200,000	$125,000
2007 sales			$300,000

Accounting entries are made for steps 1 and 2 above using this data; the following computations are required for steps 3-6:

Step 3 — Compute the current year's gross profit rate.

	2005	*2006*	*2007*
Gross profit on sales / Installment sales revenue	$120,000 / $400,000	$112,500 / $450,000	$200,000 / $600,000
Gross profit rate	30%	25%	33 1/3%

Step 4 — Apply the current year's gross profit rate to cash collections from current year's sales.

Year	*Cash collections*		*Gross profit rate*		*Realized gross profit*
2005	$150,000	x	30%	=	$ 45,000
2006	200,000	x	25%	=	50,000
2007	300,000	x	33 1/3%	=	100,000

Step 5 — Separately apply each of the previous years' gross profit rates to cash collections from that year's installment sales.

In Year 2006

From year	*Cash collections*		*Gross profit rate*		*Realized gross profit*
2005	$175,000	x	30%	=	$52,500

In Year 2007

From year	*Cash collections*		*Gross profit rate*		*Realized gross profit*
2005	$ 75,000	x	30%	=	$22,500
2006	125,000	x	25%	=	31,250
					$53,750

Step 6 — Defer the current year's unrealized gross profit to future years.

12/31/05		
Deferred gross profit (2005) = ($400,000 – 150,000) x 30%	=	$ 75,000
12/31/06		
Deferred gross profit (2006) = ($450,000 – 200,000) x 25%	=	$ 62,500
Deferred gross profit (2005) = ($400,000 – 150,000 – 175,000) x 30%	=	22,500
		$ 85,000
12/31/07		
Deferred gross profit (2007) = ($600,000 – 300,000) x 33 1/3%	=	$100,000
Deferred gross profit (2006) = ($450,000 – 200,000 – 125,000) x 25%	=	31,250
		$131,250

Financial statement presentation. If installment sales transactions represent a significant portion of the company's total sales, the following three items of gross profit would, theoretically, be reported on the company's income statement:

1. Total gross profit from current year's sales
2. Realized gross profit from current year's sales
3. Realized gross profit from prior years' sales

An income statement using the previous example would be presented as follows (assume all sales are accounted for by the installment method):

Jordan Equipment Company
Partial Income Statement
For the Years Ending December 31

	2005	*2006*	*2007*
Sales	$400,000	$450,000	$600,000
Cost of sales	(280,000)	(337,500)	(400,000)
Gross profit on current year's sales	120,000	112,500	200,000
Less deferred gross profit on current year's sales	(75,000)	(62,500)	(100,000)
Realized gross profit on current year's sales	45,000	50,000	100,000
Plus gross profit realized on prior years' sales	--	52,500	53,750
Total gross profit on sales	$ 45,000	$102,500	$153,750

However, when a company recognizes only a small portion of its revenues using the installment method, the illustrated presentation of revenue and gross profit may be confusing. Therefore, in practice, some companies simply report the realized gross profit from installment sales by displaying it as a single line item on the income statement as follows:

Stevens Furniture Company
Partial Income Statement
For the Year Ended December 31, 2005

Sales	$ 2,250,000
Cost of sales	(1,350,000)
Gross profit on sales	900,000
Gross profit realized on installment sales	35,000
Total gross profit on sales	$ 935,000

The balance sheet presentation of installment accounts receivable depends upon whether installment sales are a normal part of operations. If a company sells most of its products on an installment basis, installment accounts receivable are classified as a current asset because the operating cycle of the business (the length of which is to be disclosed in the notes to the financial statements) is the average period of time covered by its installment contracts. If installment sales are not a normal part of operations, installment accounts receivable that are not to be collected for more than a year (or the length of the company's operating cycle, if different than a year) are reported as noncurrent assets. In all cases, to avoid confusion, it is desirable to fully disclose the year of maturity next to each group of installment accounts receivable as illustrated by the following example:

Current assets:		
Accounts receivable		
Customers	$180,035	
Less allowance for uncollectible accounts	(4,200)	
	175,835	
Installment accounts—collectible in 2006	26,678	
Installment accounts—collectible in 2007	42,234	$244,747

Accounting for deferred gross profit is addressed in CON 3 which states that deferred gross profit is not a liability. The reason is that the seller company is not obligated to pay cash or provide services to the customer. Rather, the deferral arose because of the uncertainty surrounding the collectibility of the sales price. CON 3 goes on to say, "deferred gross profit on installment sales is conceptually an asset valuation—that is, a reduction of an asset." However, in practice, deferred gross profit is generally presented either as unearned revenue classified in the current liability section of the balance sheet or as a deferred credit displayed between liabilities and equity.

Following the guideline in CON 3, the current asset section would be presented as follows (using information from the Jordan Equipment example and assuming a 12/31/07 balance sheet):

Installment accounts receivable	(2006)	$125,000		
Installment accounts receivable	(2007)	300,000	$ 425,000	
Less: Deferred gross profit	(2006)	$ 31,250		
Deferred gross profit	(2007)	100,000	(131,250)	$293,750

Interest on installment method receivables. The previous examples ignored interest, a major component of most installment sales contracts. It is customary for the seller to charge interest to the buyer on the unpaid installment receivable balance. Generally, installment contracts call for equal payments, each with an amount attributable to interest on the unpaid balance and the remainder to the installment receivable balance. As the maturity date nears, a smaller amount of each installment payment is attributable to interest and a larger amount is attributable to principal. Therefore, to determine the amount of gross profit to recognize, the interest must first be deducted from the installment payment and then the difference (representing the principal portion of the payment) is multiplied by the gross profit rate as follows:

Realized gross profit = (Installment payment – Interest portion) x Gross profit rate

The interest portion of the installment payment is recorded as interest revenue at the time of the cash receipt. Appropriate accounting entries are required to accrue interest revenue when the collection dates do not correspond with the period end.

To illustrate the accounting for installment sales contracts involving interest, assume that Genrich Equipment Company sells a machine for $5,000 on December 31, 2004, to a customer with a dubious credit history. The machine cost Genrich $3,750. The terms of the agreement require a $1,000 down payment on the date of the sale. The remaining $4,000 is payable in equal annual installments of $1,401.06, including 15% annual interest, at the end of each of the next four years.

For each payment it receives, Genrich must compute the portion to record as interest revenue with the remaining portion of the payment (the principal) to be applied to reduce the installment account receivable balance. Gross profit is only recognized on the principal portion of each payment that is applied to reduce the installment receivable balance. The following schedule illustrates that gross profit is recognized on the entire down payment (which contains no element of interest revenue), whereas the annual installment payments are separated into their interest and principal portions with gross profit only being recognized on the latter portion.

Schedule of Cash Receipts

Date	Cash *(debit)*	Interest revenue *(credit)*	Installment accounts receivable *(credit)*	Installment accounts receivable balance	Realized gross profit
12/31/04				$5,000.00	
12/31/04	$1,000.00	$ --	$1,000.00	4,000.00	$ 250.00*a*
12/31/05	1,401.06	600.00*b*	801.06*c*	3,198.94*d*	200.27*e*
12/31/06	1,401.06	479.84	921.22	2,277.72	230.31
12/31/07	1,401.06	341.66	1,059.40	1,218.32	264.85
12/31/08	1,401.06	182.74	1,218.32	--	304.57
	$6,604.24	$1,604.24	$5,000.00		
			Total realized gross profit		$1,250.00

Gross profit rate = 1 – ($3,750/5,000) = 25%

[a] *$1,000 x 25% = $250*
[b] *$4,000 x 15% = $600*
[c] *$1,401.06 – 600 = $801.06*
[d] *$4,000 – 801.06 = $3,198.94*
[e] *$801.06 x 25% = $200.27*

Bad debts and repossessions. The standard accounting treatment for uncollectible accounts is to accrue a bad debt loss in the year of sale by estimating the amount expected to be uncollectible. This treatment is consistent with the accrual and matching concepts. However, just as revenue recognition under the accrual basis is sometimes abandoned for certain installment basis sales, the accrual basis of recognizing bad debts is also sometimes abandoned.

When the installment method is used, it is usually appropriate to recognize bad debts by the direct write-off method (i.e., bad debts are not recognized until the receivable has been determined to be uncollectible). This practice is acceptable because most installment contracts contain a provision that allows the seller to repossess the merchandise when the buyer defaults on the installment payments. The loss on the account may be eliminated or reduced because the seller has the option of reselling the repossessed merchandise. To write off an uncollectible installment receivable, the following three steps are followed:

1. The installment account receivable and the deferred gross profit are eliminated.
2. The repossessed merchandise is recorded as used inventory at its **net realizable value**. Net realizable value is resale value less any selling or reconditioning costs. The repossessed asset is recorded at this fair value because any asset acquired is recorded at the best approximation of its fair value.
3. Bad debt expense, and a gain or loss on repossession are recognized. The bad debt expense or repossession gain or loss is the difference between the unrecovered cost (Installment account receivable—Deferred gross profit) and the net realizable value of the repossessed merchandise.

To illustrate, assume that Marcie Company determined that a $3,000 installment receivable is uncollectible. The deferred gross profit ratio on the original sale was 30%; thus, $900 deferred gross profit exists ($3,000 x 30%). If the repossessed equipment has a $1,500 net realizable value, a $600 repossession loss (or bad debt expense) would need to be recorded.

Installment account receivable	$ 3,000
Less deferred gross profit	(900)
Unrecovered cost	2,100
Less net realizable value of repossessed equipment	(1,500)
Repossession loss	$ 600

Marcie Company would record this loss by making the following entry:

Deferred gross profit	900	
Inventory—repossessed merchandise	1,500	
Repossession loss	600	
Installment account receivable		3,000

The Cost Recovery Method

The cost recovery method does not recognize any income on a sale until the cost of the item sold has been fully recovered through cash receipts. Once the seller has recovered all costs, any subsequent cash receipts are included in income. The cost recovery method is used when the uncertainty of collection of the sales price is so great that even use of the installment method cannot be justified.

Under the cost recovery method, both revenues and cost of sales are recognized at the point of sale, but the related gross profit is deferred until all costs of sales have been recovered. Each installment must also be divided between principal and interest, but unlike the installment method where a portion of the principal recovers the cost of sales and the remainder is recognized as gross profit, all of the principal is first applied to recover the cost of the asset sold. After all costs of sales have been recovered, any subsequent cash receipts are realized as gross profit. The cost recovery method can be illustrated by using the information from the Genrich Company example used in the section "interest on installment method receivables." If Genrich used the cost recovery method, gross profit would be realized as follows:

Schedule of Cash Receipts

Date	Cash (debit)	Deferred interest income (credit)*	Installment accounts receivable (credit)	Installment accounts receivable balance	Unrecovered cost	Realized gross profit	Realized interest revenue
12/31/04				$5,000.00	$3,750.00		
12/31/04	$1,000.00	$ --	$1,000.00	4,000.00	2,750.00	$ --	$ --
12/31/05	1,401.06	600.00	801.06	3,198.94	1,948.94	--	--
12/31/06	1,401.06	479.84	921.22	2,277.72	1,027.72	--	--
12/31/07	1,401.06	(31.68)	1,059.40	1,218.32	--	--	373.34**
12/31/08	1,401.06	(1,048.16)	1,218.32	--	--	1,250.00	1,230.90***
	$6,604.24		$5,000.00			$1,250.00	$1,604.24

* *Interest received in 2005 and 2006 is credited to deferred interest income since the cost of the asset was not recovered until 2007.*

** *Computed as cash received of $1,401.06 less the portion representing unrecovered cost of $1,027.72 = $373.34. Since this amount exceeds the interest paid by the customer for the year of $341.66, the remaining $31.68 reduces deferred interest income.*

*** *Computed as cash received of $1,401.06 less the portion applied to principal of $1,218.32 = $182.74 plus the remaining deferred interest income of $1,048.16.*

The accounting entries to record the foregoing are as follows (in whole dollars):

	Debit (Credit) 2004	2005	2006	2007	2008	Totals
Initial Sale and Downpayment:						
Cash	1,000					
Installment accounts receivable	4,000					
Inventory	(3,750)					
Deferred gross profit	(1,250)					
Annual Payments:						
Cash		1,401	1,401	1,401	1,401	5,604
Installment accounts receivable		(801)	(921)	(1,059)	(1,219)	(4,000)
Deferred interest income		(600)	(480)	32	1,048	--
Interest income				(374)	(1,230)	(1,604)
Deferred gross profit					1,250	1,250
Recognized gross profit (revenue)					(1,250)	(1,250)

REVENUE RECOGNITION WHEN RIGHT OF RETURN EXISTS

PERSPECTIVE AND ISSUES

In some industries it is common practice for customers to have the right to return a product to the seller for a credit or refund. However, for companies that experience a high ratio of returned merchandise to sales, the recognition of the original sale as revenue is questionable. In fact, certain industries have found it necessary to defer revenue recognition until the return privilege has substantially expired. Sometimes the return privilege expires soon after the sale, as in the newspaper and perishable food industries. In other cases, the return privilege may last over an extended period of time, as in magazine and textbook publishing and equipment manufacturing. The rate of return normally is directly related to the length of the return privilege. An accounting issue arises when the recognition of revenue occurs in one period while substantial returns occur in later periods.

FAS 48, *Revenue Recognition When Right of Return Exists,* reduced the diversity in the accounting for revenue recognition when such rights exist.

Sources of GAAP
<u>*FAS*</u>
5, 48

DEFINITIONS OF TERMS

Deferred gross profit. The gross profit from a sale that is recognized in future periods because of the uncertainty surrounding the collection of the sales price.

Return privilege. A right granted to a buyer by express agreement with a seller or by customary industry practice that allows the buyer to return merchandise to the seller within a stated period of time.

CONCEPTS, RULES, AND EXAMPLES

FAS 48 provides criteria for recognizing revenue on a sale in which a product may be returned (as a matter of contract or a matter of industry practice), either by the ultimate consumer or by a party who resells the product to others. Paragraph 6 states the following:

> *If an enterprise sells its product but gives the buyer the right to return the product, revenue from the sales transaction [is] recognized at time of sale only if all of the following conditions are met:*
>
> *a. The seller's price to the buyer is substantially fixed or determinable at the date of sale.*
> *b. The buyer has paid the seller, or the buyer is obligated to pay the seller and the obligation is not contingent on resale of the product.*
> *c. The buyer's obligation to the seller would not be changed in the event of theft or physical destruction or damage of the product.*
> *d. The buyer acquiring the product for resale has economic substance apart from that provided by the seller.*
> *e. The seller does not have significant obligations for future performance to directly bring about the resale of the product by the buyer.*
> *f. The amount of future returns can be reasonably estimated. For purposes of this statement "returns" do not include exchanges by ultimate customers of one item for another of the same kind, quality, and price.*

If all of the above conditions are met, the seller recognizes revenue from the sales transaction at the time of the sale and any costs or losses expected in connection with returns are accrued in accordance with FAS 5, *Accounting for Contingencies*." FAS 5 states that estimated losses from contingencies are accrued and charged to income when it is probable that an asset has been impaired or a liability incurred, and the amount of loss can be reasonably estimated.

The interplay between FAS 48 and FAS 5 needs further explanation. Although FAS 48 requires under condition f. that the amount of returns be reasonably estimated, it does not reference the standard to the FAS 5 loss accrual criteria (see Chapter 12). Accordingly, a strict interpretation of both FAS 48 and FAS 5 would indicate that only when the conditions for loss accrual under FAS 5 are met (i.e., the loss is both probable and reasonably estimable) would the condition f. above under FAS 48 also be met, and both sales and estimated returns can be recognized. However, a more literal interpretation of FAS 48 indicates that, by not cross-referencing FAS 5, the FASB intended that the sole criterion for return accrual under FAS 48 be the "reasonably estimated" condition f. Then, whether losses are probable or reasonably possible, they would be accrued under FAS 48 and the sales would also be recognized. If the likelihood of losses is remote, no disclosure is required under FAS 5, and condition f. under FAS 48 would be achieved and revenue would be recognized with no need to record an allowance for estimated returns. Under this theory, only if returns cannot be reasonably estimated, would recognition of revenue be precluded under FAS 48, regardless of whether losses are probable or reasonably possible.

Example of sale with right of return

Assume that Lipkis, Inc. began the sale of its new textbook on computer programming in 2005 with the following results: On December 1, 2005, 2,000 textbooks with a sales price of $45 each and total manufacturing costs of $30 each are delivered to school bookstores on account. The bookstores have the right to return the textbooks within four months of delivery date. Payments when the books are sold. Payments and returns for the initial deliveries are as follows:

	Cash receipts		Returns	
	Units	Amount	Units	Amount
November 2005				
December 2005	600	$27,000	--	--
January 2006	500	22,500	40	$1,800
February 2006	400	18,000	90	4,050
March 2006	300	13,500	30	1,350
	1,800	$81,000	160	$7,200

Lipkis, Inc. has had similar agreements with the bookstores in the past and has experienced a 15% return rate on similar sales.

Requirements for revenue recognition met. If all six of the requirements were met, the following journal entries would be appropriate:

12/1/05	Accounts receivable	90,000	
	Sales (2,000 units x $45 per unit)		90,000
	To record sale of 2,000 textbooks		
12/31/05	Cash (600 units x $45 per unit)	27,000	
	Accounts receivable		27,000
	To record cash receipts for the month		
	Cost of sales	60,000	
	Inventory (2,000 units x $30 per unit)		60,000
	To record cost of goods sold for the month		
	Sales (15% x 2,000 units x $45 per unit)	13,500	
	Cost of sales (15% x 2,000 units x $30 per unit)		9,000
	Deferred gross profit on estimated returns (15% x 2,000 units x $15 per unit)		4,500
	To record estimate of returns		
1/1/06 to 3/31/06	Cash	54,000	
	Accounts receivable		54,000
	To record cash receipts		
	Inventory (160 units x $30 per unit)	4,800	
	Deferred gross profit on estimated returns	2,400	
	Accounts receivable (160 units x $45 per unit)		7,200
	To record actual returns		
3/31/06	Cost of sales (140 units x $30 per unit)	4,200	
	Deferred gross profit on estimated returns	2,100	
	Sales (140 units x $45 per unit)		6,300
	To record expiration of return privileges and adjust estimate to actual		

The revenue and cost of goods sold recognized in 2005 are based on the number of units expected to be returned, 300 (15% x 2,000 units). The net revenue recognized is $76,500 (85% x 2,000 units x $45 per unit) and the cost of goods sold recognized is $51,000 (85% x 2,000 units x $30 per unit). The deferred gross profit balance is carried forward until either the textbooks are returned or the return privilege expires.

Requirements for revenue recognition not met. If all six conditions are not met, revenue and cost of sales from the sales transactions must be deferred until either the return privilege has substantially expired or the point when all the conditions are subsequently met, whichever comes first.

If the facts in the Lipkis case were altered so that the bookstores were not required to pay Lipkis until the later of the date the books were actually sold, or the expiration date of the return privilege, condition b. would not be met until the store remitted payment. The following entries would be required. The return privilege is, of course, assumed to be lost by the store when the books are sold to final customers.

Date	Account	Debit	Credit
12/1/05	Inventory on consignment	60,000	
	Inventory		60,000
	To record shipment of 2,000 units to retail bookstores on consignment (2,000 units x $30 = $60,000)		
12/31/05	Cash (600 units x $45 per unit)	27,000	
	Sales		27,000
	To record cash receipts for December		
	Cost of sales (600 units x $30 per unit)	18,000	
	Inventory on consignment		18,000
	To record cost of goods sold for December		
1/1/06	Cash	54,000	
to	Sales (1,200* units x $45 per unit)		54,000
3/31/06	*To record cash receipts*		
	Cost of sales (1,200 units x $30 per unit)	36,000	
	Inventory on consignment		36,000
	To record cost of goods sold on cash receipts		
	Inventory (160 units x $30 per unit)	4,800	
	Inventory on consignment		4,800
	To record product returns		
3/31/06	Accounts receivable (40 units x $45 per unit)	1,800	
	Sales		1,800
	To record expiration of return privilege on remaining units		
	Cost of sales (40** units x $30 per unit)	1,200	
	Inventory on consignment		1,200
	To record cost of goods sold on products for which return privilege expired		

* *1,800 units paid for – 600 units paid for in December*
** *2,000 units sold – 160 units returned – 1,800 units paid for*

PROFIT RECOGNITION ON REAL ESTATE SALES

PERSPECTIVE AND ISSUES

The substance of a sale of any asset is that the transaction unconditionally transfers the risks and rewards of ownership to the buyer. However, the economic substance of many real estate sales is that the risks and rewards of ownership have not been clearly transferred. The turbulent and cyclical environments in the real estate and debt markets have led to the evolution of many complex methods of financing real estate transactions. For example, in some transactions the seller, rather than an independent third party, finances the buyer, while in others, the seller may be required to guarantee a minimum return to the buyer or continue to operate the property for a specified period of time. In many of these complex transactions, the seller still has some association with the property even after the property has been sold. The question that must be answered in these transactions is: At what point does the seller become disassociated enough from the property that profit may be recognized on the transaction?

Accounting for sales of real estate is governed by FAS 66. FIN 43 clarifies that sales of real estate under FAS 66 include property that has improvements or integral equipment not movable without incurring significant costs. Due to the complex nature of these real estate transactions, FAS 66 is very detailed and complex. The purpose of this section is to present the guidelines that need to be considered when analyzing nonretail real estate transactions. FAS 98 dealing with sales-type real estate leases and sales-leaseback real estate transactions is covered in Chapter 14.

A specialized situation involving the sale of real estate pertains to time-share projects. There have been several attempts over many years to develop comprehensive guidance to time-share project accounting, and there is currently a draft SOP on this topic being considered. A brief synopsis of the guidance in that draft SOP is included in the summaries at the end of this section.

Sources of GAAP

FAS	FIN	EITF	FSP	SOP
66, 98	43	00-13	144-1	*

* Draft SOP, *Accounting for Real Estate Time Sharing Transactions*

DEFINITIONS OF TERMS

Continuing investment. Payments that the buyer is contractually required to pay on its total debt for the purchase price of the property.

Cost recovery method. A method which defers the recognition of gross profit on a real estate sale until the seller recovers the cost of the property sold.

Deposit method. A method which records payments by the buyer as deposits rather than a sale. The seller continues to report the asset and related debt on the balance sheet until the contract is canceled or until the sale has been achieved.

First mortgage (primary debt). The senior debt the seller has on the property at the time the buyer purchases the property. A first mortgage lender (mortgagee) has foreclosure rights superior to those of second (or junior) mortgage lenders (i.e., proceeds from sale of the foreclosed property are used first to repay the first mortgage lender in full with only the remainder available to satisfy the junior lenders' balances).

Full accrual method. A method that recognizes all profit from a real estate sale at the time of sale.

Initial investment. The sales value received by the seller at the time of sale. It includes a cash down payment, buyer's notes supported by an irrevocable letter of credit, and payments by the buyer to third parties to reduce or eliminate the seller's indebtedness on the property.

Installment method. A method that recognizes revenue on the basis of payments made by the buyer on debt owed to the seller and payments by the buyer to the holder of primary debt. Each payment is apportioned between profit and cost recovery.

Lien. A claim or charge a creditor has on property which serves as security for payment of debt by the debtor.

Minimum initial investment. The minimum amount that an initial investment must equal or exceed so that the criterion for using the full accrual method is met.

Partial sale. A sale in which the seller retains an equity interest in the property or has an equity interest in the buyer.

Property improvements. An addition made to real estate, usually consisting of buildings but that may also include any permanent structure such as streets, sidewalks, sewers, utilities, etc.

Reduced profit method. A method which recognizes profit at the point of sale, but only a reduced amount. The remaining profit is deferred to future periods.

Release provision. An agreement that provides for the release of property to the buyer. This agreement releases the property to the buyer free of any previous liens.

Sales value. The sales price of the property increased or decreased for other consideration in the sales transaction that are, in substance, additional sales proceeds to the seller.

Subordination. The process by which a party's rights are ranked below the rights of others.

CONCEPTS, RULES, AND EXAMPLES

Real Estate Sales other than Retail Land Sales

FAS 66 scope. FAS 66, *Accounting for Sales of Real Estate*, established standards applicable to all real estate sales for all types of businesses. However, variations in applying this Statement in practice suggested that additional guidance was needed. FIN 43 clarified that FAS 66 is consistent with the sale-leaseback requirements of FAS 98, *Accounting for Sales and Leasebacks*.

FIN 43 explicitly states that real estate sales transactions under FAS 66 include real estate with property enhancements or integral equipment. This Interpretation defines property improvements and integral equipment as "any physical structure or equipment attached to real estate or other parts thereof, that cannot be removed and used separately without incurring significant cost." Examples include an office building or manufacturing plant.

This interpretation also identifies transactions excluded from the provisions of FAS 66 as follows:

1. A sale of improvements or integral equipment with no sale or plans for a sale of the land.
2. A sale of stock, net assets of a business, or a segment of a business which contain real estate except in cases in which an "in-substance" real estate sale occurs.
3. Securities accounted for under FAS 115.

Profit recognition methods. Profit from real estate sales is recognized in full, provided the following:

1. The profit is determinable (i.e., the collectibility of the sales price is reasonably assured or the amount that will not be collectible can be estimated).
2. The earnings process is virtually complete, that is, the seller is not obliged to perform significant activities after the sale to earn the profit.

When both of these conditions are satisfied, the method used to recognize profits on real estate sales is referred to as the **full accrual method**. If both of these conditions are not satisfied, recognition of all or part of the profit is postponed.

For real estate sales, the collectibility of the sales price is reasonably assured when the buyer has demonstrated a commitment to pay. This commitment is supported by a substantial **initial investment,** along with **continuing investments** that give the buyer a sufficient stake in the property such that the risk of loss through default motivates the buyer to honor its obligations to the seller. Collectibility of the sales price is also assessed by examining the conditions surrounding the sale (e.g., credit history of the buyer; age, condition, and location of the property; and history of cash flows generated by the property).

The full accrual method is appropriate and profit is recognized in full at the point of sale for real estate transactions when all of the following criteria are met:

1. A sale is consummated.
2. The buyer's initial and continuing investments are adequate to demonstrate a commitment to pay for the property.
3. The seller's receivable is not subject to future **subordination**.
4. The seller has transferred to the buyer the usual risks and rewards of ownership in a transaction that is in substance a sale, and the seller does not have a substantial continuing involvement in the property.

On sales in which an independent third party provides all of the financing for the buyer, the seller is most concerned that criterion 1. is met. For such sales, the sale is usually consummated on the closing date. When the seller finances the buyer, the seller must analyze the economic substance of the agreement to ascertain that criteria 2., 3., and 4. are also met (i.e., whether the transaction clearly transfers the risks and rewards of ownership to the buyer).

The FASB Emerging Issues Task Force (EITF) reached a consensus in its Issue 88-24 that provides the following guidelines for a seller of real estate to follow when considering the various forms of financing that may be applicable to the transaction:

1. The FAS 66 conditions for obtaining sufficient initial and continuing investment from the buyer before full accrual profit recognition is allowed must be applied unless the seller receives as the full sales value of the property
   a. Cash without any seller contingent liability on any debt on the property incurred or assumed by the buyer,
   b. The buyer's assumption of the seller's existing nonrecourse debt on the property,
   c. The buyer's assumption of all recourse debt on the property with the complete release of the seller from those obligations, or
   d. Any combination of such cash and debt assumption.
2. In computing the buyer's initial investment, debt incurred by the buyer that is secured by the property is not considered part of the buyer's initial investment. This is true whether the debt was incurred directly from the seller or other parties or indirectly through assumption. Payments to the seller from the proceeds of such indebtedness are not included as part of the buyer's initial investment.
3. If the transaction does not qualify for full accrual accounting and, consequently, is being accounted for using installment, cost recovery or reduced profit methods, payments made on debt described in 2. above are not considered to be buyer's cash payments. However, if the profit deferred under the applicable method exceeds the outstanding amount of seller financing and the outstanding amount of buyer's debt secured by the property for which the seller is contingently liable, the seller recognizes the excess in income.

Consummation of a sale. A sale is considered consummated when the following conditions are met:

1. The parties are bound by the terms of a contract.
2. All consideration has been exchanged.
3. Any permanent financing for which the seller is responsible has been arranged.
4. All conditions precedent to closing have been performed.

When a seller is constructing office buildings, condominiums, shopping centers, or similar structures, item 4. may be applied to individual units rather than the entire project. These four conditions are usually met on or after closing, not at the point the agreement to sell is signed or at a preclosing meeting. Closing refers to the final steps of the transaction (i.e., when consideration is paid, the mortgage is secured, and the deed is delivered or placed in escrow). If the consummation criteria **have not** been satisfied, the seller uses the deposit method of accounting until all of the criteria are met (i.e., the sale has been consummated).

Adequacy of the buyer's initial investment. Once the sale is consummated, the next step is to determine whether the buyer's initial investment adequately demonstrates a commitment to pay for the property and the reasonable likelihood that the seller will collect it. This determination is made by comparing the buyer's initial investment to the sales value of the property. FAS 66 specifically details items that are includable as the initial investment and the minimum percentages that the initial investment must bear to the sales value of the property. In order to make the determination of whether the initial investment is adequate, the sales value of the property must also be computed.

Computation of sales value. The sales value of property in a real estate transaction is computed as follows:

	Stated sales price
+	Proceeds from the issuance of an **exercised** purchase option
+	Other payments that are, in substance, additional sales proceeds (e.g., management fees, points, prepaid interest, or fees required to be maintained in advance of the sale that will be applied against amounts due to the seller at a later point)
–	A discount that reduces the buyer's note to its present value
–	Net present value of services seller agrees to perform without compensation
–	Excess of net present value of services seller performs over compensation that seller will receive
=	Sales value of the property

Composition of the initial investment. Sales transactions are characterized by many different types of payments and commitments made between the seller, buyer, and third parties; however, the buyer's initial investment only includes the following:

1. Cash paid to the seller as a down payment
2. Buyer's notes given to the seller that are supported by irrevocable letters of credit from independent lending institutions
3. Payments by the buyer to third parties that reduce existing indebtedness the seller has on the property
4. Other amounts paid by the buyer that are part of the sales value
5. Other consideration received by the seller that can be converted to cash without recourse to the seller; for example, other notes of the buyer

FAS 66 specifically states that the following items are not included as initial investment:

1. Payments by the buyer to third parties for improvements to the property
2. A permanent loan commitment by an independent third party to replace a loan made by the seller
3. Funds that have been or will be loaned, refunded, or directly or indirectly provided to the buyer by the seller or loans guaranteed or collateralized by the seller for the buyer

Size of initial investment. Once the initial investment is computed, its size must be compared to the sales value of the property. To qualify as an adequate initial investment, the initial investment must be equal to at least a major part of the difference between usual loan limits established by independent lending institutions and the sales value of the property. The **minimum initial investment** requirements for real estate sales (other than retail land sales) vary depending upon the type of property being sold. The following table from FAS 66 provides the limits for the various properties:

Type of property	Minimum initial investment expressed as a percentage of sales value
Land	
Held for commercial, industrial, or residential development to commence within two years after sale	20
Held for commercial, industrial, or residential development to commence more than two years after sale	25
Commercial and Industrial Property	
Office and industrial buildings, shopping centers, and so forth:	
Properties subject to lease on a long-term lease basis to parties with satisfactory credit rating; cash flow currently sufficient to service all indebtedness	10
Single-tenancy properties sold to a buyer with a satisfactory credit rating	15
All other	20
Other income-producing properties (hotels, motels, marinas, mobile home parks, and so forth):	
Cash flow currently sufficient to service all indebtedness	15
Start-up situations or current deficiencies in cash flow	25
Multifamily Residential Property	
Primary residence:	
Cash flow currently sufficient to service all indebtedness	10
Start-up situations or current deficiencies in cash flow	15
Secondary or recreational residence:	
Cash flow currently sufficient to service all indebtedness	15
Start-up situations or current deficiencies in cash flow	25
Single-Family Residential Property (including condominium or cooperative housing)	
Primary residence of the buyer	5[a]
Secondary or recreational residence	10[a]

[a] *If collectibility of the remaining portion of the sales price cannot be supported by reliable evidence of collection experience, the minimum initial investment [is to] be at least 60% of the difference between the sales value and the financing available from loans guaranteed by regulatory bodies such as the Federal Housing Authority (FHA) or the Veterans Administration (VA), or from independent, established lending institutions. This 60% test applies when independent first-mortgage financing is not utilized and the seller takes a receivable from the buyer for the difference between the sales value and the initial investment. If independent first mortgage financing is utilized, the adequacy of the initial investment on sales of single-family residential property [is] determined [as described in the next paragraph].*

Lenders' appraisals of specific properties often differ. Therefore, if the buyer has obtained a permanent loan or firm permanent loan commitment for maximum financing of the property from an independent lending institution, the minimum initial investment must be the **greater** of the following:

1. The minimum percentage of the sales value of the property specified in the above table or
2. The **lesser** of
    a. The amount of the sales value of the property in excess of 115% of the amount of a newly placed permanent loan or firm loan commitment from a primary lender that is an independent established lending institution
    b. 25% of the sales value

To illustrate the determination of whether an initial investment adequately demonstrates a commitment to pay for property, consider the following example:

Example determining adequacy of initial investment

Marcus, Inc. exercised a $2,000 option for the purchase of an apartment building from Rubin, Inc. The terms of the sales contract required Marcus to pay $3,000 of delinquent property taxes, pay a $300,000 cash down payment, assume Rubin's recently issued **first mortgage** of $1,200,000, and give Rubin a second mortgage of $500,000 at a prevailing interest rate.

Step 1 — Compute the sales value of the property.

Payment of back taxes to reduce Rubin's liability to local municipality	$ 3,000
Proceeds from exercised option	2,000
Cash down payment	300,000
First mortgage assumed by Marcus	1,200,000
Second mortgage given to Rubin	500,000
Sales value of the apartment complex	$2,005,000

Step 2 — Compute the initial investment.

Cash down payment	$300,000
Payment of back taxes to reduce Rubin's liability to local municipality	3,000
Proceeds from exercised option	2,000
	$ 305,000

Step 3 — Compute the minimum initial investment required.

a. The minimum percentage of the sales value of the property as specified in the table is $200,500 ($2,005,000 x 10%).

b. 1. The amount of the sales value of the property in excess of 115% of the recently placed permanent mortgage is $625,000 (sales value of $2,005,000 – $1,380,000 [115% of $1,200,000]).

2. 25% of the sales value ($2,005,000) is $501,250.

The lesser of b.1 and b.2 is b.2, $501,250. The greater of a. and b. is b., $501,250. Therefore, to record this transaction under the full accrual method (assuming all other criteria are met), the minimum initial investment must be equal to or greater than $501,250. Since the actual initial investment is only $305,000, all or part of the recognition of profit from the transaction must be postponed.

If the sale has been consummated but the buyer's initial investment does not adequately demonstrate a commitment to pay, the transaction is accounted for using the **installment method** when the seller is reasonably assured of **recovering the cost** of the property if the buyer defaults. However, if the recovery of the cost of the property is not reasonably assured should the buyer default or if the cost has been recovered and the collection of additional amounts is uncertain, the cost recovery or deposit method is used.

Adequacy of the buyer's continuing investments. The collectibility of the buyer's receivable must be reasonably assured; therefore, for full profit recognition under the full accrual method, the buyer must be contractually required to pay each year on its total debt for the purchase price of the property an amount at least equal to the level annual payment that would be needed to pay that debt (both principal and interest) over a specified period. This period is no more than twenty years for land, and no more than the customary amortization term of a first mortgage loan by an independent lender for other types of real estate. For continuing investment purposes, the contractually required payments must be in a form that is acceptable for an initial investment. If the seller provides funds to the buyer, either directly or indirectly, these funds must be subtracted from the buyer's payments in determining whether the continuing investments are adequate.

The indebtedness on the property does not have to be reduced proportionately. A lump-sum (balloon) payment will not affect the amortization of the receivable as long as the level annual payments still meet the minimum annual amortization requirement. For example, a land real estate sale may require the buyer to make level annual payments at the end of each of the first five years and then a balloon payment at the end of the sixth year. The continuing investment criterion is met provided the level annual payment required in each of the first five years is greater than or equal to the level annual payment that would be made if the receivable were amortized over the maximum twenty-year (land's specified term) period.

Continuing investment not qualifying. If the sale has been consummated and the minimum initial investment criteria have been satisfied but the continuing investment by the buyer does not meet the stated criterion, the seller recognizes profit by the **reduced profit method** at the time of sale if payments by the buyer each year will at least cover both of the following:

1. The interest and principal amortization on the maximum first mortgage loan that could be obtained on the property
2. Interest, at an appropriate rate, on the excess of the aggregate actual debt on the property over such a maximum first mortgage loan

If the payments by the buyer do not cover both of the above, the seller recognizes profit by either the **installment** or **cost recovery** method.

Release provisions. An agreement to sell real estate may provide that part or all of the property sold will be released from liens by payment of an amount sufficient to release the debt or by an assignment of the buyer's payments until release. In order to meet the criteria of an adequate initial investment, the investment must be sufficient both to pay the release on property released and to meet the initial investment requirements on property not released. If not, profit is recognized on each released portion as if it were a separate sale when a sale has been deemed to have taken place.

Seller's receivable subject to future subordination. The seller's receivable should not be subject to future subordination. Future subordination by a primary lender would permit the lender to obtain a **lien** on the property, giving the seller only a secondary residual claim. This subordination criterion does not apply if either of the following occur:

1. A receivable is subordinate to a first mortgage on the property existing at the time of sale.
2. A future loan, including an existing permanent loan commitment, is provided for by the terms of the sale and the proceeds of the loan will be applied first to the payment of the seller's receivable.

If the seller's receivable is subject to future subordination, profit is recognized using the **cost recovery method**. The cost recovery method is justified because the collectibility of the sales price is not reasonably assured in circumstances when the receivable may be subordinated to amounts due to other creditors.

Seller's continuing involvement. Sometimes sellers continue to be involved with property for periods of time even though the property has been legally sold. The seller's involvement often takes the form of profit participation, management services, financing, guarantees of return, construction, etc. The seller does not have a substantial continuing involvement with property unless the risks and rewards of ownership have been clearly transferred to the buyer.

If the seller has some continuing involvement with the property and does not clearly transfer substantially all of the risks and rewards of ownership, profit is recognized by a method other than the full accrual method. The method chosen is determined by the nature and extent of the seller's continuing involvement. As a general rule, profit is only recognized at the time of sale if the amount of the seller's loss due to the continued involvement with the property is limited by the terms of the sales contract. In this event, the profit recognized at this time is reduced by the maximum possible loss from the continued involvement.

Leases involving real estate. FAS 98 dealing with sales-type real estate leases and sale-leaseback real estate transactions is covered in Chapter 14.

Profit-sharing, financing, and leasing arrangements. In real estate sales, it is often the case that economic substance takes precedence over legal form. Certain transactions, though possibly called sales, are in substance profit-sharing, financing, or leasing arrangements and are accounted for as such. These include situations in which

1. The seller has an obligation to repurchase the property, or the terms of the transaction allow the buyer to compel the seller to repurchase the property or give the seller an option to do so.
2. The seller is a general partner in a limited partnership that acquires an interest in the property sold and holds a receivable from the buyer for a significant part (15% of the maximum first-lien financing) of the sales price.
3. The seller guarantees the return of the buyer's investment or a return on that investment for an **extended** period of time.
4. The seller is required to initiate or support operations, or continue to operate the property at its own risk for an **extended** period of time.

Options to purchase real estate property. Often a buyer will buy an option to purchase land from a seller with the hopeful intention of obtaining a zoning change, building permit, or some other contingency specified in the option agreement. Proceeds from the issue of an option by a property owner (seller) are accounted for by the **deposit method**. If the option is exercised, the seller includes the option proceeds in the computation of the sales value of the property. If the option is not exercised, the seller recognizes the option proceeds as income at the time the option expires.

Partial sales of property. Per FAS 66, "a sale is a partial sale if the seller retains an equity interest in the property or has an equity interest in the buyer." Profit on a partial sale may be recognized on the date of sale if the following occur:

1. The buyer is independent of the seller.
2. Collection of the sales price is reasonably assured.
3. The seller will not be required to support the operations of the property on its related obligations to an extent greater than its proportionate interest.

If the buyer is not independent of the seller, the seller may not be able to recognize any profit that is measured at the date of sale.

If the seller is not reasonably assured of collecting the sales price, the **cost recovery** or **installment method** is used to recognize profit on the partial sale.

A seller who separately sells individual units in condominium projects or time-sharing interests recognizes profit by the percentage-of-completion method on the sale of individual units or interests if all of the following criteria are met:

1. Construction is beyond a preliminary stage (i.e., engineering and design work, execution of construction contracts, site clearance and preparation, excavation, and completion of the building foundation have all been completed).
2. The buyer is unable to obtain a refund except for nondelivery of the units or interest.
3. Sufficient units have been sold to assure that the entire property will not revert to being rental property.
4. Sales prices are collectible.
5. Aggregate sales proceeds and costs can be reasonably estimated.

The **deposit** method is used to account for these sales up to the point all the criteria are met for recognition of a sale.

Selection of method. If a loss is apparent (e.g., the carrying value of the property exceeds the sum of the deposit, fair value of unrecorded note receivable, and the debt assumed by the buyer), then immediate recognition of the loss is required.

The installment method is used if the full accrual method cannot be used due to an inadequate initial investment by the buyer, provided that recovery of cost is reasonably assured if the buyer defaults. The cost recovery method or the deposit method are used if such cost recovery is not assured.

The reduced profit method is used when the buyer's initial investment is adequate but the continuing investment is not adequate, and payments by the buyer at least cover the sum of (1) the amortization (principal and interest) on the maximum first mortgage that could be obtained on the property and (2) the interest, at an appropriate rate, on the excess of aggregate debt over the maximum first mortgage.

Methods of Accounting for Real Estate Sales other than Retail Land Sales

Full accrual method. This method of accounting for nonretail sales of real estate is appropriate when all four of the recognition criteria have been satisfied. The full accrual method is simply the application of the revenue recognition principle. A real estate sale is recognized in full when the profit is determinable and the earnings process is virtually complete. The profit is determinable when the first three criteria have been met (the sale is consummated, the buyer has demonstrated a commitment to pay, and the seller's receivable is not subject to future subordination). The earnings process is virtually complete when the fourth criterion has been met (the seller has transferred the risks and rewards of ownership and does not have a substantial continuing involvement with the property). If all of the criteria have not been met, the seller records the transaction by one of the following methods as indicated by FAS 66:

1. Deposit
2. Cost recovery
3. Installment
4. Reduced profit
5. Percentage-of-completion (see the section on Long-Term Construction Contracts in this chapter)

Profit under the full accrual method is computed by subtracting the cost basis of the property surrendered from the sales value given by the buyer. Also, the computation of profit on the sale includes all costs incurred that are directly related to the sale, such as accounting and legal fees.

Installment method. Under the installment method, each cash receipt and principal payment by the buyer on debt assumed with recourse to the seller consists of part recovery of cost and part recovery of profit. The apportionment between cost recovery and profit is in the same ratio as total cost and total profit bear to the sales value of the property sold. Therefore, under the installment method, the seller recognizes profit on each payment that the buyer makes to the seller and on each payment the buyer makes to the holder of the primary debt. When a buyer assumes debt that is without recourse to the seller, the seller recognizes profit on each payment made to the seller and on the entire debt assumed by the buyer. The accounting treatment differs because the seller is subject to substantially different levels of risk under the alternative conditions. For debt that is without recourse, the seller recovers a portion, if not all, of the cost of the asset surrendered at the time the buyer assumes the debt.

Example of the installment method

Assume Tucker sells to Price a plot of undeveloped land for $2,000,000. Price will assume, with recourse, Tucker's existing first mortgage of $1,000,000 and also pay Tucker a $300,000 cash down payment. Price will pay the balance of $700,000 by giving Tucker a second mortgage payable in equal installments of principal and interest over a ten-year period. The cost of the land to Tucker was $1,200,000 and Price will commence development of the land immediately.

1. Computation of sales value:

Cash down payment	$ 300,000
First mortgage	1,000,000
Second mortgage	700,000
Sales value	$2,000,000

2. Computation of the initial investment:

Cash down payment	$ 300,000

3. Computation of the minimum required initial investment:
   a. $400,000 ($2,000,000 x 20%)
   b. 1. $850,000 [$2,000,000 – (115% x 1,000,000)]
      2. $500,000 ($2,000,000 x 25%)

   The minimum initial investment is $500,000 since b.2. is less than b.1. and b.2. is greater than a.

The initial investment criterion has not been satisfied because the actual initial investment is less than the minimum initial investment. Therefore, assuming the sale has been consummated and Tucker is reasonably assured of recovering the cost of the land from Price, the installment method is to be used. The gross profit to be recognized over the installment payment period by Tucker is computed as follows:

Sales value	$ 2,000,000
Cost of land	(1,200,000)
Gross profit	$ 800,000

The gross profit percentage to apply to each payment by Price to Tucker and the primary debt holder is 40% ($800,000/$2,000,000).

If Price also pays $50,000 of principal on the first mortgage and $70,000 of principal on the second mortgage in the year of sale, Tucker would recognize the following profit in the year of sale:

Profit recognized on the down payment ($300,000 x 40%)	$120,000
Profit recognized on the principal payments:	
First mortgage ($50,000 x 40%)	20,000
Second mortgage ($70,000 x 40%)	28,000
Total profit recognized in year of sale	$168,000

Note that Tucker recognizes profit only on the **payment** applicable to the first mortgage. This is because Tucker may be called upon to satisfy the liability on the first mortgage if Price defaults.

If Tucker's first mortgage was assumed without recourse, Tucker would recognize the following profit in the year of sale:

Profit recognized on the down payment ($300,000 x 40%)	$120,000
Profit recognized on Price's assumption of Tucker's first mortgage without recourse ($1,000,000 x 40%)	400,000
Profit recognized on the principal payment of the second mortgage ($70,000 x 40%)	28,000
Total profit recognized in year of sale	$548,000

The income statement (or related footnotes) for the period of sale includes the sales value received, the gross profit recognized, the gross profit deferred, and the costs of sale. In future periods when further payments are made to the buyer, the seller realizes gross profit on these payments. This amount is presented as a single line item in the revenue section of the income statement.

If, in the future, the transaction meets the requirements for the full accrual method of recognizing profit, the seller may change to that method and recognize the remaining deferred profit as income at that time.

Cost recovery method. When the cost recovery method is used (e.g., when the seller's receivable is subject to subordination or the seller is not reasonably assured of recovering the cost of the property if the buyer defaults), no profit is recognized on the sales transaction until the seller has recovered the cost of the property sold. If the buyer assumes debt that is with recourse to the seller, profit is not recognized by the seller until the cash payments by the buyer, including both principal and interest on debt due the seller and on debt assumed by the buyer, exceed the seller's cost of the property sold. If the buyer assumes debt that is without recourse to the seller, profit may be recognized by the seller when the cash payments by the buyer, including both principal and interest on debt due the seller, exceed the difference between the seller's cost of the property and the nonrecourse debt assumed by the buyer.

For the cost recovery method, principal collections reduce the seller's related receivable, and interest collections on such receivable increase the deferred gross profit on the balance sheet.

Example of the cost recovery method

Assume that on January 1, 2005, Simon, Inc. purchased undeveloped land with a sales value of $365,000 from Davis Co. The sales value is represented by a $15,000 cash down payment, Simon assuming Davis's $200,000 first mortgage (10%, payable in equal annual installments over the next twenty years), and Simon giving Davis a second mortgage of $150,000 (12%, payable in equal annual installments over the next ten years). The sale has been consummated, but the initial investment is below the minimum required amount and Davis is not reasonably assured of recovering the cost of the property if Simon defaults. The cost of the land to Davis was $300,000. The circumstances indicate the cost recovery method is appropriate. The transaction is recorded by Davis as follows:

1/1/05	Notes receivable	150,000	
	First mortgage payable	200,000	
	Cash	15,000	
	Revenue from sale of land		365,000
	Revenue from sale of land	365,000	
	Land		300,000
	Deferred gross profit		65,000

Case 1 — The first mortgage was assumed with recourse to Davis. Immediately after the sale, the unrecovered cost of the land is computed as follows:

Land	$300,000
Less: Cash down payment	(15,000)
Unrecovered cost	$285,000

The note (second mortgage) is reported as follows:

Note receivable	$150,000	
Less: Deferred gross profit	(65,000)	$ 85,000

At the end of the year Simon pays $26,547.64 ($8,547.64 principal and $18,000.00 interest) on the second mortgage note and $23,491.94 ($3,491.94 principal and $20,000.00 interest) on the first mortgage. At 12/31/05 the unrecovered cost of the land is computed as follows:

Previous unrecovered cost		$285,000.00
Less: Note receivable payment	$26,547.64	
First mortgage payment	23,491.94	(50,039.58)
Unrecovered cost		$234,960.42

The receivable is reported on the 12/31/05 balance sheet as follows:

Note receivable ($150,000 – 8,547.64)	$141,452.36	
Less: Deferred gross profit ($65,000 + 18,000)	83,000.00	$58,452.36

Case 2 — The first mortgage is assumed without recourse to Davis. The reporting of the note is the same as Case 1; however, the unrecovered cost of the property is different. Immediately after the sale, the unrecovered cost of the property is computed as follows:

Land	$300,000
Less: Cash down payment	(15,000)
Nonrecourse debt assumed by Simon	(200,000)
Unrecovered cost	$ 85,000

After Simon makes the payments at the end of the year, the unrecovered cost is computed as follows:

Previous unrecovered cost	$85,000.00
Less: Notes receivable payment	26,547.64
Unrecovered cost	$58,452.36

For the cost recovery method, the income statement for the year the real estate sale occurs includes the sales value received, the cost of the property given up, and the gross profit deferred. In future periods, after the cost of the property has been recovered, the income statement includes the gross profit earned as a separate revenue item.

If, after accounting for the sale by the cost recovery method, circumstances indicate that the criteria for the full accrual method are satisfied, the seller may change to the full accrual method and recognize any remaining deferred gross profit in full.

Deposit method. When the deposit method is used (e.g., when the sale is, in substance, the sale of an option and not real estate), the seller does not recognize any profit, does not record a receivable, continues to report in its financial statements the property and the related existing debt even if the debt has been assumed by the buyer, and discloses that those items are subject to a sales contract. The seller also continues to recognize depreciation expense on the property for which the deposits have been received. Cash received from the buyer (initial and continuing investments) is reported as a deposit on the contract. However, some amounts of cash may be received that are not subject to refund, such as interest on the unrecorded principal. These amounts are used to offset any carrying charges on the property (e.g., property taxes and interest on the existing debt). If the interest collected on the unrecorded receivable is refundable, the seller records this interest as a deposit before the sale is consummated and then includes it as a part of the initial investment once the sale is consummated. For contracts that are cancelled, the nonrefundable amounts are recognized as income and the refundable amounts returned to the depositor at the time of cancellation.

As stated, the seller's balance sheet continues to present the debt assumed by the buyer (this includes nonrecourse debt) among its other liabilities. However, the seller reports any principal payments on the mortgage debt assumed as additional deposits, while correspondingly reducing the carrying amount of the mortgage debt.

Reduced profit method. The reduced profit method is appropriate when the sale has been consummated and the initial investment is adequate but the continuing investment does not clearly demonstrate the buyer's willing commitment to pay the remaining balance of the receivable. For example, a buyer may purchase land under an agreement in which the seller will finance the sale over a thirty-year period. FAS 66 specifically states twenty years as the maximum amortization period for the purchase of land; therefore, the agreement fails to meet the continuing investment criteria.

Under the reduced profit method, the seller recognizes a portion of the profit at the time of sale with the remaining portion recognized in future periods. The amount of reduced profit recognized at the time of sale is determined by discounting the receivable from the buyer to the present value of the lowest level of annual payments required by the sales contract over the maximum period of time specified for that type of real estate property (twenty years for land and the customary term of a first mortgage loan set by an independent lending institution for other types of real estate). The remaining profit is recognized in the periods that lump-sum or other payments are made.

Example of the reduced profit method

Assume Levinson, Inc. sells a parcel of land to Raemer Co. Levinson receives sales value of $2,000,000. The land cost $1,600,000. Raemer gave Levinson the following consideration:

Cash down payment	$ 500,000
First mortgage note payable to an independent lending institution (payable in equal installments of principal and 12% interest, $133,887 payable at the end of each of the next twenty years)	1,000,000
Second mortgage note payable to Levinson (payable in equal installments of principal and 10% interest, $53,039 payable at the end of each of the next thirty years)	500,000
Total sales value	$2,000,000

The amortization term of the second mortgage (seller's receivable) exceeds the twenty-year maximum permitted by FAS 66. It is assumed that the payments by the buyer will cover the interest and principal on the maximum first mortgage loan that could be obtained on the property and interest on the excess aggregate debt on the property over such a maximum first mortgage loan; consequently, the reduced profit method is appropriate. It is also assumed that the market interest rate on similar agreements is 14%.

The present value of $53,039 per year for twenty years at the market rate of 14% is $351,278 ($53,039 x 6.623).

The gross profit on the sale ($400,000) is reduced by the difference between the face amount of the seller's receivable ($500,000) and the reduced amount ($351,278) or $148,722. The profit recognized at the time of sale is the sales value less the cost of the land less the difference between the face amount of the receivable and the reduced amount. Therefore, the reduced profit recognized on the date of sale is computed as follows:

Sales value		$ 2,000,000
Less:	Cost of land	(1,600,000)
	Excess	(148,722)
Reduced profit		$ 251,278

Under the reduced profit method, the seller amortizes its receivable at the market rate, not the rate given on the second mortgage. The receivable's carrying balance is zero after the specified term expires (in this case, twenty years). The remaining profit of $148,722 is recognized in the years after the specified term expires as the buyer makes payments on the second mortgage (years twenty-one through thirty).

Profit Recognition on Retail Land Sales

A single method of recognizing profit is applied to all consummated sales transactions within a project.

Full accrual method. The full accrual method of accounting is applied if **all** of the following conditions are met and a sale can be recorded:

1. **Expiration of refund period.** The buyer has made the down payment and each required subsequent payment until the period of cancellation with refund has expired. That period is the longest period of those required by local law, established by the seller's policy, or specified in the contract.
2. **Sufficient cumulative payments.** The cumulative payments of principal and interest equal or exceed 10% of the contract sales price.
3. **Collectibility of receivables.** Collection experience for the project in which the sale is made or for the seller's prior projects indicates that at least 90% of the con-

tracts in the project in which the sale is made that are in force six months after sale will be collected in full. The collection experience with the seller's prior projects may be applied to a new project if the prior projects have

a. The same characteristics (type of land, environment, clientele, contract terms, sales methods) as the new project
b. A sufficiently long collection period to indicate the percentage of current sales of the new project that will be collected to maturity

A down payment of at least 20% is an acceptable indication of collectibility.

4. **Nonsubordination of receivables.** The receivable from the sale is not subject to subordination to new loans on the property except that subordination by an individual lot buyer for home construction purposes is permissible if the collection experience on those contracts is the same as on contracts not subordinated.
5. **Completion of development.** The seller is not obligated to complete improvements of lots sold or to construct amenities or other facilities applicable to lots sold.

Percentage-of-completion method. The percentage-of-completion method is used if criteria 1., 2., 3., and 4. above are met, and full accrual criteria are not met (criterion 5. is not satisfied). However, additional criteria (6. and 7.) must be satisfied.

6. **There has been progress on improvements.** The project's improvements progressed beyond preliminary stages and the work apparently will be completed according to plan. Some indications of progress are

   a. The expenditure of funds
   b. Initiation of work
   c. Existence of engineering plans and work commitments
   d. Completion of access roads and amenities such as golf courses, clubs, and swimming pools

   Additionally, there should be no indication of significant delaying factors, such as the inability to obtain permits, contractors, personnel, or equipment. Finally, estimates of costs to complete and extent of progress toward completion should be reasonably dependable.
7. **Development is practical.** There is an expectation that the land can be developed for the purposes, represented and the properties will be useful for those purposes; restrictions, including environmental restrictions, will not seriously hamper development; and that improvements such as access roads, water supply, and sewage treatment or removal are feasible within a reasonable time period.

Installment method. The installment method is appropriate if criteria a. and b. are met, full accrual criteria are not met, and the seller is financially capable, as shown by capital structure, cash flow, or borrowing capacity. If the transaction subsequently meets the requirements for the full accrual method, the seller is permitted to change to that method. This would be a change in accounting estimate. This method may be changed to the percentage-of-completion method when all of the criteria are met.

Deposit method. If a retail land sale transaction does not meet any of the above, the deposit method is appropriate.

EMERGING ISSUES TASK FORCE ISSUES SUMMARIES

00-13 Determining Whether Equipment is "Integral Equipment" Subject to FASB Statement No. 66, *Accounting for Sales of Real Estate*, and No. 98, *Accounting for Leases*

Because FIN 43 states that sales of integral equipment are within the scope of FAS 66, *Accounting for Sales of Real Estate*, the determination of whether equipment is integral has increased in importance. A determination of whether equipment to be leased is integral is also necessary to enable lessors to determine the proper accounting for sales-type leases. This issue discusses how the determination is to be made.

The determination of whether equipment is integral is made based on two factors. First is the significance of the cost to remove the equipment from its existing location (which would include the costs of repairing the damage done to that location by the removal). Second is the decrease in value of the equipment that results from its removal (which is, at a minimum, the cost to ship and reinstall the equipment at a new site). The nature of the equipment and whether others can use it is considered in determining whether there is further diminution in fair value. When the combined total of the cost to remove and any further diminution of value exceeds 10% of the fair value of the equipment (installed), the equipment is integral equipment.

FASB STAFF POSITION

144-1 Determination of Cost Basis for Foreclosed Assets under FASB Statement No. 15, *Accounting by Debtors and Creditors for Troubled Debt Restructurings,* and the Measurement of Cumulative Losses Previously Recognized under Paragraph 37 of FASB Statement No. 144, *Accounting for the Impairment or Disposal of Long-Lived Assets*

When a loan collateralized by a long-lived asset is foreclosed, any valuation allowance established for the foreclosed loan should not be carried over as a separate element of the cost basis for purposes of accounting for the long-lived assets under FAS 144. Upon foreclosure, the lender must measure the long-lived asset received in full satisfaction of a receivable at fair value less cost to sell as prescribed by FAS 15. Application of that standard results in the measurement of a new cost basis for the long-lived asset received in full satisfaction of a receivable. Thus, the valuation allowance should not be carried over as a separate element of the cost basis for purposes of accounting for the long-lived asset under FAS 144 subsequent to foreclosure.

FAS 144 states that "a loss shall be recognized for any initial or subsequent write-down to fair value less cost to sell. A gain shall be recognized for any subsequent increase in fair value less cost to sell, but not in excess of the cumulative loss previously recognized (for a write-down to fair value less cost to sell)." Accordingly, the standard limits gain recognition to the extent that cumulative losses have been recognized and measured, while the assets were accounted for as long-lived assets under FAS 144. Put differently, FAS 144 does not allow the lender to "look back" to lending impairments measured and recognized under FAS 5, FAS 15, or FAS 114, for purposes of measuring the cumulative loss previously recognized.

STATEMENTS OF POSITION

Draft SOP Accounting for Real Estate Time-Sharing Transactions

This proposed Statement of Position (SOP) would provide guidance on a seller's accounting for real estate time-sharing transactions. For a time-sharing transaction to be accounted for as a sale, it would have to meet the following criteria:

1. The seller transfers nonreversionary title to the time-share;
2. The transaction is *consummated*;
3. The buyer makes cumulative payments (excluding interest) of at least 10% of the sales value of the time-share; and
4. Sufficient time-shares would have been sold to reasonably assure that the units will not become rental property.

If the seller does not transfer nonreversionary title, the draft SOP would require that the transaction be accounted for in the same manner as an operating lease.

If a time-sharing transaction accounted for as a sale met certain criteria, the seller would recognize revenue immediately using the full accrual method of accounting. But if the transaction did not meet the criteria, the seller would have to delay recognition of revenue, which would be recognized as revenue over time, based on methods that address the criterion causing the initial delay of revenue recognition.

The seller would apply the full accrual method if

1. The time-sharing receivable was not subject to future subordination;
2. The seller was able to demonstrate collectibility of the receivable;
3. The seller could estimate credit losses with reasonable reliability; and
4. Development of the project was complete.

The seller would instead apply the percentage-of-completion method if the first three conditions for full accrual accounting were met, but development of the project was not complete and, in addition, the following conditions were met:

1. Sales and costs of the project could be estimated with reasonable reliability; and
2. Construction of the project had progressed beyond preliminary stages and completion of the planned work was indicated.

Under the draft SOP, if any of the first three conditions for full accrual accounting was not met, but development was complete, the seller would apply the cash-received method. If any of the first three conditions for full accrual accounting was not met and development was not complete, however, the seller would apply the combined method (a combination of the percentage-of-completion and cash-received methods) in certain limited situations, or the deposit method.

If a transaction previously accounted for under the deposit, cash-received, or combination method of accounting later met the criteria for a "higher" revenue recognition method, the seller would change to the applicable accounting method for that transaction in the period in which the criteria are met.

Certain sales incentives the seller provides to a buyer in order to consummate a transaction would be recorded by reducing the stated sales price of the time-share by the excess of the fair value of the incentive over the amount the buyer pays and recording the incentive separately. For purposes of the 10% cumulative payments test for sale accounting or the 25% cumulative payments test for collectibility (under FAS 66), the seller would reduce the buyer's cumulative payments by the excess of the fair value of the incentive over the stated amount the buyer pays, except in certain situations in which, to receive the incentive, the buyer is required to make specific payments on its note.

All costs incurred to sell time-shares would be charged to expense as incurred except for certain costs that are

1. Incurred for tangible assets used directly in selling the time-shares;
2. Incurred for services performed to obtain regulatory approval of sales; or
3. Direct and incremental costs of successful sales efforts under the percentage-of-completion or deposit methods of accounting.

The seller would be required to account for cost of sales and time-sharing inventory in accordance with the relative sales value method.

The draft SOP stipulates that the term *credit losses* would be interpreted broadly to include all situations in which, as a result of credit concerns, a time-share seller collects less than 100% of the contractual cash payments of a note receivable, except for certain transfers of receivables to independent third parties by the seller. The amount of current sales that, historically and statistically, are expected to result in a credit loss would be recorded as estimated uncollectible receivables and presented in the seller's statement of operations as a deduction from revenues. Subsequent changes in estimated losses resulting from credit losses would be recorded as an adjustment to estimated uncollectible receivables and as an adjustment to revenues.

Under the relative sales value method, the seller effectively does not record revenue, cost of sales, or inventory relief for amounts not expected to be collected. There generally is no accounting effect on inventory when, as expected, a time-share is repossessed or otherwise reacquired.

Rental and other operations during holding periods, including sampler programs and minivacations, would be accounted for as incidental operations, under which any excess of revenues over costs is recorded as a reduction of inventory cost.

The accounting treatment for more complex time-sharing structures such as time-sharing special-purpose entities (SPE), points systems, and vacation clubs would be determined using the same sale and revenue recognition guidance as for simpler structures, provided that the time-sharing interest has been sold to the end user. For balance sheet presentation purposes, an SPE should be viewed as an entity lacking economic substance and established for the purpose of facilitating sales if the SPE structure is legally required for purposes of the developer being able to sell intervals to the class of nonresident customers to which the developer wishes to sell, and the SPE has no assets other than the time-sharing intervals and has no debt. In those circumstances, the seller should present on its balance sheet as time-sharing inventory the interests in the SPE not yet sold to end users.

If the seller, seller's affiliate, or related party operated an exchange, points, affinity, or similar program, the program's operations constitute continuing involvement by the seller, and the seller would have to determine its accounting based on an evaluation of whether it will receive compensation at prevailing market rates for its program services.

A reload transaction would be considered to be a separate sale of a second interval, and the accounting for the second interval is determined via application of the sale and revenue recognition guidance of the proposed SOP. For an upgrade transaction, the accounting for the upgraded interval would be determined via application of that guidance to the incremental sales value.

The SOP was proposed to be effective for financial statements for fiscal years beginning after June 15, 2004, with earlier application encouraged. However as of mid-2004 this has not yet been finalized.

REAL ESTATE OPERATIONS

PERSPECTIVE AND ISSUES

FAS 67, *Real Estate: Accounting for Costs and Initial Rental Operations of Real Estate Projects,* specifies the accounting for various costs in acquiring and developing real estate projects. It does not apply to

1. Real estate developed by an entity for its own use rather than for sale or rental
2. Initial direct costs of leases (discussed in Chapter 14)
3. Costs directly related to manufacturing, merchandising or service activities rather than real estate activities
4. Rental operations in which the predominant rental period is less than a month

FAS 67 does address the accounting for costs of real estate whether rented or sold.

Sources of GAAP

FAS	*EITF*	*SOP*	*FSP*
67, 144	84-17, 85-27, 86-6, 86-7, 87-9, 88-12, 88-24, 89-14, 90-20, 91-2, 94-2, 95-6, 95-7, 97-11, 98-8	75-2, 78-9, 92-1	144-1

DEFINITIONS OF TERMS

Amenities. Features of or enhancements made to real estate projects that enhance the attractiveness of the property to potential tenants or purchasers. Amenities include golf courses, utility plants, clubhouses, swimming pools, tennis courts, indoor recreational facilities, and parking facilities.

Common costs. Costs that relate to two or more units within a real estate project.

Costs incurred to rent real estate projects. Includes costs of model units and their furnishings, rental facilities, semipermanent signs, rental brochures, advertising, "grand openings," and rental overhead including rental salaries.

Costs incurred to sell real estate projects. Includes costs of model units and their furnishings, sales facilities, sales brochures, legal fees for preparation of prospectuses, semipermanent signs, advertising, "grand openings," and sales overhead including sales salaries.

Fair value. The amount in cash or cash equivalent value of other consideration that a real estate parcel would yield in a current sale between a willing buyer and a willing seller (other than in a forced or liquidation sale). The fair value of a parcel is affected by its physical characteristics, ultimate use, and the time required to make such use of the property considering access, development plans, zoning restrictions, and market absorption factors.

Incidental operations. Revenue-producing activities engaged in during the holding or development period to reduce the cost of developing the property for its intended use, as distinguished from activities designed to generate a profit or a return from the use of the property.

Incremental costs of incidental operations. Costs that would not be incurred except in relation to the conduct of incidental operations. Interest, taxes, insurance, security, and similar costs that would be incurred during the development of a real estate project regardless of whether incidental operations were conducted are not incremental costs.

Incremental revenue from incidental operations. Revenues that would not be earned except in relation to the conduct of incidental operations.

Indirect project costs. Costs incurred after the acquisition of the property, such as construction administration, legal fees, and various office costs, that clearly relate to projects under development or construction.

Net realizable value. The estimated selling price in the ordinary course of business less estimated costs of completion, holding, and disposal.

Phase. A parcel on which units are to be constructed concurrently.

Preacquisition costs. Costs related to a property that are incurred for the express purpose of, but prior to, obtaining that property. Examples may be costs of surveying, zoning or traffic studies, or payments to obtain an option on the property.

Project costs. Costs clearly associated with the acquisition, development, and construction of a real estate project.

Relative fair value before construction. The fair value of each land parcel in a real estate project in relation to the fair value of the other parcels in the project, exclusive of value added by on-site development and construction activities.

CONCEPTS, RULES, AND EXAMPLES

Preacquisition Costs

Payments are generally capitalized if they relate to an option to obtain the real property or if all of the following conditions are met:

1. Costs are directly identified with the property.
2. Costs would be capitalized if the property already were acquired.
3. Acquisition of the option or property is probable. The purchaser wants the property and believes it to be available for sale and has the ability to finance its acquisition.

Once capitalized, these costs are project costs which, if not receivable in the future, or if the property is not acquired are to be recognized as expense.

Taxes and Insurance

Real estate taxes and insurance are capitalized as property costs only when the property is undergoing activities necessary to get the property ready for its intended use. After the property is substantially complete and ready for its intended use such items are expensed.

Project Costs

Costs that are identifiable and clearly associated with acquisition, development, and construction of a real estate project are capitalized as a cost of the project.

Indirect costs that relate to several projects are capitalized and allocated to these projects. Overhead costs that do not clearly relate to any project (i.e., general and administrative expenses) are expensed as incurred.

Amenities

The costs in excess of anticipated proceeds of amenities that are to be sold or transferred in connection with the sale of individual units are treated as **common costs** of the project.

The costs of amenities that are to be sold separately or retained by the developer are capitalized with those costs in excess of estimated fair value treated as common costs. **Fair value** is determined as of the expected date of substantial physical completion and the amounts allocated to the amenity are not to be revised later. The sale of the amenity results in a gain or loss when the selling price differs from the fair value less accumulated depreciation.

Costs of amenities are allocated among land parcels benefited for which development is probable. Before completion and availability for use, operating income or loss is an adjustment to common costs. After such date, operating income or loss is included in the income statement.

Incidental Operations

Revenue from incidental operations is netted with the costs of such operations and any excess of incremental revenue over incremental costs reduces capitalized project costs. If such costs exceed revenues, the excess is recognized as expense as incurred.

Allocation of Costs

Capitalized costs are allocated by specific identification. If this is not feasible, then costs prior to construction are allocated by the relative fair value of each parcel before construction and construction costs are allocated by the relative sales value of each unit.

If estimation of relative values is impractical, allocation may be based on square footage or another area method, or by using other appropriate methods.

Revisions of Estimates

Estimates made and cost allocations are to be reviewed at least annually until the project is substantially complete and available for sale. Costs are revised and reallocated as required for changes in current estimates.

Abandonment and Change in Use

Abandonment of a project requires all capitalized costs to be expensed and not reallocated to other components of the project or other projects. Real estate dedicated to governmental units is not deemed abandoned and its costs are treated as project common costs.

Changes in use require that costs incurred and expected to be incurred that exceed the estimated value of the required project (when substantially complete and ready for intended use) be charged to expense. If no formal plan for the project exists, then project costs in excess of current net realizable value are expensed.

Selling Costs

Costs incurred to sell are capitalized if they are

1. Reasonably expected to be recovered from sale of the project or from incidental operations, and
2. Incurred for tangible assets used directly throughout the selling period to assist the selling process or incurred for services required to obtain regulatory approval of sales.

Other costs may be capitalized as prepaid expenses if directly associated with sales, cost recovery is reasonably expected from sales and the full accrual method cannot be used.

All other costs are expensed in the period incurred. Capitalized costs are expensed in the period in which the related revenue is earned.

Rental Costs

Costs related to and reasonably expected to be recoverable from future rental operations are capitalized. This excludes initial direct costs as defined and described in accounting for leases. Costs that do not qualify for capitalization are expensed as incurred.

Capitalized costs are amortized over the term of the lease, if directly related to a specific operating lease, or over the period of expected benefit. Amortization begins when the project is substantially completed and available for occupancy. Estimated unrecoverable amounts are expensed when it is probable that the lease will be terminated.

A project is substantially completed and available for occupancy when tenant improvements are completed or after one year from the end of major construction activity. Then normal operations take place with all revenues and costs (including depreciation and other amortized costs) recognized in the income statement. If part of a project is occupied but other parts are not yet complete, completed portions are considered separate projects.

Impairment and Recoverability

As discussed in Chapter 9, real estate projects must be evaluated, when warranted by events and circumstances, to determine whether their carrying value is recoverable from estimated future cash flows. FAS 144 provides guidance on grouping assets that are being held and used into "asset groups" and assets being held for sale into "disposal groups" for the purpose of the evaluation of recoverability and impairment computations. FAS 144 applies to real estate held for development and sale, property to be developed in the future, and property currently undergoing development.

Generally, under FAS 144, recoverability is evaluated at the "lowest level for which identifiable cash flows are largely independent of the cash flows of other assets and liabilities." If a project has identifiable elements with separate cash flows such as residential and commercial, or houses and condominiums, then each element is evaluated separately and not combined for the whole project. Projects are not combined in order to avoid recognizing impairment of one of the components.

Once impairment losses are recognized on property, similar to inventory, a new cost basis is adopted and future recoveries in value are not recognized.

EMERGING ISSUES TASK FORCE ISSUES SUMMARIES

84-17 Profit Recognition on Sales of Real Estate with Graduated Payment Mortgages and Insured Mortgages

This issue discusses the application of FAS 66 to graduated payment mortgages. Graduated payment mortgages for which negative principal amortization is recognized do not meet the continuing investment tests in FAS 66 and thus full profit is **not** to be recognized immediately. No consensus was reached regarding partially or fully insured mortgages. See EITF 87-9 for further discussion of this issue.

85-27 Recognition of Receipts from Made-up Rentals Shortfalls

When a seller of real estate agrees to make up any rental shortfalls for a period of time, the Task Force reached a consensus that payments to and receipts from the seller are adjustments to the cost of the property and will affect future depreciation.

86-6 Antispeculation Clauses in Real Estate Sales Contracts

Land sale agreements may contain an "antispeculation" clause requiring the buyer to develop the land in a specific manner or within a specific period of time or the seller has the right, but not the obligation, to reacquire the property. The Task Force concluded that this option would not preclude recognition of a sale if the probability of the buyer not complying is remote.

86-7 Recognition by Homebuilders of Profit from Sales of Land and Related Construction Contracts

A homebuilder enters into a contract to build a home on its own lot, relinquishing title to both the lot and the home at closing. The Task Force determined that FAS 66 guidance provides that profit recognition is not appropriate until the conditions specified in that pronouncement are met. Deposit accounting is to be used for both the land and building activity until that point.

87-9 Profit Recognition on Sales of Real Estate with Insured Mortgages or Surety Bonds

For sales of real estate, the EITF in 84-17 reached a consensus that a sale with a graduated payment mortgage that does not meet the continuing investment test in FAS 66 does not result in full, immediate profit recognition.

In 87-9, on a related matter, the Task Force reached a consensus that mortgage insurance is not to be considered the equivalent of an irrevocable letter of credit in determining whether profit is to be recognized. Purchase of such insurance is not in itself a demonstration of commitment by the buyer to honor its obligation to pay for the property. The sole exception to this rule is that for all FHA (Federal Housing Administration) and VA (Veteran's Administration) insured loans, profits may be recognized under the full accrual method.

88-12 Transfer of Ownership Interest as Part of Down Payment under FASB Statement 66

The Task Force reached a consensus that the buyer's ownership interest in a purchased property that is pledged as security for a note cannot be included as part of the buyer's initial investment in determining whether profit can be recognized under FAS 66.

88-24 Effect of Various Forms of Financing under FASB Statement 66

The EITF reached a consensus that the following guidelines be used by a seller of real estate in applying FAS 66:

1. In determining whether a transaction qualifies for accounting using the full accrual method of profit recognition, the initial and continuing investment requirements of FAS 66 must be considered unless the seller has unconditionally received all amounts due and is not at risk related to the financing.
2. In determining the buyer's initial investment, payments made on debt incurred by the buyer that is secured by the property (irrespective of whether the debt is incurred directly from the seller or other parties or indirectly by assumption), is not part of the initial investment. Also excluded from the initial investment are payments made to the seller out of the proceeds from debt described in the preceding sentence.
3. Under the installment method, cost recovery method, and reduced-profit recognition methods, payments described in 2. above are not considered to be cash payments from the buyer. If, however, the deferred profit under the method applied under FAS 66 exceeds the sum of (1) the outstanding amount of seller financing, and (2) the outstanding amount of the buyer's debt secured by the property for which the seller is contingently liable, the excess amount is recognized as income by the seller.

89-14 Valuation of Repossessed Real Estate

Foreclosed property is recorded at the lower of the net receivable due to the seller at foreclosure or the fair value of the property. SOP 92-3 provides further guidance and states that, after foreclosure, foreclosed assets are carried at the lower of fair value (less costs to sell) or cost.

90-20 Impact of an Uncollateralized Irrevocable Letter of Credit on a Real Estate Sale-Leaseback Transaction

The Task Force concluded that an uncollateralized irrevocable letter of credit is not a form of continuing involvement that precludes sale-leaseback accounting under FAS 98. However, all written contracts between the seller-lessee and the issuer of the letter of credit must be evaluated since the latter may have other forms of collateral (e.g., right of offset of amounts on deposit).

91-2 Debtor's Accounting for Forfeiture of Real Estate Subject to a Nonrecourse Mortgage

The Task Force concluded that FAS 15 applies when a nonrecourse borrower transfers property to lender in full satisfaction of the lien even though fair value of the property is less than the balance due the lender.

94-2 Treatment of Minority Interests in Certain Real Estate Investment Trusts

A sponsor's interest in an operating partnership is reported as a minority interest in the REIT's consolidated financial statements. The net equity of the operating partnership (after the contributions of the sponsor and the REIT) multiplied by the sponsor's ownership percentage in the operating partnership represents the amount to be initially reported as the minority interest in the REIT's consolidated financial statements. See related Issue 95-7 below.

95-6 Accounting by a Real Estate Investment Trust for an Investment in a Service Corporation

In determining a REIT's accounting for its investment in a service corporation (SC), the SC must be evaluated as a potential variable interest entity (VIE) under FIN 46 (discussed in detail in Chapter 11). If the SC is subject to FIN 46, this consensus does not apply to the determination of the REIT's accounting. If, however, the SC is not subject to FIN 46, this consensus continues to apply to the determination of the method of accounting that the REIT should use to record its investment (consolidation, equity method, or cost method). The EITF includes a list of factors that indicate that the equity method of accounting is to be used.

Regardless of the method of accounting used by a REIT for its investment in an SC, the SC is not considered an independent third party for the purpose of capitalizing lessor initial direct costs under FAS 91. Consequently, leasing costs capitalized by a REIT as initial direct costs may not exceed the amounts allowable if the REIT had incurred the costs directly.

95-7 Implementation Issues Related to the Treatment of Minority Interests in Certain Real Estate Investment Trusts

This is follow-up to Issue 94-2. If a minority interest balance is negative, the related charge in the REIT's income statement would be the greater of the minority interest holder's share of current earnings or the amount of distributions to the minority interest holder during the year; any excess is credited directly to equity until elimination of the minority interest deficit that existed at the formation of the REIT. Other REIT accounting matters are also addressed, including a consensus that subsequent acquisitions by the REIT, for cash, of a sponsor's minority interest in an operating partnership are accounted for consistent with the accounting for formation of the REIT.

97-11 Accounting for Internal Costs Relating to Real Estate Property Acquisitions

Internal costs of preacquisition activities incurred in connection with the acquisition of a property that will be classified as nonoperating at the date of acquisition, that are (1) directly identifiable with the acquired property, and (2) incurred subsequent to the time that acquisition of that specific property was considered probable are capitalized as part of the cost of that acquisition. If the entity later determines that the property will be classified as operating at the date of acquisition, the costs previously capitalized are charged to expense and any additional costs are to be expensed as incurred.

Internal costs of preacquisition activities incurred in connection with the acquisition of a property that is expected to be classified as operating at the date of acquisition are expensed as incurred. If the entity subsequently determines that the property will be classified as nonoperating at the date of acquisition, previously expensed costs are not to be restored and capitalized as part of the cost of that acquisition.

A property would be considered operating if, at the date of acquisition, major construction activity is substantially completed on the property and it will either (1) be held available for occupancy upon completion of tenant improvements by the acquirer, or (2) already be income producing. Internal preacquisition costs incurred are to be allocated between portions still under construction and portions substantially completed and occupied (or held available for occupancy).

98-8 Accounting for Transfers of Investments That Are in Substance Real Estate

A consensus was reached that when investments in the form of financial assets that are in substance real estate are transferred, the accounting is to follow FAS 66. Per the EITF, the implications of this consensus are

1. Transfers of acquisition, development, and construction loans (ADC loans) deemed in substance real estate under Issue 84-4 are subject to this consensus.
2. Marketable investments in a REIT accounted for under FAS 115 are accounted for per FAS 140.

STATEMENTS OF POSITION ON REAL ESTATE

75-2 Accounting Practices of Real Estate Investment Trusts

Interest income is not to be recorded when it is unreasonable to expect collection. Commitment fees are amortized over the combined commitment and loan period. The provisions dealing with loan losses and property valuation have been effectively superseded by FAS 114 and FAS 144 respectively.

78-9 Accounting for Investments in Real Estate Ventures

Owners of real estate ventures should generally use the equity method of accounting to account for their investments. However, limited partners may have such a minor interest and have no influence or control, in which case, the cost method is appropriate.

If losses exceed the investment, the losses are recorded regardless of any increase in the estimated fair value of the venture's assets. Losses in excess of investment are a liability. Losses which cannot be borne by certain investors require the remaining investors to use FAS 5, *Accounting for Contingencies*, to determine their share of any additional loss. Limited partners are not required to record losses in excess of investment. If investors do not recognize losses in excess of investment, the equity method is resumed only after the investor's share of net income exceeds the cumulative net losses not recognized previously.

Venture agreements may designate different allocations for profits, losses, cash distributions and cash from liquidation. Accounting for equity in profits and losses requires careful consideration of allocation formulas because the substance over form concept requires equity method accounting to follow the ultimate cash allocations.

Contributions of real estate to a venture as capital are recorded by the investor at cost and are not to result in recognition of a gain since a capital contribution is not the culmination of the earning process.

Interest on loans and advances that are, in substance, capital contributions are accounted for as distributions and not interest.

92-1 Accounting for Real Estate Syndication Income

This SOP applies to all income recognition from real estate syndication activities. FAS 66 applies to profit and loss recognition on sales of real estate by syndicators to partnerships. This SOP requires that the same concepts be applied to syndicators even though they may have never owned the property.

All fees charged by syndicators are includable in determination of sales value as required by FAS 66 except for syndication fees and fees for which future services must be performed. Syndication fees are recognized as income when the earning process is complete and collectibility is reasonably assured. If fees are unreasonable, they are to be adjusted and the sales price of the real estate appropriately adjusted as well. If a partnership interest is received by the syndicator, the value is included in the test of fee reasonableness. If it is part of the fee, the syndicators are to account for this interest as a retained interest from the partial sale of real estate in conformity with FAS 66. Fees for future services are recognized when the service is rendered.

Fees received from blind pool transactions are recognized ratably as the syndication partnership invests in property but only to the extent that the fees are nonrefundable. If syndicators are exposed to future losses from material involvement or from uncertainties regarding collectibility, income is deferred until the losses can be reasonably estimated. For purposes of determining the FAS 66 requirement concerning the buyer's initial and continuing investment for profit recognition, before cash received by syndicators can be allocated to initial and continuing investment, it is allocated to (1) unpaid syndication fees until such fees are paid in full, and (2) amounts previously allocated to fees for future services (to the extent such services have already been performed when the cash is collected). If syndicators receive or retain partnership interests that are subordinated, these are accounted for as participations in future profits without risk of loss.

FRANCHISING: ACCOUNTING BY FRANCHISORS

PERSPECTIVE AND ISSUES

Franchising has become a popular growth industry with many businesses seeking to sell franchises as their primary income source and individuals seeking to buy franchises and become entrepreneurs. How to recognize revenue on the individual sale of franchise territories and on the transactions that arise in connection with the continuing relationship between the franchisor and franchisee are prime accounting issues.

Originally, in 1973, the AICPA published an industry accounting guide, *Accounting for Franchise Fee Revenue,* from which the FASB extracted the principles in FAS 45 with the same title.

Sources of GAAP
FAS
45

DEFINITIONS OF TERMS

Area franchise. An agreement that transfers franchise rights within a geographical area permitting the opening of a number of franchised outlets. The number of outlets, specific locations, and so forth are decisions usually made by the franchisee.

Bargain purchase. A transaction in which the franchisee is allowed to purchase equipment or supplies for a price that is significantly lower than their fair value.

Continuing franchise fee. Consideration for the continuing rights granted by the franchise agreement and for general or specific services during its term.

Franchise agreement. A written business agreement that meets the following principal criteria:

1. The relation between the franchisor and franchisee is contractual, and an agreement, confirming the rights and responsibilities of each party, is in force for a specified period.
2. The continuing relation has as its purpose the distribution of a product or service, or an entire business concept, within a particular market area.
3. Both the franchisor and the franchisee contribute resources for establishing and maintaining the franchise. The franchisor's contribution may be a trademark, a company reputation, products, procedures, labor, equipment, or a process. The franchisee usually contributes operating capital as well as the managerial and operational resources required for opening and continuing the franchised outlet.
4. The franchise agreement outlines and describes the specific marketing practices to be followed, specifies the contribution of each party to the operation of the business, and sets forth certain operating procedures that both parties agree to comply with.
5. The establishment of the franchised outlet creates a business entity that will, in most cases, require and support the full-time business activity of the franchisee.
6. Both the franchisee and the franchisor have a common public identity. This identity is achieved most often through the use of common trade names or trademarks and is frequently reinforced through advertising programs designed to promote the recognition and acceptance of the common identity within the franchisee's market area.

Franchisee. The party who has been granted business rights (the franchise) to operate the franchised business.

Franchisor. The party who grants business rights (the franchise) to the party (the franchisee) who will operate the franchised business.

Initial franchise fee. Consideration for establishing the franchise relationship and providing some agreed-upon initial services. Occasionally, the fee includes consideration for initially required equipment and inventory, but those items usually are the subject of separate consideration. The payment of an initial franchise fee or a continuing royalty fee is not a necessary criterion for an agreement to be considered a franchise agreement.

Initial services. Common provision of a franchise agreement in which the franchisor usually will agree to provide a variety of services and advice to the franchisee, such as the following:

1. Assistance in the selection of a site. The assistance may be based on experience with factors such as traffic patterns, residential configurations, and competition.
2. Assistance in obtaining facilities, including related financing and architectural and engineering services. The facilities may be purchased or leased by the franchisee, and lease payments may be guaranteed by the franchisor.
3. Assistance in advertising, either for the individual franchisee or as part of a general program
4. Training of the franchisee's personnel
5. Preparation and distribution of manuals and similar material concerning operations, administration, and recordkeeping
6. Bookkeeping and advisory services, including setting up the franchisee's records and advising the franchisee about income taxes, real estate taxes, and other taxes, or about local regulations affecting the franchisee's business
7. Inspection, testing, and other quality control programs

CONCEPTS AND RULES

Franchise Sales

Franchise operations are generally subject to the same accounting principles as other commercial enterprises. Special issues arise out of **franchise agreements,** however, which require the application of special accounting rules.

Revenue is recognized, with an appropriate provision for bad debts, when the franchisor has substantially performed all material services or conditions. Only when revenue is collected over an extended period of time and collectibility cannot be predicted in advance would the use of the cost recovery or installment methods of revenue recognition be appropriate. Substantial performance means

1. The **franchisor** has no remaining obligation to either refund cash or forgive any unpaid balance due.
2. Substantially all **initial services** required by the agreement have been performed.
3. No material obligations or conditions remain.

Even if the contract does not require initial services, the pattern of performance by the franchisor in other franchise sales will impact the time period of revenue recognition. This can delay such recognition until services are either performed or it can reasonably be assured they will not be performed. The **franchisee** operations will be considered as started when such substantial performance has occurred.

If **initial franchise fees** are large compared to services rendered and **continuing franchise fees** are small compared to services to be rendered, then a portion of the initial fee is deferred in an amount sufficient to cover the costs of future services plus a reasonable profit, after considering the impact of the continuing franchise fee.

Area Franchise Sales

Sometimes franchisors sell territories rather than individual locations. In this event, the franchisor may render services to the area independent of the number of individual franchises to be established. Under this circumstance, revenue recognition for the franchisor is the same as stated above. If, however, substantial services are performed by the franchisor for each individual franchise established, then revenue is recognized in proportion to mandatory service. The general rule is that when the franchisee has no right to receive a refund, all revenue is recognized. It may be necessary for revenue recognition purposes to treat a franchise agreement as a divisible contract and allocate revenue among existing and estimated locations. Future revisions to these estimates will require that remaining unrecognized revenue be recorded in proportion to remaining services expected to be performed.

Other Relationships

Franchisors may guarantee debt of the franchisee, continue to own a portion of the franchise, or control the franchisee's operations. Revenue is not recognized until all services, conditions, and obligations have been performed.

In addition, the franchisor may have an option to reacquire the location. Accounting for initial revenue is to consider the probability of exercise of the option. If the expectation at the time of the agreement is that the option is likely to be exercised, the entire franchise fee is deferred and not recognized as income. Upon exercise, the deferral reduces the recorded investment of the franchisor.

An initial fee may cover both franchise rights and property rights, including equipment, signs, and inventory. A portion of the fee applicable to property rights is recognized to the extent of the fair value of these assets. However, fees relating to different services rendered by franchisors are generally not allocated to these different services because segregating the amounts applicable to each service could not be performed objectively. The rule of revenue recognition when all services are substantially performed is generally upheld. If objectively determinable separate fees are charged for separate services, then recognition of revenue can be determined and recorded for each service performed.

Franchisors may act as agents for the franchisee by issuing purchase orders to suppliers for inventory and equipment. These are not recorded as sales and purchases by the franchisor; instead, consistent with the agency relationship, receivables from the franchisee and payables to the supplier are reported on the balance sheet of the franchisor. There is, of course, no right of offset associated with these amounts, which are to be presented gross.

Continuing Franchise and Other Fees

Continuing franchise fees are recognized as revenue as the fees are earned. Related costs are expensed as incurred. Regardless of the purpose of the fees, revenue is recognized when the fee is earned and receivable. The exception is when a portion of the fee is required to be segregated and used for a specific purpose, such as advertising. The franchisor defers this amount and records it as a liability. This liability is reduced by the cost of the services received.

Sometimes, the franchisee has a period of time where **bargain purchases** of equipment or supplies are granted by the contract. If the bargain price is lower than other customers pay or denies a reasonable profit to the franchisor, a portion of the initial franchise fee is deferred and accounted for as an adjustment of the selling price when the franchisee makes the purchase. The deferred amount is either the difference in the selling price among customers and the bargain price, or an amount sufficient to provide a reasonable profit to the franchisor.

Costs

Direct and incremental costs related to franchise sales are deferred and recognized when revenue is recorded. However, deferred costs cannot exceed anticipated future revenue, net of additional expected costs.

Indirect costs are expensed as incurred. These usually are regular and recurring costs that bear no relationship to sales.

Repossessed Franchises

If, for any reason, the franchisor refunds the franchise fee and obtains the location, previously recognized revenue is reversed in the period of repossession. If a repossession is made without a refund, there is no adjustment of revenue previously recognized. However, any estimated uncollectible amounts are to be provided for and any remaining collected funds are recorded as revenue.

Business Combinations

Business combinations where the franchisor acquires the business of a franchisee are accounted for in accordance with the rules of FAS 141.

No adjustment of prior revenue is made since the financial statements are not retroactively consolidated in recording a business combination. Care must be taken to ensure that the purchase is not a repossession. If the transaction is deemed to be a repossession, it is accounted for as described in the above section.

OTHER SPECIAL ACCOUNTING AND REPORTING ISSUES

Sources of GAAP
EITF
99-19, 00-8, 00-21, 01-9, 02-16, 3-10

EMERGING ISSUES TASK FORCE ISSUES SUMMARIES

99-19 Reporting Revenue Gross as a Principal versus Net as an Agent

This issue provides guidance on whether an entity is an agent for a vendor-manufacturer, and thus recognizes the net retainage (commission) for serving in that capacity, or whether that entity is a seller of goods (principal), and thus recognizes revenue for the gross amount billed to a customer and an expense for the amount paid to the vendor-manufacturer.

The following factors are to be considered when determining whether revenue is to be reported as the net retainage (hereinafter, "net") or the gross amount billed to a customer ("gross"). None of the indicators are presumptive or determinative, although the relative strength of each indicator is to be considered.

- Is the company the primary obligor in the arrangement; that is, is the company responsible for the fulfillment of the order, including the acceptability of the product or service to the customer? If the company, rather than a supplier, is responsible, that fact is a strong indicator that the company record revenue gross. Responsibility for arranging transportation for the product is not responsibility for fulfillment. If a supplier is responsible for fulfillment, including the acceptability to the customer, that fact indicates that the company recognize only the net retainage.
- Does the company have general inventory risk? General inventory risk exists if a company takes title to a product before the product is ordered by a customer or will take title to the product if the customer returns it (provided that the customer has a right of return). In considering this indicator, arrangements with a supplier that reduce or mitigate the company's risk level are to be considered. Unmiti-

gated general inventory risk is a strong indicator that the company recognize revenue gross.

- Does the company have physical loss inventory risk? Physical loss inventory risk exists if the title to the product is transferred to the company at the shipping point and then transferred to the customer upon delivery. Physical loss inventory risk also exists if a company takes title to the product after the order is received but before the product is transferred to the shipper. While less persuasive than general inventory risk, this indicator provides some evidence that a company record revenue gross.
- Does the company establish the selling price? If a company establishes the selling price, that fact may indicate that the company recognize revenue gross.
- Is the amount earned by the company fixed? If a company earns a fixed amount per transaction or if it earns a percentage of the selling price, that fact may indicate that the company report revenue net.
- Does the company change the product or perform part of the service? If a company changes the product (beyond packaging) or performs part of the service ordered by the customer such that the selling price is greater as a result of the company's efforts, that fact is indicative that a company recognize revenue gross. Marketing skills, market coverage, distribution system, or reputation are not to be evaluated in determining whether the company changes the product or performs part of the service.
- Does the company have multiple suppliers for the product or service ordered by the customer? If a company has the discretion to select the supplier, that fact may indicate that the company record revenue gross.
- Is the company involved in determining the nature, type, characteristics or specifications of the product or service by the customer? If so, that fact may indicate that the company record revenue gross.
- Does the company have credit risk for the amount billed to the customer? Credit risk exists if a company must pay the supplier after the supplier performs, regardless of whether the customer has paid. If the company has credit risk, this fact provides weak evidence that the company record revenue gross. If the supplier assumes the credit risk, the company is to record revenue net.

The EITF consensus includes thirteen examples to assist in its implementation.

00-8 Accounting by a Grantee for an Equity Instrument to Be Received in Conjunction with Providing Goods or Services

In exchange for goods or services, an entity (the grantee) may receive equity instruments that have conversion or exercisability terms that vary based on future events, such as attainment of sales levels or a successful initial public offering. This issue describes the appropriate accounting if FAS 133 does not apply because the instruments received have underlyings based on either the grantee's or issuer's performance.

The grantee measures the fair value of the equity instruments received using the stock price and measurement assumptions as of the earlier of two dates. The first date is the date on which the grantee and the issuer reach a mutual understanding of both the terms of the equity-based compensation and the goods to be delivered (or services to be performed). The second date is the date at which the performance necessary to earn the equity is completed by the grantee, that is, the grantee's rights have vested.

If the terms of the equity agreement are dependent on the achievement of a market condition, the fair value of the instrument is to include the effects on fair value of the commitment to change the terms if the market condition is met. Pricing models are available to value path-dependent equity instruments.

If the terms of the equity agreement are dependent on the achievement of certain performance goals (beyond those that initially established the goods to be delivered or services to be performed), the fair value of the instrument is computed without the effects of the commitment to change the terms if the goals are met. If those goals are subsequently met, the fair value is adjusted to reflect the new terms and the adjustment is reported as additional revenue (similar to modification accounting described on page 814).

00-21 Revenue Arrangements with Multiple Deliverables

Perspective and Issues

Vendors may offer customers many related and unrelated products and services sold together ("bundled") or separately. The prices assigned to the various elements of a particular transaction or series of transactions on the seller's invoices and the timing of issuing those invoices are not always indicative of the actual earning of revenue on the various elements of these transactions. This consensus provides guidance on how to measure consideration received from complex, multi-element arrangements and how to allocate that consideration between the different deliverables contained in the arrangement.

Definitions of Terms

Contingent amount. The portion of the total consideration to be received by a vendor under a multiple deliverable arrangement that would be realized by the vendor only if specified performance conditions were met or additional deliverables were provided to the customer.

Noncontingent amount. The portion of the total consideration to be received by a vendor under a multiple deliverable arrangement that is not subject to any additional performance requirements that the vendor must meet.

Refund rights. The legal right of a customer to obtain a concession or recover all or a portion of the consideration paid to a vendor under a multiple deliverable arrangement.

Relative fair value method. A technique for allocating the total consideration to be received by a vendor under a multiple deliverable arrangement to each separate unit of accounting based on the ratio of the fair value of each separate unit of accounting to the total fair values of all of the separate units of accounting.

Residual method. A technique for determining the portion of the total consideration to be received by a vendor under a multiple deliverable arrangement to be allocated to the units of accounting that have been delivered by subtracting the fair values of the undelivered items from the total consideration to be received.

Stand-alone value. The value that a specific product or service (deliverable) has to a customer without considering other products or services that might accompany it as part of a multiple deliverable arrangement. In order to have value to a customer on a stand-alone basis, a deliverable must be either sold separately by any vendor or be separately resalable by the customer whether or not there is an observable market for the deliverable.

Vendor-specific objective evidence (VSOE). The price that a vendor charges for a specific product or service (deliverable) when it is sold separately. If the deliverable is not currently being sold separately, a price that is established by management possessing the authority may be used under the condition that it is considered probable that the established price will not change prior to the separate market introduction of the deliverable.

Pronouncement Summary

Arrangements between vendors and their customers often include the sale of multiple products and services (deliverables). A multiple deliverable arrangement (MDA) can be structured using fixed, variable, or contingent pricing or combinations thereof. Product delivery and service performance can occur at different times, and in different locations and customer acceptance can be subject to various return privileges, or performance guarantees.

Scope

The consensuses in this issue provide guidance on

1. How a vendor determines whether an MDA consists of a single unit of accounting or multiple units of accounting.
2. Allocating MDA consideration to multiple units of accounting.
3. Measuring MDA consideration.

In applying the consensuses, it is to be presumed that separate contracts executed at or near the same time with the same entity or related parties were negotiated as a package and are to be considered together in determining how many units of accounting are contained in an MDA. That presumption can be overcome by sufficient contradictory evidence.

The consensuses collectively apply to all deliverables (i.e., products, services, and rights to use assets) covered by contractually binding written, oral, or implied arrangements.

Excluded from the scope of the consensus are the following:

1. Criteria for the timing of revenue recognition for a unit of accounting. Existing authoritative literature governs these determinations.
2. Arrangements where, conditioned upon the vendor's revenue from the customer exceeding certain cumulative levels or the customer continuing its relationship with the vendor for a specified time period
   a. The vendor offers free or discounted products or services in the future or
   b. The vendor provides specified future cash rebates or refunds.
3. Arrangements involving the sale of award credits by a "broad-based loyalty program operator" (presumably this exception refers to airline frequent-flyer or similar customer loyalty programs).
4. Accounting for the direct costs incurred by a vendor relative to an MDA.

Specialized accounting pronouncements govern the recognition of revenue associated with many types of deliverables. In accordance with the GAAP hierarchy discussed in Chapter 1, some of these rules are more authoritative than an EITF consensus. Examples of deliverables whose accounting is governed by such pronouncements include long-term construction contracts; separately priced extended warranty and maintenance contracts; leases; computer software developed for sale, lease or license; motion pictures; franchise fees; and real estate.

If the accounting rules for whether and/or how to separate a particular deliverable from an MDA and how to allocate consideration to the resulting units of accounting are contained in a higher-level pronouncement, then the accounting for that particular deliverable is to be in accordance with the higher-level pronouncement. The remaining deliverables that are not covered by such a pronouncement, however, are subject to evaluation under these consensuses.

Basic Principles

In general, the EITF set forth three basic principles the application of which are subject to the discussion that follows:

1. MDA are divided into separate *units of accounting* if the deliverables included in the arrangement meet all three of the criteria presented in the table below.
2. Subject to certain limits regarding contingent amounts to be received under the MDA, *relative fair values* are used to allocate MDA proceeds to the separate units of accounting.
3. The revenue recognition criteria to be applied are determined *separately* for each unit of accounting.

Units of Accounting

The following table summarizes the criteria used in determining units of accounting for MDA within the scope of these consensuses and is adapted from a decision diagram contained in the EITF Abstract:

Criteria	*Outcome*	*Result*
1. Does the delivered item have stand-alone value to the customer?	Yes	Go to criteria 2
	No	Do not separate item
2. Does objective and reliable evidence exist regarding the fair value of the undelivered items?	Yes	Go to criteria 3
	No	Do not separate item
3. If the MDA includes a general right of return with respect to the delivered item, is delivery of the undelivered items probable and substantially controlled by the vendor?	Yes or Not Applicable	Delivered item is a separate unit of accounting
	No	Do not separate item

This separability evaluation is to be applied consistently to MDA that arise under similar circumstances or that possess similar characteristics. The evaluation is to be performed at the inception of the MDA and upon delivery of each item.

If consideration is allocated to a deliverable that does not qualify as a separate unit of accounting

1. Combine the amount allocated to the deliverable with the amounts allocated to all other undelivered items included in the MDA and
2. Determine revenue recognition for the combined items as a single unit of accounting.

Measurement and Allocation of MDA Consideration

The following decision diagram summarizes the factors to consider in measuring and allocating MDA consideration:

Measuring and Allocating MDA Consideration

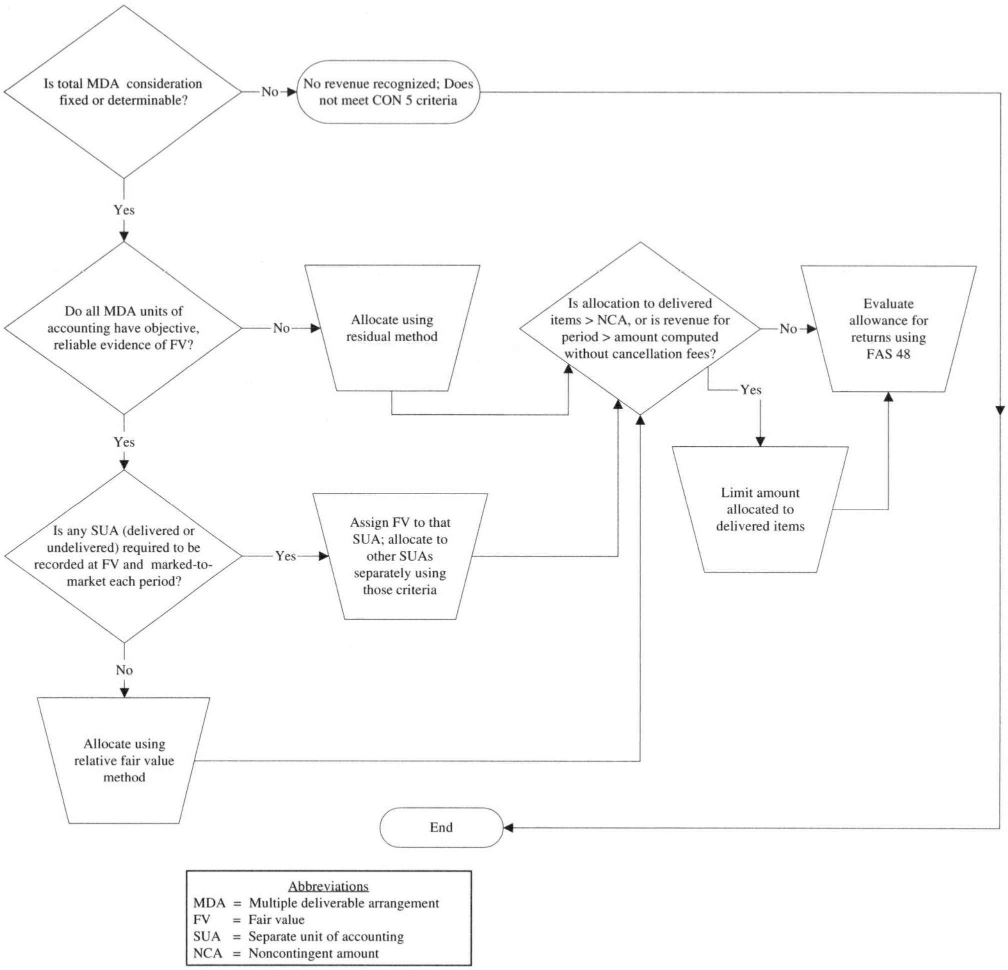

The determination of whether total MDA consideration is fixed or determinable disregards the effects of refund rights or performance bonuses, if any.

After applying the criteria set forth in the decision diagram, the vendor may recognize an asset representing the cumulative difference, from inception of the MDA, between amounts recognized as revenue and amounts received or receivable from the customer (this is analogous to the asset "costs and estimated earnings in excess of billings" which is used in long-term construction accounting). The amount of such assets may not exceed the total amounts to which the vendor is legally entitled under the MDA including fees that would be earned upon customer cancellation. The amount recognized as an asset would be further limited if the vendor did not intend to enforce its contractual rights to obtain such cancellation fees from the customer.

In measuring fair value, it is presumed that a separately stated sales price included in the sales contract for a deliverable is not representative of that deliverable's separate fair value. Rather, the best evidence of fair value is vendor-specific objective evidence (VSOE) of the sales price of the deliverable on a stand-alone basis. Use of VSOE, when available, to determine fair value is always preferable. Otherwise, third-party evidence of fair value is an acceptable substitute.

Disclosures

The financial statements of a vendor are to include the following disclosures, when applicable:

1. The nature of the vendor's MDAs including provisions relative to performance, cancellation, termination, or refund.
2. The vendor's accounting policy with respect to the recognition of revenue from MDAs (e.g., whether deliverables are separable into units of accounting).

Transition

The guidance in EITF 00-21 was effective for transactions entered into in fiscal periods beginning after June 15, 2003. In May 2003, EITF clarified the application of the consensus in situations in which higher-level GAAP guidance also exists, particularly when higher-level guidance deals with certain of the deliverables in a given MDA, but not with others. To the extent that a reporting entity had applied the guidance of EITF 00-21 prior to the May 2003 additions, implementation of the new guidance would be accounted for as implementation of a new standard, with appropriate transition accounting as the cumulative effect of an accounting change (as described in EITF Topic D-1).

With regard to the guidance in EITF 00-21, the consensus holds that when higher-level accounting literature offers guidance to parts of the MDA, the following rules apply:

1. Higher-level literature provides guidance regarding the determination of separate units of accounting and how to allocate arrangement consideration to those separate units of accounting, the arrangements or the deliverable(s) that is within the scope of that literature should be accounted for in accordance therewith, rather than the guidance in EITF 00-21.
2. If higher-level literature provides guidance requiring separation of deliverables within the scope of higher-level literature from deliverables not within the scope of higher-level literature, but does not specify how to allocate total consideration to each separate unit of accounting, the allocation is to be performed according to relative fair values, using the reporting entity's best estimate of the fair value of those deliverable(s) within the scope of higher-level literature and those not within its scope. Subsequent accounting (i.e., the identification of separate units of accounting and the allocation of values) for the value allocated to the deliverable(s) not subject to higher-level literature would be governed by the provisions of EITF 00-21.
3. If higher-level literature provides no guidance regarding the separation of the deliverables within the scope of higher-level literature from those deliverables that are not or the allocation of arrangement consideration to deliverables within the scope of the higher-level literature and to those that are not, then the guidance in EITF 00-21 should be followed for purposes of such separation and allocation. In that case, it is possible that a deliverable subject to the guidance of higher-level literature does not meet the criteria set forth by EITF 00-21 to be considered a separate unit of accounting. If so, the arrangement consideration allocable to such deliverable should be combined with the amount allocable to the other applicable undelivered item(s) within the arrangement. The

appropriate recognition of revenue would then be determined for those combined deliverables as a single unit of accounting.

01-9 Accounting for Consideration Given by a Vendor to a Customer (Including a Reseller of the Vendor's Products)

Codification of:

00-14 Accounting for Certain Sales Incentives
00-22 Accounting for Points and Certain Other Time-Based or Volume-Based Sales Incentive Offers, and Offers for Free Products or Services to Be Delivered in the Future.
00-25 Vendor Income Statement Characterization of Consideration Paid to a Reseller of the Vendor's Products

This issue provides guidance regarding the recognition, measurement, and income statement display of consideration given by a vendor to purchasers of the vendor's products. This consideration can be provided to a purchaser at any point along the distribution chain, irrespective of whether the purchaser receiving the consideration is a direct or indirect customer of the vendor. Examples of arrangements include, but are not limited to, sales incentive offers labeled as discounts, coupons, rebates, and "free" products or services as well as arrangements referred to as slotting fees, cooperative advertising, and buydowns. The issue does not apply to

1. Coupons, rebates, and other forms of rights for free or significantly discounted products or services received by a customer in a prior exchange transaction that were accounted for by the vendor as a separate deliverable in that prior exchange, or
2. An offer to a customer, in connection with a current revenue transaction, for free or discounted products or services that is redeemable by the customer at a future date without a further exchange transaction with the vendor. Covered by EITF 00-21, summarized above.

The issue also does not discuss the accounting for offers of free or discounted products or services that are exercisable after a customer has completed a specified cumulative level of revenue transactions or remained a customer for a specified time period (for example, "point" and loyalty programs).

This issue has six subissues.

1. Cash consideration given by a vendor to a customer is presumed to be a reduction of selling price and is classified as a reduction of revenue when recognized in the vendor's income statement. That presumption is overcome and the consideration is classified as a cost incurred if, and to the extent that, both of the following conditions are met:
   a. The vendor receives, or will receive, an identifiable benefit (goods or services) in exchange for the consideration. In order to meet this condition, the identified benefit must be of a type that the vendor could have acquired in an exchange transaction with a party other than a purchaser of its products or services, that is, that the benefit must be separable from the sale of the vendor's goods or services, and
   b. The vendor can reasonably estimate the fair value of that identifiable benefit. If the amount of consideration paid by the vendor exceeds the esti-

mated fair value of the benefit received, that excess amount is classified as a reduction of revenue when recognized in the vendor's income statement.

If the consideration is a "free" product or service or anything other than cash (including "credits" that the customer can apply against trade amounts owed to the vendor) or equity instruments, the cost of the consideration is characterized as an expense (as opposed to a reduction of revenue) when recognized in the vendor's income statement. The consensus contains fifteen examples of subissue 1.

2. The amounts representing reduced revenue are classified as expense only if a vendor can demonstrate that classification of those amounts as a reduction of revenue results in negative revenue for a specific customer on a cumulative basis (that is, since the inception of the overall relationship between the vendor and the customer). However, classification as an expense would not be appropriate if a supply arrangement exists that either
   a. Provides the vendor with the right to be a provider of a certain type or class of goods or services for a specified period of time and it is probable that the customer will order the vendor's goods or services, or
   b. Requires the customer to order a minimum amount of goods or services from the vendor in the future, except to the extent that the consideration given exceeds future revenue from the customer under the arrangement.
3. If the consideration offered voluntarily by a vendor and without charge to customers can be used or becomes exercisable by a customer as a result of a single exchange transaction, and that consideration will not result in a loss on the sale, the vendor recognizes the "cost" of the consideration at the later of the following:
   a. The date the related revenue is recognized by the vendor, or
   b. The date the sales incentive is offered. (For example, a vendor recognizes a liability for a mail-in rebate coupon that requires proof of purchase, based on the estimated amount of refunds or rebates that will be claimed by customers.)
4. If the consideration offered voluntarily by a vendor and without charge to customers can be used or becomes exercisable by a customer as a result of a single exchange transaction, and that consideration results in a loss on the sale, a vendor does not recognize a liability prior to the date on which the related revenue is recognized (this would be improper matching). However, the offer of consideration in an amount that will result in a loss on the sale of a product may indicate an impairment of existing inventory.
5. If a vendor offers a customer a rebate or refund of a specified amount of cash consideration that is redeemable only if the customer completes a specified cumulative level of purchases or remains a customer for a specified time, the vendor recognizes the cost of the offer in a systematic and rational manner over the period in which the underlying revenue transactions that qualify the customer for the rebate or refund take place. Measurement of the total rebate or refund obligation is based on the estimated number of customers that will ultimately earn and claim rebates or refunds under the offer. If the amount cannot be reasonably estimated, the maximum potential amount is to be recognized.
6. Without reaching consensus, the Task Force agreed to discontinue discussion of whether up-front nonrefundable consideration given by a vendor to a customer

results in an asset or is immediately recognizable as an expense in the vendor's income statement.

02-16 Accounting by a Customer (Including a Reseller) for Certain Consideration Received from a Vendor

This issue addresses accounting issues similar to Issue 01-9 from the standpoint of how the vendor's customer, either the end user or a reseller of the vendor's products or services, is to account for cash consideration it receives from its vendor.

In general, there is a rebuttable presumption that cash consideration received from a vendor is a purchase-price concession that should be recognized by the customer as a reduction of cost of goods sold (and/or the inventory of unsold units). This presumption is overcome if payment of the consideration is for either

1. **Delivery of goods and/or services.** Payment to the customer in exchange for goods or services delivered to the vendor is accounted for by the customer as revenue. In order for the customer to recognize revenue, the goods and/or services must be "sufficiently separable" from the customer's purchase of the vendor's products by meeting two criteria.
   a. The customer would have obtained the goods and/or services from a party other than the vendor **and**
   b. The customer is able to reasonably estimate the fair value of the goods and/or services provided to the vendor.

Any excess of cash consideration received by the customer over the fair value of the goods and/or services delivered to the vendor reduces the customer's cost of sales.

2. **Reimbursement of costs.** A reimbursement of the customer's specific incremental, identifiable costs incurred to sell the vendor's products or services which is accounted for by the customer as a reduction of that cost. To the extent the cash consideration received exceeds the actual cost being reimbursed, the excess reduces cost of sales and/or inventory.

Vendors sometimes enter into binding arrangements that offer customers specified amounts of cash rebates or refunds payable in the future only if the customer remains a customer for a specified period of time, or purchases a specified cumulative dollar amount of goods or services from the vendor. In general, these arrangements are to be recorded by the customer as reductions of cost of sales by systematically allocating a portion of the benefits to be received to each transaction that results in progress toward meeting the target that results in earning the benefit. In order to use this pro rata accounting, however, the amount of the refund must be both probable and reasonably estimable (as those terms are defined in FAS 5). EITF provided indicators that, if present, **may** impair the customer's ability to determine that the refund is both probable and estimable.

1. The rebate or refund applies to purchases that are to occur over a "relatively long period" (undefined in the consensus).
2. An absence of historical experience with similar products or changed circumstances that make historical experience irrelevant.
3. A past history of significant adjustments to expected rebates or refunds.
4. Susceptibility of the product to significant external factors such as technological obsolescence or changes in demand.

If the rebate or refund is not considered both probable and estimable, it is not recognized by the customer until it is fully earned by reaching the specified milestone (e.g., the dollar amount of cumulative purchases is reached or the time period for remaining a customer has expired).

Changes in a customer's estimate of the amount of future rebates or refunds, and retroactive changes by a vendor to a previous offer are recognized using a "cumulative catch-up adjustment." This is accomplished by the customer immediately charging or crediting cost of sales in an amount that will adjust the cumulative amounts recognized under the arrangement to the changed terms. Of course, if any portion of the adjustment impacts goods still in the customer's inventory, that portion would adjust the valuation of the inventory and not cost of sales.

The SEC observer to the EITF's proceedings cautioned registrants to consider whether certain transactions between vendors and customers (e.g., simultaneous agreements between the parties to purchase equal amounts of each other's goods) are covered by the provisions of APB 29 regarding nonmonetary exchanges that are not the culmination of an earning process.

03-10 Application of Issue No. 02-16 by Resellers to Sales Incentives Offered to Consumers by Manufacturers

EITF 02-16 (above) requires that cash consideration received by a customer from a vendor be presumed to be a reduction of the prices of the vendor's products or services and, therefore, is to be characterized as a reduction of cost of sales when recognized in the customer's income statement. However, in other instances the consideration is reimbursement for incentives offered to end users (e.g., retail customers) honored by the vendor's customer (retailer). The common example is coupons given to end users to be redeemed at the retailers offering the vendor's products for sale.

The EITF reached a consensus that sales incentive arrangements that meet all of certain defined criteria are not subject to the guidance in Issue 02-16. The criteria are

1. The incentive can be tendered by a consumer at resellers that accept manufacturer's incentives in partial (or full) payment of the price charged by the reseller for the vendor's product;
2. The reseller receives a direct reimbursement from the vendor (or a clearinghouse authorized by the vendor) based on the face amount of the incentive;
3. The terms of reimbursement to the reseller for the vendor's sales incentive offered to the consumer are not influenced by or negotiated in conjunction with any other incentive arrangements between the vendor and the reseller, but rather, may only be determined by the terms of the incentive offered to consumers; and
4. The reseller is subject to an agency relationship with the vendor, whether expressed or implied, in the sales incentive transaction between the vendor and the consumer.

Sales incentives that do not meet all of the foregoing criteria are subject to the guidance in EITF 01-09 and EITF 02-16, as applicable.

9 LONG-LIVED ASSETS

PERSPECTIVE AND ISSUES

Long-lived assets provide an economic benefit to the enterprise for a number of future periods. GAAP regarding long-lived assets involves the determination of the appropriate amount at which to initially record the asset. This initial cost includes costs associated with the legal obligation to eventually retire the asset and the costs of interest incurred during its construction. In addition, determinations must be made of the appropriate method to be used to allocate those amounts over the periods benefiting, subsequent increases in carrying value attributable to changes in the estimate of the retirement cost, the measurement of impairment losses, and the accounting for assets to be disposed of.

These assets are primarily operational assets and are broken down into two basic types: tangible and intangible. Tangible assets have physical substance and are categorized as follows:

1. Depreciable
2. Depletable
3. Other tangible assets

Intangible assets have no physical substance. Their value is based on the rights or privileges that they grant to the business enterprise.

Most of the accounting issues associated with long-lived assets involve proper measurement and timing of the transactions. Adequate consideration must be given to the economic substance of the transaction.

All entities are required to review long-lived assets and certain identifiable intangible assets for impairment whenever circumstances and situations change such that there is an indication that the carrying amount may not be recoverable. If, upon review, the undiscounted future cash flows (without interest charges) are less than the carrying amount, the carrying amount is reduced to fair value and an impairment loss is recognized. This fair value is considered the new cost basis and is not subject to subsequent adjustment except for depreciation and further impairment. Thus, there is no restoration of previously recognized impairment losses. With some exceptions, this standard also applies to rate-regulated assets. Thus, costs excluded by a regulator from the enterprise's rate base would be recognized as an impairment.

Long-lived assets to be disposed of by sale are presented on the balance sheet as "held for sale" and valued at their carrying amount, or their fair value less cost to sell, whichever is less. In subsequent periods, increases in value may be recognized but only to the extent of cumulative losses recognized in the past. Depreciation is not recorded for assets held for sale.

Current Developments

Asset retirement obligations. In April 2004, FASB announced its intent to issue an Exposure Draft of a proposed interpretation (ED) to FAS 143, *Accounting for Asset Retirement Obligations*. This would clarify that a reporting entity is required to recognize an asset retirement obligation even when the legal obligation is conditioned on the occurrence of a future event. In making its probability weighted estimates of future cash flow outcomes for this purpose, management is to incorporate the probability of nonoccurrence of the future event. FASB expects to issue the ED during the second quarter of 2004, with the intention that the interpretation, if adopted, will be effective for calendar year 2005 and fiscal year 2006 financial statements. Initial application would be as of the end of the adopting entity's fiscal year.

Certain costs and activities related to property, plant and equipment. In 2001, AcSEC and FASB jointly issued Exposure Drafts (collectively referred to as the "ED"), the objective of which was to resolve diverse accounting practices for different types of costs incurred at various stages in the life cycle of tangible long-lived assets (referred to in the ED as "property, plant, and equipment" or "PP&E") as well as for the determination of estimated useful lives for assets which have multiple components.

In late 2002, changes in the US accounting standards-setting framework were announced by FASB that limited future AcSEC Statements of Position to specialized industry standards. As part of the transition, FASB had permitted AcSEC to continue deliberations with respect to certain aspects of the ED based on three overarching principles AcSEC had previously established as a part of the project.

1. PP&E assets should be depreciated over their expected useful lives.
2. Replacement assets and the assets that they replace should not be simultaneously recognized as assets on an entity's books.
3. PP&E assets should be recorded at cost.

However, in April 2004, FASB asked AcSEC to discontinue work on the project and removed the project from its own agenda. Additionally, FASB directed its staff to consider whether portions of the ED should be issued as future FASB Staff Positions (FSP). Due to the possibility that portions of the ED may yet be adopted as future FSP, the discussion related to it has been retained in this chapter in the section covering outstanding Exposure Drafts.

Exchanges of productive assets. In December 2003, FASB issued an ED proposing that all nonmonetary exchanges be accounted for at fair value unless the transaction does not have commercial substance, as that term is defined in the draft. If finalized as written, this will eliminate the APB 29 exception to fair value accounting for assets that are not similar productive assets.

Sources of GAAP

ARB	*APB*	*FAS*	*FIN*	*EITF*	*SOP*	*FSP*
43, Ch. 9; 44	1, 6, 17, 29, 30	2, 34, 42, 58, 62, 68, 109, 141, 142, 143 144, 146, 147	30, 33	89-13, 90-8, 91-10, 93-11, 95-23, 98-3, 99-5, 99-9, 99-16, 00-2,01-2, 01-5, 02-7, 02-13, 02-17, D-45, D-104, 04-2, 04-3	88-1, 92-3, 93-7 98-1	FAS 141-1 FAS 142-1 FAS 144-1 FAS 146-1

Other: Accounting Research Monograph 1

DEFINITIONS OF TERMS

Amortization. The periodic charge to income that results from a systematic and rational allocation of cost over the life of an intangible asset. Analogous to depreciation of tangible assets.

Asset group. The lowest level for which identifiable cash flows are largely independent of the cash flows associated with other assets and liabilities.

Asset retirement obligation. A legal obligation associated with the retirement of a tangible long-lived asset that results from its acquisition, construction, development, and/or normal operation.

Book value. The cost of a long-lived asset less the related accumulated depreciation or amortization to the date of measurement. Sometimes referred to as *net* book value.

Boot. The monetary consideration given or received in an asset exchange.

Depreciation. The periodic charge to income that results from a systematic and rational allocation of cost over the life of a tangible asset. Analogous to amortization of intangible assets.

Disposal group. A group of assets to be disposed of in a single transaction as a group, and the liabilities directly associated with those assets that will be transferred with them.

Dividends-in-kind. Dividends paid to stockholders from assets of the corporation other than cash.

Exchange. A reciprocal transfer between an enterprise and another entity that results in the acquisition of assets or services, or the satisfaction of liabilities through a transfer of assets, services, or obligations.

Fixed assets. Those assets that are used in a productive capacity, have physical substance, are relatively long-lived, and provide future benefit that is readily measurable. Sometimes referred to as property, plant, and equipment.

Impairment. The condition that exists when a long-lived asset's carrying amount is not expected to be recoverable over the remainder of its expected life. Fixed assets and intangibles with a finite useful life are evaluated for impairment under FAS 144. Goodwill and indefinite life intangibles are evaluated for impairment under FAS 142.

Implied fair value. The excess of the fair value of a reporting unit, as a whole, over the fair values that would be assigned to its assets and liabilities in a purchase business combination at the date of measurement.

Intangible assets. Those assets that provide future economic benefit but have no physical substance. Examples include goodwill, patents, copyrights, etc.

Legal obligation. An obligation that a party is required to settle as a result of an existing or enacted law, statue, ordinance, or written or oral contract or by legal construction of a contract under the doctrine of promissory estoppel (see definition below).

Monetary assets. Assets whose amounts are fixed in terms of units of currency. Examples are cash, accounts receivable, and notes receivable.

Nonmonetary assets. Assets other than monetary assets. Examples are inventories; investments in common stock; and property, plant, and equipment.

Nonmonetary transactions. Exchanges and nonreciprocal transfers that involve little or no monetary assets or liabilities.

Nonreciprocal transfer. A transfer of assets or services in one direction, either from an enterprise to its owners or another entity, or from owners or another entity to the enterprise. An enterprise's reacquisition of its outstanding stock is a nonreciprocal transfer.

Primary asset. The depreciable long-lived asset (or amortizable intangible asset) that is the most significant component asset from which an asset group derives its cash-flow generating capacity.

Productive assets. Assets held for or used in the production of goods or services. Productive assets include an investment in another entity if the investment is accounted for by the equity method but exclude an investment not accounted for by that method.

Promissory estoppel. A legal doctrine whereby a court of law will enforce a promise made by one party (the promisor) to another party who relied on the promise (the promisee) even though no formal contract exists between the two parties or no consideration was exchanged.

Retirement. The removal from service of a long-lived asset by sale, abandonment, recycling, or other disposal on an other-than-temporary basis. Retirement can occur before or at the end of the asset's useful life. However, retirement does not include the temporary idling of an asset.

Similar productive assets. Productive assets that are of the same general type, that perform the same function, or that are employed in the same line of business.

CONCEPTS, RULES, AND EXAMPLES

Fixed Assets

Fixed assets, sometimes referred to as "property, plant and equipment," are tangible property used in a productive capacity that will benefit the enterprise for a period longer than one year.

Three issues in accounting for fixed assets are

1. The amount at which the assets are recorded
2. The rate and pattern to be used to allocate that amount to future periods
3. The recording of subsequent disposal of the assets

Recorded cost. Costs that are capitalized upon acquisition are any reasonable cost involved in bringing the asset to the buyer and incurred prior to using the asset in actual production. Examples include sales taxes, finders' fees, freight costs, installation costs, breaking-in costs, and setup costs. These costs are *not* expensed in the period in which they are incurred.

Costs incurred subsequent to purchase. Costs that occur subsequent to the initial purchase such as repairs, maintenance, or betterments are treated in one of the following ways:

1. Expensed
2. Capitalized
3. Reduced accumulated depreciation

Ordinary maintenance and repair expenditures are charged to expense as incurred.

Major repairs or maintenance increase the value (utility) of the asset or increase the estimated useful life of the asset. Those costs that increase the value of the asset are recorded as an increase in the asset's carrying amount, while those costs that extend the useful life of the asset decrease previously recorded accumulated depreciation.

The chart on the following page summarizes the treatment of expenditures subsequent to acquisition.

Construction of tangible assets for internal use. All direct costs (labor, materials, payroll, and related benefit costs) of constructing an entity's own tangible fixed assets are capitalized. However, a controversy exists regarding the proper treatment of overhead and the types of costs that qualify to be capitalized. A degree of judgment is involved in allocating costs between indirect costs, a reasonable portion of which are allocable to construction costs, and general and administrative costs, which are treated under GAAP as period costs.

To date, the FASB has not addressed this issue. The AICPA has issued conflicting guidance regarding cost capitalization. In SOP 81-1, the AICPA (in the context of long-term construction contracts) indicated that, in order for costs to be capitalized (rather than be treated as period costs), they should be "… clearly related to production either directly or by an allocation based on their discernible future benefits." Later in that same pronouncement, illustrative examples of capitalizable costs are provided with a qualifier "in *some circumstances*, support costs such as central preparation and processing of payrolls [are allocable as indirect costs]."

Subsequently, in SOP 98-1, (addressing the capitalization of costs of software self-developed for internal use, discussed in detail later in this chapter), the AICPA indicated that "general and administrative costs *and overhead costs* should not be capitalized as costs of internal-use software." The distinction between the two conflicting rules may be due to the former being applicable to tangible assets and the latter to intangible software costs, yet both types of internally constructed assets are subject to interest capitalization during the production period.

Prudence suggests that management establish a carefully reasoned policy that is consistently followed and fully disclosed in the notes to the financial statements in sufficient detail to unambiguously inform the user about the methods used and amounts involved.

Depreciation. The costs of fixed assets are allocated to the periods they benefit through depreciation. The method of depreciation chosen is that which results in a systematic and rational allocation of the cost of the asset (less its residual or salvage value) over the asset's expected useful life. The estimation of useful life takes a number of factors into consideration, including technological change, normal deterioration, and actual physical usage. The method of depreciation to be selected is based on either a function of time (e.g., technological change or normal deterioration) or as a function of actual physical usage.

Depreciation methods based on time. Each of the examples below is based on the following facts:

> Michele Corporation purchased a production machine and placed it in service on January 1, 2005. The machine cost $100,000, has an estimated salvage value of $10,000, and an estimated useful life of five years.

Accounting for Costs Incurred Subsequent to Acquisition of Property, Plant, and Equipment

		Normal accounting treatment			
			Capitalize		
Type of expenditure	*Characteristics*	*Expense when incurred*	*Charge to asset*	*Charge to accum. deprec.*	*Other*
1. Additions	• Extensions, enlargements, or expansions made to an existing asset		x		
2. Repairs and maintenance					
a. Ordinary	• Recurring, relatively small expenditures				
	1. Maintain normal operating condition	x			
	2. **Do not** add materially to use value	x			
	3. **Do not** extend useful life	x			
b. Major	• Not recurring, relatively large expenditures				
	1. Primarily increase the use value		x		
	2. Primarily extend the useful life			x	
3. Replacements and betterments	• Major component of asset is removed and replaced with the same type of component with comparable performance capabilities (replacement) or a different type of component having superior performance capabilities (betterment)				
a. Book value of old component is known					• Remove old asset cost and accum. deprec. • Recognize any loss (or gain) on old asset • Charge asset for replacement component
b. Book value of old component is not known	1. Primarily increase the use value		x		
	2. Primarily extend the useful life			x	
4. Reinstallations and rearrangements	• Provide greater efficiency in production or reduce production costs				
	1. Material costs incurred; benefits extend into future accounting periods		x		
	2. No measurable future benefit	x			
5. Relocations	• Costs of dismantlement, crating, shipping, and reinstallation • Same functionality in new location that existed at old location	x			

1. Straight-line method—Depreciation expense is recognized evenly over the estimated useful life of the asset.

   Formula

   a. Compute the straight-line depreciation rate as

   $$\frac{1}{\text{Estimated useful life}}$$

   b. Multiply the depreciation rate by the cost less estimated salvage value.

   Example

   a. Straight-line depreciation = $\frac{1}{5}$ = 20% per year

   b. 20% x ($100,000 – $10,000) = $18,000 annual depreciation

2. Accelerated methods—Depreciation expense is higher in the early years of the asset's useful life and lower in the later years. These methods are more appropriate than straight-line if the asset depreciates more quickly or has greater production capacity in the earlier years than it does as it ages. They are also sometimes used on the theory that maintenance and repair costs typically increase as assets age; therefore, in conjunction with accelerated depreciation total ownership costs (depreciation, maintenance and repairs) will approximate straight-line.

   a. Declining balance—Annual depreciation is computed by multiplying the book value at the beginning of the fiscal year by a multiple of the straight-line rate of depreciation as computed above.

   Formula

   Double-declining balance (ceases when the book value = the estimated salvage value)

   2 x Straight-line depreciation rate x Book value at the beginning of the year

   Example

Year	*Net book value, beginning of year*	*Double-declining balance depreciation computed as 2 x SL rate x beginning NBV*	*Net book value, end of year*
1	$100,000	$40,000	$60,000
2	60,000	24,000	36,000
3	36,000	14,400	21,600
4	21,600	8,640	12,960
5	12,960	2,960	10,000 limited by salvage value
Total		$90,000	

   b. Sum-of-the-years' digits (SYD) depreciation

   Formula

   (Cost – Estimated salvage value) x Applicable percentage

   $$\text{Applicable percentage} = \frac{\text{Number of years of estimated life remaining at the beginning of the year}}{\text{SYD}}$$

   $$\text{SYD} \quad \frac{n(n+1)}{2} \quad \text{where n = estimated useful life}$$

Example

$$SYD = \frac{5(5+1)}{2} = 15$$

This formula yields the sum of each year of the estimated useful life

$$1 + 2 + 3 + 4 + 5 = 15$$

Year	*Remaining estimated useful life at beginning of year*	*SYD*	*Applicable percentage*	*Annual depreciation*
1	5	15	33.33%	$30,000
2	4	15	26.67	24,000
3	3	15	20.00	18,000
4	2	15	13.33	12,000
5	1	15	6.67	6,000
Totals			100.00%	$90,000

3. Present value methods—Depreciation expense is lower in the early years and higher in the later years. The rate of return on the investment remains constant over the life of the asset. Time value of money formulas are used.
   a. Sinking fund—Uses the future value of an annuity formula.
   b. Annuity fund—Uses the present value of an annuity formula.

Partial-year depreciation. When an asset is either acquired or disposed of during the year, the full-year depreciation calculation is prorated between the accounting periods involved.

Example of partial-year depreciation

Ginger Corporation, a calendar-year entity, acquired a machine on June 1, 2005, which cost $40,000 with an estimated useful life of four years and a $2,500 salvage value. The depreciation expense for each full year of the asset's life is calculated as

	Straight-line	*Double-declining balance*	*Sum-of-years' digits*
Year 1	37,500* ÷ 4 = 9,375	50% x 40,000 = 20,000	4/10 x 37,500* = 15,000
Year 2	9,375	50% x 20,000 = 10,000	3/10 x 37,500 = 11,250
Year 3	9,375	50% x 10,000 = 5,000	2/10 x 37,500 = 7,500
Year 4	9,375	50% x 5,000 = 2,500	1/10 x 37,500 = 3,750
	37,500	37,500	37,500

* *(40,000 – 2,500)*

Because the first full year of the asset's life does not coincide with the company's fiscal year, the amounts shown above must be prorated as follows:

	Straight-line	*Double-declining balance*	*Sum-of-years' digits*
2005	7/12 x 9,375 = 5,469	7/12 x 20,000 = 11,667	7/12 x 15,000 = 8,750
2006	9,375	5/12 x 20,000 = 8,333	5/12 x 15,000 = 6,250
		7/12 x 10,000 = 5,833	7/12 x 11,250 = 6,563
		14,166	12,813
2007	9,375	5/12 x 10,000 = 4,167	5/12 x 11,250 = 4,687
		7/12 x 5,000 = 2,917	7/12 x 7,500 = 4,375
		7,084	9,062
2008	9,375	5/12 x 5,000 = 2,083	5/12 x 7,500 = 3,125
		7/12 x 2,500 = 1,458	7/12 x 3,750 = 2,188
		3,541	5,313
2009	5/12 x 9,375 = 3,906	5/12 x 2,500 = 1,042	5/12 x 3,750 = 1,562
	37,500	37,500	37,500

As an alternative to proration, an entity may follow any one of several simplified conventions.

1. Record a full year's depreciation in the year of acquisition and none in the year of disposal.
2. Record one-half year's depreciation in the year of acquisition and one-half year's depreciation in the year of disposal.

Depreciation method based on actual physical usage—Units of production. Depreciation is based upon the number of units produced by the asset in a given year.

$$\text{Depreciation rate} = \frac{\text{Cost less salvage value}}{\text{Estimated number of units to be produced by the asset over its estimated useful life}}$$

$$\text{Units of production depreciation} = \text{Depreciation rate} \times \text{Number of units produced during the current year}$$

Other depreciation methods. In addition to the foregoing, a group (composite) method is sometimes used. This method averages the service lives of a number of assets using a weighted-average of the units and depreciates the group or composite as if it were a single unit. A group consists of similar assets, while a composite is made up of dissimilar assets.

Depreciation rate:

$$\frac{\text{Sum of the straight-line depreciation of individual assets}}{\text{Total asset cost}}$$

Depreciation expense:

$$\text{Depreciation rate} \times \text{Total group (composite) cost}$$

Gains and losses are not recognized on the disposal of an asset but are netted into accumulated depreciation.

Income tax methods.

Pre-1981 depreciation. Assets placed in service prior to 1981 are depreciated based on the asset's useful life and cannot be depreciated below their salvage value. The depreciation method used depends upon the type of property and whether it was new or used when it was placed in service.

Accelerated Cost Recovery System. Assets placed in service between 1981 and 1986 are depreciated under the Accelerated Cost Recovery System (ACRS). ACRS ignores salvage value. Thus, the asset's entire income tax basis is depreciable over the specified recovery period to be used for each class of asset. Property is placed into classes and the depreciation method and life for each class is specified. Election of optional depreciation methods was also permitted. Depreciation deductions are calculated by multiplying the asset's unadjusted basis by the specified depreciation percentage for the related time period. The depreciation percentage will depend upon the asset's class, recovery year, depreciation method and convention.

Modified Accelerated Cost Recovery System. For assets placed in service after 1986, income tax depreciation is calculated using the Modified Accelerated Cost Recovery System (MACRS) which also ignores salvage value and divides assets into classes. Depreciation deductions are calculated by multiplying the asset's unadjusted basis by the appropriate depreciation percentage. The percentages are based on the type of property, class life, depreciation method, and convention. Depreciation deductions are limited for certain assets such as listed property (primarily automobiles). Optional depreciation methods may also be elected.

Additional deductions available in year placed in service. In order to provide incentives to businesses to invest in long-lived, tangible assets, the Internal Revenue Code (IRC) includes provisions that provide for aggressive deductibility of their costs in the year of acquisition. These deductions are taken prior to computing depreciation as described above and, of course, the amount of the deductions reduces the depreciable basis of the affected assets.

1. Internal Revenue Code Section 179 allows taxpayers to deduct, in the tax year placed in service, up to $100,000 of costs of qualified acquisitions. The availability of this benefit begins phasing out for companies acquiring more than $400,000 of qualified property during the tax year. The benefit fully phases out when qualified acquisitions reach $500,000. This deduction is currently scheduled to revert to an annual limit of $25,000 in 2006.
2. Two successive tax acts passed by Congress established an additional first-year "bonus" depreciation provision that permits a taxpayer to elect to deduct additional depreciation in the year qualifying property is placed in service as follows:

Date placed in service	%Bonus depreciation
Between 9/10/01 and 5/5/03	30%
Between 5/6/03 and 12/31/04	50%

Income tax depreciation will differ in amount from financial statement depreciation because of differences in treatment of salvage value, recovery methods, recovery periods, and the use of conventions for assets placed in service during the year.

The difference between income tax depreciation and financial statement depreciation is reported as a reconciling item (referred to as a "Schedule M-1 adjustment") on a corporation's US federal income tax return.

Income tax deductions for depreciation, including accelerated deductions under Section 179 and bonus depreciation are not in accordance with generally accepted accounting principles because, in general, they are not based on estimated useful lives and do not allocate cost to future periods benefited on a systematic and rational basis. Therefore, differences between financial statement and income tax depreciation result in temporary differences between the carrying values of the long-lived assets for income tax and financial reporting purposes. These temporary differences are taken into account in the calculation of deferred income taxes, as discussed in Chapter 15.

Asset retirement obligations. FAS 143 established standards for measuring the future cost to retire an asset and recognizing that cost in the financial statements as a liability, and correspondingly, as part of the depreciable cost of the asset.

The provisions of the statement do not apply to

1. Temporary idling of long-lived assets
2. Obligations arising solely from a plan to sell or otherwise dispose of long-lived assets covered by FAS 144 (discussed later in this chapter)
3. Obligations resulting from the improper operation of assets (e.g., penalties and fines such as those described in SOP 96-1, *Environmental Remediation Liabilities*
4. Minimum lease payments or contingent rentals of a lessee under FAS 13
5. Activities required to prepare an asset for an alternative use
6. The costs of replacement parts (unless there is a legal obligation to dispose of them)

The standard applies to *legal obligations* associated with the *retirement* of tangible long-lived assets that result from their acquisition, construction, development, and/or normal operation. Lessee capital lease assets and lessor assets that are leased under operating leases are also subject to these rules.

For the purposes of applying FAS 143, a legal obligation is "an obligation that a party is required to settle as a result of an existing or enacted law, statue, ordinance, or written or oral contract or by legal construction of a contract under the doctrine of *promissory estoppel*." Promissory estoppel is a legal doctrine whereby a court of law will enforce a promise made by one party (the promisor) to another party (the promisee) even though no formal contract exists between the two parties or no consideration was exchanged. This situation can arise when a party (the promisee) relies on a promise to his or her detriment and the person making the promise (the promisor) should have reasonably expected the promisee to rely on the promise. The court will, in these cases, "estop" (prevent) the promisor from asserting that s/he has no obligation because s/he should have anticipated that the promise would be relied upon.

Asset retirement obligations requiring recognition. When an entity acquires, constructs, and operates assets, it often incurs obligations that are unavoidable. Much of the discussion in FAS 143 pertains to specialized industry applications such as offshore oil platforms, nuclear power plants, mining operations, landfills, and underground storage tanks. However, in the authors' opinion, the criteria of the statement appear to apply to situations encountered more frequently in practice, such as in the following examples.

Examples of the scope of FAS 143

Example 1—Leased premises. In accordance with the terms of a lease, the lessee is obligated to remove its specialized machinery from the leased premises prior to vacating those premises, or to compensate the lessor accordingly. The lease imposes a legal obligation on the lessee to remove the asset at the end of the asset's useful life or upon vacating the premises, and therefore this situation would be covered by FAS 143.

Example 2—Owned premises. The same machinery described in example 1 is installed in a factory that the entity owns. At the end of the useful life of the machinery, the entity will either incur costs to dismantle and remove the asset or will leave it idle in place. If the entity chooses to do nothing and not remove the equipment, this would adversely affect the fair value of the premises should the entity choose to sell the premises on an "as is" basis. Conceptually, to apply the matching principle in a manner consistent with example 1, the cost of asset retirement should be recognized systematically and rationally over the productive life of the asset and not in the period of retirement. However, in this example, there is no *legal obligation* on the part of the owner of the factory and equipment to retire the asset and, thus, this would *not* be covered by FAS 143.

Example 3—Promissory estoppel. Assume the same facts as in example 2. In this case, however, the owner of the property sold to a third party an option to purchase the factory, exercisable at the end of five years. In offering the option to the third party, the owner verbally represented that the factory would be completely vacant at the end of the five-year option period and that all machinery, furniture and fixtures would be removed from the premises. The property owner would reasonably expect that the purchaser of the option relied to the purchaser's detriment (as evidenced by the financial sacrifice of consideration made in exchange for the option) on the representation that the factory would be vacant. This would trigger promissory estoppel and the owner's obligation would be covered by FAS 143.

Example of timing of recognition

Phyl Corporation owns and operates a chemical company. At its premises, it maintains underground tanks used to store various types of chemicals. The tanks were installed when Phyl Corporation purchased its facilities seven years prior. On February 1, 2005, the governor of the state signed a law passed by the state legislature which requires removal of such tanks when they are no longer being used. Since the law imposes a legal obligation on Phyl Corporation, upon enactment, recognition of an asset retirement obligation (ARO) would be required.

Example of ongoing additions to the obligation

Joyce Manufacturing Corporation (JMC) operates a factory. As part of its normal operations it stores production byproducts and used cleaning solvents on site in a reservoir specifically designed for that purpose. The reservoir and surrounding land, all owned by JMC, are contaminated with these chemicals. On February 1, 2005, the governor of the state signed a law passed by the state legislature which requires cleanup and disposal of hazardous waste from an already existing production process upon retirement of the facility. Upon the enactment of the law, immediate recognition would be required for the ARO associated with the contamination that had already occurred. In addition, liabilities will continue to be recognized over the remaining life of the facility as additional contamination occurs.

Accounting considerations. This standard raises several important accounting issues that require careful consideration.

Recognition and allocation. Upon initial recognition, the entity records an increase to the carrying amount of the related long-lived asset and an offsetting liability. The entity then depreciates the combined cost of the asset and the capitalized asset retirement obligation using a systematic and rational allocation method over the period during which the long-lived asset is expected to provide benefits, taking into consideration any expected salvage value. Conceptually, this standard is an application of the matching principle in that the total investment in the asset, including its eventual retirement, is charged to expense over the periods benefited. Depending on the pattern and timing of obligating events, an entity could, under this standard, capitalize an amount of asset retirement cost during a period and, in the same period, allocate an equal amount to depreciation expense. It is important to note that the amount added to the carrying amount of the long-lived asset does not constitute an expenditure for the purpose of capitalizing interest under the provisions of FAS 34.

Impairment. Retirement obligations added to the carrying amounts of long-lived assets are, obviously, to be included in those carrying amounts for the purpose of testing those assets for impairment. In estimating future cash flows under the impairment standard, the cash flows related to settling the liability for an asset retirement obligation are to be excluded from both the undiscounted cash flows used to assess the recoverability of the asset's carrying amount and the discounted cash flows used to measure the asset's fair value.

Measurement. Asset retirement obligations are initially measured at fair value. Fair value is defined as the amount that the entity would be required to pay in an active market to settle the obligation in a current transaction in circumstances other than a forced or liquidation settlement. From the perspective of the entity, fair value is the amount that would be demanded by a willing third party with a credit standing comparable to that of the entity, to assume all of the duties, risks, and uncertainties inherent in the entity's obligation. FASB acknowledged that, due to the risks involved, and the number of years expected to elapse between the date that the obligation is incurred and the date that it is expected to be settled, such current settlement may not be available. In addition, some entities may have the internal resources or expertise to discharge the liability by performing the necessary work using their internal workforce rather than contracting with third parties. Nevertheless, the standard requires this "third-party" market-based approach (i.e., even if the entity can and will retire the asset using internal resources, the obligation must be computed as if a third party will be retained to perform the work, including provisions for recovery of the contractor's overhead and profit).

Expected present value. In general, active markets do not exist for the settlement of an ARO. Consequently, FASB expects that most entities will use the *expected present value* technique set forth in CON 7 to compute fair value (see the discussion in Chapter 1). Under this technique, management estimates the range of estimated cash flows associated with settlement of the ARO and computes the sum of these cash flows on a probability-weighted basis. The statement acknowledges the fact that marketplace data may not be available on which to base assumptions regarding future cash flows. Management is, therefore, permitted to use information and assumptions that are available "without undue cost and effort" based on its own expectations. If, however, data is available regarding assumptions that marketplace participants would make that contradicts management's own assumptions, management must adjust its assumptions accordingly. For example, if the costs of labor in the marketplace exceed those of the entity, the higher marketplace costs are to be used in the cash flow estimates. Again, even if the entity expects to settle the ARO by use of its own labor force the cash flows to be used in the estimates of the expected present value are those that would be required to contract with third parties to do the work.

Initially applying the expected present value method. Management begins by estimating a series of cash flows that reflect its marketplace estimates of the cost and timing of performing the required retirement activities. Marketplace amounts are those amounts that would be expended by the entity to hire a third party to perform the work or to pay a third party to fully settle the ARO should a market to do so exist. Explicit assumptions are to be developed and incorporated in the estimates about all of the following matters:

1. The costs that a third party would incur in performing the necessary tasks associated with retiring the asset.
2. Additional amounts that the third party would include in pricing the work (or the settlement) related to such factors as inflation, overhead, equipment charges, profit margins, anticipated technological advances, and offsetting cash inflows, if any.
3. The extent to which the amount of the third party's costs or their timing might differ under various different future scenarios and the relative probabilities of those scenarios actually occurring.
4. The price that the third party would demand and could expect to receive for bearing the uncertainties and unforeseeable circumstances inherent in the obligation. This is referred to as *market risk premium.*

The discount rate to be used in the present value calculations is the *credit-adjusted risk-free rate* that adjusts a risk-free rate of interest for the credit standing of the entity. The risk-free interest rate is the market interest rate on monetary assets that are essentially risk-free, and that have maturity dates that coincide with the expected timing of the estimated cash flows required to satisfy the ARO. In the United States, this is the rate available for zero-coupon US Treasury instruments.

In adjusting the risk-free rate for the entity's credit standing, the entity takes into account the effects of all terms, collateral, and existing guarantees that would affect the amount required to settle the liability.

As a practical matter, for companies whose debt is not rated by a bond-rating agency, the adjustment for credit standing may be difficult to establish. For such companies, the incremental borrowing rate used for lease testing (see Chapter 14) may serve as an acceptable approximation of the credit-adjusted risk-free rate.

The ARO may be incurred in one or more of the entity's reporting periods. Each period's incremental liability incurred is recognized as a separate liability and is estimated using these principles based on market and interest rate assumptions existing in the period of subsequent recognition.

Accounting in subsequent periods. After the initial period of ARO recognition, the liability will change as a result of either the passage of time or revisions to the original estimates of either the amounts of estimated cash flows or their timing. Such changes can arise due to the effects of inflation, changes in the probabilities used in the original estimate, changes in interest rates, changes in laws, regulations, statutes, and contracts.

The entity recognizes these changes to the liability by first adjusting the carrying amount of the liability for changes due to the passage of time and then, if applicable, for changes due to revisions in either amounts or timing of estimated cash flows. Changes due to the passage of time increase the carrying amount of the liability because there are fewer periods remaining from the initial measurement date until the settlement date and, thus, the present value of the discounted future settlement amount increases. These changes are recorded as a period cost called *accretion expense* and classified separately in the operating section of the statement of income (or not-for-profit statement of activities). Accretion is computed using an interest method of allocation which results in periodic accretion expense that represents a level effective interest rate applied to the carrying amount of the liability at the beginning of each period. The effective interest rate used to calculate accretion is the credit-adjusted risk-free rate or rates (or incremental borrowing rate) applied when the liability or portion of the liability (as explained below) was initially measured and recognized. Accretion expense is not combined with interest expense, and is not considered interest cost for the purpose of applying the interest capitalization criteria of FAS 34.

Changes in the ARO that result from changes in the estimates of the timing or amounts of future cash flows are accounted for using different techniques for increases and decreases. If the expected present value increases, the increase gives rise to a new obligation accounted for separately just as the ARO was originally measured but using current market value assumptions, and the current credit-adjusted risk-free rate. Thus, over time, a particular long-lived asset may have multiple layers of obligations associated with it which are based on different assumptions measured at different dates during the asset's useful life. The incremental obligation is recorded by increasing the recorded ARO and capitalizing the additional cost as a part of the carrying amount of the related long-lived asset. If multiple layers have been recorded and it is not practicable to separately identify the period (or layer) to which subsequent revisions in estimated cash flows relate, the statement permits the use of a *weighted-average credit-adjusted risk-free rate* to measure the change in the liability resulting from that revision.

If, however, the expected present value subsequently decreases, the difference between the remeasured amount and the carrying amount of the liability (after adjustment for inception-to-date accretion) is recorded as a gain in the current period. In this case, the previously recognized layers of liabilities are reduced pro rata so as not to affect the overall effective rate of accretion over the remaining life of the obligation.

For the purposes of measurement in subsequent periods, an entity that originally determined its ARO based on available market prices rather than using the expected present value method, is required to determine the undiscounted cash flows embedded in that market price. This process is analogous to computing the rate of interest implicit in a lease.

FAS 143 does not require detailed cash flow estimates every reporting period but rather allows the entity to exercise judgment as to when facts and circumstances indicate that the initial estimate requires updating.

If the increase in carrying amount of the affected long-lived asset resulting from the remeasurement of ARO in a subsequent period impacts only that period, then the increase is fully depreciated in that period. Otherwise, the increase is depreciated in the period of change and future periods as a change in estimate in accordance with APB 20 (see Chapter 21). Both depreciation and accretion are classified as operating expenses in the statement of income.

Other provisions. Other provisions of FAS 143 affect the calculation of the credit-adjusted rate as well as how it is to be applied by rate-regulated entities.

Funding and assurance provisions. Factors such as laws, regulations, public policy, the entity's creditworthiness, or the sheer magnitude of the future obligation may cause an entity to be required to provide third parties with assurance that the entity will be able to satisfy its ARO in the future. Such assurance is provided using such instruments as surety bonds, insurance policies, letters of credit, guarantees by other entities, establishment of trust funds, or by custodial arrangements segregating other assets dedicated to satisfying the ARO. Although providing such means of assurance does not satisfy the underlying obligation, the credit-adjusted interest rate used in calculating the expected present value is adjusted for the effect on the entity's credit standing of employing one or more of these techniques.

Rate-regulated entities. Many rate-regulated entities (as defined in FAS 71 and discussed in Chapter 24) follow current specialized accounting that capitalizes costs not otherwise afforded that treatment under GAAP. These entities recover these additional costs in the rates that they charge their customers. These additional capitalized costs may or may not meet the definition of ARO under FAS 143. The differences in the amounts and timing of assets and liabilities between GAAP and regulatory accounting used for rate-making purposes give rise to temporary differences and the resultant deferred income tax accounting.

FAS 143 provides that, if the criteria in FAS 71 are met, the rate-regulated entity is to recognize a regulatory asset or liability for differences in the timing of recognition of the period costs associated with ARO for financial reporting and rate-making purposes. Accounting for the ARO arising from closed or abandoned long-lived assets of rate-regulated entities is covered by FAS 90.

Disclosures. The following information about ARO is required to be disclosed in the financial statements.

1. A general description of the ARO and the related long-lived assets.
2. A description of how the fair value of the ARO was determined (e.g., by using an expected present value method or some other market-based valuation technique).
3. The funding policy, if any, for ARO.
4. The fair value of assets dedicated to satisfy the liability, if any.
5. A reconciliation of the beginning and ending aggregate carrying amount of the liability showing separately the changes attributable to
   a. The liability incurred in the current period
   b. The liability settled in the current period
   c. Accretion expense, and
   d. Revisions in expected cash flows.
6. An explanation of any significant changes in the ARO not otherwise apparent in other disclosures required by the statement.

Example—initial measurement and recognition

Gerald Corporation constructs and places into service on January 1, 2005, specialized machinery on premises that it leases under a fifteen-year lease. The machinery cost $1,750,000 and has an estimated useful life of ten years. Gerald Corporation is contractually obligated, under the terms of the lease, to remove the machinery from the premises when it is no longer functional. Gerald is unable to obtain current market-related information regarding the costs of settling the liability at inception and, therefore, chooses to estimate the initial fair value of the ARO using an expected present value technique. The significant assumptions used by Gerald in applying this technique are as follows:

1. Labor costs are based on prevailing wage rates in that geographic area that a contractor would pay to hire qualified workers. Gerald assigns probability assessments to the range of cash flow estimates as follows:

Cash flow estimate	*Probability assessment*	*Expected cash flows for labor costs*
$40,000	25%	$10,000
60,000	50	30,000
75,000	25	18,750
	100%	$58,750

2. Based on its own experience, which Gerald believes is indicative of local market conditions, Gerald estimates that a contractor will apply a 75% burden rate to labor costs to charge for overhead and equipment usage and that, based on published industry statistics for the region, a contractor would add a markup of 8% to the combined labor, overhead, and equipment costs.
3. Since the eventual dismantlement and removal will be occurring ten years later, Gerald expects that a contractor would receive a market-risk premium of 5% of the estimated inflation-adjusted cash flows. This premium is to compensate the contractor for assuming the risks and uncertainties of contracting now for a project ten years later.
4. The risk-free rate of interest as evidenced by the price of zero-coupon US Treasury instruments that mature in ten years is 4.5%. Gerald adjusts that rate by 2.5% to reflect the effect of its credit standing as evidenced by its incremental borrowing rate of 7%. Therefore, the credit-adjusted risk-free rate used to compute the expected present value is 7%.
5. Gerald assumes an average rate of inflation of 3.5% over the ten-year period.

The ARO is initially measured as follows as of January 1, 2005:

	Expected cash flows as of January 1, 2005
Expected cash flows for labor costs	$ 58,750
Allocated overhead and equipment charges (75% x $58,750)	44,063
Contractor's markup [8% x ($58,750 + $44,063)]	8,225
Expected cash flows before inflation adjustment	111,038
Average annual compounded inflation rate of 3.5% for 10 years (1.035^{10})	x 1.4106
Inflation-adjusted expected cash flows	156,630
Market-risk premium (5% x $156,630)	7,832
Inflation adjusted expected cash flows adjusted for market risk	164,462
Present value using credit-adjusted risk-free rate of 7% for 10 years, compounded annually	$ 83,604

On January 1, 2005, Gerald would record the initial ARO as follows:

Machinery and equipment	83,604	
ARO liability		83,604

Example—accounting in subsequent periods

Assuming the same facts as above, during the ten year life of the machinery, Gerald would record entries to recognize accretion and depreciation as follows (assuming no remeasurement of the ARO is required):

Year	*Liability balance as of January 1*	*Annual accretion*	*Liability balance as of December 31*
2005	$ 83,604	$ 5,852	$ 89,456
2006	89,456	6,262	95,718
2007	95,718	6,700	102,418
2008	102,418	7,169	109,587
2009	109,587	7,671	117,258
2010	117,258	8,208	125,466
2011	125,466	8,783	134,249
2012	134,249	9,397	143,646
2013	143,646	10,055	153,701
2014	153,701	10,761	164,462

Entries to record annual accretion

The accretion for each year presented in the table is recorded as follows:

Accretion expense (presented on the income statement as part of operating expense)	xx,xxx	
Asset retirement obligation		xx,xxx

Depreciation computations

Acquisition cost of asset	$ 1,750,000
Capitalized ARO	83,604
Adjusted carrying amount of asset	$ 1,833,604
Estimated salvage value (assumed)	100,000
	$ 1,733,604
Estimated useful life	÷ 10 years
Annual depreciation expense	$ 173,360

Entry to record annual depreciation

Depreciation expense	173,360	
Accumulated depreciation		173,360

Settlement of ARO

On December 31, 2014, Gerald uses its internal workforce to dismantle and dispose of the machinery and incurred costs as follows:

Labor	$ 70,000
Internally allocated overhead and equipment charges (75% of labor)	52,500
Total costs incurred	122,500
ARO liability	164,462
Gain on settlement of ARO obligation	$ 41,962

Note that, because Gerald chose to perform the retirement activities using its own workforce, the "market approach" mandated by FAS 143 does not achieve an even matching of the total costs of acquisition and retirement to the periods benefited. The period of the retirement reflects a gain on settlement that would not have occurred had Gerald hired a contractor to perform the work instead of using its own employees.

Depletion. Depletion is the annual charge for the use of natural resources. The depletion base includes all development costs such as exploring, drilling, excavating, and other preparatory costs. The amount of the depletion base charged to periodic income is determined by the following formula:

$$\frac{1}{\text{Total expected recoverable units}} \quad \text{x} \quad \text{Depletion base} \quad \text{x} \quad \text{Units sold}$$

The unit depletion rate is revised frequently due to the uncertainties surrounding the recovery of natural resources. The revision is made prospectively; the remaining undepleted cost is allocated over the remaining expected recoverable units.

Nonmonetary transactions. Note that the following discussion covers the rules in effect under APB 29, which constituted current GAAP at the Wiley GAAP '05 publication date, as well as the changes that will result if an Exposure Draft (ED) of a proposed FAS that would amend APB 29 is ultimately adopted. The ED, entitled *Exchanges of Productive Assets, an amendment of APB Opinion No. 29*, was issued in December 2003, with a comment deadline of April 13, 2004. The FASB expects to issue the final FAS in the third quarter of 2004, to become effective prospectively for exchanges occurring during fiscal years beginning after December 15, 2004. Under provisions of the ED, prior exchanges would not be subject to remeasurement.

Scope. The following types of transactions are not treated as nonmonetary transactions:

1. Exchanges of businesses that are required to be accounted for as business combinations under FAS 141.
2. Transfers between reporting entities under common control such as between a parent company and its subsidiaries; between two subsidiaries of the same parent; or between a corporate joint venture and the venturers.

3. Issuance of equity in exchange for nonmonetary assets or the performance of services (governed, instead, by the provisions of FAS 123).
4. Stock dividends or stock splits.
5. Involuntary conversions where monetary proceeds are received for the nonmonetary assets stolen, seized, or destroyed and reinvested in other nonmonetary assets.

The ED would make technical corrections to APB 29 to add these additional scope exceptions:

6. Assets exchanged for interests in an entity.
7. Transfers that result in the transferor having continuing involvement in the transferred asset such that not all of the risks and rewards of ownership have been transferred to the transferee.
8. Transfers of financial assets within the scope of FAS 140, *Accounting for Transfers and Servicing of Financial Assets and Extinguishments of Liabilities.*
9. Certain types of transactions of oil and gas producing companies whose accounting is included in the scope of FAS 19, *Financial Accounting and Reporting by Oil and Gas Producing Companies.*

Types of nonmonetary transactions. There are three types of nonmonetary transactions.

1. *Nonreciprocal transfers with owners*—Examples include dividends-in-kind, nonmonetary assets exchanged for common stock, split-ups, and spin-offs.
2. *Nonreciprocal transfers with nonowners*—Examples include charitable donations of property either made or received by the enterprise, and contributions of land by a state or local government to a private enterprise for the purpose of construction of a specified structure.
3. *Nonmonetary exchanges*—Examples include exchanges of inventory for productive assets, exchange of inventory for similar products, and exchanges of productive assets.

General rule. The primary accounting issue in nonmonetary transactions is the determination of the amount to assign to the nonmonetary assets transferred to or from the enterprise.

The general rule is that the accounting for nonmonetary transactions is based on the fair values of the assets involved. The fair value to be used is that of the asset surrendered unless the fair value of the asset received is "more clearly evident." Fair value in this context is defined in APB 29 as

> *...the estimated realizable values in cash transactions of the same or similar assets, quoted market prices, independent appraisals, estimated fair values of assets or services received in exchange, and other available evidence.*

Exceptions to the general rule. If any of the following conditions apply, the accounting for the nonmonetary transaction is based on the recorded amount of the nonmonetary asset relinquished, reduced, if applicable, by any impairment in its value.

1. If the fair value is not reasonably determinable, the recorded amount (i.e., book value) may be the only amount available to measure the transaction. The fair value is not considered determinable within reasonable limits if there are major uncertainties with respect to the amount that would be realized for an asset.
2. An exchange of a product or property held for sale in the ordinary course of business for a product or property to be sold in the same line of business to facilitate sales to customers other than the parties to the exchange.

3. An exchange of a productive asset not held for sale in the ordinary course of business for a similar productive asset or an equivalent interest in the same or similar productive asset in the same line of business. This exception only applies when all of the exchanged assets are used in production. A product or property held-for-sale exchanged for a productive asset (even in the same line of business) is recorded at fair value.

   NOTE: The ED would eliminate this exception and replace it with a more limited exception for transactions that lack commercial substance, as discussed below. The ED also clarifies that a transfer of a nonmonetary asset does not qualify as an exchange if the transferor has continuing involvement in the transferred assets that results in the transferor retaining some of the risks or rewards associated with the transferred assets.

APB 29 includes yet another exception to the general rule of using fair value to account for nonmonetary exchanges that would be eliminated by the ED. This exception applies in the case of an exchange that is not essentially the culmination of the earnings process. When this is the case, the method used to value and record the transaction is dependent on the analysis of facts surrounding the transaction (see the decision diagram later in this chapter).

The discussion of EITF 01-2 (which would be partially nullified by the ED) later in this chapter contains interpretive guidance regarding exchanges of similar productive assets.

Nonreciprocal transfers. The valuation of most nonreciprocal transfers is based upon the fair value of the asset given (or received if the fair value of the nonmonetary asset is both objectively measurable and would be clearly recognizable). However, the valuation of nonmonetary assets distributed to owners of an enterprise in a spin-off or other form of reorganization or liquidation is based on the recorded amounts. Where there is no asset given, the valuation of the transaction is based upon the fair value of the asset received.

Example of accounting for a nonreciprocal transfer with a nonowner

1. Jacobs Corporation donated depreciable property with a book value of $10,000 (cost of $25,000 less accumulated depreciation of $15,000) to a charity during the current year.
2. The property had a fair value of $17,000 at the date of the transfer.

The transaction is valued at the fair value of the property transferred, and any gain or loss on the transaction is recognized on the date of the transfer. Thus, Jacobs recognizes a gain of $7,000 ($17,000 – $10,000) in the determination of the current period's net income. The entry to record the transaction would be as follows:

Charitable donations	17,000	
Accumulated depreciation	15,000	
Property		25,000
Gain on donation of property		7,000

Note that the gain on disposition of the donated property is reported as operating income in accordance with FAS 146 and is not to be presented in the "other income" section of the income statement.

Nonmonetary exchanges. An exchange of nonmonetary assets can take two basic forms.

1. Dissimilar assets
2. Similar assets (discussed below in the context of APB 29 and as proposed under the ED)

The recognition of a gain or loss on the exchange is dependent upon whether or not the gain or loss is deemed to be realized. If an exchange is considered to be the culmination of the earnings process, then the resulting gain or loss will be recognized. If the exchange is not considered to be the culmination of the earnings process, the resulting gain will not be recognized.

Dissimilar assets. An exchange involving dissimilar assets is considered the culmination of the earnings process. The general rule is to value the transaction at the *fair value* of the asset given up (*unless the fair value of the asset received is more clearly evident*) and to recognize gain or loss on the difference between the fair value and carrying value of the asset.

Example of an exchange involving dissimilar assets and no boot

1. Brian, Inc. exchanges a forklift with a book value of $2,500 with Emma & Co. for tooling with a fair value of $3,200.
2. No boot is exchanged in the transaction.
3. The fair value of the forklift is not readily determinable.

In this case, Brian, Inc. has a realized gain of $700 ($3,200 – $2,500) on the exchange. Because the exchange involves dissimilar assets, the earnings process has culminated and the gain is included in the determination of Brian's net income. The entry to record the transaction is as follows:

Tooling	3,200	
Forklift		2,500
Gain on exchange of forklift (operating)		700

Exchanges of similar assets under APB 29. Similar assets are those that are used for the same general purpose, are of the same general type, and are employed in the same line of business. It is not necessary for the assets exchanged to be identical to be considered similar. The treatment described applies to those assets which are exchanged as a result of technological advancement as well as to those which are exchanged as a result of wearing out (trade-ins). The general rule involving the exchange of *similar* assets involving a gain is to value the transaction at the *book value* of the asset given up. In this situation, the gain is effectively deferred over the life of the new asset. Annual depreciation continues to be recognized on the basis of the book value of the asset given up and will typically be lower than it would have been had the fair value of the new asset been recorded on the date of the exchange.

A single exception to the nonrecognition rule for similar assets occurs when the exchange involves both a monetary and nonmonetary asset being exchanged for a similar nonmonetary asset. The monetary portion of the exchange is termed *boot.* When boot is at least 25% of the fair value of the exchange, the exchange is considered a monetary transaction and both parties record the exchange at fair value. When boot less than 25% is received in an exchange, only the boot portion of the earnings process is considered to have culminated. The portion of the gain applicable to the boot is considered realized and is recognized in the determination of net income in the period of the exchange.

The formula for the recognition of the gain in an exchange involving boot of less than 25% of fair value is expressed as follows:

$$\frac{\text{Boot}}{\text{Boot + Fair value of nonmonetary asset received}} \times \text{Total gain indicated} = \text{Gain recognized}$$

Example of an exchange involving similar assets and boot

Amanda Excavating exchanges one of its underutilized front loaders with Dorothy Diggers, another excavator, for a bulldozer.

These assets are carried on the respective companies' balance sheets as follows:

	Amanda (Front loader)	*Dorothy (Bulldozer)*
Cost	$75,000	$90,000
Accumulated depreciation	7,500	15,000
Net book value	$67,500	$75,000
Fair (appraised) value	$60,000	$78,000

The terms of the exchange require Amanda to pay Dorothy $18,000 cash (boot). Boot represents approximately 23% of the fair value of the exchange computed as follows:

	Amount	*Percent of total*
Fair value of front loader	$60,000	77%
Cash consideration (boot)	18,000	23%
Total consideration	$78,000	100%

Note that as the payer of boot, Amanda does not recognize a gain. As a receiver of boot that is less than 25% of the fair value of the consideration received, Dorothy recognizes a pro rata gain that is computed as follows:

Total gain = $78,000 consideration – $75,000 net book value of bulldozer = $3,000

Portion of gain to be recognized by Dorothy:

$$\frac{\$18{,}000 \text{ boot}}{(\$18{,}000 \text{ boot} + \$60{,}000 \text{ fair value of nonmonetary asset received} = \$78{,}000)} = 23\% \text{ x } \$3{,}000 \text{ gain} = \$690 \text{ gain recognized}$$

The accounting entries to record this transaction by Amanda and Dorothy are as follows (see discussion of EITF 01-2 for interpretive guidance on exchanges involving monetary consideration):

	Amanda		*Dorothy*	
	Debit	*Credit*	*Debit*	*Credit*
Excavating equipment	10,500			32,310
Accum. depreciation—excavating equipment	7,500		15,000	
Cash		18,000	18,000	
Recognized gain	--	--	--	690
	18,000	18,000	33,000	33,000

Amanda records the increase in the carrying value of its excavating equipment to account for the difference between the $78,000 fair value of the bulldozer received and the $67,500 carrying value of the front loader exchanged. The accumulated depreciation on the front loader is reversed since, from the standpoint of Amanda, it has no accumulated depreciation on the bulldozer at the date of the exchange.

Dorothy records the cash received, removes the previously recorded accumulated depreciation on the bulldozer, records the $690 gain attributable to the boot as computed above and records the difference as an adjustment to the carrying value of its excavating equipment.

After recording the entries above, the carrying values of the exchanged equipment would be as follows:

	Amanda (bulldozer)	*Dorothy (front loader)*
Net book value exchanged	$67,500	$75,000
Cash paid (received)	18,000	(18,000)
Gain recognized	--	690
Carrying value of asset received	$85,500	$57,690

An exchange is considered the culmination of the earnings process when a loss results from the exchange of similar assets. While the earnings process is not generally considered complete when dealing with the exchange of similar assets, to record the asset at anything greater than the fair value would be imprudent.

There has been some difficulty noted in practice in distinguishing exchanges of similar assets (and also simple acquisitions of productive assets not involving exchanges) from exchanges of businesses (and direct purchase of businesses). The rules governing accounting for exchanges or purchases of productive assets materially differ from acquisitions of businesses (e.g., goodwill would only be recognized in connection with the latter class of transaction, and under APB 29 certain nonmonetary exchanges are recorded at book value) and thus clarification was required.

EITF 98-3 addresses this issue. If defines a business as a self-sustaining integrated set of activities and assets conducted and managed for the purpose of providing a return to investors. A business consists of (1) inputs, (2) processes applied to those inputs, and (3) resulting outputs that are used to generate revenues. Each of these criteria is further defined by EITF 98-3 (see detailed discussion in Chapter 11). For a transferred set of activities and assets to be deemed a business, it must contain essentially all of the inputs and processes necessary for it to continue to conduct normal operations after the transferred set is separated from the transferor, which includes the ability to sustain a revenue stream by providing its outputs to customers. If these criteria are not satisfied, the assets do not comprise a business and FAS 141 would not apply to the acquisition.

Exchanges of similar assets under the ED. The ED proposes to eliminate the "similar productive asset" exception mandated by APB 29. Instead, a nonmonetary exchange of productive assets would be subjected to a test to determine whether the exchange has "commercial substance." If determined to have commercial substance, the transaction would be recorded at the fair value of the transferred asset. If the transaction was determined not to have commercial substance, the exchange would be recognized using the recorded amount of the exchanged asset or assets, reduced for any applicable impairment of value.

To determine commercial substance, the reporting entity would have to estimate whether, after the exchange, it will experience changes in (1) its expected cash flows because of changes in their amounts, timing, and or risks (these factors are collectively referred to as the "configuration" of the expected future cash flows) *or* (2) the entity-specific value of the portion of the reporting entity's operations affected by the exchange. If the changes in either (1) or (2) are significant relative to the fair values of the assets exchanged, the transaction would be considered to have commercial substance. *Entity-specific value* is a fair value concept, defined in CON 7, that substitutes assumptions that an entity makes with respect to its own future cash flows for the corresponding assumptions that marketplace participants would make with respect to cash flows. The commercial substance criterion would not be met if a transaction is structured to achieve tax benefits in order to achieve a specific outcome for financial reporting purposes.

Involuntary conversions. An involuntary conversion results from the forced disposition of property due to casualty, theft, condemnation, or threat of condemnation. Upon involuntary conversion, the owner of the asset forfeits it and potentially receives proceeds from filing a property/casualty insurance claim or from condemnation awards.

Certain conditions may occur which necessitate the involuntary conversion of a nonmonetary asset into a monetary asset. Involuntary conversions of nonmonetary assets to monetary assets are monetary transactions, and the resulting gain or loss is recognized in the period of conversion. It makes no difference that the monetary assets received are immediately reinvested in nonmonetary assets.

This rule does not apply to the involuntary conversion of LIFO inventories that are intended to be replaced but have not yet been replaced by year-end (discussed in detail in Chapter 19).

Summary. In some situations, the fair value of the asset cannot be determined. If the fair value is not determinable, the book values of the assets involved are to be used as the valuation measure.

The situations involving the exchange of nonmonetary assets are summarized in the diagram on the next page.

Deferred income taxes. A difference between the amount of gain or loss recognized for financial reporting purposes and that recognized for income tax purposes constitutes a temporary difference. The difference in the gain or loss recognized results in a difference between the income tax basis and the financial reporting basis of the asset received. The difference in the gain or loss reverses as a result of the annual charge to depreciation. The proper treatment of temporary differences is discussed in Chapter 15.

ACCOUNTING FOR NONMONETARY EXCHANGES

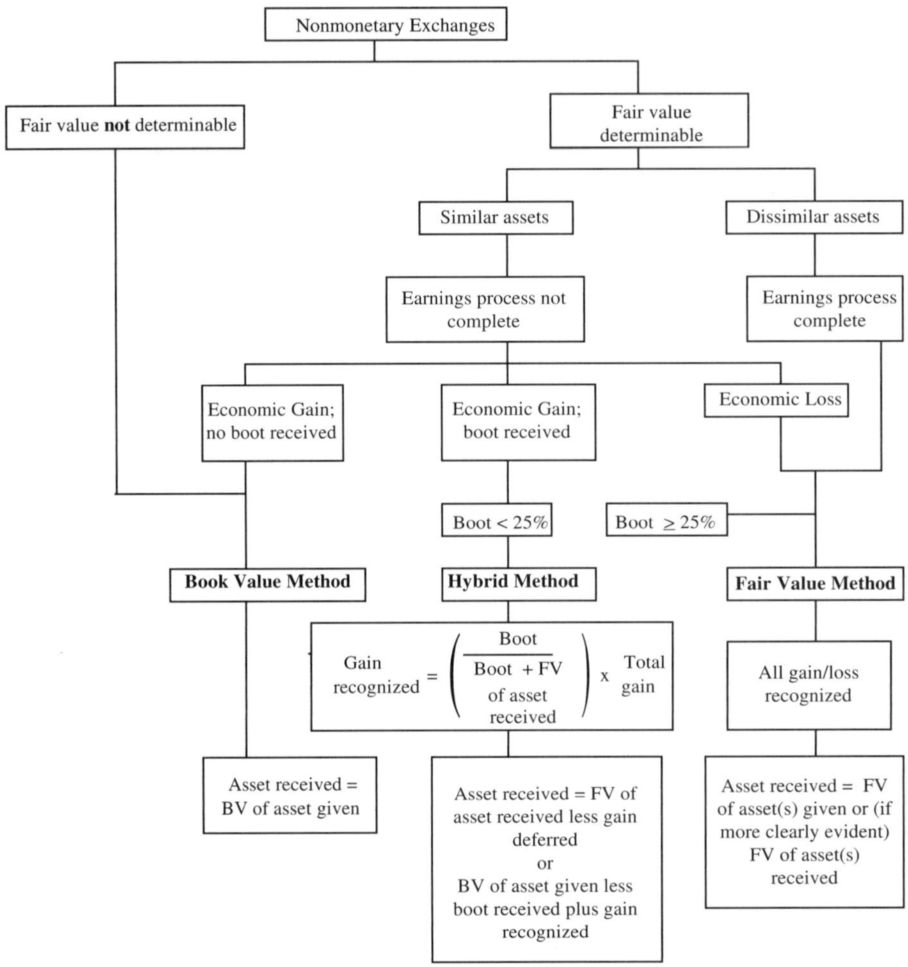

Impairment and disposal. FAS 144, *Accounting for the Impairment or Disposal of Long-Lived Assets,* applies to long-lived assets of business enterprises and not-for-profit organizations. Long-lived assets include assets to be held or used, or to be disposed of.

The GAAP rules for measuring and recording impairment of assets are not uniform for all assets or for all specialized industries. The table below distinguishes between those assets subject to the general impairment standard and those for which different, specialized rules apply.

Subject to General Impairment Standard (FAS 144)

Assets associated with discontinued operations
Cable television plant
Capitalized interest costs
Capitalized motion picture film costs

Development stage enterprises' assets
Financial institutions' depositor-relationship, borrower-relationship, and credit cardholder intangibles (These intangibles had been subject to specialized impairment standards prior to the issuance of FAS 147 in October 2002)
Real estate
Title plant costs of title insurance and title abstract companies, and title agents

Subject to Specialized Impairment Standard(s)

Broadcasters' program rights
Computer software to be sold, leased, or otherwise marketed
Deferred income tax assets
Equity method or cost method investments
Financial institutions' servicing assets
Financial instruments
Goodwill
Intangible assets of motor carriers
Loans receivable
Mortgage servicing rights
Recording masters in the recorded music industry

Split between General and Specialized Impairment Standards

Subject to General Impairment Standard	*Subject to Specialized Impairment Standard*
Public utilities and certain other regulated enterprises	Abandoned plants and disallowed plant costs of regulated enterprises
Intangibles that are amortized	Intangibles that are **not** amortized
Lessee capital leases Lessor assets subject to operating leases	Lessor direct financing, sales-type, and leveraged leases
Proved properties and wells of oil and gas producing companies with related facilities and equipment that are accounted for using the successful efforts method of accounting	Unproved properties of oil and gas producing companies
All insurance assets except deferred insurance policy acquisition costs	Deferred insurance policy acquisition costs

Impairment of long-lived assets to be held and used. *Impairment* is the condition that exists when the carrying amount of a long-lived asset (or asset group, as defined in the statement) exceeds its fair value. Impairment losses are only recognized when the carrying amount of the impaired asset (or asset group) is not recoverable. Recoverability is determined by comparing the carrying amount of the asset (or asset group) on the date it is being evaluated for recoverability to the sum of the *undiscounted* cash flows expected to result from its use and eventual disposition. It is important to note that under FAS 144, an asset's carrying value can exceed its fair value (thus technically it could be considered to be impaired) and yet, if the carrying value is recoverable from expected future cash flows from its use and disposition, as defined, no impairment loss is recognized.

FAS 144 uses "events and circumstances" criteria to determine when, if at all, an asset (or asset group) is evaluated for recoverability. Thus, there is no set interval or frequency for recoverability evaluation, unlike the annual requirement for testing goodwill for impairment. The FAS provides a list of examples of events or changes in circumstances that indicate the carrying amount of an asset (asset group) *may* not be recoverable and thus is to be evaluated for recoverability.

1. A significant decrease in the market price of a long-lived asset (asset group)
2. A significant adverse change in the extent or manner in which a long-lived asset (asset group) is being used or in its physical condition

3. A significant adverse change in legal factors or in the business climate that could affect the value of a long-lived asset (asset group), including an adverse action or assessment by a regulator
4. An accumulation of costs significantly in excess of the amount originally expected for the acquisition or construction of a long-lived asset (asset group)
5. A current period operating or cash flow loss combined with a history of operating or cash flow losses or a projection or forecast that demonstrates continuing losses associated with the use of a long-lived asset (asset group)
6. A current expectation that, more likely than not, a long-lived asset (asset group) will be sold or otherwise disposed of significantly before the end of its previously estimated useful life

The list of events and circumstances above is not intended to be all-inclusive. Rather, it is intended to provide examples of situations that warrant evaluation of an asset or group of assets for recoverability to determine whether an impairment loss must be recognized.

Under the FAS, if the carrying amount of an asset or asset group (in use or under development) is evaluated and found not to be recoverable (carrying amount exceeds the gross, undiscounted cash flows from use and disposition), then an impairment loss must be recognized. The impairment loss is measured as the excess of the carrying amount over the asset's (or asset group's) fair value. Fair value is determined using quoted market prices in active markets, when available. Otherwise, the entity estimates fair value based on the best information available such as market prices for similar assets (groups of assets), or using valuation techniques such as the expected present value of future cash flows as set forth in FASB Concepts Statement 7 (see Chapter 1).

In conjunction with the recoverability evaluation, it may also be necessary to review the appropriateness of the method of depreciation (amortization) and depreciable (amortizable) lives of the asset or group of assets. If, as a result of that review the remaining useful life of the asset (group) is revised, the revised useful life is used to develop the cash flow estimates used to evaluate recoverability. Changes to the accounting method (e.g., from straight-line to accelerated depreciation), however, would be made prospectively **after** the application of FAS 144.

FAS 144 introduced the concept of the *asset group*, defined as the lowest level for which identifiable cash flows are largely independent of the cash flows of other assets and liabilities.

An asset group could be

- The whole company
- An operating segment as defined by FAS 131
- A reporting unit as defined by FAS 142
- A business
- A part of a business (such as a division or department)

By reference to asset groups shown in the diagram in the appendix to Chapter 2

- Asset group (a) is a single division of a subsidiary
- Asset groups (b) and (c) are each separate businesses that comprise another division of the same subsidiary
- Asset group (d) is an entire subsidiary consisting of a single business
- Asset group (e) is a product line that is part of a larger business and, after the disposal of disposal group (f), will constitute an entire operating segment
- Asset groups (g) and (h) are each separate businesses that comprise a subsidiary

If a long-lived asset cannot be assigned to any asset group because it does not have identifiable cash flows largely independent of other long-lived assets individually or in asset groups (such as a corporate headquarters), then that asset is evaluated for recoverability by reference to all assets and liabilities of the entity.

The assets and liabilities in the group that are neither long-lived assets nor goodwill are separately identified. Since those assets and liabilities are not subject to the provisions of FAS 144, the GAAP applicable to their valuation is applied *before* applying FAS 144 to the group. For example, allowances for uncollectible accounts receivable and inventory obsolescence are recorded as necessary.

In assessing the composition of asset groups, there must be awareness of the interrelationship between FAS 144 and FAS 142, *Goodwill and Other Intangible Assets*. Goodwill can only be assigned to an asset group that is being evaluated for recoverability if the asset group is either a reporting unit or includes a reporting unit.

For the purposes of recoverability evaluation, future cash flows are defined as cash inflows less the associated cash outflows directly associated with and that are expected to arise as a direct result of the use and eventual disposition of the asset group excluding interest that is recognized as a period expense when incurred.

The estimate of future cash flows

- Is based on all available evidence
- Incorporates assumptions made by the entity regarding the use of the asset (group)
- Is to be consistent with assumptions used by the entity for comparable periods such as internal budgets and projections, accruals related to incentive compensation plans, or information communicated to others
- Incorporates assumptions that marketplace participants would use in their estimates of fair value when that information is available without undue cost or effort; otherwise, the entity incorporates its own assumptions
- Is made for the remaining estimated useful life of the asset (or the primary asset of an asset group) to the entity

  NOTE: The ***primary asset*** *is the long-lived asset being depreciated (or intangible asset being amortized) that is the most significant component asset from which the group derives its cash-flow generating capacity. The primary asset cannot be land or nonamortized intangible assets. If the primary asset does not have the longest useful life of the long-lived assets in the group, cash flow estimates must assume that the entire group will be sold at the end of the primary asset's useful life.*

- Takes into account future expenditures necessary to complete an asset under development including interest capitalized under FAS 34
- Includes future outflows necessary to maintain the existing service potential of all or a component of the asset or group of assets
- Excludes cash flows for future capital expenditures that increase the service potential of a long-lived asset or group of assets
- Is required to take into account the likelihood of possible cash flow outcomes if alternative courses of action are being contemplated, or if ranges of cash flows are estimated to occur under different scenarios

  NOTE: FAS 144 stops short of requiring the expected present value method set forth in CON 7, but does recommend and illustrate its use.

If an asset group is found to have sustained an impairment loss, the loss is only applied to reduce the carrying amounts of the long-lived asset or assets in the group. In general, the loss is allocated to the long-lived assets in the group based on their relative carrying values. However, the carrying value of any individual asset in the group that has a fair value that is separately identifiable without "undue cost or effort" is not to be reduced below that fair value.

After recognition of impairment losses, the adjusted carrying amounts of the impaired long-lived assets constitute their new cost bases. Depreciation (amortization) is recognized prospectively over their remaining estimated useful lives. The adjustment to carrying values to reflect an impairment loss may never be restored.

Example of impairment (Refer to the diagram in the appendix to Chapter 2)

The Parent Holding Company (PHC) owns and operates seven businesses, primarily engaged in the manufacturing and distribution of food and beverages. All of the businesses are headquartered in the same building that is owned by PHC. Additional facts are as follows:

- Due to general economic conditions and the failure, in 2005, of several high-tech startups in the city in which PHC is headquartered, the local commercial real estate market is depressed. PHC's headquarters building has eight years remaining in its expected useful life and its carrying value is $4,500,000. PHC has substantial excess space in the building, which it does not expect to need in the foreseeable future. PHC management expects the real estate market to remain depressed for the next two years and when the market recovers, it will consider selling the building and either leasing or purchasing a smaller facility in the area.
- Subsidiary 2 operates a South American bottling plant that produces a line of carbonated beverages that is sold exclusively on that continent. A large increase in sugar prices during 2005 has resulted in lower margins and, due to partial price increases, a 30% decrease in units sold during the year. The plant operates in a building that Subsidiary 2 leases under an operating lease with five years remaining. The primary asset owned by Subsidiary 2 is what it refers to as its "bottling line" which consists of equipment that mixes ingredients, adds carbon dioxide, and fills and caps the bottles. The bottling line has a remaining useful life of four years. The other assets in the asset group have remaining useful lives of seven years. Subsidiary 2 has been profitable for the past three years (2002 – 2004) but is showing a small operating loss for 2005. Additional information regarding Subsidiary 2 follows:

	Bottling line (primary asset)	*Asset B*	*Asset C*	*Totals*
Net book value	$87,000	$19,000	$17,000	$123,000
Remaining life	4 years	7 years	7 years	
Expected cash inflows, net of outflows				
2006				4,000
2007				6,000
2008				7,000
2009				8,000
From assumed disposition—end of 2009				75,000
Total expected net operating cash flows				$100,000

- PHC is in the process of preparing its consolidated financial statements for the year ended December 31, 2005. Thus far, normal depreciation of PHC and its subsidiaries' fixed assets has been recorded and impairment has not yet been considered.

Analysis.

Step 1—*Identify asset groups.* This has been diagrammed in the exhibit in the appendix to Chapter 2. Note that the headquarters building cannot be assigned to any specific asset group since it does not generate independent cash flows. Therefore, its potential impairment is assessed at the PHC level on a consolidated basis.

Step 2—*Consider the applicability of impairment indicators.* Assess each of PHC's asset groups (and on a consolidated basis), as to whether the example events and circumstances provided by FAS 144 or any other events and circumstances indicate that PHC's long-lived assets may be impaired. Based on the decline in the local real estate market, it would be presumed that the market price of the headquarters building has declined, and thus the building should be evaluated for recoverability. Analysis of the situation of Subsidiary 2 is more complex. Two of the factors in FAS 144 warrant consideration. First, it could be argued that the increase in sugar prices constitutes a significant adverse change in the business climate. This might be mitigated if management believed the price increase to be a short-term condition and assuming this belief was supportable by past experience. Second, the current period operating loss should be considered. Since there has not been a history of such losses, the relevance of this factor depends on management's forecast of future results. If Subsidiary 2 were forecast to continue to experience operating losses, this would indicate that the asset group needs to be evaluated for recoverability. For the purposes of this example, we will assume that continuing losses are forecast.

Step 3—*Evaluate recoverability*. Two recoverability evaluations are required, one for the headquarters building and the other for the asset group represented by Subsidiary 2. Since the headquarters building is not allocable to an asset group, its recoverability is evaluated using consolidated cash flows that include the cash flows of Subsidiary 2. Thus, the recoverability evaluation for Subsidiary 2 is performed first.

Subsidiary 2's recoverability evaluation is performed by reference to the four-year remaining useful life of the bottling line, its primary asset. The cash flows used to evaluate recoverability are required to assume that the asset group will be sold in its entirety at the end of four years.

Comparison of the sum of the undiscounted expected cash flows from use and disposition of $100,000 to the carrying amount of $123,000 indicates that the carrying amount of the asset group will not be fully recoverable. Therefore, the asset group is impaired.

The recoverability evaluation for the building is performed using a probability-weighted expected cash flow estimate. This estimate considers the likelihood that management will pursue the sale of the facility when the local economy recovers in two years, versus retaining it for the remaining eight years of its expected useful life. In addition, depending on different scenarios of future economic conditions and business performance by PHC's businesses, different levels of cash flows could result both from operations and from disposition. Acknowledging the inherent uncertainties associated with predicting future results and the subjectivity involved in the estimation process, management formulated its best judgment regarding the probabilities of the best, worst, and most-likely scenarios.

Estimate of Future Cash Flows

Course of action	*Use of the asset (consolidated basis)*	*Disposition of the asset*	*Total*	*Probability assessment*	*Probability-weighted cash flows*
Sale at the end of 2 years	$100,000	$3,500,000	$3,600,000	20%	$720,000
	130,000	4,600,000	4,730,000	60%	2,838,000
	150,000	4,600,000	4,750,000	20%	950,000
				100%	$4,508,000
Sale at the end of 8 years	$410,000	$4,000,000	$4,410,000	20%	$882,000
	550,000	4,700,000	5,250,000	60%	3,150,000
	620,000	4,800,000	5,420,000	20%	1,084,000
				100%	$5,116,000

Upon review of the analysis above, management determined that it is 70% probable that it will sell the building at the end of two years. Consequently, the probability-weighted expected cash flows from the use and disposition of the building are as follows:

Course of action	*Probability-weighted cash flows*	*Probability assessment for course of action*	*Expected cash flows*
Sale at the end of 2 years	$4,508,000	70%	$3,155,600
Sale at the end of 8 years	5,116,000	30%	1,534,800
		100%	$4,690,400

Comparison of the probability-weighted expected cash flows or $4,690,400 per above to the $4,500,000 carrying value of the building at December 31, 2005, indicates that the carrying value of the building is expected to be fully recoverable and thus is not impaired.

As a result of the above analysis, management may decide upon one of the alternative courses of action. If so, the expected cash flows from that course of action would be used in the recoverability evaluation since it would no longer be necessary to probability-weight the outcomes.

Step 4—*Compute impairment, if any.* Market value information regarding the asset group of Subsidiary 2 is not available "without undue cost and effort." Management elects to use the traditional present value of estimated cash flows method to estimate fair value because it believes that uncertainty regarding the timing and amounts of cash flows is minimal (but, if this were not the case, management would use the probability-weighted expected cash flow method to make this estimate). The 8% interest rate used for this illustration of the traditional present value computation is assumed to be a rate commensurate with the risks involved (unlike the risk-free rate used in the expected present value method). The computation is as follows:

Year	*Net cash flows*	*Present value at 8%*	*Carrying value of asset group*	*Impairment adjustment required*
2006	$ 4,000	$ 3,704		
2007	6,000	5,144		
2008	7,000	5,557		
2009–Use	8,000	5,880		
2009–Sale	75,000	55,127		
	$100,000	$75,412	$123,000	$47,588

Asset	*Carrying value*	*Pro rata allocation factor*	*Allocation of impairment loss*	*Tentative adjusted carrying amount*
Bottling line	$ 87,000	71%	$33,660	$53,340
Asset B	19,000	15%	7,351	11,649
Asset C	17,000	14%	6,577	10,423
Total	$123,000	100%	$47,588	$75,412

Note that the adjusted carrying amount is captioned "tentative." This is because Subsidiary 2 was able to obtain a quoted market price of $16,000 for Asset B. FAS 144 specifies that assets are not to be reduced to an amount below their fair value. To obtain the proper result, the impairment loss requires reallocation among the assets comprising the asset group.

Asset	*Tentative adjusted carrying amount*	*Pro rata reallocation factor*	*Reallocation of excess impairment loss*	*Adjusted carrying amount*
Bottling line	$53,340	84%	$(3,640)	$49,700
Asset C	10,423	16%	(711)	9,712
Subtotal	63,763	100%	(4,351)	
Asset B	11,649		4,351	16,000
Total	$75,412		$ --	$75,412

Step 5—*Record the impairment adjustment.* The entry to record impairment in the accounting records of Subsidiary 2 is as follows:

Impairment loss (operating section of income statement)	47,588	
Accumulated depreciation—Machinery and equipment		47,588

To adjust the carrying value of the bottling line and related assets to reflect an impairment loss for 2005.

Other impairment considerations. Besides the foregoing, other issues arise as a consequence of applying the impairment rules.

Going concern. The example above included an estimate of cash flows at the entity level to assess whether the building was impaired. If the estimate had indicated that the building was impaired, management must consider whether the cash flows estimated for at least the ensuing year will be sufficient for the entity to continue as a going concern. Disclosure in the financial statements of management's plans may be required under SAS 59, *The Auditor's Consideration of an Entity's Ability to Continue as a Going Concern.*

Significant estimates. If, in the example above, the expected cash flows used to assess the recoverability of the building were closer to the building's $4,500,000 carrying value, consideration is given to the applicability of SOP 94-6, *Disclosure of Certain Significant Risks and Uncertainties.* The assumptions used in the cash flow estimates could be considered, under that SOP, significant estimates for which it is reasonably possible changes could occur in the near term (the ensuing year) and, consequently, disclosure would be required.

Deferred income taxes. Impairment losses are not deductible for US federal income tax purposes. Consequently, financial statement recognition of these losses will result in differences between the carrying amounts of the impaired assets used for financial reporting purposes and income tax purposes. These differences are considered temporary differences and are accounted for under the provisions of FAS 109 as discussed in Chapter 15.

Comparison of accounting and impairment rules. See the Appendix to this chapter for a summarization and comparison of the rules affecting the accounting for tangible and intangible long-lived assets.

Long-lived assets to be disposed of by sale. An asset may be disposed of individually or as part of a disposal group. A disposal group is a group of assets to be disposed of in a single transaction as a group and the liabilities directly associated with those assets that will be transferred with those assets (e.g., environmental obligations, warranty obligations associated with a product line, etc.).

Long-lived assets (or disposal groups) are classified as held-for-sale in the period in which *all* of the following six criteria are met:

1. Management possessing the necessary authority commits to a plan to sell the asset (disposal group)
2. The asset (disposal group) is immediately available for sale on an "as is" basis (i.e., in its present condition subject only to usual and customary terms for the sale of such assets)
3. An active program to find a buyer and other actions required to execute the plan to sell the asset (disposal group) have commenced
4. An assessment of remaining actions required to complete the plan indicates that it is unlikely that significant changes will be made to the plan or that the plan will be withdrawn
5. Sale of the asset (disposal group) is probable, as that term is used in the context of FAS 5 (i.e., likely to occur), and transfer of the asset (disposal group) is expected to qualify for recognition as a completed sale within one year

   NOTE: Certain exceptions to the one-year requirement are set forth in FAS 144 for events and circumstances beyond the entity's control that extend the period required to complete the sale.

6. The asset (disposal group) is being actively marketed for sale at a price that is reasonable in relation to its current fair value

A newly acquired long-lived asset (disposal group) that is being held for sale is to be classified as held-for-sale on the date of acquisition if

- It meets criteria 5. above (subject to the same exceptions noted in 5.), *and*
- Any other of the required criteria that are not met at the date of acquisition are probable of being met within a short period (approximately three months or less) of acquisition

If the criteria are met after the balance sheet date but prior to issuance of the entity's financial statements, the long-lived asset is to continue to be classified as held-and-used at the balance sheet date. Appropriate subsequent events disclosures would be included in the financial statements in accordance with AICPA Statement on Auditing Standards 1, AU Section 560, *Subsequent Events.*

Long-lived assets (disposal groups) classified as held-for-sale are measured at the lower of their carrying amount or fair value less cost to sell. A loss is recognized for any initial or subsequent write-down to fair value less cost to sell. A gain is recognized for any subsequent increase in fair value less cost to sell, but recognized gains may not exceed the cumulative losses previously recognized. Long-lived assets that are classified as held-for-sale are presented separately on the balance sheet.

Cost to sell consists of costs that directly result from the sales transaction that would not have been incurred if no sale were transacted. Cost to sell includes brokerage commissions, legal fees, title transfer fees, and other closing costs that must be incurred prior to transfer of legal title to assets. Prior to measurement of fair value less cost to sell, the entity adjusts the carrying amounts of any assets included in the disposal group not covered by FAS 144 including any goodwill.

The entity may not accrue, as part of cost to sell, expected future losses associated with operating the long-lived asset (disposal group) while it is classified as held-for-sale. Costs associated with the disposal, including costs of consolidating or closing facilities are only recognized when the actual costs are incurred. If the exception to the one-year requirement applies (permitted when there are certain events and circumstances beyond the entity's control), and the sale is expected to occur in more than one year, the cost to sell is discounted to its present value.

Long-lived assets (disposal groups) held for sale are not to be depreciated (amortized) while being presented under the held-for-sale classification. Interest and other expenses related to the liabilities of a held-for-sale disposal group are accrued as incurred.

If, at any time after meeting the criteria to be classified as held-for-sale, the asset (disposal group) no longer meets those criteria, the long-lived asset (disposal group) is to be reclassified from held-for-sale to held-and-used, measured at the *lower of*

- Carrying value prior to classification as held-for-sale, adjusted for any depreciation (amortization) that would have been recognized had the asset (disposal group) continued to be classified as held-and-used, or
- Fair value at the date of the subsequent decision not to sell the asset (disposal group).

The adjustment required to the carrying amount of an asset (disposal group) being reclassified from held-for-sale to held-and-used is included in income from continuing operations in the period that the decision is made not to sell. FASB concluded that impairment losses from long-lived assets to be held and used, gains or losses recognized on long-lived assets to be sold, and other costs associated with exit or disposal activities (as defined in FAS 146 and discussed in detail in Chapter 3) should be accounted for consistently. Therefore, if the entity reports a measure of operations (e.g., income from operations), these amounts are reported in operations unless they qualify as discontinued operations, as explained below. The income statement classification of these amounts should be consistent with the accounting policy for classifying the depreciation of the underlying assets per the following examples:

Machinery and equipment used in production	Cost of goods sold
Office equipment	General and administrative

Trucks and delivery equipment	General and administrative or, if a separate category of expenses, selling expense
Combination factory/office building	Allocate between cost of goods sold, and general and administrative in the same manner as depreciation

If a component of an entity (as defined below) is reclassified as held-and-used, the results of that component that had previously been reported in discontinued operations are reclassified and included in income from continuing operations for all periods presented.

Upon removal of an individual asset or liability from a disposal group classified as held-for-sale, the remaining part of the group is to be evaluated as to whether it still meets all six of the criteria to be classified as held-for-sale. If all of the criteria are still met, then the remaining assets and liabilities will continue to be measured and accounted for as a group. If not all of the criteria are met, then the remaining long-lived assets are to be measured individually at the lower of their carrying amounts or fair value less cost to sell at that date. Any assets that will not be sold are reclassified as held-and-used as described above.

Long-lived assets to be disposed of other than by sale. Long-lived assets may be abandoned, exchanged, or distributed to owners in a spin-off. Until the actual disposal occurs, the assets continue to be classified on the balance sheet as "held and used." During that period prior to disposal, they are subject to conventional impairment rules applicable to assets held and used.

Abandoned assets are considered disposed of under FAS 144 when they cease to be used. Temporary idling of an asset, however, is not considered abandonment. At the time an asset is abandoned, FAS 144 prescribes that its carrying amount be adjusted to its salvage value, if any, but not less than zero (i.e., a liability cannot be recorded upon abandonment).

If the entity commits to a plan to abandon the asset before the end of its previously estimated useful life, the depreciable life is revised in accordance with the rules governing a change in estimate under APB 20 and depreciation of the asset continues until the end of its shortened useful life.

If a long-lived asset is to be disposed of either by spinning it off to owners of the company or in an exchange transaction for a similar productive long-lived asset, the disposal is recognized when the actual exchange or spin-off occurs. If that asset (group) is evaluated for recoverability while held and used and before the disposal, the estimates of future cash flows are to assume that the disposal will not occur and that the asset will continue to be held and used for the remainder of its useful life. Two separate impairment losses might be recognized in this scenario.

1. An impairment loss for the asset while it is held and used
2. An additional impairment loss if, upon exchange or spin-off, which are recorded under APB 29 at the asset's recorded amount, the recorded amount/carrying value exceeds fair value

Discontinued operations. FASB believed that financial statement users would benefit from expanded application of the accounting and disclosure provisions for discontinued operations originally set forth in APB Opinion 30. Consequently, FAS 144 eliminated the previous requirement that a discontinued operation qualify as a segment of the business. To facilitate this change, FAS 144 introduced the concept of a "component of an entity." A component of an entity is distinguishable from the rest of the entity because it has its own operations and cash flows. It may be a reportable segment or operating segment (as defined by FAS 131), a reporting unit (as defined by FAS 142), a subsidiary, or an asset group.

If a component of an entity is either classified as held-for-sale or has been disposed of during the period, the results of its operations are to be reported in discontinued operations if *both* of the following conditions are met:

- The operations and cash flows of the component have been or will be removed from the ongoing operations of the entity as a result of the disposal transaction
- The entity will have no significant continuing involvement in the operations of the component after the disposal transaction

In a period in which a component of an entity is either classified on the balance sheet as held-for-sale or has been disposed of, the entity's income statement *for current and prior periods* is to report the component's results of operations (including gains or losses related to transfer of the asset from the held and used to the held-for-sale category) as discontinued operations, net of applicable income taxes or benefit. Future losses may not be anticipated and accrued and are to be recognized in the period in which they are incurred. Placement in the income statement is illustrated in Chapter 3.

The gain or loss on disposal is permitted to be disclosed either on the face of the statement of income or in the notes to the financial statements.

In subsequent periods, certain adjustments may arise that affect amounts previously reported in discontinued operations. Examples of such adjustments include

- Resolution of contingencies associated with the terms of the disposal such as purchase price adjustments and indemnification issues with the purchaser
- Resolution of contingencies associated with the operation of the component prior to its disposal such as environmental or product warranty obligations retained by the seller
- Settlement of employee benefit plan obligations directly associated with the disposal transaction (generally settlements and curtailments of plan liabilities as contemplated by FAS 88)

When adjustments of this nature occur, they are classified separately in discontinued operations of the current period and the notes to the financial statements are to disclose the nature and amount of these adjustments.

Assets and liabilities of a disposal group classified as held-for-sale are presented separately in their respective sections of the balance sheet. Offsetting of these amounts is not permitted.

Long-lived assets temporarily idled. The only reference in FAS 144 to the temporary idling of long-lived assets is the provision that prohibits recognizing temporary idling as abandonment. At a minimum, however, if material assets are temporarily idled, the following considerations apply:

1. Idling constitutes a "significant adverse change in the extent or manner in which . ." the asset (or asset group) is being used, which is an indicator requiring a recoverability evaluation under FAS 144
2. The estimates of future cash flows used in performing the recoverability evaluation are to consider, on a probability-weighted basis, the range of outcomes under consideration by management regarding when the asset will be returned to service, sold, or abandoned
3. Idle property and equipment is to be clearly and unambiguously captioned and segregated on the balance sheet from both the "held-and-used" and "held-for-sale" categories since it does not qualify for either classification, with appropriate disclosure of the relevant circumstances
4. As part of the ongoing review of the appropriateness of useful lives, the remaining useful life of the idle equipment is to be reassessed

5. Temporary suspension of depreciation or amortization of the asset until it is returned to service is considered.

Reporting and disclosures. With respect to the impairment of long-lived assets to be held and used, the following disclosures are required:

1. A description of the impaired long-lived asset (or asset group) and the facts and circumstances that led to the impairment
2. The amount of the impairment loss and the caption in the income statement (or not-for-profit statement of activities) in which it is included, if not presented separately on the face of the income statement
3. The method or methods used to determine fair value (e.g., quoted market prices, market prices for similar assets, or other valuation techniques)
4. For public companies, the segment in which the impaired long-lived asset or asset group is reported under FAS 131

With respect to long-lived assets and disposal groups to be disposed of, and other exit and disposal activities, disclosures for the period in which the activity is initiated and any subsequent periods until completion of the activity are to include

1. A description of the exit or disposal activity, including
   a. The facts and circumstances that led to the expected exit or disposal,
   b. The expected manner and timing of the activity, including its expected date of completion,
   c. If not separately presented on the face of the balance sheet, the carrying amount or amounts of the major classes of assets and liabilities included as part of a disposal group (public companies are also required to disclose which segment or segments includes each disposal group)
2. The gain or loss recognized for any initial or subsequent write-downs to fair value less cost to sell and, if not separately presented on the face of the income statement, the caption in the income statement or the statement of activities that includes the gain or loss
3. The following information for each major category of costs to be incurred in connection with the activity (e.g., onetime termination benefits, contract termination costs, and other costs):
   a. Costs incurred during the period
   b. Cumulative costs incurred from inception to balance sheet date
   c. Total costs expected to be incurred
   d. A reconciliation of changes in the liability during the period including
      (1) Liability at the beginning of the period
      (2) Costs incurred and charged to expense during the period
      (3) Costs paid or otherwise settled during the period
      (4) Adjustments made to the liability, if any, and the reasons the adjustments were necessary
4. The income statement (or statement of activities) captions that include the costs in 3.
5. If any costs incurred that are associated with exit or disposal activities have not been accrued because the fair value of the liability is not reasonably estimable, that fact and the reasons such an estimate cannot be made
6. If applicable, the amounts of revenue and pretax profit or loss reported in discontinued operations

7. If assets are reclassified from the held-for-sale category to the held-and-used category during the period, a description of the facts and circumstances that led to the decision to change the plan to sell the asset or group of assets and the effect on the results of operations for the period in which the decision is made and any prior periods presented
8. For each reportable segment of a public company, the following information about the costs of exit or disposal activities:
   a. Costs incurred during the period
   b. Cumulative costs incurred from inception to balance sheet date, net of any adjustments to the liability, with the reasons the adjustments were necessary
   c. Total costs expected to be incurred

Capitalization of interest costs. The recorded amount of an asset includes all of the costs necessary to get the asset set up and functioning properly for its intended use including interest.

The principal purposes accomplished by the capitalization of interest costs are

1. To obtain a more accurate original asset investment cost
2. To achieve a better matching of costs related to the acquisition, construction, and development of productive assets to the future periods that will benefit from the revenues that the assets generate

All assets that require a time period to get ready for their intended use should include a capitalized amount of interest costs. However, accomplishing this level of capitalization would usually violate a reasonable cost/benefit test because of the added accounting and administrative costs generated. In many situations, the effect of interest capitalization would be immaterial. Thus, interest costs are only capitalized as a part of the historical cost of the following qualifying assets when the costs are considered to be material:

1. Assets constructed for an entity's own use or for which deposit or progress payments are made
2. Assets produced as discrete projects that are intended for lease or sale
3. Equity method investments when the investee is using funds to acquire qualifying assets for its principal operations that have not yet begun

Generally, inventories and land that are not undergoing preparation for intended use are not qualifying assets. When land is being developed, it is a qualifying asset. If land is developed for lots, the capitalized interest cost is added to the cost of the *land*. The interest is then matched against revenues when the lots are sold. If, however, the land is developed for a building, then the capitalized interest cost is added to the cost of the *building*. The interest is then matched against revenues as the building is depreciated.

The capitalization of interest costs does not apply to the following situations:

1. When routine inventories are produced in large quantities on a repetitive basis
2. When the effects of capitalization would not be material, compared to the effect of expensing interest
3. When qualifying assets are already in use or ready for use
4. When qualifying assets are not being used and are not awaiting activities to get them ready for use
5. When qualifying assets are not included in a consolidated balance sheet
6. When principal operations of an investee accounted for under the equity method have already begun
7. When regulated investees capitalize both the cost of debt and equity capital

8. When assets are acquired with grants and gifts restricted by the donor to the extent that funds are available from those grants and gifts

The amount of interest capitalized. Interest cost includes the following:

1. Interest on debt having explicit interest rates (fixed or floating)
2. Interest related to capital leases
3. Interest required to be imputed on payables

The most appropriate rate to use as the capitalization rate is the rate applicable to specific new debt resulting from the need to finance the acquired assets. If there is no specific new debt, the capitalization rate is a weighted-average of the rates of the other borrowings of the entity. This latter case reflects the fact that the previously incurred debt of the entity could be repaid if not for the acquisition of the qualifying asset. Thus, indirectly, the previous debt is financing the acquisition of the new asset and its interest is part of the cost of the new asset. The selection of borrowings to be used in the calculation of the weighted-average of rates requires judgment. The amount of interest to be capitalized is that portion which could have been avoided if the qualifying asset had not been acquired. Thus, the capitalized amount is the incremental amount of interest cost incurred by the entity to finance the acquired asset.

The base used to multiply by the rate is the average amount of accumulated net capital *expenditures* incurred for qualifying assets during the relevant time frame. Capitalized costs and expenditures are not the same terms. Theoretically, a capitalized cost financed by a trade payable for which no interest is recognized is not a capital expenditure to which the capitalization rate is applied. Reasonable approximations of net capital expenditures are acceptable, however, and capitalized costs are generally used in place of capital expenditures unless there is expected to be a material difference.

If the average capitalized expenditures exceed the specific new borrowings for the time frame involved, then the *excess* expenditures are multiplied by the weighted-average of rates and not by the rate associated with the specific debt. This requirement more accurately reflects the interest cost incurred by the entity to acquire the fixed asset.

The interest being paid on the debt may be simple or compound. Simple interest is computed on the principal alone, whereas compound interest is computed on the principal *and* on any interest that has not been paid. Most fixed assets will be acquired with debt subject to compound interest. Compound interest can be computed using compound interest tables or computer software (electronic spreadsheets or specialized software applications that compute the time value of money).

The total amount of interest actually incurred by the entity is the ceiling for the amount of interest cost capitalized. The amount capitalized cannot exceed the amount actually incurred during the period involved. On a consolidated basis, the ceiling is defined as the total of the parent's interest cost plus that of the consolidated subsidiaries. If financial statements are issued separately, the interest cost capitalized is limited to the amount that the separate entity has incurred, and that amount includes interest on intercompany borrowings. The interest incurred is a gross amount and is not netted against interest earned except in cases involving externally restricted tax-exempt borrowings.

Example of accounting for capitalized interest costs

1. On January 1, 2005, Daniel Corp. contracted with Rukin Company to construct a building for $2,000,000 on land that Daniel had purchased years earlier.
2. Daniel Corp. was to make five payments in 2005 with the last payment scheduled for the date of completion, December 31, 2005.
3. Daniel Corp. made the following payments during 2005:

January 1, 2005	$ 200,000
March 31, 2005	400,000
June 30, 2005	610,000
September 30, 2005	440,000
December 31, 2005	350,000
	$2,000,000

4. Daniel Corp. had the following debt outstanding at December 31, 2005:

a.	A 12%, three-year note dated 1/1/05 with interest compounded quarterly. Both principal and interest due 12/31/07 (relates specifically to building project).	$850,000
b.	A 10%, ten-year note dated 12/31/99 with simple interest payable annually on December 31.	$600,000
c.	A 12%, five-year note dated 12/31/01 with simple interest payable annually on December 31.	$700,000

The amount of interest to be capitalized during 2005 is computed as follows:

Average Accumulated Expenditures

Date	Expenditure	Capitalization period*	Average accumulated expenditures
1/1/05	$ 200,000	12/12	$200,000
3/31/05	400,000	9/12	300,000
6/30/05	610,000	6/12	305,000
9/30/05	440,000	3/12	110,000
12/31/05	350,000	0/12	--
	$2,000,000		$915,000

* *The number of months between the date expenditures were made and the date interest capitalization stops (December 31, 2005).*

Potential Interest Cost to Be Capitalized

($850,000 x 1.12551)* – $850,000	=	$106,684
65,000 x .1108**	=	7,202
$915,000		$113,886

* *The principal, $850,000, is multiplied by the factor for the future amount of $1 for four periods (quarterly compounding) at 3% to determine the amount of principal and interest due in 2005.*

** *Weighted-average interest rate:*

	Principal	*Interest*
10%, ten-year note	*$ 600,000*	*$ 60,000*
12%, five-year note	*700,000*	*84,000*
	$1,300,000	*$144,000*

$$\frac{\textit{Total interest}}{\textit{Total principal}} = \frac{\$144,000}{\$1,300,000} = \underline{11.08}\% \textit{ weighted-average interest rate}$$

The actual interest is

12%, three-year note [($850,000 x 1.12551) – $850,000]	=	$106,684
10%, ten-year note ($600,000 x 10%)	=	60,000
12%, five-year note ($700,000 x 12%)	=	84,000
Total interest		$250,684

The interest cost to be capitalized is the lesser of $113,886 (avoidable interest) or $250,684 (actual interest), which, of course, is $113,886. The remaining $136,798 ($250,684 – $113,886) is expensed during 2005.

Determining the time period for interest capitalization. Three conditions must be met before the capitalization period begins.

1. Necessary activities are in progress to get the asset ready to function as intended
2. Qualifying asset expenditures have been made
3. Interest costs are being incurred

As long as these conditions continue, interest costs are capitalized.

Necessary activities are interpreted in a very *broad* manner. They start with the planning process and continue until the qualifying asset is substantially complete and ready to function. Brief, normal interruptions do not stop the capitalization of interest costs. However, if the entity intentionally suspends or delays the activities for some reason, interest costs are not capitalized from the point of suspension or delay until substantial activities regarding the asset resume.

If the asset is completed in parts, the capitalization of interest costs stops for each part as it becomes ready. An asset that must be entirely complete before the parts can be used capitalizes interest costs until the total asset becomes ready.

Interest costs continue to be capitalized until the asset is ready to function as intended, even in cases where lower of cost or market rules are applicable and market is lower than cost. The required write-down is increased accordingly.

Capitalization of interest costs incurred on tax-exempt borrowings. If qualifying assets have been financed with the proceeds from tax-exempt, *externally restricted* borrowings and if temporary investments have been purchased with those proceeds, a modification is required. The interest costs incurred from the date of borrowing must be reduced by the interest earned on the temporary investment in order to calculate the ceiling for the capitalization of interest costs. This procedure is followed until the assets financed in this manner are ready. When the specified assets are functioning as intended, the interest cost of the tax-exempt borrowing becomes available to be capitalized by other qualifying assets of the entity. Portions of the tax-exempt borrowings that are not restricted are eligible for capitalization in the normal manner.

Assets acquired with gifts or grants. Qualifying assets that are acquired with externally restricted gifts or grants are not subject to capitalization of interest. The principal reason for this treatment is the concept that there is no economic cost of financing when a gift or grant is used in the acquisition.

Summary of interest capitalization requirements. The diagram on the following page summarizes the accounting for interest capitalization.

Intangible Assets

Goodwill and other acquired intangibles. Intangible assets are defined as both current and noncurrent assets that lack physical substance. Specifically excluded, however, are financial instruments and deferred income tax assets. Goodwill is not considered an identifiable intangible asset, and accordingly, under FAS 142, is accounted for differently from identifiable intangibles. Goodwill is the preeminent unidentifiable intangible, and this characteristic (i.e., the lack of identifiability) has been determined by the FASB to be the critical element in the definition of goodwill. Accordingly, identifiable intangible assets that are reliably measurable are recognized separately from goodwill.

Identifiable intangibles. Acquired intangibles are recognized separately from goodwill if they meet either of the following criteria:

1. *Legal/contractual criterion.* Control over the future economic benefits of the asset is obtained through contractual or other legal rights irrespective of whether those rights are transferable or separable from other rights and obligations.
2. *Separability criterion.* The asset is capable of being separated or divided and sold, transferred, licensed, rented, or exchanged irrespective of whether the acquirer intends to do so. This criterion is met if the asset can be sold, transferred, licensed, rented or exchanged along with a related contract, asset, or liability.

SUMMARY OF ACCOUNTING FOR INTEREST CAPITALIZATION

Capitalization of Interest during Construction

Qualifying assets
a. Assets constructed for use in operations
b. Assets for sale or lease which are constructed as discrete projects (ships, real estate), but not inventory
c. Certain equity method investments

When to capitalize interest (all three must be met)
a. Expenditures for asset have been made
b. Activities intended to get asset ready are in progress
c. Interest cost is being incurred

Applicable interest (net of discounts, premiums, and issue costs)
a. Interest obligations having explicit rates
b. Imputed interest on certain payables/receivables
c. Interest related to capital leases

Amount of interest to capitalize

Average accumulated expenditures

(Specific borrowings x Applicable interest rate) + (Other borrowings x Weighted-average interest rate*)

Qualifications
a. Amount of interest to be capitalized cannot exceed total interest costs incurred during the period
b. Interest earned on temporarily invested borrowings may not be offset against interest to be capitalized (except externally restricted tax-exempt borrowings)

$$* \text{ Weighted-average interest rate} = \frac{\text{Total interest on other borrowings}}{\text{Average outstanding principal during period}}$$

Identifiable intangible assets having indefinite useful economic lives supported by clearly identifiable cash flows are not subject to regular periodic amortization. Instead, the carrying amount of the intangible is to be tested for impairment annually, and again between annual tests if events or circumstances warrant such a test. An impairment loss is recognized if the carrying amount exceeds the fair value. Furthermore, amortization of the asset is to commence when evidence suggests that its useful economic life is no longer deemed indefinite.

The decision to permit the recognition of "indefinite-life" intangibles was likely based in part on the growing ubiquity of intellectual assets and the phenomenon of "knowledge-based businesses." The range of intangibles is perhaps more clearly understood today than it was in the past, and there is more pressure to improve the relevance of financial reporting in light of changing business and economic conditions. For manufacturing companies the primary assets typically are tangible ones, such as buildings and equipment. For financial institutions the major assets are financial instruments. For high technology, knowledge-based companies, however, the primary assets are intangible ones such as patents and copyrights, and for professional service firms the key assets may be "soft" resources such as knowledge bases and client relationships. Overall, enterprises for which intangible assets constitute a large and growing component of total assets are a rapidly growing part of the economy.

Many intangible assets are based on rights that are conveyed legally by contract, statute, or similar means. For example, governments grant franchises or similar rights to taxi companies, cable companies, and hydroelectric plants; and companies and other private-sector organizations grant franchises to automobile dealers, fast-food outlets, and professional sports teams. Other rights, such as airport landing rights, are granted by contract. Some of those franchises or similar rights are for finite terms, while others are perpetual. Many of those with finite terms are routinely renewed, absent violations of the terms of the agreement, and the costs incurred for renewal are minimal. Many such assets are also exchangeable, and the prices at which they trade reflect expectations of renewal at minimal cost. However, for others, renewal is not assured, and their renewal may entail substantial cost.

Other similar intangible assets include trademarks, service marks, trade names, copyrights, and patents. Trademarks, service marks, and trade names may be registered with the government for a period of twenty years and are renewable for additional twenty-year periods as long as the trademark, service mark, or trade name is used continuously. (Brand names, often used synonymously with trademarks, are typically not registered and thus the required attribute of control will be absent.) The US government now grants copyrights for the life of the creator plus fifty years. Patents are granted by the government for a period of seventeen years but may be effectively renewed by adding minor modifications that are patented for additional seventeen-year periods. Such assets also are commonly exchangeable.

Furthermore, not all identifiable intangible assets are based on rights that have been conveyed by legal means; some may have been developed internally. Some of those assets may be in the form of knowledge or databases, such as title plant or customer lists. Others may relate to human factors, such as customer relationships and work forces. Some of those assets may be exchangeable while others may not. Title plant and customer lists are examples of intangible assets that are exchangeable, whereas customer relationships and work forces generally are not.

In recognition of the vast diversity of intangible assets and their central role in modern business operations, the FASB concluded that exchangeability is a useful basis for distinguishing different types of intangible assets because those that are capable of being sold or otherwise transferred constitute a potential source of cash flow. FAS 142 provides guidance in the form of a comprehensive listing of intangibles that the FASB stipulates will generally meet the criteria for recognition separate from goodwill. Some of the major items are noted in the following paragraphs.

Customer- or market-based intangibles include those that relate to customer structure or market factors of the business, such as various lists (advertising, customer, dealer, mailing, subscription); the customer base; depositor or borrower relationships (of financial institutions); customer routes; the delivery system and distribution channels; customer service capability and product or service support; effective advertising programs; trademarked brand names; newspaper mastheads; a presence in specific geographic locations or markets; the value of insurance-in-force and insurance expirations; production backlog; concession stands; airport gates and slots; retail shelf space; and files and records (e.g., credit or medical).

Contract-based intangibles have a fixed or definite term, such as many types of agreements (e.g., consulting, income, licensing, manufacturing, royalty, or standstill); contracts (such as those for advertising, construction, consulting, customer, employment, insurance, maintenance, management, marketing, mortgage, purchase, service, and supply); covenants (e.g., not to compete); easements; leases (if containing valuable or favorable terms); permits (such as those for construction); and various rights (e.g., for broadcasting, development, gas allocation, landing, lease, mortgage servicing, reacquired franchise, servicing, timber cutting, use, or water).

Technology-based intangibles relate to innovations or technological advances within the business. These could include computer software and license, computer programs, information systems, program formats, and Internet domain names and portals; secret formulas and processes, and recipes; technical drawings, technical and procedural manuals, and blueprints; databases and certain types of title plants; manufacturing processes, procedures, and production lines; research and development; and technological know-how.

Statutory-based intangibles have statutorily established useful lives. The most traditional of all intangible assets, these include patents, copyrights (e.g., for manuscripts, literary works, and musical compositions), franchises (for cable, radio, and television), and trademarks and trade names.

Identifiable intangible assets, such as franchise rights, customer lists, trademarks, patents and copyrights, and licenses are to be amortized over the expected useful economic life, even if that life exceeds the former forty-year ceiling, with required evaluations of their recoverability when necessitated by changes in facts and circumstances in the same manner as set forth in FAS 144 for tangible long-lived assets. The Statement also requires consideration of the intangible's residual value (analogous to salvage value for a tangible asset) in determining the amount of the intangible to amortize. The Statement defines residual value as the value of the intangible to the entity at the end of its (entity-specific) useful life reduced by any estimated disposition costs. The residual value of an amortizable intangible is assumed to be zero unless the intangible will continue to have a useful life to another party after the end of its useful life to its current holder, and one or both of the following criteria are met:

1. The current holder has received a third-party commitment to purchase the intangible at the end of its useful life, *or*
2. A market for the intangible exists and is expected to continue to exist at the end of the asset's useful life as a means of determining the residual value of the intangible by reference to marketplace transactions.

A broadcast license which, while nominally subject to expiration in five years, might be indefinitely renewable at little additional cost to the broadcaster. If cash flows can be projected indefinitely, and assuming a market exists for the license, no amortization is to be recorded until such time as a finite life is predicted. However, impairment is required to be tested at least annually to ensure that the asset is carried at no more than its fair value.

The foregoing examples all addressed identifiable intangibles, which are recognized in the financial statements when purchased separately or in connection with a business combination. There are other intangibles, which are deemed to not be identifiable because they cannot be reliably measured. The Statement uses technological know-how and an assembled workforce as examples of such intangible assets. Intangibles that cannot be separately identified are considered integral components of goodwill.

Goodwill. Goodwill is generally afforded special treatment under FAS 142 because it is neither separately identifiable nor transferable. The Statement contains a temporary exemption for goodwill arising from combinations between two or more not-for-profit organizations or in an acquisition of a for-profit enterprise by a not-for-profit organization. This exemption is necessary while FASB continues work on separate projects currently on its agenda regarding these types of entities.

Also exempted is the special accounting for unidentifiable intangible assets recognized in an acquisition of a bank or thrift institution under FAS 72.

Initially, goodwill is recognized as the excess of the cost of an acquired entity over the net of the amounts assigned to identifiable assets acquired (including identifiable intangibles) and liabilities assumed.

Goodwill is not to be amortized. Goodwill is, however, subject to unique impairment testing techniques. Therefore, FAS 144 is not applied to goodwill and goodwill associated with acquisitions of tangible property and equipment is not tested for impairment in tandem with that property and equipment.

The impairment test for goodwill is performed at the level of the reporting unit. A reporting unit is an operating segment or one level below an operating segment. The diagram in the appendix to Chapter 2 illustrates how different groupings in a business can be characterized as reporting units and is accompanied by definitions of reporting units, operating segments, and other organizational groupings. The enterprise may internally refer to reporting units by such terms as business units, operating units, or divisions. Determination of reporting units is largely dependent on how the business is managed and its structure for reporting and management accountability. The Statement acknowledges that an entity may have only one reporting unit which would, of course, result in the goodwill impairment test being performed at the entity level. This can occur when the entity has acquired a business that it has integrated with its existing business in such a manner that the acquired business is not separately distinguishable as a reporting unit.

On the date an asset is acquired or a liability is assumed, it is to be assigned to a reporting unit if it meets **both** of the following conditions:

1. The asset will be used in or the liability is related to the operations of a reporting unit
2. The asset or liability will be considered in determining the fair value of the reporting unit

The methodology used is to be reasonable and supportable and is to be applied similarly to how aggregate goodwill is determined in a purchase business combination. Net assets include assets and liabilities that are recognized as "corporate" items if they, in fact, relate to the operations of the reporting unit (e.g., environmental liabilities associated with land owned by a reporting unit, and pension assets and liabilities attributable to employees of a reporting unit). Executory contracts (e.g., operating leases, contracts for purchase or sale, construction contracts) are considered part of net assets only if the amount reflected in the acquirer's financial statements is based on a fair value measurement subsequent to entering into the contract. To illustrate, if an acquiree had a preexisting operating lease on either favorable or unfavorable terms as compared to its fair value on the date of acquisition, the acquirer would recognize, in its purchase price allocations, an asset or liability for the fair value of the favorable or unfavorable terms, respectively. FAS 142 distinguishes between accounting for this fair value of an otherwise unrecognized executory contract and prepaid rent or rent payable which generally have carrying values that approximate their fair values.

The annual goodwill impairment test may be performed at any time during the fiscal year as long as it is done consistently at the same time each year. Each reporting unit is permitted to establish its own annual testing date. Additional impairment tests are required between annual impairment tests if: (1) warranted by a change in events and circumstances, *and* (2) it is more likely than not that the fair value of the reporting unit is below its carrying amount. If indicators exist requiring impairment testing of goodwill, impairment testing of nonamortizable intangibles, and/or recoverability evaluation of tangible long-lived assets or amortizable intangibles, the other assets are tested/evaluated first and any impairment loss recognized prior to testing goodwill for impairment.

FAS 142 provides examples of events or circumstances that require goodwill of a reporting unit to be tested for impairment between annual tests.

1. A significant adverse change in legal factors or in the business climate
2. An adverse action or assessment by a regulator
3. Unanticipated competition
4. A loss of key personnel
5. An expectation that it is more likely than not that a reporting unit or a significant portion of it will be sold or otherwise disposed of **or** the allocation of a portion of goodwill to a business to be disposed of
6. The necessity of performing an FAS 144 recoverability test of a significant asset group within a reporting unit
7. The recognition of a goodwill impairment loss in the financial statements of a subsidiary that is a component of a reporting unit

Similar to the list of events and circumstances in FAS 144, this list is not intended to be all-inclusive. Other indicators may come to the attention of management that would indicate that goodwill impairment testing be performed between annual tests.

Performing the impairment test. Goodwill is impaired when its implied fair value is less than its carrying amount. The actual determination of whether goodwill is impaired is made as follows:

1. Compare the fair value of the reporting unit as a whole to its carrying value including goodwill. If the reporting unit's fair value exceeds its carrying value, goodwill is not impaired and no further computations are required. If, however, the carrying value of the reporting unit exceeds its fair value, the second step of the impairment test is required.
2. Determine whether and by how much goodwill is impaired as follows:
   a. Estimate the *implied fair value* of goodwill
   b. Compare the implied fair value of goodwill to its carrying amount
   c. If the carrying amount of goodwill exceeds its implied value, it is impaired and is written down to the implied fair value.

The implied fair value of goodwill is the excess of the fair value of the reporting unit as a whole, over the fair values that would be assigned to its assets and liabilities in a purchase business combination.

Consistent with long-standing practice in GAAP, upon recognition of an impairment loss, the adjusted carrying amount of goodwill becomes its new cost basis, and future restoration of the written down amount is prohibited.

The *fair value of a reporting unit* is defined as the amount at which the unit as a whole could be bought or sold in a current transaction between willing parties. The determination of the implied fair value of goodwill is based on the assumption that the fair value of a reporting unit as a whole will differ from the fair value of its identifiable net assets. This is the general principle that gives rise to goodwill in the first place. The acquirer assigns additional value to the acquiree (as evidenced by a purchase price that exceeds the collective fair values of the assets and liabilities to be acquired) based on the acquirer's perceived ability to take advantage of synergies and other benefits that flow from its control over the acquiree.

Market capitalization of a publicly traded business unit is computed based on a quoted market price per share that does not consider any advantages that might inure to an acquirer in a situation where control is obtained. For this reason, the Statement cautions that the market capitalization of a reporting unit with publicly traded stock may not be representative of its fair value. Presumably, estimating the fair value of a privately held business using earnings multiples derived from publicly traded companies in the same line of business might have the same limitation.

The Statement also prescribes that when a significant portion of a reporting unit is comprised of an acquired entity, the same techniques and assumptions used to determine the purchase price of the acquisition are to be used to measure the fair value of the reporting unit unless such techniques and assumptions are not consistent with the objective of measuring fair value.

FAS 142 permits the carryforward of a previous determination of the fair value of the reporting unit if *all three* of the following conditions are met:

1. There has been no significant change in the composition of the assets and liabilities of the reporting unit.
2. The previously computed fair value of the reporting unit exceeded its carrying amount by a substantial margin (undefined in the FAS).
3. Based on any events occurring or changes in circumstances since the previous computation, the likelihood is remote that the reporting unit's current value is below its carrying amount.

The *fair value of an asset (or liability)* is the amount at which the asset (or liability) could be bought (incurred) or sold (settled) in a current transaction between willing parties other than in a forced or liquidation sale. Quoted market prices in active markets are considered the best evidence of fair value and are to be used if available. If quoted market prices are not available, the estimate of fair value is to be based on the best information available including prices for similar assets and liabilities or the results of applying available valuation techniques. Such techniques include present value of expected cash flows, option pricing models, matrix pricing, option-adjusted spread models, and fundamental analysis. The weight to be given to evidence gathered in the valuation process is to be proportional to the ability to objectively verify it. When an estimate is in the form of a range of either the amount or timing of estimated future cash flows, the likelihood of possible outcomes is to be considered (i.e., probability weightings are assigned in order to estimate the most likely outcome). Unrecognized intangibles (including in-process research and development) are included in the computation of the fair value of the reporting unit's assets and liabilities. FAS 142 retains certain exceptions to this method of determining fair values for certain assets and liabilities to be consistent with APB 16, the previous standard (e.g., deferred income taxes recorded by the acquiree prior to the acquisition). The Statement acknowledges cost/benefit considerations by providing that "all evidence available without undue cost and effort [is to] be considered in developing those estimates." Greater weight is always given to evidence that is more objectively verifiable.

The measurement techniques and assumptions used to estimate the fair values of the reporting unit's net assets are to be consistent with those used to measure the fair value of the reporting unit as a whole. For example, estimates of the amounts and timing of cash flows used to value the significant assets of the reporting unit are to be consistent with those assumptions used to estimate such cash flows at the reporting unit level when a cash flow model is used to estimate the reporting unit's fair value as a whole.

Negative goodwill. Negative goodwill results from situations (sometimes referred to as "bargain purchases") where the fair values of the net assets acquired in a business combination exceed the purchase price and is discussed in detail in Chapter 11. FAS 141 requires that negative goodwill first be allocated pro rata to reduce amounts assigned to the acquired assets including in-process research and development. Assets that are not reduced by negative goodwill are

- Financial assets (except equity method investments)
- Assets to be disposed of by sale
- Deferred income tax assets
- Prepaid assets related to pension or other postretirement benefit plans
- Any other current assets

After applying the negative goodwill to reduce the values assigned to the assets permitted to be adjusted, if negative goodwill still remains, FAS 141 prescribes that it be recognized as an extraordinary gain in the period in which the business combination is initially recognized. However, two exceptions are provided to this general rule.

- When an extraordinary gain is recognized prior to completion of the purchase price allocations, the subsequent change necessitated by completion of the allocations is also recognized as either an extraordinary gain or loss in the period that the purchase price allocation is finalized.
- If the purchase price includes a provision for contingent consideration (e.g., a subsequent adjustment to the purchase price based on the acquiree attaining certain postacquisition levels of sales or pretax income), the remaining negative goodwill is recorded as a deferred credit until the contingency is resolved. In the period in which the contingency is resolved, any remaining negative goodwill is reclassified from the deferred credit to an extraordinary gain.

Other goodwill considerations. Other provisions included in FAS 142 include the following:

- Equity method goodwill continues to be recognized under APB 18 and is not subject to amortization. This goodwill is not tested for impairment under FAS 142, but rather, is tested under APB 18. This test considers whether the fair value of the underlying investment has declined and whether that decline is "other than temporary."
- Goodwill of a reporting unit that is fully disposed of is included in the carrying amount of the net assets disposed of in computing the gain or loss on disposal.
- If a significant portion of a reporting unit is disposed of, the goodwill of that unit is required to be tested for impairment. In performing the impairment test, only the net assets to be retained after the disposal are included in the computation. If, as a result of the test, the carrying amount of goodwill exceeds its implied fair value, the excess carrying amount is allocated to the carrying amount of the net assets disposed of in computing the gain or loss on disposal and, consequently, is not considered an impairment loss.

In order to provide financial statement users with transparent information about goodwill, separate line item treatment is required as follows:

- **Balance sheet (statement of financial position)**—The aggregate amount of goodwill included in assets is captioned separately from other assets and may not be combined with other intangibles.
- **Income statement**—The aggregate amount of goodwill impairment losses is captioned separately in the operating section unless associated with discontinued operations.

Software developed for internal use. SOP 98-1 provides guidance on accounting for the costs of internally developed software. Software must meet two criteria to be accounted for as internally developed software. First, the software's specifications must be designed or modified to meet the reporting entity's internal needs, including costs to customize purchased software. Second, during the period in which the software is being developed, there can be no plan or intent to market the software externally, although development of the software can be jointly funded by several entities that each plan to use the software internally.

In order to justify capitalization of related costs, it is necessary for management to conclude that it is probable that the project will be completed and that the software will be used as intended. Absent that level of expectation, costs must be expensed currently as research and development costs (discussed in detail later in this chapter). Entities which engage in both research and development of software for internal use and for sale to others must carefully identify costs with one or the other activity, since the former is (if all conditions are met) subject to capitalization, while the latter is expensed as research and development costs until technological feasibility is demonstrated, per FAS 86. (See Chapter 24 for a discussion of software developed internally for sale or lease.)

Costs subject to capitalization. Cost capitalization commences when an entity has completed the conceptual formulation, design, and testing of possible project alternatives, including the process of vendor selection for purchased software, if any. These early-phase costs (referred to as "preliminary project stage" in SOP 98-1) are analogous to research and development costs and must be expensed as incurred. These cannot be later restored as assets if the development proves to be successful.

Costs incurred subsequent to the preliminary project stage that meet the criteria under GAAP as long-lived assets are capitalized and amortized over the asset's expected economic life. Capitalization of costs begins when both of two conditions are met. *First,* management having the relevant authority authorizes and commits to funding the project and believes that it is probable that it will be completed and that the resulting software will be used as intended. *Second,* the conceptual formulation, design, and testing of possible software project alternatives (i.e., the preliminary project stage) have all been completed.

Costs capitalized include those of the application development stage of the software development process. These include coding and testing activities and various implementation costs. In particular, the SOP notes that such costs are limited to (1) external direct costs of materials and services consumed in developing or obtaining internal-use computer software; (2) payroll and payroll-related costs for employees who are directly associated with and who devote time to the internal-use computer software project to the extent of the time spent directly on the project; and (3) interest costs incurred while developing internal-use computer software, consistent with the provisions of FAS 34.

General and administrative costs, overhead costs, and training costs are expensed as incurred. Even though these may be costs which are associated with the internal development or acquisition of software for internal use, under GAAP those costs relate to the period in which incurred. The issue of training costs is particularly important, since internal-use computer software purchased from third parties often includes, as part of the purchase price, training for the software (and often fees for routine maintenance as well). Per the SOP, when the amount of training or maintenance fees is not specified in the contract, entities are required to allocate the cost among training, maintenance, and amounts representing the capitalizable cost of computer software. Training costs are recognized as expense as incurred. Maintenance fees are recognized as expense ratably over the maintenance period.

The SOP provides examples of when computer software is acquired or developed for internal use. Some of these are: when modifications are made to software controlling robots acquired for use in the manufacturing process; software is developed for cash management, payroll processing, or accounts payable system purposes; a bank develops an on-line account status inquiry system for customers to utilize; a travel agency invests in software to give it access to an airline reservation system; a communications provider develops computerized systems to manage customer services such as voice mail; or when a publisher invests in computerized systems to produce a product which is then sold to customers.

On the other hand, software which does not qualify under the standard as being for internal use includes software sold by a robot manufacturer to purchasers of its products; the cost of developing programs for microchips used in automobile electronic systems; software developed for both sale to customers and internal use; computer programs written for use in research and development efforts; and costs of developing software under contract with another entity.

Impairment. Impairment of capitalized internal-use software is recognized and measured in accordance with the provisions of FAS 144 in the same manner as tangible long-lived assets and other amortizable intangible assets. Circumstances which might suggest that an impairment has occurred and that would trigger a recoverability evaluation include (1) a realization that the internal-use computer software is not expected to provide substantive service potential; (2) a significant change in the extent or manner in which the software is used; (3) a significant change has been made or is being anticipated to the software program; or (4) the costs of developing or modifying the internal-use computer software significantly exceed the amount originally expected. These conditions are analogous to those generically provided in FAS 144.

In some instances, ongoing software development projects will become troubled before being discontinued. The SOP provides that management needs to assess the likelihood of successful completion of projects in progress. When it becomes no longer probable that the computer software being developed will be completed and placed in service, the asset should be written down to the lower of the carrying amount or fair value, if any, less costs to sell. Importantly, it is a rebuttable presumption that any uncompleted software has a zero fair value. The SOP provides indicators that the software is no longer expected to be completed and placed in service. These include (1) a lack of expenditures budgeted or incurred for the project; (2) programming difficulties that cannot be resolved on a timely basis; (3) significant cost overruns; (4) information indicating that the costs of internally developed software will significantly exceed the cost of comparable third-party software or software products, suggesting that management intends to obtain the third-party software instead of completing the internal development effort; (5) the introduction of new technologies which increase the likelihood that management will elect to obtain third-party software instead of completing the internal project, and (6) a lack of profitability of the business segment or unit to which the software relates or actual or potential discontinuation of the segment.

Amortization of capitalized costs of software for internal use. As for other long-lived assets, the cost of computer software developed or obtained for internal use should be amortized in a systematic and rational manner over its estimated useful life. The nature of the asset exacerbates the difficulty of developing a meaningful estimate, however. Among the factors to be weighed are the effects of obsolescence, new technology, and competition. Entities would especially need to consider if rapid changes are occurring in the development of software products, software operating systems, or computer hardware, and whether management has intentions to replace any technologically obsolete software or hardware.

Amortization of each module or component of a software project commences when the computer software is ready for its intended use, without regard to whether the software is to be placed in service in planned stages that might extend beyond a single reporting period. The SOP stipulates that computer software is deemed ready for its intended use after substantially all testing has been completed.

Other matters. In some cases internal-use software is later sold or licensed to third parties, notwithstanding the original intention of management that the software was acquired or developed solely for internal use. In such cases, the SOP provides that any proceeds received are to be applied first as a reduction of the carrying amount of the software. No profit is recognized until the aggregate proceeds from sales exceed the carrying amount of the software. After the carrying value is fully recovered, any subsequent proceeds are recognized in revenue as earned.

Leasehold improvements. Leasehold improvements represent physical enhancements made to property by or on behalf of the property's lessee. By law, when improvements are made to real property and those improvements are permanently affixed to the property, the title to those improvements automatically transfers to the owner of the property. The rationale behind this is that the improvements, when permanently affixed, are inseparable from the rest of the real estate.

As a result of this automatic title transfer, the lessee's interest in the improvements is not a direct ownership interest but rather it is an intangible right to use and benefit from the improvements during the term of the lease. Consequently, the capitalized costs incurred by a lessee in constructing improvements to property that it leases represent an intangible asset analogous to a license to use them. Thus, when allocating the costs of leasehold improvements to the periods benefited, the expense is referred to as amortization (as used in the context of amortization of intangibles) and not depreciation.

A frequently encountered issue with respect to leasehold improvements relates to determination of the period over which they are to be amortized. Normally, the cost of long-lived assets is charged to expense over the estimated useful lives of the assets. However, the right to use a leasehold improvement expires when the related lease expires, irrespective of whether the improvement has any remaining useful life. Thus, the appropriate useful life for a leasehold improvement is the **lesser of** the useful life of the improvement or the term of the underlying lease.

Some leases contain a fixed, noncancelable term and additional renewal options. When considering the term of the lease for the purposes of amortizing leasehold improvements, normally only the initial fixed noncancelable term is included. There are exceptions to this general rule that arise out of the application of GAAP to the lessee's accounting for the lease. If a renewal option is a bargain renewal option, then it is probable at the inception of the lease that it will be exercised and, therefore, the option period is included in the lease term for purposes of determining the amortizable life of the leasehold improvements. Additionally, under the definition of the lease term there are other situations where it is probable that an option to renew for an additional period would be exercised. These situations include periods for which failure to renew the lease imposes a penalty on the lessee in such amount that a renewal appears, at the inception of the lease, to be reasonably assured. Other situations of this kind arise when an otherwise excludable renewal period precedes a provision for a bargain purchase of the leased asset or when, during periods covered by ordinary renewal options, the lessee has guaranteed the lessor's debt on the leased property.

It is important to note that, in deciding whether to include the period covered by a renewal option in the calculation of the amortizable life of the leasehold improvements, the lessee must be consistent with the interpretation of renewal options included in the minimum lease payment calculations made to determine whether the lease is a capital or operating lease.

Example

Marcie Corporation occupies a warehouse under a five-year operating lease commencing January 1, 2005, and expiring December 31, 2009. The lease contains three successive options to renew the lease for additional five-year periods. The options are not bargain renewals as they call for fixed rentals at the prevailing fair market rents that will be in effect at the time of exercise. When the initial calculation was made to determine whether the lease is an operating lease or a capital lease, only the initial noncancelable term of five years was included in the calculation. Consequently, for the purpose of determining the amortizable life of any leasehold improvements made by Marcie Corporation, only the initial five-year term is used. If Marcie Corporation decides, at the beginning of year four of the lease, to make a substantial amount of leasehold improvements to the leased property, it could be argued that it would now be probable that Marcie would exercise one or more of the renewal periods, since not doing so would impose the substantial financial penalty of abandoning expensive leasehold improvements. This would trigger accounting for the lease by treating the period or periods for which it is likely that the lessee will renew as a new agreement and require testing to determine whether the lease, prospectively, qualifies as a capital or operating lease.

Research and Development Costs

Research and development (R&D) are defined as follows:

1. Research is the planned search or critical investigation aimed at the discovery of new knowledge with the hope that such knowledge will be useful in developing a new product or service or a new process or technique or in bringing about a significant improvement to an existing product or process.
2. Development is the translation of research findings or other knowledge into a plan or design for a new product or process or for a significant improvement to an existing product or process whether intended for sale or use.

There are three ways in which R&D costs are incurred by a business.

1. Purchase of R&D from other entities
2. Conducting R&D for others under a contractual arrangement
3. Conducting R&D activities for the benefit of the enterprise

The accounting treatment relative to R&D depends upon the nature of the cost. R&D costs incurred in the ordinary course of operations consist of materials, equipment, facilities, personnel, and indirect costs that can be attributed to research or development activities. These costs are expensed in the period in which they are incurred unless they have alternative future uses.

Examples of such R&D costs include

1. Laboratory research to discover new knowledge
2. Formulation and design of product alternatives
    a. Testing for product alternatives
    b. Modification of products or processes
3. Preproduction prototypes and models
    a. Tools, dies, etc. for new technology
    b. Pilot plants not capable of commercial production
4. Engineering activity until the product is ready for manufacture

Examples of costs that are not considered R&D would include

1. Engineering during an early phase of commercial production
2. Quality control for commercial production
3. Troubleshooting during a commercial production breakdown
4. Routine, ongoing efforts to improve products
5. Adaptation of existing capacity for a specific customer or other requirements
6. Seasonal design changes to products
7. Routine design of tools, dies, etc.
8. Design, construction, startup, etc. of equipment except that used solely for R&D

In many cases, entities will pay other parties to perform R&D activities on their behalf. In applying substance over form in evaluating these arrangements, a financial reporting result cannot be obtained indirectly if it would not have been permitted if accomplished directly. Thus, if costs incurred to engage others to perform R&D activities that, in substance, could have been performed by the reporting entity itself, those costs must be expensed as incurred. On the other hand, if the payment is to acquire intangibles for use in R&D activities, and these assets have other uses, then the expenditure is capitalized and accounted for in accordance with FAS 142.

When R&D costs are incurred as a result of contractual arrangements, the nature of the agreement dictates the accounting treatment of the costs involved. The key determinant is the transfer of the risk associated with the R&D expenditures. If the business receives funds from another party to perform R&D and is obligated to repay those funds regardless of the outcome, a liability must be recorded and the R&D costs expensed as incurred. In order to conclude that a liability does not exist, the transfer of the financial risk must be substantive and genuine.

In-process research and development. There is an ongoing concern that acquirers are aggressively allocating large portions of the purchase price of the acquiree company to in-process R&D that is then written off at acquisition date. To the extent that this practice results in mischaracterizing these costs, it results in a reduction of the goodwill recorded in connection with the business combination. This practice can result in distorted earnings in future periods that potentially could have borne goodwill impairment costs. It also distorts future periods' performance measurements such as return on assets and return on equity.

All parties associated with the preparation of (and/or, under new SEC rules, the certification of) the financial statements should consider the reasonableness of any such write-offs and the possibility of a challenge by the SEC.

The FASB has decided that R&D costs should be dealt with in a comprehensive manner in a future project. Until then, immediate write-off of purchased in-process research and development costs is required.

EMERGING ISSUES TASK FORCE ISSUES SUMMARIES

89-13 Accounting for the Cost of Asbestos Removal

The cost of treating property acquired with a known asbestos problem is capitalized. In the case of an existing property, asbestos treatment costs are recorded as a betterment. Both capitalizations are subject to an impairment test.

When removal costs incurred due to the anticipation of the sale of property can be recovered from the sale, these costs are deferred and recognized in computing gain or loss at the time of sale.

Expensed asbestos costs are not considered extraordinary items. SEC registrants are to disclose any significant exposure for asbestos treatment in the management discussion and analysis (MD&A).

90-8 Capitalization of Costs to Treat Environmental Contamination

In general, environmental contamination treatment costs are charged to expense. Costs may be capitalized if recoverable, but only if one of the following criteria is met:

1. The costs extend the life, increase the capacity, or improve the safety or efficiency of property owned by the company.
2. The costs mitigate or prevent future environmental contamination while also improving the property.

3. The costs are incurred in preparing for sale a property that is currently held for sale.

91-10 Accounting for Special Assessments and Tax Increment Financing Entities

A property owner recognizes an obligation for special assessments levied by a municipality or by a Tax Increment Financing Entity (TIFE) that are for a fixed or determinable amount for a fixed or determinable period. A company may be contingently liable under FAS 5 if

1. It must satisfy any shortfall in annual debt service.
2. It has pledged its assets.
3. It provides a letter of credit or other credit enhancements in support of the TIFE's debt.

If constructing facilities for its own use, the presence of these factors creates a presumption that the TIFE debt is a liability.

93-11 Accounting for Barter Transactions Involving Barter Credits

A consensus was reached that APB 29 applies to these transactions and that the basis for recording them is the fair value of the nonmonetary asset given up. Ordinarily, this fair value measurement should not be higher than its carrying value.

Impairment, if applicable, is to be recorded before the exchange. Thus, a new cost basis is established and a loss is recognized on the income statement. If an operating lease is involved, impairment is measured as the amount of remaining lease costs in excess of the fair value of the probable sublease rentals for the remaining lease term. FAS 15 provides helpful guidance for determining fair value.

The value of barter credits are not used to measure fair value unless they can be converted to cash in the short term or there are independent existing market prices available for items to be received for the barter credits.

After the exchange, impairment is recorded if the carrying amount exceeds the fair value of the barter credits or if the business determines that it will not be able to use the barter credits.

95-23 Treatment of Certain Site Restoration/Environmental Exit Costs When Testing a Long-Lived Asset for Impairment

The issue summary discusses how, for the purpose of performing the recoverability evaluation under FAS 144, to treat the costs of future site restoration or closure (referred to as "environmental exit costs") that may be incurred if the asset is sold, abandoned, or ceases operations. To conform to FAS 144, references to an "asset" are also applicable to an "asset group."

FAS 143 requires asset retirement obligations recognized as liabilities to be included as part of the capitalized cost of the related asset and, to avoid double-counting, the cash settlement of those liabilities to be excluded from the expected future cash flows used to evaluate recoverability under FAS 144. If the asset retirement costs have not yet been recognized under FAS 143 because the obligation is being incurred over more than one reporting period during the useful life of the asset, then the cash flows for those unrecognized costs are to be included in the expected future cash flows.

The cash flows for environmental exit costs that are not recorded as liabilities under SOP 96-1, *Environmental Remediation Liabilities,* may not occur until the end of the asset's life if the asset ceases to be used or may be delayed indefinitely as long as management retains ownership of the asset and chooses not to sell or abandon it. Consequently, the EITF reached a consensus that management's intent regarding future actions with respect to the asset is to be taken into account in determining whether to include or exclude these cash flows from the computation of the expected future cash flows used to evaluate recoverability under FAS 144. If management is contemplating alternative courses of action to recover the carrying amount of the asset or if a range is estimated for the amount of possible future cash flows, the likelihood (probability) of these possible outcomes is to be considered in connection with the recoverability evaluation under FAS 144.

The consensus provides examples illustrating situations where cash flows for environmental exit costs not recognized as liabilities under SOP 96-1 are either included in or excluded from the undiscounted expected future cash flows used to evaluate a long-lived asset or group of assets for recoverability under FAS 144.

99-5 Accounting for Preproduction Costs Related to Long-Term Supply Arrangements

Manufacturers often incur costs referred to as preproduction costs, related to products that they will supply to their customers under long-term supply arrangements. The following consensuses were reached with respect to these costs:

1. Design and development costs are expensed as incurred.
2. Design and development costs for molds, dies, and other tools that a supplier will own and that will be used in producing the products under the long-term supply arrangement are capitalized as part of the molds, dies, and other tools (subject to a FAS 144 recoverability assessment when one or more impairment indicators is present). There is an exception, however, for molds, dies, and other tools involving new technology which are expensed as incurred as research and development costs under FAS 2.
3. If the molds, dies, and other tools described in 2. above are *not to be owned* by the supplier, then their costs are expensed as incurred unless the supply arrangement provides the supplier the noncancelable right (as long as the supplier is performing under the terms of the supply arrangement) to use the molds, dies, and other tools during the supply arrangement.
4. If there is a legally enforceable contractual guarantee for reimbursement of design and development costs that would otherwise be expensed under these consensuses, the costs are recognized as an asset as incurred. Such a guarantee must contain reimbursement provisions that are objectively measurable and verifiable. The consensus contains examples that illustrate the application of this provision.

Under these consensuses, preparers are encouraged to disclose (SEC registrants are required to disclose)

1. The accounting policy for preproduction design and development costs.
2. The aggregate amounts of
    a. Assets recognized pursuant to agreements providing for contractual reimbursement of preproduction design and development costs.
    b. Assets recognized for molds, dies, and other tools that the supplier owns.
    c. Assets recognized for molds, dies, and other tools that the supplier does not own.

99-9 Effect of Derivative Gains and Losses on the Capitalization of Interest

The interest rate to use in capitalizing interest under FAS 34 is to be the effective yield that takes into account gains and losses on the effective portion of a derivative instrument that qualifies as a fair value hedge of fixed interest rate debt. The amount of interest subject to capitalization could include amortization of the adjustments of the carrying amount of the hedged liability under FAS 133, if the entity elects to begin amortization of those adjustments during the period in which interest is eligible for capitalization. Any ineffective portion of the fair value hedge is not reflected in the capitalization rate.

During the EITF's deliberations, the FASB staff expressed a belief that when variable-rate interest on a specific borrowing is associated with an asset under construction and capitalized as part of the cost of that asset, the amounts in accumulated other comprehensive income related to a cash flow hedge of the variability of that interest are to be reclassified into earnings over the depreciable life of the constructed asset, since that depreciable life coincides with the amortization period for the capitalized interest cost on the debt.

99-16 Accounting for Transactions with Elements of Research and Development Arrangements

This issue discusses the accounting for a transaction in which a sponsor creates a wholly owned subsidiary with cash and rights to certain technology originally developed by the sponsor, and receives from the newly created subsidiary two classes of stock. The sponsor then distributes one of the classes of stock (e.g., Class A) to its stockholders. This class of stock has voting rights. Under a purchase option, the sponsor has the right, for a specified period of time, to repurchase all the Class A stock distributed to the stockholders for an exercise price approximating the fair value of the Class A shares. The class retained by the sponsor (e.g., Class B) conveys essentially no financial interest to the sponsor and has no voting rights other than certain blocking rights. The certificate of incorporation prohibits the subsidiary from changing its capital structure, from selling any significant portion of its assets, and from liquidating or merging during the term the purchase option is outstanding.

The sponsor and the subsidiary enter into a development contract that requires the subsidiary to spend all the cash contributed by the sponsor for research and development activities mutually agreed upon with the sponsor. The subsidiary has no employees other than its CEO. The subsidiary contracts with the sponsor to perform, on behalf of the sponsor, all of the research and development activities under the development contract.

The sponsor accounts for the research and development contract as follows:

- The sponsor reclassifies the cash contributed to the subsidiary as restricted cash when the Class A shares are distributed to its stockholders.
- The distribution of the Class A shares by the sponsor to its stockholders is accounted for as a dividend based on the fair value of the shares distributed.
- In the financial statements of the sponsor, the Class A shares are presented similar to a minority interest.
- The sponsor recognizes research and development expense as the research and development activities are conducted.
- The research and development expense recognized by the sponsor is not allocated to the Class A shares in determining net income or in calculating earnings per share.
- If the Class A purchase option is exercised, the sponsor accounts for the purchase as the acquisition of a minority interest.

- If the Class A purchase option is not exercised by its expiration date, the sponsor reclassifies the Class A stock to additional paid-in capital as an adjustment of the original dividend.

The effect of the above guidance is quite similar to what would be achieved by consolidating the subsidiary.

The EITF consensus contains an example of the application of the above guidance.

00-2 Accounting for Web Site Development Costs

The costs of developing a Web site, including the costs of developing services that are offered to visitors (e.g., chat rooms, search engines, e-mail, calendars, and so forth), are often quite significant. The SEC staff had expressed the opinion that a large portion of those costs should be accounted for in accordance with AICPA SOP 98-1, *Accounting for the Costs of Computer Software Developed or Obtained for Internal Use*, which sets forth certain conditions which must be met before costs may be capitalized.

In this consensus, the EITF held that costs incurred in the planning stage must be expensed as incurred. The cost of software used to operate a website must be accounted for consistent with SOP 98-1, unless a plan exists to market the software externally, in which case FAS 86 governs. Costs incurred to develop graphics (broadly defined as the "look and feel" of the Web page) are included in software costs, and thus accounted for under SOP 98-1 or FAS 86, as noted in the foregoing. However, the accounting for costs of content development will be addressed as a separate EITF issue. Costs of operating Web sites are accounted for in the same manner as other operating costs analogous to repairs and maintenance.

Issue 00-2 includes a detailed exhibit stipulating how a variety of specific costs are to be accounted for consistent with this consensus.

01-02 Interpretations of APB Opinion No. 29, *Nonmonetary Transactions*

This issue codifies and reconciles prior guidance provided by the EITF in the following issues:

86-29	Nonmonetary Transactions: Magnitude of Boot and the Exceptions to the Use of Fair Value
87-17	Spin-offs or Other Distributions of Loans Receivable to Shareholders
87-29	Exchange of Real Estate Involving Boot
89-7	Exchange of Assets or Interest in a Subsidiary for a Noncontrolling Equity Interest in a New Entity
96-2	Impairment Recognition When a Nonmonetary Asset Is Exchanged or Is Distributed to Owners and Is Accounted for at the Asset's Recorded Amount
96-4	Accounting for Reorganizations Involving a Non-Pro-Rata Split-Off of Certain Nonmonetary Assets to Owners
98-7	Accounting for Exchanges of Similar Equity Method Instruments
00-5	Determining Whether a Nonmonetary Transaction Is an Exchange of Similar Productive Assets

Exchanges of similar productive assets. Generally, under APB Opinion 29, fair value is used to measure noncash transactions. An exception, however, applies to the exchange of a productive asset for a similar productive asset or assets (SPA) or an ownership interest therein. Exchange transactions of this nature do not result in the "culmination of an earning process," and consequently, are recorded at the carrying value of the asset relinquished, adjusted for any impairment in its value. Productive assets, as defined by APB 29, include assets held or used in the production of goods or services *including* equity method investments. "Similar productive assets" are productive assets of the same general type, that perform the same general function or that are employed in the same line of business.

A series of issues was addressed by the EITF regarding how to assess whether or not two productive assets are similar productive assets (the "SPA assessment"). Specifically excluded from the scope of these issues, however, are

1. Transfers between a joint venture and its venturers
2. Contributions of real estate in return for an unconsolidated real estate investment (the accounting for these transactions is governed by SOP 78-9)
3. Transfers of real estate in exchange for nonmonetary assets other than real estate (covered by FAS 66)
4. Transfers of assets used in oil and gas producing activities (including both proved and unproved properties) in exchange for other assets also used in those activities (covered by FAS 19)

The EITF provided the following guidance relative to the SPA assessment:

1. In general, assets or groups of assets exchanged in a business transaction or an acquisition of an equity method minority interest are accounted for under the applicable guidance in FAS 141 and APB 18, respectively, and not under the provisions of APB 29.
2. The exchange of an equity method investment for a similar equity method investment does not result in the culmination of an earning process and is recorded at the carrying value of the asset relinquished adjusted for impairment, if any.
3. The criteria under APB 29 that SPAs be of the same general type or perform the same function applies only to singular assets or "multiple singular assets" (e.g., ten delivery trucks).
4. The criteria under APB 29 that SPAs be employed in the same line of business only applies to a productive asset that consists of a group of assets. Further, in order to conclude that two SPAs are in the same line of business they must be similar with regard to both the nature of their output (products and services) *and* the nature of the process used to manufacture, develop, or provide those products and services.
5. When the SPA consists of more than one asset, the SPA assessment is done at the group level.
6. The SPA assessment is based on the intent of the entity with respect to the asset received if *both* of the following conditions exist:
   a. The activities necessary to convert the productive asset from one line of business to another line of business must be initiated by management possessing the appropriate level of authority no later than the end of the quarter immediately following the quarter in which the closing of the exchange transaction occurs and must be completed within a reasonable period of time (not defined by the EITF).
   b. The cost to convert the productive asset received from one line of business to another cannot exceed 25% of the fair value of that productive asset.

   If either of these conditions is not met, the entity's intent with respect to the productive asset received is not a factor in the SPA assessment.

7. A *nonmonetary* exchange of ownership interests may involve the transfer by one entity (Entity A) of the ownership of either a controlled productive asset or group of assets or the transfer of a controlled business to another entity (Entity B) in exchange for a noncontrolling ownership interest in Entity B. The EITF reached a consensus that if the carrying value of the asset(s) given up by Entity A exceed their fair value, the difference is recognized as a loss by Entity A. If the fair value of the ownership interest received is more readily determinable, that fair value is used instead. If, instead, the fair value of the asset(s) given up exceeds their carrying value, then the difference is recognized as a gain by Entity A if it uses the cost method to account for the noncontrolling ownership interest received. If Entity A uses the equity method to account for the noncontrolling ownership interest received, it recognizes a partial gain. The partial gain is computed as the difference between the fair value of the assets given up and their carrying value reduced by the portion of the gain represented by the economic interest (which may be different from the voting interest) in Entity B that is obtained.

Exchange of product or property held for sale for productive assets. An exchange for property and equipment, even if they pertain to the same line of business, is recorded at fair value.

Exchanges involving monetary consideration (boot). If boot is 25% or more of the fair value of an exchange, the transaction is considered a monetary transaction. In that case, both parties record the transaction at fair value. If the boot is less than 25%, the payer of the boot does not recognize a gain and the receiver of the boot must follow the pro rata recognition guidance in APB 29, paragraph 22. See below for rules regarding exchanges with boot involving real estate.

Gain on a *monetary* exchange that involves transfer by one entity of its ownership of a controlled asset, group of assets, or business to another entity in exchange for a noncontrolling ownership interest in the other entity is accounted for consistent with the guidance in 7. above for similar *nonmonetary* exchanges.

Exchanges of real estate involving monetary consideration (boot). A transaction that involves the exchange of similar real estate and boot of 25% or more of the fair value of the exchange is recorded with two separate components, a monetary component and a nonmonetary component. The allocation is made based on the relative fair values of the monetary and nonmonetary portions at the time of the transaction. The party that receives the boot accounts for the monetary component of the transaction under FAS 66 as the equivalent of a sale of an interest in the underlying real estate and the nonmonetary component of the transaction based on the recorded amount (reduced, if applicable, for any impairment in value) of the nonmonetary asset relinquished. For the party that pays the boot, the monetary component is accounted for as an acquisition of real estate, and the nonmonetary component is accounted for based on the recorded amount (reduced, if applicable, for any impairment in value).

02-7 Unit of Accounting for Testing Impairment of Indefinite-Lived Intangible Assets

The EITF reached a consensus about when it is appropriate to combine into a single "unit of accounting" for impairment testing purposes, separately recorded indefinite-life intangibles, whether acquired or internally developed.

The assets may be combined into a single unit of accounting for impairment testing if they are operated as a single asset and, as such, are inseparable from one another. The EITF provided indicators to use in evaluating the individual facts and circumstances to exercise judgment.

Indicators that indefinite-lived intangibles are to be combined as a single unit of accounting.

1. The intangibles will be used together to construct or enhance a single asset.
2. If the intangibles had been part of the same acquisition, they would have been recorded as a single asset.
3. The intangibles, as a group, represent "the highest and best use of the assets" (e.g., they could probably realize a higher sales price if sold together than if they were sold separately). Indicators pointing to this situation are
    a. The unlikelihood that a substantial portion of the assets would be sold separately, or
    b. The fact that, should a substantial portion of the intangibles be sold individually, there would be a significant reduction in the fair value of the remaining assets in the group.
4. The marketing or branding strategy of the entity treats the assets as being complementary (e.g., a trademark and its related trade name, formulas, recipes, and patented or unpatented technology can all be complementary to an entity's brand name).

Indicators that indefinite-lived intangibles are not to be combined as a single unit of accounting.

1. Each separate intangible generates independent cash flows.
2. In a sale, it would be likely that the intangibles would be sold separately. If the entity had previously sold similar assets separately, this would constitute evidence that combining the assets would not be appropriate.
3. The entity is either considering or has already adopted a plan to dispose of one or more of the intangibles separately.
4. The intangibles are used exclusively by different asset groups (as defined in FAS 144).
5. Differing useful economic lives.

The EITF provided additional guidance regarding the "unit of accounting" determination.

1. Goodwill and finite-lived intangibles are not permitted to be combined in the "unit of accounting" since they are subject to different impairment rules.
2. If the intangibles collectively constitute a business, they may not be combined into a unit of accounting.
3. If the unit of accounting includes intangibles recorded in the separate financial statements of consolidated subsidiaries, it is possible that the sum of impairment losses recognized in the separate financial statements of the subsidiaries will not equal the consolidated impairment loss.

    NOTE: Although counterintuitive, this situation can occur when

    1. *At the separate subsidiary level, an intangible asset is impaired since the cash flows from the other intangibles included in the unit of accounting that reside in other subsidiaries cannot be considered in determining impairment, and*
    2. *At the consolidated level, when the intangibles are considered as a single unit of accounting, they are not impaired.*

4. Should a unit of accounting be included in a single reporting unit, that same unit of accounting and associated fair value are to be used in computing the implied fair value of goodwill for measuring any goodwill impairment loss.

02-13 Deferred Income Tax Considerations in Applying the Goodwill Impairment Test in FASB Statement No. 142

The two-step goodwill impairment test required by FAS 142 requires the annual determination of the fair value of a reporting unit and, when required by the results of the performance of the first step of the test, the implied fair value of the reporting unit's goodwill. In making these measurements, it is unclear as to how deferred income taxes are to be treated.

For the purposes of determination of the fair value of a reporting unit, the relevant facts and circumstances are to be carefully evaluated with respect to whether to assume that the reporting unit could be bought or sold in a taxable or nontaxable transaction. The factors to consider in making the evaluation are

1. The assumptions that marketplace participants would make in estimating fair value
2. The feasibility of the assumed structure considering
    a. The ability to sell the reporting unit in a nontaxable transaction, and
    b. Any limits on the entity's ability to treat a sale as a nontaxable transaction imposed by income tax laws or regulations, or corporate governance requirements.
3. Whether the assumed structure would yield the best economic after-tax return to the (hypothetical) seller for the reporting unit.

For the purpose of goodwill impairment testing, the carrying value of a reporting unit is to include deferred income taxes irrespective of whether fair value of the reporting unit was determined assuming taxable or nontaxable treatment.

For the purpose of computing the implied fair value of reporting unit goodwill (step 2 of the goodwill impairment test), assumptions must be made as to the income tax bases of the reporting unit's assets and liabilities in order to compute any relevant deferred income taxes. If the computation of the reporting unit's fair value in step 1 of the goodwill impairment test assumed that the reporting unit was structured as a taxable transaction, then new income tax bases are used, otherwise the existing income tax bases are used.

02-17 Recognition of Customer Relationship Intangible Assets Acquired in a Business Combination

FAS 141 provides two criteria for recognizing intangible assets acquired in a business combination separately from goodwill, the legal/contractual criterion and the separability criterion. If the requirements of either of these criteria are met, an intangible is recognized apart from goodwill.

One of the categories of intangible assets identified by FAS 141 is "customer-related intangible assets." Included in this category are the following intangibles with parenthetical reference to the FAS 141 criterion that generally applies:

1. Customer lists or databases (separability).
2. Order or production backlog evidenced by cancelable or noncancelable contracts such as purchase orders or sales orders (legal).
3. Customer contracts and the related customer relationships (legal).

EITF reached the following consensuses with respect to applying FAS 141 to customer-related intangible assets acquired in a business combination:

1. A customer contract and the related customer relationship may represent two distinct intangible assets to be recognized separately. Consequently the two assets may have different useful lives and may be amortizable using different methods depending on how the economic benefits of the assets are consumed.
2. In estimating the fair value of intangible assets, the particular criterion that required separate recognition (legal or separability) does not restrict the assumptions used to estimate the intangible's fair value. The criteria are not intended to prescribe measurement; rather, their purpose is solely for determining whether an acquired intangible is to be recognized separately from goodwill. The determination of fair value is to take into account the assumptions that would be made by marketplace participants, including expectations regarding future contract renewals and other benefits that are related to an intangible asset.
3. If an entity establishes relationships with its customers via contracts, the intangible asset arising from those relationships meets the legal criterion, even if a contract was not in existence at the date of acquisition. Lack of contractual rights or separability could conceivably affect the fair value of the customer relationship asset, however.

Order and production backlog originating from cancelable or noncancelable sales orders or purchase orders are considered contractual in nature and thus the customer relationship intangible with respect to those customers also meets the legal/contractual criterion for recognition separate from goodwill.

04-2 Whether Mineral Rights are Tangible or Intangible Assets

This consensus and the associated FSP FAS 141-1 and FAS 142-2 (see below) eliminate an inconsistency in FAS 141 as to whether mineral rights are to be treated as a tangible asset or intangible asset. For the purpose of its deliberations, the EITF defined mineral rights as "the legal right to explore, extract, and retain at least a portion of the benefits from mineral deposits."

The EITF decided to follow the common practice followed by mining entities and consequently reached a consensus that mineral rights, as defined above, are to be characterized as *tangible* assets.

The EITF also concluded that the mining entity is to disclose (either on the face of its balance sheet or in the notes to the financial statements) the aggregate carrying amount of mineral rights as a separate component of property, plant, and equipment.

This consensus applies to mining entities other than oil and gas producing entities covered by FAS 19, *Financial Accounting and Reporting by Oil and Gas Producing Companies*.

04-3 Mining Assets: Impairment and Business Combinations

This EITF consensus provides interpretive guidance regarding whether a mining company (excluding oil- and gas-producing entities within the scope of FAS 19) is to factor into business combination asset allocations and into asset impairment recoverability reviews the "value beyond proven and probable reserves" (VBPP), and anticipated fluctuations in the future market price of minerals in business combination allocations.

The EITF concluded that

1. Mining entities are to include *both* VBPP and anticipated future mineral market price fluctuations in the values allocated to mining assets in a business combination to the extent that a market participant would do so in determining the assets' fair values.
2. Mining entities are to include the effects of *both* VBPP and anticipated future mineral market price fluctuations in estimates of future cash flows used for determining future recoverability of assets (undiscounted) and for measuring impairment (discounted). For this purpose, the EITF reminded constituents that such estimates must also include future estimated cash outflows necessary to develop and extract the VBPP.

D-104 Clarification of Transition Guidance in Paragraph 41 of FASB Statement No. 144

The FASB staff provides guidance relating to certain situations where a company initiated the abandonment of a segment of its business prior to initial application of FAS 144. When the segment is required by contract or regulation to continue to provide services after it ceases the acceptance of new business, and consequently, the abandonment will be affected through the liquidation or "run-off" of operations, the one-year limitation in paragraph 51 of FAS 144 does not apply. The segment (and any segment being accounted for as a discontinued operation prior to initial application of FAS 144) will continue to be accounted for under APB 30 for the remainder of the run-off period. If, however, after the initial application of FAS 144, a component of an entity is abandoned through liquidation or run-off of operations, that component is not to be reported as discontinued operations until the cessation of all operations including the run-off.

STATEMENTS OF POSITION

88-1 Accounting for Developmental and Preoperating Costs, Purchases and Exchanges of Takeoff and Landing Slots, and Airframe Modifications

Preoperating costs related to the integration of new types of aircraft and developmental costs (other than advertising costs) are charged to expense as incurred.

Takeoff and landing slots purchased by an airline are recorded as identifiable intangibles in accordance with FAS 142. If the slots are acquired via an exchange transaction, they are nonmonetary assets to be recorded in accordance with APB 29.

The cost of modifications to the interior of an aircraft that increase the usefulness of the plane are capitalized and depreciated over the lesser of the life of the aircraft or the life of the modifications. When such modifications are made, the net book value (less salvage value) of the assets being replaced is charged to expense.

92-3 Accounting for Foreclosed Assets

This SOP applies to all reporting entities (except those that account for assets at fair value) and applies to all assets obtained through foreclosure or repossession (except inventories, marketable equity securities and real estate owned by the lender and accounted for under FAS 67). Foreclosed assets held for sale are measured on an individual asset basis on the balance sheet at the lower of (1) cost or (2) fair value less estimated selling costs. A valuation allowance is used to show an amount less than cost.

If the asset is subject to senior debt, that debt is not deducted from carrying value but rather is reported as a liability. Payments are deducted from the liability. After foreclosure, accrued interest is recognized as interest expense.

For foreclosed assets used in the production of income, the accounting is the same as for any other nonforeclosed acquired asset in their category. If assets that have been foreclosed and classified as held for sale are to be used in the production of income, reclassification of the asset's carrying amount is required. The adjustment is the amount necessary to adjust the asset to the value at which it would have been carried if it had been used in the production of income since foreclosure. Selling costs included in the valuation allowance are reversed and the net effect included in income from continuing operations in the period of reclassification.

93-7 Reporting on Advertising Costs

The costs of advertising are expensed either as incurred or the first time the advertising takes place. However, there are two exceptions.

1. Direct-response advertising
   a. Whose primary purpose is to elicit sales to customers who could be shown to have responded specifically to the advertising and
   b. That results in probable future economic benefits; and
2. Expenditures for advertising costs that are made subsequent to recognizing revenues related to those costs.

Expenditures for direct-response advertising are capitalized if both of the conditions listed above are met. The future benefits to be received are the future revenues arising as a direct result of the advertising. The company is required to provide entity-specific persuasive evidence that there is a linkage between the direct-response advertising and these future benefits. These costs are then amortized over the period in which the future benefits are to be received. Advertising expenditures are sometimes made subsequent to the recognition of revenue (such as in "cooperative advertising" arrangements with customers). In order to achieve proper matching, these costs are to be estimated, accrued, and charged to expense when the related revenues are recognized.

FASB STAFF POSITIONS

FSP FAS 144-1 Determination of Cost Basis for Foreclosed Assets under FASB Statement No. 15, *Accounting by Debtors and Creditors for Troubled Debt Restructurings*, and the Measurement of Cumulative Losses Previously Recognized under Paragraph 37 of FASB Statement No. 144, *Accounting for the Impairment or Disposal of Long-Lived Assets*

The valuation allowance for a loan collateralized by a long-lived asset should not be carried over as a separate element of the cost basis of a long-lived asset received in full satisfaction of a receivable in a troubled debt restructuring. The valuation allowance for the loan also should not be included in the amount of cumulative losses previously recognized when computing the amount of gain that can be recognized under FAS 144 if the value of the collateral subsequently increases.

FSP FAS 141-1 and 142-1 **Interaction of FASB Statements No. 141, *Business Combinations*, and No. 142, *Goodwill and Other Intangible Assets*, and EITF Issue No. 04-2, *Whether Mineral Rights Are Tangible or Intangible Assets***

Amends the two pronouncements referenced in the title to eliminate an inconsistency regarding whether mineral rights, as defined, are tangible assets or intangible assets. Consistent with EITF 04-2, mineral rights, as defined in that consensus, are considered to be tangible assets.

FSP FAS 146-1 **Determining Whether a One-Time Termination Benefit Offered in Connection with an Exit or Disposal Activity Is, in Substance, an Enhancement to an Ongoing Benefit Arrangement**

This FSP provides guidance on determining if termination benefits newly offered to employees in connection with an exit or disposal activity are one-time termination benefits to be accounted for under FAS 146 or enhancements to ongoing benefit arrangements which are accounted for under other authoritative pronouncements.

If the newly offered benefits represent a revision to an ongoing arrangement that is not limited to a specified termination event or to a specified future period, the benefits represent an enhancement to an ongoing benefit arrangement and, thus, are to be accounted for under the provisions of one or more of the following pronouncements:

- FAS 87—Pensions
- FAS 88—Settlements and Curtailments
- FAS 106—Postretirement Benefits other than Pensions
- FAS 112—Postemployment Benefits

EXPOSURE DRAFTS OUTSTANDING

Proposed Statement of Position: Accounting for Certain Costs and Activities Related to Property, Plant, and Equipment

Proposed FAS: Accounting in Interim and Annual Financial Statements for Certain Costs and Activities Related to Property, Plant, and Equipment

In 2001, AcSEC and FASB jointly issued these Exposure Drafts (collectively referred to as the "ED"). Their objective was to resolve diverse accounting practices for different types of costs incurred at various stages in the life cycle of fixed assets (referred to in the ED as "property, plant, and equipment" or "PP&E") as well as for the determination of estimated useful lives for assets which have multiple components. The proposed FAS amends existing literature in "level A" GAAP that conflicts with the guidance in the proposed SOP which contains the substantive aspects of the proposal.

In late 2002, changes in the US accounting standards-setting framework were announced by FASB. As a result of these changes and after a transition period, AcSEC Statements of Position relative to general accounting standards would no longer be issued (AcSEC will continue to have a role in setting specialized industry standards). As part of the transition, FASB had permitted AcSEC to continue deliberations with respect to certain aspects of the ED based on three overarching principles AcSEC had previously established as a part of the project.

1. PP&E assets should be depreciated over their expected useful lives.
2. Replacement assets and the assets that they replace should not be simultaneously recognized as assets on an entity's books.
3. PP&E assets should be recorded at cost.

In April 2004, FASB directed AcSEC to discontinue work on the project and removed the project from its own agenda. Additionally, FASB directed its staff to consider whether portions of the ED should be issued as future FASB Staff Positions. Due to the possibility of portions of the ED being adopted as future FSP, the discussion related to it has been retained below.

To monitor developments in this area, visit the FASB Web site as well as the Wiley GAAP update page at http://www.wiley.com.

Scope. If adopted, the ED would have applied to

1. All nongovernmental entities including
   a. Not-for-profit organizations
   b. Regulated entities
   c. Development stage entities
   d. Entities that report substantially all assets at fair value
2. Railroad track structures
3. Lessors of assets subject to operating leases
4. Lessees of assets subject to capital leases (except with respect to the measurement of the amount at which to record a capital lease)

The ED would *not* have applied to

1. Lessor's accounting for assets subject to sales-type or direct financing leases
2. Lessor or lessee accounting for lessor costs reimbursed by the lessee
3. Internal use software costs
4. Insurance proceeds
5. Allocation of purchase price to PP&E under FAS 141

Stages of PP&E life cycle. The ED breaks the life cycle of PP&E into four discrete stages.

1. Preliminary
2. Preacquisition
3. Acquisition or construction
4. In-service

These are addressed in the following discussion.

Preliminary stage.

Activities that occur during the stage. Exploration of opportunities for acquisition or construction, feasibility studies, purchase of options, surveying, zoning, engineering studies, design layouts, traffic studies, costs associated with obtaining management's approval to proceed with acquisition or construction.

Accounting. Capitalize payments to obtain an option to acquire PP&E. All other internal and external costs are expensed as incurred. If the option is a derivative, account for it using FAS 133; otherwise, carry it at lower of cost or fair value less cost to sell.

Boundary. Acquisition or construction is probable as evidenced by *all three* of the following criteria:

1. Management possessing the relevant authority implicitly or explicitly authorizes and commits to funding.
2. The financial resources are available to provide the necessary funding.
3. The entity has the ability to meet all applicable local and other governmental regulations.

Preacquisition stage.

Activities that occur during the stage. The same or similar to those activities that occur during the preliminary stage. The only difference is the crossing of the boundary making the acquisition or construction probable.

Accounting. Payments to obtain an option to acquire PP&E are accounted for as described above in the preliminary stage. Internal and external costs are expensed as incurred unless directly identifiable with the specific PP&E. Directly identifiable costs are limited to

1. Incremental direct costs of preacquisition activities transacted with independent third parties and incurred for the specific PP&E
2. Costs of entity-specific (or indirectly through nonindependent third parties) payroll and related benefits (e.g., health insurance) of employees who devote time to PP&E preacquisition stage activity. These costs are allocated to PP&E to the extent of time spent on the activity and in proportion to the total hours employed (including compensated absences). Specifically excluded, however, are rent, depreciation, and other occupancy costs associated with the physical space occupied by these employees.

General and administrative costs and overhead are expensed as incurred. These include the costs of all support functions including executive management, corporate accounting, acquisitions, purchasing, corporate legal, office management and administration, marketing, human resources, and information systems. These costs are expensed as incurred irrespective of whether they are incurred directly by the entity or indirectly through an outsourcing arrangement by another enterprise on the entity's behalf. The entity is not expected, however, to quantify and exclude the administrative overhead portion of incremental direct costs incurred with independent third parties. These costs qualify for capitalization.

The costs capitalized during the preacquisition stage are included in the cost of the specific PP&E upon acquisition. If it becomes no longer probable that the acquisition of the specific PP&E will occur, the costs capitalized during the preacquisition stage are written down to the lower of cost or fair value less cost to sell. There is a rebuttable presumption that this would be zero (excluding option costs). This presumption can be overcome **only** if management possessing the requisite approval authority has committed to a plan to sell the asset **and** the proceeds can be reasonably estimated.

Boundary. The entity obtains ownership or the right to use the PP&E through an agreement (e.g., a lease).

Acquisition or construction stage.

Activities that occur during the stage. Acquisition, construction (including supervision), and installation.

Accounting. Capitalize costs incurred during this stage if they are directly identifiable with specific PP&E. Directly identifiable costs are limited to

1. Incremental direct costs transacted with independent third parties and incurred for the acquisition, construction, or installation of the specific PP&E
2. Costs incurred directly by the entity (or indirectly through nonindependent third parties) of acquiring, constructing, or installing the specific PP&E. These costs include costs directly related to preproduction test runs of the PP&E that are necessary to ready the PP&E for its intended use. Such costs are limited to

    a. Payroll and payroll benefit-related costs of employees devoting time to PP&E construction-stage activity. As is the case in the preacquisition stage, the costs of rent, depreciation, and other occupancy costs associated with space occupied by these employees are excluded from "directly identifiable costs" and are expensed as incurred.

b. Depreciation of machinery and equipment (M&E) used directly in the construction or installation of PP&E to the extent of time the M&E is used directly in those activities as a percentage of its useful life

c. Incremental costs of the M&E described above, such as fuel for the machinery

d. Inventory (including spare parts) used directly in the construction and installation of the PP&E

General and administrative costs and overhead are expensed as incurred. These include the costs of all of the support functions described in the accounting for preacquisition phase costs whether incurred directly or indirectly through third-party outsourcing.

3. When real estate PP&E is being acquired, leased, or constructed

   a. Costs incurred for property taxes, insurance and ground rentals are capitalized. These costs are allocated to the portion of the property under construction during the time period that activities are in progress that are necessary to ready the asset for its intended use. Capitalization of these costs ceases at the date that the building or structure is substantially complete and ready for its intended use but no later than the date that initial operations commence in any portion of the building or structure

   b. Demolition costs incurred by an owner or lessor are expensed as incurred except when the demolition

      (1) Was contemplated as part of the acquisition or at lease inception, **and**

      (2) Occurs within a reasonable time after acquisition or inception or is subject to delay that is beyond the control of the owner/lessor (e.g., when demolition cannot occur until the present tenant vacates the premises at the end of its lease, or until government permits are obtained).

      Demolition costs meeting both criteria (1) and (2) are capitalized as either part of the land or the new building, depending on the nature of the costs. For example, costs of razing a building to prepare for the construction of a new building would be capitalized as part of the cost of the land, whereas costs of gutting parts of an existing building in preparation for converting the space to a different use would be capitalized as part of the building.

Upon substantial completion of PP&E and readiness for its intended use, all expenses associated with the PP&E (including carrying costs such as property taxes, insurance, and ground rentals) are recorded as operating expense as accrued. PP&E is considered substantially complete and ready for its intended use at the *earlier of* the date of completion of all major construction and installation activities or the date when related revenue recognition commences.

If a portion of a PP&E project is substantially complete and ready for its intended use and can be operated independently from the other portions of the project, it is accounted for as a separate project. Irrespective of this separate project accounting, however, the project continues to be considered collectively for the purpose of capitalization of property taxes, ground rentals, and insurance.

With respect to production machinery requiring preproduction test runs, the PP&E is considered ready for its intended use when it is first capable of producing a unit of product that is either saleable or usable internally by the entity. Any costs incurred subsequently that enhance the production efficiency of the PP&E are expensed as incurred.

Boundary. PP&E is substantially complete and ready for its intended use (FAS 34, para 18).

In-service stage.

Activities that occur during the stage. All activities occurring during this stage are to be categorized as either

1. Repairs and maintenance (R&M) of existing components, or
2. Replacement of existing components, or
3. Acquisition of additional components.

Accounting. Normal, recurring, or periodic R&M and all other costs related to PP&E in this stage are to be expensed as incurred **unless** incurred for

1. Acquisition of additional components, or
2. Replacement of existing components. Replacement costs, except *removal costs,* are accounted for in the same manner as prescribed for acquisition or construction of PP&E in the ED.

Removal costs associated with replacement of PP&E, including costs of disassembling a component to gain access to a subcomponent being replaced, are to be expensed as incurred. Demolition costs are not considered removal costs and are accounted for separately as described previously.

If existing PP&E (or a component thereof) is removed from service due to a replacement, its remaining net book value (or a reasonable estimate, if not separately determinable from the accounting records) is charged to depreciation expense of the period of replacement. In addition, management is to consider the need to reevaluate the associated lives of the components of the remaining PP&E asset. Changes necessitated by this reevaluation are accounted for as changes in accounting estimates, as prescribed by APB 20.

Relocation costs are directly identifiable costs of dismantlement, crating, shipping, and reinstallation of existing PP&E (or a component of PP&E) that has been in service. Relocation costs are expensed as incurred.

Planned major maintenance activities. To keep its PP&E properly maintained and operating efficiently, entities frequently must incur costs for R&M activities such as cleaning, servicing, repair, replacement, minor parts, fluids, belts, hoses, gears, etc. When incurred, these costs are not to be treated as a separate PP&E project or component. Rather, they are evaluated by management to determine whether they represent (1) the acquisition of additional components, or (2) the replacement of existing components. If these costs do not represent either of these types of expenditures, they are to be expensed as incurred. The ED specifically prohibits

1. Accruing as a liability the estimated costs of a planned major maintenance activity prior to the actual costs being incurred
2. Deferral and amortization of the entire cost of a planned major maintenance activity, and
3. Current recognition of additional depreciation or amortization to cover the future costs of a planned major maintenance activity (sometimes referred to as the "built-in overhaul method).

Retooling and change of use. Machinery is often converted to change the nature of what it is producing, such as for new models or products with different specifications. Costs of such changes are evaluated in accordance with the guidance provided for the in-service stage. Therefore, unless the costs are incurred for acquiring additional components or replacing existing components, they are expensed as incurred.

Entities that report substantially all assets at fair value. PP&E costs are to be accounted for in accordance with the ED *prior* to adjustments for changes in fair value. The adjustment for fair value is recorded as a change in unrealized appreciation or depreciation in the statement of operations.

Conversion of inventory to PP&E. Entities sometimes convert inventory to PP&E either directly or by using the inventory in the process of internally constructing PP&E. Some entities only do this occasionally or with a small portion of large quantities of fungible units that they produce (e.g., a manufacturer of industrial cleaning equipment converting one of its units for use in cleaning its own premises). In such situations, the carrying value of the inventory being converted to PP&E is evaluated for impairment under FAS 144 and the provisions of the ED are applied prospectively.

Other entities follow a consistent pattern of changing the intended use of significant amounts of inventory to PP&E during the acquisition or in-service stages. In these situations, there will be a rebuttable presumption that the entity intends to hold and use any such subsequently produced assets as PP&E. As such, the inventory is subject to the accounting prescribed by the ED and not to the accounting in the relevant literature on inventory.

Liquidated damages. In the event that liquidated damages are recovered by a buyer of PP&E from the seller, they are recorded as a reduction in the cost of the related PP&E. If the proceeds exceed the total cost of the PP&E, the excess is reported as income.

Component accounting. A *component* is defined as a tangible portion of PP&E that can be separately identified as an asset and depreciated or amortized over its own separate expected useful life of more than one year. A component is accounted for separately if it has an expected useful life that differs from that of the asset to which it relates.

The process of identifying components occurs at the time of acquisition, construction, or replacement. The preferred method of assigning costs to components is specific identification. If specific identification is not practicable, relative fair values when the asset is placed in service or other reasonable methods of allocation are used, such as relative square footage for real estate.

If the entity replaces a portion of a PP&E asset for which component accounting had not been used when originally recorded (assuming that the replacement meets the definition of a component), the cost of the replacement is capitalized and accounted for as a separate component prospectively. In addition, the entity charges the estimated net book value of the replaced item to depreciation expense in the period of replacement. The net book value of the replaced item is calculated by estimating the previously capitalized costs of the replaced PP&E component and subtracting an estimate of accumulated depreciation attributable to that component using the same depreciation method and expected useful life used to depreciate the total PP&E asset. When an item is replaced that was not previously accounted for as a separate component, management is required to reevaluate the level of component accounting and associated lives of the components of the remaining PP&E asset and similar assets. Any changes resulting from this reevaluation are to be treated prospectively as a change in accounting estimate.

Note that application of the above methodology penalizes the company for not having previously applied component accounting to the PP&E affected. The charge against depreciation for the net book value of the replaced component would not have been necessary in the period of replacement if the component had been separately accounted for over its useful life.

Although the component accounting provisions of the ED apply to amounts capitalized by a lessor or lessee, they do not modify the application of the lease classification criteria of FAS 13, which continue to be applied to the leased asset as a single unit.

The ED requires that management assess the estimated useful lives of all of its PP&E on an ongoing basis with any changes to those lives accounted for prospectively as changes in accounting estimates.

Presentation and disclosure. The ED supplements existing GAAP disclosure requirements as follows:

The carrying amounts of the following categories of PP&E are to be included either on the face of the basic financial statements or in the notes to the financial statements

1. Land and land improvements
2. Buildings and building improvements
3. Machinery and equipment, and
4. Construction in progress

If costs within a major category are significant in relation to that category and have expected useful lives significantly different from that of the category as a whole, they are broken down further into subcategories (either in the basic financial statements, or more likely, in the notes). For each category and subcategory, the entity is required to disclose the range of useful lives.

Costs capitalized in the preliminary stage (options) and preacquisition stage are included in the caption "construction in progress" until substantial completion and readiness for their intended use.

Finally, the nature and amount of costs characterized as repairs and maintenance expense are to be disclosed for each period for which an income statement is presented. If the entity changes the types or nature of costs included in repairs and maintenance expense from previous reporting periods, the details of the change are to be disclosed.

Proposed FAS: Exchanges of Productive Assets and Amendment of APB Opinion No. 29

This ED, part of the effort to converge US GAAP and International Accounting Standards, proposes to eliminate the "similar productive asset" provision of APB 29, *Accounting for Nonmonetary Transactions,* and substitute a test of "commercial substance" to determine whether a nonmonetary exchange is to be accounted for at fair value. This provision is discussed in greater detail in the text of this chapter.

APPENDIX

SUMMARY AND COMPARISON OF ACCOUNTING AND IMPAIRMENT RULES

<table>
<tr><th>Attribute</th><th>PP&E*</th><th>Amortizable intangibles</th><th>Nonamortizable intangibles</th><th>Goodwill</th></tr>
<tr><td>Useful life?</td><td colspan="2">Estimated useful life or, for leasehold improvements, the lesser of that life or the term of the lease</td><td colspan="2">Indefinite</td></tr>
<tr><td>Consider Residual or Salvage Value?</td><td>Yes</td><td>Yes—with either 3rd party commitment or ready market</td><td colspan="2">No</td></tr>
<tr><td>Capitalize Interest if Self-Constructed?</td><td>Yes</td><td colspan="3"></td></tr>
<tr><td>Recoverability Evaluation or Impairment Test?</td><td colspan="2">Recoverability evaluation</td><td>Impairment Test</td><td>Special 2-step impairment test</td></tr>
<tr><td>Frequency</td><td colspan="2">When events and circumstances warrant</td><td colspan="2">At least annually; more often if events and circumstances warrant</td></tr>
<tr><td>Change between Amortizable and Nonamortizable</td><td></td><td colspan="2">Test for impairment, adjust if required</td><td></td></tr>
<tr><td>Subsequent Increases Recognized?</td><td colspan="4">No</td></tr>
<tr><td>Level of Aggregation for Impairment Purposes</td><td colspan="2">Asset group or disposal group</td><td>Unit of accounting as specified by EITF 02-7</td><td>Reporting unit</td></tr>
</table>

* *Includes property, plant, and equipment, internal-use software, and Web site development costs.*

10 INVESTMENTS

PERSPECTIVE AND ISSUES

The appropriate accounting for noncurrent (or long-term) investments in equity and debt securities is dependent upon the degree of marketability, management's intentions regarding the holding period, and (in the case of equity investments, only) the investor's ownership percentage.

For "passive" investments in marketable equity securities, generally defined as those circumstances where the investor holds less than a 20% interest in the investee, FAS 115 requires that the investment be reported at fair market value. Such equity investments must be classified at the acquisition date as being held for trading or as being "available-for-sale." While what is often called "mark-to-market" accounting is prescribed in either case, only for trading securities will the change in fair value be reflected on the income statement in the current period. For investments in equity securities that are considered to be "available-for-sale," unrealized gains and losses are to be carried in an equity account referred to as accumulated other comprehensive income, after being reported as a component of other comprehensive income per FAS 130. However, if there is a permanent decline in the "available-for-sale" securities, this adjustment will be taken to income in the current period.

A special situation arises when an entity acquires loans that had been originated by another entity, and there had been a decline in the obligor's creditworthiness prior to this transfer. Under SOP 03-3, the accounting for such acquired loans—which may be either loans receivable or debt securities—will be based on the expected future cash flows to be received, rather than on the nominal or contractual amounts of the obligations. The acquirees of such loans will often be financial institutions, but the requirements of SOP 03-3 are equally applicable to all entities, including not-for-profit enterprises that invest in loans or debt securities.

When an investor has **significant influence** over an investee, it is no longer a passive investor, and the equity method must be used to account for the investment. Generally, significant influence is deemed to exist when the investor owns from 20 to 50% of the investee's voting shares, although APB 18 contemplates circumstances where such influence is present with under 20% ownership, or conversely is absent with holdings of 20% or greater. (Over 50%, of course, signals **control,** and under the provisions of FAS 94, full consolidation of financial statements is mandatory unless the investor lacks control over the investee. The equity method involves increasing the original cost of the investment by the investor's pro rata share of the investee's earnings, and decreasing it for the investor's share of the investee's losses and for dividends paid.

Equity method accounting has been referred to as "one-line consolidation," because the net result of applying APB 18 on reported net earnings and on net worth should be identical to what would have occurred had full consolidation been applied. Thus, to the extent that the cost of acquiring the intercorporate investment exceeds the fair value of the investor's share of the investee's underlying net assets, the excess must be accounted for in a manner analogous to the accounting prescribed for goodwill. Therefore, FAS 142 impacts the application of the equity method of accounting because the portion of the purchase cost identified as representing goodwill will no longer be subject to amortization, but must instead be tested, as conditions warrant, for impairment.

This chapter also discusses the accounting for investments in marketable equity securities and in debt securities as prescribed by FAS 115. Under current GAAP, fair value-based reporting is embraced to a greater extent than previously, although the use of the accumulated other comprehensive income account does postpone income statement recognition of some of these changes in value. Debt securities that are to be held to maturity are still accounted for at amortized historical cost; and while unrealized gains and losses on these investments are still excluded from reported earnings, they are subject to more disclosure in the financial statements than had been the case in the past. The major criticism of the requirements under FAS 115 is that management intentions still govern the choice of financial reporting modes, and intentions are difficult to objectively and definitely demonstrate. Also problematic is the determination of whether a given decline in value is temporary or other than temporary in nature, an issue which for available-for-sale and held-to-maturity investments results in substantially differing financial reporting consequences.

FAS 115 applies to most industries and superseded the specialized industry guidance (e.g., for the banking and thrift industries) previously found in AICPA audit and accounting guides. It does not apply to those industries for which fair value reporting is strictly required, such as brokers and dealers in securities. Furthermore, FAS 115 does not apply to not-for-profits, the accounting for which is governed by the provisions of FAS 124, which prescribes fair value reporting for all categories of investments, including debt instruments being held to maturity.

The graphic below summarizes the distinctions for financial reporting purposes of varying levels of ownership in an investee entity. These requirements have not changed since the promulgation of FAS 115; consolidation is still required when the parent owns over 50% of the subsidiary, unless control is absent.

Percentage of Outstanding Voting Stock Acquired

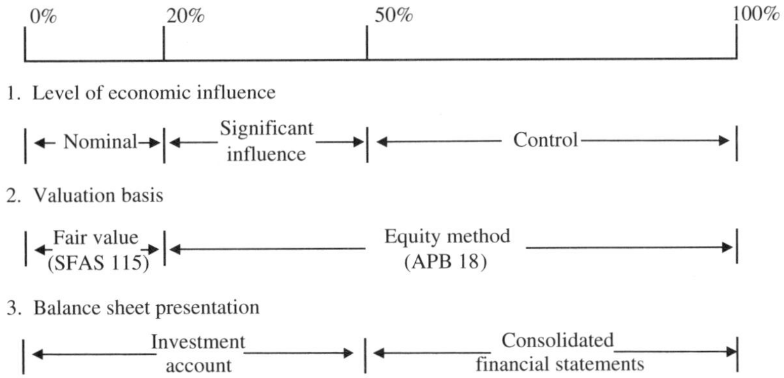

Sources of GAAP

APB	*ARB*	*FAS*	*FIN*	*EITF*	*SOP*	*FSP*
17, 18, 23	43	52, 94, 107, 109, 115, 126, 130, 133, 140, 142, 144	35	84-5, 85-40, 89-4, 96-10, 96-16, 97-7, 98-7, 98-13, 98-15, 99-8, 99-10, 99-20, 00-1, 00-6, 02-14, 02-18, 03-1, 03-16, D-11, D-39, D-44, D-46, D-68	03-3	144-1

DEFINITIONS OF TERMS

Available-for-sale securities. Investments (debt or equity) that are not classifiable as held-to-maturity or as trading.

Corporate joint venture. A corporate business owned equally by two or more investor entities; it is typically accounted for by the equity method or, less commonly, by the proportional consolidation method by the investors.

Cost method. A method of accounting for investment whereby the investor recognizes only dividends received from investee as income.

Differential. The difference between the carrying value of common stock investment and book value of underlying net assets of the investee; it should be allocated between excess (deficiency) of fair value over (under) book value of net assets, with any remainder accounted for as goodwill (or negative goodwill), and tested periodically for impairment (if positive goodwill) or allocated against the underlying investee assets and, if necessary, recognized as an extraordinary income item (if negative goodwill).

Equity method. A method that includes recognition of a percentage share of income or loss, dividends, and any changes in the investment percentage in an investee by an investor. This method recognizes the effects of any intercompany transactions between the investor and investee.

Goodwill. The excess of the cost of the acquired interest in an investee over the sum of the amounts assigned to identifiable assets acquired less liabilities assumed.

Held-to-maturity securities. Investments in debt securities that the entity has both the ability and the intent to hold to maturity.

Investee. An enterprise that issued voting stock that is held by an investor.

Investee capital transaction. The purchase or sale by the investee of its own common shares, which alters the investor's ownership interest and is accounted for by the investor as if the investee were a consolidated subsidiary.

Investor. A business enterprise that holds an investment in voting stock of another enterprise.

Other comprehensive income. Revenues, expenses, gains and losses that under generally accepted accounting principles are included in comprehensive income but excluded from earnings.

Significant influence. The ability of the investor to affect the financial or operating policies of the investee; it is presumed to exist when there is at least 20% voting common stock ownership by the investor.

Trading securities. Investments (debt or equity) which the entity intends to sell in the near term, and which are usually acquired as part of an established strategy to buy and sell, thereby generating profits based on short-term price movements.

Undistributed investee earnings. The investor's share of investee earnings in excess of dividends paid.

CONCEPTS, RULES, AND EXAMPLES

Accounting for Marketable Equity Securities

The accounting for long-term investments in equity securities was debated for many years. Historical cost had traditionally been prescribed for investments where the **investor** did not exercise control (i.e., had no more than a 50% voting interest). The threshold for the use of historical cost was later reduced to only those circumstances where **significant influence** was not a factor, presumptively defined as under a 20% voting interest. The **equity method,** promulgated by APB 18, is the prescribed method of accounting for investments where significant influence over **investee** actions is held by the investor.

Over the past decade, the trend in accounting thought has begun to favor a market (or fair) value approach. There are many reasons why users of financial statements as well as standard setters (including the SEC) have increasingly focused on the fair market value approach, including the enhanced availability of fair market value information, and the concern that adherence to the historical cost model provided management and investors with less relevant decision information, which may have contributed to certain business failures of recent years, particularly those of financial institutions.

FAS 115 is applicable to almost all reporting entities, except those whose specialized accounting practice has already been to account for all investments at market value. FAS 115 is also inapplicable to not-for-profit enterprises, although a separate standard, FAS 124, requires not-for-profits to account for all investments in debt and equity securities at fair value, with the changes in value taken into reported changes in net assets currently. All marketable equity securities (except those accounted for by the equity method, discussed later in this chapter) are to be classified at acquisition as being either for trading purposes or as available-for-sale. **Trading securities** are those that are bought with the intention of being sold in the near term with the general objective of realizing profits from short-term price movements. While a time criterion is not established, a persistent practice of active and frequent trading would be suggestive of the fact that new acquisitions of marketable equity securities are intended to be traded. If management does not admit an intention to trade, and it cannot be demonstrated that the securities are being held for trading, the investments are to be categorized as **available-for-sale**.

The distinction between these classifications is important. While equity securities in either category are reported at fair value, it is only the changes in value for the trading account that are recognized in earnings in the current period. Thus, holding gains and losses are accounted for as if realized, in the case of trading securities. In contract, changes in value for securities held in the available-for-sale portfolio are not recognized in earnings. The only exceptions will be the relatively few entities, such as securities broker-dealers, for which specialized industry accounting practices have long prescribed a pure mark-to-market approach, with all changes in value reflected in current income.

Under FAS 115, fair value of an equity security is considered to be determinable if it is quoted in an organized trading exchange or, generally, in over-the-counter trading. Restricted stock is, by definition, not traded and hence fair values are not readily determinable, but stock that is subject to "Rule 144" or similar restrictions, which are due to expire within one year, is not deemed to be restricted for purposes of applying FAS 115. Stock traded only on foreign exchanges is included in the definition if the markets are comparable in breadth and scope to those in the US. Fair values for investments in mutual funds are generally considered to be determinable.

For available-for-sale equity securities, balance sheet presentation is identical to that for trading securities—current fair value. However, unless there has been a permanent impairment to the value of those securities, the change in fair value is excluded from earnings. Instead, the change in value is reported in a separate stockholders' equity account, with the current period's change in this account being included in other comprehensive income.

FAS 115 imposed this mode of reporting changes in the fair value of available-for-sale equity securities because of the expectation that most changes in investments intended to be held for an indeterminate period will experience predominantly temporary fluctuations that, over time, may tend to largely offset. Thus, the belief is that interim fluctuations in value would not necessarily be indicative of the long-term economic impact from holding the investments, and accordingly, that including these changes in earnings could be misleading.

While others have argued that the goal of periodic financial reporting should be to report the economic events of the period being presented, without concealing or "smoothing" the results, FASB ultimately agreed with those who favored the longer-term view. Notwithstanding substantial sentiment in favor of adopting a pure fair value approach, with gains and losses on all financial instruments being reported in current period earnings, FASB's deliberations resulted in a standard that preserved many attributes of traditional historical cost concepts; the subsequent adoption of FAS 130, requiring the display of comprehensive income, somewhat ameliorated the potentially misleading implications of omitting these changes from earnings. However, making the determination of the accounting for certain transactions dependent upon management intent, rather than on objectively verifiable circumstances, remains a concern for the accounting profession, as well as posing a challenge for auditors.

Example of accounting for investments in equity securities

Assume that Ralph Corporation purchases the following equity securities for investment purposes during 2005:

Security description	Acquisition cost	Value at year-end
1,000 sh. Bell Steel common	$ 34,500	$ 37,000
2,000 sh. Whammer pfd. "A"	125,000	109,500
1,000 sh. Hilltopper common	74,250	88,750

Assume that, at the respective dates of acquisition, management of Ralph Corporation designated the Bell Steel and Hilltopper investments as being for trading purposes, while the Whammer shares were designated as having been purchased for long term investment purposes. Accordingly, the entries to record the purchases were as follows:

Investment in equity securities—held-for-trading	108,750	
Cash		108,750
Investment in equity securities—available-for-sale	125,000	
Cash		125,000

At year-end, both portfolios are adjusted to fair market value; the decline in Whammer preferred stock, series A, is judged to be a temporary market fluctuation rather than a permanent decline. The entries to adjust the investment accounts at December 31, 2005, are

Investment in equity securities—held-for-trading	17,000	
Gain on holding equity securities		17,000
Unrealized loss on securities—available-for-sale (other comprehensive income)	15,500	
Investment in equity securities—available-for-sale		15,500

Thus, the change in value of the portfolio of trading securities is recognized in earnings, whereas the change in the value of the available-for-sale securities is reflected directly in stockholders' equity, after being reported in other comprehensive income.

Other than Temporary Impairments of Investments Available for Sale

Temporary changes in fair value of available-for-sale investments are reported in comprehensive income, not in earnings. *Other than temporary* impairments in value of equity securities classified as available-for-sale must be reflected in earnings. Absent an ability to demonstrate that a decline is temporary, the conclusion must be that the loss in value is other than temporary, in which case it must be recognized in income. Declines are measured at the individual security level and thus losses in one security's value cannot be offset by gains in another's value.

Once an other than temporary impairment is recognized, the reduced carrying amount becomes the new cost basis from which other increases or decreases in value are measured. Increases or decreases in value that are temporary are recognized in other comprehensive income and then included in stockholders' equity in accumulated other comprehensive income, not in earnings. Further other than temporary declines in value are recognized in earnings. Recoveries in value in available-for-sale securities that have previously suffered a decline that was judged to be other than temporary cannot be recognized in earnings until the investment is liquidated. The fact that an equity investment once suffered an other than temporary decline in value does not prevent a subsequent decline from being judged to be only temporary in character.

Assume now that in January 2006 new information comes to Ralph Corporation management regarding the viability of Whammer Corp. Based on this information, it is determined that the decline in Whammer preferred stock is probably not a temporary one, but rather is other than temporary (i.e., the asset is impaired). FAS 115 prescribes that such a decline be reflected in earnings, and the written down value be treated as the new cost basis. The fair value has remained at the amount last reported, $109,500. Accordingly, the entry to recognize the fact of the investment's permanent impairment is as follows:

Loss on holding equity securities	15,500	
Unrealized loss on securities—available-for-sale (other comprehensive income)		15,500

Any subsequent recovery in this value would not be recognized in earnings unless realized through a sale of the investment to an unrelated entity in an arm's-length transaction, as long as the investment continues to be categorized as "available-for-sale," as distinct from "held-for-trading." However, if there is an increase in value (not limited to just a recovery of the amount of the loss recognized above, of course) the increase will be added to the investment account and shown in a separate account in stockholders' equity, since the asset is to be marked to fair value on the balance sheet.

It should be noted that the issue of permanent impairment does not arise in the context of investments held-for-trading purposes, inasmuch as unrealized holding gains and losses are immediately recognized without limitation. In effect, the distinction between realized and unrealized gains or losses does not exist for trading securities. To illustrate this point, consider now that in March 2006 further information comes to management's attention, which now suggests that the decline in Whammer preferred was indeed only a temporary decline; in fact, the value of Whammer now rises to $112,000. Since the carrying value after the recognition of the impairment was $109,500, which is treated as the cost basis for purposes of measuring further declines or recoveries, the increase to $112,000 will be accounted for as an increase to be reflected in the additional stockholders' equity account, as follows:

Investment in equity securities—available-for-sale	2,500	
Unrealized gain on securities—available-for-sale (other comprehensive income)		2,500

Note that this increase in value is not taken into earnings, since the investment is still considered to be available-for-sale, rather than a part of the trading portfolio. Even though the previous decline in Whammer stock was realized in current earnings, because judged at the time to be a permanent impairment in value, the recovery cannot be recognized in earnings. Rather, the change in value will be included in other comprehensive income and then displayed in an additional equity account.

While the term "other than temporary" is used in the standards dealing both with passive investments (FAS 115) and those where significant influence over the investee exists (APB 18), this term is not actually defined in the authoritative literature. An EITF issue currently being discussed, 03-1, is attempting to determine the meaning of this oft-employed expression and to develop guidelines for ascertaining when such impairment has occurred. The proposed guidance includes the following underlying principle for determining whether an impairment is other than temporary: an impairment will be deemed other than temporary unless positive evidence indicating that an investment's carrying amount is recoverable within a reasonable period of time outweighs negative evidence to the contrary. In other words, it will be a refutable presumption that any impairment is other than temporary—and thus requires current recognition in income.

Transfers between Available-for-Sale and Trading Investments

A major reason for the development of FAS 115 was concern that under the prior rules there had been too many instances where management had been able to deliberately affect reported earnings by careful selection of portfolio securities to be sold in a given period. The practice, typically known as "gains trading," was widely blamed for misleading financial reporting, primarily by financial institutions (which generally hold much more substantial investment portfolios than do industrial enterprises). In a gains trading situation, reporting entities seeking additional earnings would sell securities from the nontrading portfolio having low carrying values versus current market values; since these had not previously been marked-to-market, the gain would be reported in current income. In a variation on this process, securities held in a trading account, but suffering declining value, would be transferred to a nontrading portfolio, thus averting a charge against earnings.

FAS 115 was intended to curtail the abuses described above. However, by basing accounting on management's expression of its intent, FAS 115 failed to fully preclude such abuses, apart from imposing more stringent limitations on transfers among classifications and prohibiting the use of the "held-to-maturity" classification once it has been "tainted" by sales out of that portfolio.

Under FAS 115, transfers from one of the three portfolio classifications to any other are expected to be very uncommon. Thus, securities purchased for the trading portfolio would be so classified because it was management's intent to seek advantage in short-term price movements; the fact that management does not in fact dispose of those investments quickly would not necessarily mean that the original categorization was improper or that an expressed changed intent should be honored by an accounting entry. While transfers out of the trading category are not completely prohibited, these would have to be supported by facts and circumstances making the assertion of changed intent highly credible.

Transfers among portfolios are accounted for at fair value as of the date of the transfer. Generally, investments in the trading category transferred to the available-for-sale category warrant no further recognition of gain or loss, as the investments have been marked to market value already. The only exception is that, if the investment accounts, as a practical matter, have not been updated for fair values since the latest balance sheet date, any changes since that time will need to be recognized at the date the transfer occurs. The fair value at the date of transfer becomes the new "cost" of the equity security to the available-for-sale portfolio.

To illustrate, consider Ralph Corporation's investment in Hilltopper common stock, which was assigned to the trading portfolio and at December 31, 2005, was marked to fair value of $88,750. Assume that in April 2006 management now determines that this investment will not be traded, but rather will continue to be held indefinitely. Under the criterion established by FAS 115, this investment now belongs in the available-for-sale portfolio. Assume also that the value at the date this decision is made is $92,000, and that no book adjustments have been made since the one that recognized the value increase to $88,750. The entry to record the transfer from the trading to the available-for-sale portfolio is

Investment in equity securities—available-for-sale	92,000	
Investment in equity securities—held-for-trading		88,750
Gain on holding equity securities		3,250

Unrealized gains and losses on trading securities are always recognized in income, and in this example the additional increase in fair value since the last "mark-to-market" adjustment, $3,250, is recognized at the time of the transfer to the available-for-sale portfolio. Further gains after this date, however, will not be recognized in earnings, but rather will be included in other comprehensive income per FAS 130.

For securities being transferred into the trading category, any unrealized gain or loss (recorded in the accumulated other comprehensive income account, as illustrated above) is deemed to be realized at the date of the transfer. Also, any fair value changes since the date of the most recent balance sheet may need to be recognized at this time. To illustrate, consider the investment in Whammer preferred stock, which was held in the available-for-sale portfolio, and which in March 2006 was adjusted to a fair value of $112,000 (as illustrated above). The increase from adjusted cost ($109,500, after a permanent impairment in value had been recognized) was reflected in other comprehensive income, rather than in earnings, given that the security was not at the time being held for trading. Now assume that, in June 2006, a decision is made to try to sell the investment in the short term. This means that the holding of Whammer stock will be treated as being in the trading portfolio. Further, the value of the shares held at the date of this decision is $114,700. The entry to record the transfer from available-for-sale to trading and the "realization" of the increased value at that date is as follows:

Investment in equity securities—held-for-trading	114,700	
Unrealized gain on securities—available-for-sale (other comprehensive income)	2,500	
Investment in equity securities—available-for-sale		112,000
Gain on holding equity securities (an income statement account)		5,200

The recognized gain at the time of transfer, in this case, is the sum of the previously unrecognized gain that had been recorded in the additional equity account ($2,500) plus the further gain not yet given any recognition in the investor's financial statements ($2,700). Note that the elimination of the additional equity representing the previously reported unrealized gain will be included in comprehensive income in the current period as a debit, since the additional equity account is being reversed at this time. On the other hand, had there been a decline since the date of the last balance sheet, the gain to be recognized at the date of this transfer would have been the net of the previous, unrecognized gain, and the later loss; if the loss exceeded the earlier gain, a net loss would be recognized at this point. Any further gains or losses after the transfer to the trading portfolio will be handled as earlier described (i.e., recognized in income currently).

Presentation of Investments in Marketable Equity Securities

Investments in equity securities that are held for trading should be presented as current assets in classified balance sheets. Investments that are available for sale may be either current or noncurrent, depending upon the reporting entity's intentions. For purposes of reporting in the statement of cash flows, all purchases and sales of trading securities must be included in the operations section, while those of available-for-sale investments are to be shown as part of investing activities.

FAS 115 requires specific disclosures of the components of a reporting entity's portfolios of investments. For available-for-sale securities, a classification by type of security is necessary: equity securities will be grouped together in this disclosure, and thus distinguished from debt securities. Furthermore, aggregate fair values, gross unrealized holding gains and gross unrealized holding losses are also to be disclosed as of the date of each balance sheet being presented.

For each income statement presented, proceeds from the sales of available-for-sale securities and gross realized gains and losses must be disclosed. Further, the basis upon which the gains or losses were determined (e.g., average cost, specific identification, etc.) must be disclosed. In addition, the notes must identify gross gains or losses included in earnings resulting from transfers of securities from the available-for-sale to the trading portfolio, and the net change in unrealized gains or losses recognized by an adjustment of the accumulated other comprehensive income account.

Changes in Fair Value After the Balance Sheet Date

Under GAAP, events occurring after the balance sheet date are generally not reflected in the balance sheet. However, disclosure may be necessary if, absent that information, the user of the financial statements would be misled. While not addressed explicitly by FAS 115, presumably material changes in fair value occurring subsequent to the date of the balance sheet but prior to issuance of the financial statements should be disclosed.

Sometimes changes in value can be indicative of the underlying cause of the price fluctuations. Of most interest here would be declines in value of available-for-sale securities held at the balance sheet date which suggest that an "other than temporary" impairment has occurred. If the decline actually occurred after year-end as evidenced by a bankruptcy filing, then the event would be disclosed but not reflected in the year-end balance sheet. However, in some instances, the subsequent decline would be seen as a "confirming event" which provided evidence that the classification or other treatment of an item on the balance sheet was incorrect. Thus, if a decline in the fair value of available-for-sale securities at the balance sheet date had been accounted for as temporary (and hence reported in other comprehensive income) a further decline after the balance sheet date might suggest that the decline **as of the balance sheet date** had, in fact, been a permanent impairment. Note that any further value decline after year-end would not be recorded in the financial statements; the only question to be addressed is whether the decline that occurred **prior to year-end** should have been treated as a permanent impairment rather than as a temporary market fluctuation.

If it is clear that the impairment at year-end had, in fact, been other than temporary in nature, then the financial statements should be adjusted to reflect this loss in earnings. Absent sufficient basis to reach this conclusion, the appropriate course of action is to not adjust the statements, but merely to disclose the (material) change in fair value that occurred subsequent to year-end including, if appropriate, a statement to the effect that the later decline was deemed to be an other than temporary impairment, and will be reflected in the earnings of the next year's financial statements. It should also be made clear that the decline occurring prior to year-end was not considered to be an other than temporary impairment at that time.

The FASB staff noted that when an entity has decided to sell a security classified as available-for-sale having a fair value less than cost at year-end, and it does not reasonably expect a recovery in value before the sale is to occur, then a write-down for an other than temporary decline is prescribed. This would most obviously be necessary if the actual sales transaction, anticipated at year-end, occurs prior to the issuance of the financial statements.

Deferred Tax Effects of Changes in Fair Value of Marketable Equity Securities

Unrealized gains or losses on holdings of marketable securities are not recognized for income tax purposes until realized through a sale. Thus, the gains or losses that are included in the financial statements (either in the income statement or in other comprehensive income) are temporary differences as defined by FAS 109. Under this standard, the tax effects of all temporary differences are recognized in the financial statements as deferred tax benefits or deferred tax liabilities, with an additional requirement that an allowance be provided for deferred tax benefits that are "more likely than not" not going to be realized. Accordingly, adjustments to the carrying value of debt or equity investments included in either the trading or available-for-sale portfolios for changes in fair value will give rise to deferred taxes, as will any recognition of "other than temporary" declines in the value of debt securities being held to maturity.

For gains or losses recognized in connection with holdings of investments classified as trading, since the fair value changes are recognized in earnings currently, the deferred tax effects of those changes will also be presented in the income statement. For example, assume that Odessa Corp. purchased Zeta Company bonds as a short-term speculation, at a cost of $100,000. At year-end, the bonds had a fair value of $75,000. Odessa has a 40% effective tax rate. The entries to record the fair value adjustment and tax effect thereof are

Loss on holding of trading securities	25,000	
Investment in debt securities—trading portfolios		25,000
Deferred tax benefit	10,000	
Provision for income taxes		10,000

On the other hand, if the investment in Zeta Company bonds had been classified (at the date of acquisition, or subsequently if the intentions had been revised) as available-for-sale, the adjustment to fair value would have been reported in other comprehensive income, and not included in earnings. Accordingly, the tax effect of the adjustment would also have been included in other comprehensive income. The entries would have been as follows:

Unrealized loss on securities—available-for-sale	25,000	
Investment in debt securities—available-for-sale (other comprehensive income)		25,000
Deferred tax benefit	10,000	
Unrealized loss on securities—available-for-sale (other comprehensive income)		10,000

Finally, if the investment in Zeta Company bonds had been made with the intention and ability to hold to maturity, recognition of the decline in value would have depended upon whether it was judged to be temporary or other than temporary in nature. If the former, no recognition would be given to the decline, and hence there would be no deferred tax effect either. If deemed to be other than temporary, the investment would need to be written down, with the loss included in earnings. Accordingly, the tax effect would also be reported in the income statement. The entries would be as follows:

Loss on decline of securities—held-to-maturity	25,000	
Investment in debt securities—held-to-maturity		25,000
Deferred tax benefit	10,000	
Provision for income taxes		10,000

An other than temporary decline in value in securities available for sale would also have been recognized in earnings (not merely in other comprehensive income), and accordingly the tax effect of that loss would have been reported in earnings.

As with all other transactions or events giving rise to deferred tax assets, an evaluation must be made as to whether the entity would be "more likely than not" to ultimately realize the tax benefit so recorded. To the extent that it was concluded that some or all of the deferred tax asset would not be realized, an allowance would be recorded, with the offset being either to the current tax provision (if the tax effect of the timing difference was reported in earnings) or to other comprehensive income (if the tax effect had been reported there).

Deferred taxes will also be recorded in connection with unrealized gains recognized due to changes in the fair value of debt or equity investments. Deferred tax liabilities will be reported in the balance sheet, and the corresponding tax provision will be reported in the income statement (for fair value gains arising from holdings of securities in the trading portfolio) or in other comprehensive income (for value changes relative to available-for-sale investments).

Accounting for Investments in Debt Securities

Historically, accounting for marketable investments in debt securities was not well developed in the professional literature. In fact, the principal guidance concerning long-term investments in debt instruments was found in ARB 43, which stipulated that the amortized **cost method** be used, absent a substantial, other than temporary decline in value.

FAS 115 applies to both equity and debt instruments held as investments, and prescribes fair market value accounting for all except debt instruments being held to maturity. For those investments, amortized historical cost is generally preserved as the measurement principle.

FAS 115 requires that investments in debt securities be classified upon acquisition as belonging to one of three portfolios: trading, available-for-sale, or held-to-maturity. The first of these is characterized by frequent purchase and sale activities, with the general objective of realizing profits from short-term price movements, which in the case of investments in debt instruments will largely be the result of changes in market interest rates but which may also be affected by market perceptions of credit risk. Since intention is the prime criterion applied, even a paucity of sales activity does not necessarily mean that specific debt securities acquired during a period do not belong in the trading portfolio.

The held-to-maturity category is the most restrictive of the three; debt instruments can be so classified only if the reporting entity has both the positive intent and the ability to hold the securities for that length of time. A mere intent to hold an investment for an indefinite period is not adequate to permit such a classification. On the other hand, a variety of isolated causes may necessitate transferring an investment in a debt security from the held-to-maturity category without calling into question the investor's general intention to hold other similarly classified investments to maturity. Among these are declines in the creditworthiness of a particular investment's issuer or a change in tax law or regulatory rules. On the other hand, sales of investments that were classified as held-to-maturity for other reasons will raise doubts about the entity's assertions regarding these and other similarly categorized securities. For this reason, transfers from or sales of held-to-maturity securities will be very rare indeed.

Accounting for debt securities that are held for trading and those that are available for sale is based on fair value. For balance sheet purposes, increases or decreases in value are reflected by adjustments to the asset account; such adjustments are to be determined on an individual security basis. Changes in the values of debt securities in the trading portfolio are recognized in earnings immediately, while most changes in the values of debt securities in the available-for-sale category are reported in other comprehensive income rather than being included in earnings. The only exception is for declines that are deemed to be other than temporary, in which case the loss is recognized currently in earnings. Once the investment is written down for a decline that is other than temporary, subsequent increases are reported only in changes to the contra equity account; increases cannot be accounted for as "recoveries" of previous declines. (See "Other than Temporary Impairments of Investments Available for Sale" in the discussion of equity investments, above, for an example.)

There had been some confusion regarding the applicability of FAS 115, which was resolved by the issuance of FTB 94-1. The problem arose from the "grandfathering" provision of FAS 114, permitting debt restructured prior to that standard's effective date to be accounted for consistent with the provisions of FAS 15, which FAS 114 superseded. The concern was that this might have suggested that FAS 115 could not be applied to restructured loans that qualified as debt securities. However, FTB 94-1 made it clear that FAS 115 applies to all loans which qualify as debt securities, and that the "grandfathering" provision would not be applicable in such circumstances. In other words, the provisions of FAS 115 take precedence over those of FAS 114, in situations where FAS 115 applies.

Presentation in the Financial Statements

Trading securities must always be grouped with current assets in classified balance sheets, and held-to-maturity investments will be noncurrent (unless the maturity date is within one year). Available-for-sale securities may conceivably be classified as either current or noncurrent.

If declines in value are deemed to meet FAS 115's definition of other than temporary, then these are to be included in earnings in the current period. However, subsequent recoveries cannot be recognized in earnings. If available-for-sale investments are written down for such impairments that later reverse, the recovery is accounted for as an increase in fair value to be reflected in other comprehensive income account on the balance sheet only. If held-to-maturity investments are similarly written down and later recover some or all of the lost value, the fair value increase will not be reported in the balance sheet at all, although disclosure will generally be made in the notes.

For purposes of reporting in the statement of cash flows, all purchases and sales of trading securities must be included in the operations section, while those of available-for-sale and held-to-maturity investments are to be shown as part of investing activities.

FAS 115 requires specific disclosures of the components of a reporting entity's portfolios of investments. For available-for-sale securities and (separately) for **held-to-maturity securities,** classification by type of security is necessary; categories of issuers, such as US Treasury, other US agencies, state and municipal governmental units, foreign governmental units, corporations, mortgage-backed, and others are suggested. Aggregate fair values, gross unrealized holding gains, and gross unrealized holding losses must also be disclosed, by major security type, as of the date of each balance sheet being presented.

For the available-for-sale and held-to-maturity portfolios, information about contractual maturities must be presented as of the date of the latest balance sheet presented and must be grouped into at least four categories: within one year; one to five years; five to ten years; and, over ten years. Both fair values and amortized cost of debt securities in each maturity category must be presented.

For each income statement presented, proceeds from the sales of available-for-sale securities, and the gross realized gains and losses therefrom, also must be disclosed. Further, the basis upon which the gains or losses were determined, (e.g., average cost, specific identification, etc.) must be disclosed. In addition, the notes must identify gross gains or losses included in earnings resulting from transfers of securities from the available-for-sale to the trading portfolio, and the net change in unrealized gains or losses recognized by an adjustment of the contra equity account.

For sales or transfers from securities categorized as held-to-maturity, the amortized cost amounts, the related gains or losses realized or unrealized, and the circumstances surrounding the decision to sell or to reclassify the investment, are all to be disclosed in the notes to the financial statements for each period for which an income statement is being presented. There is, of course, a presumption that sales or transfers from the held-to-maturity portfolio will be rare occurrences.

Transfers of Debt Securities among Portfolios

Transfers of any given security between classifications is accounted for at fair market value. If the transfer is from the trading portfolio, there is no further income statement effect since the fair market value-based gains or losses have already been reported. If the transfer is to the trading portfolio, the unrealized gain or loss is recognized immediately. Depending on whether the transfer is from the available-for-sale or the held-to-maturity category, such unrealized gain or loss would have been included in the accumulated other comprehensive income account on the balance sheet, after having been reported as an element of other comprehensive income, or would not have been reported at all prior to the transfer.

If the debt security is being transferred from held-to-maturity to the available-for-sale portfolio, the unrealized gain or loss, not previously reflected in the investment account, will be added to the appropriate accumulated other comprehensive income account at the date of transfer and reported in other comprehensive income. If a security is being transferred from available-for-sale to held-to-maturity, the unrealized holding gain or loss previously accrued will continue to be maintained in the accumulated other comprehensive income account, but now will be amortized to income over the period until maturity as an adjustment of yield, using the effective interest method. The fair value as of the date of transfer to the held-to-maturity classification, net of any subsequent amortization of the discrepancy between fair value and maturity or par value as of the transfer date, will be the "cost" for purposes of the disclosures required by FAS 115.

Example of accounting for debt securities

Marcy Corporation purchases the following debt securities as investments in 2005:

Issue	*Face value*	*Price paid**
Dukane Chemical 8% due 2009	$200,000	$190,000
Forwall Pharmaceutical 9.90% due 2021	500,000	575,000
Luckystrike Mining 4% due 2007	100,000	65,000

* *Accrued interest is ignored in these amounts; the normal entries for interest accrual and receipt are assumed.*

Management has informed us that Marcy's objectives differed among the various investments; the Dukane bonds are considered to be suitable as a long-term investment, with the intention that they will be held until maturity. The Luckystrike bonds are a speculation; the significant discount from par value was seen as very attractive, despite the low coupon rate. Management believes the bonds were depressed because mining stocks and bonds have been out of favor, but believes the economic recovery will lead to a surge in market value, at which point the bonds will be sold for a quick profit. The Forwall Pharmaceutical bonds are deemed a good investment, but with a maturity date sixteen years in the future, management is unable to commit to holding these to maturity.

Based on the foregoing, the appropriate accounting for the three investments in bonds would be as follows:

Dukane Chemical 8% due 2009

Account for these as held-to-maturity; maintain at historical cost, with discount ($10,000) to be amortized over term to maturity (assumed to be four years, for an amortization of $2,500 per year).

Forwall Pharmaceutical 9.90% due 2021

Account for these as available-for-sale, since neither the held-for-trading nor held-to-maturity criteria apply. These should be reported at fair market value at each balance sheet date, with any unrealized gain or loss included in the additional/contra equity account, unless an "other than temporary" decline occurs.

Luckystrike Mining 4% due 2007

As an admitted speculation, these should be accounted for as part of the trading portfolio, and also reported at fair market value on the balance sheet. All adjustments to carrying value will be included in earnings each year, whether the fluctuations are temporary or permanent in nature.

Transfers between portfolio categories are to be accounted for at fair market value at the date of the transfer. Consider the following events.

1. Marcy management decides in 2006, when the Forwall bonds have a market (fair) value of $604,500, that the bonds will be disposed of in the short term, hopefully when the price hits $605,000. The bonds are presently carried on the books at $580,000, which was the fair value at the time the year-end 2005 financial statements were being prepared. Based on this description of the decision, the bonds should be transferred to the trading portfolio at a "cost" of $604,500. The entry to record this would be the following:

Investment in debt securities—held-for-trading	604,500	
Unrealized gain on holding debt securities as investment	5,000	
Investment in debt securities—available-for-sale		580,000
Gain on holding debt securities		29,500

The previously unrealized gain (reflected in the write-up of the investment from original cost, $575,000, to the fair market value at year-end 2005, $580,000) is now "realized" for financial reporting purposes, as is the further rise in value from $580,000 to $604,500 at the time the portfolio transfer takes place.

2. Assume that at year-end 2005 the investment in the Forwall bonds is still held, and the fair value has declined to $602,000. Management's intentions regarding this holding have not changed since the decision to transfer to held-for-trading. The year-end adjustment will be

Loss on holding debt securities	2,500	
Investment in debt securities—held-for-trading		2,500

The market decline is reflected in earnings in 2005, since the bonds are in the held-for-trading portfolio.

3. Now, assume that in 2006, management determines that a major investment in plant renewal and expansion will likely be necessary by the year 2008, based on a detailed capital budget prepared. With this in mind, Marcy Corporation determines that the holding of Forwall Pharmaceutical bonds would be an excellent vehicle to provide for these future cash needs, and accordingly concludes to hold these to maturity. At the time this decision is made, the fair market value of the bonds is quoted at $603,000. The entry to record the transfer from held-for-trading to held-to-maturity is as follows:

Investment in debt securities—held-to-maturity	603,000	
Investment in debt securities held-for-trading		602,000
Gain on holding debt securities		1,000

The bonds are again transferred at fair market value, which in this case gives rise to a $1,000 recognized gain.

4. In 2006 Marcy management also made a decision about its investment in Dukane Chemical bonds. These bonds, which were originally designated as held-to-maturity, were accounted for at amortized historical cost. Assume the amortization in 2005 was $2,000 (because the bonds were not held for a full year), so that the book value of the investment at year-end 2005 was $192,000. In 2006, at a time when the value of these bonds was $198,000, management concluded that it was no longer certain that they would be held to maturity, and therefore transferred this holding to the available-for-sale portfolio. The entry to record this would be

Investment in debt securities—available-for-sale	198,000	
Unrealized gain on holding debt securities as investment		6,000
Investment in debt securities—held-to-maturity		192,000

The transfer is at fair market value, but since the bonds are being transferred into the available-for-sale category (for which unrealized gains and losses are recorded in an additional or contra equity account), the gain at this date, $6,000, is not recognized in earnings, but rather will be reported in other comprehensive income.

5. In 2007, for the same reason management determined to hold the Forwall Pharmaceuticals bonds to maturity, it also reverses its prior decision regarding the Dukane Chemical bond holding. It now professes an intention to hold these until their maturity, in 2009. At the date this decision is made, the Dukane bonds are quoted at $195,000. Assume that the fair market value at year-end 2006 had been $198,000, so no adjustment was needed at that time to the carrying value of the investment. Again the transfer will be recorded at fair market value.

Investment in debt securities—held-to-maturity	195,000	
Unrealized gain on holding debt securities as investment	3,000	
Investment in debt securities—available-for-sale		198,000

The unrealized gain previously recognized in an equity account is partially eliminated, since fair value at the date of this transfer is less than the previously recorded amount. The change in this equity account must be reported as other comprehensive income for the period in which this portfolio reclassification occurs. The remaining balance in the additional/contra equity account (whether a net debit or credit) is accounted for as **additional** premium or discount, and is amortized over the remaining term to maturity. GAAP mandates that the effective yield method be used, but for this example, assume that the discount will be amortized over the remaining two years on the straight-line basis (if this difference from the effective yield method is not material, it is an acceptable practice). Thus, the actual discount as measured by the spread between the new carrying value, $195,000, and face value to be received at maturity, $200,000, **plus the additional discount** measured by the unrealized gain reported in the equity section of $3,000, gives a total discount amounting to $8,000 to be amortized over the remaining two years. This $8,000, when added to the $2,000 discount amortized in 2006 (when the bonds were in the original held-to-maturity portfolio), equals $10,000, which is the discount between the face value, $200,000 and the price paid by Marcy Corporation ($190,000).

Note that the illustrated reclassification of the Dukane Chemical bonds from the held-to-maturity to the available-for-sale portfolios would, in most instances, have serious adverse consequences for Marcy. Under FAS 115, classification as held-to-maturity can only occur when, at acquisition, management has both the intent and the ability to maintain the investment until maturity. A sale prior to maturity is taken as an indication that its intent was not truly present, and accordingly, use of the held-to-maturity classification for any other investments will be precluded, unless the sale before maturity is precipitated by certain events. These are

1. Evidence of a substantial deterioration in the issuer's creditworthiness, placing the entity at jeopardy from any further holding of the investment
2. A tax law change affecting the tax-exempt status of the investment holding
3. A major business acquisition or disposition necessitating portfolio changes to maintain the entity's interest rate risk posture
4. For banks or thrifts, a change in regulatory capital requirements such that a significant downsizing is necessitated, including disposition of the bond portfolio, and
5. A significant increase in risk weighting (under bank and thrift capital rules) of the held-to-maturity investments, again necessitating dispositions of these investments

Other isolated, nonrecurring, and unusual events and circumstances might also suffice to justify disposal of these investments without "tainting" the remaining held-to-maturity portfolio or precluding its future use by the entity, but these would be rare occurrences.

While a transfer from the held-to-maturity to the available-for-sale portfolios would not be a sale, it would be demonstrative of an intent or willingness to dispose of the investment, which would be equally suggestive of an earlier misrepresentation of management's intent regarding those investments. While FAS 115 is silent on this, the same strictures affecting an outright sale of these portfolio investments should be assumed to apply to a transfer to the available-for-sale category. In other words, while not prohibited, such transfers would be very rare and carry an accounting risk for the reporting entity.

Implications of Accounting for Investments on Reporting of Comprehensive Income

Under the provisions of FAS 130, there is expanded reporting of the changes in items (other than investments by or distributions to owners) that are reported in the equity section of the balance sheet. Among these items are unrealized gains or losses on securities held in the available-for-sale portfolio, and accordingly **changes** in these gains or losses must be reported in the statement of comprehensive income or via the other allowable reporting mechanisms described in Chapter 3. These changes may be reported net of tax or gross, with the tax effect separately presented within other comprehensive income.

The major complicating factor arising from reporting changes in the unrealized gains or losses of available-for-sale securities derives from the "recycling" of gains or losses when the underlying securities are later sold or transferred into the trading portfolio; either of these events necessitates recognition of the entire gain or loss in earnings, including any unrealized gain or loss that might have previously been reported in other comprehensive income (but not in earnings). To avoid "double counting" the gain or loss, the amount of gain or loss previously reported in other comprehensive income must be reversed simultaneously with the recognition in earnings.

To illustrate the "recycling" problem, consider an investment by Zenobia Co. in $500,000 face amount of Vaught Corp. bonds due July 1, 2015, carrying coupons of 8%. The purchase, for a total of $530,000, occurs on July 1, 2005, and the bonds are deemed available for sale, as defined by FAS 115. Per that standard, periodic interest income must be computed by the effective yield method based on the acquisition cost (i.e., the face value net of any premium or discount), but the difference, if any, between amortized cost and fair value as of the balance sheet date must be reported as a contra or additional equity account, with changes being taken into other comprehensive income for the period.

The yield to maturity on the Zenobia bonds is approximately 7.15%; for simplicity, the premium will be amortized straight-line ($1,500 per semiannual interest payment period) in this example, rather than by the effective yield method as is actually required.

Assume that the bonds have a fair value of $522,000 as of year-end 2005 and $527,000 as of year-end 2006. As of March 31, 2007, the value of the bonds is $528,000, at which time they are in fact sold.

Given the foregoing, as of December 31, 2005, the amortized cost basis of the investment would be $530,000 – $1,500 = $528,500. Since the fair value at that date is $522,000, an unrealized loss of $528,500 – $522,000 = $6,500 must be recorded in other comprehensive income, before any tax effects (which will be ignored here, again for simplicity). Interest income for the half-year ended December 31, 2005, was $20,000 – $1,500 = $18,500 under the simplifying assumption of straight-line amortization, and this would be included in earnings.

At year-end 2006, the bonds have an amortized cost basis of $528,500 – $3,000 = $525,500 vs. a fair value of $527,000. Interest income for the year ended December 31, 2006, included in earnings, was $40,000 – $3,000 = $37,000. A **positive** adjustment (i.e., income) of $8,000 must be reported in other comprehensive income for 2006 in order to carry the bonds at fair value as of the year-end.

For the three-month period ended March 31, 2007, further premium amortization of $750 must be recorded (along with an interest accrual), which will reduce the bond's amortized cost basis to $525,500 – $750 = $524,750 as of the date of the sale, which is made at the market value of $528,000. For purposes of reporting results of operations for the quarter ended March 31, 2007, a positive other comprehensive income adjustment of $1,750 must be reflected—this is necessary to bring the carrying value of the bonds up to their fair value as of that date. However, since the bonds are sold and a realized gain of $3,250 is to be reported in earnings, a "reclassification adjustment" of the same amount must be included as a **negative** (i.e., expense) item in other comprehensive income for that period, which will thus cause the **net** other comprehensive income item pertaining to the bonds held in the available-for-sale portfolio to be a **negative** $1,500 for the period ended March 31, 2007.

The foregoing is summarized in the following table (it is assumed that the 2007 transaction is reported at year-end):

Zenobia Co.
Selected Portions of Combined Statements of Earnings and Comprehensive Income
(ignoring tax effects)
December 31, 2005, 2006, and 2007

December 31, 2005

	$ --
Other income and expense:	
Interest income (net of premium amortization, $1,500)	18,500
	--
Net earnings	--

Other comprehensive income:		
Unrealized loss on bonds available for sale		(6,500)
Total other comprehensive income		--
Comprehensive income		$ --
December 31, 2006		
		$ --
Other income and expense:		
Interest income (net of premium amortization, $3,000)		37,000
		--
Net earnings		--
Other comprehensive income:		
Unrealized gain on bonds available for sale		8,000
Total other comprehensive income		--
Comprehensive income		$ --
December 31, 2007		
		$ --
Other income and expense:		
Interest income (net of premium amortization, $750)		9,250
Gain on sale of bonds		3,250
		--
Net earnings		--
Other comprehensive income:		
Unrealized loss on bonds available for sale	1,750	
Less: Reclassification adjustment for gain realized on sale	(3,250)	(1,500)
Total other comprehensive income		--
Comprehensive income		$ --

Disclosure of Fair Value Information

The basic disclosure requirements pertaining to investments in debt and marketable equity securities are set forth in FAS 107 and 115. FAS 133 contains certain amendments to FAS 107, primarily with regard to disclosures of concentrations of credit risk and the optional disclosures that are encouraged concerning market risk. It should be noted that, since under FAS 115 both trading and available-for-sale investments are marked to fair value, the impact of FAS 107 is largely felt on investments in the held-to-maturity portfolio; even though these are maintained at amortized historical cost, per FAS 107 fair value information must also be presented, and this is typically accomplished via the informative notes to the financial statements, although it can also be presented on the face of the financials, parenthetically. (Per FAS 126, nonpublic entities having under $100 million in total assets are exempted from these extended disclosure requirements, however.)

Certain Loans or Debt Securities Acquired in Transfers

The preceding discussion has not differentiated between securities investments acquired directly from the issuer and those obtained on the secondary market, since this distinction has not heretofore held implications for financial reporting. However, a new accounting standard, SOP 03-3, *Accounting for Certain Loans or Debt Securities Acquired in a Transfer*, imposes for the first time new accounting requirements for debt instruments acquired in transfers when the purchase price reflects a change in the debtor's credit standing since the original issuance of the instrument. This standard is applicable to **all** acquirers of loans or debt securities (bonds, securitized loans, etc.), not merely financial institutions, although relatively fewer of commercial or industrial entities would tend to be making such purchases.

Debt instruments (whole loans or loan participations, as well as securities) will generally trade in the secondary market at prices that vary from the amount at which they were issued originally. The prices may be higher or lower than the face amount, depending on the confluence of several factors. Because interest rates change almost continually, it is rare that market rates will correspond to the nominal rate on any given loan or debt security, even if the loan or instrument originally carried a market yield. Furthermore, many instruments are issued at premiums or discounts at inception, for various reasons. In the secondary market, prices will be adjusted continually to reflect current market conditions as they pertain to the loan's (or security's) **coupon rate** and the credit standing of the issuer/borrower, within the context of market rates of interest and other factors. If current rates are higher than the instrument's coupon (i.e., contractual) rate, it will trade at a discount from par value, while if the current rates are below the coupon rate, it will sell for a premium, if other variables are held constant.

Furthermore, the borrower's creditworthiness may well have changed since the loan was originated or the debt instrument was issued. This also impacts the price at which the loan or security will trade, with a decline in credit standing resulting in a drop in value, and an improvement in credit standing causing a rise in the value of the entity's debt. Creditworthiness pertains to the risk of default, and a number of well-regarded private sector companies closely monitor the outstanding debt of publicly held and private corporations and various governmental agencies and political subdivisions. Examples of rating agencies or measures are Moody's, Standard & Poor's and Fitch's, for publicly held companies and the Fair Isaac credit score for private companies.

Yields on debt instruments may also vary because of macrolevel factors, such as market concerns over industry developments, rather than a change in a given issuer's specific risk of default or a change in general interest rates. For example, during the telecom industry bust of the late 1990s and early 2000s, even well-regarded entities saw prices of their traded debt securities drop substantially due to industry-wide concerns.

Loans or debt securities may trade in the secondary market at their original issuance prices as the coincidental result of offsetting changes in the above-noted variables. Thus, market yields may have declined—which, taken alone, would cause a rise in the price of fixed coupon debt instruments—but concurrently the issuer's creditworthiness may have been reassessed downward by rating agencies—which, absent other events, would cause the price of the debt to decline. In tandem, the credit downgrade may have essentially negated the price response to lower market interest rates. In applying SOP 03-3, it is necessary to refer not simply to the price at which the loan or security has been transferred, in relation to its "par" or original issuance price, but also to examine whether there is information to suggest that there has been a change in the issuer's credit quality since inception of the obligation. Only in the latter circumstance will the provisions of this new standard be applied.

SOP 03-3 in greater detail. The purpose of SOP 03-3 is to prescribe the accounting for debt instruments (comprising most loans and debt securities, with certain exceptions) which are acquired via a transfer (i.e., in the secondary market) and which have been affected by changes in credit quality. The standard requires that the **accretable yield** be determined. This is derived from the relationship between the future cash flows expected to be collected and the price paid for the acquired instrument. The accretable yield is distinguished from the **nonaccretable difference,** which is generally the excess of the total of contractual future cash flows over the expected cash flows.

Neither the accretable yield nor the nonaccretable difference can be displayed in the financial statements. For example, consider a loan that contractually is obligated to pay a total of $85,000 in future interest and principal, but which can be purchased for $50,000 and is expected to provide future cash flows of only $73,500. The $23,500 ($73,500 – 50,000) spread between the purchase price and the undiscounted expected future cash flows is the accretable yield. The further $11,500 ($85,000 – 73,500) spread between expected and contractual cash flows, however, is the nonaccretable difference, which cannot be given accounting recognition under SOP 03-3. That is, the loan (which is an investment in the hands of the transferee) cannot be recorded or displayed at the higher, $85,000 amount, with a contra account or valuation allowance pertaining to the pretransfer estimated uncollectible amount being reported. Instead, the purchase cost, $50,000, must be the initial representation of this acquired asset, which is later increased by virtue of the accretion of yield (and reduced by collections).

While SOP 03-3 applies to loans and debt securities, there are important exceptions. Derivative instruments are excluded entirely from the scope of the standard, although debt instruments that contain embedded derivatives are not excluded. Also, debt securities that are accounted for at fair value with changes taken into income currently (i.e., those held in trading portfolios) are exempted, since these are not accreted to face value or to an expected level of future cash flows. Similarly, since changes in the fair values of trading and available-for-sale securities held by not-for-profit organizations both are reflected currently in the changes in net assets (the parallel performance measure for not-for-profit entities, roughly corresponding to net income), these are also exempted. Mortgage loans classified by mortgage bankers as held-for-sale (and presented at fair value) are also exempted from the provisions of SOP 03-3.

SOP 03-3 applies to both specific acquisitions of loans or debt securities (e.g., purchases of single loans, pools of loans, or debt securities) and to acquisitions as part of a business combination accounted for under FAS 141. In the case of business acquisitions, while it was sometimes observed in past practice that the gross amount of the loan would be recorded, together with a contra or valuation allowance for the estimated uncollectible portion, this is no longer permitted. SOP 03-3 is explicit that "carryover" of the selling entity's book values is not permitted. A new cost basis is established and, at the date of acquisition, the asset (investment) must reflect the actual cost of the loan or other instrument, without any "grossing up" and without any contra asset being recorded. Any valuation allowance (contra asset) provided *after* acquisition will reflect only the change in value occurring after that date. The transferee's valuation allowance cannot include any changes in value arising while the asset was in the hands of the former owner/transferor of the loan or security.

Upon acquisition the effective yield is to be computed, based on the expected pattern (i.e., timings and amounts) of future cash flows, so that interest can be accreted on the **level-yield** basis (a constant rate on a changing base). Over the holding term of the investment, expected cash flows may be altered: they may decline due to perceived impairment or may increase due to upgrading of creditworthiness. The accounting for such changes will vary, with decreases in expectations triggering immediate impairment loss recognition, while increases will generally be reported prospectively over the holding period of the instrument. The precise accounting for changes in expected future cash flows also depends, per SOP 03-3, on whether the instrument is accounted for as a loan (under FAS 114), or as a debt security (under FAS 115). These matters are addressed in the following sections.

SOP 03-3 amends PB 6, *Amortization of Discounts on Certain Acquired Loans*, which provided similar guidance. However, under PB 6, changes in expected future cash collections for qualifying loans (described below) resulted in changes to yields recognized prospectively, whereas under the newly established guidance of SOP 03-3, reductions in expected future cash flows will trigger the recognition of a loss in the current reporting period.

Accounting for investments in loans acquired by transfers. Loans acquired by transfer (i.e., in the secondary market) are recorded initially at acquisition cost, consistent with a fundamental tenet of GAAP. If the acquisition price differs from the par or face amount (i.e., there is a premium or a discount) the effective yield has to be computed and used to accrete the discount (or, if a premium, amortize it) over the expected term of the instrument. This process is well established under GAAP and is not new with SOP 03-3.

However, if there is evidence of a decline in creditworthiness since the instrument's inception, such that it is deemed probable at the date of transfer that the full amount of contractual cash flows will not be received, the provisions of SOP 03-3 must be applied. In this context, **probable** is used in the same way as it is under FAS 5, and only if that rather high threshold criterion is satisfied will this standard be invoked. In such cases, the transferee must estimate cash flows to be received, and accrete the initial carrying amount to that amount, rather than to the gross amount of future contractual cash flows. An uncertainty regarding future cash flows that suggests only a **possible** shortfall versus contractual amounts owed would not qualify under the standard for the accounting set forth in this discussion. (In such a situation, there would be disclosure of reasonably possible contingent losses, and if at a later date the loss is deemed to have become probable, a loss accrual would be recognized per FAS 5.)

The estimation of the amounts of expected future cash flows, and the timing of those cash flows, is obviously a matter of some complexity and inevitable subjectivity. For example, if payments from a credit-impaired obligor are expected to be made, say, fifteen days late on average, this will impact the computed effective yield on the loan and should be given explicit consideration in ascertaining the effective yield, subject to the usual materiality threshold concerns. The calculation of accretable yield is made at the acquisition date, but, as described below, may later have to be adjusted as expectations regarding future cash flow amounts change. Subsequent reduced expectations of cash flows will result in the recognition of impairment, while expectations of enhanced or improved cash flows may result in reversal of previously recognized impairment (if any), or increased effective yield over the instrument's remaining holding period.

Basic example

Assume that Investor Co. acquires a loan with a remaining principal balance of $650,000 on January 1, 2005. The contractual terms of the loan call for interest-only payments, at 9%, annually through December 31, 2009, at which time the full principal balance is due. The debtor's credit rating has been reduced subsequent to the initiation of the borrowing, and the 2004 interest payment was not made when due. Investor Co. pays $500,000 (flat) for the loan and any unpaid interest. The expectation is that the debtor will pay $40,000 at the end of 2005, $60,000 at the end of years 2006 and 2007 (each year), $70,000 at the end of 2008, and $600,000 at the end of 2009. Total projected cash inflows, $830,000, are lower than the contractually due amount, $1,001,000 (including the arrearage for 2004), and the effective yield will be about 12.6%. At transfer, the investment is recorded at cost, as follows:

Investment in loan receivable	500,000	
Cash		500,000

At the end of 2005, immediately prior to receipt of the payment, the entry to record the accretion for the year, at the effective yield, is

Investment in loan receivable	62,974	
Accretion (interest income)		62,974

The collection of the anticipated amount at December 31, 2005, is recorded thusly

Cash	40,000	
Investment in loan receivable		40,000

Entries for subsequent years' accretion and collections would follow in the same manner. This presumes, of course, that amounts expected to be received indeed are received, and that expectations about the future receipts do not depart from what had been anticipated when the loan was purchased.

The changes in carrying amount and recognition of income over the full five-year period are illustrated in the following chart.

	A	*B*	*C*	*D*	*E*
Year ending December 31	*Beginning carrying amount*	*Cash flows expected to be collected*	*Interest income*	*Reduction (increase) in carrying amount (B–C)*	*Ending carrying amount of loan (A–D)*
2005	$500,000	$ 40,000	$ 62,974	$ (22,974)	$522,974
2006	522,974	60,000	65,867	(5,867)	528,841
2007	528,841	60,000	66,606	(6,606)	535,447
2008	535,447	70,000	67,438	2,562	532,885
2009	532,885	600,000	67,115	532,885	--
		$830,000	$330,000	$500,000	

It will be observed in the foregoing chart that total cash collected, $830,000, consisted of $330,000 in interest, accreted at the 12.6% computed yield, and $500,000 return of investment in the loan receivable. This should be contrasted with the examples that follow.

Example with decrease in expected cash flows

If, subsequent to acquisition and computation of effective yield, the expected cash flows associated with a loan are revised downward, SOP 03-3 directs that this be accounted for as an impairment, with the adjustment being such that the previously determined yield percentage is maintained in future periods by applying the constant return to a downwardly adjusted carrying value. While some might argue that a diminished expectation of cash flows would imply a new, lower rate of return, SOP 03-3 instead opts for recognizing an immediate impairment, measured as the then-present value of the stream of cash flow shortfalls being projected. This results in a continuing rate of return equal to the original estimate, but with a step-down in the carrying value of the loan.

To illustrate, using the same basic facts above, assume now that immediately after the 2007 payment is made, Investor Co., revises its expectation of cash flows to be received in 2008 and 2009. It now anticipates zero cash collection in 2008, and only $500,000 at year-end 2009. The present value of these shortfalls—a $70,000 shortage one year hence, followed by a $100,000 shortfall two years later—discounted at the 12.6% yield on the investment computed at the date of transfer, reveals an impairment of $141,039 as of the start of 2008. The entry to record this, given that the investment is treated as a loan rather than as a debt security, is as follows:

Bad debt expense	141,039	
Allowance for uncollectible loan receivable		141,039

The reduced net carrying value of the loan receivable, which is $394,408 immediately following this adjustment, will continue to accrete at 12.6%, as the following table illustrates:

	A	*B*	*C*	*D*	*E*
Year ending December 31	*Beginning carrying amount of loan*	*Cash flows expected to be collected*	*Interest income*	*Reduction (increase) in carrying amount (B–C)*	*Ending carrying amount of loan (A–D)*
2005	$500,000	$ 40,000	$ 62,974	$ (22,974)	$522,974
2006	522,974	60,000	65,867	(5,867)	528,841
2007	528,841	60,000	66,606	(6,606)	
2007*				141,039	394,408
2008	394,408	--	49,675	(49,675)	444,083
2009	444,083	500,000	55,917	444,083	--
		$660,000	$301,039	$500,000	

* *Provision of allowance for estimated uncollectible future cash flows, computed at present value using the effective yield on the loan.*

It will be observed in the foregoing chart that total cash collected, $660,000, consisted of $301,039 in interest, accreted at the 12.6% computed yield, and the recovery of only $358,961 of the $500,000 investment in the loan receivable. In other words, SOP 03-3 treats the decrease in expected cash flows as a loss of principal, accounted for as a bad debt and a provision of a valuation allowance against the $500,000 loan receivable. Note that the decreased cash flow expectation was *not* accounted for as a lowered future return on the investment (which would have resulted in lower interest income recognition in years 2008 and 2009, in this example, coupled with a full recovery of the principal invested).

Example with decrease in expected cash flows followed by increase in expected cash flows (recovery of uncollectible loan receivable)

If Investor Co., above, first lowers its expectation regarding future cash flows and then partially reverses its estimate, so that some or all (but not more than all) of the allowance of the uncollectible loan receivable proves unneeded, this is accounted for under SOP 03-3 as a reversal of the valuation allowance account (i.e., as a change in an accounting estimate).

To illustrate, consider again the facts in the basic example, and now assume that in 2007 Investor Co. has the expectation that no interest will be collected in 2008 and that only $500,000 will be collected in 2009. In 2008, however, $20,000 is in fact collected, and Investor Co. then expects a full collection of the $600,000 in 2009 (but no recovery of the $50,000 missed payment in 2008).

The entry to record the reduced expectation of future cash flows at the end of 2006 or beginning of 2007 is as shown previously.

Bad debt expense	141,039	
Allowance for uncollectible loan receivable		141,039

In 2008, the collection of the $20,000 (when no collection at all was anticipated) coupled with the renewed expectation of collecting $600,000 in 2009 required that some of the previously provided valuation allowance be reversed. The amount of valuation allowance to be restored, per SOP 03-3, is that amount which will result in interest accretion thereafter at the previously determined 12.6% yield through the final collection of the loan. Assuming that the $20,000 collection in December 2008 came as a surprise, the adjustment will be computed with reference to the final remaining collection, $600,000, expected in December 2009, and to the $20,000 unexpected 2008 collection.

The entry to partially restore the carrying value of the loan, net of the valuation allowance, is as follows:

Allowance for uncollectible loan receivable	108,802	
Bad debt expense		108,802

The computation of the foregoing amount may be somewhat confusing, unless one keeps in mind that the objective of SOP 03-3 is to provide for the reporting of interest income over the full carrying term of the loan receivable, at a constant rate on a changing balance, with that rate being the rate computed at the date of transfer. The only exception, which will be illustrated later in this section, is for situations where the total cash to be collected exceeds the estimate made at the date of transfer; in that case, a higher rate of return is reported in periods after the change in estimate, to avoid the alternative of reporting a gain at the date the new estimate is made. In this example, the anticipated "extra" 2009 collection of $100,000 ($600,000 – $500,000) has a present value at the end of 2008 of $88,802, so this previously provided valuation allowance is no longer needed. Furthermore, the $20,000 collection in 2008 was unexpected, and had previously been fully included in the valuation allowance as being uncollectible, so this too must be reversed. Therefore, the total reversal of valuation allowance is the sum of these two amounts, or $108,802. Alternatively, this can be computed as the adjustment necessary to bring the net carrying value of the loan receivable to the amount of "principal" to be collected in December 2009 (i.e., the present value, discounting at 12.6%, of the expected $600,000 collection).

The net carrying value of the loan receivable will continue to accrete at 12.6%, both after the recognition of the valuation allowance at the end of 2007 and after the partial elimination of the valuation allowance in 2008, as the following table illustrates:

	A	B	C	D	E
Year ending December 31	Beginning carrying amount of loan	Cash flows expected to be collected	Interest income	Reduction (increase) in carrying amount (B–C)	Ending carrying amount of loan (A–D)
2005	$500,000	$ 40,000	$ 62,974	$ (22,974)	$522,974
2006	522,974	60,000	65,867	(5,867)	528,841
2007	528,841	60,000	66,606	(6,606)	
2007*				141,039	394,408
2008	394,408	20,000	49,675	(29,675)	
2008**				(108,802)	532,885
2009	532,885	600,000	67,115	532,885	--
		$780,000	$312,237	$500,000	

* *Provision of allowance for estimated uncollectible future cash flows, computed at present value using the effective yield on the loan.*

** *Restoration of a portion of the previously provided allowance, computed at present value using the effective yield on the loan, relative to expected 2009 collection, plus the $20,000 unanticipated collection in 2008 at full accreted amount.*

It will be observed in the foregoing chart that total cash collected, $780,000, consisted of $312,237 in interest, accreted at the 12.6% computed yield, and the recovery of only $467,763 of the $500,000 investment in the loan receivable. As in the immediately preceding example, SOP 03-3 treats the decrease in expected cash flows as a loss of principal, accounted for as a bad debt and a provision of a valuation allowance against the $500,000 loan receivable. In this case, $32,237 of "principal" (i.e., of the amount recognized at the time of transfer) was lost, which is the net of the $141,039 valuation allowance provision in 2007 and the $108,802 recovery recognized in 2008.

Note that in all of the preceding examples the carrying value of the loan receivable continues to earn the computed 12.6% yield throughout the holding period. This was true if the initially estimated future cash flows were all collected as planned, or if changes to the estimated amounts or timings later were made—as long as the total cash to be collected did not exceed the amount originally (i.e., upon transfer to Invest Co.) estimated. In the next example, the collections exceed what was anticipated when the loan was acquired, and this necessitates a different approach to accounting for the interest yield on the investment.

In all cases where an allowance for uncollectible loan amounts has been provided, if the loan is subsequently foreclosed, the lender must measure the long-lived asset received in full satisfaction of a receivable at fair value less cost to sell as prescribed FAS 15. That standard prescribes that after a troubled debt restructuring, the creditor must account for assets received in satisfaction of a receivable the same as if the assets had been acquired for cash. Accordingly there will be a new cost basis for the long-lived asset received in full satisfaction of a receivable; the valuation allowance would not be carried over as a separate element of the cost basis for purposes of accounting for the long-lived asset under FAS 144 subsequent to foreclosure. This treatment has been confirmed by FSP 144-1, issued in 2003.

Example with increase in expected cash flows

Assume again the basic facts of the investment in the loan receivable made by Investor Co. However, after fully collecting the anticipated amounts in 2005 and 2006, Investor revises its estimates of the amounts to be collected in 2007, 2008, and 2009. Specifically, it now expects to receive $75,000 at the end of 2007 and again at the end of 2008, and to collect the full remaining balance, $650,000, at the end of 2009. SOP 03-3 does not permit recognition of a gain or other income upon making this new estimate, but does instead require that the effective yield be recomputed and that future receipts be allocated between interest income and principal reduction consistent with the new accretable yield.

Note that no entry is required at the time of the new estimate of future cash flows because no gain or loss (or reversal of previously recognized loss) is being affected. As with changes in accounting estimates under APB 20, this is handled strictly on a prospective basis.

	A	*B*	*C*	*D*	*E*
Year ending December 31	*Beginning carrying amount of loan*	*Cash flows expected to be collected*	*Interest income*	*Reduction (increase) in carrying amount (B–C)*	*Ending carrying amount of loan (A–D)*
2005	$500,000	$ 40,000	$ 62,974	$ (22,974)	$522,974
2006	522,974	60,000	65,867	(5,867)	528,841
2007*					
2007	528,841	75,000	88,086	(13,086)	541,927
2008	541,927	75,000	90,265	(15,265)	557,192
2009	557,192	650,000	92,808	557,192	--
		$900,000	$400,000	$500,000	

* *Based on new expectations regarding future cash flows, a new yield is computed in an amount that equates the present value of expected receipts in 2007-9 to the carrying value at the end of 2006, $528,841. This yield is about 16.7%.*

In the foregoing example, $900,000 in cash is ultimately collected, allocated $400,000 to interest income and $500,000 to recovery of the amount recorded at the date of transfer, which was the sum paid for the loan receivable.

Accounting for investments in pools of loans acquired by transfers. Loans that are acquired as a pool present special accounting considerations. Each individual loan must meet the criteria of SOP 03-3 in order to apply the accounting set forth in this standard. Thus, if a group of loans are acquired together and in the aggregate have expected future cash flows in an amount lower than the aggregate contractual cash flows, this does not qualify each of the loans to be accounted for under SOP 03-3. Rather, each loan must be reviewed for impairment due to credit quality, and only those individual loans exhibiting the defined characteristic would be subject to the specified accounting.

After making a determination that each loan in a proposed pool has met the threshold conditions set forth under SOP 03-3 (i.e., that there has been evidence of credit quality deterioration subsequent to the origination, and that it is probable that, as of the transfer date, the transferee will not collect all the contractually required payments), a further determination must be made that the loans share common risk characteristics. Under provisions of SOP 03-3, loans with similar credit risk or risk ratings, and one or more predominant risk characteristics, such as financial asset type, collateral type, size, interest rate, date of origination, term, and geographic location, will be considered to have common risk characteristics. Credit risk can be assessed by reference to publicly available ratings of publicly held companies or by automated ratings such as that produced by Fair Isaac Corporation (FICO scores).

The aggregate cost of the loans to be aggregated is to be apportioned to the loans in the pool in proportion to their respective fair values at date of acquisition. The aggregate accretable yield of the pool is allocated among the loans in this same manner.

Only loans acquired in a given fiscal *quarter* (not year!) are subject to aggregation for financial reporting purposes. Once a pool is established, its integrity must be maintained, and thus loans can only be removed from the pool upon sale, foreclosure, write-off, or settlement. New loans cannot be added to an existing pool. The excess of contractually required cash flows over the acquisition cost of the pool may not be used to offset or absorb changes to anticipated cash flows associated with other loans or pools of loans having other common risk characteristics.

Removal of a loan from a portfolio is effected at the loan's then-carrying value, and accordingly a gain or loss would be reflected in income of the period, measured as the difference between the carrying value and the fair value of the amount received in settlement (e.g., cash or collateral). Any difference between the carrying amount of the loan being removed from the pool and the fair value of the amount received will not impact the percentage yield being used to accrete value on the remainder of the pool.

Accounting for investments in debt securities acquired by transfers. If the debt instrument acquired in a transfer to be accounted for under SOP 03-3 meets the definition of a **security,** as set forth in FAS 115 (namely, that it constitutes a share, participation, or other interest that is represented by a registered or bearer instrument or by book entry, and is one of a class or series of participations, interests or obligations), then SOP 03-3 prescribes a slightly different mode of accounting for changes in expected cash flows. In order to conform to FAS 115's requirements, an anticipated downward change in expected future cash flows must be examined to determine whether merely a temporary change in value has occurred, or whether an other than temporary decline has been signaled. While temporary impairment is not impossible, if in fact the transferee of debt securities—the issuer of which had suffered an adverse change in creditworthiness prior to the transfer—now anticipates further reduced cash flows from the security, there is substantial likelihood that the impairment in value is other than temporary. Under FAS 115, other than temporary impairment must be recognized by writing down the carrying value of the investment and reflecting the charge in current earnings, whether the security is being held in the available-for-sale portfolio or is being held to maturity.

If, on the other hand, the estimated future cash flows from the debt security are increased from the amounts anticipated at transfer, then similar to what was illustrated above, the accretable yield should be recomputed and periodic interest income thereafter would be appropriately adjusted. This would be a change in accounting estimate under APB 20.

To illustrate, consider the same facts as set forth above, except now assume that the loan was instead a debt security meeting the definition set forth in FAS 115. When acquired, it was treated as being available for sale, but for this example no changes in value are addressed other than that associated with the changed expectation of cash flows.

Example of reduction in cash flow expectations

The anticipated cash flows occurred in 2005, 2006, and 2007 but at the beginning of 2008 Investor Co. revises its expectations, and now believes that there will be a zero cash collection in 2008, and only $500,000 at year-end 2009. The present value of these shortfalls—a $70,000 shortage at year-end 2008, followed by a $100,000 gap at year-end 2009—discounted at the same 12.6% rate computed as the yield on the investment at transfer, reveals an impairment of $141,039 as of the start of 2008. The entry to record this, given that the investment is treated as a debt security, rather than as a loan, is as follows:

Loss on impairment of investment	141,039	
Investment in available-for-sale debt securities		141,039

Apart from the bookkeeping (writing down the investment directly rather than crediting a contra asset account), the treatment is very similar to that previously presented. Most importantly, the reduced net carrying value of the debt security held as an available for sale security will continue to accrete at 12.6%, as the following table illustrates:

	A	*B*	*C*	*D*	*E*
Year ending December 31	*Beginning carrying amount of investment*	*Cash flows expected to be collected*	*Interest income*	*Reduction (increase) in carrying amount (B–C)*	*Ending carrying amount of investment (A–D)*
2005	$500,000	$ 40,000	$ 62,974	$ (22,974)	$522,974
2006	522,974	60,000	65,867	(5,867)	528,841
2007	528,841	60,000	66,606	(6,606)	
2007*				141,039	394,408
2008	394,408	--	49,675	(49,675)	444,083
2009	444,083	500,000	55,917	444,083	--
		$660,000	$301,039	$500,000	

* *Write-down of carrying value of investment in debt security, due to reduced expectation of future cash flows, which is judged to be an other than temporary impairment, computed at present value using the effective yield on the loan.*

The total cash collected, $660,000, is accounted for as interest income, in the total amount $301,039, and recovery of the "principal" of the investment, net of the impairment recorded in 2007, amounting to $358,961.

Example with decrease in expected cash flows followed by increase in expected cash flows

Unlike in the earlier examples, where the investment was accounted for as a loan receivable, here the investment is in a debt security accounted for under FAS 115, which prohibits restoring an other than temporary decline in value. For this reason, the write-down was not effected through a contra asset (allowance) account, and a later improvement in the outlook for future cash flows must instead be accounted for prospectively as a yield adjustment.

Assume, therefore, that Investor Co., first lowers its expectation regarding future cash flows and then partially reverses its estimate, so that some or all of the amount of future cash flow thought not to be forthcoming now again is expected to be received. Specifically, assume that in 2007 Investor Co. has the expectation that no interest will be collected in 2008 and that only $500,000 will be collected in 2009. In 2008, however, $20,000 is in fact collected, and Investor Co. then expects a full collection of the $600,000 in 2009 (but no recovery of the $50,000 missed payment in 2008).

The entry to record the reduced expectation of future cash flows at the end of 2006 or beginning of 2007 is as shown below.

Loss on impairment of investment	141,039	
Investment in available-for-sale debt securities		141,039

In 2008, the collection of the $20,000 (when no collection at all was anticipated), coupled with the renewed expectation of collecting $600,000 in 2009, requires that the yield through the end of the expected holding period (final payoff, in this case) be recomputed. Assuming that the $20,000 payment for 2008 was received before the financial statements for 2008 have been prepared, it would be appropriate to recompute accretable yield as of the beginning of that year, so that both 2008 and 2009 will report interest income consistent with the pattern of cash flows over that two-year period. The calculated yield on an investment equal to the carrying value at the beginning of 2008 ($394,408), which is expected to generate cash inflows of $20,000 at the end of that year and $600,000 at the end of the next year, is 25.9%, and this is used to accrete yield over the remaining term.

Since this will be reported prospectively, no entry is made as of the beginning of the year (nor would the necessary information have been available), but the entry to record interest income and the accretion for uncollected interest would be as follows:

Cash	20,000	
Investment in available-for-sale debt securities	82,156	
Interest income		102,156

The accretion of value is akin to an amortization of discount, and represents interest earned but not received, based on the most recent estimates of future cash flows. It does not represent a recovery of the previously written down carrying value of the investment because of permanent impairment. The complete analysis can be seen in the chart below.

	A	*B*	*C*	*D*	*E*
Year ending December 31	*Beginning carrying amount of investment*	*Cash flows expected to be collected*	*Interest income*	*Reduction (increase) in carrying amount (B–C)*	*Ending carrying amount of investment (A–D)*
2005	$500,000	$ 40,000	$ 62,974	$ (22,974)	$522,974
2006	522,974	60,000	65,867	(5,867)	528,841
2007	528,841	60,000	66,606	(6,606)	
2007*				141,039	394,408
2008**	394,408	20,000	102,156	(82,156)	476,564
2009	476,564	600,000	123,436	476,564	--
		$780,000	$421,039	$500,000	

* *Write-down of carrying value of investment in debt security, due to reduced expectation of future cash flows, which is judged to be an other than temporary impairment, computed at present value using the effective yield on the loan.*

** *Interest is accreted at the new rate of 25.9% hereafter.*

It will be observed in the foregoing chart that total cash collected, $780,000, consisted of $421,039 in interest, accreted, first, at the 12.6% computed yield through the end of 2007, and then at the 25.9% computed yield in light of higher expected cash flows for 2008 and 2009. The remainder of the cash flows, totaling $358,961, was attributable to the recovery of the investment, net of the write-down for impairment in 2007.

In contrast to the example where the investment was accounted for as a loan receivable, here the yield is adjusted prospectively when a recovery in value is observed, and this causes relatively more of the future cash flows to be treated as interest income, and relatively less as recovery of the investment principal.

Note that if no reduction in future cash flows had been anticipated, but if an increase in cash flows was expected at some point during the holding period of the investment, the result, from an accounting standpoint, would be as shown immediately above. The accretable yield would have been computed and recognized prospectively over the remaining holding period of the security.

Disclosure requirements under SOP 03-3. The standard sets forth expanded disclosure requirements pertaining to accounting for prepayments. In addition, disclosure is required, separately for instruments accounted for as loans and for those accounted for as debt securities, of outstanding balances and related carrying amounts at the beginning and end of each reporting period; and of the amount of accretable yield at the beginning and end of each period, with reconciliation of additions, accretion, and disposals of loans and for any reclassification between accretable and nonaccretable yields. Also, for loans acquired during the reporting period, disclosure is required of the contractually required payments receivable, expected cash flows associated therewith, and fair values at acquisition dates. For instruments accounted for as loans (not debt securities), the investor must disclose provisions for uncollectible amounts and reversals thereto made during the period, and the amount of the allowance for uncollectible amounts at both the beginning and end of the reporting period.

Finally, if the income recognition method set forth in SOP 03-3 is not applied to any loans within the scope of the standard—because subsequent developments result in placing the loan on nonaccrual status, or because an indeterminate foreclosure date makes computation of accretable yield impossible, for example—disclosure is required of the carrying amount at acquisition and at the end of the reporting date.

The Equity Method of Accounting for Investments

The equity method, sometimes referred to as "one-line consolidation," permits an entity (investor) owning a percentage of the common stock of another entity (investee) to incorporate its pro rata share of the investee's operating results into its earnings. However, rather than include its share of each component (e.g., sales, cost of sales, operating expenses, etc.) in its financial statements, the **investor** shall only include its share of the investee's **net** income as a separate line item in its income. Note that there are exceptions to this one-line rule. The investor's share of **investee** extraordinary items and prior period adjustments retain their identities in the investor's income and retained earnings statements and are separately reported if material in relation to the investor's income. It should be noted that the final bottom-line impact on the investor's financial statements is **identical** whether the equity method or full consolidation is employed; only the amount of detail presented within the statements will differ.

The equity method is generally **not** a substitute for consolidation; it is employed where the investor has **significant influence** over the operations of the investee but lacks control. In general, significant influence is inferred when the investor owns between 20% and 50% of the investee's voting common stock. Any ownership percentage over 50% presumably gives the investor actual control, making full consolidation of financial statements necessary. The 20% threshold stipulated in APB 18 is not absolute; circumstances may suggest that significant influence exists even though the investor's level of ownership is less than 20%, or that it is absent despite a level of ownership above 20%. In considering whether significant influence exists, FIN 35 identifies the following factors: (1) opposition by the investee, (2) agreements under which the investor surrenders shareholder rights, (3) majority ownership by a small group of shareholders, (4) inability to obtain desired information from the investee, (5) inability to obtain representation on investee board of directors, etc. Whether sufficient contrary evidence exists to negate the presumption of significant influence is a matter of judgment. Judgment requires a careful evaluation of all pertinent facts and circumstances, over an extended period of time in some cases.

Prior to the issuance of FAS 94, some investors used the equity method in those rare instances in which the investor owned over 50% of the investee's voting common shares but consolidated statements were deemed to be inappropriate (usually because consolidated statements would mask important differences in the financial or operating characteristics as between the investor-parent and the investee-subsidiary). However, FAS 94 eliminated this once popular "nonhomogeneity" justification for nonconsolidation. This left only temporary control, noncontrol, and foreign exchange restrictions and related reasons as justification for not consolidating majority-owned subsidiaries. FAS 144 eliminated temporary control as a justification for nonconsolidation. As a practical matter, absence of control by the parent is the only remaining reason to not consolidate a majority-owned investee. The equity method continues to be used in accounting for nonconsolidated majority-owned subsidiaries (see Chapter 11).

Complexities in the use of the equity method arise in two areas. First, the cost of the investment to the investor might not be equal to the fair value of the investor's share of investee net assets; this is analogous to the existence of **goodwill** in a purchase business combination. Or the fair value of the investor's share of the investee's net assets may not be equal to the book value thereof; this situation is analogous to the purchase cost allocation problem in consolidations. Since the ultimate income statement result from the use of equity method accounting must generally be the same as full consolidation, an adjustment must be made for each of these **differentials**.

The second major complexity relates to interperiod income tax allocation. The equity method causes the investor to reflect current earnings based on the investee's operating results; however, for income tax purposes the investor reports only dividends received and gains or losses on disposal of the investment. Thus, temporary differences result, and FAS 109 provides guidance as to the appropriate method of computing the deferred tax effects of these differences.

In the absence of these complicating factors, the use of the equity method by the investor is straightforward: the original cost of the investment is increased by the investor's share of the investee's earnings and is decreased by its share of the investee's losses and by dividends received. The basic procedure is illustrated below.

Example of a simple case ignoring deferred taxes

Assume the following information. On January 2, 2005, R Corporation (the investor) acquired 40% of E Company's (the investee) voting common stock on the open market for $100,000. Unless demonstrated otherwise, it is assumed that R Corporation can exercise significant influence over E Company's operating and financing policies. On January 2, E's stockholders' equity consists of the following accounts:

Common stock, par $1, 100,000 shares authorized, 50,000 shares issued and outstanding	$ 50,000
Additional paid-in capital	150,000
Retained earnings	50,000
Total stockholders' equity	$250,000

Note that the cost of E Company common stock was equal to 40% of the book value of E's net assets. Assume also that there is no difference between the book value and the fair value of E Company's assets and liabilities. Accordingly, the balance in the investment account in R's records represents exactly 40% of E's stockholders' equity (net assets). Assume further that E Company reported a 2005 net income of $30,000 and paid cash dividends of $10,000. Its stockholders' equity at year-end would be as follows:

Common stock, par $1, 100,000 shares authorized, 50,000 shares issued and outstanding	$ 50,000
Additional paid-in capital	150,000
Retained earnings	70,000
Total stockholders' equity	$270,000

R Corporation would record its share of the increase in E Company's net assets during 2005 as follows:

Investment in E Company	12,000	
Equity in E income		12,000
($30,000 x 40%)		
Cash	4,000	
Investment in E Company		4,000
($10,000 x 40%)		

When R's balance sheet is prepared at December 31, 2005, the balance reported in the investment account would be $108,000 ($100,000 + $12,000 – $4,000). This amount represents 40% of the book value of E's net assets at the end of the year (40% x $270,000). Note also that the equity in E income is reported as one amount on R's income statement under the caption "Other income and expense."

In computing the deferred tax effects of income recognized by the equity method, the investor must make an assumption regarding the means by which the **undistributed earnings of the investee** will be realized by the investor. The earnings can be realized either through later dividend receipts or by disposition of the investment at a gain. The former assumption would result in taxes at the investor's marginal tax rate on ordinary income (net of the 80% dividends received deduction permitted by the Internal Revenue Code for intercorporate investments of less than 80% but at least 20%; a lower deduction of 70% applies if ownership is below 20%). The latter option would be treated as a capital gain, which is currently taxed at the full corporate tax rate, since the preferential capital gain rate was eliminated by the 1986 Tax Reform.

Example of a simple case including deferred taxes

Assume the same information as in the example above. In addition, assume that R Corporation has a combined (federal, state, and local) marginal tax rate of 34% on ordinary income and that it anticipates realization of E Company earnings through future dividend receipts. R Corporation's entries at year-end 2005 will be as follows:

1.	Investment in E Company	12,000	
	Equity in E income		12,000
2.	Income tax expense	816	
	Deferred taxes		816
	Taxable portion of investee earnings to be received in the future as dividends times marginal tax rate: $12,000 x 20% x 34% = $816		
3.	Cash	4,000	
	Investment in E Company		4,000
4.	Deferred taxes	272	
	Taxes payable—current		272
	Fraction of investee earnings currently taxed ($4,000/$12,000) x $816 = $272		

FAS 109 employs the "asset and liability approach" in contrast to the approach of predecessor standard APB 11. The deferred tax liability is originally computed with reference to the **projected** tax effect of the "temporary difference reversal." It may be subsequently adjusted for a variety of reasons, including changed tax rates and altered management expectations (see Chapter 15 for a complete discussion).

Notwithstanding FAS 109's requirement that deferred taxes be adjusted for changed expectations at each subsequent balance sheet date, the actual tax effect of the temporary difference reversal may still differ from the deferred tax provided. This difference may occur because the actual tax effect is a function of the entity's other current items of income and expense in the year of reversal (while FAS 109 requires the use of a projected effective tax rate, actual rates may differ). It may also result from a realization of the investee's earnings in a manner other than anticipated (assuming that tax rates on "ordinary" income differ from those on capital gains).

To illustrate this last point, assume that in 2005, before any further earnings or dividends are reported by the investee, the investor sells the entire investment for $115,000. The tax impact is

Selling price	$115,000
Less cost	100,000
Gain	$ 15,000
Capital gain rate (marginal corporate rate)	x 34%
Tax liability	$ 5,100

The entries to record the sale, the tax thereon, and the amortization of previously provided deferred taxes on the undistributed 2005 earnings are as follows:

1.	Cash	115,000	
	Investment in E Company		108,000
	Gain on sale of investment		7,000
2.	Income tax expense	4,556	
	Deferred tax liability	544	
	Taxes payable—current		5,100

The income tax expense of $4,556 is the sum of two factors: (1) the capital gains rate of 34% applied to the actual **book** gain realized ($115,000 selling price less $108,000 carrying value), for a tax of $2,380, and (2) the difference between the capital gains tax rate (34%) and the effective rate on dividend income (20% x 34% = 6.8%) on the undistributed 2005 earnings of E Company previously recognized as ordinary income by R Corporation [$8,000 x (34% – 6.8%) = $2,176].

Note that if the realization through a sale of the investment had been anticipated at the time the 2005 balance sheet was being prepared, the deferred tax liability account would have been adjusted (possibly to reflect the entire $5,100 amount of the ultimate obligation), with the offset included in 2005's ordinary tax expense. The above example explicitly assumes that the sale of the investment was **not** anticipated prior to 2006.

Accounting for a differential between cost and book value of equity method investments. The preceding examples ignored one of the major complexities of the equity method; namely, the requirement that the investor account for any differential between its cost and its share of the fair value of the investee's net identifiable assets consistent with the accounting for goodwill in a purchase business combination. This rule is found in APB 18, but has probably been imperfectly applied over the past thirty years. Since the issuance of FAS 142, replacing APB 17, there is a renewed emphasis on the proper implementation of this mandate.

In almost all instances, the price paid by an investor to acquire shares in an investee will differ from the underlying book value (i.e., the investee's net assets per its financial statements) it represents. In most cases, this differential relates to both discrepancies between the investee's recognized net assets at book values and at current fair values, and also to both unrecognized assets and the premium paid (i.e., goodwill) by the investor to acquire the investment. Under APB 18, the investment cost must be assigned to the various underlying assets and liabilities precisely in the manner that purchase cost is allocated in a business combination originally under APB 16 and now under FAS 141. Clearly, this means that premiums or discounts versus underlying book values must be identified and dealt with, and also that assets or liabilities **not** recognized by the investee must be identified and assigned the appropriate shares of the investor's purchase cost.

In the simplest example of applying this principle, if plant assets having appreciated values are identified, part of the price paid by the investor must be allocated (in a notational sense only—the entire investment is presented as a single caption in the investor's financial statements, consistent with the "one-line consolidation" aspect of equity method accounting) to the "step-up" in the values of those assets. Since those assets (other than land) are subject to depreciation, the investor must amortize a part of the investment cost against its share of investee earnings. This can require a mighty effort on the part of the investor, particularly when a range of assets having varying depreciable lives is involved, as would almost always be the case.

Under APB 18, any premium paid by the investor, which is analogous to goodwill, must also be identified. The amount paid by the investor could also imply that there had been a discount, although this is highly unusual in practice; in such rare instances, this would be treated as negative goodwill. While under prior rules this goodwill component would have been amortized, under FAS 142 this is subject not to amortization but rather to impairment testing. The impairment testing regime to be applied is not, however, that specified in FAS 142, which only pertains to testing by entities which actually record an asset explicitly as goodwill (i.e., the acquirer in a business combination accounted for under FAS 141 as a purchase). Equity method investors will continue to assess impairment of investments in investees by considering whether declines in the fair values of those investments, versus carrying values, may be other than temporary in nature. This matter is discussed later in this chapter.

Under FAS 141 and 142, there is an enhanced requirement, applicable to both purchase business combinations and equity method investments, to identify intangible assets that must be given separate recognition from goodwill. Previous practice was less stringent, because all intangibles were subject to amortization, with the result that many would-be identifiable intangibles, such as customer relationships, were not identified. These overlooked but nevertheless existent intangibles were effectively merged with goodwill and amortized over the period, not exceeding forty years, assigned as the economic life of goodwill. This is no longer permissible. Accordingly, in assigning purchase cost of an equity method investment, an investor may need to identify the portions of the premium paid that relate to identifiable intangibles per FAS 142, as well as to goodwill, with appropriate treatments regarding varying depreciable lives or, in some instances, nondepreciation due to the assets having indefinite lives.

Equity method investors are required, as of the implementation date for FAS 142, to identify the components of investments that represent embedded goodwill. (If APB 18 had been carefully adhered to, of course, this would have already been done when the investments were made, and the goodwill component would have been undergoing periodic amortization.) As of that date, goodwill-component amortization ceases. In addition, amortization of any portion of the investment cost that was allocable to indefinite-life identifiable intangibles was to terminate. Logically, if the amount previously assigned to goodwill was a "catch-all" residual, part of which should have been allocated to identifiable intangibles, whether or not identified by the investee entity, this also must be addressed.

Under FAS 142's transition rules, goodwill amortization ceases, but previous amortization is not restored. The remaining amount assigned (notationally) to goodwill will remain unless impairment is later determined to have occurred.

On the other hand, any negative goodwill remaining unamortized at the transition date must be removed; for negative goodwill embedded in the investor's basis of its equity method investments, this should be reported as the cumulative effect of a change in accounting principle during the first interim reporting period (or annual period, if interim reporting is not done) following the implementation date.

In the following examples, the accounting for equity method investments involving both positive goodwill and negative goodwill are presented.

Example of complex case ignoring deferred taxes—goodwill

Assume again that R Corporation acquired 40% of E Company's shares on January 2, 2005, but that the price paid was $140,000. E Company's assets and liabilities at that date had the following book and fair values:

	Book values	*Fair values*
Cash	$ 10,000	$ 10,000
Accounts receivable (net)	40,000	40,000
Inventories (FIFO cost)	80,000	90,000
Land	50,000	40,000
Plant and equipment (net of accumulated depreciation)	140,000	220,000
Total assets	$320,000	$400,000
Liabilities	$ (70,000)	$ (70,000)
Net assets (stockholders' equity)	$250,000	$330,000

The first order of business is the calculation of the differential, as follows:

R's cost for 40% of E's common	$140,000
Book value of 40% of E's net assets ($250,000 x 40%)	(100,000)
Total differential	$ 40,000

Next, the $40,000 is allocated to those individual assets and liabilities for which fair value differs from book value. In the example, the differential is allocated to inventories, land, and plant and equipment, as follows:

Item	*Book value*	*Fair value*	*Difference debit (credit)*	*40% of difference debit (credit)*
Inventories	$ 80,000	$ 90,000	$10,000	$ 4,000
Land	50,000	40,000	(10,000)	(4,000)
Plant and equipment	140,000	220,000	80,000	32,000
Differential allocated				$32,000

The difference between the allocated differential of $32,000 and the total differential of $40,000 is goodwill of $8,000. Goodwill, as shown by the following computation, represents the excess of the cost of the investment over the fair value of the net assets acquired.

R's cost for 40% of E's common	$140,000
40% of the fair value of E's net assets ($330,000 x 40%)	(132,000)
Excess of cost over fair value (goodwill)	$ 8,000

It is important to note that the allocation of the differential is not recorded formally by either R Corporation or E Company. Furthermore, R does not remove the differential from the investment account and allocate it to the respective assets, since the use of the equity method (one-line consolidation) does not involve the recording of individual assets and liabilities. R leaves the differential of $40,000 in the investment account, as a part of the balance of $140,000 at January 2, 2005. Accordingly, information pertaining to the allocation of the differential is maintained by the investor, but this information is outside the formal accounting system, which is comprised of journal entries and account balances.

After the differential has been allocated, the amortization pattern is developed. To develop the pattern in this example, assume that E's plant and equipment have ten years of useful life remaining and that E depreciates its fixed assets on a straight-line basis. Under recently promulgated standards, goodwill is no longer subject to amortization, but must be tested annually for impairment. R would prepare the following amortization schedule:

Item	*Differential debit (credit)*	*Useful life*	*Amortization* 2005	2006	2007
Inventories (FIFO)	$ 4,000	Sold in 2005	$4,000	$ --	$ --
Land	(4,000)	Indefinite	--	--	--
Plant and equipment (net)	32,000	10 years	3,200	3,200	3,200
Goodwill	8,000	Not relevant	--	--	--
Totals	$40,000		$7,200	$3,200	$3,200

Note that the entire differential allocated to inventories is amortized in 2005 because the cost flow assumption used by E is FIFO. If E had been using LIFO instead of FIFO, no amortization would take place until E sold some of the inventory that existed at January 2, 2005. Since this sale could be delayed for many years under LIFO, the differential allocated to LIFO inventories would not be amortized until E sold more inventory than it manufactured/purchased. Note, also, that the differential (in this example, a negative valuation amount) allocated to E's land is not amortized, because land is not a depreciable asset. In a complete break with past practice, the goodwill component of the differential will not be amortized, but must be tested for impairment annually, as described further below.

The **amortization** of the differential is recorded formally in the accounting system of R Corporation. Recording the amortization adjusts the equity in E's income that R recorded based upon E's income statement. E's income must be adjusted because it is based upon E's book values, not upon the cost that R incurred to acquire E. R would make the following entries in 2005, assuming that E reported net income of $30,000 and paid cash dividends of $10,000:

		Debit	Credit
1.	Investment in E Company	12,000	
	Equity in E income		12,000
	$30,000 x 40%		
2.	Equity in E income (amortization of differential)	7,200	
	Investment in E Company		7,200
3.	Cash	4,000	
	Investment in E Company		4,000
	$10,000 x 40%		

The balance in the investment account on R's records at the end of 2005 is $140,800 [$140,000 + $12,000 – ($7,200 + $4,000)], and E's stockholders' equity, as shown previously, is $270,000. The investment account balance of $140,800 is not equal to 40% of $270,000. However, this difference can easily be explained, as follows:

Balance in investment account at December 31, 2005		$140,800
40% of E's net assets at December 31, 2005		108,000
Difference at December 31, 2005		$ 32,800
Differential at January 2, 2005	$40,000	
Differential amortized during 2005	(7,200)	
Unamortized differential at December 31, 2005		$ 32,800

With the passing years, the balance in the investment account approaches the amount representing 40% of the book value of E's net assets, as the differential is amortized to equity method income or loss. However, since a part of the differential was allocated to land, which is not depreciating, and to goodwill, which is no longer subject to amortization, the carrying value will most likely never equal the equity in the investee's net assets. However, if the investee disposes of the land, the investor must also eliminate the associated portion of the differential. If the carrying value of the investment becomes impaired, as described below, the goodwill portion of the differential may also be eliminated. Thus, under certain conditions the investor's carrying value may subsequently be adjusted to equal the underlying net asset value, although this outcome is relatively unlikely to occur.

To illustrate how the sale of land would affect equity method procedures, assume that E sold the land in the year 2011 for $80,000. Since E's cost for the land was $50,000, it would report a gain of $30,000, of which $12,000 ($30,000 x 40%) would be recorded by R, when it records its 40% share of E's reported net income, ignoring income taxes. However, from R's viewpoint, the gain on sale of land should have been $40,000 ($80,000 – $40,000) because the cost of the land from R's perspective was $40,000 at January 2, 2005 (since the allocated fair value of the land was below its book value). Therefore, in addition to the $12,000 share of the gain recorded above, R should record an additional $4,000 gain [($40,000 – $30,000) x 40%] by debiting the investment account and crediting the equity in E's income account. This $4,000 debit to the investment account will negate the $4,000 differential allocated to land on January 2, 2005, since the original differential was a credit (the fair market value of the land was $10,000 less than its book value).

Adjustments to the goodwill portion of the differential are somewhat more complex. APB 18 requires that that difference between cost and underlying book value be accounted for as if the investee were a consolidated subsidiary. An investor is therefore required to complete a purchase price allocation, as illustrated above, and this may result in the identification of part of the difference as goodwill (referred to as "equity method goodwill"). Under new goodwill accounting standards, this is no longer to be amortized, but rather to be evaluated for impairment. However, FASB decided that equity method investments should continue to be tested for impairment in accordance with APB 18 (i.e., the equity investment as a whole, not the underlying net assets, should be tested for impairment) and that equity method goodwill will not be treated as being separable from the related investment. Accordingly, goodwill should not be tested for impairment in accordance with the new goodwill and intangible assets standard, FAS 142.

To illustrate, consider the following assumed facts (ignoring income taxes). E Company's reported earnings in 2006 and loss in 2007 are $15,000 and ($12,000), respectively. No dividends are paid by E after 2005. R's carrying value, before considering possible impairment in value, as of year end 2006 is computed as follows:

Carrying value of investment, December 31, 2005	$140,800
R's interest in E's 2006 net income	6,000
Amortization of carrying value	(3,200)
Carrying value, December 31, 2006	143,600
R's interest in E's 2007 net loss	(4,800)
Amortization of carrying value	(3,200)
Carrying value, December 31, 2007, before considering additional charge for impairment	$135,600

If, at December 31, 2007, R determines that the fair value of its investment in E has declined to $130,000, and this decline in value is other than temporary in nature, then it must, per APB 18, recognize a further loss amounting to $5,600 for the year. Notice that this fair value decline is assessed with reference to the fair (presumably, but not necessarily, market) value of the investment in E Company. It would not be determined with specific reference to the value of E's business operations, in the manner that goodwill is assessed in connection with purchase business combinations accounted for by the presentation of consolidated financial statements, although a permanent decline in value of the investment would likely be related to the value of E's operations.

While the standard is silent on this issue, it is reasonable that any recognized decline in value be assigned first to the implicit goodwill component of the investment account. In this example, since the value decline, $5,600, is less than the goodwill component of the differential, it will be fully absorbed, and future periods' amortization of the differential assigned to other assets will not be affected. On the other hand, if the value decline had exceeded $8,000, the excess would logically have been allocated to the underlying nonmonetary assets of the investee, such that the remaining differential previously identified with plant and equipment might have been reduced or eliminated, thereby altering future amortization.

Example of complex case including deferred taxes—goodwill

The impact of interperiod income tax allocation in the foregoing example is similar to that demonstrated earlier in the simplified example. Under prior GAAP, a complication arose with regard to the portion of the differential allocated to goodwill: since equity method goodwill is not amortizable for tax purposes it represented a permanent (not a temporary) difference that would not give rise to deferred taxes. Under the new goodwill rules, since amortization will no longer be applied to equity method goodwill, there will be no book-tax difference and hence no deferred tax issue to be addressed. The other components of the differential in the foregoing example are all temporary differences, with normal deferred tax implications.

The entries recorded by R Corporation in 2005 would be

		Debit	Credit
1.	Investment in E Company	12,000	
	Equity in E income		12,000
2.	Income tax expense	816	
	Deferred tax liability		816
	$12,000 x 20% x 34%		
3.	Cash	4,000	
	Investment in E Company		4,000
4.	Deferred tax liability	272	
	Taxes payable—current		272
	$4,000/$12,000 x $816		
5.	Equity in E income	7,200	
	Investment in E Company		7,200
6.	Deferred tax liability	490	
	Income tax expense		490
	$7,200 x 20% x 34%		

Example of complex case ignoring deferred taxes—negative goodwill

The facts in this example are similar to those in the immediately preceding examples, but in this instance the price paid by the investor, Lucky Corp., is less than the proportionate share of the investee's net assets, at fair value. This is analogous to negative goodwill in a purchase business combination, and the accounting for the negative differential between cost and fair value should follow that mandated for bargain purchases under the business combinations and goodwill standards recently promulgated FAS 141 and 142.

Assume that Lucky Corp. acquired 40% of Compliant Company's shares on January 2, 2005, for a cash payment of $120,000. Compliant Company's assets and liabilities at that date had the following book and fair values:

	Book values	*Fair values*
Cash	$ 10,000	$ 10,000
Accounts receivable (net)	40,000	40,000
Inventories (FIFO cost)	80,000	90,000
Land	50,000	40,000
Plant and equipment (net of accumulated depreciation)	140,000	220,000
Total assets	$320,000	$400,000
Liabilities	$ (70,000)	$ (70,000)
Net assets (stockholders' equity)	$250,000	$330,000

The first step is to compute the differential, which is as follows:

Lucky's cost for 40% of Compliant's common	$120,000
Book value of 40% of E's net assets ($250,000 x 40%)	(100,000)
Total differential	$ 20,000

Next, the $20,000 is allocated, on a preliminary basis, to those individual assets and liabilities for which fair value differs from book value. In the example, the differential is initially allocated to inventories, land, and plant and equipment, as follows:

Item	*Book value*	*Fair value*	*Difference debit (credit)*	*40% of difference debit (credit)*
Inventories	$ 80,000	$ 90,000	$10,000	$ 4,000
Land	50,000	40,000	(10,000)	(4,000)
Plant and equipment	140,000	220,000	80,000	32,000
Differential allocated				$32,000

The difference between the allocated differential of $32,000 and the net differential of $20,000 is negative goodwill of $12,000. Negative goodwill, as shown by the following computation, represents the excess of the fair value of the net assets acquired over the cost of the investment.

Lucky's cost for 40% of Compliant's common	$120,000
40% of the fair value of Compliant's net assets ($330,000 x 40%)	(132,000)
Excess of fair value over cost (negative goodwill)	$ 12,000

Although the topic is not addressed explicitly by FAS 142, the investor's handling of negative goodwill should track how this would be dealt with by a parent company preparing consolidated financial statements following a "bargain purchase" business combination. Under GAAP, the amount preliminarily identified as negative goodwill is to be offset, on a pro rata basis, against all of the acquired assets other than cash and cash equivalents, trade receivables, inventory, financial instruments that are required by U.S. generally accepted accounting principles (GAAP) to be carried on the balance sheet at fair value, assets to be disposed of by sale, and deferred tax assets. In the present example, the assets qualifying for having negative goodwill allocated against their respective fair values are land and plant and equipment. The negative goodwill, $12,000, will therefore be assigned as follows:

Item	*Preliminary value assignment*	*Differential assigned*	*Proportion of qualified costs*	*Allocation of negative goodwill*	*Net differential*
Inventories	$ 36,000	$ 4,000	0.0%	0	4,000
Land	16,000	(4,000)	15.4%	(1,848)	(5,848)
Plant and equipment	88,000	32,000	84.6%	(10,152)	21,848
Total	$140,000	$32,000	100.0%	(12,000)	$20,000

It will be noted in the above table that inventories are not qualified to be assigned a portion of the negative goodwill. Both land and plant and equipment, however, will be allocated some of the amount preliminarily identified as negative goodwill, notwithstanding that land has already been written down because its fair value was lower than the investee's carrying (i.e., book) value for that asset. The net differential, after offsetting of negative goodwill, is $20,000, which is the excess of the purchase cost, $120,000, over the book value of the underlying net assets of Compliant Company at the date of the transaction.

In this example, the net differential assigned to plant and equipment, $21,848, will be amortized over the next ten years (the average life of that asset group), for a charge of $2,185 per year against the earnings from the investee. Land, of course, is not depreciable and thus the total differential, a negative $5,848, will remain until the investee disposes of the land. The amount assigned to inventory, $4,000, will be taken into earnings in 2005 because of the FIFO costing convention.

Since the entire amount preliminarily identified as negative goodwill has been successfully offset against qualifying assets, no amount remains to be recognized as an extraordinary gain in 2005, the year in which the investment is made. In the (extremely unlikely) event that the bargain purchase was of such a magnitude that even after offsetting the preliminary amount determined to be negative goodwill there remained an unabsorbed balance, that would have to be reported by Lucky Corp. as an extraordinary gain in 2005, in order to conform to the requirements of the new goodwill standard.

Item	*Differential debit (credit)*	*Useful life*	*Amortization* 2005	2006	2007
Inventories (FIFO)	$ 4,000	Sold in 2005	$4,000	$ --	$ --
Land	(5,848)	Indefinite	--	--	--
Plant and equipment (net)	21,848	10 years	2,185	2,185	2,185
Totals	$20,000		$6,185	$2,185	$2,185

Again, the entire differential allocated to inventories is amortized in 2005 because the cost flow assumption used by Compliant is FIFO. If Compliant had been using LIFO instead of FIFO, no amortization would take place until Compliant sold some of the inventory that existed at January 2, 2005. Since this sale could be delayed for many years under LIFO, the differential allocated to LIFO inventories would not be amortized until Compliant sold more inventory than it manufactured/purchased. Note, also, that the differential allocated to Compliant's land is not amortized, because land is not a depreciable asset.

The amortization of the differential is recorded formally in the accounting system of Lucky Corp. Recording the amortization adjusts the equity in Compliant's income that Lucky Corp. recorded based upon Compliant's income statement. Compliant's income must be adjusted because it is based upon Compliant's book values, not upon the cost that Lucky Corp. incurred to acquire Compliant. Lucky Corp. would make the following entries in 2005, assuming that Compliant reported net income of $30,000 and paid cash dividends of $10,000:

1.	Investment in Compliant Company	12,000	
	Equity in Compliant Company's income		12,000
	$30,000 x 40%		
2.	Equity in Compliant Company's income (amortization of differential)	6,185	
	Investment in Compliant Company		6,185
3.	Cash	4,000	
	Investment in Compliant Company		4,000
	$10,000 x 40%		

The balance in the investment account on Lucky's records at the end of 2005 is $121,815 [$120,000 + $12,000 – ($6,185 + $4,000)], and Compliant's stockholders' equity, as shown previously, is $270,000. The investment account balance of $121,815 is not equal to 40% of $270,000. However, this difference can easily be explained, as follows:

Balance in investment account at December 31, 2005		$121,815
40% of E's net assets at December 31, 2005		108,000
Difference at December 31, 2005		$ 13,815
Differential at January 2, 2005	$20,000	
Differential amortized during 2005	(6,185)	
Unamortized differential at December 31, 2005		$ 13,815

As with the case of positive equity method goodwill, illustrated in the previous example, as the years pass the balance in the investment account will approach that representing 40% of the book value of E's net assets. In this case, the adjustment to land (consisting of both a fair value adjustment and an allocation of negative goodwill) will persist until the land is disposed of. This will be handled as in the prior (positive goodwill) illustration, above.

Example of complex case including deferred taxes—negative goodwill

The impact of interperiod income tax allocation in the foregoing example is similar to that demonstrated earlier in the simplified example.

The entries recorded by Lucky Corp. in 2005 would be

1.	Investment in Compliant Company	12,000	
	Equity in Compliant income		12,000
2.	Income tax expense	816	
	Deferred tax liability		816
	$12,000 x 20% x 34%		
3.	Cash	4,000	
	Investment in Compliant Company		4,000
4.	Deferred tax liability	272	
	Taxes payable—current		272
	$4,000/$12,000 x $816		
5.	Equity in Compliant income	6,185	
	Investment in Compliant Company		6,185
6.	Deferred tax liability	421	
	Income tax expense		421
	$6,185 x 20% x 34%		

Investor share of investee losses in excess of the carrying value of investment. As demonstrated in the foregoing paragraphs, the carrying value of an investment which is accounted for by the equity method is increased by the investor's share of investee earnings and reduced by its share of investee losses and by dividends received from the investee. Sometimes the losses are so large that the carrying value is reduced to zero, and this raises the question of whether the investment account should be allowed to "go negative," or whether losses in excess of the investment account should be recognized in some other manner.

In general, an equity method investment would not be permitted to have a negative (i.e., credit) balance, since this would imply that it represented a liability. In the case of normal corporate investments, the investor would enjoy limited liability and would not be held liable to the investee's creditors should, for instance, the investee become insolvent. For this reason, excess losses of the investee would not be reflected in the financial statements of the investor. The practice is to discontinue application of the equity method when the investment account reaches a zero balance, with adequate disclosure being made of the fact that further investee losses are not being reflected in the investor's earnings. If the investee later returns to profitability, the investor should ignore its share of earnings until the previously ignored losses have been fully offset; thereafter, normal application of the equity method can be resumed.

There are, however, limited circumstances in which further investee losses would be reflected. Often the investor has guaranteed or otherwise committed to indemnify creditors or other investors in the investee entity for losses incurred, or to fund continuing operations of the investee. Having placed itself at risk in the case of the investee's insolvency, continued application of the equity method is deemed to be appropriate, since the net credit balance in the investment account (reportable as a liability entitled "losses in excess of investment made in investee") would indeed represent an obligation of the investor.

The other situation in which investee losses in excess of the investor's actual investment in common stock of the investee are to be reflected is somewhat more complicated. When the investor has investments consisting of both common stock holdings accounted for under APB 18, and other investments in or loans to the investee, such as in its preference shares (including mandatorily redeemable preferred stock) or debt obligations of the investee, there will not only be further application of APB 18, but also possible interaction between the provisions of APB 18 and those of FAS 114 and/or FAS 115. In addition, there will be the question of the appropriate proportion of the investee's loss to be recognized by the investor—that is, should the investor's share of further investee losses be computed based only on its common stock ownership interest, or would some other measure of economic interest be more relevant?

The Emerging Issues Task Force (in Issues 98-13 and 99-10) has attempted to address the accounting to be applied under the circumstances described in the foregoing paragraph. A principal concern was that an anomaly could develop if, for example, the common shareholdings were being accounted for by application of the equity method (including a suspension of the method when the carrying value declined to zero due to investee losses) while investments in the same investee's debt or preferred shares were being carried at fair value per FAS 115 (assuming that the debt was not being carried at amortized cost due to classification as a held-to-maturity investment). A parallel concern invokes the accounting for loans under FAS 114 when investee debt is being held by the investor.

According to EITF 98-13, the adjusted basis of the other investments (preferred stock, debt, etc.) should be adjusted for the equity method losses, after which the investor should apply FAS 114 and 115 to the other investments, as applicable. Those equity method losses should be applied to the other investments in reverse order of seniority (that is, the respective priority in liquidation). This sequence is logical because it tracks the risk of investor loss: common shareholders' interests are the first to be eliminated, followed by those of the preferred shareholders, and so on—with debt having the highest claim to investee assets in the event of liquidation. If the investee later becomes profitable, equity method income subsequently recorded (if, as described earlier, any unrecognized losses have first been exceeded) should be applied to the adjusted basis of the other investments in reverse order of the application of the equity method losses (i.e., equity method income is applied to the more senior securities first).

In applying this standard, the **cost basis** of the other investments is taken to mean the original cost of those investments adjusted for the effects of other than temporary writedowns, unrealized holding gains and losses on FAS 115 securities classified as trading, and amortization of any discount or premium on debt securities or loans. The **adjusted basis** is defined as the cost basis adjusted for the FAS 114 valuation allowance account for an investee loan and the cumulative equity method losses applied to the other investments.

The interaction of APB 18 and FAS 114 and 115 could mean, for example, that investee losses are recognized via a reduction in carrying value of preferred shares, which might then be immediately upwardly adjusted to recognize fair value as of the balance sheet date in accordance with FAS 115. In a situation such as this, the equity method downward adjustment would be a loss recognized currently in earnings, while the upward revaluation to fair value would typically be credited to other comprehensive income, and thus excluded from current period earnings (unless defined as being held for trading purposes, which would be unusual).

EITF 98-13 addressed only the situation where the investor had the same percentage interests in common stock and all the other equity or debt securities of the investee. However, a further complication can arise when the investor's share in the common stock of the investee is not mirrored in its investment in the other debt or equity securities of the investee that it also holds. While this is discussed in EITF 99-10, GAAP is not definitive regarding the mechanism by which the investor's share of further losses should be recognized in such situations. What is clear, however, is that merely applying the investor's percentage interest in the investee's common stock to the period's loss would **not** be appropriate in these cases.

Two approaches are deemed to be justifiable. The first is to eliminate the carrying value of first, the common stock and then, the other securities of the investee (including loans made to the investee), in reverse order of seniority, as set forth under EITF 98-13. The percentage of the investee's loss to be absorbed against each class of investment other than common stock would be governed by the proportion of **that investment** held by the investor—**not** its common stock ownership percentage. The logic is that, if the investor entity were to be harmed by the investee's further losses (once the common stock investment were reduced to zero carrying value), the harm would derive from being forced to take a reduced settlement in a liquidation of the investee, at which point the percentage ownership in separate classes of stock or in holdings of classes of debt would determine the amount of the investor's losses.

The second acceptable approach also takes into account the investor's varying percentage interests in the different equity and debt holdings, but rather than being driven by the investee's reported loss for the period, the investor's loss recognition is determined by the period-to-period change in its claim on the net assets of the investee, measured by book value. This approach implicitly assumes that fair values upon a hypothetical liquidation of the investee would equal book values—an assumption which is obviously unlikely to be borne out, but given the enormous difficulty of applying this measurement technique to the fair value of the investee's assets and liabilities, a necessary compromise.

Thus, both methods of computing the excess investee losses to be recognized by an investor having more than just a common stock interest in the investee depend on the varying levels of those other investment vehicles. These two alternative, acceptable approaches are described and illustrated below.

Example of accounting for excess loss of investee when other investments are also held in same entity, when proportions of all investments are identical

Assume the following facts: Dardanelles Corporation owns 25% of the common stock of Bosporus Company. Dardanelles also owns 25% of Bosporus' preferred shares, and 25% of its commercial debt. Bosporus has $50,000 of debt and $100,000 of preferred stock outstanding.

As of 1/1/2005 the carrying (i.e., book) value of Dardanelles' investment in Bosporus common stock was $12,000, after having applied the equity method of accounting in prior periods, per APB 18. In 2005, 2006, and 2007, Bosporus incurs net losses of $140,000, $50,000 and $30,000, respectively.

As of 1/1/2005, the carrying (book) values of Dardanelles' investment in Bosporus' preferred stock and commercial debt were $25,000 and $12,500, respectively. Due to its continuing losses, the market or fair value of Dardanelles' outstanding preferred shares and its commercial debt decline over the years 2005-2007; Bosporus' portion of these values are as follows:

	Fair value of preferred shares, consistent with FAS 115	*Fair value of commercial debt, consistent with FAS 114*
1/1/2005	N/A	N/A
12/31/2005	$20,000	$12,000
12/31/2006	9,500	8,000
12/31/2007	2,000	7,000

The following table indicates the adjustments that would be made on the books of Dardanelles to record its share of Bosporus' losses in 2005-2007:

	Common stock	*Preferred stock*		*Commercial debt*	
	(Book value)	*Book value*	*Fair value*	*Book value*	*Fair value*
1/1/2005	$ 12,000	$ 25,000	N/A	$ 12,500	N/A
2005 loss (25% x 140,000 = 35,000)	(12,000)	(23,000)		--	
		2,000	$20,000	12,500	$12,000
Adjust pfd. stk. to FMV and debt to FV		18,000		(500)	
12/31/2005 values	0	20,000		12,000	
2006 loss (25% x 50,000 = 12,500)		(2,000)		(10,500)	
		18,000	9,500	1,500	8,000
Adjust pfd. stk. to FMV and debt to FV		(8,500)		--	
12/31/2006 values	0	9,500		1,500	
2007 loss (25% x 30,000 = 7,500)		--		(1,500)	
		9,500	2,000	0	7,000
Adjust pfd. stk. to FMV and debt to FV		(7,500)		--	
12/31/2007 values	$ 0	$ 2,000		$ 0	

Actual journal entries and explanations for the foregoing are given as follows:

		Debit	Credit
12/31/05	Investee losses	35,000	
	Investment in Bosporus common stock		12,000
	Investment in Bosporus preferred stock		23,000

To record Dardanelles' share of Bosporus' loss for the year; the excess over the carrying value of the common stock is used to reduce the carrying value of the preferred shares

	Debit	Credit
Investment in Bosporus preferred stock	18,000	
Unrealized gain on securities available for sale (other comprehensive income)		18,000

Since the fair market value of the preferred shares is $20,000, per FAS 115 the carrying value must be upwardly revalued and the adjustment is included in other comprehensive income for the year

Date	Account	Debit	Credit
	Loss from impairment of loan	500	
	Investment in Bosporus commercial debt		500
	As required by FAS 114, the impairment of the loan to Bosporus must be recognized by a charge against current period earnings		
12/31/06	Investee losses	12,500	
	Investment in Bosporus preferred stock		2,000
	Investment in Bosporus commercial debt		10,500
	To record Dardanelles' share of Bosporus' loss for the year; the excess over the remaining carrying value of the preferred stock (without consideration of the FAS 115 adjustment) is used to reduce the carrying value of the commercial debt held		
	Unrealized gain on securities available for sale (other comprehensive income)	8,500	
	Investment in Bosporus preferred stock		8,500
	Since the fair market value of the preferred shares is not $9,500, the adjustment booked in the prior period must be partially reversed, this adjustment is included in other comprehensive income for the year		
12/31/07	Investee losses	1,500	
	Investment in Bosporus commercial debt		1,500
	To record Dardanelles' share of Bosporus' loss for the year; the maximum to be recognized is the carrying value of the commercial debt since the carrying value of common and preferred stock investments have already been reduced to zero		
	Unrealized gain on securities available for sale (other comprehensive income)	7,500	
	Investment in Bosporus preferred stock		7,500
	Since the fair value of the preferred shares are now $2,000, the carrying value must be further reduced, with the adjustment included in other comprehensive income		

It should be noted in the foregoing example that in year 2007 there will be $6,000 of unrecognized investee losses, since as of the end of that year the carrying value of all the investor's investments in the investee will have been reduced to zero, except for the fair value of the preferred stock which is presented pursuant to FAS 115. Also note that the carrying value of the commercial debt is reduced for an impairment in 2005 because the fair value is lower than the cost basis; in later years the fair value exceeds the cost basis, but under FAS 114 net upward adjustments would not be permitted.

Example of accounting for excess loss of investee when other investments are also held in same entity, when proportions of investments vary—first method: investee's reported loss used as basis for recognition

When the percentage interest in common stock of the investee is not mirrored by the level of ownership in its other securities, the process of recognizing the investor's share of investee losses becomes much more complex. Per EITF 99-10, there are two acceptable approaches, both of which are illustrated here. The first approach is to recognize the investor's share of investee losses by reducing the various investments held in the investee (common and preferred stock and commercial debt, in this example) by the relevant percentages applicable to each class of investment.

In the following, the same facts as in the preceding example are continued, **except** that the percentage of ownership in the equity and debt instruments is as follows:

	Percentage ownership by Dardanelles Corporation
Common stock	25%
Preferred stock	50%
Commercial debt	100%

Note that the fair values of the securities held (using the new assumed percentages of ownership of each class) are as follows:

	Fair value of preferred shares, consistent with FAS 115	*Fair value of commercial debt, consistent with FAS 114*
1/1/2005	N/A	N/A
12/31/2005	$40,000	$48,000
12/31/2006	19,000	32,000
12/31/2007	4,000	28,000

Given the foregoing, the period-by-period adjustments are summarized in the following table:

	Common stock	*Preferred stock*		*Commercial debt*	
	Book value	*Book value*	*Fair value*	*Book value*	*Fair value*
1/1/2005	$ 12,000	$ 50,000	N/A	$50,000	N/A
2005 loss = $140,000					
Eliminate @ 25% ratio	(12,000)				
Reduce preferred @ 50% ratio		(46,000)			
		4,000	$40,000		$48,000
Adjust pfd. stk. to FMV and debt to FV		36,000		(2,000)	
12/31/2005 values	0	40,000		48,000	
2006 loss = $50,000					
Eliminate preferred @50% ratio		(4,000)			
Reduce commercial debt @ 100% ratio				(42,000)	
		36,000	19,000	6,000	32,000
Adjust pfd. stk. to FMV and debt to FV		17,000		--	
12/31/2006 values	0	19,000		6,000	
2007 loss = $30,000					
Reduce commercial debt @ 100% ratio				(6,000)	
			4,000	0	7,000
Adjust pfd. stk. to FMV and debt to FV		(15,000)		--	
12/31/2007 values	$ 0	$ 4,000		$ 0	

Journal entries and explanations for the adjustments that would be made consistent with the foregoing fact pattern are as follows:

12/31/05	Investee losses	58,000	
	Investment in Bosporus common stock		12,000
	Investment in Bosporus preferred stock		46,000
	To record Dardanelles' share of Bosporus' loss for the year; the excess over the carrying value of the common stock is used to reduce the carrying value of the preferred shares based on Dardanelles' 50% ownership interest in the preferred stock outstanding		
	Investment in Bosporus preferred stock	36,000	
	Unrealized gain on securities available for sale (other comprehensive income)		36,000
	Since the fair market value of the preferred shares is $40,000, per FAS 115 the carrying value must be upwardly revalued and the adjustment is included in other comprehensive income for the year		
	Loss from impairment of loan	2,000	
	Investment in Bosporus commercial debt		2,000
	As required by FAS 114, the impairment of the loan to Bosporus must be recognized by a charge against current period earnings		
12/31/06	Investee losses	46,000	
	Investment in Bosporus preferred stock		4,000
	Investment in Bosporus commercial debt		42,000
	To record Dardanelles' share of Bosporus' loss for the year; the excess over the remaining carrying value of the preferred stock (without consideration of the FAS 115 adjustment) is used to reduce the carrying value of the commercial debt held		

	Unrealized gain on securities available for sale (other comprehensive income)	17,000	
	Investment in Bosporus preferred stock		17,000
	Since the fair market value of the preferred shares is not $19,000, the adjustment booked in the prior period must be partially reversed, this adjustment is included in other comprehensive income for the year		
12/31/07	Investee losses	6,000	
	Investment in Bosporus commercial debt		6,000
	To record Dardanelles' share of Bosporus' loss for the year; the maximum to be recognized is the carrying value of the commercial debt since the carrying value of common and preferred stock investments have already been reduced to zero		
	Unrealized gain on securities available for sale (other comprehensive income)	15,000	
	Investment in Bosporus preferred stock		15,000
	Since the fair value of the preferred shares are now $4,000, the carrying value must be further reduced, with the adjustment included in other comprehensive income		

It should be noted in the foregoing example that the limitation on loss recognition each year is given by reference to the investor's percentage interests in the various classes of equity or debt held. The 2005 loss is allocated between the common and preferred interests. A $12,000, 25% interest in the common stock equates to a total of $48,000 of common stock ($12,000 ÷ 25%). Therefore, if the full $140,000 loss were first allocated to reduce the book value of the common stock, $48,000 would have been applied to reduce that book value to zero. That would leave $92,000 of loss ($140,000 – $48,000) that remains to be allocated to the preferred interests. $92,000 x the 50% preferred interest of the investor is $48,000. Since the carrying value of the preferred stock investment is greater than this amount, the full loss is recognized by the investor proportional to its interest.

Similarly, the investee loss of $50,000 in 2006 is first used to eliminate the remaining carrying value (**before** the FAS 115 adjustment) of the preferred stock investment, at a 50% ratio. The total of the preferred interests is computed by dividing the remaining carrying value of the preferred stock, $4,000, by the 50% interest that it represents. Therefore, the $8,000 of the $50,000 loss would be allocated to the preferred interests, thus leaving $42,000 to allocate to the commercial debt. Since Dardanelles owns all of this debt issue, the limitation on loss recognition would be the lesser of the remaining loss ($42,000) or the carrying value of the debt (**before** the FAS 114 adjustment) of $48,000.

Finally, note that in year 2007 there will be $24,000 of unrecognized investee losses, since as of the end of that year the carrying value of all the investor's investments in the investee will have been reduced to zero (except for the fair value of the preferred stock which is presented pursuant to FAS 115).

Example of accounting for excess loss of investee when other investments are also held in same entity, when proportions of investments vary—second method: investee's reported change in net assets used as basis for recognition

The alternative, acceptable approach to investee loss recognition when various equity and debt interests are held in the investee, at varying percentage ownership levels, ignores the investee's reported loss for the period in favor of an indirect approach, making reference to the change in the investor's interest in the investee's reported net assets (net book value). In theory, the results will often be very similar if not identical, but investee capital transactions with other owners (e.g., issuing another series of preferred shares) could impact the loss recognition by the investor under some circumstances. Furthermore, since the investor's cost of its investments in the investee will normally vary from the investee's book value of those investments (e.g., if the investments were acquired in the secondary market), the losses computed by this method may differ from those computed by the first of the two alternative approaches.

To illustrate, again assume all the facts above, including the percentage interests in the immediately preceding example. Also, the condensed balance sheets of Bosporus Corporation as of the relevant dates are given as follows:

	1/1/05	12/31/05	12/31/06	12/31/07
Total assets	$270,000	$135,000	$ 90,000	$ 50,000
Commercial debt	50,000	50,000	50,000	50,000
Other liabilities	20,000	25,000	30,000	20,000
Preferred stock	100,000	100,000	100,000	100,000
Common stock + retained earnings	100,000	(40,000)	(90,000)	(120,000)
Total liabilities and equity	$270,000	$135,000	$ 90,000	$ 50,000

The investor's share of the investee's net assets at these respective dates and the changes to be recognized therein as the investor's share of investee losses for the years 2005–2007 are given below.

	1/1/05	12/31/05 (At investee's book values)	12/31/06 (At investee's book values)	12/31/07
Investor's shares of:				
Commercial debt (100%)	$ 50,000	$ 50,000	$ 50,000	$ 30,000
Preferred stock (50%)	50,000	30,000	5,000	0
Common stock + retained earnings (25%)	25,000	0	0	0
Total share of investee's net assets	$125,000	$ 80,000	$ 55,000	$ 30,000
Change in share from prior year (investor's share of investee loss for year)		$(45,000)	$(25,000)	$(25,000)

In terms of how the actual investee losses should be recorded by the investor, the EITF guidance is not explicit, but there is no reason to depart from the approach illustrated above. Thus, the investment in Bosporus common stock would be eliminated first, then the investment in the preferred stock, and finally the investment in the debt securities. The provisions of FAS 114 and 115 would have to be adhered to as well, again similar to the illustration above.

One part of the foregoing analysis that may need elaboration is the decision, in 2007, to absorb all the excess investee losses against the investor's interest in the commercial debt. In many cases the commercial debt will be secured or for other reasons have preference over the other liabilities (which would tend to include accruals, trade payables, etc.). Therefore, in an actual liquidation situation the unsecured creditors would be eliminated before the commercial debtholders. However, the purpose of this computation—determining how much of the investee's losses should be reported by the investor—is not predicated on an actual liquidation, but rather is based on a going concern assumption and conservatism. Since the investor in this example owns a major position in the common stock, half of the preferred stock, and all of the debt, presumably if the ongoing losses were indicative of imminent demise the investor would have already put the investee into liquidation or taken other dramatic steps. Since this has not occurred, the appropriate computational strategy, it is believed, is to allocate further losses against the investor's remaining interest, which is in the commercial debt. (If actual liquidation were being contemplated, it would be necessary to consider an even greater write-down of the carrying value of this investment.)

Note that the loss recognized each period differs from that under the previous approach, since the allocation is based on the book values of the various interests on the investee's balance sheet, not the cost basis from the investor's perspective, as detailed below.

	Common stock	Preferred stock		Commercial debt	
	Book value	Book value	Fair value	Book value	Fair value
1/1/2005	$12,000	$50,000	N/A	$ 50,000	N/A
2005 change in investor's share of investee's net book value = –45,000					
Eliminate carrying value of common	(12,000)				
Reduce carrying value of preferred		(33,000)			
		17,000	$40,000		$48,000
Adjust pfd. stk. to FMV and debt to FV		23,000		(2,000)	
12/31/2005 values	0	40,000		48,000	
2006 change in investor's share of investee's net book value = –25,000					
Reduce carrying value of commercial debt		(17,000)		(8,000)	
		23,000	19,000	40,000	32,000
Adjust pfd. stk. to FMV and debt to FV		(4,000)		(8,000)	

12/31/2006 values	0	19,000		32,000	
2007 change in investor's share of investee's net book value = –25,000					
Reduce carrying value of commercial debt				(25,000)	
			4,000	7,000	7,000
Adjust pfd. stk. to FMV and debt to FV		(15,000)		--	
12/31/2007 values	$ 0	$ 4,000		$ 7,000	

Journal entries and explanations for the adjustments that would be made consistent with the foregoing fact pattern would be similar to those shown earlier in this section and therefore will not be repeated here.

Accounting for subsequent investments in an investee after suspension of equity method loss recognition. As discussed, recognition of investee losses by the investor is suspended when the investment account is reduced to zero, subject to the further reduction in the carrying value of any other investments (preferred stock, debt, etc.) in that investee, as circumstances warrant. In come cases, after the recognition of investee losses is suspended, the investor will make a further investment in the investee, and the question arises whether recognition of some or all of the previously unrecognized investee losses should immediately be given recognition, up to the amount of the additional investment.

The EITF previously addressed (in Topic D-84) the situation where the increased investment in the equity method investee triggered a need to consolidate (i.e., the 50% ownership threshold was exceeded), and cited the SEC's position against further loss recognition. More recently, in EITF 02-18, the situation where the increased investment did not cause control to be assumed, but rather where equity method accounting was specified both before and after the further investment is made (e.g., the investor owned 30% of the investee's common stock previously, and then increased the interest to 35%) has been dealt with.

EITF 02-18 holds that recognition of some or all of the previously unrecognized ("suspended") losses is conditioned on whether the new investment represents funding of prior investee losses. To the extent that it does, the previously unrecognized share of prior losses will be given recognition (i.e., reported in the investor's current period earnings). Making this determination requires the use of judgment and is fact-specific, but some of the considerations would be as follows:

- Whether the additional investment is acquired from a third party or directly from the investee, since it is unlikely that funding of prior losses occurs unless funds are infused into the investee;
- The fair value of the consideration received in relation to the value of the consideration paid for the additional investment, with an indicated excess of consideration paid over that received being suggestive of a funding of prior losses;
- Whether the additional investment results in an increase in ownership percentage of the investee, with investments being made without a corresponding increase in ownership or other interests (or, alternatively, a pro rata equity investment made by all existing investors) being indicative of the funding of prior losses; and
- The seniority of the additional investment relative to existing equity of the investee, with investment in subordinate instruments being suggestive of the funding of prior losses.

When additional investments are made in an investee that has experienced losses, the corollary issue of whether the investor has committed to further investments may arise. If such is the case, then yet-unrecognized (suspended) investee losses may also need to be recognized in investor earnings currently—in effect, as a loss contingency which is deemed probable of occurrence.

To illustrate the foregoing, consider an investor, R Corp., which invested $500,000 in an investee, E Company, representing a 40% ownership interest. Investee losses caused R Corp. to completely eliminate the carrying value of this investment, and the recognition of R Corp.'s share of a further $200,000 of E Company losses ($200,000 x 40% = $80,000) was suspended. Later, R Corp. invested another $100,000 in E Company. Application of the criteria above led to the conclusion that one-half of its investment was in excess of the value of the consideration received, and thus the entry to record the further investment would be

Investment in E Company stock	50,000	
Loss on equity method investment in E Company	50,000	
Cash		100,000

If it is determined, however, that R Corp. has "otherwise committed" to further investment in E Company, the investor might have to recognize losses up to the full amount of the suspended losses. The entry might therefore be

Investment in E Company stock	20,000	
Loss on equity method investment in E Company	80,000	
Cash		100,000

Intercompany transactions between investor and investee. Transactions between the investor and the investee **may** require that the investor make certain adjustments when it records its share of the investee earnings. According to the realization concept, profits can be recognized by an entity only when realized through a sale to outside (unrelated) parties in arm's-length transactions (sales and purchases) between the investor and investee. Similar problems, however, can arise when sales of fixed assets between the parties occur. In all cases, there is **no** need for any adjustment when the transfers are made at book value (i.e., without either party recognizing a profit or loss in its separate accounting records).

In preparing consolidated financial statements, all intercompany (parent-subsidiary) transactions are eliminated. However, when the equity method is used to account for investments, only the **profit component** of intercompany (investor-investee) transactions is eliminated. This is because the equity method does not result in the combining of all income statement accounts (such as sales and cost of sales), and therefore will not cause the financial statements to contain redundancies. In contrast, consolidated statements would include redundancies if the gross amounts of all intercompany transactions were not eliminated.

Another distinction between the consolidation and equity method situations pertains to the percentage of intercompany profit to be eliminated. In the case of consolidated statements, the entire intercompany profit is eliminated, regardless of the percentage ownership of the subsidiary. However, according to Accounting Interpretation 1 of APB 18, only the **investor's pro rata share** of intercompany profit would be eliminated in equity accounting, whether the transaction giving rise to the profit is "downstream" (a sale to the investee) or "upstream" (a sale to the investor). An exception is made when the transaction is not "arm's-length" or if the investee company was created by or for the benefit of the investor. In these cases, 100% profit elimination would be required, unless realized through a sale to a third party before year-end.

Example of accounting for intercompany transactions

Continue with the basic facts set forth in an earlier example and also assume that E Company sold inventory to R Corporation in 2006 for $2,000 above E's cost. Thirty percent of this inventory remains unsold by R at the end of 2006. E's net income for 2006, including the gross profit on the inventory sold to R, is $15,000; E's income tax rate is 34%. R should make the following journal entries for 2006 (ignoring deferred taxes):

1.	Investment in E Company	6,000	
	Equity in E income		6,000
	$15,000 x 40%		
2.	Equity in E income (amortization of differential)	3,200	
	Investment in E Company		3,200
3.	Equity in E income	158	
	Investment in E Company		158
	$2,000 x 30% x 66% x 40%		

The amount in the last entry needs further elaboration. Since 30% of the inventory remains unsold, only $600 of the intercompany profit remains unrealized at year-end. This profit, net of income taxes, is $396. R's share of this profit ($158) is included in the first ($6,000) entry recorded. Accordingly, the third entry is needed to adjust or correct the equity in the reported net income of the investee.

Eliminating entries for intercompany profits in fixed assets are similar to those in the examples above. However, intercompany profit is realized only as the assets are depreciated by the purchasing entity. In other words, if an investor buys or sells fixed assets from or to an investee at a price above book value, the gain would only be realized piecemeal over the asset's remaining depreciable life. Accordingly, in the year of sale the pro rata share (based on the investor's percentage ownership interest in the investee, regardless of whether the sale is upstream or downstream) of the unrealized portion of the intercompany profit would have to be eliminated. In each subsequent year during the asset's life, the pro rata share of the gain realized in the period would be added to income from the investee.

Example of eliminating intercompany profit on fixed assets

Assume that Investor Co., which owns 25% of Investee Co., sold to Investee a fixed asset, having a five-year remaining life, at a gain of $100,000. Investor Co. is in the 34% marginal tax bracket. The sale occurred at the end of 2005; Investee Co. will use straight-line depreciation to amortize the asset over the years 2006 through 2010.

The entries related to the foregoing are

2005

1.	Gain on sale of fixed asset	25,000	
	Deferred gain		25,000
	To defer the unrealized portion of the gain		
2.	Deferred tax benefit	8,500	
	Income tax expense		8,500
	Tax effect of gain deferral		

Alternatively, the 2005 events could have been reported by this single entry.

Equity in investee income	16,500	
Investment in Investee Co.		16,500

2006 through 2010 (each year)

1.	Deferred gain	5,000	
	Gain on sale of fixed assets		5,000
	To amortize deferred gain		
2.	Income tax expense	1,700	
	Deferred tax benefit		1,700
	Tax effect of gain realization		

The alternative treatment would be

Investment in Investee Co.	3,300	
Equity in investee income		3,300

In the above example, the tax currently paid by Investor Co. (34% x $25,000 taxable gain on the transaction) is recorded as a deferred tax benefit in 2005 since taxes will not be due on the book gain recognized in the years 2006 through 2010. Under provisions of FAS 109, deferred tax benefits are recorded to reflect the tax effects of all deductible temporary differences. Unless Investor Co. could demonstrate that future taxable amounts arising from existing temporary differences exist (or, alternatively, that a NOL carryback could have been elected), this deferred tax benefit will be offset by an equivalent valuation allowance in Investor Co.'s balance sheet at year-end 2005. Thus, the deferred tax benefit might not be recognizable, net of the valuation allowance, for financial reporting purposes unless other temporary differences not specified in the example provided future taxable amounts to offset the net **deductible** effect of the deferred gain.

NOTE: The deferred tax impact of an item of income for book purposes in excess of tax is the same as a deduction for tax purposes in excess of book.

Investee income items separately reportable by investor. In the examples thus far, the investor has reported its share of investee income, and the adjustments to this income, as a single item described as equity in investee income. However, when the investee has extraordinary items and/or prior period adjustments that are material, the investor should report its share of these items separately on its income and retained earnings statements.

Example of accounting for separately reportable items

Assume that both an extraordinary item and a prior period adjustment reported in an investee's income and retained earnings statements are individually considered material from the investor's viewpoint.

Income statement	
Income before extraordinary item	$ 80,000
Extraordinary loss from earthquake (net of taxes of $12,000)	(18,000)
Net income	$ 62,000
Retained earnings statement	
Retained earnings at January 1, 2005, as originally reported	250,000
Add prior period adjustment—correction of an error made in 2004 (net of taxes of $10,000)	20,000
Retained earnings at January 1, 2005, restated	$270,000

If an investor owned 30% of the voting common stock of this investee, the investor would make the following journal entries in 2005:

		Debit	Credit
1.	Investment in investee company	24,000	
	Equity in investee income before extraordinary item		24,000
	$80,000 x 30%		
2.	Equity in investee extraordinary loss	5,400	
	Investment in investee company		5,400
	$18,000 x 30%		
3.	Investment in investee company	6,000	
	Equity in investee prior period adjustment		6,000
	$20,000 x 30%		

The equity in the investee's prior period adjustment should be reported on the investor's retained earnings statement, and the equity in the extraordinary loss should be reported separately in the appropriate section on the investor's income statement.

Accounting for a partial sale or additional purchase of the equity investment. This section covers the accounting issues that arise when the investor sells some or all of its equity in the investee, or acquires additional equity in the investee.

Example of accounting for a discontinuance of the equity method

Assume that an investor owns 10,000 shares (30%) of XYZ Company common stock for which it paid $250,000 ten years ago. On July 1, 2005, the investor sells 5,000 XYZ shares for

$375,000. The balance in the investment in XYZ Company account at January 1, 2005, was $600,000. Assume that all the original differential between cost and book value has been amortized. To calculate the gain (loss) upon this sale of 5,000 shares, it is first necessary to adjust the investment account so that it is current as of the date of sale. Assuming that the investee had net income of $100,000 for the six months ended June 30, 2005, the investor should record the following entries:

1.	Investment in XYZ Company	30,000	
	Equity in XYZ income		30,000
	$100,000 x 30%		
2.	Income tax expense	2,040	
	Deferred tax liability		2,040
	$30,000 x 20% x 34%		

The gain upon sale can now be computed, as follows:

Proceeds upon sale of 5,000 shares	$375,000
Book value of the 5,000 shares ($630,000 x 50%)	315,000
Gain from sale of XYZ common	$ 60,000

Two entries will be needed to reflect the sale: one to record the proceeds, the reduction in the investment account, and the gain (or loss) and the other to record the tax effects thereof. Remember that the investor must have computed the deferred tax effect of the undistributed earnings of the investee that it had recorded each year, on the basis that those earnings either would eventually be paid as dividends or would be realized as capital gains. When those dividends are ultimately received or when the investment is disposed of, the previously recorded deferred tax liability must be amortized.

To illustrate, assume that the investor in this example provided deferred taxes at an effective rate for dividends (considering the 80% exclusion) of 6.8%. The realized capital gain will be taxed at an assumed 34%. For tax purposes, this gain is computed as $375,000 – $125,000 = $250,000, yielding a tax effect of $85,000. For accounting purposes, the deferred taxes already provided are 6.8% x ($315,000 – $125,000), or $12,920. Accordingly, an **additional** tax expense of $72,080 is incurred upon the sale, due to the fact that an additional gain was realized for book purposes ($375,000 – $315,000 = $60,000; tax at 34% = $20,400) **and** that the tax previously provided for at dividend income rates was lower than the real capital gains rate [$190,000 x (34% – 6.8%) = $51,680 extra tax due]. The entries are as follows:

1.	Cash	375,000	
	Investment in XYZ Company		315,000
	Gain on sale of XYZ Company stock		60,000
2.	Deferred tax liability	12,920	
	Income tax expense	72,080	
	Taxes payable—current		85,000

The gains (losses) from sales of investee stock are reported on the investor's income statement in the "Other income and expense" section, assuming that a multistep income statement is presented.

In this example, the sale of investee stock reduced the percentage owned by the investor to 15%. In such a situation, the investor should discontinue use of the equity method. The balance in the investment account on the date the equity method is suspended ($315,000 in the example) will be accounted for on the basis of fair value, under FAS 115; presumably being reported in the available-for-sale investment portfolio. This accounting principle change does **not** require the computation of a cumulative effect or any retroactive disclosures in the investor's financial statements. In periods subsequent to this principles change, the investor records cash dividends received from the investment as dividend revenue and places the security in its long-term marketable equity securities portfolio where it will be subjected to the lower of aggregate cost or market calculation. Any dividends received in excess of the investor's share of postdisposal earnings of the investee should be credits to the investment account, rather than to income.

The process of discontinuing the use of the equity method and adopting FAS 115, as necessitated by a reduction in ownership below the significant influence threshold level, does not require a retroactive restatement. However, the opposite situation having the 20% ownership level equaled or exceeded again (or for the first time) is more complex. APB 18 stipulates that this change in accounting principle (**to** the equity method) requires that the investment account, results of operations (all periods being presented, current and prior), and retained earnings of the investor company be retroactively adjusted.

Example of accounting for a return to the equity method of accounting

Continuing the same example, XYZ Company reported earnings for the second half of 2005 and all of 2006 respectively, of $150,000 and $350,000; XYZ paid dividends of $100,000 and $150,000 in December of those years. In January 2007, the investor purchased 10,000 XYZ shares for $700,000, increasing its ownership to 45% and thereby necessitating a return for equity method accounting, including retroactive adjustment. The relevant entries are as follows:

		Debit	Credit
1.	Cash	15,000	
	Income from XYZ dividends		15,000
2.	Income tax expense	1,020	
	Taxes payable—current		1,020
	To record dividend income and taxes thereon at current effective tax rate ($15,000 x .068) in 2005		
3.	Cash	22,500	
	Income from XYZ dividends		22,500
4.	Income tax expense	1,530	
	Taxes payable—current		1,530
	To record dividend income and taxes thereon ($22,500 x .068) in 2005		
5.	Investment in XYZ Company	700,000	
	Cash		700,000
	To record additional investment in XYZ Company		
6.	Investment in XYZ Company	37,500	
	Retained earnings		34,950
	Deferred tax liability		2,550
	To adjust investment to reflect equity method accounting		

Entry 6. is the cumulative effect adjustment for 15% of XYZ Company's **undistributed** earnings for the second half of 2005 and all of 2006. This adjustment is computed as follows:

Income earned in 2005 subject to equity method	
2005 income ($100,000 + $150,000)	$250,000
Less income earned through June 30 which is reflected in the investment account through previous use of equity method	(100,000)
2005 income subject to equity method adjustment	$150,000
Income earned in 2006 subject to equity method	350,000
Total income subject to equity method	$500,000
Less dividends declared in 2005 and 2006	(250,000)
Increase in investee equity since suspension of equity method (undistributed income)	$250,000
Investor's equity during the period July 1, 2005, through December 31, 2006 (cumulative effect) ($250,000 x 15%)	$ 37,500

Besides showing the cumulative effect as a prior period adjustment on the retained earnings statement, the investor also must retroactively adjust the 2005 and 2006 financial statements to reflect use of the equity method. This means that the dividend income of $15,000 in 2005 and $22,500 in 2006 should be eliminated to reflect the equity method. Accordingly, the term "dividend income" is eliminated and "equity in investee income" is substituted. Since the equity method was used for half of the year 2005 and equity in investee income was accrued through June 30, the term should already appear on 2005's income statement. However, the equity in investee income should be increased by $22,500, the investor's share of the income for the last six months of 2005 ($150,000 x 15%). The net effect on 2005's income **before taxes** is a $7,500 increase ($22,500 increase in equity in investee income less a $15,000 decrease in dividend income). For 2006, the net effect on income before taxes is $30,000. This results from adding equity in investee income of $52,500 ($350,000 x 15%) and eliminating dividend income of $22,500. In addition to the income statement, the balance sheets at December 31, 2005 and 2006, are adjusted as follows (before income tax effects):

1. Add $7,500 to the investment in investee and the retained earnings balances at December 31, 2005.
2. Add $37,500 to the investment in investee and the retained earnings balances at December 31, 2006.

Investor accounting for investee capital transactions. According to APB 18, investee transactions of a capital nature that affect the investor's share of the investee's stockholders' equity shall be accounted for as if the investee were a consolidated subsidiary. These transactions principally include situations where the investee purchases treasury stock from, or sells unissued shares or shares held in the treasury to, outside shareholders. (If the investor participates in these transactions on a pro rata basis, its percentage ownership will not change and no special accounting will be necessary.) Similar results will be obtained when holders of outstanding options or convertible securities acquire investee common shares.

When the investee engages in one of the above capital transactions, the investor's ownership percentage is changed. This gives rise to a gain or loss, depending on whether the price paid (for treasury shares acquired) or received (for shares issued) is greater or lesser than the per share carrying value of the investor's interest in the investee. However, since no gain or loss can be recognized on capital transactions, these purchases or sales will affect paid-in capital and/or retained earnings directly, without being reflected in the investor's income statement. This method is consistent with the treatment that would be accorded to a consolidated subsidiary's capital transaction. An exception is that, under certain circumstances, the SEC will permit income recognition based on the concept that the investor is essentially selling part of its investment.

Example of accounting for an investee capital transaction

Assume R Corp. purchases, on 1/2/05, 25% (2,000 shares) of E Corp.'s outstanding shares for $80,000. The cost is equal to both the book and fair values of R's interest in E's underlying net assets (i.e., there is no differential to be accounted for). One week later, E Corp. buys 1,000 shares of its stock from other shareholders for $50,000. Since the price paid ($50/share) exceeded R Corp.'s per share carrying value of its interest, $40, R Corp. has in fact suffered an economic loss by the transaction. Also, its percentage ownership of E Corp. has increased as the number of shares held by third parties has been reduced.

R Corp.'s new interest in E's net assets is

$$\frac{\text{2,000 shares held by R}}{\text{7,000 shares outstanding}} \times \text{E Corp. net assets}$$

$$.2857 \times (\$320{,}000 - \$50{,}000) = \$77{,}143$$

The interest held by R Corp. has thus been diminished by $80,000 – $77,143 = $2,857. Therefore, R Corp. should make the following entry:

Paid-in capital (or retained earnings)	2,857	
Investment in E Corp.		2,857

R Corp. should charge the loss against paid-in capital if paid-in capital from past transactions of a similar nature exists; otherwise the debit is to retained earnings. Had the transaction given rise to a gain it would have been credited to paid-in capital only (never to retained earnings) following the prescription in APB 6 that transactions in one's own shares cannot produce earnings.

Note that the amount of the charge to paid-in capital (or retained earnings) in the entry above can be verified as follows: R Corp.'s share of the posttransaction net equity (2/7) times the "excess" price paid ($50 – $40 = $10) times the number of shares purchased = 2/7 x $10 x 1,000 = $2,857.

EMERGING ISSUES TASK FORCE ISSUES SUMMARIES

84-5 Sale of Marketable Securities with a Put Option

The original consensus held that accounting, as a sale or as secured borrowing, depended upon the assessed probability of the put being exercised by the holder. FAS 125 replaced this probability assessment with an evaluation of whether the transferor has surrendered control and whether it has received consideration other than a beneficial interest in the asset transferred. If control has been transferred, even a high likelihood of exercise of the put option would not result in secured borrowing accounting treatment. If accounted for as a sale, the gain is determined with reference to all assets received and liabilities incurred by transferor to be recorded at fair value—including the put option liability, which would reflect its likelihood of exercise. FAS 140 restores the need for probability assessment, but only if transfer qualifies for sale treatment and the security is not readily available. The assessment of likelihood of exercise of the put is at transaction date only; FAS 140 does not address any subsequent reassessment.

85-40 Comprehensive Review of Sales of Marketable Securities with Put Arrangements

In general, the existence of put option does not affect accounting for sales of marketable securities, to be accounted for as sales if control is transferred, and as secured borrowings otherwise. However, per FAS 140, probability of exercise becomes relevant when sale accounting was used and security is not readily obtainable. If a put option is granted to transferee, it is recorded at fair value as a liability by the transferor, thus affecting the computation of gain or loss to be recognized on the sale.

96-10 Impact of Certain Transactions on the Held-to-Maturity Classification under FASB Statement No. 115

Transactions involving held to maturity investments that are not accounted for as sales (e.g., wash sales) do not call into question the classification of investments as held-to-maturity. A similar conclusion would result from bond swaps. However, if intent is to not hold the new security received until maturity, then intent regarding other bond holdings, etc., may be questioned. The issuance of FAS 140 had the effect of partially nullifying this consensus: Unless the closing side of the wash sale transaction is a concurrently entered contract, the opening side must be accounted for as a sale, which then would trigger the concern over the classification as held-to-maturity. FAS 140 does not affect conclusion on desecuritizations, however.

96-16 Investor's Accounting for an Investee When the Investor Has Majority of the Voting Interest but the Majority Shareholder or Shareholders Have Certain Approval or Veto Rights

This consensus deals with situations in which the majority owner of an entity does not exercise control and thus, under FAS 94, potentially should not consolidate the investee. The situation arises when the minority owners have rights such as approval of management compensation, selection or termination of management, or the establishment of operating and capital policies and procedures. Collectively, these approval or veto powers are referred to as "substantive participating rights," and are contrasted to "protective rights" such as those relating to entering bankruptcy proceedings, or to major acquisitions or dispositions of assets. The EITF concluded that a finding that the majority owner lacks control depends on the facts and circumstances, and that its lack of control is generally related to the minority owner's ability to effectively participate in decisions in the "ordinary course of business." In its view, a minority owner's protective rights would not be sufficient to overcome the presumption of majority control, while substantive participating rights would overcome that presumption.

The Task Force further concluded that a number of other factors must be given consideration in reaching a conclusion on the matter of a possible negating of majority owner control. Among these are the relative size of majority and minority interests (the greater the disparity, the more likely the minority's rights are only protective in nature); the mechanisms of governance (which decisions are reserved to stockholders as opposed to being made by the directors); other possible relationships between the majority and minority owners; and the likelihood of occurrence of decision-making situations in which the minority would have the right to significantly participate.

97-7 Accounting for Hedges of the Foreign Currency Risk Inherent in an Available-for-Sale Marketable Equity Security

This issue relates to some investments, such as those registered on foreign exchanges, which have inherent foreign exchange risk associated with them. If these investments are categorized as available-for-sale, value changes may include the effects of both market and exchange rate changes. In some cases, the entity will enter into foreign exchange hedging to protect against exchange rate risk; the issue then is whether transaction gains or losses on forward contract should be included in contra equity account for available-for-sale securities' unrealized gains or losses. The consensus was in support of this treatment: The gain or loss should be shown in the same account if it is associated with the securities' price change. Foreign exchange risk is inherent only if two conditions are met: securities are not traded on exchange denominated in investor's functional currency; and dividends or other cash flows are all denominated in foreign currency. This consensus has been affected by the later promulgation of FAS 130 and 133.

98-7 Accounting for Exchanges of Similar Equity Method Investments

A consensus was reached that exchanges of similar equity method investments should be accounted for per APB 29. EITF 86-29 provides guidelines for determining similarity/nonsimilarity of productive assets.

98-13 Accounting by an Equity Method Investor for Investee Losses When the Investor Has Loans to and Investments in Other Securities of the Investee

This considers how the loss recognized under the equity method per APB 18 should be recorded by the investor when the carrying amount of the common stock has already been reduced to zero, and how that interacts with the applicable literature relating to investments in the other securities of the investee (either FAS 114 or 115). In its consensus, the Task Force found that in situations where (1) an investor is not required to advance additional funds to the investee and (2) previous losses have reduced the common stock investment account to zero, the investor should continue to report its share of equity method losses in its statement of operations to the extent of, and as an adjustment to, the adjusted basis of the other investments in the investee. The order in which those equity method losses should be applied to the other investments should follow the seniority (i.e., priority in liquidation) of the other investments.

The adjusted basis of the other investments should be adjusted for the equity method losses, then the investor should apply FAS 114 and 115 to the other investments, as applicable. The cost basis of the other investments is the original cost of those investments adjusted for the effects of other than temporary write-downs, unrealized holding gains and losses on FAS 115 securities classified as trading, and amortization of any discount or premium on debt securities or loans. The adjusted basis is the cost basis adjusted for the FAS 114 valuation allowance account for an investee loan and the cumulative equity method losses applied to the other investments. When the investee later becomes profitable, equity method income subsequently recorded should be applied to the adjusted basis of the other investments in reverse order of the application of the equity method losses, that is, equity method income is applied to the more senior securities first.

A detailed example of this standard is set forth in the body of this chapter. Also note that EITF 99-10 (below) further addresses this matter.

98-15 Structured Notes Acquired for a Specified Investment Strategy

Structured notes are debt obligations that are coupled with derivatives, typically related to interest rates or foreign currency exchange rates, such that a prescribed increase or decrease in the reference rate will have a large impact on some defined attribute of the debt obligation, such as its interest rate, maturity value or maturity date. In some instances, two or more such instruments may be acquired, having essentially opposite characteristics, such that, for example, a change in a reference interest rate will cause the fair value on one holding to increase and the other to decrease, by equal amounts. In some instances, this may have been arranged in order to be able to achieve a recognizable loss on the one (losing) investment by selling it, while holding the other (winning) one as an available-for-sale security with unrealized gains reported in other comprehensive income. This consensus effectively ends this practice by requiring that the related investments be accounted for as a unit while held, but if one is sold the (joint) carrying amount must be allocated based on relative fair values as of the date of sale, consistent with guidance in FAS 140. The result will be that neither gain nor loss, recognized or included in stockholders' equity, will be realized from such transactions.

99-8 Accounting for Transfers of Assets That Are Derivative Instruments but That Are Not Financial Assets

This pertains to certain assets that meet the definition of a derivative instrument under FAS 133 but that are not financial assets as defined in FAS 140. The definitions of financial asset and financial liability in FAS 140 are derived from those in FAS 105. FAS 140 applies only to transfers of financial assets even though it is used to account for extinguishments of all liabilities (both financial and nonfinancial). It is unclear how transfers of assets that are derivative instruments but that are not financial assets should be accounted for. The Task Force consensus is that transfers of assets that are derivative instruments and subject to the requirements of FAS 133, but that are not financial assets, should be accounted for by analogy to FAS 140. An example would be a transfer to another entity of a derivative instrument, such as a forward contract to purchase gold that requires physical settlement and is or will be subject to the requirements of FAS 133.

99-10 Percentage Used to Determine the Amount of Equity Method Losses

This expands upon the material presented in Issue 98-13, which addresses the situation where an investor owns common stock and "other investments" in an investee and the investor is not required to advance additional funds to the investee and previous losses have reduced the common stock investment account to zero. The issue is how additional equity method losses should be measured and recognized by the investor in such a circumstance.

The consensus is that an investor should not recognize equity method losses based solely on the percentage of investee common stock held by the investor. As to whether an investor should recognize equity method losses based on (1) the ownership level of the particular investee security or loan/advance held by the investor to which the equity method losses are being applied or (2) the change in the investor's claim on the investee's book value, the Task Force was not asked to reach a consensus.

See the body of this chapter for a comprehensive example of how investee losses should be accounted for under these circumstances.

99-20 Recognition of Interest Income and Impairment on Purchased and Retained Beneficial Interests in Securitized Financial Assets

If an entity sells a portion of an asset that it owns, the portion retained becomes an asset separate from the portion sold and separate from the assets obtained in exchange. This is the situation when financial assets such as loans are securitized with certain interests being retained. The entity must allocate the previous carrying amount of the assets sold based on the relative fair values of each component at the date of sale. In most cases, the initial carrying amount (allocated cost) of the retained interest will be different from the fair value of the instrument. Furthermore, cash flows from those instruments may be delayed depending on the contractual provisions of the entire structure (for example, cash may be retained in a trust to fund a cash collateral account). The issue for the EITF was how interest income and impairment should be recognized for retained interests in securitizations classified as available-for-sale or as held-to-maturity.

The consensus was that the holder of the beneficial interest should recognize the excess of all cash flows anticipated at the acquisition transaction date over the initial investment as interest income using the effective yield method. The holder should update the estimate of cash flows over the life of the beneficial interest. If the estimated cash flows change (but there is still an excess over the carrying amount), the adjustment should be accounted for as a change in estimate with the amount of the periodic accretion adjusted over the life of the beneficial interest. If the fair value of the beneficial interest declines below its carrying amount, the holder should apply the impairment guidance in FAS 115. If it is not practicable for a holder/transferor to estimate the fair value of the beneficial interest at the securitization date, interest income should be recognized using the cash basis rather than the effective yield method.

Subsequently, certain revisions were made to clarify that if, based on current information and events that the holder of the beneficial interest anticipates a market participant will use in determining the current fair value of the beneficial interest, there is a change in estimated cash flows, the amount of accretable yield should be recalculated and if the change in estimated cash flows is adverse, an other than temporary impairment should be considered to have occurred. The change in estimated cash flows need not be "probable" as is currently stated (which has led to some confusion in practice).

00-1 Investor Balance Sheet and Income Statement Display under the Equity Method for Investments in Certain Partnerships and Other Unincorporated Noncontrolled Ventures

Under some circumstances, investor-venturers account for undivided interests in assets by means of pro rata consolidation, including a fraction of each asset category of the investee in the investor's balance sheet, typically commingled with the investor's own assets. The issue is whether this method can be used to account for an investment in a partnership or a joint venture, rather than by means of either full consolidation, the equity method, or historical cost. In its consensus, the EITF concluded that the pro rata method of consolidation is not appropriate for an investment in an unincorporated legal entity, except when the investee is in either the construction industry or the extractive industry (where this methodology has long been in use).

00-6 Accounting for Freestanding Derivative Financial Instruments Indexed to, and Potentially Settled in, the Stock of a Consolidated Subsidiary

EITF Issue 96-13 establishes a framework for accounting for freestanding derivative instruments that are indexed to, and potentially settled in, a company's own stock. That consensus did not, however, provide guidance on how to account for freestanding derivative instruments that are indexed to, and potentially settled in, a subsidiary's stock. The issue addressed here is how such contracts should be classified and measured in the consolidated financial statements.

A consensus exists that stock of a subsidiary is not equity of the parent; therefore, derivatives indexed to and to be settled in stock of a subsidiary do not meet FAS 133's exclusion criteria. If derivatives meeting the criteria of FAS 133 (e.g., for net settlement, etc.), these must be accounted for under the provisions of FAS 133, and not of Issue 96-13. The consensus also discusses a number of exceptions based on the criteria set forth in FAS 133.

The EITF reached several consensuses regarding derivatives not within the scope of FAS 133, while also noting that option or forward strike prices and premiums could be indicative of impairments of the parent's investment in subsidiaries—to be assessed using FAS 144. A parent's contract to purchase a subsidiary's (minority held) common stock should not be recorded until settled; during the period of the contract, income should continue to be allocated to the minority interest. A contract to sell shares in a subsidiary, likewise, should be recorded when settled; until that time, income would not be allocated to outside interests (counter parties to the derivative). No consensus was reached regarding written options.

02-14 Whether the Equity Method of Accounting Applies When an Investor Does Not Have an Investment in Voting Stock of an Investee but Exercises Significant Influence through Other Means

APB 18 was written to apply to investments in voting common stock of an investee, and authoritative guidance has been lacking regarding the accounting for investments in other vehicles, such as options and warrants, and complex licensing and/or management agreements, where significant influence might also be present. These nontraditional modes of investment providing the investor with significant influence have become more common over the years, thus need for guidance has become acute. EITF is developing the concept of **in-substance common stock** to address the accounting for these alternative investments. This issue is subject to further consideration by EITF, but the idea of **residual interest** is likely to be central to any consensus on accounting for such investments (i.e., if the investor possesses residual interests in the entity, it should be determined if it also has the ability to exercise significant influence over the investee; if it does, then APB 18 should be applied). Tentatively identified characteristics of a residual interest include an ownership interest that conveys certain rights; is dependent on the enterprise's profitability for distributions of enterprise assets (for example, dividends); and does not obligate the enterprise to transfer something of value to holders except in the case of liquidation or by formal act. Liquidation preferences and participation rights would be important factors to consider in making the determination of this existence.

While final consensus does not exist, it is clear that application of the equity method under APB 18 should not have been deemed limited to investments in voting common stock.

02-18 Accounting for Subsequent Investments in an Investee after Suspension of Equity Method Loss Recognition

An investor accounting for its investment under the equity method, making a further investment after it suspended loss recognition due to having reduced the former carrying value of its investment to zero, generally would not recognize the previously suspended losses. However, when the additional investment, in whole or in part, is made to fund the previous losses, loss recognition by the investor is appropriate. The previously suspended losses would be recognized only up to the amount of the additional investment determined to represent the funding of prior losses. The consensus sets forth certain factors to consider in making the determination of what fraction of the losses are to be recognized upon making the additional investment (discussed in the body of this chapter). Furthermore, if the investor becomes "otherwise committed" to provide financial support to an equity method investee, additional loss recognition may be appropriate; further guidance regarding the identification of this further level of commitment is said to be forthcoming.

03-01 The Meaning of Other than Temporary Impairment and Its Application to Certain Investments

This Issue addresses the meaning of the long-employed criterion, other than temporary. Essentially, it is to be the refutable presumption that impairments of investments are indeed other than temporary, and thus (in the case of available-for-sale and held-to-maturity investments) are to be reported currently in results of operations, unless there is positive evidence to support the alternative contention—that the impairment is instead only temporary, and thus (for held-to-maturity investments) not to be recognized at all. A similar approach is also applicable to evaluation of impairments to equity method investments.

While no consensus has yet been achieved, the proposed guidance would hold that an investment would be considered impaired if its fair value is less than its amortized cost basis (hereinafter referred to as its carrying amount). For an investment with no readily determinable fair value, the fair value of the investment would be measured when an impairment indicator is present. Certain underlying principles would be established for determining whether an impairment is other than temporary. Thus, unless positive evidence indicating that an investment's carrying amount is recoverable within a reasonable period of time outweighs negative evidence to the contrary, an impairment would be deemed other than temporary.

Under the proposed guidance, if an investment has been impaired for one year, it would be unlikely that sufficient objective and verifiable positive evidence would be available to support the recoverability of the investment's carrying value to overcome the extent of the negative evidence, except for certain investments with noncontingent contractual future cash flows. That one-year period would not be a "bright line" for purposes of determining whether an impairment is other than temporary.

Other guidance is expected to be developed to address impairment of debt securities, and how impairment criteria intersect with the classification of investments (i.e., whether the presumption that impairment continuing for longer than one year is other than temporary may be inconsistent with the held-to-maturity classification when there is not substantial doubt that the investor will collect all contractual interest and principal payments).

03-16 Accounting for Investments in Limited Liability Companies

Limited liability companies (LLC) have ownership characteristics of both limited partnerships and corporations. APB 18, while not explicitly applicable to noncorporate investments, is generally applied by analogy to various other forms of investment (such as limited partnerships), and SOP 78-9 specifically extends the equity method of accounting to real estate limited partnerships. (EITF Topic D-46 expressed the belief that the guidance in SOP 78-9 should be applied to all limited partnerships.)

This issue addresses whether equity method accounting should be applied to noncontrolling investments in LLC. The conclusion reached in March 2004 was that investments in a LLC that maintains a "specific ownership account" for each investor should be viewed as similar to a limited partnership for purposes of determining whether a noncontrolling investment should be accounted for using the cost method or the equity method of accounting. A specific ownership account is similar to a partnership capital account structure in which each member has a specific ownership account in the entity to which the member's share of profits and losses, contributions, and distributions accrues directly.

If the FASB ratifies the consensus on this issue, it will be required that the accounting for equity investments in existing LLC is conformed to the foregoing. The effect of this consensus will therefore be applied to the accounting for existing investments in LLC as of the beginning of the first fiscal period beginning after FASB ratification of the consensus (the first quarter beginning after June 15, 2004), by recognizing the cumulative effect of retroactive application. If, upon adoption of the consensus, this transition is not practicable, entities should record a change in accounting principle with a cumulative effect reflected in the current period income statement based on the book account balances in the ownership accounts. Thereafter, the consensus will be followed.

STATEMENTS OF POSITION

03-03 Accounting for Certain Loans or Debt Securities Acquired in a Transfer

This comprehensive statement of position is applicable to all reporting entities and addresses accounting for loans acquired in transfers where there has been a deterioration in credit quality prior to the acquisition, such that expected cash flows to the investor do not equal the contractual cash flows under the terms of the loan or debt security. The SOP requires that an *accretable yield* be computed based on the price paid and the expected future cash flows, and—with limited exceptions—this yield is maintained throughout the holding period of the loan or security. If expected cash flows are reassessed downward, a loss will be recognized in current earnings, but if reassessed upward (other than when this is a recovery or reversal of a previous downward revision) gain is not recognized, but rather a new accretable yield is computed and recognized prospectively. The precise accounting for changes in estimated future cash flows depends on whether the investment is a loan receivable or a debt security. (Comprehensive examples of each are included in the body of Chapter 10.)

11 BUSINESS COMBINATIONS AND CONSOLIDATED FINANCIAL STATEMENTS

PERSPECTIVE AND ISSUES

US GAAP had long permitted two distinct methods of accounting for business combinations. The purchase accounting method required that the actual cost of the acquisition be recognized, including any excess over the amounts allocable to the fair value of identifiable net assets, commonly known as goodwill. The pooling of interests methods, available only when a set of stringent criteria were all met, resulted in combining the book values of the merging entities, without any adjustment to reflect fair values of acquired assets and liabilities, and without any recognition of goodwill. Since pooling of interests accounting required that the mergers be achieved by means of exchanges of common stock, the use of this method was largely restricted to publicly-held acquirers, which greatly preferred poolings since this averted step-ups in carrying value of depreciable assets and goodwill recognition, the amortization of which would reduce future reported earnings.

Pooling accounting was widely seen as not being indicative of economic reality, since mergers which were "marriages of equals" rarely, if ever, occurred, notwithstanding the presumption that this was the theoretical basis for this method of accounting's use. The effort to make purchase accounting universally required involved much debate and a very lengthy FASB project. Ultimately, gaining acceptance for the elimination of pooling required a significant compromise on the related matter of goodwill accounting, so that under the rules established in 2001 (FAS 141 and FAS 142) goodwill is no longer amortized and the impact on reported income will often more closely resemble that of the now-banned pooling method than the traditional purchase accounting method. However, although periodic amortization is no longer reported, goodwill must be tested annually for impairment and, when impairment is found to have occurred, goodwill must be written down to fair value, with the adjustment reflected in operating income of that period.

Currently, all business combinations, except for those involving not-for-profit entities and combinations of entities under common control (e.g., parent/subsidiary and brother/sister mergers), must be accounted for as purchases. Goodwill arising from earlier purchase business combinations is not restored, but the unamortized balance as of the effective date of the new standards was no longer to be amortized. Poolings completed before the effective date of FAS 141 did not, however, need to be restated. The accounting for mergers or acquisitions of not-for-profit and mutual organizations was not resolved by FAS 141, but FASB is currently addressing these situations (discussed in this chapter).

While goodwill impairment must be regularly assessed, the actual application of FAS 142 results in recognizing goodwill created by the reporting entity subsequent to the purchase combination, to the extent that this replaces or offsets impaired goodwill, so in many cases impairments will not be recognized even when the value of the acquired operations has declined. This approach—which reverses the longstanding ban on recognizing internally created (as opposed to purchased) goodwill—was necessitated by the virtual impossibility of separately identifying elements of goodwill having alternative derivations. Even with this simplifying approach, measurement of goodwill impairment is a fairly difficult task, often requiring the services of independent valuation consultants.

This chapter will address purchase accounting for business combinations in detail, and the accounting for goodwill to a lesser extent. Chapter 9 addresses the accounting for all intangible assets, including goodwill, with greater specificity.

When the acquired entity is merged into the acquiring entity or when both entities are consolidated into a new (third) entity, all assets and liabilities are recorded directly in the accounting records of the surviving organization. However, when the acquirer obtains a majority (or all) of the common stock of the acquired entity (which maintains a separate legal existence), the assets and liabilities of the acquired company will not be recorded in the acquirer's accounting records. In this case, GAAP normally requires that consolidated financial statements be prepared (i.e., that an accounting consolidation be effected). In either case, under FAS 141, purchase accounting must be applied, which normally will result in the recognition of goodwill. In the case of accounting consolidations, goodwill does not appear in the acquirer's (or acquiree's) accounting records, but rather will arise from the consolidation entries made to generate the financial statements.

As was also the case under predecessor standard APB 16, the purchase method of FAS 141 does not apply to combinations of entities under common control. In such instances, those transactions are accounted for by a method essentially identical to pooling of interests accounting. While **common control** is not defined by FAS 141, the EITF addressed this in Issue 02-5, as detailed later in this chapter.

Consolidated financial reporting is required when the parent entity owns a majority of the voting common shares of the subsidiary. Former exceptions to this requirement (with the "nonhomogeneity" of operations traditionally being the most popular justification for nonconsolidation) have been eliminated in several stages. Most recently, FAS 144 ended the exception for temporary control, so that only lack of control over the subsidiary by the parent now remains a legitimate reason to exclude a subsidiary from full consolidation.

While the presentation of consolidated financial statements is required under GAAP, there is no parallel requirement to present combined financial statements for entities under common control (brother/sister entities). However, in certain cases, it is desirable that combined financial statements be prepared for such entities. This process is very similar to an accounting consolidation using pooling accounting, except that the equity accounts for the combining entities are carried forward intact.

The major accounting issues in business combinations and in the preparation and presentation of consolidated or combined financial statements are as follows:

1. The proper accounting basis for the assets and liabilities of the combining entities
2. The accounting for goodwill or negative goodwill, if any exists
3. The elimination of intercompany balances and transactions in the preparation of consolidated or combined statements

Consolidation of many of what were formerly called "special purpose entities" (SPE)—recently renamed "variable interest entities" (VIE) by FIN 46(R)—will increase substantially under these recently imposed requirements, which were spurred on by the financial reporting scandals of the early 2000s. Rules governing consolidation of VIE are complex and will likely evolve further, but it is clear that many formerly "off the books" transactions, even those involving closely held enterprises, will now be subject to inclusion in the "primary beneficiary's" financial statements.

Sources of GAAP

APB	*ARB*	*FAS*	*FTB*	*EITF*
16, 18, 29	51	94, 140, 141, 142	85-5, 85-6	84-13, 84-33, 84-35, 85-12, 85-28, 85-45, 86-29, 86-32, 87-11, 87-17, 87-21, 87-27, 88-16, 89-7, 90-5, 90-6, 90-12, 90-13, 91-5, 93-7, 95-3, 95-8, 95-14, 95-19, 95-21, 96-4, 96-5, 96-7, 96-20, 97-2, 97-6, 97-8, 97-15, 98-1, 98-2, 98-3, 98-4, 99-6, 99-12, 99-15, 01-3, 02-5, 02-11, 02-17, D-54, D-58, D-81, D-100, D-101, D-105
FIN		*FSP*		*SOP*
46(R)		46-1, 46-2, 46-3, 46-4, 46-5, 46-6, 46-7, 46-8, 46(R)-1, 46(R)-2, 46(R)-3, 46(R)-4		03-3

DEFINITIONS OF TERMS

Accounting consolidation. The process of combining the financial statements of a parent company and one or more legally separate and distinct subsidiaries.

Acquisition. One enterprise pays cash, or issues stock or debt, for all or part of the voting stock of another enterprise. The acquired enterprise remains intact as a separate legal entity. The parent-subsidiary relationship is accounted for as a purchase, and it is referred to as an acquisition.

Combination. Any transaction whereby one enterprise obtains control over the assets and properties of another enterprise, regardless of the resulting form of the enterprise emerging from the combination transaction.

Combined financial statements. Financial statements presenting the financial position and/or results of operations of legally separate entities, related by common ownership, as if they were a single entity.

Consolidated financial statements. Consolidated statements presenting, primarily for the benefit of the shareholders and creditors of the parent company, the results of operations and the financial position of a parent company and its subsidiaries essentially as if the group were a single enterprise with one or more branches or divisions.

Consolidation. A new enterprise is formed to acquire two or more other enterprises through an exchange of voting stock. The acquired enterprises then cease to exist as separate legal entities.

Control. Generally, the ability of one entity to direct the activities of another, so as to accomplish the former's objectives. Control may be present even absent majority ownership.

Controlling financial interest. The at-risk equity investors hold a controlling financial interest in an entity if they collectively

1. Have voting or similar rights (such as the rights of a common stockholder, general partner, or LLC member) to make decisions, directly or indirectly, about the entity's activities that significantly affect the entity's success.

   NOTE: If none of the investors hold these rights, this criterion is not satisfied. In addition, if some investors' voting rights are not proportional to their obligations to absorb the entity's expected losses, or to receive the entity's expected residual rewards, or both ***and*** *substantially all of the entity's activities involve or are conducted on behalf of an investor that has disproportionately few voting rights, this criterion is not satisfied.*

2. Are obligated to absorb the entity's expected losses. If the investors are directly or indirectly protected from these losses or guaranteed a return by the entity (or by other parties involved with the entity), this criterion is not satisfied.
3. Are entitled to receive the entity's expected residual returns. If the investors' return is limited by (a) the entity's governing documents, (b) arrangements with other variable interest holders (e.g., holders of debt, beneficial interests, etc.) or (c) the entity itself, this criterion is not satisfied.

If **any** one of these three criteria is absent, the at-risk equity investors collectively lack a controlling financial interest and, therefore, only have a controlling voting interest.

Entity concept. A method of preparing consolidated financial statements of a parent and majority-owned subsidiary that involves restatement of net assets of the subsidiary to fair value at the date of acquisition for **both** majority and noncontrolling interests.

Equity investment. An interest in an entity that, under GAAP, is reportable as equity on the entity's balance sheet. The practical application of this definition to certain types of instruments (e.g., mandatorily redeemable preferred stock) was affected by the issuance in May 2003 of FAS 150, *Accounting for Certain Financial Instruments with Characteristics of Both Liabilities and Equity*.

Expected losses and expected residual returns. Expected losses represent the expected negative variability in the fair value of an enterprise's net assets exclusive of variable interests. Expected residual returns represent the expected positive variability in the fair value of an enterprise's net assets exclusive of variable interests. The expected variability (separately defined below and illustrated in this chapter) in an enterprise's net income or loss is included in the determination of expected losses and expected residual returns.

Expected variability. When estimating an entity's expected future cash flows in accordance with CON 7, *Using Cash Flow Information and Present Value in Accounting Measurements* (discussed more fully in Chapter 1), a range of probability-weighted expected outcomes is used. Mathematically, this is simply a weighted-average calculation. The expected variability of the cash flows included in that calculation is computed by: (1) computing the difference between each individual estimated outcome and the weighted-average, (2) multiplying each difference computed in the previous step by the probability of occurrence assigned to that individual outcome, and (3) separately summing the positive variations (expected residual returns) and negative variations (expected losses). The absolute value of the expected residual returns will always equal the absolute value of the expected losses. The sum of the absolute values of the expected residual returns and the expected losses represents the expected variability in both directions associated with that estimate of probability-weighted expected cash flows.

Goodwill. The excess of the cost of an acquisition price over the fair value of acquired net assets which is recorded as an asset and written down only when, and if, impairment is identified and measured, based on future events and conditions.

Merger. One enterprise acquires all of the net assets of one or more other enterprises through an exchange of stock, payment of cash or other property, or the issue of debt instruments.

Negative goodwill. Properly known as the "excess of fair value over cost of acquired net assets." This amount represents the **net** excess of fair value of the net assets of a business acquisition, after allocation as a pro rata reduction of the amounts that otherwise would be assigned to all of the acquired assets other than cash and cash equivalents, trade receivables, inventory, financial instruments that are required to be carried on the balance sheet at fair value, assets to be disposed of by sale, and deferred tax assets. This excess is generally reported as an extraordinary gain in the period in which the business combination is initially recognized, unless the purchase price involves contingent consideration, in which case it is reported as a deferred credit until the contingency is resolved.

Noncontrolling interest. Sometimes referred to as minority interest, any remaining outstanding voting stock of a subsidiary not purchased by the acquiring enterprise.

Parent company concept. A method of preparing consolidated financial statements of a parent and majority-owned subsidiary that involves restatement of net assets of the subsidiary to fair value at the date of acquisition for **only** the majority interest.

Preacquisition contingencies. Uncertainties existing at the date of an acquisition accounted for by the purchase method that, if resolved within one year of the acquisition, result in a reallocation of the purchase price.

Primary beneficiary. A variable interest holder that is required to consolidate a variable interest entity (VIE). Consolidation is required when the holder of one or more variable interests would absorb a majority of the VIE's expected losses, receive a majority of the VIE's expected residual returns, or both. If one holder would absorb a majority of the VIE's expected losses and another holder would receive a majority of the VIE's expected residual returns, the holder absorbing the majority of the expected losses is the primary beneficiary and is thus required to consolidate the VIE.

Purchase method. The accounting method used for a business combination that recognizes that one combining entity was acquired by another. It establishes a new basis of accountability for the acquiree.

Purchased preacquisition earnings. An account used to report the earnings of a subsidiary attributable to percentage ownership acquired at the interim date in the current reporting period.

Related parties and de facto principals and agents. In determining whether a holder of an interest in a variable interest entity (VIE) is the VIE's primary beneficiary, the holder and its related parties are treated collectively as a single party. For this purpose, FIN 46(R) expands the definition of related parties from FAS 57 to include additional parties that act as "de facto agents or principals" of the variable interest holder including

1. A party unable to finance its operations without receiving subordinated financial support from the VIE interest holder such as another VIE of which the holder is the primary beneficiary.
2. A party the received its interests in the VIE as a contribution or loan from the holder.
3. An officer, employee, or member of the governing board of the holder.
4. A party that has agreed not to sell, transfer, or encumber its interest in the entity without prior approval of the holder when that agreement could constrain that party's ability to manage the economic risks or realize the economic rewards with respect to its interests in the VIE to which it would otherwise be entitled.
5. A party with a close business relationship to the holder such as the relationship between a professional service provider (e.g., an attorney, accountant, banker, consultant, etc.) and one of its significant clients.

Upon the application of this related-party attribution rule, if two or more related parties (including de facto agents or principals) hold variable interests in the same VIE for which the parties collectively would be the primary beneficiary, a determination is required of which party will individually be considered the primary beneficiary (i.e., will consolidate the VIE in its financial statements). The party whose activities are most closely associated with the VIE is deemed to be the primary beneficiary. Among the factors that are to be considered when making this determination are

1. The existence of principal/agency relationships between members of the related-party group.
2. The significance of the VIE's activities to the members of the related-party group.
3. The relationship of the members of the related-party group to the VIE's activities.
4. The exposure of a member of the related-party group to the VIE's expected losses.
5. The design (structure) of the VIE.

Reporting unit. An operating segment or one level below that (called a component), that is used to perform goodwill impairment testing.

Reverse acquisition. An acquisition when one entity, nominally the acquirer, issues so many shares to the former owners of the target entity that they become the majority owners of the successor entity.

Reverse spin-off. A spin-off transaction in which the nominal or legal spinnor is to be accounted for as the spinnee, in order to best reflect the economic reality of the spin-off transaction.

Subordinated financial support. Variable interests that absorb some or all of an entity's expected losses.

Subsidiary. An enterprise that is controlled, directly or indirectly, by another enterprise.

Total at-risk equity investment. The following criteria are set forth in FIN 46(R) for determining the total at-risk equity investment in an entity:

1. **Include** only equity investments that participate significantly in profits and losses, even if the investments have no voting rights.
2. **Exclude** equity interests issued by the entity in exchange for subordinated interests in other variable interest entities.
3. **Exclude** amounts provided to the equity investor (e.g., fees, charitable contributions, or other payments) directly or indirectly by the entity or other parties involved with the entity unless the provider is a parent, subsidiary, or affiliate of the investor that is required to be included in the same set of consolidated financial statements as the investor.
4. **Exclude** amounts financed for the equity investor (e.g., by loans or guarantees of loans) directly by the entity or by other parties involved with the entity, unless the party is a parent, subsidiary, or affiliate of the investor that is required to be included in the same set of consolidated financial statements as the investor.

There is a rebuttable presumption that an equity investment of less than 10% of an entity's total assets is insufficient to permit the entity to finance its activities without additional subordinated financial support. In order to overcome this presumption, one or more of the following conditions must be present:

1. **Performance**—The entity has demonstrated that it can finance its activities without additional subordinated financial support.
2. **Comparability**—The entity's invested equity is at least as much as other entities holding similar assets of similar quality in similar amounts and who operate without additional subordinated financial support.
3. **Reasonable forecast**—Based on reasonable quantitative evidence, the entity's invested equity exceeds the estimate of the entity's expected losses.

This 10% threshold was intended by FASB to apply only in one direction (i.e., a less than 10% investment is considered insufficient but a 10% or more investment is not necessarily presumed to be sufficient). Many entities engaged in high-risk activities, holding high-risk assets, or carrying significant off-balance-sheet exposures require more than 10% equity investment in order to finance their activities. Consequently, irrespective of the 10% threshold, an evaluation must be done to determine whether a particular entity with which the enterprise is involved requires an equity investment of 10% or greater in order to finance its activities without additional subordinated financial support.

Unrealized intercompany profit. The excess of the transaction price over the carrying value of an item (usually inventory or plant assets) transferred from (or to) a parent to (or from) the subsidiary (or among subsidiaries) and not sold to an outside entity. For purposes of consolidated financial statements, recognition must be deferred until subsequent realization through a transaction with an unrelated party.

Variable interest. Ownership, contractual, or other monetary interests in an entity that are either entitled to receive expected positive variability (referred to as expected residual returns) or obligated to absorb expected negative variability (referred to as expected losses).

Variable interest entity. An entity for which an analysis of the at-risk investments of the holders of its voting interests would not be effective in establishing the party or parties that hold a controlling financial interest in the entity. This situation arises either because (1) the entity is not adequately capitalized by at-risk equity sufficient to absorb its expected losses **or** (2) because the at-risk equity holders do not receive or bear all of the financial benefits or detriments that would provide those holders with a controlling financial interest in the entity.

CONCEPTS, RULES, AND EXAMPLES

Purchase Accounting under FAS 141

Business combinations (of whatever legal form) involving unrelated entities (i.e., those not under common control), are required to be accounted for using the purchase method of accounting. The only current exceptions to this rule are not-for-profit entities or mutual enterprises, whose consolidation accounting is currently being deliberated by FASB. The long-standing option in US GAAP to treat certain transactions, meeting a series of restrictive criteria, as "poolings of interests" no longer exists for newly transacted business combinations. Purchase accounting is an application of the cost principle, whereby assets obtained are accounted for at the price that was paid. A purchase transaction gives rise to a **new basis of accounting** for the purchased assets and liabilities.

Pooling, which had become subject to growing criticism from the SEC, from some academicians, and to a much lesser extent, from some in the corporate and public accounting realms, has finally been banned outright, effective for transactions **initiated** after June 30, 2001. The use of grossly disparate methods of accounting for what could be almost identical economic transactions was no longer seen as being conceptually defensible, despite widespread use not only in the U.S. but in many other nations as well (although, in recent years, the use of pooling had been sharply curtailed by many nations' accounting standards). Though defended by some (principally publicly held entities that generally were able to structure stock-swap acquisitions and which were often very driven by the desire to avert future goodwill amortization charges that would reduce reported earnings) all transactions must now be accounted for as purchases.

FAS 141, *Business Combinations*, continues the definition of "initiated" originally found in APB 16: it is the earlier of (1) the date that the major terms of a plan, including the ratio of exchange of stock, are announced publicly or otherwise formally made known to the stockholders of any one of the combining companies, or (2) the date that stockholders of a combining company are notified in writing of an exchange offer. Purchase accounting must be used for acquisitions initiated after June 30, 2001. The other provisions of FAS 141 (e.g., strengthened rules for identification and separate recognition of intangibles other than goodwill, discussed later in this chapter) are effective for acquisitions **completed** after June 30, 2001; thus these requirements are applicable to transactions that may have been initiated earlier.

FAS 141 replaced APB 16, while largely retaining the guidance in that standard pertaining to purchase business combinations. FAS 142, *Goodwill and Other Intangible Assets,* superseded APB 17 and arguably mitigates to a great extent the perceived negative impact of banning pooling by dropping the requirement to amortize goodwill arising from business acquisitions accounted for as purchases. (Goodwill is addressed later in this chapter and also in Chapter 9.)

Cost allocation, goodwill, and negative goodwill. The major purchase business combinations accounting issue is how to allocate the purchase cost to the various assets and liabilities acquired. Where the legal form of combination is a merger or consolidation, the acquirer records all the acquired assets and assumed liabilities at their **fair values** (**not** the acquired entity's book values). If the actual cost exceeds the fair value of the identifiable tangible and intangible net assets acquired, this excess is recorded as an intangible asset (**goodwill**). Under FAS 142, goodwill is no longer subject to periodic amortization, but rather, will be subject to periodic evaluation for impairment. It is expected that many, if not most, purchase business combinations will involve the recognition of goodwill.

Requirements for goodwill accounting now differ markedly from what was mandated under the prior rules (APB 17). They also differ from what appeared to be the goal of the FASB's proposal made in 1999, under which pooling accounting was to have been eliminated and goodwill arising from purchases was to have been amortized over twenty years or less. At that time, FASB rejected the notion of not subjecting goodwill to periodic amortization, and it noted that the conceptual alternative, conducting periodic assessments of goodwill impairment, would be hindered by the absence of cash flows directly identifiable with goodwill. Nonetheless, faced with strident opposition to the proposed elimination of pooling of interests accounting, FASB first proposed a compromise that would have retained goodwill amortization and reported it "below the line" (i.e., as a nonoperating expense). Ultimately FASB reached an accommodation which eliminated the longstanding requirement to amortize goodwill, substituting impairment testing, which it had earlier said would be unworkable.

Far less common than transactions giving rise to goodwill are "bargain purchases," where the cost of the acquisition is actually less than the fair value of the net assets acquired. Under FAS 142, this deficiency of cost under fair value is first allocated as a pro rata reduction of the amounts that otherwise would be assigned to the acquired assets other than cash and cash equivalents, trade receivables, inventory, financial instruments that are required to be carried on the balance sheet at fair value, assets to be disposed of by sale, and deferred income tax assets.

If the initially recorded amounts of these acquired assets are entirely eliminated, the excess, commonly called **negative goodwill,** is generally recognized immediately as an extraordinary gain. In cases in which there are contingent consideration issues (discussed below), however, the negative goodwill will be carried as a deferred credit on the balance sheet, until the contingency is resolved.

NOTE: Under prior GAAP, the offset was against all noncurrent assets, other than marketable securities, with any residual being deferred and amortized in the manner of positive goodwill. In practical terms, the new requirement is very close to the superseded one. On the other hand, FASB's 1999 proposal would have offset negative goodwill first against intangible assets acquired having no observable market; second, against acquired depreciable nonfinancial assets and to any other acquired intangible assets; and finally, any excess would have been recognized immediately as an extraordinary gain.

The logical foundation for gain recognition in bargain purchases is the belief that the very act of consummating the acquisition gives rise to income. This contradicts the principle that income results only from the use of assets, not their mere purchase. However, if care is given to accurate measurement of fair values, and the bargain is of such a great magnitude (unlikely to occur, in reality) that the allocated fair values of most noncurrent assets is entirely offset by the negative goodwill, with an excess yet remaining, then a gain has probably indeed been achieved by the acquirer. By giving this residual gain prominence in the income statement by requiring that it be categorized as extraordinary, rather than included in operations or in other income, the risk of misleading users of the financial statements is reduced.

Accounting for mergers. If the acquisition form of combination is used, the acquired entity maintains a separate legal and accounting existence and all assets and liabilities remain, in the records of the acquiree, at their premerger book values. However, when an **accounting consolidation** is performed (i.e., when consolidated financial statements are prepared), exactly the same results are obtained as those outlined above (i.e., assets and liabilities are adjusted to fair values, and goodwill is recorded, as noted above). In terms of how the parent-level (i.e., consolidated) financial statements are presented, there is absolutely no difference between acquisition combinations and outright mergers.

When less than 100% of the stock of the acquired entity is owned by the acquirer, a complication arises in the preparation of consolidated statements, and a noncontrolling interest (discussed below) must be computed.

When one entity is acquired by another, whether by outright merger or via a stock holding, a distinguishing characteristic of the purchase accounting method is that none of the equity accounts of the acquired entity (including its retained earnings) will appear on the acquirer's accounting records or on the consolidated financial statements. In other words, ownership interests of the acquired entity's shareholders are not continued after the merger, consolidation, or combination (acquisition) takes place.

In some transactions there is a continuity of ownership, as when, for example, shareholders in one entity exchange their shares for stock of the other (acquiring) entity. Previously, if a number of restrictive conditions were met, these transactions would be accounted for as poolings of interests, and (with some limitations) the equity of both combining enterprises would be carried forward to the postcombination balance sheets. Despite the appearance of being "mergers of equals," however, the vast preponderance of these transactions were acquisitions of one entity by the other. Under current GAAP, pooling accounting has been eliminated (for transactions after June 30, 2001), and the acquiree's equity accounts cannot be carried forward under any circumstances.

In determining which entity is the acquirer in transactions involving two or more enterprises, the new standard stresses that consideration be given to all pertinent facts, with emphasis on the relative voting rights in the combined enterprise and the composition of the board of directors and the senior management of the combined enterprise. In determining which of the shareholder groups retained or received the larger portion of the voting rights in the combined enterprise, the existence of any major voting blocks, unusual or special voting arrangements, and options, warrants, or convertible securities needs to be considered. Even if a new enterprise is formed to issue stock to effect a business combination (sometimes referred to as a consolidation), one of the existing combining enterprises must, on the basis of the evidence available, be deemed the acquirer.

Determining fair values. The purchase method requires that a determination be made of the fair value of each of the acquired company's identifiable tangible and intangible assets and of each of its liabilities, as of the date of combination. The determination of these fair values is crucial for proper application of the purchase method. FAS 141 carried forward the guidance previously found in APB 16, with some elaboration. The list below indicates how this is to be accomplished for various assets and liabilities.

1. **Marketable securities**—Fair values, which, for trading and available for sale securities, are already reflected in the acquiree's balance sheet
2. **Receivables**—Present values of amounts to be received determined by using current interest rates, less allowances for uncollectible accounts and collection costs, if applicable
3. **Inventories**
    a. Finished goods and merchandise inventories—Estimated selling prices less the sum of the costs of disposal and a normal profit
    b. Work in process inventories—Estimated selling prices less the sum of the costs of completion, costs of disposal, and a normal profit
    c. Raw material inventories—Current replacement cost
4. **Property, plant, and equipment**
    a. If expected to be used in operations—Current replacement costs for similar capacity unless the expected future use of the assets indicates a lower value to the acquirer
    b. If expected to be sold—Fair value less cost to sell
5. **Identifiable intangible assets and other assets** (such as land, natural resources, and nonmarketable securities)—Appraised (fair) value
6. **Liabilities** (such as notes and accounts payable, long-term debt, warranties, claims payable)—Present value of amounts to be paid determined at appropriate current interest rates
7. **Single-employer defined benefit pension plans**—Liabilities for a projected benefit obligation (PBO) in excess of the fair value of plan assets (or, conversely, assets representing the fair value of plant assets in excess of PBO) are to be determined pursuant to FAS 87, *Employers' Accounting for Pensions*
8. **Single-employer defined benefit postretirement plans**—Liabilities for accumulated postretirement benefit obligations (APBO) in excess of the fair value of plan assets (or, conversely, assets representing the fair value of plan assets in excess of APBO) are to be determined pursuant to FAS 106, *Employers' Accounting for Postretirement Benefits other than Pensions*

In-process research and development. One of the more controversial items acquired in business combinations is often "in-process research and development." Under GAAP, research and development costs (R&D) must be expensed as incurred. However, an acquirer can purchase another enterprise that has previously incurred and expensed substantial sums for research and development; in some instances, much or most of the price paid for the acquisition is for the value of the acquiree's previous R&D efforts. FIN 4 clearly states that the acquirer must expense that portion of the purchase price since, were this to be recorded as an acquired asset, it would create a "back door" for R&D capitalization which is prohibited by FAS 2.

While the traditional concern had been that acquiring entities would attempt to capitalize in-process research and development, in more recent years the opposite situation has more frequently arisen; that is, excessive portions of purchase premiums were attributed to in-process research and development and then immediately expensed, thereby reducing the allocation to goodwill and averting future amortization charges. With the new "no amortization" requirement, the expectation is that the motivation for exaggerated allocations to in-process research and development will abate. However, the new standard emphasizes again that appropriate allocation of the purchase cost to in-process research and development is required, and that this must be immediately expensed by the acquiring entity.

While in-process research and development costs must be expensed immediately upon acquisition, the value of this R&D does continue to play an important financial reporting role due to the new requirement that goodwill be regularly tested for impairment. Specifically, under the provision of FAS 142, a determination must be made of the implied fair value of goodwill, which is compared to the recorded amount of goodwill for purposes of ascertaining whether, and by how much, goodwill has been impaired. The process, which is identical to the purchase price allocation procedure used in a purchase business combination, involves the allocation of the overall fair value of a reporting unit to all assets and liabilities and **unrecognized intangibles** (including in-process R&D) as if the unit had been acquired as of the date of the impairment test.

Thus, the value of in-process R&D remains of vital concern to those responsible for accurate financial reporting as long as goodwill remains a recognized asset. Only to the extent that there is an excess of the aggregate fair value over amounts assigned to individual assets/liabilities will there be an implied fair value of goodwill. Were the analysis not done in this manner, the entire (and overstated) residual amount would be allocated to goodwill, which logically would not be truly comparable to the recorded amount of the goodwill, thereby impeding the impairment testing of goodwill.

Example

Purchaser Corp. acquired Attractive Co. in 2004 for $3.4 million. The purchase price was properly allocated to assets acquired and liabilities assumed, including an allocation of $240,000 to in-process R&D, which was properly expensed as of the acquisition date. A residual value of $500,000 was assigned to goodwill. The operations of the former Attractive Co. became a separate reporting unit within the consolidated company.

In 2005, to test for possible impairment, Purchaser management assessed the fair value of the former Attractive Co. operations—using information about comparable operations and economic characteristics, including market multiples of earnings—at $2.75 million. As of that date, the recorded (book) value of the reporting unit's net assets, **excluding** goodwill, was $2,400,000, and goodwill continued at its original $500,000 recorded value. Due to the fact that the estimated fair value of the reporting unit is less than its book value, FAS 142 requires the computation of the fair values of the individual assets and liabilities of the reporting unit to determine if its goodwill is impaired.

Management assigns an aggregate fair value of $2.4 million to the net identifiable tangible and intangible assets excluding goodwill, and also estimates that the in-process R&D has an economic (fair) value of $210,000. Since the residual fair value, [$2.75 million less ($2.4 million + $210,000) = $140,000], is less than the recorded amount of goodwill ($500,000), an impairment of ($500,000 – $140,000 =) $360,000 must be recognized by Purchaser Corp. as an operating expense in 2005.

Note that had the fair value of acquired in-process R&D, $210,000, been excluded from the foregoing analysis, the residual fair value would have been computed as $2.75 million – $2.4 million = $350,000; in that case, since recorded goodwill was $500,000, the impairment of goodwill would have only been $150,000. This result would have been erroneous because it would have ignored a real, albeit unrecognized, asset of the reporting unit (i.e., the in-process R&D). This would result in overstating goodwill by the $210,000 of in-process R&D, recognizing and erroneously captioning an asset for which such recognition is prohibited by GAAP.

Identifying all intangibles. Prior to undertaking the purchase price allocation, the acquiring enterprise must review the purchase consideration, if other than cash, to ensure that it has been appropriately valued. It must also carefully identify **all** of the assets acquired and liabilities assumed, including intangible assets. As the move to a "knowledge-based economy" accelerates, an increasing share of the purchase cost for business acquisitions will pertain to intangible assets, adding to valuation challenges as time goes on.

Intangibles cannot expediently be classified as part of goodwill, as was often done under prior standards, since the newly prescribed treatment for goodwill is not mirrored in the accounting for other intangibles. An identifiable intangible asset will be recognized separately from goodwill if it meets the asset recognition criteria in CON 5, and if either (1) control over the future economic benefits of the asset results from contractual or other legal rights (referred to as the "legal/contractual" criterion) or (2) the intangible asset is capable of being separated or divided and sold, transferred, licensed, rented, or exchanged (referred to as the "separability" criterion). Furthermore, even if the intangible asset cannot be sold, transferred, licensed, rented, or exchanged individually, it would still meet the separability criterion if it could be sold, transferred, licensed, rented, or exchanged along with a related contract, asset, or liability.

FAS 141 sets forth a lengthy listing of intangibles which are to be separately recognized, along with the terms over which amortization is generally to be applied, with certain exceptions for those intangibles having indefinite lives, such as perpetually renewable broadcast licenses, which are maintained at cost (subject to potential impairment write-downs) until a finite life can be ascertained, if ever. These intangibles generally fall into one of a set of categories, such as customer- or market-based assets (e.g., customer lists, newspaper mastheads, and trademarked brand names); contract-based assets (e.g., covenants not to compete, broadcast rights); artistic-based assets (e.g., plays, other literary works, musical compositions); and technology-based assets (e.g., title plant, databases, computer software). Except for indefinite life intangibles, identifiable intangibles are to be amortized over their estimated useful lives, defined as the period over which the intangible asset is expected to directly or indirectly generate cash flows for the entity. (See Chapter 9 for a complete discussion.)

The standards demand that all identifiable assets acquired and liabilities assumed in a business combination**, whether or not recorded separately in the financial statements of the acquired enterprise,** are to be assigned a portion of the total cost of the acquisition, based on their respective fair values as of the date of acquisition. Fair value—the amount a willing buyer would pay for the asset—will not necessarily correspond to the perceived value to the acquirer, based on the acquirer's planned use of the asset, which was the implicit cost allocation basis under APB 16. Independent appraisals and actuarial or other valuations may be useful in determining those fair values, but interestingly, the income tax basis of an asset or liability is not to be considered in determining its fair value. Given that the residual asset, goodwill, will not be amortized, the emphasis on accurate and complete valuation of all other identifiable intangibles is necessary to prevent its overstatement.

Identifiable intangibles under FAS 141. Acquired intangible assets are separately recognized if the benefit conferred is obtained through contractual or other legal rights, or if the intangible asset can be sold, transferred, licensed, rented, or exchanged, regardless of the acquirer's intent to do so. Thus, more intangible assets, such as unpatented technology and database content, are being separated from goodwill than previously was the case.

Appendix A to FAS 141 presents a comprehensive listing of intangible assets that FASB believes have characteristics that meet one of these two criteria (legal/contractual or separability), although it was also acknowledged that depending upon the facts and circumstances a specific acquired intangible asset might not meet the criteria. In practice, it would be logical to first consider whether the acquired intangibles are those specifically described by the FASB, and then to consider whether other intangibles also meeting the two criteria for separate capitalization might also be present.

The identified intangibles can be grouped into permits, intellectual property, technology tools, procurement rights, competitor arrangements, and customer arrangements.

Among the permits are

1. Broadcast rights, defined as being a license to transmit over certain bandwidths in the radio frequency spectrum, granted by the operation of communication laws
2. Certification marks, or right to be able to assert that a product or service meets certain standards of quality or origin, such as "ISO 9000 Certified"
3. Collective marks, or rights to signify membership in an association
4. Construction permits, which are rights to build a specified structure at a specified location
5. Franchise rights, or permits to engage in a trade-named business, to sell a trademarked good, or to sell a service-marked service in a particular geographic area
6. Internet domain names
7. Operating rights, permits to operate in a certain manner, such as that granted to a carrier to transport specified commodities, and
8. Use rights, which are permits to use specified land, property, or air space in a particular manner, such as the right to cut timber, expel emissions, or land airplanes

Intellectual property includes items such as

1. Copyrights, or the rights to reproduce, distribute, etc. an original work of literature, music, art, photography, or film
2. Newspaper mastheads, the rights to use the information that is displayed on the top of the first pages of newspapers
3. Patents, which are rights to make, use, or sell an invention for a specified period
4. Service marks, rights to use the name or symbol that distinguishes a service
5. Trade dress, defined as access to the overall appearance and image (unique color, shape, or package design) of a product; trademarks, which are rights to use the word, logo, or symbol that distinguishes a product; tradenames, or the right to use the name or symbol that distinguishes a business; trade secrets, which consist of information, such as a formula, process, or recipe, that is kept confidential; and unpatented technology, or access to the knowledge about the manner of accomplishing a task

Technology tools may consist of computer software, including programs, procedures, and documentation associated with computer hardware, as well as databases, which are collections of a particular type of information, such as scientific data or credit information.

Procurement rights include

1. Construction contracts, which are rights to acquire the subject of the contract in exchange for taking over the remaining obligations (including any payments)
2. Employment contracts, or rights to take the seller's place as the employer under the contract and thus obtain the employee's services in exchange for fulfilling the employer's remaining duties, such as payment of salaries and benefits, under the contract
3. Lease agreements, which, when they are assignable, are rights to step into the shoes of the lessee and thus obtain the rights to use assets that are the subject of the agreement, in exchange for making the remaining lease payments

4. License agreements, rights to access or use properties that are the subjects of licenses in exchange for making any remaining license payments and adhering to other responsibilities as licensee
5. Royalty agreements, which are rights to take the place of payors and thus assume the payors' remaining rights and duties under the agreements
6. Service or supply contracts, or rights to become the customer of particular contracts and thus purchase the specified products or services for the prices specified in those contracts

Competitor arrangements may include noncompete agreements, which are rights to assurances that companies or individuals will refrain from conducting similar businesses or selling to specific customers for an agreed-upon period; and standstill agreements, which convey rights to assurances that companies or individuals will refrain from engaging in certain activities for specified periods.

Finally, customer arrangements are items such as

1. Customer lists, defined as information about companies' customers, including names, contact information, and order histories that a third party, such as a competitor or a telemarketing firm would want to use in its own business
2. Customer relationships, or relationships between entities and their customers for which
    a. The entities have information about the customers and have regular contacts with the customers, and
    b. The customers have the ability to make direct contact with the entity
3. Contracts and related customer relationships which arise through contracts and are of value to buyers who can "step into the shoes" of the sellers and assume their remaining rights and duties under the contracts, and which hold the promise that the customers will place future orders with the entity
4. Noncontractual customer relationships, arising through means such as regular contacts by sales or service representatives, the value of which are derived from the prospect of the customers placing future orders with the entities
5. Order or production backlogs, providing buyers rights to step into the shoes of sellers on unfilled sales orders for services and for goods in amounts that exceed the quantity of finished goods and work-in-process on hand for filling the orders

One commonly cited intangible asset which was deliberately omitted by the FASB from its census of identifiable intangibles is the assembled workforce. Reportedly, FASB decided that the replacement cost technique that is often used to measure the fair value of an assembled workforce is not a representationally faithful measure of the fair value of the intellectual capital acquired. It was thus decided that an exception to the recognition criteria would be made, and that the fair value of an acquired assembled workforce would remain part of goodwill.

Duplicate assets and assets to be disposed of. While all assets are to be carefully evaluated, it is equally important to note that assets having no value are to be assigned no allocated cost. A typical example arises when facilities of the acquired entity duplicate those of the acquirer and accordingly are to be disposed of. The cost allocated to these facilities is equal to the estimated net salvage value, zero if no salvage value is expected, or a negative amount equal to the estimated costs of disposal, if warranted. The EITF has approved the allocation of "holding costs" to assets to be disposed of when debt from the business acquisition is to be paid down from the proceeds of such asset sales. In effect, the value assigned to such assets to be sold is the present value of the estimated selling price; interest incurred on debt used to finance these assets is then charged to the asset rather than to interest expense until the disposition actually occurs. On the other hand, if facilities of the acquired entity duplicate and are superior to facilities of the purchaser, with the intention that the latter will be disposed of, fair value must be allocated to the former. Eventual disposition of the redundant facilities of the acquirer may later result in a recognized gain or loss. This would fall into the general category of indirect costs of acquisition, which are not capitalizable or allocable to assets acquired in the purchase business combination.

The EITF has reached a similar conclusion with regard to entire subsidiaries of acquired entities (EITF 87-11 and 90-6). In such situations, the expected cash flows from the subsidiary's operations, through the expected date of disposition (but not longer than one year from the acquisition date), are considered in the purchase price allocation process. Ideally, operations of the subsidiary, including the cost of borrowed funds, if relevant, will **not** impact the acquirer's income statement, absent changes in estimates or altered plans for its disposition. Failure to achieve the planned disposition within one year, however, will result in all further operating results, including borrowing costs, being reported in the consolidated statement of income for future periods. Any difference between the subsidiary's carrying value at the disposition date and the proceeds of the disposition is treated as a re-allocation of the original purchase price of the business combination. If, however, the difference arises from identifiable events that occur after the merger date, gain or loss is reported at the disposition date.

Income tax accounting implications of purchase business combinations. Accounting for the income tax implications of purchase business combinations changed substantially with the issuance of FAS 109. Prior to that, any existing deferred income tax benefits or liabilities of the acquired entity, or any deferred income tax effects created by the purchase transaction itself (e.g., due to different income tax and financial reporting bases of the acquired assets or liabilities), were not recognized **as such** in the postacquisition consolidated balance sheet of the acquirer. Instead, these income tax effects were deemed to be components of the valuation process whereby the total purchase cost was allocated to the acquired identifiable assets and liabilities and, when necessary, to goodwill or negative goodwill. Accordingly, purchased assets and liabilities were recorded on a net-of-tax basis under APB 16.

Under FAS 109, the net-of-tax method was eliminated. Instead, asset and liability fair values are assigned "gross," and income tax effects, if any, are recorded as deferred income tax assets and/or liabilities. Under the FAS 109 "asset and liability" approach to deferred income tax accounting (detailed in Chapter 15), deferred income tax assets and liabilities are computed and adjusted at the date of each balance sheet. Therefore, any deferred income taxes of an acquired entity, or any deferred income taxes generated by the acquisition transaction itself, are recognized in recording the purchase business combination.

If an acquired entity has unrecorded deferred income tax benefits that can be used to offset the acquirer's deferred income tax liabilities, these benefits will be recognized in the postacquisition balance sheet. Similarly, under the provisions of FAS 109, the net operating loss carryforward (NOL) benefits of an acquired entity will also be recognized in the balance sheet of the acquirer if the acquirer can utilize those benefits under existing income tax law. The gross amount of the income tax benefits will always be recorded if the benefits are available to the acquirer. An offsetting valuation allowance will also be recorded if it is **more likely than not** that a deferred income tax asset will not be realized by the reporting entity (for example, if it is estimated that there will not be sufficient future taxable income to utilize the NOL).

The subsequent realization of unrecognized NOL benefits of an acquired entity will affect only goodwill and other noncurrent intangible assets, which are adjusted on a prospective basis when NOL benefits are subsequently recognized. Benefits exceeding recorded goodwill and other intangibles are credited to income tax expense (not, as under earlier GAAP, to extraordinary income) in the period when first recognized. (See Chapter 15 for details.)

The 1993 Tax Reconciliation Act provided for the amortization of goodwill over a fifteen-year period (previously, goodwill amortization was not deductible). If, before the new standard on goodwill was promulgated, the management of an enterprise had selected a longer or shorter amortization period, a temporary difference would have resulted. Under the new standard, there is no amortization of goodwill, but the tax requirement continues as before. This also creates a temporary difference, and thus deferred tax effects must be reported.

Other costs of business combinations. Direct costs of a business acquisition (e.g., finders' fees) are part of the cost to be allocated to tangible and intangible assets, including goodwill. However, stock registration and related expenses are offset against the proceeds (credits) of the stock issuance. Indirect costs are simply expensed in the period when the combination is effected.

In some instances, there are alternative ways to handle certain costs, influencing their treatment as either direct or indirect costs of a business acquisition. For example, if a prospective acquiree company has employee stock options outstanding, and it pays the employees to settle the options prior to the acquisition, then (per APB 25, as later interpreted by the EITF in 84-13 and 85-45) compensation expense must be recognized. On the other hand, if the employees exercise their options and then have their shares purchased by the acquirer (or exchanged for stock in the acquirer), there is no compensation expense, but instead this is reported as an additional cost of the purchase.

Costs related to a takeover defense by a prospective acquiree company are not capitalized, but are expenses of the period incurred. However, the EITF has suggested that if the costs are related to a "going private" transaction, these expenses may be classified as an extraordinary item in the statement of income.

In some takeover defense strategies, a target company will repurchase some of its own shares, generally at a price higher than that being offered by the prospective acquirer. Although generally the cost of repurchased stock is simply charged to treasury stock, there is the recognition that excessive repurchase costs are not always related to the "fair value" of the stock. When the price paid explicitly contains consideration for the seller's agreement not to purchase any further shares (a "standstill agreement"), this excess cost must be expensed (per FTB 85-6), with only the fair value of the shares themselves being charged to the treasury stock account. The EITF did not reach a consensus about the treatment of excessive costs of treasury shares absent explicit payment for other services. However, the SEC favors expensing any excess costs. As a general rule, judgment should be applied in evaluating each circumstance.

Example of purchase transaction—goodwill

Jorie Corp. acquired all of the common stock of Balkin Boiler Manufacturing Co. on January 2, 2003, at a cost of $32 million, consisting of $15 million in cash and the balance represented by a long-term note to former Balkin stockholders. As of January 2, 2003, immediately prior to the transaction, Balkin's balance sheet is as follows, with both book and fair values indicated ($000 omitted):

	Book value	Fair value		Book value	Fair value
Cash	$ 1,000	$ 1,000	Current liabilities	$26,200	$26,200
Accounts receivable, net	12,200	12,000	Long-term debt	46,000	41,500
Inventory	8,500	9,750	Guarantee of debt	--	75
Other current assets	500	500			
Property, plant, and equipment, net	38,500	52,400			
Customer list	--	1,400			
Patents	2,400	3,900			
In-process research and development	--	8,600	Stockholders' equity (deficit)	(9,100)	21,775
Totals	$63,100	$89,550		$63,100	$89,550

The fair value of inventory exceeded the corresponding book value because Balkin had been using LIFO for many years to cost its inventory, and actual replacement cost was therefore somewhat higher than carrying value at the date of the acquisition. The long term debt's fair value was slightly lower than carrying value (cost) because the debt carries a fixed interest rate and the market rates have risen since the debt was incurred. Consequently, Balkin benefits economically by having future debt service requirements that are less than they would be if it were to borrow at current rates. Conversely, of course, the fair value of the lender's note receivable has declined since it now represents a loan payable at less than market rates. Finally, the fair value of Balkin's receivables have also declined from their carrying amount, due to both the higher market rates of interest and to the greater risk of uncollectibility because of the change in ownership. The higher interest rates impact the valuation in two ways: (1) when computing the discounted present value of the amounts to be received, the higher interest rate reduces the computed present value, and (2) the higher interest rates may serve as an incentive for customers to delay payments to Balkin rather than borrow the money to repay the receivables, with that delay resulting in cash flows being received later than anticipated thus causing the present value to decline.

Balkin's customer list has been appraised at $1.4 million and is a major reason for the company's acquisition by Jorie. Having been internally developed over many years, the customer list is not recorded as an asset by Balkin, however. The patents have been amortized down to $2.4 million in Balkin's accounting records, consistent with GAAP, but an appraisal finds that on a fair value basis the value is somewhat higher.

Similarly, property, plant, and equipment has been depreciated down to a book value of $38.5 million, but has been appraised at a sound value (that is, replacement cost new adjusted for the fraction of the useful life already elapsed) of $52.4 million.

A key asset being acquired by Jorie, albeit one not formally recognized by Balkin, is the in-process research and development (IPR&D), which pertains to activities undertaken over a period of several years aimed at making significant process and product improvements which would enhance Balkin's market position and will be captured by the new combined operations. It has been determined that duplicating the benefits of this ongoing R&D work would cost Jorie $8.6 million. The strong motivation to make this acquisition, and to pay a substantial premium over book value, is based on Balkin's customer list and its IPR&D. Balkin has previously expensed all R&D costs incurred, as required under GAAP (FAS 2).

Balkin had guaranteed a $1.5 million bank debt of a former affiliated entity, but this was an "off the books" event since, under FIN 45, guarantees issued between corporations under common control are exempt from recognition. The actual contingent obligation has been appraised as having a fair value (considering both the amount and likelihood of having to honor the commitment) of $75,000.

Thus, although Balkin's balance sheet reflects a stockholders' deficit (including the par value of common stock issued and outstanding, additional paid-in capital, and accumulated deficit) of $9.1 million, the value of the acquisition, including the IPR&D, is much higher. The preliminary computation of goodwill is as follows:

Purchase price		$32,000,000
Net working capital	$(2,950,000)	
Property, plant, and equipment	52,400,000	
Customer list	1,400,000	
Patents	3,900,000	
In-process research and development	8,600,000	
Guarantee of indebtedness of others	(75,000)	
Long-term debt	(41,500,000)	21,775,000
Goodwill (excess of cost over fair value)		$10,225,000

Under GAAP (FIN 4), the fair value allocated to the in-process research and development must be immediately expensed. All other assets and liabilities are recorded by Jorie at the allocated fair values, with the excess cost being assigned to goodwill. The entry to record the purchase (for preparation of consolidated financial statements, for example) is as follows:

Cash	1,000,000	
Accounts receivable, net	12,000,000	
Inventory	9,750,000	
Other current assets	500,000	
Property, plant, and equipment	52,400,000	
Customer list	1,400,000	
Patents	3,900,000	
Goodwill	10,225,000	
Research and development expense	8,600,000	
Current liabilities		26,200,000
Guarantee of indebtedness of others		75,000
Long-term debt		41,500,000
Notes payable to former stockholders		17,000,000
Cash		15,000,000

Note that, while the foregoing example is for a stock acquisition, an asset and liability acquisition would be accounted for in the exact same manner. Also, since the debt is recorded at fair value, which will often differ from face (maturity) value, the differential (premium or discount) must be amortized using the effective yield method from acquisition date to the maturity date of the debt, and thus there will be differences between actual payments of interest and the amounts recognized in the income statements as interest expense. Finally, note that property, plant, and equipment is recorded "net"—that is, the allocated fair value becomes the "cost" of these assets; accumulated depreciation previously recorded in the accounting records of the acquired entity does not carry forward to the postacquisition financial statements of the consolidated entity.

Example of purchase transaction—negative goodwill

Haglund Corp. acquires, on March 4, 2003, all the capital stock of Foster Co. for $800,000 in cash. A formerly successful enterprise, Foster had recently suffered from declining sales and demands for repayment of its outstanding bank debt, which were threatening its continued existence. Haglund management perceived an opportunity to make a favorable purchase of a company operating in a related line of business, and accordingly made this modest offer, which was accepted by the stockholders of Foster, the acquiree. Foster's balance sheet at the date of acquisition is as follows, with both book and fair values indicated ($000 omitted):

	Book value	*Fair value*		*Book value*	*Fair value*
Cash	$ 800	$ 800	Current liabilities	$ 2,875	$ 2,875
Accounts receivable, net	3,600	3,400	Long-term debt	11,155	11,155
Inventory	1,850	1,800			
Property, plant, and equipment	6,800	7,200	Stockholders' equity		
Net operating loss carryforwards	--	2,400	(deficit)	(980)	1,570
Totals	$13,050	$15,600		$13,050	$15,600

Foster had provided a valuation allowance for the deferred income tax asset attributable to the net operating loss carryforward benefit, since recurring and increasing losses made it more likely than not that these benefits would not be realized, consistent with GAAP (FAS 109). Haglund Corp., which is highly profitable, is in the same line of business, and intends to continue

Foster's operations, expects to be able to realize these benefits, and therefore will have no valuation allowance against this asset.

Thus, although Foster's balance sheet reflects a stockholders' deficit (including outstanding common stock, additional paid-in capital and accumulated deficit) of $980,000, the value of the acquisition is much higher, and furthermore the acquirer is able to negotiate a bargain purchase. The preliminary computation of negative goodwill is as follows:

Net working capital	$ 3,125,000	
Property, plant, and equipment	7,200,000	
Net operating loss carryforward	2,400,000	
Long-term debt	(11,155,000)	1,570,000
Purchase price		800,000
Negative goodwill (excess of fair value over cost)		$ 770,000

Under GAAP, the negative goodwill is first offset against all of the acquired assets other than cash and cash equivalents, trade receivables, inventory, financial instruments that are required to be carried on the balance sheet at fair value, assets to be disposed of by sale, and deferred income tax assets, on a pro rata basis. In the present instance, only the property, plant, and equipment are available for this offsetting (the NOL benefits are equivalent to deferred income tax assets under FAS 109; see further discussion in Chapter 15). The entry to record the purchase before allocating negative goodwill is therefore as follows:

Cash	800,000	
Accounts receivable, net	3,400,000	
Inventory	1,800,000	
Property, plant, and equipment	7,200,000	
Deferred income tax asset	2,400,000	
Current liabilities		2,875,000
Long-term debt		11,155,000
Cash		800,000
Negative goodwill		770,000

The entry to record the offsetting of the negative goodwill is as follows:

Negative goodwill	770,000	
Property, plant, and equipment, net		770,000

Since the negative goodwill is fully absorbed by the property, plant, and equipment, there will be no residual to recognize in earnings.

Example of purchase transaction—excess negative goodwill

The facts are similar to the immediately preceding example, except that Foster Co.'s long-term debt amounts to only $3,155,000 (book and fair values) as of the date of the acquisition transaction. This results in such a large amount of negative goodwill that an excess remains after property, plant, and equipment are reduced to zero. This excess negative goodwill is reported in the period in which the acquisition occurs as an extraordinary gain.

Foster's balance sheet at the date of acquisition is as follows, with both book and fair values indicated ($000 omitted):

	Book Value	*Fair Value*		*Book Value*	*Fair Value*
Cash	$ 800	$ 800	Current liabilities	$ 2,875	$ 2,875
Accounts receivable, net	3,600	3,400	Long-term debt	3,155	3,155
Inventory	1,850	1,800			
Property, plant, and equipment, net	6,800	7,200			
Net operating loss carryforwards	--	2,400	Stockholders' equity	7,020	9,570
Totals	$13,050	$15,600		$13,050	$15,600

The preliminary computation of negative goodwill is as follows:

Net working capital	$3,125,000	
Property, plant, and equipment	7,200,000	
Net operating loss carryforward	2,400,000	
Long-term debt	(3,155,000)	9,570,000
Purchase price		800,000
Negative goodwill (excess of fair value over cost)		$8,770,000

The entry to record the purchase before allocating negative goodwill is therefore as follows:

Cash	800,000	
Accounts receivable, net	3,400,000	
Inventory	1,800,000	
Property, plant, and equipment	7,200,000	
Deferred income tax asset	2,400,000	
Current liabilities		2,875,000
Long-term debt		3,155,000
Cash		800,000
Negative goodwill		8,770,000

The entry to record the offsetting of the negative goodwill is as follows:

Negative goodwill	8,770,000	
Property, plant, and equipment, net		7,200,000
Extraordinary item—gain on purchase		1,570,000

Since the negative goodwill is not fully absorbed by the property, plant, and equipment, there will be a residual to recognize in earnings. Under GAAP, this is presented as an extraordinary item (net of the related income tax effects, not computed here) in the income statement.

However, if the transaction provided for a contingent purchase price (e.g., based on meeting earnings targets over the next several years), the excess negative goodwill ($1,570,000 in this example) would be recorded on the balance sheet as a deferred credit, not subject to amortization, until the contingency was resolved. To the extent an increase in the purchase price resulted, that would reduce (or, in the extreme, even eliminate) the negative goodwill. Any remaining negative goodwill after the contingent purchase price has been resolved will be reported in the period of final resolution as an extraordinary gain.

Determining if an Acquisition Is a Business Combination

Before applying FAS 141 it is necessary to conclude that the acquisition constitutes a business, as opposed to being a group of productive assets. EITF 98-3 addresses this particular issue and offers a set of criteria, all of which must be met in order for the acquiree to meet the definition of a business. A business is defined as

> *...a self-sustaining integrated set of activities and assets conducted and managed for the purpose of providing a return to investors. A business consists of (a) inputs, (b) processes applied to those inputs, and (c) resulting outputs that are used to generate revenues. For a transferred set of activities and assets to be deemed a business, it must contain all of the inputs and processes necessary for it to continue to conduct normal operations after the transferred set is separated from the transferor, which includes the ability to sustain a revenue stream by providing its outputs to customers.*

According to EITF 98-3, the necessary **inputs** include (1) long-lived assets, including intangible assets, or right to the use of long-lived assets; (2) intellectual property; (3) the ability to obtain access to necessary materials or rights; and (4) employees. Note that the presence of intellectual property does not necessarily imply that intangible assets had been recognized for financial reporting purposes by the acquiree, and in many cases intangibles might not even be assigned values by the acquirer applying FAS 141.

Processes represent the existence of systems, standards, protocols, conventions, and rules that act to define the processes necessary for normal, self-sustaining operations, such as

(1) strategic management processes, (2) operational processes, and (3) resource management processes.

Outputs are the ability to obtain access to the customers that purchase the outputs of the transferred set.

According to EITF 98-3, a transferred set of activities and assets fails the definition of a business if it excludes one or more of the above items such that it is not possible for the set to continue normal operations and sustain a revenue stream by providing its products and/or services to customers. Exclusion of minor items that does not prevent the transferred set from continuing normal operations does not prevent classification of the acquired assets and activities as a business. The assessment of whether excluded items are only minor should be made without regard to the attributes of the transferee and should consider such factors as the uniqueness or scarcity of the missing element, the time frame, the level of effort, and the cost required to obtain the missing element. If goodwill is present in a transferred set of activities and assets, it should be presumed that the excluded items are minor and that the transferred set is a business, since goodwill is associated with an ongoing business and not with individual productive assets.

Importantly, the assessment of whether a transferred set of assets and operations constitutes a business should be made without regard to how the acquirer intends to use the transferred set. It is not relevant whether the transferee will actually operate the transferred set of assets and operations on a stand-alone basis or intends to continue using the transferred set in the same manner as did the transferor. The acquired operations can be restructured, integrated with the acquirer's operations, and reengineered in various ways without interfering with the determination that it was a business combination, if all criteria are satisfied.

There is also no threshold for numbers of individual assets to be obtained to qualify as a business. However, EITF 98-3 notes that if essentially all but a *de minimis* amount of the fair value of the transferred set of activities and assets is represented by a single tangible or identifiable intangible asset, the concentration of value is an indicator that an asset rather than a business is being received. It cites 3% as being a working definition of *de minimis*.

As described by EITF 98-3, the actual determination of whether a transferred set of assets and activities is or is not a business is a three-step process. These are

1. Identify the elements included in the transferred set of assets and activities
2. Compare the identified elements in the transferred set to the complete set of elements necessary for the transferred set to conduct normal operations, to identify any missing elements.
3. If there are missing elements, make an assessment as to whether the missing elements lead to a conclusion that the transferred set is not a business. That assessment is based on the degree of difficulty or the level of investment (relative to the fair value of the transferred set) necessary to obtain access to or to acquire the missing elements.

If the degree of difficulty and level of investment necessary to obtain access to or to acquire the missing elements are not significant, the missing elements may be deemed minor, thus not impeding classification as a business acquisition. The determination requires the exercise of judgment and is dependent on the particular facts and circumstances. EITF 98-3 offers a series of illustrative examples to suggest how to apply the three-step test to determine if an acquisition is a business combination or merely the purchase of assets.

Goodwill

Identifiable and unidentifiable intangible assets. Ending the acceptability of pooling of interests accounting was accompanied by an even more fundamental change in the accounting for goodwill. After FASB first prepared to demand accelerating amortization of goodwill over a period shorter than the previously permitted forty years while precluding impairment testing, and then changed their mind and decided to prohibit any form of amortization in favor of the formerly rejected intermittent testing for impairment—an entirely new methodology was introduced.

The asset commonly known as goodwill is a subset of the broader topic, intangible asset accounting. FAS 142 addresses the accounting for all intangibles and raises the bar for delineating among different types of intangibles (i.e., distinguishing those separately identifiable intangibles having finite lives, those arguably having indefinite lives, and goodwill, which is unique in being "unidentifiable" and having an indeterminate life which makes periodic amortization impossible, in the FASB's current view). Chapter 9 discusses intangibles other than goodwill in great detail. Accordingly, this subject will only be addressed in the present chapter to the extent that the recognition and measurement of **identifiable** intangibles acquired in a purchase business combination impacts upon the measurement of goodwill, which is normally seen as being a residual asset following the assignment of purchase cost to all other assets and liabilities.

CON 5, *Recognition and Measurement in Financial Statements of Business Enterprises*, states that an asset is recognized if it meets the definition of an asset (found in CON 6, *Elements of Financial Statements*), has a relevant attribute measurable with sufficient reliability, and the information about it is representationally faithful, verifiable, neutral (i.e., it is reliable), and capable of making a difference in user decisions (i.e., it is relevant). In a business acquisition, any acquired **identifiable** intangible asset (e.g., patents, customer lists, etc.) must be recognized separately from goodwill when it meets these CON 5 asset recognition criteria, and additionally meets **either** of the following two criteria:

1. ***Legal/contractual***—Control over the future economic benefits of the asset results from contractual or other legal rights (regardless of whether those rights are transferable or separable from other rights and obligations), or
2. ***Separability***—The asset is capable of being separated or divided and sold, transferred, licensed, rented, or exchanged (regardless of whether there is an intent to do so or whether a market currently exists for that asset)—or, if it cannot be individually sold, etc., it is capable of being sold, transferred, licensed, rented or exchanged along with a related contract, asset, or liability.

All intangible assets acquired from other enterprises or individuals, whether singly, in groups, or as part of a business combination, are recognized initially and are measured based on their respective fair values. (Note that the initially determined fair value may be reduced in the case of business combinations with which negative goodwill is associated, as illustrated above.) Under the provisions of FAS 142 (but, arguably, as was also the case under the predecessor standard APB 17), serious effort must be directed to identifying the various intangibles acquired.

Useful economic life. Reliably measurable identifiable intangible assets, with the exception of those meeting the criteria for nonamortization (explained below), must be amortized over their respective useful economic lives. Useful economic life is the period over which the asset is expected to contribute (whether directly or indirectly) to cash flows of the entity. Factors to be considered in estimating the useful economic life of an intangible asset to an enterprise include

1. Legal, regulatory, or contractual provisions that may limit the maximum useful life;
2. Legal, regulatory, or contractual provisions that may enable renewal or extension of the asset's legal or contractual life (provided there is evidence to support renewal or extension without substantial cost and without materially modifying the original terms);
3. The effects of obsolescence, demand, competition, and other economic factors (such as the stability of the industry, the rate of technological change, expected changes in distribution channels, and the existence of uncertainty over future legal and/or regulatory changes);
4. The expected useful life of assets or groups of assets of the enterprise to which the useful life of the asset may parallel (such as mineral rights to depleting assets);
5. The expected use of the intangible asset by the enterprise; and
6. The level of maintenance expenditure required to obtain the expected future economic benefits from the asset.

In those instances where an intangible asset is determined to have an indefinite useful economic life, it will not be amortized until its life is determined to be finite at a later date. An example of such an asset would be a broadcast license, expiring in five years, but which may be renewed indefinitely at little cost. If the acquirer intends to renew the license indefinitely, and there is evidence to support its ability to do so, and the cash flows related to that license are expected to continue indefinitely, then no amortization would be recognized until such time as these criteria are no longer met.

Residual value. Typically, the entire fair value assigned to an intangible asset will be subject to amortization, although in some instances a residual value may be determined, which reduces the amortizable basis. The residual value of an amortizable intangible is assumed to be zero unless the useful life to the acquiring enterprise is shorter than the intangible asset's useful economic life, and either (1) the acquiring enterprise has a commitment from a third party to purchase the asset at the end of its useful life, or (2) the residual value can be determined by reference to an observable market for that asset and that market is expected to exist at the end of the asset's useful life. The method of amortization is to reflect the pattern in which the economic benefits of the intangible asset are to be consumed; absent the ability to ascertain this, straight-line amortization is applied. However, if impairment (determined by application of the FAS 144 criteria) is later determined, the carrying amount will be written down to the impaired amount.

Allocation to goodwill. After completing the purchase price allocation, any residual of cost over fair value of the net identifiable assets and liabilities is assigned to the unidentifiable asset, goodwill. Formerly subject to mandatory amortization, this now is not permitted to be amortized at all, by **any** allocation scheme and over **any** useful life. Impairment testing, using a methodology at variance with that set forth in FAS 144 (which, however, continues in effect for all other types of long-lived assets and intangibles other than goodwill), must be applied periodically, and any computed impairment will be presented as a separate line item in that period's income statement, as a component of income from continuing operations (unless associated with discontinued operations, in which case, the impairment would, net of income tax effects, be combined with the remaining effects of the discontinued operations).

The FASB had proposed an elaborate typology of constituent elements that often are incorporated into goodwill, possibly hoping to narrow the definition of that portion of goodwill that would be deemed a nonamortizing asset. This proved to be impractical, in much the way that the conceptual definition of goodwill, as the excess earnings power of the acquiree's operations, has not provided a workable blueprint for direct measurement. Thus, goodwill

will continue to be computed indirectly, by reference to the residual cost of the purchase transaction. If all other acquired assets have been identified (including, at the moment the transactions occurs, in-process research and development, which is then immediately expensed) and properly valued, by process of elimination. the remaining excess purchase price can be assigned to no asset other than goodwill.

The decision to eliminate the requirement for amortization was based on the recognition that **any** assigned useful life would be entirely arbitrary. The FASB recognized that not all goodwill declines in value and that any decline in value would rarely occur on a straight-line basis. Furthermore, FASB found during its field testing of the revised proposal that the estimation (albeit, indirectly) of future cash flows associated with goodwill (which is critical to implementation of an impairment testing approach) was feasible, contrary to earlier doubts. Finally, elimination of periodic amortization charges against earnings was a political price the FASB was willing to pay in order to secure its primary goal, elimination of the pooling-of-interests method of accounting for business combinations.

Impairment of goodwill. Given the decision to end the practice of amortization of goodwill, it became necessary to develop a mechanism for ensuring that the amount presented in the financial statements would not exceed the goodwill's estimated fair value at any point in time. This goal is generally consistent with the rules underlying those governing the balance sheet presentation of other long-lived assets.

For example, unlike tangible fixed assets, goodwill is impossible to separately identify and, if the ongoing business is successful, will tend to regenerate itself or be replaced by new internally generated goodwill. Historically, of course, goodwill could only achieve financial statement recognition in the limited situation of being purchased (i.e., internally generated goodwill was not recognizable for financial reporting purposes). However, any strategy for testing for impairment will inevitably be confounded by the existence, along with the purchased goodwill, of internally generated goodwill created subsequent to the date of the business combination. FASB concluded that it would be impossible to track "acquisition-specific" goodwill for impairment testing purposes and has, accordingly, endorsed a major departure from the traditional prohibition against recognition of internally generated intangibles. This approach still results in an inconsistency, however, since only entities that have purchased goodwill in the past will be permitted to recognize the internally generated replacement goodwill to avoid impairment write-downs. Entities that internally generate goodwill that have not entered into prior purchase business combinations are still prohibited from capitalizing that new goodwill and from presenting it as an asset on their balance sheets.

The impairment testing approach endorsed by FAS 142 reasons that "anomalies that result from the differences in how acquired goodwill and internally generated goodwill are accounted for…justify a departure from the current model of accounting." Thus, it concluded, as long as the total goodwill identifiable with the "reporting unit" to which acquisition-based goodwill was assigned can be shown to have a fair value exceeding the book value of the goodwill arising from the acquisition (which means apples are to be compared with oranges), no impairment will be found. This represents a major departure from prior accounting practice.

A reporting unit is defined in FAS 142 as an operating segment or a component of an operating segment that is one level below the operating segment as a whole. In order for a component to be considered a reporting unit it must

1. Constitute a business as defined in EITF 98-3, *Determining Whether a Nonmonetary Transaction Involves Receipt of Productive Assets or of a Business*, and

2. Have available discrete financial information regarding its operating results that is regularly reviewed by segment management.

A reporting unit is defined by reference to an operating segment, which is a term that is used in FAS 131. It is important to note that this definition applies equally to publicly held and privately held companies. This is true even though nonpublic entities are exempted from reporting segment information.

The appendix to Chapter 2 provides a diagram of how an organizational structure could be analyzed to determine its reporting units and provides definitional guidance regarding terminology used in the authoritative GAAP literature.

Measurement procedures for impairment. FASB recognized that goodwill impairment testing could not be effected by the same mechanical approach as FAS 144 sets forth for other long-lived assets. The reason is that the potentially very long-enduring cash flows emanating from goodwill would obviate the usefulness of FAS 144's "undiscounted cash flows" threshold test for impairment. In other words, it is computationally impossible to forecast undiscounted cash flows from the use and eventual disposition of an asset that has an indefinite life. In essence, the cash flows would continue into perpetuity and, thus, goodwill would never be deemed to be impaired.

Accordingly, FASB devised a unique impairment testing protocol for goodwill. Since direct measurement of the fair value of goodwill is clearly impossible, FASB concluded that a method similar to the method of allocating the purchase price to the net assets acquired in a business combination would need to be used to indirectly measure the value of goodwill subsequent to its acquisition date. Thus, it decided that the fair value of the net assets of a reporting unit be subtracted from the fair value of that reporting unit to determine the implied fair value of goodwill.

The fair value of the net assets of the reporting unit can be measured in a variety of ways. Direct market observation is certainly the most objective method, but in the absence of that information, other techniques can be substituted. CON 7 sets forth an "expected present value technique" which uses the sum of probability-weighted present values in a range of estimated cash flows adjusted for risk, all discounted using the same interest rate convention. FASB has indicated that such a technique is a more effective measurement tool than was the traditional present value approach, especially in situations in which the timing or the amount of estimated cash flows is uncertain, as is the case in measuring nonfinancial assets and liabilities.

In order to operationalize an approach that incorporates the values of the recognized assets and liabilities, the FASB concluded that all of the assets and liabilities of an acquired entity (including goodwill) that will be used in the operations of a reporting unit would have to be allocated to that reporting unit as of the acquisition date. For many business enterprises, this required changes to the internal, management accounting: for example, many entities had not previously allocated liabilities such as pension and environmental obligations below the corporate or entity level. To the extent these liabilities relate to one or more reporting unit or units, they are now included in the determination of the fair value of the recognized net assets of that unit or units.

Under FAS 131, the standard that sets forth the segment reporting required of publicly held corporations, "corporate" assets and liabilities are not assigned to any operating segment. Goodwill had often been included in these nonallocated corporate assets. The impairment testing process, however, could not proceed if a similar approach were adhered to, and accordingly under FAS 142 goodwill and all other related assets and liabilities are assigned to reporting units for purposes of testing goodwill for impairment. The amount of goodwill allocated to each segment is required to be disclosed in the notes to the financial statements of publicly held enterprises.

Goodwill impairment testing is a two-step process (as is impairment testing under FAS 144, although these two standards differ fundamentally in their respective approaches). In the first step, the possibility of impairment is assessed by comparing the fair value of the "reporting unit" taken as a whole to its carrying (book) value. If the fair value of the reporting unit exceeds its book value, there is no need for further analysis, since no impairment will be found to have occurred.

If, however, the carrying value exceeds fair value, a second step must be performed to indicate whether goodwill is impaired and, it if is impaired, by how much. In the second step, the recorded goodwill is compared to its implied fair value, computed in the same manner as when completing a business combination's "purchase price allocation." Thus, the fair value of the reporting unit is allocated to all the unit's assets and liabilities (including any unrecognized intangibles, according to the standard, even though this raises a question of noncomparability with book value), including, as a residual, goodwill. If the amount thus assigned to goodwill (its implied fair value) is less than its carrying value, the excess book value must be written off as an impairment expense. No other adjustments are to be made to the carrying values of any of the reporting unit's other assets or liabilities.

Unlike FAS 144's impairment measurement requirements, which use net (i.e., discounted) present values (or, when there is uncertainty regarding amounts or timing of future cash flows, probability-weighted expected present values) to actually measure the magnitude of any indicated impairment, the goodwill impairment approach uses a pseudo-purchase price allocation methodology. Implicitly, of course, the present value of future cash flow estimation techniques described above are incorporated in the impairment model, since the overall fair value of the reporting unit, and the fair values of some or all of the individual assets and liabilities, may be measured using these techniques.

Initial assessment of goodwill's fair value. In order to facilitate periodic assessments of possible impairment, it is necessary that a "benchmark assessment" be made. This benchmark assessment is performed in conjunction with most significant acquisitions, regardless of how much goodwill arises from that acquisition. Similarly, a benchmark assessment is performed in conjunction with a reorganization of an entity's reporting structure.

The **benchmark assessment** involves identifying the valuation model to be used, documenting key assumptions, and measuring the fair value of the reporting unit. In determining how goodwill is to be assigned to "reporting units," a reasonable and supportable approach must be adopted. In general, goodwill is assigned consistent with previous recognition of goodwill and with the reporting units to which the acquired assets and liabilities had been assigned. Goodwill assigned to a reporting unit is measured by the difference between the fair value of the entire reporting unit and the collective sum of the fair values of the reporting unit's assets, net of its liabilities.

In practice, consideration of the "synergistic" effects of business acquisitions may also be necessary (i.e., if other reporting units are expected to benefit from an acquired reporting unit, some or all of the acquired goodwill might be assignable to the other units). For example, a purchase may give a division of the acquirer access to a market niche benefiting one of its existing operating units, even if all the tangible and other intangible assets are assigned to other parts of the enterprise. If the goodwill allocation is based on the existence of such synergies, a "with and without" calculation is then used (i.e., it will be necessary to compare the fair value of the reporting unit before the acquisition to that after it).

Goodwill may also be split among two or more reporting units of the acquirer. Any allocation method used is to be consistently applied and the logic for doing so documented.

While it may be costly to accomplish, this benchmark assessment is necessary to ensure that the entity has identified and documented all key assumptions and tested the outputs of the selected valuation model for reasonableness prior to actually testing goodwill for impairment. Furthermore, measuring the fair value of the reporting unit as part of the benchmark assessment will provide management with a "reality check" on whether the amount of goodwill assigned to the reporting unit is reasonable, by comparing the fair value of the reporting unit with its carrying (book) value. If the fair value of the reporting unit is found to be less than its carrying amount, the goodwill allocation methodology should be reassessed, and the selected valuation model and the assumptions underpinning the initial valuation critically reexamined. In those cases where the indicated fair value of the reporting unit is still less than its carrying amount, goodwill would be tested for impairment.

Under FAS 142, a two-step testing protocol is prescribed. The first step is to compare the reporting unit's carrying amount (book value) to the unit's fair value. If fair value exceeds carrying value, there is no impairment and no need for further analysis. On the other hand, if carrying value exceeds estimated fair value, it becomes necessary to formally test for impairment; that is, to apply the second step as described in the following section.

Ongoing testing for impairment of goodwill. FASB's original intent was to mandate goodwill impairment testing on an "events and circumstances" basis, similar to the approach used in FAS 144 for depreciable or amortizable long-lived assets. This approach was discarded in favor of a requirement for annual impairment testing, although interim testing also remains necessary when an event or circumstance occurs between annual tests that suggests that the fair value of a reporting unit might have declined below its carrying value. Examples of such occurrences include an adverse change in the business climate or market, a legal factor, an action by regulators, the introduction of new competition, or a loss of key personnel. Goodwill is also required to be tested for impairment on an interim basis when it is deemed "more likely than not" that a reporting unit or a significant portion of a reporting unit will be sold or otherwise disposed of, and furthermore, when a significant asset group within a reporting unit is required to be reviewed for recoverability because of the events and circumstances triggers included in FAS 144. Annual testing, however, is not triggered by such circumstances, but rather, is required in all cases.

Assuming the step-one analysis (comparing fair value to carrying value for any reporting unit which includes goodwill) reveals the possibility of impairment, the step-two exercise, impairment testing, must be performed. Because of the nature of goodwill, FASB rejected the use of the impairment testing technique of FAS 144 (formerly FAS 121) and instead crafted a unique methodology.

The two-step testing regime requires as the first step that a threshold test be applied: is the fair value of the reporting unit greater than, or less than, its carrying value? If the fair value is lower than the carrying value, impairment is suggested. The impairment, however, is **not** validly measured by the shortfall computed in step one, because to do so would effectively be to adjust the carrying value of the entire reporting unit to the lower of cost or market.

Under FAS 142, impairment is the condition that exists when the carrying amount of goodwill exceeds its implied fair value. Implied fair value, in turn, is the excess of the fair value of a reporting unit as a whole over the individual fair values assigned to its assets and liabilities. Once the fair value of a reporting unit is determined, the fair value of the goodwill component of that unit's net assets must be computed; this is then compared to the carrying value of that goodwill, to ascertain if any impairment loss is to be recognized. For the purpose of making this determination, fair value of a reporting unit is the amount at which the unit as a whole could be bought or sold in a current transaction between willing parties.

The second step of the process is as follows:

1. It is necessary to allocate the fair value of the reporting unit to all assets and liabilities, and to any unrecognized intangibles (including in-process R&D), as if the unit had been acquired at the measurement date. Any excess of fair value over amounts assigned to net assets (including the unrecognized assets such as in-process research and development) is the implied fair value of goodwill.
2. The implied fair value of goodwill is compared to its carrying amount (book value). If the carrying amount of the goodwill is greater than its implied fair value, a write-down of the carrying amount is required. Once written down, goodwill cannot later be written back up, even if later tests show that the fair value has recovered and exceeds carrying value.

Example of goodwill impairment testing

Armand Heavy Industries is a holding company that has two reporting units that were acquired as wholly owned subsidiaries consequent to purchase business combinations after the effective date of FAS 142. Armand's relevant reporting units are Bardige Diesel Engines and Ciarcia Transmissions. Upon acquisition of the two businesses (which are operated as subsidiaries), Armand recorded the assets and liabilities at fair values and recognized the excess of the purchase prices over these assigned fair values as goodwill.

At December 31, 2005, the carrying values of the assets and liabilities are as follows:

	(Amounts in millions)	
	Bardige Diesel	*Ciarcia Transmissions*
Cash	$ 20	$ 10
Accounts receivable	100	20
Inventories	10	700
Land, buildings, and equipment	1,400	1,800
Identifiable intangibles	300	0
Goodwill	400	200
Accounts payable	(80)	(300)
Long-term debt	(300)	(400)
Totals	$1,850	$2,030

Summary income statement information for the two companies for the year ended December 31, 2005 is as follows:

	(Amounts in millions)	
	Bardige Diesel	*Ciarcia Transmissions*
Revenues	$1,000	$800
Pre-tax income	$ 200	$120
Net income	$ 120	$ 30

It is Armand's policy to perform its annual goodwill impairment testing for both reporting units as of December 31.

The following data is available, at reasonable cost, to management of Armand:

Bardige Diesel

There are no comparable publicly held companies that have similar economic characteristics to this operation. However, management is able to develop reasonably supportable estimates of expected future cash flows associated with the group of assets. That computation yielded a fair value for Bardige Diesel of $1,700.

Ciarcia Transmissions

A competitor of Ciarcia Transmissions, the Gaffen Gearbox Company, is publicly held and traded on the NASDAQ. Its stock has consistently sold at a multiple of 3 times revenues. Management of Armand Heavy Industries believes that the stock price is fairly representative of the fair value of Gaffen Gearbox, and accordingly that using the multiple in assessing the value of Ciarcia will result in a fair estimate.

	(Amounts in millions)	
	Bardige Diesel	Ciarcia Transmissions
Fair value of reporting unit	$1,700	$2,400
Carrying amount of reporting unit including goodwill	1,850	2,030
Fair value over (under) carrying value	$ (150)	$ 370

Step 1—Test for potential impairment. Compare fair value of the reporting unit to its carrying amount, including goodwill.

a. In the case of Bardige Diesel, the carrying amount exceeds the fair value of the reporting unit, and thus the goodwill of this reporting unit must be tested further to determine whether it is impaired.

b. In the case of Ciarcia Transmissions, the fair value of the reporting unit exceeds the carrying value, and thus the goodwill of this reporting unit is not impaired and no further testing is required.

Step 2—Measure the amount of the impairment loss. For Bardige Diesel, management used the guidance in FAS 141 on business combinations and computed the implied value of goodwill and resulting impairment loss as follows:

	(Amounts in millions)	
	Carrying value	Fair value
Cash	$ 20	$ 20
Accounts receivable	100	90
Inventories	10	8
Land, buildings, and equipment	1,400	1,200
In-process research and development	--	100
Identifiable intangibles	300	350
Customer lists	--	100
Goodwill	400	NA
Accounts payable	(80)	(80)
Long-term debt	(300)	(280)
Total (net) carrying value	$1,850	
Total (net) fair value assigned to assets and liabilities		1,508
Fair value of reporting unit		1,700
Implied fair value of goodwill		192
Carrying value of goodwill		400
Impairment loss		$ 208

As indicated above, Ciarcia Transmissions does not have to proceed to Step 2 because its goodwill was found in Step 1 not to be impaired.

Circumstances under which detailed annual testing may be waived. Obviously, annual assessments of impairment can become very extended, and possibly expensive, exercises. In recognition of this fact, the FASB prescribed limited circumstances in which the risk of impairment would be quite low, and therefore the fair value of each reporting unit would not have to be recomputed in a year when they apply. To qualify for this exception, there must not have been changes to the components of the reporting unit since the previous fair value computation; when last measured, the fair value amount must have exceeded the carrying amount of the reporting unit by a substantial margin; and there must be no evidence to suggest that the current fair value of the reporting unit may be less than its current carrying amount.

Timing of annual testing. The annual impairment tests need not be performed at fiscal year-ends. Instead, the fair value measurement for each reporting unit could be performed any time during the fiscal year, as long as that measurement date is used consistently from year to year. Different measurement dates can be used for different reporting units. Once elected, however, a reporting unit's annual impairment measurement date is not permitted to be changed.

Other impairment testing considerations.

Impairment of identifiable long-lived assets. Testing for impairment of goodwill in accordance with FAS 142 may intersect with evaluating long-lived assets for impairment, as prescribed by FAS 144. GAAP requires that assets other than goodwill be evaluated for impairment **first,** and any adjustments necessitated by this evaluation made before testing for goodwill impairment. In some cases, possible impairment of long-lived assets may only be discovered as the goodwill impairment testing is progressing; in such instances, the goodwill impairment testing is ceased and other impairment issues fully addressed before returning to the goodwill impairment testing procedures.

Example—Evaluation of other assets necessitated by goodwill impairment testing

Using the same facts as given above for Armand Heavy Industries, the step two comparison of fair values to carrying values yielded a fair value of land, buildings, and equipment of $1,200 which is less than the carrying value of those assets. FAS 144 (as discussed in detail in Chapter 9) requires management to evaluate whether the carrying values of long-lived assets are recoverable when events or changes in circumstances indicate that this may be in doubt. One of the triggering events given as an example in FAS 144 is a significant decrease in the market price of a long-lived asset or asset group. Therefore, since this factor is present, management is required to evaluate the recoverability of those assets.

Management ceased its goodwill impairment testing and estimated the future cash flows (without discounting) from using and disposing of its long-lived assets (which consisted of a single asset group) and determined that these future cash flows aggregated $1,500,000 for the remaining estimated useful lives of the assets. The following comparison was made to the assets' carrying values:

Future cash flows over remaining estimated lives from use and disposition	$1,500,000
Carrying value	1,400,000
Excess (deficiency) of cash flows over carrying value	$ 100,000

Note the following anomalies that arise from this set of facts:

1. Because the gross, undiscounted cash flows from use and disposition of the asset group exceed the carrying value of the asset group, the group is not considered to be impaired even though its fair value has declined below its carrying value.
2. If the amount of the estimated future cash flows had been even slightly below the carrying value, say $1,390,000, the assets would be considered impaired.
3. If the assets were determined to be impaired, the carrying value would be required to be written down to fair value, which in this example is $1,200,000, and this write-down would be recognized prior to the resumption of goodwill impairment testing.

Tiered structures. Another possibly complicating factor is the existence of "tiered" structures, with goodwill reflected in the financial statements of a subsidiary entity. In such a circumstance, it is necessary to test for goodwill impairment at the subsidiary reporting unit level in the same manner as goodwill is tested by the parent entity. This subsidiary level test is required to be made prior to making the test at the parent company level. If an impairment loss is recognized at the subsidiary level, consideration must be given to the question of whether it is "more likely than not" that the event that gave rise to the impairment loss at the subsidiary level would also reduce the fair value of the consolidated reporting unit or units in which the subsidiary's reporting unit with impaired goodwill resides, to an amount below its carrying amounts. If this is deemed not "more likely than not" to have occurred, then there is no need to test further. On the other hand, if it is deemed to be "more likely than not" that a fair value deficit might also impact the consolidated reporting unit(s), then there is a need to test for impairment at the consolidated reporting unit level. It is possible for the subsidiary to recognize an impairment loss but for the consolidated reporting unit not to recognize a further loss—if the excess fair value of the other operations included in the consolidated reporting unit effectively offsets the deficit value flowing from the subsidiary's portion of that unit.

Display of goodwill and of goodwill impairment. The aggregate amount of goodwill is to be presented as a separate line item in the statement of financial position (balance sheet). Traditionally, in classified balance sheets, goodwill is an "other" noncurrent asset, distinguished from property, plant, and equipment.

The aggregate amount of goodwill impairment losses is generally to be presented as a separate line item in the operating section of the income statement. The exception to this rule is when the goodwill impairment loss is associated with a discontinued operation, in which case the impairment loss will be included, on a net-of-tax basis, within the results of discontinued operations. The portion of goodwill associated with net assets to be disposed of is recognized as part of the gain or loss on disposal and is not included in the calculation of impairment loss.

Disclosures about business combinations are to include the primary reason for the acquisition, including a description of the factors that contributed to a purchase price that reflects a premium that results in recognition of goodwill or a discount that results in recognition of an extraordinary gain (negative goodwill). If goodwill is material in relation to the total cost of a business acquisition, disclosure is required of the amount of acquired goodwill. The amount of acquired goodwill related to each segment (only for those entities that are required to report segment information) and the amount of acquired goodwill that is deductible for income tax purposes must also be disclosed.

For each period for which a balance sheet is presented, the notes to the financial statements must disclose the changes in the carrying amount of goodwill during the period. This must include the amount of goodwill acquired, the amount of impairment loss recognized, and the amount of goodwill included in the gain or loss on disposal of all or a portion of a reporting unit. For publicly held entities, this information is to be provided for each segment, and disclosure is to be made of any significant changes in the allocation of goodwill by segment.

For each goodwill impairment loss recognized, disclosure must be made of the following information: a description of the facts and circumstances leading to the impairment; a description of the reporting unit for which the impairment loss is recognized, the adjusted carrying amount of goodwill of that reporting unit, and the amount of the impairment loss; if applicable, the fact that the impairment loss is an estimate that has not yet been finalized, with the reasons therefore and, in subsequent periods, the nature and amount of any significant adjustments made to the initial estimate of the impairment loss; and, when salient, the segment to which the impaired goodwill pertains.

In the period in which an excess over cost related to an acquisition (i.e., negative goodwill) is recognized as an extraordinary gain, it will be shown net of income tax, as set forth by APB 30.

Special requirements for disposal of segments or other operations containing goodwill. When a significant portion of a reporting unit is disposed of, goodwill is allocated based on the relative fair values of the portion of the reporting unit being disposed of and the portion of the reporting unit remaining. An impairment test of the goodwill in the remaining (i.e., not disposed of) portion of the reporting unit would be required after the allocation of goodwill to ensure that the reporting unit can support the remaining goodwill.

Goodwill is allocated to a portion of a reporting unit being disposed of only when that portion constitutes a business. However, the allocation approach is not to be used when the business being disposed of is not classified as held-for-sale and was never integrated into the reporting unit. In that scenario, since the operating unit's identity and the original goodwill are still intact, all of the goodwill associated with that business would be included in the determination of the gain or loss on disposal.

The relative fair value allocation approach is also used to determine how goodwill is to be allocated when an entity reorganizes its reporting structure.

Other impairment considerations. In some instances a reporting unit may consist of multiple asset groups, and an event might occur that would necessitate an evaluation to determine if the carrying values of some, but not all, long-lived assets of that reporting unit are fully recoverable, per FAS 144. In between required annual goodwill impairment tests, that same event that triggered the recoverability review of an asset group under FAS 144, might or might not require an interim impairment test of reporting unit goodwill, since the criteria differ between the two pertinent standards. Under FAS 142, should a recoverability review be required for a significant asset **group** within the reporting unit, management must assess whether the triggering event would, more likely than not, also result in a reduction of the fair value of that reporting unit.

Under FAS 142, the reporting unit is the unit of measurement for goodwill, and thus the reporting unit is the lowest level of assets with which goodwill can be associated. Therefore, goodwill cannot be associated with lower-level asset groups, and there is no need to allocate or otherwise associate reporting unit goodwill with asset groups when those assets are tested for impairment.

Example of the interrelationship between FAS 142 and FAS 144

By reference to the diagram in the Appendix to Chapter 2, the Parent Holding Company's (PHC) Subsidiaries 5 and 6 include two asset groups. PHC's last annual goodwill impairment testing date for Subsidiaries 5 and 6 was November 30, 2004. At March 31, 2005, an evaluation for recoverability is required for Asset Group (j) due to the incurrence of an operating loss for business ix that contains those assets coupled with the forecasted continuation of such losses for the foreseeable future. When PHC initially made the benchmark assessment of its goodwill and allocated the portion of goodwill that relates to reporting unit (5), all of that goodwill was related to Business viii, which is a self-contained asset group whose assets are not required to be reviewed for recoverability at March 31, 2005, and which has significantly outperformed the expectations that PHC originally had for it upon its initial acquisition. Consequently, management believes it unlikely that the poor financial results of business ix which contains Asset Group (j) would result in a reduction in the fair value of the reporting unit as a whole to an amount below its carrying value. Consequently, it is not necessary for PHC to perform a goodwill impairment test at March 31, 2005.

Goodwill may be an asset of a consolidated subsidiary, and the subsidiary may also prepare and present financial statements on a stand-alone basis (for example, to provide to creditors of, and noncontrolling stockholders in, that subsidiary). The subsidiary might constitute part of a reporting unit at the parent company level (by reference to the diagram in the Appendix to Chapter 2, for example, this is the case with Subsidiary 5). Per FAS 142, impairment must be tested annually at the subsidiary level when stand-alone financial statements of the subsidiary are produced, whether the subsidiary is publicly held or private. As discussed earlier, for consolidated financial reporting purposes, an impairment loss at the subsidiary level would not automatically be "pushed up," but testing for impairment at the level of the parent's reporting unit that contains that subsidiary would require consideration due to the indicator of possible impairment. If management considers it more likely than not that the goodwill impairment loss recognized by the subsidiary that is a component of a reporting unit would reduce the fair value of that reporting unit to an amount less than its carrying amount, then the goodwill of that reporting unit is to be tested for impairment at the date the subsidiary recognizes its goodwill impairment loss. Upon testing, however, it might be the case that impairment would be found not to exist; this would be the result of the reporting unit's fair value exceeding its carrying value, probably because other component parts of that reporting unit had appreciated in value offsetting the reduction in value of the subsidiary.

Noncontrolling Interests

When a company acquires some, but not all, of the voting stock of another entity, the shares held by third parties represent a **minority or noncontrolling interest** in the acquired company. This occurs when the acquisition form of business combination is employed. A legal merger or consolidation would give the acquirer a 100% interest in whatever assets it obtained from the selling entity. Under GAAP, if a parent company owns more than half of another entity, the two are to be consolidated for financial statement purposes unless the parent company does not have control over the subsidiary such as in situations where the subsidiary is in bankruptcy or reorganization, or subject to severe restrictions imposed by a domestic or foreign government. The noncontrolling interest in the assets and earnings of the consolidated entity must also be accounted for.

When consolidated statements are prepared, the full amount of assets and liabilities (in the balance sheet) and income and expenses (in the income statement) of the subsidiary are generally presented. Accordingly, offsetting amounts must be shown for the portion of these items that does not belong to the parent company. In the balance sheet this offset is normally a credit shown as a separate caption in stockholders' equity, representing the noncontrolling interest in consolidated net assets equal to the noncontrolling percentage ownership in the net assets of the subsidiary. Some entities choose to present this caption between liabilities and stockholders' equity; however CON 6, *Elements of Financial Statements*, points out that such noncontrolling interests do not meet the definition of a liability and that they represent residual interests in components of the consolidated entity.

Although less likely, a debit balance in noncontrolling interest could result when the subsidiary has a deficit in its stockholders' equity **and** when there is reason to believe that the noncontrolling owners will make additional capital contributions to erase that deficit. This situation sometimes occurs where the entities are closely held and the noncontrolling owners are related parties having other business relationships with the parent company and/or its stockholders. In most other circumstances, a debit in noncontrolling interest would be charged against parent company retained earnings under the concept that the loss will be borne by that company. Although some believe that this debit should be added to goodwill on the consolidated balance sheet instead, it might be difficult to demonstrate that this would not result in an overstatement of total assets.

In the income statement, the noncontrolling interest in the income (or loss) of a consolidated subsidiary is shown as a deduction from (or an addition to) consolidated net income. As above, if the noncontrolling interest in the net assets of the subsidiary has already been reduced to zero, and if a net debit noncontrolling interest will **not** be recorded (the usual case), then the noncontrolling interest in any further losses is also **not** recorded. (However, this must be explained in the notes to the financial statements.) Furthermore, if past noncontrolling losses have not been recorded, the noncontrolling interest in current profits will not be recognized until the aggregate of such profits equals the aggregate unrecognized losses. This closely parallels the rule for equity method accounting recognition of profits and losses.

There are two alternative theories of consolidation that are used in practice, the entity theory and the parent company theory. When a noncontrolling interest exists, as in this example, the consolidation theory embraced and the related method employed will determine whether the consolidated balance sheet reflects the full excess of fair values over book values of the subsidiary's net assets, or only the parent company's percentage share of the excess.

Under the entity theory of consolidation, the purchase of a majority interest in a subsidiary for a stated price implies that the purchase of 100% of the subsidiary would be priced proportionally higher than the percentage actually purchased and, consequently, the acquiree's goodwill is imputed to be the amount that a purchaser of a 100% interest would pay for it. The computational approach used to implement the entity theory is called the full goodwill method. Under this method, the noncontrolling interest in the acquiree's net assets is reported based on the fair value of the acquiree's net assets.

Under the alternative parent company theory of consolidation, goodwill arising from a purchase of less than 100% of the acquiree is valued at the difference between the purchase price paid by the acquirer and the acquirer's proportionate share of the fair values of the identifiable net assets acquired. The computational approach used to implement the parent company theory is called the partial goodwill method. Under this method, the noncontrolling interest is reported based on the book value of the subsidiary.

Under current GAAP, both methods are acceptable, but in its current project on business combinations and noncontrolling interests, FASB has tentatively endorsed use of the entity theory/full goodwill method to recognize goodwill in the acquisition of less than a 100% controlling interest in the acquired entity. Both methods will be illustrated in the following example.

Example of consolidation involving a noncontrolling interest—Entity theory/full goodwill method

On January 1, 2005, Andes Company acquires a 90% interest in Baker Company in exchange for 5,400 shares of its $10 par value stock having a total market value of $120,600.

Details regarding the book values and fair values of the net assets acquired are as follows:

Item	*Book value (BV)*	*Fair value (FV)*	*Difference between BV and FV*
Cash	$ 37,400	$ 37,400	$ --
Accounts receivable (net)	9,100	9,100	--
Inventories	16,100	17,100	1,000
Equipment	50,000	60,000	10,000
Accumulated depreciation	(10,000)	(12,000)	(2,000)
Patents	10,000	13,000	3,000
Accounts payable	(6,600)	(6,600)	--
Total	$106,000	$118,000	$12,000

Note that the book value of the net assets of Baker Company may be computed by one of the following two methods:

1. Subtract the book value of the liability from the book values of the assets.

   $112,600 – $6,600 = $106,000

2. Add the book values of the components of Baker Company stockholders' equity.

   $50,000 + $15,000 + $41,000 = $106,000

The balance sheets of Andes and Baker are presented below as of January 1, 2005, immediately preceding the purchase:

Andes Company and Baker Company
Balance Sheets at 1/1/05
(Immediately before combination)

	Andes Company	*Baker Company*
Assets		
Cash	$ 30,900	$ 37,400
Accounts receivable (net)	34,200	9,100
Inventories	22,900	16,100
Equipment	200,000	50,000
Less accumulated depreciation	(21,000)	(10,000)
Patents	--	10,000
Total assets	$267,000	$112,600

	Andes Company	*Baker Company*
Liabilities and stockholders' equity		
Accounts payable	$ 4,000	$ 6,600
Bonds payable, 10%	100,000	--
Common stock, $10 par value	100,000	50,000
Additional paid-in capital	15,000	15,000
Retained earnings	48,000	41,000
Total liabilities and stockholders' equity	$267,000	$112,600

The workpaper for preparing a consolidated balance sheet at the date of acquisition is presented below. The first two columns are the trial balances of Andes Company and Baker Company immediately following the acquisition.

Andes Company and Baker Company Consolidated Working Papers
For Date of Combination—1/1/05

Entity theory/full goodwill method
90% interest

	[1] Andes Company	*[2]* Baker Company (book value)	*[3]* Consolidating and eliminating entries Debit	*[4]* Consolidating and eliminating entries Credit	*[5]* Consolidated balances
Balance sheet, 1/1/05					
Cash	$ 30,900	$ 37,400			$ 68,300
Accounts receivable, net	34,200	9,100			43,300
Inventories	22,900	16,100	$ 1,000		40,000
Equipment	200,000	50,000	10,000		260,000
Accumulated depreciation	(21,000)	(10,000)		$ 2,000	(33,000)
Investment in stock of Baker Company	120,600			120,600	
Excess of cost over fair value (goodwill)			16,000		16,000
Patents		10,000	3,000		13,000
Total assets	$387,600	$112,600			$407,600
Accounts payable	$ 4,000	$ 6,600			$ 10,600
10% Bonds payable	100,000				100,000
Common stock, $10 par	154,000	50,000	50,000		154,000
Additional paid-in capital	81,600	15,000	15,000		81,600
Retained earnings	48,000	41,000	41,000		48,000
Noncontrolling interest				13,400	13,400
Total liabilities and equity	$387,600	$112,600	$136,000	$136,000	$407,600

1. Record investment in Andes Company's accounting records (entry already reflected in column [1] above).

   The entry by Andes Company to record the 90% purchase-acquisition was

Investment in stock of Baker Company	120,600	
Common stock		54,000
Additional paid-in capital		66,600

To record the issuance of 5,400 shares of $10 par value stock to acquire a 90% interest in Baker Company

Although common stock is used as consideration in our example, Andes Company could have used debentures, cash, or any other form of consideration acceptable to Baker Company's stockholders to make the purchase.

2. Revaluation and elimination entry

Under the entity theory, goodwill and noncontrolling interest are recorded based on the aggregate fair value of 100% of the net assets of the subsidiary.

Purchase price for 90% of Baker	$120,600
Divided by percentage ownership purchased	÷ 90%
Implied fair value of 100% of Baker's net assets	134,000
Aggregate fair value of Baker's identifiable net assets	118,000
Imputed value of Baker goodwill	$ 16,000

Implied fair value of 100% of Baker's net assets	$134,000
x percentage ownership of noncontrolling interest	x 10%
	$ 13,400

	Debit	Credit
Goodwill	$ 16,000	
Inventories	1,000	
Equipment	10,000	
Patents	3,000	
Common stock—Baker Company	50,000	
Additional paid-in capital—Baker company	15,000	
Retained earnings—Baker Company	41,000	
Accumulated depreciation		$ 2,000
Noncontrolling interest		13,400
Investment in Baker		120,600
	$136,000	$136,000

To record the revaluation of Baker Company net assets to their aggregate fair values, eliminate the stockholders' equity accounts of Baker Company, reflect 100% of the implied goodwill associated with the acquisition, eliminate Andes' investment in Baker, and record the fair value of the minority interest retained by Baker's former controlling stockholders.

Example of consolidation involving a noncontrolling interest—Parent company theory/ partial goodwill method

Assuming the same facts as the preceding example, the workpaper for preparing a consolidated balance sheet at the date of acquisition is presented below. The first two columns are the trial balances of Andes Company and Baker Company following the acquisition.

Andes Company and Baker Company Consolidated Working Papers
For Date of Combination—1/1/05

Parent company theory/partial goodwill method
90% interest

	[1] Andes Company	[2] Baker Company (book value)	[3] Adjustments and eliminations Debit	[4] Adjustments and eliminations Credit	[5] Noncontrolling interest	[6] Consolidated balances
Balance sheet, 1/1/05						
Cash	$ 30,900	$ 37,400				$ 68,300
Accounts receivable, net	34,200	9,100				43,300
Inventories	22,900	16,100	$ 900b			39,900
Equipment	200,000	50,000	9,000b			259,000
Accumulated depreciation	(21,000)	(10,000)		$ 1,800b		(32,800)
Investment in stock of Baker Company	120,600			120,600a		
Difference between cost and book value			25,200b	25,200b		
Excess of cost over fair value (goodwill)			14,400b			14,400
Patents		10,000	2,700b			12,700
Total assets	$387,600	$112,600				$404,800

	[1] Andes Company	[2] Baker Company (book value)	[3] Adjustments and eliminations Debit	[4] Credit	[5] Noncontrolling interest	[6] Consolidated balances
Accounts payable	$ 4,000	$ 6,600				$ 10,600
Bonds payable	100,000					100,000
Common stock	154,000	50,000	45,000a		$ 5,000	154,000
Additional paid-in capital	81,600	15,000	13,500a		1,500	81,600
Retained earnings	48,000	41,000	36,900a		4,100	48,000
Noncontrolling interest					$10,600	10,600
Total liabilities and equity	$387,600	$112,600	$147,600	$147,600		$404,800

1. Record investment in Andes Company's accounting records (entry already reflected in column [1] above).

   The entry by Andes Company to record the 90% purchase-acquisition was

Investment in stock of Baker Company	120,600	
Common stock		54,000
Additional paid-in capital		66,600

   To record the issuance of 5,400 shares of $10 par value stock to acquire a 90% interest in Baker Company

   Although common stock is used for the consideration in our example, Andes Company could have used debentures, cash, or any other form of consideration acceptable to Baker Company's stockholders to make the purchase. This entry is identical to the first entry in the preceding example using the entity theory/full goodwill method.

2. Difference between investment cost and book value

   The difference between the investment cost and the parent company's equity in the net assets of the subsidiary is computed as follows:

Investment—FV of 5,400 shares of Andes issued		$120,600
Common stock	$50,000 x 90% =	45,000
Additional paid-in capital	15,000 x 90% =	13,500
Retained earnings	41,000 x 90% =	36,900
Andes' share—Baker net assets/stockholders' equity		95,400
Differential		$25,200

   This difference is due to several undervalued assets and to unrecorded goodwill. The allocation procedure is similar to that for a 100% purchase; however, in this case, the parent company obtained a 90% interest and, thus, under the parent company theory will only recognize 90% of the difference between the fair values and book values of the subsidiary's assets, not 100% as was the case in the preceding example. The allocation is presented as follows:

Allocation of the Differential

Item	Book value (BV)	Fair value (FV)	Difference between BV and FV	Ownership percentage	Percentage share of difference between BV and FV
Cash	$ 37,400	$ 37,400	$ --		
Accounts receivable (net)	9,100	9,100	--		
Inventories	16,100	17,100	1,000	90%	$ 900
Equipment	50,000	60,000	10,000	90%	9,000
Accumulated depreciation	(10,000)	(12,000)	(2,000)	90%	(1,800)
Patents	10,000	13,000	3,000	90%	2,700
Accounts payable	(6,600)	(6,600)	--		
Total	$106,000	$118,000	$12,000		
Amount of difference between purchase price and share of book value allocated to revaluation of net assets					10,800
Total differential per above					25,200
Remainder allocated to goodwill					$14,400

The equipment has a book value of $40,000 ($50,000 less 20% depreciation of $10,000). An appraisal concluded that the equipment's replacement cost new was $60,000 less 20% accumulated depreciation of $12,000 resulting in a net fair value of $48,000.

Goodwill is proven by the following computation:

Purchase price paid by Andes		$120,600
Fair value of net assets acquired	$118,000	
Percentage interest acquired	x 90%	106,200
Excess of purchase price over fair value of net assets acquired		$ 14,400

Noncontrolling interest is proven by the following computation:

Fair value of net assets acquired	$118,000
Percentage interest retained by former controlling stockholders	x 10%
Noncontrolling interest	$ 11,800

3. Consolidating entries on workpaper

The basic reciprocal accounts are the investment in subsidiary account on the parent's books and the subsidiary's stockholders' equity accounts. Only the parent's share of the subsidiary's accounts may be eliminated as reciprocal accounts. The remaining 10% portion is allocated to the noncontrolling interest. The workpaper entry to eliminate the basic reciprocal accounts is as follows:

Entry a:

Capital stock—Baker Co.	45,000	
Additional paid-in capital—Baker Co.	13,500	
Retained earnings—Baker Co.	36,900*	
Differential	25,200	
Investment in stock of Baker Co.—Andes Co.		120,600

* *($41,000 x 90% = $36,900)*

Note that only 90% of Baker Company's stockholders' equity accounts are eliminated. Also, an account called differential is debited in the workpaper entry. The differential account is a temporary account to record the difference between the cost of the investment in Baker Company in the parent's accounting records and the book value of the parent's interest (90% in this case) from the subsidiary's accounting records.

The next step is to allocate the differential to the specific assets by making the following workpaper entry:

Entry b:

Inventory	900	
Equipment	9,000	
Patents	2,700	
Goodwill	14,400	
Accumulated depreciation		1,800
Differential		25,200

This entry reflects the allocations prepared in step 2. and recognizes the parent's share of the asset revaluations. The noncontrolling interest column is the 10% interest of Baker Company's net assets owned by outside, third parties.

Comparison of the two consolidation methods

Consolidated balance sheet, 1/1/05	[1] Consolidated Entity theory/full goodwill method	[2] Consolidated Parent company theory/ partial goodwill method	[3] Difference
Cash	$ 68,300	$ 68,300	
Accounts receivable	43,300	43,300	
Inventories	40,000	39,900	$100
Equipment	260,000	259,000	1,000
Accumulated depreciation	(33,000)	(32,800)	(200)
Goodwill	16,000	14,400	1,600
Patents	13,000	12,700	300
Total assets	$407,600	$404,800	$2,800
Accounts payable	$ 10,600	$10,600	
Bonds payable	100,000	100,000	
Common stock	154,000	154,000	
Additional paid-in capital	81,600	81,600	
Retained earnings	48,000	48,000	
Noncontrolling interest	13,400	10,600	$2,800
Total liabilities and equity	$407,600	$404,800	$2,800

The comparison above highlights the difference between the two methods. Under the full goodwill method, the assets and liabilities including goodwill are recorded at 100% of their fair values and the noncontrolling interest included in equity includes a proportionate share of the increase in fair values resulting from the revaluation. Under the partial goodwill method, the consolidated balance sheet reflects only the portion of the increase in fair values of the assets and liabilities, including goodwill, that is allocable to the new majority owner, with the portion of the increase attributable to the noncontrolling stockholders remaining unrecognized. The $2,800 difference in the noncontrolling interest results from the following computation:

Implied fair value of 100% of Baker's net assets	$134,000
x percentage ownership of noncontrolling interest	x 10%
Noncontrolling interest in fair value of net assets	13,400
Excess of implied fair value over book value of net assets ($134,000 – $106,000)	28,000
x percentage ownership of noncontrolling interest	x 10%
Noncontrolling interest share of revaluation	2,800
Noncontrolling interest share of book value of net assets	$ 10,600

These examples do not include any other intercompany balances as of the date of consolidation. If any existed, they would be eliminated to fairly present the financial position of the consolidated entity. Several examples of the elimination of other reciprocal amounts will be shown later in the illustration of the preparation of consolidated financial statements subsequent to the date of acquisition.

Consolidated Statements in Subsequent Periods

The same concepts employed to prepare a consolidated balance sheet at the date of acquisition are applicable to later consolidated statements. Where a noncontrolling interest exists, income in subsequent periods must be allocated to it. The exact nature of the worksheet entries depends on whether the parent is maintaining its accounting records of the investment in subsidiary using the cost method or equity method (which are acceptable alternatives since the consolidated financial statements will be identical under either method). The equity method is often used when a separate, parent-only column is included in consolidating financial statements.

In addition to the eliminating entries for the parent's recorded investment and subsidiary stockholders' equity, other eliminations will be needed when there are intercompany balances or transactions resulting from parent-subsidiary loans (advances), sales of inventory items (whether or not these occurred at a profit to the seller), sales of fixed assets at other than net book value, and bond transactions or transactions in stock other than voting common shares. The selected items in the following example will demonstrate the accounting issues applicable to all such intercompany items and the proper handling of these items in the consolidation workpapers.

Example of a consolidation in subsequent periods

The basic facts of the Andes Company-Baker Company case have already been presented. Additional information is as follows:

1. Andes Company uses the equity method to record changes in the value of its investment in Baker.
2. During 2005, Andes Company sold merchandise to Baker Company for $20,000 that originally cost Andes Company $15,000. This is referred to as a downstream sale. On December 31, 2005, Baker Company's inventory included merchandise purchased from Andes Company at a cost to Baker Company of $12,000.
3. Also during 2005, Andes Company purchased $18,000 of merchandise from Baker Company. This is referred to as an upstream sale. Baker Company uses a normal markup of 25% above its cost. Andes Company's ending inventory includes $10,000 of the merchandise acquired from Baker Company.
4. Baker Company reduced its intercompany account payable to Andes Company to a balance of $4,000 as of December 31, 2005, by making a payment of $1,000 on December 30. This $1,000 payment was still in transit on December 31, 2005 and, thus, had not yet been received by Andes.
5. On January 2, 2005, Baker Company acquired equipment from Andes Company for $7,000. The equipment was originally purchased by Andes Company for $5,000 and had a book value of $4,000 at the date of sale to Baker Company. The equipment had an estimated remaining life of four years as of January 2, 2005 and is being depreciated using the straight-line method, with no estimated salvage value.
6. On December 31, 2005, Baker Company purchased for $44,000, 50% of the outstanding bonds issued by Andes Company. The bonds mature on December 31, 2010, and were originally issued at par. The bonds pay interest annually on December 31 of each year, and the interest was paid to the prior investor immediately before Baker Company's purchase of the bonds.

The worksheet for the preparation of consolidated financial statements as of December 31, 2005, is presented below.

The balance shown in the parent's accounting records as "investment in subsidiary" at the financial statement date should be reconciled to ensure the parent company made the proper entries under the method of accounting used to account for its investment.

An analysis of the investment in Baker at December 31, 2005, is as follows:

	Investment in Stock of Baker Company		
Original cost, 1/1/05	120,600		
% of Baker Co.'s 2005 income ($9,400 x 90%)	8,460	3,600	% of Baker Co.'s 2005 dividends paid ($4,000 x 90%)
Balance, 12/31/05	125,460		

Any errors would require correcting entries before the consolidation process is continued. Correcting entries are posted by the appropriate company; eliminating entries are **not** recorded by either company.

The difference between the cost of the investment and the book value of the net assets acquired was determined and allocated in the preparation of the date of acquisition consolidated balance sheet presented earlier. The same computations are used in preparing financial statements for as long as the investment is owned. Since FASB has currently expressed its preference for the entity theory/full goodwill method, the illustration of that method is carried forward for the purpose of this example.

The following adjusting and eliminating entries are required to prepare consolidated financial statements as of December 31, 2005, and for the year then ended. The number or letter in parentheses to the left of the entry corresponds to the key used on the worksheet.

Step 1 —Complete the transaction for any intercompany items in transit at the end of the year.

(1)	Cash	1,000	
	Accounts receivable—subsidiary		1,000

This adjusting entry will now properly present the financial positions of both companies by eliminating the timing difference.

Step 2 —Prepare the eliminating entries.

(a)	Sales	38,000	
	Cost of sales		38,000

Total intercompany sales of $38,000 include $20,000 in a downstream transaction sold from Andes Company to Baker Company and $18,000 in an upstream transaction sold from Baker Company to Andes Company.

(b)	Cost of sales	5,000	
	Inventory		5,000

The ending inventories are overstated because of the unrealized gross profit from the intercompany sales. The debit to cost of goods sold is required because a decrease in ending inventory will increase cost of goods sold to be deducted on the income statement. Supporting computations for the entry are as follows:

	In ending inventory of	
	Andes Company	*Baker Company*
Intercompany sales not resold, at selling price	$10,000	$12,000
Cost basis of remaining intercompany merchandise		
From Baker to Andes (÷ 125%)	(8,000)	
From Andes to Baker (÷ 133 1/3%)		(9,000)
Unrealized gross profit	$ 2,000	$ 3,000

NOTE: When preparing consolidated workpapers for 2006 (the next fiscal period), an additional eliminating entry will be required if the goods in 2005's ending inventory are sold to outsiders during 2006. The additional entry will recognize the profit for 2006 that was eliminated as unrealized in 2005. This entry is necessary since the entry at the end of 2005 was made only on the worksheet and not recorded in the accounting records of either Andes or Baker. The 2006 entry would be as follows:

Retained earnings—Baker Co., 1/1/06	2,000	
Retained earnings—Andes Co., 1/1/06	3,000	
Cost of goods sold, 2006		5,000

(c)	Accounts payable—Parent	4,000	
	Accounts receivable—Subsidiary		4,000

This entry eliminates the remaining intercompany receivable/payable owed by Baker Company to Andes Company. This eliminating entry is necessary to avoid overstating the consolidated entity's balance sheet. The receivable/payable is not extinguished, and Baker Company must still transfer $4,000 to Andes Company in the future.

(d)	Gain on sale of equipment	3,000	
	Equipment		2,000
	Accumulated depreciation		250
	Depreciation expense		750

This entry eliminates the gain on the intercompany sale of the equipment, eliminates the overstatement of equipment, and removes the excess depreciation taken on the gain. Supporting computations for the entry are as follows:

	Cost	*At date of intercompany sale accum. depr.*	*2005 depr. ex.*	*End-of-period accum. depr.*
Original basis (to seller, Andes Co.)	$5,000	$(1,000)	$ 1,000	$(2,000)
New basis (to buyer, Baker Co.)	7,000	--	1,750	(1,750)
Difference	$(2,000)		$(750)	$ 250

If the intercompany sale had not occurred, Andes Company would have depreciated the remaining book value of $4,000 over the estimated remaining life of four years. However, since Baker Company's acquisition price ($7,000) was more than Andes Company's undepreciated basis in the asset ($4,000), the depreciation recorded by Baker Company will include part of the unrealized intercompany profit. The equipment must be reflected on the consolidated balance sheet at its original cost to the consolidated entity. Therefore, the write-up of $2,000 in the equipment, the excess depreciation of $750, and the gain of $3,000 all must be eliminated in consolidation. The ending balance of accumulated depreciation must be shown at what it would have been if the intercompany equipment transaction had not occurred. In future periods, a retained earnings adjustment will be used instead of adjusting the gain since the gain is a 2005 transaction; however, concepts with respect to adjusting accumulated depreciation and the related expense will be extended to include the additional periods.

		Debit	Credit
(e)	Bonds payable	50,000	
	Investment in bonds of Andes Company		44,000
	Gain on debt extinguishment		6,000

This entry eliminates the book value (the par value of the bonds) of Andes Company's debt against the bond investment account of Baker Company. To the consolidated entity, this transaction is shown as a retirement of debt even though Andes Company still owes the outstanding intercompany debt to Baker Company. For the purpose of this example, it is assumed that Baker Company is accounting for its investment in the bonds as being held-to-maturity under FAS 115 and, therefore, accounting for the investment at amortized cost. In future periods, Baker Company will amortize the discount, ultimately, upon maturity, bringing the recorded investment up to its par (maturity) value. Retained earnings will be used in future eliminating entries instead of the gain since the gain is a 2005 event.

		Debit	Credit
(f)	Equity in subsidiary's net income—Andes Co.	8,460	
	Dividends paid—Baker Co.		3,600
	Investment in stock of Baker Co.		4,860

This eliminating entry adjusts the carrying value of the investment in Baker back to its balance at the beginning of the period and also eliminates the subsidiary's net income. The elimination is computed as follows:

Baker's net income of $9,400 x 90% attributable to Andes	=	$ 8,460
Baker's dividends paid of $4,000 x Andes' 90% share	=	$ 3,600
Andes' investment in Baker at 12/31/05		$125,460
Andes' original recorded investment in Baker		120,600
Effects of Andes' 2005 equity method accounting		$ 4,860

(g)

	Debit	Credit
Goodwill	16,000	
Inventories	1,000	
Equipment	10,000	
Patents	3,000	
Common stock—Baker Company	50,000	
Additional paid-in capital—Baker Company	15,000	
Retained earnings—Baker Company	41,000	
Accumulated depreciation		2,000
Noncontrolling interest		13,400
Investment in Baker		120,600

This entry eliminates Baker Company's stockholders' equity at the beginning of the year, 1/1/05, reflects 100% of the imputed goodwill associated with Baker, revalues the acquired assets at their acquisition date fair values, reflects the noncontrolling interests of the formerly controlling stockholders of Baker, and eliminates Andes' 1/1/05 investment in Baker. Note that the changes in these amounts during the year were eliminated in entry (f) above. Also note that this entry is identical with the 1/1/05 revaluation and elimination entry 2. in the example of recording the acquisition at 1/1/05 using the entity theory/full goodwill method.

(h)

	Debit	Credit
Cost of sales	1,000	
Depreciation expense	2,000	
Other operating expenses—patent amortization	300	
Inventory		1,000
Accumulated depreciation		2,000
Patents (or contra asset, accumulated amortization)		300

The elimination entry amortizes the revaluations to fair value made in entry (g). The inventory has been sold and, therefore, becomes part of cost of goods sold. Goodwill is not amortized, but will be tested annually for possible impairment. The remaining revaluations will be amortized as follows:

	Revaluation	*Amortization period*	*Annual amortization*
Equipment (net)	$8,000	4 years	$2,000
Patents	3,000	10 years	300

Amortization will continue to be made on future worksheets. For example, at the end of the next year (2006), the amortization entry (h) would be as follows:

	Debit	Credit
Retained earnings	3,300	
Depreciation expense	2,000	
Other operating expenses—patent amortization	300	
Inventory		1,000
Accumulated depreciation		4,000
Patents (or contra asset, accumulated amortization)		600

The $3,300 debit to retained earnings is an aggregation of the prior period's charges affecting the income statement ($1,000 + $2,000 + $300). During subsequent years, some accountants prefer reducing the allocated amounts in entry (g) for prior periods' charges. In this case, the amortization entry in future periods would reflect just that period's amortization.

In adjusting for the noncontrolling interest in the consolidated entity's equity and earnings, the following guidelines are to be observed:

1. The entire subsidiary's stockholders' equity section is eliminated in the basic eliminating entry. The noncontrolling interest's share of the subsidiary's stockholders' equity is presented separately.
2. The entire amounts of intercompany transactions and balances are eliminated. For example, all receivables/payables and sales/cost of sales with a 90% subsidiary are eliminated.

3. For intercompany transactions in inventory and fixed assets, the possible effect on noncontrolling interest depends on whether the original transaction affected the subsidiary's income statement. Noncontrolling interest is adjusted only if the subsidiary is the selling entity (upstream sales). In this case, the noncontrolling interest is adjusted for its percentage ownership of the common stock of the subsidiary. The noncontrolling interest is **not** adjusted for unrealized profits on downstream sales. The effects of downstream transactions are confined solely to the parent's (i.e., controlling) ownership interests.

The noncontrolling interest's share of the subsidiary's net income is shown as a deduction on the consolidated income statement since 100% of the subsidiary's revenues and expenses are consolidated, even though the parent company owns less than a 100% interest. For this example, the noncontrolling interest deduction on the income statement is computed as follows:

Baker Company's reported income	$9,400
Less unrealized profit on an upstream inventory sale	(2,000)
Baker Company's income for consolidated financial statement purposes	7,400
Noncontrolling interest share	x 10%
Noncontrolling interest share of Baker net income	$ 740

Andes Company and Baker Company Consolidated Working Papers
Year Ended December 31, 2005

Consolidation of 90% owned subsidiary
first year, subsequent to acquisition, equity method used by Parent; Entity theory/full goodwill method

	Andes Company	*Baker Company*	*Adjustments and eliminations* Debit	*Adjustments and eliminations* Credit	*Noncontrolling interest*	*Consolidated balances*
Income statements for year ended 12/31/05						
Sales	$750,000	$420,000	$ 38,000[a]			$1,132,000
Cost of sales	581,000	266,000	5,000[b] 1,000[h]	$ 38,000[a]		815,000
Gross profit	169,000	154,000				317,000
Depreciation and interest expense	28,400	16,200	2,000[h]	750[d]		45,850
(Gain) loss on sale of equipment	(3,000)		3,000[d]			
Other operating expenses	117,000	128,400	300[h]			245,700
Total operating expenses and gain	142,400	144,600				291,550
Income from operations	26,600	9,400				25,450
Gain on debt extinguishment				6,000[e]		6,000
Equity in subsidiary's income	8,460		8,460[f]			
Noncontrolling income ($7,400 x 10%)					$ 740	(740)
Net income	$ 35,060	$ 9,400	$ 57,760	$ 44,750	$ 740	$ 30,710
Statement of retained earnings for the year ended 12/31/05						
1/1/05 retained earnings						
Andes Company	$ 48,000					$ 48,000
Baker Company		$ 41,000	$ 41,000[g]			
Add net income (from above)	35,060	9,400	57,760	$ 44,750	$ 740	30,710
Total	83,060	50,400	98,760	44,750	740	78,710
Deduct dividends paid	15,000	4,000		3,600[f]	400	15,000
Balance, 12/31/05	$ 68,060	$ 46,400	$ 98,760	$ 48,350	$ 340	$ 63,710

	Andes Company	*Baker Company*	*Adjustments and eliminations* Debit	Credit	*Noncontrolling interest*	*Consolidated balances*
Balance sheet, 12/31/05						
Cash	$ 45,300	$ 6,400	$ 1,000[l]			$ 52,700
Accounts receivable, trade (net)	38,700	12,100				50,800
Accounts receivable, subsidiary	5,000			$ 1,000[l] 4,000[c]		
Inventories	38,300	20,750	1,000[g]	5,000[b] 1,000[h]		54,050
Equipment	195,000	57,000	10,000[g]	2,000[d]		260,000
Accumulated depreciation	(35,200)	(18,900)		250[d] 2,000[g] 2,000[h]		(58,350)
Investment in stock of Baker Company	125,460			4,860[f] 120,600[g]		
Goodwill			16,000[g]			16,000
Investment in held-to-maturity bonds of Andes Company		44,000		44,000[e]		
Patents (net)		9,000	3,000[g]	300[h]		11,700
Total assets	$412,560	$130,350				$386,900
Accounts payable, trade	$ 8,900	$ 14,950				$ 23,850
Accounts payable, parent		4,000	4,000[c]			
Bonds payable	100,000		50,000[e]			50,000
Total liabilities	108,900	18,950				73,850
Common stock	154,000	50,000	50,000[g]			154,000
Additional paid-in capital	81,600	15,000	15,000[g]			81,600
Retained earnings (from above)	68,060	46,400	98,760	48,350	$340	63,710
Noncontrolling interest				13,400[g]	$340	13,740
Total stockholders' equity	303,660	111,400				313,050
Total liabilities and stockholders' equity	$412,560	$130,350	$48,760	$48,760		$386,900

Other Accounting Issues in Business Combinations

Contingent consideration. Many business acquisitions include contingent consideration features, which require, if specified conditions are later met, that additions to the purchase price be paid either in cash, or in shares of the acquiring entity. The presence of contingent consideration provisions in an acquisition arrangement must be addressed, both at the time of the acquisition and later, if and when contingent consideration is earned and paid.

At the date of the acquisition, contingent consideration is important to the extent that it precludes immediate recognition of an extraordinary gain arising from the excess of "negative goodwill" over the amounts allocable to reduce the carrying values of various assets (all assets other than cash, receivables, inventory, financial instruments carried on the balance sheet at fair value, assets to be disposed of by sale, and deferred income tax assets). Under GAAP, if such an excess exists, it is to be classified as a deferred credit, not taken into earnings, until the contingency regarding the purchase price has been resolved. Only a small fraction of business combinations are true "bargain purchases," and of these, it is expected that only a minute portion will result in such a large amount of negative goodwill that an excess will remain after offsetting against the qualified assets. Of those, an even smaller proportion will relate to transactions in which contingent consideration is to be paid, and thus for which the deferral of what otherwise would be immediately recognized as extraordinary gain would be prescribed.

The accounting for the subsequent payment of the added consideration depends upon whether the contingency was related to the earnings of the acquired entity or to the fair value of the original consideration package given by the acquirer.

In the former instance, a subsequent payment of added cash, stock, or any other valuable consideration will require a revaluation of the purchase price. This revaluation possibly could alter the amounts allocable to certain (mostly noncurrent) assets (where cost in the original purchase transaction was less than fair value acquired (i.e., a "bargain purchase") and the difference was offset against those assets), or could result in an increased amount of goodwill being recognized. The effects of a revaluation are handled prospectively (i.e., the additional depreciation of fixed assets is allocated to the remaining economic lives of those items) without making any adjustment to postacquisition periods' results already reported.

In the latter case, the event triggering the issuance of additional shares is a decline in fair value of the original purchase package. Additional shares of the acquirer's stock are issued in order to increase the value of the consideration to the amount intended by the parties at the date of the transaction. According to APB 16, this does not alter the total cost of the transaction for accounting recognition purposes, even though, obviously, further consideration is later transferred to the former owners of the acquiree. The total value of the purchase would **not** be changed and, thus, no alteration of amounts allocated to the various assets and liabilities acquired would be needed. However, the issuance of extra shares of common stock will typically require that the allocation between the common stock and the additional paid-in capital accounts be adjusted.

In rare instances, contingent consideration based on the value of the securities used to effect the acquisition may involve transactions in which common stock was not used. If part of the original purchase price had been paid in bonds or other debt instruments, the reallocation might affect the premium or discount recognized on the debt, which would have an impact on future earnings as these accounts are subsequently amortized.

Net operating loss carryforwards of an acquired entity. An entity acquired in a purchase business combination may have a net operating loss carryforward (NOL) that will be available for use by the acquiring entity. While prior GAAP generally prohibited recognition of the income tax benefit of NOL, under FAS 109, deferred income tax assets including NOL are given recognition. Under this standard, benefits related to acquired NOL are reported in the acquirer's balance sheet (as are deferred income tax assets arising from any other future deductible temporary differences). A valuation allowance is also recorded if realization of the NOL is not considered "more likely than not."

As discussed more fully in Chapter 15, recognition "for the first time" of the benefits of NOL (acquired in a purchase business combination at a date subsequent to the purchase) is accomplished by reducing recorded goodwill to zero. Next, if further acquired NOL are realized, other identifiable intangible assets acquired in the same transaction are reduced to zero. Any excess over this amount is reflected as an adjustment to current period deferred income tax expense or benefit. "For the first time" means that a valuation allowance has been reduced or eliminated, either because the probability of realization has been reassessed or because the income tax benefits have, in fact, been realized in the current period.

Preacquisition contingencies. At the time a business combination is consummated, the purchase price must be allocated to acquired assets and assumed liabilities in accordance with their respective fair values, with any excess purchase price being assigned to goodwill (if fair value exceeds cost, the cost deficiency is allocated primarily against noncurrent assets, with any remainder treated as "negative goodwill" and, in general, recognized as an extraordinary gain at the date of the acquisition). In some cases, however, the fair values of certain assets (e.g., those to be disposed of) may not be known with precision, and the amounts of certain estimated or contingent liabilities (such as outstanding warranty or litigation claims) may also be subject to a high degree of uncertainty. FAS 141 provides for a "look back" to reallocate the purchase price when these contingencies are ultimately resolved. However, under FAS 141 there is a limited allocation period, usually deemed to be one year, during which a reallocation can be effected; thereafter, resolutions of preacquisition contingencies are treated as current period events and reported in net income of that period.

An exception to this rule exists in the case of income tax uncertainties existing at the date of the business combination. Resolution of these must be accounted for in accordance with FAS 109, which stipulates that such adjustments are to be applied to increase or decrease the remaining balance of goodwill attributable to that business combination; if goodwill is reduced to zero, the remaining amount is first used to reduce other noncurrent intangible assets from the same acquisition to zero, and any excess beyond that amount is recorded as an adjustment to the deferred income tax expense or benefit for the period of resolution. Thus, the resolution of these specific income tax uncertainties cannot result in a general reallocation of the purchase price, as are other resolutions of preacquisition contingencies.

Changes in majority interest. The parent's ownership interest can change as a result of purchases or sales of the subsidiary's common shares by the parent, or as a consequence of capital transactions of the subsidiary. The latter circumstance is generally handled precisely as demonstrated in the equity method discussion in Chapter 10, (see pages 405-408). If the parent's relative book value interest in the subsidiary changes, gains or losses are treated as incurred in an entity's own treasury stock transactions. Gains are credited to additional paid-in capital; losses are charged to any previously created additional paid-in capital or to retained earnings. However, in financial statements of its registrants, the SEC requires that the parent company recognize a gain on a transaction when a subsidiary sells shares to outside interests at a price greater than the parent's carrying amount.

When the parent's share of ownership increases through the purchase of additional stock in the subsidiary, the cost of the newly acquired stock is debited to the asset, investment in subsidiary with a corresponding credit to cash. An issue arises in the preparation of consolidated income statements when the change in ownership takes place midperiod. Consolidated statements are to be prepared based on the ending ownership level.

Example of a consolidation with a change in the majority interest

Assume that Andes Company increased its ownership of Baker Company from 90% to 95% on October 1, 2005. The investment was acquired at book value of $5,452.50 determined as follows:

Baker Company common stock outstanding at 10/1/05		$50,000
Additional paid-in capital, 10/1/05		15,000
Retained earnings at 10/1/05		
Balance, 1/1/05	$41,000	
Net income for nine months ($9,400 x .75)	7,050*	
Preacquisition dividends paid	(4,000)	44,050
		109,050
		x 5%
Book value acquired		$5,452.50

* *Assumes income was earned evenly over the year.*

The consolidated net income attributable to Andes' interests for 2005 would reflect a net of

90%	x	$9,400	x	12/12	=	$8,460.00
5%	x	$9,400	x	3/12	=	117.50
95%						$8,577.50

The preacquisition dividends ($4,000 x 90%) would have been recorded by Andes as follows:

Cash	3,600.00	
Investment in Baker company		3,600.00

Andes would apply the equity method to record its share of the consolidated net income as follows:

Investment in Baker company	8,577.50	
Equity in subsidiary's income		8,577.50

The interim stock purchase results in a new caption, **purchased preacquisition earnings**, being presented on the consolidated income statement. This caption represents the percentage of the subsidiary's income earned, in this case, on the 5% stock interest from January 1, 2005, to October 1, 2005. The basic eliminating entries would be based on the 95% ownership as follows:

Equity in subsidiary's income—Andes Co.	8,577.50	
Dividends paid—Baker Co.		3,600.00
Investment in Baker Co.		4,977.50
Goodwill	16,000.00	
Inventories	1,000.00	
Equipment	10,000.00	
Patents	3,000.00	
Common stock—Baker Co.	50,000.00	
Additional paid-in capital—Baker Co.	15,000.00	
Retained earnings—Baker Co. **	40,800.00	
Purchased preacquisition earnings***	352.50	
Accumulated depreciation		2,000.00
Investment in stock of Baker Co.—Andes Co. ****		120,600.00
Noncontrolling interest		13,552.50
** *$41,000 beginning 2005 balance*	*$41,000*	
Less preacquisition dividend of 5% x $4,000	*(200)*	
Retained earnings available, as adjusted	*$40,800*	
*** *5% x $9,400 x 9/12 = $352.50*		
**** *Original cost, 1/1/05, for 90% interest*	*$120,600*	
***** *Noncontrolling interest consists of:*		
Originally recognized amount	*$13,400.00*	
Allocated share of earnings 1/1/05 – 10/1/05 ($9,400 x 75% x 10% = $705)	*705.00*	
Share of preacquisition dividends through 10/1/05 ($4,000 x 10% = $400)	*(400.00)*	
Sale of ½ preacquisition retained net income to Andes [($705 – $400) x ½ = $152.50]	*(152.50)*	
	$13,552.50	

Purchased preacquisition earnings are shown as a deduction, along with noncontrolling interest, to arrive at consolidated net income. Purchased preacquisition earnings are used only with interim acquisitions when applying the purchase accounting method.

Requirement that all majority-owned subsidiaries be consolidated. It has been a general assumption under GAAP that when one entity is owned outright or a majority of its voting interests controlled by another entity (the parent company), the most meaningful representation of the parent company's real financial position and economic performance will be through the presentation of consolidated financial statements. This presumption dates from the issuance in 1959 of ARB 51, *Consolidated Financial Statements*, which stopped short of absolutely requiring that consolidated financial reporting be employed. Over the ensuing years, a number of excuses for not fully consolidating certain subsidiaries arose, leading to substantial diversity of reporting practices. This in turn resulted in FASB issuance of FAS 94, *Consolidation of All Majority-Owned Subsidiaries*.

The practice of excluding some or all subsidiaries from the parent company's financial statements was variously justified due to the parent's lack of absolute control over the affairs of the subsidiary, whether because of legal restrictions or due to the relationship with noncontrolling owners, as well as when control was present but expected to be only temporary. More controversial, if less widely understood, were situations where "off-balance-sheet financing" was accomplished through the use of majority or wholly owned leasing, factoring, or other financing subsidiaries that were then excluded from the parent's financial statements. The actual justification given for excluding these entities from the consolidated financial statements, particularly in the cases of highly leveraged financing subsidiaries, was that consolidation of such "nonhomogeneous" operations would distort the parent's key financial and operating statistics, such as the working capital ratio and gross profit margin.

FAS 94 significantly narrowed, but did not totally eliminate, the ability of entities to exclude majority-owned subsidiaries from parent company financial statements. Most importantly, the "nonhomogeneity" argument could no longer be used to exclude leasing, real estate, financing, insurance, or other subsidiary operations. Under FAS 94, all majority-owned subsidiaries were to be consolidated, unless (1) control over the subsidiary was expected to be temporary in nature, or (2) control could be shown to not reside with the majority owner.

FAS 144 further restricted decisions to not consolidate majority-owned subsidiaries, by eliminating the "temporary control" exception. Thus, currently, only demonstrable lack of ability to control the majority-owned subsidiary can justify excluding it from the parent company's consolidated financial statements.

Separate financial statements of entities that are majority owned by other companies (i.e., its subsidiaries) are still permitted to be issued. In fact, noncontrolling stockholders and other interested parties (creditors, vendors, or customers, as well as regulatory authorities) might, in many instances, receive little useful disaggregated information from the parent company's consolidated financial statements. However, if the reporting subsidiary itself had one or more majority-owned subsidiaries of its own, these would be consolidated in the financial statements of the first-tier subsidiary.

Majority-owned subsidiaries that are not consolidated due to the absence of control by a parent company will generally be accounted for using the equity method (discussed in detail in Chapter 10). Analysis of the specific facts and circumstances (e.g., whether the parent has significant influence, even if not actual control) will determine whether the equity method is appropriate.

Combined Financial Statements

When a group of entities is under common ownership, control, or management, it is often useful to present combined (or combining—showing the separate as well as the combined entities) financial statements. In this situation, the economic substance of the nominally independent entities' combined operations may be more important to financial statement users than is the legal form of those enterprises. When consolidated statements are not presented, combined statements may be used to show the financial position, or operating results, of a group of companies that are each subsidiaries of a common parent.

According to ARB 51, the process of preparing combined statements is virtually the same as consolidations employing the previously permitted pooling-of-interests method. The major exception is that the equity section of the combined balance sheet will incorporate the equity sections of both of the combining entities. However, only a single combined retained earnings amount need be presented.

Example of the stockholders' equity section of a combined financial statement

Lanushka Ltd. and Scully Enterprises, Inc.
Combined Balance Sheet
December 31, 2005

Stockholders' equity	
Capital stock:	
Preferred, $100 par, authorized 90,000 shares, issued 5,000 shares	$ 500,000
Common, $50 par, authorized 100,000 shares, issued 60,000 shares	3,000,000
Common, $10 par, authorized 250,000 shares, issued 100,000 shares	1,000,000
Additional paid-in capital	650,000
Retained earnings	3,825,000
	$8,975,000

Combinations of Entities under Common Control

FAS 141 explicitly does **not** apply to combinations of entities under common control (parent and subsidiary, brother-sister corporations, etc.). Mergers among such affiliated entities must be accounted for "as if" poolings. This treatment is consistent with the concept of poolings as combinations of common stockholder interests. Notwithstanding the banning of pooling of interests accounting under current GAAP, this prescription still remains in effect.

A question arises, however, when a parent (Company P) transfers ownership in one of its subsidiaries (Company B) to another of its subsidiaries (Company A) in exchange for additional shares of Company A. If P's carrying value of its investment in B differs from B's book value, there appears to be a requirement for A to reflect its new investment in B at B's book value, rather than at P's cost (or equity) basis.

EITF 90-5 resolved this apparent conflict by stating that A's carrying value for the investment in B is to be P's basis, not B's book value. Furthermore, if A subsequently retires the interests of noncontrolling owners of B, the transaction is to be accounted for as a purchase, whether it is effected through a stock issuance by A or by a cash payment to the selling shareholders.

The EITF further concluded (in Issue 90-13) that when a purchase transaction is closely followed by a "sale" of the parent's subsidiary to the newly acquired (target) entity, these two transactions are to be viewed as a single transaction. Accordingly, the parent recognizes gain or loss on the sale of its subsidiary to the target company, to the extent of noncontrolling interest in the target entity. As a result, there will be a new basis (step-up) not only for the target company's assets and liabilities, but also for the subsidiary company's net assets. Basis is stepped up to the extent of noncontrolling participation in the target entity to which the subsidiary company was transferred.

Combinations of Mutual Enterprises and Not-for-Profit Organizations

The accounting procedures for combinations of mutual enterprises and for combinations of not-for-profit organizations were not addressed by FAS 141 and 142. FASB has continued with separate projects on these topics, however, and is expected to issue Exposure Drafts on each of these before year-end 2004.

Mutual enterprises. Historically, combinations of mutual enterprises (of which mutually owned savings and loan associations had been the most prominent) had been accounted for as poolings of interests, since there was normally no exchange of cash or other assets as consideration for the transaction. Also, the identity of the "acquirer" was difficult to ascertain in such transactions. Under the provisions of FAS 141, pooling accounting has been eliminated, and in every business combination one party must be identified as the acquirer. FASB is attempting to determine whether combinations involving mutual enterprises have special attributes that demand an accounting treatment other than that stipulated by FAS 141.

This project addresses only combinations of two or more mutual enterprises, since acquisitions of an investor-owned entity by a mutual enterprise and acquisitions of a mutual enterprise by an investor-owned entity are each already subject to the requirements of FAS 141. The FASB was seeking to ascertain whether there were any unique attributes of mutual enterprises to justify an accounting treatment different from that provided by the general standard. Pending the outcome of this investigation, the requirements of APB 16 and 17 continued to be applicable to combinations of two or more mutual enterprises. FASB has since reached decisions on (1) the applicability of the purchase method to combinations of mutual enterprise, (2) identification of an acquirer, and (3) identification of acquired intangible assets. It continues to contemplate measurement of the fair value of an acquired mutual enterprise, as well as the fair value of certain assets acquired and liabilities assumed.

FASB has concluded that the requirement of FAS 141, that all business combinations be accounted for using the purchase method, is also applicable to business combinations for mutual enterprises. In such combinations, the fair value of the acquired enterprise taken as a whole is to be used for the initial measurement of the value of the acquired enterprise. This complies with the guidance contained in FAS 141. The fair value of the acquired mutual enterprise is reported in the financial statements of the acquirer as a direct addition to a capital or equity account and appropriately labeled and identified as capital or equity arising from the acquisition of a mutual enterprise. Disclosure is to be made of the amount and nature of the addition to capital or equity, as well as the basis for determining the fair value of the acquired mutual enterprise. The criteria in FAS 141 are used to identify the acquiring enterprise. The criteria set forth in FAS 141 for recognizing identifiable intangible assets are applied in the recording of combinations of mutual enterprises.

Given the conclusion that FAS 141 applies to combinations among two or more mutual enterprises, FASB decided to (1) amend FAS 141 to remove its delayed effectiveness for combinations between mutual enterprises; and (2) amend FAS 142 to remove its delayed effectiveness provisions for combinations between mutual enterprises. Thus, the provisions of FAS 141 would thus (including its transition) apply to combinations **initiated** after a final Statement is issued. The provisions of FAS 142 (including its transition) would apply to mutual enterprises effective with fiscal years beginning after the date that a final Statement is issued.

FASB has also directed its staff to explore fair value measurement issues related to applying the purchase method to combinations between mutual enterprises, and to develop a proposal for additional guidance that can be provided as part of the project. In particular, a proposal for additional guidance related to measuring the fair value of an acquired mutual enterprise and the fair value of certain assets acquired and liabilities assumed, some of which may be subject to marketability restrictions, is to be developed. An Exposure Draft is promised for late 2004.

Not-for-profit organizations. As with mutual enterprise mergers, many not-for-profit organization combinations are characterized by an absence of cash or other consideration being paid by the presumptive acquirer. Also, many of these combinations have traditionally been accounted for as poolings, which is banned under FAS 141. FASB's deliberations have resulted in the conclusion that, while FAS 141 should apply to combinations of not-for-profit organizations in general, there may be circumstances unique to such combinations that could be identified and that would justify a different accounting treatment. Such an approach is being referred to as being **differences-based**.

The definition of a not-for-profit organization set forth in FAS 116 will be used for the FASB's project. Its scope is to include (1) combinations between two or more not-for-profit organizations and (2) the acquisition of a for-profit business enterprise by a not-for-profit organization. The scope will include combinations in which no combining entity dominates the process of selecting a voting majority of the combined entity's governing board (transactions which are sometimes referred to as mergers of equals). The acquisition of a not-for-profit organization by a business enterprise is already within the scope of FAS 141.

The scope of the proposed Statement will exclude the following transactions:

1. A transaction in which control is obtained through means other than an acquisition by purchase or gift of net assets or equity interests;
2. The formation of a joint venture;
3. The acquisition of noncontrolling interests; and
4. A transfer of net assets or exchange of equity interests between entities under common control.

FASB has concluded that a combination occurs when a not-for-profit organization acquires assets and liabilities that constitute an activity or acquires equity interests of one or more other entities and obtains control over that entity or entities. These would be distinguished from acquisitions of assets subject to certain liabilities based on whether the transferred set of processes and assets represents an **activity**—defined as an integrated set of processes conducted and assets managed for the purpose of providing goods and services to beneficiaries, customers, or members that fulfill the purpose or mission for which an organization exists. An activity consists of (1) inputs, (2) processes applied to those inputs, and (3) resulting outputs that are used to provide goods and services to beneficiaries, customers, or members. For a transferred set of processes and assets to be an activity, it must contain all of the inputs and processes necessary for it to continue to conduct normal operations after the transferred set is separated from the transferor. While the notion of **control** is implicit, it will not be a term defined in the proposed new standard.

FASB has observed that combinations in which the acquiring entity is a not-for-profit organization, rather than a business enterprise, cannot be assumed to be an exchange of commensurate value. Acquired not-for-profit organizations lack owners who are concerned with receipts of a return on and return of their investment. Also, the parent or governing body of an acquired not-for-profit organization may place its mission effectiveness ahead of achieving maximum price when negotiating a combination agreement, and it may approve a combination at a price less than fair value if that action would maximize the resources available to further its mission going forward. In some instances, an owner of a business enterprise may be motivated by donative intent to make a contribution to a not-for-profit organization by transferring ownership interests for less than a fair price. If an entity voluntarily transfers its net assets or equity to a not-for-profit organization in exchange for assets of substantially lower value or without receiving consideration and no unstated rights or privileges are involved, the contribution inherent in that combination is to be reported in accordance with FAS 116. However, if a not-for-profit organization acquires another entity in an exchange of commensurate value, the combination is reported similarly to the standards of FAS 141. Accordingly, a determination of whether a combination is reciprocal (involving an exchange of commensurate value) or nonreciprocal (containing an inherent contribution) will have to be made in every combination in which the acquired entity is a not-for-profit organization.

Under the proposed approach to not-for-profit acquisition accounting, when the acquired entity is a not-for-profit organization, the contribution recognized by the acquirer would be measured as the excess of the net fair value of the identifiable assets acquired and the liabilities assumed over the fair value of the assets transferred as consideration. In those rare cases in which the sum of the fair value of the liabilities assumed exceeds the sum of the fair values of the identifiable assets acquired, the acquiring organization would initially recognize that excess as goodwill.

If the acquired entity is a business enterprise, the contribution inherent in a combination would be measured as the excess of the fair value of the acquired business enterprise over the cost of that business enterprise.

FASB has concluded that, since communities neither own nor control not-for-profit organizations, a community's relationship with a not-for-profit organization has no effect on the accounting for a combination of not-for-profit organizations.

In an actual combination situation, it may be difficult to ascertain whether the transaction is reciprocal or not. FASB will suggest certain factors to consider in making the determination that a combination is partly an exchange and partly a contribution, including

1. The net fair value of the assets acquired and liabilities assumed substantially exceeds the fair value of the consideration exchanged and no unstated rights or privileges are involved; and
2. A review of the facts and circumstances surrounding the combination, including careful study of the negotiations, provides evidence that the participants were acting as a donor and a donee in addition to acting as a buyer and a seller.

Factors suggesting that combination is purely reciprocal would include

1. The organization or business enterprise is acquired through a competitive bidding process involving multiple potential acquirers;
2. The amount of consideration offered by the acquiring organization was developed in consultation with acquisition advisors, was based on an estimate of the acquired entity's fair value, or both—whether the estimate of the acquired entity's fair value may have been developed internally by the acquiring organization or by independent valuation experts;
3. The acquired entity's former parent or predecessor board of directors retained outside specialists to assist in negotiating the combination, used estimates of the organization's fair value to evaluate the adequacy of the offers received, or both;
4. One or both parties to the combination retained consultants to provide an opinion on the fairness of the consideration paid and received; and
5. The provisions of not-for-profit corporation law or involvement of a state attorney general or other regulatory body influenced the terms or structure of the combination transaction to ensure that fair value consideration is obtained when the acquired organization's parent approves the combination.

When not-for-profit organizations combine, there may be difficulty in determining which was the acquirer. FASB will state that all pertinent facts and circumstances are to be considered. When the combination is effected solely through the distribution of cash or other assets or by incurring liabilities, the organization that distributes cash or other assets or incurs liabilities is generally the acquiring organization. In a not-for-profit combination in which no consideration is exchanged, the not-for-profit organization that is able to dominate the process of selecting a voting majority of the combined organization's initial governing body is the acquirer. In making that determination, consideration would be given to (1) the existence of rights provided by the combined organizations' articles of incorporation, its bylaws, or by provisions in the combination agreement to elect or appoint members to the combined organization's governing body, and (2) the ability to dominate the selection process through other means. Other factors will be identified in the proposed standard.

For those combinations of not-for-profit organizations giving rise to goodwill recognition, FASB will propose a two-path method of accounting subsequent to acquisition if the acquired entity is another not-for-profit organization or is a business enterprise that will be converted to a not-for-profit organization.

1. Reporting units primarily supported by fees or other charges to third parties for goods and services would test goodwill for impairment using the fair value method required by FAS 142; but
2. Reporting units not primarily supported by fees or other charges to third parties would test goodwill for impairment using a trigger-based approach that writes off goodwill **in its entirety** if certain triggering events occur. At acquisition, the acquiring organization would have to identify the reasons goodwill arose in the transaction and determine what triggering events related to those reasons would signal significant impairment.

The final standard may contain variations on the above, as this matter is subject to further deliberations. For combinations in which a not-for-profit organization acquires a business enterprise that will continue to be operated as a business enterprise, goodwill will be recognized subsequent to acquisition in accordance with FAS 142.

Regarding financial statement presentation, FASB has reached the following tentative conclusions:

1. The contribution resulting from a nonreciprocal combination transaction would be reported in the statement of activities as a separate line item. The contribution would be reported as increases in permanently restricted net assets, temporarily restricted net assets, and unrestricted net assets depending on the type of donor-imposed restrictions assumed by the acquiring organization.
2. Limitations placed on net assets by the governing board of an entity acquired in a nonreciprocal combination would be reported as donor-imposed restrictions only if those limitations are (a) imposed as conditions of the combination transaction, (b) are irrevocable, and (c) are not self-imposed. Limitations imposed by the governing board of an acquired entity as a condition of the combination will be deemed self-imposed if members of the governing board of the acquired entity make up a significant portion of the governing board of the combined organization. Limitations placed by the governing board of an acquired entity as a condition of the combination would be deemed not self-imposed if the acquired entity was only a portion of another entity and that other entity continues to survive as an unaffiliated entity. Limitations on the acquired net assets that are placed by the governing board of the acquiring entity would not be reported as donor-imposed restrictions.
3. An acquiring organization would not apply the reporting exception in FAS 116. Instead, an acquiring organization would report its assumption of fiduciary responsibilities for the restricted net assets of the acquired entity separately from any expiration of those restrictions that occurs after the date of acquisition and before the end of the reporting period.
4. For reciprocal combinations, an acquiring organization would report changes in net assets that result from its assumption of fiduciary responsibilities for the restricted net assts of the acquired entity in the statement of activities as a reclassification, separate from other reclassifications.
5. A nonreciprocal combination in which no consideration is exchanged would be reported as a noncash activity in the statement of cash flows. If cash is received as one of the assets acquired in the nonreciprocal combination, it would be reported as an investing activity inflow.

6. The net cash outflow for a reciprocal combination would be reported as an investing activity outflow.
7. If the combination transaction is in part a purchase and in part a contribution, the net cash outflow would be reported as an investing activity outflow and the noncash portion reported as a noncash activity.

Disclosures to be made in the context of not-for-profit combinations would replicate those required under FAS 141, tailored to reflect the unique attributes of such transactions. The proposal will detail these disclosures with specificity.

The proposed statement will be effective upon issuance, to apply prospectively to all combinations initiated after the effective date. It will preclude adjustments of amounts recognized in combinations occurring before the issuance date regardless of whether the combination was originally accounted for by the purchase or pooling-of-interests methods. The statement will include transition provisions for intangible assets and negative goodwill consistent with the transition provisions for business enterprises in FAS 141.

Accounting for Leveraged Buyouts

Possibly one of the most complex accounting issues to have arisen over the past two decades has been the appropriate accounting for a leveraged buyout (LBO). At the center of this issue is the question of whether a **new basis** of accountability has been created by the LBO transaction. If so, then a step-up in the reported value of assets and/or liabilities is warranted. If not, the carryforward bases of the predecessor entity continues to be reported in the company's financial statements.

The EITF has addressed leveraged buyouts, first in 86-16, then in 88-16 and 90-12. The task force's conclusion was that partial or complete new basis accounting is appropriate only when the transaction is characterized by a **change in control of voting interest**. Consensus 88-16 established a series of mechanical tests by which this change in interest is to be measured. The EITF identified three groups of interests: shareholders in the newly created company, management, and shareholders in the old company (who may or may not also have an interest in the new company). Depending upon the relative interests of these groups in the old entity (OLDCO) and in the new enterprise (NEWCO), there will be **either,** (1) a finding that the transaction was a purchase (new basis accounting applies) or (2) that it was a recapitalization or a restructuring (carryforward basis accounting applies).

Among the tests that the EITF decreed to determine proper accounting for any given LBO transaction is the "monetary test." This test requires that at least 80% of the net consideration paid to acquire OLDCO interests must be **monetary**. In this context, monetary means cash, debt, and the fair value of any equity by securities given by NEWCO to selling shareholders of OLDCO. Loan proceeds provided OLDCO to assist in the acquisition of NEWCO shares by NEWCO shareholders are excluded from this definition. If the portion of the purchase that is effected through monetary consideration is less than 80%, but other criteria of EITF 88-16 are satisfied, there will be a step up. This step up will be limited to the percentage of the transaction represented by monetary consideration.

EITF 88-16 presents an extensive series of examples illustrating the circumstances that would and would not meet the purchase accounting criteria to be employed in LBO. These examples should be consulted as needed when addressing an actual LBO transaction accounting issue.

Reverse Acquisitions

Reverse acquisitions occur when one entity (the nominal acquirer) issues so many shares to the former owners of another entity (the nominal acquiree) that they become the majority owners of the resultant combined enterprise. The result of this event is that the legal and accounting treatments of the transaction will diverge, with the nominal acquiree being the acquirer for financial reporting purposes. While often the nominal acquirer will adopt the acquiree's name, thus alerting users of the statements to the nature of the organizational change, this does not necessarily occur, and, in any event, it will be critical that the financial statements contain sufficient disclosure so that users are not misled. This will be important particularly in the periods immediately following the transaction, and especially when comparative financial statements are presented which include some periods prior to the acquisition, since comparability will be affected.

A typical reverse acquisition would occur when a "shell" enterprise, which often is a publicly held but dormant company, merges with an operating company, which often will be nonpublic. The objective is for the operating entity to "go public" without the usual time consuming and expensive registration process. However, reverse acquisitions are not limited to such situations, and there have been many such transactions involving two public or two nonpublic companies. The nominal acquirer may have substantial operations of its own, although of lesser scope or with lower growth prospects than those of the nominal acquiree.

A number of difficult questions arise in reverse acquisitions, and GAAP does not provide definitive guidance on these important issues. The SEC has provided some direction that, under the hierarchy of GAAP, are viewed as definitive absent higher level "official" indicators from other standard setters. Among the matters to be considered, and which will be discussed in the following paragraphs, are these.

1. What circumstances signal a reverse acquisition?
2. How should the consolidated financial statements be presented in the subsequent periods?
3. How should the purchase cost be computed and allocated in a reverse acquisition?
4. What would the shareholders' equity section of the balance sheet be immediately following the reverse acquisition?
5. What would be the impact on computation of earnings per share?
6. How will noncontrolling interest be presented in the financial statements?

Reverse acquisitions occur when the former shareholders of the nominal acquiree become the majority owners of the postacquisition consolidated enterprise, and most commonly this will result when a stock-for-stock swap occurs. Under prior rules, if all of the twelve restrictive conditions set forth in APB 16 were met, the transaction would be accounted for as a pooling, thus obviating the concerns noted above. Under recently promulgated GAAP, however, poolings are prohibited and all business combinations will be accounted for as purchases. Unless the combining entities were under common control prior to the transaction (in which case the transaction is accounted for in the manner of a pooling, continuing the exception first established by Interpretation 39 under APB 16), purchase accounting is required for all reverse acquisitions.

If the former owners of the nominal acquiree in a purchase business combination become the majority owners of the consolidated enterprise following the transactions, it will be deemed to have been a reverse acquisition. Following a reverse acquisition, consolidated financial statements will be presented. Although the financial statements will be identified as being those of the nominal acquirer (which will be the legal owner of the nominal acquiree), in substance these will be the financial statements of the acquiree company, with the assets and liabilities, and revenues and expenses, of the nominal acquirer being included effective with the date of the transaction. Put another way, the legal parent company will be deemed to be a continuation of the business of the legal subsidiary, notwithstanding the formal structure of the transaction or the name of the successor enterprise. For this reason, if the legal parent (nominally the acquirer) does not change its name to that of the acquiree, it would be appropriate for the financial statement titles to be captioned in a way that most clearly communicates the substance of the transaction to the readers. For example, the statements may be headed "ABC Company, Inc.—successor to XYZ Corporation."

Given the foregoing, it is clear that the stockholders' equity section of the posttransaction consolidated balance sheet is to be that of the acquiree, not the acquirer, with appropriate modification for the new shares issued in the transaction and ancillary adjustments, if any. Comparative financial statements for earlier periods, if presented, are to be consistent, meaning that these would be the financial statements of the nominal acquiree. Since in some instances the acquiree's name is different than that shown in the heading, care must be taken to fully communicate with the readers. The fact that the prior period's financial information identified as being that of the legal parent is really that of the nominal acquiree obviously is extremely pertinent to a reader's understanding of these statements.

Consistent with the accounting imposed on other purchase business combinations, the cost of reverse acquisitions is measured at the fair value of the net assets acquired, or the value of the consideration paid, if more apparent. A special rule is that, if fair value cannot be determined for the issuer's stock, and the transaction is valued at the fair value of the issuer's net assets, no goodwill is recognized in the transaction. In addition, in the special case of a publicly held shell company and a privately held acquiree, the SEC has ruled that no goodwill can be recognized in any event. Clearly, in such instances there is substantial doubt about the true existence of goodwill and unusual difficulty in valuing the transaction, and this prohibition is prudent under the circumstances.

If the fair value of the shares of the nominal acquiree (which becomes the legal subsidiary after the transaction is completed) is used to determine the cost of the purchase, it is suggested that a calculation be made to determine the number of shares that the acquiree would have issued in order to provide the same level of ownership in the combined entity to the shareholders of the nominal acquirer as they have as a consequence of the reverse acquisition. The fair value of the number of shares thus determined is used to value the transaction, as illustrated later in this section.

In some instances, the market price of acquiree shares may not be fairly indicative of the value of the transaction. In such cases, the most feasible alternative would be to use the fair value of all the outstanding shares of the ostensible acquirer, prior to the transaction, to value the purchase transaction. In some instances, adjustments would have to be made for trading volume, price fluctuations, etc., to most accurately reflect the substance of the acquisition.

In other cases, particularly where the acquirer is a dormant shell entity, market price of its shares may not be meaningful. If possible to determine, utilizing the fair value of the net assets of the acquirer may be a more meaningful technique.

Whatever specific technique is employed under the circumstances, the total purchase cost is to be allocated to the net assets of the acquirer (not the acquiree) following the principles set forth in FAS 141. If the purchase cost exceeds the fair value of net identifiable assets, the excess is allocated to goodwill, which will be tested for impairment as explained elsewhere in this chapter, and written down or eliminated when and if impairment is detected. The financial statements of the consolidated enterprise following the reverse acquisition would reflect the assets and liabilities of the nominal acquirer at fair value, and those of the nominal acquiree at historical cost.

Since for financial reporting purposes the nominal acquiree is the parent company, the retained earnings or deficit of the acquiree will be carried forward in the equity section of the successor entity's balance sheet. The retained earnings or deficit of the nominal acquirer will not be presented. The amount shown for paid-in capital would be valued in terms of the issued capital of the nominal acquiree (the new subsidiary), plus the cost of the acquisition as described above and illustrated below. However, in the actual financial statement, which must reflect the legal structure of the transaction, paid-in capital would be expressed in terms of the legal parent company, which was the nominal acquirer. An example of accounting for a reverse acquisition follows.

Assume that Agoura Corp., which is the nominal acquirer that becomes the legal parent company, issues shares in exchange for the outstanding common stock of Belmar Co., Inc., which is the nominal acquiree which becomes the legal subsidiary of Agoura. For accounting purposes, this will be a reverse acquisition such that Belmar is the actual acquirer.

The balance sheets of the two entities at the end of 2004 and as of September 30, 2005, the date of the transaction, are given as follows:

	Agoura Corporation	
	December 31, 2004	September 30, 2005
Current assets	$ 800,000	$1,000,000
Plant, property, and equipment, net	2,400,000	2,600,000
	$3,200,000	$3,600,000
Current liabilities	$ 400,000	$ 600,000
Long-term debt	600,000	400,000
Deferred tax liabilities	200,000	200,000
	1,200,000	1,200,000
Stockholders' equity		
8% redeemable preferred stock, 2,000 shs.	200,000	200,000
Common stock, 100,000 shs.	600,000	600,000
Retained earnings	1,200,000	1,600,000
	$3,200,000	$3,600,000

	Belmar Company, Inc	
	December 31, 2004	September 30, 2005
Current assets	$2,500,000	$1,750,000
Plant, property and equipment, net	5,000,000	7,500,000
	$7,500,000	$9,250,000
Current liabilities	$1,250,000	$1,500,000
Long-term debt	1,750,000	2,000,000
Deferred tax liabilities	500,000	750,000
	3,500,000	4,250,000
Stockholders' equity		
Common stock, 60,000 shs.	1,500,000	1,500,000
Retained earnings	2,500,000	3,500,000
	$7,500,000	$9,250,000

Agoura had net income of $400,000 for the nine months ended September 30, 2005, while Belmar Co. enjoyed earnings of $1,000,000 for that period. Neither company paid any dividends during this period.

The fair value of each share of Belmar common stock was $100 at the date of the acquisition. Agoura shares were quoted at $24 on the date.

Agoura's identifiable net assets had fair values equal to their respective book values, with the exception of the plant, property and equipment, which were appraised at $3,000,000 at September 30, 2005.

In effecting the acquisition, Agoura issues 150,000 new shares of its common stock to the owners of Belmar in exchange for all outstanding Belmar shares. Thus, former Belmar owners become the owners of a majority of the common stock of Agoura after this transaction.

To compute the cost of the reverse acquisition, the number of shares of the nominal acquiree entity, Belmar, which would have had to have been issued to acquire the nominal acquirer, Agoura, must be computed. This is done as follows:

Actual Agoura shares issued to former Belmar owners	150,000
Agoura shares outstanding prior to transaction	100,000
Total Agoura shares outstanding after transaction	250,000
Fraction held by former Belmar owners (150,000/250,000)	60%
Number of Belmar shares outstanding before transaction	60,000
Number of Belmar shares that could have been issued in transaction if 60% of total would have remained with original Belmar shareholders	40,000

If Belmar had issued 40,000 of its shares to effect the acquisition of Agoura, the cost would have been (given the fair value of Belmar shares at September 30, 2005) $100 x 40,000 = $4,000,000. This purchase cost would have been allocated to Agoura's assets and liabilities as follows:

Current assets		$1,000,000
Plant, property and equipment		3,000,000
		$4,000,000
Current liabilities	$600,000	
Long-term debt	400,000	
Deferred tax liabilities	200,000	1,200,000
		2,800,000
8% redeemable preferred stock, 2,000 shs.		200,000
		2,600,000
Cost of purchase (from above)		4,000,000
Goodwill to be recognized		$1,400,000

From the foregoing, the information needed to construct a consolidated balance sheet as of the date of the transaction, September 30, 2005, can be determined.

Agoura Corporation
Consolidated Balance Sheet
September 30, 2005

Current assets	$ 2,750,000
Plant, property and equipment, net	10,500,000
Goodwill	1,400,000
	$14,650,000
Current liabilities	$ 2,100,000
Long-term debt	2,400,000
Deferred tax liabilities	950,000
	5,450,000
Stockholders' equity	
8% redeemable preferred stock, 2,000 shs.	200,000
Common stock, 100,000 shs.	5,500,000
Retained earnings	3,500,000
	9,200,000
	$14,650,000

Computing earnings per share after a reverse acquisition poses special problems, particularly so in the year in which the transaction occurs and in any subsequent years when comparative financial statements are presented that include those of pretransaction periods. For this purpose, the number of shares outstanding for the period from the beginning of the current reporting year until the date of the reverse acquisition is the number of shares issued by the nominal acquirer (the legal parent company) to the shareholders of the nominal acquiree. For the period after the transaction, the number of shares considered to be outstanding is the actual number of shares of the legal parent company outstanding during that period. The average number of shares outstanding for the full year being reported upon would be computed by averaging these two amounts. Other appropriate adjustments would be made to deal with changes in numbers of shares issued during the period, as is done under other circumstances (as described in Chapter 18), if necessary. Under the current standard for computing earnings per share (FAS 128), the calculation of basic earnings per share (replacing the former measure, primary earnings per share) is simplified for all entities.

Earnings per share for any earlier periods presented for comparative purposes is likewise complicated by the occurrence of a reverse acquisition. The number of shares issued by the legal parent (nominal acquirer) in the reverse acquisition transaction would be used to make this calculation.

Continuing with the Agoura-Belmar acquisition example above, earnings per share can be computed. Assume that consolidated net income for the year ended December 31, 2005, after deducting preferred dividends, equals $1,600,000. This includes Belmar Co., Inc. earnings for the full year 2005, plus Agoura Corp. earnings from the date of acquisition, September 30, 2005, until year-end. Remember that, notwithstanding that the new entity is called Agoura, from an accounting perspective this is Belmar Company.

Earnings per share would thus be computed as follows:

Number of shares outstanding from September 30, 2005	250,000
Number of shares deemed outstanding before September 30—the number of Agoura shares issued to Belmar	150,000

Average number of shares

[(150,000 x 9) + (250,000 x 3)] ÷ 12 = 175,000

Earnings per share for 2005

$1,600,000 ÷ 175,000 = $9.14 per share

For 2005, assuming Belmar alone had earnings of $1,400,000 for the year, earnings per share would be

$1,400,000 ÷ 150,000 = $9.33 per share

Finally, there is the question of noncontrolling interest. In a reverse acquisition situation, the noncontrolling is comprised of the former shareholders of the legal subsidiary who do not exchange their shares for those of the new parent company, but continue on as stockholders in the legal subsidiary entity. Note that this holds even though from the accounting perspective they are shareholders in an entity that acquired another company. In other words, the identity of the noncontrolling interest is determined by the legal structure of the transaction, not the accounting substance. Since the net assets of the legal subsidiary (but substantive parent) are included in the consolidated financial statements at the old book values, noncontrolling interest is likewise computed based on the book value of the legal subsidiary's net assets.

For example, in the present case all shareholders of Belmar might not agree to tender their shares in exchange for Agoura stock, and if so they will continue on as noncontrolling owners of the legal subsidiary, Belmar, after it is nominally acquired by Agoura Corp. To illustrate, consider these assumed facts.

Agoura offered 2.5 shares for each share of Belmar common stock. In the example above, 150,000 shares of Agoura were exchanged for 60,000 Belmar shares. Now, however, assume that owners of 4,000 Belmar shares decline to participate in this transaction, so Agoura issues only 140,000 shares in exchange for 56,000 Belmar shares. After the exchange, former Belmar owners hold 140,000 of a total of 240,000 Agoura Corp. shares, or 58.33% of the total outstanding; still a majority and thus enough to define this as a reverse acquisition.

The cost of the purchase is computed similar to what was illustrated above. Since the owners of 56,000 Belmar shares participated and the transaction resulted in these owners obtaining a 58.33% interest in the successor entity, the calculation of the number of Belmar shares that hypothetically would have had to have been issued in a "straight" acquisition of Agoura is as follows:

56,000 shares outstanding ÷ .5833 = 96,000 total shares after transaction

96,000 total shares – 56,000 shares outstanding = 40,000 new shares to be issued

Thus, it can be seen that the cost of the purchase, determined in the manner that is necessary when a reverse acquisition takes place, remains 40,000 x \$100 = \$4,000,000 even given the existence of the noncontrolling interest.

The noncontrolling interest is 4,000 shares ÷ 60,000 shares = 6.6667%. It consists, as of the acquisition date, of 6.6667% of the book value of Belmar common stock and retained earnings, as follows:

6.6667% x \$1,500,000	=	\$100,000
6.6667% x \$3,500,000	=	233,310
Total noncontrolling interest		\$333,310

The consolidated balance sheet at acquisition date would differ from that shown above only as follows: a noncontrolling interest of \$333,310 would be presented (under current GAAP, as a liability, as equity, or in a semiequity account); common stock would be only \$5,400,000, comprised of 93.33% (1 – 6.66667%) of Belmar's \$1,500,000, plus the \$4 million purchase cost); and retained earnings would be only 93.33% or Belmar's pretransaction balance of \$3.5 million, or \$3,266,655. All other asset and liability account balances would be identical to the presentation above.

Spin-Offs

Occasionally an entity disposes of a wholly or partially owned subsidiary or of an investee by transferring it unilaterally to the entity's shareholders. The proper accounting for such a transaction, generally known as a spin-off, depends upon the percentage of the company that is owned.

If the ownership percentage is relatively minor, 25% for example, the transfer to stockholders would be viewed as a "dividend in kind" and would be accounted for at the fair value of the property (i.e., shares in the investee) transferred.

However, when the entity whose shares are distributed is majority or wholly-owned, the effect is not merely to transfer a passive investment, but to remove the operations from the former parent and to vest them with the parent's shareholders. This transaction is a true spin-off transaction, not merely a property dividend. APB 29 requires that spin-offs and other similar nonreciprocal transfers to owners be accounted for at the recorded book values of the assets and liabilities transferred.

If the operations (or subsidiary) being spun off are distributed during a fiscal period, it may be necessary to estimate the results of operations for the elapsed period prior to spin-off in order to ascertain the net book value as of the date of the transfer. Stated another way, the operating results of the subsidiary to be disposed of are included in the reported results of the parent through the actual date of the spin-off.

In most instances, the subsidiary being spun off will have a positive net book value. This net worth represents the cost of the nonreciprocal transfer to the owners, and, like a dividend, will be reflected as a charge against the parent's retained earnings at the date of spin-off. In other situations, the operations (or subsidiary) will have a net deficit (negative net book value). Since it is unacceptable to recognize a credit to the parent's retained earnings for other than a culmination of an earnings process, the spin-off is recorded as a credit to the parent's paid-in capital. In effect, the stockholders (the recipients of the spun-off subsidiary) have made a capital contribution to the parent company by accepting the operations having a negative book value. As with other capital transactions, this would **not** be presented in the income statement, but only in the statement of changes in stockholders' equity (and in the statement of cash flows).

Reverse Spin-Offs

The preceding section has discussed the normal spin-off situation, where an entity (now being referred to as the spinnor) transfers assets into a new legal spun-off entity (the spinnee) and distributes the shares of the spinnee to its shareholders, without the surrender by the shareholders of any stock of the spinnor. As noted, this transaction is accounted for at book value under APB 29.

In other situations, the spinnee will be the continuing entity. The issue is whether to account for a spin-off as a reverse spin-off based on the substance instead of the legal form of the transaction. In a reverse spin-off, the legal spinnee is treated as though it were the spinnor for accounting purposes (accounting spinnor). This parallels the considerations applicable to reverse acquisitions, discussed earlier in this chapter. It is further complicated, however, by the fact that the determination of the accounting spinnor and spinnee may have significant implications with regard to the reporting of discontinued operations in accordance with FAS 144. The accounting spinnee is reported as a discontinued operation by the accounting spinnor if the spinnee is a **component of an entity** and meets the conditions for such reporting contained in FAS 144.

In EITF 02-11, a consensus was expressed that reverse spin-off accounting (whereby the legal spinnee is treated as the accounting spinnor, etc.) is appropriate when it results in the most accurate depiction of the substance of the transaction for shareholders and other users of the financial statements. Whether this is appropriate however, is a matter of judgment and must be based on all the facts and circumstances. Absent convincing evidence of the existence of a reverse spin-off, the presumption will be that normal spin-off accounting (whereby the legal spinnee is treated as the accounting spinnee, etc.) is to be applied.

Factors that suggest that reverse spin-off accounting is warranted would include factors such as these.

Relative size. Generally, in a reverse spin-off, the accounting spinnor (legal spinnee) is larger than the accounting spinnee (legal spinnor). This determination will be based on a comparison of the assets, revenues, and earnings of the two entities. There are no established "bright lines" that are used to determine which entity is the larger of the two, however.

Relative fair values. Generally, in a reverse spin-off, the fair value of the accounting spinnor (legal spinnee) is greater than that of the accounting spinnee (legal spinnor).

Senior management. Typically, in a reverse spin-off, the accounting spinnor (legal spinnee) retains the senior management of the formerly combined entity, defined to include the chairman of the board, chief executive officer, chief operating officer, chief financial officer, and those divisional heads reporting directly to them, or the executive committee if one exists.

Length of time to be held. Normally, in a reverse spin-off, the accounting spinnor (legal spinnee) is held for a longer period than the accounting spinnee (legal spinnor). A proposed or approved plan of sale for one of the separate entities concurrent with the spin-off may, therefore, identify that entity as the accounting spinnee.

The determination of which entities are the accounting spinnor and spinnee, respectively, has significant implications. In a spin-off, the net book value of the spinnee is treated, in effect, as a dividend distribution to the shareholders of the spinnor. Since the net book value of these entities will differ from each other, the amount of the reduction to retained earnings of the surviving reporting entity (the accounting spinnor) will be affected by this determination. EITF 02-11 offers several examples of fact patterns which support spin-off or reverse spin-off determinations.

Push-Down Accounting

For a number of years, the matter of what is commonly called "push down" accounting (but which is also known as "new basis accounting") had been on the FASB's technical agenda. It received scant attention notwithstanding the SEC's long-held position that, under narrowly defined circumstances, push-down accounting is to be applied. After being temporarily dropped as a project, in 1996 the topic was again added to the FASB's agenda as part of its business combinations project. Since 2000 this matter has received renewed attention and may be jointly dealt with by the FASB and the International Accounting Standards Board.

Under new basis accounting, the amounts allocated to various assets and liabilities can be adjusted to reflect the arm's-length valuation reflected in a significant transaction, such as the sale of a majority interest in the entity. For example, the sale of 90% of the shares of a company by one shareholder to a new investor—which under the entity concept would not alter the accounting by the company itself—would, under new basis accounting, be "pushed down" to the entity. The logic is that, as under purchase method accounting for business combinations, the most objective gauge of "cost" is that arising from a recent arm's-length transaction.

Traditionally, GAAP has not permitted new basis accounting, in part because of the practical difficulty of demonstrating that the reference transaction was indeed arm's-length in nature. (Obviously, the risk is that a series of sham transactions could be used to grossly distort the "cost" and hence carrying values of the entity's assets, resulting in fraudulent financial reporting.) Also heavily debated has been where the threshold should be set (a 50% change in ownership, an 80% change, etc.) to denote when a significant event had occurred that would provide valid information on the valuation of the entity's assets and liabilities for financial reporting purposes.

In its recent deliberations, the FASB has agreed that a transfer of control over assets from one entity to a joint venture is an event which should result in gain recognition (where warranted) in the financial statements of the transferor, and that a new basis of accountability would be established for those assets. This is a marked departure from past practice, under which a transfer of appreciated assets to a joint venture or partnership (e.g., a transfer of land to a building partnership) was to be accounted for at book value.

Many of the more general issues of push-down accounting (those applicable to traditional business acquisitions) have yet to be dealt with. For example, proponents of push-down accounting point out that in a purchase business combination a new basis of accounting is established, and that this new basis should be pushed down to the acquired entity and should be used when presenting that entity's own, separate financial statements. However, practical problems remain: for example, while push-down makes some sense in the case where a major block of the investee's shares is acquired in a single free-market transaction, if new basis accounting were to be used in the context of a series of step transactions, continual adjustment of the investee's carrying values for assets and liabilities would be necessary. Furthermore, the price paid for a fractional share of ownership of an investee may not always be meaningfully extrapolated to a value for the investee company as a whole.

The SEC's position has been that push-down accounting would be required if 95% or more of the shares of the company have been acquired (unless the company has outstanding public debt or preferred stock that may impact the acquirer's ability to control the form of ownership of the company); that it would be permitted, but not mandated, if 80% to 95% has been acquired; and it would be prohibited if less than 80% of the company is acquired.

While there is no requirement under GAAP to apply the push-down concept, the SEC position is substantial authoritative support and can be referenced even for nonpublic company financial reporting. It would be defensible in any instance where there is a change in control and/or a change in ownership of a majority of the common shares, when separate financial statements of the subsidiary are to be presented. Full disclosure is to be made of the circumstances whenever push-down accounting is applied.

Example of push-down accounting

Assume that Pullup Corp. acquires, in an open market arm's-length transaction, 90% of the common stock of Pushdown Co. for $464.61 million. At that time, Pushdown Co.'s net book value was $274.78 million (for the entire company). Book and fair values of selected assets and liabilities of Pushdown Co. as of the transaction date are summarized as follows ($000,000 omitted):

	Book value		*Fair value of*	*Excess of*
	100% of entity	*90% interest*	*90% interest*	*FV over book*
Assets				
Receivables	$ 24.6	$ 22.14	$ 29.75	$ 7.61
Inventory	21.9	19.71	24.80	5.09
Property, plant & equipment, net	434.2	390.78	488.20	97.42
All others	223.4	201.06	201.06	0.00
Add'l goodwill			120.00	120.00
Total assets	$704.1	$633.69	$863.81	$230.12
Liabilities				
Bonds payable	104.9	94.41	88.65	5.76
All other liabilities	325.0	292.50	310.55	18.05
Total liabilities	429.9	386.91	399.20	12.29
Equity				
Preferred stock	40.0	36.00	36.00	0.00
Common stock	87.4	78.66	78.66	0.00
Revaluation surplus*			217.83	217.83
Retained earnings	146.8	132.12	132.12	0.00
Total equity	274.2	246.88	464.61	217.83
Liabilities + Equity	$704.1	$633.69	$863.81	$230.12

* *Net premium paid over book value by arm's-length of "almost all" common stock*

Assuming that "new basis" accounting is deemed to be acceptable and meaningful, since Pushdown Co. must continue to issue separate financial statements to its creditors and holders of its preferred stock, and also assuming that a revaluation of the share of ownership that did **not** change hands (i.e., the 10% noncontrolling interest in this example) should **not** be revalued based on the majority transaction, the entries by the subsidiary (Pushdown Co.) for purposes only of preparing stand-alone financial statements would be as follows:

Accounts receivable	7,610,000	
Inventory	5,090,000	
Plant, property and equipment (net)	97,420,000	
Goodwill	120,000,000	
Discount on bonds payable	5,760,000	
Other liabilities		18,050,000
Paid-in capital from revaluation		217,830,000

The foregoing entry would only be made for purposes of preparing separate financial statements of Pushdown Co. If consolidated financial statements of Pullup Corp. are also presented, essentially the same result will be obtained. The additional paid-in capital account would be eliminated against the parent's investment account, however, since in the context of the consolidated financial statements this would be a cash transaction rather than a mere accounting revaluation.

There is also a body of opinion that says that the separate financial statements of Pushdown Co. in this example should be "grossed up" for the imputed premium that would have been achieved on the transfer of the remaining 10% ownership interest. This is less appealing, however, given the absence of a "real" transaction involving that last 10% ownership stake, making the price at which it would have traded somewhat speculative.

The foregoing example obviously also ignored the tax effects of the transaction. Since the step-ups in carrying value would not, in all likelihood, alter the corresponding tax bases of the assets and liabilities, deferred tax effects would have also had to be recognized. This would be done following the procedures set forth at FAS 109, as described fully in Chapter 15.

Non-Sub Subsidiaries

Another issue that has concerned accountants and the Securities and Exchange Commission is the sudden popularity of what have been called "non-sub subsidiaries." This situation arises when an entity plays a major role in the creation and financing of what is often a start-up or experimental operation, but does not take an equity position at the outset. For example, the sponsor might finance the entity by means of convertible debt or debt with warrants entitling it to the later purchase of common shares. The original equity in such arrangements is often provided by the creative or managerial talent engaged in the new entity's operations, who generally exchange their talents for an equity interest. If the operation prospers, the sponsor will exercise its rights and obtain a majority voting stock position; if the operation fails, the sponsor presumably avoids reflecting the losses in its financial statements.

While this strategy may seem to avoid the requirements of equity method accounting or consolidation based on majority voting ownership, the economic substance of the arrangement clearly suggests that the operating results of the sponsored entity be reflected as a subsidiary in the consolidated financial statements of the sponsor who, in substance, is fulfilling the customary role of a parent, even absent ownership of voting stock.

The entities described above are often similar in structure and purpose to the "special-purpose entities" or "special-purpose vehicles." These SPE have been widely discussed in recent years, as their use has grown exponentially for such valid purposes as securitizations, and also for less worthy objectives, including concealing the existence of debt which might represent moral, if not legal, obligations of the reporting entity. These matters are described in the next section.

Variable Interest Entities

Introduction and background information. As previously discussed, ARB 51, *Consolidated Financial Statements*, issued over 40 years ago, provides the primary authority for determining when consolidated financial statements are required to be presented. The rationale underlying ARB 51 is that consolidated financial statements are more informative to users when one enterprise directly or indirectly holds a "controlling financial interest" in one or more other enterprises. ARB 51 went on to stipulate that the usual condition that best evidenced which party held a controlling financial interest was the party that held a majority voting interest.

This general rule requiring consolidation by a party holding a majority of the voting interests is still operational today and the foregoing discussion of consolidations and business combinations provided extensive guidance regarding parent/subsidiary relationships in the context of the parent holding a majority voting interest in the subsidiary. The subsidiary in this relationship is sometimes referred to as a **voting interest entity**.

Since the issuance of ARB 51, however, managers and their advisors have devised many new and creative types of ownership structures, financing arrangements, financial instruments, and business relationships. Many, if not most of these arrangements were originated to accomplish legitimate business objectives. Some of the arrangements were designed with the express intent of establishing financial control over assets or operations while the sponsoring entity avoided the establishment of voting control that served as the determinant of consolidation.

Examples of such arrangements abound and have been discussed in previous sections of this chapter. Perhaps no such type of financial arrangement or structure, however, has received the level of recent negative publicity as the special-purpose entity (SPE). The primary authoritative pronouncement that discusses SPE, is FAS 140, *Accounting for Transfers and Servicing of Financial Assets and Extinguishments of Liabilities*, which is discussed in detail in Chapter 5. In the context of FAS 140 (and the predecessor standard, FAS 125, in which the definition originated) an SPE is narrowly defined as a trust or other legal vehicle to which a transferor transfers a portfolio of financial assets (such as mortgage loans, commercial loans, credit card debt, automobile loans, and other groups of homogenous borrowings). Commonly SPE have been organized as trusts or partnerships (flow-through entities, in order to avoid double incidence of corporate income taxation), and the outside equity participant was ultimately defined as having as little as 3% of the total assets of the SPE at risk (this was not established by GAAP, but rather evolved somewhat by default and has been subject to varying interpretation under different sets of conditions). The SPE typically issues and sells securities that represent beneficial interests in the cash flows from the portfolio. This process is called a securitization. The proceeds the SPE receives from the sale of the securities are used to purchase the portfolio from the transferor. The cash flows received by the SPE from the dividends, interest, redemptions, principal repayments, and/or realized gains on the financial assets are used to pay a return to the investors in the SPE's securities. By transferring packages of such loans to an SPE, these assets can be legally isolated and made "bankruptcy proof" (and thus made more valuable as collateral for other borrowings); various types of debt instruments can thus be used, providing the sponsor with fresh resources to fund future lending activities. SPE within the scope of FAS 140 are limited to entities that hold financial assets. SPE are sometimes used, however, to hold nonfinancial assets such as real estate, machinery, or energy contracts.

Use of special-purpose entities under prior GAAP. SPE had their origin in the rules for consolidation, which historically were based on the existence of majority ownership of one enterprise by another. While the substitution of **control** for **ownership** had been contemplated as a means of limiting the use of SPE to evade consolidation requirements, practical difficulties in defining control had kept this project from fruition for many years.

As discussed previously, SPE achieved "level A GAAP" status by virtue of being somewhat obliquely addressed in FAS 125, which dealt with transfers of financial assets (and later was superseded by the very similar FAS 140). The concept of a "qualified" SPE (QSPE) also arose from this standard, denoting that SPE can participate in "true sales" of financial assets under FAS 125/140, to be accounted for as sales rather than as secured borrowings.

Importantly, in order for the sponsor to avoid consolidating the SPE, the outside equity participant was required to have **control,** which—although customarily not invoked under GAAP as the criterion for consolidation—was established as the key determinant for sponsor nonconsolidation of an SPE. Where an SPE was controlled by parties other than the sponsor, and there was significant risk capital invested by them, consolidation of the SPE in the sponsor's financial statements could be avoided.

Problems in past practice. With benefit of hindsight, it is clear that the rules for SPE evolved in a way that left too much to chance and to the influence of highly interested parties. As a result, notwithstanding the arguably important role that SPE may have played in the financial marketplace, SPE came to be widely used to accomplish financial reporting manipulations. Thus, the "outside" equity participants often funded their "independent capital contributions" with debt obtained from lenders to the sponsor, or via debt indirectly guaranteed by the sponsor, some of whom evaded disclosure of their positions as guarantors by means of imaginative interpretations of GAAP, particularly of FAS 5.

Furthermore, sponsors engaged in transactions with SPE that often resulted in the sponsors recognizing large amounts of income. In some instances, complex sets of guarantees and option arrangements had the effect of causing these gains to be reversible. In the most egregious transactions, sponsors were able to recoup reportable gains from economic events and transactions that could never have supported income recognition if engaged in directly by the entity, even extending to recognizing fair value changes in the sponsor's own capital stock.

It is clear that SPE do serve various tax, legal, and strategic corporate objectives, but whether the exclusion of SPE from their sponsor's consolidated financial statements had, under prior rules, any accounting legitimacy, remains an open question. In other words, in setting forth a representation of an entity's economic position and the results of its operations, the validity of excluding events or transactions that are in fact integral to the entity's current position and future prospects, merely because these have been "walled off" by a legal structure, was doubtful. Simply put, the issue is whether economic substance is to be presented, regardless of legal form.

FASB's response. After the revelations became public regarding Enron and its use of SPE to hide its true financial condition, FASB recognized the need to augment the existing consolidations model to take into account financial arrangements where parties other than the holders of a majority of the voting interests exercise financial control over another entity. Thus, it undertook a project to issue an interpretation of ARB 51 to broaden its scope.

In its deliberations on these issues, FASB decided not to refer to entities within the scope of the eventual interpretation as SPE. This decision underscores the fact that the type of entity to which the interpretation applies is more broadly defined than entities that qualify as SPE involved in securitization transactions or even SPE that hold nonfinancial assets. Thus, an entity within the scope of the interpretation may or may not have formerly been referred to as an SPE.

FASB coined the term variable interest entity (VIE) to designate an entity that is financially controlled by one or more parties that do not hold a majority voting interest. A party that possesses the majority of this financial control, if there is one, is referred to as the VIE's primary beneficiary.

To provide guidance on a timely basis, FASB undertook an ambitious schedule in an attempt to balance the needs of the user community with its own due process procedures. The following chronology illustrates how this rushed approach impacted the standards-setting process:

July 2002	Issuance of proposed interpretation, *Consolidation of Certain Special Purpose Entities*
September 2002	FASB holds two public roundtables to elicit feedback
January 17, 2003	FASB Interpretation No. 46 (FIN 46), *Consolidation of Variable Interest Entities*, issued
February 2003	FIN 46 disclosure requirements become effective for financial statements issued after January 31, 2003
	Primary beneficiaries of VIE created after January 31, 2003, were to immediately consolidate those entities in accordance with FIN 46
July 24, 2003	Five FASB Staff Positions (FSP) issued to interpret FIN 46

September 30, 2003	Financial statements of publicly held companies for fiscal quarters ending on or after this date were to consolidate any VIE created before February 1, 2003
October 9, 2003	FSP FIN 46-6 issued deferring the effective date for applying the consolidation provisions of FIN 46 (the disclosure provisions were unaffected) for public companies holding interests in VIE created prior to February 1, 2003, and nonregistered investment companies
October 2003	FASB issues an Exposure Draft of a proposed interpretation of FIN 46
November 26, 2003	Another FSP issued
December 19, 2003	Another FSP issued
December 23, 2003	FIN 46(R) issued to interpret FIN 46; FIN 46(R) superseded FIN 46 and further delayed its implementation as discussed in this section. (The "R" stands for "revised" as FIN 46(R) indicates on its cover that it was revised in December 2003)
February 12, 2004	Three FSP issued to replace three previous FSP due to the issuance of FIN 46(R)
June 30, 2004	Privately held companies were initially required to consolidate VIE created prior to February 1, 2003, in year-end financial statements for fiscal years ending on or after this date

Effective date matrix. The table set forth on the following page provides the most recent implementation and effective date provisions contained in FIN 46(R).

Scope exceptions. The following are excluded from the scope of FIN 46(R):

1. Not-for-profit organizations as defined in FAS 117, para 168, unless the organization was organized to avoid VIE status.
2. Employer/sponsors of employee benefit plans including ESOP, pension, profit sharing, 401(k), postretirement, and postemployment plans.
3. Enterprises subject to SEC Regulation S-X Rule 6-03(c)(1) (investment companies, mutual funds) may only consolidate an entity subject to the same regulation.
4. Separate accounts of life insurance entities.
5. A "Qualifying special-purpose entity" (QSPE) or a "formerly qualifying SPE" (FQSPE) under the provisions of FAS 140, *Accounting for Transfers and Servicing of Financial Assets and Extinguishments of Liabilities*, are not to be consolidated by entities and their affiliates who transfer financial assets to them.
6. Enterprises holding variable interests in a QSPE or FQSPE are not to consolidate that entity unless the holder has the unilateral ability to cause the entity's liquidation or change the entity so that it ceases to meet the conditions of FAS 140 to be considered a QSPE or FQSPE.
7. A governmental organization.
8. A nongovernmental financing entity established by a governmental organization unless the financing entity is being used to circumvent FIN 46(R) to avoid consolidation.
9. An entity created prior to December 31, 2003, for which, after expending "exhaustive efforts," management of the variable interest holder is unable to obtain information needed to determine whether the entity is a VIE, determine whether the holder is the primary beneficiary, or make the required consolidating/eliminating entries required by FIN 46(R).

Effective Date Matrix—FIN 46(R)—Issued December 2003

Accounting provisions	*Newly adopting nonpublic companies*	*Newly adopting public companies*		*All entities that already adopted FIN 46*
		Small business issuers[1]	*Nonsmall business issuers*	
VIE or potential VIE created on or after January 1, 2004	Immediately	For SPE[2], apply **either** FIN 46 or FIN 46(R) end of 1st reporting period ending after 12/15/03, (i.e., as of 12/31/03 for 12/31/03 year-ends)	For SPE[2], end of 1st reporting period ending after 12/15/03, (i.e., as of 12/31/03 for 12/31/03 year-ends)	Either continue to apply FIN 46 until FIN 46(R) becomes effective or adopt FIN 46(R) early
All other VIE or potential VIE	End of 1st annual period beginning after 12/15/04 (i.e., end of calendar year 2005)	All other VIE or potential VIE—end of 1st reporting period ending after 12/15/04 (i.e., as of 12/31/04 for calendar year-ends)	All other VIE or potential VIE—end of 1st reporting period ending after 3/15/04 (i.e., 1st calendar quarter for calendar year-end 12/31/04)	
Investment companies not subject to SEC Reg. S-X, Rule 6-03(c)(1) that are currently accounting for investments according to AAG, *Audits of Investment Companies*	Effective date delayed pending AICPA/AcSEC issuance (with required FASB clearance) of an SOP clarifying the scope of the guide			
Disclosure provisions	**Immediately:** If reasonably possible that evaluator will initially consolidate or disclose information about a VIE when FIN 46(R) becomes effective, all financial statements initially **issued** after December 31, 2003, irrespective of the date on which the VIE was created or that the enterprise obtained its interest.			

[1] *SEC Regulation S-B §228.10(a)(1)*

[2] *Entities previously characterized as Special Purpose Entities (SPE) are generally lessors to single lessees and entities involved in activities related to securitizations or other asset-backed financings.*

> *NOTE: With respect to this exception, however, management of the variable interest holder is required to continue to make these efforts after initial adoption of FIN 46(R). If the variable interest holder significantly participated in the design/redesign of the entity, it would be unusual for it to be able to contend that it was unable to obtain the necessary information.*

10. An entity that qualifies to be treated as a business, as defined below (the definition included in FIN 46(R) was adapted from EITF 98-3, *Determining Whether a Nonmonetary Transaction Involves Receipt of Productive Assets or a Business*). However, this scope exception **does not apply** and the entity would be required to be evaluated as to whether it is a VIE by the holders of its variable interests if **any one or more** of the following conditions exists:
    a. The variable interest holder and/or its related parties/de facto agents[1] (de facto agents are discussed later in this chapter) participated significantly in the design or redesign of the entity. This factor is not considered when the entity is an operating joint venture jointly controlled by the variable interest holder, and either an independent party or a franchisee.
    b. The design of the entity results in substantially all of its activities either involving or being conducted on behalf of the variable interest holder and its related parties.
    c. Based on the relative fair values of interests in the entity, the variable interest holder and its related parties provide more than half of its total equity, subordinated debt, and other forms of subordinated financial support.
    d. The entity's activities relate primarily to one or both of the following:
        (1) Single-lessee leases
        (2) Securitizations or other forms of asset-backed financings

Definition of a business. A business is defined, in the context of FIN 46(R) as

> *...a self-sustaining integrated set of activities and assets conducted and managed for the purpose of providing a return to investors. A business consists of (a) inputs, (b) processes applied to those inputs, and (c) resulting outputs that are used to generate revenues. For a set of activities and assets to be a business, it must contain all of the inputs and processes necessary for it to conduct normal operations, which include the ability to sustain a revenue stream by providing its outputs to customers.*

In evaluating whether an entity is a business, consideration must be given to unique factors relating to the industry and the activities being performed including

Inputs

1. Fixed assets either owned or leased
2. Intangibles either owned or licensed
3. Access to materials or rights needed to perform its activities
4. Employees

Processes

1. Strategic management
2. Operations
3. Resource management

---

[1] *Only for the purposes of applying factor a. above, de facto agents exclude parties that require the variable interest holder's prior approval to sell, transfer, or encumber their interest in the entity.*

Outputs

1. Access to customers (clients)

A three-step process is provided in order to assess whether a set of activities ("set") qualifies as a business.

1. Identify elements included in the "set" (i.e., determine the existing inputs, processes, and outputs).
2. Compare the elements identified in 1. with the elements necessary for the set of activities to be conducted as a normal business operation.
3. If any elements are missing, assess the degree of effort or investment relative to the fair value of the set of activities needed to acquire or gain access to the missing elements. If a significant effort or investment would be required, it can be concluded that the set of activities is not a business; conversely, a de minimis amount of effort or investment to supply the missing elements would lead to the conclusion that the set of activities is a business.

Interpretation 46(R): accounting for variable interest entities (VIE). FIN 46(R) substantially alters the consolidations model to which accountants had long been accustomed. Under FIN 46(R), variable interest entities that have a primary beneficiary, as defined, must be consolidated in the general-purpose financial statements of that primary beneficiary, regardless of the extent of ownership (or lack of it) by that entity. FIN 46(R) introduces a number of new terms and concepts in the attempt to explain and operationalize the accounting for VIE.

Expected variability. When estimating an entity's expected future cash flows in accordance with CON 7, *Using Cash Flow Information and Present Value in Accounting Measurements* (discussed more fully in Chapter 1), a range of probability-weighted expected outcomes is used. Mathematically, this is simply a weighted-average calculation. The following example illustrates the mathematical concept of expected variability:

Example of expected variability of cash flows

Mided Mining Company is computing the probability-weighted expected future cash flows from operating and disposing of a tunnel boring machine that has a remaining estimated useful life of three years. This estimate was necessitated by FAS 144 which requires an evaluation, when certain events or circumstances occur, of whether the future cash flows associated with the use and disposal of long-lives assets are sufficient to recover their carrying value over their estimated remaining depreciable lives. Because of uncertainty regarding the amounts and timing of the cash flows, Mided's management used the CON 7 probability-weighted expected cash flow model with the following results:

	2005	2006	2007	3-year outcome	Probability of occurrence	Probability-weighted expected outcome
Expected outcome 1	$3,500	$3,200	$2,700	$9,400	20%	$1,880
Expected outcome 2	4,000	3,900	3,700	11,600	45%	5,220
Expected outcome 3	4,300	4,100	4,000	12,400	30%	3,720
Expected outcome 4	4,400	4,700	--	9,100	5%	455
					100%	
Probability-weighted expected cash flows (weighted-average)						$11,275

The $11,275 weighted average, undiscounted, is compared to the carrying value of the tunnel boring machine to determine whether or not the carrying value is fully recoverable. The weighted-average consists of four different outcomes, each with its own estimated probability of occurrence. Since these amounts represent management's best estimates, management deems it possible that, at the end of the three-year period, any one of these outcomes could actually occur.

When management considers the individual probability of occurrence for each of the four outcomes estimated above, the analysis yields the following results:

	[1]	[2]	[3]	[4]	[5]		
	3-year outcome	*Probability weighted expected outcome*	*[1] – [2] Variation*	*Probability of occurrence*	*[3] x [4] Probability weighted variation*	*Positive variation*	*Negative variation*
Expected outcome 1	$9,400	$11,275	$(1,875)	20%	$(375)	$ --	$(375)
Expected outcome 2	11,600	11,275	325	45%	146	146	--
Expected outcome 3	12,400	11,275	1,125	30%	338	338	--
Expected outcome 4	9,100	11,275	(2,175)	5%	(109)	--	(109)
				100%		$484	$(484)

Careful examination of the above analysis yields the following conclusions:

1. Variations naturally occur between expected outcomes and actual outcomes.
2. Because the expected outcome is calculated as an average, some of the amounts used to compute it will be higher than the average and some will be lower than the average.
3. When the individual variations are computed and each is multiplied by its probability of occurrence, the absolute value of the sum of the positive variations will exactly equal the absolute value of the sum of the negative variations.
4. When these two absolute values are summed ($484 + $484 = $968 in the example above), the result, the total variability in both directions is called the **expected variability** of the cash flows.
5. The higher the expected variability of a set of cash flow estimates, the higher the level of risk and uncertainty associated with the estimate.

Variable interests. Ownership, contractual, or other monetary interests in an entity that are either entitled to receive expected positive variability (referred to as expected residual returns) or obligated to absorb expected negative variability (referred to as expected losses). Variable interests are identified by thoroughly analyzing the assets, liabilities, and contractual arrangements of an entity to determine whether each item being analyzed creates variability or absorbs/receives variability. Favorable changes in the fair value of the entity's net assets and contractual arrangements that create variability comprise expected residual returns which result from estimated outcomes in which the entity outperforms the probability-weighted expected results. Unfavorable changes in the fair value of the entity's net assets and contractual arrangements that create variability comprise expected losses which result from estimated outcomes in which the entity underperforms the probability-weighted expected results.

Appendix B of FIN 46(R) (this appendix was extensively revised since the original issuance of FIN 46 in January 2003) provides examples of potential variable interests. Each of the items below is **potentially** a variable interest in an entity or in specified assets of an entity. Upon analysis of the specific facts, circumstances, and contract terms, the financial statement preparer is charged with determining whether a particular item either absorbs expected losses or receives expected residual returns (collectively referred to as expected variability) or both. The absorbing/receiving of variability is the sole determinant of whether an interest is a variable interest and, in analyzing specific situations, the degree of variability can differ widely for each item.

1. At-risk equity investments in a VIE
2. Investments in subordinated debt instruments issued by a VIE
3. Investments in subordinated beneficial interests issued by a VIE
4. Guarantees of the value of VIE assets or liabilities
5. Written put options on the assets of a VIE or similar obligations that protect senior interests from suffering losses
6. Forward contracts to sell assets owned by the entity at a fixed price
7. Stand-alone or embedded derivative instruments including total return swaps and similar arrangements
8. Contracts or agreements for fees to be paid to a decision maker (these are generally deemed to absorb variability unless the relationship between the entity and the decision maker meets specified criteria to be considered an employee/employer relationship or a "hired service provider" relationship, in which case the arrangement would not be deemed to create a variable interest. In this case, the fees would be included in computations of expected variability)
9. Other service contracts with nondecision makers
10. Operating leases that include residual value guarantees and/or lessee option to purchase the leased property at a specified price
11. Variable interests of one VIE in another VIE
12. Interests retained by a transferor of financial assets to a VIE

As previously stated, although all of these examples potentially qualify as variable interests, they differ widely in terms of the extent of their variability which has a direct effect on the likelihood of their causing their holders to be considered the primary beneficiary of the VIE. Note that an interest can qualify as a variable interest but the entity in which the interest is held not qualify as a variable interest entity. Careful analysis of the facts and circumstances is necessary to determine the economics of a particular situation.

Expected losses and expected residual returns. Expected losses represent the expected negative variability in the fair value of an enterprise's net assets exclusive of variable interests. Expected residual returns represent the expected positive variability in the fair value of an enterprise's net assets exclusive of variable interests. The expected variability in an enterprise's net income or loss is included in the determination of its expected losses and expected residual returns.

VIE defined. Variable interest entities include, under FIN 46(R), any entity which, by design, satisfies **one** of the following characteristics:

1. The total equity investment at risk is not sufficient to permit the entity to finance its activities without additional subordinated financial support from either the existing equity holders or other parties. That is, the equity investment at risk is **not** sufficient to absorb all of the expected losses of the entity. For this purpose, the total equity investment at risk

    a. Includes only equity investments in the entity that participate significantly in profits and losses even if those investments do not carry voting rights.
    b. Does not include equity interests that the entity issued in exchange for subordinated interests in other variable interest entities.
    c. Does not include amounts provided to the equity investor directly or indirectly by the entity or by other parties involved with the entity (for example, by fees, charitable contributions, or other payments), unless the provider is a parent, subsidiary, or affiliate of the investor that is required to be included in the same set of consolidated financial statements as the investor.

   d. Does not include amounts financed for the equity investor (for example, by loans or guarantees of loans) directly by the entity or by other parties involved with the entity, unless that party is a parent, subsidiary, or affiliate of the investor that is required to be included in the same set of consolidated financial statements as the investor.

or

2. As a group the holders of the equity investment at risk lack **any one** of the following three characteristics of a controlling financial interest:
   a. The direct or indirect ability through voting or similar rights to make decisions about an entity's activities that affect the entity's success. The investors do not have that ability through voting rights or similar rights if no owners hold voting rights or similar rights (such as those of a common stockholder in a corporation or a general partner in a partnership).
   b. The obligation to absorb the expected losses of the entity. The investor or investors do not have that obligation if they are directly or indirectly protected from absorbing the expected losses or are guaranteed a return by the entity itself or by other parties with whom the entity is involved.
   c. The right to receive the expected residual returns of the entity. The investors do not have that right if their return is limited to a specified maximum amount by the entity's governing documents or arrangements with other variable interest holders or with the entity.

   The equity investors as a group also are considered to lack characteristic 2.a. if, upon consideration of those investors' at-risk equity investments and all other interests in the entity

   (1) The voting rights of some investors are not proportional to their obligations to absorb the entity's expected losses, to receive the entity's expected residual returns, or both, **and**
   (2) Substantially all of the entity's activities (for example, lending activities, or asset acquisitions) either involve or are conducted on behalf of an investor that has disproportionately few voting rights.

In other words, VIE are generally thinly capitalized entities which carry risks of economic loses or possibilities of economic gains beyond what the nominal owner (the "equity participant") could absorb or will be able to benefit from, respectively. If a party provides "subordinated financial support" to the entity that exposes it to absorbing the majority of the VIE's expected losses, or entitles it to receive the majority of the VIE's expected residual returns, or both, it is generally deemed to be the primary beneficiary of that VIE and will be required to consolidate the VIE as its subsidiary, irrespective of how much, if any equity investment it has in the VIE.

Initial determination of VIE status. Whether or not an entity qualifies as a VIE is initially determined when an entity obtains its variable interest in that entity. This determination is based on the circumstances existing at that date, taking into account future changes that are required in existing governing documents and contractual arrangements. It is not necessary, however, for an interest holder to make this determination if both of the following conditions exist:

1. It is apparent that the holder's interest would not be a significant variable interest, and

2. The holder, its related parties, and its de facto agents (as specified below) were not significant participants in the design or redesign of the entity.

Related-party considerations in determining the primary beneficiary. Many SPE structures made use of related-party relationships, which did not, however, automatically necessitate consolidation (although disclosures were required under GAAP). For the purpose of a variable interest holder determining whether it is the primary beneficiary of a VIE, FIN 46(R) expands the definition of related parties that is set forth in FAS 57, *Related Party Disclosures*, to include additional parties that act as "de facto agents" or "de facto principals" of the variable interest holder. The following table sets forth the related parties as prescribed by FAS 57 as well as additional related parties designated by FIN 46(R) for this purpose:

Related parties FAS 57

- Affiliates—Parties that directly or indirectly, through one or more intermediaries control, are controlled by, or are under common control with the variable interest holder
- Equity method investees of the variable interest holder
- Employee benefit trusts (e.g., pension and profit-sharing trusts) when the variable interest holder/plan sponsor or members of its management manage the plan or serve as the plan trustee
- Principal owners of the variable interest holder (owners of record or beneficial owners of > 10% of the variable interest holder's voting interests) and members of their immediate families
- Management of the variable interest holder and members of their immediate families
- Transacting parties where one party controls or significantly influences the management or operating policies of the other to the extent that it might be prevented from fully pursuing its own separate interests
- Other parties that have an ownership interest in one of the transacting parties; or control, or significantly influence the management or operating policies of the transacting parties to the extent that one or more of the transacting parties might be prevented from fully pursuing its own separate interests

De facto principals/agents FIN 46(R)

- Parties that cannot finance their operations without subordinated financial support from the variable interest holder (e.g., another VIE of which the variable interest holder is the primary beneficiary)
- Parties that received their interest in the VIE as a contribution or loan from the variable interest holder
- Officers and employees of the variable interest holder
- Members of the governing board of the variable interest holder
- Parties that have agreements not to sell, transfer, or pledge their interests in the VIE as collateral without the prior approval of the variable interest holder where that prior approval right constrains that party's ability to manage the economic risks or realize the economic rewards from its interests
- Parties with a close business relationship to the variable interest holder such as the relationship of a professional service provider to one of its significant clients.

These related-party attribution rules under FIN 46(R) will require consolidation of many of the currently popular SPE structures, unless the VIE is well capitalized and such subordinated support vehicles as loan guarantees are dispensed with.

If two or more related parties (including de facto principals/agents specified above) hold variable interests in the same VIE, and the aggregate variable interests held by those parties would, if held by a single party, identify that party as the primary beneficiary, then the member of the related-party group that is most closely associated with the VIE is the primary beneficiary that is required to consolidate the VIE as a subsidiary in its financial statements. In determining which party is most closely associated with the VIE, all relevant facts and circumstances are to be considered including

1. Whether there is a principal/agent relationship between parties within the related-party group.
2. The relationship of the activities of the VIE to each of the parties in the related-party group.
3. The significance of the VIE's activities to each of the parties in the related-party group
4. The extent of a party's exposure to the expected losses of the VIE
5. The structure of the VIE

Reconsideration of VIE status. Once an initial determination is made as to whether an entity is a variable interest entity (as opposed to a voting interest entity), that initial determination need not be reconsidered unless one or more of the following circumstances occurs:

1. A change is made to the VIE's governing documents or contractual arrangements that results in changes in either the characteristics or sufficiency of the at-risk equity investment in the VIE.
2. As a result of a return of some or all of the equity investment to the equity investors, other interests become exposed to the VIE's expected losses.
3. There is an **increase** in the VIE's expected losses that results from the entity engaging in activities or acquiring assets that were not anticipated at either the inception of the entity or a later reconsideration date.
4. There is a **decrease** in the VIE's expected losses due to the entity modifying or curtailing its activities.
5. Additional at-risk equity is invested in the VIE.

FIN 46(R) specifically excludes a troubled debt restructuring (as defined and discussed in Chapter 13) from being an event requiring reconsideration of VIE status.

Determination and redetermination of whether an interest holder is the primary beneficiary. A holder of a variable interest initially determines whether it is the primary beneficiary of a VIE in conjunction with the initial determination that the entity is a VIE, that is, when the holder initially obtains its interest in the entity. This initial determination of whether an interest holder is the primary beneficiary (irrespective of whether the holder is or is not considered to be the primary beneficiary) needs to be reconsidered when the changes are made to the entity's governing documents or contractual arrangements that result in a reallocation of the obligation to absorb expected losses or the right to receive expected residual returns of the VIE between the existing primary beneficiary and other unrelated parties. A variable interest holder that had previously determined that it was the VIE's primary beneficiary is required to reconsider its initial decision to consolidate that VIE if (1) it sells or otherwise disposes of all or part of its variable interest to unrelated parties, or (2) if the VIE issues new variable interests to parties other than the primary beneficiary or the primary beneficiary's related parties.

If a variable interest holder had, upon obtaining its interest, determined that it was **not** the primary beneficiary of a VIE, it is to reconsider this determination it if obtains additional variable interests in the VIE.

As is the case with the determination of whether an entity is a VIE, the initial or subsequent determination of its primary beneficiary is not affected by a troubled debt restructuring.

Variable interests in "silos." A party may hold a variable interest in specific assets of a VIE (e.g., a guarantee or a subordinated residual interest). In computing expected losses and expected residual returns, a holder of a variable interest in specified assets of a VIE must determine if the interest it holds qualifies as an interest in the VIE itself. The variable interest is considered an interest in the VIE itself if **either** (1) the fair value of the specific assets is more than half of the total fair value of the VIE's assets **or** (2) the interest holder has another significant variable interest in the entity as a whole.

If the interests are deemed to be interests in the VIE itself, the expected losses and expected residual returns associated with the variable interest in the specified assets are treated as being associated with the VIE.

If the interests are not deemed to be interests in the VIE itself, the interests in the specified assets are treated as a separate VIE (referred to as a "silo") if the expected cash flows from the specified assets (and any associated credit enhancements, if applicable) are essentially the sole source of payment for specified liabilities or specified other interests. Under this scenario, expected losses and expected residual returns associated with the silo assets are accounted for separately to the extent that the interest holder either absorbs the VIE's expected losses or is entitled to receive its expected residual returns. Any excess of expected losses or expected residual returns not borne by (received by) the variable interest holder is considered attributable to the entity as a whole.

If one interest holder is required to consolidate a silo of a VIE, other VIE interest holders are to exclude the silo from the remaining VIE.

Consolidation requirements. An entity must consolidate a VIE of which it is the primary beneficiary. The variable interest holder that is the primary beneficiary of a VIE holds a variable interest (or combination of variable interests) that will absorb a majority of the entity's expected losses, receive a majority of the entity's expected residual returns, or both. The rights and obligations conveyed by the reporting entity's variable interests and the relationship of its variable interests with variable interests held by other parties must be weighed to determine whether its variable interests will absorb a majority of a VIE's expected losses, receive a majority of the entity's expected residual returns, or both. Note that absorbing losses is more important than receiving residual returns: thus, if one entity will absorb a majority of a VIE's expected losses and another (unrelated) entity will receive a majority of the VIE's expected residual returns, the entity absorbing a majority of the losses must consolidate the VIE.

If there are other (noncontrolling) interests, which are analogous to minority interests, these are shown in the consolidated balance sheet just as minority interests are under GAAP, and likewise a share of the operating results of the VIE are allocated to the noncontrolling interests in the consolidated statements of income (operations).

FIN 46(R) provides a 10% equity threshold test which in practice is confusing and unworkable. The interpretation indicates that an at-risk equity investment of less than 10% of the entity's total assets is presumptively **not** considered sufficient to permit the entity to finance its activities without obtaining additional subordinated financial support but then goes on to provide that the presumption of insufficiency can be overcome by either quantitative analysis, qualitative analysis, or both. Consequently, financial statement preparers could mistakenly rely on the 10% presumption to conclude that an entity with less than 10% at-risk equity is a VIE, when in fact, further analysis would contradict that conclusion. Conversely, the interpretation indicates that it is also possible that an entity can require at-risk equity of more than 10% in order to sufficiently finance its activities. Consequently, the financial statement preparer also cannot rely on meeting or exceeding the 10% threshold as conclusive proof that the entity is sufficiently capitalized to avoid being characterized as a VIE.

FIN 46(R) will change past practice greatly. Currently, enterprises generally have been consolidated in financial statements because one enterprise controls the other through a majority of voting interests. FIN 46(R) requires existing unconsolidated variable interest entities to be consolidated by their primary beneficiaries if the entities do not effectively disperse risks among parties involved. Variable interest entities that effectively disperse risks will not be consolidated unless a single party holds an interest or combination of interests that effectively recombines risks that were previously dispersed.

Example of application of FIN 46(R). To explain the approach required by FIN 46(R), consider one of the more common SPE situations under prior GAAP, that of a synthetic lease. A **synthetic lease** is a financing transaction whereby an independent third-party lessor (i.e., unrelated to the lessee) constructs or acquires an existing single-tenant property and leases it to a lessee. The synthetic lease transaction is generally structured with a short lease term so that the lessee accounts for it as an operating lease under GAAP notwithstanding the fact that, for federal income tax purposes, it is treated as a "financing" which results in the lessee/taxpayer capitalizing the leased asset and deducting depreciation and interest. This arrangement achieves the lessee's objective by removing the related debt obligation from its balance sheet. The lessee commits to a fixed schedule of rental payments, say for five years, so over that time there will be only a single amount for annual cash flows paid each year. The lease calls for the lessor to pay the lessee any excess of the fair value of the asset at lease termination date, over its book value plus a fixed rate of return to the lessor's owners. However, if the fair value of the asset is less than the book value plus the fixed rate of return, the lessee agrees to pay the lessor for any shortfall. Thus, there is cash flow variability created by this residual value guarantee by the lessee, making the lease structure potentially a VIE.

Assume the rental will be $50,000 per year for this example. Thus, the average (expected) cash flow each of those years will be the contractual amount. The **fair value** of the annual cash flow in any year will be the amount defined under CON 7, which is essentially the discounted present value of the lease payment. Assume 6% is the relevant discount rate, and rents are paid annually in arrears. The fair value of year one rent is then $\$50,000 \div 1.06 = \$47,170$; the corresponding amount for year two rent is $\$50,000 \div 1.06^2 = \$44,500$; etc. Since this amount is fixed, there are no expected residual rewards or expected losses from the rental stream in each of the years one through five.

NOTE: See Chapter 14 for more complex lease examples involving VIE and decision diagrams useful in analyzing VIE.

However, it is estimated that at the lease termination date there may be a range of fair values for the asset. Also, the lessor is entitled to a cumulative return on investment. It is now necessary to compute, **separately**, the expected (i.e., probability-weighted) fair values of the shortfall amount and the excess value amount. For simplicity, assume only three discrete outcomes are estimated to be possible.

1. The asset is sold for an amount that falls short of the book value plus the promised rate of return, for a net shortfall of $20,000;
2. The asset is sold for a net gain, after guaranteed return to the lessor, of $10,000; or
3. The asset is sold for a net gain of $40,000.

The relative probabilities of the three outcomes have been assessed at 40%, 35%, and 25%, respectively.

The expected residual cash flow to (or from) the lessee is given as $-20,000(.40) + $10,000(.35) + $40,000(.25) = $5,500

Using these amounts, the expected loss (the single negative outcome) and the expected residual return (the sum of the two positive outcomes) can be computed. These are the foregoing individual cash flow amounts less the expected cash flows, weighted by the respective probabilities.

Expected loss = $-20,000 – $5,500 = $-25,500(.40) = $-10,200.

Expected residual return = [$10,000 – $5,500 = $4,500(.35) = $1,575] + [$40,000 – $5,500 = $34,500(.25) = $8,625] = $10,200.

Note that the expected loss equals the expected residual returns, as it must, since the arithmetic average (mean) was used to compute the deviations of each projected outcome. Since the expected loss based on expected cash flow will be borne by the lessee if it occurs, and the expected residual based on expected cash flows will be paid to the lessee if one or the other occurs, the lessee is the primary beneficiary.

The actual computation would be based on the **fair value of the expected cash flows**. In this case, the expected fair value of the loss is given as $-10,200 ÷ $(1.06)^5$ = $-7,622. The expected fair value of the expected residual rewards is $7,622.

The total expected variability of the lease arrangement is therefore $15,244 (all earlier years' rental streams had zero variability), and the lessee absorbs all of this.

Note that in real-life situations there may be many other complications, such as rentals based on variables such as sales of product, etc. In an actual situation, with a wide range of possible cash flows each period, the computations will be more challenging. However, it might be possible in many cases to immediately conclude qualitatively, based on analysis of the risks, rewards, and relationships that the VIE is indeed to be consolidated, in which case these calculations will be unnecessary. Also, in some situations the VIE will have a range of assets and multiple parties with whom it is in contractual arrangements, which is a complication addressed somewhat by the standard, but which will require more analysis.

Initial measurement. Assets, liabilities, and noncontrolling interests of newly consolidated VIE generally will be initially measured at their fair values. However, there is a (logical) exception for assets and liabilities transferred to a VIE by its primary beneficiary; these will continue to be measured as if they had not been transferred (i.e., at book value in the transferor/primary beneficiary's hands). Were this rule not imposed, a reporting entity could create gains merely by transfer of assets to a VIE, violating a basic principle of revenue recognition.

In general, FIN 46(R) applies the concepts regarding initial measurement and recognition of goodwill or negative goodwill that are found in FAS 141, *Business Combinations*, summarized as follows:

	Measurement or recognition issue	*Applicable requirement per FIN 46(R) to be followed by primary beneficiary (PB)*
1.	Measurement date	Date that holder of variable interest(s) first becomes the primary beneficiary
2.	Measurement amount for assets, liabilities and noncontrolling interests	Fair value (FV) on measurement date
3.	Measurement amount exception for enterprises under common control and assets and liabilities consolidated shortly after transfer from primary beneficiary to the VIE	Carrying value (net book value or NBV) in the accounting records of the enterprise that controls the VIE with no gain or loss recognized on account of transfer to a VIE
4.	Excess of FV of VIE assets + NBV of assets transferred by the PB to the VIE *Over* FV of consideration paid + NBV of previously held interests + FV of VIE liabilities and noncontrolling interests	Pro rata adjustment to newly consolidated VIE nonmonetary assets, as required by FAS 141 when negative goodwill results from a business combination. Any remaining amount, after the pro rata adjustment, is an extraordinary gain in the period of initial consolidation
5.	Excess of FV of consideration paid + NBV of previously held interests + FV of VIE liabilities and noncontrolling interests *Over* FV of VIE identifiable assets + NBV of identifiable assets transferred by the PB to the VIE	If the VIE is a business, as defined, recognized as goodwill If the VIE is not a business, recognized as an extraordinary loss in the period of initial consolidation

The following examples clarify application of the rules described in the preceding paragraphs:

Case One

First, assume that Client Corporation enters into an operating lease with an unrelated VIE, Non-Affiliate Corp., and that Non-Affiliate Corporation has a building with book value of $12,000,000, fair value of $10,500,000 and an outstanding mortgage balance of $11,000,000 (assumed to be the mortgage's fair value). Assume that, due to the terms of the lease arrangement, the criteria for consolidation under FIN 46(R) are met, and that Client Corporation has no equity interest (even using the FIN 46(R) related-party criteria) in Non-Affiliate Corp. Client Corporation would consolidate the building on its balance sheet at its fair value of $10.5 million, reflect debt of $11 million, and because Non-Affiliate Corp. qualifies as a business under the definition provided by FIN 46(R), record goodwill of $500,000. Noncontrolling interest would be recorded at zero, since at this date there is no value to its interest.

Case Two

If, instead, the fair value of the building were $12.5 million, then the consolidation entry would reflect the building at $12.5 million, the debt at $11 million, and the noncontrolling interest (which happens to also be the 100% equity holder in the VIE) at $1.5 million, since all residual interest will go to those parties.

Case Three

Same facts as above, but now assume Client Corporation has a 25% interest in Non-Affiliate Corporation, and again the fair value of the building is $12.5 million. At first blush, recordation as follows would seem appropriate: debit building $12.5 million, credit mortgage payable $11 million, credit noncontrolling interest ($1.5 million x .75 =) $1.125 million, credit Client Corporation's equity (paid-in capital, representing the investment made in the building corporation) for ($1.5 million x .25 =) $375,000. However, this is wrong, since it effectively recognizes a gain on the increase in value of the building ($12.5 million fair value less $12 million book value). Under FIN 46(R) the primary beneficiary cannot recognize this gain, and therefore the primary beneficiary's percentage share of the excess fair value over its carrying value ($500,000 x .25 =) $125,000, must be used to reduce the recorded value of the building. The proper entry is: debit building $12,375,000 ($12,500,000 fair value – Primary beneficiary share of appreciation of $125,000 = $12,375,000), credit mortgage payable $11 million, credit noncontrolling interest ($1.5 million x .75 =) $1.125 million, and credit Client Corporation's equity ($375,000 – $125,000 =) $250,000.

After initial measurement, the assets, liabilities, and noncontrolling interests of a consolidated variable interest entity will be accounted for as if the entity were consolidated based on majority voting interests. In some circumstances, earnings of the variable interest entity attributed to the primary beneficiary arise from sources other than investments in equity of the entity.

Disclosures. The primary beneficiary of a VIE is required to disclose (1) the nature, purpose, size, and activities of the VIE, (2) the carrying amount and classification of consolidated assets that are collateral for the VIE's obligations, and (3) any lack of recourse by creditors (or beneficial interest holders) of a consolidated VIE to the general credit of the primary beneficiary. If an enterprise holds a significant variable interest in a VIE of which it is not the primary beneficiary, it is required to disclose (1) the nature of its involvement with the VIE and when that involvement began, (2) the nature, purpose, size, and activities of the VIE, and (3) the reporting enterprise's maximum exposure to loss as a result of its involvement with the VIE.

If a reporting enterprise does not consolidate a VIE because it is unable, after exhaustive efforts, to obtain the necessary information, it is required to make the following disclosures:

1. The number of entities to which FIN 46(R) is not being applied and the reason why the required information is unavailable
2. The nature, purpose, size (if available), and activities of the entity or entities excluded and the nature of the reporting enterprise's involvement with them
3. The reporting enterprise's maximum exposure to loss due to its involvement with the entity or entities, and
4. The amounts of income, expense, purchases, sales, or other measures of activity between the reporting enterprise and the VIE for all periods presented. If, in the first set of financial statements to which FIN 46(R) applies, it is not practicable to provide the information for prior periods that are presented for comparative purposes, then that information may be omitted.

If the reporting enterprise consolidates multiple, similarly structured VIE, the informative disclosures may be aggregated for these similar VIE as long as separate information would not be deemed to provide material information to a financial statement user.

If the VIE engages in activities covered by FAS 140, *Accounting for Transfers and Servicing of Financial Assets and Extinguishments of Liabilities*, the disclosures required by FAS 140 regarding the VIE are required to be in the same note to the financial statements as the disclosures enumerated above.

Exceptions to VIE consolidation requirements. While FIN 46(R) is expected to require the consolidation of VIE engaged in leasing, and in a wide range of other transactions, including financial transactions, such as securitizations, it specifically permits off-balance-sheet financial vehicles known as **qualified special purpose entities** (QSPE) to continue to be nonconsolidated entities. These are widely used by corporations and financial institutions and consolidation of QSPE would have been enormously disruptive to the capital markets.

Prior to the issuance of FAS 125, the accounting for financial SPE was guided by analogizing from EITF 90-15, although that standard specifically stated that it applied only to leasing transactions. In fact, SPE were not even formally defined in the accounting literature. In practice, it was generally observed that SPE were designated as any entity that does not qualify as a "business" as that term is defined in EITF 98-3 (and has been adapted in FIN 46(R), as described earlier in this chapter). Generally, if an entity meets the definition of a business, the special nonconsolidation rules for SPE did **not** apply. However, this was not universally agreed, and an entity that qualified as a business under Issue 98-3 could also have been an SPE, at least in the opinion of some of those involved in standard setting.

Around 1990, the SEC decreed that for an SPE to remain unconsolidated by the sponsor, and for sale recognition (where relevant) by the sponsor/transferor to be appropriate, "the majority owner of the SPE must be an independent third party who has made a substantive capital investment in the SPE, has control of the SPE, and has substantive risks and rewards of ownership of the assets of the SPE (including residuals). This became known as the "risks and rewards" analysis approach, which became the de facto standard until the issuance of FAS 125.

Rules regarding SPE changed again with the issuance of a comprehensive standard, FAS 125, which in turn was shortly thereafter replaced by yet another comprehensive standard, FAS 140. These deal with **financial** assets only, and establish the new concept of a **qualifying** SPE.

FAS 125, issued in mid-1996, replaced the "risks and rewards" approach with a focus on "control over financial assets." Note that FAS 125 addressed transfers of **financial** assets, and was not germane to transfers of other operating assets (plant and equipment, patents and copyrights, etc.). It introduced the concept of the qualifying SPE (QSPE), which was an SPE which

1. *Is a trust, corporation, or other legal vehicle whose activities are permanently limited by the legal documents establishing the SPE to*

   -Holding title to transferred financial assets
   -Issuing beneficial interests
   -Collecting cash proceeds from and otherwise servicing the assets held
   -Distributing proceeds to the holders of its beneficial interests

2. *Has standing at law distinct from the transferor*

Thus, one could say that QSPE were intended as a subset of SPE. In order for transfers of financial assets to SPE to be accounted for as sales (true sales), and thus for gain recognition to be appropriate (when otherwise warranted by the facts), the SPE transferee must be a QSPE. The consolidation requirements under EITF 90-15 and EITF Topic D-14 remained in effect for all transactions other than those involving QSPE or subject to FAS 125 (e.g., for nonfinancial assets, for transfers to related parties, etc.). FAS 125 did not explicitly address the need for sponsors to consolidate QSPE, but clearly if gain recognition would be appropriate consolidation could not be mandated, since that would obviate gain recognition (because upon consolidation, intercompany transactions, gains, etc., are all eliminated).

FAS 140, issued in late 2000, entirely replaced FAS 125, although most of the guidance remained identical. One reason for issuing the new standard was dissatisfaction with FAS 125's treatment of SPE. FAS 140 added new guidance with regard to defining the circumstances in which an SPE can be considered qualifying; circumstances in which the assets held by a qualifying SPE are to appear in the consolidated financial statements of the transferor; circumstances in which sale accounting is precluded if transferred financial assets can be removed from an SPE by the transferor; and other matters.

QSPE under FAS 140 were more narrowly defined. To be deemed a QSPE

A qualifying SPE is a trust or other legal vehicle that meets all of the following conditions:

a. *It is demonstrably distinct from the transferor,*
b. *Its permitted activities (1) are significantly limited, (2) were entirely specified in the legal documents that established the SPE or created the beneficial interests in the transferred assets that it holds, and (3) may be significantly changed only with the approval of the holders of at least a majority of the beneficial interests held by entities other than any transferor, its affiliates, and its agents,*
c. *It may hold only*
   i) *Financial assets transferred to it that are passive in nature;*
   ii) *Passive derivative financial instruments that pertain to beneficial interests (other than another derivative financial instrument) issued or sold to parties other than the transferor, its affiliate, or its agents;*
   iii) *Financial assets (for example, guarantees or rights to collateral) that would reimburse it if others were to fail to adequately service financial assets transferred to it or to timely pay obligations due to it and that it entered into when it was established, when assets were transferred to it, or when beneficial interests (other than derivative financial instruments) were issued by the SPE;*
   iv) *Servicing rights related to financial assets that it holds;*
   v) *Temporarily, nonfinancial assets obtained in connection with the collection of financial assets that it holds; and*
   vi) *Cash collected from assets that it holds and investments purchased with that cash pending distribution to holders of beneficial interests that are appropriate for that purpose (that is, money-market or other relatively risk-free instruments without options and with maturities no later than the expected distribution date).*
d. *If it can sell or otherwise dispose of noncash financial assets, it can do so only in automatic response to one of the following conditions:*
   i) *Occurrence of an event or circumstance that (a) is specified in the legal documents that established the SPE or created the beneficial interests in the transferred assets that it holds; (b) is outside the control of the transferor, its affiliates, or its agents; and (c) causes, or is expected at the date of transfer to cause, the fair value of those financial assets to decline by a specified degree below the fair value of those assets when the SPE obtained them;*
   ii) *Exercise by a beneficial interest holder (other than the transferor, its affiliates, or its agents) of a right to put that holder's beneficial interest back to the SPE;*
   iii) *Exercise by the transferor of a call or "replacement of accounts provision" specified in the legal documents that established the SPE, transferred assets to the SPE, or created the beneficial interests in the transferred assets that it holds; or*
   iv) *Termination of the SPE or maturity of the beneficial interests in those financial assets on a fixed or determinable date that is specified at inception.*

FAS 140 provided detailed guidance addressing the matters of the QSPE's need to be demonstrably distinct from the transferor; the necessary limitation on its permitted activities; limitations on what assets the QSPE can hold; and the limitations on sales or other dispositions of the assets by the QSPE. When all conditions are met, the QSPE is not consolidated in the financial statements of the sponsor.

Of interest is that fact that the threshold level of outside equity under FAS 140 was set at 10%. As the FASB stated, "if at least 10% of the interests in the transferred assets (or 10% of the interests in a series in the master trust) were currently held by third parties and if the transferor could not unilaterally dissolve the SPE, that is sufficient evidence to demonstrate that the SPE is demonstrably distinct from the transferor, its affiliates, or its agents." FASB settled on the 10% level "not because it was grounded in any particular literature, but because it appeared sufficient to demonstrate that the transferee is distinct from the transferor." FAS 140 was effective for transfers and servicing of financial assets and extinguishments of liabilities occurring after March 31, 2001.

The accounting for VIE meeting the QSPE rules of FAS 140 continue to be governed by that standard and are not impacted by the imposition of FIN 46(R). However, FASB may further revise VIE accounting, and this area is ripe for ongoing evolution.

Purchase Method Procedures

FASB is currently pursuing a project that will broadly reconsider existing purchase accounting guidance, including that issued by the FASB, its predecessor (APB), and the EITF, as well as other developed practices. It determined that the project was necessary since some current purchase accounting rules and practices do not provide transparent information to users and are sometimes inconsistent with the Conceptual Framework. FASB has defined several aspects to this project, identified as "milestones." These are

- Milestone 1—The Working Principle and Scope
- Milestone 2—Preacquisition Contingencies
- Milestone 3—Measuring the Fair Value of the Exchange
- Milestone 4—Recognition and Measurement of Acquired Assets and Assumed Liabilities
- Milestone 5—Noncontrolling Interest Issues
- Milestone 6—Other Issues and Transition

Milestone 1. As a basis for considering issues relating to the application of the purchase method, FASB (in conjunction with IASB, which is collaborating on this entire project) tentatively agreed on a working principle (Milestone 1). Elements of this include the following:

- The accounting for a business combination is to be based on the assumption that the transaction is arm's-length, in which independent and willing parties exchange equal values, and accordingly, absent evidence to the contrary, the consideration paid by the acquirer is representative of the fair value of the acquirer's interest in the business over which it obtains control (the acquiree).
- In a business combination, the total amount to be recognized by the acquirer would be the fair value of the business acquired (the acquiree). Assuming an exchange of equal values, that amount may be measured through direct measurement of the fair value of the business acquired (the acquiree) or based on the fair value of the consideration paid, whichever is more clearly evident of the fair value of the business acquired (the acquiree).
- In a business combination in which the acquirer obtains control of all or substantially all of the ownership interest of an acquired business (an acquiree)
    - If the consideration paid is cash or other financial assets (or liabilities incurred) of the acquirer, the fair value of the consideration paid generally is more clearly evident than the fair value of the business acquired (the acquiree) and thus, absent evidence to the contrary, is used to determine the total amount to be recognized in the financial statements of the acquirer.

- If the consideration paid is in the form of marketable equity instruments of the acquirer, the fair value of the equity instruments generally is more clearly evident than the fair value of the business acquired (the acquiree) and thus, absent evidence to the contrary, is used to determine the total amount to be recognized in the financial statements of the acquirer.

- In a business combination, the acquirer obtains control over the acquired entity (the acquiree) and therefore is responsible for the assets and liabilities of the acquired entity (the acquiree). The acquired assets and assumed liabilities are recognized on the date control is obtained, and measured at their fair values at that date.
  - If the fair value of the acquired business (the acquiree) exceeds the sum of the fair values of the recognized identifiable assets acquired and liabilities assumed, that excess amount (which is the **implied fair value** of goodwill) is recognized as an asset.
  - In those rare circumstances in which the business combination is not an exchange of equal values (i.e., a forced liquidation sale), if the fair value of the acquired business (the acquiree) exceeds the consideration paid for the acquirer's interest, that excess (1) would first reduce the amount of the implied fair value of goodwill, and (2) any remaining excess would be recognized as a gain in the income statement for the period of the acquisition.

In considering the foregoing, FASB concluded that FAS 141 is to be amended (following the FASB's new numbering convention for revisions, this would be FAS 141[R]) to include in the definition of business combinations those events and circumstances in which an entity obtains control over a business through means other than a transaction involving an acquisition of the net assets or equity interests in that business. This will also result in amending FIN 46(R). The proposed FAS 141(R) would continue to exclude joint venture formation and transactions between entities under common control from its scope.

FASB also concluded that certain items not be subject to the recognition and fair value measurement standards under the working principle. These include deferred income taxes, most benefit plan obligations, "basket purchases" of assets and related liabilities that do not meet the definition of a business, as proposed as a part of this project, and operating leases.

In conjunction with the Milestone 1 decisions, FASB decided to modify the definition of a business first set forth in EITF 98-3 (which will be superseded upon the effective date of proposed FAS 141[R]), and adapted in Appendix C of FIN 46(R) so that

1. An integrated set of activities that is not self-sustaining or will not continue in normal operations will, nevertheless, qualify as a business.
2. A development stage entity that has not commenced planned principal operations will be considered to be a business.
3. The presence of goodwill is not a conclusive indicator that an integrated set of activities qualifies as a business.

In addition, FASB clarified that the assessment of whether a set of assets and activities is a business is to be made in the context of a hypothetical potential acquirer rather than only from the standpoint of the specific actual acquirer.

Other expected amendments to FIN 46(R) would

1. Specifically reference FAS 141(R) as the authoritative guidance for recognition, measurement, and disclosure when an enterprise becomes the primary beneficiary of a VIE that meets the revised definition of a business.
2. Provide that when an enterprise initially becomes the primary beneficiary of a VIE that is not a business, the primary beneficiary would follow the guidance in

FAS 141(R) with respect to recognition and measurement of assets and liabilities **other than goodwill** unless those assets or liabilities were transferred by the enterprise at, after, or shortly before the initial consolidation. If a VIE is not a business, no goodwill would be recognized and the difference between consideration paid and amounts recognized in the consolidated financial statements would be recorded as a gain or loss with separate disclosure in the notes to the consolidated financial statements.

Milestone 2. Preacquisition contingencies (consisting of various contingent assets and liabilities) are to be initially recognized at acquisition based on fair values. FAS 5 principles will no longer be applied to initial recognition of preacquisition contingencies, nor to the subsequent remeasurement of those assets and liabilities. Among other things, this implies that contingent gains arising from purchase transactions will be given recognition, unlike under current GAAP (FAS 5). Contingent assets acquired and contingent liabilities assumed in a business combination that are financial instruments will be accounted for in accordance with applicable financial instruments accounting guidance. Contingent liabilities assumed in a business combination that are not financial instruments will be subsequently measured on a fresh-start (fair value) basis, while contingent assets acquired that are not financial instruments will be classified as intangible assets as defined in FAS 142 and, therefore, will be accounted for under that standard.

Milestone 3. Contingent consideration given in exchange in a business combination is an obligation of the acquirer as of the acquisition date, and therefore is to be recognized as part of the purchase price on that date. Consistent with the working principle, the initial measurement of contingent consideration is to be its fair value. This implies that future "earn out" payments, which are common aspects of purchase business acquisitions, will need to be estimated, valued and recognized at acquisition date, contrary to present practice. If the contingent consideration involves issuance of equity instruments, this would be recorded as equity, not as a liability. If recognized as a liability, remeasurement will be on a fresh-start (fair value) basis, with any adjustment thereto taken into current income and not used to revalue the purchase transaction; if classified as equity, however, no remeasurement would be permitted.

FASB has also concluded that the acquisition date is the date that the acquirer gains control over the target entity. Equity securities issued as consideration in a business combination would be measured at their fair value on the acquisition date. Acquisition-related costs paid to third parties (i.e., finder's, advisory, legal, accounting, and other professional fees) are not part of the exchange transaction and would be expensed as incurred. This, too, is a departure from current GAAP.

In a business combination in which consideration in the form of a business or other assets (which often includes nonmonetary assets carried at other than fair value) are transferred to an entity (acquiree) in exchange for shares issued by that entity, the business combination would be accounted for at fair value. The fair value measurement would be based on the fair value of the consideration paid or the fair value of the business acquired, whichever is more clearly evident. However, from the consolidated group's perspective, the business or other asset transferred by the acquiring entity to the acquired entity is not viewed as part of the assets acquired and liabilities assumed. Therefore, the amount of any gain or loss arising from the transfer to the acquiree of the business or other asset would be eliminated in the consolidated financial statements.

Milestone 4. FASB's working definition of fair value defines it as "the amount at which an asset or liability could be exchanged or settled in a current transaction between knowledgeable unrelated willing parties when neither is acting under compulsion." The measurement of identifiable assets and liabilities initially recorded at fair value by the acquirer in a business combination would be determined under the following fair value measurement hierarchy:

Level 1 — Determination of fair value by reference to observable prices of market transactions for identical assets or liabilities at or near the measurement date, whenever that information is available.

Level 2 — In the absence of observable prices of market transactions for identical assets or liabilities at or near the measurement date, the estimate of fair value is to be determined by adjusting observable prices of market transactions for similar assets or liabilities that occur at or near the measurement date. A similar asset or liability is one that is reasonably comparable (i.e., one having similar patterns of cash flows that can be expected to respond similarly to those of the item being measured to changes in economic conditions). Generally, when an asset or liability is sufficiently similar to an asset or liability being measured, adjustments for any differences are objectively determinable.

Level 3 — In the absence of observable prices of market transactions for identical or similar assets or liabilities at or near the measurement date, the estimate of fair value is to be determined using other valuation techniques which generally are variants of the market, income, and cost approaches to valuation. FASB indicates that it is preferable to use multiple valuation techniques when the necessary information to do so is available "without undue cost and effort." Valuation techniques are to be consistent with the objective of estimating fair value and incorporate assumptions that marketplace participants would use whenever market-based information is available without undue cost and effort. If market-based information is not available without undue cost and effort, an entity may use as inputs its own assumptions as a practical expedient. In any event, for any valuation technique, market inputs are to be maximized and use of internal estimates and assumptions are to be minimized. Any entity-specific assumptions that incorporate advantages or disadvantages possessed by the entity are to be adjusted to negate the effects of these advantages or disadvantages in order to meet the objective of fair value measurement.

FASB concluded that the business combination is to account for assets and liabilities of the acquiree, plus any assets and liabilities exchanged among the parties to the combination **as a condition of the agreement** that are directly related to and essential to the business combination, subject to certain conditions.

In a change from past practice, but consistent with provisions of FAS 146, *Accounting for Costs Associated with Exit and Disposal Activities*, FASB concluded that costs expected to be incurred by the acquiring entity pursuant to a plan to (1) exit an activity of an acquired entity, (2) involuntarily terminate employees of an acquired entity, or (3) relocate employees of an acquired entity, are not assumed liabilities, and therefore would not be recognized as liabilities at the time of the business combination. Previously recorded liabilities for such costs, if assumed by the acquirer, would qualify as a liability at the acquisition date, however. Acquired assets to be disposed of would be recorded at fair value less disposition costs, consistent with FAS 146. The fair values of assets acquired that are to be held and used are to be determined using an "in-use" valuation premise. The fair values of assets acquired that are to be held for disposal are to be determined using an "in-exchange" valuation premise.

FASB has also agreed on measurement approaches to be applied to various categories of assets and liabilities obtained in the purchase. Surprisingly, it has decided to require capitalization of acquired in-process research and developments assets—said to be a gesture toward convergence with International Accounting Standards—but to subject these costs to impairment testing in subsequent periods. Another change is to the treatment of subsequently realized deferred income tax benefits not recognized at the date of the acquisition. FAS 109 currently requires, in turn, the reduction of goodwill, reduction of other noncurrent intangible assets, and reduction of income tax expense; the expected new standard will impose a rebuttable presumption that goodwill be adjusted for benefits realized by reduction of a valuation allowance for acquired deferred income tax assets within one year of the acquisition date. That presumption could be overcome if recognition of the acquired deferred income tax benefit results from an identifiable event or circumstance occurring after the acquisition date. This would provide evidence that the event giving rise to the recognition of the benefit would not have been considered by the acquirer in assessing the amount of the valuation allowance needed at the acquisition date and, thus, the deferred income tax benefit would be appropriately reported as a reduction of income tax expense (or increase in income tax benefit) of that subsequent period.

As noted earlier in this chapter, FASB is expected to require the use of the full goodwill method (entity theory), under which the amount of goodwill recognized upon a business combination will be grossed up to include the portion attributable to the noncontrolling interest. This method is permitted, but not required, under current GAAP.

Under the FASB's anticipated standard, the treatment of negative goodwill is expected to be altered: instead of being offset against most categories of nonmonetary acquired assets, as is currently done, negative goodwill would be fully reported as a gain in the period of the acquisition transaction but it would no longer be characterized as an extraordinary gain. Offsetting of negative goodwill against assets would no longer be permitted.

Finally, the current one-year period for reallocation of purchase price following resolution of preacquisition contingencies would be modified to end at the earlier of one year from the acquisition date or when the acquiring entity is no longer waiting for information that it has arranged to obtain and that is known to be available or obtainable. The FASB has concluded that since the objective of obtaining information during the measurement period is to measure the assets acquired and liabilities assumed at their fair values as of the acquisition date, the only information that would be considered in recording assets acquired and liabilities assumed is information that would affect the determination of their fair values as of the acquisition date. Therefore, discovery during the measurement period of the need for an adjustment to the measurement of an acquired asset for an event that had not occurred as of the acquisition date would not be reflected as an adjustment of the initial measurement of that asset, but would be reported in current earnings.

Milestone 5. The FASB project will also address certain matters being debated in the FASB's liabilities vs. equity project, and in fact may reverse some of the decisions reached there. Noncontrolling (minority) interests will be required to be displayed in the equity section, as currently permitted but not required. In another unexpected conclusion, the FASB has determined that, in step acquisitions, preacquisition investments held by the acquirer at the date control is ultimately obtained are to be remeasured at their fair value, with any unrealized holding gains or losses on those investments to be recognized in consolidated net income for that period (effectively making the acquisition of a subsidiary an income-generating event).

After control is achieved, subsequent changes in the parent's interest, whether by virtue of its further purchase or sale of shares, or by other means, leaving control with the parent entity, would not result in recognized gains or losses. However, if the parent's interest decreases so that control is no longer present, whether by sale or by other means (e.g., issuance of new shares by subsidiary to third parties), gain or loss would be recognized in income currently. Any such gain or loss would be recognized in the income statement for the period, and calculated as the difference between (1) the proceeds, if any, from the sale of ownership interests in the subsidiary that resulted in the loss of control, and (2) the parent's share of the carrying amount of the subsidiary's net assets in the consolidated financial statements less the fair value of any investment remaining in the former subsidiary. Also, the noncontrolling interests' share of the carrying amount of the subsidiary's net assets would be derecognized with a corresponding reduction in the carrying amount of the noncontrolling interests.

The following decisions were made with respect to display and disclosure of noncontrolling interests:

1. The amounts of net income attributable to both controlling and noncontrolling interests are to be presented on the face of the consolidated statement of income in addition to presenting consolidated net income.
2. The amounts of comprehensive income attributable to both controlling and noncontrolling interests are to be presented on the face of the financial statement in which consolidated comprehensive income is presented in addition to presenting consolidated comprehensive income.
3. Individual line items in the consolidated statement of income and the individual components of other comprehensive income are to be presented on a consolidated basis on the face of the relevant financial statements with individual amounts attributable to controlling and noncontrolling interests not required to be presented.

These changes would not affect the computation of earnings per share under FAS 128.

Milestone 6. FASB decided that it will issue in the third quarter of 2004 a two-part Exposure Draft that includes (1) a proposed statement on business combinations, and (2) a proposed statement on noncontrolling interests. The current FASB agenda calls for statements to be finalized in the second quarter of 2005. Tentatively, the proposed changes would be effective for fiscal periods beginning after December 15, 2005, with early adoption encouraged. However, the FASB staff has indicated that they plan to address with the Board a possible postponement of the effective date at a Board meeting prior to issuance of the proposed statements. The proposed changes to the accounting for business combinations would be applied prospectively with retroactive application prohibited. Portions of the proposed changes to the accounting for noncontrolling interests would be retroactive and other portions prospective.

Disclosure Requirements

In the period in which a material business combination is completed, the notes to the acquirer's financial statements must disclose the following information:

1. The name and a brief description of the acquiree, together with the percentage of voting shares acquired;
2. The period for which the results of the acquiree's operations are included in the income statement of the acquirer;
3. The cost of the transaction and, if applicable, the number of shares of stock issued or issuable, the value assigned to those shares, and the basis for determining that value;
4. Contingent payments, options, or commitments specified in the acquisition agreement and the accounting treatment that will be followed should any such contingency occur;

5. A condensed balance sheet disclosing the following for each major asset and liability caption of the acquiree:
   a. The book value as reflected in the acquiree's financial records at the date of acquisition before fair value adjustments
   b. The fair values assigned at the date of acquisition (including, if pertinent, how negative goodwill was allocated to preliminarily determined asset fair values).
6. For any purchase price allocation that has not been finalized, that fact and the reasons therefore and, in subsequent periods, the nature and amount of any material adjustments made to the initial allocation of the purchase price; and
7. If the amount assigned to goodwill or to other intangible assets acquired is significant in relation to the total cost of the acquired enterprise:
   a. The amount of acquired goodwill
   b. The amount of acquired goodwill related to each segment (for entities that are required to report segment information in accordance with FAS 131)
   c. The amount of acquired goodwill that is deductible for income tax purposes

The notes to the financial statements of the acquirer also must disclose the following information in the period in which individually **immaterial** business combinations have been completed, if material in the aggregate:

1. The number of entities acquired and a brief description of the acquirees;
2. The aggregate cost of the acquisitions, the number of shares of stock issued or issuable, and the value assigned to those shares;
3. The aggregate amount of any contingent payments, options, or commitments and the accounting treatment that will be followed should any such contingency occur (if potentially significant in relation to the aggregate cost of the acquirees); and
4. Information pertaining to recorded goodwill, if the aggregate amount assigned to goodwill or to other intangible assets acquired is significant in relation to the aggregate cost of the acquirees.

Notes to the financial statements also must disclose, for any material business combination completed **after** the balance sheet date but before the financial statements are issued, information similar to that for completed transactions, above.

For each period for which a statement of financial position is presented, the notes to the financial statements also are to disclose the changes in the carrying amount of goodwill during the period. That would include the amount of goodwill acquired, the amount of impairment loss recognized, and the amount of goodwill included in the gain or loss on disposal of all or a portion of a reporting unit. Entities that report segment information in accordance with FAS 131 are to provide that information for each segment, disclosing any significant changes in the allocation of goodwill by segment.

When goodwill impairment losses are recognized, disclosure is required of

1. The facts and circumstances leading to the impairment;
2. The reporting unit for which the impairment loss is recognized, the adjusted carrying amount of goodwill of that reporting unit, and the amount of the impairment loss;
3. If relevant, the fact that the impairment loss estimate has yet to be finalized, the reasons therefore and, in subsequent periods, the nature and amount of any significant adjustments made to the initial estimate of the impairment loss; and
4. The segment to which the impaired goodwill relates (for entities that are required to report segment information in accordance with FAS 131).

In the period in which an excess over cost related to an acquisition is recognized as an extraordinary gain, it will be presented net of tax, as required under the provisions of APB 30, with appropriate disclosure in the notes to the financial statements.

EMERGING ISSUES TASK FORCE ISSUES SUMMARIES

84-13 Purchase of Stock Options with Stock Appreciation Rights in a Leveraged Buyout

This pronouncement addressed the question of whether options and similar rights which are purchased by a target company before completion of a leveraged buyout, with or without funds advanced by acquirer, should be deemed as compensation or as part of the cost of the buyout. The consensus was that GAAP (APB 25) requires that this be accounted for as compensation.

84-33 Acquisition of a Tax Loss Carryforward—Temporary Parent-Subsidiary Relationship

Assume that Company X has a large NOL carryforward while Company Y is profitable. In a highly leveraged purchase combination, Company X acquires 80% of Company Y while giving Y's owners the option to repurchase a 60% interest in Y at a fixed price. The Task Force concurred that in such a situation the companies' financial statements are not to be consolidated and that income is to be recognized on the equity method only until the carrying amount of the investment equals the probable repurchase price.

85-12 Retention of Specialized Accounting for Investments in Consolidation

A consensus was reached that specialized accounting principles that are appropriately applied at a subsidiary company level are also to be used in the consolidated financial statements.

85-28 Consolidation Issues Relating to Collateralized Mortgage Obligations

A special purpose subsidiary, created to originate collateralized mortgage obligations, must be consolidated, if it was formed by a parent company that normally originates mortgages and then transfers them to the subsidiary.

85-45 Business Combinations: Settlement of Stock Options and Awards

This pronouncement extends the consensus of 84-13. If a target company in an LBO (leveraged buyout) settles options voluntarily, the payments must be accounted for as compensation expense in the separate financial statement of the target company. However, no consensus was reached on how the target should account for a reimbursement of costs received from the acquirer.

86-29 Nonmonetary Transactions: Magnitude of Boot and the Exceptions to the Use of Fair Value

This consensus primarily addresses APB 29 issues, but also offers interpretation on exchanges of investments that are accounted for under the provisions of either APB 16 or 18. A consensus was reached that an entity is to account for an exchange of securities in which it acquires control of a subsidiary as an acquisition to be accounted for per APB 16. If control is not achieved but the investment will be accounted for by the equity method, the exchange is treated as a monetary transaction per APB 29. However, this accounting would not apply to the acquisition of a noncontrolling interest.

86-32 Early Extinguishment of a Subsidiary's Mandatorily Redeemable Preferred Stock

This extinguishment is a capital stock transaction with no gain or loss recognized. Dividends would be included in noncontrolling interest as a charge against income.

87-11 Allocation of Purchase Price to Assets to Be Sold

A consensus was reached that earnings or losses of a division which is to be sold, as well as interest on any incremental debt used to acquire it, and the gain or loss on the ultimate sale of the division, is not to be included in income, if the sale is within one year. Under the provisions of FAS 38, these are accounted for as reallocations of the purchase price, inasmuch as they effectively are resolutions of preacquisition contingencies.

87-17 The Spin-Offs or Other Distributions of Loans Receivable to Shareholders

A consensus was reached that a transfer of loans receivable to a newly formed subsidiary in consideration for stock of the subsidiary is to be recorded at fair value by the enterprise and the recipient. The transaction would be classified as a dividend-in-kind rather than a spin-off because the subsidiary is not an operating company.

87-21 Change of Accounting Basis in Master Limited Partnership Transactions

This pronouncement addressed the variety of transactions that are used to create master limited partnerships, and specifically was intended to specify when a new basis of accounting is to be recognized. The consensus was that a new basis of accounting is not appropriate in "roll-ups" where the general partner was the general partner in all of the predecessors. Similarly, new basis of accounting is not appropriate in a "drop down" in which the sponsor is the corporate parent that maintains effective control after the restructuring. Also, a new basis of accounting is not appropriate in a "rollout" or in a reorganization. Likewise, even if the general partner was the general partner in only some of the predecessors, no new basis could be established. Transaction costs incurred in connection with a roll-up are to be expensed, not capitalized, in a manner similar to the accounting for poolings under APB 16.

88-16 Basis in Leveraged Buyout Transactions

One of the most complex accounting areas, first addressed in EITF 86-16, this pronouncement stipulates how to compute the new cost basis after an LBO transaction. A consensus was reached that a new basis is to be recognized only when there is a change in the voting control from the former entity to the post-LBO entity; that a "substance over form" rule applies when seeking to determine if there had in fact been a change in control; and that a "monetary test" is established whereby fair value can only be used if at least 80% of the fair value of consideration paid to make the acquisition is monetary in nature.

89-7 Exchange of Assets or Interest in a Subsidiary for a Noncontrolling Equity Interest in a New Entity

The Task Force analyzed two example transactions and reached a consensus that full gain recognition is not appropriate for either transaction. The specific facts of the transactions are described in the EITF. The Task Force did note that because of the many possible variations, the specific facts and circumstances of each transaction would affect gain or loss recognition.

90-5 Exchanges of Ownership Interests between Entities under Common Control

This consensus stipulates that there is no step up in a transfer of a subsidiary from a parent company to another of its subsidiaries, and that the subsidiary's basis in the new subsidiary will be the same as was the parent company's. However, a buyout of noncontrolling interests by the subsidiary is to be accounted for as a purchase transaction, whether effected by cash or by a stock transaction.

90-6 Accounting for Certain Events Relating to an Acquired Operating Unit to Be Sold

This pronouncement addresses circumstances in which a division of an acquired company is expected to be sold within one year of the acquisition transaction, but the disposition does not occur in a timely manner. The consensus was that a strict interpretation of FAS 38 is to be applied; therefore, after one year, further changes must be included in earnings, and no longer by a reallocation of the purchase price. If the decision to sell is reversed, the accounting to be employed depends upon whether this occurs before or after the one-year time horizon is reached. If before, a reallocation of the purchase price is prescribed, including a cumulative restatement for depreciation, etc. If the decision to sell is reversed after one-year period elapses, then a fair value adjustment is to be made to the assets and liabilities as of the date of the decision: if this is a write-down, it is to be taken to income, while if it is a write-up, the adjustment will be to goodwill and amortization prospectively.

90-12 Allocating Basis to Individual Assets and Liabilities for Transactions within the Scope of EITF 88-16

This consensus prescribes the use of the partial purchase (step acquisition accounting) method, even if retained earnings are eliminated as a consequence.

90-13 Accounting for Simultaneous Common Control Mergers

This consensus addresses situations in which a parent company obtains control of a target, then spins one of its previously owned subsidiaries off to the target in exchange for more shares in the target (i.e., the old subsidiary becomes a "grandson" after the series of transactions). A consensus was reached that this latter step must be viewed as an integral part of the acquisition, not as an "Interpretation 39" transfer among entities under common control. A step-up in basis would be permitted to the extent of a change in control, both upon the acquisition of the target and on the sale of the subsidiary to the new target subsidiary. The accounting for a spin-off of the old subsidiary to the target company is to be accounted for as "reverse acquisition" of the target by the subsidiary, per APB 16.

91-5 Nonmonetary Exchanges of Cost-Method Investments

The Task Force reached consensus on three issues regarding how an investor accounts for its investment in a company, subsequent to a business combination, if the cost method is used. The first consensus reached was that the cost-method investor in the acquired company would record the transaction at fair value. The second consensus reached was that the cost-method investor in the acquiring company would continue to carry the investment at historical cost. The third consensus was that if an investor in the acquired company also possessed a cost-method investment in the acquiring company, the first two conclusions would still apply.

93-7 Uncertainties Related to Income Taxes in a Purchase Business Combination

The consensus was that all income tax uncertainties (such as uncertainties about the allocation of purchase price to individual assets and liabilities for tax purposes in a taxable business combination, uncertainties about carryforwards in a nontaxable combination, and uncertainties about preacquisition tax returns of the acquired entity) existing at the time of a purchase business combination are to be accounted for under the provisions of FAS 109, not under the provisions of FAS 38 (preacquisition contingencies). Any such adjustments are to be applied to increase or decrease the remaining balance of goodwill attributable to that business combination; if goodwill is reduced to zero, the remaining amount is used to reduce other noncurrent intangible assets from the same acquisition to zero, with any excess taken to income.

95-3 Recognition of Liabilities in Connection with a Purchase Business Combination

If costs to exit an activity of an acquiree and involuntary termination or relocation costs relative to employees of an acquiree are anticipated at or very shortly after the acquisition, they are to be reflected in the allocation of the purchase price, unless the costs are incurred to generate revenue of the combined entity after the acquisition, in which case these would be period costs. (This is analogous to Issue 94-3 and examples in that consensus apply here also.) If later settled for amounts are less than accrued, the savings are used to reduce the purchase price of the entity, which usually means goodwill recorded on the acquisition would be reduced; these adjustments are **not** preacquisition contingencies as defined by FAS 38, and thus the one-year limit is probably not applicable. Costs not identified timely would be period costs of the postacquisition entity. Costs related to assets or employees of the acquirer are not costs of the acquisition and cannot be part of the purchase price allocation process; these must be reflected in the income statement in all cases. A number of restrictions on the use of accrued liability treatment are prescribed—generally, to avoid a "big bath" by anticipating vague future costs. Costs of activities or employees of the acquirer are not allocable to the purchase price, per FTB 85-5. The consensus also identified certain disclosures to be made under these circumstances, including a description of plans to exit activities, possible reallocation of purchase transaction, etc.

95-8 Accounting for Contingent Consideration Paid to the Shareholders of an Acquired Company in a Purchase Business Combination

Whether contingent consideration based on earnings is to be accounted for as an adjustment of the purchase price or as compensation for services, for the use of property, or for profit sharing depends on the facts and circumstances of each case. Some of the factors that can assist in making this determination relate to the terms of continuing employment, components of shareholder group, reasons for the contingent payment provisions, the formula used for determining contingent consideration, and other agreements and issues. For example, if compensation other than contingent payments is set at a reasonable level, this supports treatment of the contingent payments as an additional purchase price.

95-14 Recognition of Liabilities in Anticipation of a Business Combination

The issue involves contingency plans for exiting businesses and/or terminating employees if a business combination is consummated. The specific questions are whether the conditions specified in Issue 94-3 will be met only if the combination does occur. The consensus was that the commitment date for exit plan costs, and the recognition date for involuntary termination benefits, cannot occur prior to consummation.

95-19 Determination of the Measurement Date for the Market Price of Securities Issued in a Purchase Business Combination

Where there is conflicting guidance on which market price is to be considered in determining cost of acquisition using stock, the guidance in APB 16 is to be relied upon: market price for a reasonable period before and after the event is to be considered, although this span is usually brief (i.e., a few days). If number of shares to be exchanged is subsequently changed, this creates a new measurement date for valuation.

95-21 Accounting for Assets to Be Disposed of Acquired in a Purchase Business Combination

This involves the interaction among Issue 87-11 (allocation of purchase cost to assets to be sold), APB 16, FAS 121, and a proposed standard on consolidation. There was no attempt to reach a consensus, and further consideration at a later date is likely. The key issue is whether expected cash flows from operation of assets to be sold off should be considered, per 87-11, or whether assets should simply be booked at fair value less costs to sell, as suggested by proposed FAS on consolidations, which builds on the FAS 121 rule.

96-4 Accounting for Reorganizations Involving a Non-Pro-Rata Split-Off of Certain Nonmonetary Assets to Owners

The EITF's consensus was that a non-pro-rata split-off in a corporate plan of organization be accounted for at fair value. With regard to a pro rata basis distribution in the split-off of a targeted business, the distribution to holders of related targeted stock is accounted for at historical cost.

96-5 Recognition of Liabilities for Contractual Termination Benefits or Changing Benefit Plan Assumptions in Anticipation of a Business Combination

Termination costs to be incurred from business combination are not to be accrued when business combination is merely deemed probable, but only when it is actually consummated.

96-7 Accounting for Deferred Taxes on In-Process Research and Development Activities Acquired in a Purchase Business Combination

Per FIN 4, the purchase price allocated in a purchase business combination to research and development costs must be expensed immediately. At issue is whether, under FAS 109, a deferred tax liability must be allocated to the initial (pre-write-off) basis difference between tax and book bases. The consensus was that since write-off occurs prior to the measurement of deferred taxes, no deferred taxes are to be assigned.

97-2 Application of FASB Statement No. 94 and APB Opinion No. 16 to Physician Practice Management Entities and Certain Other Entities with Contractual Management Arrangements

A physician practice management can establish a controlling financial interest in physician practices via contractual management agreement, and thus trigger FAS 94 consolidation requirement, if six criteria are met: life of ten years minimum or remaining life of entity; not terminable by physicians under normal conditions; control over all ongoing, major central operations except for dispensing medical services; control over compensation of professionals, hiring and firing, etc.; financial interest is salable or transferable; and right to receive income based on performance risk and change in fair value.

97-8 Accounting for Contingent Consideration Issued in a Purchase Business Combination

This EITF deals with indirect contingent consideration arrangements, such as those that are embedded in a security or are part of a separate financial instrument. At issue was the timing of recognition of the cost of the contingent consideration. The consensus was that the fair value of the instrument is to be recognized at the date of acquisition as part of purchase cost to be allocated if the instrument is traded or indexed to an instrument that is traded. Subsequent changes in value are to be ignored. On the other hand, if the instrument is not traded, contingent cost would be measured only when contingency is resolved, per APB 16. Other related accounting issues are addressed in EITF 86-28 and 96-13.

97-15 Accounting for Contingency Arrangements Based on Security Prices in a Purchase Business Combination

This issue relates to "below market" or "above market" guarantees of market value of securities issued in purchase transaction; under APB 16 the normal type of market value guarantee does not get reflected in purchase cost. The consensus is that for below market value guarantee, there would be no purchase cost adjustment, as cost is fair value of unconditional securities given at date of combination only. On the other hand, in an above market contingent issuance (e.g., issue more shares if price three years hence is not at least $x, where $x > $y [price at deal date]), there will be a requirement to issue more shares if the price exceeds some defined threshold, perhaps with a declining number of shares up to price of $z, where $z > $x. In these cases, the cost of the purchase is the maximum number of additional shares times price as of the date of transaction, with no later adjustments to be recognized.

98-1 Valuation of Debt Assumed in a Purchase Business Combination

APB 16 directs cost allocation based on fair values of assets and liabilities, with fair value of liabilities being computed using present value. Issue arises because present value ≠ fair value in some cases, such as when prepayment option affects fair value but present value would often ignore this contingent change in future cash flows. Consensus was to use fair value, even if ≠ present value of cash flows. Since market values may not be available, some use of present value method may be required, but the value of option features, etc. must be included in the calculation.

98-2 Accounting by a Subsidiary for an Investment in Its Parent Company's Stock

This issue relates to the display of an investment by subsidiary in parent's or joint venture partner's stock in separate statements of the subsidiary or the joint venture specifically, how; FAS 115 rules affect this presentation. Questions to be answered are how to account for initial purchase and subsequent accounting for such investments. Possible answers are to account for the investment as an asset to be accounted for at fair value; a distribution to the parent or joint venture partner (similar to treasury stock); or as an asset measured by the equity method, with an elimination of reciprocal ownership investments. No consensus has been reached on this issue yet.

98-3 Determining Whether a Transaction Is an Exchange of Similar Productive Assets or a Business Combination

APB 29 states that nonmonetary exchanges should generally be reported at fair value, but the exchange of productive assets are to be recorded at carrying value or assets relinquished (although a current ED would end this exception—see Chapter 9). FAS 141, however, uses a fair value approach, to account for business combinations. Some exchanges (e.g., of radio stations or other groups of operating assets) may be viewed as being either nonmonetary exchanges or business combinations. In this consensus, EITF defined a business as a self-sustaining integrated set of activities and assets conducted and managed for the purpose of providing a return to investors. It consists of (1) inputs, (2) processes applied to those inputs, and (3) resulting outputs that are used to generate revenues. Each of these criteria is further defined by EITF 98-3 (see discussion in body of this chapter). For a transferred set of activities and assets to be deemed a business, it must contain all of the inputs and processes necessary for it to continue to conduct normal operations after the transferred set is separated from the transferor, which includes the ability to sustain a revenue stream by providing its outputs to customers. If these criteria are not satisfied, the assets do not comprise a business and FAS 141 would not apply to an acquisition.

98-4 Accounting by a Joint Venture or Businesses Received at Its Formation

At issue is how a joint venture should record, in stand-alone financial statements, businesses received from venture partner, in situations where either the relationship between joint venturer and venturers has none of the five attributes of a corporate joint venture set forth in APB 18 but there is joint control, or where all five attributes exist and there is joint control. In common practice, the carryforward basis is used. A need for definition of joint control is noted, and this will be further pursued by EITF. SEC supports the APB 16 treatment for contributions to newly formed, jointly controlled entity if entity is not joint venture (presumably means carryforward basis); and also would object to the conclusion that joint control is the only defining characteristic of a joint venture. More discussion of these matters is anticipated.

99-6 Impact of Acceleration Provisions in Grants Made between Initiation and Consummation of a Pooling-of-Interests Business Combination

The issue is whether granting stock options (or restricted stock) that provide for automatic vesting upon a change in control, after initiation of a business combination, violates the change-in-equity-interests condition and thus precludes pooling treatment for that business combination. The consensus is that this would not violate the change-in-equity-interests condition, provided the option grant is consistent with a pattern of past grants made prior to initiation of the business combination, and the change in control provision was not added to the plan in contemplation of the business combination. To the contrary, the removal of such a provision in contemplation of the business combination would be an alteration of equity interests that would preclude pooling-of-interests accounting.

99-12 Accounting for Formula Arrangements under Issue No. 95-19

A consensus on Issue 95-19 stipulated that if the purchase price, including the number of shares, is subsequently changed, a new measurement date is established for valuing the equity securities to be issued. That guidance applies to changes in the number of shares or amount of other consideration when the change is pursuant to a formula in the initial acquisition agreement that could adjust the number of shares or amount of other consideration as a result of changes in the market price of the acquirer's common stock. There is the further issue of which date is to be used as the measurement date to value equity securities issued in a purchase business combination if the number of shares or amount of other consideration to be issued could change pursuant to a formula in the initial acquisition agreement. There is no consensus yet, but the tentative conclusion is that if the number of shares or amount of other consideration could change pursuant to a formula in the initial acquisition agreement, the date on which the number of shares and amount of other consideration become fixed as a result of the final application of the formula is the measurement date.

A further issue is: once a measurement date is determined pursuant to the foregoing, how should the guidance in Issue 95-19 that requires the shares to be valued based on market prices "a few days before and after" the measurement date be applied? The Task Force reached a tentative conclusion that the securities be valued based on market prices a few days before and after the measurement date determined in the foregoing, provided that the measurement period would not include any dates after the date the business combination is consummated. Appropriate changes will be made to Issue 95-19; this will apply prospectively to purchase business combinations initiated after the date final consensuses are reached.

99-15 Accounting for Decreases in Deferred Tax Asset Valuation Allowances Established in a Purchase Business Combination as a Result of a Change in Tax Regulations

This issue arises as a result of new consolidated tax return regulations issued in 1999, which changed the rules for utilizing certain net operating loss carryovers and carrybacks (NOLC) by eliminating the requirement to apply the limitations on the separate return limitation year losses to situations in which a change in ownership as defined in Section 382 of the Internal Revenue Code has occurred within six months of a target company becoming a member of a consolidated group.

The change in tax regulations requires an entity to reevaluate the need for an existing valuation allowance for deferred tax assets relating to NOLC acquired in a prior purchase business combination. The specific question is whether the effect of the adjustment should be (1) included in operations or (2) applied first to reduce to zero any goodwill related to the acquisition, second to reduce to zero other noncurrent intangible assets related to the acquisition, and third to reduce income tax expense.

The Task Force consensus is that the effect of a change in tax law or regulation that results in a decrease in a valuation allowance that initially was recorded in the allocation of the purchase price in a purchase business combination is to be included in income from continuing operations. The consensus applies to any reduction in the valuation allowance that otherwise would not have been recognized except for the change in tax law or regulation, regardless of whether the valuation allowance is reduced in the period of the tax law change or in a subsequent period.

00-4 Majority Owner's Accounting for a Transaction in the Shares of a Consolidated Subsidiary and a Derivative Indexed to the Minority Interest in That Subsidiary

This issue addresses how a majority owner is to account for entering into a derivative financial instrument with the noncontrolling owner, if the derivative instrument provides the majority owner with substantially all the risks and rewards of the ownership of the noncontrolling share. The consensus was that the derivative instrument and the noncontrolling interest be combined and accounted for as a financing. After combination, the derivative will not be subject to the provisions of FAS 133.

01-3 Accounting in a Purchase Business Combination for Deferred Revenue of an Acquiree

This consensus addresses recognition by an acquirer of deferred revenue previously accounted for by an acquired entity as a liability under GAAP, noting that the threshold for liability recognition under APB 16 (now FAS 141) does not correspond to revenue recognition rules. In the case of revenue deferred because the acquiree entity had a performance obligation, the conclusion was that in the context of a purchase business combination, recognition of a performance obligation liability would only be appropriate when the acquirer has a legal obligation to provide concessions or goods or services to customers. Absent such an obligation, the deferred revenue would not be recognized as a liability of the acquirer in a business combination. Revenue arrangements in business combinations might also result in the recognition of an asset (for the customer relationship) and a liability (deferred revenue); these are not to be netted.

02-5 Definition of "Common Control" in Relation to FASB Statement 141, *Business Combinations*

FAS 141 excludes combinations of entities under common control from purchase accounting requirements, as did its predecessor, APB 16. Neither standard defined what was meant by common control, however. In discussion (no consensus reached yet), the EITF acknowledged that common control exists when one person owns over 50% of two or more entities, and also when immediate family members vote their shares in concert so as to effect control. However, the idea that different companies owned by individuals that are not members of an immediate family are under common control was rejected, unless there is contemporaneous written evidence of an agreement to vote a majority of an entity's shares in concert. Further development of guidelines to identify common control is expected to be produced as part of the FASB's new basis project, which is now in progress.

02-11 Accounting for Reverse Spinoffs

Spin-off transactions are accounted for as distributions to shareholders, at book value, per APB 29. In some instances, the legal form of the transaction does not accurately describe the economic substance, and the legal spinnor is to be accounted for as the accounting spinnee (and vice versa).

02-17 Recognition of Customer Relationship Intangible Assets Acquired in a Business Combination

This consensus addresses the propriety of separate recognition of customer relationship intangibles in business combinations. EITF concluded that the contractual-legal and the separability criteria do not restrict the use of certain assumptions that would be used in estimating the fair value of an intangible asset. Thus, if the parties to the business combination believe that an existing contractual relationship with a customer will be renewed, this is considered in making the purchase price allocation to that asset, once the threshold for recognition (i.e., the contractual right) has been identified. It furthermore concluded that the guidance in FAS 141 that states "if an entity establishes relationships with its customers through contracts, those customer relationships would arise from contractual rights," applies if an entity has a practice of establishing contracts with customers, regardless of whether a contract is in existence at the date of acquisition. However, in assigning fair value to the relationship, the lack of a current contract would likely be considered, even if recognition is warranted. Finally, consensus was reached that an order or a production backlog arising from contracts such as purchase or sales orders (even if the purchase or sales orders are cancelable) would be considered a contract.

D-100 Clarification of Paragraph 61(b) of FASB Statement 141 and Paragraph 49(b) of FASB Statement 142

Under FAS 141, intangible assets other than goodwill resulting from business combinations are to be separately accounted for, but under prior GAAP (APB 17) it was not uncommon for intangibles thus obtained to be aggregated as goodwill, since the accounting was identical. The transition provisions for FAS 142 permit disaggregating intangibles, but only to the extent that separate accounting records (even if aggregated for financial reporting purposes) had been maintained. The amount of purchase cost allocated to goodwill and other intangible assets cannot be redetermined as part of this process, however. A failure to properly separate formerly aggregated intangibles would potentially distort subsequent determinations of goodwill impairment, since under FAS 141 this determination is based on the value of goodwill after fully assigning purchase cost to all intangibles, including those not formally recognized.

D-101 Clarification of Reporting Unit Guidance in Paragraph 30 of FASB Statement 142

Whether a component of an operating segment is a reporting unit for purposes of applying FAS 142, for purposes of applying the requirement to determine goodwill impairment depends on whether the component functions as a business, whether discrete financial information is available about that component, whether it is accountable to and in regular contact with segment managers, and whether it is qualitatively distinct from other components of the operating segment. It is possible that components aggregated for purposes of reporting under FAS 131 could be separate for purposes of applying FAS 142.

D-105 Accounting in Consolidation for Energy Trading Contracts between Affiliated Entities When the Activities of One but Not Both Affiliates Are within the Scope of Issue 98-10

This addresses the need to eliminate intercompany profits resulting from market-to-market accounting for energy trading contracts among affiliates of a consolidated entity, when not all of these entities' activities are governed by EITF 98-10. Energy trading concerns often do not distinguish derivatives from nonderivatives, since all are accounted for at fair value, although the disclosure requirements of FAS 133 still apply to the derivatives. All gains and loses arising from intercompany transactions must be eliminated in consolidation. It is also possible that the characterization of a given contract (as a hedge or not) can change between the stand-alone and the consolidated financial statements.

FASB STAFF POSITIONS

FIN 46-1 Applicability of FASB Interpretation No. 46, *Consolidation of Variable Interest Entities*, to Entities Subject to the AICPA Audit and Accounting Guide, *Health Care Organizations*

This FSP clarifies that the scope exception in FIN 46 for not-for-profit organizations applies to all such organizations as defined in FAS 117, including health care organizations subject to the AAG, *Health Care Organizations*. The guidance in this FSP was incorporated into paragraph 4(a) of FIN 46(R) issued in December 2003.

FIN 46-2 Reporting Variable Interests in Specified Assets of Variable Interest Entities as Separate Variable Interest Entities under Paragraph 13 of FASB Interpretation No. 46, *Consolidation of Variable Interest Entities*

Certain variable interests in specified assets of a variable interest entity (VIE) are required to be treated by their holder as separate variable interest entities, sometimes referred to as "silos" or "deemed entities." This FSP specifies that if any parties other than the variable interest holder and the secured lender have rights or obligations with respect to the specified assets or the cash flows from those assets, the specified assets and related liabilities are not to be treated as a silo for accounting purposes.

The guidance in this FSP was carried forward with conforming changes as FSP FIN 46(R)-1 when FIN 46(R) was issued in December 2003.

FIN 46-3 Application of Paragraph 5 of FASB Interpretation No. 46, *Consolidation of Variable Interest Entities* When Variable Interests in Specified Assets of a Variable Interest Entity Are Not Considered Interests in the Entity under Paragraph 12 of Interpretation 46

In estimating expected losses for the purpose of determining whether an entity is a VIE, expected losses associated with specified assets are to be excluded from the estimate if those assets do not represent at least a majority of the entity's assets.

FIN 46-4 Transition Requirements for Initial Application of FASB Interpretation No. 46, *Consolidation of Variable Interest Entities*

Upon initial adoption of FIN 46, the determinations of whether an entity is a VIE, and which entity (if any) is the VIE's primary beneficiary, are to be made as of the later of the date the interest holder became involved with the entity or the date that an event requiring reconsideration of the entity's status or the status of its interest holders has occurred. If one or more reconsideration events have occurred, the determinations are each to be made as of the most recent date at which FIN 46 would have required reconsideration.

An exception is provided for enterprises for which, at transition to FIN 46, it is not practicable to obtain the necessary information to make the determinations on the applicable dates. In this case, the determinations are to be made as of the date on which FIN 46 is initially applied and the VIE assets, liabilities, and noncontrolling interests are to be measured at their respective fair values as of the date of initial FIN 46 application.

The guidance in this FSP was incorporated into paragraph 38 of FIN 46(R), which was issued in December 2003.

FIN 46-5 Calculation of Expected Losses under FASB Interpretation No. 46, *Consolidation of Variable Interest Entities*

This FSP clarifies and illustrates the fact that all entities have "expected losses" as that term is defined in FIN 46; even when the entity has never experienced a net loss and does not expect to ever experience one. The word "loss" as used in the context of an "expected loss" is not the same as an accounting loss used in the context of an income statement. In the language of VIE, an expected loss is experienced by an entity whenever an estimated outcome (irrespective of its probability) is monetarily less than the probability-weighted expected outcome. To express this in different terms, a probability-weighted expected cash flow estimate is a weighted-average. In computing averages, some of the outcomes are above the average (or mean) and some are below the average. When an outcome is below the average, this is an expected loss.

The guidance in this FSP is superseded by FSP 46(R)-2 for entities that have adopted FIN 46(R), which was issued in December 2003.

FIN 46-6 Effective Date of FASB Interpretation No 46, *Consolidation of Variable Interest Entities*

This FSP was issued on October 9, 2003, for the purpose of deferring the effective date for applying the consolidation provisions of FIN 46 to (1) nonregistered investment companies that account for their investments in accordance with the AICPA Audit and Accounting Guide, *Audits of Investment Companies*, and (2) interests held by public entities in VIE or potential VIE that were created before February 1, 2003. However, if a public entity had issued financial statements reporting VIE in accordance with FIN 46, it was not permitted to reverse those effects. Instead, it was required to continue to use FIN 46 to report those interests. The disclosures required by paragraph 26 of FIN 46 were not deferred. The effective date of provisions of FIN 46(R), issued in December 2003, superseded the effective date provisions of this FSP.

FIN 46-7 Exclusion of Certain Decision Maker Fees from Paragraph 8(c) of FASB Interpretation No. 46, *Consolidation of Variable Interest Entities*

This FSP provides needed clarification regarding the treatment of fees to decision makers in determining variability and in determining the parties that absorb variability. The guidance included in the FSP was incorporated in paragraphs B18-B21 of FIN 46(R), issued in December 2003.

When evaluating VIE or potential VIE, the evaluator must exercise care in examining the relationship between a decision maker and the entity being evaluated. The objective of this examination is to determine whether the decision maker's role with respect to the entity is, in substance, that of a hired service provider (or employee) or instead its role is in substance that of a variable interest holder who potentially qualifies as the VIE's primary beneficiary.

Decision maker fees are required to be included in computations of expected losses and expected residual returns and are **not** treated as variable interests if the fees meet the characteristics of a **hired service provider** or employee meeting **all** of the following criteria:

1. The fees represent charges for services priced consistently with the level of effort required to provide those services. Presence of the following indicators may lead to the conclusion that the fees exceed the efforts required to provide the services:
    a. Terms, conditions, or amounts included in the service arrangement that would not customarily be included in an arms-length agreement.
    b. The amount of the expected fees from the arrangement is proportionally large when compared to the total amount of expected return from the entity to the holders of its variable interests.
    c. The variability expected to be associated with the fees is proportionally large when compared to the total expected variability of the entity's net assets.
2. The decision maker fees have the same or higher level of seniority as other operating liabilities of the entity such as trade accounts payable.
3. Exclusive of fees meeting the criteria in 1. and 2. above, the decision maker and its related parties (including de facto principals and agents) do not hold interests in the entity that individually or in the aggregate would absorb more than a trivial amount of the entity's expected losses or would receive more than a trivial amount of the entity's expected residual returns.
4. The arrangement with the decision maker includes "kick-out rights" that are substantive. In order for such rights to be considered substantive, they must meet **both** of the following criteria:
    a. Removal of the decision maker can be accomplished by a simple majority vote of the voting interest holders excluding the decision maker and its related parties (including de facto agents/principals).

b. The kick-out rights are not subject to significant barriers that would prevent their exercise including, but not limited to
   (1) Narrow time limits or other limiting conditions that make exercise of the rights unlikely
   (2) Financial penalties or operational barriers that would make the kick-out unlikely due to cost considerations.
   (3) An inadequate rate of compensation that would make it unlikely that a qualified replacement could be found.
   (4) Unavailability of an adequate number of qualified replacement decision makers.
   (5) Lack of provisions in the contractual arrangements, or in laws and regulations, that specifically provide a reasonable means for the parties possessing the kick-out rights to arrange for and conduct a vote for their exercise.
   (6) The holders of the kick-out rights lacking access to the necessary information needed to exercise those rights.

If all four of the above criteria are **not met,** fees paid to decision makers are excluded from the computation of a VIE's expected losses or expected residual returns because rather than creating those expected losses or residual returns, those decision maker fees qualify as variable interests that either absorb expected losses or receive expected residual returns. In that case, the decision maker is **potentially** the party that has financial control as the entity's primary beneficiary.

FIN 46-8 Evaluating Whether as a Group the Holders of the Equity Investment at Risk Lack the Direct or Indirect Ability to Make Decisions about an Entity's Activities through Voting Rights or Similar Rights under FASB Interpretation No. 46, *Consolidation of Variable Interest Entities*

The holders of the equity investment at risk (the equity group) have the ability to make decisions about an entity's activities if they hold **all** voting or similar rights. Conversely, the equity group would lack the ability to make decisions if it holds **no** voting or similar rights.

In situations in which the equity group and another party (or parties) outside the equity group have the ability to make or participate in making decisions about the entity, emphasis should be placed on (1) the ability of the equity group to make decisions that have a significant impact on the success of the entity, and (2) the extent to which the equity group absorbs expected losses and receives expected residual returns of the entity. If the equity group has the ability to make decisions that have a significant impact on the success of the entity and the equity group has an obligation to absorb expected losses and the right to receive expected residual returns, the equity group likely has the "direct or indirect ability to make decisions about an entity's activities through voting rights or similar rights." The greater the equity as compared to the expected losses of the entity, the less likely that the equity group would surrender the direct or indirect ability to make decisions about an entity's activities to another party outside the equity group. Further, if the amount of at-risk equity is sufficient to absorb expected losses, the risks of another party outside the equity group may be significantly mitigated by the amount of the equity group's investment.

The FSP also clarifies that it was not the intent of FASB that all franchisor/franchisee relationships qualify as VIE. A distinction is drawn between the decision-making authority that a franchisee typically holds with respect to the success of the business and the decision-making authority that a franchisor typically retains with respect to the protection of its brand image. The latter authority does not generally limit the franchisee's authority over the normal operations of its business and thus would not preclude the franchisee's investors from being judged to hold decision-making authority through voting or other rights.

The guidance in this FSP was carried forward with conforming changes as FSP FIN 46(R)-3 when FIN 46(R) was issued in December 2003.

FIN 46(R)-1 Reporting Variable Interests in Specified Assets of Variable Interest Entities as Separate Variable Interest Entities under Paragraph 13 of FASB Interpretation No. 46 (revised December 2003), *Consolidation of Variable Interest Entities*

This FSP replaces FSP FIN 46-2 for entities that have adopted FIN 46(R). The guidance was carried forward without significant changes; see the discussion of FSP FIN 46-2 above.

FIN 46(R)-2 Calculation of Expected Losses under FASB Interpretation No. 46, *Consolidation of Variable Interest Entities*

This FSP replaces FSP FIN 46-5 for entities that have adopted FIN 46(R). This FSP clarifies and illustrates the fact that all entities have "expected losses" as that term is defined in FIN 46(R), even when the entity has never experienced a net loss and does not expect to ever experience one. The term "expected losses" is based on the variability in the fair value of the entity's net assets exclusive of variable interest and not on the anticipated amount or variability of the net income or loss.

FIN 46(R)-3 Evaluating Whether as a Group the Holders of the Equity Investment at Risk Lack the Direct or Indirect Ability to Make Decisions about an Entity's Activities through Voting Rights or Similar Rights under FASB Interpretation No. 46, *Consolidation of Variable Interest Entities*

This FSP replaces FSP FIN 46-8 for entities that have adopted FIN 46(R). The guidance was carried forward without significant changes; see the discussion above for FSP FIN 46-8

FIN 46(R)-4 Technical Correction of FASB Interpretation No. 46 (Revised December 2003), *Consolidation of Variable Interest Entities*, Relating to Its Effects on Question No. 12 of EITF Issue No. 96-21, "Implementation Issues in Accounting for Leasing Transactions Involving Special-Purpose Entities"

This FSP clarifies the applicability of the accounting guidance provided in EITF 96-21 with respect to the accounting for contingent loss accruals by a lessee who has guaranteed the lessor's residual under an operating lease. The guidance in the EITF continues to be applicable when the lessee is **not** the primary beneficiary of a VIE lessor. If the lessee is the primary beneficiary, the EITF guidance does not apply since any such loss accrual would eliminate in consolidation.

12 CURRENT LIABILITIES AND CONTINGENCIES

PERSPECTIVE AND ISSUES

The division of assets and liabilities into current and noncurrent allows working capital (current assets minus current liabilities) to be calculated. Working capital, which is the relatively liquid portion of total entity capital, can be used to determine the ability of an entity to repay obligations. Working capital assumes a going-concern concept. If the entity is to be liquidated in the near future, classification of assets and liabilities is inappropriate.

ARB 43, Chapter 3, defines current liabilities as those obligations whose liquidation is reasonably expected to require the use of existing resources properly classifiable as current assets or the creation of other current liabilities. This definition excludes from the current liability classification any currently maturing obligations that will be satisfied by using long-term assets and currently maturing obligations expected to be refinanced.

The offsetting of assets and liabilities is generally prohibited under GAAP. However, under certain narrowly defined circumstances, where a right of setoff actually exists, netting for financial reporting purposes can be done, as described in this chapter.

FASB has declared, as its long-term goal, that all financial liabilities are to be recognized in the balance sheet at fair values, rather than at amounts based on their historical cost. Fair value is an estimated market exit price (i.e., an estimate of the amount that would have been paid if the entity had settled the liability on the balance sheet date). Currently, however, many current liabilities are measured at settlement value, which is the amount of cash (or its equivalent amount of other assets) that will be paid to the creditor to liquidate the obligation during the current operating cycle. Accounts payable, dividends payable, salaries payable, and other current obligations are measured at settlement value because they require the entity to pay a determinable amount of cash. If a current liability is near its payment date, there will be only an insignificant risk of changes in fair value because of changes in market conditions or the entity's credit standing, and settlement value and fair value will be essentially the same.

Other current liabilities are measured at the proceeds received when the obligation arose. Liabilities that are measured this way generally require the entity to discharge the obligation by providing goods or services rather than by paying cash. Liabilities that require the entity to provide goods or services, rather than cash, are not financial instruments and thus are not subject to FASB's fair value measurement goal. Subscriptions payable, deposits payable, and deferred revenues are examples of current liabilities measured by reference to proceeds received.

Although measurement of current liabilities is generally straightforward, some liabilities are difficult to measure because of uncertainties. Uncertainties regarding whether an obligation exists, how much of an entity's assets will be needed to settle the obligation, and when the settlement will take place can impact whether, when, and for how much an obligation will be recognized in the financial statements. FAS 5 is the primary standard that describes accounting for potential liabilities in circumstances involving uncertainties. It requires a liability to be recognized if it is (1) probable that an obligation has been incurred because of a transaction or event happening on or before the date of the financial statements and (2) the amount of the obligation can be reasonably estimated. Thus, uncertainties about the existence of an obligation need not be resolved before the liability is recorded. For example, estimated settlement amounts for ongoing lawsuits are recognized prior to a court's decision if it is probable that the outcome will be unfavorable. Further, difficulty in measuring an obligation is not, by itself, a reason for not recording a liability if the amount can be estimated. For example, warranty obligations are commonly recognized as liabilities even though the number of claims and the amount of each claim are unknown at the time of the sale of the warrantied item. Although future events will eventually resolve the uncertainties (the warranty claims will be paid and the lawsuit will be settled), the liabilities are required to be recognized before all of the uncertainties are resolved so that relevant information is provided on a timely basis.

FAS 5, as interpreted by FIN 34, requires disclosures about direct and indirect guarantees of the indebtedness of others. In late 2002, FASB promulgated FIN 45, which requires that certain obligations arising from guarantees be recorded as liabilities. FIN 45 is discussed in detail in this chapter.

Sources of GAAP

ARB	APB	FAS	FIN	FTB	EITF	SOP	FSP
43, Ch. 3, 50	6, 10, 21	5, 6, 11, 43, 48, 78, 112	8, 14, 39, 41, 45	79-3	85-20, 86-5, 86-12, 86-15, 86-30, 93-14, 95-22, 00-23, 03-3, 03-8, 03-12, D-77, D-79	96-1	FIN 45-1, FIN 45-2

DEFINITIONS OF TERMS

Accumulated benefits. Employee benefits that can be carried over into the next year but that expire upon termination of employment.

Contingency. An existing condition, situation, or set of circumstances involving uncertainty as to possible gain or loss that will ultimately be resolved when one or more future events occur or fail to occur.

Current liabilities. Obligations whose liquidation is reasonably expected to require the use of existing resources properly classified as current assets or the creation of other current liabilities. Obligations that are due on demand or will be due on demand within one year or the operating cycle, if longer, are current liabilities. Long-term obligations callable because of the debtor's violation of a provision of the debt agreement are current liabilities unless specific FAS 78 conditions are met.

FICA. Social security taxes levied upon both employees and employers.

FUTA. Social security tax levied upon employers to finance the administration of federal unemployment benefit programs.

Indirect guarantee of indebtedness of others. A guarantee under an agreement that obligates one entity to transfer funds to a second entity upon the occurrence of specified events under conditions whereby (1) the funds are legally available to the creditors of the second entity, and (2) those creditors may enforce the second entity's claims against the first entity.

Operating cycle. The average length of time necessary for an enterprise to convert inventory to receivables to cash.

CONCEPTS, RULES, AND EXAMPLES

ARB 43, Chapter 3, contains several examples of current liabilities. It also contains broad general descriptions of the types of items to be shown as current liabilities. These obligations can be divided into those where

1. Both the amount and the payee are known;
2. The payee is known but the amount may have to be estimated;
3. The payee is unknown and the amount may have to be estimated; and
4. The liability has been incurred due to a loss contingency.

Amount and Payee Known

Accounts payable arise primarily from the acquisition of materials and supplies to be used in the production of goods or in conjunction with the providing of services. APB 21 states that payables that arise from transactions with suppliers in the normal course of business and that are due in customary trade terms not to exceed one year may be stated at their face amount rather than at the present value of the required future cash flows.

Notes payable are more formalized obligations that may arise from the acquisition of materials and supplies used in operations or from the use of short-term credit to purchase capital assets (APB 21 also applies to short-term notes payable).

Dividends payable become a liability of the enterprise when the board of directors declares a cash dividend. Since declared dividends are usually paid within a short period of time after the declaration date, they are classified as current liabilities.

Unearned revenues or advances result from customer prepayments for either performance of services or delivery of product. They may be required by the selling enterprise as a condition of the sale or may be made by the buyer as a means of guaranteeing that the seller will perform the desired service or deliver the product. Unearned revenues and advances should be classified as current liabilities at the balance sheet date if the services are to be performed or the products are to be delivered within one year or the **operating cycle,** whichever is longer.

Refundable deposits may be received to cover possible future damage to property. Many utility companies require security deposits. A deposit may be required for the use of a reusable container. Refundable deposits are classified as current liabilities if the firm expects to refund them during the current operating cycle or within one year, whichever is longer.

Accrued liabilities have their origin in the end-of-period adjustment process required by accrual accounting. Commonly accrued liabilities include wages and salaries payable, benefits payable, interest payable, and taxes payable. In addition an employer may have a current obligation for the employer portion of **FICA** tax and **FUTA** (unemployment) tax. Payroll taxes are not legal liabilities until the associated payroll is actually paid.

Agency liabilities result from the legal obligation of the enterprise to act as the collection agent for customer or employee taxes owed to various federal, state, or local government units. Examples of agency liabilities include sales taxes, income taxes withheld from employee paychecks, and employee **FICA** contributions.

Product financing liabilities originate when an entity sells and agrees to repurchase its inventory with the repurchase price equal to the original sales price plus the carrying and financing costs. The purpose of this transaction is to allow the seller to arrange financing on the original purchase of the inventory. The transaction is accounted for as a borrowing rather than as a sale. Chapter 7 provides more information about product financing arrangements.

Current maturing portion of long-term debt is shown as a current liability if the obligation is to be liquidated by using assets classified as current. However, if the currently maturing debt is to be liquidated by using other than current assets (i.e., by using a sinking fund that is properly classified as a noncurrent investment), then these obligations should be classified as long-term liabilities.

Obligations that, by their terms, are due on demand (FAS 78) or will be due on demand within one year (or operating cycle, if longer) from the balance sheet date, even if liquidation is not expected to occur within that period, are classified as current liabilities.

FAS 78 also requires that **long-term obligations that contain call provisions** be classified as current liabilities, if as of the balance sheet date one of the following occurs:

1. The debtor is in violation of the agreement and that violation makes the obligation callable.
2. The debtor is in violation of the agreement and that violation, unless cured within the grace period specified in the agreement, makes the obligation callable.

However, if circumstances arise that effectively negate the creditor's right to call the obligation, the obligation may be classified as long-term. Examples are

1. The creditor has waived the right to call the obligation caused by the debtor's violation or the creditor has subsequently lost the right to demand repayment for more than one year (or operating cycle, if longer) from the balance sheet date.
2. Obligations contain a grace period for remedying the violation, and it is probable that the violation will be cured within the grace period. In these situations, the circumstances must be disclosed.

Long-term obligations that contain subjective acceleration clauses are classified as current liabilities if circumstances (such as recurring losses or liquidity problems) indicate that the clause will be exercised and payment will be due within one year (or one operating cycle). If, instead, the likelihood of the acceleration of the due date were remote, the obligation would be reported as long-term debt. Situations between the two extremes require disclosure (FTB 79-3).

Short-term obligations expected to be refinanced may be classified as noncurrent liabilities if the conditions specified in FAS 6 are met. FAS 6 states that an entity may reclassify currently maturing debt (other than obligations arising from transactions in the normal course of business that are due in customary terms) as long-term, provided that the entity intends to refinance the obligation on a long-term basis **and** its intent is supported by **either** of the following:

1. Post-balance-sheet-date issuance of a long-term obligation or equity securities. After the date of the entity's balance sheet but before that balance sheet is issued, long-term obligations or equity securities have been issued for the purpose of refinancing the short-term obligations on a long-term basis.
2. Refinancing agreement. Before the balance sheet is issued, the entity has entered into a financing agreement that clearly permits the entity to refinance the short-term obligation on a long-term basis on terms that are readily determinable.

If reclassification of the maturing debt is based upon the existence of a refinancing agreement, then FAS 6 requires the following:

1. The refinancing agreement is noncancelable and will not expire within one year or operating cycle of the balance sheet date.
2. The replacement debt will not be callable except for violation of a provision of the refinancing agreement with which compliance is objectively determinable or measurable.
3. The entity is not in violation of the terms of the refinancing agreement.
4. The lender or investor is financially capable of honoring the refinancing agreement.

Under the provisions of FAS 6, the amount of currently maturing debt to be reclassified cannot exceed the amount raised by the replacement debt or equity issuance nor can it exceed the amount specified in the refinancing agreement. If the amount specified in the refinancing agreement can fluctuate, then the maximum amount of debt that can be reclassified is equal to a reasonable estimate of the minimum amount expected to be available on any date from the due date of the maturing obligation to the end of the fiscal year. If no estimate can be made of the minimum amount available under the financing agreement, then none of the maturing debt can be reclassified as long-term. If debt or other agreements limit the ability of the organization to fully utilize the proceeds of the refinancing agreement (for example, a clause in another debt agreement sets a maximum debt-to-equity ratio), then only the amount that can be drawn without violating the limitations expressed in those other agreements can be reclassified to long-term. FIN 8 states that if an entity uses current assets after the balance sheet date to liquidate a current obligation, and then replaces those current assets by issuing either equity securities or long-term debt before the issuance of the balance sheet, the currently maturing debt must still be classified as a current liability.

Payee Known but Amount May Have to Be Estimated

Taxes payable include federal, state, and local income taxes. The amount of income taxes payable is an estimate because the tax laws and rates in effect when the accrual is determined may differ from the tax laws and rates in effect when the taxes ultimately are paid. Temporary differences in recognition and measurement between accounting standards and tax laws create deferred tax liabilities (and deferred tax assets). The portion deemed currently payable must be classified as a current liability. The remaining amount is classified as a long-term liability.

Property taxes payable represent the unpaid portion of an entity's obligation to a state or other taxing authority that arises from ownership of real property. ARB 43, Chapter 10 indicates that the most acceptable method of accounting for property taxes is a monthly accrual of property tax expense during the fiscal period of the taxing authority for which the taxes are levied. The fiscal period of the taxing authority is the fiscal period that includes the assessment or lien date.

A liability for property taxes payable arises when the fiscal year of the taxing authority and the fiscal year of the entity do not coincide or when the assessment or lien date and the actual payment date do not fall within the same fiscal year. For example, XYZ Corporation is a calendar-year corporation that owns real estate in a state that operates on a June 30 fiscal year. In this state, property taxes are assessed and become a lien against property on July 1, although they are not payable until April 1 and August 1 of the next calendar year. XYZ Corporation would accrue an expense and a liability on a monthly basis beginning on July 1. At year-end (December 31), the firm would have an expense for six months' property tax on their income statement and a current liability for the same amount.

Bonus payments may require estimation since the amount of the bonus may be affected by the entity's net income for the year, by the income taxes currently payable, or by other factors. Additional estimation is necessary if bonus payments are accrued on a monthly basis for purposes of interim financial reporting but are determinable only annually by using a formula whose values are uncertain until shortly before payment.

Compensated absences refer to paid vacation, paid holidays, paid sick leave, and other paid leaves of absence. FAS 43 states that an employer must accrue a liability for employee's compensation of future absences if all of the following conditions are met:

1. The employee's right to receive compensation for future absences is attributable to employee services already rendered.
2. The right vests or accumulates.
3. Payment of the compensation is probable.
4. The amount of the payment can be reasonably estimated.

If an employer is required to compensate an employee for unused vacation, holidays, or sick days even if employment is terminated, then the employee's right to this compensation is said to vest. Accrual of a liability for nonvesting rights depends on whether the unused rights expire at the end of the year in which earned or accumulate and are carried forward to succeeding years. If the rights expire, a liability for future absences should not be accrued at year-end because the benefits to be paid in subsequent years would not be attributable to employee services rendered in prior years. If unused rights accumulate and increase the benefits otherwise available in subsequent years, a liability should be accrued at year-end to the extent that it is probable that employees will be paid in subsequent years for the increased benefits attributable to the accumulated rights and the amount can be reasonably estimated.

FAS 43 allows an exception for employee paid sick days that accumulate but do not vest. No accrued liability is required for sick days that only accumulate. However, an accrual may be made. The Board stated that these amounts are rarely material and the low reliability of estimates of future illness coupled with the high cost of developing these estimates indicates that accrual is not necessary. The required accounting should be determined by the employer's actual administration of sick pay benefits. If the employer routinely lets employees take time off when they are not ill and allows that time to be charged as sick pay, then an accrual should be made.

Pay for other employee leaves of absence that represent time off for past services (jury duty, personal days) should be considered compensation subject to accrual. Pay for employee leaves of absence that will provide future benefits and that are not attributable to past services rendered would not be subject to accrual. FAS 43 does not provide guidance as to whether accruals should be based on current pay rates or expected future rates of pay and does not provide guidance regarding discounting of the accrual amounts.

FAS 112 uses the four conditions of FAS 43 to accrue an obligation for postemployment benefits other than pensions. Postemployment benefits other than pensions are benefits paid after termination of employment but before retirement to or on behalf of former or inactive employees, their beneficiaries, and covered dependents. Examples of those benefits are salary continuation agreements, supplemental unemployment compensation, severance benefits, workers' compensation and other disability-related payments, job training or job placement services and continuation of health care or life insurance benefits after employment. If the four conditions in FAS 43 are met, a liability is accrued. If one or more of the conditions are not met, the employer should assess whether a liability should be accrued under FAS 5. If neither FAS 43 nor FAS 5 is applicable because the amount cannot be reasonably estimated, this fact must be disclosed.

Payee Unknown and the Amount May Have to Be Estimated

Sales incentives are usually offered by an enterprise to increase product sales. They may require the purchaser to accumulate a specified number of miles, points, box tops, wrappers, or other proofs of purchase. They may or may not require the payment of a cash amount. If the incentive offer terminates at the end of the current period but has not been completely accounted for, or if it extends into the next accounting period, a current liability for the estimated number of redemptions that are expected in the future period would be recorded. If the incentive offer extends for more than one accounting period, the estimated liability must be divided into a current portion and a long-term portion. See EITF 00-22 and EITF 01-9, included in Chapter 8, for additional information about accounting for and disclosure of sales incentives.

Product warranties providing for repair or replacement of defective products may be sold separately or may be included in the sale price of the product. If the warranty extends into the next accounting period, a current liability for the estimated amount of warranty expense expected in the next period must be recorded. If the warranty spans more than the next period, the estimated liability must be partitioned into a current and long-term portion. FIN 45, discussed more fully later in this chapter, requires disclosure of product warranties in the notes to financial statements. Entities are required to disclose the following information:

1. The nature of the product warranty, including how the warranty arose and the events or circumstances in which the entity must perform under the warranty.
2. The entity's accounting policy and methodology used to determine its liability for the product warranty, including any liability (such as deferred revenue) associated with an extended warranty.
3. A reconciliation of the changes in the aggregate product warranty liability for the reporting period. The reconciliation must include five components: (1) the beginning aggregate balance of the liability, (2) the reductions in the liability caused by payments under the warranty, (3) the increase in the liability for new warranties issued during the period, (4) the change in the liability for adjustments to estimated amounts to be paid under preexisting warranties, and (5) the ending aggregate balance of the liability.
4. The nature and extent of any recourse provisions or available collateral that would enable the entity to recover the amounts paid under the warranties, and an indication (if estimable) of the approximate extent to which the proceeds from recovery or liquidation would be expected to cover the maximum potential amount of future payments under the warranty.
5. The disclosures required by FAS 57 if the warranties are made to benefit related parties. (See Chapter 2 for a discussion of related-party disclosures.)

A proposed FASB staff position would also require the above disclosures for an indemnification clause included by a software vendor-licensor in a software licensing agreement that indemnifies the licensee against liability and damages (including legal defense costs) arising from any claims of patent, copyright, trademark or trade secret infringement by the software vendor's software.

Future product returns are accrued if a buyer has a right to return the product purchased and the sale is recognized in accordance with FAS 48. If an entity is unable to make a reasonable estimate of the amount of future returns, the sale cannot be recognized until the return privilege has expired or conditions permit the loss to be estimated. Examples of factors that might impair the ability to reasonably estimate a loss are

1. Susceptibility of the product to technological or other obsolescence
2. A lengthy period over which returns are permitted
3. Absence of experience with returns on similar products sold to similar markets

4. Sales are few, significant, and have unique terms (rather than a large number of relatively homogeneous sales of small dollar amounts).

Contingencies

FAS 5 defines a **contingency** as an existing condition, situation, or set of circumstances involving uncertainty as to possible gain or loss. The uncertainty will ultimately be resolved when one or more future events occur or fail to occur. FAS 5 defines the different levels of probability as to whether or not future events will confirm the existence of a loss as follows:

1. **Probable**—The future event or events are likely to occur.
2. **Reasonably possible**—The chance of the future event or events occurring is more than remote but less than likely.
3. **Remote**—The chance of the future event or events occurring is slight.

Professional judgment is required to classify the likelihood of the future events occurring. All relevant information that can be acquired concerning the uncertain set of circumstances needs to be obtained and used to determine the classification.

FAS 5 states that a loss must be accrued if **both** of the following conditions are met:

1. It is **probable** that an asset has been impaired or a liability has been incurred at the date of the financial statements.
2. The amount of loss can be reasonably estimated.

Loss contingency. Loss contingencies are recognized only if there is an impairment of an asset or the incurrence of a liability as of the balance sheet date. Examples of possible loss contingencies include

1. Collectibility of receivables
2. Warranty liabilities and product defects
3. Loss due to fire, explosion, or other hazards
4. Expropriation of assets
5. Litigation, claims, and assessments
6. Incurred but not reported (IBNR) claims if the entity insures its risk of loss with a claims-made policy
7. Exposures under multiple-year retrospectively rated insurance contacts
8. Catastrophic losses by insurance and reinsurance entities
9. The contingent obligations under guarantees
10. Obligations under standby letters of credit
11. Repurchase agreements
12. Withdrawal from a multiemployer plan

Events that give rise to loss contingencies that occur after the balance sheet date (i.e., bankruptcy or expropriation) but before issuance of the financial statements may require disclosure so that statement users are not misled. Note disclosures or pro forma financial statements may be prepared as supplemental information to show the effect of the loss.

It is not necessary that a single amount be identified. A range of amounts is sufficient to indicate that some amount of loss has been incurred and should be accrued. The amount accrued is the amount within the range that appears to be the best estimate. If there is no best estimate, the minimum amount in the range should be accrued since it is probable that the loss will be at least this amount (FIN 14). The maximum amount of loss should be disclosed. If future events indicate that the minimum loss originally accrued is inadequate, an additional loss should be accrued in the period when this fact becomes known. This accrual is a change in estimate, not a prior period adjustment.

When a loss is probable and no estimate is possible, these facts should be disclosed in the current period. The accrual of the loss should be made in the earliest period in which the amount of the loss can be estimated. Accrual of that loss in future periods is a change in estimate. It is not a prior period adjustment.

If the occurrence of the loss is reasonably possible, the facts and circumstances of the possible loss and an estimate of the amount, if determinable, should be disclosed. (See also Chapter 2.) If the occurrence of the loss is remote, no accrual or disclosure is usually required.

Unasserted claims or assessments. It is not necessary to disclose loss contingencies for an unasserted claim or assessment where there has been no manifestation of an awareness of possible claim or assessment by a potential claimant unless it is deemed probable that a claim will be asserted and a reasonable possibility of an unfavorable outcome exists. Under the provisions of FAS 5, general or unspecified business risks are not loss contingencies and, therefore, no accrual is necessary. Appropriations of retained earnings may be used for these risks as long as no charge to income is made to establish the appropriation. Disclosure of these business risks may be required under SOP 94-6 (see Chapter 2).

Estimate vs. contingency. Distinguishing between an estimate and a contingency can be difficult because both involve an uncertainty that will be resolved by future events. However, an estimate exists because of uncertainty about the amount of a loss resulting from an event requiring an acknowledged accounting recognition. The event has occurred and the effect is known, but the amount itself is uncertain. For example, depreciation is an estimate, but not a contingency because the actual fact of physical depreciation is acknowledged, although the amount is obtained by an assumed accounting method.

In a contingency, the amount is also usually uncertain, although that is not an essential characteristic. Instead, the uncertainty lies in whether the event has occurred (or will) and what the effect, if any, on the enterprise would be. Collectibility of receivables is a contingency because it is uncertain whether a customer will not pay at a future date, although it is probable that some customers will not pay. Similar logic would hold for obligations related to product warranties. That is, it is uncertain whether a product will fail, but it is probable that some will fail within the warranty period.

Other contingencies are rarely recognized until specific events confirming their existence occur. Every business risks loss by fire, explosion, government expropriation or casualties in the ordinary course of business. To the extent those losses are not (or cannot be) insured, the risks are contingencies. Because those events are often random in their occurrence, uncertainty surrounds whether the future event confirming the loss will or will not take place. The passage of time usually resolves the uncertainty. Until the event confirming the loss occurs (or is probable of occurrence) and the amount of the loss can be reasonably estimated, the potential loss is not recognized in financial statements.

The most difficult area of contingencies is litigation. Accountants must rely on attorneys' assessments concerning the likelihood of such events. Unless the attorney indicates that the risk of loss is remote or slight, or that the loss if it occurs would be immaterial to the company, disclosure in financial statements is necessary and an accrual may also be necessary. For example, in cases where judgments have been entered against the entity, or where the attorney gives a range of expected losses or other amounts and indicates that an unfavorable outcome is probable, accruals of loss contingencies for at least the minimum point of the range must be made. In most cases, however, an estimate of the contingency is unknown and the contingency is reflected only in footnotes.

Guarantees

While disclosures of at least some guarantees had been common under provisions of FAS 5, the economic significance of such arrangements had rarely been measured or disclosed in the past. In late 2002, FASB issued FIN 45, which significantly alters past practice by requiring that the fair value of guarantees be recognized as a liability. Subsequently, FASB has issued two staff positions (FSP) interpreting the guidance of FIN 45.

FIN 45 applies to guarantee contracts that contingently require the guarantor to make payments (either in cash, financial instruments, shares of its stock, other assets, or in services) to the guaranteed party based on any of the following circumstances:

1. Changes in a specified interest rate, security price, commodity price, foreign exchange rate, index of prices or rates, or any other variable, including the occurrence or nonoccurrence of a specified event that is related to an asset or liability of the guaranteed party. For example, the provisions apply to the following:
   a. A financial standby letter of credit
   b. A market value guarantee on either securities (including the common stock of the guaranteed party) or a nonfinancial asset owned by the guaranteed party
   c. A guarantee of the collection of the scheduled contractual cash flows from individual financial assets held by a variable interest entity (VIE)
2. Another entity's failure to perform under an obligating agreement. For example, the provisions apply to a performance standby letter of credit, which obligates the guarantor to make a payment if the specified entity fails to perform its nonfinancial obligation.
3. The occurrence of a specified event or circumstance (an indemnification agreement), such as an adverse judgment in a lawsuit or the imposition of additional taxes due to either a change in the tax law or an adverse interpretation of the tax law, provided that the guarantor is an entity other than an insurance or reinsurance company.
4. The occurrence of specified events under conditions whereby payments are legally available to creditors of the guaranteed party and those creditors may enforce the guaranteed party's claims against the guarantor under the agreement (an indirect guarantee of the indebtedness of others).

When a guarantor enters into a guarantee agreement, it assumes two distinct obligations having different accounting implications. The first, which is a **noncontingent** obligation, is the obligation to stand ready to perform over the term of the guarantee in the event that the specified triggering events or conditions occur. The second obligation, which is a **contingent** obligation, is the obligation to make future payments if those triggering events or conditions occur. At the inception of a guarantee, the guarantor would recognize a liability for **both** the noncontingent and contingent obligations at their fair values. However, in the unusual circumstance that a liability is recognized under FAS 5 for the contingent obligation (i.e., because it is deemed probable of occurrence and reasonable of estimation that the guarantor will pay), the liability to be initially recognized for the noncontingent obligation would only be the portion, if any, of the guarantee's fair value not recognized under FAS 5.

It is important to stress that this does not mean that the guarantor records the entire face amount of the guarantee; rather, it is the **fair value** that would be recognized. When a guarantee is issued in a stand-alone, arm's-length transaction with an unrelated party, the fair value of the guarantee (and thus the amount to be recognized as a liability) is the premium received by the guarantor. When a guarantee is issued as part of another transaction (such as the sale or lease of an asset) or as a contribution to an unrelated party, the fair value of the liability is measured by the premium that would be required by the guarantor to issue the same guarantee in a stand-alone, arm's-length transaction with an unrelated party. In the absence of such stand-alone transactions, an estimate of fair value will result from the application of the expected present value measurements set forth in CON 7. (See Appendix to Chapter 1.)

In practice, if the likelihood that the guarantor will have to perform is judged to be only "possible" or "remote," the only amount to be reported will be the fair value of the **noncontingent** obligation to stand ready to perform. If, however, the contingency is probable of occurrence and can be reasonably estimated under FAS 5, that amount must be reported and the liability to be reported, in total, under the guarantee arrangement will be the greater of (1) the fair value computed as explained above (and illustrated below), or (2) the amount computed in accordance with FAS 5's provisions.

Example of estimating the fair value of a guarantee using CON 7 when recognition under FAS 5 would not be otherwise required

Big Red Company guarantees a $1,000,000 debt of Little Blue Company for the next three years in conjunction with selling equipment to Little Blue. Big Red evaluates its risk of payment as follows:

(1) There is no possibility that Big Red will pay during year 1.
(2) There is a 15% chance that Big Red will pay during year 2. If it has to pay, there is a 30% chance that it will have to pay $500,000 and a 70% chance that it will have to pay $250,000.
(3) There is a 20% chance that Big Red will pay during year 3. If it has to pay, there is a 25% chance that it will have to pay $600,000 and a 75% chance that it will have to pay $300,000.

The expected cash flows are computed as follows:

Year 1	100% chance of paying $0 = $0
Year 2	85% chance of paying $0 and a 15% chance of paying (.30 x $500,000 + .70 x $250,000 =) $325,000 = $48,750
Year 3	80% chance of paying $0 and a 20% chance of paying (.25 x $600,000 + .75 x $300,000 =) $375,000 = $75,000

The present value of the expected cash flows is computed as the sum of the years' probability-weighted cash flows, here assuming an appropriate discount rate of 8%.

Year 1	$0 x 1/1.08 =	$ 0
Year 2	$48,750 x $1/(1.08)^2$ =	41,795
Year 3	$75,000 x $1/(1.08)^3$ =	59,537
Fair value of the guarantee		$101,332

Based on the foregoing, a liability of $101,332 would be recognized at inception. This would reduce the net selling price of the equipment sold to Little Blue, thereby reducing the profit to be reported on the sale transaction.

Example of estimating the fair value of a guarantee using CON 7 when recognition under FAS 5 is also required

Assume the same basic facts as in the foregoing example, but now also assume that it has been determined that there is a 60% likelihood that the buyer will eventually default and, after legal process, Big Red will have to repay debt amounting to $400,000 at the end of the fifth year. Assume also that a likelihood of 60% is deemed to make this contingent obligation "probable" under FAS 5. The present value of that payment is $272,233, but FAS 5 does not address or seemingly anticipate the application of present value methods. Thus, it would appear that accrual of the full $400,000 expected loss is required, unaffected by expected timing or by the probability

(60%, in this example) that it will occur. Since this amount exceeds the amount computed under FIN 45, no additional amount would be recognized in connection with the noncontingent obligation to stand ready to perform.

If, instead of the immediate foregoing facts, the probable repayments were estimated to be $75,000, then the liabilities to be recognized would total $101,322, of which $75,000 would be required to satisfy the provisions of FAS 5, and the incremental amount, $26,332 would be attributed to the noncontingent obligation.

The entry to record the liability depends upon the circumstances under which the guarantee arose. If the guarantee was issued in a stand-alone transaction for a premium, the offset would be to the asset accepted for the premium's payment (most likely, cash or a receivable). If the guarantee was issued in conjunction with the sale of assets, the proceeds would be allocated between the sale of the asset and the guarantee obligation, so that the profit (loss) on the sale of the asset would be reduced (increased). If the guarantee was issued in conjunction with the formation of a business accounted for under the equity method, the offset would be an increase in the carrying amount of the investment. If the guarantee was issued to an unrelated party for no consideration, an immediate expense would be recognized. If a residual value guarantee was provided by a lessee-guarantor, the offset would be reported as prepaid rent and then amortized over the term of the lease to rent expense. The residual value of equipment by the manufacturer is recognized by the manufacturer as an asset (included in the seller/lessor's net investment in lease).

After initial recognition, the liability is adjusted as the guarantor either is released from risk or is subject to increased risk. FIN 45 does not specify the accounting for guarantees subsequent to initial recognition, and there is no requirement to reassess the fair value of the guarantee after inception. In fact, according to FSP 45-2, *Whether FASB Interpretation No. 45, "Guarantor's Accounting and Disclosure Requirements for Guarantees, Including Indirect Guarantees of Indebtedness of Others," Provides Support for Subsequently Accounting for a Guarantor's Liability at Fair Value,* FIN 45 only addresses measurement of a guarantor's liability at the inception of the guarantee and fair value should only be used in subsequent accounting for the guarantee if the use of that method can be justified under other authoritative guidance. FIN 45 cannot be cited to support adjustments to fair value subsequent to initial recognition.

However, if the guarantor is subsequently released from risk, that logically could be recognized in one of three ways, in the authors' opinion, although no guidance is provided by FIN 45. First, the liability could simply be written off at its expiration or settlement. Second, the liability could be amortized systematically over the guarantee period. Third, the liability might be adjusted to reflect changing fair value, which presumably declines over time as the risk of having to perform decreases. Furthermore, changes dictated by the provisions of FAS 5 (e.g., as a previously "remote" contingency becomes a "probable" one) must be accounted for under that standard, apart from the requirements of FIN 45.

FIN 45 does *not* apply to

1. Commercial letters of credit and other loan commitments
2. Subordination arrangements in securitization transactions
3. A lessee's guarantee of the residual value of the leased property
4. A guarantee contract or an indemnification agreement that is issued by either an insurance or a reinsurance company
5. Contingent rents
6. Vendor rebates (by the guarantor) based on either the sales revenues of or the number of units sold by the guaranteed party.
7. Guarantees that prevent the guarantor from recognizing either the sale of the asset underlying the guarantee or the profits from that sale.

8. Guarantees arising from pension plans, vacation pay arrangement, deferred compensation contracts, and stock issued to employees.

FIN 45's requirement to recognize an initial liability does not apply to the following types of guarantees (i.e., these guarantees are subject only to FIN 45's disclosure requirements):

1. A guarantee that is accounted for as a derivative instrument at fair value
2. A contract that guarantees the functionality of nonfinancial assets that are owned by the guaranteed party (product warranties)
3. Contingent consideration in a business combination
4. A guarantee that requires the guarantor to issue its own equity shares
5. A guarantee by an original lessee that has become secondarily liable under a new lease that relieved the original lessee of the primary obligation under the original lease
6. A guarantee issued between parents and their subsidiaries or between corporations under common control
7. A parent's guarantee of a subsidiary's debt to a third party
8. A subsidiary's guarantee of a parent's debt to a third party or the debt of another subsidiary of the parent
9. Software licenses which contain an "indemnification clause" protecting the licensee from liabilities and damages that might arise if the licensor's software is subject to a claim of patent, copyright, or trade secret infringement (per FSP 45-2, *Accounting for Intellectual Property Infringement Indemnifications under FASB Interpretation No. 45, "Guarantor's Accounting and Disclosure requirements for Guarantees, Including Indirect Guarantees of Indebtedness of Others"*).

A guarantor is now required to disclose the following information about each guarantee, or each group of similar guarantees, even if the likelihood of the guarantor's having to make any payments under the guarantee were deemed remote:

1. The nature of the guarantee, including how the guarantee arose and the events or circumstances that would require the guarantor to perform under the guarantee
2. The maximum potential amount of future payments (undiscounted) under the guarantee
3. The carrying amount of the liability, if any, for the guarantor's obligations under the guarantee, including any amount recognized under FAS 5
4. The nature and extent of any recourse provisions or available collateral that would enable the guarantor to recover the amounts paid under the guarantee, and an indication of the approximate extent to which the proceeds from recoveries or liquidation would be expected to cover the maximum potential amount of future payments under the guarantee
5. The fair value of financial guarantees issued, if the entity is required to disclose the fair value of financial instruments under the provisions of FAS 107 as amended by FAS 126. (See Chapter 6 for a discussion of which entities are required to disclose the fair value of financial instruments.)
6. The disclosures required by FAS 57 if the guarantees are made to benefit related parties. (See Chapter 2 for a discussion of related-party disclosures.)

Offsetting of Assets and Liabilities

APB 10 states that offsetting of assets and liabilities is improper except where a right of setoff exists. A right of setoff is a debtor's legal right to discharge debt owed to another party by applying against the debt an amount the other party owes to the debtor. FIN 39 and FIN 41 describe certain conditions, which if met, allow but do not require an entity to offset the amounts recognized. The entity's choice to offset or not must be applied consistently. (FIN 39 and FIN 41 are discussed further in Chapter 2.)

EMERGING ISSUES TASK FORCE ISSUES SUMMARIES

85-20 Recognition of Fees for Guaranteeing a Loan (partially nullified by FASB Intepretation 45)

A guarantor should perform ongoing assessments of the probability of loss related to the guarantee and recognize a liability if the conditions in FAS 5 are met. (FIN 45 requires initial recognition of the stand-ready obligation under the guarantee. The contingent aspect of the guarantee would be recognized if the conditions in FAS 5 are met.)

86-5 Classifying Demand Notes with Repayment Terms

An obligation is considered due on demand even if a debt agreement specifies repayment terms if the creditor can demand payment at any time. For example, for an agreement that says "due in monthly installments of principal and interest...or on demand, whichever is earlier," the obligation is a current liability.

86-15 Increasing-Rate Debt

Notes that mature in three months but can be continually extended for up to five years are known as "increasing-rate notes." The outstanding term of the debt should be estimated after considering plans, ability and intent to service the debt. Based upon this term, the borrower's periodic interest rate should be determined by the use of the interest method.

Debt interest costs should be amortized over the estimated outstanding term of the debt. Any excess accrued interest resulting from paying the debt before the estimated maturity date is an adjustment of interest expense. It is not an extraordinary item under FAS 4.

The classification of the debt as to current or noncurrent should be based on the source of repayment. Thus, this classification need not be consistent with the period used to determine the periodic interest cost. For example, the time frame used for the estimated outstanding term of the debt could be a year or less, but because of a planned long-term refinancing agreement the noncurrent classification could be used.

86-30 Classification of Obligations When a Violation Is Waived by the Creditor

A borrower violates a covenant of a long-term debt agreement on one of the quarterly or semiannual compliance dates, giving the lender the right to call the debt. If the lender waives that right for a period greater than one year (but retains the requirements to meet the covenant in the future), the borrower should classify the debt as noncurrent unless both (1) a covenant violation has occurred at the balance sheet date or would have occurred absent a loan modification and (2) it is probable that the borrower will be unable to comply with the covenant at measurement dates within the next twelve months.

93-14 Accounting for Multiple-Year Retrospectively Rated Insurance Contracts by Insurance Enterprises and Other Enterprises (also see FASB Interpretation 45)

An entity that enters into a multiple-year retrospectively rated contract with an insurance company should recognize a liability to the extent that it has an obligation to pay cash (or other consideration) to the insurer that would not have had to be paid if it were not for the experience under the contract. The amount recognized in the current period is the total contract costs as of the reporting date with and without the experience under the contact. The amount recognized should include premium adjustments, settlement adjustments, and impairments of coverage. However, if the insurance policy does not transfer risk, the policy premiums are accounted for as a deposit by the insured. Special provisions apply if the insured could terminate the contract prior to the end of its term and that termination would change the amounts paid.

95-22 Balance Sheet Classification of Borrowings Outstanding under Revolving Credit Agreements That Include Both a Subjective Acceleration Clause and a Lockbox Agreement

This consensus applies to borrowings outstanding under a revolving credit agreement that includes both a subjective acceleration clause and a requirement to maintain a lockbox into which the borrower's customers send remittances that are then used to reduce the debt outstanding. These borrowings are short-term obligations and are classified as current liabilities unless the entity has the intent and ability to refinance the revolving credit agreement on a long-term basis (i.e., the conditions in FAS 6 are met). However, if the lockbox is a "springing" lockbox, which is a lockbox agreement in which remittances from the borrower's customers are forwarded to its general bank account and do not reduce the debt outstanding until and unless the lender exercises the subjective acceleration clause, the obligations are long-term since the remittances do not automatically reduce the debt outstanding if the acceleration clause has not been exercised.

00-23 Issues Related to the Accounting for Stock Compensation under APB Opinion No. 25 and FASB Interpretation No. 44

If a company grants a stock option to an employee and guarantees that if the option does not have an intrinsic value of at least $X at a future date, the company will pay a bonus equal to the shortfall, the "guaranteed" minimum amount should be recognized as compensation expense and a bonus liability over the period of service. Any amount recognized as a bonus liability that exceeds the amount paid to the employee should be reclassified to equity. The recognized cost should not be reversed unless the employee fails to fulfill his or her service obligation.

If a company grants a stock option to an employee and loans money to that employee at the same time, agreeing that the loan will be forgiven over the next three years unless the option has an intrinsic value of $X, the arrangement should be accounted for on a combined basis with the recognition of compensation cost over the service period equal to the "guaranteed" minimum (generally, the loan amount). Any amount of the loan that an employee repays as a result of the performance of the stock underlying the options should be credited to equity. The recognized cost should not be reversed unless the employee fails to fulfill a service obligation.

If a contingent cash bonus and a stock option award are granted at the same time, but the payment of the cash bonus does not depend upon the exercise of the stock option, the cash bonus should be accounted for as a separate element of compensation. For example, if the cash bonus will be paid only if the stock option vests and the stock price exceeds the exercise price at the vesting date, the cash bonus is a separate element of compensation because the bonus will be paid regardless of whether the option is exercised.

Chapter 17 provides additional discussion of this EITF Issue.

03-3 Applicability of EITF *Abstracts*, Topic No. D-79 to Claims-Made Insurance Policies

If a claims-made insurance policy contains a retroactive provision, the retroactive and prospective provisions of the policy should be accounted for separately, if practicable. If it is not practicable to separate those provisions, the claims-made insurance policy should be accounted for entirely as a retroactive contract. A claims-made insurance policy that contains no retroactive provisions should be accounted for on a prospective basis.

A claims-made insurance policy that provides coverage for specific, known claims that were reportable by the insured to the insurance carrier prior to the policy period contains a retroactive provision. The italicized phrase would encompass asserted claims, known unasserted claims, and any known previous event or circumstance that might result in a specific claim (whether asserted or unasserted), regardless of whether the insured has recognized a loss contingency for those claims. It also includes claims that were not reported, but would have been reportable had a claims-made policy been in place in a prior period. A recognized liability for IBNR (claims for losses related to events that the insured is not specifically aware of but expects to be reported) generally would not be determinative in concluding that the claims-made insurance policy contains a retroactive provision.

The Task Force also provided a list of conditions indicating that a claims-made insurance policy does not contain a retroactive provision and, therefore, should be accounted for on a prospective basis.

03-8 Accounting for Claims-Made Insurance and Retroactive Insurance Contracts by the Insured Entity

This was issued to codify and conform the guidance formerly found in

EITF Topic D-79	Accounting for Retroactive Insurance Contracts Purchased by Entities other than Insurance Enterprises to Claims-Made Insurance Policies
EITF 86-12	Accounting by Insureds for Claims-Made Insurance Policies
EITF 03-3	Applicability of EITF Abstracts Topic No. D-79

The EITF reached consensuses on a number of matters pertaining to "claims-made" insurance polices. First, when insurance is purchased which will provide coverage for an occurrence of a prior period, and a contingent loss had been recorded per FAS 5, the purchased retroactive insurance contracts that indemnify the insured should be accounted for in a manner similar to the manner in which retroactive reinsurance contracts are accounted for under FAS 113. The amounts paid will be expensed immediately, while a receivable will be established for the expected recoveries related to the underlying insured event. If the receivable exceeds the amounts paid for the insurance, the resulting gain is to be deferred. If the amounts and timing of the insurance recoveries can be reasonably estimated, the deferred gain should be amortized using the interest method over the estimated period over which the entity expects to recover substantially all amounts due under the terms of the insurance contract. If reasonable estimation is not possible, however, the proportion of actual recoveries to total estimated recoveries will be used to determine the amount of the amortization. Immediate gain recognition and liability derecognition are not appropriate because the liability has not been extinguished, and offsetting conditions set forth by FIN 39 would not be met.

Second, EITF concluded that a claims-made insurance policy contains a retroactive provision if it provides coverage for specific, known claims that were reportable prior to the policy period. Those include asserted claims, known unasserted claims, and any known previous event or circumstances that might result in a specific claim (whether asserted or unasserted), regardless of whether the insured has recognized a loss contingency for those claims. If a claims-made insurance policy contains such a provision, the retroactive and prospective provisions must be accounted for separately, if practicable. If it is not practicable to separate the provisions, the claims-made policy should be accounted for entirely as a retroactive contract in accordance with FAS 113.

The consensus cites several factors to be considered in assessing whether a claims-made policy does or does not contain retroactive provisions.

Third, EITF reached a consensus that FAS 5 requires insured entities (except for those within the scope of FAS 113), including those that use a claims-made approach for insuring certain risks, to recognize a liability for the probable losses from IBNR claims and incidents, if both the pertinent criteria of FAS 5 are met. Unless the conditions of FIN 39 are met, however, offsetting prepaid insurance and receivables for expected recoveries from insurers against a recognized IBNR liability or the liability incurred as a result of a past insurable event would not be appropriate.

In some instances, it would not be possible to reasonably estimate IBNR claims. EITF rejected a suggestion that the cost of "tail" coverage insurance could be used as a surrogate for this estimate. However, it concluded that if the insured entity had the unilateral option to purchase tail coverage at a premium not to exceed a specified fixed maximum, then the insured entity could record a receivable for expected insurance recoveries for the portion of the IBNR liability that is insurable under the tail coverage. EITF agreed that the purchase of tail coverage does not eliminate the need to determine if an additional liability should be accrued because of policy limits or other factors.

Fourth, regarding interim financial reporting, EITF reached a consensus that when the entity's fiscal year and policy year coincide, an appropriate method would be to recognize expense through a combination of (1) accruing the IBNR liability, (2) accruing any expected increase in insurance recoverables, and (3) amortizing the insurance premium on a pro rata basis over the year. The liability for any unusual claims or incidents, as well as any applicable insurance recoverable related thereto, would be recognized in the interim period in which they become known.

Consistent with GAAP for interim reporting, the approach treats usual recurring losses as integral to annual reporting, and, therefore, any expected changes in the IBNR liability and related insurance recoverables that are not related to specific events can be spread over the entire year. However, material unusual losses must be accounted for as discrete items and recognized as they occur. This assumes the recurring purchase of a claims-made insurance policy with a one-year term and the payment of premiums on the first day of each policy year. Additional guidance is also provided regarding other accounting matters, including changes in estimates during the reporting period.

03-12 Impact of FASB Interpretation No. 45, *Guarantor's Accounting and Disclosure Requirements for Guarantees, Including Indirect Guarantees of Indebtedness of Others*, on EITF Issue No. 95-1, *Revenue Recognition on Sales with a Guaranteed Minimum Resale Value*

EITF Abstracts had been erroneously changed to indicate that FIN 45 partially nullified EITF 95-1. FIN 45 does not apply to a guarantee for which the underlying is related to an asset of the guarantor. The residual value of equipment guaranteed by the manufacturer is recognized by the manufacturer as an asset (included in the seller/lessor's net investment in the lease); thus, the accounting prescribed in EITF 95-1 is unaffected by FIN 45.

D-79 Accounting for Retroactive Insurance Contracts Purchased by Entities other than Insurance Enterprises

This announcement discusses how a noninsurance entity should account for a purchased retroactive insurance policy if the purchased policy covers a past event for which the entity has recognized a liability in accordance with FAS 5. The insurance policy does not extinguish the entity's liability and it meets the indemnification against loss or liability conditions of FAS 5. The amount paid for the retroactive policy should be reported as a receivable to the extent that the amount does not exceed the recorded liabilities relating to the underlying insured event. If the recorded liabilities exceed the amounts paid for the insurance, the insurance receivable should be increased to reflect the resulting gain deferred (i.e., the difference). If the amounts and timing of the insurance recoveries can be reasonably estimated, the deferred gain should be amortized using the interest method over the estimated period over which the entity expects to recover substantially all amounts due under the terms of the insurance contract. If the amounts and timing of the insurance recoveries cannot be reasonably estimated, then the proportion of actual recoveries to total estimated recoveries should be used to determine the amount of the amortization. Immediate gain recognition is not appropriate because the liability has not been extinguished (the entity is not entirely relieved of its obligation). The effect of this announcement is to apply FAS 113 to noninsurance companies in this circumstance. (FAS 113 is discussed further in "Insurance" section of Chapter 24.)

If the purchased insurance policy includes coverage for legal and other costs, the accounting for legal and other costs should be consistent between the asset and the liability. That is, if the entity's accounting policy is to accrue for those costs, then the insurance receivable also should reflect those costs. If an entity's accounting policy is not to accrue for those costs, then the insurance receivable should not reflect those costs.

STATEMENTS OF POSITION

96-1 Environmental Remediation Liabilities

This SOP includes a very detailed description of relevant laws, remediation provisions and other pertinent information, which is useful to auditors as well as to reporting entities. In terms of accounting guidance, the SOP provides that FAS 5 is the principal standard to be interpreted in the context of environmental obligations (e.g., determining the threshold for accrual of a liability, etc.) and its sets "benchmarks" for liability recognition. The benchmarks for the accrual and evaluation of the estimated liability (i.e., the stages which are deemed to be important to ascertaining the existence and amount of the liability) are

1. The identification and verification of an entity as a potentially responsible party (PRP), since the SOP stipulates that accrual should be based on the premise that expected costs will be borne by only the "participating potentially responsible parties" and that the "recalcitrant, unproven and unidentified" PRP will not contribute to costs of remediation
2. The receipt of a "unilateral administrative order"
3. Participation, as a PRP, in the remedial investigation/feasibility study (RI/FS)
4. Completion of the feasibility study
5. Issuance of the Record of Decision (RoD)
6. The remedial design through operation and maintenance, including postremediation monitoring

The amount of the liability that is to be accrued is affected by the entity's allocable share of liability for a specific site, and by its share of the amounts related to the site that will not be paid by the other PRP or the government. The categories of costs to be included in the accrued liability include incremental direct costs of the remediation effort itself, as well as the costs of compensation and benefits for employees directly involved in the remediation effort. The SOP indicates that costs are to be estimated based on existing laws and technologies, and are not to be discounted to estimated present values unless timing of cash payments is fixed or reliability determinable.

Incremental direct costs will include such items as fees paid to outside law firms for work related to the remediation effort, costs relating to completing the RI/FS, fees to outside consulting and engineering firms for site investigations and development of remedial action plans and remedial actions, costs of contractors performing remedial actions, government oversight costs and past costs, the cost of machinery and equipment dedicated to the remedial actions that do not have an alternative use, assessments by a PRP group covering costs incurred by the group in dealing with a site, and the costs of operation and maintenance of the remedial action, including costs of postremediation monitoring required by remedial action plan.

As was first set forth by EITF 93-5, *Accounting for Environmental Liabilities*, the SOP states that potential recoveries cannot be offset against the estimated liability, and further notes that any recovery recognized as an asset should be reflected at fair value, which implies that only the present value of future recoveries can be recorded. It also stipulates that environmental clean up costs are not unusual in nature, and thus cannot be shown as extraordinary items in the income statement. Furthermore, it is presumed that the costs are operating in nature, and thus cannot normally be included in "other income and expense" category of the income statement, either. Disclosure of accounting policies regarding recognition of liability and of related asset (for recoveries from third parties) are also needed, where pertinent.

13 LONG-TERM DEBT

PERSPECTIVE AND ISSUES

Long-term liabilities are liabilities that will be paid or otherwise settled over a period of more than one year, or if longer, more than one operating cycle. This chapter discusses accounting for bonds, long-term notes payable, mandatorily redeemable shares, and obligations to issue or repurchase the entity's own shares. Other common types of long-term liabilities are lease obligations (Chapter 14), deferred income taxes (Chapter 15), pension and deferred compensation plan obligations (Chapter 16), and contingencies (Chapter 12).

The appropriate valuation of long-term debt at the date of issuance is the present value of the future payments, using an interest rate commensurate with the risks involved. In many situations the interest rate commensurate with the risks involved is the rate stated in the agreement between the borrower and the creditor. However, in other situations the debt may be noninterest-bearing, or the rate stated in the agreement may not be indicative of the rate applicable to a borrower having similar creditworthiness and debt having similar terms. In other words, the rate stated in the agreement is not commensurate with the risks involved. To reflect the liability at the appropriate value, interest must be imputed at the market rate, and the resulting premium or discount is amortized as interest over the life of the agreement (per APB 21).

Debt remains on the books of the debtor until it is extinguished. In most cases, a debt is extinguished at maturity, when the required principal and interest payments have been made and the debtor has no further obligation to the creditor. In other cases, the debtor may desire to extinguish the debt before its maturity. For example, if market interest rates are falling, a debtor may chose to issue debt at the new lower rate and use the proceeds to retire older higher-interest-rate debt. FAS 140 states that a debt is extinguished if either of two conditions is met.

1. The debtor pays the creditor and is relieved of its obligation for the liability.
2. The debtor is legally released from being the primary obligor under the liability, either judicially or by the creditor.

FASB is currently pursuing a project addressing several liability extinguishment issues. Among these is the possible clarification or replacement of the FAS 140 criterion, above, that directs extinguishment accounting when the debtor is "legally released from being the primary obligor," since this expression is not legally defined. The project will also consider whether FAS 140 criteria should be applied to liabilities which are not within the scope of that standard.

FAS 140 ended the once-acceptable practice of removing debt from the balance sheet via an in-substance defeasance of debt. In-substance defeasances recognized prior to the date FAS 140 became effective were allowed to remain off the balance sheet.

If a debtor experiences financial difficulties before the debt is paid, a creditor may need to recognize an impairment of the debt. Under FAS 114, an impairment of the debt is recognized when the present value of the expected future cash flows discounted at the debt's original effective interest rate is less than the recorded investment in the debt. If for economic or legal reasons related to the debtor's financial difficulties, the creditor grants the debtor concessions that would not otherwise have been granted, the debtor must determine how to recognize the effects of the troubled debt restructuring (FAS 15).

Some debt is issued with terms that allow it to be converted to an equity instrument (common or preferred stock) at a future date. When issued, under current GAAP, no value is apportioned to the conversion feature. When the debt is converted, the stock issued is generally valued at the carrying value of the debt (APB 14). In certain situations, a debtor will modify the conversion privileges after issuance of the debt in order to induce prompt conversion of the debt into equity, in which case the debtor must recognize an expense for this consideration (FAS 84).

Debt can also be issued with stock warrants, which allow the holder to purchase a stated number of common shares at a certain price within a defined time period. If debt is issued with detachable warrants, the proceeds of issuance are allocated between the two financial instruments (APB 14).

FAS 150 requires an issuer to report (1) mandatorily redeemable shares, (2) financial instruments that obligate the issuer to repurchase its shares, and (3) financial instruments that obligate the issuer to issue a variable number of shares as liabilities. FAS 150 was effective for instruments issued after May 31, 2003. For previously issued instruments, FAS 150 was effective for fiscal periods beginning after June 15, 2003 (except for mandatorily redeemable shares of nonpublic companies, as to which it became effective for periods beginning after December 15, 2003).

The issuance of FAS 150 concluded the first phase of the Board's redeliberations of an Exposure Draft which had been issued several years earlier. Other aspects of the proposed standards would require a compound instrument, such as convertible debt or debt issued with warrants, to be divided into its liability components and equity components, with the components separately presented in the balance sheet. FASB believes that such a presentation provides a more faithful representation of the rights and obligations embedded in compound instruments than does the current practice of presenting the instruments entirely as liabilities or entirely as equity. A discussion of the proposed standard is found later in this chapter.

FASB is also pursuing a project examining whether long-term debt should continue to be measured at the amount recorded at the date of issuance, reduced by payments subsequently received and adjusted by amortization. FASB has declared that its long-term goal is to have all financial liabilities recognized in the balance sheet at their fair values, rather than at amounts based on their historical cost. This very contentious FASB project is discussed at the end of this chapter.

Through-put contracts, take-or-pay contracts, and other unconditional purchase obligations are sometimes used instead of debt to finance a capital project or a joint venture. These agreements may or may not be recognized on the balance sheet. Entities are required to disclose information about those types of obligations in the notes to the financial statements (FAS 47).

Short-term obligations that are expected to be refinanced and therefore classified as long-term debt per FAS 6 are discussed in Chapter 12.

Sources of GAAP

APB	*FAS*	*FIN*	*FTB*	*EITF*	*SOP*	*FSP*
14, 21, 26	5, 6, 15, 47, 84, 114, 118, 140, 145, 150	8	79-3, 80-1, 80-2, 81-6	85-17, 85-29, 86-36, 87-19, 88-18, 90-19, 94-8, 96-19, 96-22, 98-5, 99-1, 00-27, 01-1, 02-4, 02-15, 03-7,D-10, D-23, D-61, D-98	97-1	129-1, 150-1, 150-2, 150-3

DEFINITIONS OF TERMS

Amortization. The process of allocating an amount to expense over the periods benefited.

Bond. A written agreement whereby a borrower agrees to pay a sum of money at a designated future date plus periodic interest payments at the stated rate.

Bond issue costs. Costs related to issuing a bond (i.e., legal, accounting, underwriting fees, printing, and registration costs).

Book value approach. Recording the stock issued from a bond conversion at the carrying value of the bonds converted.

Callable bond. A bond in which the issuer reserves the right to call and retire the bond prior to its maturity.

Carrying value. The face amount of a debt issue increased or decreased by the applicable unamortized premium or discount plus unamortized issue costs.

Collateral. Asset(s) pledged to settle the obligation to repay a loan.

Convertible debt. Debt that may be converted into common or preferred stock at the holder's option after specific criteria are met.

Covenant. A clause in a debt contract written for the protection of the lender that outlines the rights and actions of the parties involved when certain conditions occur (e.g., when the debtor's current ratio declines beyond a specified level).

Debenture. Long-term debt not secured by collateral.

Discount. Created when a debt instrument is issued for less than face value and occurs when the stated rate on the instrument is less than the market rate at the time of issue.

Effective interest method. Amortizing the discount or premium to interest expense so as to result in a constant rate of interest when applied to the amount of debt outstanding at the beginning of any given period.

Effective rate. See **market rate**.

Face value. The stated amount or principal due on the maturity date.

Freestanding financial instrument. A financial instrument that is entered into separately and apart from any of the entity's other financial instruments or equity transactions, or that is entered into in conjunction with some other transaction and is legally detachable and separately exercisable.

Imputation. The process of interest rate approximation that is accomplished by examining the circumstances under which the note was issued.

Issuer. The entity that issued a financial instrument or may be required under the terms of a financial instrument to issue its equity shares.

Long-term debt. Probable future sacrifices of economic benefits arising from present obligations that are not currently payable within one year or the operating cycle of the business, whichever is longer.

Mandatorily redeemable shares. Any of various financial instruments issued in the form of shares that embody an unconditional obligation requiring the issuer to redeem the instrument by transferring its assets at a specified or determinable date (or dates) or upon an event that is certain to occur.

Market rate. The current rate of interest available for obligations issued under the same terms and conditions by an issuer of similar credit standing.

Market value approach. Recording the stock issued from a bond conversion at the current market price of the bonds converted or the stock issued.

Maturity date. The date on which the face value (principal) of the bond or note becomes due.

Maturity value. See **face value**.

Monetary value. What the fair value of the cash, shares, or other instruments that a financial instrument obligates the issuer to convey to the holder would be at the settlement date under specified market conditions.

Net settlement. A form of settling a financial instrument under which the party with a loss delivers to the party with a gain cash (net cash settlement) or shares of stock (net share settlement) with a current fair value equal to the gain.

Physical settlement. A form of settling a financial instrument under which (1) the party designated in the contract as the buyer delivers the full stated amount of cash or other financial instruments to the seller and (2) the seller delivers the full stated number of shares of stock or other financial instruments or nonfinancial instruments to the buyer.

Premium. Created when a debt instrument is issued for more than its face value and occurs when the stated rate on the instrument is greater than the market rate at the time of issue.

Principal. See **face value**.

Secured debt. Debt that has collateral to satisfy the obligation if not repaid (e.g., a mortgage on specific property).

Serial bond. Debt whose face value matures in installments.

Stated rate. The interest rate written on the face of the debt instrument.

Straight-line method. The method of amortizing the premium or discount to interest expense such that there is an even allocation of interest expense over the life of the debt.

Take-or-pay contract. A contract in which a purchaser of goods agrees to pay specified fixed or minimum amounts periodically in return for products, even if delivery is not taken. It results from a project financing arrangement where the project produces the products.

Through-put agreement. An agreement similar to a take-or-pay contract except a service is provided by the project under the financing arrangement.

Troubled debt restructure. Occurs when the creditor, for economic or legal reasons related to the debtor's financial difficulties, grants a concession to the debtor (deferment or reduction of interest or principal) that it would not otherwise consider.

Unconditional purchase obligation. An obligation to transfer a fixed or minimum amount of funds in the future or to transfer goods or services at fixed or minimum prices.

Yield rate. See **market rate**.

CONCEPTS, RULES, AND EXAMPLES

Notes and Bonds

Notes are a common form of exchange in business transactions for cash, property, goods, and services. Notes represent debt issued to a single investor without intending for the debt to be broken up among many investors. A note's maturity, usually lasting one to seven years, tends to be shorter than that of a bond.

Bonds are primarily used to borrow funds from the general public or institutional investors when a contract for a single amount (a note) is too large for any one lender to supply. Dividing up the amount needed into $1,000 or $10,000 units makes it easier to sell the bonds. Bonds also result from a single agreement.

Notes and bonds share common characteristics. They both are promises to pay a sum of money at a designated maturity date plus periodic interest payments at a stated rate. They include a written agreement stating the amount of the **principal,** the interest rate, when the interest and principal are to be paid, and the restrictive **covenants,** if any, that must be met.

The interest rate is affected by many factors, including the cost of money, the business risk factors, and the inflationary expectations associated with the business. The **stated rate** on a note or bond often differs from the **market rate** at the time of issuance. When this occurs, the present value of the interest and principal payments will differ from the maturity, or **face value**. (For a complete discussion of present value techniques see Chapter 1.) If the market rate exceeds the stated rate, the cash proceeds will be less than the face value of the debt because the present value of the total interest and principal payments discounted back to the present yields an amount that is less than the face value. Because an investor is rarely willing to pay more than the present value, the bonds must be issued at a discount. The **discount** is the difference between the issuance price (present value) and the face, or stated, value of the bonds. This discount is then amortized over the life of the bonds to increase the recognized interest expense so that the total amount of the expense represents the actual bond yield. When the stated rate exceeds the market rate, the bond will sell for more than its face value (at a **premium**) to bring the effective rate to the market rate. Amortization of the premium over the life of the bonds will decrease the total interest expense.

When the market and stated rates are equivalent at the time of issuance, no discount or premium exists and the instrument will sell at its face value. Changes in the market rate subsequent to issuance are irrelevant in determining the discount or premium or its **amortization**.

All commitments to pay (and receive) money at a determinable future date are subject to present value techniques and, if necessary, interest imputation with the exception of the following:

1. Normal accounts payable due within one year
2. Amounts to be applied to purchase price of goods or services or that provide security to an agreement (e.g., advances, progress payments, security deposits, and retainages)
3. Transactions between parent and subsidiary

4. Obligations payable at some indeterminable future date (e.g., warranties)
5. Lending and depositor savings activities of financial institutions whose primary business is lending money
6. Transactions where interest rates are affected by prescriptions of a governmental agency (e.g., revenue bonds, tax exempt obligations, etc.)

APB 21 specifies when and how interest is to be imputed when a debt is noninterest-bearing or the stated rate is not reasonable. APB 21 divides debt into three categories for discussion. The diagram below illustrates the accounting treatment for the three types of debt.

ACCOUNTING FOR MONETARY ASSETS AND LIABILITIES

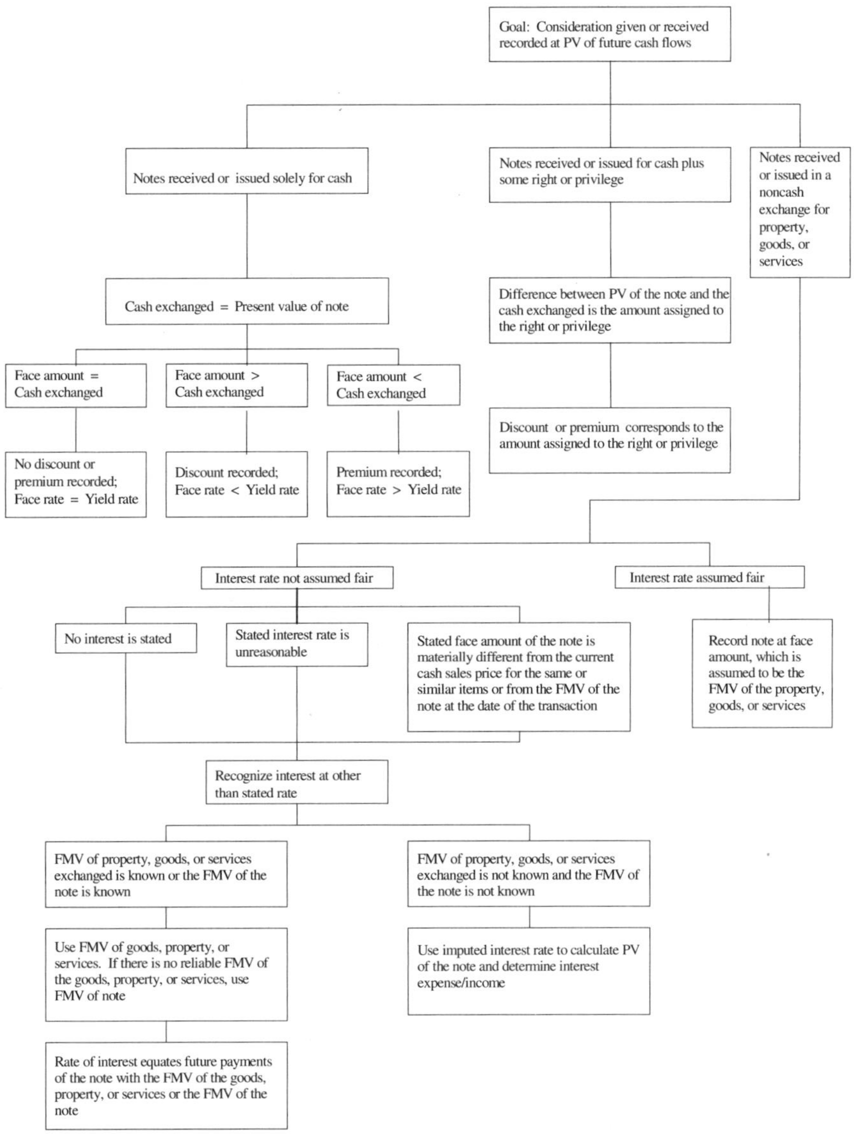

Notes issued solely for cash. When a note is issued solely for cash, its present value is assumed to be equal to the cash proceeds. The interest rate is that rate that equates the cash proceeds to the amounts to be paid in the future. For example, a $1,000 note due in three years that sells for $889 has an implicit rate of 4% ($1,000 x .889, where .889 is the present value factor of a lump sum at 4% for three years). This rate is to be used when amortizing the discount.

In most situations, a bond is issued at a price other than its face value. The amount of the cash exchanged is equal to the total of the present value of the interest and principal payments. The difference between the cash proceeds and the face value is recorded as a premium if the cash proceeds are greater than the face value or a discount if they are less. The journal entry to record a bond issued at a premium follows:

Cash	(proceeds)	
Bonds payable		(face value)
Premium on bonds payable		(difference)

Example of bonds issued for cash

Enterprise Autos issues $100,000 of 10-year bonds bearing interest at 10%, paid semiannually, at a time when the market demands a 12% return from issuers with similar credit standings. The proceeds of the bond issuance would be $88,500, which is computed as follows:

Present value of 20 semiannual interest payments of $5,000 discounted at 12% (6% semiannually: factor = 11.4699)	$57,300
Present value of $100,000 due in 10 years, discounted at 12% compounded semiannually (factor = .31180)	31,200
Present value of bond issuance	$88,500

The journal entry would be

Cash	88,500	
Discount on bonds payable	11,500	
Bonds payable		100,000

Notes issued for cash and a right or privilege. Often when a note bearing an unrealistic rate of interest is issued in exchange for cash, an additional right or privilege is granted, such as the issuer agreeing to sell merchandise to the purchaser at a reduced rate. The difference between the present value of the receivable and the cash loaned is regarded as an addition to the cost of the products purchased for the purchaser/lender and as unearned revenue to the seller/issuer. This treatment stems from an attempt to match revenue and expense in the proper periods and to differentiate between those factors that affect income from operations and income or expense from nonoperating sources. In the situation above, the purchaser/lender will amortize the discount (difference between the cash loaned and the present value of the note) to interest income over the life of the note, and the contractual right to purchase inventory at a reduced rate will be allocated to inventory (or cost of sales) as the right expires. The seller/issuer of the note will amortize the discount to interest expense over the life of the note, and the unearned revenue will be recognized in sales as the products are sold to the purchaser/lender at the reduced price. Because the discount is amortized on a different basis than the contractual right, net income for the period is also affected.

Example of accounting for a note issued for both cash and a contractual right

1. Miller borrows $10,000 via a noninterest-bearing three-year note from Krueger.
2. Miller agrees to sell $50,000 of merchandise to Krueger at less than the ordinary retail price for the duration of the note.
3. The market rate of interest on a note with similar payment terms and a borrower of similar creditworthiness is 10%.

According to APB 21, the difference between the present value of the note and the face value of the loan is to be regarded as part of the cost of the products purchased under the agreement.

The present value factor for an amount due in three years at 10% is .75132. Therefore, the present value of the note is $7,513 ($10,000 x .75132). The $2,487 ($10,000 – $7,513) difference between the face value and the present value is to be recorded as a discount on the note payable and as unearned revenue on the future purchases by the debtor. The following entries would be made by the debtor (Miller) and the creditor (Krueger) to record the transaction:

Miller			*Krueger*		
Cash	10,000		Note receivable	10,000	
Discount on note payable	2,487		Contract right with supplier	2,487	
Note payable		10,000	Cash		10,000
Unearned revenue		2,487	Discount on note receivable		2,487

The discount on note payable (and note receivable) is to be amortized using the effective interest method, while the unearned revenue account and contract right with supplier account are amortized on a pro rata basis as the right to purchase merchandise is used up. Thus, if Krueger purchased $20,000 of merchandise from Miller in the first year, the following entries would be necessary:

Miller			*Krueger*		
Unearned revenue [$2,487 x (20,000/50,000)]	995		Inventory (or cost of sales)	995	
Sales		995	Contract right with supplier		995
Interest expense	751		Discount on note receivable	751	
Discount on note payable ($7,513 x 10%)		751	Interest revenue		751

The amortization of unearned revenue and contract right with supplier accounts will fluctuate with the amount of purchases made. If there is a balance remaining in the account at the end of the loan term, it is amortized to the appropriate account in that final year.

Noncash transactions. When a note is issued for consideration such as property, goods, or services, and the transaction is entered into at arm's length, the stated interest rate is presumed to be fair unless (1) no interest rate is stated; (2) the stated rate is unreasonable; or (3) the face value of the debt is materially different from the consideration involved or the current market value of the note at the date of the transaction. According to APB 21, when the rate on the note is **not** considered fair, the note is to be recorded at the "fair market value of the property, goods, or services received or at an amount that reasonably approximates the market value of the note, whichever is the more clearly determinable." When this amount differs from the face value of the note, the difference is to be recorded as a discount or premium and amortized to interest expense.

Example of accounting for a note exchanged for property

1. A sells B a machine that has a fair market value of $7,510.
2. A receives a three-year noninterest-bearing note having a face value of $10,000.

In this situation, the fair market value of the consideration is readily determinable and, thus, represents the amount at which the note is to be recorded. The following entry by B is necessary:

Machine	7,510	
Discount on notes payable	2,490	
Notes payable		10,000

The discount will be amortized to interest expense over the three-year period using the interest rate **implied** in the transaction. The interest rate implied is 10%, because the factor for an amount due in three years is .75132, which when applied to the $10,000 face value results in an amount equal to the fair value of the machine.

If the fair market value of the consideration or note is not determinable, then the present value of the note must be determined using an **imputed** interest rate. This rate will then be used to establish the present value of the note by discounting all future payments on the note at this rate. General guidelines for imputing the interest rate, which are provided by APB 21, include the prevailing rates of similar instruments from creditors with similar credit ratings and the rate the debtor could obtain for similar financing from other sources. Other determining factors include any collateral or restrictive covenants involved, the current and expected prime rate, and other terms pertaining to the instrument. The objective is to approximate the rate of interest that would have resulted if an independent borrower and lender had negotiated a similar transaction under comparable terms and conditions. This determination is as of the issuance date, and any subsequent changes in interest rates would be irrelevant.

Example of accounting for a note exchanged to property

1. A sells B a used machine. The fair market value is not readily determinable.
2. A receives a three-year noninterest-bearing note having a face value of $20,000. The market value of the note is not known.
3. B could have borrowed the money for the machine's purchase from a bank at a rate of 10%.

In this situation, the fair market value of the consideration is not readily determinable, so the present value of the note is determined using an imputed interest rate. The rate used is the rate at which B could have borrowed the money—10%. The factor for an amount due in three years at 10% is .75132, so the present value of the note is $15,026. The following entry by B is necessary:

Machine	15,026	
Discount on notes payable	4,974	
Notes payable		20,000

Effective Interest Method

The **effective interest method** is the preferred method of accounting for a discount or premium arising from a note or bond. Under the effective interest method, the discount or premium is amortized over the life of the debt in such a way as to result in a constant rate of interest when applied to the amount outstanding at the beginning of any given period. Therefore, interest expense is equal to the market rate of interest at the time of issuance multiplied by this beginning figure. The difference between the interest expense and the cash paid represents the amortization of the discount or premium.

Amortization tables are often created at the time of the bond's issuance to provide amounts necessary when recording the entries relating to the debt issue. They also provide a check of accuracy since the final values in the unamortized discount or premium and carrying value columns should be equal to zero and the bond's face value, respectively.

Example of applying the effective interest method

1. A 3-year, 12%, $10,000 bond is issued at 1/1/X7, with interest payments semiannually.
2. The market rate is 10%.

The amortization table would appear as follows:

Date	*Credit cash*	*Debit int. exp.*	*Debit prem.*	*Unamort. prem. bal.*	*Carrying value*
1/1/X7				$507.61	$10,507.61(a)
7/1/X7	$ 600.00(b)	$ 525.38(c)	$ 74.62(d)	432.99(e)	10,432.99(f)
1/1/X8	600.00	521.65	78.35	354.64	10,354.64
7/1/X8	600.00	517.73	82.27	272.37	10,272.37
1/1/X9	600.00	513.62	86.38	185.99	10,185.99
7/1/X9	600.00	509.30	90.70	95.29	10,095.29
1/1/X0	600.00	504.71(g)	95.29	--	10,000.00
	$3,600.00	$3,092.39	$507.61		

(a) PV of principal and interest payments at 5% for 6 periods			*(c) $10,507.61 x .10 x one-half year*
$10,000(.74622)	=	*$ 7,462.20*	*(d) $600.00 – $525.38*
$ 600(5.07569)	=	*3,045.41*	*(e) $507.61 – $74.62*
		$10,507.61	*(f) $10,507.61 – $74.62 (or $10,000 + $432.99)*
(b) $10,000.00 x .12 x one-half year			*(g) Rounding error = $.05*

Although the effective interest method is the preferred method of amortizing a discount or premium, the **straight-line method** may be used if the results are not materially different. The amortized portion is equal to the total amount of the discount or premium divided by the life of the debt from issuance in months multiplied by the number of months the debt has been outstanding that year. Interest expense under the straight-line method is equal to the cash interest paid plus the amortized portion of the discount or minus the amortized portion of the premium.

When the **interest date does not coincide with the year-end,** an adjusting entry must be made to recognize the proportional share of interest payable and the amortization of the discount or premium. Within the amortization period, the discount or premium can be amortized using the straight-line method.

If **bonds or notes are issued between interest payment dates,** the interest and the amortization must be computed for the period between the sale date and the next interest date. The purchaser usually pays the issuer for the amount of interest that has accrued since the last payment date. That payment is recorded as a payable by the issuer. At the next interest date, the issuer pays the purchaser as though the bond had been outstanding for the entire interest period. The discount or premium is also amortized for the short period.

Example of note issued between payment dates

On June 1, 20X0, Acme Manufacturing issues a $100,000 7% bond with a three-year life at 104 (i.e. at 104% of face value). Interest is payable on July 1 and January 1. The computation of the premium would be

Proceeds	$104,000
Face value	100,000
Premium	$ 4,000

The entry to record the bond issuance and the receipt of interest from the purchaser would be

Cash	106,967	
Bonds payable		100,000
Premium on bonds		4,000
Interest payable		2,967

The bonds will be outstanding for two years and seven months. An effective interest rate must be computed that will equate the present value of the future principal and interest payments to the cash received. Using a spreadsheet facilitates the trial and error process. Many inexpensive calculators with financial functions also do this calculation. Alternatively, present value tables can be used to compute the value, as shown below.

First, compute the present value of the interest and principal payments as of 7/1/X0 using a guess of 5% annually.

Present value of an annuity due of $3,500 for six periods @ 2.5% = 3,500 x 5.6458 =	19,760
Present value of a single payment of $100,000 in five periods @2.5% =100,000 x .88385 =	88,385
	108,145

Then, compute the present value of that result one month earlier (at June 1, 20X0) using the same interest rate.

Present value of a single payment of $108,145 in one month = 108,145/[1+(.05/12)] = 107,696

The result is more than the cash received ($106,967), so we know that the interest rate must be higher than 5%. Repeat the calculation at a 6% annual rate:

Present value of an annuity due of $3,500 for six periods @3% = 3,500 x 5.5797 =	19,529
Present value of a single payment of $100,000 in five periods @3% =100,000 x .86261 =	86,261
	105,790

Present value of a single payment of $105,790 in one month = 105,790/[1+(.06/12)] = 105,263

The result is less than the cash received ($106,967), so we know the rate is between 5 and 6%. By interpolation, we determine that the rate is 5.3%.

$$\frac{107{,}696 - 106{,}967}{107{,}696 - 105{,}263} \times (6\% - 5\%) = .299$$, which is added to 5% to get t he effective rate.

The amortization of the $4,000 premium would be as follows:

	Cash paid (received)	*Interest at 5.3% annually*	*Amortization*	*Interest payable*	*Bond payable*
					104,000
06/01/X0	(2,967)			2,967	104,000
07/01/X0	3,500	459	74	(2,967)	103,926
01/01/X1	3,500	2,754	746		103,180
07/01/X1	3,500	2,734	765		102,415
01/01/X2	3,500	2,714	786		101,629
07/01/X2	3,500	2,693	807		100,822
01/01/X3	103,500	2,672	822		100,000

The entry to record the first interest payment would be

Interest payable	2,967	
Interest expense	459	
Premium on bonds	74	
Cash		3,500

Costs may be incurred in connection with issuing bonds. Examples include legal, accounting, and underwriting fees; commissions; and engraving, printing, and registration costs. These costs theoretically should be treated as either an expense in the period incurred or a reduction in the related amount of debt, in much the same manner as a discount (CON 6). These costs do not provide any future economic benefit and, therefore, should not be an asset. Since these costs reduce the amount of cash proceeds, they in effect increase the effective interest rate and probably should be accounted for the same as an unamortized discount. However, in practice, issue costs are treated as deferred charges and amortized using the straight-line method. (FASB, as part of its convergence project with the IASB, has proposed that issuance costs be defined as the incremental costs directly attributable to issuance of an instrument that would not have been incurred if the instrument had not been issued. It would also require that the issuance costs be accounted for as a reduction of the proceeds of issuance.)

Extinguishment of Debt

Management may reacquire or retire outstanding debt before its scheduled maturity. This decision is usually caused by changes in present or expected interest rates or in cash flows.

In-substance defeasance (irrevocably placing assets in a trust that is to be used solely to service the remaining debt payments) does not result in the extinguishment of a liability. Except for items excluded by FAS 140, a liability is removed from the balance sheet only if

1. The creditor is paid and the debtor is relieved of the obligation.
2. The debtor is released legally either by the creditor or judicially from being the primary obligor.

FASB is pursuing a project to clarify the phrase "legally released from being the primary obligor," which is not a legally defined term and thus may be subject to varying interpretations. Although the FASB staff has made recommendations for improved language, FASB has not acted on these and has instead indicated that it will pursue this issue in the context of a broader review of FAS 140's extinguishment criteria. This project is in the early stages and interested parties should monitor subsequent developments.

If a debtor becomes secondarily liable, through a third-party assumption and a release by the creditor, the original debtor becomes a guarantor. A guarantee obligation, based on the probability that the third party will pay, is to be recognized and initially measured at fair value. The amount of guarantee obligation increases the loss or reduces the gain recognized on extinguishments. Guarantees are discussed in Chapter 12.

Some financial instruments can have characteristics of either assets or liabilities depending on market conditions (forward contracts, swap contracts, and written commodity options). To be derecognized, those instruments must not only meet the two criteria above, but must also meet the surrender of control criteria of FAS 140 (Chapter 5).

Gain or loss. According to APB 26, the difference between the net carrying value and the price paid to acquire the debt instruments is to be recorded as a gain or loss. If the acquisition price is greater than the carrying value, a loss exists. A gain is generated if the acquisition price is less than the carrying value. These gains or losses are to be recognized in the period in which the retirement took place. Previously, material gains and losses from debt extinguishment were classified as extraordinary in the income statement. However, FAS 145, issued in April 2002, changed that requirement. Those gains and losses now will be reported as extraordinary only if the criteria of APB 30 are met—that is, if the event creating the gain or loss is both unusual and infrequently occurring. It is expected that extinguishments of debt will rarely, if ever, meet these dual criteria. Hence, gains and losses on debt extinguishments will be reported in earnings before extraordinary items.

The unamortized premium or discount and issue costs should be amortized to the acquisition date and recorded prior to the determination of the gain or loss. If the extinguishment of debt does not occur on the interest date, the interest payable accruing between the last interest date and the acquisition date must also be recorded.

Example of accounting for the extinguishment of debt

1. A 10%, 10-year, $200,000 bond is dated and issued on 1/1/01 at 98, with the interest payable semiannually.
2. Associated bond issue costs of $14,000 are incurred.
3. Four years later, on 1/1/05, the entire bond issue is repurchased at 102 (i.e., 102% of face value) and is retired.
4. At 1/1/05 the unamortized discount using the effective interest rate of 10.325% is $2,858.

Reacquisition price [(102%) x $200,000]		$204,000
Net carrying amount:		
Face value	$200,000	
Unamortized discount	(2,858)	
Unamortized issue costs [14,000 x (6/10)]	(8,400)	188,742
Loss on bond repurchase		$ 15,258

Troubled Debt Restructurings

Troubled debt restructurings are defined by FAS 15 as situations where the creditor, for economic or legal reasons related to the debtor's financial difficulties, grants the debtor a concession that would not otherwise be granted. As explained in EITF 02-4, no single characteristic or factor, taken alone, is determinative of whether a modification of terms or an exchange of a debt instrument is a troubled debt restructuring under FAS 15. Thus, making this determination requires the exercise of judgment. EITF 02-4 poses the following two questions to help answer the question of whether FAS 15 applies in a particular instance:

- Is the debtor experiencing financial difficulty?
- Has the creditor granted a concession?

If the answer to **either** of those questions is "no," the modification of terms or exchange of debt instruments is not within the scope of FAS 15.

Is the debtor experiencing financial difficulty? If the debtor's creditworthiness has deteriorated since the debt was originally issued, the debtor should evaluate whether it is experiencing financial difficulties. The following factors are indicators that the debtor is experiencing financial difficulties:

- The debtor is in default on some of its debt
- The debtor has declared, or is in the process of declaring, bankruptcy
- There is doubt as to whether the debtor is a going concern
- The debtor's securities have been or are likely to be delisted
- The debtor forecasts that its entity-specific cash flows are insufficient to service the debt through its maturity in accordance with its terms
- The debtor cannot obtain resources at the current market rates for nontroubled debtors except through existing creditors

If **both** of the following factors are present, the debtor is **not** experiencing financial difficulty:

- The creditors agree to restructure the old debt solely to reflect either (1) a decrease in the current interest rates for the debtor, or (2) an increase in the debtor's creditworthiness
- The debtor is currently servicing the old debt and can obtain funds to repay the old debt at the current market rate for a nontroubled debtor

Has the creditor granted a concession? The creditor has granted a concession if the debtor's effective borrowing rate on the restructured debt is less than the effective borrowing rate immediately prior to the restructuring. The effective borrowing rate should give effect to all the terms of the restructured debt, including options, warrants, guarantees, and so forth. If the debtor is restructuring the debt for a second time, the effective borrowing rate of the new debt should be compared to the effective borrowing rate of the original debt.

However, in any of the following four situations, a concession granted by the creditor does not automatically qualify as a restructuring:

1. The fair value of the assets or equity interest accepted by a creditor from a debtor in full satisfaction of its receivable is at least equal to the creditor's recorded investment in the receivable.
2. The fair value of the assets or equity interest transferred by a debtor to a creditor in full settlement of its payable is at least equal to the carrying value of the payable.
3. The creditor reduces the effective interest rate to reflect a decrease in current interest rates or a decrease in the risk, in order to maintain the relationship.
4. The debtor, in exchange for old debt, issues new debt with an interest rate that reflects current market rates.

FTB 81-6 notes that FAS 15 does not apply to debtors in bankruptcy unless the restructuring does not result from a general restatement of the debtor's liabilities in bankruptcy proceedings. That is, FAS 15 applies only if the debt restructuring is isolated to the creditor.

A troubled debt restructuring can occur one of two ways. The first is a settlement of the debt at less than the carrying amount. The second is a continuation of the debt with a modification of terms (i.e., a reduction in the interest rate, face amount, accrued interest owed, or an extension of the payment date for interest or face amount). Accounting for such restructurings is prescribed for both debtors and creditors. FTB 80-2 points out that the debtor and creditor must individually apply FAS 15 to the specific situation since the tests are not necessarily symmetrical and it is possible for one or the other, but not both, to have a troubled debt restructuring when the debtor's carrying amount and the creditor's recorded investment differ. FAS 114 as amended by FAS 118 specifies the accounting by creditors for troubled debt restructurings involving a modification of terms.

Debtors. If the debt is settled by the exchange of assets, a gain is recognized in the period of transfer for the difference between the carrying amount of the debt (defined as the face amount of the debt increased or decreased by applicable accrued interest and applicable unamortized premium, discount, or issue costs) and the consideration given to extinguish the debt. A two-step process is used: (1) any noncash assets used to settle the debt are revalued at fair market value and the associated ordinary gain or loss is recognized and (2) the debt restructuring gain is determined and recognized. The gain or loss is evaluated under the unusual and infrequent criteria of APB 30, which are discussed in Chapter 3. (Automatically classifying the gain on loss as an extraordinary item was eliminated by FAS 145.) If stock is issued to settle the liability, the stock is recorded at its fair market value (FAS 15).

Example 1: Settlement of debt by exchange of assets

Assume the debtor company transfers land having a book value of $70,000 and a fair market value of $80,000 in full settlement of its note payable. The note has a remaining life of five years, a principal balance of $90,000, and related accrued interest of $10,000 is recorded. The following entries are required to record the settlement:

Debtor		
Land	10,000	
Gain on transfer of assets		10,000
Note payable	90,000	
Interest payable	10,000	
Land		80,000
Gain on settlement of debt		20,000

If the debt is continued with a modification of terms, it is necessary to compare the total future cash flows of the restructured debt (both principal and stated interest) with the carrying value of the original debt. If the total amount of future cash payments is greater than the carrying value, no adjustment is made to the carrying value of the debt. However, a new lower effective interest rate must be computed. This rate makes the present value of the total future cash payments equal to the present carrying value of debt and is used to determine interest expense in future periods. The effective interest method must be used to compute the expense. If the total future cash payments of the restructured debt are less than the present carrying value, the current debt should be reduced to the amount of the future cash flows and a gain should be recognized. No interest expense would be recognized in subsequent periods, since only the principal is being repaid.

According to FAS 15, a troubled debt restructuring that involves only a modification of terms is accounted for prospectively. Thus, there is no change in the carrying value of the liability **unless** the carrying amount of the original debt exceeds the total future cash payments specified by the new agreement.

If the restructuring consists of part settlement and part modification of payments, the part settlement is accounted for first and then the modification of payments.

Example 2: Restructuring with gain/loss recognized (payments are less than carrying value)

Assume that the note has a principal balance of $90,000, accrued interest of $10,000, an interest rate of 5%, and a remaining life of five years. The interest rate is reduced to 4%, the principal is reduced to $72,500, and the accrued interest at date of restructure is forgiven.

Future cash flows (after restructuring):

Principal	$ 72,500
Interest (5 years x $72,500 x 4%)	14,500
Total cash to be paid	$ 87,000
Amount prior to restructure	
($90,000 principal + $10,000 accrued interest)	(100,000)
Debtor's gain	$ 13,000

The following entries need to be recorded by the debtor to reflect the terms of the agreement:

Beginning of Year 1

Interest payable	10,000	
Note payable	3,000	
Gain on restructure of debt		13,000

End of Years 1-5

Note payable	2,900	
Cash		2,900

NOTE: $14,500 ÷ 5 yrs. = $2,900; No interest expense is recorded in this case.

End of Year 5

Note payable	72,500	
Cash		72,500

Example 3: Restructuring with no gain/loss recognized (payments exceed carrying value)

Modify Example 2 as follows:

Assume the $100,000 owed is reduced to a principal balance of $95,000. The interest rate of 5% is reduced to 4%.

Future cash flows (after restructuring):	
Principal	$ 95,000
Interest (5 years x $95,000 x 4%)	19,000
Total cash to be received	$ 114,000
Amount prior to restructure	
($90,000 principal + $10,000 accrued interest)	(100,000)
Interest expense/revenue over 5 years	$ 14,000

In this example, a new effective interest rate must be computed such that the present value of the future payments equals $100,000. A trial and error approach is used to calculate the effective interest rate that discounts the $95,000 principal and the $3,800 annual interest payments to $100,000, the amount owed prior to restructuring.

Trial and Error Calculation

	(n = 5, i = 2.5%)	(n = 5, i = 3%)
PV of ordinary annuity	4.64583	4.57971
PV of 1	.88385	.86261

2.5%: (.88385 x $95,000) + (4.64583 x $3,800) = $101,620

3%: (.86261 x $95,000) + (4.57971 x $3,800) = $ 99,351

Interpolation:

$$\left[\frac{101{,}620 - 100{,}000}{101{,}620 - 99{,}351}\right] \times (3\% - 2.5\%) = .357$$

New effective rate = 2.5% + .357% = 2.857%

Interest amortization schedule:

Year	*Cash*	*Interest at effective rate*	*Reduction in carrying value*	*Carrying amount*
				$100,000
1	$ 3,800(a)	$2,857(b)	$ 943(c)	99,057
2	3,800	2,830	970	98,087
3	3,800	2,802	998	97,089
4	3,800	2,774	1,026	96,063
5	3,800	2,745	1,055	95,000*
	$19,000			

* *Rounded*
(a) *$3,800 = $95,000 x .04*
(b) *$2,857 = $100,000 x 2.857%*
(c) *$943 = $3,800 – $2,857*

The following entries are made by the debtor to recognize the cash payments in the subsequent periods:

End of Year 1		
Note payable ($3,800 – $2,857)	943	
Interest expense ($100,000 x .02857)	2,857	
Cash		3,800
End of Year 5		
Note payable	95,000	
Cash		95,000

When the total future cash payments **may** exceed the carrying amount of the liability, no gain or loss is recognized on the books of the debtor unless the maximum future cash payments are less than the carrying amount of the debt. For example, if the debtor is required to make interest payments at a higher rate if its financial condition improves before the maturity of the debt, the debtor should assume that the larger payments would have to be made. The contingent payments would be included in the total future cash payments for comparison with the carrying amount of the debt. If the future cash payments exceed the carrying amount, a new effective interest rate should be determined. The new rate should be the rate that equates the present value of the future cash payments with the carrying amount of the liability. Interest expense and principal reduction are then recognized as the future cash payments are made.

Example 4: Contingent payments

Modify Example 2 as follows: The new agreement states that if financial condition at maturity improves as specified, an additional principal payment of $15,000 is required and additional 1% of interest must be paid in arrears for years 4 and 5.

Future cash payments:	
Required principal per agreement	$ 72,500
Required interest per agreement (5 years x $72,500 x 4%)	14,500
Contingent principal payment	15,000
Contingent interest payments (2 years x 72,500 x 1%)	1,450
	$103,450
Amount prior to restructure ($90,000 + $10,000)	(100,000)
	$ 3,450

When computing the new effective interest rate, only as many contingent payments as are needed to make the future cash payments exceed the carrying value are included in the calculation. Thus, the contingent principal payment would be included, but the contingent interest would not. The contingent interest payments would be recognized using the same criteria as are used in FAS 5; that is, the payments are recognized when they are both probable and reasonably estimable.

FAS 114 creditors. FAS 114, as amended by FAS 118, applies to all creditors, to all troubled debt restructurings involving a modification of terms, and to all loans except

1. Groups of similar small balance loans that are collectively evaluated
2. Loans measured at fair value or lower of cost or fair value
3. Leases
4. FAS 115 debt securities

If it is probable that a creditor will not collect all amounts (principal and interest) owed to the degree specified in the loan agreement, a loan is considered impaired. A delay does not impair the loan if the creditor collects all amounts due (including accrued interest during the delay at the contractual rate).

An impaired loan can be measured on a loan-by-loan basis in any of the following ways:

1. Present value of expected future cash flows using the loan's original effective interest rate (the contractual interest rate adjusted for premium or discount and net deferred loan costs or fees at acquisition or origination)
2. Loans' observable market price
3. Fair value of the collateral if the loan is collateral dependent (repayment expected to be provided by the collateral). If foreclosure is probable, this measurement must be used.

Other measurement considerations include

1. Costs to sell, on a discounted basis, if they will reduce cash flows to satisfy the loan
2. Creation of or adjustment to a valuation allowance account with the offset to bad-debt expense if the recorded investment is greater than the impaired loan measurement
3. If the contractual interest rate varies based on changes in an independent factor, the creditor can choose between
   a. Calculating the effective interest on the factor as it changes over the loan's life, or
   b. Calculating the effective interest as fixed at the rate in effect at the date of impairment.

   The choice must be consistently applied. Projections of factor changes should not be made.
4. Cash flow estimates should be the creditors' best estimate based on reasonable and supportable assumptions
5. Significant changes occurring in measurement values require recalculation and adjustment of the valuation allowance. Net carrying amount of the loan should not exceed the recorded investment.

After impairment, creditors use existing methods to record, measure, and display interest income. If the existing policy results in a recorded investment less than fair value, no additional impairment is recognized.

Under FAS 114, the creditor would account for the earlier examples as follows:

Example 1

Land	80,000	
Bad debt expense	20,000	
Note receivable		90,000
Interest receivable		10,000

Example 2

Future cash flows (after restructuring) at the agreement's original effective interest rate

		5% 5 yrs PV Factor
Principal	$ 56,806	($72,500 x .78353)
Interest	12,555	($ 2,900 x 4.32948)
Total present value	$ 69,361	
Amount prior to restructure ($90,000 principal + $10,000 accrued interest)	(100,000)	
Creditor's loss	$(30,639)	

Beginning of Year 1		
Bad debt expense	30,639	
Interest receivable		10,000
Valuation allowance		20,639
End of Year 1		
Cash	2,900	
Valuation allowance	568	
Bad debt expense (or interest income)		3,468 (69,361 x .05)
End of Year 2		
Cash	2,900	
Valuation allowance	596	
Bad debt expense (or interest income)		3,496 [(69,361 + 568) = 69,929 x .05]
End of Year 3		
Cash	2,900	
Valuation allowance	626	
Bad debt expense (or interest income)		3,526 [(69,929 + 596) = 70,525 x .05]
End of Year 4		
Cash	2,900	
Valuation allowance	658	
Bad debt expense (or interest income)		3,558 [(70,525 + 626) = 71,151 x .05]
End of Year 5		
Cash	2,900	
Valuation allowance	691	
Bad debt expense (or interest income)		3,591 [(71,151 + 658) = 71,809 x .05]
Cash	72,500	
Valuation allowance	17,500	
Note receivable		90,000

Example 3

Future cash flows (after restructuring) at the agreement's original effective interest rate

		5% 5 yrs PV Factor
Principal	$ 74,435	($95,000 x .78353)
Interest	16,452	($ 3,800 x 4.32948)
Total present value	$ 90,887	
Amount prior to restructure ($90,000 principal + $10,000 accrued interest)	(100,000)	
Creditor's loss	$(9,113)	

Beginning of Year 1		
Bad debt expense	9,113	
Note receivable—new	95,000	
Note receivable—old		90,000
Interest receivable		10,000
Valuation allowance		4,113

End of Year 1		
Cash	3,800	
Valuation allowance	744	
Bad debt expense (or interest income)		4,544 (90,887 x .05)
End of Year 2		
Cash	3,800	
Valuation allowance	781	
Bad debt expense (or interest income)		4,581 [(90,887 + 744) = 91,631 x .05]
End of Year 3		
Cash	3,800	
Valuation allowance	821	
Bad debt expense (or interest income)		4,621 [(91,631 + 781) = 92,412 x .05]
End of Year 4		
Cash	3,800	
Valuation allowance	862	
Bad debt expense (or interest income)		4,662 [(92,412 + 821) = 93,233 x .05]
End of Year 5		
Cash	3,800	
Valuation allowance	905	
Bad debt expense (or interest income)		4,705 [(93,233 + 862) = 94,095 x .05]
Cash	95,000	
Note receivable		95,000

Convertible Debt

Bonds are frequently issued with the right to convert them into common stock of the company at the holder's option. **Convertible debt** is used for two reasons. First, when a specific amount of funds is needed, convertible debt often allows a lesser number of shares to be issued (assuming conversion) than if the funds were raised by directly issuing the shares. Thus, less dilution occurs. Second, the conversion feature allows debt to be issued at a lower interest rate and with fewer restrictive covenants than if the debt was issued without it.

This dual nature of debt and equity, however, creates a question as to whether the equity element should receive separate recognition. Support for separate treatment is based on the assumption that this equity element has economic value. Since the convertible feature tends to lower the rate of interest, a portion of the proceeds should be allocated to this equity feature. FASB agrees with that view, and in October 2000 it issued proposed standards that would require convertible debt to be divided into its liability components and equity components. Those components would be separately presented in the balance sheet. If issued, those standards would replace the current standards of APB 14, which require that the instrument be reported as either all debt or all equity. For more details, see the discussion of the proposed standards later in this chapter.

Features of convertible debt typically include (1) a conversion price 15-20% greater than the market value of the stock when the debt is issued; (2) conversion features (price and number of shares) which protect against dilution from stock dividends, splits, etc.; and (3) a callable feature at the issuer's option, which is usually exercised once the conversion price is reached (thus forcing conversion or redemption).

Convertible debt also has its disadvantages. If the stock price increases significantly after the debt is issued, the issuer would have been better off by simply issuing the stock. Additionally, if the price of the stock does not reach the conversion price, the debt will never be converted (a condition known as overhanging debt).

When convertible debt is issued and the conversion price is greater than the market value of the stock on the issuance date, no value is apportioned to the conversion feature when recording the issue (APB 14). The debt and its interest are reported as if it were a nonconvertible debt. Upon conversion, the stock may be valued at either the book value or the market value of the bonds.

If the **book value approach** is used, the new stock is valued at the carrying value of the converted bonds. This method is widely used since no gain or loss is recognized upon conversion, and the conversion represents the transformation of contingent shareholders into shareholders. It does not represent the culmination of an earnings cycle. The primary weakness of this method is that the total value attributed to the equity security by the investors is not given accounting recognition.

Example of book value method

Assume that a $1,000 bond with an unamortized discount of $50 and a market value of $970 is converted into 10 shares of $10 par common stock whose market value is $97 per share. Conversion using the book value method is recorded as follows:

Bonds payable	1,000	
Discount on bonds payable		50
Common stock		100
Additional paid-in capital		850

The **market value approach** assumes the new stock issued is valued at market (i.e., the market price of the stock issued or the market price of the bonds converted, whichever is more easily determinable). A gain (loss) occurs when the market value of the stocks or bonds is less (greater) than the carrying value of the bond.

Example of the market value method

Assume the same facts as the example above. The entry to record the conversion is

Bonds payable	1,000	
Loss on redemption (ordinary)	20	
Discount on bonds payable		50
Common stock		100
Additional paid-in capital		870

The weakness of this method is that a gain or loss can be reported as a result of an equity transaction. Only the existing shareholders are affected, as their equity will increase or decrease, but the firm as a whole is unaffected. For this reason, the market value approach is not widely used.

When convertible debt is retired, the transaction is handled in the same manner as nonconvertible debt: the difference between the acquisition price and the carrying value of the bond is reported currently as a gain or loss.

Embedded beneficial conversion features. APB 14 does not discuss situations in which the conversion feature is in-the-money at the date the bonds are issued or situations in which the conversion terms vary based on specified future events. EITF Issues 98-5 and 00-27 provide guidance for those types of situations.

EITF Issue 98-5 requires recognition of a conversion feature that is in-the-money at issuance as additional paid-in-capital, measured by allocating a portion of the proceeds equal to the intrinsic value of that feature. The intrinsic value of the feature is the difference between the conversion price and the fair value of the stock into which the security is convertible, multiplied by the number of shares into which the security is convertible. According to EITF 00-27, the issuance proceeds should not be reduced by issuance costs when calculating the intrinsic value of the conversion feature. Rather, the amount allocated to the conversion feature is a discount on the issuance of the bonds, to be amortized over the period from issuance to the stated maturity date. If the holder of the bond converts the bond prior to the maturity date, the unamortized discount is recognized immediately as interest expense.

Example 1: Intrinsic value of a conversion feature—fixed dollar terms

Software Solutions issues $1,000,000 of convertible debt, which is convertible into $10 par common stock at a price of $50 per share. The fair value of the common stock on the commitment date of the issue is $60. The intrinsic value of the conversion feature is computed as follows:

$1,000,000/$50 per share = 20,000 shares to be issued upon conversion
($60 fair value – $50 conversion price) x 20,000 shares = $200,000 intrinsic value

Software Solutions would make the following entry to recognize the issuance of the bonds at 100:

Cash	1,000,000	
Discount on bonds payable	200,000	
Bonds payable		1,000,000
Additional paid-in capital		200,000

If the price at which the bond is convertible to stock changes over the life of the bond, the intrinsic value should be computed using the terms that are most beneficial to the holder. The most favorable conversion price that would be in effect assuming that there are no changes to the current circumstances except for the passing of time should be used to measure the intrinsic value.

Example 2: Intrinsic value of a conversion feature—variable terms

American National Biotech issues $1,000,000 of convertible debt, convertible into $10 par common stock at a price 15% below the commitment date market price for years 1 and 2, 20% below the commitment date market price for years 3 to 5, and 25% below the commitment date market price for years 6 to maturity. The fair value of the common stock on the commitment date of the issue is $50. The intrinsic value of the conversion feature is computed as follows:

The most beneficial price is the 25% discount available in years 6 to maturity
That price would be $37.50 ($50 x .75)
$1,000,000/$37.50 per share = 26,667 shares to be issued upon conversion
($50 fair value – $37.50 conversion price) x 26,667 shares = $333,337 intrinsic value

American National Biotech would make the following entry to recognize the issuance of the bonds at 100:

Cash	1,000,000	
Discount on bonds payable	333,337	
Bonds payable		1,000,000
Additional paid-in capital		333,337

In some cases the conversion price will be dependent on a future event, or the bond becomes convertible only upon the occurrence of a future event. In those cases, the contingent beneficial conversion feature should be measured at the commitment date but not recognized in earnings until the contingency is resolved.

Example 3: Intrinsic value of a conversion feature—contingent price terms

Major Manufacturing Co. issues $1,000,000 of convertible debt, which is convertible into $10 par common stock at a discount of 20% off of the conversion date market price. The fair value of the common stock on the commitment date of the issue is $50. The intrinsic value of the conversion feature is computed as follows:

Because the conversion percentage is fixed, the intrinsic value is always $250,000.

Market price at conversion	$40	$50	$60	$70
Conversion price	$32	$40	$48	$56
Number of shares issued	31,250	25,000	20,833	17,857
Discount	$8	$10	$12	$14
Intrinsic value	$250,000	$250,000	$250,000	$250,000

Major Manufacturing Co. would make the following entry to recognize the issuance of bonds at 100:

Cash	1,000,000	
Discount on bonds payable	250,000	
Bonds payable		1,000,000
Additional paid-in capital		250,000

Example 4: Intrinsic value of a conversion feature—contingent conversion

Shoemaker Co. issues $1,000,000 of convertible debt, which is convertible into $10 par common stock at a discount of 25% below the commitment date market price. The fair value of the common stock on the commitment date of the issue is $60, so the conversion price is $45. The debt is convertible only upon an initial public offering. The intrinsic value of the conversion feature is computed as follows:

$1,000,000/$45 per share = 22,222 shares to be issued upon conversion
($60 fair value – $45 conversion price) x 22,222 shares = $333,330 intrinsic value

Shoemaker Co. would not allocate any portion of the proceeds to the conversion feature at issuance. It would make the following entry to recognize the issuance of the bonds at 100:

Cash	1,000,000	
Bonds payable		1,000,000

Upon the occurrence of an initial public offering, Shoemaker would make the following entry:

Discount on bonds payable	333,330	
Additional paid-in capital		333,330

Example 5: Intrinsic value of a conversion feature—contingent conversion with variable terms

Food Franchisers issues $1,000,000 of convertible debt, which is convertible into $10 par common stock at a price of $50. The fair value of the common stock on the commitment date of the issue is $60. The debt is convertible only upon an initial public offering. If the stock's market price is at least 20% higher than the IPO price one year after the IPO, the conversion price will be 70% of the then market price. The intrinsic value of the contingent conversion feature at issuance is computed as follows:

$1,000,000/$50 per share = 20,000 shares to be issued upon conversion
($60 fair value – $50 conversion price) x 20,000 shares = 250,000 intrinsic value

The intrinsic value of the contingent conversion price change is also computed at the commitment date using the assumptions that the IPO price will be the same as the current market price and that the stock price one year after the IPO is 20% higher, as follows:

Contingent conversion price = $60 x 120% x 70% = $50.40
$1,000,000/$50.40 per share = 19,841 shares to be issued upon conversion
($72 fair value – $50.40 conversion price) x 19,841 shares = $428,565 intrinsic value

Food Franchisers would not allocate any portion of the proceeds to the conversion feature at issuance. It would make the following entry to recognize the issuance of the bonds at 100:

Cash	1,000,000	
Bonds payable		1,000,000

Upon the occurrence of an initial public offering at $55, Food Franchisers would make the following entry:

Discount on bonds payable	250,000	
Additional paid-in capital		250,000

If the stock price increased to $66 ($55 x 120%), Food Franchisers would make the following entry for the difference between the two intrinsic values:

Discount on bonds payable	178,565	
Additional paid-in capital		178,565

If a bond with an embedded beneficial conversion feature is extinguished prior to conversion, a portion of the reacquisition price is allocated to the repurchase of the conversion feature. That portion is the intrinsic value of the conversion feature at the extinguishment date, which would be recorded as a decrease in additional paid-in capital. That accounting may result in a reduction in additional paid-in capital that is larger than the amount originally recorded in paid-in capital at issuance. However, no portion of the reacquisition price should be allocated to the conversion feature if that feature had no intrinsic value at the issuance date.

Example of extinguishment of debt with an embedded conversion feature

Software Solutions (Example 1, above) repurchases $500,000 face of its debt at 140. At the date of issuance, the following entry had been made relating to the debt later extinguished.

Cash	500,000	
Discount on bonds payable	100,000	
Bonds payable		500,000
Additional paid-in capital		100,000

At the date of the repurchase, the market value of the stock is $85, and the unamortized discount on the debt was $20,000. The intrinsic value of the conversion feature at the date of the repurchase is computed as follows:

$500,000/$50 per share = 10,000 shares to be issued upon conversion
($85 fair value – $50 conversion price) x 10,000 shares = $350,000 intrinsic value

Software Solutions would make the following entry to recognize the retirement of the bonds:

Bonds payable	500,000	
Additional paid-in capital	350,000	
Discount on bonds payable		20,000
Gain on extinguishment of debt		130,000
Cash		700,000

Questions have arisen regarding the accounting for the settlement of this instrument partially in cash (the recognized liability) and partially in stock (the unrecognized equity instrument). EITF 03-7 reached a consensus that only the cash payment is to be considered in computing gain or loss on settlement of the recognized liability. Shares transferred to the holder to settle the excess conversion spread represented by the embedded equity instrument are not considered part of the settlement of the debt component of the instrument.

Disclosure of contingently convertible securities. Allegations had been raised that disclosures regarding contingently convertible securities have often been inconsistent across companies, and often have been inadequate. To address this problem, FSP 129-1 interprets how the disclosure provisions of FAS 129 apply to contingently convertible securities. FAS 129 applies to all contingently convertible securities, even those that are not included in the computation of diluted EPS. The FSP identifies the qualitative and quantitative terms that must be disclosed so that users can understand the potential impact of conversion, including: events or changes in circumstances that would cause the contingency to be met and features necessary to understand the conversion rights, the conversion price and number of shares, events or changes that could adjust or change any features of the securities, and the manner of settlement upon conversion. Disclosures should indicate whether shares that would be issued upon conversion are included in the calculation of EPS. Disclosures should also include information about derivative transactions related to the securities.

Induced Conversion of Debt

A special situation exists in which the conversion privileges of convertible debt are modified after issuance. These modifications may take the form of reduced conversion prices or additional consideration paid to the convertible debt holder. The debtor offers these modifications or "sweeteners" to induce prompt conversion of the outstanding debt.

FAS 84 specifies the accounting method used in these situations and only applies when the convertible debt is converted into equity securities. Upon conversion, the debtor must recognize an expense for the excess of the fair value of all the securities and other consideration given over the fair value of the securities specified in the original conversion terms. The reported expense should not be classified as an extraordinary item.

Example of induced conversion expense

1. January 1, 2001, XYZ Company issued ten 8% convertible bonds at $1,000 par value without a discount or premium, maturing December 31, 2011.
2. The bonds are initially convertible into no par common stock of XYZ at a conversion price of $25.
3. On July 1, 2005, the convertible bonds have a market value of $600 each.
4. To induce the convertible bondholders to quickly convert their bonds, XYZ reduces the conversion price to $20 for bondholders who convert before July 21, 2005 (within twenty days).
5. The market price of XYZ Company's common stock on the date of conversion is $15 per share.

The fair value of the incremental consideration paid by XYZ upon conversion is calculated for each bond converted before July 21, 2005.

Value of securities issued to debt holders:		
Face amount	$1,000	per bond
÷ New conversion price	÷ $20	per share
Number of common shares issued upon conversion	50	shares
x Price per common share	x $15	per share
Value of securities issued	$ 750	(a)
Face amount	$1,000	per bond
÷ Original conversion price	÷ $25	per share
Number of common shares issuable pursuant to original conversion privilege	40	shares
x Price per share	x $15	per share
Value of securities issuable pursuant to original conversion privileges	$ 600	(b)
Value of securities issued	$ 750	(a)
Value of securities issuable pursuant to the original conversion privileges	600	(b)
Fair value of incremental consideration	$ 150	

The entry to record the debt conversion for each bond is

Convertible debt	1,000	
Debt conversion expense	150	
Common stock—no par		1,150

Debt Issued with Stock Warrants

Warrants are certificates enabling the holder to purchase a stated number of shares of stock at a certain price within a certain time period. They are often issued with bonds to enhance the marketability of the bonds and to lower the bond's interest rate.

When bonds with detachable warrants are issued, the purchase price must be allocated between the debt and the stock warrants based on relative market values (APB 14). Since two separate instruments are involved, a market value must be determined for each. However, if one value cannot be determined, the market value of the other should be deducted from the total value to determine the unknown value.

Example of accounting for a bond with a detachable warrant

1. A $1,000 bond with a detachable warrant to buy 10 shares of $10 par common stock at $50 per share is issued for $1,025.
2. Immediately after the issuance the bonds trade at $995 and the warrants at $35.
3. The market value of the stock is $48.

The relative market value of the bonds is 96.6% [995/(995 + 35)] and the warrant is 3.4% [35/(995 + 35)]. Thus, $34.85(3.4% x $1,025) of the issuance price is assigned to the warrants. The journal entry to record the issuance is

Cash	1,025.00	
Discount on bonds payable	9.85	
Bonds payable		1,000.00
Paid-in capital—warrants (or "Stock options outstanding")		34.85

The discount is the difference between the purchase price assigned to the bond, $990.15 (96.6% x $1,025), and its face value, $1,000. The debt itself is accounted for in the normal fashion.

The entry to record the subsequent future exercise of the warrant would be

Cash	500.00	
Paid-in capital—warrants	34.85	
Common stock		100.00
Paid-in capital		434.85 (difference)

Assuming the warrants are not exercised, the journal entry is

Paid-in capital—warrants	34.85	
Paid-in capital—expired warrants		34.85

Debt Issued with Conversion Features and Stock Warrants

EITF 00-27 states that when a debt instrument includes both detachable instruments such as warrants, and an embedded beneficial conversion option, the proceeds of issuance should first be allocated among the convertible instrument and the other detachable instruments based on their relative fair values. Then, the EITF 98-5 model should be applied to the amount allocated to the convertible instrument to determine if the embedded conversion option has an intrinsic value.

Example of convertible debt issued with stock warrants

Cellular Communicators issues $1,000,000 of convertible debt with 100,000 detachable warrants. The debt is convertible into $10 par common stock at a price of $50 per share. At the commitment date of this issuance, the common stock is trading at $46 per share. Immediately after the issuance, the bonds trade at 85 and the warrants trade at $2. The issuance proceeds of $1,000,000 is allocated to the two instruments as follows:

$850,000 /($850,000 + $200,000) x $1,000,000 = $809,524 to the debt
$200,000/($850,000 + $200,000) x $1,000,000 = $190,476 to the warrants

The intrinsic value of the conversion feature is next computed as follows:

$1,000,000/$50 per share = 20,000 shares to be issued upon conversion

The effective conversion price is the bond's allocated proceeds of $809,524 divided by 20,000 shares or $40.48

($46 current fair value of the stock – $40.48 effective conversion price) x 20,000 shares = $110,476, which is the implied discount granted on the bonds in connection with the conversion feature

Cellular Communicators would make the following entry to recognize the issuance of the bonds with warrants at 100:

Cash	1,000,000	
Discount on bonds payable	110,476	
Bonds payable		809,524
Additional paid-in capital		110,476
Paid-in capital—warrants		190,476

There are a wide range of features that may be incorporated into stock purchase warrants and it will often be a challenge to identify the substance of these features, and to then prescribe the proper accounting for each feature. One such example involves warrants that are issued with put options, sometimes called "puttable warrants." Such warrants allow the holder to purchase a fixed number of the issuer's shares at a fixed price (common to all warrants), but also are puttable by the holder at a specified date for a fixed monetary amount that the holder could require the issuer to pay in cash. For example, assume the warrants are issued when the entity's shares are trading at $12, and each warrant permits the purchase of 100 shares at $15 through April 30, 2006. If not previously exercised, the warrant holders can put each warrant back to the issuer for the equivalent of $14 per share, that is, for 100 ($14 – $12) = $200 per warrant. The warrant holder is thus assured (given the underlying stock price at inception) of at least $2 per share income, and of course may reap a much larger reward if the share price has risen beyond $15 by the expiration date.

FAS 150 applies to all freestanding instruments including those composed of more than one option or forward contract embodying obligations that require or that may require settlement by transfer of assets. The embedded put option in the foregoing example of a warrant does create a liability, since the issuer (the reporting entity) may be called upon to distribute assets (cash) to the holders of those put options. FSP 150-1 states that this is a liability even if the repurchase feature is conditional on a defined contingency in addition to the level of the issuer's share price. The warrant is not an outstanding share and therefore does not meet the exception for outstanding shares set forth by FAS 150.

FSP 150-1 provides examples of put options which are subject to only cash payment and also of those which could be settled by an issuance of stock. The former case is straightforward: the instrument must be classified as a liability if the share price at the reporting date is such that a cash payment would be demanded by the holders of the puttable warrants. If the share price at that date is such that exercise of the warrant would be elected over exercise of the put option, then the warrant would be included in equity, not in liabilities. In other words, classification would depend on current stock price and could change from period to period, although FSP 150-1 is not explicit on this point.

Other put arrangements call for settlement in shares. That is, if advantageous to do so, the warrant holders exercise the warrants and acquire shares, but if the strike price has not been attained at expiration date, the put is exercised and the reporting entity would have to settle, but instead of paying cash it would issue shares having an aggregate value equal to the put amount. Thus, at inception, the number of shares that the puttable warrant obligates the reporting entity to issue can vary, and the instrument must be examined under the provisions of FAS 150 that deal with obligations to issue a variable number of shares. The facts and circumstances must be considered in judging whether the *monetary value* of the obligation to issue a number of shares that varies is predominantly based on a fixed monetary amount known at inception; if so; it is a liability under FAS 150.

Yet another variation, also illustrated by FSP 150-1, is the warrant for the purchase of shares, which shares are puttable. The holder can exercise the warrant and then immediately force the issuer to repurchase the shares thereby issued. The price at which the shares could be put would be defined in the warrant, and the likelihood that the put option would be exercised would vary with the market value of the shares. Obviously, if the shares acquired by exercise of the warrant had a greater market value than the put price, the put would not be invoked. Accordingly, whether these warrants would be classified as equity or liability would depend on the market value of the underlying shares, and this could change from one balance sheet date to the next. However if the shares to be issued upon warrant exercise were to have a mandatory redemption feature, then the warrants would be reportable as liabilities in any case.

FSP 150-1 offers several other examples, illustrating more complex features that may be found in stock purchase warrants which, depending on circumstances, might necessitate classification as liabilities in the balance sheet.

Through-Put and Take-or-Pay Contracts

Through-put and take-or-pay contracts are sometimes used to help a supplier pay for new facilities, machines, or other expenditures. They are negotiated as a way of arranging financing for the facilities that will produce the goods or provide the services desired by a purchaser. A through-put contract is an agreement between the owner of a transportation facility or manufacturing facility (such as a pipeline) and a purchaser (such as an oil processor) that requires the purchaser to pay specified amounts at future dates to the owner in return for the transportation or manufacture of a product. A take-or-pay contract is similar. It is an agreement between a purchaser and a supplier that requires the purchaser to pay specified amounts at future dates in return for products or services. In both types of contracts, the purchaser is required to make the specified payments even if it does not receive goods or services.

Some of these contracts are reported on the balance sheet as an asset and a liability. Others are not reported. Other than standards relating to recognition of losses on unconditional purchase obligations (ARB 43, chap. 4), there are no standards that require the contracts to be recognized on the balance sheet. However, FAS 47 requires certain disclosures to be made.

Mandatorily Redeemable Shares and Similar Instructions

FAS 150, issued in May 2003, requires that shares of stock (typically, but not necessarily, preferred shares) that are issued with mandatory redemption features be reported as liabilities rather than equity instruments. Payments or accruals of "dividends" and other amounts to be paid to holders of such shares are to be reported as interest expense. The only exception to those rules is for shares that are required to be redeemed only upon the liquidation or termination of the issuer.

FAS 150 is effective for shares issued or modified after May 31, 2003. For previously issued shares of public entities, FAS 150 was effective at the beginning of the first interim period beginning after June 15, 2003. For previously issued shares of nonpublic entities, FAS 150 became effective for the first fiscal period beginning after December 15, 2003. FAS 150 was to be implemented by reporting the cumulative effect of a change in an accounting principle for shares issued before May 15, 2003, and still existing at the beginning of the interim period of adoption. Restatement is not permitted.

After issuance, FAS 150 was the object of concern and criticism, particularly due to the perceived lack of opportunity to educate financial statement users regarding the potentially large impact on entities' balance sheets—at the extreme, eliminating all (or even *more than all)* of previously reported equity. In response, FASB issued FSP 150-3, which delayed the effective date for nonpublic reporting entities. Specifically, for instruments that are mandatorily redeemable on fixed dates for amounts that either are fixed or are determined by reference to an interest rate index, currency index, or another external index, the classification, measurement, and disclosure provisions of FAS 150 was deferred and will be effective for fiscal periods beginning after December 15, 2004.

For all other financial instruments that are mandatorily redeemable, the classification, measurement, and disclosure provisions of FAS 150 have been deferred *indefinitely*, pending further FASB action. During that deferral period, FASB expressed its plans to reconsider implementation issues and, perhaps, classification or measurement guidance for those instruments in conjunction with its larger, ongoing project on liabilities and equity.

In the authors' opinion, financial statement preparers should not presume that this application of FAS 150 will be rescinded, although that is a possibility. There would not appear to be a conceptually sound argument for why public entities having such mandatorily redeemable instruments would be required to report these as liabilities, while granting nonpublic ones an exemption. Accordingly, at minimum, nonpublic entities having mandatorily redeemable shares should educate lenders and other financial statement users to the implications of the new standard and, where necessary and feasible, arrange to amend loan agreements containing covenants which would be violated by a sudden, major change in apparent debt/equity ratios. In other cases, it might be wise, or necessary, to revise the underlying shareholder agreements that define the mandatory redemption provisions. For example, "buy sell" agreements might be superseded by agreements between the individual shareholders themselves, providing for buyouts of retiring or deceased shareholders by the other owners, rather than by the entity itself, and thereby averting liability classification.

Note also (as also set forth in FSP 150-3) that deferral of the disclosure requirements under FAS 150, as described above, does not remove the requirements under FAS 129, which requires the disclosure of information about the pertinent rights and privileges of the various securities outstanding, including mandatory redemption requirements.

FSP 150-3 has also deferred indefinitely the *measurement* provisions of FAS 150, both as to the parent in consolidated financial statements and as to the subsidiary that issued the instruments that resulted in mandatorily redeemable noncontrolling interests before November 5, 2003. For those instruments, the measurement guidance for redeemable shares and noncontrolling interests under GAAP (e.g., EITF D-98) continues to apply during the deferral period. However, the *classification* provisions are not deferred. (See discussion of D-98 at the end of this chapter.)

If on the date of adoption the redemption price is greater than the book value of the shares, the company would *recognize a liability* for the redemption price of the shares that are subject to mandatory redemption, reclassifying amounts previously recognized in equity accounts. The difference between the redemption price and amounts previously recorded in equity is reported on the income statement as a cumulative effect transition adjustment loss. If the redemption price exceeds the company's equity balance, the cumulative transition loss should be reported as an excess of liabilities over assets (a deficit in the stockholders' equity section). In the opposite case, it is reported as an excess of assets over liabilities (i.e., as positive equity).

Shares are mandatorily redeemable if the issuer has an unconditional obligation to redeem the shares by transferring its assets at a specified or determinable date (or dates) or upon an event certain to occur (for example, the death of the holder). The obligation to transfer assets must be unconditional—that is, there is no specified event that is outside the control of the issuer that will release the issuer from its obligation. Thus, callable preferred shares, which are redeemable at the issuer's option, and convertible preferred shares, which are redeemable at the holder's option, are not mandatorily redeemable shares.

FAS 150 requires this reporting for all mandatorily redeemable financial instruments, unless the redemption is required to occur only upon the liquidation or termination of the reporting entity. The exception exists because the fundamental *going concern* assumption underlying GAAP financial reporting would be violated if a classification was imposed in GAAP financial statements that presumed or was conditioned on the reporting entity's cessation as a going concern. However, the exception under FAS 150 did not, as issued, extend to mandatorily redeemable financial instruments of a consolidated subsidiary, in the consolidated financial statements of its parent entity. Since it is the *going concern* status of the reporting entity (i.e., the parent) that is of significance, the mandatory redemption feature of the subsidiary's instruments, albeit conditional, was to be reported consistent with FAS 150's provisions. However, subsequently FSP 150-3 has indefinitely postponed the effective date of this provision for noncontrolling interests. This deferral is applicable to both publicly held and nonpublic reporting entities.

Example of mandatorily redeemable preferred shares

On June 1, 2004, Verde Corporation issues 1,000 shares of mandatorily redeemable 5% preferred stock with a par value $100 for $110,330. The shares are redeemable at $150 on May 31, 2011. At issuance, Verde Corporation recognizes a liability of $110,330.

Some corporations and partnerships, primarily closely held ones, issue shares or units that are redeemed at the death of the holder. If those shares or units represents the only shares or units in the entity, the entity reports those instruments as liabilities and describes them in its statement of financial position as shares (or units) subject to mandatory redemption, to distinguish them from other liabilities. The classification is unaffected by any insurance policies that the entity may have on the holders' lives. The entity presents interest expense and payments to holders of those instruments separately, apart from interest and payments to other creditors in its statements of income and cash flows. The entity also discloses that the instruments are mandatorily redeemable upon the death of the holders.

Example of shares that are mandatorily redeemable at the death of the holder

Mike and Ike are equal shareholders in M&I's Auto Repair, Inc. Upon the death of either shareholder, the corporation will redeem shares of the deceased for half of the book value of the corporation. The following information would be disclosed in the notes to the financial statements:

All of the corporation's shares are subject to mandatory redemption upon death of the shareholders, and are thus reported as a liability. The liability amount consists of

Common stock—$100 par value, 1,000 shares authorized, issued and outstanding	$100,000
Undistributed earnings attributable to those shares	50,000
Accumulated other comprehensive income	(2,000)
Total liability	$148,000

After issuance, the amount of the liability for the mandatorily redeemable shares should be adjusted using the effective interest method if both the amount to be paid and the settlement date are fixed. If either the amount to be paid or the settlement date varies based on specified conditions, the liability is measured subsequently at the amount of cash that would be paid under the conditions specified in the contract if settlement occurred at the reporting date, recognizing the resulting change in that amount from the previous reporting date as interest cost.

Example of mandatorily redeemable preferred shares (continued)

The effective interest rate, calculated as described in the "Effective Interest Method" section of this chapter, is 8.5%. Verde Corporation would recognize the following annual interest expense and liability amounts:

	Cash paid	*Interest at 8.5% annually*	*Change in liability*	*Ending liability*
06/01/04				110,330
05/31/05	5,000	9,378	4,378	114,708
05/31/06	5,000	9,750	4,750	119,458
05/31/07	5,000	10,154	5,154	124,612
05/31/08	5,000	10,592	5,592	130,204
05/31/09	5,000	11,067	6,068	136,271
05/31/10	5,000	11,583	6,583	142,854
05/31/11	155,000	12,146	(142,854)	0

The entry to record the first "dividend" payment would be

Interest expense	9,378	
Liability		4,378
Cash		5,000

If shares have a conditional redemption feature, which requires the issuer to redeem the shares by transferring its assets upon an event not certain to occur, the shares become mandatorily redeemable—and, therefore, become a liability—if that event occurs, the event becomes certain to occur, or the condition is otherwise resolved. The fair value of the shares is reclassified as a liability, and equity is reduced by that amount, recognizing no gain or loss.

Note that when redemption value is based on a notion of fair value, defined in the underlying agreement, the initial recognition of the difference between this computed amount and the corresponding book value will almost inevitably result in a surplus or deficit. In other words, the promised redemption amount, measured at transition and again at each balance sheet date, will not equal the book value of the equity which is subject to redemption. This discrepancy must be reflected in stockholders' equity, even though the redeemable equity is reclassified to a liability. In effect, the redemption arrangement will result in either a residual in equity (assuming redemption were to fully occur at the balance sheet date) or a deficit, because the agreement provides that redeeming shareholders are entitled to more or less than their respective pro rata shares of the book value of their equity claims. This point is reiterated by FSP 150-2, which states that if the redemption price of mandatorily redeemable shares is greater than the book value of those shares, the company should report the excess as a deficit (equity), even though the mandatorily redeemable shares are reported as a liability.

Common shares that are mandatorily redeemable are not included in the denominator when computing basic or diluted earnings per share. If any amounts, including contractual (accumulated) dividends, attributable to shares that are to be redeemed or repurchased have not been recognized as interest expense, those amounts are deducted in computing income available to common shareholders (the numerator of the calculation), consistently with the "two-class" method set forth in FAS 128 (Chapter 18). The redemption requirements for mandatorily redeemable shares for each of the next five years are required to be disclosed in the notes to the financial statements.

Obligations to Issue or Repurchase Shares

FAS 150 also requires that certain financial instruments that require an entity to purchase or issue its own equity shares be reported as liabilities. FAS 150 does not apply to financial instruments that are issued as contingent consideration in a business combination (Chapter 11) or obligations under stock-based compensation plans that are accounted for under FAS 123, APB 25, or SOP 93-6 (Chapter 17). It also does not apply to an embedded feature of a financial instrument unless that financial instrument is a derivative in its entirety.

Additional discussion and examples of FAS 150 are found in Chapter 17.

Obligations to issue shares. If an entity enters into a contract that requires it or permits it at its discretion to issue a variable number of shares upon settlement, that contract is recognized as a liability if at inception the monetary value of the obligation is based solely or predominantly on one of the following criteria:

1. A fixed monetary amount known at inception (e.g., a $100,000 payable can be settled by issuing shares worth $100,000 at the then-current market value).
2. An amount that varies based on something other than the fair value of the issuer's equity shares (for example, a financial instrument indexed to the Dow that can be settled by issuing shares worth the index-adjusted amount at the then-current market value).
3. Variations inversely related to changes in the fair value of the entity's equity shares (i.e., a written put option that could be net share settled).

Contracts that meet one of the above criteria are recognized at fair value at the date of issuance and at every measurement date afterwards. The changes in the fair value are recognized in earnings unless the contract falls within the scope of FAS 133 and that statement requires the changes to be recognized elsewhere.

Example of a contract with a fixed monetary amount known at inception

Numero Uno Corp. purchases equipment worth $100,000 and agrees to pay $110,000 at the end of one year or, at its option, to issue shares worth $112,000. The contract is recognized as a liability at issuance of $100,000. Subsequent to issuance the liability is remeasured at the fair value of the contract, which would be the accreted value of the cash payment amount ($110,000).

Obligations to repurchase shares. If an entity (the issuer) enters into a contract that obligates it to transfer assets to either repurchase its own equity shares or to pay an amount that is indexed to the price of its own shares, the contract is to be reported as a liability (or in certain cases, as an asset, if the fair value of the contract is favorable to the issuer). Examples of that type of financial instrument are written put options on the option writer's (issuer's) equity shares, and forward contracts to repurchase an issuer's own equity shares if those instruments require physical or net cash settlement. (If the repurchase obligation is a redemption feature of common or preferred shares issued, see "Mandatorily Redeemable Shares" in this chapter.)

FAS 150 requires that an issuer classify a financial instrument that is within its scope as a liability (or as an asset in some circumstances) because that financial instrument embodies an obligation of the issuer. FAS 150 addresses three types of freestanding financial instruments that embody obligations of the issuer: mandatorily redeemable financial instruments, obligations to repurchase the issuer's equity shares by transferring assets, and certain obligations to issue a variable number of shares. Instruments within the scope of FAS 150 should be classified and measured in accordance with FAS 150 per EITF D-98.

Written put options are measured initially and subsequently at fair value. Forward contracts are initially measured at the fair value of the shares to be repurchased (adjusted by any consideration or unstated rights or privileges) if the contract requires physical settlement for cash. The offset to the liability entry is a debit to equity. Subsequent to issuance, forward contracts are remeasured in one of two ways.

1. If both the amount to be paid and the settlement date are fixed, the contract is measured at the present value of the amount to be paid, computed using the rate implicit in the contract at inception.

2. If either the amount to be paid or the settlement date varies based on specified conditions, the contract is measured at the amount of cash that would be paid under the conditions specified in the contract if settlement occurred at the reporting date.

Under either measure, the amount of the change from the previous reporting date is recognized as interest cost.

Example of a written put option on a fixed number of shares

Numero Dos Corp. writes a put allowing the purchaser to sell 100 shares of Numero Dos common stock at $20 per share in six months. The purchaser pays Numero Dos $300 for the right to put the 100 shares. Numero Dos's common stock is currently trading at $23. Numero Dos reports a liability of $300. The liability is subsequently remeasured at the fair value of the put option.

Example of a forward contract with a variable settlement date

Numero Tres Corp. enters into a contract to purchase 200 shares of its subsidiary at $25 in two years. However, if the holder of the shares dies before the settlement date, Numero Tres agrees to purchase the shares at the present value of $25 at the settlement date computed using the then-current prime rate. The shares are currently trading at $22. The liability to repurchase shares is initially reported at $4,400. At each subsequent measurement date, Numero Tres would adjust the liability to the present value of $25 at settlement date using the discount rate implicit in the contract, unless the holder of the shares had died. If the holder of the shares had died, Numero Tres would adjust the liability to the present value of $25 at settlement date using the then-current prime rate. For example, if one year from issuance date the holder is still alive, the liability would be adjusted to $4,690 using the 6.6% rate implicit in the agreement. The adjustment amount of $290 would be charged to interest expense. If instead the holder had died and the prime rate was 5%, the liability would be adjusted to $4,762 ($5,000/1.05) and the adjustment of $362 would be charged to interest expense.

An entity that has entered into a forward contract that requires physical settlement by repurchase of a fixed number of its equity shares of common stock in exchange for cash does not include those shares in the denominator when computing basic or diluted earnings per share. If any amounts, including contractual (accumulated) dividends, attributable to shares that are to be redeemed or repurchased have not been recognized as interest expense, those amounts are deducted in computing income available to common shareholders (the numerator of the calculation), consistently with the "two-class" method set forth in FAS 128 (Chapter 18).

Measuring Liabilities at Fair Value

Under GAAP, until extinguished, long-term debt is measured at the amount recorded at the date of issuance, reduced by payments made and adjusted for any amortization since issuance. This historical cost-based approach is not, however, universally viewed as contributing to the most meaningful financial reporting. In recent years, FASB has indicated its belief that more appropriate financial reporting would result if all financial liabilities (and assets) were reported at their respective fair values, rather than at amounts based on historical cost. Fair value of a liability is an estimated market exit price, that is, an estimate of the amount that would have been paid if the entity had settled the liability on the balance sheet date.

Many preparers and users of financial statements question the relevance of information about the fair value of a financial liability, given that management does not intend, and may not even be able, to settle the obligation before the stated maturity. In effect, the fair value amounts are purely hypothetical and do not alter the real obligation represented by the cost-based carrying amount of the liability at issue.

On the other hand, under the current reporting model it is entirely possible that an entity will report gains from debt extinguishment as a result of the early retirement of a debt obligation carrying a below-market interest rate, even if that extinguishment is funded by the immediate issuance of debt bearing the current market rate. Notwithstanding that the entity's real economic position has not been improved (and may have been diminished), a gain has been reported, which many would agree is misleading. The following example illustrates this problem.

Example

Company A and Company B are competitors, they both are publicly held, and both have bonds outstanding. On December 31, 2005, Company A owes $2,000,000 due in 6 years that carries a fixed interest rate of 10%. Company B also owes $2,000,000 due in 6 years, but Company B issued its bonds in a less favorable interest rate environment. Its debt carries an interest rate of 14%. The two companies have equivalent credit ratings. The prevailing market interest rate for both companies changes to 12% on December 31, 2005. Under historical cost-based GAAP, each company will report $2,000,000 of outstanding debt in its statement of financial position dated December 31, 2005. The fair value of Company A's debt at that date is $1,835,500, while the fair value of Company B's debt is $2,164,500—both fair values computed at the present value of the interest and principal payments at the prevailing market rate of 12%.

If Company A paid off its bonds, it would recognize a gain of $164,500 ($2,000,000 – $1,835,500). But for Company A to recognize its gain, it would have had to repay debt that carried a favorable interest rate. Company A would lose its economically advantageous position of being a company with below-market financing. In addition, if Company A had not used $1,835,500 to repay the debt, it could have invested that amount in its own operations and perhaps earned a higher return. Moreover, if Company A continues to need financing, it will have to refinance at the higher current interest rate. Repurchasing its bonds might not have been the best way for Company A to invest its resources, and might have been motivated, in part, by the desire to manage reported earnings in 2005.

If Company B retired its bonds, it would recognize a loss of $164,500 ($2,000,000 – $2,164,500). As an alternative, Company B could leave its bonds outstanding and realize its loss by paying above-market rates during the remaining 6 years of their term. Depending on the available alternative uses of its money, repaying the bonds and relieving future operations of the burden of above-market interest payments may be the best use of its resources, but Company B would suffer a loss as a result—a loss that can be avoided simply by choosing to not repay its debt.

Company A's gain and Company B's loss would be caused by changes in interest rates—not by a decision to repay debt. The existing measurement model for liabilities sometimes provides an incentive for unwise actions. If Company A wanted to report a gain, it could pay off its debt, even though that might not have been the best use of its resources. If Company B wanted to avoid a loss, it could allow its bonds to remain outstanding, even though the best economic decision would have been to retire them.

The effects of financing decisions, including that of leaving existing financing in place, whether made actively or indirectly through inattention, can significantly impact entity performance. Investors and creditors need information that will help them evaluate the effects of an entity's decision to settle a liability or allow it to remain outstanding. From this perspective, it is logical that information based on prices that reflect the market's assessment, under current conditions, of the present values of the future cash flows embodied in an entity's financial instruments would be more relevant for investors' and creditors' decisions than information based on historic, superseded market prices. Those older market prices reflect both an old interest rate and an outdated assessment of the amounts, timing, and uncertainty of future cash flows.

The project to replace historical data about financial liabilities with fair value data continues to be very controversial. Among opponents are financial institutions that would have to reprice virtually the entire balance sheet at each reporting date and that might see a significant increase in periodic earnings volatility (albeit, reflecting economic reality). It is not clear whether FASB will be successful in changing this longstanding tradition of reporting essentially all financial liabilities at historical cost.

Proposed Standards for Convertible Debt and Debt Issued with Warrants

FASB has proposed (in its *Liabilities and Equity* project) new standards for the issuers of convertible debt and other compound financial instruments. It believes that separate balance sheet presentation of liability components and equity components of a compound instrument more faithfully represents the rights and obligations embedded in that instrument than does presenting the instrument entirely as a liability or entirely as equity.

With certain exceptions, the proposed standard would require that proceeds received from the issuance of a compound financial instrument be allocated to its components based on the relative fair values of those components. Under a **relative-fair-value method,** the fair value of each of the separately classified components is determined independently of the fair values of the other components. The proceeds of issuing the compound financial instrument are then allocated to the components on a pro rata basis.

If it is impracticable to apply the relative-fair-value method because the fair value of one of the components cannot be reliably determined, the proceeds would be allocated to the components using the **with-and-without method**. Under that method, the fair value of the compound financial instrument is compared to the fair value of a hypothetical financial instrument that contains all the same components except the specific component being valued. The value of the component or components that can be reliably measured is measured at its fair value determined as if it were freestanding. The value of the remaining component is the difference between the amount assigned to the component(s) that can be reliably measured and the proceeds of issuance of the compound financial instrument.

If a financial instrument contains a **component that is a derivative,** the proceeds of issuing that financial instrument would be allocated to its components using the with-and-without method, first allocating to the derivative component the amount of proceeds that would be equal to its fair value as if it were freestanding. That is, the value of the nonderivative component is the difference between the amount assigned to the derivative component and the proceeds of issuance of the compound financial instrument.

Because APB 14, which would be superseded by the proposed standards, required use of the relative-fair-value method for allocating the proceeds of debt issued with stock purchase warrants, no changes in accounting for those compound instruments are expected.

Certain financial instruments, in addition to containing a liability component, an equity component, or both, also contain a component that, freestanding, would be classified as an asset. An example of that type of financial instrument is callable convertible debt, which contains a call option, a debt, and a conversion option. Unless the asset component is required by GAAP to be separated (e.g., per FAS 133), the effect of the asset component would be incorporated into the determination of the fair values of the liability component and the equity component.

For purposes of initial measurement of the components of compound financial instruments, the following general rules would be applied under the proposed standard:

- If a compound financial instrument has no component that is an outstanding share of stock, the obligation that is classified as a liability would be considered an unconditional obligation, and the obligation that is classified as equity would be considered a conditional obligation.

- If a compound financial instrument has a component that is an outstanding share of stock (other than mandatorily redeemable stock), the instrument would be considered to be (1) an outstanding equity share and (2) a conditional obligation.

Example comparing existing and proposed standards—issuance of convertible debt

An entity issues at par 10,000 noncallable bonds, for a total issue proceeds of $10,000,000. Each bond can be converted by the holder into 100 shares of the entity's $10 par common stock. The noncallable bonds contain the following components:

1. An obligation to repay principal
2. An obligation to pay interest periodically
3. An obligation to issue equity shares if the conversion option is exercised

The first two components are liabilities. The third component is an equity component because it requires the issuance of a fixed number of shares. Because none of the components are outstanding shares of stock, the liability components are unconditional. The fair value of comparable nonconvertible debt is $850; the fair value of the conversion feature is $150.

Entry upon issuance of the bonds	*Proposed standards*		*Existing standards*	
Cash	10,000,000		10,000,000	
Discounts on bonds payable	1,500,000			
Bonds payable		10,000,000		10,000,000
Paid-in capital from conversion option		1,500,000		

The discount on the bonds payable would be amortized over the life of the debt instrument using the effective interest method.

The proposed standard also provides guidance on the accounting for costs incurred to issue a financial instrument. Costs incurred to issue a financial instrument would be accounted for as a reduction of the proceeds of issuance before allocation of those proceeds to the components. Issuance costs are only the incremental costs directly attributable to issuance of an instrument that would not have been incurred if the instrument had not been issued.

It would also be required that a gain or loss, if any, on the liability component of convertible debt be recognized in earnings if the debt were extinguished by repayment or by conversion. That gain or loss would be calculated as the difference between the portion of the consideration paid (or in the case of conversion, the fair value of the compound convertible debt instrument at the date of conversion) that is attributed to the liability component and its carrying amount at the date it is extinguished. The amount of consideration or fair value that is attributed to the liability component would be determined using the relative-fair-value method unless the use of that method is impracticable, in which case the with-and-without method would be used.

Example comparing existing and proposed standards—conversion of convertible debt

Assume that $50,000 face value of the bonds in the previous example are converted when the market price of the convertible bonds is $55,500, the market price of the common stock is $11 per share, and the unamortized discount on those bonds is $6,500. The fair value of comparable nonconvertible debt is $850 per bond; the fair value of the conversion feature is $250.

	Proposed		*Existing standards using*			
Entry upon conversion of the bonds	*standards*		*Book value*		*Market value*	
Bonds payable	50,000		50,000		50,000	
Paid-in capital from conversion option	7,114					
Loss on conversion shares					12,000	
Discount on bonds payable		6,500				6,500
Common stock		50,000		50,000		50,000
Additional paid-in capital						5,500
Gain on conversion of shares		614				

The gain on conversion under the proposed standards is the difference between the fair value of the liability component on the date of conversion and the carrying value of the liability component. The fair value of the liability component is computed as follows:

$$\$850/(\$850 + \$250) \times \$55{,}500 = \$42{,}886$$

The book value of the liability component is $50,000 – $6,500 = $43,500. The gain is $614. The proceeds from issuing the common shares are $50,386, which is the $7,500 from issuance plus the $42,886 value of the liability component surrendered. Those proceeds are recorded in the common stock account ($50,000) and paid-in capital from conversion option ($386, which is the $7,500 initially recorded less the adjustment of $7,114 at the time of conversion).

The proposal discussed above was to have been adopted for implementation in mid-2002, but a number of contentious issues remain unresolved as of mid-2004. Accordingly, it is not possible to predict when, or if, this standard will be adopted. For more information about this proposed standard, see Chapter 17.

EMERGING ISSUES TASK FORCE ISSUES SUMMARIES

85-17 Accrued Interest upon Conversion of Convertible Debt

If terms of the debt instrument provide that any accrued interest at the date of conversion is forfeited by the former debt holder, the accrued interest (net of income tax) from the last payment date to the conversion date should be charged to interest expense and credited to capital as a part of the cost of the securities issued.

85-29 Convertible Bonds with a "Premium Put"

A liability for the put premium should be accrued over the period from the date of issuance to the initial put date. Accrual should continue regardless of market value changes. If the put expires unexercised and if the market value of the common stock exceeds the put price at expiration date, the put premium should be credited to additional paid-in capital. If the put expires unexercised and if the put price exceeds the market value of the common stock, the put premium should be amortized as a yield adjustment over the remaining term of the debt. The embedded put is a derivative instrument subject to FAS 133. However, because FAS 133 permits entities not to account separately for convertible bonds issued at par with a "premium put" embedded in pre-1998 or pre-1999 hybrid instruments, the consensus in this Issue would continue to apply if the entity elects not to separately account for the embedded derivative.

86-36 Invasion of a Defeasance Trust

Removal of assets from a defeasance trust does not affect the entity's prior recognition of the extinguishment of debt if at the same time a proportional amount of the outstanding bonds are purchased in the marketplace. Any resulting gain or loss would not be classified as extraordinary.

NOTE: Although FAS 140 does not permit in-substance defeasance of debt, it allowed those already recognized to remain off the balance sheet. Thus, this opinion applies to those preexisting defeasance trusts.

87-19 Substituted Debtors in a Troubled Debt Restructuring

Given the sale of real estate collateral (present value less than the net investment) with the requirement for the purchaser to make direct payment to the creditor, the creditor is still required to recognize a loss in the amount by which the net investment in the loan exceeds the fair value of the payments to be received. The fair value of the payments should be recorded as an asset.

88-18 Sales of Future Revenue

Classification of the proceeds from an investor to obtain a right to a specified amount of revenues or a measure of income in the future would be classified as either debt or deferred income by the investee, based upon the specific facts and circumstances of the transaction. This EITF identifies six factors that would cause the amounts to be recorded as debt. They are

1. The transaction does not purport to be a sale.
2. The entity has significant continuing involvement in the generation of the cash flows due the investor.
3. The transaction is cancelable by either party through payment of a lump sum or other transfer of assets by the entity.
4. The investor's rate of return is implicitly or explicitly limited by the terms of the transaction.
5. Variations in the entity's revenue or income underlying the transaction have only a trifling impact on the investor's rate of return.
6. The investor has any recourse to the entity relating to the payments due the investor.

Amounts recorded as debt should be amortized under the interest method and amounts recorded as deferred income should be amortized under the units-of-revenue method. The proceeds classified as foreign-currency-denominated debt would be subject to recognition of foreign currency transaction gains and losses under FAS 52. FAS 133 established cash flow hedge accounting for hedges of the variability of the functional currency equivalent of future foreign-currency-denominated cash flows. Classification of the proceeds as deferred income would be a nonmonetary liability. Thus, no foreign exchange gains or losses would arise under FAS 52. The Task Force did not address any situations when immediate income recognition would be appropriate.

90-19 Convertible Bonds with Issuer Option to Settle for Cash upon Conversion

If a convertible bond is issued with terms that require the issuer to satisfy the obligation entirely in cash based on the fixed number of shares multiplied by the stock price on the date of conversion, FAS 133 requires the embedded derivative (the conversion option, which is a cash-settled written call option to the issuer) to be separated from the debt host contract and accounted for by the issuer separately as a derivative instrument.

If a convertible bond is issued with terms that require the issuer to satisfy the obligation (the amount accrued to the benefit of the holder exclusive of the conversion spread) in cash and to satisfy the conversion spread (the excess conversion value over the accreted value) in either cash or stock, the bond should be accounted for like convertible debt (that is, as a combined instrument) if the conversion spread meets the requirements of EITF 00-19. If the conversion spread feature does not meet those provisions, FAS 133 requires that the embedded derivative be separated from the debt host contract and accounted for by the issuer separately as a derivative instrument.

If a convertible bond is issued with terms that permit the issuer to satisfy the entire obligation in either stock or cash, the bond should be accounted for as conventional convertible debt. If the holder exercises the conversion and the issuer pays cash, the debt is extinguished and the issuer should account for the transaction in accordance with APB 26.

If the issuer must satisfy the obligation entirely with cash, the only EPS effect is the charge to income for the conversion spread. If the entire obligation may be satisfied in either stock or cash, the bond should be considered a common stock equivalent. If the issuer must satisfy the accreted value of the obligation in cash and may satisfy the conversion spread in either cash or stock, there is no adjustment to then numerator in the EPS computation for the cash-settled portion because that portion of the instrument will always be settled in cash. The conversion spread should be included in diluted earnings per share and accounted for in accordance with FAS 128.

94-8 Accounting for Conversion of a Loan into a Debt Security in a Debt Restructuring

The initial cost basis of a debt security of the original debtor received as part of a debt restructuring should be the security's fair value at the date of the restructuring. Any excess fair value of the security over the net carrying amount of the loan should be recorded as a recovery on the loan. Any excess net carrying value amount of the loan over the fair value of the security should be recorded as a charge-off to the allowance for credit losses. Additionally, securities received in a restructuring for only past-due interest on a loan should be measured at the date of the restructuring and accounted for with the entity's policy for recognizing cash received for past-due interest. After the restructuring, the securities should be accounted for according to the provisions of FAS 115.

96-19 Debtor's Accounting for a Modification or Exchange of Debt Instruments

An exchange of debt instruments with substantially different terms is a debt extinguishment and should be accounted for in accordance with FAS 140. Any substantial modification in the terms of an existing debt, other than for a troubled debt restructuring, should similarly be reported as a debt extinguishment.

An exchange or modification is considered substantial when the present value of cash flows under the new debt instrument is at least 10% different from the present value of the remaining cash flows under the terms of the original instrument. For the purpose of the 10% test, the effective interest rate of the original debt instrument is used as the discount rate.

Cash flows can be affected by changes in principal amounts, interest rates, maturity, or by fees exchanged to effect changes in

1. Recourse or nonrecourse features
2. Priority of the obligation
3. Collateralized or noncollateralized features
4. Debt covenants and/or waivers
5. The guarantor
6. Option features

Assuming the 10% test is met and the debt instrument are deemed to be substantially different, the new investment should be initially recorded at fair value and that amount should be used to determine debt extinguishment gain or loss to be recognized, as well as the effective rate of the new instrument. Fees paid by the debtor to the creditor or received by the debtor from the creditor should be included in determining debt extinguishment gain or loss. Additionally, any costs incurred with third parties should be amortized using the interest method in a manner similar to that used for debt issue costs.

Assuming the 10% test is not met and the debt instruments are not deemed to be substantially different, then the new effective interest is to be determined based on the carrying amount of the original instrument and the revised cash flows. Fees paid by the debtor to the creditor or received by the debtor from the creditor should be amortized as an adjustment to interest expense over the remaining term of the modified debt instrument using the interest method. Additionally, any costs incurred with third parties should be expensed as incurred.

96-22 Applicability of the Disclosures Required by FASB Statement 114 When a Loan Is Restructured in a Troubled Debt Restructuring into Two (or More) Loans

Since they are legally distinct from the original loan, restructuring loans should be considered separately in years after restructuring when addressing the applicability of disclosures. The measure of loan impairment would continue to be based on the terms of the original agreement. For SEC reporting purposes, the impact of multiple loan structures on the disclosure of impaired loans should be made clear to users.

98-5 Accounting for Convertible Securities with Beneficial Conversion Features or Contingently Adjustable Conversion Ratios

This consensus applies to convertible securities (debt or preferred stock) that are convertible to common stock (or other securities) via a nondetachable conversion right that is in the money at the date that the investor is committed to purchase the convertible securities. That type of conversion feature is called an "embedded beneficial conversion feature." The securities may be converted at a fixed price, a fixed discount to the market price at date of conversion, a variable discount to the market price at conversion, or the conversion price may be dependent upon future events. In addition, the conversion feature can be exercisable at issuance, at a stated date in the future, or upon the happening of a future event (such as an IPO).

Embedded beneficial conversion features are valued separately at issuance. The feature is recognized as additional paid-in capital by allocating a portion of the proceeds equal to the intrinsic value of the feature. The intrinsic value is computed at the commitment date as (1) the difference between the conversion price and the fair value of the common stock (or other securities) into which the security is convertible, multiplied by (2) the number of shares into which the security is convertible.

For convertible debt securities, a discount on the debt may result from the allocation of a portion of the proceeds to the conversion feature. That discount should be amortized over the period to the stated redemption date (modified by EITF 00-27). For convertible preferred securities, any "discount" on issuance is analogous to a dividend to the preferred shareholder and should be recognized using the effective interest method through the date of the earliest conversion.

If the conversion feature has multiple steps, the computation of the intrinsic value is made using the conversion terms most beneficial to the investor. For example, if the security was convertible at market price after three months and at a 25% discount to market price after one year, the 25% discount terms would be used to measure the intrinsic value. However, at any financial statement date, the cumulative amortization recorded must be the greater of (1) the amount computed using the effective interest method of amortization or (2) the amount of the benefit the investor would receive if the securities were converted at that date. If the securities are converted prior to the full amortization of the discount, the unamortized discount is included in the amount transferred to equity upon conversion.

If the security becomes convertible only upon occurrence (or failure to occur) of a future event outside the control of the investor or if the conversion terms change based on the occurrence (or failure to occur) of a future event, the value of the contingent beneficial conversion feature should be measured as of the commitment date, but it is not recognized in the financial statements until the contingency is resolved.

If a convertible debt security is extinguished prior to conversion, a portion of the reacquisition price of the debt security is allocated to the beneficial conversion feature. That portion is measured as the intrinsic value of the conversion feature at the extinguishment date. Any residual would be allocated to the debt security, and a gain or loss on extinguishment would be recorded.

99-1 Accounting for Debt Convertible into the Stock of a Consolidated Subsidiary

In the consolidated financial statements, (1) debt issued by a consolidated subsidiary that is convertible into that subsidiary's stock and (2) debt issued by a parent company that is convertible into the stock of a consolidated subsidiary should be accounted for in accordance with APB 14. That is, no portion of the proceeds from the issuance of the debt should be accounted for as attributable to the conversion feature. This Issue does not apply to convertible debt instruments that require a cash settlement by the issuer of an in-the-money conversion feature, that provide the holder an option to receive cash for an in-the-money conversion feature, or that have a beneficial conversion feature.

00-27 Application for EITF Issue 98-5, "Accounting for Convertible Securities with Beneficial Conversion Features or Contingently Adjustable Conversion Ratios" to Certain Convertible Instruments

This consensus addresses a number of issues about the application of EITF 98-5 in specific situations.

If an instrument includes both detachable instruments and an embedded beneficial conversion option, the proceeds of issuance should first be allocated among the convertible instrument and the other detachable instruments based on their relative fair values. Then, the Issue 98-5 model should be applied to the amount allocated to the convertible instrument to determine if the embedded conversion option has an intrinsic value.

If the conversion price could change upon the occurrence of a future event, assume that there are no changes to the current circumstances except the passage of time. Use the most favorable price that would be in effect if nothing were changed at the conversion date to measure the intrinsic value of an embedded conversion option. Changes to the conversion terms that are caused by future events not controlled by the issuer are recognized if and when the trigger event occurs.

If there is no intrinsic value to a conversion clause at issuance, but the conversion price resets after the commitment date and, upon reset, the conversion price is greater than the fair market value of the underlying stock, the beneficial conversion amount is recognized when the reset occurs. The beneficial conversion amount is measured by the number of shares that will be issued upon conversion multiplied by the decrease in price between the original conversion price and the reset price.

The definition of commitment date for purposes of applying EITF 98-5 is the same as the definition of a firm commitment in FAS 133. If an instrument includes both detachable instruments and an embedded beneficial conversion option, the commitment date should also be used when determining the relative fair values of all the instruments issued.

If a convertible instrument has a stated redemption date, a discount resulting from recording a beneficial conversion option should be amortized from the date of issuance to the stated redemption date, regardless of when the earliest conversion occurs. If the instrument has beneficial conversion features, the unamortized discount remaining at the date of conversion should be immediately recognized as interest expense or as a dividend, as appropriate.

If the terms of a contingent conversion option do not permit an issuer to compute the number of shares that the holder would receive upon conversion, the issuer should wait until the contingent event occurs and then compute the number of shares that would be received. The number of shares that would be received is compared to the number of shares that would have been received if the contingent event had not occurred to determine the excess number of shares. The number of excess shares multiplied by the stock price as of the commitment date equals the incremental intrinsic value that should be recognized.

If an instrument includes a beneficial conversion option that expires at the end of a stated period and the instrument then becomes mandatorily redeemable at a premium, the proceeds of issuance should be allocated between the debt and the embedded beneficial conversion features. The debt amount is then accreted to the redemption amount over the period to the required redemption date.

If interest or dividends are paid in kind, the commitment date for the paid-in-kind securities is the commitment date for the original instrument if the payment in kind is not discretionary. The payment is not discretionary if (1) neither the issuer nor the holder can elect other forms of payment for the interest or dividends and (2) if the original instrument was converted before dividends were declared or interest was accrued, the holder will receive the number of shares as if the accumulated dividends or interest have been paid in kind. If the payment in kind is discretionary, the commitment date for the paid-in-kind securities is the date that the interest is accrued or the dividends are declared.

If an issuer issues a convertible instrument as repayment of a nonconvertible instrument, the fair value of the newly issued convertible instrument equals the redemption amount owed at the maturity date of the old debt. That is, the carrying amount of the old debt is the proceeds received for applying EITF 98-5 to the new debt.

Several tentative conclusions that will be reconsidered at a future meeting are described below.

If a convertible instrument is extinguished prior to its maturity date, no portion of the reacquisition price should be allocated to the conversion option if that option had no intrinsic value at the issuance date.

The intrinsic value of a conversion feature at an early extinguishment date of convertible debt is recorded as a decrease in additional paid-in capital, which may result in a reduction in additional paid-in capital that is larger than the amount originally recorded in paid-in capital at issuance.

If an entity redeems convertible preferred stock with a beneficial conversion feature, the intrinsic value of the conversion feature that was recorded at issuance is reversed, and the remaining reacquisition price is allocated to the reacquisition of the stock. Any excess of that portion over the carrying amount of the stock is an adjustment to earnings available to common shareholders.

If a company issues a warrant that allows the holder to acquire a convertible instrument for a stated price and that warrant is classified as equity, the date used to measure the intrinsic value of the conversion option is the commitment date for the warrant, not its exercise date, provided that the issuer received fair value for the warrant when issued. The deemed proceeds for determining whether a beneficial conversion option exists are equal to the sum of the proceeds received for the warrant and the exercise price of the warrant. If that sum is less than the fair value of the common stock that would be received upon exercise of the convertible instrument that would be obtained upon exercise of the warrant, the excess represents a deemed distribution to the holder of the warrant, which is to be recognized over the life of the warrant. The deemed distribution is limited to the proceeds received for the warrant; that is, if the deemed distribution is larger than the proceeds received, the difference is not recognized until the warrant is exercised. If the issuer received less than fair value for the warrant upon issuance, the exercise date of the warrant should be used to measure the intrinsic value of the conversion option.

If a company issues a warrant that allows the holder to acquire a convertible instrument for a stated price and that warrant is classified as a liability, the date used to measure the intrinsic value of the conversion option is the exercise date for the warrant, not its commitment date. The deemed proceeds for determining whether a beneficial conversion option exists are equal to the sum of the fair value of the warrant on the exercise date and the exercise price of the warrant.

If a conversion feature permits the holder to receive both common stock and warrants to acquire common stock, the intrinsic value of the conversion option is measured as the difference between (1) the proceeds allocated to the common stock portion of the conversion feature and (2) the fair value at the commitment date of the common stock to be received by the holder upon conversion.

The guidance in EITF 00-19 should be used to evaluate whether the issuer controls settlement of the conversion feature of convertible preferred stock. If the issuer does not control settlement, the convertible preferred stock is considered temporary equity.

This Issue describes several other situations on which the EITF has not yet reached consensus.

01-1 Accounting for a Convertible Instrument Granted or Issued to a Nonemployee for Goods or Services or a Combination of Goods or Services and Cash

This issue describes the accounting for a convertible instrument that is used to pay a nonemployee for goods or services if that instrument contains a nondetachable conversion option. The measurement date under EITF 96-18 should be used to measure the intrinsic value of the conversion option rather than the commitment date. The proceeds from issuing the instrument for purposes of determining whether a beneficial conversion option exists is the fair value of the instrument or the fair value of the goods and services received, whichever is more reliably measured. The fair value of the convertible instrument can be measured by applying FAS 123, as interpreted by EITF 96-18. (For details, see Chapter 17.) Once the convertible instrument is issued, distributions paid or payable are financing costs rather than adjustments of the cost of the goods or services received.

If a purchaser of a convertible instrument that contains an embedded beneficial conversion option provides goods or services to the issuer under a separate contract, the contracts should be considered separately unless the separately stated pricing is not equal to fair value. If not equal to fair value, the terms of the respective transactions should be adjusted. The convertible instrument should be recognized at its fair value with a corresponding increase or decrease to the purchase price of the goods or services.

02-4 Determining Whether a Debtor's Modification or Exchange of Debt Instrument is within the Scope of FASB Statement No. 15

This consensus sets forth criteria to determine whether debt instrument modifications or exchanges of debt obligations should be deemed troubled debt restructurings. It is incorporated into the discussion of "Troubled Debt Restructuring" in this chapter.

02-15 Determining Whether Certain Conversions of Convertible Debt to Equity Securities Are within the Scope of FASB Statement No. 84

FAS 84 applies to all conversions of convertible debts that (1) occur pursuant to changed conversion privileges, (2) are exercisable only for a limited period of time, and (3) include the issuance of all of the equity securities issuable pursuant to conversion privileges included in the terms of the debt at issuance for each debt instrument that is converted, regardless of the party that initiates the offer or whether the offer relates to all debt holders.

03-7 Accounting for the Settlement of the Equity-Settled Portion of a Convertible Debt Instrument That Permits or Requires the Conversion Spread to Be Settled in Stock (Instrument C of EITF Issue No. 90-19, "Convertible Bonds with Issuer Options to Settle for Cash upon Conversion")

EITF 90-19 discusses issues relative to several variations of convertible debt instruments. That EITF Issue provided accounting guidance with respect to an "Instrument C" which contained the following provisions:

- Instrument is convertible at the option of its holder into a fixed number of shares of the issuer's common stock.
- At conversion, the issuer must settle the obligation to the holder as follows:
  - Payment in cash for the accreted value of the obligation (for a zero-coupon obligation, the accreted value is the amount received from the holder at issuance plus interest accreted from date of issuance to date of settlement)
  - Payment in either cash or stock to satisfy the conversion spread (the difference between the conversion value over the accreted value)
- If the holder does not exercise the conversion option, the issuer is obligated to settle the accreted value of the debt in cash at maturity

Questions have arisen regarding the accounting for the *settlement* of this instrument partially in cash (the recognized liability) and partially in stock (the unrecognized equity instrument). EITF 03-7 reached a consensus that only the cash payment is to be considered in computing gain or loss on settlement of the recognized liability. Shares transferred to the holder to settle the excess conversion spread represented by the embedded equity instrument are not considered part of the settlement of the debt component of the instrument.

D-98 Classification and Measurement of Redeemable Securities

In May 2003, the EITF added the following subsequent developments to EITF D-98 in response to FAS 150.

- FAS 150 requires that an issuer classify a financial instrument that is within its scope as a liability (or as an asset in some circumstances) because that financial instrument embodies an obligation of the issuer.
- FAS 150 addresses three types of freestanding financial instruments that embody obligations of the issuer: mandatorily redeemable financial instruments, obligations to repurchase the issuer's equity shares by transferring assets, and certain obligations to issue a variable number of shares. Instruments within the scope of FAS 150 should be classified and measured in accordance with that Statement. ASR 268 (Rule 5-02.28 of Regulation S-X) and the interpretive guidance in this staff announcement no longer apply for those instruments after the effective date of FAS 150.

STATEMENTS OF POSITION

97-1 Accounting by Participating Mortgage Loan Borrowers

This SOP establishes the borrower's accounting for a participating mortgage loan if the lender participates in increases in the market value of the mortgaged real estate project, the results of operations of that mortgaged real estate project, or both. It requires that certain disclosures be made in the financial statements. In addition, this SOP requires the following:

1. At origination, if the lender is entitled to participate in appreciation in the market value of the mortgaged real estate project, the borrower should determine the fair value of the participation feature and should recognize a participation liability for that amount. A corresponding debit should then be recorded to a debt-discount account. The debt discount should be amortized by the interest method, using the effective interest rate.
2. At the end of each reporting period, the balance of the participation liability should be adjusted if necessary, so that the liability equals the fair value of the participation feature at that point in time. The corresponding debit or credit should be adjusted to the related debt-discount account. The revised debt discount should then be amortized prospectively.

FASB STAFF POSITIONS

129-1 Disclosure Requirements under FASB Statement No. 129, *Disclosure of Information about Capital Structure*, Relating to Contingently Convertible Securities

This FSP identifies the qualitative and quantitative terms that must be disclosed so that users can understand the potential impact of conversion, including: events or changes in circumstances that would cause the contingency to be met and features necessary to understand the conversion rights, the conversion price and number of shares, events or changes that could adjust or change any features of the securities, and the manner of settlement upon conversion.

150-1 Issuer's Accounting for Freestanding Financial Instruments Composed of More Than One Option or Forward Contract Embodying Obligations under FASB Statement No. 150, *Accounting for Certain Financial Instruments with Characteristics of Both Liabilities and Equity*

This FSP provides illustrations of several types of stock purchase warrants which contain provisions which might necessitate presentation as liabilities in the issuers' balance sheets, under defined conditions. Several of the more common of these situations are described in this chapter.

150-2 Accounting for Mandatorily Redeemable Shares Requiring Redemption by Payment of an Amount That Differs from the Book Value of Those Shares, under FASB Statement No. 150, *Accounting for Certain Financial Instruments with Characteristics of Both Liabilities and Equity*

As explained in the chapter, this FSP further emphasized the FAS 150 provision that requires the difference between fair value and book value of stock that is subject to mandatory redemption at fair value to be presented in stockholders' equity.

150-3 Effective Date, Disclosures, and Transition for Mandatorily Redeemable Financial Instruments of Certain Nonpublic Entities and Certain Mandatorily Redeemable Noncontrolling Interests under FASB Statement No. 150, *Accounting for Certain Financial Instruments with Characteristics of Both Liabilities and Equity*

This postponed the effective date of certain provisions of FAS 150 and, for certain mandatory redemption arrangements of stock issued by nonpublic companies, indefinitely postponed implementation, pending the outcome of further FASB deliberations on a range of liability and equity issues.

14 LEASES

PERSPECTIVE AND ISSUES

Lease transactions have grown in popularity over the years as businesses look for new ways to finance their fixed asset additions. A lease agreement involves at least two parties, a lessor and a lessee, and an asset that is to be leased. The lessor, who owns the asset, agrees to grant the lessee the right to use it for a specified period of time in return for periodic rent payments.

There are several economic reasons why the lease transaction is considered. They are as follows:

1. The lessee (borrower) is able to obtain 100% financing
2. Income tax benefits available to one or both of the parties

3. The lessor receives the equivalent of interest as well as an asset with some remaining value at the end of the lease term

The lease transaction derives its accounting complexity from the number of alternatives available to the parties involved. Leases can be structured to allow differing income tax benefits associated with the leased asset that meet the objectives of the transacting parties. Leases can be used to transfer ownership of the leased asset, and they can be used to transfer the risks and rewards of ownership. In any event, the substance of the transaction dictates the accounting treatment, irrespective of its legal form. The lease transaction is probably the best example of the accounting profession's substance over form argument. If the transaction effectively transfers ownership to the lessee, then the substance of the transaction is that of a sale and, accordingly, it is recognized as such even though the transaction is legally structured as a lease.

FAS 13 sets forth the GAAP for lease accounting. Numerous pronouncements have followed which expand upon the base set by FAS 13. As a result of the extensive additions to the principles related to lease accounting, and the number and extent of changes made to the original pronouncement, it is cumbersome, if not impossible, to research a lease accounting issue by attempting to use the original pronouncements and the amendments thereto. Therefore, we recommend using the codified discussion of leases contained in the FASB Current Text (Section L10) as the basis for such research.

In January 2003, FASB issued its FIN 46, *Consolidation of Variable Interest Entities,* which was then closely followed by the issuance of a series of interpretive FASB Staff Positions (FSP), and then, in December 2003 it was superseded and replaced by FIN 46(R) which attempts to clear up much of the confusion inherent in the original interpretation. A comprehensive discussion of variable interest entities and FIN 46(R) is included in Chapter 11. FIN 46(R) supersedes EITF 90-15 which previously was used to determine whether a lessee under an operating lease was required to consolidate a "nonsubstantive" lessor. Under the provisions of FIN 46(R), many more lessor entities will be required to be consolidated with the financial statements of the lessee, especially in situations where the lessor and lessee have common or related-party ownership.

It is necessary for the lessee to first apply FIN 46(R) to evaluate its relationship with the lessor and, in that respect, FIN 46(R) takes precedence over FAS 13 and its many amendments. This is because if FIN 46(R) requires the lessee to consolidate the lessor, the effects of the lease transaction between the parties will be removed from the consolidated financial statements via an eliminating entry and, consequently, the consolidated reporting entity will depreciate the leased asset and reflect all of the costs of acquiring, holding, maintaining, and disposing of the asset. The lessor will, of course, in any separately issued financial statements, account for the lease in accordance with the appropriate lease accounting requirements that would apply absent FIN 46(R). Certain concepts and definitions discussed herein are also explained in Chapter 11 but are repeated and expanded upon here for the sake of completeness and further clarification in the specific context of lease transactions.

Sources of GAAP

FAS	*FIN*	*FTB*	*EITF*
13, 22, 23, 27, 28, 29, 66, 77, 91, 98, 140, 144, 145, 146	19, 21, 23, 24, 26, 27, 43, 45, 46(R)	79-10, 79-12, 79-13, 79-14, 79-15, 79-16, 82-1, 86-2, 88-1	85-16, 86-17, 86-33, 87-7, 88-10, 88-21, 89-16, 89-20, 90-14, 90-20, 92-1, 93-8, 95-1, 95-4, 95-17, 96-21, 97-1, 97-10, 98-9, 99-13, 00-11, 00-13, 01-8, 03-12, D-8, D-24

DEFINITIONS OF TERMS

Bargain purchase option. A provision allowing the lessee the option of purchasing the leased property for an amount, exclusive of lease payments, which is sufficiently lower than the expected fair value of the property at the date the option becomes exercisable. Exercise of the option must appear reasonably assured at the inception of the lease. GAAP does not offer additional guidance defining "sufficiently lower," in which many factors such as the time value of money, usage, and technological changes influence whether the option fulfills the criteria for a bargain.

Bargain renewal option. A provision allowing the lessee the option to renew the lease agreement for a rental payment sufficiently lower than the expected fair rental of the property at the date the option becomes exercisable. Exercise of the option must appear reasonably assured at the inception of the lease.

Contingent rentals. Rentals that represent the increases or decreases in lease payments that result from changes in the factors on which the lease payments are based occurring subsequent to the inception of the lease. However, changes due to the pass-through of increases in the construction or acquisition cost of the leased property or for increases in some measure of cost during the construction or preconstruction period are excluded from contingent rentals. Also, provisions that are dependent only upon the passage of time are excluded from contingent rentals. A lease payment that is based upon an existing index or rate, such as the consumer price index or the prime rate, is a contingent payment, and the computation of the minimum lease payments is based upon the index or rate applicable at the inception of the lease.

Controlling financial interest. The at-risk equity investors hold a controlling financial interest in an entity if they collectively

1. Have voting or similar rights (such as the rights of a common stockholder or general partner, or LLC member) to make decisions, directly or indirectly, about the entity's activities that significantly affect the entity's success.

   NOTE: If none of the investors hold these rights this criterion is not satisfied. In addition, if some investors' voting rights are not proportional to their obligations to absorb the entity's expected losses, or to receive the entity's expected residual rewards, or both, ***and*** *substantially all of the entity's activities involve or are conducted on behalf of an investor that has disproportionately few voting rights, this criterion is not satisfied.*

2. Are obligated to absorb the entity's **expected losses**. If the investors are directly or indirectly protected from these losses or guaranteed a return by the entity (or by other parties involved with the entity) this criterion is not satisfied.
3. Are entitled to receive the entity's **expected residual returns**. If the investors' return is limited by (a) the entity's governing documents, (b) arrangements with other variable interest holders (e.g., holders of debt, beneficial interests, etc.), or (c) with the entity itself, this criterion is not satisfied.

If **any** one of these three criteria is absent, the at-risk equity investors collectively lack a controlling financial interest and, therefore, only have a controlling voting interest.

Estimated economic life of leased property. At the inception of the lease, the estimated remaining time, with normal maintenance and repairs, that the property is expected to be economically usable for its intended purpose by one or more users. The economic life will be affected by such factors as technological changes, normal deterioration, and physical usage. Judgments regarding these matters are influenced by knowledge gained from previous experience. The estimated time period is not limited by the lease term.

Estimated residual value of leased property. The estimated fair value of the leased property at the end of the lease term.

Equity investment. An interest in an entity that under GAAP is reportable as equity on the entity's balance sheet. The practical application of this definition to certain types of instruments (e.g., mandatorily redeemable preferred stock) has been affected by the issuance in May 2003 of FAS 150, *Accounting for Certain Financial Instruments with Characteristics of Both Liabilities and Equity*.

Executory costs. Those costs such as insurance, maintenance, and taxes incurred for the leased property, whether paid by the lessor or lessee. Amounts paid by a lessee as consideration for a guarantee from an unrelated third party of the residual value are also executory costs. If executory costs are paid by the lessor, any lessor's profit on those costs is considered the same as executory costs.

Expected losses and expected residual returns. Expected losses represent the expected negative variability in the fair value of an enterprise's net assets exclusive of variable interests. Expected residual returns represent the expected positive variability in the fair value of an enterprise's net assets exclusive of variable interests. The expected variability (separately defined below and illustrated in this chapter and Chapter 11) in an enterprise's net income or loss is included in the determination of expected losses and expected residual returns.

Expected variability. When estimating an entity's expected future cash flows in accordance with CON 7, *Using Cash Flow Information and Present Value in Accounting Measurements* (discussed more fully in Chapter 1), a range of probability-weighted expected outcomes is used. Mathematically, this is simply a weighted-average calculation. The expected variability of the cash flows included in that calculation is computed by: (1) computing the difference between each individual estimated outcome and the weighted-average, (2) multiplying each difference computed in the previous step by the probability of occurrence assigned to that individual outcome, and (3) separately summing the positive variations (expected residual returns) and negative variations (expected losses). The absolute value of the expected residual returns will always equal the absolute value of the expected losses. The sum of the absolute values of the expected residual returns and the expected losses represents the expected variability in both directions associated with that estimate of probability-weighted expected cash flows.

Fair value of leased property. The property's selling price in an arm's-length transaction between unrelated parties.

When the lessor is a **manufacturer or dealer,** the fair value of the property at the inception of the lease will ordinarily be its normal selling price net of volume or trade discounts. In some cases, due to market conditions, fair value may be less than the normal selling price or even the cost of the property.

When the lessor is **not a manufacturer or dealer,** the fair value of the property at the inception of the lease will ordinarily be its costs net of volume or trade discounts. However, if a significant amount of time has lapsed between the acquisition of the property by the lessor and the inception of the lease, fair value is determined in light of market conditions prevailing at the inception of the lease. Thus, fair value may be greater or less than the cost or carrying amount of the property.

Implicit interest rate. The discount rate that, when applied to the minimum lease payments, excluding that portion of the payments representing executory costs to be paid by the lessor, together with any profit thereon, and the unguaranteed residual value accruing to the benefit of the lessor, causes the aggregate present value at the beginning of the lease term to be equal to the fair value of the leased property to the lessor at the inception of the lease, minus any investment tax credit retained and expected to be realized by the lessor (and plus initial direct costs in the case of direct financing leases).

Inception of the lease. The date of the written lease agreement or commitment (if earlier) wherein all principal provisions are fixed and no principal provisions remain to be negotiated.

Incremental borrowing rate. The rate that, at the inception of the lease, the lessee would have incurred to borrow over a similar term (i.e., a loan term equal to the lease term) the funds necessary to purchase the leased asset.

Initial direct costs.[1] Only those costs incurred by the lessor that are (1) costs to originate a lease incurred in transactions with independent third parties that (a) result directly from and are essential to acquire that lease and (b) would not have been incurred had that leasing transaction not occurred and (2) certain costs directly related to specified activities performed by the lessor for that lease. Those activities are: evaluating the prospective lessee's financial condition; evaluating and recording guarantees, collateral, and other security arrangements; negotiating lease terms; preparing and processing lease documents; and closing the transaction. The costs directly related to those activities include only that portion of the employees' total compensation and payroll-related fringe benefits directly related to time spent performing those activities for that lease and other costs related to those activities that would not have been incurred but for that lease. Initial direct costs do not include costs related to activities performed by the lessor for advertising, soliciting potential lessees, servicing existing leases, and other ancillary activities related to establishing and monitoring credit policies, supervision, and administration. Initial direct costs do not include administrative costs, rent, depreciation, any other occupancy and equipment costs and employees' compensation and fringe benefits related to activities described in the previous sentence, unsuccessful origination efforts, and idle time.

Lease. An agreement conveying the right to use property, plant, or equipment (land or depreciable assets or both) usually for a stated period of time.

Lease term. The fixed noncancelable term of the lease plus the following:

1. Periods covered by bargain renewal options
2. Periods for which failure to renew the lease imposes a penalty on the lessee in an amount such that renewal appears, at the inception of the lease, to be reasonably assured
3. Periods covered by ordinary renewal options during which a guarantee by the lessee of the lessor's debt directly or indirectly related to the leased property is expected to be in effect or a loan from the lessee to the lessor directly or indirectly related to the leased property is expected to be outstanding
4. Periods covered by ordinary renewal options preceding the date that a bargain purchase option is exercisable
5. Periods representing renewals or extensions of the lease at the lessor's option

However, the lease term does not extend beyond the date a bargain purchase option becomes exercisable or beyond the useful life of the leased asset.

Minimum lease payments. For the **lessee:** The payments that the lessee is or can be required to make in connection with the leased property. Contingent rental guarantees by the lessee of the lessor's debt, and the lessee's obligation to pay executory costs are excluded from minimum lease payments. Additionally, if a portion of the minimum lease payments

---

[1] *Initial direct costs are offset by nonrefundable fees that are yield adjustments as prescribed in FAS 91, **Accounting for Nonrefundable Fees and Costs Associated with Originating or Acquiring Loans and Initial Direct Costs of Leases**.*

representing executory costs is not determinable from the provisions of the lease, an estimate of executory costs is excluded from the calculation of the minimum lease payments. If the lease contains a bargain purchase option, only the minimum rental payments over the lease term and the payment called for in the bargain purchase option are included in minimum lease payments. Otherwise, minimum lease payments include the following:

1. The **minimum rental payments** called for by the lease over the lease term
2. Any **guarantee of residual value** at the expiration of the lease term made by the lessee (or any party related to the lessee), whether or not the guarantee payment constitutes a purchase of the leased property. When the lessor has the right to require the lessee to purchase the property at termination of the lease for a certain or determinable amount, that amount is considered a lessee guarantee. When the lessee agrees to make up any deficiency below a stated amount in the lessor's realization of the residual value, the guarantee to be included in the MLP is the stated amount rather than an estimate of the deficiency to be made up. FIN 19 provides additional guidance regarding residual guarantees, as follows:
    a. Lease provisions requiring the lessee to reimburse the lessor for residual value deficiencies due to damage, extraordinary wear and tear, or excessive usage are analogous to contingent rentals since, at the inception of the lease, the amount of the deficiency is not determinable. Therefore, these payments are not included in the MLP as residual value guarantees.
    b. Some leases contain provisions limiting the lessee's obligation to reimburse the lessor for residual value deficiencies to an amount less than the stipulated residual value of the leased property at the end of the lease term. In computing the MLP associated with these leases, the amount of the lessee's guarantee is limited to the specified maximum deficiency the lessee can be required to reimburse to the lessor.
    c. A lessee may contract with an unrelated third party to guarantee the residual for the benefit of the lessor. The MLP can only be reduced by the third party guarantee to the extent that the lessor explicitly releases the lessee from the obligation to make up the deficiency, even if the guarantor defaults. Amounts paid by the lessee to the guarantor are executory costs and are not included in the MLP, and
3. Any payment that the lessee must or can be required to make upon **failure to renew or extend** the lease at the expiration of the lease term, whether or not the payment would constitute a purchase of the leased property

For the **lessor:** The payments described above plus any guarantee of the residual value or of the rental payments beyond the lease term by a third party unrelated to either the lessee or lessor (provided the third party is financially capable of discharging the guaranteed obligation).

Noncancelable in this context is a lease that is cancelable only upon one of the following conditions:

1. The occurrence of some remote contingency
2. The permission of the lessor
3. The lessee enters into a new lease with the same lessor
4. Payment by the lessee of a penalty in an amount such that continuation of the lease appears, at inception, reasonably assured

Nonrecourse financing. Lending or borrowing activities in which, in the event of default, the collateral available to the creditor is limited to certain assets specifically agreed to in the loan agreement and does not include the general assets of the debtor.

Penalty. Any requirement that is imposed or can be imposed on the lessee by the lease agreement or by factors outside the lease agreement to pay cash, incur or assume a liability, perform services, surrender or transfer an asset or rights to an asset or otherwise forego an economic benefit, or suffer an economic detriment.

Primary beneficiary. A variable interest holder that is required to consolidate a variable interest entity (VIE). Consolidation is required when the holder of one or more variable interests would absorb a majority of the VIE's expected losses, receive a majority of the VIE's expected residual returns, or both. If one holder would absorb a majority of the VIE's expected losses and another holder would receive a majority of the VIE's expected residual returns, the holder absorbing the majority of the expected losses is the primary beneficiary and is thus required to consolidate the VIE.

Profit recognition. Any method to record a transaction involving real estate, other than the deposit method, or the methods to record transactions accounted for as financing, leasing, or profit-sharing arrangements. Profit recognition methods commonly used to record transactions involving real estate include, but are not limited to, the full accrual method, the installment method, the cost recovery method, and the reduced profit method.

Related parties. Entities that are in a relationship where one party has the ability to exercise significant influence over the operating and financial policies of the related party. Examples include the following:

1. A parent company and its subsidiaries
2. An owner company and its joint ventures and partnerships
3. An investor and its investees

The ability to exercise significant influence must be present before the parties can be considered related. Significant influence may also be exercised through guarantees of indebtedness, extensions of credit, or through ownership of debt obligations, warrants, or other securities. If two or more entities are subject to the significant influence of a parent, owner, investor, or common officers or directors, then those entities are considered related to each other.

Related parties and de facto principals and agents. In determining whether a holder of an interest in a variable interest entity (VIE) is the VIE's primary beneficiary, the holder and its related parties are treated collectively as a single party. For this purpose, FIN 46(R) expands the definition of related parties from FAS 57 to include additional parties that act as "de facto agents or principals" of the variable interest holder including

1. A party unable to finance its operations without receiving subordinated financial support from the VIE interest holder such as another VIE of which the holder is the primary beneficiary.
2. A party that received its interests in the VIE as a contribution or loan from the holder.
3. An officer, employee, or member of the governing board of the holder.
4. A party that has agreed not to sell, transfer, or encumber its interest in the VIE without prior approval of the holder when that agreement could constrain the party's ability to manage the economic risks or realize the economic rewards with respect to its interests in the VIE to which it would otherwise be entitled.

5. A party with a close business relationship to the holder such as the relationship between a professional service provider (e.g., attorney, accountant, banker, consultant, etc.) and one of its significant clients.

Upon the application of this related-party attribution rule, if two or more related parties (including de facto agents or principals) hold variable interests in the same VIE for which the parties collectively would be the primary beneficiary, a determination is required of which party will individually be considered the primary beneficiary (i.e., will consolidate the VIE in its financial statements). The party whose activities are most closely associated with the VIE is deemed to be the primary beneficiary. Among the factors that are to be considered when making this determination are

1. The existence of principal/agency relationships between members of the related-party group.
2. The significance of the VIE's activities to the members of the related-party group.
3. The relationship of the members of the related-party group to the VIE's activities.
4. The exposure of a member of the related-party group to the VIE's expected losses.
5. The design (structure) of the VIE.

Renewal or extension of a lease. The continuation of a lease agreement beyond the original lease term, including a new lease where the lessee continues to use the same property.

Sale-leaseback accounting. A method of accounting for a sale-leaseback transaction in which the seller-lessee records the sale, removes all property and related liabilities from its balance sheet, recognizes gain or loss from the sale, and classifies the leaseback in accordance with this section.

Total at-risk investment. The following criteria are set forth in FIN 46(R) for determining the total at-risk equity investment in an entity:

1. **Include** only equity investments that participate significantly in profits and losses, even if the investments have no voting rights.
2. **Exclude** equity interests issued by the entity in exchange for subordinated interests in other variable interest entities.
3. **Exclude** amounts provided to the equity investor (e.g., fees, charitable contributions, or other payments) directly or indirectly by the entity or other parties involved with the entity unless the provider is a parent, subsidiary, or affiliate of the investor that is required to be included in the same set of consolidated financial statements as the investor.
4. **Exclude** amounts financed for the equity investor (e.g., by loans or guarantees of loans) directly by the entity or by other parties involved with the entity, unless the party is a parent, subsidiary, or affiliate of the investor that is required to be included in the same set of consolidated financial statements as the investor.

There is a rebuttable presumption that an equity investment of less than 10% of an entity's total assets is insufficient to permit the entity to finance its activities without additional subordinated financial support. In order to overcome this presumption, one or more of the following conditions must be present:

1. **Performance**—The entity has demonstrated that it can finance its activities without additional subordinated financial support.

2. **Comparability**—The entity's invested equity is at least as much as other entities holding similar assets of similar quality in similar amounts and who operate without additional subordinated financial support.
3. **Reasonable forecast**—Based on reasonable quantitative evidence, the entity's invested equity exceeds the estimate of the entity's expected losses.

This 10% threshold was intended by FASB to apply only in one direction (i.e., a less-than 10% investment is considered insufficient but a 10% or more investment is not necessarily presumed to be sufficient). Many entities engaged in high-risk activities, holding high-risk assets, or carrying significant off-balance-sheet exposures require more than 10% equity investment in order to finance their activities. Consequently, irrespective of the 10% threshold, an evaluation must be done to determine whether a particular entity with which the enterprise is involved requires an equity investment of 10% or greater in order to finance its activities without additional subordinated financial support.

Unguaranteed residual value. The estimated residual value of the leased property exclusive of any portion guaranteed by the lessee, by any party related to the lessee, or any party unrelated to the lessee. If the guarantor is related to the lessor, the residual value is considered unguaranteed.

Unrelated parties. All parties that are not related parties as defined above.

Variable interest. Ownership, contractual, or other monetary interests in an entity that are either entitled to received expected positive variability (referred to as expected residual returns) or obligated to absorb expected negative variability (referred to as expected losses).

Variable interest entity. An entity for which an analysis of the at-risk investments of the holders of its voting interests would not be effective in establishing the party or parties that hold a controlling financial interest in the entity. This situation arises either because (1) the entity is not adequately capitalized by at-risk equity sufficient to absorb its expected losses *or* (2) because the at-risk equity holders do not receive or bear all of the financial benefits or detriments that would provide those holders with a controlling financial interest in the entity.

CONCEPTS, RULES, AND EXAMPLES

Variable Interest Entities

The complex and evolving rules for lease accounting from the standpoint of the lessee and of the lessor are set forth in this chapter. From the standpoint of the lessee, it is critical for the accountant to first determine whether the relationship between the entities requires consolidation as a **variable interest entity** under FIN 46(R), which is discussed in detail in Chapter 11. If consolidation is required, the lease transaction recorded by the lessor will be eliminated in the consolidated financial statements and the lease accounting will, in effect, be moot from the standpoint of the lessee.

Effective date provisions. Due to the replacement of FIN 46 with FIN 46(R), changes were made to the initial effective date of FIN 46. A matrix is provided in Chapter 11 summarizing the revised effective date provisions.

Decision diagrams. The following decision diagrams will be used to discuss the illustrative examples of leasing transactions presented in this chapter.

APPLYING FASB INTERPRETATION 46(R)

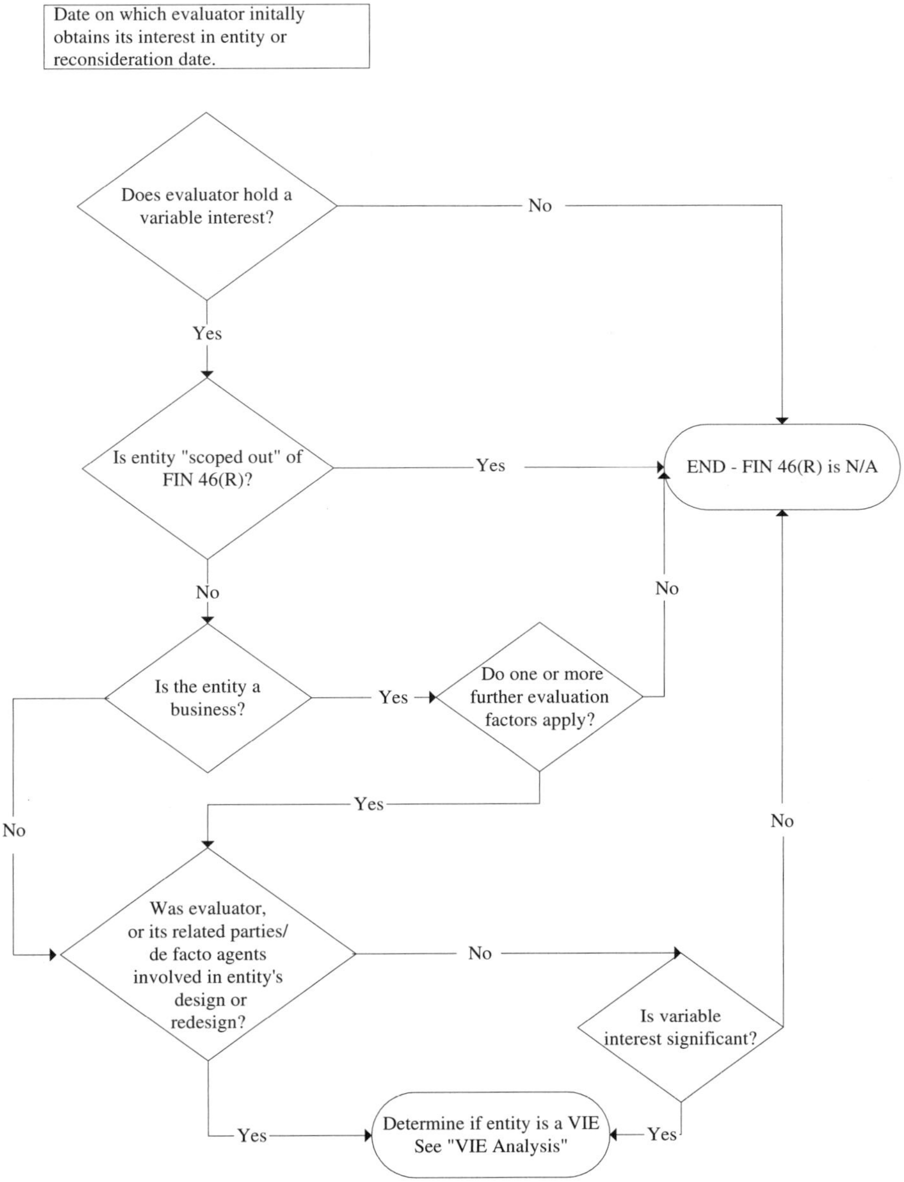

VIE ANALYSIS

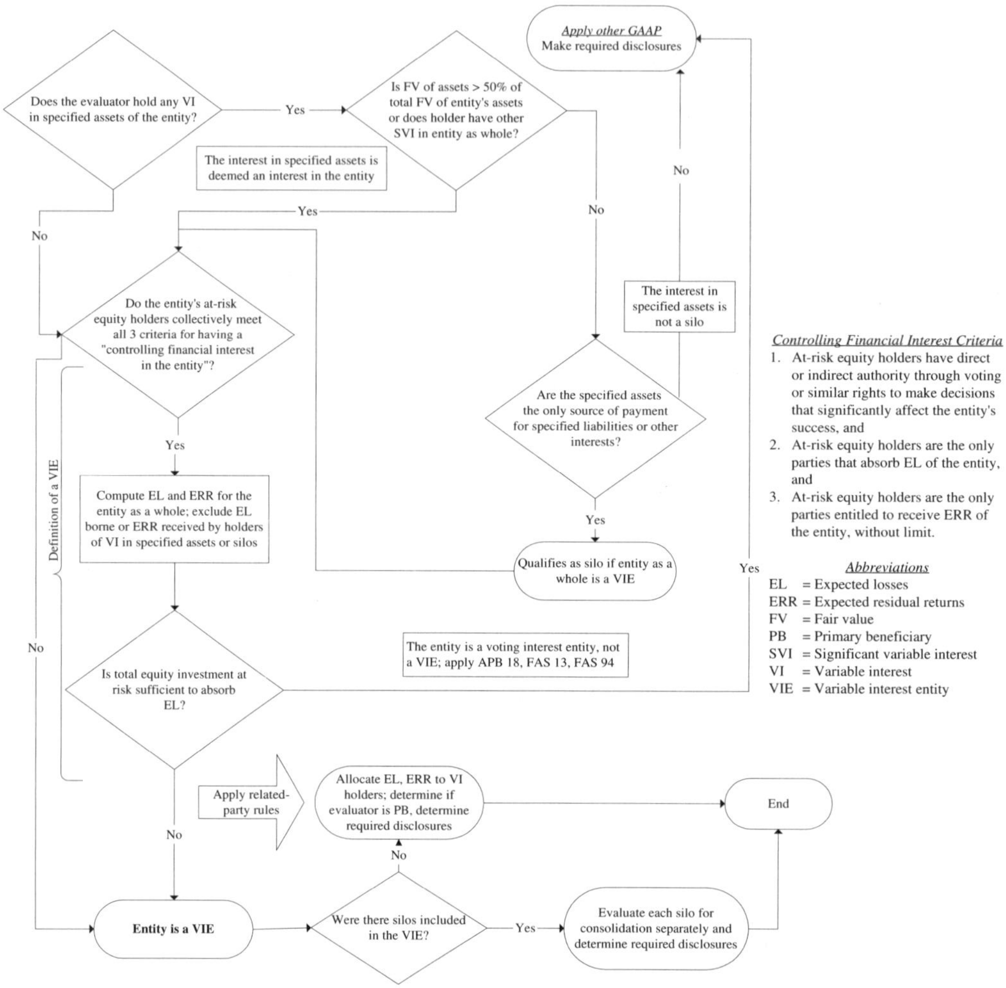

Entities "scoped out" of FIN 46(R). The following are excluded from the scope of FIN 46(R):

1. Not-for-profit organizations as defined in FAS 117, para. 168, unless the organization was organized to avoid VIE status.
2. Employer/sponsors of employee benefit plans including ESOP, pension, profit sharing, 401(k), postretirement, and postemployment plans.
3. Enterprises subject to SEC Regulation S-X Rule 6-03(c)(1) (investment companies, mutual funds) may only consolidate an entity subject to the same regulation.
4. Separate accounts of life insurance entities.
5. A "Qualifying special-purpose entity" (QSPE) or a "formerly qualifying SPE" (FQSPE) under the provisions of FAS 140, *Accounting for Transfers and Servicing of Financial Assets and Extinguishments of Liabilities,* are not to be consolidated by entities and their affiliates who transfer financial assets to them.

6. Enterprises holding variable interests in a QSPE or FQSPE are not to consolidate that entity unless the holder has the unilateral ability to cause the entity's liquidation or change the entity so that it ceases to meet the conditions of FAS 140 to be considered a QSPE or FQSPE.
7. A governmental organization.
8. A nongovernmental financing entity established by a governmental organization unless the financing entity is being used to circumvent FIN 46(R) to avoid consolidation.
9. An entity created prior to December 31, 2003, for which, after expending "exhaustive efforts," management of the variable interest holder is unable to obtain information needed to determine whether the entity is a VIE, determine whether the holder is the primary beneficiary, or make the required consolidating/eliminating entries required by FIN 46(R).

   NOTE: With respect to this exception, however, management of the variable interest holder is required to continue to make these efforts after initial adoption of FIN 46(R). If the variable interest holder significantly participated in the design/redesign of the entity, it would be unusual for it to be able to contend that it was unable to obtain the necessary information.

10. An entity that qualifies to be treated as a business, as defined below (the definition included in FIN 46(R) was adapted from EITF 98-3, *Determining Whether a Nonmonetary Transaction Involves Receipt of Productive Assets or a Business").* However, this scope exception *does not apply* and the entity would be required to be evaluated as to whether it is a VIE by the holders of its variable interests if *any one or more* of the following conditions exists (these are referred to in the decision diagram as "further evaluation factors" for ease of understanding:
    a. The variable interest holder and/or its related parties/de facto agents[2] (de facto agents are discussed later in this chapter) participated significantly in the design or redesign of the entity. This factor is not considered when the entity is an operating joint venture jointly controlled by the variable interest holder, and either an independent party or a franchisee.
    b. The design of the entity results in substantially all of its activities either involving or being conducted on behalf of the variable interest holder and its related parties.
    c. Based on the relative fair values of interests in the entity, the variable interest holder and its related parties provide more than half of its total equity, subordinated debt, and other forms of subordinated financial support.
    d. The entity's activities relate primarily to one or both of the following:
       (1) Single-lessee leases
       (2) Securitizations or other forms of asset-backed financings.

Definition of a business. A business is defined, in the context of FIN 46(R) as

> *...a self-sustaining integrated set of activities and assets conducted and managed for the purpose of providing a return to investors. A business consists of (a) inputs, (b) processes applied to those inputs, and (c) resulting outputs that are used to generate revenues. For a set of activities and assets to*

---

[2] *Only for the purposes of applying factor a. above, de facto agents exclude parties that require the variable interest holder's prior approval to sell, transfer, or encumber their interest in the entity.*

> *be a business, it must contain all of the inputs and processes necessary for it to conduct normal operations, which include the ability to sustain a revenue stream by providing its outputs to customers.*

In evaluating whether an entity is a business, consideration must be given to unique factors relating to the industry and the activities being performed including

Inputs

1. Fixed assets either owned or leased
2. Intangibles either owned or licensed
3. Access to materials or rights needed to perform its activities
4. Employees

Processes

1. Strategic management
2. Operations
3. Resource management

Outputs

1. Access to customers (clients)

A three-step process is provided in order to assess whether a set of activities ("set") qualifies as a business:

1. Identify elements included in the "set" (i.e., determine the existing inputs, processes, and outputs.)
2. Compare the elements identified in 1. with the elements necessary for the set of activities to be conducted as a normal business operation.
3. If any elements are missing, assess the degree of effort or investment relative to the fair value of the set of activities needed to acquire or gain access to the missing elements. If a significant effort or investment would be required, it can be concluded that the set of activities is not a business; conversely, a de minimis amount of effort or investment to supply the missing elements would lead to the conclusion that the set of activities is a business.

Variable interests in "silos." A party may hold a variable interest in specific assets of a VIE (e.g., a guarantee or a subordinated residual interest). In computing expected losses and expected residual returns, as defined above, a holder of a variable interest in specified assets of a VIE must determine if the interest it holds qualifies as an interest in the VIE itself. The variable interest is considered an interest in the VIE itself if **either** (1) the fair value of the specific assets is more than half of the total fair value of the VIE's assets, or (2) the interest holder has another significant variable interest in the entity as a whole.

If the interests are deemed to be interests in the VIE itself, the expected losses and expected residual returns associated with the variable interest in the specified assets are treated as being associated with the VIE.

If the interests are not deemed to be interests in the VIE itself, the interests in the specified assets are treated as a separate VIE (referred to as a "silo") if the expected cash flows from the specified assets (and any associated credit enhancements, if applicable) are essentially the sole source of payment for specified liabilities or specified other interests. Under this scenario, expected losses and expected residual returns associated with the silo assets are accounted for separately to the extent that the interest holder either bears the expected losses or is entitled to receive the expected returns. Any excess of expected losses or residual returns not borne by (received by) the variable interest holder is considered attributable to the entity as a whole.

If one interest holder is required to consolidate a silo of a VIE, other VIE interest holders are to exclude the silo from the remaining VIE.

Example of application of FIN 46(R) to related-party leases

The most commonly encountered potential VIE situations that occur in practice involve related-party leases. Business owners often organize a partnership or LLC (for this discussion we will assume an LLC) to own property that is leased to a business with the same or similar ownership. The transaction is structured in this manner for a number of reasons that include avoidance of double taxation of the gain on the eventual sale of the property and legal protection of the building from creditors of the operating business in the event of business bankruptcy.

In attempting to avoid lessee capitalization, the lease is often structured with a short initial term (e.g., three years) with the lessee having successive options to renew the lease at similar terms. The building is pledged as collateral under a mortgage with a third-party lender. The lessor entity is thinly capitalized (i.e., it has very little owner-invested equity). Consequently, the lender, besides holding a mortgage on the building as collateral, has further protected its interests by obtaining a loan guarantee from the lessee, an assignment of rents, and a personal guarantee of the owner.

These relationships are illustrated in the following diagram:

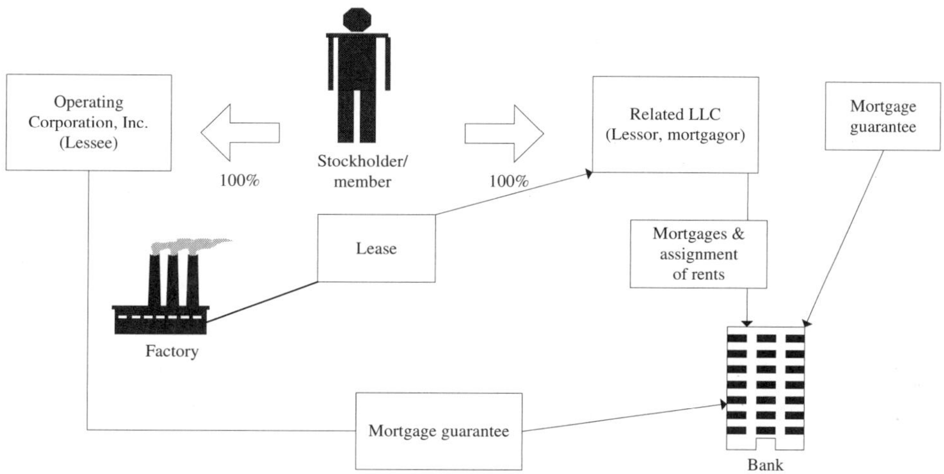

Pre-FIN 46(R) GAAP

An analysis of the above facts yields the following economic conclusions:

1. The arrangement, in substance, most likely qualifies as a capital lease under FAS 13, as amended. The computation of the noncancelable lease term would include periods for which "failure to renew the lease imposes a penalty on the lessee [that makes renewal]...reasonably assured." Clearly, as long as the lessee's guarantee of the lessor's debt is outstanding, failure to renew the lease would impose an economic penalty on the lessee. Consequently, in lengthening the period of the lease term, the lease would be more likely to qualify as a capital lease under either the "75% of economic life test" or the "90% test" of the discounted present value of the minimum lease payments.
2. The risks associated with the property have been primarily assumed by the lessee corporation since, if the lessor defaulted on the mortgage payments, the lender would enforce the guarantee against the lessee.

3. The lessor has retained the rights to the residual rewards from the property upon its eventual sale. The lessee would not share in any appreciation of the property under the scenario described above.

Under GAAP prior to FIN 46(R), the above arrangement would have required capitalization by the lessee if the guarantee of the mortgage was in effect for a period sufficiently long under the 75% and 90% tests.

If for some reason the lease qualified for operating lease treatment, previous GAAP (EITF 90-15 which is superseded by FIN 46[R]) would have required an evaluation of whether substantially all of the risks *and* rewards resided directly or indirectly with the lessee. If this were the case and certain other conditions were met, the lessee would have been required to combine (consolidate) the lessor in its financial statements.

The loophole in EITF 90-15 that allowed a lessee to avoid consolidating the lessor in an arrangement of this type is the fact that the lessor retained the residual rewards upon sale of the property (i.e., the lessee had no right to share in the appreciation of the property). EITF 90-15 only required consolidation (combination) when both all of the substantive residual risks and residual rewards of the leased asset along with the risks associated with the lessor's mortgage debt resided directly or indirectly with the lessee. Consequently, when this was not the case, consolidation was not required.

Post-FIN 46(R) GAAP

Following the decision diagrams and using the related-party/de facto principal and agent rules included in FIN 46(R)

1. The lessee holds a variable interest in the lessor in the form of the lease and the related guarantee of the lessor's mortgage debt.
2. The lessor entity is not "scoped out" of FIN 46(R).
3. The lessor entity is a business. It has inputs (owned fixed assets), processes for managing its investment, and outputs relative to access to the lessee.
4. The following "further evaluation factors" apply:
    a. The lessee/variable interest holder and its related parties participated significantly in the design of the lessor
    b. The design of the lessor LLC results in all of its activities involving and being conducted on behalf of the lessee/variable interest holder.
    c. The lesser/variable interest holder and its related parties provided 100% of the subordinated financial support for the lessor entity.
    d. The lessor entity's activities relate to a single-lessee lease.
5. The lessee/evaluator and its related-party owner were involved in the design of the lessor entity.
6. The lessee's variable interest is assumed to be significant.
7. The lessee's variable interest is in the leased asset.
8. The fair value of the leased asset represents 100% of the total fair value of the lessor's assets and thus is deemed to be an interest in the lessor as a whole versus an interest in just the specified assets of the lessor.
9. The at-risk equity holder of the lessor does not meet the second criterion for being considered to hold a controlling financial interest (i.e., the variable interest holder/lessee could potentially absorb expected losses of the lessor should the lessee be called upon by the lender to perform under the guarantee of the lessor's indebtedness). Note that, in this case, the other two criteria for controlling interest are met.

10. As a result of the analysis up to this point, it can be concluded that the lessor is a variable interest entity.
11. No silos exist, since 100% of the fair value of the assets are leased to the single lessee.
12. Application of the related-party/de facto principal and agent rules to the variable interests in the lessor indicate that 100% of the expected losses and expected residual returns from the lessor are allocable to the members of the related-party group (the lessee, the lessor, and the related-party owner of both). Thus, collectively, they are the primary beneficiary. The party most closely associated with the leased property is the lessee who, consequently, would be considered the primary beneficiary that is required to consolidate the lessor in its financial statements.

Other lease terms and provisions. The following discussion will examine the effect that certain changes to the above facts would have on the foregoing conclusions:

1. What if the stockholder/member's guarantee of the mortgage was not required by the lender and only the lessee guaranteed the debt?

   The analysis would be identical. Due to the fact that the lessee/variable interest holder is exposed to the expected losses of the lessor under the terms of the guarantee, the lessor/LLC's sole member (and at-risk equity holder) is not the only party that potentially would absorb expected losses of the lessor.

2. What if the rentals due under the lease exceed arm's-length market rentals because the owner is using the lessor as a conduit for the lessee to indirectly provided additional salary or dividends to the owner (characterized as the excess rent)?

   A lease itself qualifies as a variable interest under FIN 46(R). Normally, if the lease terms are at market rentals at lease inception and the lease does not contain a guarantee of the lessor's residual value in the leased asset or a similar provision, the lease would not be a factor in determining the VIE's primary beneficiary. Under this scenario however, the lease would be considered in determining the primary beneficiary because the expected losses of the lessor that would be borne by the lessee (the excess of the rentals required over the fair value of the right to use the leased property) exceed the amounts that would have been expected had the rentals been at fair value. Thus, the stockholder/member would not be considered to have a controlling financial interest since s/he was not the only party exposed to the lessor's expected losses.

3. What if neither the lessee nor the owner was required to guarantee the debt?

   A prudent lender would probably not waive both guarantees unless the lessor was sufficiently capitalized by the owner's at-risk equity. Consequently, under this scenario the lessee would perform the quantitative analysis required to estimate expected losses and estimated residual returns to determine whether the lessor is a VIE and, if it is, whether they are collectively the primary beneficiary.

4. If a lessee otherwise was not considered a primary beneficiary of a related-party VIE lessor, what other lease provisions could potentially trigger that result and require that the lessee and its related parties estimate expected losses and expected residual returns?

   It would be impractical to list all such provisions. However, common provisions would include the existence of lessee guarantees of the lessor's residual value, options to purchase the property, management, marketing, brokerage, or other types of service agreements with related parties, etc.

5. What if the leased property were owned directly by the owner rather than in an LLC or other entity?

   This *potentially* is a loophole in FIN 46(R). The FIN 46(R) definition of a VIE requires that the VIE be a "legal structure used to conduct activities or to hold assets." Examples of these structures included in FIN 46(R) include corporations, partnerships, limited liability companies, grantor trusts, and other trusts. In the authors' opinion, the examples given in the interpretations can cause conceptual substance-over-form arguments. The financial statement preparer should be asking questions such as the following regarding such an arrangement:

   a. If the same leasing arrangements that would have existed between the lessee and a legal entity exist instead between the lessee and its owner—the party that would have owned the legal entity if the transaction had been structured in that manner—what economic justification could there be for the lessee not to account for the arrangement in the same manner?
   b. Under US income tax law, a grantor trust is ignored and its assets, income, and deductions are attributed to its grantor. The only practical difference between a grantor trust and a proprietorship is the fact that the trust may have a legal governing document whereas the proprietorship does not. How does this type of arrangement differ from a proprietorship which essentially is not a legal entity but is treated identically for income tax purposes?
   c. What financial statement treatment would be most transparent and informative for users? Conversely, would a user be misled by failing to consolidate the property whether owned by a formal entity or not?

      All parties affected by these transactions should seek expert professional advice prior to either structuring a new transaction or modifying an existing transaction. For example, adverse income tax consequences could result from the transfer of property from one form of ownership to another.

Example: Arm's length leases—Computing Expected Losses and Expected Residual Returns

The application of FIN 46(R) is, of course, not limited to related-party arrangements. The following is an example of the quantitative analysis (versus the qualitative analysis illustrated in the related-party example above) that might be necessary in an arm's-length leasing arrangement.

NOTE: The terms of the leases below are not intended to represent current market conditions, but rather have been designed to best illustrate the concepts of FIN 46(R).

Lawrence Lessor, LLC (referred to herein as "the Entity" since it is the entity that the variable interest holders will be evaluating as to whether it is a VIE) is a limited liability company organized specifically for the purpose of building, owning, and operating a single-lessee retail discount warehouse club store on land that it has recently acquired. The store is the only asset owned by the Entity. The 148,000 square foot store will be occupied by Clubco, a nationally known chain that is unrelated to Lawrence Lessor.

The Entity's voting owners (the LLC members) wish only to invest a minimal amount of equity in the Entity and, consequently, the mortgage lender insisted on obtaining a third-party guarantee of the mortgage which Lawrence obtained from an unrelated third-party and paid a premium for.

The terms of the lease with the retailer are as follows: (assumed to be an operating lease):

Description of space	148,000 square foot retail discount warehouse club store
Lessee	Clubco Stores, Inc.
Initial lease term	Three years
Lease commencement date	1/1/05
Annual base rent	$600,000
Contingent rent	1% of annual sales over $30 million
Purchase options:	$9 million–not a bargain purchase option in accordance with FAS 13
Residual guarantee	Lessee guarantees to lessor that residual value of the building at the end of the lease term will be at least equal to the $7,500,000 fair value of the store land and building at inception or it will pay the lessor the difference
Executory costs	All real estate taxes, maintenance, insurance, and common area expenses are to be borne by the lessee

The construction has been completed, the occupancy permits issued, and the construction financing settled with the proceeds of a 25-year, 6% mortgage loan on December 1, 2004. The mortgage loan is guaranteed by an unrelated third-party guarantor. The store is opening and commencing business on January 1, 2005.

Mortgage details are as follows:

Summary Amortization Schedule for Mortgage

25-year, 6% mortgage, original principal amount of $7,275,750

Year	*Payments*	*Interest*	*Principal*	*Balance*
Original loan				$ 7,275,750
1	$ 562,533	$ 433,022	$ 129,511	7,146,239
2	562,533	425,034	137,499	7,008,740
3	562,533	416,553	145,980	6,862,760
	$ 1,687,599	$ 1,274,609	$ 412,990	

The Entity's recorded aggregate carrying amount of $7,500,000 for the land and building represents the fair value at lease inception with the land's fair value representing 10%, or $750,000.

The rental terms for the store are considered to be at market rates. If the terms were not at market rates, additional expected variability would be assigned to the lease (in addition to the expected variability resulting from the purchase option and residual value guarantee).

Expected cash flows are discounted to their present value using an assumed 3% interest rate representing the interest rate available on risk-free investments. To simplify the example, cash flows are assumed to occur at the end of each annual period for the purpose of discounting them to present value. A copy of the balance sheet from the Entity's annual partnership return at lease inception is as follows:

Schedule L	Balance Sheets per Books			
	Beginning of tax year		End of tax year	
Assets	(a)	(b)	(c)	(d)
1. Cash				1,000
2. a. Trade notes and accounts receivable				
b. Less allowance for bad debts				
3. Inventories				
4. US government obligations				
5. Tax-exempt securities				
6. Other current assets (*attach schedule*)				
7. Mortgage and real estate loans				
8. Other investments (*attach schedule*)				
9. a. Buildings and other depreciable assets			6,750,000	
b. Less accumulated depreciation				6,750,000
10. a. Depletable assets				
b. Less accumulated depletion				
11. Land (net of any amortization)				750,000
12. a Intangible assets (amortizable only)				
b Less accumulated amortization				
13. Other assets (*attach schedule*)				
14. Total assets				7,501,000
Liabilities and Capital				
15. Accounts payable				
16. Mortgages, notes, bonds payable in less than 1 year				
17. Other current liabilities (*attach schedule*)				
18. All nonrecourse loans				7,275,750
19. Mortgages, notes, bonds payable in 1 year or more				
20. Other liabilities (*attach schedule*)				
21. Partners' capital accounts				225,250
22. **Total** liabilities and capital				7,501,000

Analysis by Clubco-(See the decision diagrams earlier in this chapter)

1. Clubco holds a variable interest in Lawrence Lessor ("the Entity") in the from of the lease. Expected variability results from the purchase option and the residual value guarantee.
2. The Entity is not scoped out of FIN 46(R).
3. The Entity is a business.
4. Further evaluation factor d. applies; that is, this is a single-lessee lease.
5. Clubco was not involved in the design of the Entity.
6. For illustrative purposes, assume that the purchase option is significant to Clubco.
7. Clubco holds a variable interest in the leased store (the specified assets) in the form of the lease containing a purchase option and residual value guarantee.
8. The fair value of the building leased by Clubco is 100% of the fair value of the Entity's assets. Therefore, Clubco is deemed to hold a variable interest in the Entity as a whole.
9. In applying the test to determine if the members of the LLC/entity have a controlling financial interest (distinguished from a controlling voting interest, which they clearly have), the following results are determined:
   a. The LLC members are the sole voting interest holders and, therefore, meet the voting test.
   b. The LLC members are *not* the only parties that absorb expected losses of the lessor due to the existence of the residual value guarantee provision in the lease that potentially could result in Clubco bearing a portion of the expected losses.

c. The LLC members are also *not* the only parties entitled to receive the expected residual returns from the property due to the existence of the purchase option provision in the lease that potentially could result in Clubco receiving a portion of the expected residual returns.

10. As a consequence of the analysis up to this point, Clubco can conclude that its variable interest is in a lessor that is a VIE.
11. Since Clubco leases 100% of the fair value of the assets held by entity, there are no silos included therein.
12. To determine whether or not it is the primary beneficiary of the VIE/lessor, Clubco must determine if it either will bear the majority of the expected losses, or receive the majority of the expected residual returns. One form this calculation might take is illustrated below.

Computation of expected cash flow possibilities for the lease term

	Year 1					
Probability	5%	15%	30%	35%	10%	5%
Assumptions						
Annual store sales	$25,000,000	$30,000,000	$40,000,000	$50,000,000	$55,000,000	$60,000,000
Percentage rent base	$30,000,000	$30,000,000	$30,000,000	$30,000,000	$30,000,000	$30,000,000
Percentage rent rate	1%	1%	1%	1%	1%	1%
Possible cash flow outcomes						
Rent—Base	$ 600,000	$ 600,000	$ 600,000	$ 600,000	$ 600,000	$ 600,000
Rent—Percentage	--	--	100,000	200,000	250,000	300,000
Total rental income	600,000	600,000	700,000	800,000	850,000	900,000
Mortgage payments	562,533	562,533	562,533	562,533	562,533	562,533
Possible net cash flow	$ 37,467	$ 37,467	$ 137,467	$ 237,467	$ 287,467	$ 337,467
Present value, discounted at 3%	$ 36,376	$ 36,376	$ 133,463	$ 230,550	$ 279,094	$ 327,638

	Year 2					
Probability	5%	15%	30%	35%	10%	5%
Assumptions						
Estimated percentage change in sales	-2.00%	0.00%	2.00%	2.50%	3.00%	4.00%
Annual store sales	$24,500,000	$30,000,000	$40,800,000	$51,250,000	$56,650,000	$62,400,000
Percentage rent base	$30,000,000	$30,000,000	$30,000,000	$30,000,000	$30,000,000	$30,000,000
Percentage rent rate	1%	1%	1%	1%	1%	1%
Possible cash flow outcomes						
Rent—Base	$ 600,000	$ 600,000	$ 600,000	$ 600,000	$ 600,000	$ 600,000
Rent—Percentage	--	--	108,000	212,500	266,500	324,000
Total rental income	600,000	600,000	708,000	812,500	866,500	924,000
Mortgage payments	562,533	562,533	562,533	562,533	562,533	562,533
Possible net cash flow	$ 37,467	$ 37,467	$ 145,467	$ 249,967	$ 303,967	$ 361,467
Present value, discounted at 3%	$ 35,316	$ 35,316	$ 137,117	$ 235,618	$ 286,518	$ 340,717

	Year 3					
Probability	5%	15%	30%	35%	10%	5%
Assumptions						
Estimated percentage change in sales	-1.00%	0.00%	2.50%	3.50%	3.75%	5.00%
Annual store sales	$24,255,000	$30,000,000	$41,820,000	$53,043,750	$58,774,375	$65,520,000
Percentage rent base	$30,000,000	$30,000,000	$30,000,000	$30,000,000	$30,000,000	$30,000,000
Percentage rent rate	1%	1%	1%	1%	1%	1%
Possible cash flow outcomes						
Rent—Base	$ 600,000	$ 600,000	$ 600,000	$ 600,000	$ 600,000	$ 600,000
Rent—Percentage	--	--	118,200	230,438	287,744	355,200
Total rental income	600,000	600,000	718,200	830,438	887,744	955,200
Mortgage payments	562,533	562,533	562,533	562,533	562,533	562,533
Possible net cash flow, operations	37,467	37,467	155,667	267,905	325,211	392,667
Estimated residual amount	7,000,000	8,000,000	9,000,000	10,000,000	12,000,000	13,000,000
Mortgage repayment	6,862,760	6,862,760	6,862,760	6,862,760	6,862,760	6,862,760
Possible net sales proceeds	137,240	1,137,240	2,137,240	3,137,240	5,137,240	6,137,240
Possible net cash flow	$ 174,707	$1,174,707	$2,292,907	$3,405,144	$5,462,451	$6,529,907
Present value, discounted at 3%	$ 159,881	$1,075,023	$2,098,334	$3,116,189	$4,998,916	$5,975,790
3-year totals of present value of possible cash flows discounted at 3%	$ 231,573	$1,146,715	$2,368,914	$3,582,357	$5,564,528	$6,644,145

Note that, in the forecast for Year 3, the effects of the purchase option and residual value guarantee are ignored. They are considered later in the analysis of which variable interest holders participate in expected losses and expected residual returns.

13. Calculation of probability-weighted discounted expected cash flows.

Scenario	*Present value of possible cash flows*	*Estimated probability*	*Discounted probability-weighted expected cash flows*
1	$ 231,573	5%	11,579
2	1,146,715	15%	172,007
3	2,368,914	30%	710,674
4	3,582,357	35%	1,253,825
5	5,564,528	10%	556,453
6	6,644,145	5%	332,207
		100%	$3,036,745

This computation uses the expected cash flow methodology prescribed by CON 7, which is also used in estimation of fair value for the purposes of impairment testing of goodwill and tangible long-lived assets, and in computing asset retirement obligations.

14. Calculations of expected losses and expected residual returns (and the related expected variability).

Scenario	*Present value of possible cash flows*	*Discounted/ probability-weighted expected cash flows*	*Variance from expected outcome*	*Estimated probability*	*Expected losses*	*Expected residual returns*
1	$ 231,573	$3,036,745	$(2,805,172)	5%	$(140,259)	
2	1,146,715	3,036,745	(1,890,030)	15%	(283,505)	
3	2,368,914	3,036,745	(667,831)	30%	(200,349)	
4	3,582,357	3,036,745	545,612	35%		$190,965
5	5,564,528	3,036,745	2,527,783	10%		252,778
6	6,644,145	3,036,745	3,607,400	5%		180,370
				100%	$(624,113)	$624,113

FIN 46(R) requires consideration of the "expected variability" inherent in the estimate of probability-weighted expected cash flows, in this case $3,036,745. This amount represents a weighted-average of the various expected outcomes multiplied by their respective probabilities. As is always the case when averaging numbers, the sums of the positive and negative differences between each value included in the average and the average itself are always equal. This explains why the expected losses and expected residual returns both equal $624,113. Therefore, the expected variability in both directions is the sum of the two absolute values (i.e., $624,113 + $624,113 = $1,248,226).

Another important point to note is that the terms "expected losses" and "expected residual returns" are not associated with traditional GAAP income or cash flow measures. The entity illustrated above has positive expected cash flows under all six scenarios for all three years. Notwithstanding that fact, the computation shows that it will experience expected losses and expected residual returns—variations from expectation, positive or negative, that could occur as a result of operations or of changes in the fair value of the property. This will always be the case, irrespective of how profitable an entity is or how much cash flow it generates.

15. For each scenario, the facts are analyzed to determine which of the variable interest holders will bear the expected losses. There were no silos included in the VIE, therefore only a single primary beneficiary determination is required. The results of the analysis are aggregated as follows:

	Expected losses
Scenario 1	$(140,259)
Scenario 2	(283,505)
Scenario 3	(200,349)
	$(624,113)

Scenario	*Estimated residual value of store*	*Expected losses*	*Clubco*	*3rd-party guarantor*	*At-risk equity holders of entity*	*Mortgage lender*	*Notes*
1	7,000,000	$(140,259)	$(140,259)				$7.5MM guarantee $7 MM residual
2	8,000,000	(283,505)			$(283,505)		
3	9,000,000	(200,349)			(200,349)		
Excess of share of losses over equity				(258,604)	(258,604)		
		$(624,113)	$(140,259)	$(258,604)	$(225,250)	$ --	
		100%	22%	42%	36%	0%	

Total equity at risk is $225,250 which would not be sufficient for the entity to absorb the expected losses of $624,113 without receiving additional subordinated financial support. Consequently, the Entity (Lawrence Lessor, LLC) by definition is a variable interest entity.

Note that, based on the analysis of the expected losses, no variable interest holder will absorb a majority (>50%) of the Entity's losses. Consequently, the expected residual returns need to be analyzed.

Scenario	*Estimated residual value of store*	*Expected residual returns*	*Clubco*	*At-risk equity holders of entity*	*Guarantor*	*Notes*
4	$10,000,000	$190,965	$190,965			Exercise of $9MM Option
5	12,000,000	252,778	252,778			Exercise of $9MM Option
6	13,000,000	180,370	180,370			Exercise of $9MM Option
		$624,113	$624,113			
		100%	100%			

16. Since 100% of the expected residual returns will be received by Clubco, it is the primary beneficiary, the party that is required to consolidate Lawrence Lessor, LLC in its financial statements.

Classification of Leases—Lessee

For accounting and reporting purposes the lessee has two possible classifications for a lease.

1. Operating
2. Capital

The proper classification of a **lease** is determined by the circumstances surrounding the transaction. According to FAS 13, if substantially all of the benefits and risks of ownership have been transferred to the lessee, the lessee records the lease as a capital lease at its inception. Substantially all of the risks or benefits of ownership are deemed to have been transferred if **any one** of the following criteria is met:

1. The lease transfers ownership to the lessee by the end of the **lease term**
2. The lease contains a **bargain purchase option**
3. The lease term is equal to 75% or more of the **estimated economic life** of the leased property, and the beginning of the lease term does not fall within the last 25% of the total economic life of the leased property
4. The present value (PV) of the minimum lease payments at the beginning of the lease term is 90% or more of the fair value to the lessor less any investment credit retained by the lessor. This requirement cannot be used if the lease's inception is in the last 25% of the useful economic life of the leased asset. The interest rate, used to compute the PV, is the **incremental borrowing rate** of the lessee unless the **implicit rate** is available and lower.

If a lease agreement meets none of the four criteria set forth above, it is classified as an operating lease by the lessee.

Classification of Leases—Lessor

The are four possible classifications that apply to a lease from the standpoint of the lessor.

1. Operating
2. Sales-type
3. Direct financing
4. Leveraged

The conditions surrounding the origination of the lease determine its classification by the lessor. If the lease meets **any one** of the four criteria specified above for lessees and **both** of the qualifications set forth below, the lease is classified as either a sales-type lease, direct financing lease, or leveraged lease depending upon the conditions present at the inception of the lease.

1. Collectibility of the minimum lease payments is reasonably predictable
2. No important uncertainties surround the amount of unreimbursable costs yet to be incurred by the lessor under the lease

If a lease transaction does not meet the criteria for classification as a sales-type lease, a direct financing lease, or a leveraged lease as specified above, it is classified by the lessor as an operating lease. The classification testing is performed prior to considering the proper accounting treatment.

Distinction between Sales-Type, Direct Financing, and Leveraged Leases

A lease is classified as a sales-type lease when the criteria set forth above have been met and the lease transaction is structured in such a way that the lessor (generally a **manufacturer or dealer**) recognizes a profit or loss on the transaction in addition to interest income. In order for this to occur, the **fair value of the property (FV)** must be different from the cost (carrying value). The essential substance of this transaction is that of a sale, and thus its name. Common examples of sales-type leases: (1) when a customer of an automobile dealership opts to lease a car in lieu of an outright purchase, and (2) the re-lease of equipment coming off an expiring lease. Note however, that a lease involving real estate must transfer title (i.e., criterion 1. above) by the end of the lease term for the lessor to classify the lease as a sales-type lease.

A direct financing lease differs from a sales-type lease in that the lessor does not realize a profit or loss on the transaction other than interest income. In a direct financing lease, the fair value of the property at the inception of the lease is equal to the cost (carrying value). This type of lease transaction most often involves lessor entities engaged in financing operations. The lessor (a bank, or other financial institution) purchases the asset and then leases the asset to the lessee. This transaction merely replaces the conventional lending transaction where the borrower uses the borrowed funds to purchase the asset. There are many economic reasons why the lease transaction is considered. They are as follows:

1. The lessee (borrower) is able to obtain 100% financing
2. Flexibility of use for the tax benefits
3. The lessor receives the equivalent of interest as well as an asset with some remaining value at the end of the lease term

In summary, it may help to visualize the following chart when considering the classification of a lease from the lessor's standpoint:

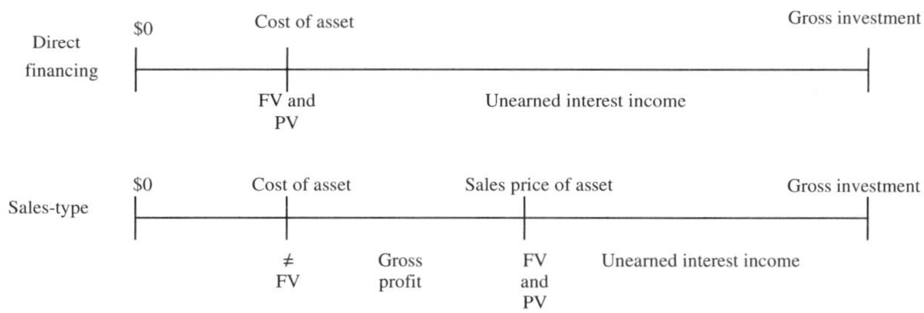

One form of a direct financing lease is a leveraged lease. This type is mentioned separately because it receives a different accounting treatment by a lessor. A leveraged lease meets all the definitional criteria of a direct financing lease, but differs because it involves at least three parties: a lessee, a long-term creditor, and a lessor (commonly referred to as the equity participant). Other characteristics of a leveraged lease are as follows:

1. The financing provided by the long-term creditor must be without recourse as to the general credit of the lessor, although the creditor may hold recourse with respect to the leased property. The amount of the financing must provide the lessor with substantial "leverage" in the transaction.
2. The lessor's net investment declines during the early years and rises during the later years of the lease term before its elimination (See Appendix).

Accounting for Leases—Lessee

As discussed in the preceding section, there are two classifications that apply to a lease transaction from the standpoint of the lessee, operating or capital.

Operating leases. The accounting treatment accorded an operating lease is relatively simple; the rental payments are charged to expense as the payments are made or become payable. This assumes that the lease payments are being made on a straight-line basis (i.e., an equal payment per period over the lease term). If the lease agreement calls for either an alternative payment schedule or a scheduled rent increase over the lease term, per FASB Technical Bulletin 85-3, the lease expense is recognized on a straight-line basis unless another systematic and rational basis is a better representation of the actual physical usage of the leased property. In such an instance it is necessary to record either a prepaid asset or a liability depending upon the structure of the payment schedule. If the scheduled increase(s) is due to additional leased property, recognition should be proportional to the leased property with the increased rents recognized over the years that the lessee has control over the use of the additional leased property.

Notice that in the case of an operating lease there is no balance sheet recognition of the leased asset because the substance of the lease is merely that of a rental. There is no reason to expect that the lessee will derive any future economic benefit from the leased asset beyond the lease term.

Capital leases. Recall that the classification of a lease is determined prior to the consideration of the accounting treatment. Therefore, it is necessary to first examine the lease transaction against the four criteria (transfer of title, bargain purchase option, 75% of useful life, or 90% of net FV). Should the lease agreement satisfy one of these, it is accounted for as a capital lease.

The lessee records a capital lease as an asset and an obligation (liability) at an amount equal to the present value of the **minimum lease payments** at the beginning of the lease term. The asset is recorded at the lower of the present value of the minimum lease payments or the fair value of the asset. When the fair value of the leased asset is less than the present value of the minimum lease payments, the interest rate used to amortize the lease obligation will differ from the interest rate used in the 90% test. The interest rate used in the amortization will be the same as that used in the 90% test when the fair value is greater than or equal to the present value of the minimum lease payments. For purposes of this computation, the minimum lease payments are considered to be the payments that the lessee is obligated to make or can be required to make excluding **executory costs** such as insurance, maintenance, and taxes. The minimum lease payments generally include the **minimum rental payments,** any **guarantee of the residual value** made by the lessee, and the **penalty** for **failure to renew** the lease, if applicable. If the lease includes a bargain purchase option (BPO), the amount required to be paid under the BPO is also included in the minimum lease payments. The present value is computed using the incremental borrowing rate of the lessee **unless** it is practicable for the lessee to determine the implicit rate used by the lessor, **and** the implicit rate is less than the incremental borrowing rate. The lease term used in this present value computation is the fixed, **noncancelable** term of the lease plus the following:

1. All periods covered by **bargain renewal options**
2. All periods for which failure to renew the lease imposes a penalty on the lessee
3. All periods covered by ordinary renewal options during which the lessee guarantees the lessor's debt on the leased property
4. All periods covered by ordinary renewals or extensions up to the date a BPO is exercisable

5. All periods representing renewals or extensions of the lease at the lessor's option

Remember, if the amount computed as the present value of the minimum lease payments exceeds the fair value of the leased property at the **inception of the lease,** the amount recorded is limited to the fair value.

The amortization of the leased asset will depend upon how the lease qualifies as a capital lease. If the lease transaction meets the criteria of either transferring ownership, or containing a bargain purchase option, then the asset arising from the transaction is amortized over the estimated useful life of the leased property. If the transaction qualifies as a capital lease because it meets either the 75% of useful life or 90% of FV criteria, the asset is amortized over the lease term. The conceptual rationale for this differentiated treatment arises because of the substance of the transaction. Under the first two criteria, the asset actually becomes the property of the lessee at the end of the lease term (or upon exercise of the BPO). In the latter situations, the title to the property remains with the lessor, and thus, the lessee ceases to have the right to use the property at the conclusion of the lease term.

The leased asset is amortized (depreciated) over the lease term if title does not transfer to the lessee, while the asset is depreciated in a manner consistent with the lessee's normal depreciation policy if the title is to eventually transfer to the lessee. This latter situation can be interpreted to mean that the asset is depreciated over the useful economic life of the leased asset. The treatment and method used to amortize (depreciate) the leased asset is very similar to that used for any other long-lived asset. The amortization entry requires a debit to amortization expense and a credit to accumulated amortization. The leased asset is not amortized below the estimated residual value.

In some instances when the property is to revert back to the lessor, there may be a guaranteed residual value. This is an amount that the lessee guarantees to the lessor. If the FV of the asset at the end of the lease term is greater than or equal to the guaranteed residual amount, the lessee incurs no additional obligation. On the other hand, if the FV of the leased asset is less than the guaranteed residual value, then the lessee must make up the difference, usually with a cash payment. The guaranteed residual value is often used as a tool to reduce the periodic payments by substituting the lump-sum amount at the end of the term that results from the guarantee. In any event the amortization must still take place based on the **estimated residual value**. This results in a rational and systematic allocation of the expense to the periods of usage and avoids a large loss (or expense) in the last period as a result of the guarantee.

The annual (periodic) rent payments made during the lease term are allocated between a reduction in the obligation and interest expense in a manner such that the interest expense represents the application of a constant periodic rate of interest to the remaining balance of the lease obligation. This is commonly referred to as the effective interest method and is described in APB 21.

The following examples illustrate the treatment described in the foregoing paragraphs.

Example of accounting for a capital lease—Asset returned to lessor

1. The lease is initiated on 1/1/05 for equipment with an expected useful life of three years. The equipment reverts back to the lessor upon expiration of the lease agreement.
2. The FV of the equipment at lease inception is $135,000.
3. Three payments are due to the lessor in the amount of $50,000 per year beginning 12/31/05. An additional sum of $1,000 is to be paid annually by the lessee for insurance.
4. The lessee guarantees a $10,000 residual value on 12/31/07 to the lessor.
5. Irrespective of the $10,000 residual value guarantee, the leased asset is expected to have only a $1,000 salvage value on 12/31/07.

6. The lessee's incremental borrowing rate is 10%. (The lessor's implicit rate is unknown.)
7. The present value of the lease obligation is as follows:

PV of guaranteed residual value	=	$10,000	x	.7513 *	=	$ 7,513
PV of annual payments	=	$50,000	x	2.4869 **	=	124,345
						$131,858

* *The present value of an amount of $1 due in three periods at 10% is .7513.*
** *The present value of an ordinary annuity of $1 for three periods at 10% is 2.4869.*

The first step in dealing with any lease transaction is to classify the lease. In this case, the lease term is for three years, which is equal to 100% of the expected useful life of the asset. Note that the 90% test is also fulfilled as the PV of the minimum lease payments ($131,858) is greater than 90% of the FV (90% x $135,000 = $121,500). Thus, the lessee accounts for the lease as a capital lease.

In number 7. (above) the present value of the lease obligation is computed. Note that the executory costs (insurance) are not included in the minimum lease payments and that the incremental borrowing rate of the lessee was used to determine the present value. This rate was used because the lessor's implicit rate was not determinable.

NOTE: In order to have used the implicit rate it would have to have been less than the incremental borrowing rate.

The entry necessary to record the lease on 1/1/05 is

Leased equipment	131,858	
Lease obligation		131,858

Note that the lease is recorded at the present value of the minimum lease payments that, in this case, is less than the FV. If the present value of the minimum lease payments had exceeded the FV, the lease would have been recorded at the FV.

The next step is to determine the proper allocation between interest and reduction of the lease obligation for each lease payment. This is done using the effective interest method as illustrated below.

Year	*Cash payment*	*Interest expense*	*Reduction in lease obligation*	*Balance of lease obligation*
Inception of lease				$131,858
1	$50,000	$13,186	$36,814	95,044
2	50,000	9,504	40,496	54,548
3	50,000	5,452	44,548	10,000

The interest is calculated at 10% (the incremental borrowing rate) of the balance of the lease obligation for each period, and the remainder of each $50,000 payment is allocated as a reduction in the lease obligation. The lessee is also required to pay $1,000 for insurance on an annual basis. The entries necessary to record all payments relative to the lease for each of the three years are shown below.

	12/31/05		*12/31/06*		*12/31/07*	
Insurance expense	1,000		1,000		1,000	
Interest expense	13,186		9,504		5,452	
Lease obligation	36,814		40,496		44,548	
Cash		51,000		51,000		51,000

The leased equipment recorded as an asset must also be amortized (depreciated). The initial unamortized balance is $131,858; however, as with any other long-lived asset, it cannot be amortized below the estimated residual value of $1,000 (note that it is amortized down to the actual estimated residual value, **not** the guaranteed residual value). In this case, the straight-line amortization method is applied over a period of three years. This three-year period represents the lease term, **not** the life of the asset, because the asset reverts back to the lessor at the end of the lease term. Therefore, the following entry will be made at the end of each year:

Amortization expense	43,619		
Accumulated amortization		43,619	[($131,858 – 1,000) ÷ 3]

Finally, on 12/31/07 we must recognize the fact that ownership of the property has reverted back to the owner (lessor). The lessee made a guarantee that the residual value would be $10,000 on 12/31/07; as a result, the lessee must make up the difference between the guaranteed residual value and the actual residual value with a cash payment to the lessor. The following entry illustrates the removal of the leased asset and obligation from the lessee's accounting records:

Lease obligation	10,000	
Accumulated amortization	130,858	
Cash		9,000
Leased equipment		131,858

The foregoing example illustrated a situation where the asset was to be returned to the lessor. Another situation exists (under BPO or transfer of title) where ownership of the asset is expected to transfer to the lessee at the end of the lease term. Remember that leased assets are amortized over their useful life when title transfers or a bargain purchase option exists. At the end of the lease, the balance of the lease obligation should equal the guaranteed residual value, the bargain purchase option price, or termination penalty for failure to renew the lease.

Example of accounting for a capital lease—Asset ownership transferred to lessee

1. A three-year lease is initiated on 1/1/05 for equipment with an expected useful life of five years.
2. Three annual lease payments of $52,000 are required beginning on 1/1/05 (note that the payment at the beginning of the year changes the PV computation from the previous example). The lessee pays $2,000 per year for insurance on the equipment and this amount is included in the annual payments.
3. The lessee can exercise a bargain purchase option on 12/31/07 for $10,000. The expected residual value at 12/31/07 is $18,000.
4. The lessee's incremental borrowing rate is 10% (the lessor's implicit rate is unknown).
5. The fair value of the leased property at the inception of the lease is $140,000.

Once again, the classification of the lease must be determined prior to computing the accounting entries to record it. This lease is classified as a capital lease because it contains a BPO. In this case, the 90% test is also fulfilled.

The PV of the lease obligation is computed as follows:

PV of bargain purchase option	= $10,000 x	.7513*	= $ 7,513
PV of annual payments	= ($52,000 – $2,000) x	2.7355**	= 136,755
			$144,268

* *.7513 is the PV of an amount due in three periods at 10%.*
** *2.7355 is the PV of an annuity due for three periods at 10%.*

Since the lessee pays $2,000 a year for insurance, this payment is treated as executory costs and excluded from the calculation of the present value of the annual payments. Note that the present value of the lease obligation is greater than the FV of the asset. Because of this, the lease obligation must be recorded at the FV of the leased asset.

1/1/05 Leased equipment	140,000	
Obligation under capital lease		140,000

According to FAS 13, the allocation between interest and principal is determined so that interest expense is computed using a constant periodic rate of interest applied to the remaining balance of the obligation. If the FV of the leased asset is greater than or equal to the PV of the lease obligation, the interest rate used is the same as that used to compute the PV (i.e., the incremental borrowing rate or the implicit rate). In cases such as this when the PV exceeds the FV of the leased asset, a new rate must be computed through a series of manual trial and error calculations. Alternatively, spreadsheet or loan amortization software can be used to solve for the unknown effective interest rate. In this situation the interest rate used was 13.267%. The amortization of the lease takes place as follows:

Date	*Cash payment*	*Interest expense*	*Reduction in lease obligation*	*Balance of lease obligation*
Inception of lease				$140,000
1/1/05	$50,000	$ --	$50,000	90,000
1/1/06	50,000	11,940	38,060	51,940
1/1/07	50,000	6,891	43,109	8,831
12/31/07	10,000	1,169	8,831	--

The following entries are required in years 2005 through 2007 to recognize the payment and amortization.

		2005		2006		2007	
1/1	Insurance expense	2,000		2,000		2,000	
	Obligation under capital lease	50,000		38,060		43,109	
	Accrued interest payable			11,940		6,891	
	Cash		52,000		52,000		52,000
12/31	Interest expense	11,940		6,891		1,169	
	Accrued interest payable		11,940		6,891		1,169
12/31	Amortization expense	24,400		24,400		24,400	
	Accumulated amortization [($140,000 – $18,000) ÷ 5 years)]		24,400		24,400		24,400
12/31	Obligation under capital lease					10,000	
	Cash						10,000

Accounting for Leases—Lessor

As previously noted, there are four classifications of leases with which a lessor must be concerned. They are operating, sales-type, direct financing, and leveraged.

Operating leases. As in the case of the lessee, the operating lease requires a less complex accounting treatment. The payments received by the lessor are recorded as rent revenues in the period in which the payment is received or becomes receivable. As with the lessee, if either the rentals vary from a straight-line basis or the lease agreement contains a scheduled rent increase over the lease term, the revenue is recorded on a straight-line basis unless an alternative basis of systematic and rational allocation is more representative of the time pattern of physical usage of the leased property. If the scheduled increase(s) is due to the lessee leasing additional property under a master lease agreement, the increase is allocated proportionally to the additional leased property and recognized on a straight-line basis over the years that the lessee has control over the additional leased property. FTB 88-1 prescribes that, in this case, the total revised rent be allocated between the previously leased property and the additional leased property based on their relative fair values.

The lessor presents the leased property on the balance sheet under the caption "Investment in leased property." This caption is shown with or near the fixed assets of the lessor, and depreciated in the same manner as the lessor's other fixed assets.

Any **initial direct costs** are amortized over the lease term as the related lease revenue is recognized (i.e., on a straight-line basis unless another method is more representative). However, these costs may be charged to expense as incurred if the effect is not materially different from straight-line amortization.

Any incentives made by the lessor to the lessee are treated as reductions of rent and recognized on a straight-line basis over the term of the lease.

In most operating leases, the lessor recognizes rental income over the lease term and does not measure or recognize any gain or loss on any differential between the fair value of the property and its carrying value. One exception to this rule is set forth in FAS 98. The exception applies when an operating lease involving real estate is not classified as a sales-type lease because ownership to the property does not transfer to the lessee at the end of the lease term. In this case, if at the inception of the lease the fair value of the property is less than its carrying amount, the lessor must recognize a loss equal to that difference at the inception of the lease.

Sales-type leases. In accounting for a sales-type lease, it is necessary for the lessor to determine the following amounts:

1. Gross investment
2. Fair value of the leased asset
3. Cost

From these amounts, the remainder of the computations necessary to record and account for the lease transaction can be made. The first objective is to determine the numbers necessary to complete the following entry:

Lease receivable	xx	
Cost of goods sold	xx	
Sales		xx
Inventory		xx
Unearned interest		xx

The gross investment (lease receivable) of the lessor is equal to the sum of the minimum lease payments (excluding executory costs) plus the **un**guaranteed residual value. The difference between the gross investment and the present value of the two components of gross investment (minimum lease payments and unguaranteed residual value) is recorded as the unearned interest revenue. The present value is computed using the lease term and implicit interest rate (both of which were discussed earlier). The lease term used in this computation includes any renewal options exercisable at the discretion of the lessor. The resulting unearned interest revenue is to be amortized into income using the effective interest method. This will result in a constant periodic rate of return on the net investment (the net investment is the gross investment less the unearned income).

Recall from our earlier discussion that the fair value (FV) of the leased property is, by definition, equal to the normal selling price of the asset adjusted by any residual amount retained (this amount retained can be exemplified by an unguaranteed residual value, investment credit, etc.). The adjusted selling price used for a sales-type lease is equal to the present value of the minimum lease payments. Thus, we can say that the normal selling price less the residual amount retained is equal to the PV of the minimum lease payments.

The cost of goods sold to be charged against income in the period of the sale is computed as the historic cost or carrying value of the asset (most likely inventory) plus any initial direct costs, less the present value of the unguaranteed residual value. The difference between the adjusted selling price and the amount computed as the cost of goods sold is the gross profit recognized by the lessor at the inception of the lease (sale). Thus, a sales-type lease generates two types of revenue for the lessor.

1. The gross profit on the sale
2. The interest earned on the lease receivable

Note that if the sales-type lease involves real estate, the lessor must account for the transaction under the provisions of FAS 66 in the same manner as a seller of the same property (see Chapter 8).

The application of these points is illustrated in the example below.

Example of accounting for a sales-type lease

Price Inc. is a manufacturer of specialized equipment. Many of its customers do not have the necessary funds or financing available for outright purchase. Because of this, Price offers a leasing alternative. The data relative to a typical lease are as follows:

1. The noncancelable fixed portion of the lease term is five years. The lessor has the option to renew the lease for an additional three years at the same rental. The estimated useful life of the asset is ten years.
2. The lessor is to receive equal annual payments over the term of the lease. The leased property reverts back to the lessor upon termination of the lease.
3. The lease is initiated on 1/1/05. Payments are due annually on 12/31 for the duration of the lease term.
4. The cost of the equipment to Price Inc. is $100,000. The lessor incurs costs associated with the inception of the lease in the amount of $2,500.
5. The selling price of the equipment for an outright purchase is $150,000.
6. The equipment is expected to have a residual value of $15,000 at the end of five years and $10,000 at the end of eight years.
7. The lessor desires a return of 12% (the implicit rate).

The first step is to calculate the annual payment due to the lessor. In order to yield the lessor's desired return, the present value (PV) of the minimum lease payments must equal the selling price adjusted for the present value of the residual amount. The present value is computed using the implicit interest rate and the lease term. In this case, the implicit rate is given as 12% and the lease term is eight years (the fixed noncancelable portion plus the renewal period). Thus, the computation would be as follows:

Normal selling price – PV of residual value = PV of minimum lease payments

Or, in this case,

$150,000 – (.40388* x $10,000 = $4,038.80) = 4.96764** x Annual minimum lease payment

$$\frac{\$145,961.20}{4.96764} = \text{Annual minimum lease payment}$$

$ 29,382.40 = Annual minimum lease payment

* *.40388 is the present value of an amount of $1 due in eight periods at a 12% interest rate.*

** *4.96764 is the present value of an annuity of $1 for eight periods at a 12% interest rate.*

Prior to examining the accounting implications of the lease, we must first determine the lease classification. Assume that there are no uncertainties regarding the lessor's costs, and the collectibility of the lease payments is reasonably assured. In this example, the lease term is eight years (discussed above) while the estimated useful life of the asset is ten years; thus, this lease is not an operating lease because the lease term covers 80% of the asset's estimated useful life. This exceeds the previously discussed 75% criterion. (Note that it also meets the 90% of FV criterion because the PV of the minimum lease payments of $145,961.20 is greater than 90% of the FV [90% x $150,000 = $135,000]). Next it must be determined if this is a sales-type, direct financing, or leveraged lease. To do this, examine the FV or selling price of the asset and compare it to the cost. Because the two are not equal, this is a sales-type lease.

Next, obtain the figures necessary for the lessor to record the entry. The gross investment is the total minimum lease payments plus the unguaranteed residual value or

($29,382.40 x 8 = $235,059.20) + $10,000 = $245,059.20

The cost of goods sold is the historical cost of the inventory ($100,000) plus any initial direct costs ($2,500) less the PV of the unguaranteed residual value ($10,000 x .40388 = $4,038.80). Thus, the cost of goods sold amount is $98,461.20 ($100,000 + $2,500 – $4,038.80). Note that the initial direct costs will require a credit entry to record their accrual (accounts payable) or payment (cash). The inventory account is credited for the carrying value of the asset, in this case $100,000.

The adjusted selling price is equal to the PV of the minimum payments, or $145,961.20. Finally, the unearned interest revenue is equal to the gross investment (i.e., lease receivable) less the present value of the components making up the gross investment (the present values of the minimum annual lease payments of $29,382.40 and the unguaranteed residual of $10,000). The computation is [$245,059.20 – ($29,382.40 x 4.96764 = $145,961.20) – ($10,000 x .40388 = 4,038.80) = $95,059.20]. Therefore, the entry necessary for the lessor to record the lease is

Lease receivable	245,059.20	
Cost of goods sold	98,461.20	
Inventory		100,000.00
Sales		145,961.20
Unearned interest		95,059.20
Accounts payable (initial direct costs)		2,500.00

The next step in accounting for a sales-type lease is to determine the proper handling of each payment. Both principal and interest are included in each payment. Interest is recognized using the effective interest rate method so that an equal rate of return is earned each period over the term of the lease. This will require setting up an amortization schedule as illustrated below.

Year	*Cash payment*	*Interest*	*Reduction in principal*	*Balance of net investment*
Inception of lease				$150,000.00
1	$ 29,382.40	$18,000.00	$ 11,382.40	138,617.00
2	29,382.40	16,634.11	12,748.29	125,869.31
3	29,382.40	15,104.32	14,278.08	111,591.23
4	29,382.40	13,390.95	15,991.45	95,599.78
5	29,382.40	11,471.97	17,910.43	77,689.35
6	29,382.40	9,322.72	20,059.68	57,629.67
7	29,382.40	6,915.56	22,466.84	35,162.83
8	29,382.40	4,219.57	25,162.83	10,000.00
	$235,059.20	$95,059.20	$140,000.00	

A few of the columns need to be elaborated upon. First, the net investment is the gross investment (lease receivable) less the unearned interest. Note that at the end of the lease term, the net investment is equal to the estimated residual value. Also note that the total interest earned over the lease term is equal to the unearned interest at the beginning of the lease term.

The entries below illustrate the proper accounting for the receipt of the lease payment and the amortization of the unearned interest in the first year.

Cash	29,382.40	
Lease receivable		29,382.40
Unearned interest	18,000.00	
Interest revenue		18,000.00

Note that there is no entry to recognize the principal reduction. This is done automatically when the net investment is reduced by decreasing the lease receivable (gross investment) by $29,382.40 and the unearned interest account by only $18,000. The $18,000 is 12% (implicit rate) of the net investment. These entries are to be made over the life of the lease.

At the end of the lease term the asset is returned to the lessor and the following entry is required:

Asset	10,000	
Lease receivable		10,000

Direct financing leases. The accounting for a direct financing lease holds many similarities to that for a sales-type lease. Of particular importance is that the terminology used is much the same; however, the treatment accorded these items varies greatly. Again, it is best to preface our discussion by determining our objectives in the accounting for a direct financing lease. Once the lease has been classified, it must be recorded. In order to do this, the following numbers must be obtained:

1. Gross investment
2. Cost
3. Residual value

As mentioned earlier, a direct financing lease generally involves a leasing company or other financial institution and results in only interest income being earned by the lessor. This is because the FV (selling price) and the cost are equal and, therefore, no profit is recognized on the actual lease transaction. Note how this is different from a sales-type lease that involves both a profit on the transaction and interest income over the lease term. The reason for this difference is derived from the conceptual nature underlying the purpose of the lease transaction. In a sales-type lease, **the manufacturer** (distributor, dealer) is seeking an alternative means to finance the sale of the product, whereas a direct financing lease is a result of the consumer's need to finance an equipment purchase through a third party. Because the consumer is unable to obtain conventional financing, he or she turns to a leasing company that will purchase the desired asset and then lease it to the consumer. Here the profit on the transaction remains with the manufacturer while the interest income is earned by the leasing company.

Like a sales-type lease, the first objective is to determine the amounts necessary to complete the following entry:

Lease receivable	xxx	
Asset		xxx
Unearned interest		xx

The gross investment is still defined as the minimum amount of lease payments exclusive of any executory costs plus the unguaranteed residual value. The difference between the gross investment as determined above and the cost (carrying value) of the asset is to be recorded as the unearned interest income because there is no manufacturer's/dealer's profit earned on the transaction. The following entry would be made to record the initial direct costs:

Initial direct costs	xx	
Cash (or accounts payable)		xx

The net investment in the lease is defined as the gross investment less the unearned interest income plus the unamortized initial direct costs related to the lease. Initial direct costs are defined in the same way that they were for purposes of the sales-type lease; however, the accounting treatment is different. For a direct financing lease, the unearned lease (interest) income and the initial direct costs are amortized to income over the lease term to yield a constant effective rate of interest on the net investment. Thus, the effect of the initial direct costs is to reduce the implicit interest rate, or yield, to the lessor over the life of the lease.

An example follows that illustrates the preceding principles.

Example of accounting for a direct financing lease

Edwards, Inc. needs new equipment to expand its manufacturing operation; however, it does not have sufficient capital to purchase the asset at this time. Because of this, Edwards has employed Samuels Leasing to purchase the asset. In turn, Edwards (the lessee) will lease the asset from Samuels (the lessor). The following information applies to the terms of the lease:

Lease information

1. A three-year lease is initiated on 1/1/05 for equipment costing $131,858 with an expected useful life of five years. FV at 1/1/05 of the equipment is $131,858.
2. Three annual payments are due to the lessor beginning 12/31/05. The property reverts back to the lessor upon termination of the lease.
3. The unguaranteed residual value at the end of year three is estimated to be $10,000.
4. The annual payments are calculated to give the lessor a 10% return (implicit rate).
5. The lease payments and unguaranteed residual value have a PV equal to $131,858 (FMV of asset) at the stipulated discount rate.
6. The annual payment to the lessor is computed as follows:

PV of residual value	=	$10,000 x .7513* = $7,513
PV of lease payments	=	Selling price – PV of residual value
	=	$131,858 – 7,513 = $124,345

$$\text{Annual payment} = \frac{\$124,345}{PV_{3,}10\%} = \frac{\$124,345}{2.4869^{**}} = \$50,000$$

* *.7513 is the PV of an amount due in three periods at 10%.*
** *2.4869 is the PV of an annuity of $1 for three periods at a 10% interest rate.*

7. Initial direct costs of $7,500 are incurred by Samuels in the lease transaction.

As with any lease transaction, the first step must be to determine the proper classification of the lease. In this case, the PV of the lease payments ($124,345) exceeds 90% of the FV (90% x $131,858 = $118,672). Assume that the lease payments are reasonably assured and that there are no uncertainties surrounding the costs yet to be incurred by the lessor.

Next, determine the unearned interest and the net investment in the lease.

Gross investment in lease [(3 x $50,000) + $10,000]	$160,000
Cost of leased property	131,858
Unearned interest	$ 28,142

The unamortized initial direct costs are to be added to the gross investment in the lease and the unearned interest income is to be deducted to arrive at the net investment in the lease. The net investment in the lease for this example is determined as follows:

Gross investment in lease	$160,000
Add: Unamortized initial direct costs	7,500
	$167,500
Less: Unearned interest income	28,142
Net investment in lease	$139,358

The net investment in the lease (Gross investment – Unearned revenue) has been increased by the amount of initial direct costs. Therefore, **the implicit rate is no longer 10%**. We must recompute the implicit rate. The implicit rate is really the result of an internal rate of return calculation. We know that the lease payments are to be $50,000 per annum and that a residual value of $10,000 is expected at the end of the lease term. In return for these payments (inflows) we are giving up equipment (outflow) and incurring initial direct costs (outflows) with a net investment of $139,358 ($131,858 + $7,500). The only way to manually obtain the new implicit rate is through a trial and error calculation as set up below.

$$\frac{50,000}{(1+i)^1} + \frac{50,000}{(1+i)^2} + \frac{50,000}{(1+i)^3} + \frac{10,000}{(1+i)^3} = \$139,358$$

Where i = implicit rate of interest

This computation is most efficiently performed using either spreadsheet or present value software. In doing so, the $139,358 is entered as the present value, the contractual payment stream and residual value are entered, and the software iteratively solves for the unknown implicit interest rate.

In this case, the implicit rate is equal to 7.008%. Thus, the amortization table would be set up as follows:

	(a) Lease payments	*(b)* Reduction in unearned interest	*(c)* PV x implicit rate (7.008%)	*(d)* Reduction in initial direct costs (b-c)	*(e)* Reduction in PVI net invest. (a-b + d)	*(f)* PVI net invest. in lease (f)(n+1) = (f)n – (e)
0						$139,358
1	$ 50,000	$13,186 (1)	$ 9,766	$3,420	$ 40,234	99,124
2	50,000	9,504 (2)	6,947	2,557	43,053	56,071
3	50,000	5,455 (3)	3,929	1,526	46,071	10,000
	$150,000	$28,145*	$20,642	$7,503	$129,358	

* *Rounded*

(b.1) $131,858 x10% = $13,186
(b.2) [$131,858 – ($50,000 – 13,186)] x 10% = $9,504
(b.3) {$131,858 – [($50,000 – 9,504) + ($50,000 – 13,186)]} x 10% = $5,455

Here the interest is computed as 7.008% of the net investment. Note again that the net investment at the end of the lease term is equal to the estimated residual value.

The entry made to initially record the lease is as follows:

Lease receivable* [($50,000 x 3) + 10,000]	160,000	
Asset acquired for leasing		131,858
Unearned interest		28,142

* *Also the "gross investment in lease."*

When the payment of (or obligation to pay) the initial direct costs occurs, the following entry must be made:

Initial direct costs	7,500	
Cash (or accounts payable)		7,500

Using the schedule above, the following entries would be made during each of the indicated years:

	2005		*2006*		*2007*	
Cash	50,000		50,000		50,000	
Lease receivable*		50,000		50,000		50,000
Unearned interest	13,186		9,504		5,455	
Initial direct costs		3,420		2,557		1,526
Interest revenue		9,766		6,947		3,929

* *Also the "gross investment in lease."*

Finally, when the asset is returned to the lessor at the end of the lease term, it must be recorded by the following entry:

Used asset	10,000	
Lease receivable*		10,000

* *Also the "gross investment in lease."*

Leveraged leases. Leveraged leases are discussed in detail in the Appendix of this chapter because of the complexity involved in the accounting treatment.

Special Situations

Change in residual value. For any of the foregoing types of leases, the lessor is to review the estimated residual value at least annually. If there is a decline in the estimated residual value, the lessor must make a determination as to whether this decline is temporary or permanent. If temporary, no adjustment is required; however, if the decline is other than temporary, then the estimated residual value must be revised to conform to the revised estimate. The loss that arises in the net investment is recognized in the period of decline. Under no circumstance is the estimated residual value to be adjusted to reflect an increase in the estimate.

Change in the provisions of a lease. Accounting issues arise when the lessee and lessor agree, subsequent to its inception, to change the provisions of the lease (other than by renewals or term extensions that are discussed later). If, from the standpoint of the lessee, the revised lease terms would have, at the inception of the original lease, resulted in a different lease classification (e.g., operating lease versus capital lease or vice versa), the revised agreement is considered to be a new agreement.

If the original lease was accounted for as a capital lease and the revised lease qualifies for treatment as an operating lease, FAS 13 originally provided that the recorded asset and obligation be eliminated with a gain or loss recognized for the difference. This treatment was amended by FAS 145, effective for transactions occurring after May 15, 2002. Leases subject to the new rules are to be accounted for as sale-leaseback transactions (discussed later in this chapter).

If the original lease was accounted for as an operating lease and the revised lease is a capital lease, then on the date of the revision, the lessee records an asset and an obligation based on the present value of the remaining lease payments (or the fair value of the leased property, if less).

Finally, if the original and revised leases are both capital leases, then the lessee adjusts the recorded asset and obligation by an amount equal to the difference between the present value of the future minimum lease payments under the revised agreement and the recorded balance of the obligation. For the purposes of this calculation, the rate of interest to be used is the rate that was used to record the lease initially. The adjustment is recognized as a gain or loss of the period in which the revision is made.

In the case of either a sales-type or direct financing lease where there is a change in the provisions of a lease, the lease is accounted for by the lessor as discussed below.

We are basically concerned with changes in the provisions that affect the amount of the remaining minimum lease payments. When a change of this type occurs, one of the following three things can happen:

1. The change does not give rise to a new agreement. A new agreement is defined as a change that, if in effect at the inception of the lease, would have resulted in a different classification.
2. The change does give rise to a new agreement that would be classified as a direct financing lease
3. The change gives rise to a new agreement that would be classified as an operating lease

If either 1. or 2. occurs, the balance of the minimum lease payments receivable and the estimated residual value (if affected) are adjusted to reflect the effect of the change. The net adjustment is charged (or credited) to unearned income, and the accounting for the lease over its remaining term is adjusted to reflect the change.

If the new agreement is an operating lease, then the remaining net investment (lease receivable less unearned income) is written off and the leased asset is recorded by the lessor at the lower of its cost, present fair value, or carrying value. The net adjustment resulting from these entries is charged (or credited) to income of the period in which the revision is made. Thereafter, the new lease is accounted for as any other operating lease.

Early termination of a lease. Accounting for premature lease termination from the standpoints of the lessee and lessor follows:

Lessee accounting. Discontinuation of business activities in a particular location is considered an exit activity, the accounting for which is specified in FAS 146 (see Chapter 3).

Operating leases. In connection with lease termination the lessee may incur (1) costs to terminate the lease prior to the end of its noncancelable term and/or (2) continuing lease costs incurred during the remainder of the lease term for which the lessee receives no economic benefit because the premises are no longer in use. On the date the lessee terminates the lease, the lessee recognizes a liability for the fair value of the termination costs. The termination date is the date that the lessee provides written notice to the lessor in accordance with the notification requirements contained in the lease or the date the lessee and lessor agree to a negotiated early termination.

The fair value of rentals that continue to be incurred under the lease during its remaining term without benefit to the lessee is recognized as a liability on the date that the lessee ceases to use the property (referred to as the cease-use date). Fair value is computed based on the remaining rentals due under the lease, adjusted for any prepaid or deferred rent under the lease, and reduced by estimated sublease rentals that are reasonable to expect for the property. The fair value measurement requires that reasonable sublease rentals be included in the computation **even if the lessee does not intend to sublease the property**.

In periods subsequent to the recognition of these liabilities but prior to their settlement, changes in fair value are measured using the credit-adjusted risk-free rate of interest (in essence, the lessee's incremental borrowing rate) used to initially measure the liability.

Upon initial recognition of these liabilities, the related costs are recognized in the lessee's income statement as operating expense (or income from continuing operations if no measure of operations is presented) unless required to be presented as part of discontinued operations. The cumulative effects of any subsequent period changes in liabilities that result from changes in the estimates of either the amounts or timing of cash flows are reported in the same income statement caption used to initially recognize the costs. Changes to the liabilities as a result of the passage of time increase their carrying amount and are recorded as accretion expense, which is also considered an operating expense.

Capital leases. If the lease is a capital lease, it is subject to the provisions of FAS 144 with respect to long-lived assets to be disposed of other than by sale (see Chapter 9) either individually (in which case the gain or loss is recorded as a component of operating expense) or as part of a disposal group (in which case the gain or loss is presented as a part of discontinued operations). During the time period between the termination date and the cease-use date, the capital lease asset continues to be classified as "held and used," is subject to impairment evaluation, and its remaining carrying value is amortized over that shortened time period.

Lessor accounting. Lessor accounting for an early lease termination is as follows:

Sales-type and direct financing leases. The lessor records the leased equipment as an asset at the lower of its original cost, present fair value, or current carrying value. The difference between the remaining net investment in the lease and the amount of the adjustment to recognize the leased equipment is reflected in income of the period in which the lease is terminated.

Operating leases. Accounting for the leased asset is subject to the provisions of FAS 144. Between the termination date and the cease-use date, the leased asset continues to be presented as held-and-used and depreciated subject to an impairment evaluation that considers the likelihood and timing of replacing the tenant and market rents that would be realized. On the cease-use date, the leased asset is reclassified from held-and-used to the category of idle property and equipment with the associated temporary suspension of depreciation.

Upon receiving notice of termination, the lessor recognizes a receivable for the fair value of any termination fees to be received from the lessee as a result of early cancellation and a corresponding deferred rent liability that is recorded as an adjustment to any previously recorded deferred rent liability or prepaid rent. The remaining rental stream to be received thereafter is recognized on a straight-line basis over the remainder of the time period during which such payments were agreed to continue by adjusting any remaining prepaid rent, deferred rent, and/or unamortized initial direct costs so that they will be fully amortized by the date on which the lessee's payment obligation is fully satisfied.

Renewal or extension of an existing lease. The renewal or extension of an existing lease agreement affects the accounting of both the lessee and the lessor. There are two basic situations: (1) the renewal occurs and makes a residual guarantee or penalty provision inoperative or (2) the renewal agreement does not do the foregoing and the renewal is treated as a new agreement. The accounting treatment prescribed under the latter situation for a lessee is as follows:

1. If the renewal or extension is classified as a capital lease, then the (present) current balances of the asset and related obligation are adjusted by the difference between the present value of the future minimum lease payments under the revised agreement and the (present) current balance of the obligation. The present value of the minimum lease payments under the revised agreement is computed using the interest rate in effect at the inception of the original lease.
2. If the renewal or extension is classified as an operating lease, then the current balances of the asset and liability are written off and a gain (loss) recognized for the difference. The new lease agreement resulting from a renewal or extension is accounted for in the same manner as other operating leases.

Under the same circumstances, the following treatment is followed by the lessor:

1. If the renewal or extension is classified as a direct financing lease, then the existing balances of the lease receivable and the estimated residual value are adjusted for the changes resulting from the revised agreement.

   NOTE: Remember that an upward adjustment to the estimated residual value is not allowed.

   The net adjustment is charged or credited to unearned income.
2. If the renewal or extension is classified as an operating lease, then the remaining net investment under the existing sales-type lease or direct financing lease is written off and the leased asset is recorded as an asset at the lower of its original cost, present fair value, or current carrying amount. The difference between the net investment and the amount recorded for the leased asset is charged to income of the period that includes the renewal or extension date. The renewal or extension is then accounted for prospectively as any other operating lease.
3. If the renewal or extension is classified as a sales-type lease **and** it occurs at or near the end of the existing lease term, then the renewal or extension is accounted for as a sales-type lease.

   NOTE: A renewal or extension that occurs in the last few months of an existing lease is considered to have occurred at or near the end of the existing lease term.

If the renewal or extension causes the guarantee or penalty provision to be inoperative, the **lessee** adjusts the current balance of the leased asset and the lease obligation to the present value of the future minimum lease payments (according to FAS 13 "by an amount equal to the difference between the PV of the future minimum lease payments under the revised agreement and the present balance of the obligation"). The PV of the future minimum lease payments is computed using the rate used in the original lease agreement.

Given the same circumstances, the **lessor** adjusts the existing balance of the lease receivable and estimated residual value to reflect the changes of the revised agreement (remember, no upward adjustments to the residual value). The net adjustment is charged (or credited) to unearned income.

Leases between related parties. Leases between related parties are classified and accounted for as though the parties are unrelated, except in cases where it is certain that the terms and conditions of the agreement have been influenced significantly by the fact that the lessor and lessee are related. When this is the case, the classification and/or accounting is modified to reflect the true economic substance of the transaction rather than the legal form. Under FIN 46(R), discussed earlier in this chapter, many related-party lessors will qualify as variable interest entities (VIE). When this is the case, the lessee will present consolidated financial statements that include the lessor's assets, liabilities, and results of operations. The elimination of intercompany transactions and balances will result in the rental expense and rental income being removed from the consolidated financial statements, which will instead reflect the depreciation of the leased asset and the interest expense on any related debt.

FAS 57 requires that the nature and extent of leasing activities between related parties be disclosed. FIN 46(R) requires the following disclosures by the primary beneficiary of a VIE:

1. The nature, purpose, size, and activities of the VIE
2. The carrying amount and classification of consolidated assets that collateralize the VIE's obligations
3. Any lack of recourse that VIE creditors or holders of VIE beneficial interests have to the general credit of the primary beneficiary

Accounting for leases in a business combination. A business combination, in and of itself, has no effect upon the classification of a lease. However, if, in connection with a business combination, a lease agreement is modified to change the original classification of the lease, it is considered a new agreement and accounted for as previously discussed.

In most cases, a business combination will not affect the previous classification of a lease unless the provisions have been modified as indicated in the preceding paragraph.

The acquiring company applies the following procedures to account for a leveraged lease in a business combination:

1. The classification as a leveraged lease is retained.
2. The net investment in the leveraged lease is assigned a fair value (present value, net of income taxes) based upon the remaining future cash flows. Also, the estimated income tax effects of the cash flows are recognized.
3. The net investment is broken down into three components: net rentals receivable, estimated residual value, and unearned income.
4. Thereafter, the leveraged lease is accounted for as described in the Appendix to this chapter.

In a business combination where a lease is acquired that does not conform to FAS 13 (pre-1979), the acquiring company accounts for the lease by retroactively applying FAS 13 at the date of combination.

Accounting for changes in lease agreements resulting from refunding of tax-exempt debt. Tax-exempt debt is often "refunded" by the issuer of the debt instruments. Refunding is a refinancing that enables the issuer (i.e., a municipality that issued bonds) to take advantage of favorable interest rates. A **current refunding** is effected when the debt becomes callable and the issuer issues new debt in order to use the proceeds to retire the original debt. An **advance refunding** is a more complex variation that occurs prior to the call date of the original instruments. It entails issuance of new tax-exempt debt at the lower interest rate with a similar maturity to the original issuance. The proceeds of the new debt are invested in a portfolio of market-traded US Treasury securities and other obligations that effectively "defease" the original bonds (see Chapter 13 for a discussion of debt defeasance). If, during the lease term, a change in the lease results from a refunding by the lessor of tax-exempt debt (including an advance refunding) and (1) the lessee receives the economic advantages of the refunding and (2) the revised agreement can be classified as a capital lease by the lessee and a direct financing lease by the lessor, the change is accounted for as follows:

1. If the change is accounted for as an extinguishment of debt
   a. Lessee accounting. The lessee adjusts the lease obligation to the present value of the future minimum lease payments under the revised agreement. The present value of the minimum lease payments is computed using the interest rate applicable to the revised agreement. Any gain or loss is recognized currently

as a gain or loss on the extinguishment of debt in accordance with the provisions of FAS 145 (discussed in detail in Chapter 13).

b. Lessor accounting. The lessor adjusts the balance of the lease receivable and the estimated residual value, if affected, for the difference in present values between the old and revised agreements. Any resulting gain or loss is recognized currently.

2. If the change is not accounted for as an extinguishment of debt

   a. Lessee accounting. The lessee accrues any costs in connection with the debt refunding that are obligated to be reimbursed to the lessor. These costs are amortized by the interest method over the period from the date of refunding to the call date of the debt to be refunded.

   b. Lessor accounting. The lessor recognizes as revenue any reimbursements to be received from the lessee, for costs paid in relation to the debt refunding. This revenue is recognized in a systematic manner over the period from the date of refunding to the call date of the debt to be refunded.

Sale or assignment to third parties; nonrecourse financing. The sale or assignment of a lease or of property subject to a lease that was originally accounted for as a sales-type lease or a direct financing lease will not affect the original accounting treatment of the lease. Any profit or loss on the sale or assignment is recognized at the time of the transaction except under the following two circumstances:

1. When the sale or assignment is between related parties, apply substance versus form provisions presented above under "leases between related parties"
2. When the sale or assignment is with recourse, it is accounted for using the provisions of FAS 77 or FAS 140.

The sale of property subject to an operating lease is not treated as a sale if the seller (or any related party to the seller) retains "substantial risks of ownership" in the leased property. A seller may retain "substantial risks of ownership" by various arrangements. For example, if the lessee defaults upon the lease agreement or if the lease terminates, the seller may arrange to do one of the following:

1. Acquire the property or the lease
2. Substitute an existing lease
3. Secure a replacement lessee or a buyer for the property under a remarketing agreement

A seller does **not** retain substantial risks of ownership by arrangements where one of the following occurs:

1. A remarketing agreement includes a reasonable fee to be paid to the seller
2. The seller is not required to give priority to the releasing or disposition of the property owned by the third party over similar property owned by the seller

When the sale of property subject to an operating lease is not accounted for as a sale because the substantial risk factor is present, it is accounted for as a borrowing. The proceeds are recorded by the seller as an obligation. Rental payments made by the lessee under the operating lease are recorded as revenue by the seller even if the payments are paid to the third-party purchaser. The seller accounts for each rental payment by allocating a portion to interest expense (to be imputed in accordance with the provisions of APB 21), and the remainder to reduce the existing obligation. Other normal accounting procedures for operating leases are applied except that the depreciation term for the leased asset is limited to the amortization period of the obligation.

The sale or assignment of lease payments under an operating lease by the lessor are accounted for as a borrowing as described above.

Nonrecourse financing is a common occurrence in the leasing industry, whereby the stream of lease payments on a lease is discounted on a nonrecourse basis at a financial institution with the lease payments collateralizing the debt. The proceeds are then used to finance future leasing transactions. Even though the discounting is on a nonrecourse basis, FTB 86-2 prohibits the offsetting of the debt against the related lease receivable unless a legal right of offset exists or the lease qualified as a leveraged lease at its inception. The SEC in a Staff Accounting Bulletin has also affirmed this position.

Money-over-money lease transactions. In cases where a lessor obtains nonrecourse financing in excess of the leased asset's cost, FTB 88-1 states that the borrowing and leasing are separate transactions and are not to be offset against each other unless a legal right of offset exists. Only dealer profit on sales-type leases may be recognized at the beginning of the lease term.

Transfers of residual value (FAS 140 and FTB 86-2). Recently, there has been an increase in the acquisition of interests in residual values of leased assets by companies whose primary business is other than leasing or financing. This generally occurs through the outright purchase of the right to own the leased asset or the right to receive the proceeds from the sale of a leased asset at the end of its lease term.

In instances such as these, the rights are generally recorded by the purchaser at the fair value of the assets surrendered unless the fair value of the residual is more objectively determinable. Increases in the estimated value of the interest in the residual (i.e., residual value accretion) to the end of the lease term are permitted to be recognized only for guaranteed residual values because they are financial assets. However, recognition of such increases is prohibited for unguaranteed residual values. A nontemporary write-down of a residual value interest (guaranteed/unguaranteed) is recognized as a loss and is not permitted to be subsequently restored. This guidance also applies to lessors who sell the related minimum lease payments but retain the interest in the residual value irrespective of whether the residual is guaranteed.

Leases involving government units. Leases that involve government units (i.e., airport facilities, bus terminal space, etc.) usually contain special provisions that prevent the agreements from being classified as anything but operating leases. These special provisions, referred to as fiscal funding clauses, include the governmental body's authority to abandon a facility at any time during the lease term, thus making its economic life indeterminable. These leases also do not contain a BPO or transfer ownership. The fair value is generally indeterminable because neither the leased property nor similar property is available for sale.

However, leases involving government units are subject to the same classification criteria as nongovernment units, except when all of the following six criteria are met:

NOTE: If all six conditions are met, the agreement is classified as an operating lease by both lessee and lessor.

1. A government unit or authority owns the leased property
2. The leased property is part of a larger facility operated by or on behalf of the lessor
3. The leased property is a permanent structure or part of a permanent structure that normally cannot be moved to another location
4. The lessor, or a higher governmental authority, has the right to terminate the lease at any time under the lease agreement or existing statutes or regulations

5. The lease neither transfers ownership nor allows the lessee to purchase or acquire the leased property
6. The leased property or similar property in the same area cannot be purchased or leased from anyone else

If any of the six conditions that qualify the lease for automatic operating lease treatment is not met, then the lease is evaluated to determine the likelihood of future cancellation. Using the loss contingency criteria from FAS 5, if it is remote (i.e., the chances are slight) that the lease will be canceled, then the lease agreement qualifies as a noncancelable lease and is classified the same as any other such lease with a nongovernmental lessee. Otherwise, the lease is considered to be cancelable and accounted for as an operating lease.

Accounting for a sublease. A sublease is an arrangement where the original lessee re-leases the leased property to a third party (the sublessee), and the original lessee acts as a sublessor. Normally, the nature of a sublease agreement does not affect the original lease agreement, and the original lessee/sublessor retains primary liability to the lessor.

The original lease remains in effect, and the original lessor continues to account for the lease as before. The original lessee/sublessor accounts for the lease as follows:

1. If the original lease agreement transfers ownership or contains a BPO and if the new lease meets any one of the four specified criteria (i.e., transfers ownership, BPO, 75% test, or 90% test) and both the collectibility and uncertainties criteria, then the sublessor classifies the new lease as a sales-type or direct financing lease; otherwise as an operating lease. In either situation, the original lessee/sublessor continues accounting for the original lease obligation as before.
2. If the original lease agreement does not transfer ownership or contain a BPO, but it still qualifies as a capital lease, then the original lessee/sublessor (with one exception) applies the usual criteria in classifying the new agreement. If the new lease qualifies, the original lessee/sublessor accounts for it as a direct financing lease, with the unamortized balance of the asset under the original lease being treated as the cost of the leased property. The one exception arises when the circumstances surrounding the sublease suggest that the sublease agreement was an important part of a predetermined plan in which the original lessee played only an intermediate role between the original lessor and the sublessee. In this situation, the sublease is classified by the 75% and 90% criteria as well as collectibility and uncertainties criteria. In applying the 90% criterion, the fair value for the leased property is the fair value to the original lessor at the inception of the original lease. Under all circumstances, the original lessee continues accounting for the original lease obligation as before. If the new lease agreement (sublease) does not meet the capitalization requirements imposed for subleases, then the new lease is accounted for as an operating lease.
3. If the original lease is an operating lease, the original lessee/sublessor accounts for the new lease as an operating lease and accounts for the original operating lease as before.

Sale-Leaseback Transactions

Sale-leaseback describes a transaction where the owner of property (seller-lessee) sells the property, and then immediately leases all or part of it back from the new owner (buyer-lessor). These transactions may occur when the seller-lessee is experiencing cash flow or financing problems or because of available income tax advantages. The important consideration in this type of transaction is the recognition of two separate and distinct economic events. It is important to note, however, that in a sale-leaseback there is not a transfer of property. First, there is a sale of property, and second, there is a lease agreement for the same property in which the original seller is the lessee and the original buyer is the lessor. This is illustrated below.

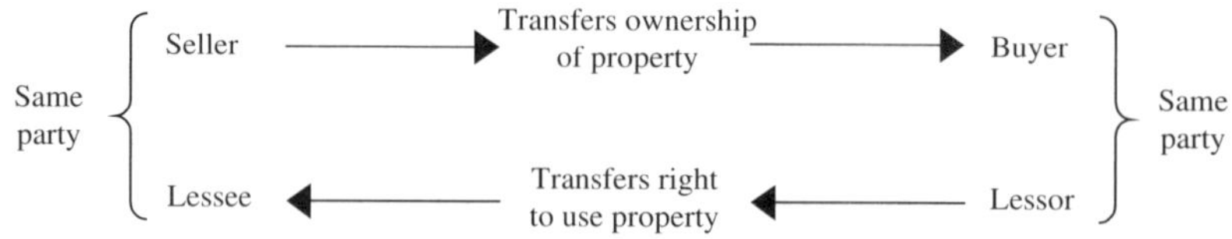

If an entity owns property and is also a lessee of it (e.g., the entity invests in a partnership that owns the leased property), and sells the property while remaining a lessee, the transaction is accounted for as a sale-leaseback, if the existing lease terms are modified.

A sale-leaseback transaction is usually structured with the sales price of the asset greater than or equal to the current market value. The result of this higher sales price is higher periodic rental payments over the lease term. The transaction is usually attractive because of the income tax benefits associated with it. The seller-lessee benefits from the higher price because of the increased gain on the sale of the property and the deductibility of the lease payments that are usually larger than the depreciation that was previously being deducted. The buyer-lessor benefits from both the higher rental payments and the larger depreciable income tax basis.

The accounting treatment from the seller-lessee's point of view will depend upon the degree of rights to use that it retains. The degree of rights to use retained may be categorized as follows:

1. Substantially all
2. Minor
3. More than minor but less than substantially all

The guideline for the determination of substantially all is based upon the classification criteria presented for the lease transaction. For example, a test based upon the 90% recovery criterion seems appropriate. That is, if the present value of fair rental payments is equal to 90% or more of the fair value of the asset sold, the seller-lessee is presumed to have retained **substantially all** of the rights to use the sold property. The test for retaining **minor** rights would be to substitute 10% or less for 90% or more in the preceding sentence.

If substantially all the rights to use the property are retained by the seller-lessee, and the agreement meets at least one of the criteria for capital lease treatment, the seller-lessee accounts for the leaseback as a capital lease and any profit on the sale is deferred and amortized in proportion to amortization of the leased asset. If the leaseback is classified as an operating lease, it is accounted for as such, and any profit on the sale is deferred and amortized over the lease term in proportion to gross rental charges. Any loss on the sale would also be deferred unless the loss were perceived to be a real economic loss, in which case the loss would be immediately recognized and not deferred.

If only a **minor portion** of the rights to use are retained by the seller-lessee, the sale and the leaseback are accounted for separately. However, if the rental payments appear unreasonable based upon the existing market conditions at the inception of the lease, the profit or loss is adjusted so the rentals are at a reasonable amount. The amount created by the adjustment is deferred and amortized over the life of the property if a capital lease is involved or over the lease term if an operating lease is involved.

If the seller-lessee retains **more than a minor portion but less than substantially all** the rights to use the property, any excess profit on the sale is recognized on the date of the sale. For purposes of this paragraph, excess profit is derived as follows:

1. If the leaseback is classified as an operating lease, the excess profit is the profit that exceeds the present value of the minimum lease payments over the lease term. The seller-lessee uses its incremental borrowing rate to compute the present value of the minimum lease payments. If the implicit rate of interest in the lease is known and lower, it is substituted for the incremental borrowing rate in computing the present value of the minimum lease payments.
2. If the leaseback is classified as a capital lease, the excess profit is the amount that exceeds the recorded amount of the leased asset.

When the fair value of the property at the time of the leaseback is less than its undepreciated cost, the seller-lessee immediately recognizes a loss for the difference. In the example below, the sales price is less than the book value of the property. However, there is no economic loss because the FV is greater than the book value.

Sales price	Book value	FV and PV
\$85,000	\$90,000	\$100,000

(\$5,000)
Artificial loss

The artificial loss is deferred and amortized as an addition to depreciation.

The diagram below summarizes the accounting for sale-leaseback transactions.

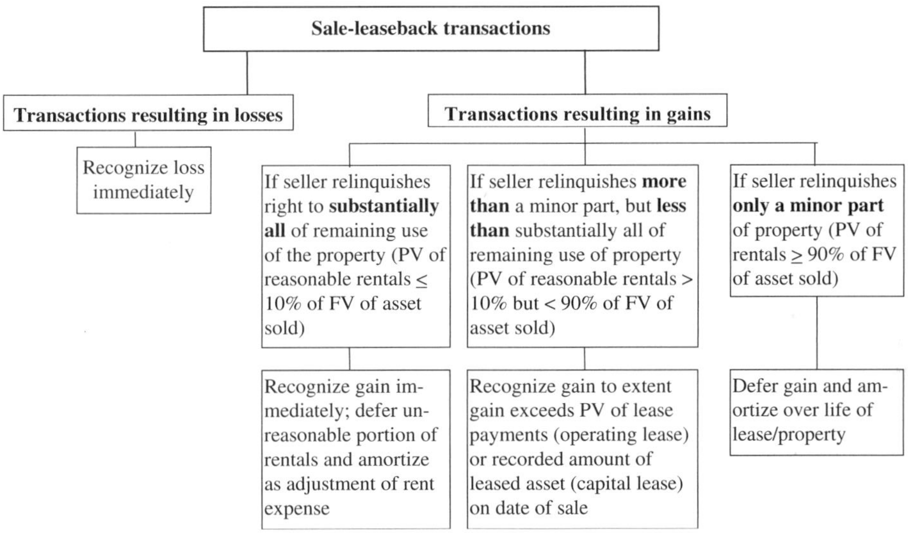

In the above circumstances, when the leased asset is land only, any amortization is recognized on a straight-line basis over the lease term, regardless of whether the lease is classified as a capital or operating lease.

Executory costs are not to be included in the calculation of profit to be deferred in a sale-leaseback transaction.

The buyer-lessor accounts for the transaction as a purchase and a direct financing lease if the agreement meets the criteria of **either** a direct financing lease **or** a sales-type lease. Otherwise, the agreement is accounted for as a purchase and an operating lease.

Sale-leaseback involving real estate. Three requirements are necessary for a sale-leaseback involving real estate (including real estate with equipment) to qualify for sale-leaseback accounting treatment. Those sale-leaseback transactions not meeting the three requirements are accounted for using the deposit method (see Chapter 8) or as a financing. The three requirements are

1. The lease must be a normal leaseback (explained below)
2. Payment terms and provisions must adequately demonstrate the buyer-lessor's initial and continuing investment in the property
3. Payment terms and provisions must transfer all the risks and rewards of ownership as demonstrated by a lack of continuing involvement by the seller-lessee

A normal leaseback involves active use of the leased property in the seller-lessee's trade or business during the lease term.

The buyer-lessor's initial investment is adequate if it demonstrates the buyer-lessor's commitment to pay for the property and indicates a reasonable likelihood that the seller-lessee will collect any receivable related to the leased property. The buyer-lessor's continuing investment is adequate if the buyer is contractually obligated to pay an annual amount at least equal to the amount of the annual payment sufficient to repay the principal and interest over no more than twenty years for land or the customary term of a first mortgage for other real estate.

Any continuing involvement by the seller-lessee other than normal leaseback disqualifies the lease from sale-leaseback accounting treatment. Some examples of continuing involvement other than normal leaseback include

1. The seller-lessee has an obligation or option (excluding the right of first refusal) to repurchase the property
2. The seller-lessee (or party related to the seller-lessee) guarantees the buyer-lessor's investment or debt related to that investment or a specified return on that investment
3. The seller-lessee is required to reimburse the buyer-lessor for a decline in the fair value of the property below estimated residual value at the end of the lease term based on other than excess wear and tear
4. The seller-lessee remains liable for an existing debt related to the property
5. The seller-lessee's rental payments are contingent on some predetermined level of future operations of the buyer-lessor
6. The seller-lessee provides collateral on behalf of the buyer-lessor other than the property directly involved in the sale-leaseback
7. The seller-lessee provides nonrecourse financing to the buyer-lessor for any portion of the sales proceeds or provides recourse financing in which the only recourse is the leased asset
8. The seller-lessee enters into a sale-leaseback involving property improvements or integral equipment without leasing the underlying land to the buyer-lessor
9. The buyer-lessor is obligated to share any portion of the appreciation of the property with the seller-lessee
10. Any other provision or circumstance that allows the seller-lessee to participate in any future profits of the buyer-lessor or the appreciation of the leased property

Example of accounting for a sale-leaseback transaction

To illustrate the accounting treatment in a sale-leaseback transaction, suppose that Seller/Lessee Corporation sells equipment that has a book value of $80,000 and a fair value of $100,000 to Buyer/Lessor Corporation for $100,000 in cash, and then immediately leases it back under the following conditions:

1. The sale date is January 1, 2005, and the equipment has a fair value of $100,000 on that date and an estimated remaining useful life of fifteen years.
2. The lease term is fifteen years, noncancelable, and requires equal rental payments of $13,109 at the beginning of each year.

3. Seller/Lessee Corp. has the option to annually renew the lease at the same rental payments upon expiration of the original lease.
4. Seller/Lessee Corp. has the obligation to pay all executory costs.
5. The annual rental payments provide the Buyer/Lessor Corp. with a 12% return on investment.
6. The incremental borrowing rate of Seller/Lessee Corp. is 12%.
7. Seller/Lessee Corp. depreciates similar equipment on a straight-line basis.

Seller/Lessee Corp. will classify the agreement as a capital lease since the lease term exceeds 75% of the estimated remaining economic life of the equipment, and because the present value of the lease payments ($13,109 x 7.62817[3] = $100,000) is greater than 90% of the fair value of the equipment. Assuming that collectibility of the lease payments is reasonably predictable and that no important uncertainties exist concerning the amount of unreimbursable costs yet to be incurred by Buyer/Lessor Corp., Buyer/Lessor Corp. will classify the transaction as a direct financing lease because the present value of the minimum lease payments is equal to the fair value of $100,000.

Seller/Lessee Corp. and Buyer/Lessor Corp. would make the following journal entries during the first year:

Upon Sale of Equipment on January 1, 2005

Seller/Lessee Corp.			*Buyer/Lessor Corp.*		
Cash	100,000		Equipment	100,000	
Equipment*		80,000	Cash		100,000
Unearned profit on sale-leaseback		20,000			
Leased equipment	100,000		Lease receivable		
Lease obligations		100,000	($13,109 x 15)	196,635	
			Equipment		100,000
			Unearned interest		96,635

* *Assumes new equipment; for used equipment the accumulated depreciation would also be debited to remove it.*

To Record First Payment on January 1, 2005**

Seller/Lessee Corp.			*Buyer/Lessor Corp.*		
Lease obligations	13,109		Cash	13,109	
Cash		13,109	Lease receivable		13,109

** *No interest is recorded in connection with the first payment since it is made at the inception of the lease.*

To Record Incurrence and Payment of Executory Costs

Seller/Lessee Corp.			*Buyer/Lessor Corp.*
Insurance, taxes, etc.	xxx		(No entry)
Cash (or accounts payable)		xxx	

To Record Amortization Expense on the Equipment, December 31, 2005

Seller/Lessee Corp.			*Buyer/Lessor Corp.*
Amortization expense	6,667		(No entry)
Accum. amort.— capital leases ($100,000 ÷ 15)		6,667	

To Amortize Profit on Sale-Leaseback by Seller/Lessee Corp., December 31, 2005

Seller/Lessee Corp.			*Buyer/Lessor Corp.*
Unearned profit on sale-leaseback	1,333		(No entry)
Amortization expense ($20,000 ÷ 15)		1,333	

To Record Interest for 2005, December 31, 2005

Seller/Lessee Corp.			*Buyer/Lessor Corp.*		
Interest expense	10,427		Unearned interest	10,427	
Accrued interest payable		10,427	Interest income		10,427

---

[3] *7.62817 is the present value of an annuity due for fifteen periods at a 12% interest rate.*

Partial Lease Amortization Schedule**

Date	*Cash payment*	*Interest expense*	*Reduction of obligation*	*Lease obligation*
Inception of lease				$100,000
1/1/05	$13,109	$ --	$13,109	86,891
1/1/06	13,109	10,427	2,682	84,209

** *No interest is recorded in connection with the first payment since it is made at the inception of the lease.*

Leases Involving Real Estate

Leases involving real estate can be divided into the following four categories:

1. Leases involving land only
2. Leases involving land and building(s)
3. Leases involving real estate and equipment
4. Leases involving only part of a building

Leases Involving Land Only

Lessee accounting. If the lease agreement transfers ownership or contains a bargain purchase option, the lessee accounts for the lease as a capital lease, and records an asset and related liability equal to the present value of the minimum lease payments. If the lease agreement does not transfer ownership or contain a bargain purchase option, the lessee accounts for the lease as an operating lease.

Lessor accounting. If the lease gives rise to dealer's profit (or loss) and transfers ownership (i.e., title), the lease is classified as a sales-type lease and accounted for under the provisions of FAS 66 in the same manner as a seller of the same property (profit recognition on real estate sales is discussed in detail in Chapter 8). If the lease transfers ownership, both the collectibility and no material uncertainties criteria are met, but does not give rise to dealer's profit (or loss), the lease is accounted for as a direct financing or leveraged lease as appropriate. If the lease does not transfer ownership, but it contains a bargain purchase option and both the collectibility and no material uncertainties criteria are met, the lease is accounted for as a direct financing, leveraged, or operating lease using the same lessor classification criteria as any other lease. If the lease does not meet the collectibility and/or no material uncertainties criteria, the lease is accounted for as an operating lease.

Leases Involving Land and Building

Lessee accounting. If the agreement transfers title or contains a bargain purchase option, the lessee accounts for the agreement by separating the land and building components and capitalizing each separately. The land and building elements are allocated on the basis of their relative fair values measured at the inception of the lease. The land and building components are separately accounted for because the lessee is expected to own the real estate by the end of the lease term. The building is amortized over its estimated useful life without regard to the lease term.

When the lease agreement neither transfers title nor contains a bargain purchase option, the fair value of the land must be determined in relation to the fair value of the aggregate property included in the lease agreement. If the fair value of the land is less than 25% of the aggregate fair value of the leased property, then the land is considered immaterial. Conversely, if the fair value of the land is 25% or greater of the fair value of the aggregate leased property, then the land is considered material.

When the land component of the lease agreement is considered immaterial (FV land < 25% of the total FV), the lease is accounted for as a single unit. The lessee capitalizes the lease if one of the following applies:

1. The term of the lease is 75% or more of the economic useful life of the building
2. The present value of the minimum lease payments equals 90% or more of the fair value of the leased real estate less any lessor investment tax credit

If neither of the above two criteria is met, the lessee accounts for the lease agreement as a single operating lease.

When the land component of the lease agreement is considered material (FV land ≥ 25% of the total FV), the land and building components are separated. By applying the lessee's incremental borrowing rate to the fair value of the land, the annual minimum lease payment attributed to land is computed. The remaining payments are attributed to the building. The division of minimum lease payments between land and building is essential for both the lessee and lessor. The portion of the lease involving the land is **always** accounted for as an operating lease. The lease involving the building(s) must meet either the 75% or 90% test to be treated as a capital lease. If neither of the two criteria is met, the building(s) are also accounted for as an operating lease.

Lessor accounting. The lessor's accounting depends on whether the lease transfers ownership, contains a bargain purchase option, or does neither of the two.

If the lease transfers ownership and gives rise to dealer's profit (or loss), the lessor classifies the lease as a sales-type lease and accounts for the lease as a single unit under the provisions of FAS 66 in the same manner as a seller of the same property (see Chapter 8). If the lease transfers ownership, meets both the collectibility and no important uncertainties criteria, but does not give rise to dealer's profit (or loss), the lease is accounted for as a direct financing or leveraged lease as appropriate.

If the lease contains a bargain purchase option and gives rise to dealer's profit (or loss), the lease is classified as an operating lease. If the lease contains a bargain purchase option, meets both the collectibility and no material uncertainties criteria, but does not give rise to dealer's profit (or loss), the lease is accounted for as a direct financing lease or a leveraged lease as appropriate.

If the lease agreement neither transfers ownership nor contains a bargain purchase option, the lessor should follow the same rules as the lessee in accounting for real estate leases involving land and building(s).

However, the collectibility and the no material uncertainties criteria must be met before the lessor can account for the agreement as a direct financing lease, and in no such case may the lease be classified as a sales-type lease (i.e., ownership must be transferred).

The treatment of a lease involving both land and building can be illustrated in the following examples.

Example of lessee accounting for land and building lease containing transfer of title

1. The lessee enters into a ten-year noncancelable lease for a parcel of land and a building for use in its operations. The building has an estimated remaining useful life of twelve years.
2. The FV of the land is $75,000, while the FV of the building is $310,000.
3. A payment of $50,000 is due to the lessor at the beginning of each of the ten years of the lease.
4. The lessee's incremental borrowing rate is 10%. (The lessor's implicit rate is unknown.)
5. Ownership will transfer to the lessee at the end of the lease.

The present value of the minimum lease payments is $337,951 ($50,000 x 6.75902[4]). The portion of the present value of the minimum lease payments to be capitalized for each of the two components of the lease is computed as follows:

FV of land			$ 75,000		
FV of building			310,000		
Total FV of leased property			$385,000		
Portion of PV allocated to land	$337,951	x	75,000 / 385,000	=	$ 65,835
Portion of PV allocated to building	$337,951	x	310,000 / 385,000	=	272,116
Total PV to be capitalized					$337,951

The entry made to initially record the lease is as follows:

Leased land	65,835	
Leased building	272,116	
Lease obligation		337,951

Subsequently, the obligation will be decreased using the effective interest method. The leased building will be amortized over its expected useful life.

Example of lessee accounting for land and building lease without transfer of title or bargain purchase option

Assume the same facts as the previous example except that title does not transfer at the end of the lease.

The lease is still a capital lease because the lease term is more than 75% of the remaining useful life of the building. Since the FV of the land is less than 25% of the aggregate fair value of the leased property, (75,000/385,000 = 19%), the land component is considered immaterial and the lease is accounted for as a single unit. The entry to record the lease is as follows:

Leased property	337,951	
Lease obligation		337,951

Assume the same facts as the previous example except that the FV of the land is $110,000 and the FV of the building is $275,000. Once again title does not transfer.

Because the FV of the land exceeds 25% of the aggregate FV of the leased property (110,000/385,000 = 29%), the land component is considered material and the lease is separated into two components. The annual minimum lease payment attributed to the land is computed as follows:

$$\frac{\text{FV of land}}{\text{PV factor}} \quad \frac{\$110{,}000}{6.75902^{*}} = \$16{,}275$$

* *6.75902 is the PV of an annuity due for ten periods at 10%.*

The remaining portion of the annual payment is attributed to the building.

Annual payment	$ 50,000
Less amount attributed to land	(16,275)
Annual payment attributed to building	$ 33,725

The present value of the minimum annual lease payments attributed to the building is then computed as follows:

Minimum annual lease payment attributed to building	$ 33,725
PV factor	x 6.75902[4]
PV of minimum annual lease payments attributed to building	$227,948

The entry to record the capital portion of the lease is as follows:

Leased building	227,948	
Lease obligation		227,948

---

[4] *6.75902 is the PV of an annuity due for ten periods at 10%.*

There is no computation of the present value of the minimum annual lease payment attributed to the land since the land component of the lease is treated as an operating lease. For this reason, each year $16,275 of the $50,000 lease payment will be recorded as land rental expense. The remainder of the annual payment ($33,725) will be applied against the lease obligation using the effective interest method.

Leases Involving Real Estate and Equipment

When real estate leases also involve equipment or machinery, the equipment component is separated and accounted for as a separate lease agreement by both lessees and lessors. "The portion of the minimum lease payments applicable to the equipment element of the lease shall be estimated by whatever means are appropriate in the circumstances." The lessee and lessor apply the capitalization requirements to the equipment lease independently of accounting for the real estate lease(s). The real estate leases are handled as discussed in the preceding two sections. In a sale-leaseback transaction involving real estate with equipment, the equipment and land are not separated.

Refer to the Profit Recognition on Real Estate Sales section of Chapter 8 for a discussion of FIN 43, *Real Estate Sales*.

Leases Involving Only Part of a Building

It is common to find lease agreements that involve only part of a building as, for example, when leasing a floor of an office building or a store in a shopping mall. A difficulty that arises in this situation is that the cost and/or fair value of the leased portion of the whole may not be objectively determinable.

Lessee accounting. If the fair value of the leased property is objectively determinable, then the lessee follows the rules and accounts for the lease as described in "Leases involving land and building." If the fair value of the leased property cannot be objectively determined, consider whether the agreement satisfies the 75% test. This calculation is made using the estimated remaining economic life of the building in which the leased premises are located. If the test is met (i.e. the term of the lease is 75% or more of the estimated remaining economic life of the building), the lease is accounted for as a capital lease. If the test is not met, the lease is accounted for as an operating lease.

Lessor accounting. From the lessor's position, **both the cost and fair value** of the leased property must be objectively determinable before the procedures described under "Leases involving land and building" will apply. If either the cost or the fair value cannot be determined objectively, the lessor accounts for the agreement as an operating lease.

Wrap-Lease Transactions

A wrap-lease transaction occurs when the lessor of an asset obtains nonrecourse financing using the lease rentals and asset as collateral, sells the underlying asset and nonrecourse debt and then leases the asset back while remaining the substantive lessor under the original lease. When this occurs and the asset is real estate, the specialized rules with respect to sale-leaseback of real estate apply, otherwise the transaction is treated as a sales-leaseback with the lease to the end user treated as a sublease.

Wrap-Lease Transaction

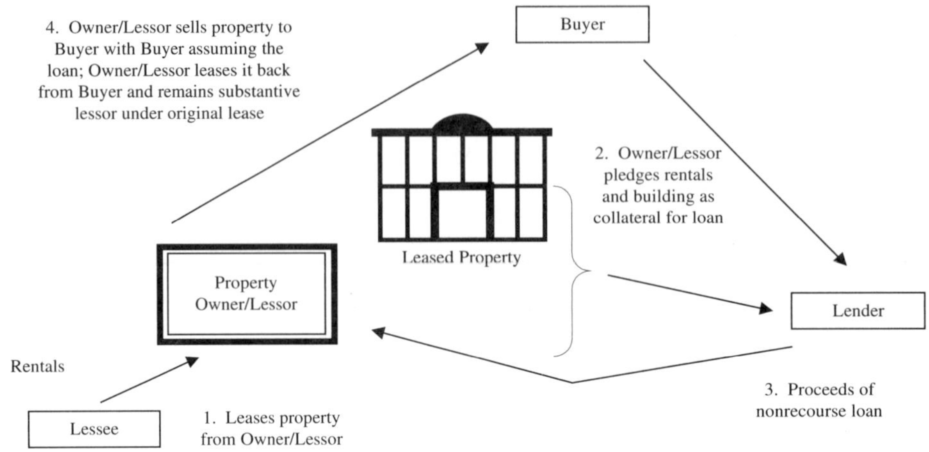

Cash Flows

Lessee pays rentals to Lessor.
Lessor pays rentals to Buyer.
Buyer pays loan principal and interest to Lender.

Summary of Accounting for Selected Items (See following page)

Reporting of Current and Noncurrent Lease Receivable (Lessor) and Lease Obligations (Lessee)

The balance of the lease payments receivable (lessor) and the lease obligation (lessee) must be allocated between the current and noncurrent portions. First, the current portion is computed at the date of the financial statements as the present value of the lease payments/receipts to be paid/received within twelve months of the balance sheet date. The noncurrent portion is computed as the difference between the current portion determined and the balance of the lease obligation at the end of the period. The conceptual justification for this treatment is the fact that the total lease obligation is equal to the present value of the future minimum lease payments. Therefore, it follows that the current portion is the present value of the lease payments due within one year while the noncurrent portion is the present value of all other remaining lease payments.

EMERGING ISSUES TASK FORCE ISSUES SUMMARIES

85-16 Leveraged Leases

- Real estate leases and sale-leaseback transactions
- Delayed equity contributions by lessors

Under the provisions of FAS 13, real estate leases can be accounted for as a leveraged lease if the requirements discussed in the appendix to this chapter are met. Furthermore, the Task Force reached a consensus that recourse debt originating from the delayed equity investment can be accounted for as a leveraged lease if the other requirements for

TREATMENT OF SELECTED ITEMS IN ACCOUNTING FOR LEASES

	Lessor		Lessee	
	Operating	*Direct financing and sales-type*	*Operating*	*Capital*
Initial direct costs	Capitalize and amortize over lease term in proportion to rent revenue recognized (normally SL basis)	Direct financing: Record in separate account Add to net investment in lease Compute new effective rate that equates gross amt. of min. lease payments and unguar. residual value with net invest. Amortize so as to produce constant rate of return over lease term Sales-type: Expense in period incurred as part of cost of sales	N/A	N/A
Investment tax credit retained by lessor	N/A	Reduces FV of leased asset for 90% test	N/A	Reduces FV of leased asset for 90% test
Bargain purchase option	N/A	Include in: Minimum lease payments 90% test	N/A	Include in: Minimum lease payments 90% test
Guaranteed residual value	N/A	Include in: Minimum lease payments 90% test Sales-type: Include PV in sales revenues	N/A	Include in: Minimum lease payments 90% test
Unguaranteed residual value	N/A	Include in: "Gross investment in lease" Not included in: 90% test Sales-type: Exclude from sales revenue Deduct PV from cost of sales	N/A	N/A
Contingent rentals	Revenue in period earned	Not part of minimum lease payments; revenue in period earned	Expense in period incurred	Not part of minimum lease payments; expense in period incurred
Amortization period	Amortize down to estimated residual value over estimated economic life of asset	N/A	N/A	Amortize down to estimated residual value over lease term or estimated economic life[b]
Revenue (expense)[a]	Rent revenue (normally SL basis) Amortization (depreciation expense)	Direct financing: Interest revenue on net investment in lease (gross investment less unearned interest income) Sales-type: Dealer profit in period of sale (sales revenue less cost of leased asset) Interest revenue on net investment in lease	Rent expense (normally SL basis)[c]	Interest expense and amortization (depreciation) expense

[a] *Elements of revenue (expense) listed for the above items are not repeated here (e.g., treatment of initial direct costs).*

[b] *If lease has automatic passage of title or bargain purchase option, use estimated economic life; otherwise, use the lease term.*

[c] *If payments are not on a SL basis, recognize rent expense on a SL basis unless another systematic and rational method is more representative of use or benefit obtained from the property, in which case, the other method should be used.*

such treatment are fulfilled. Finally, the lessor's related obligation is accounted for as a liability at its present value at the inception of the lease.

86-17 Deferred Profit on Sale-Leaseback with Lessee Guarantee of Residual Value

A consensus was reached that the profit equal to the present value of periodic rents plus the gross amount of the guaranteed residual value is deferred for sale-leaseback transactions classified as involving more than minor but less than substantially all the use of the property. The present value of the rents is amortized over the lease term while the guaranteed residual is deferred until resolution at the end of the lease term. The use of sale-leaseback accounting is limited to transactions in which all risks and rewards of ownership, other than the leaseback, are transferred to the buyer-lessor. FAS 98 lists examples of continuing involvement by the seller-lessee that indicate the risks and rewards of ownership have not been transferred.

86-33 Tax Indemnification in Lease Agreements

A consensus was reached that tax indemnification payments do not meet the definition of contingent rentals. These payments are allocated by lessors to: (1) amount resulting from any lost investment tax credit (ITC) and (2) amount linked to all other tax effects.

Amounts associated with lost ITC[5] are accounted for based on the lessor's normal accounting policy for accounting for ITC (the flow-through or deferral methods).

Amounts associated with other tax effects are accounted for in accordance with the classification of the underlying lease. Consequently, lessors would adjust their recorded investment in a sales-type or direct financing lease or amortize the payment ratably over the term of an operating lease. Lessees would adjust the basis in the leased asset under a capital lease or recognize the payment on a straight-line basis over the remaining lease term under an operating lease.

87-7 Sale of an Asset Subject to a Lease and Nonrecourse Financing: "Wrap-Lease Transactions"

A consensus was reached that the original lessor is to separate revenue directly associated with future remarketing rights and defer recognition of income until the remarketing services are performed. A consensus was also reached that the original lessor should record any retained interest in the residual value of the leased asset as an asset in their financial statements. No consensus was reached on how to account for the proceeds other than the revenue from the remarketing rights.

88-10 Costs Associated with Lease Modification or Termination

A consensus was reached regarding situations where a lessee enters into a new lease for replacement property prior to the expiration of a preexisting property lease. If the preexisting lease is terminated, all costs related to the preexisting lease are expensed when the leased property has no future benefit to the lessee. When the lease is not terminated, the expense is reduced by any actual or probable sublease income. In addition if the preexisting lease is assumed by the new lessor, any payments to the lessee or assumption of loss by the lessor are considered incentives. These incentives are amortized on a straight-line basis to rent expense or rent revenue over the life of the new lease. The amount of the incentive is

---

[5] *ITC was a tax credit afforded business under the Internal Revenue Code prior to 1986 as an economic incentive to purchase qualifying productive equipment. The incentive was designed to stimulate business expansion and economic growth.*

determined separately by the lessee and lessor. No consensus was reached on the issue of deferring the costs of moving from one lease to another (moving) however; generally moving costs are expensed as incurred.

88-21 Accounting for the Sale of Property Subject to the Seller's Preexisting Lease

A consensus was reached regarding situations where an entity sells property in which it has an ownership interest, and continues to lease the property under a preexisting operating lease. The consensus requires recognition of the transaction as a sale-leaseback if the preexisting lease is modified in connection with the sale. If no changes are made or changes are insignificant, profit is deferred and recognized in accordance with FAS 28, 66, or 98 as appropriate. Any deferred profit is not affected by the seller-lessee's prior ownership. In addition, exercise of renewal options or sublease provisions contained in the preexisting lease do not affect the accounting for the transaction. FAS 98 only applies to renewal options not contained in the original lease term. Finally, leases between parties under common control are not considered preexisting leases and FAS 98 applies unless one of the parties is a regulated enterprise.

89-16 Consideration of Executory Costs in Sale-Leaseback Transactions

A consensus was reached that in the calculation of deferred profit in a sale-leaseback transaction executory costs are to be excluded.

89-20 Accounting for Cross-Border Tax Benefit Leases

A consensus was reached regarding the recognition of income for cash received by the US enterprise for the foreign investor's tax benefits in situations where a US enterprise gives ownership interest in an asset to a foreign investor to allow the foreign investor tax benefits. In exchange, the US enterprise receives cash for the fair value of the ownership interest plus consideration for the tax benefit. The US enterprise may agree to indemnify the foreign investor for future loss of the tax benefit. The income may be recognized immediately or deferred unless there is more than a remote possibility of loss of the cash consideration due to indemnification or other contingencies. In this case, income must be deferred.

90-14 Unsecured Guarantee by Parent of Subsidiary's Lease Payments in a Sale-Leaseback Transaction

The Task Force reached a consensus that when one member of a consolidated group provides an unsecured guarantee of lease payments for another member of the consolidated group, such additional collateral does not reduce the buyer-lessor's risk of loss, except in the event of the seller-lessee's bankruptcy. The unsecured guarantee would, therefore, not constitute a form of continuing involvement. Thus, sale-leaseback accounting would be permitted in the **consolidated financial statements**.

The Task Force reached a different consensus with respect to treatment of the guarantee in the **separate financial statements** of the seller-lessee. Since the guarantee was from a party, albeit related, outside the reporting entity, it would be deemed to represent additional collateral that reduces the risk of loss to the buyer-lessor. Therefore, in the separate financial statements, sale-leaseback accounting would be prohibited due to the "continuing involvement" rules.

90-15 Impact of Nonsubstantive Lessors, Residual Value Guarantees, and Other Provisions in Leasing Transactions

NOTE: The consensus reached in EITF Issue 90-15 was nullified by the January 2003 issuance of FIN 46(R), ***Consolidation of Variable Interest Entities****. This discussion of EITF Issue 90-15 has been retained in the text because certain nonpublic companies will not be required to fully implement the provisions of FIN 46(R), (discussed in this chapter and in Chapter 11) until the issuance of annual financial statements for years ending on or after June 30, 2004.*

The terms of leases are often deliberately structured to qualify as operating leases in the financial statements of the lessee. The lessee may desire this treatment for a variety of reasons such as to comply with restrictive covenants in loan agreements that limit capital expenditures or simply to avoid the added complexity of capital lease accounting. Although many such leases are true operating leases in both letter and spirit, others have characteristics that make such a classification questionable.

A common technique used to obtain the desired accounting treatment is for the property to be owned and leased by a Special Purpose Entity (SPE). The SPE lacks economic substance because all of the following conditions exist:

1. Substantially all of its activities involve assets leased to a single lessee.
2. The owner or owners of the SPE have not made a substantive equity capital investment that is at risk during the entire term of the lease.
3. The lessee is obligated with substantially all of the risks and will benefit from substantially all of the rewards from the leased property.

The Task Force reached a consensus that when all of the preceding conditions exist, the lessee is required to consolidate the SPE lessor in its financial statements. This consolidation has the same effect as treating the lease as a capital lease since the consolidated financial statements will present the leased asset, related accumulated depreciation and depreciation expense, the underlying third-party debt used to finance the leased asset and interest expense thereon.

The consensus also provides interpretive guidance on whether the risks and rewards reside in the lessee and, accordingly whether a lessor is considered to be an SPE.

90-20 Impact of an Uncollateralized Irrevocable Letter of Credit on a Real Estate Sale-Leaseback Transaction

A consensus was reached that an uncollateralized, irrevocable letter of credit is not considered a form of continuing involvement that would preclude sale-leaseback accounting unless a contract exists between the seller-lessee and third-party guarantor that would create collateral. The existence of collateral relating to the letter of credit is a form of continuing involvement that precludes sale-leaseback accounting.

92-1 Allocation of Residual Value or First-Loss Guarantee to Minimum Lease Payments in Leases Involving Land and Building(s)

A consensus was reached that for both the lessor and lessee the portion of the minimum lease payments attributable to the land is the land's fair value times the lessee's incremental borrowing rate. Therefore, the remaining part of the minimum lease payments, including the total guaranteed amount are assigned to the building.

93-8 Accounting for the Sale and Leaseback of an Asset That Is Leased to Another Party

A consensus was reached that when a leaseback involves an asset that is personal property falling outside coverage of FAS 98 and (1) subject to an operating lease or (2) subleased or intended to be subleased to another entity under an operating lease, FAS 28 is to be followed.

95-1 Revenue Recognition on Sales with a Guaranteed Minimum Resale Value

In order to provide sales incentives, manufacturers sometimes include in a sales contract, a guarantee that the purchaser will, upon disposition of the property, receive a minimum resale amount. Upon disposition, the manufacturer either reacquires the property at the agreed-upon minimum price or reimburses the purchaser for any shortfall between the actual sales proceeds and the guaranteed amount. The EITF reached a consensus that transactions containing guarantees of resale value of equipment by a manufacturer are to be accounted for as leases and not as sales. The minimum lease payments used to determine if the criteria have been met for lessor sales-type lease accounting are computed as the difference between the proceeds received from the transferee/lessee upon initial transfer of the equipment and the amount of the residual value guarantee on its first contractual exercise date.

If the lease is accounted for as an operating lease because it does not qualify for sales-type lease accounting, the manufacturer/lessor is to record the proceeds received at inception as a liability which is subsequently reduced by crediting revenue pro rata from the inception of the lease until the first guarantee exercise date so that, on that exercise date, the remaining liability is the guaranteed residual amount. If the lessee elects, under the terms of the arrangement, to continue to use the leased asset after the first exercise date, the manufacturer/lessor will continue to amortize the liability for the remaining residual amount to revenue to reduce it further to any remaining guarantee, if applicable.

The foregoing prescribed accounting is followed by manufacturers even when there is dealer involvement in the transaction when it is the manufacturer who is responsible for the guarantee to the purchaser.

In EITF 03-12, the Task Force reached a consensus that FIN 45, *Guarantor's Accounting and Disclosure Requirements for Guarantees, Including Indirect Guarantees of Indebtedness of Others,* does not apply to these transactions irrespective of whether they are accounted for as operating leases or sales-type leases because, in either case, the underlying of such a guarantee is an asset owned by the guarantor.

95-4 Revenue Recognition on Equipment Sold and Subsequently Repurchased Subject to an Operating Lease

This consensus determined that a manufacturer can recognize a sale at the time its product is transferred to a dealer for subsequent sale to a third-party customer even if this ultimate customer enters into an operating lease agreement with the same manufacturer or the manufacturer's finance affiliate if four conditions are satisfied:

1. The dealer must be an independent entity that conducts business separately with manufacturers and customers
2. The passage of the product from the manufacturer to the dealer fully transfers ownership
3. The manufacturer (or finance affiliate) has no obligation to provide a lease arrangement for the customer of the dealer

4. The customer is in control of selecting which of the many financing options available will be used.

95-17 Accounting for Modifications to an Operating Lease That Do Not Change the Lease Classification

A consensus was reached that when the lessee and the lessor agree to shorten the lease term and increase the lease payments over the revised lease term, the nature of the modification is a matter of judgment that depends on the relevant facts and circumstances. If the modification is deemed only a change in future lease payments, the increase is amortized over the remaining term of the modified lease. On the other hand, a modification deemed a termination penalty is to be recognized in the period of modification. Termination penalties are calculated as the excess of the modified lease payments over the original lease payments that would have been required during the shortened lease term. To determine if the modification is a termination penalty, consider: (1) the length of the modified lease period compared to the remaining term of the original lease, and (2) the difference between the modified lease payments and comparable market rents.

96-21 Implementation Issues in Accounting for Leasing Transactions Involving Special-Purpose Entities (SPE)

This issue followed up EITF 90-15, to provide criteria concerning lessors with single lessees, and the failure of the owner of record of the SPE to have made a substantial initial investment in the SPE. Consensuses were reached on a number of matters involving, among others, multitiered SPE structures, multiple leases within a single SPE, fees paid to owners of record of an SPE, and sources of initial investment in the SPE. This last item is a commonly encountered problem in related entity lessors. This consensus should be reviewed carefully because FIN 46(R), *Consolidation of Variable Interest Entities,* nullified its SPE-related consensuses, and in light of recent publicity regarding abuses concerning the use of SPE.

The following guidance remains in this issue after FIN 46(R) is fully effective:

1. Payments made by a lessee during construction of the leased asset in connection with a build-to-suit lease transaction are considered part of the minimum lease payments for the purpose of the 90% of fair value test used to determine whether the lease is a capital lease. These advance payments are to be included in minimum lease payments at their future value, at the beginning of the lease term, with interest accreted using the same interest rate used to discount payments made during the lease term. If the lease is an operating lease, these payments are accounted for as prepaid rent and amortized to expense along with other rent costs over the term of the lease, normally using the straight-line method.
2. Lease structuring fees or lease administration fees paid by a lessee are included as part of the minimum lease payments for the purpose of the 90% of fair value test.
3. Lessees sometimes incur real estate development or construction costs prior to executing a lease with the developer/lessor. The lessee records these costs as construction in progress on its balance sheet and any subsequent lease arrangement is accounted for as a sale-leaseback transaction under FAS 98.

Under FIN 45, a lessee guarantee of the residual value of an operating lease is to be recognized by the lessee as a liability at the inception of the guarantee.

97-1 Implementation Issues in Accounting for Lease Transactions, Including Those Involving Special-Purpose Entities (SPE)

Yet another follow-up to Issue 90-15 that was subsequently superseded by FIN 46(R), this one is a follow-up to certain responses in Issue 96-21 and focuses on environmental risk indemnifications by lessees, non-performance-related default covenants, and depreciation. Consensuses were reached on these, which impact upon determining whether consolidation of the SPE would be required under various circumstances. After the effective date of FIN 46(R), the remaining consensuses provide that

1. An indemnification by the lessee to the lessor for any environmental contamination that the lessee causes during the lease term does not affect the lessee's classification of the lease as capital or operating.
2. If (a) a lessee indemnifies the lessor for environmental contamination that occurred **prior** to the lessee's occupancy of the property, (b) the lessor has the right to put the property to the lessee in the event of loss or damage, and (c) loss is reasonably possible or probable, the transaction is governed under the sale-leaseback rules and the lessee is considered to have purchased, sold, and then leased back the property.
3. A lessee providing an indemnification that meets certain criteria under FIN 45 is required to record the indemnification as a guarantee and is subject to that pronouncement's disclosure provisions.
4. Leases sometimes contain financial covenants obligating the lessee to maintain certain financial ratios. Should the lessee violate these covenants, it is considered an event of default under the lease and the lessor may have a right to put the property to the lessee or require the lessee to make a payment to the lessor. In this case, for the purpose of the 90% of fair value test, the lessee includes in the minimum lease payments the maximum amount it would be required to pay in the event of default unless **all** of the following conditions exist:

    a. The default covenant provision is customary in financing arrangements,
    b. The occurrence of the event of default is objectively determinable and is not at the subjective whim of the lessor,
    c. The event of default is based on predefined criteria that relate solely to the lessee and its operations, and
    d. It is reasonable to assume at the inception of the lease and in considering recent lessee operating trends that the event of default will not occur.

    The inclusion of a put provision in the lease as a remedy violates the continuing involvement criteria in FAS 98 if the transaction is part of a sale-leaseback transaction. This would necessitate accounting for the transaction using the deposit method or as a financing depending on the application of FAS 66 to the circumstances.

97-10 The Effect of Lessee Involvement in Asset Construction

The Task Force reached a consensus that a lessee is to be considered the owner of a real estate project during its construction period if the lessee has substantially all of the construction period risks. The test to be used in determining if a lessee has substantially all of the construction period risks is virtually the same as the 90% of fair value test for determining if a lease is to be classified as a capital lease by a lessee. Beginning with the earlier of the date of the inception of the lease or the date that the construction terms are agreed to, if at any time during the construction period the documents governing the construction project could require, under any circumstance, that the lessee pay 90% or more of the total project costs, excluding land acquisition costs, then the lessee is considered to be the owner of the real estate project during its construction period.

The lessee's maximum guarantee includes any payments the lessee could be required to make in connection with a construction project. The lessee's maximum guarantee includes, but is not limited to

1. Lease payments that must be made regardless of when or whether the project is complete
2. Guarantees of the construction financing
3. Equity investments made in the owner-lessor or any party related to the owner-lessor
4. Loans or advances made to the owner-lessor or any party related to the owner-lessor
5. Payments made by the lessee in the capacity of a developer, a general contractor, or a construction manager/agent that are reimbursed less frequently than is normal or customary
6. Primary or secondary obligations to pay project costs under construction contracts
7. Obligations that could arise from being the developer or general contractor
8. An obligation to purchase the real estate project under any circumstances
9. An obligation to fund construction cost overruns
10. Rent or fees of any kind, such as transaction costs, to be paid to or on behalf of the lessor by the lessee during the construction period
11. Payments that might be made with respect to providing indemnities or guarantees to the owner-lessor

Six examples are provided for when a lessee is considered the owner of a real estate project despite the present value of the lessee's maximum guarantee being less than 90% of total project costs.

98-9 Accounting for Contingent Rent

The issues are

1. A lessor's appropriate accounting for contingent rental revenue that is based on future specified targets.
2. A lessee's appropriate accounting for contingent rental expense that is based on future specified targets.

A consensus was reached that contingent rentals based on achievement of specified targets are to be recognized by the lessee during interim periods if it is probable that the target will be reached by the end of the fiscal year. If the specified target is not met, previously recorded expense is reversed at the time it becomes probable that the target will not be met. A consensus was reached that lessors are to defer recognition of contingent rental income until specified targets have been met.

99-13 Application of Issue No. 97-10 and FASB Interpretation No. 23 to Entities That Enter into Leases with Governmental Entities

A consensus was reached that a government-owned property that is being constructed and is subject to a future lease of the completed improvements is included in the scope of EITF Issue 97-10. If, under Issue 97-10, the lessee is deemed to bear substantially all of the construction period risks, then the lessee is considered the owner of the property for accounting purposes. Under that scenario, the transaction is accounted for under the sale-leaseback rules discussed previously in this chapter.

00-11 Lessors' Evaluation of Whether Leases of Certain Integral Equipment Meet the Ownership Transfer Requirements of FASB Statement No. 13

FIN 43, *Real Estate Sales,* clarifies that FAS 66, *Accounting for Sales of Real Estate,* applies to all sales of real estate including real estate with accompanying property improvements or integral equipment. The EITF reached a consensus that, when evaluating a lease that includes integral equipment to determine the classification of the lease under FAS 13 (as amended by FAS 98), the equipment is to be evaluated as real estate. The consensus also provides guidance on evaluating how to determine transfer of ownership of integral equipment when no statutory title registration system exists in the jurisdiction.

00-13 Determining Whether Equipment is "Integral Equipment" Subject to FASB Statement No. 66, *Accounting for Sales of Real Estate*, and No. 98, *Accounting for Leases*

Because FIN 43, issued in June 1999, states that sales of integral equipment are within the scope of FAS 66, *Accounting for Sales of Real Estate*, the determination of whether equipment is integral has increased in importance. A determination of whether equipment to be leased is integral is also necessary for proper accounting for sales-type leases by lessors. This issue discusses how the determination is made.

The determination of whether equipment is integral is made based on two factors. The first is the significance of the cost to remove the equipment from its existing location (which would include the costs of repairing the damage done to that location by the removal). The second factor is the decrease in value of the equipment that results from its removal (which is, at a minimum, the cost to ship and reinstall the equipment at the new site). The nature of the equipment and whether others can use it are considered in determining whether there is further diminution in fair value. When the combined total of the cost to remove and any further diminution of value exceeds 10% of the fair value of the equipment (installed), the equipment is integral equipment.

01-8 Determining Whether an Arrangement Contains a Lease

FAS 13 defines a lease as "an agreement conveying the right to use property, plant, or equipment (land and/or depreciable assets) usually for a stated period of time." This Issue provides guidance on determining when all or part of an arrangement constitutes a lease.

Scope. Property, plant, or equipment, as used in FAS 13, includes only land and/or depreciable assets. Therefore, inventory (including equipment parts inventory) cannot be the subject of a lease because inventory is not depreciable. Although specific property, plant, or equipment may be explicitly identified in an arrangement, it is not the subject of a lease if the arrangement can be fulfilled without using the specified property, plant, or equipment. For example, if the owner/seller is obligated to deliver a specified quantity of goods or services but can provide those goods or services using property, plant, or equipment other than that specified in the arrangement, then the arrangement does not contain a lease.

In addition, FAS 13 contains specific scope exceptions with respect to agreements concerning

1. Exploration or exploitation of natural resources (e.g., oil, gas, minerals, and timber).

2. Intangible licensing rights (e.g., motion pictures, plays, manuscripts, patents, and copyrights).

Lease treatment is not precluded in situations where the owner or manufacturer of the property has extended a product warranty that includes a provision for replacement of the property if it is not operating adequately. Similarly, if the arrangement includes a provision permitting the equipment owner the right to substitute other equipment on or after a specified date, irrespective of the reason, the arrangement can still qualify as a lease.

Right to use property, plant, or equipment. The right to use the specified property, plant, or equipment is conveyed if any one of the following conditions is met:

- A *party* (for the purpose of this discussion, we will refer to this party, the potential lessee, as "the recipient" of the rights) has the ability or right to operate the property, plant, or equipment or direct others to do so as the recipient specifies, while attaining or controlling more than a minor portion of the output (or service utility),
- The recipient has the ability or right to control physical access to the specified property, plant, or equipment while attaining or controlling more than a minor portion of the output (or other service utility) or
- Analysis of the relevant facts and circumstances indicates that it is remote (as that term is used in FAS 5) that a party (or parties) other than the recipient will attain more than a minor amount of the output (or other service utility) that will be produced or generated by the specified property, plant, or equipment during the term of the arrangement, *and* the price that the recipient will pay for the output is neither contractually fixed per unit of output nor equal to the market price per unit of output at the time delivery of the output is received.

Timing of initial assessment and subsequent reassessments. The assessment of whether an arrangement contains a lease is to be made at the inception of the arrangement. A reassessment of whether the arrangement contains a lease is to be made only if (a) the contractual terms are modified, (b) a renewal option is exercised or the parties to the arrangement agree on an extension of its term, (c) there is a change in the determination as to whether or not fulfillment of the arrangement is dependent on the property, plant, or equipment that was originally specified, or (d) the originally specified property and equipment undergoes a substantial physical change. Remeasurement/redetermination is not permitted merely because of a change in an estimate made at inception (e.g., the number of expected units of output or the useful life of the equipment).

Aggregation of separate contracts. In applying the EITF guidance, there is a rebuttable presumption that separate contracts between the same parties (or related parties) that are executed on or near the same date were negotiated together as a package.

This issue also provides accounting guidance for any recognized assets and liabilities existing at the time that an arrangement (or a portion of an arrangement) either ceases to qualify as a lease or commences to qualify as a lease due to a reassessment in the circumstances as described above.

03-12 Impact of FASB Interpretation No. 45, *Guarantor's Accounting and Disclosure Requirements for Guarantees, Including Indirect Guarantees of Indebtedness of Others,* on EITF Issue No. 95-1, *Revenue Recognition on Sales with a Guaranteed Minimum Resale Value*

The "status" section of EITF 95-1 had been erroneously changed to indicate that FIN 45 partially nullified EITF 95-1. This consensus clarifies that FIN 45 *does not apply* to a guarantee for which the underlying is related to an asset of the guarantor. See the related discussion of EITF 95-1 earlier in this chapter.

D-107 Lessor Consideration of Third-Party Residual Value Guarantees

It is a common practice in equipment leasing transactions for the lessor to obtain, from an unrelated third party, a full or partial guarantee of the residual value of a portfolio of leased assets. These transactions are structured in such a manner that the third-party guarantor provides a guarantee of the aggregate residual value of the portfolio but does not individually guarantee the residual value of any of the individually leased assets included in that portfolio. To the extent that a specific leased asset's residual value exceeds the guaranteed minimum amount, that excess is used to offset shortfalls relating to other specific leased assets whose residual values are below the guaranteed minimum amount.

The SEC staff observer announced the SEC staff's position that the expected proceeds from these types of portfolio residual guarantees are to be *excluded* from minimum lease payments in computing the present value of the minimum lease payments for the purpose of determining the lessor's classification of the lease transaction. The SEC believes this treatment to be appropriate because, under the terms of this portfolio guarantee, the lessor is unable to determine, at lease inception, the guaranteed residual amount of any individually leased asset.

FASB TECHNICAL BULLETINS

79-10 Fiscal Funding Clauses in Lease Agreements

Issue: The effect a fiscal funding clause present in a lease agreement has on the classification of the lease under FAS 13.

Background: Fiscal funding clauses are common in lease agreements with governmental units under which the lease is contingent upon fund appropriations.

Resolution: If the likelihood of a fiscal funding clause being exercised is remote, the lease agreement is considered noncancelable. Otherwise, the lease is considered cancelable and classified as an operating lease.

79-12 Interest Rate Used in Calculating the Present Value of Minimum Lease Payments

Issue: The allowability of the use of the secured borrowing rate by a lessee in computing the present value of minimum lease payments.

Background: FAS 13 requires the lessee to use its incremental borrowing rate or the lessor's implicit rate if it is lower and known by the lessee.

Resolution: The lessee may use its secured borrowing rate as its incremental borrowing rate if that rate appears reasonable.

79-13 Applicability of FASB Statement No. 13 to Current Value Financial Statements

Issue: Applicability of FAS 13 to current value financial statements.

Resolution: The provisions of FAS 13 apply to current value financial statements.

79-14 Upward Adjustment of Guaranteed Residual Values

Issue: Allowability of upward adjustments resulting from renegotiations of guaranteed residual values.

Resolution: Upward adjustments of guaranteed residual values in lease agreements are not allowed.

79-15 Accounting for Loss on a Sublease Not Involving the Disposal of a Segment

Issue: How to determine and whether to recognize a loss on a sublease.

Resolution: The general principles for recognition of losses are to be followed with respect to expected losses on subleases.

79-16 Effect of a Change in Income Tax Rate on the Accounting for Leveraged Leases

Issue: The effect of a change in income tax rate on the accounting for leveraged leases.

Background: FAS 13 requires that the rate of return and allocation of income be recalculated from the date of inception of a lease and a gain or loss recognized when an important assumption is changed.

Resolution: The effect on a leveraged lease of a change in the income tax rate is recognized as a gain or loss in the accounting period in which the rate changes. Deferred income taxes relating to the change are recognized in accordance with FAS 109.

82-1 Disclosure of the Sale or Purchase of Tax Benefits through Tax Leases

Issue: Required disclosures for the sale or purchase of income tax benefits through tax leases.

Background: Disclosure is required for transactions involving solely the sale or purchase of income tax benefits through tax leases.

Resolution: Information regarding the accounting policies followed for such transactions is to be disclosed. The disclosure is to include the method of recognizing revenue and allocating the income tax benefits and asset costs to current and future periods. In addition, in conformity with the disclosure requirements of FAS 109, these transactions may result in significant reconciling items between income taxes computed at the domestic federal statutory tax rate and income taxes computed at the effective tax rate applied to pretax income from continuing operations. If such transactions are considered unusual or infrequent to the enterprise, they may warrant separate line-item treatment on the face of the income statement or disclosure in the accompanying notes. Finally, the necessity of disclosure of any loss contingencies associated with the transaction is to be evaluated under FAS 5.

86-2 Accounting for an Interest in the Residual Value of a Leased Asset:

- **Acquired by a Third Party or**
- **Retained by a Lessor That Sells the Related Minimum Rental Payments**

Issues: Various issues have been raised concerning the accounting for and valuation of an interest in the residual value of a leased asset acquired by a third party or retained by a lessor that sells the related minimum lease payments.

Resolution: An interest in the residual value of a leased asset is recorded as an asset at the amount of cash disbursed, the fair value of other consideration given, and the present value of liabilities assumed at the date the right is acquired, unless the fair value of the interest in the residual value is more clearly evident. A lessor retaining an interest in the residual value of the leased asset does not recognize increases in value, but does recognize other-than-temporary declines in value. (FAS 140, which superseded only this provision of FTB 86-2, permits recognition of such increases for guaranteed residual values, but not for unguaranteed residual values.)

88-1 Issues Relating to Accounting for Leases

Provides guidance on five issues relating to leases.

1. Issue: How to account for escalating rents when the physical use of the property changes under an operating lease.

Resolution: When a lessee controls the use of the leased property, recognition of rental expense or rental revenue is not affected by the extent to which the lessee utilizes that property. Escalating rents under agreements giving the lessee the right to control the use of the entire leased property at the beginning of the lease term are included in the minimum lease payments and recognized on a straight-line basis over the term of the lease.

2. Issue: How to account for lease incentives in an operating lease.

Resolution: Incentives paid to or incurred on behalf of the lessee by the lessor are an inseparable part of the new lease agreement. These costs are recognized as reductions to rental expense or rental revenue on a straight-line basis over the term of a new lease.

3. Issue: The applicability of leveraged lease accounting to existing assets of the lessor.

Resolution: At the inception of a lease, the cost or carrying value and the fair value of an asset must be the same for the lease to be classified as a direct financing lease which is a necessary condition for leveraged lease treatment. The carrying amount of an existing asset before any write-down must equal its fair value in order for the lease to be classified as a leveraged lease.

4. Issue: Whether to recognize income on a money-over-money lease transaction.

Resolution: If an enterprise manufactures or purchases an asset, leases the asset to a lessee and obtains nonrecourse financing in excess of the asset's cost using the leased asset and the future lease rentals as collateral (a money-over-money lease transaction), a lease broker may recognize income at the beginning of the lease term for the cash received in excess of the carrying amount of the leased asset provided four criteria are met. Some modification of the presentation of the nonrecourse debt and lease receivable is appropriate for leasing transactions meeting all of the criteria for leveraged leases.

5. Issue: How to account for wrap-lease transactions.

Resolution: If an enterprise purchases an asset, leases the asset to a lessee, obtains nonrecourse financing using the lease rentals or the lease rentals and the asset as collateral, sells the asset subject to the lease and the nonrecourse debt to a third-party investor, and leases the asset back while remaining the substantive principal lessor under the original lease, the transaction is accounted for as a sale-leaseback transaction. The subleased asset and the related nonrecourse debt are not offset on the balance sheet unless a right of setoff exists.

FASB STAFF POSITIONS

The FASB Staff has issued a series of FASB Staff Positions (FSP) providing guidance on the implementation of FIN 46 and its revision, FIN 46(R) that was issued in the December 2003. Full coverage of these FSP is provided in Chapter 11, *Business Combinations and Consolidated Financial Statements.*

APPENDIX

LEVERAGED LEASES

One of the more complex accounting subjects regarding leases is the accounting for a leveraged lease. Once again, as with both the sales-type and direct financing, the classification of the lease by the lessor has no impact on the accounting treatment accorded the lease by the lessee. The lessee simply treats it as any other lease and, thus, is only interested in whether the lease qualifies as an operating or capital lease. The lessor's accounting problem is substantially more complex than that of the lessee.

In order to qualify as a leveraged lease, a lease agreement must meet the following requirements, and the lessor must account for the investment tax credit (when in effect) in the manner described below.

NOTE: Failure to do so will result in the lease being classified as a direct financing lease.

1. The lease must meet the definition of a direct financing lease (the 90% of FV criterion does not apply).[6]
2. The lease must involve at least three parties.
    a. An owner-lessor (equity participant)
    b. A lessee
    c. A long-term creditor (debt participant)
3. The financing provided by the creditor is nonrecourse as to the general credit of the lessor and is sufficient to provide the lessor with substantial leverage.
4. The lessor's net investment (defined below) decreases in the early years and increases in the later years until it is eliminated.

This last characteristic poses the accounting issue.

The leveraged lease arose as a result of an effort to maximize the tax benefits associated with a lease transaction. In order to accomplish this, it was necessary to involve a third party to the lease transaction (in addition to the lessor and lessee); a long-term creditor. The following diagram[7] illustrates the relationships in a leveraged lease agreement:

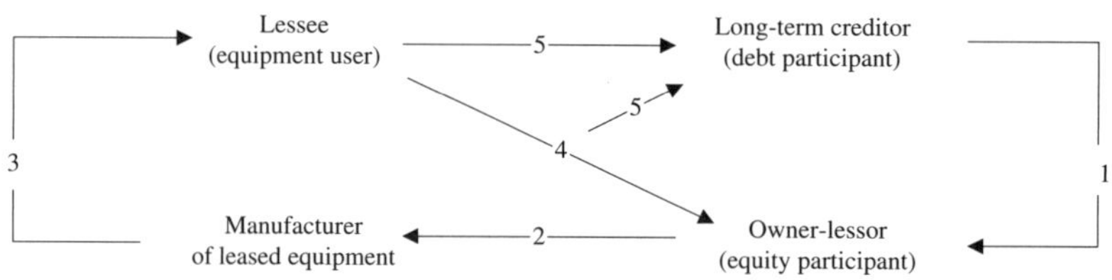

1. The owner-lessor obtains long-term financing from the creditor, generally in excess of 50% of the purchase price. FAS 13 indicates that the lessor must be provided with sufficient leverage in the transaction, therefore the 50%.
2. The owner then uses this financing along with his/her own funds to purchase the asset from the manufacturer
3. The manufacturer delivers the asset to the lessee

---

[6] *A direct financing lease must have its cost or carrying value equal to the fair value of the asset at the lease's inception. So even if the amounts are not significantly different, leveraged lease accounting may not be used.*

[7] *Adapted from "A Straightforward Approach to Leveraged Leasing" by Pierce R. Smith,* ***The Journal of Commercial Bank Lending,*** *July 1973, pp. 40-47.*

4. The lessee remits the periodic rent to the lessor
5. The debt is guaranteed by either using the equipment as collateral, the assignment of the lease payments, or both, depending on the demands established by the creditor

The FASB concluded that the entire lease agreement be accounted for as a single transaction and not a direct financing lease plus a debt transaction. The feeling was that the latter did not readily convey the lessor's net investment in the lease to the user of the financial statements. Thus, the lessor records the investment as a net amount. The gross investment is calculated as a combination of the following amounts:

1. The rentals receivable from the lessee, net of the principal and interest payments due to the long-term creditor
2. A receivable for the amount of the investment tax credit (ITC) to be realized on the transaction[8]
3. The estimated residual value of the leased asset
4. The unearned and deferred income consisting of
   a. The estimated pretax lease income (or loss), after deducting initial direct costs, remaining to be allocated to income
   b. The ITC remaining to be allocated to income over the remaining term of the lease[8]

The first three amounts described above are readily obtainable; however, the last amount, the unearned and deferred income, requires additional computations. In order to compute this amount, it is necessary to create a cash flow (income) analysis by year for the entire lease term. As described in 4. above, the unearned and deferred income consists of the pretax lease income (Gross lease rentals – Depreciation – Loan interest) and the unamortized investment tax credit. The total of these two amounts for all of the periods in the lease term represents the unearned and deferred income at the inception of the lease.

The amount computed as the gross investment in the lease (foregoing paragraphs) less the deferred taxes relative to the difference between pretax lease income and taxable lease income is the net investment for purposes of computing the net income for the period. In order to compute the periodic net income, another schedule must be completed that uses the cash flows derived in the first schedule and allocates them between income and a reduction in the net investment.

The amount of income is first determined by applying a rate to the net investment. The rate to be used is the rate that will allocate the entire amount of cash flow (income) when applied in the years in which the net investment is positive. In other words, the rate is derived in much the same way as the implicit rate (trial and error), except that only the years in which there is a positive net investment are considered. Thus, income is recognized only in the years in which there is a positive net investment.

The income recognized is divided among the following three elements:

1. Pretax accounting income
2. Amortization of investment tax credit
3. The tax effect of the pretax accounting income

The first two are allocated in proportionate amounts from the unearned and deferred income included in the calculation of the net investment. In other words, the unearned and deferred

---

[8] *The investment tax credit was repealed, effective January 1, 1986. ITC is relevant only for property placed in service prior to this date. We continue to discuss these concepts because Congress has historically reinstated this credit during economic downturns to provide economic stimulus.*

income consists of pretax lease accounting income and ITC. Each of these is recognized during the period in the proportion that the current period's allocated income is to the total income (cash flow). The last item, the tax effect, is recognized in tax expense for the year. The tax effect of any difference between pretax lease accounting income and taxable lease income is charged (or credited) to deferred taxes.

When tax rates change, all components of a leveraged lease must be recalculated from the inception of the lease using the revised after-tax cash flows arising from the revised tax rates.

If, in any case, the projected cash receipts (income) are less than the initial investment, the deficiency is to be recognized as a loss at the inception of the lease. Similarly, if at any time during the lease period the aforementioned method of recognizing income would result in a future period loss, the loss is to be recognized immediately.

This situation may arise as a result of the circumstances surrounding the lease changing. Therefore, any estimated residual value and other important assumptions must be reviewed on a periodic basis (at least annually). Any change is to be incorporated into the income computations; however, there is to be no upward revision of the estimated residual value.

The following example illustrates the application of these principles to a leveraged lease:

Example of simplified leveraged lease

1. A lessor acquires an asset for $100,000 with an estimated useful life of three years in exchange for a $25,000 down payment and a $75,000 three-year note with equal payments due on 12/31 each year. The interest rate is 18%.
2. The asset has no residual value.
3. The PV of an ordinary annuity of $1 for three years at 18% is 2.17427.
4. The asset is leased for three years with annual payments due to the lessor on 12/31 in the amount of $45,000.
5. The lessor uses the ACRS method of depreciation (150% declining balance with a half-year convention in the year placed in service) for tax purposes and elects to reduce the ITC rate to 4% as opposed to reducing the depreciable basis.
6. Assume a constant tax rate throughout the life of the lease of 40%.

Chart 1 analyzes the cash flows generated by the leveraged leasing activities. Chart 2 allocates the cash flows between the investment in leveraged leased assets and income from leveraged leasing activities. The allocation requires finding that rate of return, which when applied to the investment balance at the beginning of each year that the investment amount is positive, will allocate the net cash flow fully to net income over the term of the lease. This rate can be found only by a computer program or by an iterative trial and error process. The example that follows has a positive investment value in each of the three years, and thus the allocation takes place in each time period. Leveraged leases usually have periods where the investment account turns negative and is below zero.

Allocating principal and interest on the loan payments is as follows:

($75,000 ÷ 2.17427 = $34,494)

Year	*Payment*	*Interest 18%*	*Principal*	*Balance*
Inception of lease	$ --	$ --	$ --	$75,000
1	34,494	13,500	20,994	54,006
2	34,494	9,721	24,773	29,233
3	34,494	5,261	29,233	--

Chart 1

	A	B	C	D	E	F	G	H	I
	Rent	Depr.	Interest on loan	Taxable income (loss) (A-B-C)	Income tax payable (rcvbl.) Dx40%	Loan principal payments	ITC	Cash flow (A+G-C-E-F)	Cumulative cash flow
Initial	$ --	$ --	$ --	$ --	$ --	$ --	$ --	$(25,000)	$(25,000)
Year 1	45,000	25,000	13,500	6,500	2,600	20,994	4,000	11,906	(13,094)
Year 2	45,000	38,000	9,721	(2,721)	(1,088)	24,773	--	11,594	(1,500)
Year 3	45,000	37,000	5,261	2,739	1,096	29,233	--	9,410	7,910
Total	$135,000	$100,000	$28,482	$ 6,518	$ 2,608	$75,000	$4,000	$ 7,910	

The chart below allocates the cash flows determined above between the net investment in the lease and income. Recall that the income is then allocated between pretax accounting income and the amortization of the investment credit. The income tax expense for the period is a result of applying the tax rate to the current periodic pretax accounting income.

The amount to be allocated in total in each period is the net cash flow determined in column H above. The investment at the beginning of year one is the initial down payment of $25,000. This investment is then reduced on an annual basis by the amount of the cash flow not allocated to income.

Chart 2

	1	2	3	4	5	6	7
		Cash Flow Assumption				*Income Analysis*	
	Investment beginning of year	Cash flow	Allocated to investment	Allocated to income	Pretax income	Income tax expense	Investment tax credit
Year 1	$25,000	$11,906	$ 7,964	$3,942	$3,248	$1,300	$1,994
Year 2	17,036	11,594	8,908	2,686	2,213	885	1,358
Year 3	8,128	9,410	8,128	1,282	1,057	423	648
		$32,910	$25,000	$7,910	$6,518	$2,608	$4,000

Rate of return = 15.77%

1. Column 2 is the net cash flow after the initial investment, and columns 3 and 4 are the allocation based upon the 15.77% rate of return. The total of column 4 is the same as the total of column H in Chart 1.
2. Column 5 allocates column D in Chart 1 based upon the allocations in column 4. Column 6 allocates column E in Chart 1, (and, of course, is computed as 40% of column 5) and column 7 allocates column G in Chart 1 on the same basis.

The journal entries below illustrate the proper recording and accounting for the leveraged lease transaction. The initial entry represents the cash down payment, investment tax credit receivable, the unearned and deferred revenue, and the net cash to be received over the term of the lease.

The remaining journal entries recognize the annual transactions which include the net receipt of cash and the amortization of income.

	Year 1		*Year 2*		*Year 3*	
Rents receivable [Chart 1 (A-C-F)]	31,518					
Investment tax credit receivable	4,000					
Cash		25,000				
Unearned and deferred income		10,518				
Initial investment, Chart 2 (5+7) totals						
Cash	10,506		10,506		10,506	
Rent receivable		10,506		10,506		10,506
Net for all cash transactions, Chart 1 (A-C-F) line by line for each year						

	Year 1		*Year 2*		*Year 3*	
Income tax receivable (cash)	4,000					
Investment tax credit receivable		4,000				
Unearned and deferred income	5,242		3,571		1,705	
Income from leveraged leases		5,242		3,571		1,705

Amortization of unearned income, Chart 2 (5+7) line by line for each year

The following schedules illustrate the computation of deferred income tax amount. The annual amount is a result of the temporary difference created due to the difference in the timing of the recognition of income for GAAP and tax purposes. The income for tax purposes can be found in column D in Chart 1, while the income for GAAP purposes is found in column 5 of Chart 2. The actual amount of deferred tax is the difference between the tax computed with the temporary difference and the tax computed without the temporary difference. These amounts are represented by the income tax payable or receivable as shown in column E of Chart 1 and the income tax expense as shown in column 6 of Chart 2. A check of this figure is provided by multiplying the difference between GAAP and tax income by the annual rate.

Year 1		
Income tax payable	$ 2,600	
Income tax expense	(1,300)	
Deferred income tax (Dr)		$1,300
Taxable income	$ 6,500	
Pretax accounting income	(3,248)	
Difference	$ 3,252	
$3,252 x 40% = $1,300		

Year 2		
Income tax receivable	$ 1,088	
Income tax expense	885	
Deferred income tax (Cr)		$1,973
Taxable loss	$ 2,721	
Pretax accounting income	2,213	
Difference	$ 4,934	
$4,934 x 40% = $1,973		

Year 3		
Income tax payable	$ 1,096	
Income tax expense	(423)	
Deferred income tax (Dr)		$ 673
Taxable income	$ 2,739	
Pretax accounting income	(1,057)	
Difference	$ 1,682	
$1,682 x 40% = $673		

15 INCOME TAXES

PERSPECTIVE AND ISSUES

The computation of taxable income for the purpose of filing federal, state, and local income tax returns differs from the computation of net income under GAAP for a variety of reasons. In some instances, referred to as **temporary differences,** the **timing** of income or expense recognition varies. In other instances, referred to as **permanent differences,** income or expense recognized for income tax purposes is never recognized under GAAP, or vice versa. The objective under the GAAP matching principle is to recognize the income tax effects of transactions in the period that those transactions occur. Consequently, deferred income tax benefits and obligations may arise in financial statements. The methodology of determining the amounts of these assets and liabilities is the subject of this chapter.

The process of *inter*period income tax allocation, which is the process that gives rise to deferred income tax assets and liabilities, has been required under GAAP for decades. As with many accounting measurements, the prescribed methodology will vary depending upon whether the primary objective is accuracy of the balance sheet or of the income statement. While the income statement had historically been viewed as being of greatest concern, since the completion of the FASB's conceptual framework the emphasis has shifted to the balance sheet. This ultimately precipitated a major change in the interperiod income tax allocation rules culminating in the issuance of FAS 109 in 1992, which currently remains in effect.

Under FAS 109 all temporary differences result in deferred income tax assets or liabilities, although deferred income tax assets may need to be reduced by a valuation allowance unless it is "more likely than not" that the benefit will be realized in the future. Purchase price allocations made pursuant to purchase business combinations are made gross of income tax effects, and any associated income tax benefit or obligation is recognized separately. The income tax effects of net operating loss or tax credit carryforwards are treated as deferred income tax assets just like any other deferred income tax benefit. FAS 109 discontinued the previous requirements that the effect of utilizing a net operating loss in a subsequent year be treated as an extraordinary item in the income statement.

With its balance sheet orientation, FAS 109 requires that the amounts presented be based on the amounts expected to be realized, or obligations expected to be incurred. An average effective income tax rate convention is permitted to be used, thereby avoiding the computational complexity that made FAS 109's immediate predecessor so unpopular. The effects of all changes in the balance sheet deferred income tax assets and liabilities flow through the income tax provision; consequently, income tax expense is normally not directly calculable based on pretax accounting income in other than the simplest situation.

Discounting of deferred income taxes has never been permitted under GAAP, even though the ultimate realization of deferred income tax assets and liabilities is often far in the future. The promulgation of CON 7, which deals with the use of present value in accounting measurements, has not changed this prohibition. In any event, the inability to predict accurately the timing of the realization of deferred income tax benefits or payments would make discounting very difficult to accomplish.

Sources of GAAP

APB	*FAS*	*Q&A*	*FIN*	*FTB*	*EITF*
16, 17, 20, 23, 28	5, 6, 12, 37, 52, 109	109	18	82-1	86-9, 86-43, 86-44, 88-4, 93-12, 93-13, 93-16, 93-17, 94-10, 95-10, 95-20, 96-7, 98-11, 99-15, 00-15, 02-13, D-30, D-31, D-32, D-33

DEFINITIONS OF TERMS

Deferred income tax asset. The asset recognized to reflect the expected future benefit available to be realized upon the reversal of deductible temporary differences.

Deferred income tax liability. The liability recognized to reflect the expected future income taxes that will be payable upon the reversal of taxable temporary differences.

Future deductible temporary difference. The difference between the GAAP carrying amount and income tax basis of an asset or liability that will reverse in the future and result in future income tax deductions; these give rise to deferred income tax assets.

Future taxable temporary difference. Temporary differences that result in future taxable amounts; thee give rise to deferred income tax liabilities.

Gains and losses included in comprehensive income but excluded from net income. Certain items which, under GAAP, are events occurring currently but that are reported directly in equity as accumulated other comprehensive income, such as changes in the fair values of available-for-sale portfolios of marketable equity securities.

Interperiod tax allocation. The process of apportioning income tax expense among reporting periods without regard to the timing of the actual cash payments for income taxes. The objective is to reflect fully the income tax consequences of all economic events reported in current or prior financial statements and, in particular, to report the expected future income tax effects of the reversals of temporary differences existing at the reporting date.

Intraperiod tax allocation. The process of apportioning income tax expense applicable to a given period between income before extraordinary items and those items required to be shown net of tax such as extraordinary items, discontinued operations, and prior period adjustments.

Operating loss carryback or carryforward. The excess of income tax deductions over taxable income. To the extent that this results in a carryforward, the income tax effect is included in the reporting entity's deferred income tax asset.

Ordinary income or loss (used in interim accounting for income taxes). In GAAP this term is defined differently than it is for income tax purposes. For GAAP purposes, ordinary income or loss is computed as pretax income (loss) from continuing operations less: (1) extraordinary items, (2) discontinued operations, (3) cumulative effects of changes in accounting principle, and (4) significant unusual or infrequently occurring items.

Permanent differences. Differences between pretax accounting income and taxable income as a result of the treatment accorded certain transactions by the income tax laws and regulations that differ from the accounting treatment. Permanent differences will not reverse in subsequent periods.

Pretax accounting income. Income or loss for the accounting period as determined in accordance with GAAP without regard to the income tax expense for the period.

Taxable income. The difference between the taxable revenue and deductible expenses as defined by the Internal Revenue Code for a tax period without regard to special deductions (e.g., net operating loss or contribution carrybacks and carryforwards).

Tax credits. Reductions in income tax liability as a result of certain expenditures accorded special treatment under the Internal Revenue Code. Examples of such credits are: the Investment Tax Credit, investment in certain depreciable property; the Jobs Credit, payment of wages to targeted groups; the Research and Development Credit, an increase in qualifying R&D expenditures; and others.

Tax planning strategy. A representation by management of a planned transaction or series of transactions that would affect the particular future years in which temporary differences will result in taxable or deductible amounts.

Temporary differences. In general, differences between income tax and financial reporting bases of assets and liabilities that will result in taxable or deductible amounts in future periods. Temporary differences include "timing differences" as defined by prior GAAP as well as certain other differences, such as those arising from business combinations. Some temporary differences cannot be associated with particular assets or liabilities, but nonetheless do result from events that received financial statement recognition and will have income tax effects in future periods.

Unrecognized tax benefits. Deferred income tax benefits against which a valuation allowance had been provided as of the date of the financial statements.

Valuation allowance. The contra asset which is to be reflected to the extent that, in management's judgment, it is "more likely than not" that the deferred income tax asset will not be realized.

CONCEPTS, RULES, AND EXAMPLES

Evolution of Accounting for Income Taxes

The differences in the timing of recognition of certain expenses and revenues for income tax reporting purposes versus the timing under GAAP had always been a subject for debates in the accounting profession. The first of these debates was over the matter of whether or not income tax effects of timing difference should be recognized in the financial statements. At one extreme were those who believed that only the amount of income tax currently owed (as shown on the income tax return for the period) should be reported as periodic income tax expense, on the grounds that potential changes in tax law and the vagaries of the entity's future financial performance would make any projection to future periods speculative. This was the "no allocation" or "flow-through" position. At the other extreme were those who held that the matching principle demanded that reported periodic income tax expense be mechanically related to pretax accounting income, regardless of the amount of income taxes actually currently payable. This was the "comprehensive allocation" argument. The middle ground approach, known as "partial allocation," acknowledged the need for some deferred income tax provision, but only when actual future income tax payments or benefits could be accurately predicted. This debate was settled in the late 1960s: comprehensive income tax allocation became GAAP.

The other key debate was over the measurement strategy to be applied to interperiod income tax allocation. When, in the 1960s and 1970s, accounting theory placed paramount importance on the income statement, with much less interest in the balance sheet, the method of choice was the "deferred method," which invoked the matching principle. The annual income tax provision (consisting of current and deferred portions) was calculated so that it would bear the expected relationship to pretax accounting income; any excess or deficiency of the income tax provision over income taxes payable was recorded as an adjustment to the deferred income tax amounts reflected on the balance sheet. This practice, when applied, resulted in a net deferred income tax debit (subject to some limitations on asset realization) or a net deferred income tax credit, which did not necessarily mean that an asset or liability, as defined under GAAP, actually existed for that reported amount.

By the late 1970s, accounting theory (reflected in FASB's conceptual framework project) made the financial reporting priority the statement of financial position (balance sheet). Primary emphasis was placed on the measurement of assets and liabilities—which, under CON 6's definitions, clearly would not include certain deferred income tax benefits or obligations as these were then measured. To compute deferred income taxes consistent with a balance sheet orientation requires use of the "liability method." This essentially ascertains, as of each balance sheet date, the amount of future income tax benefits or obligations that are associated with the reporting entity's assets and liabilities existing at that time. Any adjustments necessary to increase or decrease deferred income taxes to the computed balance, plus or minus the amount of income taxes owed currently, determines the periodic income tax expense or benefit to be reported in the income statement. Put another way, income tax expense is the residual result of several other balance-sheet-oriented computations.

Movement to a balance-sheet-oriented measurement approach began with issuance of FAS 96. This unpopular standard embraced the inherently more straightforward liability approach, but added a number of major complexities to the computation of deferred income taxes, and proved to be unwieldy in practice. It was replaced with FAS 109, under which all deferred income tax assets are given full recognition, whether arising from deductible temporary differences or from net operating loss or tax credit carryforwards.

Under FAS 109 it is necessary to assess whether the deferred income tax asset is realizable. Testing for realization is accomplished by means of a "more-likely-than-not" criterion that indicates whether an allowance is needed to offset some or all of the recorded deferred income tax asset. While the determination of the amount of the allowance may make use of the scheduling of future expected reversals, other methods may also be employed and, in general, FAS 109 is a less rigorous, more flexible standard in regard to the financial statement presentation of deferred income tax assets than was its predecessor.

In summary, interperiod income tax allocation under GAAP is currently based on the liability method, using comprehensive allocation. While this basic principle may be straightforward, there are a number of computational complexities to be addressed. These will be presented in the remainder of this chapter.

An example of application of the liability method of deferred income tax accounting follows.

Simplified example of interperiod income tax allocation using the liability method

Caitlyn International has no permanent differences in years 2005 through 2007 (these are discussed later in this chapter). The company has only two balance sheet amounts with temporary differences between their income tax and financial reporting bases, property and equipment; and prepaid rent. No consideration is given to the classification of the deferred income tax amounts (i.e., current or long-term) as it is not considered necessary for purposes of this example.

Details of Caitlyn's temporary differences are as follows:

Caitlyn International Temporary Differences

Prepaid rent future deductible temporary differences

Basis at December 31	*Tax*	*GAAP*	*Future (taxable) deductible amount*
2005	--	$(100,000)	$100,000
2006	--	(80,000)	80,000
2007	--	(125,000)	125,000

Property and equipment future taxable temporary difference

On January 1, 2005, Caitlyn International purchased property and equipment with a 10-year estimated useful life which, under its normal accounting policy, it depreciates using the straight-line method. For income tax purposes, these assets qualify as 5-year personal property under the General Depreciation System (GDS) and consequently income tax depreciation is computed using the Modified Accelerated Cost Recovery System (MACRS) which is equivalent to double-declining balance depreciation with a half-year assumed for the year placed in service and changing to straight-line depreciation when advantageous to the taxpayer. In addition, the property is eligible for a 50% special depreciation allowance in 2005, the year placed in service, under the provisions of the Jobs and Growth Tax Relief Reconciliation Act of 2003 (JGTRRA).

	2005	*Tax*	*GAAP*	*Future (taxable) deductible amount*
A	Purchase price of assets	$950,000	$950,000	
B	Special first-year depreciation	475,000	--	
C	Adjusted depreciable basis (A – B)	475,000	950,000	
D	Depreciation rate	x 20%	x 10%	
E	2005 depreciation (C x D)	95,000	95,000	
F	Special first-year depreciation (B)	475,000	--	
G	2005 depreciation and first-year allowance (E + F)	570,000	95,000	
H	Basis at 12/31/05 (A – G)	$380,000	$855,000	$(475,000)
	2006			
I	Depreciation rate	x 32%	x 10%	
J	2006 Depreciation (C x I)	152,000	95,000	
K	Basis at 12/31/06 (H – J)	$228,000	$760,000	$(532,000)

	2007			
L	Depreciation rate	x 19.2%	x 10%	
M	2007 Depreciation (C x L)	91,200	95,000	
N	Basis at 12/31/06 (K – M)	$136,800	$665,000	$(528,200)

The computation of deferred income taxes is as follows:

	12/31/2005	*12/31/2006*	*12/31/2007*
Future deductible temporary difference			
Prepaid rent	$ 100,000	$ 80,000	$125,000
Future (taxable) temporary difference			
Property and equipment	(475,000)	(532,000)	(528,200)
Net (taxable) deductible temporary difference	(375,000)	(452,000)	(403,200)
Effective tax rate	34%	34%	37%
Ending deferred income tax asset (liability)	(127,500)	(153,680)	(149,184)
Beginning deferred income tax asset (liability)	--	(127,500)	(153,680)
Deferred income tax (expense) benefit	$(127,500)	$ (26,180)	$ 4,496

Note from the computations that, under the liability method, deferred income tax expense is the amount necessary to adjust the balance sheet to the computed balance. No attempt is made to correlate the amount of deferred income tax expense to pretax accounting income. Nor is it necessary, as it was under APB 11, to track the amounts of each temporary difference that originate or reverse during the year.

FAS 109 in Greater Detail

While the liability method is conceptually straightforward, in practice there are a number of complexities to be addressed. Income tax accounting remains one of the more difficult areas of accounting practice. In the following pages, these measurement and reporting issues will be discussed in greater detail:

1. The nature of temporary differences
2. Treatment of net operating loss carryforwards
3. Measurement of deferred income tax assets and liabilities
4. Considering whether a valuation allowance is needed
5. The effect of tax law changes on previously recorded deferred income tax assets and liabilities
6. The effect of a change in the tax status of the reporting entity from taxable to nontaxable or vice versa on previously recognized deferred income tax assets and liabilities
7. The income tax effects of business combinations
8. Intercorporate income tax allocation
9. Exceptions to the general rules of FAS 109

Detailed examples of deferred income tax accounting under FAS 109 are presented throughout the following discussion of these issues.

The Nature of Temporary Differences

While many typical business transactions are accounted for identically for income tax and financial reporting purposes, there are many others subject to different income tax and accounting treatments, often leading to their being reported in different periods in financial statements than they are reported on income tax returns. The term "timing differences," used under prior GAAP, has been superseded by the broader term "temporary differences" under current rules. Under income statement oriented GAAP, timing differences were said to originate in one period and to reverse in a later period. These involved such common items as alternative depreciation methods, deferred compensation plans, percentage-of-completion accounting for long-term construction contracts, and cash basis versus accrual basis accounting.

The more comprehensive concept of temporary differences, consistent with the modern balance sheet orientation of GAAP, includes all differences between the income tax and financial reporting bases of assets and liabilities, if those differences will result in taxable or deductible amounts in future years. Temporary differences include all the items formerly defined as timing differences, and other additional items. Deferred income taxes are provided for all temporary differences, but not for permanent differences, which are book-tax differences in asset or liability bases that will never reverse.

Temporary differences under FAS 109 that were defined as timing differences under prior GAAP include the following:

Revenue recognized for financial reporting purposes before being recognized for income tax purposes. Revenue accounted for by the installment method for income tax purposes, but currently reflected in GAAP income; certain construction-related revenue recognized using the completed-contract method for income tax purposes, but recognized using the percentage-of-completion method for financial reporting purposes; earnings from investees recognized using the equity method for accounting purposes but taxed only when later distributed as dividends to the investor. These are future taxable temporary differences because future periods' taxable income will exceed GAAP income as the differences reverse; thus they give rise to deferred income tax liabilities.

Revenue recognized for income tax purposes prior to recognition in the financial statements. Certain taxable revenue received in advance, such as prepaid rental income and service contract revenue not recognized in the financial statements until later periods. These are future deductible temporary differences, because the costs of future performance will be deductible in the future years when incurred without being reduced by the amount of revenue deferred for GAAP purposes. Consequently, the income tax benefit to be realized in future years from deducting those future costs is a deferred income tax asset.

Expenses deductible for income tax purposes prior to recognition in the financial statements. Accelerated depreciation methods or shorter statutory useful lives used for income tax purposes, while straight-line depreciation or longer useful economic lives are used for financial reporting; amortization of goodwill and nonamortizable intangible assets over a 15-year life for income tax purposes while not amortizing them for financial reporting purposes unless they are impaired. Upon reversal in the future, the effect would be to increase taxable income without a corresponding increase in GAAP income. Therefore, these items are future taxable temporary differences, and give rise to deferred income tax liabilities.

Expenses recognized in the financial statements prior to becoming deductible for income tax purposes. Certain estimated expenses, such as warranty costs, as well as such contingent losses as accruals of litigation expenses, are not tax deductible until the obligation becomes fixed. In those future periods, those expenses will give rise to deductions on the reporting entity's income tax return. Thus, these are deductible temporary differences that give rise to deferred income tax assets.

In addition to these familiar and well-understood timing differences, temporary differences include a number of other categories that also involve differences between the income tax and financial reporting bases of assets or liabilities. These are

Reductions in tax-deductible asset bases arising in connection with tax credits. Under the provisions of the 1982 tax act, taxpayers were permitted a choice of either full ACRS depreciation coupled with a reduced investment tax credit, or a full investment tax credit coupled with reduced depreciation allowances. If the taxpayer chose the latter option, the asset basis was reduced for tax depreciation, but was still fully depreciable for financial reporting purposes. Accordingly, this election was accounted for as a future taxable temporary difference, and gave rise to a deferred income tax liability.

Investment tax credits accounted for by the deferral method. Under GAAP, investment tax credits could be accounted for by either the "flow through" method (full recognition in the period the asset is placed in service, by far the most common method in practice), or by the "deferral" method (recognition in income over the useful lives of the assets giving rise to the credit). Thus, a future deductible temporary difference existed, with which a deferred income tax asset would be associated.

The two categories discussed immediately above are no longer of much interest since the investment tax credit was eliminated under current tax law. In the past, however, Congress has reinstated the credit to provide an incentive for businesses to invest in productive equipment. Future reinstatement always remains a possibility, given the cyclical nature of the US economy.

Increases in the income tax bases of assets resulting from the indexing of asset costs for the effects of inflation. Occasionally proposed but never enacted, enacting such a provision to income tax law would allow taxpaying entities to finance the replacement of depreciable assets through depreciation based on current costs, as computed by the application of indices to the historical costs of the assets being remeasured. This reevaluation of asset costs would give rise to future deductible temporary differences that would be associated with deferred income tax benefits.

Certain business combinations accounted for by the purchase method. Under certain circumstances, the amounts assignable to assets or liabilities acquired in purchase business combinations will differ from their tax bases. Such differences may be either taxable or deductible in the future and, accordingly, may give rise to deferred income tax liabilities or assets. These differences are explicitly recognized by the reporting of deferred income taxes in the consolidated financial statements of the acquiring entity. Note that these differences are no longer allocable to the financial reporting bases of the underlying assets or liabilities themselves, as was the case under APB 11's **net of tax** method.

A financial reporting situation in which deferred income taxes may or may not be appropriate would include life insurance (such as key person insurance) under which the reporting entity is the beneficiary. Since proceeds of life insurance are not subject to income tax under present law, the excess of cash surrender values over the sum of premiums paid will **not** be a temporary difference under the provisions of FAS 109, if the intention is to hold the policy until death benefits are received. On the other hand, if the entity intends to cash in (surrender) the policy at some point prior to the death of the insured (i.e., it is holding the insurance contract as an investment), which would be a taxable event, then the excess surrender value is in fact a temporary difference, and deferred income taxes are to be provided thereon.

Treatment of Net Operating Loss Carryforwards

The recognition and measurement of the income tax effects of net operating loss carryforwards under FAS 109 differs materially from how this was dealt with under earlier standards. Historically, it had been presumed that net operating losses would generally not be realizable; accordingly, the income tax effects of carryforwards were not recognized in the financial statements until the future period in which the benefits were realized for income tax purposes. That is, the provision for income taxes in the loss year only reflected the benefit derived, if any, from carrying back the net operating loss to prior years to obtain a refund. Any excess net operating loss available to offset future years' taxable income was not recognized until actually realized. Consequently, the balance sheet would not display a deferred income tax asset relating to the net operating loss carryforward. Such treatment was justified in order to report the entity's assets at amounts that did not exceed net realizable value. (In exceptional cases, when realization of the benefits was deemed to be assured beyond a reasonable doubt, recognition in the loss period was permitted.)

FAS 96, the first replacement for APB 11, entirely prohibited recognition of net deferred income tax assets to the extent that they exceeded amounts currently refundable through net operating loss carrybacks as of the balance sheet date. This proscription was based on the view that the display of deferred income tax assets for these benefits would have been tantamount to anticipating future income. Even the narrow "assured beyond a reasonable doubt" exception previously provided was foreclosed.

With the imposition of FAS 109, however, all temporary differences and carryforwards have been conferred identical status, and their income tax effects are to be given full recognition on the balance sheet. Specifically, the income tax effects of net operating loss carryforwards are equivalent to the income tax effects of future deductible temporary differences, and the once important distinction between the two has been eliminated. The deferred income tax effects of net operating losses are computed and recorded, but as is the case for all other deferred income tax assets, the need for a valuation allowance must also be assessed (as discussed below). The income tax effects of income tax credit carryforwards (e.g., general business credits, alternative minimum tax credits) are used to increase deferred income tax assets dollar-for-dollar versus being treated in the same manner as future deductible temporary differences as illustrated below.

Example—Net operating loss carryforwards and income tax credit carryforwards

Casey Corporation has the following future deductible temporary differences and available carryforwards at December 31, 2005:

Inventory costs capitalized under Internal Revenue Code §263A	$40,000
Allowance for uncollectible accounts receivable	20,000
Net operating loss carryforward	18,000
General business credit carryforward	14,000

Casey's computation of deferred income taxes at December 31, 2005, is as follows:

Capitalized inventory costs	$40,000
Allowance for uncollectible accounts receivable	20,000
Net operating loss carryforward	18,000
	78,000
Assumed income tax rate	x 34%
	26,520
General business credit carryforward	14,000
Deferred income tax asset	$40,520

Note the net operating loss is multiplied by the income tax rate to compute its effect on the deferred income tax asset since it is available to reduce future years' *taxable income*. In contrast, the general business credit carryforward is not multiplied by the *income tax* rate since it is available to be used to offset future years' income tax.

The reporting of the current income tax benefit of carrying back net operating losses has also been changed by the current standard. FAS 109 provides that the income tax benefits of net operating loss carrybacks and carryforwards, with limited exceptions (discussed below), are to be reported in the same manner as the source of either income or loss in the current year. As used in the standard, the phrase "in the same manner" refers to the classification of the income tax benefit in the income statement (i.e., as income taxes on income from continuing operations, discontinued operations, extraordinary items, etc.) or as the income tax effect of gains included in other comprehensive income but excluded from net income on the income statement. The income tax benefits are **not** reported in the same manner as the source of the net operating loss carryforward or income taxes paid in a prior year, or as the source of the expected future taxable income that will permit the realization of the carryforward.

For example, if the income tax benefit of a loss that arose in a prior year in connection with an extraordinary item is first given recognition in the current year, the benefit would be allocated to income taxes on income from continuing operations if the benefit offsets income taxes on income from continuing operations in the current year. The expression "first given recognition" means that the **net** deferred income tax asset, after deducting the valuation allowance, reflects the income tax effect of the loss carryforward for the first time.

Under FAS 109, of course, the **gross** deferred income tax asset will always reflect all future deductible temporary differences and net operating loss carryforwards in the periods they arise. Thus, first given recognition means that the valuation allowance is eliminated for the first time. If it offsets income taxes on extraordinary income in the current year, then the benefits would be reported in extraordinary items. As another example, the tax benefit arising from the entity's loss from continuing operations in the current year would be allocated to continuing operations, regardless of whether it might be realized as a carryback against income taxes paid on extraordinary items in prior years. The income tax benefit would also be allocated to continuing operations in cases where it is anticipated that the benefit will be realized through the reduction of income taxes to be due on extraordinary gains in future years. (See the discussion of intraperiod income tax allocation later in this chapter.)

Thus, the general rule is that the reporting of income tax effects of net operating losses are driven by the source of the tax benefits in the current period. There are only two exceptions to the foregoing rule. The first exception relates to existing future deductible temporary differences and net operating loss carryforwards which arise in connection with purchase business combinations and for which income tax benefits are first recognized. This exception will be discussed below (see income tax effects of business combinations). As in the preceding paragraph, first recognized means that a valuation allowance (as discussed more fully later in this chapter) provided previously is being eliminated for the first time.

The second exception to the aforementioned general rule is that certain income tax benefits allocable to stockholders' equity are **not** to be reflected in the income statement. Specifically, income tax benefits arising in connection with contributed capital, employee stock options, dividends paid on unallocated ESOP shares, or temporary differences existing at the date of a quasi reorganization are reported as accumulated other comprehensive income in the stockholders' equity section of the balance sheet and are not included in the income statement.

Measurement of Deferred Income Tax Assets and Liabilities

Under FAS 109 there is no need to forecast (or "schedule") the future years in which temporary differences are expected to reverse except in the most exceptional circumstances. To eliminate the scheduling requirement of FAS 96, it was necessary to endorse the use of the expected average (i.e., effective) income tax rate to measure the deferred income tax assets and liabilities, and to forgo a more precise measure of marginal tax effects. Scheduling will now be encountered primarily (1) when income tax rate changes are to be phased in over multiple years, and (2) in order to determine the classification (current or noncurrent) of a deferred income tax asset arising from a net operating loss carryforward or income tax credit carryforward or to determine whether such a carryforward might expire unused for the purpose of determining the amount of valuation allowance needed (as discussed in the following section of this chapter).

Currently, C corporations with taxable income between $335,000 and $10,000,000 are taxed at an expected income tax rate equal to the 34% marginal rate, since the effect of the surtax exemption has fully phased out at that level, effectively resulting in a flat tax. Thus, the computation of deferred income taxes for these entities is accomplished simply by applying the 34% top marginal rate to all temporary differences and net operating loss carryforwards outstanding at the balance sheet date. This technique is applied to future taxable temporary differences (producing deferred income tax liabilities), and to future deductible temporary differences and net operating loss carryforwards (giving rise to deferred income tax assets). The deferred income tax assets computed must still be evaluated for realizability; some, or all, of the projected income tax benefits may fail the "more-likely-than-not" test and consequently may need to be offset by a valuation allowance.

On the other hand, reporting entities that have historically been taxed at an effective federal income tax rate lower than the top marginal rate compute their deferred income tax assets and liabilities by using their expected future effective income tax rates. Consistent with the goal of simplifying the process of calculating deferred income taxes, reporting entities are permitted to apply a single, long-term expected income tax rate, without attempting to differentiate among the years when temporary difference reversals are expected to occur. In any event, the inherent imprecision of forecasting future income levels and the patterns of temporary difference reversals makes it unlikely that a more sophisticated computational effort would produce better financial statements. Therefore, absent such factors as the phasing in of new income tax rates, it will not be necessary to consider whether the reporting entity's effective income tax rate will vary from year to year.

The effective income tax rate convention obviates the need to predict the impact of the alternative minimum tax (AMT) on future years. In determining an entity's deferred income taxes, the number of computations may be as few as one, which contrasts markedly with FAS 96, the standard's immediate predecessor.

The procedure to compute the gross deferred income tax provision (i.e., before addressing the possible need for a valuation allowance) is as follows:

1. Identify all temporary differences existing as of the reporting date. This process is simplified if the reporting entity maintains both GAAP and income tax balance sheets for comparison purposes.
2. Segregate the temporary differences into future taxable differences and future deductible differences. This step is necessary because a valuation allowance may be required to be provided to offset the income tax effects of the future deductible temporary differences and carryforwards, but not against the income tax effects of the future taxable temporary differences.
3. Accumulate information about available net operating loss and tax credit carryforwards as well as their expiration dates or other types of limitations, if any.
4. Measure the income tax effect of aggregate future taxable temporary differences by separately applying the appropriate expected income tax rates (federal plus any state, local, and foreign rates that are applicable under the circumstances). Ensure that consideration is given in making these computations to the federal income tax deductibility of income taxes payable to other jurisdictions.
5. Similarly, measure the income tax effects of future deductible temporary differences, including net operating loss carryforwards.

FAS 109 prescribes that separate computations be made for each taxing jurisdiction. In many cases, this level of complexity is not needed and a single, combined effective income tax rate can be used. However, in assessing the need for valuation allowances, it is necessary to consider the entity's ability to absorb deferred income tax benefits against income tax liabilities. Inasmuch as benefits from one tax jurisdiction will not reduce income taxes payable to another tax jurisdiction, separate calculations will be needed in these situations. Also, for purposes of balance sheet presentation (discussed below), offsetting of deferred income tax assets and liabilities is only permissible within the same jurisdiction.

Separate computations are made for each taxpaying component of the primary reporting entity: if a parent company and its subsidiaries are consolidated for financial reporting purposes but file separate income tax returns, the reporting entity comprises a number of components, and the income tax benefits of any one will be unavailable to reduce the income tax obligations of the others.

The principles set forth above are illustrated by the following example.

Computation of deferred income tax liability and asset—Basic example

Assume that Humfeld Company has a total of $28,000 of future taxable temporary differences, and a total of $8,000 of future deductible temporary differences. There are no available operating loss or tax credit carryforwards. Taxable income is $230,000 and the income tax rate is a flat (i.e., not graduated) 34% for the current year and not anticipated to change in the future. Also assume that there were no deferred income tax liabilities or assets in prior years.

Current income tax expense and income taxes currently payable are computed as taxable income times the current rate ($230,000 x 34% = $78,200). The deferred income tax asset is computed as $2,720 representing 34% of future deductible temporary differences of $8,000. The deferred income tax liability of $9,520 is calculated as 34% of future taxable temporary differences of $28,000. The deferred income tax expense of $6,800 is the net of the deferred income tax liability of $9,520 and the deferred income tax asset of $2,720.

The journal entry to record the required amounts is

Current income tax expense	78,200	
Deferred income tax asset	2,720	
Income tax expense—deferred	6,800	
Deferred income tax liability		9,520
Income taxes currently payable		78,200

In 2006, Humfeld Company has taxable income of $411,000, aggregate future taxable and future deductible temporary differences are $75,000 and $36,000, respectively, and the income tax rate remains a flat 34%.

Current income tax expense and income taxes currently payable each are $139,740 ($411,000 x 34%).

Deferred amounts are calculated as follows:

	Deferred tax liability	*Deferred tax asset*	*Income tax expense—deferred*
Required balance at 12/31/06			
$75,000 x 34%	$25,500		--
$36,000 x 34%		$12,240	--
Balances at 12/31/05	9,520	2,720	--
Adjustment required	$15,980	$9,520	$6,460

The journal entry to record the deferred amounts is

Deferred income tax asset	9,520	
Income tax expense—deferred	6,460	
Deferred income tax liability		15,980

Because the **increase** in the liability in 2006 is larger (by $6,460) than the increase in the asset for that year, the result is a deferred income tax **expense** for 2006.

The Valuation Allowance for Deferred Income Tax Assets Expected to Be Unrealizable

Under prior GAAP, the presentation of deferred income tax assets in the balance sheet was constrained or prohibited entirely. FAS 109 requires that all deferred income tax assets be given full recognition, subject to the possible provision of an allowance when it is determined that this asset is unlikely to be realized. This approach (providing full recognition on a gross basis, but also providing for a valuation allowance to reduce the recorded asset to the expected realizable amount) conveys the greatest amount of useful information to the users of the financial statements.

In dealing with the question of measurement of the valuation account, FASB could well have been guided by FAS 5, which established the standard for recognizing contingent incurrences of obligations and impairments of assets. Under FAS 5, the threshold for recognition of impairment would have been that the impairment was deemed to be "probable" of realization. FASB rejected the notion of applying that standard to this measurement situation, and instead developed a new measure, the "more-likely-than-not" criterion. (To date, this criterion has been applied exclusively to the deferred income tax asset issue.)

Under this provision of FAS 109, a valuation allowance is to be provided for that fraction of the computed year-end balances of the deferred income tax assets for which it has been determined that it is more likely than not that the reported asset amount will **not** be realized. As used in this context, "more likely than not" represents a probability of just over 50%. Since it is widely agreed that the term probable, as used in FAS 5, denotes a much higher probability (perhaps 85% to 90%), the threshold for reflecting an impairment of deferred income tax assets is much lower than the threshold for other assets (i.e., in most cases, the likelihood of a valuation allowance being required is greater than, say, the likelihood that a long-lived asset is impaired).

If a higher threshold had been set (such as FAS 5's "probable"), great diversity could have developed in practice as to the amount of valuation allowances offsetting deferred income tax assets, which would not have been consistent with the goal of comparability of financial statements over time and across entities.

Establishment of a valuation allowance

Assume that Couch Corporation has a future deductible temporary difference of $60,000 at December 31, 2005. The tax rate is a flat 34%. Based on available evidence, management of Couch Corporation concludes that it is more likely than not that all sources will not result in future taxable income sufficient to realize an income tax benefit of more than $15,000 (25% of the future deductible temporary difference). Also assume that there were no deferred income tax assets in previous years and that prior years' taxable income was inconsequential.

At 12/31/05 Couch Corporation records a deferred income tax asset in the amount of $20,400 ($60,000 x 34%) and a valuation allowance of $15,300 (34% of the $45,000 difference between the $60,000 of future deductible temporary differences and the $15,000 of future taxable income expected to absorb the future tax deduction arising from the reversal of the temporary difference).

The journal entry at 12/31/05 is

Deferred income tax asset	20,400	
Valuation allowance		15,300
Income tax benefit—deferred		5,100

The deferred income tax benefit of $5,100 represents that portion of the deferred income tax asset (25%) that, more likely than not, is realizable.

Assume that at the end of 2006, Couch Corporation's future deductible temporary difference has decreased to $50,000 and that Couch now has a net operating loss carryforward of $42,000. The total of the net operating loss carryforward ($42,000) plus the amount of the future deductible temporary difference ($50,000) is $92,000. A deferred income tax asset of $31,280 ($92,000 x 34%) is recognized at the end of 2006. Also assume that management of Couch Corporation concludes that it is more likely than not that $25,000 of the tax asset will **not** be realized. Thus, a valuation allowance in that amount is required, and the balance in the allowance account of $15,300 must be increased by $9,700 ($25,000 – $15,300).

The journal entry at 12/31/06 is

Deferred income tax asset	10,880	
Valuation allowance		9,700
Income tax benefit—deferred		1,180

The deferred income tax asset is debited $10,880 to increase it from $20,400 at the end of 2005 to its required balance of $31,280 at the end of 2006. The deferred income tax **benefit** of $1,180 represents the **net** of the $10,880 increase in the deferred income tax asset and the $9,700 increase in the valuation allowance.

While the meaning of the more-likely-than-not criterion is clear (more than 50%), the practical difficulty of assessing whether or not this threshold test is met in a given situation remains. A number of positive and negative factors need to be evaluated in reaching a conclusion as to the necessity of a valuation allowance. Positive factors (those suggesting that an allowance is not necessary) include

1. Evidence of sufficient future taxable income, exclusive of reversing temporary differences and carryforwards, to realize the benefit of the deferred income tax asset
2. Evidence of sufficient future taxable income arising from the reversals of existing future taxable temporary differences (deferred income tax liabilities) to realize the benefit of the deferred income tax asset
3. Evidence of sufficient taxable income in prior year(s) available for realization of a net operating loss carryback under existing statutory limitations.
4. Evidence of the existence of prudent, feasible **tax planning strategies** under management control that, if implemented, would permit the realization of the deferred income tax asset
5. An excess of appreciated asset values over their tax bases, in an amount sufficient to realize the deferred income tax asset
6. A strong earnings history exclusive of the loss that created the deferred income tax asset

While the foregoing may suggest that the reporting entity will be able to realize the benefits of the future deductible temporary differences outstanding as of the balance sheet date, certain negative factors must also be considered in determining whether a valuation allowance needs to be established against deferred income tax assets. These factors include

1. A cumulative recent history of losses
2. A history of operating losses, or of net operating loss or tax credit carryforwards that have expired unused
3. Losses that are anticipated in the near future years, despite a history of profitable operations

Thus, the process of evaluating whether a valuation allowance is needed involves the weighing of both positive and negative factors to determine whether, based on the preponderance of available evidence, it is more likely than not that the deferred income tax assets will be realized.

To illustrate the determination of the valuation allowance required in a specific situation, assume the following facts:

1. Foy Corporation reports on a calendar year, and it commenced operations and began applying FAS 109 in 2002.
2. As of the December 31, 2005 balance sheet, it has future taxable temporary differences of $85,000 relating to income earned on equity method investments; future deductible temporary differences of $12,000 relating to deferred compensation arrangements; a net operating loss carryforward (which arose in 2002) of $40,000; and a capital loss carryforward of $10,000 (which arose in 2005).
3. Foy's expected effective income tax rate for future years is 34% for both ordinary income and net long-term capital gains. Capital losses cannot be offset against ordinary income.

The first steps are to compute the deferred income tax asset and/or liability without consideration of the possible need for a valuation allowance. The computations would proceed as follows:

Deferred income tax liability:	
Future taxable temporary difference (equity method investment)	$85,000
Effective tax rate	x 34%
Required balance	$28,900
Deferred income tax asset:	
Future deductible temporary differences and carryforwards:	
Deferred compensation	$12,000
Net operating loss carryforward	40,000
	52,000
Effective tax rate	x 34%
Required balance (a)	$17,680
Capital loss	$10,000
Effective tax rate	x 34%
Required balance (b)	$ 3,400
Total deferred income tax asset: (a) + (b)	
Ordinary	$17,680
Capital	3,400
Total required balance	$21,080

The next step would be to consider the need for a valuation allowance to partially or completely offset the deferred income tax asset, based on a "more likely than not" assessment of the asset's realizability. Foy management must evaluate both positive and negative evidence to determine the need for a valuation allowance, if any. Assume that management identifies the following factors that may affect this need:

1. Before the net operating loss (NOL) deduction, Foy reported taxable income of $5,000 in 2005. Management believes that taxable income in future years, apart from NOL deductions, should continue at approximately the same level experienced in 2005.
2. The future taxable temporary differences are not expected to reverse in the foreseeable future as the equity method investee is not expected to incur losses or pay dividends to Foy.
3. The capital loss arose in connection with a securities transaction of a type that is unlikely to recur. The company does not generally engage in activities that have the potential to result in capital gains or losses.
4. Management estimates that certain productive assets have a fair value exceeding their respective income tax bases by about $30,000. The entire gain, if realized for income tax purposes, would result in recapture of depreciation previously taken. Since the current plans call for a substantial upgrading of the company's plant assets, management feels it could easily accelerate those actions in order to realize taxable gains, should it be desirable to do so for income tax planning purposes.

Based on the foregoing information, Foy Corporation management concludes that a $3,400 valuation allowance is required. The reasoning is as follows:

1. There will be some taxable operating income generated in future years ($5,000 annually, based on the earnings experienced in 2005), which will absorb a modest portion of the reversal of the deductible temporary difference ($12,000) and net operating loss carryforward ($40,000) existing at year-end 2005.
2. More importantly, the feasible tax planning strategy of accelerating the taxable gain relating to appreciated assets ($30,000) would certainly be sufficient, in conjunction

with operating income over several years, to permit Foy to fully realize the income tax benefits of the future deductible temporary difference and NOL carryover.

3. However, since capital losses can only be carried forward for five years, are only usable to offset future capital gains, and Foy management is unable to project future realization of capital gains, it is more likely than not that the associated tax benefit accrued ($3,400) will not be realized, and thus a valuation allowance must be recorded.

Based on this analysis, an allowance for unrealizable deferred income tax benefits in the amount of $3,400 is established by a charge against the current (2005) tax provision.

Among the foregoing positive and negative factors to be considered, perhaps the most difficult to fully grasp is that of available income tax planning strategies. Since FAS 109 requires that all available evidence be assessed to determine the need for a valuation allowance, the matter of the cost of implementing those strategies is irrelevant. In fact, there is no limitation regarding strategies that may involve significant costs of implementation, although in computing the amount of valuation allowance needed, any costs of implementation must be netted against the benefits to be derived.

For example, if a gross deferred income tax asset of $50,000 is recorded, and certain strategies have been identified by management which would protect realization of the future deductible item associated with the computed income tax benefit, at an implementation cost of $10,000, then the net amount of income tax benefit which is more likely than not to be realizable would not be $50,000. Rather, it may be only $43,400, which is the gross benefit less the after-tax cost of implementation, assuming a 34% tax rate ($50,000 – [$10,000 x (1 – .34)]). Accordingly, a valuation allowance of $6,600 is established in this example.

Impact of a qualifying tax strategy

Assume that Kruse Company has a $180,000 net operating loss carryforward as of 12/31/05, scheduled to expire at the end of the following year. Future taxable temporary differences of $240,000 exist that are expected to reverse in approximately equal amounts of $80,000 in 2006, 2007, and 2008. Kruse Company estimates that taxable income for 2006 (exclusive of the reversal of existing temporary differences and the operating loss carryforward) will be $20,000. Kruse Company expects to implement a qualifying income tax planning strategy that will accelerate the total of $240,000 of taxable temporary differences to 2006. Expenses to implement the strategy are estimated to approximate $30,000. The tax rate is 34%.

In the absence of the income tax planning strategy, $100,000 of the net operating loss carryforward could be realized in 2006 based on estimated taxable income of $20,000 plus $80,000 of the reversal of future taxable temporary differences. Thus, $80,000 would expire unused at the end of 2006 and the net amount of the deferred income tax asset at 12/31/05 would be recognized at $34,000, computed as $61,200 ($180,000 x 34%) minus the valuation allowance of $27,200 ($80,000 x 34%).

However, by implementing the income tax planning strategy, the deferred income tax asset is calculated as follows:

Taxable income for 2006:	
Expected amount without reversal of taxable temporary differences	$ 20,000
Reversal of taxable temporary differences due to tax-planning strategy, net of costs	210,000
	230,000
Net operating loss to be carried forward	(180,000)
Net operating loss expiring unused at 12/31/06	$ --

The gross deferred income tax asset thus can be recorded at the full benefit amount of $61,200 ($180,000 x 34%). However, a valuation allowance is required for $19,800, representing the net-of-tax effect of the $30,000 in anticipated expenses related to implementation of the strategy. The **net** deferred income tax asset at 12/31/05 is $41,400 ($61,200 – $19,800). Kruse Company will also recognize a deferred income tax liability of $81,600 at the end of 2005 (34% of the taxable temporary differences of $240,000).

The adequacy of the valuation allowance must be assessed as of each balance sheet date. Adjustments to the amount of the valuation allowance are recorded by a charge against, or a credit to, current earnings, via the current period income tax expense or benefit. Thus, even if the gross amount of future deductible temporary differences has remained constant during a year, income tax expense for that year might be increased or decreased as a consequence of reassessing the adequacy of the valuation allowance at year-end. It is important that these two computational steps be separately addressed: **first** the computation of the gross deferred income tax assets (the product of the expected effective income tax rate and the total amount of future deductible temporary differences) must be made; **then** the amount of the valuation allowance to be provided to offset the deferred income tax asset must be assessed (using the criteria set forth above). Although changes in both the deferred income tax asset and valuation allowance affect current period income tax expense, the processes of measuring these two amounts are distinct. Furthermore, FAS 109 requires disclosure of both the gross deferred income tax asset (and also the gross deferred income tax liability) and the change in the valuation allowance for the year. These disclosure requirements underline the need to separately measure these items without offsetting.

The Effect of Tax Law Changes on Previously Recorded Deferred Income Tax Assets and Liabilities

The balance-sheet-oriented measurement approach of FAS 109 makes it necessary to reevaluate the deferred income tax asset and liability balances at each year-end. If changes to income tax rates or other provisions of the income tax law (e.g., deductibility of items) are enacted, the effect of these changes must be recognized so that the deferred income tax assets and liabilities are fairly presented on the balance sheet. Any offsetting adjustments are made through the current period's income tax expense or benefit on the income statement; that is, current income tax expense or benefit reflects the income tax effect of current transactions **and** the revision of previously provided income tax effects for transactions which have yet to reverse.

It might have been argued that the change in the deferred income tax balances should be recognized when first anticipated (e.g., when income tax rate changes are proposed in Congress). However, FASB concluded that it would be more meaningful to report the effects of such changes in the period when the proposed changes in the income tax law have been enacted into law. Enactment is defined by the various taxing jurisdictions; thus for example, federal laws are enacted when the president signs the legislation into law or congress overrides a presidential veto.

This provides a more reliable measure of the impact of such changes and is more consistent with the informational needs of financial statement users.

When income tax rates are revised, this may impact not only the unreversed effects of items which were originally reported in the continuing operations section of the income statement, but also the unreversed effects of items first presented as discontinued operations, extraordinary items, or in other income statement captions. Furthermore, the impact of changes in income tax rates on the accumulated balance of deferred income tax assets or liabilities that arose through charges or credits to other comprehensive income (under FAS 130) is included in income tax expense associated with continuing operations.

For example, if an entity has unrealized gains on holding available-for-sale securities at a time when relevant income tax rates (presumably, the capital gains rates) are lowered, the reduction in the deferred income tax liability associated with these unrealized gains will reduce current period income tax expense associated with continuing operations, despite the fact that the income tax provision was originally reported in other comprehensive income (not net income) and in the equity section of the balance sheet as accumulated other comprehensive income.

When income tax law changes occur during an interim reporting period, the effects are to be reported in the interim period in which enactment occurs. The effects of the changes are included in continuing operations, whatever the source of the temporary differences being impacted. For example, if in the first fiscal quarter of a year an entity accrued a loss relating to discontinued operations, which is not tax deductible until realized, the income tax effect would be shown in the discontinued operations section of the income statement for that quarter. If income tax rates are changed in the third quarter of the same year, the deferred income tax asset recognized in connection with the loss from discontinued operations would then need to be adjusted upward or downward, based on the difference between the newly enacted income tax rates and the previously effective income tax rates. The income statement effect of this adjustment is included with income tax expense pertaining to income from continuing operations in the third quarter.

Computation of a deferred income tax asset with a change in rates

Assume Campione Company has $80,000 of future deductible temporary differences at the end of 2005, which are expected to result in income tax deductions of approximately $40,000 each on tax returns for 2006-2007. Enacted tax rates were 50% for years 2002-2005, and are 40% for 2006 and thereafter.

The deferred income tax asset is computed at 12/31/05 under each of the following independent assumptions:

1. If Campione Company expects to offset the future deductible temporary differences against taxable income in years 2006-2007, the deferred income tax asset is $32,000 ($80,000 x 40%).
2. If Campione Company expects to realize an income tax benefit for the future deductible temporary differences by carrying back a loss to pre-2006 tax years to obtain a refund of income taxes previously paid at the higher 50% rate, the deferred income tax asset is $40,000 ($80,000 x 50%).

Assume that Campione Company expects, at the end of 2005, to realize a deferred income tax asset of $32,000 (the first scenario above). Also assume that income taxes payable in **each** of the years 2002-2004 were $8,000 (or 50% of taxable income of $16,000 in each year). Realization of $24,000 (3 years x $8,000 per year) of the $32,000 deferred income tax asset is assured through carryback refunds even if no taxable income is earned in years 2006-2007. Whether a valuation allowance for the remaining $8,000 is needed depends on Campione Company's assessment of the levels of future taxable income.

The foregoing estimate of the **certain** tax benefit, based on a loss carryback to periods of higher tax rates than are statutorily in effect for future periods, should only be utilized when future losses (for income tax purposes) are expected. This restriction applies since the benefit thus recognized (net of any valuation allowance) exceeds benefits that would be available in future periods, when tax rates will be lower.

Reporting the Effect of Changes in an Entity's Income Tax Status

The reporting of changes in an entity's income tax status is entirely analogous to the reporting of newly enacted income tax rate changes. Such adjustments typically arise from a change from (or to) taxable status to (or from) "flow through" or nontaxable status. When a previously taxable C corporation elects to become a flow-through entity (an S corporation), the stockholders become personally liable for income taxes on the company's earnings. This liability occurs whether the earnings are distributed to them or not, similar to the taxation of partnerships and limited liability companies.

When the income tax status change becomes effective, the effect of any consequent adjustments to deferred income tax assets and liabilities is reported in current income tax expense. This is always included in the income tax provision relating to continuing operations.

Under FAS 109, deferred income taxes are to be eliminated by reversal through current period income tax expense. Thus, if an entity with a net deferred income tax liability elects S corporation status, it will report an income tax benefit in the continuing operations section of its current income statement.

Similarly, if an S corporation elects to convert to a C corporation, the effect is to assume a net income tax benefit or obligation for unreversed temporary differences existing at the date the change becomes effective. Accordingly, the financial statements for the period in which the change becomes effective will include the effects of the event in current income tax expense. For example, if the entity has unreversed future taxable temporary differences at the date its income tax status change became effective, it reports income tax expense for that period. Conversely, if it had unreversed future deductible temporary differences, a deferred income tax asset (subject to the effects of any valuation allowance necessitated by applying the more-likely-than-not criterion) would be recorded, with a corresponding credit to the current period's income tax expense or benefit in the income statement.

Any entity eliminating an existing deferred income tax asset or liability, or recording an initial deferred income tax asset or liability, must fully explain the nature of the events that transpired to cause this adjustment. This is disclosed in the notes to the financial statements for the reporting period.

S corporation elections may be made prospectively at any time during the year preceding the tax year in which the election is intended to be effective and retroactively up to the 16th day of the 3rd month of the tax year in which the election is intended to be effective. The Internal Revenue Service (IRS) normally informs the electing corporation of whether or not its election has been accepted within 60 days of filing. In practice, however, the IRS seldom denies a timely filed election and such elections are considered essentially automatic. Consequently, if a reporting entity files an election before the end of its current fiscal year to be effective at the start of the following year, it is logical that the income tax effects be reported in current year income. For example, an election by a C corporation to become an S corporation that is filed in December 2005, to be effective at the beginning of the company's next fiscal year, January 1, 2006, would give rise to the elimination of the deferred income tax assets and liabilities at the date of filing, the effect of which would be reported in the 2005 financial statements. No deferred income tax assets or liabilities would appear on the December 31, 2005 balance sheet, and income tax expense or benefit for 2005 would include the effects of the reversals of deferred income tax assets and liabilities that had been previously recognized.

There are two situations that could result in an S corporation continuing to recognize deferred income taxes. The first situation arises when the S corporation operates in one or more states that impose state income taxes on the S corporation in an amount that is material to the financial statements. In this situation, the S corporation should compute and recognize deferred state income tax assets and liabilities in the same manner that a C corporation recognizes them for federal income taxes.

The second situation is "built-in gains tax." Under current income tax law, a C corporation electing to become an S corporation may have built-in gains, which could result in a future corporate income tax liability, under defined circumstances. In such cases the reporting entity, even though it has become an S corporation, will continue to report a deferred income tax liability related to this built-in gain.

Reporting the Effect of Accounting Changes for Tax Purposes

Occasionally an entity will initiate or be required to adopt changes in accounting that affect income tax reporting, but which will not impact financial statement reporting. Examples from the recent past have included the change to the direct write-off method of bad debt recognition (mandated by a change in the income tax law, while the GAAP requirement to recognize an allowance for uncollectible accounts receivable continued in effect for financial reporting); and the adoption of uniform capitalization for valuing inventory for income tax purposes, while continuing to expense currently certain administrative costs not inventoriable under GAAP for financial reporting.

Generally, these mandated changes involve two distinct types of temporary differences. The first of these changes is the onetime, catch-up adjustment which either immediately or over a prescribed time period impacts the income tax basis of the asset or liability in question (net receivables or inventory, in the examples above), and which then reverses as these assets or liabilities are later realized or settled and are eliminated from the balance sheet. The second change is the ongoing differential in the amount of newly acquired assets or incurred liabilities recognized for income tax and financial reporting purposes; these differences also eventually reverse, when the inventory is ultimately depleted or the receivables are ultimately collected. This second type of change is the normal temporary difference that has already been discussed. It is the first type of change which differs from those previously discussed in this chapter, and which will now be explained.

As an example, consider that Blakey Corporation has, at December 31, 2005, gross receivables of $12,000,000 and an allowance for bad debts in the amount of $600,000. Also assume that expected future taxes will be at a 34% rate and that, effective January 1, 2006, the income tax law is revised to eliminate deductions for accrued bad debts, with existing allowances to be taken into income ratably over four years (a four-year spread). A balance sheet of Blakey Corporation prepared on January 1, 2005, would report a deferred income tax *benefit* in the amount of $204,000 (i.e., $600,000 x 34%, which is the income tax effect of future deductions taken when specific receivables are written off and bad debts are incurred for tax purposes); a current income tax liability of $51,000 (one-fourth of the tax obligation); and a noncurrent income tax liability of $153,000 (three-fourths of the tax obligation).

The deferred income tax benefit is *not* deemed to be identified with the contra asset allowance for doubtful accounts (if it were, it would all be reported as a current asset), but rather with the future specific bad debts expected to be incurred. Accordingly, the deferred income tax benefit is categorized as current and noncurrent according to Blakey Corporation's best estimate of the timing of those future bad debts (much or most of which will, in all likelihood, occur within one year).

Income Tax Effects of Dividends Paid on Shares Held by Employee Stock Ownership Plans (ESOP)

FAS 109 affects the accounting for certain ESOP transactions. Under SOP 93-6, dividends paid on **unallocated** shares are not considered to be dividends for financial reporting purposes. If used to pay down ESOP debt, these dividends are reported as reductions of debt or of accrued interest; if paid to plan participants, such dividends are reported as compensation cost. GAAP requires that the income tax benefits arising from dividends paid on unallocated shares be consistent with the reporting of those dividends. Thus, if the dividends were included in compensation cost, the tax benefit would be included in the income tax provision associated with continuing operations.

Dividends paid on **allocated** shares are treated as normal dividends for financial reporting purposes. However, per SOP 93-6, any income tax benefits resulting from these dividend payments are also to be credited to income tax expense reported in continuing operations. In FASB's view, income tax deductible dividends for **other than unallocated** ESOP-held shares represent an exemption from income tax of an equivalent amount of the payor's earnings. For that reason, it concluded that the income tax effects be reported in continuing operations.

FASB's decision regarding the presentation of the income tax effects of ESOP and other stock compensation plans are fully analogous. Given that both types of plans sometimes result in income tax deductions for amounts not recognized as compensation expense under GAAP, it was determined that the resulting income tax benefits be accounted for consistently.

Accounting for Income Taxes: Business Combinations

Accounting for the income tax effects of business combinations reported as purchases under FAS 141 is one of the more complex aspects of interperiod income tax accounting. The principal complexity relates to the recognition, at the date of the purchase, of the deferred income tax effects of the differences between the income tax and financial reporting bases of the assets and liabilities acquired. Further difficulties arise in connection with the recognition of goodwill and of negative goodwill. In some instances, the reporting entity expects that the ultimate income tax allocation will differ from the initial one (such as when the taxpayer anticipates disallowance by the tax authorities of an allocation made to identifiable intangibles), and this creates yet another complex accounting matter to be dealt with.

Under prior GAAP, a "net of tax" method of valuation of acquired assets and liabilities was prescribed, which effectively assigned the income tax effects of differing income tax and GAAP bases to the corresponding assets and liabilities. Under FAS 109, however, purchase price is allocated on a "gross of tax effects" basis, with separate recognition of the deferred income tax assets and obligations.

Purchase business combinations can be either taxable or nontaxable in nature. In a taxable business combination, the total purchase price is allocated to assets and liabilities for both income tax and financial reporting purposes, although under some circumstances these allocations may differ. In a nontaxable business combination, the predecessor entity's income tax bases for the various assets and liabilities are carried forward, while for financial reporting the purchase price is allocated to the assets and liabilities acquired. Thus, in most cases, there will be some significant differences between the income tax and financial reporting bases. Accordingly, both taxable and nontaxable purchase business combinations can involve the application of deferred income tax accounting.

Accounting for Purchase Business Combinations at Acquisition Date

FAS 109 requires that the income tax effects of the income tax and GAAP basis differences of all assets and liabilities generally be presented as deferred income tax assets and liabilities as of the acquisition date. In general, this "grossing up" of the balance sheet is a straightforward matter. An example, in the context of a nontaxable purchase business combination, follows:

Facts:
1. The income tax rate is a flat 34%.
2. The acquisition of a business is effected at a cost of $500,000.
3. The fair values of assets acquired total $750,000.
4. The carryforward income tax bases of assets acquired total $600,000.
5. The fair and carryforward income tax bases of the liabilities assumed in the purchase are $250,000.

6. The difference between the income tax basis and fair values of the assets acquired, \$150,000, consists of future taxable temporary differences of \$200,000 and future deductible temporary differences of \$50,000.
7. There is no doubt as to the realizability of the future deductible temporary differences in this case.

Based on these facts, the GAAP allocation of the purchase price is as follows:

Gross purchase price	\$500,000
Allocation to identifiable assets and (liabilities):	
Assets, other than goodwill and deferred income tax asset	750,000
Deferred income tax asset (34% x \$50,000)	17,000
Liabilities, other than deferred income tax obligations	(250,000)
Deferred income tax liability (34% x \$200,000)	(68,000)
Net of the above allocations	449,000
Allocation to goodwill	\$ 51,000

Although goodwill will be amortized for income tax purposes but not for financial reporting and thus could create a future taxable temporary difference, it is not "grossed up" in the balance sheet for two reasons. First, at the date on which the business combination is consummated, the income tax and financial reporting bases of goodwill are generally the same, since income tax amortization has not yet begun. Second, recognition of deferred income taxes in connection with goodwill would have the effect of increasing the gross amount of goodwill that would be reported in the financial statements in most cases, and this is not generally seen as being a desirable outcome.

Goodwill and negative goodwill. Goodwill arises when a portion of the price paid in a business combination accounted for as a purchase cannot be allocated to identifiable assets, including intangibles. This excess cost is deemed to relate to the unidentifiable intangible asset, known as goodwill, that connotes the acquired entity's excess earning power. Historically, goodwill has been subject to mandatory amortization for purposes of GAAP financial reporting, and until 1993 such amortization was not deductible for income tax purposes. The 1993 income tax law change provided that goodwill would be income tax-deductible, with a mandatory fifteen-year amortization period. In 2001, the FASB promulgated new business combinations and goodwill accounting requirements (FAS 141 and 142), mandating that goodwill no longer be amortized for financial reporting purposes, but rather be subject to periodic impairment testing. (See Chapters 9 and 11 for complete discussions.) Thus, the relationship of GAAP and income tax accounting for goodwill has varied considerably over the years.

Prior to the 1993 income tax law change, goodwill was generally considered to embody a permanent difference, rather than a temporary difference, since recovery would come, if at all, only upon sale or dissolution of the entity as a whole. Accordingly, deferred income tax was not provided.

When goodwill became statutorily amortizable over fifteen years, the income tax/GAAP difference was deemed to be a temporary difference (unless being amortized for financial reporting purposes over the same fifteen-year life used for income tax purposes), with deferred income tax effects to be recognized for financial reporting under GAAP.

Under FAS 141 and 142, the pre-1993 situation has effectively been reversed. Goodwill is now deductible for income tax purposes but no longer amortizable for GAAP basis financial reporting. Goodwill may be charged to expense on a sporadic basis, however, since it must be regularly tested for impairment and to the extent impaired it must be written down or off immediately.

Since, per FAS 109, temporary differences are those arising from differences between the income tax and financial reporting bases of assets and liabilities, it is clear that deferred income tax effects should be measured and reported for goodwill. In general, deductible income tax amortization of goodwill will create a deferred income tax liability in the financial statements, analogous to that arising from the use of accelerated income tax depreciation. If GAAP goodwill is subsequently reduced to reflect an impairment, a portion of the deferred income tax liability will be reversed. Some part of the deferred income tax liability will remain on the balance sheet until the goodwill is ultimately eliminated either through full impairment or when the reporting unit is disposed of or ceases operations.

In some purchase business combination situations, "negative goodwill" results from what are often referred to as bargain purchases. These are situations in which the fair value of the net identifiable assets acquired exceeds the purchase price. Under FAS 141 and 142, this excess is first allocated on a pro rata basis to all acquired assets other than cash and cash equivalents, trade receivables, inventory, financial instruments that are required to be carried on the balance sheet at fair value, assets to be disposed of by sale, and deferred income tax assets. This will tend to affect the carrying value of long-lived, mostly depreciable, assets, which will reduce future depreciation charges over the respective lives of those assets. Any excess negative goodwill would then be immediately recognized as an extraordinary gain, as distinct from the earlier requirement that this negative goodwill be amortized over up to forty years.

For income tax purposes, negative goodwill is handled in a manner similar to that under GAAP—the cost bases of nonmonetary long-lived assets are proportionally reduced, and any excess is immediately taxable. Thus, a temporary difference will probably no longer arise from the accounting treatment applied to negative goodwill for income tax and GAAP purposes. In the past, temporary differences arose from the differential treatments (immediate taxability versus amortization for financial reporting), creating deferred income tax assets in many instances.

The accounting for a taxable purchase business combination is similar to that for a nontaxable one. However, unlike the previous example, in which there were numerous assets with different income tax and financial reporting bases, there are likely to be only a few differences in the case of taxable purchases. Previously, because goodwill was not deductible, attempts were often made by the purchaser to allocate, for income tax purposes, excess purchase cost to other intangibles, such as covenants not to compete. Since the 1993 income tax act makes all such intangibles including goodwill amortizable over fifteen years, this motive should no longer be encountered. Accordingly, income tax/GAAP differences in taxable business combinations are likely to be less common.

Accounting for Purchase Business Combinations after the Acquisition

One of the attributes which distinguishes FAS 109 from its predecessors is that net deferred income tax benefits are now fully recognized, subject to the possible need for a valuation allowance. This requirement has a major impact on the accounting for business combinations.

In the example presented above, it was stated that all future deductible temporary differences were assumed to be fully realizable, and therefore the deferred income tax benefits associated with those temporary differences were recorded as of the acquisition date, with no need for an offsetting valuation allowance. However, in other situations, there may be substantial doubt concerning realizability (i.e., it may be considered more likely than not that the future benefits are unrealizable) and accordingly a valuation allowance would be recognized at the date of the purchase business combination. In such an instance, the allocation of the purchase price would reflect this fact, which would result in the allocation of a greater share of the purchase cost to goodwill than would otherwise be the case. Under current GAAP goodwill cannot be amortized for financial reporting purposes, and the difference in accounting for goodwill under GAAP and income tax reporting rules will add to the deferred income tax implications of the business combination.

If, at a date subsequent to the business combination transaction, it is determined that the valuation account be reduced or eliminated, FAS 109 stipulates that the effect of this reduction is applied first to eliminate any goodwill recorded in connection with that business combination. Once goodwill has been reduced to zero, the excess is applied to eliminate any noncurrent identifiable intangible assets acquired in that business combination, and any further excess is reflected in the current period income tax expense or benefit. Thus, in this situation the general rule that changes in the allowance are mated to debits or credits in current period income tax expense from continuing operations is not followed.

Subsequent realization of a deferred income tax asset in a purchase business combination

Assume that Michael Company (acquirer) acquired Reba Enterprises (acquiree) on January 1, 2005, for $2,000,000. There was no goodwill in the transaction. The income tax basis of the net assets is $6,000,000 (i.e., future deductible temporary differences equal $4,000,000).

Income tax and GAAP bases at acquisition date, 1/1/05

	Income tax basis	*GAAP basis*
Assets	$6,000,000	$6,000,000
Accrued warranty costs	--	(4,000,000)
Basis, net	$6,000,000	$2,000,000

The $4,000,000 of accrued warranty costs (which is not deductible for income tax purposes until actually paid) is expected to reverse as follows: 2005—$1,500,000; 2006—$1,000,000; After 2006—$1,500,000.

The income tax rate is 34% and the law restricts use of the acquiree's deductible temporary differences and carryforwards to its own future taxable income. The acquiree has incurred tax losses in the past three years and 2005 is also expected to result in a tax loss. Thus, Michael Company concludes that a valuation allowance for the full amount of the deferred income tax asset is required. However, at the end of 2006, Michael Company, due to improved results, decides that a valuation allowance is no longer necessary.

At the date of acquisition the deferred income tax asset is recorded at $1,360,000 ($4,000,000 x 34%) but with a corresponding valuation allowance for the same amount. At the end of 2005, the deferred income tax asset is $850,000 computed as 34% of $2,500,000 ($4,000,000 original warranty liability – $1,500,000 reversal in 2005), again with a corresponding valuation allowance. At the end of 2006, the deferred income tax asset is $510,000 computed as 34% of $1,500,000 ($4,000,000 original warranty liability – the 2005 reversal of $1,500,000 and the 2006 reversal of $1,000,000). At the end of 2006, when management determines that a valuation allowance is no longer necessary, elimination of the valuation allowance results in a deferred income tax benefit or in a reduction of deferred income tax expense. (Note that had goodwill arisen in the acquisition, the income tax benefit would have first been applied to reduce goodwill to zero and then to reduce acquired noncurrent intangible assets to zero.)

The foregoing facts are summarized as follows:

	Future deductible temporary difference	*Deferred income tax asset*	*Valuation allowance*	*Deferred income tax expense (benefit)*
At acquisition	$4,000,000	$1,360,000	$1,360,000	$ --
12/31/2005	2,500,000	850,000	850,000	--
12/31/2006	1,500,000	510,000	--	(510,000)

Thus, the journal entries related to deferred income taxes are

At 1-1-05 (date of acquisition)

Assets acquired	6,000,000	
Deferred income tax asset	1,360,000	
Accrued warranty costs		4,000,000
Cash		2,000,000
Valuation allowance		1,360,000

At 12-31-05		
Valuation allowancc	510,000	
Deferred income tax asset		510,000
At 12-31-06		
Valuation allowance	850,000	
Deferred income tax asset		340,000
Income tax benefit—deferred		510,000

Under FAS 109, the income tax benefits of net operating losses are not distinguished from those arising from future deductible temporary differences. Accordingly, the treatments set forth above hold here as well. If the benefits are recognized for the first time at a date after the acquisition (by reducing or eliminating the valuation allowance), then goodwill arising from the business combination is eliminated, other purchased noncurrent intangibles are reduced to zero, and current income tax expense is reduced. Negative goodwill is neither created nor increased in such circumstances, however.

Precisely the same approach is employed in connection with income tax credit carryforwards which may have existed at the date of the business combination, but which may not have been recognized due to doubtful realizability. While previously the treatments accorded net operating losses and income tax credit carryforwards were dissimilar, under FAS 109 they are identical. Under prior GAAP, recognition of benefits for net operating loss carryforwards was possible under limited circumstances, while recognition of income tax credit carryforwards was strictly prohibited.

In some instances, entities having unrecognized income tax benefits of net operating losses or income tax credits arising in connection with a purchase business combination may generate other similar income tax benefits after the date of the acquisition. A question in such a circumstance relates to whether a "FIFO" convention should be adopted to guide the recognition of these benefits. While in some instances income tax law may determine the order in which the benefits are actually realized, in other cases the law may not do so. FAS 109 provides that in those latter situations, the benefits realized are to be apportioned, for financial reporting purposes, between pre- and postacquisition income tax benefits. The former are accounted for as above, and the latter reported as reductions of current period income tax expense, consistent with the general rules of FAS 109.

Poolings of Interests

Pooling of interests accounting is prohibited by FAS 141 for business combinations initiated after June 30, 2001. FAS 141 was not retroactive, however, so that reporting entities that had previously recorded poolings were not required to restate those transactions and, consequently, poolings still exist in the financial statements of some companies. In poolings of interests, the combining entities generally do not adjust carrying values of assets and liabilities. Reissued or comparative financial statements of periods before the effective date of the combination are restated on a combined basis. However, notwithstanding the general principle of not revising asset or liability carrying amounts, a special rule applies to deferred income tax benefits for which a full or partial valuation allowance had been recognized under the more-likely-than-not criterion of FAS 109.

The standard stipulates that, if one of the combining entities had an unrecognized net deferred income tax benefit (i.e., there was a deferred income tax benefit recognized, gross, which was offset by a valuation allowance), the restated financial statements may or may not reflect the net income tax benefits as an asset. That is, the valuation allowance **may** be eliminated on a retroactive basis. This treatment depends upon whether the combined entity will be able, under provisions of the income tax laws, to utilize the net operating loss and tax credit carryforwards of the merged companies. If it can do so, then the deferred income tax benefits are recognized in any restated prior period financial statements. If, under the law, the benefits cannot be utilized in a consolidated income tax return or if a consolidated return is not expected to be filed, then the income tax benefits would not be recognized in financial statements restated for the pooling of interests.

Thus, upon recording the pooling, the need for a valuation allowance was subject to a revised analysis, but only the ability to utilize the income tax benefits in a consolidated return was to be considered; other changes in circumstances were handled as described earlier in this chapter (by adjusting the allowance through current period income tax expense or benefit). This is strictly consistent with the concept of a pooling of interests, in which financial statements are presented for current and prior periods as if the entities had always been combined; had they been combined and had the income tax benefits been available for use in a consolidated return, the valuation allowance would never have been provided.

Under some circumstances, poolings of interests were taxable, meaning that for income tax purposes there was an increase in the income tax basis (referred to as a "step-up") of the net assets of one of the merged entities. The differences between the new, stepped-up income tax bases and the carryforward GAAP bases (net book values) utilized for financial reporting purposes are future deductible temporary differences giving rise to deferred income tax assets. Whether these assets are recognized is dependent upon whether the more-likely-than-not criterion is met. If the test is not met, a valuation allowance must be established for some or all of the gross benefits recorded. If a valuation allowance is established, and it is later reduced or eliminated when the likelihood of ultimate realization exceeds the 50% probability threshold, the effect of eliminating the valuation allowance will be reflected in income tax expense or benefit for the current period.

Tax Allocation for Business Investments

As noted in Chapter 10, there are two basic methods for accounting for investments in the common stock of other corporations: (1) the fair value method as set forth in FAS 115, and (2) the equity method, as prescribed by APB 18. The cost method, previously employed for intercorporate investments lacking the attribute of "significant influence" by the investor, is no longer appropriate, except for the exceedingly rare situation when fair value information is absolutely unavailable. If the cost method is used, however, there will be no deferred income tax consequence, since this conforms to the method prescribed for income tax reporting.

The fair value method is used in instances where the investor is not considered to have significant influence over the investee. The ownership threshold generally used to denote significant influence is 20% of ownership; this level of ownership is not considered an absolute (FIN 35), but it will be used to identify the break between application of the fair value and equity methods in the illustrations which follow. In practice, the 20% ownership interest defines the point at which there is a rebuttable presumption that the investor has significant influence, and it is often noted that publicly held companies will establish investment ownership percentages very slightly over or under 20%, presumably to support their desires and decisions to use, or not use, the equity method of accounting for those investments.

Under both the cost and fair value methods, ordinary income is recognized as dividends received by the investor, and capital gains (losses) are recognized upon the disposal of the investment. For income tax purposes, no provision is made during the holding period for the allocable undistributed earnings of the investee. There is no deferred income tax computation necessary when using the cost method because there is no temporary difference. Tax allocation issues pertaining to the use of the fair value method are discussed in Chapter 10.

The equity method is generally required whenever an investor owns 20% or more of an investee or has significant influence over the investee's operations with a lower ownership percentage. Under the equity method, the investment is recorded at cost and subsequently increased by the allocable portion of the investee's net income. The investor's share of the investee's net income is then included in the investor's pretax accounting income. Dividend payments are not included in pretax accounting income but instead are considered to be a reduction in the carrying amount of the investment. For income tax purposes, however, dividends received are the only revenue realized by the investor. As a result, the investor must recognize deferred income tax expense on the undistributed net income of the investee that will be taxed in the future. The current effective GAAP in this area consists of APB 23 and FAS 109, which superseded APB 24 but continues the principles that were set forth therein. These standards are discussed below.

GAAP distinguishes between an investee and a subsidiary and prescribes different accounting treatments for each. An investee is considered to be a corporation whose stock is owned by an investor that holds between 20% and 50% of the outstanding stock. An investee situation occurs when the investor has significant influence but not control over the corporation invested in. A subsidiary, on the other hand, exists when more than 50% of the stock of a corporation is owned by another. This results in a presumption that the investor has direct control over the corporation invested in. APB 23, as amended by FAS 109, governs accounting for the income tax effects of owning subsidiaries.

Undistributed earnings of a subsidiary. These accounting requirements are set forth in APB 23, as amended by FAS 109. While the timing of distribution of a subsidiary's net income to its parent may be uncertain, it will eventually occur, whether by means of dividends, or via the disposal of the entity and realization of capital gains. Accordingly, deferred income taxes must be provided, but the amount will be dependent upon the anticipated means of realization, which of course may change over time.

Before FAS 109, an "indefinite reversal" provision in APB 23 permitted reporting entities to avoid recognizing deferred income tax liabilities associated with undistributed subsidiary net income if there was sufficient evidence available to demonstrate that the subsidiary would invest the undistributed net income indefinitely or that distribution was intended to occur in a tax-free liquidation. Under such circumstances, deferred income tax accrual was unnecessary, but expanded disclosures were required.

FAS 109 deleted this provision from APB 23 because, while management controls the timing and circumstances of the distribution of the net income of subsidiaries for income tax purposes, ultimate recognition is a certainty. The same logic also applies to the recognition of deferred income tax assets. The formerly accepted concept of "indefinite reversal" has thus been debunked. However, FAS 109 effectively "grandfathered" certain existing temporary differences for which deferred income taxes were not to be provided, including undistributed net income of domestic subsidiaries or corporate joint ventures if the differences are essentially permanent in nature and arose in fiscal years beginning on or prior to December 15, 1992. The provisions of FAS 109 were to be applied prospectively, without exception, with no need for adjustment for temporary differences arising from ownership of subsidiaries prior to the effective date of that standard.

The magnitude of the income tax effects to be provided depends upon specific application of the income tax laws and management intent. If the law provides a mechanism under which the parent can recover its investment tax-free, deferred income taxes would not be provided. For example, under §332 of the Internal Revenue Code (IRC), a parent corporation can liquidate an 80%-or-more-owned subsidiary without recognizing gain or loss for income tax purposes. Also, under IRC §368, a parent can effect a statutory merger or consolidation with its 80%-or-more-owned subsidiary, under which no taxable gain or loss would be recognized.

In other cases, the minimization or avoidance of income taxes can be achieved only if the parent company owns a stipulated share of the subsidiary's stock. A parent owning less than this threshold level of its subsidiary may express its intent to utilize a tax planning strategy to acquire the necessary additional shares to realize this benefit. In evaluating this strategy, the cost of acquiring the additional shares must be considered, and the benefits to be recognized (i.e., a reduced deferred income tax liability) must be offset by the cost of implementing the strategy as discussed earlier in this chapter.

Undistributed earnings of an investee. When an entity has an equity method investee, it is presumed to be able to exercise significant influencc, but lack control. Because the ability to indefinitely postpone income taxes on the investee's net income would be absent in such a case, in contrast to the parent-subsidiary situation above, GAAP requires full interperiod income tax allocation for the effects of undistributed investee net income. The facts and circumstances involved in each situation, however, will be the final determinant of whether this temporary difference is assumed to be a future dividend or a capital gain for purposes of computing the deferred income tax effect.

Example of income tax effects from investee company

To illustrate the application of these concepts, assume Parent Company owns 30% of the outstanding common stock of Investee Company and 70% of the outstanding common stock of Subsidiary company. Additional data for Subsidiary and Investee companies for the year 2005 are as follows:

	Investee Company	*Subsidiary Company*
Net income	$50,000	$100,000
Dividends paid	20,000	60,000

The following sections illustrate how the foregoing data are used to recognize the income tax effects of the stated events.

The pretax accounting income of Parent Company will include its equity in Investee Company net income equal to $15,000 ($50,000 x 30%). Parent's taxable income, on the other hand, will include dividend income of $6,000 ($20,000 x 30%), reduced by a deduction of 80% of the $6,000, or $4,800. This 80% dividends received deduction is a permanent difference between pretax accounting income and taxable income and is allowed for dividends received from domestic corporations in which the taxpaying corporation's ownership is less than 80% but at least 20%. A lower dividends received deduction of 70% is permitted when the ownership is less than 20%, and a 100% deduction is provided for dividends received from domestic corporations in which the ownership is 80% to 100%.

In this example, a temporary difference results from Parent's equity ($9,000) in Investee's undistributed income of $30,000 (= $50,000 net income less $20,000 dividends). The amount of the deferred income tax credit in 2005 depends upon the expectations of Parent Company regarding the manner in which the $9,000 of undistributed income will be realized. If the expectation of receipt is via dividends, then the temporary difference is 20% (the net taxable portion, after the dividends received deduction) of $9,000, or $1,800, and the deferred income tax liability associated with this temporary difference in 2005 is the expected effective income tax rate times $1,800. However, if the expectation is that receipt will be through future sale of the investment, then the temporary difference is the full $9,000 and the deferred income tax liability is the current corporate capital gains rate times the $9,000.

The entries below illustrate these alternatives. An assumed tax rate of 34% is used for ordinary income, while a rate of 20% is used for capital gains. It is also assumed that there are no pre-2005 temporary differences to consider. Note that the amounts in the entries below relate only to Investee Company's incremental impact upon Parent Company's income tax assets and liabilities.

	Expectations for undistributed income			
	Dividends		Capital gains	
Income tax expense	1,020		2,208	
Deferred income tax liability		612[b]		1,800[c]
Income taxes payable		408[a]		408[a]

[a]Computation of income taxes payable:

Dividend income—30% x ($20,000)	$6,000
Less 80% dividends received deduction	(4,800)
Amount included in Parent's taxable income	$1,200
Tax liability—34% x ($1,200)	$ 408

[b]Computation of deferred income tax liability (dividend assumption):

Temporary difference:	
Parent's share of undistributed income—30% x ($50,000 – $20,000 = $30,000)	$9,000
Less 80% dividends received deduction	(7,200)
Temporary difference	$1,800
Deferred income tax liability—34% x ($1,800)	$ 612

[c]Computation of deferred income tax liability (capital gain assumption):

Temporary difference:	
Parent's share of undistributed income—same as above	$9,000
Deferred income tax liability—20% x ($9,000)	$1,800

Example of income tax effects from subsidiary company

The pretax accounting income of Parent Company will also include equity in Subsidiary income of $70,000 (70% x $100,000). This $70,000 will be included in consolidated pretax income in the Parent's consolidated financial statements. For income tax purposes, Parent and Subsidiary cannot file a consolidated income tax return because the minimum level of control (i.e., 80%) is not present. Consequently, the taxable income of Parent will include dividend income of $42,000 (70% x $60,000), and there will be an 80% dividends received deduction of $33,600. The temporary difference discussed in APB 23 results from Parent's 70% equity ($28,000) in the Subsidiary's undistributed earnings of $40,000. The amount of the deferred income tax liability in 2005 depends upon the expectations of Parent Company as to the manner in which this $28,000 of undistributed income will be received. The same expectations can exist as previously discussed, for Parent's equity in Investee's undistributed earnings (i.e., through future dividend distributions or capital gains).

The entries below illustrate these alternatives. A marginal tax rate of 34% is assumed for dividend income, and a rate of 20% applies to capital gains. It is also assumed that there are no pre-2005 temporary differences to consider. The amounts in the entries below relate only to Subsidiary Company's incremental impact upon Parent Company's income tax assets and liabilities.

	Expectations for undistributed income			
	Dividends		Capital gains	
Income tax expense	4,760		8,456	
Deferred income tax liability		1,904[b]		5,600[c]
Income taxes payable		2,856[a]		2,856[a]

[a]Computation of income taxes payable:

Dividend income—70% x ($60,000)	$42,000
Less 80% dividends received deduction	(33,600)
Amount included in Parent's taxable income	$ 8,400
Tax liability—34% x ($8,400)	$ 2,856

[b]Computation of deferred income tax liability (dividend assumption):

Temporary difference:	
Parent's share of undistributed income—70% x ($40,000)	$28,000
Less 80% dividends received deduction	(22,400)
	$ 5,600
Deferred income tax liability—34% x ($5,600)	$ 1,904

[c]Computation of deferred income tax liability (capital gain assumption):

Temporary difference:	
Parent's share of undistributed income—70% x ($40,000)	$28,000
Deferred income tax liability—20% x ($28,000)	$ 5,600

If a parent company owns 80% or more of the voting stock of a subsidiary and the parent consolidates the subsidiary for both financial reporting and income tax purposes, then no temporary differences exist between consolidated pretax income and taxable income. If, in the circumstances noted above, consolidated financial statements are prepared but a consolidated income tax return is not, IRC §243 allows the Parent to take a 100% dividends received deduction. Accordingly, the temporary difference between consolidated pretax income and taxable income is zero if the parent assumes the undistributed income will be realized in dividends.

Summary of Temporary Differences of Investees and Subsidiaries

Level of Ownership Interest

0%	<20%	50%	>80%	100%
Accounting				
Income recognition	Fair value method	Equity Method		
Deferred income tax on undistributed earnings	No temporary difference	Temporary difference		No temporary difference
Income tax				
Dividends recognized	30% of dividends received (70% deduction)	20% of dividends received (80% deduction)		None (100% deduction)

Accounting for Income Taxes: Intraperiod Tax Allocation

FAS 109 predominantly deals with the requirements of **inter**period income tax allocation (i.e., deferred income tax accounting), but its scope also includes **intra**period income tax allocation. This relates to the matching of various categories of comprehensive income or expense (continuing operations, extraordinary items, corrections of errors, prior period adjustments, etc.) with the income tax effects of those items, as presented in the income (or other financial) statement. The general principle is that the income statement presentation of the effects of income taxes should be the same as items to which the income taxes relate; and in this regard, FAS 109 did not change prior practice. A "with and without" approach is prescribed as the mechanism by which the marginal, or incremental income tax effects of items other than those arising from continuing operations are to be measured. However, under FAS 109 there are some significant departures from past practice, as described in the following paragraphs.

Under prior GAAP, the "with and without" technique was applied in a step-by-step fashion proceeding down the face of the income statement. For example, an entity having continuing operations, discontinued operations, and extraordinary items would calculate income tax expense as follows: (1) Income tax would be computed separately for the aggregate results and for continuing operations. The difference between the two amounts would be allocated to the total of discontinued operations and extraordinary items. (2) Income tax expense would be computed on discontinued operations. The residual amount (i.e., the difference between income tax on discontinued operations and the income tax on the total of discontinued operations and extraordinary items) would then be allocated to extraordinary items. Thus, under the provisions of APB 11, the amount of income tax expense allocated to any given classification in the statement of income (and the other financial statements, if relevant) was partially a function of the location in which the item was traditionally presented in the income and retained earnings statements.

FAS 109 adopted an incremental calculation of income tax expense to be allocated to classifications other than continuing operations. However, rather than applying successive allocations on the "with and without" basis to determine income tax expense or benefit applicable to each succeeding income statement caption, the income tax effects of all items **other** than continuing operations are allocated pro rata. That is, once income tax expense or benefit allocable to continuing operations is determined, the residual income tax expense or benefit is apportioned to all the other classifications (discontinued operations, et al.) in the ratios that those other items bear, on a pretax basis, to the total of all such items. Furthermore, income tax expense or benefit on income from continuing operations includes not only income taxes on the income earned from continuing operations, as expected, but also the following items:

1. The impact of changes in income tax laws and rates, which includes the effects of such changes on items which were previously reflected directly in stockholders' equity (accumulated other comprehensive income), as described more fully below
2. The impact of changes in the entity's taxable status
3. Changes in estimates about whether the income tax benefits of future deductible temporary differences or net operating loss or tax credit carryforwards are more likely than not to be realizable (i.e., an adjustment to the valuation allowance for such items)
4. The income tax effects of tax-deductible dividends paid to stockholders, as discussed elsewhere in this chapter

Under FAS 109, stockholders' equity is charged or credited directly with the initial income tax effects of items that are reported in stockholders' equity without being presented on the income statement. These items include the following:

1. Corrections of the effects of accounting errors of previous periods
2. Gains and losses which are defined under GAAP as being part of comprehensive income but are not reported in the income statement, such as foreign currency translation adjustments under FAS 52, and the fair value adjustments applicable to available-for-sale portfolios of debt and marketable equity securities held as investments. As a result of amendments to FAS 109 made by FAS 130, *Reporting Comprehensive Income*, the income tax effects of these types of items will be reported in the same financial statement where other comprehensive income items are reported. As discussed more fully in Chapter 3, these items may be reported either in a standalone statement of comprehensive income, a combined statement of income and other comprehensive income, or in an expanded version of the statement of changes in stockholders' equity.
3. Taxable or deductible increases or decreases in contributed capital, such as offering costs reported under GAAP as reductions of the proceeds of a capital stock offering, but which are either immediately deductible or amortizable for income tax purposes
4. Increases in the income tax bases of assets acquired in a taxable business combination accounted for as a pooling of interests under GAAP, if an income tax benefit is recognized at the date of the business combination (i.e., if the income tax effects of

existing future deductible temporary differences are not fully offset by a valuation allowance at that date)

5. Expenses incurred in connection with stock issued under provisions of compensatory stock option plans, which are recognized for income tax purposes but are reported for accounting purposes in stockholders' equity under the provisions of APB 25
6. Dividends paid on unallocated shares held in an ESOP, and that are charged against retained earnings
7. Deductible temporary differences and net operating loss and tax credit carryforwards that existed at the date of a quasi reorganization

The effects of income tax rate or other income tax law changes on items for which the income tax effects were originally reported directly in stockholders' equity are reported in continuing operations, if they occur in any period after the original event. For example, assume the reporting entity recognized a deferred income tax asset related to an employee stock option program amounting to $34,000 in 2005, based on the estimated future income tax deduction it would receive at the then-current and anticipated future income tax rate of 34%. If the statutory income tax rate is reduced to 25% in 2006 before the temporary difference reverses, the adjustment to the deferred income tax asset ($34,000 – $25,000 = $9,000) is reported in income tax expense or benefit applicable to income from continuing operations in 2006.

A comprehensive example of the intraperiod income tax allocation process prescribed under FAS 109 is presented below. (This example does not include items that will, under provisions of FAS 130, be reported in other comprehensive income; the accounting for those is illustrated in Chapter 3.) Assume there was $50,000 in future deductible temporary differences at 12/31/05; these differences remain unchanged during the current year, 2006.

	2006
Income from continuing operations	$400,000
Loss from discontinued operations	(120,000)
Extraordinary gain on involuntary conversion (taxable because no replacement property purchased)	60,000
Correction of error: understatement of depreciation in 2005	(20,000)
Income tax credits	5,000

Income tax rates are: 15% on the first $100,000 of taxable income; 20% on the next $100,000; 25% on the next $100,000; 30% thereafter.

Expected future effective income tax rates were 20% at December 31, 2005, but are judged to be 28% at December 31, 2006.

Retained earnings at December 31, 2005, totaled $650,000.

Intraperiod tax allocation proceeds as follows:

Step 1 — Income tax on total taxable income of $320,000 ($400,000 – $120,000 + $60,000 – $20,000) is **$61,000** computed as follows:

Taxable income	*Income tax rate*	*Income tax*	
$100,000	15%	$15,000	
100,000	20%	20,000	
100,000	25%	25,000	
20,000	30%	6,000	
$320,000		$66,000	Income tax before credits
		(5,000)	Tax credit
		$61,000	Income tax payable

Step 2 — Income tax on income from continuing operations of $400,000 is **$85,000**, net of tax credit computed as follows.

Taxable income	*Income tax rate*	*Income tax*	
$100,000	15%	$15,000	
100,000	20%	20,000	
100,000	25%	25,000	
100,000	30%	30,000	
$400,000		$90,000	Income tax before credits
		(5,000)	Tax credit
		$85,000	Income tax payable

Step 3 — The $24,000 difference is allocated pro rata to discontinued operations, extraordinary gain, and correction of the error in prior year depreciation as follows:

	Gross amount before tax	*Relative %*	*Allocation of difference*
Discontinued operations	$(120,000)	150%	$36,000
Extraordinary gain	60,000	(75%)	(18,000)
Error correction	(20,000)	25%	6,000
	$ (80,000)	100%	$24,000

Step 4 — The adjustment of the deferred income tax asset, amounting to a $4,000 increase due to an effective tax rate estimate change [$50,000 x (.28 – .20)] is allocated to continuing operations, regardless of the source of the temporary difference.

A summary combined statement of income and retained earnings for 2006 is presented below.

Income from continuing operations, before income taxes		$400,000
Income taxes on income from continuing operations:		
Current	$90,000	
Deferred	(4,000)	
Tax credits	(5,000)	81,000
Income from continuing operations, net		319,000
Loss from discontinued operations, net of income tax benefit of $36,000		(84,000)
Extraordinary gain, net of income tax of $18,000		42,000
Net income		277,000
Retained earnings, January 1, 2006 as originally reported		650,000
Correction of accounting error, net of tax effects of $6,000		(14,000)
Retained earnings, January 1, 2006, as restated		636,000
Retained earnings, December 31, 2006		$913,000

Classification of Deferred Income Taxes

A reporting entity that presents a classified balance sheet will classify its deferred income tax liabilities and assets as either current or noncurrent consistent with the classification of the related asset or liability. A deferred income tax asset or liability that is not related to an asset or liability for financial reporting purposes, such as the deferred income tax consequences related to a net operating loss carryforward or income tax credit carryforward, is classified based on the expected reversal or utilization date. These classifications must be made for each separate tax-paying component within each taxing jurisdiction.

Within each of the separate components, the current asset and liability are offset and presented as a single amount, with similar treatment for the noncurrent items. Understandably, offsetting is not permitted for different tax-paying components or for different tax jurisdictions. Thus, a balance sheet may present current and noncurrent deferred income tax assets, along with current and noncurrent deferred income tax liabilities, under certain circumstances.

If the enterprise has recorded a valuation allowance, it must prorate the allowance between current and noncurrent according to the relative size of the gross deferred income tax asset in each classification. The FASB mandated this approach to avoid the necessity of having to estimate which deferred income tax assets would not be recovered.

Balance Sheet Disclosures

A reporting entity is required to disclose the components of the net deferred income tax liability or asset recognized in the statement of financial position as follows:

1. Total of all deferred income tax liabilities
2. Total of all deferred income tax assets
3. Total valuation allowance
4. Net change in the valuation allowance for the year
5. Narrative description of the types of temporary differences and carryforwards that cause significant portions of deferred income tax assets and liabilities. Publicly held companies are required, in addition, to disclose the approximate income tax effect (not the separate tax effect for each tax jurisdiction) of each temporary difference and carryforward (gross, without consideration of any necessary valuation allowance).

When deferred income tax liabilities are not recognized because of the exceptions provided under APB 23 the following information is to be provided:

1. The types of temporary differences and the events that would cause those temporary differences to become taxable
2. The cumulative amount of each type of temporary difference
3. The amount of unrecognized deferred income tax liability for any undistributed foreign earnings, or a statement that such a determination is not practicable
4. The amount of unrecognized deferred income tax liability for other temporary differences that arose prior to the period for which application of this statement was first required for each of those particular differences

Income Statement Disclosures

FAS 109 places primary emphasis upon the income tax expense or benefit allocated to continuing operations. All significant components of income taxes associated with continuing operations are required to be disclosed for each year for which an income statement is presented. Examples of these components include but are not limited to

1. Current income tax expense or benefit
2. Deferred income tax expense or benefit (exclusive of the effects of other components listed below)
3. General business credits, investment tax credits, or other tax credits
4. Government grants (to the extent recognized as a reduction of income tax expense)
5. The benefits of net operating loss carryforwards
6. Income tax expense that results either from allocating certain income tax benefits directly to contributed capital or from allocating them to reduce goodwill or other noncurrent intangible assets of an acquired entity
7. Adjustments to the deferred income tax liability or asset for enacted changes in income tax laws or rates or a change in the tax status of the reporting entity
8. Adjustments to the beginning of year balance of the valuation allowance because of a change in circumstances that causes a change in judgment about the realizability of the related deferred income tax asset in future years

FAS 109 also requires disclosure of the following:

1. The amounts of income tax expense or benefit allocated to financial statement elements other than continuing operations (e.g., discontinued operations, extraordinary items, other comprehensive income, and retained earnings)

2. The amounts and expiration dates of net operating loss and tax credit carryforwards under the currently enacted tax law
3. The amount of the valuation allowance for which subsequently recognized income tax benefits will reduce goodwill or other noncurrent intangible assets of an acquired entity, or will be allocated to equity
4. A narrative description of the nature of significant reconciling items between income tax expense or benefit computed on pretax income from continuing operations by applying the statutory federal income tax rate and the actual amount of such expense or benefit reflected in the financial statements. For the purpose of this disclosure, the federal statutory rate is the regular marginal rate to which ordinary taxable income is subjected (currently 34%) without consideration of the effect of graduated rates, alternative minimum tax rates, or income taxes from other state, local or foreign taxing jurisdictions.
5. Public companies are additionally required to provide a reconciliation of the differences described in 4. above using either percentages or dollar amounts.

Other Disclosures

1. If there are significant matters that affect the comparability of information between periods presented that are not apparent to a financial statement user from the disclosures described above, the nature of such matters and their effect on the financial statements for the periods presented.
2. For each period for which an income statement is presented in the separately issued financial statements of a reporting entity that is a member of an affiliated group that files a consolidated income tax return
    a. The amounts of current and deferred income tax expense included in the statement of income.
    b. The amounts of any income tax-related balances due to or from other companies in the affiliated group at each balance sheet date.
    c. A description of the method used by members of the affiliated group to allocate the consolidated current and deferred income tax expense or benefit between them and the nature of any changes, during the years presented, in this method of allocation or the method of determining amounts due to or from affiliates as described in b. above.
3. Per EITF 00-15 (described later in this chapter), the income tax benefit realized during each period presented from employees' exercise of nonqualified employee stock options. This may be presented as a separate line item in the operating section of the statement of cash flows or in the statement of changes in stockholders' equity.
4. It has become generally accepted, although not explicitly required, to disclose the fact that a reporting entity is not subject to federal income taxes (and state income taxes, if applicable) because it is a flow-through entity (e.g., an S corporation, a limited liability company, or partnership). Public companies are required to disclose this fact as well as the net differences between the income tax bases and financial reporting bases of its assets and liabilities.

EMERGING ISSUES TASK FORCE ISSUES SUMMARIES

86-9 IRC Section 338 and Push-Down Accounting

The EITF addressed a number of issues concerning whether the use of a step-up in the income tax basis of an acquired entity, as permitted by the 1982 tax law, mandated the use of push-down accounting, and the necessary allocation of the income tax provision between parent and subsidiaries if a step-up was not elected. There was a consensus that push-down accounting is not required for non-SEC registrants. In addition, a consensus was reached that, if the acquiree continues to report its net assets on their historical basis, three alternative methods of allocating consolidated income tax expense or benefit are acceptable: (1) allocation to the acquiree on the preacquisition basis; (2) crediting the income tax benefit of basis step-up to the acquiree's stockholders' equity upon realization; and (3) crediting the income tax benefit to the income of the acquirer when realized as a permanent difference.

86-43 Effect of a Change in Tax Law or Rates on Leveraged Leases

When a change in the income tax law is enacted, all components of a leveraged lease must be recalculated from the inception of the lease based upon the revised after-tax cash flows resulting from the change. Differences from the original computation are included in income in the year in which the tax law changes are enacted. Later, EITF 87-8 stipulated that assumptions regarding the effect of the alternative minimum tax must be included in leveraged lease computations.

86-44 Effect of a Change in Tax Law on Investments in Safe Harbor Leases

This issue related to two Exposure Drafts released in 1981 and 1982 of a proposed FAS, concerning accounting for tax leases. A final FAS was never issued; however the guidance is still valid, since it stipulates how an investor would account for the lease investment under the alternative accounting methods proposed by the two Exposure Drafts.

88-4 Classification of Payment Made to IRS to Retain Fiscal Year

S corporations and partnerships are permitted to elect tax fiscal years other than a calendar year. If the election is made, however, the electing entity is required to make a payment to the Internal Revenue Service in an amount that approximates the income tax that the stockholders (or partners) would have paid on the income for the period between the fiscal year-end elected and the end of the calendar year. This payment, which is not a tax, is recomputed and adjusted annually and is fully refundable to the electing entity in the future upon liquidation, conversion to a calendar tax year-end or a decline in its taxable income to zero. A consensus was reached that this "required payment" be accounted for as an asset, analogous to a deposit.

93-12 Recognition and Measurement of the Tax Benefit of Excess Tax-Deductible Goodwill Resulting from a Retroactive Change in Tax Law

Companies had the option of retroactively applying the goodwill amortization provisions of the 1993 tax act to business combinations that occurred after July 25, 1991. The consensus was that the benefit related to income tax-deductible goodwill in excess of goodwill for financial reporting purposes was to be included in income from continuing operations in the period of enactment, **if** the entity expects to elect to retroactively amortize goodwill for tax purposes. A current income tax benefit related to the effect of retroactive amortization deducted from the combination date to the enactment date; a deferred income tax benefit related to the tax-deductible goodwill (less retroactive amortization to the enactment date) in excess of the reported amount of goodwill as of the enactment date.

93-13 Effect of a Retroactive Change in Enacted Tax Rates That Is Included in Income from Continuing Operations

The income tax effect of a retroactive change in tax rates on current and deferred income tax assets and liabilities is to be determined at the enactment date, using temporary differences and currently taxable income computed as of the date of enactment. The cumulative income tax effect is included in income from continuing operations. Furthermore, the income tax effect of items not included in income from continuing operations (e.g., from discontinued operations) that arose during the current fiscal year and prior to enactment is measured based on the enacted income tax rate at the time the transaction was recognized for financial reporting purposes; the income tax effect of a retroactive change in rates on current or deferred income tax assets or liabilities related to those items, nevertheless, is included in income from continuing operations.

93-16 Application of FASB Statement 109 to Basis Differences within Foreign Subsidiaries That Meet the Indefinite Reversal Criterion of APB Opinion No. 23

The Task Force concluded that the APB 23 indefinite reversal criterion applies only to "outside basis differences," and not to "inside basis differences" arising in connection with ownership of foreign subsidiaries. Furthermore, if deferred income taxes had not previously been provided for the "inside basis differences," under FAS 109 entities would be required to provide them for differences arising in fiscal years beginning after December 15, 1992, but could elect not to provide them for temporary differences arising earlier, if this had not been done when FAS 109 was adopted.

93-17 Recognition of Deferred Income Tax Asset on Discontinued Operations

This consensus relates to the disposal of the stock of a subsidiary that is accounted for as a discontinued operation under APB 30 and FAS 144. Notwithstanding the rule in APB 30 that gain recognition at the measurement date is limited to the amount of the loss expected to be realized from the disposal, if the reporting entity has an excess of its income tax basis over its GAAP basis in the subsidiary, the APB 30 gain recognition limitations are applied on a pretax basis, and the deferred income tax asset on the "outside basis difference" is recognized as provided under FAS 109 at the measurement date, as defined in APB 30. This would only apply, of course, if the deferred income tax asset is deemed more likely than not to be realized.

94-10 Accounting by a Company for the Income Tax Effects of Transactions among or with Its Shareholders under FASB Statement No. 109

Certain transactions among stockholders that occur outside the company can affect the status of deferred income taxes. The most commonly encountered of these is the change in ownership of over 50% of the company's stock, which limits or eliminates the company's ability to utilize net operating loss carryforwards, and accordingly will necessitate a write-off of deferred income tax assets previously recognized under FAS 109. Changes in deferred income taxes caused by transactions among stockholders are to be included in current period income tax expense in the income statement, since these are analogous to changes in expectations resulting from other external events (e.g., changes in enacted income tax rates). However, the income tax effects of changes in the income tax bases of assets or liabilities caused by transactions among stockholders would be included in equity, not in the income statement, although subsequent period changes in the valuation account, if any, would be reflected in income.

95-10 Accounting for Tax Credits Related to Dividend Payments in Accordance with FASB Statement No. 109

The accounting for a tax credit in the separate financials of the entity paying the dividend is a reduction of tax expense.

95-20 Measurement in the Consolidated Financial Statements of a Parent of the Tax Effects Related to the Operations of a Foreign Subsidiary That Receives Tax Credits Related to Dividend Payments

Some foreign countries tax corporate income at rates that differ depending on whether the income is distributed as dividends or retained by the corporation. Upon subsequent distribution of the accumulated earnings, the taxpayer receives a tax credit or refund for the difference between the two rates. In the consolidated financial statements of a parent company, the future income tax credit and the deferred income tax effects related to dividends that will be paid in the future are recognized based on the distributed rate if the parent is not invoking the indefinite reversal criteria of APB 23. However, the undistributed rate is used if the parent has not provided deferred income taxes as a result of applying the APB 23 criterion.

96-7 Accounting for Deferred Income Taxes on In-Process Research and Development Activities Acquired in a Purchase Business Combination

In-process R&D acquired in a purchase business combination is to be written off before the measurement of deferred income taxes. Thus, no deferred income taxes are provided on differences in initial bases for income tax and financial reporting purposes.

98-11 Accounting for Acquired Temporary Differences in Certain Purchase Transactions That Are Not Accounted for as Business Combinations

FAS 109 established the principle that the income tax effects of temporary differences related to purchase business combinations are to be "grossed up," in contrast to the older, "net of tax" method which had been prescribed by APB 11. However, FAS 109 did not address the accounting for acquisitions of individual assets having different income tax and accounting bases. This consensus holds that the income tax attributes of such an acquisition are to be recorded in a manner similar to the accounting for the income tax effects of negative goodwill under FAS 109. Computationally, this involves the use of simultaneous equations or trial and error.

99-15 Accounting for Decreases in Deferred income tax Asset Valuation Allowances Established in a Purchase Business Combination as a Result of a Change in Tax Regulations

In mid-1999, new consolidated income tax return regulations were issued that eliminated the requirement to apply the limitations on the separate return limitation year losses to situations in which a change in ownership as defined in Section 382 of the Internal Revenue Code has occurred within six months of a target company becoming a member of a consolidated group. As a result, only the loss limitation of Section 382 applies in those circumstances. The change in income tax regulations requires an entity to reevaluate the need for an existing valuation allowance for deferred income tax assets relating to net operating loss carryforwards acquired in a prior purchase business combination.

The issue was whether, in the event that the valuation allowance is reduced or eliminated, the effect of the adjustment should be (1) included in operations or (2) applied first to reduce to zero any goodwill related to the acquisition, second to reduce to zero other noncurrent intangible assets related to the acquisition, and third to reduce income tax expense. Support for both approaches can be found in FAS 109.

The consensus is that the effect of a change in income tax law or regulation that results in a decrease in a valuation allowance that initially was recorded in the allocation of the purchase price in a purchase business combination is to be included in income from continuing operations. This applies to any reduction in the valuation allowance that otherwise would not have been recognized except for the change in income tax law or regulation, whether the valuation allowance is reduced in the period of the income tax law change or in a subsequent period.

00-15 Classification in the Statement of Cash Flows of the Income Tax Benefit Received by a Company upon Exercise of a Nonqualified Employee Stock Option

A consensus was reached that the current income tax benefit realized from a corporate income tax deduction arising from an employee's exercise of nonqualified stock options is to be classified as an operating cash flow in the statement of cash flows. If this benefit is not shown as a separate line item in either the statement of cash flows or the statement of changes in stockholders' equity, it is to be disclosed in the notes to the financial statements.

APPENDIX A

ACCOUNTING FOR INCOME TAXES IN INTERIM PERIODS

Interim Reporting

FAS 109 essentially left unchanged the principles applicable to accounting for income taxes in financial statements covering interim periods, established by APB 28 and FIN 18. As set forth in those standards, the appropriate perspective for interim period reporting is to view the interim period as an integral part of the year, rather than as a discrete period. This objective is usually achieved by projecting income for the full annual period, computing the income tax thereon, and applying the "effective rate" to the interim period income or loss, with quarterly (or monthly) revisions to the expected annual results and the income tax effects thereof, as necessary.

While the Board chose to not comprehensively address interim reporting when it deliberated FAS 109, there were certain clear contradictions between APB 28 and the principles of FAS 109, which the Board did address. As discussed in more detail below, these issues were (1) recognizing the income tax benefits of interim losses based on expected net income of later interim or annual periods, (2) reporting the benefits of net operating loss carryforwards in interim periods, and (3) reporting the effects of income tax law changes in interim periods. Other matters requiring interpretation, which were left to the user to address without official guidance, included the classification of deferred income tax assets and liabilities on interim balance sheets and allocation of interim period income tax provisions between current and deferred expense.

The annual computation of income tax expense is based upon the current income taxes payable or refundable as indicated on the income tax return, plus or minus the adjustment necessary to adjust the deferred income tax asset and liability to the proper balances as of the balance sheet date (including consideration of the need for a valuation allowance, as previously discussed). The computation of interim period income tax expense should be consistent with this asset and liability method.

FIN 18 introduced some unfortunate terminology that, although confusing, nevertheless must be understood in the context of interim tax computations. The term "ordinary income" as used in FIN 18 is not the same as that term is used in the income tax law to distinguish capital gains, for example, from operating income and deductions. The FIN 18 definition of "ordinary income" is, formulaically

Pretax income or loss from continuing operations

+/– Extraordinary items
+/– Discontinued operations
+/– Cumulative effects of changes in accounting principle
+/– Significant unusual or infrequently occurring items

This "ordinary income" is used as the denominator in calculating an effective income tax rate to be used to compute income tax expense currently payable for the interim period. Note that pretax income is *not* adjusted for the effects of permanent or temporary differences.

Below is a relatively simple example that illustrates these basic principles:

Basic example of interim period accounting for income taxes

Boffa, Inc. estimates that pretax accounting income for the full fiscal year ending June 30, 2005, will be $400,000. Boffa does not expect to have any of the items that would adjust its "ordinary income" as defined above either at year-end or during any of its interim quarters. The company expects that it will incur $60,000 of meals and entertainment expenses of which 50% are nondeductible under the current tax law, the annual premium on an officer's life insurance policy is \$12,000, and dividend income (from a less than 20% ownership interest) is expected to be \$100,000. The company recognized income of \$75,000 in the first quarter of the year. The deferred income tax liability arises solely in connection with property and equipment temporary differences; these differences totaled \$150,000 at the beginning of the year and are projected to equal \$280,000 at year-end after taking into account expected acquisitions and disposals for the remainder of the fiscal year. The graduated statutory income tax rate schedule is provided below. Boffa management used a future expected effective income tax rate of 34% to compute the beginning deferred income tax liability and does not anticipate changing that percentage at the end of the fiscal year. The change in the future taxable temporary difference during the first quarter is \$30,000.

Boffa must first calculate its estimated effective income tax rate for the year. This rate is computed using all of the tax planning alternatives available to the company (e.g., tax credits, foreign rates, capital gains rates, etc.).

Estimated annual pretax accounting income (and "ordinary income" as defined in FIN 18)		\$ 400,000
Permanent differences:		
Add: Nondeductible officers' life insurance premium	\$ 12,000	
Nondeductible meals and entertainment	30,000	42,000
		442,000
Less: Dividends received deduction (\$100,000 x 70%)		(70,000)
		372,000
Less: Change in future taxable temporary difference		(130,000)
Estimated taxable income for the year		\$ 242,000
Annual current tax on estimated taxable income (see below)		\$ 70,530
Effective income tax rate for **current** income tax expense (computed as a percentage of "ordinary income") \$70,530/400,000		17.6%

Tax rate schedule: At least	Not more than	Rate	Taxable income	Tax
\$ --	\$ 50,000	15%	\$ 50,000	\$ 7,500
50,000	75,000	25%	25,000	6,250
75,000	--	34%	167,000	56,780
				\$70,530

Computation of the first quarter **current** income tax expense.

"Ordinary income" for first quarter	\$75,000
Estimated annual effective income tax rate per above	x 17.6%
	\$13,200

This amount can be "proven" as follows:

Annualized current tax computed above	\$70,530
Portion of annual tax attributable to first quarter	
First quarter pretax income as a % of forecast \$75,000/\$400,000	x 18.75%
Result, materially the same as above	\$13,224

Computation of the first quarter **deferred** income tax expense (same method as year-end).

	Future taxable temporary difference	*Effective tax rate estimated for reversal year(s)*	*Computed deferred tax liability*
Property and equipment			
End of first quarter	\$180,000	34%	\$61,200
Beginning of fiscal year	150,000	34%	51,000
First quarter deferred income tax expense			\$10,200

Recap of first quarter income tax expense.

Current	$13,200
Deferred	10,200
Total	$23,400

Finally, the entry necessary to record the income tax expense at the end of the first quarter is as follows:

Income tax expense	23,400	
Income taxes payable—current		13,200
Deferred income tax liability		10,200

In the second quarter, Boffa, Inc. revises its estimate of income for the full fiscal year. It now anticipates only $210,000 of pretax accounting income ("ordinary income"), including only $75,000 of dividend income, because of dramatic changes in the national economy. Other permanent differences are still expected to total $42,000.

Estimated annual pretax accounting income (and "ordinary income" as defined in FIN 18)		$210,000
Permanent differences:		
Add: Nondeductible officers' life insurance premium	$12,000	
Nondeductible meals and entertainment	30,000	42,000
		252,000
Less: Dividends received deduction ($75,000 x 70%)		(52,500)
		199,500
Less: Change in future taxable temporary difference		(130,000)
Estimated taxable income for the year		$ 69,500
Annual current tax on estimated taxable income (see below)		$ 12,375
Effective income tax rate for **current** income tax expense (computed as a percentage of "ordinary income" $12,375/$210,000)		5.2%

Tax rate schedule				
At least	*Not more than*	*Rate*	*Taxable income*	*Tax*
$ --	$ 50,000	15%	$ 50,000	$ 7,500
50,000	75,000	25%	19,500	4,875
			$69,500	$12,375

The actual "ordinary income" for the second quarter was $22,000, and the change in the temporary difference was only an additional $10,000. Income tax expense for the second quarter is computed as follows:

Computation of year-to-date and second quarter **current** income tax expense (benefit).

"Ordinary income" for the half year ($75,000 + $22,000)	$97,000
Estimated annual effective income tax rate per above	x 5.2%
Year-to-date current income tax expense	$ 5,044
Less: Expense recognized in first quarter	13,200
Current income tax (benefit) for second quarter	$ (8,156)

Computation of year-to-date and second quarter **deferred** income tax expense (benefit).

	Future taxable temporary difference	*Effective tax rate estimated for reversal year(s)*	*Computed deferred tax liability*
Property and equipment			
End of second quarter	$190,000	34%	$64,600
Beginning of fiscal year	150,000	34%	51,000
Year-to-date deferred income tax expense			13,600
Less: Expense recognized in first quarter			10,200
Deferred income tax expense for second quarter			$ 3,400

Recap of second quarter income expense (benefit)

Current	$(8,156)
Deferred	3,400
Total	$(4,756)

Under APB 28, and also under the general principle that changes in estimate are reported prospectively (as stipulated by APB 20), the results of prior quarters are not restated for changes in the estimated effective annual tax rate. Given the current and deferred income tax expense that was recognized in the first quarter, shown above, the following entry is required to record the income taxes as of the end of the second quarter:

Income taxes payable—current	8,156	
Income tax expense (benefit)		4,756
Deferred income tax liability		3,400

The foregoing illustrates the basic problems encountered in applying GAAP to interim reporting. In the following paragraphs, we will discuss some of the items requiring modifications to the approach described above.

Net Operating Losses in Interim Periods

FIN 18 sets forth the appropriate accounting when losses are incurred in interim periods or when net operating loss (NOL) carryforward benefits are realized during an interim reporting period.

Carryforward from prior years. The interim accounting for the utilization of a net operating loss (NOL) carryforward is effected in one of two ways.

1. If the income tax benefit of the NOL is expected to be realized as a result of current year "ordinary income," that income tax benefit is included as an adjustment to the effective annual tax rate computation illustrated above.
2. If the income tax benefit of the NOL is not expected to be realized as described in 1., the benefit is allocated first to reduce year-to-date income tax expense from continuing operations to zero with any excess allocated to other sources of income that would provide the means to utilize the NOL (e.g., extraordinary items, discontinued operations, etc.)

When a valuation allowance is reduced or eliminated because of a revised judgment, the previously unrecognized income tax benefit is included in the income tax expense or benefit of the interim period in which the judgment is revised. An increase in the valuation allowance resulting from a revised judgment would cause a catch-up adjustment to be included in the current interim period's income tax expense from continuing operations. In either situation, the effect of the change in judgment is **not** prorated to future interim periods by means of the effective tax rate estimate.

To illustrate, consider the following example:

Camino Corporation has a previously unrecognized $50,000 net operating loss (NOL) carryforward—that is, Camino had previously established a full valuation allowance for the deferred income tax asset arising from the NOL and thus had not previously recognized any deferred income tax benefit associated with the NOL; a flat 40% tax rate for current and future periods is assumed. Income for the full year (before NOL) is projected to be $80,000, consequently, the management of Camino has revised its judgment as to the future realizability of the NOL. In the first quarter Camino will report a pretax loss of $10,000.

Projected annual income	$ 80,000
x Tax rate	40%
Projected tax liability	$ 32,000

Accordingly, in the income statement for the first fiscal quarter, the pretax operating loss of $10,000 will give rise to an income tax **benefit** of $10,000 x 40% = $4,000.

In addition, an income tax benefit of $20,000 ($50,000 NOL x 40%) is recognized, and is included in the current quarter's income tax benefit relating to continuing operations. Thus, the total income tax benefit for the first fiscal quarter will be $24,000 ($4,000 + $20,000).

If Camino's second quarter results in pretax operating income of $30,000, and the expectation for the full year remains unchanged (i.e., operating income of $80,000), the second quarter income tax expense is $12,000 ($30,000 x 40%).

The income tax provision for the fiscal first half-year will be a **benefit** of $12,000, as follows:

Cumulative pretax income through second quarter ($30,000 – $10,000)	$ 20,000
x Effective rate	40%
Income tax provision before recognition of NOL carryforward benefit	8,000
Benefit of NOL carryforward first recognized in first quarter	(20,000)
Total year-to-date tax provision (benefit)	$(12,000)
Consisting of:	
First quarter (benefit)	$(24,000)
Second quarter expense	12,000
Year-to-date benefit, per above	$(12,000)

The foregoing example assumes that during the first quarter Camino's judgment changed as to the full realizability of the previously unrecognized benefit of the $50,000 loss carryforward. Were this **not** the case, however, the benefit would have been recognized only as actual tax liabilities were incurred (through current period income) in amounts sufficient to offset the NOL benefit.

To illustrate this latter situation, assume the same facts about net income for the first two quarters, and assume now that Camino's judgment about the realizability of the prior period NOL does **not** change. Tax provisions for the first quarter and first half are as follows:

	First quarter	*First half-year*
Pretax income (loss)	$(10,000)	$ 20,000
x Effective rate	40%	40%
Tax provision before recognition of NOL carryforward benefit	$ (4,000)	$ 8,000
Benefit of NOL carryforward recognized	--	(8,000)
Tax provision (benefit)	$ (4,000)	--

Notice that recognition of an income tax benefit of $4,000 in the first quarter is based on the expectation of at least a breakeven full year's results. That is, the benefit of the first quarter's loss was deemed **more likely than not**. Otherwise, no income tax benefit would have been reported in the first quarter.

Estimated loss for the year. When the full year is expected to be profitable, it is irrelevant that one or more interim periods result in a loss, and the expected effective rate for the full year is used to record interim period income tax expense and benefits, as illustrated above. However, when the full year is expected to produce a loss, the computation of the effective annual income tax benefit rate must logically take into account the extent to which a net deferred income tax asset (i.e., the asset less any related valuation allowance) will be recognized at year-end. For the first set of examples, below, assume that the realization of income tax benefits related to NOL carryforwards are **not entirely** more likely than not. That is, the full benefits will be recognized as deferred income tax assets, but those assets will be offset partially or completely by the valuation allowance.

For each of the following examples we will assume that the Gibby Corporation is anticipating a loss of $150,000 for the fiscal year. The Company's general ledger currently reflects a deferred income tax liability of $30,000; all of the liability will reverse during the fifteen-year carryforward period. Assume **future** income taxes will be at a 40% rate.

Example 1

Assume that the company can carry back the entire $150,000 NOL to the preceding three years. The income tax potentially refundable by the carryback would (remember this is only an estimate until year-end) amount to $48,000 (an assumed amount). The effective rate is then 32% ($48,000/150,000).

	Ordinary income (loss)		*Tax (benefit) expense*		
Reporting period	*Reporting period*	*Year-to date*	*Year-to-date*	*Less previously provided*	*Reporting period*
1st qtr.	$ (50,000)	$ (50,000)	$(16,000)	$ --	$(16,000)
2nd qtr.	20,000	(30,000)	(9,600)	(16,000)	6,400
3rd qtr.	(70,000)	(100,000)	(32,000)	(9,600)	(22,400)
4th qtr.	(50,000)	(150,000)	(48,000)	(32,000)	(16,000)
Fiscal year	$(150,000)				$(48,000)

Note that both the income tax expense (2nd quarter) and benefit are computed using the estimated annual effective rate. This rate is applied to the year-to-date numbers just as in the previous examples, with any adjustment being made and realized in the current reporting period. This treatment is appropriate because the accrual of income tax benefits in the first, third and fourth quarters is consistent with the effective rate estimated at the beginning of the year, in contrast to those circumstances in which a change in estimate is made in a quarter relating to the realizability of income tax benefits not previously provided (or benefits for which full or partial valuation allowances were required).

Example 2

In this case assume that Gibby Corporation can carry back only $50,000 of the loss and that the remainder must be carried forward. Realization of future taxable income to fully utilize the NOL is not deemed to be more likely than not. The estimated carryback of $50,000 would generate an income tax refund of $12,000 (again assumed). The company is assumed to be in the 40% tax bracket (a flat rate is used to simplify the example). Although the benefit of the NOL carryforward is recognized, a valuation allowance must be provided to the extent that it is more likely than not that the benefit will not be realized. In this example, management has concluded that only 25% of the gross benefit will be realized in future years. Accordingly, a valuation allowance of $30,000 must be established, leaving a net of $10,000 as an estimated realizable income tax benefit related to the carryforward of the projected loss.

$150,000 loss – $50,000 carried back = $100,000 NOL x 40% tax rate =
$40,000 benefit x 75% portion deemed unrealizable = $30,000 valuation allowance

Considered in conjunction with the carryback refund of $12,000, the company will obtain a $22,000 income tax benefit relating to the projected current year loss, for an effective income tax benefit rate of 14.7%. The calculation of the estimated annual effective rate is as follows:

Expected annual net loss			$150,000
Tax benefit from NOL carryback		$12,000	
Tax benefit of NOL carryforward			
($100,000 x 40%)	$40,000		
Valuation allowance	(30,000)	10,000	
Total recognized benefit			$22,000
Estimated annual effective rate ($22,000 ÷ $150,000)			14.7%

	Ordinary income (loss)		*Tax (benefit) expense*			
			Year-to-date			
Reporting period	*Reporting period*	*Year-to-date*	*Computed*	*Limited to*	*Less previously provided*	*Reporting period*
1st qtr.	$ 10,000	$ 10,000	$ 1,470	$ --	$ --	$ 1,470
2nd qtr.	(80,000)	(70,000)	(10,290)	--	1,470	(11,760)
3rd qtr.	(100,000)	(170,000)	(24,990)	(22,000)	(10,290)	(11,710)
4th qtr.	20,000	(150,000)	(22,000)	--	(22,000)	--
Fiscal year	$(150,000)					$(22,000)

In the foregoing, the income tax expense (benefit) is computed by multiplying the year-to-date income or loss by the estimated annual effective rate, and then subtracting the amount of tax expense or benefit already provided in prior interim periods. It makes no difference if the current period indicates an income or a loss, assuming of course that the full-year estimated results are not being revised. However, if the cumulative loss for the interim periods to date exceeds the projected loss for the full year upon which the effective income tax benefit rate had been based, then no further tax benefits can be recorded, as is illustrated above in the benefit for the third quarter.

The foregoing examples cover most of the situations encountered in practice. The reader is referred to Appendix C of FIN 18 for additional examples.

Operating loss occurring during an interim period. An instance may occur in which the company expects net income for the year and incurs a net loss during one of the reporting periods. In this situation, the estimated annual effective rate, which was calculated based upon the expected net income figure, is applied to the year-to-date income or loss to arrive at year-to-date income tax expense. The amount previously provided is subtracted from the year-to-date expense to arrive at the expense for the current reporting period. If the current period operations resulted in a loss, then the period will reflect an income tax benefit.

Income Tax Provision Applicable to Significant Unusual or Infrequently Occurring Items, Discontinued Operations, or Extraordinary Items Occurring in Interim Periods

Unusual, infrequent, or extraordinary items. The financial statement presentation of these items and their related income tax effects are prescribed by FAS 109. Extraordinary items and discontinued operations are to be shown **net** of their related income tax effects. Unusual or infrequently occurring items are separately disclosed as a component of pretax income, and the income tax expense or benefit is included in the income tax expense from continuing operations. Presenting these items net of tax is strictly prohibited so the reader does not mistake them for extraordinary items.

The interim treatment accorded these items does not differ from the fiscal year-end reporting required by GAAP. However, according to APB 28, these items **are not** to be included in the computation of the estimated effective annual income tax rate. The opinion also requires that these items be recognized in the interim period in which they occur rather than being prorated equally throughout the year. Examples of the treatment prescribed by the opinion follow later in this section.

Recognition of the income tax effects of a loss due to any of the aforementioned situations is permitted if the benefits are expected to be realized during the year, or if they will be recognizable as a deferred income tax asset at year-end under the provisions of FAS 109.

If a situation arises where realization is not more likely than not in the period of occurrence but becomes assured in a subsequent period in the same fiscal year, the previously unrecognized income tax benefit is reported in income from continuing operations until it reduces the income tax expense to zero, with any excess reported in those other categories of income (e.g., discontinued operations) which provided a means of realization of the tax benefit.

The following examples illustrate the treatment required for reporting unusual, infrequently occurring, and extraordinary items. Again, these items are not to be used in calculating the estimated annual tax rate. For income statement presentation, the income tax expense or benefit relating to unusual or infrequently occurring items is to be included with ordinary income from continuing operations. Extraordinary items are shown net of their applicable tax provision.

The following data apply to the next two examples:

1. Irwin Industries expects fiscal year ending June 30, 2005 income to be $96,000 and net permanent differences to reduce taxable income by $25,500.

2. Irwin Industries also incurred a $30,000 extraordinary loss in the second quarter of the year.

Example 1

In this case, assume that the loss can be carried back to prior periods and, therefore, the realization of any income tax benefit is assured. Based on the information given earlier, the estimated annual effective income tax rate can be calculated as follows:

Expected pretax accounting income	$96,000
Anticipated permanent differences	(25,500)
Expected taxable income	$70,500

Income Tax Calculation "Excluding" Extraordinary Item

$50,000	x	.15	=	$ 7,500
20,500	x	.25	=	5,125
$70,500				$12,625

Effective annual rate = 13.15% ($12,625 ÷ 96,000)

No adjustment in the estimated annual effective rate is required when the extraordinary, unusual, or infrequent item occurs. The income tax (benefit) applicable to the item is computed using the estimated fiscal year ordinary income and an analysis of the incremental impact of the extraordinary item. The method illustrated below is applicable when the company anticipates operating income for the year. When a loss is anticipated but realization of benefits of NOL carryforwards is **not** more likely than not, the company computes its estimated annual effective rate based on the amount of tax to be refunded from prior years. The income tax (benefit) applicable to the extraordinary, unusual, or infrequent item is then the decrease (increase) in the refund to be received.

Computation of the income tax applicable to the extraordinary, unusual, or infrequent item is as follows:

Estimated pretax accounting income	$96,000
Permanent differences	(25,500)
Extraordinary item	(30,000)
Expected taxable income	$40,500

Income Tax Calculation "Including" Extraordinary Item

$40,500 x .15 = $6,075

Income tax "excluding" extraordinary item	$12,625
Income tax "including" extraordinary item	6,075
Income tax benefit applicable to extraordinary, unusual, or infrequent item	$ 6,550

			Income tax (benefit) applicable to				
			Ordinary income (loss)		*Unusual, infrequent, or extraordinary item*		
Reporting period	*Ordinary income (loss)*	*Unusual, infrequent, or extraordinary item*	*Reporting period*	*Year-to-date*	*Year-to-date*	*Previously provided*	*Reporting period*
1st qtr.	$10,000	$ --	$ 1,315	$ 1,315	$ --	$ --	$ --
2nd qtr.	(20,000)	(30,000)	(2,630)	(1,315)	(6,550)	--	(6,550)
3rd qtr.	40,000	--	5,260	3,945	(6,550)	(6,550)	--
4th qtr.	66,000	--	8,680	12,625	(6,550)	(6,550)	--
Fiscal year	$96,000	$(30,000)	$12,625				$ (6,550)

Example 2

Again, assume that Irwin Industries estimates net income of $96,000 for the year with permanent differences of $25,500 which reduce taxable income. The extraordinary loss of $30,000 cannot be carried back and the ability to carry it forward is not **more likely than not**. Because no net deferred income tax assets exist, the only way that the loss can be deemed to be realizable is to the extent that current year ordinary income offsets the effect of the loss. As a result, realization of the loss is assured only as, and to the extent that, there is ordinary income for the year.

			Income tax (benefit) applicable to				
			Ordinary income (loss)		*Unusual, infrequent, or extraordinary item*		
Reporting period	*Ordinary income (loss)*	*Unusual, infrequent, or extraordinary item*	*Reporting period*	*Year-to-date*	*Year-to-date*	*Previously provided*	*Reporting period*
1st qtr.	$ 5,000	$ --	$ 658	$ 658	$ --	$ --	$ --
2nd qtr.	20,000	(30,000)	2,630	3,288	(3,288)[a]	--	(3,288)
3rd qtr.	(10,000)	--	(1,315)	1,973	(1,973)[a]	(3,288)	1,315
4th qtr.	81,000	--	10,652	12,625	(6,550)[a]	(1,973)	(4,577)
Fiscal year	$96,000	$(30,000)	$12,625				$ (6,550)

[a] *The recognition of the income tax benefit to be realized relative to the unusual, infrequent, or extraordinary item is limited to the lesser of the total income tax benefit applicable to the item or the amount available to be realized. Because realization is based upon the amount of income tax applicable to ordinary income during the period, the year-to-date figures for the income tax benefit fluctuate as the year-to-date income tax expense relative to ordinary income fluctuates. Note that at no point does the amount of the income tax benefit exceed what was calculated above as being applicable to the unusual, infrequent, or extraordinary item.*

Discontinued operations in interim periods. Discontinued operations, according to APB 28, are included as significant, unusual, or extraordinary items. Therefore, the computations described for unusual, infrequent, or extraordinary items will also apply to the income (loss) from the discontinued component of the entity, including any provisions for operating gains (losses) subsequent to the measurement date.

If the decision to dispose of operations occurs in any interim period other than the first interim period, the operating income (loss) applicable to the discontinued component has already been used in computing the estimated annual effective tax rate. Therefore, a recomputation of the **total tax** is not required. However, the total tax is to be divided into two components.

1. That tax applicable to ordinary income (loss)
2. That tax applicable to the income (loss) from the discontinued component

This division is accomplished as follows: a revised estimated annual effective rate is calculated for the income (loss) from ordinary operations. This recomputation is then applied to the ordinary income (loss) from the preceding periods. The total income tax applicable to the discontinued component is then composed of two items.

1. The difference between the total income tax originally computed and the income tax recomputed on remaining ordinary income
2. The income tax computed on unusual, infrequent, or extraordinary items as described above

Example

Rochelle Corporation anticipates net income of $150,000 during the fiscal year. The net permanent differences for the year will be $10,000. The company also anticipates income tax credits of $10,000 during the fiscal year. For purposes of this example, we will assume a flat statutory rate of 50%. The estimated annual effective rate is then calculated as follows:

Estimated pretax income	$150,000
Net permanent differences	(10,000)
Taxable income	140,000
Statutory rate	50%
Income tax	70,000
Anticipated credits	(10,000)
Total estimated income tax	$ 60,000
Estimated effective rate ($60,000 ÷ 150,000)	40%

The first two quarters of operations were as follows:

	Ordinary income (loss)		*Tax expense*		
Reporting period	*Reporting period*	*Year-to-date*	*Year-to-date*	*Less previously provided*	*Reporting period*
1st qtr	$30,000	$30,000	$12,000	$ --	$12,000
2nd qtr.	25,000	55,000	22,000	12,000	10,000

In the third quarter, Rochelle made the decision to dispose of Division X. During the third quarter, the company earned a total of $60,000. Upon reclassification of Division X's property and equipment to "held-for-sale" on its balance sheet, the company expects to incur a onetime charge to income of $75,000 and estimates that current year divisional operating losses subsequent to the disposal decision will be $20,000, all of which will be incurred in the third quarter. The company estimates revised ordinary income in the fourth quarter to be $35,000. The two components of pretax accounting income (discontinued operations and revised ordinary income) are shown below.

		Division X	
Reporting period	*Revised ordinary income*	*Loss from operations*	*Asset reclassification*
1st qtr.	$ 40,000	$(10,000)	$ --
2nd qtr.	40,000	(15,000)	--
3rd qtr.	80,000	(20,000)	(75,000)
4th qtr.	35,000	--	--
Fiscal year	$195,000	$(45,000)	$(75,000)

Rochelle must now recompute the estimated annual income tax rate. Assume that all the permanent differences are related to the revised continuing operations. However, $3,300 of the tax credits were applicable to machinery used in Division X. Because of the discontinuance of operations, the credit on this machinery would not be allowed. Any recapture of prior period credits must be used as a reduction in the income tax benefit from either operations or the loss on disposal. Assume that the company must recapture $2,000 of the $3,300 investment tax credit that is related to Division X.

The recomputed estimated annual rate for continuing operations is as follows:

Estimated (revised) ordinary income	$195,000
Less net permanent differences	(10,000)
	$185,000
Tax at statutory rate of 50%	$ 92,500
Less anticipated credits from continuing operations	(6,700)
Tax provision	$ 85,800
Estimated annual effective tax rate ($85,800 ÷ 195,000)	44%

The next step is to then apply the revised rate to the quarterly income from continuing operations as illustrated below.

	Ordinary income			*Tax provision*		
Reporting period	*Reporting period*	*Year-to-date*	*Estimated annual effective rate*	*Year-to-date*	*Less previously provided*	*Reporting period*
1st qtr.	$ 40,000	$ 40,000	44%	$17,600	$ --	$17,600
2nd qtr.	40,000	80,000	44%	35,200	17,600	17,600
3rd qtr.	80,000	160,000	44%	70,400	35,200	35,200
4th qtr.	35,000	195,000	44%	85,800	70,400	15,400
Fiscal year	$195,000					$85,800

The tax benefit applicable to the operating loss from discontinued operations and the loss from the asset reclassification and remeasurement must now be calculated. The first two quarters are calculated on a differential basis as shown below.

Reporting period	*Tax applicable to ordinary income* *Previously reported*	*Recomputed (above)*	*Tax (benefit) expense applicable to Division X*
1st qtr.	$12,000	$17,600	$ (5,600)
2nd qtr.	10,000	17,600	(7,600)
			$ (13,200)

The only calculation remaining applies to the third quarter tax benefit pertaining to the operating loss and the loss on reclassification of the assets of the discontinued component. The calculation of this amount is made based on the revised estimate of annual ordinary income both including and excluding the effects of the Division X losses. This is shown below.

	Loss from operations of Division X	*Asset reclassification*
Estimated annual income from continuing operations	$195,000	$195,000
Net permanent differences	(10,000)	(10,000)
Loss from Division X operations	(45,000)	--
Provision for loss on reclassification of Division X assets	--	(75,000)
Total	$140,000	$110,000
Tax at the statutory rate of 50%	$ 70,000	$ 55,000
Anticipated credits (from continuing operations)	(6,700)	(6,700)
Recapture of previously recognized tax credits as a result of disposal	--	2,000
Taxes after effect of Division X losses	63,300	50,300
Taxes computed on estimated income before the effect of Division X losses	85,800	85,800
Tax benefit applicable to Division X	(22,500)	(35,500)
Amounts allocable to quarters one and two ($5,600 + $7,600)	(13,200)	--
Tax benefit to be recognized in the third quarter	$ (9,300)	$(35,500)

The quarterly tax provisions can be summarized as follows:

	Pretax income (loss)			*Tax (benefit) applicable to*		
Reporting period	*Continuing operations*	*Operations of Division X*	*Loss on asset reclassification*	*Continuing operations*	*Operations of Division X*	*Loss on asset reclassification*
1st qtr.	$ 40,000	$(10,000)	$ --	$17,600	$ (5,600)	$ --
2nd qtr.	40,000	(15,000)	--	17,600	(7,600)	--
3rd qtr.	80,000	(20,000)	(75,000)	35,200	(9,300)	(35,500)
4th qtr.	35,000	--	--	15,400	--	--
Fiscal year	$195,000	$(45,000)	$(75,000)	$85,800	$(22,500)	$(35,500)

The following income statement shows the proper financial statement presentation of these discontinued operations. The notes to the statement indicate which items are to be included in the calculation of the annual estimated rate.

Income Statement
(FIN 18, Appendix D)

Net sales*		$xxxx
Other income*		xxx
		xxxx
Costs and expenses		
Cost of sales*	$xxxx	
Selling, general, and administrative expenses*	xxx	
Interest expense*	xx	
Other deductions*	xx	
Unusual items*	xxx	
Infrequently occurring items*	xxx	xxxx
Income (loss) from continuing operations before income taxes and other items listed below		xxxx
Provision for income taxes (benefit)**		xxx
Income (loss) from continuing operations before items listed below		xxxx

Discontinued operations:		
Income (loss) from operations of discontinued Division X (less applicable income taxes of $xxxx)	xxxx	
Income (loss) on reclassification of assets of Division X to held-for-sale, (less applicable taxes of $xxxx)	xxxx	xxxx
Income (loss) before extraordinary items and cumulative effect of a change in accounting principle		xxxx
Extraordinary items (less applicable income taxes of $xxxx)		xxxx
Cumulative effect on prior years of a change in accounting principle (less applicable income taxes of $xxxx)***		xxxx
Net income (loss)		$xxxx

* *Components of ordinary income (loss).*

** *Consists of total income taxes (benefit) applicable to ordinary income (loss), unusual items and infrequently occurring items.*

*** *This amount is shown net of income taxes. Although the income taxes are generally disclosed (as illustrated), this is not required.*

APPENDIX B

COMMON PERMANENT AND TEMPORARY DIFFERENCES

Common Permanent Differences

Club dues. Dues assessed by business, social, athletic, luncheon, sporting, airline and hotel clubs are not deductible for federal income tax purposes.

Dividends received deduction. Depending on the percentage interest of the payer owned by the recipient, a percentage of the dividends received by a corporation are nontaxable. Different rules apply to subsidiaries. See section in chapter.

Lease inclusion amounts. Lessees of automobiles whose fair value the IRS deems to qualify as a luxury automobile are required to limit their lease deduction by adding to taxable income an amount determined by reference to a table prescribed annually in a revenue procedure.

Meals and entertainment. A percentage (currently 50%) of business meals and entertainment costs are not deductible for federal income tax purposes.

Municipal interest income. A 100% exclusion is permitted for investment in qualified municipal securities. Note that the capital gains applicable to sales of these securities **are** taxable.

Officer's life insurance premiums. Premiums paid on an officer's life insurance policy on which the company is the beneficiary are not allowed as a tax deduction, nor are any death proceeds taxable.

Organization and start-up costs. GAAP requires organization and start-up costs to be treated as expenses as incurred. Certain organization and start-up costs are not allowed amortization under the tax code. The most clearly defined are those expenditures relating to the cost of raising capital. Also see temporary differences below.

Penalties and fines. Any penalty or fine arising as a result of violation of the law is not allowed as a taxable deduction. This includes a wide range of items including parking tickets, environmental fines, and penalties assessed by the Internal Revenue Service.

Percentage depletion. The excess of percentage depletion over cost depletion is allowable as a deduction for income tax purposes.

The portion of wages or salaries used in computing the jobs credit is not allowed as a deduction for income tax purposes.

Common Temporary Differences

Installment sale method. Use of the installment sale method for income tax purposes generally results in a temporary difference because that method is generally not permitted to be used in accordance with GAAP.

Long-term construction contracts. A temporary difference will arise if different methods (e.g., completed-contract or percentage-of-completion) are used for GAAP and income tax purposes.

Depreciation. A temporary difference will occur unless the modified ACRS method is used for financial reporting over estimated useful lives that are the same as the IRS-prescribed recovery periods.

Goodwill. For income tax purposes, amortization over fifteen years is mandatory. Amortization of goodwill is no longer permitted under GAAP, but periodic write-downs for impairment may occur, with any remainder of goodwill being expensed when the reporting unit to which it pertains is ultimately disposed of.

Estimated costs (e.g., warranty expense). Estimates or provisions of this nature are not included in the determination of taxable income until the period in which they actually occur.

Accounting for investments. Use of the equity method for financial reporting while using the cost method for income tax purposes.

Prepaid income (e.g., prepaid rent). Prepaid income of this nature is includable in taxable income in the period in which it is received, while for financial reporting purposes, it is considered a liability until the revenue is earned.

Net capital loss. C corporation capital losses are recognized currently for financial reporting purposes but are carried forward to be offset against future capital gains for income tax purposes.

Organization costs. GAAP requires organization costs to be treated as expenses as incurred. Organization costs are amortized over a 60-month period for income tax purposes. Also see organization and start-up costs above.

Accrued contingent liabilities. These cannot be deducted for income tax purposes until the liability becomes fixed and determinable.

Excess charitable contributions. These can be carried over to future years for income tax purposes.

Mandatory change from cash to accrual. Generally one-fourth of this adjustment is recognized for income tax purposes each year.

Uniform cost capitalization (UNICAP). Income tax accounting rules require manufacturers and certain wholesalers to capitalize as inventory costs, certain costs that, under GAAP are considered administrative costs that are not allocable to inventory.

Cash basis versus accrual basis. Use of the cash method of accounting for income tax purposes and the accrual method for financial reporting.

Deferred compensation. Under GAAP, the present value of deferred compensation agreements must be accrued and charged to expense over the employee's remaining employment period, but cannot be deducted for income tax purposes until actually paid.

16 PENSIONS AND OTHER POSTRETIREMENT BENEFITS

PERSPECTIVE AND ISSUES

A convergence of economic and political factors in the US has had a profound impact on the tools and techniques used by businesses and their employees to plan for and fund retirees' postemployment income.

Consider the demographics of the aging "Baby Boom" generation, the resulting financial uncertainties surrounding the financial health of the Social Security retirement system, the low savings rate, and the standard of living they currently enjoy. These conditions have necessitated the establishment of a private, supplemental system for providing pension and postretirement health benefits for retirees. The growth of this system has been promoted by the generous income tax benefits available to enterprises that provide employees with such benefits and to employees for voluntarily contributing portions of their earnings to individual retirement accounts or to employer retirement plans that accept such contributions.

This chapter focuses on accounting for postretirement benefits including single-employer and multiemployer plans, defined benefit pension plans, defined contribution pension plans, and postretirement plans other than pensions that help fund retiree costs of health care benefits.

FAS 87 specifies the accrual basis of accounting for pension costs. At the time of its issuance in 1985 (it was adopted by only a 4-3 vote), FASB acknowledged that is was not likely to be the final step in the evolution of pension accounting which it characterized as being in a "transitional stage." FASB admitted in the standard that it had made a political compromise when it stated that "recognition in financial statements of [pension assets and liabilities] in their entirety would be too great a change from past practice."

While today, almost twenty years later, the accounting model remains unchanged, GASB has recently indicated that this topic may be revisited in the near future. Concerns include the impact of the mandated "smoothing" of gains and losses, the subjective selection of expected asset returns and discount rate, the common use of overfunding to affect the entity's reported earnings, and the complexity of information presented in the footnote disclosures.

FAS 87 continues three primary characteristics of the predecessor standard APB 8.

1. Delayed recognition (changes are not recognized immediately but are subsequently recognized in a gradual and systematic way)
2. Reporting net cost (various items are aggregated and reported as one net amount)
3. Offsetting assets and liabilities (assets and liabilities are sometimes shown net)

Estimates and averages may be used as long as material differences do not result. Explicit assumptions and estimates of future events must be used for each specified variable included in pension costs and disclosed in the notes to the financial statements.

FAS 87 focuses directly on the terms of the plan to assist in the recognition of compensation cost over the service period of the employees. It results in recognition of significant liabilities and recognizes a minimum liability in the case of plans that are materially underfunded.

The principal emphasis of FAS 87 is the present value of the pension obligation, and the fair value of plan assets. The main accounting issues revolve around the expense to recognize on the income statement and the liability to be accrued on the balance sheet.

FAS 88 is closely related to FAS 87. It establishes standards to be followed by employers of defined benefit pension plans when obligations are settled, plans are curtailed, or benefits are terminated.

Although there are some major differences in terminology and measurement, other postretirement benefits (OPEB) accounting basically follows the fundamental framework established for pension accounting and applies to all forms of postretirement benefits. However, in most cases, the main focus is on postretirement health care benefits. FAS 106 considers OPEB to be a form of deferred compensation and requires accrual accounting. The terms of the individual contract govern the accrual of the employer's obligation for deferred compensation and the cost is attributed to employee service periods until full eligibility to receive benefits is attained. The employer's obligation for OPEB is fully accrued when the employee attains full eligibility for all expected benefits.

FAS 132, *Employers' Disclosures about Pensions and Other Postretirement Benefits*, was issued in 1998 and revised and standardized these disclosures by using a separate but parallel format, eliminating less useful information, requiring some additional data deemed useful by analysts, and allowing some aggregation of presentation. FAS 132 did not alter the recognition and measurement aspects of FAS 87, 88, and 106, while amending the disclosure requirements of those standards. A revised version of FAS 132 was then issued in late 2003, which replaced the original FAS 132, adding further disclosure requirements, and forms the basis for the discussion in this chapter.

The recent economic environment caused financial statement users to question the suitability of the current pension accounting model. The sustained downturn in the US stock market in the early 2000s severely impacted the value of pension assets and imposed hardships on employer/sponsors who found their employee benefit plans to be inadequately funded. The problem was compounded by the fact that, at the same time that the values of plan assets were precipitously declining, many plan sponsors are continuing to use lofty assumptions based on investment performance during the 1990s regarding the expected long-term performance of their plans' investment portfolios. Even applying the smoothing technique mandated by FAS 87, which brings some portion of the discrepancy between actual returns and expected returns into the measure of pension cost, the use of unrealistic assumptions can mask the true economic obligations that are accumulating. (Note that the deliberate use of unsupported assumptions would constitute a GAAP departure. However, the range of reasonable values does often provide financial statement preparers with some ability to manipulate reported results, and this can be material to its results of operations.)

Sources of GAAP

APB	*FAS*	*EITF*	*FSP*
12, 16, 30	5, 87, 88, 106, 112, 130, 132(R), 144, 149	88-1, 88-5, 90-3, 91-7, 92-13, 93-3, 03-2, 03-4, D-36, D-92, D-106	106-1

DEFINITIONS OF TERMS

Accrued pension cost. Cumulative net pension cost accrued in excess of the employer's contributions.

Accumulated benefit obligation. Actuarial present value of benefits (whether vested or nonvested) attributed by the pension benefit formula to employee service rendered before a specified date and based on employee service and compensation (if applicable) prior to that date. The accumulated benefit obligation differs from the projected benefit obligation in that it includes no assumption about future compensation levels. For plans with flat-benefit or no-pay-related pension benefit formulas, the accumulated benefit obligation and the projected benefit obligation are the same.

Accumulated postretirement benefit obligation. The actuarial present value of benefits attributed to employee service rendered to a particular date. Prior to an employee's full eligibility date, the accumulated postretirement benefit obligation as of a particular date for an employee is the portion of the expected postretirement benefit obligation attributed to that employee's service rendered to that date. On and after the full eligibility date, the accumulated and expected postretirement benefit obligations for an employee are the same.

Actual return on plan assets component (of net periodic pension cost). Difference between fair value of plan assets at the end of the period and the fair value at the beginning of the period, adjusted for employer contributions and payments of benefits during the period.

Actuarial present value. Value, as of a specified date, of an amount or series of amounts payable or receivable thereafter, with each amount adjusted to reflect (1) the time value of money (through discounts for interest) and (2) the probability of payment (by means of decrements for events such as death, disability, withdrawal, or retirement) between the specified date and the expected date of payment.

Amortization. Usually refers to the process of reducing a recognized liability systematically by recognizing revenues or reducing a recognized asset systematically by recognizing expenses or costs. In pension accounting, amortization is also used to refer to the systematic recognition in net pension cost over several periods of previously **unrecognized** amounts, including unrecognized prior service cost and unrecognized net gain or loss.

Annuity contract. Irrevocable contract in which an insurance company[1] unconditionally undertakes a legal obligation to provide specified benefits to specific individuals in return for a fixed consideration or premium. It involves the transfer of significant risk from the employer to the insurance company. Participating annuity contracts provide that the purchaser (either the plan or the employer) may participate in the experience of the insurance company. The insurance company ordinarily pays dividends to the purchaser. If the substance of a participating annuity contract is such that the employer remains subject to all or most of the risks and rewards associated with the benefit obligation covered or the assets transferred to the insurance company, the purchase of the contract does not constitute a settlement.

Assumptions. Estimates of the occurrence of future events affecting pension costs, such as mortality, withdrawal, disablement and retirement, changes in compensation and national pension benefits, and discount rates to reflect the time value of money.

Attribution. Process of assigning pension benefits or cost to periods of employee service.

Attribution period. The period of an employee's service to which the expected postretirement benefit obligation for that employee is assigned. The beginning of the attribution period is the employee's date of hire unless the plan's benefit formula grants credit only for service from a later date, in which case the beginning of the attribution period is generally the beginning of that credited service period. The end of the attribution period is the full eligibility date. Within the attribution period, an equal amount of the expected postretirement benefit obligation is attributed to each year of service unless the plan's benefit formula attributes a disproportionate share of the expected postretirement benefit obligation to employees' early years of service. In that case, benefits are attributed in accordance with the plan's benefit formula.

Career-average-pay formula. Benefit formula that bases benefits on the employee's compensation over the entire period of service with the employer. A career-average-pay plan is a plan with such a formula.

Contributory plan. Pension plan under which employees contribute part of the cost. In some contributory plans, employees wishing to be covered must contribute. In other contributory plans, employee contributions result in increased benefits.

Curtailment. Event that significantly reduces the expected years of future service of present employees or eliminates for a significant number of employees the accrual of defined benefits for some or all of their future services. Curtailments include (1) termination of employee's services earlier than expected, which may or may not involve closing a facility or discontinuing a segment of a business and (2) termination or suspension of a plan so that employees do not earn additional defined benefits for future services. In the latter situation, future service may be counted toward vesting of benefits accumulated based on past services.

Defined benefit pension plan. Pension plan that defines an amount of pension benefit to be provided, usually as a function of one or more factors such as age, years of service, or compensation. Any pension plan that is not a defined contribution pension plan is, for purposes of FAS 87, a defined benefit pension plan.

---

[1] *If the insurance company is controlled by the employer or there is any reasonable doubt that the insurance company will meet its obligation under the contract, the purchase of the contract does not constitute a settlement for purposes of FAS 88.*

Defined contribution pension plan. Plan that provides pension benefits in return for services rendered, provides an individual account for each participant, and specifies how contributions to the individual's account are to be determined instead of specifying the amount of benefits the individual is to receive. Under a defined contribution pension plan, the benefits a participant will receive depend solely on the amount contributed to the participant's account, the returns earned on investments of those contributions, and forfeitures of other participants' benefits that may be allocated to such participant's account.

Expected long-term rate of return on plan assets. Assumption as to the rate of return on plan assets reflecting the average rate of earnings expected on the funds invested or to be invested to provide for the benefits included in the projected benefit obligation.

Expected postretirement benefit obligation. The actuarial present value as of a particular date of the benefits expected to be paid to or for an employee, the employee's beneficiaries, and any covered dependents pursuant to the terms of the postretirement benefit plan.

Expected return on plan assets. Amount calculated as a basis for determining the extent of delayed recognition of the effects of changes in the fair value of assets. The expected return on plan assets is determined based on the expected long-term rate of return on plan assets and the market-related value of plan assets.

Explicit approach to assumptions. Approach under which each significant assumption used reflects the best estimate of the plan's future experience solely with respect to that assumption.

Fair value. Amount that a pension or postretirement plan could reasonably expect to receive for an investment in a current sale between a willing buyer and a willing seller (i.e., in other than a forced or liquidation sale). Fair value of a plan investment is to be measured by its price in an active market, if available. If no active market exists for the investment, an active market price for an investment with similar characteristics may be used. Finally, if neither market exists, FAS 87 and FAS 106 permit the use of forecasted **expected cash flows.** FAS 149 clarifies that because these standards preceded the issuance of CON 7, the term "expected cash flows" as used to estimate fair value in this context does not require the use of the probability weighted expected cash flow model that FAS 7 introduced (although that model is based on sound estimation principles and is permitted to be used).

Final-pay formula. A plan with a benefit formula that bases benefits on the employee's compensation over a specified number of years near the end of the employee's service period or on the employee's highest compensation periods. For example, a plan might provide annual pension benefits equal to 1% of the employee's average salary for the last five years (or the highest consecutive five years) for each year of service.

Flat-benefit formula. A plan with a benefit formula that bases benefits on a fixed amount per year of service, such as $20 of monthly retirement income for each year of credited service.

Full eligibility (for benefits). The status of an employee having reached the employee's full eligibility date. Full eligibility for benefits is achieved by meeting specified age, service, or age and service requirements of the postretirement benefit plan.

Full eligibility date. The date at which an employee has rendered all of the service necessary to have earned the right to receive all of the benefits expected to be received by that employee (including any beneficiaries and dependents expected to receive benefits). Determination of the full eligibility date is affected by plan terms that provide incremental benefits expected to be received by or on behalf of an employee for additional years of service, unless those incremental benefits are trivial. Determination of the full eligibility date is **not** affected by plan terms that define when benefit payments commence or by an employee's current dependency status.

Fund. Used as a verb, to pay over to a funding agency (as to fund future pension benefits or to fund pension cost). Used as a noun, assets accumulated in the hands of a funding agency for the purpose of meeting pension benefits when they become due.

Funding policy. Program regarding the amounts and timing of contributions by the employer(s), participants, and any other sources (for example, state subsidies or federal grants) to provide the benefits a pension plan specifies.

Gain or loss. Change in the value of either the projected benefit obligation or the plan assets resulting from experience different from that assumed or from a change in an actuarial assumption. See also **Unrecognized net gain or loss**.

Gain or loss component (of net periodic pension cost). Sum of (1) the difference between the actual return on plan assets and the expected return on plan assets and (2) the amortization of the unrecognized net gain or loss from previous periods. The gain or loss component is the net effect of delayed recognition of gains and losses (the net change in the unrecognized net gain or loss) except that it does not include changes in the projected benefit obligation occurring during the period and deferred for later recognition.

Interest cost component (of net periodic pension cost). Increase in the projected benefit obligation due to passage of time.

Market-related value of plan assets. Balance used to calculate the expected return on plan assets. Market-related value can be either fair value or a calculated value that recognizes changes in fair value in a systematic and rational manner over not more than five years. Different ways of calculating market-related value may be used for different classes of assets, but the manner of determining market-related value must be applied consistently from year to year for each asset class.

Measurement date. Date at which plan assets and obligations are measured.

Mortality rate. Proportion of the number of deaths in a specified group to the number living at the beginning of the period in which the deaths occur. Actuaries use mortality tables, which show death rates for each age, in estimating the amount of pension benefits that will become payable.

Net periodic pension cost. Amount recognized in an employer's financial statements as the cost of a pension plan for a period. Components of net periodic pension cost are service cost, interest cost, actual return on plan assets, gain or loss, amortization of unrecognized prior service cost, and amortization of the unrecognized net obligation or asset existing at the date of initial application of FAS 87. The term **net periodic pension cost** is used instead of **net pension expense** because part of the cost recognized in a period may be capitalized as part of an asset such as inventory.

Plan amendment. Change in terms of an existing plan or the initiation of a new plan. A plan amendment may increase benefits, including those attributed to years of service already rendered. See also **Retroactive benefits**.

Postemployment benefits. Benefits provided to former and inactive employees after employment but before retirement. Postemployment benefits include, but are not limited to, salary continuation, supplemental unemployment benefits, severance benefits, disability-related benefits (including workers' compensation), job training and counseling, and continuation of benefits such as health care benefits and life insurance coverage.

Postretirement benefits. All forms of benefits, other than retirement income, provided by an employer to retirees. Those benefits may be defined in terms of specified benefits, such as health care, tuition assistance, or legal services, that are provided to retirees as the need for those benefits arises or they may be defined in terms of monetary amounts that become payable on the occurrence of a specified event, such as life insurance benefits.

Prepaid pension cost. Cumulative employer contributions in excess of accrued net pension cost.

Prior service cost. Cost of retroactive benefits granted in a plan amendment. See also **Unrecognized prior service cost**.

Projected benefit obligation. Actuarial present value as of a date of all benefits attributed by the pension benefit formula to employee service rendered prior to that date. The projected benefit obligation is measured using assumptions as to future compensation levels if the pension benefit formula is based on those future compensation levels (pay-related, final-pay, final-average-pay, or career-average-pay plans).

Retroactive benefits. Benefits granted in a plan amendment (or initiation) that are attributed by the pension benefit formula to employee services rendered in periods prior to the amendment. The cost of the retroactive benefits is referred to as prior service cost.

Service. Employment taken into consideration under a pension plan. Years of employment before the inception of a plan constitute an employee's past service. Years thereafter are classified in relation to the particular actuarial valuation being made or discussed. Years of employment (including past service) prior to the date of a particular valuation constitute prior service.

Service cost component (of net periodic pension cost). Actuarial present value of benefits attributed by the pension benefit formula to services rendered by employees during the period. The service cost component is a portion of the projected benefit obligation and is unaffected by the funded status of the plan.

Settlement. Transaction that (1) is an irrevocable action, (2) relieves the employer (or the plan) of primary responsibility for a pension benefit obligation, and (3) eliminates significant risks related to the obligation and the assets used to effect the settlement. Examples include making lump-sum cash payments to plan participants in exchange for their rights to receive specified pension benefits and purchasing nonparticipating annuity contracts to cover vested benefits. A transaction must meet all of the above three criteria to constitute a settlement.

Substantive plan. The terms of the postretirement benefit plan as understood by an employer that provides postretirement benefits and the employees who render services in exchange for those benefits. The substantive plan is the basis for the accounting for that exchange transaction. In some situations an employer's cost-sharing policy, as evidenced by past practice or by communication of intended changes to a plan's cost-sharing provisions, or a past practice of regular increases in certain monetary benefits may indicate that the substantive plan differs from the existing written plan.

Transition obligation. The unrecognized amount, as of the date FAS 106 is initially applied, of (1) the accumulated postretirement benefit obligation in excess of (2) the fair value of plan assets plus any recognized accrued postretirement benefit cost or less any recognized prepaid postretirement benefit cost.

Unfunded accumulated benefit obligation. Excess of the accumulated benefit obligation over plan assets.

Unfunded accumulated postretirement benefit obligation. The accumulated postretirement benefit obligation in excess of the fair value of plan assets.

Unrecognized net gain or loss. Cumulative net gain (loss) that has not been recognized as a part of net periodic pension cost. See **Gain or loss**.

Unrecognized prior service cost. Portion of prior service cost that has not been recognized as a part of net periodic pension cost.

CONCEPTS, RULES, AND EXAMPLES

The principal objective of FAS 87 is to measure the compensation cost associated with employees' benefits and to recognize that cost over the employees' service period. This statement is concerned only with the accounting aspects of pension costs. The **funding** (assets set aside to meet future payment obligations) of the benefits is not covered and is considered to be a financial management matter.

When an entity provides benefits that can be estimated in advance to its retired employees and their beneficiaries, the arrangement is a pension plan. The accounting for most types of retirement plans is covered by FAS 87 and 88. These plans include unfunded, insured, trust fund, **defined contribution** and **defined benefit plans,** and deferred compensation contracts, if equivalent. Independent deferred profit sharing plans and pension payments to selected employees on a case-by-case basis are not considered pension plans. The typical plan is written and the amount of benefits can be determined by reference to the associated documents. The plan and its provisions can also be implied, however, from unwritten but established past practices.

The establishment of a pension plan represents a commitment to employees that is of a long-term nature. Although some companies manage their own plans, this commitment usually takes the form of contributions to an independent trustee. These contributions are used by the trustee to invest in plan assets of various types (treasury bonds, treasury bills, certificates of deposit, annuities, marketable securities, corporate bonds, etc.). The plan assets are expected to generate a return generally in the form of interest, dividends, and/or appreciation in asset value. The return on the plan assets (and occasionally their liquidation) provides the trustee with cash to pay benefits to which the employees are entitled. These benefits, in turn, are defined by the plan's benefit formula. The benefit formula incorporates many factors including employee compensation, employee service longevity, employee age, etc. and is considered to provide the best indication of pension obligations and costs. It is used as the basis for determining the pension cost recognized in the financial statements each fiscal year.

Net Periodic Pension Cost

It is assumed that a company will continue to provide retirement benefits well into the future. The accounting for the plan's costs is reflected in the financial statements and these amounts are not discretionary. All pension costs incurred are recognized as expenses.

By their very nature, a sponsor's pension obligations are long-term liabilities. Short-term fluctuations in interest rates, market prices of plan investments, and other factors could, if recognized as incurred, cause material swings in net periodic pension cost and net income in the financial statements of the employer/sponsor that could potentially be offset by reversals in subsequent periods. As illustrated in the subsequent discussion, to avoid this volatility, the FASB permitted the use of smoothing techniques to recognize certain of these changes in a systematic and rational manner by amortizing them instead of recognizing them immediately. This practice was adopted to soften the effects of such short-term fluctuations on reported earnings.

The benefits earned and costs recognized over the employees' service periods are computed by reference to the pension plan's benefit formula. **Net periodic pension cost** consists of the sum of the following six components:

1. Service cost
2. Interest cost on projected benefit obligation
3. Actual return on plan assets
4. Gain or loss

5. Amortization of unrecognized prior service cost
6. Amortization of unrecognized net assets or net obligation existing at date of initial application of FAS 87

In order to compute net periodic pension cost, the **accumulated benefit obligation (ABO)** and the **projected benefit obligation (PBO)** must be computed. Both of these obligations are actuarially determined using the actuarial present value of benefits earned that are attributable to services rendered by the employee to the date of the computation. The ABO is computed by reference to the present compensation level of the employee. It does not consider expected compensation increases that normally occur during the remaining time that the employee is expected to work prior to retirement. The PBO adjusts the accumulated benefit obligation for expected future compensation increases. Under the provisions of most pension plans, this provides a more relevant measure of the estimated cost of the benefits to be paid upon retirement. This is because the benefit formula set forth in the plan normally results in increases in future pension benefits based on increases in the employee's compensation.

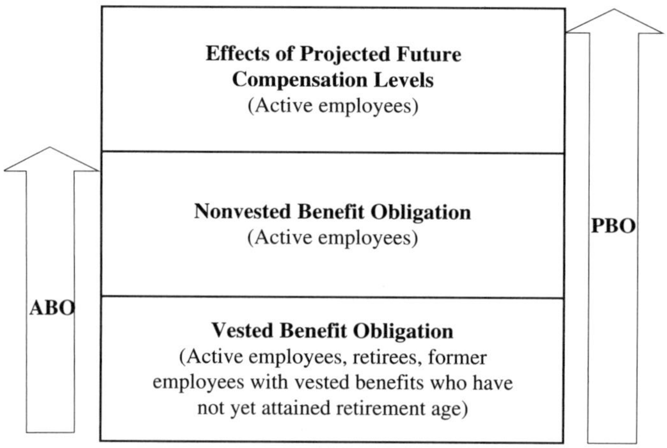

Pay-related, **final-pay,** or **career-average-pay** plans are examples of plans based on future compensation levels. These plans measure benefits based on **service** to date but include **assumptions** as to future compensation increases, turnover, etc. In non-pay-related or **flat-benefit plans,** both obligations (ABO and PBO) are the same.

The following discussion employs a componentized technique by providing a series of examples which cumulatively build to the comprehensive summary of net periodic pension costs and the sample pension disclosures that follow. Key amounts are cross-referenced between examples using parenthesized lowercase letters [(a), (b), etc.]. In accordance with accounting convention, obligations and increases thereto are presented in parentheses.

Example

	January 1, 2005
Accumulated benefit obligation	$(1,500)
Progression of salary and wages	(400)
Projected benefit obligation	$(1,900)

The expected progression of salary and wages is added to the accumulated benefit obligation to arrive at the projected benefit obligation. These amounts are provided by the actuary in a pension plan report.

Computation of the amounts to be presented on the balance sheet requires the determination of plan assets. Plan assets include contributions made by the employer that sponsors the pension plan (sponsor) plus the net earnings on the plan's investments (dividends, interest, and asset appreciation, less asset depreciation), less benefits paid to retired participants.

Example

Plan assets, January 1, 2005	$1,376
Investment earnings during 2005	158
Sponsor's contributions during 2005	145
Benefits paid to retired participants	(160)
Plan assets, December 31, 2005	$1,519

Service costs. This component of net periodic pension cost is the actuarial present value of benefits attributed during the current period. Under FAS 87, the plan's benefit formula is the key to attributing benefits to employee service periods. In most cases, this **attribution** is straightforward.

If the benefit formula is ambiguous, the accounting for pension service costs must be based on the **substantive plan**. In some cases, this means that if an employer has committed to make future **amendments** to provide benefits greater than those written in the plan, that commitment is the basis for the accounting. The relevant facts regarding that implicit commitment are disclosed.

Employers use pensions as a compensation tool to aid in the recruitment and long-term retention of employees. In order to provide incentives for employees to continue their employment with the company over time, plan participants' rights to receive present or future pension benefits are often conditioned on continued employment with the employer/plan sponsor for a specified period. As the conditions are satisfied, the employee is said to "vest" in that portion of the future benefits that become unconditional.

Vesting schedules can result in a disproportionate share of plan benefits being attributed to later years of employment. In this situation, instead of applying the benefit formula, proportions or ratios are used to attribute projected benefits to years of service in a manner that more equitably reflects the substance of timing of earning of the employee benefits. Normally, the actuary accomplishes this by attributing plan benefits to completed years of service by multiplying total benefits by the following ratio:

$$\frac{\text{Number of years of service completed by the employee}}{\text{Number of years of service required to be completed for full vesting}}$$

Certain types of benefits are not includable in vested benefits (e.g., death or disability benefit) and, thus, require a different allocation formula to attribute them to years of service. If the plan's benefit formula does not specify how to relate the benefit to years of service, the following formula is used by the actuary to attribute the benefits to years of service:

$$\frac{\text{Number of completed years of service}}{\text{Total projected years of service}}$$

FAS 87 actuarial assumptions must reflect plan continuation, must be consistent as to future economic expectations, and must be the best estimate in regard to each individual assumption. It is not acceptable to determine that the aggregate assumptions are reasonable if any of the individual assumptions are unreasonable.

The discount rate used in the calculation of service costs is the rate at which benefits could be settled. Examples include those rates in current **annuity contracts,** those published by the Pension Benefit Guaranty Corporation (PBGC), and those that reflect returns on high-quality, fixed-income investments.

Future compensation is considered in the calculation of the service cost component to the extent specified by the benefit formula. To the degree considered in the benefit formula, future compensation includes changes due to advancement, longevity, inflation, etc. Indirect effects, such as predictable bonuses based on compensation levels, and automatic increases specified by the plan also need to be considered. The effect of **retroactive amendments** is included in the calculation when the employer has contractually agreed to them. Service costs attributed during the period increase both the ABO and PBO since they result in additional benefits to be payable in the future.

Example

	January 1, 2005	*2005 Service cost*
Accumulated benefit obligation	$(1,500)	$ (90)
Progression of salary and wages	(400)	(24)
Projected benefit obligation	$(1,900)	$(114) (a)*

* *Component of net periodic pension cost*

The current period service cost component is found in the actuarial report.

Interest cost on PBO. The PBO is a discounted amount. It represents the discounted actuarial present value, at the date of the valuation, of all benefits attributed under the plan's formula to employee service rendered prior to that date. Each year, when the actuary calculates the end-of-year PBO, it is one year closer to the year in which the benefits attributed in prior years will be paid to participants. Consequently, the present value of those previously attributed benefits will have increased to take into account the time value of money. This annual increase, computed by multiplying the assumed settlement discount rate times the PBO at the beginning of the year, increases net periodic pension cost and PBO. Since this "interest" cost is accounted for as part of pension cost it is not treated as interest for the purposes of computing capitalized interest under FAS 34.

Example

	January 1, 2005	*2005 Service cost*	*2005 Interest cost*
Accumulated benefit obligation	$(1,500)	$ (90)	$(120)
Progression of salary and wages	(400)	(24)	(32)
Projected benefit obligation	$(1,900)	$(114) (a)*	$(152) (b)*

* *Component of net periodic pension cost*

The **interest cost component** is calculated by multiplying the start of the year obligation balances by an assumed 8% settlement rate. This amount is found in the actuarial report.

Benefits paid. Benefits paid to retirees are deducted from the above to arrive at the end of the year balance sheet amounts of the accumulated benefit obligation and the projected benefit obligation.

Example

	January 1, 2005	*2005 Service cost*	*2005 Interest cost*	*2005 Benefits paid*	*December 31, 2005*
Accumulated benefit obligation	$(1,500)	$ (90)	$(120)	$160	$(1,550)
Progression of salary and wages	(400)	(24)	(32)	--	(456)
Projected benefit obligation	$(1,900)	$(114) (a)	$(152) (b)	$160	$(2,006)

Benefits of $160 were paid to retirees during the current year. This amount is found in the report of the pension plan trustee.

Actual return on plan assets. This component is the difference between the **fair value** of the plan assets at the end of the period and the fair value of the plan assets at the beginning of the period adjusted for contributions and payments during the period. Another way to express the result is that it is the net (realized and unrealized) appreciation and depreciation of plan assets plus earnings from the plan assets for the period.

Example

	January 1, 2005	2005 Actual return on plan assets	2005 Sponsor funding	2005 Benefits paid	December 31, 2005
Plan assets	$1,376	$158 (c)*	$145	$(160)	$1,519

* *Component of net periodic pension cost*

The actual return on plan assets of $158, cash deposited with the trustee of $145, and benefits paid ($160) are amounts found in the report of the pension plan trustee. These items increase the plan assets to $1,519 at the end of the year. The actual return on plan assets is adjusted, however, to the expected long-term rate (9% assumed) of return on plan assets ($1,376 x 9% = $124). The difference ($158 – $124 = $34) is a return on asset adjustment and is deferred as a gain (loss). The return on asset adjustment is a component of net periodic pension cost and is discussed in detail in the following section.

Gain or loss. Gains (losses) result from (1) changes in plan assumptions, (2) changes in the amount of plan assets, and (3) changes in the amount of the projected benefit obligation. As discussed previously, even though these gains or losses are economic events that impact the sponsor's obligations under the plan, upon their occurrence, their immediate recognition in the sponsor's financial statements is not permitted by FAS 87. Instead, to provide "smoothing" of the effects of short-term fluctuations, **unrecognized net gain (loss)** is **amortized** if it meets certain criteria specified below.

Since actuarial cost methods are based on numerous assumptions (employee compensation, mortality, turnover, earnings of the pension plan, etc.), it is not unusual for one or more of these assumptions to be invalidated by changes over time. Adjustments will invariably be necessary to bring prior estimates back in line with actual events. These adjustments are known as actuarial gains (losses). The accounting issue regarding the recognition of actuarial adjustments is their timing. All pension costs must eventually be recognized as expense. Actuarial gains (losses) are not considered prior period adjustments since they result from a refinement of estimates arising from obtaining subsequent information. Thus, under APB 20, they are considered changes in an estimate to be recognized in current and future periods.

Plan asset gains (losses) result from both realized and unrealized amounts. They represent periodic differences between the actual return on assets and the expected return. The expected return is generated by multiplying the **expected long-term rate of return** by the **market-related value** of plan assets. Market-related value is a concept unique to pension accounting. It results from the previously discussed actuarial smoothing techniques under FAS 87. Market-related value consists of two components. The first component is the fair value of the plan assets. The second component is an adjustment for the unrecognized portion of previous years' market gains or losses that are being amortized over a period of five years or less using a consistently applied method. Consistently applied means from year to year for each asset class (i.e., bonds, equities), since different classes of assets may have their market-related value calculated in a different manner (i.e., fair value in one case, moving average in another case). Thus, the market-related value may be fair value, but it also may be other than fair value if all or a portion of it results from calculation.

Plan asset gains (losses) include both (1) changes in the market-related value of assets (regardless of definition) from one period to another **and** (2) any changes that are not yet reflected in market-related value (i.e., the difference between the actual fair values of assets and the calculated market-related values). Only the former changes are recognized and amortized. The latter changes are recognized over time through the calculated market-related values. Differences in the experienced amount of PBO from that assumed will also result in gain (loss).

Irrespective of the income smoothing techniques used, if this unrecognized net gain (loss) exceeds a "corridor" of 10% of the greater of the beginning balances of the market-related value of plan assets or the projected benefit obligation, a minimum amount of amortization is required. The **excess** over 10% is divided by the average remaining service period of active employees and included as a component of net pension costs. Average remaining life expectancies of inactive employees may be used if that is a better measure due to the demographics of the plan participants.

Net pension costs include only the **expected return on plan assets**. Any difference between actual and expected returns is deferred through the **gain (loss) component of net pension cost**. If actual return is greater than expected return, net pension cost is **increased** to adjust the actual return to the lower expected return. If expected return is greater than actual return, the adjustment results in a **decrease** to net pension cost to adjust the actual return to the higher expected return. If the unrecognized net gain (loss) is large enough, it is amortized. Conceptually, the expected return represents the best estimate of long-term performance of the plan's investments. In any given year, however, an unusual short-term result may occur given the volatility of financial markets.

The expected long-term rate of return used to calculate the expected return on plan assets is the average rate of return expected to be earned on invested funds to provide for pension benefits included in the PBO. Present rates of return and expected future reinvestment rates of return are considered in arriving at the rate to be used.

To summarize, net periodic pension cost includes a gain (loss) component consisting of **both** of the following, if applicable:

1. As a minimum, the portion of the unrecognized net gain (loss) from previous periods that exceeds the **greater** of 10% of the beginning balances of the market-related value of plan assets **or** the PBO, usually amortized over the average remaining service period of active employees expected to receive benefits.
2. The difference between the expected return and the actual return on plan assets.

An accelerated method of amortization of unrecognized net gain (loss) is acceptable if it is applied consistently to both gains and losses, and if the method is disclosed in the notes to the financial statements. In all cases, at least the minimum amount discussed above must be amortized.

Example

	January 1, 2005	*2005 Return on asset adjustment*	2005 *Amortization*	*December 31, 2005*
Unrecognized actuarial gain (loss)	$(210)	$34 (d)*	$2(d)*	$(174)

* *Components of net periodic pension cost*

The return on asset adjustment of $34 is the difference between the actual return of $158 and the expected return of $124 on plan assets. The actuarial loss at the start of the year ($210 assumed) is amortized if it **exceeds** a "corridor" of the larger of 10% of the projected benefit obligation at the beginning of the period ($1,900 x 10% = $190) or 10% of the fair value of plan assets ($1,376 x 10% = $138). In this example, $20 ($210 – $190) is amortized by dividing the years of average remaining service (twelve years assumed), with a result rounded to $2. The straight-line method is used, and it is assumed that market-related value is the same as fair value.

Amortization of unrecognized prior service cost. Prior service costs are incurred when the sponsor adopts plan amendments that increase plan benefits attributable to services rendered by plan participants in the past. These costs are accounted for as a change in estimate. Prior service costs are measured at the amendment date by the increase in the projected benefit obligation. The remaining service period of every active employee expected to receive benefits is estimated, and an equal amount of prior service cost is assigned to each future period. Consistent use of an accelerated amortization method is acceptable and must be disclosed if used.

If most of the plan's participants are inactive, remaining life expectancy is used as a basis for amortization instead of estimated remaining service period. If economic benefits will be realized by plan participants over a shorter period than remaining service period, amortization of costs is accelerated to recognize the costs in the periods that the participants benefit. If an amendment **reduces** the projected benefit obligation, unrecognized prior service costs are reduced to the extent that they exist and any excess is amortized in the manner described above for benefit increases.

Example

	January 1, 2005	*2005 Amortization*	*December 31, 2005*
Unrecognized prior service cost	$320	$(27) (e)*	$293

* *Component of net periodic pension cost*

Unrecognized prior service cost ($320) is amortized over the years of average remaining service (twelve years assumed) at the amendment date with a result rounded to $27. The straight-line method was used. These amounts are found in the actuarial report.

Amortization of unrecognized amount at date of initial FAS 87 application. FAS 87 has been GAAP for about fifteen years, and after this period of time has elapsed few plans still remain with unamortized transition amounts. The difference between the PBO and the fair value of plan assets minus recognized prepaid or plus accrued pension cost at the beginning of the fiscal year of the initial FAS 87 application was to be amortized using the straight-line method over the average remaining active employee service period. If the average remaining service period was less than fifteen years, the employer could elect to use a fifteen-year period. If all or almost all of a plan's participants were inactive, the employer used the inactive participants' average remaining life expectancy.

NOTE: For purposes of illustrating this, implementation of FAS 87 is assumed to be currently taking place.

Example

	January 1, 2005	*2005 Amortization*	*December 31, 2005*
Unamortized net obligation (asset) existing at FAS 87 application	$(6)	$3 (f)*	$(3)

* *Component of net periodic pension cost*

At initial adoption of FAS 87, the "transition amount" was computed as an asset of $48. This transition asset is being amortized using the straight-line method over sixteen years ($3 per year), which represents the average remaining service period of employees expected to receive benefits under the plan at transition. Thus, the unamortized balance at January 1, 2005, was $6 and the amortization for 2005 was $3. These amounts are found in the actuarial report.

Summary of net periodic pension cost. The components that were identified in the above examples are summed as follows to determine the amount defined as net periodic pension cost:

		2005
Service cost	(a)	$114
Interest cost	(b)	152
Actual return on plan assets	(c)	(158)
Gain (loss)	(d)	36
Amortization of unrecognized prior service cost	(e)	27
Amortization of unrecognized net obligation (asset) existing at FAS 87 application	(f)	(3)
Total net periodic pension cost		$168

One possible source of confusion is the actual return on plan assets ($158) and the unrecognized gain of $36 that net to $122. The actual return on plan assets reduces pension cost. This is because, to the extent that plan assets generate earnings, those earnings help the plan sponsor subsidize the cost of providing the benefits. Thus, the plan sponsor will not have to fund benefits as they become due, to the extent that plan earnings provide the plan with cash to pay those benefits. This reduction, however, is adjusted by increasing pension cost by the difference between actual and expected return of $34 and the amortization of the excess actuarial loss of $2, for a total of $36. The net result is to include the **expected** return of $124 ($158 – $34) less the amortization of the excess of $2 for a total of $122 ($158 – $36). In recognizing the components of net periodic pension costs, FAS 132 requires the **disclosure** of this expected return of $124 and the loss of $2.

Reconciliation of Beginning and Ending ABO, PBO, and Plan Assets

The following table summarizes the 2005 activity affecting ABO, PBO, and Plan Assets and reconciles the beginning and ending balances per the actuarial report:

	Accumulated benefit obligation	*Progression of salaries and wages*	*Projected benefit obligation*	*Fair value of plan assets**
Balance, January 1, 2005	$ (1,500)	$ (400)	$ (1,900)	$ 1,376
Service cost	(90)	(24)	(114) (a)	
Interest cost	(120)	(32)	(152) (b)	
Benefits paid to retired participants	160		160	(160)
Actual return on plan assets				158 (c)
Sponsor's contributions				145
Balance, December 31, 2005	$ (1,550)	$ (456)	$ (2,006)	$ 1,519

**Assumed to be the same as market-related value for this illustration.*

Employer's Liabilities and Assets

Accounting for defined benefit plans remains a controversial topic. In particular, the fact that plan assets and liabilities are, with certain exceptions, not considered to be the employers' assets and liabilities, continues to be a contentious issue. When FAS 87 was first imposed, the FASB concluded that full imposition of accrual-basis recognition rules would have caused there to be unacceptably large adjustments to the financial statements of companies whose plans were materially underfunded. The adjustments would have been necessary to recognize previously unrecognized assets or liabilities representing the differences between PBO and the fair value of plan assets. To ease the perceived burden on these plan sponsors, FASB developed a compromise **minimum liability** approach. This minimum liability is computed by reference to the excess of the ABO (which is a smaller obligation than the PBO since it does not recognize projected future compensation increases) over the fair value of the plan assets. For the purpose of this calculation, the fair value of the assets is used, not the market-related value used to calculate the expected return on plan assets. To the extent that there is a pension liability already recorded, the sponsor need only recognize the additional amount necessary to increase the recorded liability to the amount of the minimum liability.

The theory behind using the ABO is the fact that, if the pension plan were terminated at the balance sheet date, the future compensation increases would never occur and the pension obligation could be settled for the smaller amount.

Fair value is determined as of the financial statement date (or not more than three months prior to that date if used consistently—see discussion of EITF Issue D-106 for a related interpretation), and in the amount that would result from negotiations between a willing buyer and seller not in a liquidation sale. Fair value is measured in preferred order by market price, selling price of similar investments, or discounted cash flows at a rate indicative of the risk involved.

In FAS 87, the additional minimum liability is recognized by an offsetting entry to recognize an intangible asset up to the amount of unrecognized prior service cost. Any additional debit needed is considered a loss and is shown net of income tax benefits (subject to the restrictions on recognition of deferred tax assets per FAS 109) in other comprehensive income.

Several points need to be emphasized with respect to the additional minimum liability. **First,** an asset is **not** recorded if the fair value of the plan assets exceeds the accumulated benefit obligation. **Second,** the calculation of the minimum liability requires consideration of any already recorded prepaid or accrued pension cost. The net liability must be equal to at least the **unfunded accumulated benefit obligation** irrespective of the starting point. An already recorded **prepaid pension cost** will increase the amount of the recognized additional liability. An already recorded **accrued pension cost** will decrease it. **Third,** the intangible asset is **not** amortized. **Fourth,** at the time of the next calculation, the amounts are either added to or reversed out with no effect on net income. These balance sheet entries are entirely independent of net income and do not affect the calculation of net pension costs. **Fifth,** unless a significant event occurs or measures of obligations and assets as of a more current date become available, interim financial statements will show the year-end additional minimum liability adjusted for subsequent contributions and accruals. In this case, previous year-end assumptions regarding net pension cost would also carry over to the interim financial statements.

A schedule showing the variables of the above example in accordance with FAS 132 reconciling the balance sheet amounts with the funded status of the plan is shown below. Assumed activity for 2004 is provided for comparative purposes.

	2004	*2005*
Change in benefit obligation		
Projected benefit obligation, beginning of year	$1,800	$1,900
Service cost	111	114
Interest cost	144	152
Amendment (prior service cost element)	--	--
Actuarial loss (gain)	--	--
Benefits paid	(155)	(160)
Projected benefit obligation, end of year	1,900	2,006
Change in plan assets		
Fair value of plan assets, beginning of year	1,241	1,376
Actual return (loss) on plan assets	150	158
Employer contribution	140	145
Benefits paid	(155)	(160)
Fair value of plan assets, end of year	1,376	1,519
Funded status [plan over (under) funded]	(524)	(487)
Unrecognized net actuarial loss on assets	210	174
Unrecognized prior service cost	320	293
Unamortized net obligation (asset) at FAS 87 adoption	(6)	(3)
Prepaid (accrued) pension cost	$ --	$ (23)

	2004	2005
Amounts recognized on the balance sheet consist of		
Accrued benefit liability	$ (124)	$ (31)
Intangible asset	124	8
Accumulated other comprehensive income	--	--
Net amount recognized	$ --	$ (23)

The difference between the projected benefit obligation and the plan assets indicates that the plan in this example is underfunded by **$524** at the beginning of 2005. Net actuarial losses, prior service costs, and the unamortized net asset existing when FAS 87 was first applied are the remaining reconciling items to the zero amount shown on the balance sheet at the end of the prior year. **Conceptually,** the zero balance sheet amount is a journal entry netting of the following elements that would be recognized in the employer's accounting records at the end of 2004, if accounting under FAS 87 mirrored the pension plan's financial statements:

Investments	1,376	
Deferred actuarial loss	210	
Deferred prior service cost	320	
Deferred asset existing at FAS 87 application		6
Projected benefit obligation		1,900

Applying FAS 87 prescribed accounting, however, only the additional minimum liability in the case of seriously underfunded plans is required to be recognized on the balance sheet. This amount is the difference between the accumulated benefit obligation ($1,500) and the fair value of the plan assets ($1,376) plus prepaid pension cost ($0) or minus accrued pension cost ($0). In the above example, the result is $124 and the journal entry follows:

Intangible asset	124	
Pension liability		124

This journal entry is entirely independent of the calculation of pension cost and has no effect on that calculation. It only affects the balance sheet and remains until adjusted at the end of the next year. At that time, it will be decreased or increased to the extent required.

If the result of the minimum liability calculation exceeds the unrecognized prior service cost, FAS 130 requires the excess to be treated as other comprehensive income. For instance, assume that the required minimum liability in the above example were $350. In this case, the intangible asset would be recorded at the amount of the unrecognized prior service cost and the **excess** ($350 minimum liability – $320 unrecognized prior service cost = $30 excess) would be recorded as other comprehensive income. The required journal entry would be (revision of prior journal entry)

Other comprehensive income	30	
Intangible asset	320	
Pension liability		350

If not needed at the end of the next year, this entry would then be reversed.

In the following year employer/sponsor contributions of $145, net periodic pension costs of $168, and benefit payments of $160 are used in order to arrive at the end of the year balance sheet amounts. An accrued pension cost of $23 ($168 – $145) is required. This difference results from the employer funding $23 less than pension cost. **Conceptually,** this accrued amount is the netting of the following:

Investments	$1,519	
Deferred actuarial loss	174	
Deferred prior service cost	293	
Deferred assets existing at FAS 87 application		$ 3
Projected benefit obligation		2,006
Totals	$1,986	$2,009

The excess credit is shown as an accrued pension liability of $23. Note that an additional minimum liability is still required since the accumulated benefit obligation ($1,550) and the plan assets ($1,519) differ by $31 and there is only a pension liability on the balance sheet of $23. Thus, the additional minimum liability balances at the start of the year are adjusted through the following journal entry:

Pension liability	116	
Intangible asset		116

This entry does not affect pension cost.

In summary, only two journal entries are ordinarily required, if applicable. They are illustrated below based on facts from the preceding example.

1. Record net periodic pension cost and adjust associated accrued (or prepaid) pension cost.

Net periodic pension cost	168	
Accrued pension benefits		168

2. Record the minimum liability, associated intangible assets, and other comprehensive income as applicable in the circumstances (assumes the journal entry for any such prior amounts has already been reversed).

Intangible asset	8	
Accrued benefit liability		8

The net result of recording these entries on the balance sheet is summarized as follows:

Balance Sheet

Assets		*Liabilities*	
Intangible pension asset	$8	Accrued pension benefits	$31

Disclosure Requirements

FAS 132, as replaced in 2003 by FAS 132(R), provides for expanded disclosures for plans covered by FAS 87, but also created a somewhat streamlined format for the pension disclosures of nonpublic companies. After the issuance of FAS 132 in 1998, concerns were raised by financial statement users, including financial analysts, and accordingly FAS 132(R) was promulgated in 2003, with additional requirements for disclosure of information about types of plan assets, investment strategy, measurement date(s), plan obligations, cash flows, and components of the net periodic pension cost recognized in interim periods. FAS 132(R) continues to provide differential requirements for nonpublic companies, but does significantly also expand requirements to interim period financial statements, bowing to concerns bearing on public company financial reporting practices.

The following paragraphs describe the currently mandated disclosures, *with appropriate indicators of items not required of nonpublic entities.*

Reconciliation of plan benefit obligation. This reconciliation must report, if applicable, the separate effects for the period of the service cost, interest cost, contributions by plan participants, actuarial gains and losses, foreign currency exchange rate changes, benefits paid, plan amendments, business combinations, divestitures, plan curtailments, settlements, and special termination benefits. In preparing this reconciliation, for defined benefit pension plans the plan benefit obligation is to be defined as the projected benefit obligation; for defined benefit postretirement plans, it is defined as the accumulated postemployment benefit obligation. *This information is not required in financial statements of nonpublic entities.*

Reconciliation of fair value of plan assets. This reconciliation must report, if applicable, the separate effects for the period of the actual return on plan assets, foreign currency exchange rate changes, contributions made by the employer, contributions by the plan participants, benefits paid, business combinations, divestitures, and settlements. *This information is not required in financial statements of nonpublic entities.*

Funded status of the plan, amounts not recognized in the employer's balance sheet, and the amounts recognized in the balance sheet. This must report, as applicable, the amount of unamortized prior service cost, the amount of any unrecognized net gain or loss (including the asset gains or losses not yet reflected in market-related value), the amount of any remaining unamortized, unrecognized net obligation or asset arising from initial application of FAS 87, net pension or other postretirement benefit prepaid asset or accrued liabilities, and any intangible asset and the amount of accumulated other comprehensive income recognized per FAS 87. *This information is not required in financial statements of nonpublic entities.*

Information about plan assets. Per FAS 132(R), for each major category of plan assets, such as equities, debt instruments, and real estate, disclosure is required of the percentage of the fair value of total plan assets held as of the measurement date used for each balance sheet presented. A narrative description of investment policies and strategies employed is now required, which should address target allocations for major asset classes, presented on a weighted-average basis as of the measurement date, as well as other factors that are pertinent to an understanding, such as information about investment goals, risk management practices, permitted and prohibited investments (e.g., use of derivatives, diversification, and relationships between plan assets and benefit obligations). Also required is a narrative explanation of the basis upon which the expect long-term return on assets has been ascertained (e.g., the extent to which historical performance has been used to extrapolate from, what adjustments were made to anticipate future trends, etc.). The standard encourages expanded discussion and the use of greater asset categorization.

Accumulated benefit obligation. For defined benefit pension plans, disclosure is required of the accumulated benefit obligation, in addition to the aforementioned disclosures of the projected benefit obligation.

Benefits to be paid. The benefits expected to be paid in each of the next five fiscal years plus the aggregate of the five years thereafter. These estimated amounts are developed using the same assumptions that are used to measure the employer's benefit obligation, and should include benefits that will be attributable to estimated future employee service.

Contributions to be received. The amount of contributions expected to be paid into the plan during the next fiscal year; the aggregate of the amounts required by funding regulations or laws, discretionary amounts, and noncash contributions may be reported.

Periodic benefit cost. This must report separately the service cost component, interest cost component, expected return on plan assets, amortization of unrecognized transition asset or liability, the amount of recognized gain or loss, prior to service cost recognized, and gain or loss due to settlement or curtailment. *This information is not required in financial statements of nonpublic entities.*

Change in additional minimum pension liability. The amount reported within other comprehensive income for the period associated with a change in the additional minimum pension liability must be reported.

Assumptions. There must be disclosure of various assumptions used in the accounting for plans: assumed discount rates, rates of compensation increase (for pay-related plans), and expected long-term rate of return on plan assets. These must be reported in a tabular format, identifying assumptions pertaining to the reported benefit obligation and to determine net benefit cost.

Measurement dates. The measurement dates used to determine pension and other postretirement benefit measurements, for at least the plans making up a majority of plan assets and obligations.

Assumed health care cost trends. For relevant plans, disclosure is required of the assumed health care cost trend rates for the following year used to measure the expected cost of benefits, as well as a general description of the direction and pattern of change in the assumed trend rates thereafter, together with the ultimate rate and when that terminal rate is expected to be achieved.

Sensitivity date. Disclosure of the effects of a one-percentage-point increase and decrease in the assumed health care cost trend rate on the aggregate service and interest cost components of the net periodic postretirement health care benefit cost, and on the accumulated postretirement benefit obligation for health care benefits. In computing these amounts all other assumptions must be held constant. *This information is not required in financial statements of nonpublic entities.*

Other information. As applicable, other disclosures are also required. These include the amounts and types of securities of the employer and its related entities included in plan assets, the approximate amount of future annual benefits of plan participants covered by insurance contracts issued by the employer or its related entities, and any significant transactions between the employer or related entities and the plan, all of which are equally required for public and nonpublic reporting entities. For public companies only, any commitment to future benefit increases used as a basis for computing the obligation, the cost of providing special or contractual termination benefits during the reporting period, and information about any changes not otherwise apparent, are also required disclosures.

For entities having multiple plans, the information required under FAS 132(R) is to be aggregated so that all defined benefit retirement plans are combined, and all other postretirement benefit plans are likewise combined. Disclosure of amounts recognized in the balance sheet must distinguish prepaid benefit costs from accrued benefit liabilities. However, disclosures about pension plans with assets in excess of the accumulated benefit obligation generally may be aggregated with disclosures about pension plans with accumulated benefit obligations in excess of assets. When aggregation is utilized, the financial statements must disclose separately the aggregate benefit obligations and aggregate fair value of plan assets for each of the pension plans and other benefit plans with accumulated obligations in excess of assets. The reporting entity may also combine disclosures about pension plans or other postretirement benefit plans outside the US with those for US plans unless the obligations of the plans outside the US are significant relative to the entity's total benefit obligation and the non-US plans use significantly different assumptions.

The simplified disclosures permitted for nonpublic entities are illustrated by the following tabulation of comparative data:

	2004	2005
Funded status		
Projected benefit obligation at December 31	$ 1,900	$ 2,006
Fair value of Plan assets at December 31	1,376	1,519
Funded status	$ (524)	$ (487)
Amounts recognized on the balance sheet		
Prepaid (accrued) benefit cost	$ --	$ (23)
Weighted-average assumptions		
Discount rate	7.5%	7.5%
Expected return on plan assets	9.0%	9.0%
Rate of compensation increase	4.0%	4.0%
Additional pension data		
Net periodic pension cost	$ 163	$ 168
Employer contribution	140	145
Benefits paid	155	160

Most of the information used to determine the amounts in the foregoing disclosure is provided by the actuary or worksheet entries and does not appear in the entity's accounting records. Thus, accounts that reflect such events as the actuarial loss and prior service costs will usually not be found in the employer's accounting records.

Interim Financial Reporting Requirements

FAS 132(R) has imposed new requirements affecting both public and nonpublic company interim financial reporting. Beginning with the effective date of this standard, publicly traded entities must disclose, in interim financial statements that include a statement of income, details of benefit cost and contributions paid. The amount of net periodic benefit cost recognized must be set forth, showing separately the service cost component, the interest cost component, the expected return on plan assets for the period, the amortization of the unrecognized transition obligation or transition asset, the amount of recognized gains or losses, the amount of prior service cost recognized, and the amount of gain or loss recognized due to a settlement or curtailment. Additionally, the total amount of the employer's contributions paid, and expected to be paid, during the current fiscal year, must be presented, if significantly different from amounts previously disclosed pursuant to the annual reporting requirements of the standard. It is permissible to present estimated contributions in the aggregate, combining contributions required by funding regulations or laws, discretionary contributions, and noncash contributions.

For nonpublic entities, disclosure is required—in interim periods when a complete set of financial statements is presented—of the total amount of the employer's contributions paid, and expected to be paid, during the current fiscal year, if significantly different from amounts previously disclosed pursuant to the annual reporting requirements of the standard. Estimated contributions may be presented in the aggregate combining contributions required by funding regulations or laws, discretionary contributions, and noncash contributions.

Other Pension Considerations

Annuity and insurance contracts. If annuity contracts and other insurance contracts that are equivalent in substance are valid and irrevocable, if they transfer significant risks to an unrelated insurance company (not a captive insurer), and if there is no reasonable doubt as to their payment, they are excluded from plan assets and their benefits are excluded from the accumulated benefit obligation and from the projected benefit obligation. Most other contracts are not considered annuities for FAS 87 purposes. If a plan's benefit formula specifies coverage by **nonparticipating** annuity contracts, the service component of net pension costs is the cost of those contracts. In the case of a **participating** annuity contract, the cost of the participation right is recognized as an asset and measured annually at its fair value. If fair value is inestimable, the cost is systematically amortized and carried at amortized cost (not to exceed net realizable value). Benefits provided by the formula beyond those provided by annuities are accounted for in the usual FAS 87 manner. All other insurance contracts are considered investments and are usually measured at cash surrender value, conversion value, contract value, or some equivalent.

Defined contribution plans. In the typical defined contribution plan, the contribution is either discretionary or derived from a formula, and that amount is the expense in the sponsor's financial statements for the year. Benefits are generally paid from the pool of accumulated contributions and are limited to the plan assets available to pay them. If, however, the defined contribution plan has defined benefits, the provision is calculated in the usual manner under FAS 87.

Multiemployer pension plans. Participation in a multiemployer plan (two or more unrelated employers contribute such as in collectively bargained union-sponsored plans) requires that the contribution for the period be recognized as net pension cost and that any contributions due and unpaid be recognized as a liability. Assets of all the employers sponsoring this type of plan are usually commingled and not segregated or restricted. A Board of Trustees usually administers these plans. If there is a withdrawal of an employer from this type of plan and if an obligation to make up any funding deficiency is either probable or reasonably possible, FAS 5 applies.

Some plans are, in substance, a pooling or aggregation of single employer plans and are ordinarily without collective-bargaining agreements. Contributions are usually based on a specified benefit formula. These plans are not considered multiemployer, and the accounting is based on each employer's respective interest in the plan.

Non-US pension arrangements. The terms and conditions that define the amount of benefits and the nature of the obligation determine the substance of a non-US pension arrangement. If they are, in substance, similar to pension plans, FAS 87 and 88 apply.

Business combinations. When an entity that sponsors a single-employer defined benefit pension plan is purchased, the purchaser must assign part of the purchase price to an asset if plan assets exceed the projected benefit obligation, or to a liability if the projected benefit obligation exceeds plan assets. The projected benefit obligation includes the effect of any expected plan curtailment or termination as a result of the change in ownership of the sponsor. This assignment eliminates any existing unrecognized components, and any future differences between contributions and net pension cost will affect the asset or liability recognized when the purchase was initially recorded.

FAS 88

This statement is meant to be applied within the framework of FAS 87. It describes the accounting to be followed by obligors when all or part of defined benefit pension plans have been settled or curtailed. It establishes employer accounting procedures for benefits offered when employment is terminated.

Settlements include both the purchase of nonparticipating annuity contracts and lump-sum cash payments. The following three criteria must all be met in order to constitute a pension obligation settlement:

1. Must be irrevocable
2. Must relieve the obligor of primary responsibility for the obligation
3. Must eliminate significant risks associated with the obligation and the assets used to effect it

Transactions that do not meet these three criteria do not qualify for treatment as a settlement under FAS 88. For example, an obligor could invest in a portfolio of high-quality fixed-income securities that would provide cash flows of interest and return-of-principal payments on dates that approximate the dates on which settlement payments are expected to become due. This would not meet the above criteria, however, because the employer is still primarily liable for the pension obligation and the investment is not irrevocable. Such a defeasance strategy does not constitute a settlement.

Under an annuity contract settlement, an unrelated insurance company unconditionally accepts an obligation to provide the required benefits. The following criteria must be met for this type of settlement:

1. Must be irrevocable
2. Must involve transfer of material risk to the insurance company

There can be no reasonable doubt as to the ability of the insurance company to meet its contractual obligation. The substance of any **participating** annuity contract must relieve the employer of most of the risks and rewards or it does not meet the criteria.

Curtailments include early discontinuance of employee services or cessation or suspension of a plan. Additional benefits may not be earned, although future service time may be counted towards vesting. Curtailments must meet the following criteria:

1. Must materially diminish present employees' future service or
2. Must stop or materially diminish the accumulation of benefits by a significant number of employees

A curtailment and a settlement can occur separately or together.

Settlements. If the entire projected benefit obligation is settled, any FAS 87 unrecognized net gain (loss) plus any remaining unrecognized net asset existing when FAS 87 was initially applied are immediately recognized. A pro rata portion is recognized in the case of partial settlement. If the obligation is settled by purchasing **participating** annuities, the cost of the right of participation is deducted from the gain (but not from the loss) before recognition.

If the total of the interest cost and service cost components of the FAS 87 periodic pension cost is greater than or equal to the settlement costs during a given year, the recognition of the above gain (loss) is not required, but is permitted. However, a consistent policy must be followed in this regard. The settlement cost is generally the cash paid, or the cost of **nonparticipating** annuities purchased, or the cost of **participating** annuities reduced by the cost of the right of participation.

Curtailments. A curtailment results in the elimination of future years of service. The pro rata portions of any (1) unrecognized cost of retroactive plan amendments and (2) remaining unrecognized net obligation existing when FAS 87 was initially applied that is associated with the eliminated years of service are immediately recognized as a loss.

If curtailment results in a decrease in the projected benefit obligation, a gain is indicated. An increase in the projected benefit obligation (excluding termination benefits) indicates a loss. This indicated gain (loss) is then netted against the loss from unrecognized prior service cost recognized in accordance with the preceding paragraph. The net result is the **curtailment gain** or **curtailment loss**. This gain (loss) is accounted for as provided in FAS 5. A gain is recognized upon actual employee termination or plan suspension. A loss is recognized when both the curtailment is probable and the effects are reasonably estimable.

After the curtailment gain (loss) is calculated, any remaining unrecognized net asset existing when FAS 87 was initially applied is transferred from that category and combined with the gain (loss) arising after FAS 87 application. It is subsequently treated as a component of the new gain (loss) category.

Termination benefits. Termination benefits are accounted for in accordance with FAS 5. Special short time period benefits require that a loss and a liability be recognized when the offer is accepted and the amount can be reasonably estimated. Contractual termination benefits require that a loss and a liability be recognized when it is probable that employees will receive the benefits and the amount can be reasonably estimated. The cost of these benefits is the cash paid at termination and the present value of future payments. Termination benefits and curtailments can occur together.

Component disposal. Gains (losses), as calculated above, that result because of a disposal of a component of the entity are recognized according to the provisions of FAS 144.

Postretirement Benefits other than Pensions

FAS 106 establishes the standard for employers' accounting for **other** (than pension) **postretirement employee benefits** (OPEB). This standard prescribes a single method for measuring and recognizing an employer's **accumulated postretirement benefit obligation** (APBO). It applies to all forms of postretirement benefits, although the most material benefit is usually postretirement health care insurance coverage. It uses the fundamental framework established by FAS 87 and 88. To the extent that the promised benefits are similar, the accounting provisions are similar. Only when there is a compelling reason, is the accounting different.

FAS 106 requires accrual accounting and adopts the three primary characteristics of pension accounting as follows:

1. Delayed recognition (changes are not recognized immediately but are subsequently recognized in a gradual and systematic way)
2. Reporting net cost (aggregates of various items are reported as one net amount)
3. Offsetting assets and liabilities (assets and liabilities are sometimes shown net)

FAS 106 distinguishes between the **substantive** plan and the **written** plan. Although generally the same, the **substantive plan** (the one understood as evidenced by past practice or by communication of intended changes) is the basis for the accounting if it differs from the written plan.

FAS 106 focuses on accounting for a single-employer plan that defines the postretirement benefits to be provided. A defined benefit postretirement plan defines benefits in terms of (1) monetary amounts or (2) benefit coverage to be provided. Postretirement benefits can include tuition assistance, legal services, day care, housing subsidies, health insurance coverage (probably the most significant), and other benefits. The amount of benefits usually depends on a benefit formula. OPEB may be provided to current employees, former employees, beneficiaries and covered dependents. This standard applies to **settlement** of the APBO and to **curtailment** of a plan as part of a **special termination** benefit offer. It also applies to deferred compensation contracts with individuals. Taken together, these contracts are **equivalent** to an OPEB plan. FAS 106 does not apply to benefits provided through a pension plan. If part of a larger plan with active employees, the OPEB is segregated and accounted for in accordance with this standard. If not materially different, estimates, averages, and computational shortcuts may be used.

The basic tenet of FAS 106 is that accrual accounting is better than cash basis accounting. Recognition and measurement of the obligation to provide OPEB is required in order to provide relevant information to financial statement users. Although funding and cash flow information is incorporated into the statement, the overall liability is the primary focus.

The standard attempts, in accordance with the terms of the substantive plan, to account for the exchange transaction that takes place between the employer, who is ultimately responsible for providing OPEB, and the employee who provides services, in part at least, to obtain the OPEB. FAS 106 accounting requires that the liability for OPEB be fully accrued when the employee is **fully eligible** for all of the expected benefits. The fact that the employee may continue to work beyond this date is not relevant since the employee has already provided the services required to earn the OPEB.

OPEB are considered to be deferred compensation earned in an exchange transaction during the time periods that the employee provides services. The expected cost generally is attributed in equal amounts (unless the plan attributes a disproportionate share of benefits to early years) over the periods from the employee's hiring date (unless credit for the service is only granted from a later plan eligibility or entry date) to the date that the employee attains full eligibility for all benefits expected to be received. This accrual is followed even if the employee provides service beyond the **date of full eligibility**.

Accounting for postretirement benefits. The **expected postretirement benefit obligation** (EPBO) is the actuarial present value (APV) as of a specific date of the benefits expected to be paid to the employee, beneficiaries and covered dependents. This term is not used in FAS 87. Measurement of the EPBO is based on the following:

1. Expected amount and timing of future benefits
2. Expected future costs
3. Extent of cost sharing (contributions, deductibles, coinsurance provisions, etc.) between employer, employee and others (i.e., the government). The APV of employee contributions reduces the APV of the EPBO. Obligations to return employee contributions, plus interest if applicable, are recognized as a component of EPBO.

The EPBO includes an assumed salary progression for a pay-related plan. Future compensation levels represent the best estimate after considering the individual employees involved, general price levels, seniority, productivity, promotions, indirect effects, etc.

The APBO is the APV as of a specific date of all future benefits attributable to service by an employee to that date. It represents the portion of the EPBO earned to date. After full eligibility is attained, the APBO equals the EPBO.

The APBO also includes an assumed salary progression for a pay-related plan. Thus, this term is more comparable to the projected benefit obligation (PBO) under FAS 87. The accumulated benefit obligation in FAS 87 has no counterpart in FAS 106.

Net periodic postretirement benefit costs include the following components:

1. Service cost—APV of benefits attributable to the current period (i.e., the portion of the EPBO earned this period)
2. Interest cost—Interest on the APBO
3. Actual return on plan assets
4. Gain or loss
5. Amortization of unrecognized prior service cost
6. Amortization of the transition asset or obligation

The **transition obligation** was the unrecognized and **unfunded APBO** for all of the participants in the plan at the date of adoption of FAS 106. This obligation was either (1) recognized immediately as the effect of an accounting change, subject to certain limitations, or (2) elected to be recognized on a delayed basis over future service periods with disclosure of the unrecognized amount. The delayed recognition must have resulted in, at least, as rapid a recognition as would have been recognized on a pay-as-you-go (cash) basis.

Service costs and interest costs are defined and measured in the same manner by FAS 106 and 87. However, under FAS 106, interest increases the APBO while under FAS 87, interest increases the PBO.

Under FAS 106, a single method is required to be followed in measuring and recognizing the net periodic cost and the liability involved. That method attributes the EPBO to employee service rendered to the full eligibility date.

Assumptions. FAS 106 requires the use of explicit assumptions using the best estimates available of the plan's future experience, solely with regard to the individual assumption under consideration. Plan continuity can be presumed, unless there is evidence to the contrary. Principal actuarial assumptions include: discount rates, present value factors, retirement age, participation rates (**contributory plans**), salary progression (pay-related plans) and probability of payment (turnover, dependency status, mortality). Present value factors for health care

OPEB include cost trend rates, Medicare reimbursement rates and per capita claims cost by age.

Current interest rates, as of the **measurement date,** are used for discount rates in present value calculations. Examples include high-quality, fixed-income investments with similar amounts and timing and interest rates at which the postretirement benefit obligations could be settled. The EPBO, APBO, service cost and interest cost components use assumed discount rates.

The expected long-term rate of return on plan assets is an assumption about the average rate of return expected on contributions during the period and on existing plan assets. Current returns on plan assets and reinvestment returns are considered in arriving at the rate to be used. Related income taxes, if applicable, reduce the rate. Expected return on plan assets and the market-related value of plan assets use this rate in their calculation. Since ERISA does not require OPEB plans to be funded via the separate trust vehicles used for pension plans, OPEB plans are often unfunded. Thus, there are no "plan assets." Instead, the sponsor pays benefits directly, as they become due, from general corporate assets.

Example

A sample illustration of the basic accounting for OPEB as established by FAS 106 follows. Kitzes Corporation established a new OPEB plan as of January 1, 2005. Although the plan was new, it retroactively credited employees for their years of service to Kitzes prior to the establishment of the plan.

All employees had been hired at age 30 and become fully eligible for benefits at age 60. The plan is unfunded and, thus, there are no plan assets. The first calculation is the determination of the unrecognized transition obligation (UTO).

Kitzes Corporation
December 31, 2004

Employee	*Age*	*Years of service*	*Total years when fully eligible*	*Expected retirement age*	*Remaining service to retirement*	*EPBO*	*APBO*
A	35	5	30	60	25	$ 14,000	$ 2,333
B	40	10	30	60	20	22,000	7,333
C	45	15	30	60	15	30,000	15,000
D	50	20	30	60	10	38,000	25,333
E	55	25	30	65	10	46,000	38,333
F	60	30	30	65	5	54,000	54,000
G	65	RET	--		--	46,000	46,000
H	70	RET	--		--	38,000	38,000
					85	$288,000	$226,332

Explanations

1. EPBO (expected postretirement benefit obligation) is usually determined by an actuary, although it can be calculated if complete data is available.
2. APBO is calculated using the EPBO. Specifically, it is EPBO x (Years of service/Total years when fully eligible)
3. The unrecognized transition obligation (UTO) is the APBO at 12/31/04 since there are no plan assets to be deducted. The $226,332 can be amortized over the average remaining service to retirement of 14.17 (85/6) years or an optional period of 20 years, if longer. Kitzes selected the 20-year period of amortization.
4. Note that Employee F has attained full eligibility for benefits and yet plans to continue working.
5. Note that the above 2004 table is used in the calculation of the 2005 components of OPEB cost that follows.

After the establishment of the UTO, the next step is to determine the benefit cost for the year ended December 31, 2005. This calculation follows the framework established by FAS 87. The discount rate is assumed to be 10%.

Kitzes Corporation
OPEB Cost
December 31, 2005

1.	Service cost	$ 5,500
2.	Interest cost	22,633
3.	Actual return on plan assets	--
4.	Gain or loss	--
5.	Amortization of unrecognized prior service cost	--
6.	Amortization of UTO	11,317
	Total OPEB Cost	$39,450

Explanations

1. Service cost calculation uses only employees not yet fully eligible for benefits.

Employee	*[a] 12/31/03 EPBO*	*[b] Total years when fully eligible*	*[a ÷ b] Service cost*
A	$14,000	30	$ 467
B	22,000	30	733
C	30,000	30	1,000
D	38,000	30	1,267
E	46,000	30	1,533
			$5,000
	Interest for 2004 ($5,000 x 10%)		500
	Total service cost		$5,500

2. Interest cost is the 12/31/04 APBO of $226,332 x 10% = $22,633.
3. There are no plan assets so there is no return.
4. There is no gain (loss) since there are no changes yet.
5. There is no unrecognized prior service cost initially.
6. Amortization of UTO is the 12/31/04 UTO of $226,332/20-year optional election = $11,317.

After calculation of the 2005 benefit cost, the next step is to project the EPBO and APBO for December 31, 2005. Assuming no changes, it is based on the December 31, 2004 actuarial measurement and it is calculated as shown earlier in the determination of the UTO.

Kitzes Corporation
December 31, 2005

Employee	*Age*	*Years of service*	*Total years when fully eligible*	*EPBO*	*APBO*
A	36	6	30	$ 15,400	$ 3,080
B	41	11	30	24,200	8,873
C	46	16	30	33,000	17,600
D	51	21	30	41,800	29,260
E	56	26	30	50,600	43,853
F	61	31	--	59,400	59,400
G	66	RET	--	44,620	44,620
H	71	RET	--	36,860	36,860
				$305,880	$243,546

Changes in experience or assumptions will result in gains (losses). The gain (loss) is measured by the difference resulting in the APBO or the plan assets from that projected. However, except for the effects of a decision to temporarily deviate from the substantive plan, these gains or losses have no impact in the year of occurrence. They are deferred and amortized as in FAS 87. Amortization of unrecognized net gain (loss) is included as a component of net postretirement cost for a year if, as of the beginning of the year, it exceeds 10% of the **greater** of the APBO or the market-related value of plan assets. The minimum amortization is the **excess** divided by the remaining average service period of active plan participants. A systematic method of amortization that amortizes a greater amount, is applied consistently to both gains and losses and is disclosed may also be used. If gains (losses) are recognized immediately, special rules of offsetting may be required.

Other Postemployment Benefits

FAS 112 applies the criteria set forth by FAS 43 to accrue an obligation for postemployment benefits other than pensions if services have been performed by employees, employees' rights accumulate or vest, payment is probable, and the amount can be reasonably estimable. If these benefits do not vest or accumulate, FAS 5 applies. If neither FAS 43 nor FAS 5 is applicable because the amount is not reasonably estimable, this fact must be disclosed.

Deferred Compensation Contracts

If the aggregate deferred compensation contracts with individual employees are equivalent to a pension plan, the contracts are accounted for according to FAS 87 and 88. All other deferred compensation contracts are accounted for according to APB 12.

FAS 106 states that the terms of the individual contract will govern the accrual of the employee's obligation for deferred compensation and the cost is to be attributed over the employee service period until full eligibility is attained.

Per APB 12, the amount to be accrued is not to be less than the present value of the estimated payments to be made. This estimated amount is accrued in a systematic and rational manner. When elements of both current and future employment are present, only the portion attributable to the current services is accrued. All requirements of the contract, such as continued employment for a specified period, availability for consulting services, and agreements not to compete after retirement, need to be met in order for the employee to receive future payments. Finally, the total amount is amortized to expense over the period from the date the contract is signed to the point when the employee is fully eligible to receive the deferred payments.

One benefit that may be found in a deferred compensation contract is for periodic payments to employees or their beneficiaries for life, with provisions for a minimum lump-sum settlement in the event of early death of one or all of the beneficiaries. The estimated amount to be accrued is based on the life expectancy of each individual concerned or on the estimated cost of an annuity contract, not on the minimum amount payable in the event of early death.

Employee Retirement Income Security Act of 1974

Congress passed the Employee Retirement Income Security Act (ERISA) in 1974. The principal objectives of ERISA were to provide statutory law for pension plan requirements, to strengthen the financial soundness of private pension plans, to safeguard employees' pension rights, and to create the Pension Benefit Guaranty Corporation (PBGC).

Prior to ERISA, the Internal Revenue Code was the principal source of law for governing and managing pension plans. Unfortunately, the thrust of the Code emphasizes tax considerations, and the important nontax aspects of pension plans, such as vesting, funding, and employee participation, were not addressed. ERISA filled the void by mandating minimum vesting, funding, employee participation, and other requirements. Virtually every private pension plan in the United States is affected by the provisions of ERISA.

ERISA, as subsequently amended by Congress and interpreted by regulations issued by the Internal Revenue Service (IRS), provides minimum vesting periods for participants. Amounts contributed by employees must, at all times, be 100% vested. Benefits derived from employer contributions must become nonforfeitable when the employee reaches normal retirement age. Normal retirement age is the earlier of the time a participant attains normal retirement age under the plan or the later of: (1) attainment of age sixty-five, or (2) the fifth anniversary of the individual's participation in the plan.

Plans must meet one of two alternative minimum vesting standards for benefits to be derived from employer contributions prior to normal retirement age:

1. A five-year cliff schedule requiring full vesting after five years of service
2. A three-to-seven-year graded schedule requiring 20% vesting after three years of service and 20% additional vesting in each of the following years (IRC § 1.411(a)-3T)

These vesting standards were liberalized by the Economic Growth and Tax Relief Reconciliation Act of 2001 (EGTRRA). EGTRRA provides accelerated vesting for participants with accrued benefits derived from employer matching contributions that complete an hour of service under the plan in a plan year beginning after December 31, 2001. Vesting of employer matching contributions under EGTRRA is under one of three alternative vesting schedules.

1. Full and immediate vesting
2. A three-year cliff schedule requiring full vesting after three years of service
3. A six-year graded schedule requiring 20% vesting per year starting after completion of the second year of service

For plans that are determined, under a formula to provide a disproportionate share of benefits to highly compensated individuals (top-heavy plans), the minimum vesting is required to be even faster.

In addition, ERISA requires minimum funding, in accordance with an acceptable actuarial method, for private pension plans. ERISA also established standards for employee participation and has made defined contribution plans more popular.

All of the above requirements strengthen the financial soundness of employee pension funds. To further ensure the ability of a plan to pay pension obligations and to safeguard employee rights, ERISA amended the Internal Revenue Code to allow for the assessment of fines and the denial of tax deductions. The Act also requires that pension plans submit annual reports, provide a description of the plan, and make a full disclosure through the submission of various statements and schedules.

Prior to the enactment of ERISA, some employees lost pension benefits when plans were terminated because of bankruptcy or other reasons. In order to protect employee rights under these circumstances, ERISA created PBGC. The function of this agency is to guarantee employees, if the employer cannot pay, at least a minimum amount of benefits for their years of service. This guarantee is financed by an insurance premium charge that is levied on all employers with defined benefit plans. PBGC also has the right to administer terminated plans, to file liens on employers' assets, and to take over employers' assets under certain specified circumstances.

EMERGING ISSUES TASK FORCE ISSUES SUMMARIES

88-1 Determination of Vested Benefit Obligation for a Defined Benefit Pension Plan

In situations not specifically addressed by FAS 87, the vested benefit obligation can be either (1) the actuarial present value of the vested benefits that the employee is entitled to if the employee separates immediately, or (2) the actuarial present value of the vested benefits to which the employee is currently entitled but based on the employee's expected date of separation or retirement. The SEC observer indicated that the alternative selected is to be disclosed. The FASB staff favored (1) but several task force members thought (2) was more consistent with FAS 87. This issue is usually applicable to foreign defined benefit pension plans.

88-5 Recognition of Insurance Death Benefits

It is **not** appropriate for the purchaser of life insurance to recognize income from death benefits on an actuarially expected basis.

90-3 Accounting for Employers' Obligations for Future Contributions to a Multiemployer Pension Plan

Based on FAS 87, the existence of an executed agreement does not require recognition by an employer of a liability beyond currently due and unpaid contributions.

91-7 Accounting for Pension Benefits Paid by Employers After Insurance Companies Fail to Provide Annuity Benefits

A consensus was reached that a loss is recognized by an employer at the time the employer assumes the benefit obligation payments to retirees for an insolvent insurance company that held these pension obligations. The loss recognized is the lesser of any gain recognized in the original contract with the insurance company or the amount of benefit obligation payments assumed by the company. Any additional loss not recognized is recorded as a plan amendment in accordance with FAS 87.

92-13 Accounting for Estimated Payments in Connection with the Coal Industry Retiree Health Benefit Act of 1992

If the company is currently operating in the coal industry, it may account for this obligation as either part of its multiemployer plan participation or as a contingent extraordinary loss in accordance with FAS 5. If the company is no longer operating in the coal industry, the entire obligation is recorded as an extraordinary loss under FAS 5.

93-3 Plan Assets under FASB Statement No. 106

A trust established to pay postretirement benefits does not necessarily have to be "bankruptcy proof," or insulated completely from the claims of general creditors, in order to qualify as plan assets in accordance with FAS 106. Assets held in a trust that explicitly makes them available to the general creditors in bankruptcy do not qualify as plan assets under FAS 106.

03-2 Accounting for the Transfer to the Japanese Government of the Substitutional Portion of Employee Pension Fund Liabilities

Background—Effective April 1, 2002, the Japanese government amended the Japanese Welfare Pension Insurance Law (JPIL) to allow employers to transfer to the government "substitutional" obligations and related assets from employer-sponsored Employees' Pension Fund plans (EPF). The substitutional portion of the plan's benefits represents an option elected by the employer/sponsor to fund the payment of a defined benefit to retiring plan participants in lieu of the employer and employee making contributions to Japanese Pension Insurance (JPI) (a system resembling US social security).

If the employer/sponsor follows a four-phase process in accordance with the law, the Japanese government will assume the future obligation to pay the substitutional benefits and the employer and employee will commence making contributions to JPI. After the completion of the four phases, the EPF is deemed to be legally dissolved and a new Corporate Defined Benefit Pension Plan (CDBP) established with the remaining assets and obligations.

These remaining assets and obligations represent the portion of the EPF that was structured as a defined benefit plant to supplement the substitutional portion of the plan benefits. The employer may elect to transfer the remaining assets to a defined contribution plan.

Issue—How does the electing employer/sponsor account for the separation of the two parts of the EPF and the transfer of the substitutional assets and obligations to the Japanese government?

Consensus—The EITF reached the following conclusions:

- Prior to separation, the entire projected benefit obligation (PBO) is remeasured at its fair value under FAS 88 on the date that the employer/sponsor receives government approval under phase 2. The fair value determination is to take into account the effects of anticipated future salary increases.
- The four-phase process is treated as a single settlement transaction upon completion.
- The elimination of the substitutional portion of the benefit obligation is accounted for as a settlement transaction at the time the assets are transferred to the government (which is the fourth phase of the process).
- A settlement gain or loss is recognized for the proportionate amount of the FAS 87 net unrecognized gain or loss attributable to the substitutional portion of the obligation. This is computed using the ratio of the PBO settled to the total EPF PBO, both calculated excluding the previously accrued salary progression.
- The difference between the fair values of the assets transferred to the government and the obligation settled (as determined under a government-specified formula) is separately accounted for and disclosed as a government subsidy.
- The derecognition of the presettlement accrued salary progression is accounted for and disclosed separately from the government subsidy.

03-4 Determining the Classification and Benefit Attribution Method for a "Cash Balance" Pension Plan

In recent years a trend has emerged for employers to terminate classic defined benefit pension plans and replace them with "cash balance" plans, the accounting for which has not been well understood. These hybrid plans typically describe the pension benefit by reference to an account balance rather than a monthly annuity at retirement. In this issue, EITF has considered plans which are characterized by defined principal-crediting rates as percentages of salary, and offer defined, noncontingent interest-crediting rates that entitle participants to future interest credits at stated, fixed rates until retirement. The consensus reached was that "cash balance" plans with the foregoing attributes are to be deemed defined benefit plans, consistent with definitions set forth in FAS 87. This is true because an employer's contributions to a cash balance plan trust and the earnings on the invested plan assets may be unrelated to the principal and interest credits to participants' hypothetical accounts.

Given this consensus position, EITF also determined that the benefit promise in the cash balance arrangement is not pay-related as contemplated by FAS 87 and, accordingly, use of a projected unit credit method is neither required nor appropriate for purposes of measuring the benefit obligation and annual cost of benefits earned under FAS 87. The appropriate cost attribution approach, therefore, is the traditional unit credit method.

If a reporting entity had been accounting for a cash balance pension plan as a defined contribution plan, the effect of applying the consensuses (i.e., the difference between the funded status as a defined benefit plan and any existing prepaid or accrued pension cost) should be reported as the effect of adopting a new accounting principle (in a manner similar to a cumulative-effect-type adjustment) as of the beginning of the year containing the next reporting period beginning after May 28, 2003.

On the other hand, if an entity had been accounting for such a plan as a defined benefit plan, the effect of remeasuring the pension obligation using the guidance in this consensus should be calculated as of the plan's next measurement date after May 28, 2003. Any difference in the measurement of the obligation as a result of applying the consensus should be reported as a component of actuarial gains and losses under FAS 87. For an entity that has an accounting policy of immediate recognition of all gains and losses, or all gains and losses outside the 10 percent corridor described in FAS 87, the component of such gain or loss that can be attributed to the adoption of the guidance in this consensus, using a with-and-without calculation, is to be reported as the effect of adopting the consensus (in a manner similar to a cumulative-effect-type adjustment) as of the measurement date.

D-92 The Effect of FASB Statement No. 135 on the Measurement and Recognition of Net Periodic Benefit Cost under FASB Statements No. 87 and No. 106

The FASB staff announced an inadvertent error in FAS 135 that constituents had interpreted as changing the accounting for net periodic benefit costs. The announcement clarifies that this was not the intent of FASB in issuing FAS 135.

D-106 Clarification of Q&A No. 37 of FASB Special Report, *A Guide to Implementation of Statement 87 on Employers' Accounting for Pensions*

Q&A 37 provides guidance to employers who use a measurement date that precedes the financial statement date on how to determine the additional minimum liability that arises between measurement date and period end.

The FASB staff acknowledged that the original Q&A was ambiguous and that, accordingly, it had revised the wording of Q&A 37 in the implementation guide.

As newly worded (and originally intended), the additional minimum liability is computed using the following formula (assuming a measurement date of September 30 and a financial statement date of December 31):

Required minimum liability at 9/30	+	Prepaid pension cost per the 12/31 balance sheet prior to fourth quarter plan contributions	**or** –	Accrued pension cost per the 12/31 balance sheet prior to fourth quarter plan contributions

FASB STAFF Q&A

Statement 87

Q&A Impact of the Sunset Provision of the Economic Growth and Tax Relief Reconciliation Act

Although not authoritative GAAP, the FASB staff announced the following position: The Economic Growth and Tax Relief Reconciliation Act (EGTRRA) increased the maximum benefits that a defined benefit plan is permitted to pay to retirees. However, the legislation is scheduled to expire (or "sunset") after 2010. This creates a conflict with Internal Revenue Code (IRC) § 411(d)(6) which prohibits plan amendments that decrease participants' accrued benefits under a plan (anticutback provisions). This conflict presents a challenge for actuaries in estimating benefits payable in future years. The FASB staff opined management may need to consult with legal counsel regarding whether the anticutback provisions would apply to prevent the future reduction in benefits. Depending on the opinion of counsel, the actuary would either: (1) treat the sunset provision as having full impact with benefits payable in years after 2010 being reduced to the pre-EGTRRA limits, or (2) treat the sunset provision as being subject to the anticutback provisions.

FASB STAFF POSITION

FSP 106-1 Accounting and Disclosure Requirements Related to the Medicare Prescription Drug, Improvement and Modernization Act of 2003

The Medicare Prescription Drug, Improvement and Modernization Act of 2003 introduced a prescription drug benefit under Medicare (Medicare Part D), as well as a federal subsidy to sponsors of retiree health care benefit plans that provide a benefit that is at least actuarially equivalent to Medicare Part D. This gave rise to questions regarding whether an employer that provides postretirement prescription drug coverage should recognize the effects of the Act on its accumulated postretirement benefit obligation (APBO) and net postretirement benefit costs and, if so, when and how to account for those effects. This FSP permits a sponsor of a postretirement health care plan that provides a prescription drug benefit to make a onetime election to defer accounting for the effects of the Act.

FAS 106 requires presently enacted changes in relevant laws to be considered in current period measurements of postretirement benefit costs and the APBO. Under that guidance, measures of the APBO and net periodic postretirement benefit costs on or after the date of enactment should reflect the effects of the Act. However, certain accounting issues raised by the Act—in particular, how to account for the federal subsidy—are not explicitly addressed by FAS 106, and significant uncertainties may exist for a plan sponsor as to both the direct effects of the Act and its ancillary effects on plan participants' behavior and health care costs. FASB accordingly concluded that a plan sponsor or its advisors may not have sufficiently reliable information available on which to measure the effects of the Act, sufficient time before issuance of financial statements for fiscal years that include the Act's enactment date to prepare actuarial valuations that reflect the effects of the Act, or sufficient guidance to ensure that the sponsor's accounting for the effects of the Act is consistent with generally accepted accounting principles.

Therefore, FASB concluded that a plan sponsor may elect to defer recognizing the effects of the Act in the accounting for its plan under FAS 106 and in providing disclosures related to the plan required by FAS 132(R), until authoritative guidance on the accounting for the federal subsidy is issued, or until certain other events occur. Regardless of whether a plan sponsor elects that deferral, certain other disclosures are required by this FSP.

If an entity that sponsors a postretirement health care plan that provides prescription drug benefits elects the deferral provided by this FSP, it must disclose in annual or interim financial statements the existence of the Act and the fact that, in accordance with this FSP, any measures of the APBO or net periodic postretirement benefit cost in the financial statements or accompanying notes do not reflect the effects of the Act on the plan, as well as the fact that specific authoritative guidance on the accounting for the federal subsidy is pending and that guidance, when issued, could require the sponsor to change previously reported information. The entity is also encouraged to disclose additional information that it believes is appropriate for the reader to understand the Act's possible economic consequences including whether the sponsor would need to amend the plan (regardless of whether the sponsor intends to do so) in order to benefit from the new legislation. In that context, an additional disclosure could be an estimate of the cash flows that the plan sponsor believes it will be entitled to receive under the federal subsidy. If such estimates are provided, the plan sponsor should acknowledge that the issues of how and when the federal subsidy should be accounted for are not yet resolved by the FASB.

Entities that do not elect the deferral provided by this FSP must disclose in annual or interim financial statements the effects, if any, of the Act on the reported measure of the accumulated postretirement benefit obligation; how that effect has been, or will be reflected, in the net postretirement benefit costs of current or subsequent periods; the effects of any changes in estimates of participation rates or per capita claims costs as a result of the Act; and the fact that specific authoritative guidance on the accounting for the federal subsidy is pending and that guidance, when issued, could require the sponsor to change previously reported information.

To the extent a plan sponsor's accounting recognizes the effect of the federal subsidy, the sponsor should disclose the basis for concluding that its plan is at least "actuarially equivalent" (as defined) to Medicare Part D. In addition, if the plan sponsor concludes that some or all of the federal subsidy related to prescription drug costs included in the APBO should be recognized immediately as a component of income from continuing operations, any amount so recognized should be reported as a separate line item on the face of the income statement or statement of activities. The Position states that for purposes of this requirement, current period amortization of amounts measured but initially deferred as of the date of enactment of the Act does not constitute immediate recognition.

FASB Staff noted that the accounting for the subsidy is explicitly not addressed in the FSP and nothing therein could be construed as either an endorsement or rejection of any particular accounting treatment of the subsidy, pending the issuance of specific authoritative guidance. When it is ultimately issued, the guidance on accounting for the federal subsidy will include transition guidance, as applicable, for entities that elected to defer accounting for the effects of the Act and those that did not.

The FSP was effective for interim or annual financial statements of fiscal years ending after December 7, 2003. The election to defer accounting for the Act was a onetime election that must have been made before net periodic postretirement benefit costs for the period that included the Act's enactment date were first included in reported financial information pursuant to the requirements of FAS 106. For an entity that elects deferral, that election may not be changed, and the deferral continues to apply until authoritative guidance on the accounting for the federal subsidy is issued, or until the guidance in the following sentence applies. The election to defer expires if, subsequent to January 31, 2004, but prior to the issuance of additional authoritative guidance, a significant event occurs that ordinarily would call for remeasurement of a plan's assets and obligations—for example, a plan amendment, settlement, or curtailment. Upon the occurrence of such an event, the sponsor should account for that event pursuant to the guidance in FAS 106 and also should reflect in its accounting for the plan its best estimate of the effects of the Act, including the federal subsidy (if applicable based on the terms of the plan and the sponsor's analysis of generally accepted accounting principles) and any effects on participation rates and health care cost estimates.

When those costs are reported depends on the measurement date selected for the plan pursuant to FAS 106. If a public company with a December 31 fiscal year-end uses a September 30 measurement date, the net periodic postretirement benefit costs for the period that includes the Act's enactment date would be reported in the first interim period of 2004.

17 STOCKHOLDERS' EQUITY

PERSPECTIVE AND ISSUES

CON 6 defines stockholders' equity as the residual interest in the assets of an entity after deducting its liabilities. Stockholders' equity is comprised of all capital contributed to the entity plus its accumulated earnings less any distributions that have been made. There are three major categories within the equity section: paid-in capital represents equity contributed by owners; retained earnings represents the sum of all earnings less that not retained in the business (i.e., dividends); and other comprehensive income represents changes in net assets, other than by means of transactions with owners, which have not been reported in earnings under applicable GAAP rules (e.g., accumulated translation gains or losses). (Comprehensive income was discussed in Chapter 3 and is not addressed in this chapter.)

It is generally quite clear that liabilities differ from equity interests, since liabilities are claims against the assets of the reporting entity, while equity represents only residual claims to **net** assets, after all liabilities have been fully satisfied. While this conceptual distinction is straightforward enough, the evolution of complex financial instruments, some of which exhibit attributes of both liabilities and equity, has made it necessary that a formalized approach to distinguishing between these be developed.

FASB has been attempting to deal with this issue for well over a decade. A discussion memorandum, *Distinguishing between Liability and Equity Instruments and Accounting for Instruments with Characteristics of Both*, was issued in 1990, and an Exposure Draft, *Accounting for Financial Instruments with Characteristics of Liabilities, Equity, or Both,* was published in 2000. It was only in late 2001 that the FASB committed to the completion of this project, and that effort has recently culminated in the promulgation of FAS 150, *Accounting for Certain Financial Instruments with Characteristics of Liabilities and Equity.* This is a "limited scope" statement, dealing only with mandatorily redeemable financial instruments and a few other situations. Other topics remain to be addressed, as does a promised revision to the definition of liabilities presented in CON 6, to facilitate and justify the newly mandated treatment for these instruments.

Earnings are not generated by transactions in an entity's own equity (e.g., by the issuance, reacquisition, or reissuance of its common or preferred shares). Depending on the laws of the jurisdiction of incorporation, distributions to shareholders may be subject to various limitations, such as to the amount of retained (accounting basis) earnings.

A major objective of the accounting for stockholders' equity is the adequate disclosure of the **sources** from which the capital was derived. For this reason, a number of different paid-in capital accounts may be presented in the balance sheet. The rights of each class of shareholder must also be disclosed. Where shares are reserved for future issuance, such as under the terms of stock option plans, this fact must also be made known.

The longstanding controversy over accounting for stock-based compensation (employee stock options) heated up substantially in the wake of the financial reporting scandals of 2001-02 and the subsequent passage of the Sarbanes-Oxley Act. In the mid-1990s the FASB had concluded that the economic substance of such plans was to provide compensation, and that resulted in an expense that should logically be reported by the entity (the **fair value method of accounting**), in contradistinction to the **intrinsic value** method set forth by APB 25, which generally results in no compensation cost being associated with the option plans. Under extreme political and constituent pressure, FASB produced a standard (FAS 123) which, while extolling fair value accounting as preferable, permitted continued usage of the intrinsic value method with mere footnote disclosure of the effects that would have obtained under FAS 123.

Following the market declines of 2001-03 and the revelations of corporate malfeasance, popular opinion turned substantially against the practice of granting large stock awards to executives while averting income statement recognition of the corresponding costs. Additionally, the IASB announced its intention to impose a rule similar to what FAS 123 had first developed, but with mandatory rather than optional application. Finally, a number of prominent US corporations announced the intent to voluntarily switch their accounting for options to the fair value method, signaling that corporate financial reporting practices might begin to improve even absent FASB leadership. The upshot of these events was that FASB issued an Exposure Draft to deal with accounting for stock options, with the goal again being to eliminate the "off income statement" treatment of those costs. In the meanwhile, it has issued a new standard (FAS 148) offering several transition methods to those reporting entities which are making the election to embrace the fair value accounting method. As of mid-2004, it appears highly likely that mandatory expensing of stock-based compensation will be imposed under GAAP. On March 31, 2004, the FASB issued an Exposure Draft (ED) of a proposed standard that, if adopted, will significantly change the accounting for equity-based compensation. The anticipated effective date for this new statement is December 15, 2004. Potential changes as a result of this Exposure Draft are explained at the end of the chapter.

SOP 93-6 revised the accounting for employers' contributions to employee stock ownership plans (ESOP). The new standard does optionally permit "grandfathering" shares acquired prior to 1993. The major changes from the prior rules relate to the measurement of compensation cost and to the accounting for dividends paid on unallocated shares.

Sources of GAAP

ARB	*APB*	*FAS*	*FIN*	*FTB*	*EITF*	*SOP*
43, Ch. 1A, 1B, 7A, 7B, 13B; 46	6, 12, 15, 25, 29	5, 52, 87, 115, 123, 129, 130 148, 150	28, 31, 38, 44	85-6, 97-1	84-40, 85-1, 85-2, 85-46, 86-32, 87-23, 88-6, 89-11, 90-7, 95-16, 96-18, 97-14, 98-2, 98-12, 99-7, 00-6, 00-16, 00-19, 00-23, 00-27, D-18, D-42, D-43, D-60, D-72, D-90, D-91, D-93, D-98	90-7, 93-6

DEFINITIONS OF TERMS

Additional paid-in capital. Amounts received at issuance in excess of the par or stated value of capital stock and amounts received from other transactions involving the entity's stock and/or stockholders. It is classified by source.

Allocated shares. ESOP shares assigned to individual participants. These shares are usually based on length of service, compensation or a combination of both.

Appropriation (of retained earnings). A segregation of retained earnings to communicate the unavailability of a portion for dividend distributions.

Authorized shares. The maximum number of shares permitted to be issued by a corporation's charter and bylaws.

Callable. An optional characteristic of preferred stock allowing the corporation to redeem the stock at specified future dates and at specific prices. The call price is usually at or above the original issuance price.

Cliff vesting. A condition of an option or other stock award plan which provides that the employee becomes fully vested at a single point in time.

Combination plans. Awards consisting of two or more separate components, such as options and stock appreciation rights, each of which can be exercised. Each component is actually a separate plan and is accounted for as such.

Committed-to-be-released shares. ESOP shares that will be allocated to employees for service performed currently. They are usually released by payment of debt service.

Compensatory plan. A stock option or similar plan including elements of compensation which are recognized over the service period.

Comprehensive income. The change in equity of a business enterprise during a period from transactions and other events and circumstances from nonowner sources. It includes all changes in equity during a period, except those resulting from investments by and distributions to owners.

Constructive retirement method. Method of accounting for treasury shares which treats the shares as having been retired. The shares revert to authorized but unissued status. The stock and additional paid-in capital accounts are reduced, with a debit to retained earnings or a credit to a paid-in capital account for the excess or deficiency of the purchase cost over or under the original issuance proceeds.

Contributed capital. The amount of equity contributed by the corporation's shareholders. It consists of capital stock plus additional paid-in capital.

Convertible. An optional characteristic of preferred stock allowing the stockholders to exchange their preferred shares for common shares at a specified ratio.

Cost method. Method of accounting for treasury shares which presents aggregate cost of reacquired shares as a deduction from the total of paid-in capital and retained earnings.

Cumulative. An optional characteristic of preferred stock. Any dividends of prior years not paid to the preferred shareholders must be paid before any dividends can be distributed to the common shareholders.

Date of declaration. The date on which the board of directors votes that a dividend shall be paid. A legal liability (usually current) is created on this date in the case of cash, property, and scrip dividends.

Date of grant. The date on which the board of directors awards the stock to the employees in stock option plans.

Date of payment. The date on which the shareholders are paid the declared dividends.

Date of record. The date on which ownership of the shares is determined. Those owning stock on this date will be paid the declared dividends.

Deficit. A debit balance in the retained earnings account. Dividends may not generally be paid when this condition exists. Formally known as accumulated deficit.

Discount on capital stock. Occurs when the stock of a corporation is originally issued at a price below par value. The original purchasers become contingently liable to creditors for this difference.

Employee stock ownership plan (ESOP). A form of defined contribution employee benefit plan, whereby the employer facilitates the purchase of shares of stock in the company for the benefit of the employees, generally by a trust established by the company. The plan may be leveraged by borrowings either from the employer-sponsor or from third-party lenders.

Fair value. An estimate of the value of a stock option which takes into account exercise price, expected term, current stock price, expected volatility, expected dividend yield, and risk-free interest rate during expected term; used to measure compensation under FAS 123.

Fixed options. Options that grant the holder the rights to a specified numbers of shares at fixed prices. They are not dependent upon achievement of performance targets.

Graded vesting. A vesting process whereby the employee becomes entitled to a stock-based award fractionally over a period of years.

Intrinsic value. The excess of the market price of an underlying stock over the exercise price of a related stock option; used to measure compensation under APB 25.

Issued stock. The number of shares issued by the firm and owned by the shareholders and the corporation. It is the sum of outstanding shares plus treasury shares.

Junior stock. Shares with certain limitations, often as to voting rights, which are granted to employees pursuant to a performance compensation program. Such shares are generally convertible to ordinary shares upon achievement of defined goals.

Legal capital. The aggregate par or stated value of stock. It represents the amount of owners' equity that cannot be distributed to shareholders. It serves to protect the claims of the creditors.

Liquidating dividend. A dividend distribution that is not based on earnings. It represents a return of contributed capital.

Measurement date. The date on which the price that enters into the computation of the fair value of an equity instrument granted as compensation is fixed.

Minimum value. As used in FAS 123, a computed option value that does not take into account the effect of expected volatility of the price of the underlying stock. In general, not allowed in the new Exposure Draft.

Noncompensatory stock options. Options which do not include an element of compensation. Under APB 25, many stock option plans meet the prescribed criteria and thus are deemed noncompensatory; under FAS 123 most stock plans will include an element of compensation to be measured and allocated over the service periods of the employees or to be disclosed as such in the notes to the financial statements.

No-par stock. Stock that has no par value. Sometimes a stated value is determined by the board of directors. In this case, the stated value is accorded the same treatment as par value stock.

Outstanding stock. Stock issued by a corporation and held by shareholders (i.e., issued shares that are not held in the treasury).

Par value method. A method of accounting for treasury shares which charges the treasury stock account for the aggregate par or stated value of the shares acquired and charges the excess of the purchase cost over the par value to paid-in capital and/or retained earnings. A deficiency of purchase cost is credited to paid-in capital.

Participating. An optional characteristic of preferred stock whereby preferred shareholders may share ratably with the common shareholders in any profit distributions in excess of a predetermined rate. Participation may be limited to a maximum rate or may be unlimited (full).

Performance-based options. Options that are granted to employees conditional on the achievement of defined goals, such as market price of the underlying stock or earnings of the entity.

Phantom stock plan. A type of stock compensation arrangement that gives employees the right to participate in the increase in value of the company's shares (book value or market value, as stipulated in the plan), without being required to actually purchase the shares initially.

Quasi reorganization. A procedure that reclassifies amounts from contributed capital to retained earnings to eliminate a deficit in that account. All the assets and liabilities are first revalued to their current values. It represents an alternative to a legal reorganization in bankruptcy proceedings.

Retained earnings. The undistributed earnings of a firm.

Service period. The period over which a stock-based compensation award is earned by the recipient. If not otherwise defined in the plan, it is the vesting period. Under FAS 123, if performance conditions affect either exercise price or date, then the service period must be consistent with the related assumption used in estimating fair value.

Stock-based compensation. Compensation arrangements under which employees receive shares of stock, stock options, or other equity instruments, or under which the employer incurs obligations to the employees based on the price of the company's shares.

Stock options. Enable officers and employees of a corporation to purchase shares in the corporation at a predetermined price for a defined period of time.

Stock rights. Enables present shareholders to purchase additional shares of stock of the corporation. They are commonly used if a preemptive right is granted to common shareholders by some state corporation laws.

Suspense shares. ESOP shares that usually collaterize ESOP debt. They have not been allocated or committed to be released.

Tandem plans. Compensation plans under which employees receive two or more components, such as options and stock appreciation rights, whereby the exercise of one component cancels the other(s). The accounting is based on the component that is more likely to be exercised.

Treasury stock. Shares of a corporation that have been repurchased by the corporation. This stock has no voting rights and receives no cash dividends. Some states do not recognize treasury stock. In such cases, reacquired shares are treated as having been retired.

Vesting. The process whereby the recipient of a stock-based compensation award earns the right to control or exercise the award.

CONCEPTS, RULES, AND EXAMPLES

Legal Capital and Capital Stock

Legal capital typically refers to that portion of the stockholders' investment in a corporation that is permanent in nature and represents assets that will continue to be available for the satisfaction of creditor's claims. Traditionally, legal capital was comprised of the aggregate par or stated value of common and preferred shares issued. In recent years, however, many states have eliminated the requirement that corporate shares have a designated par or stated value. States which have adopted provisions of the Model Business Corporation Act have eliminated the distinction between par value and the amount contributed in excess of par.

The specific requirements regarding the preservation of legal capital are a function of the business corporation laws in the state in which a particular entity is incorporated. Accordingly, any action by the corporation that could affect the amount of legal capital (e.g., the payment of dividends in excess of retained earnings) must be considered in the context of the relevant laws of the state where the company is chartered.

Ownership interest in a corporation is made up of common, and optionally, preferred shares. The common shares represent the residual risk-taking ownership of the corporation after the satisfaction of all claims of creditors and senior classes of equity.

Preferred stock. Preferred shareholders are owners who have certain rights superior to those of common shareholders. Preferences as to earnings exist when the preferred shareholders have a stipulated dividend rate (expressed either as a dollar amount or as a percentage of the preferred stock's par or stated value). Preferences as to assets exist when the preferred shares have a stipulated liquidation value. If a corporation were to liquidate, these preferred holders would be paid a specific amount before the common shareholders would have a right to participate in any of the proceeds.

In practice, preferred shares are more likely to have preferences as to earnings than as to assets. Although unusual, preferred shares may have both preferential rights. Preferred shares may also have the following optional features: **participation** in earnings beyond the stipulated dividend rate; the **cumulative** feature, ensuring that dividends in arrears, if any, will be fully satisfied before the common shareholders participate in any earnings distribution; and **convertibility** or **callability** by the corporation. Preferences must be disclosed adequately in the financial statements, either on the face of the balance sheet or in the notes thereto.

In exchange for the preferences, the preferred shareholders' other rights or privileges are often limited. For instance, the right to vote may be restricted to common shareholders. The most important right denied to the preferred shareholders, however, is the right to participate without limitation in the earnings of the corporation. Thus, if the corporation has exceedingly large earnings for a particular period, most of these earnings would accrue to the benefit of the common shareholders. This statement is true even if the preferred stock is participating (a fairly uncommon feature) because participating preferred stock usually has some upper limitation placed upon the extent of participation.

Occasionally, several classes of stock will be categorized as common (e.g., Class A common, Class B common, etc.). Since there can be only one class of shares that represents the true residual risk-taking ownership in a corporation, it is clear that the other classes, even though described as common shareholders, must in fact have some preferential status. Typically, these preferences relate to voting rights. An example of this situation arises when a formerly closely held corporation sells shares to the public but gives the publicly held shares a disproportionately small capacity to exercise influence over the entity, thereby keeping control in the hands of the former majority owners even as they are reduced to the status of minority owners. The rights and responsibilities of each class of shareholder, even if described as common, must be fully disclosed in the financial statements.

Issuance of shares. The accounting for the sale of shares by a corporation depends upon whether the stock has a par or stated value. If there is a par or stated value, the amount of the proceeds representing the aggregate par or stated value is credited to the common or preferred stock account. The aggregate par or stated value is generally defined as legal capital not subject to distribution to shareholders. Proceeds in excess of par or stated value are credited to an additional paid-in capital account. The **additional paid-in capital** represents the amount in excess of the legal capital that may, under certain defined conditions, be distributed to shareholders.

A corporation selling stock below par value credits the capital stock account for the par value and debits an offsetting **discount account** for the difference between par value and the amount actually received. If the discount is on original issue capital stock, it serves to notify the actual and potential creditors of the contingent liability of those investors. As a practical matter, corporations avoided this problem by reducing par values to an arbitrarily low amount. This reduction in par eliminated the chance that shares would be sold for amounts below par.

Where the Model Business Corporation Act has been adopted or where corporation laws have been conformed to the guidelines of that Act, there is often no distinction made between par value and amounts in excess of par. In those jurisdictions, the entire proceeds from the sale of stock may be credited to the common stock account without distinction between the stock and the additional paid-in capital accounts. The following entries illustrate these concepts:

Facts: A corporation sells 100,000 shares of $5 par common stock for $8 per share cash.

Cash	800,000	
Common stock		500,000
Additional paid-in capital		300,000

Facts: A corporation sells 100,000 shares of no-par common stock for $8 per share cash.

Cash	800,000	
Common stock		800,000

Preferred stock will often be assigned a par value because in many cases the preferential dividend rate is defined as a percentage of par value (e.g., 10%, $25 par value preferred stock will have a required annual dividend of $2.50).

If the shares in a corporation are issued in exchange for services or property rather than for cash, the transaction should be reflected at the fair value of the property or services received. If this information is not readily available, then the transaction should be recorded at the fair value of the shares that were issued. Where necessary, appraisals should be obtained in order to properly reflect the transaction. As a final resort, a valuation of the stock issued can be made by the board of directors (APB 29). Stock issued to employees as compensation for services rendered should be accounted for at the fair value of the services performed, if determinable, or the value of the shares issued. If shares are given by a major shareholder directly to an employee for services performed for the entity, this exchange should be accounted for as a capital contribution to the company by the major shareholder and as compensation expense incurred by the company. Only when accounted for in this manner will there be conformity with the general principle that all costs incurred by an entity, including compensation, should be reflected in its financial statements.

In certain instances, common and preferred shares may be issued to investors as a unit (e.g., one share of preferred and two shares of common sold as a package). Where both of the classes of stock are publicly traded, the proceeds from a unit offering should be allocated in proportion to the relative market values of the securities. If only one of the securities is publicly traded, then the proceeds should be allocated to the one that is publicly traded based on its known market value. Any excess is allocated to the other. Where the market value of neither security is known, appraisal information may be used. The imputed fair value of one class of security, particularly the preferred shares, can be based upon the stipulated dividend rate. In this case, the amount of proceeds remaining after the imputing of a value of the preferred shares would be allocated to the common stock.

The foregoing procedures would also apply if a unit offering were made of an equity and a nonequity security such as convertible debentures. Under proposed FASB guidelines, proceeds would be apportioned on the basis of relative fair values. (See the detailed discussion later in this chapter.)

Stock Subscriptions

Occasionally, particularly in the case of a newly organized corporation, a contract is entered into between the corporation and prospective investors, whereby the latter agree to purchase specified numbers of shares to be paid for over some installment period. These stock subscriptions are not the same as actual stock issuances and the accounting differs.

The amount of stock subscriptions receivable by a corporation is occasionally accounted for as an asset on the balance sheet and is categorized as current or noncurrent in accordance with the terms of payment. However, in accordance with SEC requirements, most subscriptions receivable are shown as a reduction of stockholders' equity in the same manner as treasury stock. Since subscribed shares do not have the rights and responsibilities of actual outstanding stock, the credit is made to a stock subscribed account instead of to the capital stock accounts.

If the common stock has par or stated value, the common stock subscribed account is credited for the aggregate par or stated value of the shares subscribed. The excess over this amount is credited to additional paid-in capital. No distinction is made between additional paid-in capital relating to shares already issued and shares subscribed for. This treatment follows from the distinction between legal capital and additional paid-in capital. Where there is no par or stated value, the entire amount of the common stock subscribed is credited to the stock subscribed account.

As the amount due from the prospective shareholders is collected, the stock subscriptions receivable account is credited and the proceeds are debited to the cash account. Actual issuance of the shares, however, must await the complete payment of the stock subscription. Accordingly, the debit to common stock subscribed is not made until the subscribed shares are fully paid for and the stock is issued.

The following journal entries illustrate these concepts:

1. 10,000 shares of $50 par preferred are subscribed at a price of $65 each; a 10% down payment is received.

Cash	65,000	
Stock subscriptions receivable	585,000	
Preferred stock subscribed		500,000
Additional paid-in capital		150,000

2. 2,000 shares of no-par common shares are subscribed at a price of $85 each, with one-half received in cash.

Cash	85,000	
Stock subscriptions receivable	85,000	
Common stock subscribed		170,000

3. All preferred subscriptions are paid and subscribed preferred shares are issued, and one-half of the **remaining** common subscriptions are collected in full.

Cash [$585,000 + ($85,000 x .50)]	627,500	
Stock subscriptions receivable		627,500
Preferred stock subscribed	500,000	
Preferred stock		500,000

4. The remaining common subscriptions are collected in full.

Cash ($85,000 x .50)	42,500	
Stock subscriptions receivable		42,500
Common stock subscribed	170,000	
Common stock		170,000

When a subscriber defaults on an obligation under a stock subscription agreement, the accounting will follow the provisions of the state in which the corporation is chartered. In some jurisdictions, the subscriber is entitled to a proportionate number of shares based upon the amount already paid on the subscriptions, sometimes reduced by the cost incurred by the corporation in selling the remaining defaulted shares to other stockholders. In other jurisdictions, the subscriber forfeits the entire investment upon default. In this case, the amount already received is credited to an additional paid-in capital account that describes its source.

Additional Paid-in Capital

Additional paid-in capital represents all capital contributed to a corporation other than that defined as par, stated value, no-par stock, or donated capital. Additional paid-in capital can arise from proceeds received from the sale of common and preferred shares in excess of their par or stated values. It can also arise from transactions related to the following:

1. Sale of shares previously issued and subsequently reacquired by the corporation (treasury stock)
2. Retirement of previously outstanding shares
3. Payment of stock dividends in a manner that justifies the dividend being recorded at the market value of the shares distributed
4. Lapse of stock purchase warrants or the forfeiture of stock subscriptions, if these result in the retaining by the corporation of any partial proceeds received prior to forfeiture
5. Warrants which are detachable from bonds
6. Conversion of convertible bonds
7. Other "gains" on the company's own stock, such as that which results from certain stock option plans

When the amounts are material, the sources of additional paid-in capital should be described in the financial statements.

Donated Capital

Donated capital can result from an outright gift to the corporation (e.g., a major shareholder donates land or other assets to the company in a nonreciprocal transfer) or may result when services are provided to the corporation. Under FAS 116, such nonreciprocal transactions are recognized as revenue in the period the contribution is received. Donated capital should be adequately disclosed in the financial statements.

In these situations, historical cost is not adequate to properly reflect the substance of the transaction, since the historical cost to the corporation would be zero. Accordingly, these events should be reflected at fair market value (APB 29). If long-lived assets are donated to the corporation, they should be recorded at their fair value at the date of donation, and the amount so recorded should be depreciated over the normal useful economic life of such assets. If donations are conditional in nature, they should not be reflected formally in the accounts until the appropriate conditions have been satisfied. However, disclosure might still be required in the financial statements of both the assets donated and the conditions required to be met.

Retained Earnings

Legal capital, additional paid-in capital, and donated capital collectively represent the contributed capital of the corporation. The other major source of capital is retained earnings, which represents the accumulated amount of earnings of the corporation from the date of inception (or from the date of reorganization) less the cumulative amount of distributions made to shareholders and other charges to retained earnings (e.g., from treasury stock transactions). The distributions to shareholders generally take the form of dividend payments but may take other forms as well, such as the reacquisition of shares for amounts in excess of the original issuance proceeds.

Retained earnings are also affected by action taken by the corporation's board of directors. **Appropriation** serves disclosure purposes and restricts dividend payments, but does nothing to provide any resources for the satisfaction of the contingent loss or other underlying purpose for which the appropriation has been made. Any appropriation made from retained earnings must eventually be returned to the retained earnings account. It is not permissible to charge losses against the appropriation account nor to credit any realized gain to that account. The use of appropriated retained earnings has diminished significantly over the years.

It is axiomatic that transactions in a corporation's own stock can result in a reduction of retained earnings (i.e., a deficiency on such transactions can be charged to retained earnings) but cannot result in an increase in retained earnings (any excesses on such transactions are credited to paid-in capital, never to retained earnings).

If a series of operating losses have been incurred or distributions to shareholders in excess of accumulated earnings have been made, and if there is a debit balance in retained earnings, the account is generally referred to as **accumulated deficit**.

Dividends

Dividends are the pro rata distribution of earnings to the owners of the corporation. The amount and the allocation between the preferred and common shareholders is a function of the stipulated preferential dividend rate; the presence or absence of (1) a participation feature, (2) a cumulative feature, and (3) arrearages on the preferred stock; and the wishes of the board of directors. Dividends, even preferred stock dividends, where a cumulative feature exists, do not accrue. Dividends only become a liability of the corporation when they are declared by the board of directors.

Traditionally, corporations were not allowed to declare dividends in excess of the amount of retained earnings. Alternatively, a corporation could pay dividends out of retained earnings **and** additional paid-in capital but could not exceed the total of these categories (i.e., they could not impair legal capital by the payment of dividends). States that have adopted the Model Business Corporation Act grant more latitude to the directors. Corporations can now, in certain jurisdictions, declare and pay dividends in excess of the book amount of retained earnings if the directors conclude that, after the payment of such dividends, the fair value of the corporation's net assets will still be a positive amount. Thus, directors can declare dividends out of unrealized appreciation that, in certain industries, can be a significant source of dividends beyond the realized and recognized accumulated earnings of the corporation. This action, however, represents a major departure from traditional practice and demands both careful consideration and adequate disclosure.

Three important dividend dates are

1. The **declaration** date
2. The **record** date
3. The **payment** date

The declaration date governs the incurrence of a legal liability by the corporation. The record date refers to that point in time when a determination is made as to which specific registered stockholders will receive dividends and in what amounts. Finally, the payment date relates to the date when the distribution of the dividend takes place. These concepts are illustrated in the following example:

On May 1, 2004, the directors of River Corp. declared a $.75 per share quarterly dividend on River Corp.'s 650,000 outstanding common shares. The dividend is payable May 25 to holders of record May 15.

May 1	Retained earnings (or dividends)	487,500	
	Dividends payable		487,500
May 15	No entry		
May 25	Dividends payable	487,500	
	Cash		487,500

If a dividends account is used, it is closed to retained earnings at year-end.

Dividends may be made in the form of cash, property, or scrip. Cash dividends are either a given dollar amount per share or a percentage of par or stated value. Property dividends consist of the distribution of any assets other than cash (e.g., inventory or equipment).

Finally, scrip dividends are promissory notes due at some time in the future, sometimes bearing interest until final payment is made.

Occasionally, what appear to be disproportionate dividend distributions are paid to some, but not all, of the owners of closely held corporations. Such transactions need to be carefully analyzed. In some cases these may actually represent compensation paid to the recipients. In other instances, these may be a true dividend paid to all shareholders on a pro rata basis, to which certain shareholders have waived their rights. If the former, the distribution should not be accounted for as a dividend, but rather as compensation or some other expense category and included on the income statement. If the latter, the dividend should be "grossed up" to reflect payment on a proportional basis to all the shareholders, with an offsetting capital contribution to the company recognized as having been effectively made by those to whom payments were not made.

Property dividends. If property dividends are declared, the paying corporation may incur a gain or loss. Since the dividend should be reflected at the fair value of the assets distributed, the difference between fair value and book value is recorded at the time the dividend is declared and charged or credited to a loss or gain account.

Scrip dividends. If a corporation declares a dividend payable in scrip that is interest bearing, the interest is accrued over time as a periodic expense. The interest is **not** a part of the dividend itself.

Liquidating dividends. Liquidating dividends are not distributions of earnings, but rather a return of capital to the investing shareholders. A liquidating dividend is normally recorded by the declarer through charging additional paid-in capital rather than retained earnings. The exact accounting for a liquidating dividend is affected by the laws where the business is incorporated, and these laws vary from state to state.

Stock dividends. Stock dividends represent neither an actual distribution of the assets of the corporation nor a promise to distribute those assets. For this reason, a stock dividend is not considered a legal liability or a taxable transaction.

Despite the recognition that a stock dividend is not a distribution of earnings, the accounting treatment of relatively insignificant stock dividends (defined as being less than 20% to 25% of the outstanding shares prior to declaration) is consistent with it being a real dividend. Accordingly, retained earnings are debited for the fair market value of the shares to be paid as a dividend, and the capital stock and additional paid-in capital accounts are credited for the appropriate amounts based upon the par or stated value of the shares, if any. A stock dividend declared but not yet paid is classified as such in the stockholders' equity section of the balance sheet. Since such a dividend never reduces assets, it cannot be a liability.

The selection of 20% to 25% as the threshold for recognizing a stock dividend as an earnings distribution is arbitrary, but it is based somewhat on the empirical evidence that small stock dividends tend not to result in a reduced market price per share for outstanding shares. The aggregate value of the outstanding shares should not change, but the greater number of shares outstanding after the stock dividend should necessitate a lower per share price. As noted, however, the declaration of small stock dividends tends not to have this impact, and this phenomenon supports the accounting treatment.

On the other hand, when stock dividends are larger in magnitude, it is observed that per share market value declines after the declaration of the dividend. In such situations, it would not be valid to treat the stock dividend as an earnings distribution. Rather, it should be accounted for as a split. The precise treatment depends upon the legal requirements of the state of incorporation and upon whether the existing par value or stated value is reduced concurrent with the stock split.

If the par value is not reduced for a large stock dividend and if state law requires that earnings be capitalized in an amount equal to the aggregate of the par value of the stock dividend declared, the event should be described as a stock split effected in the form of a dividend, with a charge to retained earnings and a credit to the common stock account for the aggregate par or stated value. When the par or stated value is reduced in recognition of the split and state laws do not require treatment as a dividend, there is no formal entry to record the split but merely a notation that the number of shares outstanding has increased and the per share par or stated value has decreased accordingly. It should be noted that many companies account for stock splits as if they were a large stock dividend. By doing this, par value per share remains unchanged. The concepts of small versus large stock dividends are illustrated in the following examples:

Assume that stockholders' equity for the Wasatch Corp. on November 1, 2004, is as follows:

Common stock, $1 par, 100,000 shares outstanding	$ 100,000
Paid-in capital in excess of par	1,100,000
Retained earnings	750,000

Small Stock Dividend: On November 10, 2004, the directors of Wasatch Corp. declared a 15% stock dividend, or a dividend of 1.5 shares of common stock for every 10 shares held. Before the stock dividend, the stock is selling for $23 per share. After the 15% stock dividend, each original share worth $23 will become 1.15 shares, each with a value of $20 ($23/1.15). The stock dividend is to be recorded at the market value of the new shares issued, or $300,000 (15,000 new shares at the postdividend price of $20). The entries to record the declaration of the dividend and the issuance of stock (on November 30) by Wasatch Corp. are as follows:

Nov. 10	Retained earnings	300,000	
	Stock dividends distributable		15,000
	Paid-in capital in excess of par		285,000
Nov. 30	Stock dividends distributable	15,000	
	Common stock, $1 par		15,000

Large Stock Dividend: Because the focus of the Committee on Accounting Procedure was on reducing the number of small stock dividends, the accounting requirements for governing large stock dividends are less specific than those for small stock dividends. In practice, ARB 43 results in the par or stated value of the newly issued shares being transferred to the capital stock account from either retained earnings or paid-in capital in excess of par. To illustrate, assume that on November 10, 2004, Wasatch Corp. declares a 50% large stock dividend, a dividend of one share for every two held. Legal requirements call for the transfer to capital stock of an amount equal to the par value of the shares issued. Entries for the declaration on November 10 and the issuance of 50,000 new shares (100,000 x .50) on November 30 are as follows:

Nov. 10	Retained earnings	50,000	
	Stock dividends distributable		50,000
	OR		
	Paid-in capital in excess of par	50,000	
	Stock dividends distributable		50,000
Nov. 30	Stock dividends distributable	50,000	
	Common stock, $1 par		50,000

Treasury Stock

Treasury stock consists of a corporation's own stock which has been issued, subsequently reacquired by the firm, and not yet reissued or canceled. Treasury stock does not reduce the number of shares issued but does reduce the number of shares outstanding, as well as total stockholders' equity. These shares are not eligible to receive cash dividends. Treasury stock is **not** an asset although, in some very limited circumstances, it may be presented as an asset if adequately disclosed (ARB 43, Ch 1A). Reacquired stock that is awaiting delivery to satisfy a liability created by the firm's compensation plan or reacquired stock held in a profit-sharing trust is still considered outstanding and would not be considered treasury stock. In each case, the stock would be presented as an asset with the accompanying footnote disclosure. Accounting for excesses and deficiencies on treasury stock transactions is governed by ARB 43, Ch 1B, and APB 6.

Three approaches exist for the treatment of treasury stock: the **cost, par value,** and **constructive retirement** methods.

Cost method. Under the cost method, the gross cost of the shares reacquired is charged to a contra equity account (treasury stock). The equity accounts that were credited for the original share issuance (common stock, paid-in capital in excess of par, etc.) remain intact. When the treasury shares are reissued, proceeds in excess of **cost** are credited to a paid-in capital account. Any deficiency is charged to retained earnings (unless paid-in capital from previous treasury share transactions exists, in which case the deficiency is charged to that account, with any excess charged to retained earnings). If many treasury stock purchases are made, a cost flow assumption (e.g., FIFO or specific identification) should be adopted to compute excesses and deficiencies upon subsequent share reissuances. The advantage of the cost method is that it avoids identifying and accounting for amounts related to the original issuance of the shares and is, therefore, the simpler, more frequently used method.

The cost method is most consistent with the one-transaction concept. This concept takes the view that the classification of stockholders' equity should not be affected simply because the corporation was the middle "person" in an exchange of shares from one stockholder to another. In substance, there is only a transfer of shares between two stockholders. Since the original balances in the equity accounts are left undisturbed, its use is most acceptable when the firm acquires its stock for reasons other than its retirement, or when its ultimate disposition has not yet been decided.

Par value method. Under the par value method, the treasury stock account is charged only for the aggregate par (or stated) value of the shares reacquired. Other paid-in capital accounts (excess over par value, etc.) are relieved in proportion to the amounts recognized upon the original issuance of the shares. The treasury share acquisition is treated almost as a retirement. However, the common (or preferred) stock account continues at the original amount, thereby preserving the distinction between an actual retirement and a treasury share transaction.

When the treasury shares accounted for by the par value method are subsequently resold, the excess of the sale price over par value is credited to paid-in capital. A reissuance for a price **below** par value does not create a contingent liability for the purchaser. It is only the original purchaser who risks this obligation to the entity's creditors.

Constructive retirement method. The constructive retirement method is similar to the par value method, except that the aggregate par (or stated) value of the reacquired shares is charged to the stock account rather than to the treasury stock account. This method is superior when (1) it is management's intention not to reissue the shares within a reasonable time period or (2) the state of incorporation defines reacquired shares as having been retired. In the latter case, the constructive retirement method is probably the only method of accounting for treasury shares that is **not** inconsistent with the state Business Corporation Act, although the state law does not necessarily dictate such accounting. Certain states require that treasury stock be accounted for by this method.

The two-transaction concept is most consistent with the par value and constructive retirement methods. First, the reacquisition of the firm's shares is viewed as constituting a contraction of its capital structure. Second, the reissuance of the shares is the same as issuing new shares. There is little difference between the purchase and subsequent reissuance of treasury shares and the acquisition and retirement of previously issued shares and the issuance of new shares.

Treasury shares originally accounted for by the cost method can subsequently be restated to conform to the constructive retirement method. If shares were acquired with the intention that they would be reissued and it is later determined that such reissuance is unlikely (due, for example, to the expiration of stock options without their exercise), then it is proper to restate the transaction.

Example of accounting for treasury stock

1. 100 shares ($50 par value) that were originally sold for $60 per share are later reacquired for $70 each.
2. All 100 shares are subsequently resold for a total of $7,500.

To record the acquisition, the entry is

Cost method			*Par value method*			*Constructive retirement method*		
Treasury stock	7,000		Treasury stock	5,000		Common stock	5,000	
Cash		7,000	Additional paid-in capital—common stock	1,000		Additional paid-in capital—common stock	1,000	
			Retained earnings	1,000		Retained earnings	1,000	
			Cash		7,000	Cash		7,000

To record the resale, the entry is

Cost method			*Par value method*			*Constructive retirement method*		
Cash	7,500		Cash	7,500		Cash	7,500	
Treasury stock		7,000	Treasury stock		5,000	Common stock		5,000
Additional paid-in capital—treasury stock		500	Additional paid-in capital—common stock		2,500	Additional paid-in capital—common stock		2,500

If the shares had been resold for $6,500, the entry is

Cost method			*Par value method*			*Constructive retirement method*		
Cash	6,500		Cash	6,500		Cash	6,500	
Retained earnings*	500		Treasury stock		5,000	Common stock		5,000
Treasury stock		7,000	Additional paid-in capital—common stock		1,500	Additional paid-in capital—common stock		1,500

* *"Additional paid-in capital—treasury stock" or "Additional paid-in capital—retired stock" of that issue would be debited first to the extent it exists.*

Alternatively, under the par or constructive retirement methods, any portion of or the **entire** deficiency on the treasury stock acquisition may be debited to retained earnings without allocation to paid-in capital. Any excesses will always be credited to an "Additional paid-in capital—retired stock" account.

The laws of some states govern the circumstances under which a corporation may acquire treasury stock and may prescribe the accounting for the stock. For example, a charge to retained earnings may be required in an amount equal to the treasury stock's total cost. In such cases, the accounting per the state law prevails. Also, some states (including those that have adopted the Model Business Corporation Act) define excess purchase cost of reacquired (i.e., treasury) shares as being "distributions" to shareholders that are no different in nature than dividends. In such cases, the financial statement presentation should adequately disclose the substance of these transactions (e.g., by presenting both dividends and excess reacquisition costs together in the retained earnings statement).

When a firm decides to formally retire the treasury stock, the journal entry is dependent on the method used to account for the stock. Using the original sale and reacquisition data from the illustration above, the following entries would be made if the cost and par value methods, respectively, were employed:

Cost method			Par value method		
Common stock	5,000		Common stock	5,000	
Additional paid-in			Treasury stock		5,000
capital—common stock	1,000				
Retained earnings	1,000				
Treasury stock		7,000			

* *"Additional paid-in capital—treasury stock" may be debited to the extent it exists.*

If the constructive retirement method were used to record the treasury stock purchase, no additional entry would be necessary upon the formal retirement of the shares.

After the entry is made, the pro rata portion of all paid-in capital existing for that issue (i.e., capital stock and additional paid-in capital) will have been eliminated. If stock is purchased for immediate retirement (i.e., not put into the treasury) the entry to record the retirement is the same as that made under the constructive retirement method.

In some circumstances, shares held by current stockholders may be donated back to the enterprise, possibly to facilitate a resale to new owners who will infuse needed capital into the business. In accounting for donated treasury stock, the intentions of management regarding these reacquired shares is key; if these are to simply be retired, the common stock account should be debited for the par or stated value (if par or stated value stock) or the original proceeds received (if no-par, no-stated-value stock). The current fair value of the shares should be credited to the "donated capital" account, and the difference should be debited or credited to a suitably titled paid-in capital account, such as "additional paid-in capital from share donations."

If the donated shares are to be sold (the normal scenario), variations on the par and cost methods of treasury stock accounting can be employed, with "donated capital" being debited and credited, respectively, when shares are received and later reissued, instead of the "treasury stock" account employed in the above illustrations. Note, however, that if the cost method is used, the debit to the donated capital account should be for the fair value of the shares, not the cost (a seeming contradiction). If the constructive retirement method is utilized instead, only a memorandum entry will be recorded when the shares are received; when reissued, the entire proceeds should be credited to "donated capital."

Other Equity Accounts

In principle, modern financial reporting in conformity with GAAP subscribes to what was once known as the "all inclusive" or "clean surplus" concept, which means that all items of income, expense, gain or loss (other than transactions with owners) should flow through the income statement. In fact, there are a number of important exceptions which have been imposed by specific GAAP standards, beginning with the market value declines recognized under the now superseded FAS 12 on noncurrent portfolios of marketable equity securities, and reported directly in shareholder equity. Later standards added translation gains or losses (FAS 52), certain adjustments for minimum pension obligations (FAS 87), and unrealized gains and losses on available-for-sale portfolios of debt or equity investments (FAS 115) to the litany of recognized economic events which escaped reporting in the income statement. Most recently, hedging gains and losses qualifying under FAS 133 are also deferred for income measurement purposes. As explained in Chapter 3, the FASB concepts project had foreseen the need for a flow statement analogous to the income statement to report all such changes for the reporting period, and this was finally mandated by FAS 130, which established the concept of comprehensive income (the term which now denotes normal earnings plus the change in these other equity accounts). Comprehensive income must now be reported either in a combined statement with the income statement, as a stand-alone statement, or in an expanded statement of changes in stockholders' equity.

In the balance sheet, the various elements of other comprehensive income (i.e., the current balances of such items as translation gains and losses and unrealized gains and losses from available-for-sale securities holdings) can be aggregated into a single caption, with details reserved to the notes, or the separate items can be grouped into a subsection of the equity section. Since items of other comprehensive income are neither paid-in capital nor retained earnings, this constitutes a third major classification within the equity section of the balance sheet. Many entities will have only minor amounts of such items or none at all.

Refer to Chapter 3 for a complete discussion of other comprehensive income.

Accounting for Stock Options and Similar Compensation Arrangements

The fact that employee stock options are often sought-after by incoming executives and others strongly suggests that there is a perception of value to these. GAAP had historically ignored this perception; if certain conditions were met (as they often were), no cost was ascribed to the issuance of this form of compensation. Once this practice became ingrained, at a time when stock-based compensation was rare and measurement techniques were largely unknown, any suggestion that GAAP be revised became very contentious indeed. Under APB 25's "intrinsic vale" method, as long as option exercise prices were equal to or greater than the market values of the underlying shares as of the respective dates of the grants, no compensation cost was recognized, whereas the "time value" (the ability to wait to purchase shares until the price had risen) was a coveted asset.

The explosive growth in popularity of these compensation arrangements (arguably encouraged by the favorable accounting and tax treatments) caused increasing discomfort among financial analysts and accounting standard-setting bodies, as the fiction that no expense was incurred by employer entities offering such programs appeared unsustainable. Eventually, FASB undertook a comprehensive reexamination of the subject, with the intent of conforming financial reporting with economic reality.

Alas, FASB's efforts were strenuously and effectively opposed by the preparer community. Many, particularly in the "high technology" sector, argued that it would be competitively harmed in its ability to command top talent if it was impeded in its ability to offer sizable option awards to executives while maintaining, for financial reporting purposes, that no costs were being incurred. This well-orchestrated opposition led the FASB to accept a deeply flawed compromise. FAS 123 (detailed later in this chapter), while recommending a superior "fair value" model to measurement of stock-based compensation costs, nonetheless permitted continued application of APB 25 for measurement purposes, if coupled with supplemental (footnote) disclosure of the impact on earnings.

It had long been held true that inadequate recognition and/or measurement could not be compensated for fully by expanded disclosures. Nonetheless, FAS 123 embraced precisely such an approach. Not surprisingly, virtually all publicly held entities initially opted for this hybrid approach, even though it necessitates use of two very different and complex measures, adding to the cost of preparing financial reports. Recently, in response to such developments as the public reaction to financial reporting scandals, which were connected in the public mind, rightly or not, with highly compensated executives' lucrative stock-based compensation programs, and the IASB's announced intent to mandate use of the FAS 123-like fair value method, a number of large publicly held corporations have embraced fair value reporting of options. The FASB is currently reexamining this issue and will likely dictate that APB 25's intrinsic value method be superceded by FAS 123, although some changes to the measurement methodology are possible. In addition, the Exposure Draft (explained in more detail at the end of the chapter) amends FAS 123 as it applies to share-based compensation for employees.

FAS 123 was designated as the preferable GAAP for purposes of applying the provisions of APB 20. Thus, if an enterprise fully adopts FAS 123, it cannot later revert to APB 25 for financial reporting purposes. An entity must employ only one set of rules, APB 25 or FAS 123, for all the stock compensation programs and plans that it has in effect. It cannot use different rules to measure the impact of different plans. However, as noted, it can utilize APB 25 for the basic financial statements, relegating FAS 123 for use in preparing footnote disclosures.

In the following sections, the major distinctions between the standards will be explained. Subsequently, detailed guidance to, first, APB 25 and related literature, and second, FAS 123 will be set forth.

APB 25 versus FAS 123 in brief. APB 25 measures compensation associated with the issuance of stock options by the **intrinsic value** method, under which that cost is limited to the excess of the quoted market price of the stock at the measurement date (generally, grant date) over the option exercise price. Options are categorized, under tax law, as "incentive stock options" (sometimes referred to as qualified options), which do not result in either taxable income to the holder or tax deductions to the issuing corporation upon either grant or exercise, and "nonqualified" options, which will result in taxable income to the recipient and a tax deduction for the issuer upon exercise. The conditions for treatment as incentive stock options are very strict (e.g., limitations on length of exercise period and on maximum amount of annual exercise by each employee), and most plans are therefore nonqualified. However, nonqualified plans can also be structured to be noncompensatory (defined below), meaning that the grantees incur no taxable income at the date of the grant.

Under FAS 123, on the other hand, a **fair value** approach is prescribed for employee stock options and similar equity instruments. This gives recognition to the fact that the value of options is comprised of three elements: intrinsic value (identical to that identified under APB 25), plus the time value of money and the time value associated with the underlying stock's volatility. Thus, even if intrinsic value were zero (i.e., the option price is equal to or greater than market price at the measurement date), the sum of the other two components would nonetheless most often result in compensation being attributed to grants of fixed options.

For reporting entities that continue to apply APB 25, variable (or performance-based) options are accounted for differently than are fixed options. FIN 28 and FIN 38 address the accounting for such plans, including "junior stock" plans. Unlike plans qualifying under APB 25, these do involve the mandatory recognition of compensation cost. Entities that have fully implemented FAS 123 also recognize compensation cost for such arrangements, but the pattern of expense recognition will differ from that under APB 25 coupled with FIN 28 and FIN 38. These two sets of alternative requirements are fully explored in the following sections.

Accounting for Employee Stock Options under APB 25

The Exposure Draft issued on March 31, 2004, does not allow accounting for stock-based compensation under APB 25. However, until this is approved, which is likely by the end of 2004, APB 25 is still allowed under certain circumstances. Under the provisions of APB 25, there are two types of stock option plans: compensatory and noncompensatory. To be classified as noncompensatory, the plan must meet all of the following four tests:

1. Substantially all full-time employees meeting limited employment qualifications must be eligible to participate;
2. Shares must be offered equally or proportionate to wages earned;
3. Time to exercise must be limited; and
4. There must be no more than a reasonable discount from market price, such as that which would be granted in a typical "rights offering."

Failure to meet even one of these criteria causes the stock option plan to be categorized as compensatory in nature. However, this does not necessarily mean that compensation expense will be recognized.

Any stock option program conveys to the recipients something of value; namely, the time to decide whether or not to purchase the shares of stock at a price that was fixed at the date of the grant. However, because of the strong sentiment against the recognition of compensation, APB 25 continued the practice earlier established by ARB 43, which essentially eliminated compensation recognition from fixed stock option plans. This result had been accomplished by defining compensation as the excess of the quoted market (or fair) value of the shares optioned over the amount to be paid by the employee, determined in most cases as of the grant date. That is, if the option price was equal to or greater than the market (or fair) value as of the date the option was granted, no compensation was to be recognized, regardless of the value later achieved by the shares. Since exercise price typically was fixed at or above the market price as of the grant date, compensation was rarely to be recognized under terms of the most common fixed option plans, regardless of whatever valuable attributes the options carried.

The measurement date stipulated by APB 25 is the earliest date on which both the number of shares to which an individual employee is entitled is known, and the option price is fixed. For most fixed option plans, both of these data are known on the grant date. Note that the measurement date will be the grant date even if the employee must meet certain other conditions, such as continued employment for a specified period, before the options can be exercised. This later date, the vesting date, is used for purposes of allocating compensation, if any, but is not used to compute the amount of such compensation.

If an option plan is compensatory (because one or more of the four conditions are not met), compensation cost is measured by the difference between the **market price** (or the fair market value, for a nontraded stock) and the option price. The **cost** of the shares to the issuing corporation is not the relevant comparison, except in the very limited situation where the shares are specifically acquired to meet the requirements of the stock option plan and are delivered to option holders shortly after acquisition.

Furthermore, even if no compensation cost is deemed to have been incurred at the measurement date (usually the grant date), certain subsequent events may give rise to the recognition of compensation. The most important of these are

1. The renewal or extension of an option, in which case a new measurement date occurs, and if the market price or fair value at that date exceeds the option price, compensation cost will be recognized; and
2. The payment of cash to an employee to settle a previously made stock award or option grant, for which payment will be deemed compensation expense.

If a given option plan involves the payment of compensation to the employees, such compensation cost should be recognized in the period(s) in which the services being compensated are performed. If the grant is unconditional, which means it effectively is in recognition of past services rendered by the employees, then compensation is reported in the period of the grant. If the stock options are granted before some or all of the required services are performed, compensation cost should be recognized over the periods in which the performance is scheduled to occur. Whether compensation cost is recognized ratably over the periods or not is a function of the vesting provisions of the plan. If the plan provides for **cliff vesting,** compensation will be accrued on an essentially straight-line basis, while if it provides for **graded vesting** the pattern of recognition will be more complex.

Example of accounting for stock options—Measurement and grant date the same

Options are granted to corporate officers to purchase 10,000 shares of $1 par stock at a price of $52 per share, when the market price is $58. The options may not be exercised until five years from the grant date. The company has no reason to expect that any of the options will be forfeited by the employees to whom they are granted. The entry to record the granting of the options is

Deferred compensation expense	60,000	
Stock options outstanding		60,000

While deferred taxes are ignored for purposes of this example, in general the recognition of expense for tax purposes would be in a later period, necessitating the recording of a deferred tax benefit. Deferred compensation expense is subtracted from stock options outstanding in the paid-in capital section of owner's equity to indicate the amount of net contributed services on any date, that is, on the grant date nothing has yet been contributed by the option holders ($60,000 – $60,000 = $0). As the employees provide services to earn the options, entries are made assigning compensation expense to years one through five.

Compensation expense	12,000	($60,000 ÷ 5 years)
Deferred compensation expense		12,000

When the option is exercised, cash is received and the stock is issued. The following entry is made (assume exercise after the five-year period):

Cash	520,000 (option price)	
Stock options outstanding	60,000	
Common stock		10,000 (par)
Additional paid-in capital		570,000 (excess)

If options are forfeited as a result of an employee failing to fulfill an obligation (e.g., staying with the company), under the provisions of APB 25 compensation expense is credited in the year of forfeiture. The amount credited reflects the total compensation expense previously charged to the income statement for the employee who forfeited the options. Assume that one officer, who was granted options for 1,000 shares, leaves the company in year three, two years before the options can be exercised. The result is handled as a change in an accounting estimate and the following entry is made in year three:

Stock options outstanding	6,000	
Deferred compensation expense		3,600
Compensation expense		2,400

If the measurement date follows the grant date, it is necessary to assume compensation expense based on the market values of the common stock that exist at the end of each period until the measurement date is reached. Per FIN 28, changes in the market value of stock between the date of grant and the measurement date are adjustments to compensation expense in **the period the market value of the stock changes**. The effect of such changes is **not** spread out over future periods.

Example of accounting for stock options—Measurement and grant date the same, with graded vesting

Assume the same facts as the previous example, except that rights to 2,000 shares vest each year (i.e., the officers can exercise options for a total of 2,000 shares after one year, a total of 4,000 shares after two years, etc.). Where the option program provides for such graded vesting (as contrasted with the cliff vesting of the prior example), the allocation of compensation expense to the period until full vesting has occurred (the end of year five in this example) is to be done in a manner proportional to the number of shares to which rights to exercise the option have vested. As explained in FIN 28, the service period is determined separately for each portion of the option. Thus, the 20% which vests in the first year is deemed attributable to services performed in the first year only, while the 20% which vests in the second year is attributed to services performed in years one and two, etc. The effect of this requirement is to heavily front-load the total compensation cost, as follows:

Fraction of options	*Allocation to years of service*				
	First	*Second*	*Third*	*Fourth*	*Fifth*
1st 20%	20%	--	--	--	--
2nd 20%	10%	10%	--	--	--
3rd 20%	6.67%	6.67%	6.66%	--	--
4th 20%	5%	5%	5%	5%	--
5th 20%	4%	4%	4%	4%	4%
Total allocation	45.67%	25.67%	15.66%	9%	4%

Accordingly, the entries to record compensation in years one and two, respectively, are

Compensation expense	27,402		($60,000 x .4567)
Deferred compensation expense		27,402	
Compensation expense	15,402		($60,000 x .2567)
Deferred compensation expense		15,402	

Example of accounting for stock options—Measurement and grant date different

1. On 1/1/04, a company grants an option to purchase 100 shares of common stock at 90% of the market price at 12/31/2007 and the compensation period is **four years**. The total compensation amount per share is represented by the difference between the current market price and the estimated purchase price granted by the option (90% x Market price) or simply 10% of the current market price.
2. At 1/1/04, the number of shares is determinable, but the option price is unknown.
3. The market values of the common stock are as follows:

12/31/2004	$10
12/31/2005	13
12/31/2006	15
12/31/2007	15

The following entries for compensation expense are recorded:

	2004		*2005*		*2006*		*2007*	
Compensation expense	25		40		47.50		37.50	
Stock options outstanding		25		40		47.50		37.50

2004: ($10 x 10% x 100 shares x 1/4) = $25
2005: ($13 x 10% x 100 shares x 2/4) – expense recognized to date = $40
2006: ($15 x 10% x 100 shares x 3/4) – expense recognized to date = $47.50
2007: ($15 x 10% x 100 shares x 4/4) – expense recognized to date = $37.50

The expense recorded in 2005, 2006, and 2007 results in part from a change in estimate. Note that the market value of the stock at the end of 2004, 2005, and 2006 is used as the estimate of the market price of the stock that will exist at 12/31/2007 and that the total amount of compensation expense previously accrued is subtracted from the latest estimate of cumulative expense.

A time line depicting the actual and estimated compensation expense would appear as follows:

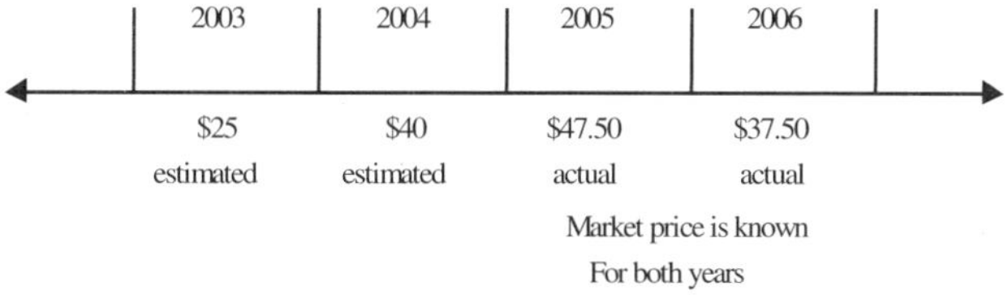

Interpretations of APB 25

APB 25, enacted in 1972, contains certain ambiguities that led to confusion regarding its application. While the FASB pursued the project that was intended to supersede APB 25, little attention was paid to correcting APB 25's deficiencies. After FAS 123 was promulgated, and it became clear that virtually all companies would continue to measure income under APB 25, several efforts were initiated to resolve the problems with the older standard. These efforts resulted in the promulgation of FIN 44 and EITF 00-23. Taken together, these interpretations address many of the areas of ambiguity in APB 25. The more broadly applicable of these matters are addressed in this section.

Much of this guidance relates to "fixed" awards. Consistency of representation (e.g., to the IRS) is required in the categorization of stock award recipients, which means that independent contractors cannot be treated as employees for purposes of applying APB 25. (FAS 123 makes it clear, furthermore, that fair value is the appropriate measure of equity instruments issued to nonemployees.) However, the FASB has elected to provide an exception in the case of independent members of an entity's board of directors; awards issued as compensation for their duties **as directors** can be accounted for under APB 25. Awards made as compensation for services as consultants, et al. however, will not qualify for this exception.

Also, while the general rule is that only stock of the employer can be issued to the employee if APB 25 is to be applied, stock of a parent corporation can be issued to employees of its subsidiaries because in consolidated financial statements the parent company is effectively the employer. To avert an inconsistency in reporting, this same position applies even in the case of stand-alone financial statements of the subsidiary.

If a recipient of stock options undergoes a change in status (e.g., from independent contractor to employee) during the vesting period, a new measurement date is required and only the portion of compensation cost applicable to the period of employee status is to be accounted for under APB 25; compensation recognized under the fair value method is not adjusted.

Some stock option plans incorporate "look-back" provisions, which adjust purchase price downward if the market price at the exercise date is lower than at the grant date. Since the Internal Revenue Code permits "look-back" options in qualified employee stock option plans, and since APB 25 defines noncompensatory plans in terms of what is permissible under the IRC, the interpretation is that such options are allowable.

FIN 44 states also that a new measurement date is required only for the following modifications to the terms of fixed options and awards: (1) a reduction in the exercise price to zero, or the exchange of a stock option award for a restricted stock award; (2) a direct extension of the award's term or one that occurs upon a future separation event beyond the maximum contractual term, provided the employee could potentially receive the term extension; and (3) an extension of the term that occurs upon a future separation event, but not beyond the award's maximum contractual term, in which case incremental compensation cost is measured at the modification date and recognized if and when the future separation event occurs.

An acceleration of the vesting date pursuant to the original terms of the award does not give rise to a new measurement date determination. Compensation expense will only be recognized if the acceleration of vesting occurs and the award is effectively reinstated as a result of the acceleration (e.g., when an award would have otherwise expired unvested without the modification).

In some cases, cash is given to the employee to settle an earlier award or to repurchase the shares after exercise. The interpretation requires that compensation cost be recognized if cash is paid to settle an earlier grant, or an option or award, or to repurchase shares shortly after exercise or issuance, based on the original intrinsic value of the option plus any cash paid in excess of that original intrinsic value, for the current intrinsic value of the award plus any excess of the current intrinsic value of the award at the settlement date.

Other interpretations would impact on "variable" awards. If the exercise price or the number of shares to be issued in what had been a "fixed" award is changed, a variable award is created. The cancellation of one fixed award, followed by the grant of what is denoted as another fixed award to the same individual(s) shortly thereafter, is to be treated effectively as a modification and as the creation of a variable award, to be accounted for consistent with FIN 28. Therefore, compensation (and possibly negative compensation) will be recognized over the vesting period.

If a stock award plan features a call privilege and it is expected that the stock will be repurchased by the issuer shortly after exercise, this must be accounted for as a variable award; the repurchase must be separately accounted for. However, for nonpublic companies variable award accounting is not required if certain conditions are present (repurchase price is equal to fair value and repurchase is not expected to occur shortly after exercise or issuance, or if for other than fair value the employee still bears risks and rewards of ownership for a reasonable period). Also, repurchase to effect tax withholding rules will not trigger variable award accounting.

In poolings of interests, exchanges of fixed stock options will not normally trigger a new measurement date, if the aggregate intrinsic value of the new awards do not exceed that of the old immediately prior to the exchange, and the ratio of exercise to market price per share is not reduced. Other modifications, if not *de minimis*, would result in a new measurement date. In purchase business combinations, exchanges involving vested options are deemed part of the purchase transaction and are to be valued as part of the purchase cost, using fair value accounting. Exchanges involving nonvested options would continue to be accounted for per APB 25, however.

The interpretation also addresses minor matters concerned with determination of grant date, accounting for related deferred tax assets, and compound cash bonus and stock-based plans. With regard to cash bonuses, those that are not fixed and that are contingent upon exercise of options result in combined variable accounting; fixed bonuses contingent upon exercise of options results in combined fixed accounting with the bonus reducing the options' stated exercise prices; and fixed or variable cash bonuses that are contingent upon vesting of awards are to be accounted for as a separate compensation element.

The EITF reached consensuses on a number of issues relating to stock compensation under APB 25 and the aforementioned FIN 44. As is typical with EITF consensuses, these address rather narrow specialized concerns, and technically are clarifications of existing GAAP (APB 25 and FIN 44), not setting new standards, which the EITF, lacking due process, is not empowered to do. In the following paragraphs, the major provisions of EITF 00-23 will be discussed.

Modifications to the terms of outstanding options are sometimes made for a range of reasons, the most common of which is that the options are "underwater," due to a significant decline in the market price of the underlying shares. The general rule is that modifications in the terms of options triggers a new measurement date; this rule was narrowed somewhat by FIN 44, as discussed above. In EITF 00-23, the conclusion reached was that if the intrinsic value is increased in connection with an exchange of options in one entity for options in another within the same consolidated group, when not part of an equity restructuring, variable accounting for the modified awards is required. For all other exchanges, such modifications result in a new measurement date.

In some instances, employers lend money to employees in association with a grant of options, with the loan to be forgiven (e.g., if the value of the options do not appreciate by some amount over a defined time horizon). The EITF decreed that the options and the loan are to be accounted for jointly, with compensation measured by reference to the guaranteed amount, usually the amount of the loan. This is to be ratably recognized over the service period.

Several of the consensuses in EITF 00-23 pertain to exchanges of options pursuant to business combinations accounted for as poolings of interests. Since pooling accounting has been banned effective mid-2001, these are no longer of concern. Many other positions pertained to purchase business combinations, however, and these remain relevant. For example, the EITF found that a subsequent repurchase of options issued as consideration in a purchase business combination, and fully vested at that time, will be deemed a treasury stock transaction (except where the settlement exceeds the fair value of the vested awards, in which case the excess will be deemed additional compensation cost). If the options were unvested at the business combination date, a portion based on the proportion of the vesting period not expired will be compensation expense to be recognized; the balance is a treasury stock transaction, subject to the caveat that if the settlement price exceeds fair value, further compensation is to be recognized (similar to the case of vested options, above). In no case would any adjustment be made to the purchase transaction from which the option grants arose, since the business combination and the later settlement are deemed separate transactions.

When employees forfeit awards prior to vesting because they fail to fulfill defined obligations, where the options were granted as compensation in a purchase business combination, compensation is reversed in the forfeiture period. Any unearned compensation (the amount not already recognized as expense since the grant date) is reversed through equity. The purchase transaction is not to be remeasured.

EITF 00-23 contains additional guidance with regard to accounting for options granted in purchase transactions, including some that address swaps involving subsidiary shares.

A number of the consensuses in EITF 00-23 pertain to changes in the status of the grantee (e.g., from employee to nonemployee) concurrent with changes to the terms of the grant. The conclusion was that the accounting should follow the grantee's status during the time the status existed. Merely temporary changes in status, reversed shortly afterward, would not precipitate such a result, however.

Under certain circumstances, option plans give grantees the right to demand that the issuer repurchase the options or shares (a put option), and in other cases the issuer may have the right to make this repurchase (a call option). The repurchase feature may either be part of the option arrangement or may be contained in a side agreement between the employees and the employer. The EITF has determined that with regard to these "immature shares" (i.e., unexercised options, unvested shares, stock purchased with a nonrecourse loan which has yet to be fully repaid, and stock obtained by means of option exercise over the past six months), a fair value repurchase feature triggers variable accounting unless management represents that it has a positive intent to **not** call the shares within the following six months, and this intent is corroborated by other facts and circumstances, such as past history regarding the calling of immature shares.

If the right to call immature shares is contingent on some event, which is assessed as being unlikely to occur and is not under the grantor's control, this condition will not necessitate variable accounting for the options. Likewise, if the grantee has the right to put the immature shares back to the grantor, and such right is contingent on some event, if the likelihood of occurrence is not probable, and the grantee does not control the event, then variable accounting is not prescribed. If the grantor, in the case of the call provision, or the grantee, in the case of the put, controls the contingent event, then variable accounting for the stock compensation is mandatory. EITF 00-23 also contains guidance on a number of other variations on the themes of put or call rights potentially resulting in the repurchase of immature shares.

If "in the money" options are granted subsequent to the cancellation of a previous award, there will be the presumption that there had been an agreement or a promise to make adjustments for possible market price increases after the cancellation; this makes variable accounting required, unless sufficient facts and circumstances exist to support the position that the new grant was unrelated to the former one. However, if the new options have an exercise price equal to or greater than the fair value at grant date, there is no requirement for variable accounting.

Under FIN 44, a modification reducing the exercise price, or increasing the number of shares, under a fixed option plan generally triggers variable plan accounting. In EITF 00-23, a consensus was reached that under such circumstances, whether a new measurement date or variable accounting is the consequence of the change is a function of all the facts and circumstances. For example, in some cases changes to terms are made to conform to regulatory mandates or to achieve tax objectives for the grantee. In such cases, fixed award accounting would still be valid, but a new measurement date would be specified.

The EITF also decreed that deferred tax benefits cannot be recognized at the time of a purchase business combination when nonqualified options were issued in a nontaxable merger and were fully vested at the date the combination was consummated. Although the entity will realize tax benefits later, that should be accounted for when realized by adjusting the purchase price allocation (generally, this will be by reducing goodwill recorded in the purchase transaction) to the extent that the deduction for tax purposes does not exceed the fair value of the awards recognized as part of the purchase price; any excess over that would be credited to paid-in capital. Examples of journal entries to be made are included in this consensus.

Finally, if short-term inducements are given to encourage exercise of options, this causes the options to be accounted for as variable awards thereafter, even if the inducements expire unused.

Stock Appreciation Rights under APB 25

The previous section dealt with stock option plans, under which the employees are given the right to purchase shares either at advantageous (i.e., below market) prices or at the market price (or higher) as of the date of the grant. Another type of stock-based compensation program gives the employees the opportunity to participate in any increase in value of the company's stock without having to incur the cost of actually purchasing the shares. Such plans may be referred to as phantom stock plans, stock appreciation rights, or variable stock award programs. A wide variety of such plans is found in practice: Some provide for the payment of cash to the employees, while others reward participants with shares of the sponsor's stock. Often such plans are granted together with compensatory stock option plans as either combination or tandem plans: The former give the employees thc rights to both the options and the phantom stock, while the latter require the employees to choose which they will exercise (simultaneously forfeiting the other).

Accounting for stock appreciation rights (SAR) and similar plans is prescribed by FIN 28. There are significant distinctions between APB 25 and FIN 28, the most important of which is the method of computing the compensation cost to be allocated to the periods over which services are provided by the employees. Under APB 25, compensation cost (if any) is determined as of the measurement date (usually the grant date), and is not affected by changes in market price thereafter. By contrast, under Interpretation 28, compensation cost incurred in connection with stock appreciation rights or other variable awards is determined prospectively until full vesting is achieved, with future increases or decreases in market price resulting in charges or credits to periodic compensation expense.

Under both standards, however, total compensation cost is allocated ratably (if cliff vesting is provided by the plan) or proportionally (if graded vesting is provided). Likewise, both standards provide that when an employee forfeits options or rights for which compensation had previously been accrued, the accrual is to be reversed against compensation expense in the period of the forfeiture.

Accounting for compensation cost under SAR that provide graded vesting involves particularly complex allocations under the provisions of FIN 28. (If an enterprise adopts FAS 123, the complexity of this computation is relaxed somewhat, but if the entity uses APB 25 for fixed option plans it must continue to apply FIN 28 and FIN 38 as well, for variable plans.)

Performance-based stock compensation plans often provide for payment in shares, instead of cash. For example, a stock appreciation rights plan may contain a provision that the increase in value will be distributed to the participant in the form of a sufficient number of shares of the sponsor's stock so that the aggregate fair market value is equal to the dollar amount of the award. If the plan provides only for payment in shares (a plan which most often is referred to as a phantom stock plan), the offset to the periodic charge for compensation cost should be to paid-in capital accounts. If the award is payable at the participant's choice in either cash or stock, a liability should be accrued, since the sponsor cannot control the means by which the obligation will be settled. If the payment will be made in cash or stock at the option of the company, the offset to compensation should be either to a liability account or to equity accounts, based on the best available information concerning the sponsor's intentions. As these intentions change from one period to another, the amounts should be reclassified as necessary.

Example of accounting for SAR under FIN 28

1. A company grants 100 SAR, payable in cash, to an employee on 1/1/05.
2. The predetermined amount for the SAR plan is $50 per right, and the market value of the stock is $55 on 12/31/05, $53 on 12/31/06, and $61 on 12/31/07.

Compensation expense recorded in each year would be

			Total expense		*Expense previously accrued*		*Current expense*
2005	100 ($55 – $50)	=	$ 500	-	$ 0	=	$ 500
2006	100 ($53 – $50)	=	$ 300	-	$500	=	$(200)
2007	100 ($61 – $50)	=	$1,100	-	$300	=	$ 800

The total expense recognized over the three-year period is $1,100 [100 x ($61 – $50)]. The required journal entries would be as follows:

2005			
	Compensation expense	500	
	Liability under SAR plan		500
2006			
	Liability under SAR plan	200	
	Compensation expense		200
2007			
	Compensation expense	800	
	Liability under SAR plan		800

If the SAR were to be redeemed in common stock, "Stock rights outstanding" (a paid-in capital account) would replace the liability account in the above entries.

The example assumes no service or vesting period, which is the period of time until the SAR become exercisable. If the above plan had a two-year service period, 50% of the total expense would be recognized at the end of the first year and 100% at the end of the second year and thereafter until exercise. The compensation would be accrued as follows:

2005:	($ 500 x 50%) = $ 250	–	$ 0	=	$250
2006:	($ 300 x 100%) = $ 300	–	$250	=	$ 50
2007:	($1,100 x 100%) = $1,100	–	$300	=	$800

Often stock option plans and SAR are joined in tandem plans, under the terms of which the exercise of one automatically cancels the other. This feature makes accounting for these types of arrangements more complex. Per FIN 28, on the basis of the available facts each period, a determination must be made as to which one of the compensation plans has the higher likelihood of exercise. Once determined, this is the plan accounted for with the other plan being ignored. In the absence of evidence to the contrary, however, the presumption is that the SAR, not the options, will be exercised.

Example of accounting for a combined stock option and stock appreciation rights

To illustrate the accounting for a combined SAR and stock option plan, consider the following facts:

1/1/05 Plan adopted; base price is $100, option price is $95; 1,000 shares exercisable on 1/1/08 **or** 1,000 SAR payable in cash on 1/1/09 on increase over 1/1/05 market value.

Market prices are as follows:

12/31/05	$ 98
12/31/06	110
12/31/07	108
12/31/08	125

Two cases are presented simultaneously, representing two alternative fact situations.

Case 1: It is assumed that only SAR will be exercised.
Case 2: It is assumed that 1/2 SAR, 1/2 options will be exercised.

The appropriate journal entries are as follows:

	Case 1	*Case 2*		
12/31/05	No entry	Compensation expense	625	
		Deferred compensation	1,875	
		Stock options outstanding (500 shares x $5)		2,500
		Compensation expense is 1/4 of projected four-year total relating to expected option exercise in Case 2.		

No SAR liability is accrued since the market price is below the base price. The compensatory part of the stock options, determined under the rules of APB 25, is $5 per share, which is allocated over the four-year vesting period on a straight-line basis.

	Case 1			*Case 2*		
12/31/06	Compensation expense	10,000		Compensation expense	5,625	
	Liability under SAR plan			Deferred compensation		625
	($10 x 1,000 SAR)		10,000	Liability under SAR plan		
				($10 x 500 SAR)		5,000
				Deferred compensation relating to options amortized ratably over option period ($2,500 x 1/4).		

SAR liability recognized for difference between year-end market value and base price for number of expected SAR exercisable.

12/31/07	Liability under SAR plan	2,000		Liability under SAR plan	1,000	
	Compensation expense		2,000	Compensation expense		375
				Deferred compensation		625
12/31/08	Compensation expense	17,000		Compensation expense	9,125	
	Liability under SAR plan		17,000	Deferred compensation		625
				Liability under SAR plan		
				($12,500 - $5,000 + $1,000)		8,500

The option holders may exercise either the options or the SAR in ratios other than those presumed as the basis for the accounting. Assume that either (a) holders elect 100% SAR; (b) holders elect 50% SAR, 50% stock; or (c) they elect to exercise only the stock options. For each of the cases above, the entries under each assumed exercise ratio are as follows:

	Case 1			*Case 2*		
(a)	Liability under SAR plan	25,000		Liability under SAR plan	12,500	
(all cash)	Cash		25,000	Stock options outstanding	2,500	
				Compensation expense	10,000	
				Cash		25,000
(b)	Liability under SAR plan	25,000		Liability under SAR plan	12,500	
(50%				Stock options outstanding	2,500	
cash,	Cash ($47,500 – $12,500)	35,000		Cash	35,000	
50%				Common stock—$20 par		10,000
stock)	Common stock—$20 par		10,000	Additional paid-in capital		40,000
	Additional paid-in capital		50,000			
				Liability under SAR plan	12,500	
				Stock options outstanding	2,500	
(c)	Liability under SAR plan	25,000		Cash	95,000	
(all stock)	Cash	95,000		Common stock—$20 par		20,000
	Common stock—$20 par		20,000	Additional paid-in capital		90,000
	Additional paid-in capital		100,000			

Notice that the proceeds of the stock issuance vary. When stock options are exercised but SAR were accrued, the cost of the shares includes the accrued SAR liability. On the other hand, when the expectation was that options would be exercised but SAR are exercised instead, additional compensation expense will be recorded (as in Case 2a). Since this is due to a change in estimate and not an accounting error, no prior period adjustment can be recorded.

An additional complication arises when there is not **cliff vesting,** as assumed here, but is graded over the years of the option/SAR plans. In such cases, the amount of compensation expense and/or liability under the SAR plan is based on the fraction of vesting at each reporting period. This has the effect of deferring much of the cost to later periods, as was illustrated earlier in the chapter for stock options with graded vesting provisions.

Essentially the same accounting procedures are employed for interim financial reporting. If in subsequent periods the presumed ratio of SAR exercise to stock option exercise in combination (or tandem) plans changes, compensation expense accrued in connection with the anticipated SAR exercise is **not** reduced even though the expected number of SAR to be exercised is diminished. On the other hand, a reduced expectation of stock option exercise may result in a reversal of compensation expense.

Accounting for Employee Stock Options under FAS 123

The failed effort to end the use of the "implicit value" approach of APB 25 has already been described. FAS 123, albeit not mandatory, at least does require the pro forma disclosure of net income and earning per share as if FAS 123 were being utilized for financial reporting purposes. Unlike APB 25, the accounting under FAS 123 for both fixed and variable awards is consistent, and almost without exception compensation cost, at least equal to a defined "minimum value," will be recognized for both types of plans, over the corresponding service period. FAS 123 measures compensation with reference to "fair value," which equals the sum of three elements—intrinsic value, time value of money, and time value associated with the stock's volatility.

NOTE: minimum value estimation of stock options is not allowed in most cases under provisions of the new Exposure Draft. See discussion in Appendix B of this chapter.

As under APB 25, intrinsic value is the amount of advantage, if any, that the holder of an option can realize by exercising the option rather than buying the underlying stock directly. The intrinsic value component equals the difference between the market price of the underlying stock and the option's exercise price. For options "at" or "out of the money" when granted, there is no intrinsic value.

The time value of money, as is well understood, arises because the holder of an option does not pay the exercise price until the exercise date. Instead, the holder can invest funds elsewhere while waiting to exercise the option. The time value of money component is determined by reference to the rate of return available on risk-free securities. If the stock pays a dividend, or is expected to pay a dividend during the life of the option, the value to the holder of the option from delaying payment of the exercise price is only the excess (if any) of the return available on a risk-free security over the return available from exercising the option today and owning the shares. The time value of money component for a dividend-paying stock equals the discounted present value of the expected interest income that could be earned less the discounted present value of the expected dividends to be forgone during the expected life of the option.

The time value associated with volatility represents the ability of the holder to profit from appreciation of the underlying stock while being exposed to the loss of only the option premium, not the full current value of the stock. A more volatile stock has a higher probability of big increases or decreases in price, compared with one having lower volatility. As a result, an option on a highly volatile stock has a higher probability of a big payoff than an option on a less volatile stock and so has a higher time value relating to volatility fair value component.

Volatility is the measure of the amount by which a stock's price fluctuates during a period. It is expressed as a percentage because it looks at stock price fluctuations during a period relative to the stock's price at the beginning of the period. Expected annualized volatility is the predicted amount that is the input to the option pricing model. This is calculated largely from the stock's historical price fluctuations.

To illustrate this basic concept, assume that the present market price of underlying stock is $20 per share, and the option plan grants the recipient the right to purchase shares at today's market price at any time during the next five years. If a risk-free rate, such as that available on Treasury notes having maturities of five years is 5%, then the present value of the future payment of $20 is $15.67 [$\$20 \div (1.05)^5$], which suggests that the option has a value of $20 – $15.67 = $4.33 per share, before considering the value of lost dividends. If the stock is expected to pay a dividend of $.40 per share per year, the present value of the dividend stream that the option holder will forego until exercise five years hence is about

$1.64, discounting again at 5%. Therefore, the **net** value of the option being granted, assuming it is expected to be held to the expiration date before being exercised, is $4.33 – $1.64 = $2.69 per share. (Although the foregoing computation was based on the full five-year life of the option, the actual requirement is to use the **expected term** of the option, which may be shorter.)

It should be noted that critics of FAS 123 have pointed out that the value models suggested by either binomial (lattice) models or closed form models (Black-Scholes) were intended to value marketable options. Employee options cannot generally be sold or traded. While there is some validity to this criticism, alternative models have rarely been proposed. In addition, readily available inexpensive commercial software is now available which greatly enhances the usability of these models. Also, the assignment of zero value to options (the APB 25 approach) cannot be reasonably defended. Thus, the FAS 123 approach, even if flawed, is conceptually superior.

FAS 123 in Greater Detail

With one exception (see below), FAS 123 applies to all stock-based compensation plans, however described, and whether the employees receive stock or cash based on the price of the stock. Included are all stock purchase plans, fixed and variable option arrangements, restricted stock, and stock appreciation rights. FAS 123 also applies to transactions in which stock is exchanged for goods and services in the normal course of business (e.g., for inventory), but the accounting for such transaction, using fair values, is essentially similar to what has long been considered GAAP.

The fair value of the equity instruments granted is used to measure each of these compensation arrangements. Fair value for publicly traded entities is to be measured by one of the recognized options pricing models, of which the Black-Scholes and binomial models are the universally recognized alternatives. These models take into consideration the term of the option (the longer the term, the greater will be the value of the right, all other factors remaining constant); the market price at grant date and the option exercise price (the greater the excess of the former over the latter, the greater will be the option value); the risk-free interest rate, measured by the rate on zero coupon Treasury debt with a term equal to the expected life of the option); the expected dividends to be paid on the stock (the option value is inversely related to expected dividends); and the expected volatility of the stock (the greater the expected volatility, the more valuable the option).

NOTE: The Black-Scholes model was most widely used under FAS 123, but the more complex binomial model, which allows for explicit consideration of more factors, is the preferred model in the Exposure Draft, which is expected to be approved by the end of 2004. Commercial software is readily available to perform either Black-Scholes or binomial model calculations.

For nonpublicly traded companies, essentially the same approach is to be used, except that the measure of volatility, which would be difficult to assess, or even meaningless, in the absence of an active market for the shares, is dispensed with. This truncated measure is referred to as the **minimum value** model.

NOTE: Under provisions of the Exposure Draft, use of minimum value models will not be allowed in most cases.

A full option pricing model approach including a factor for volatility can be used, however, if there is a desire to do so and a means of estimating it.

Exception under FAS 123 for stock purchase plans. FAS 123 does provide an exemption for stock purchase plans that meet all of a set of defined conditions. If the plan does this, it will not be deemed to be a compensatory plan. The conditions are as follows:

1. The plan contains no option features **other** than permitting employees a very limited time, no longer than thirty-one days, to enroll in the plan after the purchase price has been fixed, or permitting employees to cancel participation in a program offering stock at the market price on the purchase date and obtaining a refund of moneys already withheld or paid.
2. Any discount from market price is limited to the greater of
   a. That which would be reasonable in a recurring offer to existing shareholders or others or
   b. Stock issuance costs saved by not having a public offering. A 5% discount is assumed defensible; higher discounts would have to be justified.
3. Substantially all full-time employees, subject only to limited qualifications, are permitted to participate on an equitable basis.

With the sole exception of plans that comply with these restrictions, stock option and related programs are compensatory and subject to the measurement and disclosure requirements of FAS 123. Thus, the new standard is far more restrictive than APB 25. For example, any program which offers employees the right to a lower price at exercise date based on the then-existing market value would be compensatory, as would be one which provided for a purchase price determined as of grant date but gave participants the right to cancel before the exercise.

Measuring volatility. The volatility measure is the most difficult aspect of the option pricing model. FAS 123 addresses this at great length, and should be consulted by those attempting to apply the Black-Scholes or binomial models. In general, volatility is a measure of the variation in prices of the security over a relevant period, projected to the future period that equals the expected term of the employee options. FAS 123 stipulates that this is to be computed by reference to the annualized standard deviation of the differences in the natural logarithms of the possible future stock prices. Since future prices cannot be known, the standard suggests that historical volatility be used to forecast future volatility. In general, this will be achieved by using stock prices over a historical period of time equal to the expected life of the options being granted (e.g., for four-year options, volatility would be assessed by reference to the prior four years' stock price behavior).

If the stock is expected to pay dividends (again, this can be anticipated based on historical experience, taking into account the frequency with which dividend rates have been adjusted and the amounts of such adjustments, modified to reflect future expectations), the volatility measure will also be affected. This is because the market price of the stock reflects the declaration of dividends, and this would distort the actual price volatility unless explicitly dealt with. The market price will reflect this event on the **ex-dividend** date, which is the last date on which a seller of the shares will still have claim to the dividend. After this date, the buyer will own the dividend, therefore the price of the stock will typically drop by the per share amount of the dividend on this date.

A simple way of thinking about volatility is to relate it to the well-understood concept of the "normal distribution." The expected annualized volatility is effectively the standard deviation of the expected price of the stock. One standard deviation plus or minus from the present price, adjusted for the expected (or average) change in price over the period, will have about a 67% probability of including the actual price at the end of the term of the option. For example, if the price per share is $40 currently, and the expected return (based on past price changes) is 10% and the computed volatility measure is 25%, the price of the stock one year hence which is determined at a 67% probability is from $34.43 to $56.76. This is computed as follows: The rate of return over one year, at 67% probability (i.e., one standard deviation plus or minus), is from –15% (= 10% – 25%) to +35% (= 10% + 25%). The natural logarithms $e^{-.15}$ and $e^{.35}$ equate to .8607 and 1.4191, respectively. Thus, the likely stock price one year hence ranges from $34.43 ($40 x .8607) to $56.76 ($40 x 1.4191). For performing more complicated calculations, software is readily available.

The discount rate. FAS 123 specifies the use of a risk-free rate. The risk-free rate of return is easily ascertained as the rate on treasury bills or notes having a remaining term to maturity equal to the expected life of the options being computed. Reasonable approximations would be acceptable (e.g., it would be valid to interpolate a discount rate from published data).

The expected term of the options. The objective of FAS 123 is to allocate compensation cost to the periods in which services are provided to the entity granting the options. If the award is for past services, as indicated when the options are immediately exercisable by the holders, compensation cost must be fully expensed at the date of the grant. More typically, however, the options will not be exercisable until some later date, called the vesting date, which often will be a few years after the grant date. In such a case, the compensation element is really intended to apply to some or all of the intervening period from grant to vesting dates, and should be accrued over that time, based either on an estimate of the number of options expected to vest or on an estimate of the number of options expected to be exercised.

In some instances there is a performance condition stipulated in the option agreement, and the options will not be exercisable until the condition is met. A variation of this has the number of options dependent upon the extent to which performance is achieved. Compensation cost associated with such option arrangements is to be accrued over the expected period until the conditions will be satisfied.

In the case of either service period-based or performance-based options, provision for forfeitures may be made either at inception or as forfeitures actually occur. The former method requires that compensation cost be accrued based on the number of options that are expected to vest less those which vest but are not, for whatever reason, subsequently exercised by the holders. For example, it may be estimated based on past behavior that of 100 options granted, only 85 will vest (due to employee turnover, failure to meet performance conditions, etc.) and only 78 will be exercised; compensation cost would be based on 78 options in such a case. The latter method would have compensation determined based on the 85 options expected to vest, with compensation cost adjusted if and when some of the 7 (85-78) options are forfeited.

If the former method, basing compensation on the number of options expected to be exercised, is utilized, then changes in that expectation during the period in which compensation is being accrued is to be accounted for as a change in an accounting estimate as defined in APB 20; the effect is reported in the period in which the change occurs. Under the alternative method, the effect of forfeitures is reported in compensation as they individually occur.

Payments in lieu of dividends on options. Normally dividends are not paid on shares that have not been issued; thus, unexercised options do not gain the benefit of any dividends declared on the underlying stock. However, an entity can choose to pay dividend equivalents on options. Under the provisions of FAS 123, such dividends or dividend equivalents on options which vest are to be accounted for as other dividends, that is, charged against retained earnings. Those paid on options that do not vest are deemed to be compensation expense. The reporting entity can either estimate what fraction of options will vest, and allocate such dividend equivalents between retained earnings and compensation expense accordingly, or else can charge all to retained earnings and account for forfeitures as they occur, by reversing the charge from retained earnings to compensation cost.

Settlements of awards. Sometimes an entity that grants options to employees will repurchase the resulting shares after they are issued, or will purchase and cancel the options, by making a payment to the option holders. To the extent that shares are purchased for market value, the transaction is similar to any other treasury stock transaction, and equity accounts will be charged with the purchase price. If, however, the purchase price exceeds the market or fair value, the excess is deemed to be additional compensation expense. If the payment is made to cancel options which have not yet vested, the remaining unrecognized compensation cost must be expensed, as the options have effectively vested at that point in time. The additional compensation element, if any, is measured by the difference between the price paid and the value of the option repurchased, as computed using the methods prescribed by FAS 123 (i.e., by the fair value method).

Examples of accounting for options under FAS 123

Example where calculation of compensation expense does not consider expected forfeitures. Assume the same facts as were presented earlier in this section when APB 25 was being explained.

Options are granted to corporate officers to purchase 10,000 shares of $1 par stock at a price of $52 per share, when the market price is $58. The options may not be exercised until five years from the grant date. The company has no reason to expect that any of the options will be forfeited by the employees to whom they are granted. If the risk-free interest rate is 8% and the stock is expected to pay dividends of $2 annually, the minimum value as prescribed under FAS 123 is as follows:

Current market	$58.00
Less: Present value of exercise price ($52 x .681)	35.39
Present value of expected dividends ($2 x 3.993)	7.99
	$14.62

Thus the 10,000 options have a value of $146,200 (10,000 x $14.62), to be recognized over five years, or $29,240 per year before considering forfeitures.

The entry to record the granting of the options is

Deferred compensation expense	146,200	
Stock options outstanding		146,200

As was the case under APB 25, deferred compensation expense is subtracted from stock options outstanding in the paid-in capital section of owner's equity to indicate the amount of net contributed services on any date [i.e., on the grant date nothing has yet been contributed by the option holders ($146,200 – $146,200 = $0)]. As the employees provide services to earn the options, entries are made assigning compensation expense to years one to five.

Compensation expense	29,240 ($146,200 ÷ 5 years)	
Deferred compensation expense		29,240

When the option is exercised, cash is received and the stock is issued. The following entry is made (assume exercise after the five-year period):

Cash	520,000 (option price)	
Stock options outstanding	146,200	
Common stock		10,000 (par)
Additional paid-in capital		656,200 (excess)

If options are forfeited as a result of an employee failing to fulfill an obligation (e.g., staying with the company), under the provisions of FAS 123 compensation expense is credited in the year of forfeiture. (This is assuming that compensation expense had not been based on the **net** number of options that were expected to be exercised, which is the alternative, acceptable method under this standard.) The amount credited reflects the total compensation expense previously charged to the income statement for the employee who forfeited the options. Assume that one officer, who was granted options for 1,000 shares, leaves the company in year three, two years before the options can be exercised. The result is handled as a change in an accounting estimate and the following entry is made in year three:

Stock options outstanding	14,620	
Deferred compensation expense		8,772
Compensation expense		5,848

Next consider the case of an option plan that features graded vesting, that is, where instead of having all options vest after five years, 20% of the options granted will vest each year. Under FIN 28, which applies to entities that continue to adhere to APB 25, a rather complicated allocation pattern must be employed. These are not freely selectable alternatives, however, if fair value is determined based on different expected lives for options that vest in different years, then the FIN 28 method is required. Entities that adopt FAS 123 can either continue the FIN 28 method, illustrated earlier in this chapter, or can recognize compensation on a straight-line basis. Straight-line compensation recognition can be used only if the expected lives of the award are determined in another manner. If the straight-line method is used, the compensation cost recognized to date must be at least equal to the value of the vested portion of the award at that date. FAS 123 includes illustrations of the accounting required under such circumstances.

Accounting under FAS 123 using expected number of options to be exercised. Assume a different set of facts from the example presented immediately above. The company's stock is not publicly traded, however the company does address volatility and uses a binomial model. FAS 123 permits the computation of fair value based on the expected number of options that will vest (i.e., net of expected forfeitures). As noted above, the standard also permits accounting for forfeitures when they occur. The following assumptions and information are needed to apply the binomial model to value share options granted on January 1, 2005:

Share options granted	90,000
Employees granted options	300
Expected forfeitures per year	3.0%
Share price at the grant date	$10
Exercise price	$10
Par value per share	$1
Number of years to vest	5 years
Contractual term (CT) of options	10 years
Risk-free interest rate over CT	1.5 to 4.3%
Expected volatility over CT	40-60%
Expected dividend yield	1.0%
Suboptimal exercise factor	2

Using as inputs the last seven items from the table above, the company's binomial-lattice-based valuation model produces a fair value estimate of $4.90 per option. The company uses the binomial model because that model more fully captures and better reflects the characteristics of the instruments being valued and it has the necessary data.

With an annual forfeiture rate of 3%, the number of options expected to vest is given as

10,000 x .97 x .97 x .97 x .97 x .97 = 8,627 options

Accordingly, the total value of $42,272 (8,627 options x $4.90) will be recognized as compensation expense over the five years on a ratable basis. If the forfeiture rate changes, that would be treated as a change in an accounting estimate, and reflected in income on a prospective basis. The entry to record the granting of the options is

Deferred compensation expense	42,272	
Stock options outstanding		42,272

Stock options outstanding is an additional paid-in capital account. Deferred compensation expense is subtracted from stock options outstanding in the paid-in capital section of owners' equity to indicate the amount of net contributed services on any date [i.e., on the grant date nothing has yet been contributed by the option holders ($42,272 – $42,272 = $0)]. As the employees provide services to earn the options, entries are made assigning compensation expense to years one to five.

Compensation expense	8,454 (42,272 ÷ 5 years)	
Deferred compensation expense		8,454

When the option is exercised, cash is received and the stock is issued. The following entry is made (assume exercise after the five-year period, and that the number of forfeitures exactly equals the amount predicted):

Cash	86,270 (option price)		
Stock options outstanding	42,272		
Common stock		8,627	(par)
Additional paid-in capital		119,915	(excess)

Note that under this method the effect of forfeitures is reflected in income; that is, compensation cost is reduced on a prospective basis. If the assumption regarding the number of forfeitures changed during the service period, compensation cost attributable to prior periods is effectively adjusted in the current period by making a "catch up" adjustment as illustrated in the following paragraph.

Assume that in year three of the preceding example the holders of 5% of the remaining options leave the company (the forfeiture rate in years one and two having equaled the expected 3%). Management believes that the rate in year three was unusually high, but now expects that the forfeiture rate over the full five-year period will average 4%. Given this new insight, the number of options that it believes will eventually vest will be as follows:

10,000 x .96 x .96 x .96 x .96 x .96 = 8,154 options

The total compensation cost over five years, given this revised estimate, will be $39,953 (8,154 options x $4.90). Since aggregate compensation cost of $16,908 ($8,454 x 2) has already been recognized in years one and two, and total compensation cost for years one through three under the revised assumption should be $23,972 (3/5 x $39,953), the difference of $7,064 should be allocated to compensation expense in year three. The entry in year three is

Compensation expense	7,064	
Deferred compensation expense		7,064

The entries in years four and five, assuming no other changes in the forfeiture rate, are

Compensation expense ($39,953 ÷ 5 yrs)	7,991	
Deferred compensation expense		7,991

Also, there should be an adjustment to reduce the amounts in the deferred compensation expense and stock options outstanding accounts, based on the new expected totals, as follows:

Stock options outstanding ($42,272 – $39,953)	2,319	
Deferred compensation expense		2,319

Assuming that the average forfeiture rate does indeed equal 4% over the vesting period, and that all options are exercised at the vesting date, the entry to be made at the end of year five will be

Cash	81,540 (option price)		
Stock options outstanding	39,953		
Common stock		8,154	(par)
Additional paid-in capital		113,339	(excess)

On the other hand, if the options are not forfeited, but instead expire unexercised after first vesting with the grantees, then the accounting treatment under FAS 123 would be different. The standard provides that previously recognized compensation cost is not to be reversed if vested options expire unexercised. Thus, in such a circumstance, the stock options outstanding would be closed to another paid-in capital account, such as "capital from unexercised options."

Given the facts in the immediately preceding discussion, assume now that at the time the options vest, only 8,000 are exercised, and that, per the terms of the option agreement, the remaining 154 expire one year later, unexercised. The entries would be as follows:

For the exercise:

Cash	80,000 (option price)		
Stock options outstanding	39,200		
Common stock		8,000	(par)
Additional paid-in capital		111,200	(excess)

For the expiration one year later:

Stock options outstanding	753	
Additional paid-in capital from unexercised options		753

Accounting for stock appreciation rights (SAR) under FAS 123. One of the motivating reasons for developing FAS 123 was to eliminate the disparate treatment applied to fixed options, variable (or performance) options and other stock-based compensation schemes. Thus, under the new standard the measurement principles applicable to SAR are the same as for stock options.

One distinction that may arise in connection with SAR, however, is that the holder may have the ability to elect to receive cash in settlement of the award. In the case of such plans, the accrual of compensation expense will result in the recognition of a liability. (In some such plans, however, the settlement can only be made in shares of stock; in such cases, the accrual will be offset by paid-in capital.)

Accounting for tandem plans under FAS 123. Accounting for tandem plans has been explained earlier in this chapter for situations where APB 25 and related standards are still being utilized. The concepts are the same for tandem plans by entities that adopt FAS 123, but the accounting will be somewhat different, for several reasons. First, FAS 123 requires that when an entity incurs a substantive liability, it must be reported as such. Further, it states that when the employee has the right to receive payment in cash, a liability has been created. Only if the company can choose to settle tandem plans in stock, and past experience suggests that indeed it does choose to do so, will the compensation be based on the stock option part of the plan and will the offset to compensation expense be paid-in capital.

Second, cash SAR are measured with reference to the intrinsic value as of the exercise date, which differs from the fair value approach to measuring stock options under FAS 123. Note that time value, which is typically a major component of total value assigned to options under this standard, is not measured as part of intrinsic value as applied to SAR. For that reason, compensation cost as determined in the context of tandem plans may be significantly less than would be the case for the option portion of the plan on its own.

To illustrate, consider again the facts presented in the example of tandem plans earlier in this chapter when APB 25 was being discussed.

1/1/05	Plan adopted; base price is $100, option price is $95; 1,000 shares exercisable on 1/1/08 **or** 1,000 SAR payable in cash on 1/1/09 an increase over 1/1/05 market value.

Market prices are as follows:

12/31/05	$ 98
12/31/06	110
12/31/07	108
12/31/08	125

Assuming now a 6% risk-free rate and no dividend yield on the stock, the fair value of the options alone using the minimum value model is $100 – ($95 x .792) = $24.75 x 1,000 = $24,750. Were these options freestanding and not part of a tandem plan, compensation cost of $6,187.50 would be accrued each year.

However, since the holders have the right to choose cash payments, under FAS 123 it must be assumed that they will do this, and that the company has incurred a liability (not an equity instrument). Accordingly, compensation cost is debited or credited as the market price varies from the rights price ($100), with the limitation that the cumulative compensation cost cannot be negative (as the employees obviously have no obligation to pay the company if the market declines from the $100 per share level). Therefore the entries will be as follows:

12/31/05 No entry

No SAR liability is accrued since the market price is below the base price. The compensatory stock options are ignored since the holders have the right to demand a cash settlement.

12/31/06	Compensation expense	10,000	
	Liability under SAR plan ($10 x 1,000 SAR)		10,000

SAR liability recognized for difference between year-end market value and base price for number of expected SAR exercisable.

12/31/07	Liability under SAR plan	2,000	
	Compensation expense		2,000
12/31/08	Compensation expense	17,000	
	Liability under SAR plan		17,000

Recall that the option holders may exercise either the options or the SAR, although the accrual under FAS 123 was based on the presumption that 100% exercise of the SAR would occur. Assume that (a) holders elect 100% SAR; (b) holders elect 50% SAR, 50% stock; or (c) they elect to exercise only the stock options. For each of the cases above, the entries under each assumed exercise ratio are as follows:

(a)	Liability under SAR plan	25,000	
(all cash)	Cash		25,000
(b)	Liability under SAR plan	25,000	
(50% cash,	Cash ($47,500 – $12,500)	35,000	
50% stock)	Common stock—$20 par		10,000
	Additional paid-in capital		50,000
(c)	Liability under SAR plan	25,000	
(all stock)	Cash	95,000	
	Common stock—$20 par		20,000
	Additional paid-in capital		100,000

Reload options and other plan features. Some option arrangements permit the exercise price to be paid for by delivering shares already held by the grantee (these shares are referred to as "mature shares"), rather than with cash. These shares are valued at the market price as of the date of the exercise. Furthermore, there may be a reload feature, which provides that the holder will be granted another option equal to the number of mature shares used in the exercise, and that the exercise price for the reload option will be equal to the market at the time of exercise of the original option. This feature obviously has value, and in a fair value approach as is adopted under FAS 123 this feature should be considered in computing compensation cost. However, there are a number of subjective elements that would need to be addressed, including the expected market value at exercise and reload date and the number of options that would be exercised in this fashion. Due to this and the fact that valuation models dealing with reload features are not yet widely understood, FAS 123 has stipulated that there be no additional value assigned for such options. Rather, if and when a reload option is granted (when mature shares are used to exercise the original option), it is to be accounted for as a new option.

Other modifications of options are accounted for prospectively as exchanges of the old options for a new equity instrument. Fair value is used to account for such transactions. For example, modification of the terms of an outstanding option would be accounted for based on a comparison of the fair value of the modified option at the date it is granted and at the date of the old option that is effectively repurchased, based on the shorter of (1) the remaining initially estimated expected life or (2) the expected life of the modified option. If the fair value of the modified option exceeds that of the option that is replaced, additional compensation cost must be recognized.

Other FAS 123 Matters

The Board issued FTB 97-1 that deals with "look-back options" in the context of FAS 123. Plans with this feature permit exercise at a price that is the lower of the market price at the grant date or at the date of exercise.

Transition considerations. With the recent surge in companies voluntarily changing their accounting for stock-based compensation from the APB 25 intrinsic value method to the FAS 123 fair value approach, for both income measurement and disclosure purposes, FASB has issued FAS 148 to expand the means by which this transition may be effected.

Under FAS 123, application of the fair value method was to be **prospective,** which meant that during a lengthy transition period preexisting options would continue to be measured under the intrinsic value method while new grants would require measurement under the fair value method. This approach was imposed under FAS 123 because of the concern that relevant data needed to retroactively apply the fair value method to outstanding options would be unavailable to difficult to procure. This is less likely to be a concern now, however, since the FAS 123 disclosures have been required since that standard became effective in 1995, even when the reporting entities used APB 25 for primary reporting purposes.

Accordingly, FASB has decreed that three alternative acceptable methods are available to reporting entities which are now voluntarily changing to full FAS 123 compliance—with the original prospective application method being tolerated only until the end of 2003. These methods are

1. **Prospective.** The fair value method is applied to the recognition provisions for all employee awards granted, modified, or settled after the beginning of the fiscal year in which the recognition provisions are first applied. However, this method can only be applied if an entity elects to adopt the recognition provisions of FAS 123 for stock-based employee compensation in a fiscal year beginning before December 16, 2003.
2. **Modified prospective.** The fair value method is applied to the recognition of stock-based employee compensation cost from the beginning of the fiscal year in which the recognition provisions are first applied as if the FAS 123 method had been used to account for all employee awards granted, modified, or settled in fiscal years beginning after December 15, 1994. However, prior periods' compensation cost is not restated.

3. **Retroactive restatement.** Restate all periods presented to reflect stock-based employee compensation cost under the FAS 123 method for all employee awards granted, modified, or settled in fiscal years beginning after December 15, 1994. Restatement of periods prior to those presented is permitted but not required. The restated net income and earnings per share of prior periods is to be determined in a manner consistent with the requirements set forth in FAS 148.

When either the modified prospective or the retroactive restatement methods are elected, the reporting entity may need to report an adjustment to additional paid-in capital as of the beginning of the first period for which stock-based employee compensation cost is accounted for in accordance with the fair value based method. For awards that are unvested or which, in the case of certain variable awards, are unexercised as of the beginning of that period, that adjustment shall be determined by the following steps:

1. First, the carrying amounts of unearned or deferred compensation (contra equity accounts), stock-based compensation liabilities, and the related deferred tax balances recognized under APB 25, if any, are to be reversed.
2. Next, the stock-based compensation liabilities and related deferred tax balances determined under FAS 123 are to be recognized.
3. Finally, the difference between the amounts reversed and the amounts recognized, above, is to be reported as an adjustment to additional paid-in capital as of the beginning of the period. No cumulative effect of a change in accounting principle shall be presented.

If electing retroactive restatement, the effect on additional paid-in capital or retained earnings arising from the restatement of periods subsequent to the period of initial application of the fair value based method but prior to the earliest period for which an income statement is presented is to be reported as an adjustment to those accounts as of the beginning of the earliest period for which an income statement is presented. The transition adjustment, as well as the effect of restatement of intervening periods, if any, should be disclosed in the year of adoption.

Disclosure requirements under FAS 123. FAS 123 significantly expands the disclosures that are required by entities having stock compensation arrangements, and this expansion applies as well, for the most part, to those companies that continue to employ APB 25 for financial statement purposes. Disclosures are set forth in the Disclosure Checklist included at the end of this book.

In addition to the disclosures identified in the checklist, FAS 123 requires that for options outstanding as of the date of the latest balance sheet, the range of exercise prices, weighted-average exercise price, and weighted-average remaining contractual life must be presented. If the range is wide, exercise prices should be grouped into ranges that are more meaningful for assessing the number and timing of additional share issuances and the cash that may be received as a result of such exercises (FAS 123 suggests that the range is wide if the highest exercise price exceeds about 150% of the lowest). For each such range the following disclosures are required:

1. The number, weighted-average exercise price, and weighted-average remaining contractual life of options outstanding
2. The number and weighted-average exercise price of options currently exercisable

Furthermore, if the company grants options under a number of plans (e.g., fixed and variable plans), the income statement oriented disclosures should be appropriately segregated.

For entities that continue to apply APB 25, the company must also disclose for each year for which an income statement is provided the pro forma net income (and earnings per share, if required under FAS 128) as if fair value based measurements had been used. Thus, **all** entities will have to apply the Black-Scholes or binomial model (if publicly owned) or the minimum value model (if privately owned), whether FAS 123 is adopted or not. It should be noted that, in determining the pro forma disclosures, the tax effect of compensation differences will also have to be considered, as discussed below. This particular pro forma disclosure cannot be merged with any other pro forma calculation; it must be possible for financial statement readers to understand the impact on earnings of the choice of accounting method for stock-based compensation alone.

Finally, enterprises that use equity instruments to acquire goods or services other than employee services must also provide disclosures similar to those above (e.g., number of shares, weighted-average prices, etc.).

Expanded disclosures under FAS 148. Entities which voluntarily adopt the fair value approach of FAS 123, as well as those which continue to employ the intrinsic value methodology of APB 25, are subject to the newly imposed disclosure requirements set forth by FAS 148. The following disclosures are now mandated:

1. The method used to account for stock-based employee compensation in each period presented;
2. For entities adopting the fair value recognition provisions of FAS 123, a description of the method of reporting the change in accounting principle must be set forth for all financial statements in which the period of adoption is presented;
3. If awards of stock-based employee compensation were outstanding and accounted for under the intrinsic value method for any period for which an income statement is presented, a tabular presentation of the following information for all periods presented:
    a. Net income and basic and diluted earnings per share as reported;
    b. The stock-based employee compensation cost, net of related tax effects, included in the determination of net income as reported;
    c. The stock-based employee compensation cost, net of related tax effects, that would have been included in the determination of net income if the fair value based method had been applied to all awards (i.e., those granted, modified, or settled in fiscal periods beginning after December 15, 1994);
    d. Pro forma net income as if the fair value based method had been applied to all awards—which will reflect the difference in stock-based employee compensation cost, if any, included in net income and the total cost measured by the fair value based method, as well as additional tax effects, if any, that would have been recognized in the income statement if the fair value based method had been applied to all awards; and
    e. Pro forma basic and diluted earnings per share as if the fair value based method had been applied to all awards—which will reflect the change in the denominator of the diluted earnings per share calculation as if the assumed proceeds under the treasury stock method, including measured but unrecognized compensation cost and the excess tax benefits credited to additional paid-in capital, were determined under the fair value based method.

Expanded interim disclosures under FAS 148. The new standard also has expanded requirements for disclosures accompanying interim financial statements. Specifically, the following information about stock-based employee compensation costs must be disclosed prominently and in tabular form for all periods presented if awards of stock-based employee compensation were outstanding and accounted for under the intrinsic value method for any period for which an income statement is presented;

1. Net income and basic and diluted earnings per share as reported;
2. The stock-based employee compensation cost, net of related tax effects, included in the determination of net income as reported;
3. The stock-based employee compensation cost, net of related tax effects, that would have been included in the determination of net income if the fair value based method had been applied to all awards (i.e., awards, granted, modified, or settled in fiscal periods beginning after December 15, 1994);
4. Pro forma net income as if the fair value based method had been applied to all awards, and
5. Pro forma basic and diluted earnings per share as if the fair value based method had been applied to all awards.

Accounting for Equity Instruments Issued to other than Employees

While FAS 123 makes it very clear that stock issuances to persons or entities other than employees (e.g., vendors providing goods or services to the enterprise) are to be measured at fair value (defined by either the value of the goods or services received or the value of the equity instruments delivered in exchange, whichever is subject to more reliable measurement), it offers no specific guidance regarding measurement. (Note that the Exposure Draft that amends FAS 123 does not address instruments issued to other than employees.) The Emerging Issues Task Force supplemented this basic directive, with consensuses on EITF 96-18, dealing exclusively with those situations in which the fair value of the equity instruments delivered is more objectively ascertainable than is the value of goods or services received. EITF 96-18 is the foundation for the discussion that follows in this section.

Measurement date. For purposes of ascertaining the amounts to be assigned for these transactions, the key concern is the determination of the measurement date. Essentially, the amount of expense or the value of the asset acquired through the issuance of equity instruments is fixed as of the measurement date, although, under certain circumstances as explained below, some subsequent adjustments may need to be made.

Per the consensus on EITF 96-18, the measurement date will be the **earlier** of the date at which a commitment for performance is made or when the performance is actually completed. Whether or not there has been a "performance commitment" by the party providing the goods or services is a question of fact and must be determined from the surrounding circumstances, but in general will be deemed to exist if there is a "sufficiently large disincentive for nonperformance" to make performance probable. This disincentive must derive from the relationship between the equity instrument issuer/recipient of the goods or services and its counterparty. Mere risk of forfeiture is not enough to qualify as a disincentive, nor is the risk of being sued for nonperformance. When a sufficiently large disincentive exists, however, the measurement date will precede the completion of performance and, accordingly, when accrual of the related expense or recognition of the asset would otherwise be required under GAAP, it will be necessary to include the value of the equity instruments in such cost.

For example, if the agreed-upon price for the construction of a new power plant includes options on the utility company's stock, subject to a completion date of no longer than three years hence, **and** the contract also contains substantial financial disincentives to late completion, such as a provision for liquidated damages, then it would be concluded that there was a "performance commitment" within the meaning of EITF 96-18. On the other hand, if the price agreed to were to be fully payable even in the event of late delivery, there would be no "performance commitment" as that term is used.

In many situations in which the compensation includes significant equity instrument components, there will still be no finding of a performance commitment because the payment arrangement provides for phases of work, with payment in full for work as it is completed. For example, if a contractor agrees to build a multiplicity of sales kiosks in various air terminals for a retailing chain, with payment to be made in cash and the retailer's stock upon the completion of each kiosk, the contractor could terminate the arrangement after any intermediate completion date without significant penalty. In such cases, the measurement date would be, for each subproject, the date on which the work is completed.

When to recognize the fair value of the equity instruments. In general, the normal rules of GAAP would apply in circumstances in which stock or other equity instruments were being granted as part, or all, of the consideration for the transaction. Thus, if the services provided represented an expense of the enterprise, the expense should be recognized when incurred, which could well precede the date on which the payment was ultimately to be made.

No specific guidance has been offered regarding timing or manner of recognition. However, an EITF consensus was reached that once recognized, an asset or expense would not later be reversed if a stock option issued as consideration were to expire unexercised. This is consistent with FAS 123's treatment of expirations of options granted to employees. (It is, however, in contrast to the accounting prescribed for forfeitures under both APB 25 and FAS 123, which mandate that compensation be reversed under such circumstances.) Thus, an expense or asset measurement is made with the best information available at that time, and there is no "look back" based on subsequent events; the value assigned to the option would be credited to an appropriate paid-in capital account (e.g., "capital from expired options") if this becomes necessary.

Accounting prior to measurement date. If, under GAAP, it is necessary for the entity to recognize an expense or an asset related to the transaction involving the issuance of equity for goods or services prior to the measurement date, the then-current fair values of the equity instruments must be utilized to determine these amounts. If fair values change later, these variations are attributed to those later periods, consistent with Interpretation 28, discussed earlier in this chapter. Thus, for a transaction which calls primarily for cash payment but also, to a lesser extent, for the issuance of stock, a decline in the value of the equity portion in a later interim period would reduce the cost (or asset value) to be recognized in that period; if the stock portion is a significant component, a decline could largely eliminate the cost otherwise to be accrued or even, conceivably, cause it to become negative in a later reporting period. Of course, overall, the aggregate cost would be positive upon ultimate completion (at worst it could be zero, if the transaction were predicated only on the issuance of equity instruments, and these became worthless—an obviously unlikely scenario).

Measurement of fair value of the equity instrument portion of the transaction when certain terms are not known at inception. In some circumstances where there is a performance commitment there will also be a material uncertainty regarding the valuation of the equity instruments, either because of some question regarding the number of instruments to be delivered, the value of such instruments, or some factor dependent upon the performance of the party providing the service. For example, the arrangement may include a guarantee of the value of the instrument extending for some period subsequent to completion of performance that unless the underlying shares maintain a market price of $15 or greater for one year following delivery, or else a defined number of additional shares will be granted. This type of arrangement is referred to as a "market condition." In other circumstances there may be a condition based on the counterparty's performance, for example, when options are granted to a tax accountant structuring a tax shelter, in which the number of options ultimately deliverable depends upon successfully surviving an IRS audit. Situations such as this are denoted "counterparty performance conditions."

Where the arrangement contains market conditions, measurement of the equity instrument portion of the contracted price should be based on two elements: the first is the fair value of the basic equity instrument; the second is the fair value of the contingent commitment, such as the aforenoted promise to grant a specified number of extra shares if the market price falls below $15 during the one-year period. In practice, the valuation of these contingencies might prove to be challenging, but clearly any such promise has some positive value, and the standard requires that this be assessed. Changes in the value of the second (contingent) element subsequent to the performance commitment date would **not** be recognized since, per EITF 96-13, a derivative financial instrument to be settled in a company's own shares (as contrasted to a settlement in cash) is not to be remeasured.

Compared to market conditions, measurement when there are counterparty performance conditions is more complicated. At the measurement date, the equity instruments are valued at the lowest of the defined alternative amounts. For example, if the value of the option award to the tax accountant noted above is $20,000 (at the performance commitment date) assuming survival against IRS challenge, but only $5,000 if the IRS ultimately prevails, then the measurement of the value of the service would be based on the $5,000 amount. However, later, when the outcome of the performance condition is known, an additional cost would have to be recognized if a more favorable outcome occurred (in this example, successful defense of the tax shelter). The added cost would be based not on the values as of the performance commitment date, but rather as of the date of resolution of the condition. If the value of the options under the "success" outcome is $28,000 at that date, and the value of the "failure" outcome is $19,000, then an added cost of ($28,000 – 19,000) $9,000 would be recognized.

Where a given transaction involves both market and counterparty performance conditions, the accounting specified for situations involving only counterparty performance conditions is to be applied.

Reporting prior to the measurement date when certain terms are not known. When market conditions (e.g., the value of the stock underlying the options two years hence) are not known, and expenses must be accrued or assets recorded prior to the measurement date, the then-current fair values of the equity instruments at such dates should be used, with subsequent adjustments as necessary. When there are counterparty performance conditions, either alone or in conjunction with market conditions, then interim measurements should be based on the lowest of the alternative values as of each date, with subsequent changes in this same measure assigned to later periods.

Reporting after the measurement date when certain terms are not known. When market conditions (e.g., the value of the stock underlying the options two years hence) are not known, **after** the measurement date the principles of EITF 96-13 are to be applied, which generally would mean that changes in value would not be recognized. On the other hand, when there are counterparty performance conditions, with or without market conditions also being present, the principles of FAS 123, specifically the "modification accounting" procedures, are to be utilized. This results in reporting an adjustment in subsequent periods determined with reference to the difference between the then-current fair value of the revised equity instruments and that of the old instruments immediately prior to the recognition event. In all cases, the "then-current" values are to be determined with reference to the lowest aggregate fair values under the alternative outcomes specified by the contractual arrangement.

Accounting for the Tax Effects of Options and SAR

Generally, amounts reported as compensation expense in connection with stock option and appreciation rights plans are deductible for tax purposes, but the timing and amounts of tax deductions may differ from the amounts reportable as expenses under GAAP. (An exception: incentive stock options provide no deduction for the grantor, and only tax at the capital gains rate for the employee, when shares acquired via option exercises are ultimately sold.) Thus, both temporary and permanent differences may occur, which are accounted for differently under GAAP (FAS 109).

Timing differences occur because, for tax purposes, the company will be entitled to a deduction in the period in which the employee reports the compensation as ordinary income, whereas for financial reporting purposes the tax must be associated with any compensation expense accrued in the period(s) in which the services are provided. If APB 25 is being used, there probably will be no compensation recognized in any period in connection with the options granted; for this reason, the tax benefit flowing from the deductibility of compensation is not reported in the income statement (a result of applying the matching concept), but instead will be credited to paid-in capital.

If FAS 123 is being used, on the other hand, compensation expense is recognized, and the tax effect thereof will be included in the income statement. The ultimate amount of the tax deduction depends on the spread between exercise price and fair market value on exercise date; this will differ from the aggregate compensation recognized over the service period, which is keyed to fair value at the grant date, and not to the ultimate market price upon exercise. Accordingly, there will usually be some portion of the tax benefit that will be credited to paid-in capital (similar to that under APB 25), even if most of the tax benefits impact the income statements over the service period.

Since, for compensatory arrangements under APB 25, and for all plans if accounted for under FAS 123, the actual tax deduction occurs in a period subsequent to the service provision periods, a deferred tax benefit will be recognizable by the sponsoring corporation as compensation is expensed for GAAP reporting purposes. Under current GAAP (FAS 109), such benefits are to be recorded in every case, although when it is deemed "more likely than not" that the benefit will **not** ultimately be received by the reporting entity, an offsetting valuation account must also be recorded. (See Chapter 15.)

Example of accounting for the tax ramifications of stock options

Assume an option to purchase ten shares at $80 per share is granted to a key employee when the market price is $100 per share, exercisable over four years. The company is continuing to use APB 25 to account for such transactions. This would be deemed a compensatory option; the following entry is made to record the deferred compensation at the grant date:

Deferred compensation expense	200 [= 10 x ($100 – $80)]	
Stock options outstanding		200

Compensation, in the total amount $200, is associated with employee service in years one through four. The **annual** entry to recognize the expense is

Compensation expense	50	
Deferred compensation expense		50

Assume the tax rate remains constant at 40% and that the enterprise has been and is expected to continue to be profitable (and that hence there is no need for a reserve against the deferred tax asset). The compensation expense is not deductible for tax purposes until the option is exercised, and the amount of the ultimate deduction depends on the market price on the exercise date. The entry to record the tax effects for each of the years one to four is

Deferred tax asset	20 (= $50 x .40)	
Tax expense (benefit)		20

In year five, the options are exercised at the option price of $80 per share, at a time when the market price per share is $115. Thus, the compensation expense deductible for tax purposes in year five is $350 [= 10 shares x ($115 – $80)], having a tax effect (reducing taxes otherwise payable) of $140. No additional compensation expense is allowed as a deduction in the determination of net income. The result is a permanent difference of $150 (= $350 – $200). The journal entry to reflect the reversal of the previously deferred tax benefit as follows:

Taxes payable	140 ($350 x .40)	
Paid-in capital		60 (= $150 x .40)
Deferred tax asset		80 (= $20 x 4 yrs.)

The same approach is followed by an entity that has adopted FAS 123; however the measure of compensation cost will differ, and thus will the measure of the deferred taxes related thereto. It should be noted that the treatment illustrated above applies only to the benefit of the income tax deduction for a specific stock option award that exceeds the compensation expense recognized for that award for financial reporting purposes. Payroll taxes, even though directly related to the appreciation of stock options, are operating expenses and should be reflected as such in the statement of operations.

Finally, note that in the more typical situation found under APB 25, where the stock option plan is noncompensatory in nature, there will be no deferred taxes and only the tax effect of the exercise will be reported. In such cases, the entire tax benefit of the deductible amount (the excess of market value at exercise date over the exercise price) will be credited to paid-in capital.

Convertible Preferred Stock

The treatment of convertible preferred stock at its issuance is no different than that of nonconvertible preferred. When it is converted, the book value approach is used to account for the conversion. Use of the market value approach would entail a gain or loss for which there is no theoretical justification since the total amount of contributed capital does not change when the stock is converted. When the preferred stock is converted, the "Preferred stock" and related "Additional paid-in capital—preferred stock" accounts are debited for their original values when purchased, and "Common stock" and "Additional paid-in capital—common stock" (if an excess over par or stated value exists) are credited. If the book value of the preferred stock is less than the total par value of the common stock being issued, retained earnings is charged for the difference. This charge is supported by the rationale that the preferred shareholders are offered an additional return to facilitate their conversion to common stock. Many states require that this excess instead reduce additional paid-in capital from other sources.

Mandatorily Redeemable Common and Preferred Stock

A mandatory redemption clause requires common or preferred stock to be redeemed (retired) at a specific date(s) or upon occurrence of an event which is uncertain as to timing although ultimately certain to occur. This feature is in contrast to callable preferred stock, which is redeemed at the issuing corporation's option. Mandatory redemption features are not uncommon in practice; closely held corporations, for example, have "buy-sell" agreements to redeem the shares of retiring or deceased owners at formula prices, often book value. Historically, the mandatory redemption feature has been ignored in determining balance sheet classification for nonpublic companies. On the other hand, for publicly held companies, mandatorily redeemable shares (which are almost always preferred stock in these situations) had to be displayed as either debt or as a "mezzanine equity" item separate from stockholders' equity.

Under recently enacted FAS 150, which is discussed in greater detail later in this chapter, financial instruments with mandatory redemption features must be reported as liabilities. This means that "mezzanine" presentation of redeemable preferred stock is no longer appropriate. It also means that some entities, having "buy-sell" agreements with **all** of their respective shareholders, should report **no equity** at all and should display all of what formerly was equity within the liabilities caption of the balance sheet. This is a major change from previous GAAP practice.

The only exception to this requirement exists in the circumstance where the redemption is required to occur only upon the liquidation or termination of the reporting entity. Since financial statements are prepared under the assumption of a going concern, it would be inconsistent to classify this type of redeemable stock as a liability.

If the stock subject to mandatory redemption provisions represents the only shares in the reporting entity, it must, under FAS 150, report those instruments in the liabilities section of its balance sheet, and describe them as **shares subject to mandatory redemption,** so as to distinguish the instruments from other financial statement liabilities. Transition to this new standard may create distress, particularly in those cases where there will be a need to modify loan agreements, restrictive covenants, and so forth, since these entities' debt/equity ratios and other financial indicators will change dramatically and in many instances immediately violate existing covenants. The use of the special caption above will serve to educate financial statements users regarding the substantive meaning of this new mode of financial statement presentation.

In some cases stock is issued which is not subject to mandatory redemption provisions **currently,** but which is contingently subject to such requirements once defined events occur. An assessment must be made each reporting period to ascertain whether the triggering event has yet occurred. If it has, reclassification of the conditionally mandatorily redeemable stock to liabilities must be effected.

FAS 150 offers two such examples. First, if shares are to become mandatorily redeemable upon a change in control of the issuing corporation, these remain classified within equity until that event occurs, if ever. When it does occur, the equity is reclassified to liabilities, measured at the **fair value** at that date, with no gain or loss recognized. Any disparity between the carrying value of the equity and the amount transferred to liabilities would therefore remain in equity, as additional paid-in capital or as a reduction to paid-in capital or to retained earnings.

Another example of conditional mandatory redemption would occur when preferred stock is issued with a mandatory redemption at a date certain, say ten years hence, conditioned on the failure of the preferred stockholders to exercise the right to convert to common stock before another defined date, say five years from issuance. For the first five years, the preferred stock would be displayed as equity, since the mandatory redemption feature has yet to become activated. If the shareholders elect to exchange the preferred stock to common stock, the usual accounting for such conversions would apply. If the five-year period elapses and the preferred shares are not exchanged, the mandatory redemption provision becomes effective, and the preferred stock is to be reclassified to liabilities, measured at fair value.

Accounting for mandatorily redeemable financial instruments of a nonpublic reporting entity must be conformed to the requirements outlined above, effective for existing or new contracts for fiscal periods beginning after December 15, 2004. For all other mandatorily redeemable financial instruments issued by nonpublic entities that are not SEC registrants, the classification, measurement, and disclosure provisions are deferred indefinitely. For mandatorily redeemable noncontrolling interests that would not be classified by the subsidiary as liabilities (because they are redeemable only upon liquidation) but would be classified by the parent as liabilities on the consolidated statements, the classification and measurement provisions of FAS 150 are deferred indefinitely. For other mandatorily redeemable noncontrolling interests, the measurement provisions of FAS 150 are deferred indefinitely, but the classifications provisions are not deferred. For financial instruments created before issuance date of FAS 150 and still existing at the beginning of the interim period of adoption, transition is to be achieved by reporting the cumulative effect of a change in an accounting principle by initially measuring the financial instruments at fair value or other measurement attribute required by the statement.

In addition to the requirement of FAS 150, expanded disclosure of mandatorily redeemable common or preferred stock is required by FAS 129, which superseded a virtually identical requirement established by FAS 47. Specifically, the redemption requirements for each of the next five years must be set forth in the notes to the financial statements prepared in accordance with GAAP, if the amounts are either fixed or determinable on fixed or determinable dates. Thus, readers can interpret the cash requirements on the reporting entity in a manner similar to the drawing of inferences about other fixed commitments, such as maturities of long-term debt and lease obligations.

Book Value Stock Plans

A book value plan is intended also to be a compensation program for participating employees although there are important secondary motives in many such plans, such as the desires to generate capital and to tie the employees to the employer. Under the terms of typical book value plans, employees (or those attaining some defined level, such as manager) are given the opportunity or, in some cases, they are required to purchase shares in the company, which then must be sold back to the company upon termination of employment. EITF 87-23 and EITF 88-6 addressed different aspects of such plans.

In EITF 87-23, a consensus was reached that, if the employees participating in a nonpublic company's book value stock plan have substantive investments in the company that are at risk, then the increases in book value during the period of ownership are not to be treated as compensation. However, if the employees are granted options to purchase shares at book value, compensation is to be recognized for value increases, presumably because under the latter scenario the employee has no investment at risk and is only being given an "upside" opportunity. This interpretation is also applicable to book value options granted to employees of publicly held companies. FIN 44 affirmed the conclusions reached in EITF 87-23.

For accounting purposes, shares issued at book value to employees are simply recorded as a normal stock sale. To the extent that book value exceeds par or stated value, additional paid-in capital accounts may also be credited.

EITF 88-6 addresses the related question of book value stock plans of publicly held companies. In this consensus, the Task Force concluded that the plan was a performance plan akin to a SAR, and accordingly results in compensation expense recognition. This conclusion was reached at least in part due to SEC pressure, which arose largely in the context of initial public offerings (IPO).

Junior Stock

Another category of stock-based compensation program involves junior stock. Typically, such shares are subordinate to normal shares of common stock with respect to voting rights, dividend rate, or other attributes, and are convertible into regular common shares if and when stipulated performance goals are achieved. Like stock appreciation rights, grants of junior stock represent a performance-based program, in contrast to fixed stock options.

FIN 38 specifies that compensation cost incurred in connection with grants of junior stock is generally to be accrued in accordance with the provisions of FIN 28. However, compensation is only to be recognized when it is deemed to be probable, as that term is defined by FAS 5, that the performance goals will be achieved. It may be that achievement is not deemed probable at the time the junior stock is issued, but it later becomes clear that such achievement is indeed likely. In other circumstances, the ability to convert junior stock to regular stock is dependent upon the achievement of more than a single performance goal, and it is not probable that all such goals can be achieved, although some of them are deemed probable of achievement. In both scenarios, full accrual of compensation cost may be delayed until the estimated likelihood of achievement improves.

FIN 38 specifies that the measure of compensation is derived from the comparison of the market price of ordinary common stock with the price to be paid, if any, for the junior stock. Since the junior stock will be convertible to ordinary common stock if the defined performance goals are achieved, the compensation to be received by the employees participating in the plan is linked to the value of unrestricted common shares.

Put Warrant

A detachable put warrant can either be put back to the debt issuer for cash or can be exercised to acquire common stock. EITF 88-9 concluded that these instruments should be accounted for in the same manner as a mezzanine security. The proceeds applicable to the put warrant ordinarily are to be classified as equity and should be presented between the liability and equity sections in accordance with SEC SAR 268.

In the case of a warrant with a put price substantially higher than the value assigned to the warrant at issuance, however, the proceeds should be classified as a liability since it is likely that the warrant will be put back to the company.

The original **classification** should not be changed because of subsequent economic changes in the value of the put. The value assigned to the put warrant at issuance, however, should be adjusted to its highest redemption price, starting with the date of issuance until the earliest date of the warrants. Changes in the redemption price before the earliest put dates are changes in accounting estimates and changes after the earliest put dates should be recognized in income. If the put is classified as equity, the adjustment should be reported as a charge to retained earnings, and if the put is classified as a liability the adjustment is reported as interest expense.

Regardless of how the put is classified on the balance sheet, the primary and fully diluted EPS should be calculated on both an equity basis (warrants will be exercised) and on a debt basis (put will be exercised) and the more dilutive of the two methods should be used.

Accounting for Stock Issued to Employee Stock Ownership Plans

For over twenty-five years, it has been a government policy to encourage employee ownership of corporations. To that end, tax laws have been adopted which make this prospect attractive to employer entities. Thus, there has been a steady increase in the number of corporations which are entirely or partially employee-owned under terms of employee stock ownership plans (ESOP). The accounting for ESOP was first set forth in AICPA Statement of Position (SOP) 76-3, later superseded by SOP 93-6, which is the current source of GAAP.

Depending on what motivated the creation of the ESOP (e.g., estate planning by the controlling shareholder, expanding the capital base of the entity, rewarding and motivating the work force), the sponsor's shares may be contributed to the plan in annual installments in a block of shares from the sponsor, or shares from an existing shareholder may be purchased by the plan.

Employee stock ownership plans are defined contribution plans in which shares of the sponsoring entity are awarded to employees as additional compensation. Briefly, ESOP are created by a sponsoring corporation which either funds the plan directly (unleveraged ESOP) or, more commonly, facilitates the borrowing of money either directly from an outside lender (directly leveraged ESOP) or from the employer, which in turn will borrow from an outside lender (indirectly leveraged ESOP).

Borrowings from outside lenders may or may not be guaranteed by the sponsor. However, since effectively the only source of funds for debt repayment are future contributions by the sponsor, GAAP requires that the ESOP's debt be considered debt of the sponsor even absent a guarantee.

When recording the direct or indirect borrowings by the ESOP as debt in the sponsor's balance sheet, a debit to a contra equity account, not to an asset, is also reported. This is necessary since the borrowings represent a commitment (morally if not always legally) to make future contributions to the plan and this is certainly not a claim to resources. Significantly, this results in a "double hit" to the sponsor's balance sheet (i.e., the recording of a liability **and** the reduction of net stockholders' equity) which is often an unanticipated and unpleasant surprise to plan sponsors. This contra equity account is referred to as "unearned ESOP shares" in accordance with provisions of SOP 93-6. If the sponsor itself lends funds to the ESOP without a "mirror loan" from an outside lender, this loan should not be reported in the employer's balance sheet as debt, although the debit should still be reported as a contra equity account.

As the ESOP services the debt, using contributions made by the sponsor and/or dividends received on sponsor shares held by the plan, it reflects the reduction of the obligation by reducing both the debt and the contra equity account on its balance sheet. Simultaneously, income and thus retained earnings will be impacted as the contributions to the plan are reported in the sponsor's current statement of earnings. Thus, the "double hit" is eliminated, but net worth continues to reflect the economic fact that compensation costs have been incurred.

The interest cost component of debt service must be separated from the remaining compensation expense. That is, the sponsor's income statement should reflect the true character of the expenses being incurred, rather than aggregating the entire amount into a category which might have been denoted as "ESOP contribution."

In a leveraged ESOP, shares held serve as collateral for the debt and are not allocated to employees until the debt is retired. In general, shares must be allocated by the end of the year in which the debt is repaid. However, in order to satisfy the tax laws, the allocation of shares may take place at a faster pace than the retirement of the principal portion of the debt.

Under SOP 93-6, the cost of ESOP shares allocated is measured based upon the fair value on the release date for purposes of reporting compensation expense in the sponsor's income statements. This is in contradistinction to the actual historical cost of the shares to the plan.

Furthermore, dividends paid on unallocated shares (i.e., shares held by the ESOP) are not treated as dividends, but rather must be reported in the sponsor's income statement as compensation cost and/or as interest expense. Of less significance to nonpublic companies is the fact that under the new rules only common shares released and committed to be released are treated as being outstanding, with the resultant need to be considered in calculating both basic and diluted EPS.

Example of accounting for ESOP transactions

Assume that Intrepid Corp. establishes an ESOP, which then borrows $500,000 from Second Interstate Bank. The ESOP then purchases 50,000 shares of Intrepid no-par shares from the company; none of these shares are allocated to individual participants. The entries would be

Cash	500,000	
Bank loan payable		500,000
Unearned ESOP shares (contra equity)	500,000	
Common stock		500,000

The ESOP then borrows an additional $250,000 from the sponsor, Intrepid, and uses the cash to purchase a further 25,000 shares, all of which are allocated to participants.

Compensation	250,000	
Common stock		250,000

Intrepid Corp. contributes $50,000 to the plan, which the plan uses to service its bank debt, consisting of $40,000 principal reduction and $10,000 interest cost. The debt reduction causes 4,000 shares to be allocated to participants at a time when the average market value had been $12 per share.

Interest expense	10,000	
Bank loan payable	40,000	
Cash		50,000
Compensation	48,000	
Additional paid-in capital		8,000
Unearned ESOP shares		40,000

Dividends of $.10 per share are declared (only the ESOP shares are represented in the following entry, but dividends are paid equally on all outstanding shares)

Retained earnings (on 29,000 shares)	2,900	
Compensation (on 46,000 shares)	4,600	
Dividends payable		7,500

Note that in all the foregoing illustrations the effect of income taxes is ignored. Since the difference between the cost and fair values of shares committed to be released is analogous to differences in the expense recognized for tax and accounting purposes with regard to stock options, the same treatment should be applied. That is, the tax effect should be reported directly in stockholders' equity, rather than in earnings.

Financial Instruments with Characteristics of Both Liabilities and Equity

Standard setters have been struggling with the proper reporting for hybrid instruments—having characteristics of both liabilities and equity—for decades, and the FASB's formal project is now almost fifteen years old. Two needs had been perceived: first, to establish criteria for classification for certain instruments (e.g., mandatorily redeemable stock) that nominally are equity but have key characteristics of debt, but which will severely impact corporate balance sheets if a "substance over form" approach is strictly enforced; and second, to develop the methodology for disaggregating the constituent parts of compound instruments so that they may be accounted for as debt and as equity, respectively.

A discussion memorandum was issued in 1990; ten years later, FASB issued an Exposure Draft, *Accounting for Financial Instruments with Characteristics of Liabilities, Equity, or Both*, as well as a concomitant proposed amendment to CON 6 to revise the definition of liabilities. Later, FASB decided to restructure its efforts to engage in a multiphase project, the first part of which has come to fruition now with the recent issuance of FAS 150. This standard addresses only financial instruments issued in the form of shares that are mandatorily redeemable (i.e., that embody unconditional obligations requiring the issuer to redeem them by transferring its assets at a specified or determinable date or dates or upon an event that is certain to occur.)

According to FAS 150, the affected instruments include those, other than an outstanding share, that, at inception, embody an obligation to repurchase the issuer's equity shares, or are indexed to such an obligation, and that require or may require the issuer to settle the obligations by transferring assets (for example, a forward purchase contract or written put option on the issuer's equity shares that is to be physically settled or net cash settled). It also includes financial instruments that embody unconditional obligations, or financial instruments other than outstanding shares that embody conditional obligations, that the issuers must or may settle by issuing a variable number of equity shares, if, at inception, the monetary values of the obligations are based solely or predominantly on any of the following:

1. A fixed monetary amount known at inception, for example, a payable settleable with a variable number of the issuer's equity shares;
2. Variations in something other than the fair value of the issuer's equity shares, for example, a financial instrument indexed to the S&P 500 and settleable with a variable number of the issuer's equity shares; or
3. Variations inversely related to changes in the fair value of the issuer's equity shares, for example, a written put option that could be net share settled.

The requirements of FAS 150 apply to issuers' classification and measurement of freestanding financial instruments, including those that comprise more than one option or forward contract. It does not apply, however, to features that are embedded in financial instruments that are not derivatives in their entirety. For example, it does not alter the accounting treatment of conversion features (as found in convertible debentures), conditional redemption features, or other features embedded in financial instruments that are not derivatives in their entirety. It also does not affect the classification or measurement of convertible bonds, puttable stock, or other outstanding shares that are **conditionally** redeemable. FAS 150 also does not address certain financial instruments indexed partly to the issuer's equity shares and partly, **but not predominantly,** to another referent.

FAS 150 establishes requirements for only a limited range of financial instruments having characteristics of both liabilities and equity. FASB is now pursuing a second phase of its project and will address the accounting for various financial instruments with characteristics of both liabilities and equity not addressed in FAS 150. Guidance currently in effect under GAAP for those instruments remains in effect in the interim.

Terminology of FAS 150. This standard uses terminology that may not be familiar to most accountants but which is important to understanding when and how to apply FAS 150. Key terms include the following:

Freestanding financial instrument—A financial instrument that is entered into separately and apart from any of the entity's other financial instruments or equity transactions, or that is entered into in conjunction with some other transaction and is legally detachable and separately exercisable.

Issuer—The entity that issued a financial instrument or may be required under the terms of a financial instrument to issue its equity shares.

Mandatorily redeemable financial instrument—Any of various financial instruments issued in the form of shares that embody an unconditional obligation requiring the issuer to redeem the instrument by transferring its assets at a specified or determinable date (or dates) or upon an event that is certain to occur.

Monetary value—What the fair value of the cash, shares, or other instruments that a financial instrument obligates the issuer to convey to the holder would be at the settlement date under specified market conditions.

Net cash settlement—A form of settling a financial instrument under which the party with a loss delivers to the party with a gain cash equal to the gain.

Net share settlement—A form of settling a financial instrument under which the party with a loss delivers to the party with a gain shares of stock with a current fair value equal to the gain.

Nonpublic entity—Any entity other than one (a) whose equity securities trade in a public market either on a stock exchange (domestic or foreign) or in the over-the-counter market, including securities quoted only locally or regionally; (b) that makes a filing with a regulatory agency in preparation for the sale of equity securities in a public market; or (c) that is controlled by an entity covered by (a) or (b).

Obligation—A conditional or unconditional duty or responsibility to transfer assets or to issue equity shares.

Physical settlement—A form of settling a financial instrument under which (a) the party designated in the contract as the buyer delivers the full stated amount of cash or other financial instruments to the seller and (b) the seller delivers the full stated number of shares of stock or other financial instruments or nonfinancial instruments to the buyer.

In addition to the foregoing, **fair value and financial instrument** are used as defined in other recent FASB standards.

Applicability of FAS 150. This standard only applies to three types of freestanding financial instruments: mandatorily redeemable financial instruments; obligations to repurchase the issuer's shares by transferring assets; and certain obligations to issue a variable number of shares. Mandatorily redeemable shares were addressed earlier in this chapter; the other classes of instruments affected by FAS 150 are discussed in the following paragraphs.

Obligations to repurchase the issuer's equity shares by transferring assets include financial instruments, other than outstanding shares, that, at inception, (a) embody obligations to repurchase the issuers' equity shares, or are indexed to such obligations, and (b) require or may require the issuers to settle the obligations by transferring assets. These must be classified as liabilities (or, rarely, as assets). Such obligations could include forward purchase contracts or written put options on an issuer's equity shares that are to be physically settled or net cash settled.

Certain **obligations to issue a variable number of shares** are financial instruments that embody unconditional obligations, or financial instruments other than outstanding shares that embody conditional obligations, that the issuers must or may settle by issuing variable numbers of equity shares. These obligations also must be classified as liabilities (or, rarely, as assets) if, at inception, the monetary values of the obligations are based solely or predominantly on **any one** of the following:

1. A fixed monetary amount known at inception (e.g., a payable settleable with a variable number of the issuer's equity shares);
2. Variations in something other than the fair value of the issuer's equity shares (e.g., a financial instrument indexed to the S&P 500 and settleable with a variable number of the issuer's equity shares); or
3. Variations inversely related to changes in the fair value of the issuer's equity shares (e.g., a written put option that could be net share settled).

FAS 150 only applies to freestanding instruments, which could include those that comprise more than one option or forward contract, as, for example, an instrument that consists of a written put option for an issuer's equity shares and a purchased call option. The standard does not apply to features embedded in another financial instrument, such as an option on the issuer's equity shares that is embedded in a nonderivative host contract.

If a freestanding instrument is composed of more than one option or forward contract and one of those contracts embodies an obligation to repurchase the issuer's shares that require or may require settlement by a transfer of assets, the financial instrument is a liability. In addition, if a freestanding instrument composed of more than one option or forward contract includes an obligation to issue shares, the various component obligations must be analyzed to determine if any of them would be obligations under FAS 150. If one or more would be obligations under this standard, then judgment must be used to determine if the monetary value of the obligations that would be liabilities is collectively predominant over the other component liabilities. If so, the instrument is a liability. If not, the instrument is outside the scope of FAS 150. Following is a list of examples of these types of financial instruments:

- Puttable warrants.
- Warrant for shares that can be put by the holder immediately after exercise.
- Warrant that allows the holder to exercise the warrant or put the warrant back to the issuer on the exercise date for a variable number of shares with a fixed monetary value.
- Forward contract in which the number of shares to be issued depends on the issuer's share price on the settlement date.
- Warrant with a "liquidity make-whole" put to issue additional shares to the holder if the sales price of the shares when later sold is less than the share price when the warrant is exercised.
- Warrant that allows the holder to exercise the warrant or, if contingent event does not occur, put the warrant back to the issuer on the exercise date for a variable number of shares with a fixed monetary value.

The standard does not apply to or affect the timing of recognition of financial instruments issued as contingent consideration in a business combination, nor the measurement guidance for contingent consideration, as set forth in FAS 141. It also does not affect accounting for stock-based compensation (FAS 123), or ESOP plans (SOP 93-6), both of which are addressed earlier in this chapter.

Initial and subsequent measurements. As noted, mandatorily redeemable financial instruments, which are now to be reported as liabilities, are initially recognized at fair value. Mandatorily redeemable financial instruments are subsequently remeasured using fair value, with any adjustments to be included in the periodic determination of income. In general, the value of mandatorily redeemable financial instruments will be accreted over time and the accretion will be treated as interest expense. The method of determining subsequent fair values corresponds to that set forth in the following paragraph.

Forward contracts that require **physical settlement** by repurchase of a fixed number of the issuer's equity shares in exchange for cash are to be measured initially at the fair value of the shares, as adjusted for any consideration or unstated rights or privileges. Equity is reduced by this same amount. Fair value in this context may be determined by reference to the amount of cash that would be paid under the conditions specified in the contract if the shares were repurchased immediately. Alternatively, the settlement amount can be discounted at the rate implicit at inception after taking into account any consideration or unstated rights or privileges that may have affected the terms of the transaction.

Subsequent measurement can be effected by either accretion (which is feasible only if the amount to be paid and the settlement date are both fixed), or by determining the amount of cash that would be paid under the conditions specified in the contract if settlement occurred at the reporting date (useful when either the amount to be paid or the settlement date vary based on defined conditions and terms). In either case, the change from the amount reported in the prior period is interest expense. If accretion is appropriate, the instruments are to be measured subsequently at the present value of the amount to be paid at settlement, accruing interest cost using the rate implicit at inception.

Conditionally redeemable instruments, first classified as equity and transferred to liabilities when the condition is satisfied, are measured at fair value at that date, with no gain or loss being recognized from the reclassification. For earnings per share computation purposes, the amount of common shares that are to be redeemed or repurchased are excluded for both basic and diluted calculations.

Disclosure requirements. The nature and terms of the financial instruments to which FAS 150 applies, and the rights and obligations embodied in those instruments, must be disclosed. That would include information about settlement alternatives, if any, in the contract, and would furthermore identify the entity that controls the settlement alternatives.

Additionally, for all outstanding financial instruments within the scope of FAS 150, and for each settlement alternative, issuers are required to disclose

1. The amount that would be paid, or the number of shares that would be issued and their fair value, determined under the conditions specified in the contract if the settlement were to occur at the reporting date;
2. How changes in the fair value of the issuer's equity shares would affect those settlement amounts;
3. The maximum amount that the issuer could be required to pay to redeem the instrument by physical settlement, if applicable;
4. The maximum number of shares that could be required to be issued, if applicable;
5. The fact that a contract does not limit the amount that the issuer could be required to pay or the number of shares that the issuer could be required to issue, if applicable; and
6. For a forward contract or an option indexed to the issuer's equity shares, the forward price or option strike price, the number of issuer's shares to which the contract is indexed, and the settlement date or dates of the contract, as applicable.

The definition of **liabilities,** set forth in CON 6 (see Chapter 1), was to have been revised in conjunction with the promulgation of new standards of accounting for instruments having characteristics of both liabilities and equity. That change will not be made at this time, however, but will be addressed in a subsequent phase of this FASB project. FASB also decided against imposing new requirements to bifurcate embedded derivatives. Furthermore, to prevent the provisions of the new standard from being circumvented by the insertion for nonsubstantive or minimal features into financial instruments, any such features are to be disregarded in applying FAS 150's classification provisions.

Effective date and transition. Other than for mandatorily redeemable shares of a nonpublic entity, FAS 150 became effective for financial instruments entered into or modified after May 31, 2003. Otherwise, FAS 150 is effective beginning with the first interim period which begins after June 15, 2003.

Application of FAS 150

Example 1: Obligations that require net share settlement—monetary value changes in the same direction as the fair value of the issuer's equity shares

Algernon Corp. grants 10,000 stock appreciation rights that entitle the holder to receive a number of equity shares to be determined based on the change in the fair value of Algernon's equity shares. At the date of the grant, the fair value of Algernon's equity shares is $25 per share. Subsequently, the fair value of Algernon's equity shares increases to $28 per share. Algernon is thus required to issue shares worth $30,000 [($28 – $25) x 10,000], or 1,072 shares.

This financial instrument contains an obligation to issue a number of equity shares with a value equal to the appreciation of 10,000 equity shares. The number of shares to be issued, therefore, is not fixed. Classification will depend on whether the monetary value changes in the same direction as changes in the fair value of the equity shares. In this example, the monetary value changes in the same direction as changes in the fair value of the equity shares.

The increase in fair value of the equity shares from $25 to $28 resulted in an increase in the monetary value of the obligation from $0 to $30,000. If the fair value of the equity shares increases further, for example to $30 per share, the monetary value of the obligation increases as well to $50,000 [($30 – $25) x 10,000]. If the fair value of the equity shares then decreases, for example from $30 to $27, the monetary value of the obligation decreases to $20,000 [($27 –$25) x 10,000]. Because the monetary value of the obligation changes in the same direction as the change in fair value of the issuer's equity shares, this obligation does not qualify as a liability and the equity classification is prescribed. (Accounting for stock appreciation rights is discussed earlier in this chapter.)

Example 2: Obligations that require net share settlement—monetary value changes in opposite direction as the fair value of the issuer's equity shares

Bocephus Corp. issues equity shares to Middleboro Co. for $5 million (1 million shares at $5 each). Simultaneously, Bocephus enters into a financial instrument with Middleboro, under the terms of which, if the per share value of Bocephus' shares is greater than $5 on a specified date, Middleboro will transfer shares of Bocephus with a value of [(share price – $5) x 1,000,000] to Bocephus. If the per share is less than $5 on a specified date, Bocephus transfers shares of its own equity with a value of [($5 – share price) x 1,000,000] to Middleboro.

The 1,000,000 shares issued to Middleboro do not embody an obligation. They also do not convey to the issuer the right to receive cash or another financial instrument from the holder, or to exchange other financial instruments on potentially favorable terms with the holder. Therefore, the equity classification criteria are met and the component is classified as equity.

The financial instrument issued to Middleboro contains an obligation to issue a variable number of equity shares if the fair value of Bocephus' equity shares is less than $5 on a certain date. As a result, the classification will depend upon whether the monetary value is equal to the change in fair value of a fixed number of equity shares, and whether the changes are in the same direction as the fair value of the equity shares.

The first criterion is met because the monetary value of the obligation is equal to the appreciation of a fixed number (1,000,000) of the issuer's equity shares. However, the monetary value of the obligation changes in a direction opposite to the changes in the fair value of the issuer's equity shares. If the fair value of the equity shares increases, the monetary value of the obligation decreases (and may in fact be reduced to zero or result in a receivable from the counterparty). If the fair value of the equity shares decreases, the monetary value of the obligation increases. Because the monetary value of the obligation does not change in the same direction as the fair value of the equity shares, criterion (b) is not met; therefore, the obligation is not classified as equity.

Example 3: Written put options that require physical settlement

Calabassa Corp. writes a put option that allows a holder, Yetta Co., to put 200 shares of Calabassa stock to Calabassa for $33 per share on a specified date. The put option requires physical settlement (delivery of the shares and payment therefore). Because the put option requires Calabassa to transfer assets (cash) to settle the obligation, the component is classified as a liability.

Example 3a: Forward purchase contract that requires physical or net cash settlement

In a fact pattern slightly at variance with the preceding example, Calabassa Corp. enters into a freestanding forward purchase arrangement with Yetta Co., under which Yetta is to transfer 200 shares of Calabassa stock to Calabassa for $33 per share on a specified date. The forward purchase agreement requires physical settlement (delivery of the shares and payment therefore). Because the forward purchase arrangement requires Calabassa to transfer assets (cash) to settle the obligation, the component is classified as a liability. The same result would hold if the contract called for a net cash settlement. While a put option (the preceding example) requires that the liability be initially recorded, and subsequently remeasured, at fair value, the forward purchase arrangement is to be recorded at fair value, and then accreted to the present value of the forward purchase price at each balance sheet date, using the implicit interest rate given by the initial fair value.

Example 4: Written put option that require net share settlement

Delmarva Corp. writes a put option that allows the holder, Zitti Corp., to put 200 shares of Delmarva stock to Delmarva for $44 a share on a specified date. The put requires net share settlement (i.e., shares having a value equal to the spread between the option price and fair value must be delivered in settlement). Assume the fair value of the shares at the date the put is issued is $44. The monetary value of the obligation at that time is therefore zero.

Subsequently, the fair value of Delmarva's equity shares decreases to $36 and the put option is exercised. At this point, the monetary value of the obligation is $1,600 [200 shares x ($44 – $36)]. Delmarva would be required to issue about 45 shares ($1,600 divided by $36). The monetary value of the obligation increased because of a decrease in the fair value of Delmarva's equity shares. Because changes in the monetary value of the obligation are not in the same direction as changes in the fair value of Delmarva's equity shares, the component is not classified as equity, but rather as a liability. The contract is measured initially and subsequently at fair value, with changes in fair value recognized in current earnings.

Example 5: Unconditional obligation that must be either redeemed for cash or settled by issuing shares

If the reporting entity issues financial instruments which do not require the transfer of assets to settle the obligation, but instead, unconditionally require the issuer to settle the obligation **either** by transferring assets or by issuing a variable number of its equity shares, this may or may not create a liability. Because such instruments do not require the issuer to settle by transfer of assets, they are not automatically classified as liabilities under FAS 150. However, those instruments may still be classified as liabilities, if other stipulated conditions are met.

Assume that Garner Corp. issues one million shares of cumulative preferred stock for cash equal to the stock's liquidation preference of $25 per share. Under the terms, Garner is required either to redeem the shares on the third anniversary of the issuance, for the issuance price plus any accrued but unpaid dividends, either in cash or by issuing sufficient shares of its common stock to be worth $25 per share. This does not represent an unconditional obligation to transfer assets, and therefore the preferred stock is not a mandatorily redeemable financial instrument as that term is defined in FAS 150. However, the stock is still a liability, because the preferred shares represent an unconditional obligation that the issuer may settle by issuing a variable number of its equity shares with monetary value that is fixed and known at inception. Because the preferred shares are liabilities, payments to holders are reported as interest cost, and accrued but not-yet-paid payments are part of the liability for the shares.

If the redemption price of mandatorily redeemable shares is greater than the book value of those shares, the company should report the excess as a deficit (equity), even though the mandatorily redeemable shares are reported as a liability.

Disclosure Requirements

Under FAS 129, which consolidates requirements previously set forth in APB 10 and 15, and FAS 47, certain disclosures of an entity's capital structure are required. Under this standard, the financial statements will be required to explain, in summary form, the pertinent rights and privileges of the various equity securities outstanding, including dividend and liquidation preferences, participation rights, call prices and dates, conversion and exercise prices or rates along with pertinent dates, sinking fund requirements, unusual voting rights, and significant terms of any contractual obligations to issue additional shares.

Furthermore, the number of shares issued upon conversion, exercise, or satisfaction of required conditions, during at least the most recent annual reporting period and any subsequent interim period that is presented, must be disclosed. If preference shares have a liquidation preference considerably in excess of par or stated value in the event of involuntary liquidation, the aggregate amount must be disclosed. The amount that would be paid upon exercise of call privileges applicable to preferred shares must be disclosed also, but in this case either per share or aggregate data can be given. Any dividend arrearages on cumulative preferred shares must be stated, on **both** per share and aggregate bases. Finally, if redeemable preferred shares are outstanding, the amount of redemption requirements for each of the subsequent five years must be given, if fixed or determinable on fixed or determinable dates; if there are several series of such shares, this can be given in the aggregate.

Corporate Bankruptcy and Reorganizations

Entities operating under and emerging from protection of the bankruptcy laws. The going concern assumption is one of the basic postulates underlying generally accepted accounting principles and is responsible for, among other things, the historical cost convention in financial reporting. For entities that have entered bankruptcy proceedings, however, the going concern assumption will no longer be of central importance.

Traditionally, the basic financial statements (balance sheet, income statement, and statement of cash flows) presented by going concerns were seen as less useful for entities undergoing reorganization. Instead, the **statement of affairs,** reporting assets at estimated realizable values and liabilities at estimated liquidation amounts, was recommended for use by such organizations. In more recent years, this is less frequently encountered in practice.

SOP 90-7 sets forth certain financial reporting standards for entities undergoing and emerging from reorganization under the bankruptcy laws. Under provisions of this SOP, assets are presented at estimated realizable values. Liabilities are set forth at the estimated amounts to be allowed in the balance sheet and liabilities subject to compromise are to be distinguished from those that are not. Furthermore, the SOP requires that in both the statements of income and cash flows, normal transactions be differentiated from those which have occurred as a consequence of the entity's being in reorganization. While certain allocations to the latter category are rather obvious, such as legal and accounting fees incurred, others are less clear. For example, the standard suggests that if the entity in reorganization earns interest income on funds that would normally have been used to settle obligations owed to creditors, such income will be deemed to be income arising as a consequence of the bankruptcy action.

Another interesting aspect of this standard is the accounting to be made for the emergence from reorganization (known as **confirmation of the plan of reorganization**). SOP 90-7 provides for **fresh start** financial reporting in such instances. This accounting is similar to that applied to purchase business combinations under APB 16, with the total confirmed value of the entity upon its emergence from reorganization being analogous to the purchase price in an acquisition. In both cases, this total value is to be allocated to the identifiable assets and liabilities of the entity, with any excess being allocated to goodwill. In the case of entities emerging from bankruptcy, goodwill (reorganization value in excess of amounts allocable to identifiable assets) is measured as the **excess** of liabilities existing at the plan confirmation date, computed at present value of future amounts to be paid, over the reorganization value of assets. Reorganization value is calculated with reference to a number of factors, including forecasted operating results and cash flows of the new entity.

SOP 90-7 applies only to entities undergoing formal reorganization under the Bankruptcy Code. Less formal procedures may still be accounted for under preexisting **quasi reorganization** accounting procedures.

Quasi reorganization. Generally, this procedure is applicable during a period of declining price levels. It is termed "quasi" since the accumulated deficit is eliminated at a lower cost and with less difficulty than a legal reorganization.

Per ARB 43, Ch. 7A, the procedures in a quasi reorganization involve the

1. Proper authorization from stockholders and creditors where required
2. Revaluation of assets to their current values. All losses are charged to retained earnings, thus increasing any deficit.
3. Elimination of any deficit by charging paid-in capital
   a. First, additional paid-in capital to the extent it exists
   b. Second, capital stock when additional paid-in capital is insufficient. The par value of the stock is reduced, creating the extra additional paid-in capital to which the remaining deficit is charged.

No retained earnings may be created by a reorganization. Any excess created by the reduction of par value is credited to "Paid-in capital from quasi reorganization."

ARB 46 requires that retained earnings be dated for ten years (less than ten years may be justified under exceptional circumstances) after a quasi reorganization takes place. Disclosure similar to "since quasi reorganization of June 30, 19XX" is appropriate.

Reporting by Limited Liability Companies and Partnerships

Accounting theory and practice have overwhelmingly developed within the context of businesses organized as normal corporations. Accordingly, there is little official guidance to entities organized as partnerships or other forms of business, which is generally not a serious concern given that most transactions entered into by such entities do not differ generically from those conducted by corporations. The primary differences relate to equity transactions and to the display of the equity section of the balance sheet.

AICPA Practice Bulletin 14 addresses certain issues pertaining to accounting and reporting by limited liability companies and partnerships. This pronouncement establishes that, when an entity restructures itself as a limited liability company or a limited liability partnership, the basis of all assets and liabilities from its predecessor entity are carried forward. Also, as suggested by FAS 109, if the new entity is not a taxable one, any deferred tax assets or liabilities existing previously are to be written off at the time the change in tax status becomes effective; with the elimination of any debit or credit balance being effected by a charge or credit to current period tax expense.

With regard to financial statement display issues, the practice bulletin establishes that the headings of each statement identify the entity as being a limited liability company or a limited liability partnership, similar to the common practice of identifying partnership entities. The apparent logic is that this alerts the user to certain anomalies, such as (most commonly) an absence of income tax expense and a related liability, and the use of somewhat distinctive captions in the equity section of the balance sheet. In the case of limited liability companies and partnerships, the term "members' equity" has been prescribed, and the changes in members' equity is to be communicated either in a separate financial statement, in a combined statement of operations and changes in members' equity, or in the notes to the financial statements.

The bulletin recommends that, where there are several classes of members' equity, these be set forth separately in the equity section of the balance sheet, although this is not a firm requirement. If not set forth in the balance sheet, however, the notes must provide adequate disclosure about the different classes of equity outstanding. This is entirely analogous to the existing GAAP requirements concerning disclosure about common and preferred stock of typical corporations, which has been analogized further to apply to classes of partnership equity in limited partnerships.

A deficit, if one exists, should be reported in the members' equity account(s), even if there is limited liability for the members. This is consistent with the "going concern" assumption that underlies GAAP. It is not required to disaggregate members' equity into separate components (undistributed earnings, unallocated capital, etc.) on the face of the balance sheet or in the notes, although this is of course permissible.

Amounts due from members for capital contributions, if any remain unpaid at the balance sheet date, should be shown as deductions from members' equity. This is entirely consistent with practice for unpaid stock subscriptions receivable.

GAAP presumes that comparative financial statements are more useful than those for a single period, and accordingly that comparative statements should normally be presented. However, for such financial statements to be meaningful, the information for the earlier period must be truly comparable to that of the more recent period. If the formation of the limited liability company or the limited liability partnership results in a new reporting entity being created, the guidance of APB 20 dealing with changes in accounting entities should be consulted.

Practice Bulletin 14 sets forth certain disclosures to be made in the financial statements of limited liability companies or limited liability partnerships. There should be a description of any limitations on members' equity and of the different classes of members' interests and the respective rights, preferences, and privileges of each class and amounts thereof. If the entity will cease to exist at a stipulated date, this must be disclosed. As suggested above, any change in tax status, and the impact of eliminating any tax liability or benefit from the entity's balance sheet, must be adequately explained in the notes to the financial statements in the period the change in status occurs.

In the period in which a limited liability company or a limited liability partnership is formed by combining entities under common control, or by conversion from another type of entity, the bulletin requires disclosures about the assets and liabilities previously held by the predecessor entity or entities. Entities created by combining predecessors under common control are encouraged, but not required, to make disclosures set forth by APB 16 applicable to poolings.

EMERGING ISSUES TASK FORCE CONSENSUS SUMMARIES

84-18 Stock Option Pyramiding

This consensus held that, in cases in which an employee exercises a stock option by exchanging shares held instead of cash, some holding period of shares exchanged is necessary to avoid treating the exercise as a SAR. FIN 44 later ruled that the holding period needs to be at least six months to avoid variable plan accounting treatment.

84-40 Long-Term Debt Repayable by a Capital Stock Transaction

The Task Force was unable to reach a consensus on the issue of whether debt issued by a trust created by a subsidiary should be presented as debt or equity, when the proceeds of the debt were used to acquire parent company convertible preferred stock. The SEC's position, however, is that this should be treated as debt, not equity. In addition, there was a consensus that the trust should be consolidated in the parent's financial statements.

85-1 Classifying Notes Received for Capital Stock

A consensus was reached regarding the classification of a contribution to a company's equity in the form of a note receivable. These notes should generally not be reported as an asset unless circumstances indicate both the ability and intent to pay in a short period of time. The Task Force noted that the most widespread practice is to report these notes as a reduction of equity. However, if the cash is received prior to the issuance of the financial statements, the note may be reported as an asset.

86-32 Early Extinguishment of a Subsidiary's Mandatorily Redeemable Preferred Stock

The consensus was that when a parent entity acquires, for early retirement, the mandatorily redeemable preferred stock of a subsidiary, the transaction is to be accounted for as a capital transaction in the consolidated financial statements. No gain or loss is to be recognized in the statement of income.

88-6 Book Value Stock Plans in an Initial Public Offering

This consensus extends that set forth in EITF 87-23. For publicly held companies, a book value stock purchase plan is a performance plan akin to stock appreciation rights, and thus gives rise to compensation expense. For book value options outstanding during an initial public offering (IPO), any value change resulting from the IPO is deemed to be compensation expense, as are further value changes after the IPO. However, for book value options that are converted to fair market value option plans during an IPO, compensation is recognized only during the IPO. Book value shares that convert to market value stock issued at or within one year of IPO also give rise to compensation in the amount of any increase in value; however, no further compensation is recognized after the IPO takes place. Book value stock that remains book value stock does not result in compensation during the IPO, but if issued in contemplation of the IPO, then the book value increase would be attributable to compensation. Pure market value plans are covered under the provisions of APB 25, and are not affected by this pronouncement. FIN 44 confirmed the consensus on this Issue, and furthermore holds that, for public entities, if a repurchase feature is not based on fair value of the shares as of the repurchase date, then variable plan accounting is required.

88-9 Put Warrants

Put warrants consist of both warrants for the purchase of (common, usually) stock and a put feature which allows the holder to redeem the warrants for cash, sometimes in conjunction with the warrant exercise, sometimes as an alternative to it. Put warrants are typically issued in connection with a debt offering, and APB 14 stipulates that the proceeds of the offering must be allocated between the debt and the warrants. The Task Force concluded that the proceeds allocated to the warrants should generally be included in equity; however, a later consensus on EITF 96-13 holds that for public companies, this should be classified as a liability since the holder is given the right to elect whether or not to receive cash. If the put price is adjustable, the adjustments from issuance date until the earliest put date should be made consistent with the balance sheet classification of the put warrant: if equity, the adjustment would be by a charge to retained earnings; if as debt, then the charge would be similar to interest expense. The impact on the earnings per share computation is also addressed. FAS 133 later held that puts are derivative financial instruments and must accordingly be reported at fair value. The precise accounting depends on whether the derivative has been designated and qualifies as a hedging instrument in a given situation.

89-11 Sponsor's Balance Sheet Classification of Capital Stock with a Put Option Held by an Employee Stock Ownership Plan

This pronouncement deals with those circumstances in which an employee participant in an ESOP has a put option (i.e., a right to demand redemption by the sponsoring company). While the ESOP can substitute for the sponsor as the purchaser of the employee's shares, the sponsor cannot legally require the plan to do so; therefore, the employer is obligated to repurchase shares. The issue was: If the sponsor's shares are shown outside of the equity section as a consequence, can the contra equity (unearned compensation) also be presented there? The consensus was that the contra equity should follow the capital stock account. If the put option meets the definitions under FAS 133 as a derivative, then the appropriate rules must be applied (e.g., reporting at fair value).

90-7 Accounting for a Reload Stock Option

A reload stock option should be accounted for as a fixed plan if (1) each reload grant is for exercise at the market price on the reload grant date and (2) shares tendered satisfy the holding period in EITF 84-18. The consensus was later updated to hold that a reload feature that provides for automatic grants of new options at then-current market prices in exchange for shares tendered to satisfy tax withholding requirements is acceptable, and shares so tendered need not satisfy the holding period requirement set forth in EITF 84-18. FIN 44 has effectively limited this consensus to reload features set forth in the original option award; later modifications will result in variable award accounting.

95-16 Accounting for Stock Compensation Arrangements with Employer Loan Features under APB Opinion No. 25

This issue relates to the situation in which an employee exercises a stock option by issuing a nonrecourse note to the employer, secured by the stock itself. The question is whether, when the terms of the note include either a variable interest rate or fixed interest with a prepayment option, this in effect results in the granting of a new option. The consensus was that the exercise of the option is, in substance, the issuance of a new option having a new measurement date, unless certain conditions are met. Those conditions might include a term in the original option that permitted exercise by issuance of nonrecourse debt having a specified term, or a proviso that implies that such an exercise does not extend the original option period even where the original agreement did not address exercise with a nonrecourse note. Otherwise, there will be another measurement of the compensation implicit in the arrangement. The consensus also stated that if the terms of the original arrangement provided for exercise through the issuance of the note and the interest is determined to be part of the exercise price, then the original grant should be accounted for as a variable plan, since the exercise price is not known at grant date. Furthermore, this may cause a fixed option to be converted into a variable option at the exercise, as when interest on the note is nonrecourse and thus must be deemed part of the exercise price. Lastly, dividends paid during the term of the nonrecourse note are to be treated as additional compensation; and interest received which is deemed part of the exercise price will be accounted for as payment for the shares, not as interest income.

96-18 Accounting for Equity Instruments That Are Issued to other than Employees for Acquiring, or in Conjunction with Selling, Goods or Services

FAS 123 established the measurement principles for transactions in which equity instruments are issued in exchange for the receipt of goods or services. These are to be measured at the fair value of the consideration received or the fair value of the equity instruments issued, whichever is more reliably measurable. The measurement date was not stipulated, nor was guidance on recognition of the cost of those transactions provided by the standard. Such transactions could involve a contemporaneous exchange of the equity instruments for goods or services, or may involve an exchange that spans several financial reporting periods. Furthermore, the quantity and terms of the equity instruments to be issued may be known or only known within a range when the transaction arrangement is established.

This consensus addresses the measurement date and recognition approach for any of these transactions, if the counterparty to the transaction is other than an employee, superseding the guidance in EITF 96-3. It does not, however, address the accounting for equity instruments either issued to a lender or investor who provides financing to the issuer or issued in a business combination.

The transactions covered are those in which (1) the fair value of the equity instruments is more reliably measurable than the fair value of the goods or services received and (2) the counterparty receives shares of stock, stock options, or other equity instruments in settlement of the entire transaction or, if the transaction is part cash and part equity instruments, in settlement of the portion of the transaction for which the equity instruments constitute the consideration.

A consensus was reached that the issuer should measure the fair value of the equity instruments using the stock price and other measurement assumptions as of the earlier of either of the following: (1) the date at which a commitment for performance by the counterparty to earn the equity instruments is reached (a performance commitment) or (2) the date at which the counterparty's performance is complete. This is referred to as the measurement date.

Furthermore, a consensus was reached that an asset, expense, or sales discount would be recognized (or previous recognition reversed) in the same period(s) and in the same manner (i.e., capitalize versus expense) as if the enterprise had paid cash for the goods or services or used cash rebates as a sales discount instead of paying with or using the equity instruments. Also, a recognized asset, expense, or sales discount should not be reversed if a stock option that the counterparty has the right to exercise expires unexercised.

When it is appropriate under generally accepted accounting principles for the issuer to recognize any cost of the transaction during financial reporting periods prior to the measurement date, for purposes of recognition of costs during those periods the equity instruments should be measured at their then-current fair values at each of those interim financial reporting dates. Changes in those fair values between those interim reporting dates should be attributed in accordance with the methods illustrated in FIN 28.

If, on the measurement date, the quantity or any of the terms of the equity instruments are dependent on the achievement of market conditions, then the issuer should use the fair value of the equity instruments for recognition purposes. That fair value would be calculated as the fair value of the equity instruments without regard to the market condition plus the fair value of the issuer's commitment to change the quantity or terms of the equity instruments based on whether the market condition is met.

If, on the measurement date, the quantity or any of the terms of the equity instruments are dependent on the achievement of counterparty performance conditions that, based on the different possible outcomes, result in a range of aggregate fair values for the equity instruments as of that date, then the issuer should utilize the lowest aggregate (i.e., the variable terms times the applicable number of equity instruments) amount within that range for recognition purposes, which could be zero.

For transactions that involve both market conditions and counterparty performance conditions, the consensus was that the guidance above (i.e., to use lowest aggregate fair value) also applies. For transactions in which the quantity or any of the terms are not known up front, the accounting prior to the measurement date, which involves only market conditions, the then-current fair value also applies. For transactions that involve only counterparty performance conditions, when it is appropriate under generally accepted accounting principles for the issuer to recognize any cost of the transaction in reporting periods prior to the measurement date, the equity instruments should be measured at their then-current lowest aggregate fair value at each of those interim reporting dates. Changes in those lowest aggregate fair values between those interim reporting dates should be attributed in accordance with the methods illustrated in FIN 28.

In the case of transactions that involve both market conditions and counterparty performance conditions, the then-current lowest aggregate fair value also applies. The accounting after the measurement date for transactions that involve only market conditions and in which the quantity or any of the terms are not known up front, the issuer should recognize and classify future changes in the fair value of this commitment in accordance with any relevant accounting literature on financial instruments, such as EITF 96-13. For transactions that involve only counterparty performance conditions, the consensus is that as each quantity and term becomes known and until all the quantities and terms that stem from the counterparty's performance become known, the "lowest aggregate" fair value measure would be used to reflect additional cost of the transaction, using the "modification accounting" methodology.

In the case of transactions that involve both market conditions and counterparty performance conditions, the consensus was that through the date the last performance-related condition is resolved, the issuer should apply "modification accounting" for the resolution of both counterparty performance conditions and market conditions. If, at the time the last counterparty performance-related condition is resolved, one or more market conditions remain, then the issuer should measure the then-current fair value of the issuer's commitment to issue additional equity instruments or change the terms of the equity instruments based on whether the market condition is met.

After the issuer measures the then-current fair value of the issuer's commitment related to the market condition, the issuer should, to the extent necessary, recognize and classify future changes in the fair value of this commitment in accordance with any relevant accounting literature on financial instruments, such as EITF 96-13.

97-14 Accounting for Deferred Compensation Arrangements Where Amounts Earned Are Held in a Rabbi Trust and Invested

Assets are placed in a grantor trust representing deferred compensation, invested either in employer securities or diversified; assets in a "rabbi trust" are available to a grantor/employer's creditors in the event of bankruptcy. The tentative conclusion by the EITF is that assets of the trust should be consolidated with employer's financial statements; any employer's stock held would be treated as treasury stock. Also, before diversification of trust assets, amount of deferred compensation would be adjusted through earnings to reflect fair value of the amount owed to employee.

98-2 Accounting by a Subsidiary for an Investment in Its Parent Company's Stock

The issue relates to the display of an investment by a subsidiary in the parent's or joint venture partner's stock in separate statements of the subsidiary or the joint venture; specifically, how the FAS 115 rules affect this presentation. Questions to be answered are how to account for the investment as an asset to be accounted for at fair value; a distribution to the parent or joint venture partner (similar to treasury stock); or as an asset measured by the equity method, with an elimination of reciprocal ownership investments. No consensus has been reached on these matters, and further discussion is not planned.

99-7 Accounting for an Accelerated Share Repurchase Program

The issue pertains to accelerated share repurchase programs, which are combinations of transactions that permit an entity to purchase a targeted number of shares immediately, with the final purchase price determined by an average market price over fixed periods of time. Such programs are intended to combine the immediate share retirement benefits (boosting earnings-per-share, etc.) of tender offers with the market impacts and pricing benefits of disciplined open market stock repurchase programs. At issue were the implications of accelerated share repurchase programs on EPS calculations and entities' abilities to account for business combinations as poolings of interests.

The consensus was that an entity should account for an accelerated share repurchase program as two separate transactions: first, as shares of common stock acquired in a treasury stock transaction recorded on the acquisition date, and second, as a forward contract indexed to its own common stock. Pursuant to EITF 99-3, *Application of Issue No. 96-13 to Derivative Instruments with Multiple Settlement Alternatives*, an entity would classify the forward contract in the above example as an equity instrument because the entity will receive cash when the contract is in a gain position but pay cash or stock when the contract is in a loss position. Changes in the fair value of the forward contract would not be recorded, and the settlement of the forward contract would be recorded in equity.

The treasury stock transaction would result in an immediate reduction of the outstanding shares used to calculate the weighted-average common shares outstanding for both basic and diluted EPS. The effect of the forward contract on diluted EPS would be calculated in accordance with FAS 128, as interpreted by EITF Topic D-72.

Regarding the impact of accelerated share repurchase programs on the ability to account for a business combination as a pooling of interests, the entity should consider the share repurchase date or, with respect to postconsummation repurchases, the date on which the intent to repurchase shares is formulated to determine whether the treasury stock acquisition results in a violation of APB 16, as interpreted by the SEC's SAB 96. Any resulting preconsummation tainted treasury shares could be "cured" by issuing the same amount of common stock between the purchase date and the date of consummation of the business combination.

The issue of the possible effects of the forward contract in the accelerated share repurchase program on an entity's ability to account for a business combination as a pooling of interests was not resolved, but may be addressed later. The impact of derivative financial instruments indexed to, and potentially settled in, a company's own stock on pooling-of-interests transactions will also be addressed later.

00-6 Accounting for Freestanding Derivative Financial Instruments Indexed to, and Potentially Settled in, the Stock of a Consolidated Subsidiary

EITF 96-13, *Accounting for Derivative Financial Instruments Indexed to, and Potentially Settled in, a Company's Own Stock*, establishes a framework for accounting for freestanding derivative instruments that are indexed to, and potentially settled in, a company's own stock. That consensus did not, however, provide guidance on how to account for freestanding derivative instruments that are indexed to, and potentially settled in, a subsidiary's stock. The issue addressed here is how such contracts should be classified and measured in the consolidated financial statements.

A consensus exists that stock of a subsidiary is not equity of the parent; therefore, derivatives indexed to and to be settled in stock of a subsidiary do not meet FAS 133's exclusion criteria. If derivatives meet the criteria of FAS 133 (e.g., for net settlement, etc.), they must be accounted for under the provisions of FAS 133, and not of EITF 96-13. The consensus also discusses a number of exceptions based on the criteria set forth in FAS 133.

The EITF reached several consensuses regarding derivatives not within the scope of FAS 133, while also noting that option or forward strike prices and premiums could be indicative of impairments of the parent's investment in subsidiaries, to be assessed using FAS 121. A parent's contract to purchase a subsidiary's (minority held) common stock should not be recorded until settled; during the period of the contract, income should continue to be allocated to the minority interest. A contract to sell shares in a subsidiary, likewise, should be recorded when settled; until that time, income would not be allocated to outside interests (counterparties to the derivative). No consensus was reached regarding written options.

00-16 Recognition and Measurement of Employer Payroll Taxes on Employee Stock-Based Compensation

This issue discusses (1) when a liability for employer payroll taxes on employee stock compensation should be recognized in the employer's financial statements and (2) how that liability should be measured. The consensus was that a liability for employee payroll taxes on stock compensation should be recognized and measured on the date of the event triggering the measurement and payment of the tax to the taxing authority (which would generally be the exercise date).

00-18 Accounting Recognition for Certain Transactions Involving Equity Instruments Granted to other than Employees

EITF 96-18 and EITF 00-8, which require "symmetrical accounting," do not address the period(s) or manner in which the fair value of the transactions should be recognized, other than to observe that a transaction should be recognized in the same period(s) and in the same manner as if cash were being exchanged in the transaction instead of the equity instruments. The consensus is that where fully vested, exercisable, nonforfeitable equity instruments are issued at the date the grantor and grantee enter into an agreement, by eliminating any obligation on the part of the counterparty to earn the equity instruments, a measurement date has been reached. The majority held that the grantor should recognize the equity instruments when they are issued (in most cases, when the agreement is entered into), and generally agreed that whether the corresponding cost is an immediate expense or a prepaid asset (or whether the debit should be characterized as contra equity) depends on the specific facts and circumstances. No further consideration of this matter is planned.

Consensus was reached that, if an entity grants fully vested, nonforfeitable equity instruments that are exercisable by the grantee only after a specified period of time and the terms of the agreement provide for earlier exercisability by the grantee only after a specified period of time and the terms of the agreement provide for earlier exercisability if the grantee achieves specified performance conditions, the grantor should measure the fair value of the equity instruments at the date of grant and should recognize that measured cost under the same guidance as the foregoing. Change to EITF 96-18 should be made to eliminate a reference to **immediate exercisability**. A majority agreed that if, subsequent to the arrangement date, the grantee performs as specified and exercisability is accelerated, the grantor should measure and account for the increase in the fair value of the equity instruments resulting from the acceleration of exercisability using "modification accounting." Since, generally, option-pricing models are not sensitive to exercisability restrictions, it may be necessary to provide additional guidance on how to measure the discount attributable to the exercisability restriction.

For transactions that include a grantee performance commitment, there was general agreement that the grantee should account for the arrangement as an executory contract (that is, generally no accounting before performance) in the same manner as it would if the grantor had agreed to pay cash (upon vesting) for the goods or services. Further consideration will be directed to the accounting in cases in which the fair value at the date the equity instruments are earned is greater than or less than the fair value measured at the performance commitment date (measurement date).

Further discussion of several matters raised on EITF 00-18 is anticipated.

00-19 Accounting for Derivative Financial Instruments Indexed to, and Potentially Settled in, a Company's Own Stock

This consensus restates a number of earlier, related issues and codifies the EITF's position on this entire subject area. It applies to freestanding derivatives only—similar embedded derivatives are not covered. Also not covered are derivatives which issued to compensate employees or to acquire goods and services from nonemployees, when performance has yet to occur. It does apply, however, to derivatives issued to acquire goods and services from nonemployees, when performance has occurred.

The issue for the EITF was how certain equity derivative contracts indexed to, and potentially settled in, a company's own stock should be accounted for. Such contracts could include written puts, written calls and warrants, purchased puts, purchased calls, forward sale contracts, and forward purchase contracts.

In its consensus, the EITF reached a number of conclusions. These are summarized as follows.

1. Initial balance sheet classification is to be guided by the principle that contracts which require net cash settlements are assets or liabilities, and those that require settlement in shares are equity instruments. If the reporting entity has the choice of settlement modes, settlement in shares is to be assumed; if the counter party has the option, net cash settlement is presumed. An exception occurs if the two settlement alternatives are not of equal value, in which case the economic substance should govern.
2. Initial measurement should be at fair value. Contracts classed as equity are accounted for in permanent equity, with value changes being ignored, unless settlement expectations change. For publicly held companies, under defined circumstances, guidance is provided by analogy from ASR 268. All other contracts would be classified as assets or liabilities, to be measured continuously at fair value. If settlement in shares ultimately occurs, already recognized gains or losses are left in earnings, not reclassified or reversed.

3. Events may necessitate reclassification of contracts from assets/liabilities to equity. If a contract first classed as equity is later reclassed to assets/liabilities, any value change to the date of reclassification will be included in equity, not earnings. Thereafter, value changes will be reported in earnings. If partial net share settlement is permitted, the portion that can be so settled remains in equity. Appropriate disclosure under APB 22 may be required, if more than one contract exists and different methods are applied to them.
4. All the following conditions must be satisfied in order to classify a contract in equity:
   a. The contract permits settlement in unregistered shares (the assumption being that the issuer cannot effectively control the conditions for registration, making cash settlement likely unless unregistered shares can be delivered);
   b. There are sufficient authorized, unissued shares to settle the contact, after considering all other outstanding commitments;
   c. The contract contains an explicit limit on the number of shares to be issued;
   d. There are no required cash payments to the counter party based on the issuer's failure to make timely SEC filings;
   e. There are no "make whole" provisions to compensate the holder after he sells the shares issued in the market at a price below some defined threshold value;
   f. Requirements for net cash settlement are accompanied by similar requirements for existing shareholders;
   g. There are no provisions that indicate that the counter parties have rights greater than those of the actual shareholders; and
   h. There is no requirement for any collateral posting for any reason.
5. Contracts that are subject to this consensus cannot qualify for hedge accounting (this is based on the SEC's position on this matter).
6. Contracts offering multiple settlement alternatives that require the company to receive cash when the contract is in a gain position but pay either stock or cash at the company's option when in a loss position are to be accounted for as equity. Also, such contracts requiring payment of cash when in a loss position but receipt of either cash or stock at the company's option when in a gain position must be accounted for as assets/liabilities.
7. For EPS computation purposes, for those contracts that provide the company with a choice of settlement methods, settlement in shares is to be assumed, although this can be overcome based on past experience or stated policy. If the counterparty controls the choice, however, the more dilutive assumption must be made, irrespective of past experience or policy.

The consensus is effective for contracts entered into after September 30, 2000; for contracts in existence on that date, the requirements of the consensus are to be applied on June 30, 2001, using a cumulative-effect-type presentation. The consensus includes detailed guidance for a number of specific types of contracts.

00-23 Issues Related to the Accounting for Stock Compensation under APB Opinion No. 25 and FASB Interpretation No. 44

Many practical issues had arisen pertaining to application of APB 25 and FIN 44, which were brought to the EITF's attention by the SEC. A number of these were resolved with consensus positions by the EITF. These include the following (many others also exist; see the consensus for details):

1. When options on the stock of one entity in a consolidated group are exchanged for options in another entity in the group, variable accounting will be required if the effect is to reduce the exercise price, as discussed in Question 11 of FIN 44. Otherwise, the exchange results in a new measurement date.
2. Indirect guarantees of the value of stock option grants necessitate recognition of compensation over the service period equal to the "guaranteed" minimum.
3. Fair value repurchase features, in the case of nonpublic issuers, do not trigger variable accounting, if the repurchase is not within six months of exercise.
4. In the case of business combinations accounted for as poolings, the accounting attributes of the combining entity's awards carry forward to the awards issued or granted by the issuer in the business combination. If the combination is a purchase, however, the attributes do not carry forward to acquirer awards issued or granted in the combination.
5. Subsequent repurchase of awards fully vested as of the date of a business combination is the equivalent of reacquisition of residual equity interests, to be accounted for similar to treasury stock, unless the settlement is above fair value, in which case the excess is compensation. Several variations on this issue are also addressed in the consensus.
6. When one entity in a controlled group issues options in its shares to employees in a "sister" entity, the value should be measured at the grant date and recognize that amount as a dividend to the controlling entity. The employer entity should recognize compensation cost and a credit to paid in capital (a contribution by or on behalf of the parent or controlling entity).

Examples are presented in the consensus; other issues will be subsequently addressed.

D-90 Grantor Balance Sheet Presentation of Unvested, Forfeitable Equity Instruments Granted to a Nonemployee

EITF 96-18 discusses the appropriate balance sheet presentation of arrangements where unvested, forfeitable equity instruments are issued to an unrelated nonemployee (the counterparty) as consideration for future services. SEC staff has since addressed situations where the grantor is entitled to recover the specific consideration paid, plus a substantial mandatory penalty, as a minimum measure of damages for counterparty nonperformance. Fair value measurement under FAS 123 is required. In practice, however, it was found that some reporting entities have made no entries until performance occurs, while others have recorded the fair value of the equity instruments as equity at the measurement date and record the offset either as an asset (future services receivable) or as a reduction of stockholders' equity (contra equity).

The SEC staff believes that if the issuer receives a right to receive future services in exchange for unvested, forfeitable equity instruments, those equity instruments should be treated as unissued for accounting purposes until the future services are received (that is, the instruments are not considered issued until they vest). Consequently, there would be no recognition at the measurement date and no entry should be recorded. This does not apply to similar arrangements in which the issuer exchanges fully vested nonforfeitable equity instruments, as those types of arrangements are addressed in EITF 00-18.

D-91 Application of APB 25 and FASB Interpretation 44 to an Indirect Repricing of a Stock Option

This concerns a FASB response to a very specific set of assumed facts whereby the accounting for previously issued fixed options must be changed to variable due to the issuance of new options clearly linked to the now out-of-the-money earlier awards. In general, whether variable accounting under APB 25 and FIN 44 becomes required is highly dependent upon specific facts and circumstances.

D-93 Accounting for the Rescission of the Exercise of Employee Stock Options

For a given fact-specific scenario in which exercised options are "rescinded" during the same tax year, variable accounting would be required for any replacement options granted, since it would be presumed that the new options contained the same rescission rights, the existence of which makes variable accounting mandatory. Depending on the circumstances, there might be expanded disclosures required as well. For purposes of EPS calculations, the weighted-average number of shares outstanding must include shares issued under option arrangements which were subsequently rescinded, until the effective date of such rescission.

D-98 Classification and Measurement of Redeemable Securities

Per SEC rules, equity which is not "permanent" (i.e., which can be redeemed by the holder's demand or by conditions not under the issuer's control) must be displayed outside of the equity section of the balance sheet. (There are no similar requirements under general GAAP, however.) The potential effects of normal liquidation events, however, do not necessitate such presentation. Determining whether securities are subject to redemption at the holder's option is fact-specific and may not be obvious in some instances. If securities must be redeemed if, for example, a registration statement is not filed by a defined date, or if there is noncompliance with debt covenants, inclusion as equity would be prohibited. Similarly, if the preferred stock is subject to a change-in-control provision and the preferred holders control a majority of votes on the board of directors, the preferred stock would be excludable from equity. Where redemption values vary over time, the stock should be presented at its redemption amount at the balance sheet date, which may or may not involve accretion over time (by the interest method, generally), depending on its terms.

FASB TECHNICAL BULLETINS

85-6 Accounting for a Purchase of Treasury Shares at a Price Significantly in Excess of the Current Market Price of the Shares and the Income Statement Classification of Costs Incurred in Defending against a Takeover Attempt

Purchase of shares from a party attempting a takeover at an above-market price (sometimes referred to as "greenmail") in order to avert takeover may involve an element of cost that is not properly allocated to treasury stock. Such costs are to be expensed (but not to be reported as extraordinary) and not included in the treasury stock account.

97-1 Accounting under Statement 123 for Certain Employee Stock Purchase Plans with a Look-Back Option

This bulletin provides guidance for accounting for certain employee stock purchase plans that have a look-back option, which is a provision that sets the exercise price equal to the lesser of the market price at the grant date or the exercise date.

APPENDIX A

EXPOSURE DRAFT OUTSTANDING

Proposed FAS: Share-Based Payment—an Amendment of Statements No. 123 and 95

The development and enactment of FAS 123 in 1995 was a politically charged event that left neither users, preparers nor neutral observers satisfied. In FAS 123, FASB concluded that fair value-based reporting of stock-based compensation cost was conceptually superior but that it was impossible at that time to mandate such accounting. It therefore permitted continuing use of APB 25's discredited intrinsic value method, with supplementary footnote disclosures of the "correct" amounts of compensation expense, net income, and retained earnings as computed on a fair value basis—notwithstanding the fundamental principle that good disclosure is not a remedy for poor accounting.

Many of the financial reporting scandals of the late 1990s and early 2000s were, rightly or wrongly, often linked in the public mind to extravagant executive compensation schemes, and generous option grants that involved no reportable compensation costs were seen as having helped motivate such behaviors. Following the WorldCom debacle in 2002, a growing number of publicly held companies began to voluntarily fully embrace FAS 123; by early 2004 over 500 large public companies were reporting compensation cost determined on the basis of fair value of options. Furthermore, the international standard-setting body (IASB) undertook a project to mandate fair value accounting for share-based payments, which culminated in the issuance of IFRS 2 in February 2004. Public pressure, coupled with FASB's commitment to converge its standards with those of IASB, therefore made it almost inevitable that FAS 123's voluntary approach would be eliminated.

In March 2004 FASB issued its ED which, if enacted, will require publicly held companies to use fair value accounting for share-based payments, while permitting nonpublic entities to continue with the intrinsic value methodology. The minimum value method provided by FAS 123 (a simplified approach to fair value, ignoring volatility measures in deference to nonpublic entities' lack of share price data), would be eliminated as an option. The proposed standard amends FAS 123 and FAS 95. It would require accounting and reporting which would be similar to, but not identical with, that under IFRS 2.

The proposed standard would broadly address share-based payments. It covers plans for employees that convey shares of the employer's stock, derivatives (such as options) related to the employer's shares, or cash in amounts tied to the value of the employer's shares. All share-based plans are considered compensatory unless the benefit to employees is no greater than that available to shareholders generally. The benefit to recipients is assessed based both on the discount from market price and the number of shares they are eligible to buy. Consequently, virtually all plans will be considered compensatory for accounting purposes, including employee stock purchase plans that are noncompensatory under the federal tax laws. This represents a change from APB 25, under which noncompensatory plans for tax purposes were also noncompensatory for accounting proposes. The new rules will even be somewhat stricter than those set forth under FAS 123.

Additionally, the ED would modify FAS 123 as to (1) the prescribed pattern of compensation cost recognition, (2) the accounting for employee stock purchase plans, and (3) accounting for the income tax effects of share-based transactions. It would also amend FAS 95 to require that excess tax benefits be reported in the cash flow statement as a financing activity, rather than as an operating activity (these are currently reported as a reduction of income taxes paid).

The proposed requirements of this Standard would become effective for public and nonpublic companies that did not use the minimum-value method as of the beginning of the first fiscal year beginning after December 15, 2004. Nonpublic companies that used the minimum-value method would have an additional year to adopt the new standard. Nonpublic companies will be encouraged to use the fair value method, but this ED would permit those entities to account for their share options at intrinsic value, but it would have to be remeasured at each reporting date until exercise or other settlement.

Scope. This ED is the result of a limited scope effort to address deficiencies in FAS 123 which had become untenable in the current business climate. If adopted, the new standard would apply to

1. Public and nonpublic companies
2. Accounting for all share-based awards to employees, including employee stock purchase plans

The ED would **not** apply to

1. Accounting for employee stock ownership plan transactions (ESOP)
2. Awards to nonemployees, with an exception made in the case of awards to nonemployee members of the board of directors in their capacity as directors, a distinction first established by FIN 44.

These exclusions will be taken up in a later phase of FASB's project on equity-based compensation arrangements.

Overview of Significant Revisions Being Made to FAS 123

This statements eliminates, for publicly held entities, the alternative of continuing to account for share-based payment arrangements with employees under APB 25, which generally had resulted in having no reportable compensation cost associated with executive stock options. Because compensation cost will now be measured under the fair value approach and formally reported in the body of the income statement, the ED also eliminates the requirement to provide a pro forma disclosure of the effect of applying fair-value-based accounting methods.

In the following paragraphs, the key features of the proposed amendment to FAS 123 will be explained, followed by examples of how the provisions of the standard would be applied. The ED is proposing not merely a mandatory application of the formerly voluntary measurement requirements of FAS 123, but also certain changes in the required methodology itself. Therefore, in the following discussion, emphasis will be placed on the changes to the fair value methodology of FAS 123 which are being proposed, some of which are substantial.

Measurement of compensation cost from share-based payment arrangements with employees. The objective is to estimate, as of the grant date, the fair value of the award that an employee earns as a result of requisite service and satisfying vesting requirements. The estimate of fair value would reflect transferability and other restrictions if they are in effect when the award vests. Compensation costs would be recognized only for those awards that vest.

- **Classifying awards as liabilities or equity.** This ED amends FAS 123 to require that the classification criteria of FAS 150 be applied in determining whether an instrument granted to an employee is a liability or equity. In particular, some stock-based compensation awards that call for settlement by issuing an entity's own equity instruments may be classified as liabilities if they meet the criteria of FAS 150. Although FAS 150 did not exist when FAS 123 was promulgated, the results under the ED are expected to largely replicate those under FAS 123. Under APB 25, however, there was no attempt to distinguish between awards creating equity instruments and those creating liabilities.

- **Valuation models.** In the absence of an observable market price for an award, which is most often the case for employee share options, reporting entities will be required to use a valuation method that takes into account the factors set forth in the standard. FAS 123 explicitly cited both the Black-Scholes and binomial approaches as being among the acceptable option pricing models, but the former has been the target of criticism in the years since FAS 123's promulgation, purportedly overstating compensation cost as a consequence of not reflecting the unique characteristics of nontradable employee options. FASB believes and prefers that most companies will now use the binomial, or *lattice*, model, rather than a *closed-form* model such as the Black-Scholes, although it does not dictate selection of any particular option pricing model. The binomial model is favored, however, because it accommodates more potential postvesting behaviors than the closed-form models.

  Binomial or lattice models value options by constructing lattices or trees that represent different possible stock prices at different future points in time. The value of the option is determined at each node or branch of the tree. To determine these values, companies need to develop information about expected volatility, dividends, and risk-free rates that will apply at each of the possible branches or nodes of the model. In addition, information about employee postvesting behavior is needed to determine likely exercise dates. Note that under the revised standard it would be necessary to use *expected volatility*, whereas under FAS 123 historical volatility of share prices was typically employed as a surrogate.
- **Liability-classified awards.** The provisions dealing with share-based payments that involve liabilities, rather than equity, are affected by the issuance of FAS 150, which occurred after the original FAS 123 had been promulgated. Certain share-based payments create liabilities under FAS 150, (e.g., awards which result in the issuance of mandatorily redeemable shares, or those which require cash settlements, as do stock appreciation rights). Liability-classified awards would be remeasured at fair value each reporting period. Prior to vesting, the cumulative compensation costs would equal the proportionate amount of the award earned to date, and thus the periodic compensation cost would reflect both the passage of time (service period) and change in the fair value of the ultimate award. Subsequent to vesting, any further change in fair value would be recorded as a charge against earnings. This is similar to the result under FAS 123, but is a fundamental change from APB 25, which required liability-classified awards be accounted for using the intrinsic value method, as were equity-based awards.
- **Equity-classified awards.** Equity-classified awards that are publicly traded and have observable market prices would be valued using the market price. Few, if any, employee stock compensation awards would have this characteristic, however. If not publicly traded, equity-classified awards are valued using a valuation model such as the binomial model or the Black-Scholes (called Black-Scholes-Merton in the ED) model.
- **Valuation for graded-vesting awards.** Companies that grant awards with graded vesting will no longer be able to measure the awards as if it were a cliff-vested award. For example, a graded-vested award that vested over five years (20% each year) would have to be treated as five separate awards. The fair value of each of these awards would be separately determined, using an appropriate methodology.
- **Measurement alternatives for nonpublic companies.** FAS 123 offered nonpublic companies choosing fair value the alternative of using a minimum value model, which eliminated the volatility variable from the valuation model of choice. This was done

> because for a nontraded stock there would be no historical record of volatility of prices, and hence no reasonable way to estimate future volatility. FAS 123's minimum-value method for measuring fair value would no longer be permitted. Nonpublic companies could instead choose to use either intrinsic values or fair values to measure share-option or liability-classified awards. No such choice would be available for nonvested or vested stock awards, which would be measured using grant-date fair values. If a reporting entity chooses to use the intrinsic value alternative, the intrinsic value of an equity-classified award will have to be reestimated each reporting period. However, if a company uses the fair value alternative no reestimation is required, which would reduce fluctuations in earnings. If nonpublic companies choose the fair value approach, they will not later be able to return to the use of intrinsic value, because fair value is deemed preferable for purposes of applying APB 20 (accounting changes). These matters represent significant changes from FAS 123 as first promulgated. Furthermore, the intrinsic value method under the ED differs dramatically from the intrinsic value method under APB 25: Under the latter, intrinsic value is measured once, at grant date (generally), and typically was zero; under the former, it is remeasured at each balance sheet date and will be zero only under the unique situation where the market price never exceeds the exercise price, rendering the option, under this formulation, worthless.

Recognizing compensation. Vesting can be based on a service condition, performance condition, or a combination of both.

- Service conditions are requirements to achieve a specified duration of employment.
- Performance conditions are requirements to achieve company-specific operating or financial goals.

Compensation cost would be recognized based on the actual number of awards that eventually vest. Estimates are accrued each period and adjustments are made based on current estimates of expected future vesting until the actual number of awards that vest are known. This is a major change from FAS 123, which allowed companies to recognize compensation expense based on the assumption that all awards would vest, and then adjusting for actual forfeitures as they occurred.

Under the proposed standard, compensation cost for equity-based awards would be measured at the grant date, and not subsequently revised (apart from recognizing forfeitures). Under APB 25, the measure was generally at grant date, but when either the amount the employee would be required to pay or the number of shares the employee would be entitled to were not known, compensation was measured at a later date (so-called **variable awards,** the accounting for which was governed by FIN 28 and FIN 38, both of which will be eliminated by the ED).

Market conditions affect the exercisability of an award, not its vesting. The ED defines a market condition as an exercisability requirement based on achieving a specified share price. Market conditions can affect the grant-date fair value, and hence the compensation expense to be recognized by the reporting entity. If an employee forfeits an award because a market condition is not satisfied, compensation previously accrued is not reversed, unlike forfeitures, which necessitate reversal of previously accrued compensation cost.

Under provisions of the ED, compensation cost for liability-based awards would be measured at the exercise or settlement date, but compensation is estimated at each reporting date from grant date to exercise or settlement date, much like variable accounting under APB 25 and its interpretations. This is similar to practice under current FAS 123.

Modified awards. The incremental compensation cost resulting from a modification of an award would be measured as the excess of the fair value of the modified award over the fair value of the original award measured immediately prior to the modification. Modifications can occur because of repricing, extending the life, or changing the vesting condition of the award. Cancellations of existing awards and concurrent replacement with new ones would be accounted for as modifications. In practice, modifications will rarely result in recognized compensation costs less than the fair value of the award at the grant date, but this could conceivably result if the original service or performance vesting conditions are not expected to be satisfied at the modification date.

Income tax effects of share-based compensation. If the ultimate deductible compensation cost for an individual employee's equity instruments on the employer's tax return is less than the cumulative compensation cost recognized for financial reporting purposes, then the deferred tax asset related to this difference should be written off, net of any valuation allowance, on the income statement. FAS 123, on the other hand, reflected a portfolio rather than an individual approach and required that the deficiency be charged to paid-in capital. Thus, under the ED the reduction in the deferred tax asset would affect the income statement directly, rather than the balance sheet. If the tax benefit ultimately realized is less than the amount recognized for financial reporting purposes, the difference will now be recognized as tax expense. Contrariwise, tax benefits realized in excess of the amount recognized for financial reporting purposes would be recognized as additional paid-in capital at the time the tax benefit is realized.

Accounting for Employee Stock Options under this ED

The ED does not permit public company accounting for stock-based compensation as provided under APB 25—which, together with associated interpretations, will be fully superseded by the new standard. Under ED, fair value accounting must be applied in measuring compensation expense. Ideally, fair value would be market-based: An observable market price, if available for an option with similar features, would be used as the estimate of fair value of the employee option. However, in most cases, due to the nature of employee stock options, observable market prices will not be available. Therefore, the entity will have to estimate the fair value of the employee share option using a valuation model that meets the requirements of the ED. The valuation model (which is very similar to that set forth under FAS 123) takes into account the following factors, at a minimum:

1. Exercise price of the option
2. Expected term of the option, taking into account several things including the contractual term of the option, vesting requirements, and postvesting employee termination behaviors
3. Current price of the underlying share
4. Expected volatility of the price of the underlying share
5. Expected dividends on the underlying share
6. Risk-free interest rate(s) for the expected term of the option

In practice, there are likely to be ranges of reasonable estimates for expected volatility, dividends, and option term. The **closed form** models, of which Black-Scholes (now BSM) is the most widely regarded, are predicated on a set of deterministic assumptions, which remain invariate over the full term of the option. For this reason, current thinking is that a **lattice** model, of which the binomial model is an example, would be preferred. Lattice models explicitly identify nodes, such as the anniversaries of the grant date, at each of which new parameter values can be specified (e.g., expected dividends can be independently defined each period).

If a company changes from the Black-Scholes model to a binomial model, the change would be a change in accounting estimate. Also, changing back to a less desirable model would be discouraged, but apparently not prohibited if supportable. The presumption is that moving from a binomial model to the Black-Scholes model would not be well received.

Other features that may affect the value of the option include changes in the issuer's credit risk, if the value of the awards contains cash settlement features (liability instruments). Also, contingent features that could cause a loss of equity shares earned or reduce realized gains from sale of equity instruments earned, such as a **clawback feature** (for example, where an employee who terminates the employment relationship and begins to work for a competitor is required to transfer to the issuing enterprise shares granted and earned under a share-based payment arrangement—see the illustrations in the ED) would be factors affecting the valuation model.

Market, performance, or service conditions may affect vesting. An award becomes vested at the date the employee's right to receive or retain shares no longer has any of these conditions. Vesting may be conditional on satisfying two or more conditions. Regardless of the conditions that must be satisfied, the existence of a market condition requires recognition of compensation cost if service has been rendered, even if the market condition is never satisfied.

The definition of **an employee** used in the proposed standard is that given by Internal Revenue Service Ruling 87-41. In addition, this statement requires that nonemployee directors, acting in their role as members of the company's board of directors, be treated as employees if they were elected by the shareholders or appointed to the board and will be subject to election at the next shareholder election. Any awards granted to these individuals for their service as directors would be considered to be employee compensation.

The **grant date** is defined as the date when the employer and employee have a mutual understanding of the key terms and conditions of the share-based compensation arrangement and all necessary authorizations of those conditions have occurred. The **service inception date** is the first day of the requisite service period. Compensation cost is attributed over the service period.

If a given option plan involves the payment of compensation to the employees, such compensation cost should be recognized in the period(s) in which the services being compensated are performed. If the grant is unconditional, which means it effectively is in recognition of past services rendered by the employees and does not depend on the rendering of further service, then compensation is reported in full in the period of the grant. If the stock options are granted before the service inception date, compensation cost should be recognized over the periods in which the performance is scheduled to occur. Whether compensation cost is recognized ratably over the periods or not is a function of the vesting provisions of the plan. If the plan provides for **cliff vesting,** compensation will be accrued on an essentially straight-line basis, while if it provides for **graded vesting,** the pattern of recognition will be more complex. The accounting for graded vesting plans under the ED represents a change from current practice.

Before presenting specific examples of accounting for stock options, simple examples of calculating the fair value of options using both the Black-Scholes and the binomial/lattice methods are provided. First, an example of the Black-Scholes, closed-form model (referred to in the ED as the Black-Scholes-Merton formula or BSM model) is provided.

Example of determining the fair value of options using the Black-Scholes model

Black-Scholes is a closed-form model, meaning that it solves for an option price from an equation. It computes a theoretical call price based on five parameters—the current stock price, the option exercise price, the expected volatility of the stock price, the time until option expiration, and the short-term risk-free interest rate. Of these, expected volatility is the most difficult to ascertain. Volatility is generally computed as the standard deviation of recent historical returns on the stock. In the following example, the stock is currently selling at \$40 and the standard deviation of prices (daily closing prices can be used, among other possible choices) over the past several years was \$6.50, thus yielding an estimated volatility of \$6.50/\$40 = 16.25%.

BSM actually computes the theoretical value of a "European" call option, where exercise can occur only on the expiration date. "American" options, which include most employee stock options, can be exercised at any time until expiration. The value of an American-style option is generally greater than a European-style option since during the pre-exercise period the holder does not have a right to receive dividends that are paid on the stock. (For nondividend paying stocks, the value of American and European options will tend to be equal.) BSM ignores dividends but this is readily dealt with, as shown below, by deducting from the computed option value the present value of expected dividends over the option holding period.

BSM also is predicated on constant volatility over the option term, which available evidence suggests may not be a wholly accurate description of stock price behavior. On the other hand, the reporting entity would find it very difficult, if not impossible, to compute differing volatilities for each node in the lattice model described later in this section.

The model:

$$C = SN(d_1) - Ke^{(-rt)}N(d_2)$$

C = Theoretical call premium
S = Current stock price
t = time until option expiration
K = option striking price
r = risk-free interest rate
N = Cumulative standard normal distribution
e = exponential term (2.7183)

$$d_1 = \frac{\ln(S/K) + (r + s^2/2)^t}{s\sqrt{t}}$$

$$d_2 = d_1 - s\sqrt{t}$$

s = standard deviation of stock returns
ln = natural logarithm

The BSM valuation is illustrated with the following assumed facts; note that dividends are ignored in the initial calculation but will be addressed once the theoretical value is computed. Also note that volatility is defined in terms of the variability of the entity's stock price, measured by the standard deviation of prices over, say, the past three years, which is used as a surrogate for expected volatility over the next twelve months.

Assume the following facts:

S = \$40
t = 2 years
K = \$45
r = 3% annual rate
s = standard deviation of percentage returns = 16.25% (based on \$6.50 standard deviation of stock price compared to current \$40 price)

From the foregoing data, all of which is known information (the volatility, s, is computed or assumed, as discussed above) the factors d_1 and d_2 can be computed. The cumulative standard normal variates (N) of these values must then be determined (using a table or formula), following which the BSM option value is calculated, *before the effect of dividends*. In this example, the computed amounts are

$N(d_1) = 0.2758$
$N(d_2) = 0.2048$

With these assumptions the value of the stock options is approximately $2.35. This is derived from the BSM as follows:

$$
\begin{aligned}
C &= SN(d_1) - Ke^{(-rt)}N(d_2) \\
&= 40(.2758) - 45(.942)(.2048) \\
&= 11.032 - 8.679 \\
&= 2.35
\end{aligned}
$$

The foregone two-year stream of dividends, which in this example are projected to be $0.50 annually, have a present value of $0.96. Therefore, the net value of this option is $1.39 ($2.35 – .96).

Example of determining the fair value of options using the binomial/lattice model

In contrast to the BSM, the binomial/lattice model is an open form, inductive model. It allows for multiple branches of possible outcomes on a "tree" of possible price movements and induces the option's price. As compared to the BSM approach, this relaxes the constraint on exercise (it can be assumed that exercise occurs at any point in the option period, and past experience may guide the reporting entity to make certain such assumptions, e.g., that one-half the options will be exercised when the market price of the stock reaches 150% of the strike price, etc.). It also allows for varying dividends from period to period. It is assumed that the common (Cox, Ross, and Rubinstein) binomial model will be used in practice. To keep this preliminary example relatively simple in order to focus on the concept, a single-step binomial model is provided. Assume an option is granted on a $20 stock that will expire in one year. The option exercise price equals the stock price of $20. Also, assume there is a 50% chance that the price will jump 20% over the year and a 50% chance the stock will drop 20%, and that no other outcomes are possible. The risk-free interest rate is 4%. With these assumptions there are three basic calculations.

1. Plot the two possible future stock prices.
2. Translate these stock prices into future options values.
3. Discount these future values into a single present value.

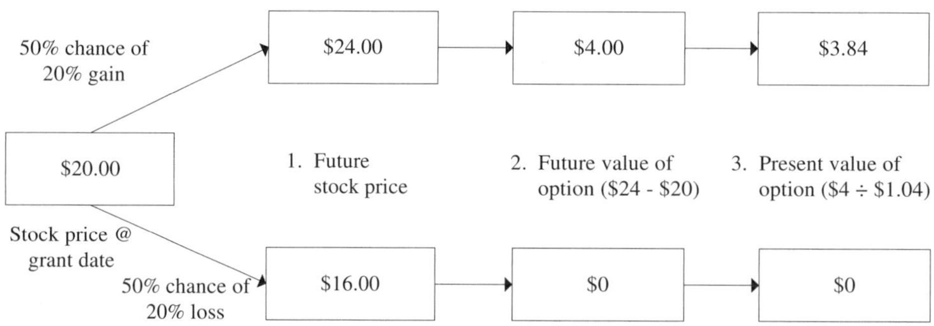

In this case, the option will only have value if the stock price increases, and otherwise the option would expire worthless and unexercised. In this simplistic example, there is only a 50% chance of the option having a value of $3.84, and therefore the option is worth $1.92 at grant date.

A more complicated binomial model simply extends this one-step model into a random walk of many steps or intervals. In theory, the time to expiration can be broken into a large number of ever-smaller time intervals, such as months, weeks, or days. The advantage is that the parameter values (volatility, etc) can then be varied with greater precision from one period to the next (assuming, of course, that there is a factual basis upon which to base these estimates). Calculating the binomial model then involves the same three calculation steps. First, the possible future stock prices are determined for each branch, using the volatility input and time to expiration (which grows shorter with each successive node in the model). This permits computation of terminal values for each branch of the tree. Second, future stock prices are translated into option values at each node of the tree. Third, these future option values are discounted and added to produce a single present value of the option, taking into account the probabilities of each series of price moves in the model.

Example of multiperiod option valuation using binomial model

Consider the following example of a 2-period binomial model. Again, certain simplifying assumptions will be made so that a manual calculation can be illustrated (in general, computer programs will be necessary to compute option values). Eager Corp. grants 10,000 options to its employees at a time when the market price of shares is $40. The options expire in 2 years; expected dividends on the stock will be $0.50 per year; and the risk-free rate is currently 3%, which is not expected to change over the 2-year horizon. The option exercise price is $43.

The entity's past experience suggests that, after 1 year (of the 2-year term) elapses, if the market price of the stock exceeds the option exercise price, one-half of the options will be exercised by the holders. The other holders will wait another year to decide. If at the end of the second year—without regard to what the stock value was at the end of the first year—the market value exceeds the exercise price, all the remaining options will be exercised. The workforce has been unusually stable and it is not anticipated that option holders will cease employment before the end the option period.

The stock price moves randomly from period to period. Based on recent experience, it is anticipated that in each period the stock may increase by $5, stay the same, or decrease by $5, with equal probability, versus the price at the period year-end. Thus, since the price is $40 at grant date, 1 year hence it might be either $45, $40, or $35. The price at the end of the second year will follow the same pattern, based on the price when the first year ends.

Logically, holders will rather exercise their options than see them expire, as long as there is gain to be realized. Since dividends are not paid on options, holders have a motive to exercise earlier than the expiration date, which explains why historically one-half the options are exercised after one year elapses, as long as the market price exceeds the exercise price at that date, even though the exercising holders risk future market declines.

The binomial model formulation requires that each sequence of events and actions be explicated. This gives rise to the commonly seen decision tree representation. In this simple example, following the grant of the options 1 of 3 possible events occur; either the stock price rises $5 over the next year, or it remains constant, or it falls by $5. Since these outcomes have equal *a priori* probabilities, p=1/3 is assigned to each outcome of this first year event. If the price does rise, one half the option holders will exercise at the end of the first year, to reap the economic gain and capture the second year's dividend. The other holders will forego this immediate gain and wait to see what the stock price does in the second year before making an exercise decision.

If the stock price in the first year either remains flat or falls by $5, no option holders are expected to exercise. However, there remains the opportunity to exercise after the second year elapses, if the stock price recovers. Of course, holding the options for the second year means that no dividends will be received.

The cost of the options granted by Eager Corp., measured by fair value using the binomial model approach, is computed by the sum of the probability-weighted outcomes, discounted to present value using the risk-free rate. In this example, the rate is expected to remain at 3% per year throughout the option period, but it could be independently specified for each period—another advantage the binomial model has over the more rigid BSM. The sum of these present value computations measures the cost of compensation incorporated in the option grant, regardless of what pattern of exercise ultimately is revealed, since at the grant date, using the available information about stock price volatility, expected dividends, exercise behavior and the risk-free rate, this best measures the value of what was promised to the employees.

The following graphic offers a visual representation of the model, although in practice it is not necessary to prepare such a document. The actual calculations can be made by computer program, but to illustrate the application of the binomial model, the computation will be presented explicitly here. There are four possible scenarios under which, in this example, holders will exercise the options, and thus the options will have value. All other scenarios (combinations of stock price movements over the 2-year horizon) will cause the holders to allow the options to expire unexercised.

First, if the stock price goes to $45 in the first year, one-half the holders will exercise at that point, paying the exercise price of $43 per share. This results in a gain of $2 ($45 – $43) per share. However, having waited until the first year-end, they lost the opportunity to receive the $0.50 per share dividend, so the net economic gain is only $1.50 ($2.00 – $0.50) per share. As this occurs after 1 year, the present value is only $1.50 x 1.03^{-1} = $1.46 per share. When this is weighted by the probability of this outcome obtaining (given that the stock price rise to $45 in the first year has only a 1/3 probability of happening, and given further that only one-half the option holders would elect to exercise under such conditions), the actual expected value of this outcome is [(1/3)(1/2)($1.46)] = $0.24. More formally,

[(1/3)(1/2)($2.00 – $0.50)] x 1.03^{-1} = $0.2427

The second potentially favorable outcome to holders would be if the stock price rises to $45 the first year and then either rises another $5 the second year or holds steady at $45 during the second year. In either event, the option holders who did not exercise after the first year's stock price rise will all exercise at the end of the second year, before the options expire. If the price goes to $50 the second year, the holders will reap a gross gain of $7 ($50 – $43) per share; if it remains constant at $45, the gross gain is only $2 per share. In either case, dividends in both years 1 and 2 will have been foregone. To calculate the compensation cost associated with these branches of the model, the first-year dividend lost must be discounted for 1 year, and the gross gain and second-year dividend must be discounted for 2 years. Also, the probabilities of the entire sequence of events must be used, taking into account the likelihood of the first year's stock price rise, the proclivity of holders to wait for a second year to elapse, and the likelihood of a second-year price rise or price stability. These computations are shown below.

For the outcome if the stock price rises again

[(1/3)(1/2)(1/3)]{[($7.00) x 1.03^{-2}] – [($0.50) x 1.03^{-1}] – [$0.50 x 1.03^{-2}]} = [0.05544]{$6.59 – $0.48 – $0.47} = $0.31276

For the outcome if the stock price remains stable

[(1/3)(1/2)(1/3)]{[($2.00) x 1.03^{-2}] – [($0.50) x 1.03^{-1}] – [($0.50) x 1.03^{-2}]} = [0.05544]{$1.88 – $0.48 – $0.47} = $0.05147

The final, favorable outcome for holders would occur if the stock price holds constant at $40 the first year but rises to $45 the second year, making exercise the right decision. Note that none of the holders would exercise after the first year given that the price, $40, was below exercise price. The calculation for this sequence of events is as follows:

[(1/3)(1/3)]{[($2.00) x 1.03^{-2}] – [($0.50) x 1.03^{-1}] – [($0.50) x 1.03^{-2}]} = [0.1111]{$1.88 – $0.48 – $0.47} = $0.10295

Summing these values yields $0.709879 ($0.2427 + $0.31276 + $0.05147 + $0.10295), which is the expected value per option granted. When this per-unit value is then multiplied by the number of options granted, 10,000, the total compensation cost to be recognized, $7,098.79, is derived. This would be attributed over the required service period, which is illustrated later in this section. (In the facts of this example, no vesting requirements were specified; in such cases, the employees would not have to provide future service in order to earn the right to the options, and the entire cost would be recognized upon grant.)

A big advantage of the binomial model is that it can value an option that is exercisable before the end of its term (an American-style option). This is the style that employee stock options normally take. FASB prefers the binomial model because it can incorporate the unique features of employee stock options. Two key features that FASB recommends that companies incorporate into the binomial model are vesting restrictions and early exercise. Doing so, however, requires that the reporting entity had previous experience with employee behaviors (e.g., with past employee option programs) that would provide it with a basis for making estimates of future behavior.

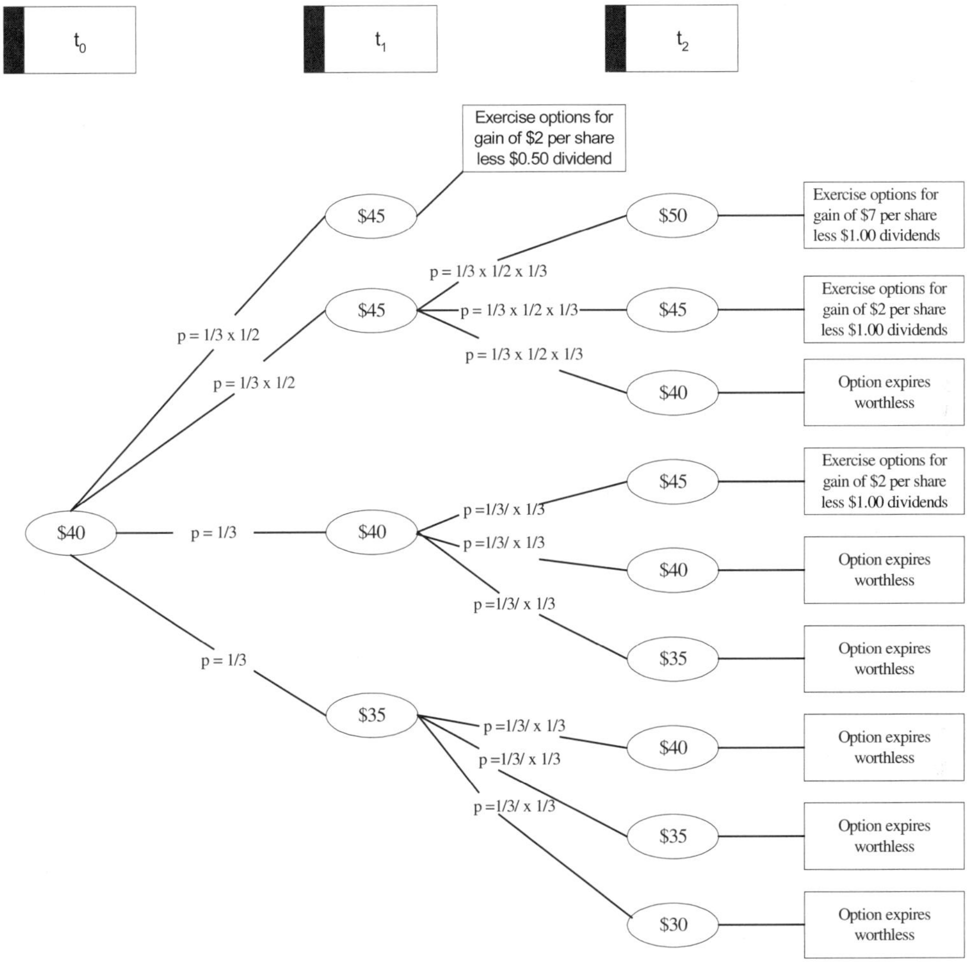

The binomial model permits the specification of more assumptions than does the BSM, which has generated the perception that the binomial will more readily be manipulated so as to result in lower option values, and hence lower compensation costs, than the BSM. But, this is not necessarily the case: switching from BSM to the binomial model can increase, maintain, or decrease the option's value. Having the ability to specify additional parameters, however, does probably give management greater flexibility and, accordingly, will present additional challenges for the auditors who must attest to the financial statement effects of management's specification of these variables.

To calculate either the BSM or binomial models without the aid of computer software would be very difficult. Fortunately, reasonably priced software is available to perform these calculations. What managers must do is determine the assumptions that should be used to create an unbiased, representative value of the options. We now turn to specific examples of accounting for share-based compensation as required under this new ED.

Example of accounting for stock options for a nonpublic entity that is not an SEC registrant and elects the intrinsic value method

Options are granted to corporate officers to purchase 10,000 shares of $1 par stock at a price of $50 per share, when the current market price is $50. The options may not be exercised until 3 years from the grant date. These options have no intrinsic value ($50 – $50 = 0) at the grant date. The intrinsic value method and fair value method require the same measurement date (grant date) for shares and similar instruments whose fair value does not differ from their intrinsic value (and instruments with no time value). This example assumes there is no forfeiture before vesting occurs. Because of the company's decision to use the intrinsic value method, its share options are recognized at intrinsic value at each reporting date through the date of settlement, and the periodic adjustment in intrinsic value, prorated over the service period, is included in compensation cost for that period. Note that this contrasts with the intrinsic value method under superseded APB 25, where only the grant date intrinsic value was relevant. Consequently, the compensation cost recognized each year of the 3-year requisite service period will vary based on changes in the share option's intrinsic value. For example, assume that at the end of year 1 stock is valued at $55 per share, resulting in a $5 ($55 – $50) intrinsic value per share—thus, a total value of $50,000 for the award. In year 1 the compensation cost would be 1/3 of $50,000.

Compensation cost	16,667	
Additional paid-in capital		16,667

Assume that at the end of year 2 the stock is valued at $53 per share, and thus the intrinsic value is $3 per share option ($53 – $50), for an intrinsic value of the award of $30,000. The intrinsic value of the award has declined by $20,000 ($50,000 – $30,000). Because services for 2 of the 3 years of service have now been rendered, the company must recognize *cumulative* compensation cost for two-thirds of the intrinsic value of the award, or $20,000 ($30,000 x 2/3). However, the company already recognized $16,667 in the first year, so only $3,333 in further compensation cost needs to be recognized in year 2.

Compensation cost	3,333	
Additional paid-in capital		3,333

Note that, depending on the change in intrinsic value from the prior reporting date, the current period could be credited with *negative* compensation expense.

Example of fair value accounting for stock options with cliff vesting—measurement and grant date the same

Options are granted to corporate officers to purchase 10,000 shares of $1 par stock at a price of $50 per share, which is also the market price on the grant date. The options may not be exercised until 3 years from the grant date. The company has no reason to expect that any of the options will be forfeited by the employees to whom they are granted. The company uses the following assumptions to apply the binomial model:

Share options granted	10,000
Employees granted options	100
Expected forfeitures per year	3.0%
Share price at the grant date	$50
Exercise price	$50
Par value per share	$1
Number of years to vest	3 years
Contractual term (CT) of options	10 years
Risk-free interest rate over CT	2 to 5%
Expected volatility over CT	40 to 700%
Expected dividend yield	1.0%
Suboptimal exercise factor	2

Given these assumptions needed to construct a binomial model to value the options, a fair value estimate of approximately $6 per option is determined (details not presented). It is estimated that 3% of employees will turn over each year and that these will not vest. The number of share options expected to vest is estimated at the grant date of 9,127 (10,000 x .97 x .97 x .97). The estimated fair value of the award on the grant date would be $54,762 (9,127 x $6). The entry to record the compensation cost [($54,762 ÷ 3) = $18,254] in each of the years 1, 2, and 3 is

Compensation cost	18,254	
Additional paid-in capital		18,254

While deferred taxes are ignored for purposes of this example, in general the recognition of expense for tax purposes would be in a later period, necessitating the recording of a deferred tax benefit.

If in year 1, the actual forfeiture rate is 6% instead of the 3% expected rate, and management determines that the forfeiture rate should change to 6%, then in year 2 an adjustment would be needed. The revised estimate of the number of options expected to vest is 8,306 (10,000 x .94 x .94 x .94). The revised cumulative compensation cost would be $49,836 (8,306 x $6). The cumulative adjustment to reflect adjustment of the forfeiture rate is the difference between two-thirds of the revised cost of the award and the cost already recognized in year 1. The related entries and computations are

Revised total compensation cost	$49,836
Revised cumulative cost as of the end of year 1	$16,112
Cost already recognized in year 1	$18,254
Adjustment to cost at the end of year 1	$(2,142)

The related journal entries are

Additional paid-in capital	2,142	
Compensation cost		2,142

Entries in years 2 and 3

Compensation cost	16,112	
Additional paid-in capital		16,112

At the end of the third year, the company would examine actual forfeitures and make any necessary adjustments to reflect compensation cost for the number of shares actually vested. Assuming vesting equals expected, the journal entry at exercise of the options would be

Cash	500,000 (option price)	
Additional paid-in capital	49,836	
Common stock		10,000 (par)
Additional paid-in capital		539,836 (excess)

The difference between the market price of the shares and the exercise price at the date of exercise is deductible for tax purposes because the share options do not qualify as incentive stock options. The realized tax benefits result in a credit to additional paid-in capital and a reduction in the deferred tax asset. (For further details on the income tax effects see the ED, Appendix B, which provides more detailed examples.)

The statement of cash flows, as amended by this ED, requires that the cash flow benefit that results from the tax benefit be classified as a cash inflow from financing activities and a cash outflow from operating activities.

Example of accounting for stock options with graded vesting—measurement and grant date the same

This ED requires that each separately vesting part of an award with a graded vesting schedule be measured and recognized as a separate award. It also requires that compensation cost for each part be recognized over the requisite service period for that part. The accounting is provided for this and assumes the same assumptions as in the previous example. The 10,000 options vest according to a graded schedule of 25% for the first and second years of service and 50% for the third year. Using the 3% annual employee turnover forfeiture rate, 300 options are expected to never vest, leaving 9,700 options expected to vest at 25% of the award—or 2,425 options vested. In the second year, another 3% are expected to be forfeited, leaving 9,409 to vest at 25% of the award—or 2,352 options vested. In the final year another 3% are forfeited and vesting occurs at 50% of the remaining—or 4,563 vested options.

Year	*Vested option*	*Value per option*	*Compensation cost*
1	2,425	$5.00	$12,125
2	2,352	$5.50	12,936
3	4,563	6.00	27,378
	9,340		$52,439

The value of the option is determined separately for different vesting periods after which exercise might occur. Thus, the compensation cost associated with the options is less in the earlier years, as reflected in the table above. Compensation cost is recognized over the periods of requisite service during which each group of share options is earned. In year 1, therefore, compensation cost is $27,719 [$12,125 + ($12,936 ÷ 2) + ($27,378 ÷ 3)]. The journal entry for year 1 would be

Compensation cost	27,719	
Additional paid-in capital		27,719

Example of accounting for SAR—share-based liabilities

The company grants SAR with the same terms and conditions used in the examples above. Each SAR entitles the holder to receive an amount in cash equal to the increase in value of one share of company stock over $50. Using the same assumptions and option-pricing model the fair value of the share options is computed to be $6 per SAR (details not presented). The awards cliff-vest at the end of 3 years. The forfeitures are expected to be 3% a year: SAR expected to vest are 9,127 (10,000 x .97 x .97 x .97). Thus the fair value of the award at the beginning of year 1 is $54,762 (9,127 x $6). We assume expected and actual forfeitures are the same. The share-based compensation liability at the end of year 1 is $18,254 ($54,762 ÷ 3). The journal entry for year 1 is

Compensation cost	18,254	
Share-based compensation SAR liability		18,254

At the end of year 2, the estimated fair value is assumed to be $10 per SAR. Therefore, the award's fair value is $91,270 (9,270 x $10) and the corresponding liability at that date is $60,847 ($91,270 x 2/3) because service has been provided for 2 of the 3 years of requisite service. Compensation cost recognized for the award in year 2 is $42,593 ($60,847 – $18,254). The journal entry for year 2 is

Compensation cost	42,593	
Share-based compensation SAR liability		42,593

At the end of year 3 the estimated fair value is assumed to be $9 per SAR. Therefore, the award's fair value is $83,430 (9,270 x $9) and the corresponding liability at that date is the same because the award is fully vested. Compensation cost for year 3 is $22,583 ($83,430 – $42,593 – $18,254). The journal entry for year 3 is

Compensation cost	22,583	
Share-based compensation SAR liability		22,583

If the SAR were to be redeemed in common stock, "Stock rights outstanding" (a paid-in capital account) would replace the liability account in the above entries. Often stock option plans and SAR are joined in tandem plans, under the terms of which the exercise of one automatically cancels the other. In the absence of evidence to the contrary, however, the presumption is that the SAR, not the options, will be exercised.

Example of a liability to equity modification

Assume the same facts as in the example above. At the end of year 1 the fair value is $10 per SAR. The share-based compensation liability is $30,423 (9,127 x $10 ÷ 3) and the journal entry would be the same as the above example at the end of year 1. On January 1 of year 2, however, the company modifies the SAR by replacing the cash-settlement feature with a net-share settlement feature, which converts the award from a liability award to an equity award because there is no longer an obligation to settle for cash, or an obligation classified as a liability per FAS 150. The estimated fair value is unchanged at $10 per SAR, nor is vesting behavior changed. At the modification date, services for 1/3 of the award have been provided. The original grant-date fair value of the award is $54,762 (9,127 x $6) and the cumulative compensation cost, had the award been classified as equity at the grant date, is $18,254. The additional compensation cost recognized at the modification date is $24,339 ($54,762 – $30,423). The journal entry would be

Compensation cost	24,339	
Share-based compensation SAR liability		24,339

Other ED Matters

The most common share-based compensation arrangements have been presented. Other more complicated awards have been and will continue to be developed. Some of these are presented below. For a further discussion with examples refer to the ED.

Share options with performance conditions and/or market conditions. Some option arrangements provide grants of share options with a performance condition. These types of plans permit employees to vest in differing numbers of options depending on the increase in market value of one of the company's products (or other condition) over a vesting period. These performance conditions can include factors such as market share increases, passing clinical trials, and other performance goals.

In addition to performance conditions, market conditions may also affect the option arrangements. These would include such things as indexing share prices to an industry group and the exercise price of options tied to this index. Therefore, the exercise price could go up or down depending on how the index performs. Arrangements exist for share units to have both performance and market conditions. These are accounted for in the same way as other options. The difficulty is in determining the fair values, as there are more factors contributing to uncertainty. These factors can, however, be modeled in a binomial valuation model.

Modifications of share option awards. A company may modify the vesting conditions of an award. The accounting treatment for these modifications depends on the probability of vesting under the original conditions or the modified conditions. Other modifications are whether SAR will be settled in cash or equity or some combination, different from the original plan assumptions. A modification of vesting conditions is accounted for based on the principles set forth in the ED. Illustrations of different potential modifications are illustrated in Appendix B of the ED.

Other types of share-based compensation awards covered in the ED. Other share awards that the ED covers are outlined below.

- Share award with a clawback feature: These are restrictions on the employee's subsequent employment with a direct competitor, which if violated cause the ex-employee to return the value of the share award to the company.
- Tandem plan—share options or cash SAR: Employees are granted awards with two separate components, in which exercise of one component cancels the other.
- Tandem plan—phantom shares or share options: Similar to the plan above, but the employee's choice of which component to exercise depends on the relative value of the components when the award is exercised.
- Look-back share options: Share options awarded under Section 423 of the Internal Revenue Code, which provides that employees will not be immediately taxed on the difference between the market price of the stock and a discounted purchase price if certain requirements are met.
- Employee share purchase plans: Employee share purchase plans are not compensatory if their terms are no more favorable than those available to all holders of the same

class of shares and if all employees that meet limited employment qualifications may participate in the plan on an equitable basis.

- Book value share purchase plans (nonpublic companies only): Companies with two classes of stock—one of which is available to all employees and the price is based on book value.
- Voluntary (or involuntary) change to fair-value-based method (nonpublic companies only): A nonpublic company elects as accounting policy the intrinsic value method and grants share awards to employees. Subsequently, the accounting for the value of these awards is changed to fair value because it is preferable under GAAP. Estimating grant date values is very difficult in hindsight. Therefore, these companies do not have to retrospectively apply fair value methods to unvested awards at the date of change.
- Certain instruments become subject to FAS 150: Certain instruments will become subject to FAS 150 when an employee could terminate service and receive or retain the fair value of the instrument for the remaining contractual term of that instrument.

Disclosure requirements under this ED. For a company to achieve the objectives of the ED the minimum information needed to achieve disclosure objectives are set forth below.

- A description of the share-based payment arrangements, including the terms of the awards. A nonpublic company should disclose its policy for measuring compensation cost.
- The most recent income statement should provide the number and weighted-average exercise prices of the share options and equity instruments.
- Each year for which an income statement is provided, a company should provide the weighted-average grant-date fair value of equity options and the intrinsic value of options exercised during the year.
- For fully vested share options and those expected to vest at the latest balance sheet date, the company should provide the number, weighted-average exercise price, aggregate intrinsic value, and contractual terms of options outstanding and currently exercisable.
- If more than one share-based plan is in effect, the information should be provided separately for different types of awards.
- For each year for which an income statement is provided, companies should provide the following:
  - Companies that do not use the intrinsic value method should provide a description of the method of determining fair value and a description of the assumptions used.
  - Total compensation cost for share-based payment arrangements, including tax benefits and capitalization of compensation costs should be stated.
  - Descriptions of significant modifications and numbers of employees affected should also be provided.
- On the latest balance sheet date the total compensation cost related to nonvested awards not yet recognized and the period over which they are expected to be recognized.
- The amount of cash received from exercise of share-based compensation and the amount of cash used to settle equity instruments should be disclosed.
- Description of the company's policy for issuing shares upon share options exercise, including the source of the shares.

APPENDIX B

FINANCIAL STATEMENT PRESENTATION

This appendix provides an illustration of the various financial statements that may be required to be presented and are related to the stockholders' equity section of the balance sheet.

Stockholders' Equity Section of a Balance Sheet

Capital stock:		
Preferred stock, $100 par, 7% cumulative, 30,000 shares authorized, issued, and outstanding		$ 3,000,000
Common stock, no par, stated value $10 per share, 500,000 shares authorized, 415,000 shares issued		4,150,000
Total capital stock		$ 7,150,000
Additional paid-in capital:		
Issued price in excess of par value—preferred	$ 150,000	
Issued price in excess of stated value—common	845,000	995,000
Total paid-in capital		$ 8,145,000
Donated capital		100,000
Retained earnings:		
Appropriated for plant expansion	$2,100,000	
Unappropriated	2,110,000	4,210,000
Accumulated other comprehensive income		165,000
Total capital, retained earnings, and accumulated other comprehensive income		$12,620,000
Less 10,000 common shares held in treasury, at cost		(120,000)
Total stockholders' equity		$12,500,000

Retained Earnings Statement

Balance at beginning of year, as reported	$ 3,800,000
Prior period adjustment—correction of an error in method of depreciation (less tax effect of $77,000)	115,000
Balance at beginning of year, restated	$ 3,915,000
Net income for the year	583,000
Cash dividends declared during the year	
Preferred stock	(210,000)
Common stock	(78,000)
Balance at end of year	$ 4,210,000

Statement of Changes in Stockholders' Equity

	Preferred stock		*Common stock*		*Additional paid-in capital*	*Donated capital*	*Retained earnings*	*Accumulated other comprehensive income**	*Treasury stock (common)*	*Total stockholders' equity*
	Shares	*Amount*	*Shares*	*Amount*						
Balance, 12/31/00, as reported	--	--	400,000	$4,000,000	$840,000	$100,000	$3,800,000	$ 56,000	$(120,000)	$ 8,676,000
Correction of an error in method of depr.	--	--	--	--	--	--	115,000		--	115,000
Balance, 12/31/00, restated	--	--	400,000	$4,000,000	$840,000	$100,000	$3,915,000		$(120,000)	$ 8,791,000
Preferred stock issued in public offering	30,000	$3,000,000	--	--	150,000	--	--		--	3,150,000
Stock options exercised	--	--	15,000	150,000	5,000	--	--		--	155,000
Net income	--	--	--	--	--	--	583,000		--	583,000
Cash dividends declared:										
Preferred, $7.00 per share	--	--	--	--	--	--	(210,000)		--	(210,000)
Common, $.20 per share	--	--	--	--	--	--	(78,000)		--	(78,000)
Unrealized holding gains on available-for-sale securities arising during period								85,000		
Less: Reclassification for adjustment of gains included in net income								(12,000)		
Foreign currency translation adjustments								36,000		
Total other comprehensive income								109,000		
Balance, 12/31/01	30,000	$3,000,000	415,000	$4,150,000	$995,000	$100,000	$4,210,000	$165,000	$(120,000)	$12,500,000

* *Comprehensive income for the period:*

Net income	*$748,000*
Other comprehensive income	*109,000*
	$857,000

18 EARNINGS PER SHARE

PERSPECTIVE AND ISSUES

Earnings per share (EPS) is an indicator widely used by both actual and prospective investors to gauge the profitability of a corporation. Its purpose is to indicate how effective an enterprise has been in using the resources provided by its common stockholders. In its simplest form, EPS is net income (loss) divided by the number of shares of outstanding common stock. The EPS computation becomes more complex with the existence of securities that are not common stock but have the potential of causing additional shares of common stock to be issued (e.g., convertible preferred stock, convertible debt, options, and warrants). Omission of an EPS number that takes into account the potential dilutive effects of such securities would be misleading. In addition, a lack of standardization in the way in which these securities are included in such an EPS computation would make comparisons among corporations extremely difficult.

In an effort to integrate with international reporting standards and to simplify reporting practices on EPS, the FASB issued FAS 128 in February 1997. FAS 128 established standards for computing and presenting EPS for public companies. If, however, a nonpublic company chooses to disclose EPS, it is required to do so in accordance with FAS 128.

Publicly traded corporations with a complex capital structure are obligated to report basic EPS and diluted EPS. The dual presentation is required on the face of the corporation's income statement even if both of these computations result in the same EPS amount. In addition, a reconciliation of the numerator and the denominator of the basic EPS computation to the numerator and denominator of the diluted EPS computation is required.

Basic EPS, which includes no dilution, is computed by dividing income available to common stockholders by the weighted-average number of shares outstanding for the period. In contrast, diluted EPS considers the potential dilution that could occur from other financial instruments that would increase the total number of outstanding shares of common stock.

FAS 129 established standards for disclosing information about an entity's capital structure. This statement consolidated the standards related to the disclosure of information about an entity's capital structure in one pronouncement. FAS 129 applies to all entities, public and nonpublic. Companies are required to disclose the rights and privileges of each type of security outstanding. Examples of disclosures include company policies on participation rights, on the liquidation of preferred stock, and on redeemable stock.

Sources of GAAP

APB	*FAS*	*FIN*	*FTB*	*EITF*
30	128, 129, 150	28	79-8	92-3, 00-19, 03-6, D-42, D-53, D-62, D-72, D-82

DEFINITIONS OF TERMS

There are a number of terms used in the discussion of earnings per share that have special meanings in that context. When used, they are intended to have the meanings given in the following definitions.

Antidilution (antidilutive). An increase in earnings per share or reduction in net loss per share resulting from the conversion, exercise, or contingent issuance of certain securities.

Basic earnings per share (basic EPS). The portion of net income available to each share of common stock outstanding during the reporting period.

Call option. A contract that allows the holder to buy a specified quantity of stock from the writer of the contract at a fixed price for a given period. Refer to **option** and **purchased call option**.

Common stock. A stock that is subordinate to all other stock of the issuer.

Contingent issuance. A possible issuance of shares of common stock that is dependent upon the exercise of conversion rights, options or warrants, the satisfaction of certain conditions, or similar arrangements.

Contingent stock agreement. An agreement to issue common stock (usually in connection with a business combination) that is dependent on the satisfaction of certain conditions.

Contingently issuable shares (contingently issuable stock). Shares issuable for little or no cash consideration upon the satisfaction of certain conditions pursuant to a contingent stock agreement.

Conversion price. The price that determines the number of shares of common stock into which a security is convertible. For example, $100 face value of debt convertible into five shares of common stock has a conversion price of $20 per share.

Conversion rate. The ratio of (1) the number of common shares issuable upon conversion to (2) a unit of convertible security. For example, a class of preferred stock may be convertible at the rate of three shares of common stock for each share of preferred stock.

Convertible security. A security that is exchangeable for another security based on a stated rate; for example, convertible preferred stock that is convertible into common stock on a two-for-one basis (two shares of common stock for each share of preferred stock).

Conversion value. The current market value of the common shares obtainable upon conversion of a convertible security, after deducting any cash payment required upon conversion.

Diluted earnings per share (diluted EPS or DEPS). The portion of net income available to each share of common stock outstanding during the reporting period and to each share that would have been outstanding assuming the issuance of common shares for all dilutive potential common shares outstanding during the reporting period.

Dilution (Dilutive). A reduction in earnings per share or an increase in net loss per share resulting from assuming that convertible securities have been converted or that options and warrants have been exercised or other shares have been issued upon the fulfillment of certain conditions.

Dual presentation. The presentation with equal prominence of two types of earnings per share amounts on the face of the income statement: one is basic earnings per share (EPS), the other is diluted earnings per share (DEPS).

Earnings per (common) share (EPS). The amount of net income attributable to each outstanding share of common stock. For convenience, the term is used in FAS 128 to refer to either net income (earnings) per share or net loss per share. The term is only permitted to be used without qualifying language when no potentially dilutive convertible securities, options, warrants, or other agreements providing for contingent issuances of common stock are outstanding during the period.

Exercise price. The amount that must be paid for a share of common stock upon exercise of a stock option or warrant.

If-converted method. A method of computing earnings per share that assumes conversion of convertible securities as of the beginning of the earliest period reported (or at the actual time of issuance, if later).

Income available to common stockholders. Income (or loss) from continuing operations or net income (or net loss) adjusted by subtracting preferred stock dividends.

Mandatorily redeemable instrument. A financial instrument, often issued in the form of a share, that requires the issuer to transfer assets to the holder in exchange for canceling the instrument on either a specified date (or dates), or upon occurrence of an event that is certain to occur. In accordance with FAS 150, such instruments are considered liabilities and are not classified as equity in the issuer's balance sheet.

Option. Unless otherwise stated in FAS 128, a call option that gives the holder the right to purchase shares of common stock in accordance with an agreement upon payment of a specified amount, including, but not limited to, options granted to and stock purchase agreements entered into with employees. Options are considered "securities" in FAS 128. Refer to **Call option**.

Potential common stock. A security or other contract that may entitle its holder to obtain common stock during the reporting period or after the end of the reporting period.

Preferred stock. A class of capital stock, typically nonvoting, whose holders have rights to receive distributions (dividends or liquidating distributions) that have a higher priority than distributions to the common stockholders. Common stockholders are not entitled to receive corporate distributions until all required higher-priority distributions to preferred stockholders have been made.

Purchased call option. A contract that allows the reporting entity to buy a specified quantity of its own stock from the writer of the contract at a fixed price for a given period. Refer to **Call option**.

Put option. A contract that allows the holder to sell a specified quantity of stock to the writer of the contract at a fixed price during a given period.

Redemption price. The amount that the issuer of a security is required to pay to the holder at maturity or under a sinking fund arrangement.

Reverse treasury stock method. A method of recognizing the dilutive effect on earnings per share of satisfying a put obligation. It assumes that the proceeds used to buy back common stock (pursuant to the terms of the put option) will be raised from issuing shares at the average market price during the period. Refer to **Put option**.

Rights issue. An offer to existing stockholders to purchase additional shares of common stock in accordance with an agreement for a specified amount (which is generally substantially less than the fair value of the shares) for a given period.

Security. The evidence of a debt or ownership or related right. For purposes of FAS 128, it includes stock options and warrants, as well as debt and stock.

Treasury stock method. A method of recognizing the use of proceeds that would be obtained upon exercise of options and warrants in computing diluted earnings per share. It assumes that any proceeds would be used to repurchase outstanding common stock at average market prices during the period.

Two-class method. A method employed for securities that cannot be accounted for by the if-converted method. This method computes earnings per share by treating participating securities as though they were common stocks with different dividend rates from that of the other common stock.

Warrant. A security issued by a corporation entitling the holder to purchase a specified number of shares of stock at a stated price, usually above the stock's market price at the time that the warrant is issued. Similar to call options, warrants are effective for a longer period of time. Warrants are often issued in tandem with another class of security (e.g., bonds or preferred stock) in order to provide an incentive to potential investors to purchase the other security.

Weighted-average number of shares. The number of shares outstanding determined by relating (1) the portion of time within a reporting period that a particular number of shares of a certain security has been outstanding to (2) the total time in that period. For example, if 100 shares of a certain security were outstanding during the first quarter of a fiscal year and 300 shares were outstanding during the balance of the year, the weighted-average number of outstanding shares would be 250 [(100 x 1/4) + (300 x 3/4)]. In computing DEPS, equivalent common shares are considered for all dilutive potential common shares.

CONCEPTS, RULES, AND EXAMPLES

Simple Capital Structure

Simple capital structures are those having no potential common shares (options, warrants, etc.). These entities will only have basic EPS. All other entities are considered to have a complex capital structure. Entities with a complex capital structure will have **potential common stock** in the form of potentially dilutive **securities, options, warrants,** or other rights that upon conversion or exercise would dilute **earnings per common share**. **Dilutive** securities have the potential upon their issuance to reduce earnings per share.

Computational guidelines. The basic EPS calculation is **income available to common stockholders** (the numerator) divided by the **weighted-average number of common shares outstanding** (the denominator) during the period. The objective of the basic EPS calculation is to measure the performance of the entity over the reporting period. Complexities arise because net income does not necessarily represent the earnings available to the common stockholder, and a simple weighted-average of common shares outstanding does not necessarily reflect the true nature of the situation.

Numerator. The income available to common stockholders used as the numerator in any of the EPS computations must be reduced by any preferential claims against it by other securities. The justification for this reduction is that the preferential claims of the other securities must be satisfied before any income is available to the common stockholder. These other securities are usually in the form of **preferred stock,** and the deduction from income is the amount of the dividend declared (whether or not paid) during the year on the preferred stock. If the preferred stock is cumulative, the dividend is deducted from income (added to the loss) whether or not declared. Dividends in arrears do not affect the calculation of EPS in the current period; such dividends have been included in prior periods' EPS computations. However, the amount in arrears is required to be disclosed, as well as the effects on the EPS calculation of the rights given to holders of preferential securities.

Denominator. The weighted-average number of common stock shares outstanding is "an arithmetical mean average of shares outstanding and assumed to be outstanding for EPS computations" (FAS 128). The difficulty in computing the weighted-average exists because of the effect that various transactions have on the computation of common shares outstanding. While it is impossible to analyze all the possibilities, FAS 128 provides discussion of some of the more common transactions affecting the number of common shares outstanding. By analogy, the theoretical model set forth in these relatively simple examples can be applied to situations that are not explicitly discussed.

If a company reacquires its stock (treasury stock), the number of shares reacquired is excluded from EPS calculations as of the date of reacquisition. The same theory holds for the issuance of common stock during the period. The number of shares newly issued is included in the computation only for the period after their issuance date. The logic for this treatment is that the proceeds from issuance of the shares were not available to the company to generate earnings until the shares were issued. This same logic applies to the reacquired shares because the cash paid to reacquire those shares was no longer available to generate earnings after the reacquisition date.

A **stock dividend or split** does not generate additional consideration, but it does increase the number of shares outstanding. FAS 128 states that the increase in shares as a result of a stock split or dividend, or decrease in shares as a result of a reverse split, is to be given retroactive recognition as an appropriate equivalent charge for all periods presented. Thus, even if a stock dividend or split occurs at the end of the period, it is considered outstanding for the entirety of **each** period presented. The reasoning is that a stock dividend or split has no effect on the ownership percentage of the common stockholder. As such, to show a dilution in the EPS reported would erroneously give the impression of a decline in profitability when in fact it was merely an increase in the shares outstanding due to the stock dividend or split. FAS 128 carries this principle one step further by requiring the retroactive adjustment of outstanding shares for stock dividends or splits occurring after the end of the period, but before the release of the financial statements. The rationale for this adjustment is that the primary interest of the financial statement user is considered to be the company's current capitalization. If this situation occurs, disclosure of both the end-of-year outstanding shares and those used to compute EPS is required.

When shares are issued in connection with a business combination that occurs during the period, they are treated as issued and outstanding as of the date of the acquisition.

Weighted-Average (WA) Computation

Transaction	*Effect on WA computation*
• Common stock outstanding at the beginning of the period	• Included in number of shares outstanding
• Issuance of common stock	• Increase number of shares outstanding by the number of shares issued times the portion of the year outstanding
• Conversion into common stock	• Increase number of shares outstanding by the number of shares converted times the portion of the year outstanding
• Reacquisition of common stock	• Decrease number of shares outstanding by number of shares reacquired times portion of the year since reacquisition
• Stock dividend or split	• Increase number of shares outstanding by number of shares issued for the dividend or resulting from the split retroactively as of the beginning of the earliest period presented
• Reverse split	• Decrease number of shares outstanding by decrease in shares retroactively as of the beginning of the earliest period presented
• Business combination	• Increase number of shares outstanding by number of shares issued times portion of year since acquisition

The table does not provide for all of the possible complexities arising in the EPS computation; however, most of the others occur under a complex capital structure. The complications arising under a complex capital structure are discussed and illustrated in detail later in this chapter and in its Appendix. The illustration below applies some of the foregoing concepts to a simple capital structure.

Example of EPS computation—Simple capital structure

Assume the following information:

	Numerator information			*Denominator information*	
a.	Income from continuing operations before extraordinary items	$130,000	a.	Common shares outstanding 1/1/04	100,000
b.	Extraordinary loss (net of income tax)	(30,000)	b.	Shares issued for cash 4/1/04	20,000
c.	Net income	100,000	c.	Shares issued in 10% stock dividend declared in July 2004	12,000
d.	6% cumulative preferred stock, $100 par, 1,000 shrs. issued and outstanding	100,000	d.	Shares of treasury stock reacquired 10/1/04	10,000

When calculating the numerator, the claims related to the preferred stock are deducted to arrive at the income available to the common stockholders. In this example, the preferred stock is cumulative. Thus, regardless of whether or not the board of directors declares a preferred dividend, holders of the preferred stock have a claim of $6,000 (1,000 shares x $100 par x 6%) against 2004 earnings. Therefore, $6,000 must be deducted from the numerator to arrive at the income available to common stockholders. Note that any cumulative preferred dividends in arrears are ignored in computing this period's EPS since they would have been incorporated into previous periods' EPS calculations. Also note that this $6,000 would have been deducted for **non**cumulative preferred stock only if a dividend of this amount had been declared during the period.

The EPS calculations follow:

Earnings per common share:

On income from continuing operations before extraordinary item $\quad \dfrac{\$130{,}000 - \$6{,}000}{\text{Common shares outstanding}}$

On net income $\frac{\$100,000 - \$6,000}{\text{Common shares outstanding}}$

The computation of the denominator is based upon the weighted-average number of common shares outstanding. A simple weighted-average is not considered appropriate because of the various complexities. Table 1 illustrates one way of computing the weighted-average number of shares outstanding.

Table 1

Item	*Actual number of shares*	*Retroactive effects of July stock dividend*	*Subtotal number of shares deemed outstanding*	*Fraction of the year deemed outstanding*	*Shares times fraction of the year deemed outstanding*
Number of shares as of beginning of the year 1/1/04	100,000	10,000 [10%(100,000)]	110,000	12/12	110,000
Shares issued 4/1/04	20,000	2,000 [10%(20,000)]	22,000	9/12	16,500
Treasury shares reacquired 10/1/04	(10,000)	--	(10,000)	3/12	(2,500)
Weighted-average number of common shares outstanding					124,000

The stock dividend declared in July is treated as being retroactive to the beginning of the year. Thus, for the period 1/1 through 4/1, 110,000 shares are considered to be outstanding. When shares are issued, they are included in the weighted-average beginning with the date of issuance. The shares issued as a result of the stock dividend applicable to the 20,000 newly issued shares are also assumed to have been outstanding for the same period as the 20,000 shares. Thus, we can see that of the 12,000-share stock dividend, 10,000 shares relate to the beginning balance and 2,000 shares to the new issuance (10% of 100,000 and 20,000, respectively). The reacquisition of the treasury stock requires that these shares be excluded from the calculation for the remainder of the period after their reacquisition date. This amount is subtracted from the calculation because the shares were reacquired from shares outstanding prior to their reacquisition.

To complete the example, we divide the previously computed numerator by the weighted-average number of common shares outstanding to arrive at EPS.

Earnings per common share:

On income from continuing operations before extraordinary item $\frac{\$130,000 - \$6,000}{124,000 \text{ common shares}} = \$1.00$

On net income $\frac{\$100,000 - \$6,000}{124,000 \text{ common shares}} = \$\ .76$

The numbers computed above are required to be presented on the face of the income statement. Reporting a $.24 extraordinary loss per share ($30,000 extraordinary item ÷ 124,000 common shares) is required either on the face of the income statement or in the notes to the financial statements.

Preferred stock dividends payable in common shares. All dividends represent distributions of accumulated earnings, and accordingly, are not reported as expenses on the income statement under GAAP. However, as illustrated above, for purposes of computing earnings per share, preferred dividends must be deducted in order to ascertain how much income is available for common stockholders. In some cases, preferred dividends are not payable in cash, but rather in common shares (based on market value as of the date of declaration, typically). In certain cases, the dividends may be payable in common shares or cash at the issuer's option.

FAS 128 defines income available to common stockholders as "income (or loss) from continuing operations or net income (or net loss) adjusted for preferred stock dividends."

Logic suggests that this adjustment be made for all preferred stock dividends, regardless of the form of payment. This adjustment in computing income available to common stockholders is consistent with the treatment of common stock issued for goods or services.

Complex Capital Structure

The computation of EPS under a complex capital structure involves all of the complexities discussed under the simple structure and many more. A complex capital structure is one that includes securities that grant rights with the potential to be exercised and **reduce** EPS (dilutive securities). Any **antidilutive** securities (those that increase EPS) are not included in the computation of EPS. Note that a complex capital structure requires **dual presentation** of basic EPS and diluted EPS (DEPS). The common stock outstanding and all other dilutive securities are used to compute DEPS.

Diluted earnings per share (DEPS). DEPS represents the earnings attributable to each share of common stock after giving effect to all potentially dilutive securities which were outstanding during the period. The computation of DEPS requires that the following steps be performed:

1. Identify all potentially dilutive securities.
2. Compute dilution, the effects that the other dilutive securities have on net income and common shares outstanding.

Identification of potentially dilutive securities. Dilutive securities are those that have the potential of being exercised and reducing the EPS figure. Some examples of dilutive securities identified by FAS 128 are convertible debt, convertible preferred stock, options, warrants, participating securities, two-class common stocks, and contingent shares.

Convertible securities. A **convertible security** is one type of potentially dilutive security. A security of this type has an inherent dual nature. Convertibles are comprised of two distinct elements: the right to receive dividends or interest, **and** the right to potentially participate in earnings by becoming a common stockholder. This security is included in the DEPS computation due to the latter right.

Options and warrants. Options, warrants, and their equivalents generally derive their value from the right to obtain common stock at specified prices over an extended period of time.

Participating securities and two-class common stocks. The capital structure of some entities includes securities that may participate in dividends with common stocks according to a predetermined formula, or a class of common stock with different dividend rates from those of another class of common stock but without prior or senior rights. EITF 03-6 nullified the option of using the **if-converted method** for those securities that are convertible into common stock if the effect is dilutive. For these securities, participating securities and two-class commons stocks, the **two-class method** of computing EPS, as described below, is used.

Financial instruments with characteristics of both liabilities and equity. FAS 150, issued in May 2003, specifies that certain freestanding financial instruments (as distinguished from compound financial instruments) that may resemble equity are nevertheless required to be classified as liabilities on the issuer's balance sheet. (See Chapter 17.) Such instruments include **mandatorily redeemable financial instruments** (including mandatorily redeemable common or preferred stock) and certain forward contracts that require physical settlement by repurchase of a fixed number of the issuer's equity shares. Issuers of these instruments are required to (1) exclude any shares of common stock that are required to be redeemed or repurchased from the denominator of the EPS and DEPS computations, and (2) apply the two-class method described below to deduct from income available to common stockholders (the numerator of EPS and DEPS computations) any amounts that are attributable to shares that are to be redeemed or repurchased, including contractual dividends and participation rights in undistributed earnings. The deduction described in (2) is limited to amounts not recognized in the issuer's financial statements as interest expense.

The two-class method. The two-class method is an earnings allocation formula that determines earnings per share for each class of common stock and participating security according to dividends declared (or accumulated) and participation rights in undistributed earnings. Under this method, income from continuing operations (or net income) is reduced by the amount of dividends declared in the current period for each class of stock and by the contractual amount of dividends that must be paid for the current period. The remaining earnings are allocated to common stock and participating securities to the extent that each security may share in earnings if all of the earnings for the period had been distributed. The total earnings allocated to each security are determined by adding together the amount allocated for dividends and the amount allocated for a participation feature. The total earnings allocated to each security are divided by the number of outstanding shares of the type of security to which the earnings are allocated to determine the earnings per share for that type of security. An example of the two-class method follows:

Participating convertible preferred stock: Assume that Timp Co. has 100,000 shares of common stock and 10,000 shares of preferred stock outstanding during 2005. Net income is $800,000 for 2005. Each share of preferred stock is convertible into 3 shares of common stock and is entitled to a noncumulative dividend of $6.00 per share. After the common stock has been paid a dividend of $4 per share, the preferred stock then participates in any additional dividends on a 30:70 per share ratio with the common stock. For 2005, the common shareholders have been paid $4.70 per share (or a total of $470,000) and the preferred shareholders have been paid $6.30 per share (or a total of $63,000). Basic earnings per share under the two-class method for 2005 would be computed as follows:

Net income		$800,000
Less dividends paid		
Common	$470,000	
Preferred	63,000	533,000
Undistributed 2005 earnings		$267,000

Allocation of undistributed earnings

To preferred

0.3(10,000) ÷ [.3(10,000 + .7(100,000)] x $267,000 = $10,970
$10,970 ÷ 10,000 shares = $1.097 per share

To common

0.7(100,000) ÷ [.3(10,000 + .7(100,000)] x $267,000 = $256,030
$256,030 ÷ 100,000 shares = $2.56 per share

	Preferred	*Common*
Distributed earning	$6.30	$4.70
Undistributed earnings	1.097	2.56
Totals	$7.397	$7.26

Contingent issuances of common stock. Another consideration is **contingent issuances** of common stock (e.g., stock subscriptions). If shares are to be issued in the future with no restrictions on issuance other than the passage of time, they are to be considered issued and treated as outstanding in the computation of DEPS. Other issuances that are dependent upon certain conditions being met are to be evaluated in a different manner. FAS 128 uses as examples the maintenance of current earnings levels and the attainment of specified earnings increases. If the contingency is to merely maintain the earnings levels currently being attained, then the shares are considered outstanding for the entire period and considered in the computation of DEPS if the effect is dilutive. If the requirement is to increase earnings over a period of time, the DEPS computation includes those shares that would be issued based on the assumption that the current amount of earnings will remain unchanged if the effect is dilutive. Previously reported DEPS are not restated to give recognition to shares issued as a result of the earnings level attainment. If a contingent issuance is based upon the lapsing of time **and** the market price of the stock (which generally affects the number of shares issued), both conditions must be met to include the contingently issuable shares in the DEPS computation. The Board prohibits restatement of DEPS data should fluctuations in the market price occur in future periods.

Computation of DEPS. The second step in the process is the actual computation of DEPS. There are basically two methods used to incorporate the effects of other dilutive securities on EPS (excluding participating and two-class common securities for which the two-class method described above is used).

1. The treasury stock method, and
2. The if-converted method

The treasury stock method. The treasury stock method, which is used for the exercise of most warrants or options, requires that DEPS be computed as if the options or warrants were exercised at the beginning of the period (or actual date of issuance, if later), and that the funds obtained from the exercise were used to purchase (reacquire) the company's common stock at the **average market price** for the period. Note that the proposed amendment to FAS 128, which is outlined at the end of this chapter, would change this computation slightly. It stipulates that the number of incremental shares included in quarterly and year-to-date diluted EPS shall be computed using the average market price of common shares for the quarterly and year-to-date periods. For example, an entity with a calendar year-end would compute the number of incremental shares used for its second quarter DEPS using the average market price of common shares during the quarter ended June 30, 2005. The number of incremental shares used to calculate year-to-date DEPS at the end of the second quarter would be determined using the average market price of common shares for the year-to-date period ending June 30, 2005. These two average market prices would most likely differ since the one is the average market price for April–June and the other is the average market price for January–June.

An example of the existing requirements under FAS 128 follows. A corporation has warrants outstanding for 1,000 shares of common stock exercisable at $10 per share and the average market price of the common stock is $16 per share, the following would occur: the company would receive $10,000 (1,000 x $10) and issue 1,000 shares from the exercise of the warrants which would enable it to repurchase 625 shares ($10,000 ÷ $16) in the open market. The net increase in the denominator (which effects a dilution in EPS) is 375 shares (1,000 issued less 625 repurchased). If the **exercise price** is greater than the average market price, the exercise is not assumed since the result would be antidilutive. In that case, DEPS of prior periods presented in comparative form are **not** restated to reflect the change in market price.

Treasury Stock Method

Denominator must be increased by net dilution, as follows:

Net dilution	= Shares issued – Shares assumed to be repurchased
where	
Shares issued	= Proceeds received ÷ Exercise price per share
Shares assumed to be repurchased	= Proceeds received ÷ Average market price per share

The if-converted method. The if-converted method is used for those securities that are currently sharing in the earnings of the company through the receipt of interest or dividends as preferential securities, but that have the **potential** for sharing in the earnings as common stock (e.g., convertible bonds or convertible preferred stock). The if-converted method logically recognizes that the convertible security can only share in the earnings of the company as one or the other, not both. Thus, the dividends or interest less income tax effects applicable to the convertible security as a preferential security are not recognized in income available to common stockholders used to compute DEPS, and the weighted-average number of shares is adjusted to reflect the assumed conversion as of the beginning of the year (or actual date of issuance, if later).

If-Converted Method

Numerator

Income available to common stockholders recomputed to reflect assumed and/or actual conversion

- Add back interest expense less income tax effects
- Convertible preferred dividends are no longer subtracted
- Add back other expenses attributable to convertible issues

Denominator

Weighted-average number of shares of common stock outstanding adjusted to reflect the assumed and/or actual conversion of convertible securities at the beginning of the period or actual date of issuance, if later

Exceptions. Generally, the if-converted method is used for convertible securities, while the treasury stock method is used for options and warrants. There are some situations specified by FAS 128 for which this does not hold true.

1. If options or warrants permit or require that debt or other securities of the issuer be tendered for all or a portion of the exercise price, the if-converted method is used.
2. If options or warrants require that the proceeds from the exercise are to be used to retire existing debt, the if-converted method is used.
3. If convertible securities require cash payment upon conversion, and are, therefore, considered equivalent to warrants, the treasury stock method is used.

Dual presentation of earnings per share. DEPS is a pro forma presentation which reflects the dilution of EPS that would have occurred if **all** contingent issuances of common stock that would individually reduce EPS had taken place at the beginning of the period (or the date actually issued, if later). The presentation of concept of dual earnings per share provides the reader with factually supportable EPS that range from no dilution to the maximum potential dilution. DEPS assumes that all issuances that have the legal right to become common stock exercise that right (unless the exercise would be antidilutive), and therefore anticipates and measures all **potential** dilution. The **dual presentation** of EPS and DEPS is prominently displayed on the face of the income statements. The underlying basis for the computation is that of conservatism. The DEPS considers all other potentially dilutive securities but only uses those securities which are dilutive. Thus, in most cases, the DEPS is less than the basic EPS. DEPS can never be greater than the basic EPS, but it could potentially be the same if all of the convertible securities were antidilutive.

NOTE: The FASB concluded that an entity that reports a discontinued operation, an extraordinary item, or the cumulative effect of an accounting change in a period is to use ***income from continuing operations*** *as the "control number" for determining whether including potential common shares in the diluted EPS computation would be dilutive or antidilutive. Income from continuing operations (or a similar line item above net income if it appears on the income statement) would be adjusted for preferred dividends. If necessary, refer to FAS 128, footnote 8 for an example.*

Examples of EPS Computation—Complex Capital Structure

Each of the following independent examples is presented to illustrate the foregoing principles. The procedural guidelines are detailed to enable the reader to understand the computation without referring back to the preceding explanatory text.

Example of the treasury stock method

Assume that net income is $50,000 and the weighted-average number of common shares outstanding has been computed as 10,000. Additional information regarding the capital structure is

1. 4% nonconvertible, cumulative preferred stock, par value of $100 per share, 1,000 shares issued and outstanding the entire year
2. Options and warrants to purchase 1,000 shares of common stock at $8 per share were outstanding all year.
3. The average market price of common stock during the year was $10.

The first step in applying this method is the determination of basic EPS. This calculation appears as follows:

$$\frac{\text{Net income} - \text{Preferred dividends}}{\text{Weighted-average number of common shares outstanding}} = \frac{\$50{,}000 - \$4{,}000}{10{,}000 \text{ shares}} = \$4.60$$

The second step is the calculation of DEPS which is based upon outstanding common stock and other dilutive securities. The options and warrants are the only potentially dilutive securities in the example. However, remember that only dilutive options (Market price > Exercise price) are included in the computation. The treasury stock method is used to compute the number of shares to be added to the denominator as illustrated below.

Proceeds from assumed exercise of options and warrants (1,000 shares x $8 per share)	$8,000
Number of shares issued	1,000
Number of shares assumed to be reacquired ($8,000 ÷ $10 average market price per share)	800
Number of shares assumed issued and not reacquired	200*

* *An alternative approach that can be used to calculate this number for DEPS is demonstrated below.*

$$\frac{\text{Average market price} - \text{Exercise price}}{\text{Average market price}} \times \text{Number of shares under options/warrants} = \text{Shares not reacquired}$$

$$\frac{\$10 - \$8}{\$10} \times 1{,}000 \text{ shares} = 200 \text{ shares}$$

DEPS can now be calculated as follows, including the effects of applying the treasury stock method:

$$\frac{\text{Net income} - \text{Preferred dividends}}{\text{Weighted-average number of common shares outstanding + Number of shares assumed issued and not reacquired with proceeds from options and warrants}} = \frac{\$50{,}000 - \$4{,}000}{10{,}200 \text{ shares}} = \$4.51$$

Note the dilutive effect of the options and warrants, as EPS of $4.60 is reduced to DEPS of $4.51.

Table 2
Computations of Basic and Diluted Earnings Per Share

Items	*EPS on outstanding common stock (Basic EPS)* Numerator		Denominator	*DEPS* Numerator		Denominator
Net income	$50,000			$50,000		
Preferred dividends	(4,000)			(4,000)		
Common shs. outstanding			10,000 shs			10,000 shs
Options and warrants						200
Totals	$46,000	÷	10,000 shs	$46,000	÷	10,200 shs
EPS		$4.60			$4.51	

Example of the if-converted method

Assume net income of $50,000 and weighted-average common shares outstanding of 10,000. Additional information regarding capital structure is

1. 7% convertible debt, 200 bonds each convertible into forty common shares. The bonds were outstanding the entire year. The income tax rate is 40%. The bonds were issued at par ($1,000 per bond). No bonds were converted during the year.
2. 4% convertible, cumulative preferred stock, par value of $100 per share, 1,000 shares issued and outstanding. Each preferred share is convertible into two common shares. The preferred stock was issued at par value and was outstanding the entire year. No shares were converted during the year.

The first step is to compute basic EPS. As in the previous example, this is $4.60. The next step is the computation of DEPS assuming conversion of the convertible debt in order to determine whether their conversion would be dilutive. The convertible bonds are assumed to have been converted to common stock at the beginning of the year since no bonds were actually converted during the year. The effects of this assumption are twofold. One, if the bonds are converted, interest expense would be reduced by $14,000 (7% x 200 bonds x $1,000 par value per bond); and two, there will be an additional 8,000 shares of common stock outstanding during the year (200 bonds x 40 common shares per bond). The effect of avoiding $14,000 of interest expense will increase net income, but it will also increase income tax expense due to the lost income tax deduction. Consequently, the net after-tax effect of avoiding interest expense of $14,000 is $8,400 [(1 – .40) x $14,000]. DEPS is computed as follows:

$$\frac{\text{Net income} - \text{Preferred dividends} + \text{Interest expense (net of tax)}}{\text{Weighted-average number of common shares outstanding} + \text{Shares issued upon conversion of bonds}} = \frac{\$50{,}000 - \$4{,}000 + \$8{,}400}{10{,}000 + 8{,}000 \text{ shares}} = \$3.02$$

The convertible debt is dilutive because EPS of $4.60 is reduced to DEPS of $3.02.

To determine the dilutive effect of the preferred stock, the preferred stock is assumed to have been converted to common stock at the beginning of the year since no shares of preferred stock were actually converted during the year. The effects of this assumption are twofold. One, if the preferred stock is converted, there will be no preferred dividends of $4,000 for the year; and two, there will be an additional 2,000 shares of common stock outstanding during the year (the **conversion rate** is 2 for 1 on 1,000 shares of outstanding preferred stock). DEPS considering the preferred stock is computed, as follows, reflecting these two assumptions:

$$\frac{\text{Net income} + \text{Interest expense (net of tax)}}{\text{Weighted-average number of common shares outstanding} + \text{Shares issued upon conversion of bonds and conversion of preferred stock}} = \frac{\$50{,}000 + \$8{,}400}{10{,}000 + 8{,}000 + 2{,}000 \text{ shares}} = \$2.92$$

The convertible preferred stock is also dilutive because DEPS of $3.02 is reduced to DEPS of $2.92.

Together, the effect of the convertible bonds and preferred stock reduces EPS of $4.60 to DEPS of $2.92. In this example the convertible bonds must be considered first, prior to the inclusion of the convertible preferred stock in the computation. For a complete explanation of the sequencing process of including multiple dilutive securities in the computations of DEPS, see the comprehensive example in Appendix A. Table 3 summarizes the computations made for this example.

Table 3
Computations of Basic and Diluted Earnings Per Share

Items	*EPS on outstanding common stock (Basic EPS)* Numerator		Denominator	*DEPS* Numerator		Denominator
Net income	$50,000			$50,000		
Preferred dividend	(4,000)					
Common shs. outstanding			10,000 shs			10,000 shs
Conversion of preferred						2,000
Conversion of bonds				8,400		8,000
Totals	$46,000	÷	10,000 shs	$58,400	÷	20,000 shs
EPS		$4.60			$2.92	

In the preceding example all of the potentially dilutive securities were outstanding the entire year and no conversions or exercises were made during the year. If a potentially dilutive security was not outstanding the entire year, then the numerator and denominator effects would have to be "time-weighted." For instance, suppose the convertible bonds in the above example were issued during the current year on July 1. If all other facts remain unchanged, DEPS would be computed as follows:

$$\frac{\text{Net income + Interest expense (net of tax)}}{\begin{array}{c}\text{Weighted-average number of common shares outstanding +}\\ \text{Shares issued upon conversion of preferred stock}\\ \text{and conversion of bonds}\end{array}} = \frac{\$50{,}000 + 1/2(8{,}400)}{10{,}000 + 2{,}000 + 1/2(8{,}000)} = \$3.39$$

Since the DEPS of $3.39 is still less than the EPS of $4.60, the convertible debt is dilutive whether or not it is outstanding the entire year.

If actual conversions or exercises take place during a period, the common shares issued upon conversion will be outstanding from their date of issuance, and therefore, will be included in the computation of the weighted-average number of common shares outstanding. These shares are then weighted from their respective dates of issuance. Assume that all the bonds in the above example are converted on July 1 into 8,000 common shares; the following effects should be noted:

1. For basic EPS, the weighted-average of common shares outstanding will be increased by (8,000 shares)(6 months outstanding/12 months in the period) or 4,000. Income will increase $4,200 net of income tax, because the bonds were only outstanding for the first half of the year.
2. For DEPS, the if-converted method is applied to the period January 1 to June 30 because it was during this period that the bonds were potentially dilutive. The interest expense, net of income tax, of $4,200 is added to the net income in the numerator, and 4,000 shares are added to the denominator.
3. Interestingly, the net effect of items 1. and 2. is the same for the period whether these dilutive bonds were outstanding the entire period or converted during the period.

Inclusions/Exclusions from Computation of DEPS

Certain types of instruments and contracts having characteristics of both liabilities and equity require special treatment using the **two-class method** described previously, if under FAS 150, they are required to be classified as liabilities on the balance sheet of the issuer. Examples of these instruments include mandatorily redeemable common or preferred stock; and forward purchase contracts or written put options on the issuer's equity shares that require physical settlement or net cash settlement.

The computations of DEPS also does **not** include contracts such as purchased put options and purchased call options (options held by the entity on its own stock). The inclusion of such contracts would be antidilutive.

Sometimes entities issue contracts that may be settled in common stock or in cash at the election of either the issuing entity or the holder. The determination of whether the contract is reflected in the computation of DEPS is based on the facts available each period. It is presumed that the contract will be settled in common stock and the resulting common shares included in DEPS if the effect is dilutive. This presumption may be overcome if past experience or a stated policy provides a reasonable basis to believe that the contract will be paid partially or wholly in cash. The new standard described in the ED at the end of this chapter would preclude the assumption that the contract would be paid in cash, in whole or part. If during the reporting period the exercise price exceeds the average market price for that period, the potential dilutive effect of the contract on EPS is computed using the **reverse treasury stock method**. Under this method

1. Issuance of sufficient common shares is assumed to have occurred at the beginning of the period (at the average market price during the period) to raise enough proceeds to satisfy the contract.
2. The proceeds from issuance of the shares are assumed to have been used to satisfy the contract (i.e., to buy back shares).
3. The denominator of the DEPS calculation includes the incremental number of shares (the difference between the number of shares assumed issued and the number of shares assumed received from satisfying the contract).

Consolidated DEPS

When computing consolidated DEPS, entities with subsidiaries that have issued common stock or potential common shares to parties other than the parent company (minority interests) follow these general guidelines.

1. Securities issued by a subsidiary that enable their holders to obtain the subsidiary's common stock are included in computing the subsidiary's EPS. Per share earnings of the subsidiary are included in the consolidated EPS calculations based on the consolidated group's holding of the subsidiary's securities.
2. For the purpose of computing consolidated DEPS, securities of a subsidiary that are convertible into its parent company's common stock, along with subsidiary's options or warrants to purchase common stock of the parent company, are all considered among the potential common shares of the parent company.

Partially Paid Shares

If an entity has common shares issued in a partially paid form and the shares are entitled to dividends in proportion to the amount paid, the common-share equivalent of those partially paid shares is included in the computation of basic EPS to the extent that they were entitled to participate in dividends. Partially paid stock subscriptions that do not share in dividends until paid in full are considered the equivalent of warrants and are included in the calculation of DEPS using the treasury stock method.

Presentation

The reason for the differentiation between simple and complex capital structures is that FAS 128 requires different financial statement presentation for each. FAS 128 mandates that EPS be shown on the face of the income statement for each of the following items (when applicable):

1. Income from continuing operations.
2. Net income.

An entity that reports a discontinued operation, an extraordinary item, or the cumulative effect of a change in accounting principle presents basic and diluted EPS amounts for these line items either on the face of the income statement or in the notes to the financial statements. These requirements must be fulfilled regardless of whether the capital structure is simple or complex. The difference in the two structures is that a simple capital structure requires presentation of only a single EPS number for each item, while a complex structure requires the dual presentation of basic EPS and DEPS for each item.

Earnings per share data is to be presented for all periods for which an income statement or summary of earnings is presented. If DEPS is reported for at least one period, it is to be reported for all periods presented, regardless of whether or not DEPS differs from basic EPS. However, if basic and diluted EPS are the same amounts for all periods presented, dual presentation may be accomplished in one line on the face of the income statement.

Rights issue. A **rights issue** whose exercise price at issuance is below the fair value of the stock contains a bonus element. If a rights issue contains a bonus element (somewhat similar to a stock dividend) and is offered to all existing stockholders, basic and diluted EPS are adjusted retroactively for the bonus element for all periods presented. However, if the ability to exercise the rights issue is contingent on some event other than the passage of time, this retroactive adjustment does not apply until the contingency is resolved.

Restated EPS. When a restatement of the results of operations of a prior period is required to be included in the income statement, EPS for the prior period(s) are also restated. The effect of the restatement, expressed in per share terms, is disclosed in the period of restatement. Restated EPS data is computed as if the restated income (loss) had been reported in the prior period(s).

Year-to-date DEPS. If an entity has year-to-date income from continuing operations (Topic D-62 in EITF Abstracts) that includes losses in one or more quarters, the calculation of year-to-date DEPS includes dilutive potential shares for all quarters on a quarterly weighted-average basis. Thus, options that are "in the money" in a quarter(s) in which a net loss(es) occur(s) are included in the year-to-date denominator in the DEPS calculation. Likewise, contingent shares excluded because of a loss from continuing operations in a quarter(s) are included in year-to-date DEPS.

Other Disclosure Requirements

The following additional items are required to be disclosed for all periods for which an income statement is presented:

1. A reconciliation of the numerators and the denominators of the basic and diluted EPS computations for income from continuing operations including the effects of all securities that affect EPS.
2. The effect of preferred dividends in arriving at income available for common stockholders in computing basic EPS.
3. Securities which could potentially dilute basic EPS in future periods but which were not included in DEPS for the period(s) presented since the results were antidilutive.

In addition, for the latest period for which an income statement is presented, a description is required for transactions occurring after the balance sheet date that result in a material change in the number of shares that were outstanding at the balance sheet date.

EMERGING ISSUES TASK FORCE ISSUES SUMMARIES

92-3 EPS Treatment of Tax Benefits for Dividends on Unallocated Stock Held by an Employee Stock Ownership Plan

Under FAS 109, the tax benefits related to dividends paid on unallocated ESOP common stock held by an ESOP that are charged to retained earnings are not deducted from net income when calculating DEPS. Also note, this consensus applies to convertible ESOP preferred stock when calculating the if-converted DEPS. However, under SOP 93-6, dividends paid on unallocated shares are not charged to retained earnings. Since the employer controls the use of dividends on unallocated shares, these dividends are not considered dividends for financial reporting purposes. Consequently, the dividends do not affect the DEPS computation. The transition provisions of SOP 93-6 do, however, allow employers to continue their current accounting methods for ESOP shares acquired on or prior to December 31, 1992.

00-19 Accounting for Derivative Financial Instruments Indexed to, and Potentially Settled in, a Company's Own Stock

NOTE: As a result of the issuance of FAS 150 in May 2003, this consensus was partially nullified. At the time this publication went to press, the EITF had not yet revised the text of this consensus. A discussion of the provisions of FAS 150 has been incorporated in this chapter and in Chapter 17. New developments that occur between annual editions are posted on the publisher's Web site at http://www.wiley.com.

This consensus, covered in detail in Chapter 17, provides criteria to apply in determining the initial balance sheet classification of certain derivative financial instruments as debt or equity as well as circumstances that would require their reclassification.

For EPS computation purposes, for those contracts that provide the company with a choice of either cash settlement or settlement in shares, settlement in shares is assumed, although this can be overcome based on past experience or stated policy. If the counterparty controls the choice, however, the more dilutive assumption must be made, irrespective of past experience or policy. The consensus includes detailed guidance for a number of specific types of contracts.

03-6 Participating Securities and the Two-Class Method under FASB Statement No. 128, *Earnings per Share*

Some reporting entities which issue securities that are entitled to participate in dividends with common shares will report lower EPS under the provisions of this consensus. This issue addresses the computation of EPS by entities that have issued securities, other than common stock, that entitle the holder to participate in dividends when, and if, dividends are declared on common stock. In addition, this issue provides further guidance on calculating EPS using a two-class method and requires companies to retroactively restate EPS amounts presented.

Participation rights are defined based solely on whether the holder is entitled to receive any dividends if the entity declares them during the period. The consensus also nullifies the guidance of D-95 by requiring the use of the two-class method for computing basic EPS when participating convertible securities exist. The use of the two-class method is also expanded to encompass other forms of participating securities, including options, warrants, forwards, and other contracts to issue an entity's common shares (except for unvested share-based compensation awards).

Presentation and disclosure. Presentation of participating securities' basic and diluted EPS is not required, but is permitted for other than common stock. What is required is adjustment to the earnings that are used to compute EPS for the common stock.

Transition. This consensus is effective for reporting periods beginning after March 31, 2004, and should be applied by restating previous periods' reported EPS. Therefore, existing instruments will need to be examined in light of the changes from this consensus.

Participating security. A participating security was difficult to apply given the description in FAS 128, so the EITF formally defined them as, "A security that may participate in undistributed earnings with common stock, whether that participation is conditioned upon the occurrence of a specified event or not, regardless of the form of participation."

Allocating earnings and losses. In addition to the amount of dividends declared in the current period, net dividends must be reduced by the contractual amount of dividends or other participation payments that are paid or accumulated for the current period. The allocation of undistributed earnings for a period should be done for a participating security based on the contractual participation rights of the security to share in the current earnings assuming all earnings for the period are distributed. The allocation process is not based on a fair-value analysis, but is based on the term on the securities. For losses, an entity would allocate to the participating securities a portion of the net losses of the entity in accordance with the contractual provisions which may require the security to have an obligation to share in the issuing entity's losses. This occurs when the participating security holder has an obligation to share in the losses of the issuing entity if the holder is obligated to fund the issuing authority's losses or if losses incurred by the issuing entity reduce the security's principal or mandatory redemption amount.

Two-class method. This is an earnings allocation formula for computing EPS. It determines EPS for each class of common stock and participating securities according to dividends declared/accumulated and participation rights in undistributed earnings. This consensus requires that the two-class method be applied for participating convertible securities when computing basic EPS. This changes earlier guidance, which permitted reporting entities to make an accounting policy election to use the if-converted method, rather than the two-class method, in the basic EPS calculation, as long as the if-converted method was not less dilutive.

D-42 The Effect on the Calculation of Earnings Per Share for the Redemption or Induced Conversion of Preferred Stock

NOTE: As a result of the issuance of EITF Topic D-42, EITF Topic D-95 has been nullified.

Companies may redeem shares of their outstanding preferred stock for noncash consideration such as in exchange for other securities. Sometimes the company "induces" conversion by offering additional securities or other consideration to the holders. Such offers are sometimes referred to as "sweeteners."

The position of the SEC staff is that any excess of the fair value of consideration transferred (excess consideration) over the carrying value of the preferred stock represents a return to the preferred stockholder and, consequently, is to be accounted for similar to dividends paid to the preferred stockholders for purposes of computing EPS, including when there is an excess of the carrying amount of the preferred stock over the fair value of the consideration transferred.

In computing the carrying amount of preferred stock that has been redeemed or been subject to an induced conversion, the carrying amount of the preferred stock is to be reduced by the related issuance costs irrespective of how those costs were classified in the stockholders' equity section of the balance sheet upon initial issuance.

D-53 Computation of Earnings Per Share for a Period That Includes a Redemption or an Induced Conversion of a Class of Preferred Stock

This topic discusses the application of the "if-converted" method to the redemption of only a portion of an outstanding class of preferred stock. The SEC's position is that any excess consideration (see discussion of Topic D-42 above) is to be attributed to the redeemed or converted shares. Thus, in applying the "if-converted" method to determine whether the stock is dilutive for the period, the redeemed or converted shares are treated separately from those shares that are still issued and outstanding.

D-82 Effect of Preferred Stock Dividends Payable in Common Shares on Computation of Income Available to Common Stockholders

At the option of the issuer, preferred stock dividends are sometimes payable in either cash or common stock. The form of payment is not a determinant in accounting for the effect of the preferred dividend on net income available to common stockholders. Therefore, for the purposes of the numerator in EPS computations, net income or loss is adjusted to compute the portion available to common stockholders.

EXPOSURE DRAFT OUTSTANDING

Proposed FAS: ***Earnings per Share—an amendment of FASB Statement No. 128***

A primary purpose of this proposed standard is to provide for convergence with the corresponding international standard, IAS 33, thereby improving comparability of EPS data on a global basis. In particular, this provision of this ED, if enacted, will do the following:

- Amend FAS 128 for calculating the number of incremental shares included in diluted shares when applying the treasury stock method.
- Eliminate the provisions of FAS 128 that allow an entity to rebut the presumption that contracts with the option of settling either in cash or stock will be settled in stock.
- Require that shares that would be issued as a result of conversion of mandatorily convertible securities would be included in the weighted-average number of ordinary shares outstanding used in computing basic earnings per share from the date that the conversion becomes mandatory.

Effective date and transition: The statement would be effective for financial statements for both interim and annual periods beginning after December 15, 2004. After the effective date, all prior period EPS data presented would be adjusted retrospectively. This retrospective adjustment would include interim financial statements, summaries of earnings, and selected financial statements, as well as the annual financial statements.

APPENDIX

COMPREHENSIVE EXAMPLE

The examples within the text used a simplified approach for determining whether or not options, warrants, convertible preferred stock, or convertible bonds have a dilutive effect on DEPS. If the DEPS number computed was lower than basic EPS, the security was considered dilutive. This approach is adequate when the company has only **one** potentially dilutive security. If the firm has more than one potentially dilutive security, a more complex ranking procedure must be employed (FAS 128).

For example, assume the following facts concerning the capital structure of a company:

1. Income from continuing operations and net income are both $50,000. Income from continuing operations is not displayed on the firm's income statement.
2. The weighted-average number of common shares outstanding is 10,000 shares.
3. The income tax rate is a flat 40%.
4. Options to purchase 1,000 shares of common stock at $8 per share were outstanding all year.
5. Options to purchase 2,000 shares of common stock at $13 per share were outstanding all year.
6. The average market price of common stock during the year was $10.
7. 7% convertible bonds, 200 bonds, each convertible into 40 common shares, were outstanding the entire year. The bonds were issued at par value ($1,000 per bond) and no bonds were converted during the year.
8. 4% convertible, **cumulative** preferred stock, par value of $100 per share, 1,000 shares issued and outstanding the entire year. Each preferred share is convertible into one common share. The preferred stock was issued at par value and no shares were converted during the year.

Note that reference is made below to some of the tables included in the body of the chapter because the facts above represent a combination of the facts used for the examples in the chapter.

In order to determine both basic EPS and DEPS, the following procedures must be performed:

1. Calculate basic EPS as if the capital structure were simple.
2. Identify other potentially dilutive securities.
3. Calculate the per share effects of assuming issuance or conversion of each potentially dilutive security on an individual basis.
4. Rank the per share effects from smallest to largest.
5. Recalculate EPS (step 1 above) adding the potentially dilutive securities one at a time in order, beginning with the security with the **smallest** per share effect.
6. Continue adding potentially dilutive securities to each successive calculation until all have been added or until the addition of a security increases EPS (antidilution) from its previous level.

Applying these procedures to the facts above

1. Basic EPS

$$\frac{\text{Net income} - \text{Preferred dividends}}{\text{Weighted-average number of common shares outstanding}} = \frac{\$50{,}000 - \$4{,}000}{10{,}000 \text{ shares}} = \$4.60$$

2. Identification of other potentially dilutive securities
   a. Options (two types)
   b. 7% convertible bonds
   c. 4% convertible cumulative preferred stock

Diluted EPS (DEPS)

3. Per share effects of conversion or issuance of other potentially dilutive securities calculated individually
   a. Options—Only the options to purchase 1,000 shares at $8.00 per share are potentially dilutive. The options to purchase 2,000 shares of common stock are antidilutive because the exercise price is greater than the average market price. Thus, they are not included in the computation.

      Proceeds if options exercised:

1,000 shares x $8 per share	=	$8,000
Shares that could be acquired:		
$8,000 ÷ $10	=	800
Dilutive shares: 1,000 – 800	=	200

      $$\frac{\text{Increase/decrease in net income}}{\text{Increase in weighted-average number of common shares outstanding}} = \frac{\$0}{200 \text{ shs.}} = \$0$$

   b. 7% convertible bonds (see Table 3)

      $$\frac{\text{Increase/decrease in net income}}{\text{Increase in weighted-average number of common shares outstanding}} = \frac{\$8,400}{8,000 \text{ shs.}} = \$1.05$$

   c. 4% convertible cumulative preferred stock—The outstanding common shares increase by 1,000 when all shares are converted. This results in total dividends of $4,000 not being paid.

      $$\frac{\text{Increase/decrease in net income}}{\text{Increase in weighted-average number of common shares outstanding}} = \frac{\$4,000}{1,000 \text{ shs.}} = \$4.00$$

4. Rank the per share effects from smallest to largest

a.	Options	$ 0
b.	7% convertible bonds	1.05
c.	4% convertible cumulative preferred stock	4.00

5. Recalculate the EPS in rank order starting from the security with the smallest per share dilution and adding one potentially dilutive security at a time
   a. DEPS—options added

      $$\frac{\text{Net income} - \text{Preferred dividends}}{\text{Weighted-average number of common shares outstanding + Shares not acquired with proceeds of options}} = \frac{\$50,000 - \$4,000}{10,000 + 200 \text{ shs.}} = \$4.51$$

   b. DEPS—options and 7% convertible bonds added

$$\frac{\text{Net income} - \text{Preferred dividends} + \text{Interest expense (net of tax)}}{\text{Weighted-average number of common shares outstanding} + \text{Shares not acquired with proceeds of options} + \text{Shares issued upon conversion of bonds}} = \frac{\$50{,}000 - \$4{,}000 + \$8{,}400}{10{,}000 + 200 + 8{,}000 \text{ shs.}} = \$2.99$$

c. DEPS—options, 7% convertible bonds and 4% convertible cumulative preferred stock added

$$\frac{\text{Net income} + \text{Interest expense (net of tax)}}{\text{Weighted-average number of common shares outstanding} + \text{Shares not acquired with proceeds of options} + \text{Shares issued upon conversion of bonds and preferred stock}} = \frac{\$50{,}000 + 8{,}400}{10{,}000 + 200 + 8{,}000 + 1{,}000 \text{ shs.}} = \$3.04$$

DEPS = $2.99

Since the addition of the 4% convertible cumulative preferred stock raises DEPS from $2.99 to $3.04, the preferred stock is antidilutive and is therefore excluded from the computation of DEPS.

A dual presentation of basic EPS and DEPS is required. The dual presentation on the face of the income statement would appear as follows:

Net income	$50,000
Earnings per common share* (Note X)	$4.60
Earnings per common share, assuming dilution*(Note X)	$2.99

* *The captions "Basic earnings per share" and "Diluted earnings per share" may be substituted, respectively.*

Note X: Earnings Per Share (illustrative disclosure based on facts from the Appendix)

The following adjustments were made to the numerators and denominators of the basic and diluted earnings per share computations:

	Year Ended December 31, 2004		
	Income (numerator)	*Weighted-average number of outstanding shares (denominator)*	*Amount per share*
Net income	$50,000		
Less: Preferred stock dividends	(4,000)		
Basic EPS			
Income available to common stockholders	46,000	10,000	$4.60
Effects of Dilutive Securities			
Options to purchase common stock		200	
7% convertible bonds	8,400	8,000	
Diluted EPS			
Income available to common stockholders adjusted for the effects of assumed exercise of options and conversion of bonds	$54,400	18,200	$2.99

There were 1,000 shares of $100 par value, 4% convertible, cumulative preferred stock issued and outstanding during the year ended December 31, 2004, that were not included in the above computation because their conversion would not have resulted in a dilution of earnings per share.

19 INTERIM REPORTING

PERSPECTIVE AND ISSUES

The term "interim reporting" refers to financial reporting for periods of less than a year. While reporting on interim periods had long been common practice, only in recent decades has it been required, and has specific guidance been provided under the authoritative literature. Since 1970, the SEC has required companies subject to its periodic reporting requirements to file quarterly condensed financial information on a Form 10-Q. It was the issuance of APB 28 in 1973, however, that established GAAP for publicly held or privately held companies issuing interim financial statements to stockholders and other users. The relevant rules are now set forth in APB 28, FAS 3, and FIN 18, which have been in place for many years without change. However, interim financial reporting is one of the topics targeted by the FASB and its international standard-setting peer, the IASB, for short-term convergence, and thus there is the possibility that current US GAAP requirements for interim reporting could be altered to more closely parallel that under IFRS.

The basic objective of interim reporting is to provide current and more timely information regarding enterprise performance to enable existing and prospective investors, lenders, and other financial statement users to act upon more relevant information in making informed decisions.

There are two distinct views of interim reporting. Under the first view, the interim period is considered to be an **integral** part of the annual accounting period. Annual operating expenses are estimated and then allocated to the interim periods based on forecasted annual activity levels such as sales volume. The results of subsequent interim periods must be adjusted to reflect the effect of estimation errors in earlier interim periods of the same fiscal year. The APB indicated a preference for the integral approach in APB 28.

Under the second view, the interim period is considered to be a **discrete** accounting period. Thus, there are no estimations or allocations made on bases different from those used for annual reporting. The same expense recognition rules apply as under annual reporting, and no special interim accruals or deferrals are necessary or permissible. Annual operating expenses are recognized in the interim period incurred, irrespective of the number of interim periods benefited.

Proponents of the **integral view** argue that unique interim expense recognition procedures are necessary to avoid misleading fluctuations in period-to-period results. Using the integral view results in interim earnings which are indicative of annual earnings and, thus, arguably more useful for predictive purposes. Proponents of the **discrete view** argue that the smoothing of interim results for purposes of forecasting annual earnings has undesirable effects. For example, a turning point during the year in an earnings trend could be obscured if smoothing techniques implied by the integral view approach were to be employed.

In response to inconsistencies in interim reporting practices and problems in implementing GAAP in interim reporting, FASB undertook a comprehensive study of the issue. In 1978, the FASB Discussion Memorandum, *Interim Financial Accounting and Reporting*, was issued. A fundamental objective of this project was to resolve the **integral/discrete** debate. However, FASB made no recommendations and ultimately removed the project from its agenda. The current convergence efforts of FASB and IASB may result in changes to US GAAP for interim reporting, inasmuch as the APB 28 requirements lean toward the integral view (while nonetheless mandating certain procedures which bespeak adherence to the discrete view), but the corresponding IFRS (IAS 34) proclaims faithfulness to the discrete view (although certain aspects of that standard hew closer to the integral view). Thus a "converged" standard, promised in the near future by both FASB and IASB, could well differ from one or both currently prescribed standards.

The debate between integral and discrete views of interim reporting is more than academic, and can result in very different interim measures of results of operations. This can occur, for example, because certain annual expenses may be concentrated in one interim period, yet benefit the entire year's operations. Examples include advertising expenses and major repairs and maintenance of equipment. Also, in the US (and many other jurisdictions) progressive (graduated) income tax rates are applied to total annual income and various tax credits may arise, all of which are computed on annual pretax earnings, making the determination of quarterly income tax expenses often complex.

Interim reporting is problematic for reasons other than the choice of an underlying reporting philosophy. As reporting periods are shortened, the effects of errors in estimation and allocation are magnified, and randomly occurring events which might not be material in the context of a full fiscal year might create major distortions in short interim period "snapshots" of entity performance. The effects of seasonal fluctuations and temporary market conditions further limit the reliability, comparability, and predictive value of interim reports.

Furthermore, technological advances and the seemingly insatiable demand for information (particularly when in the consumers' view such information is costless) are also changing how interim data is to be reported, and what level of assurance is to be provided by both preparers and independent attesting entities. Thus, the Chairman of the US Securities and Exchange Commission (SEC) has proposed an initiative to implement a "current disclosure system" that would require public companies to make "affirmative disclosures of unquestionably material information in real time, including providing updates to prior disclosures." With the advent of new technologies such as Extensible Business Reporting Language (XBRL), and such modernized accounting procedures such as the "virtual close," users will in the not-too-distant future be demanding to receive more and better information from reporting entities on a real-time basis.

Because of this evolving reporting environment, and the spate of well-publicized audit failures in the late 1990s an early 2000s, the issue of independent auditor association with interim financial reports is subject to continuing controversy. The assumption of auditing standard-setting responsibility by the Public Company Accounting Oversight Board (PCAOB), mandated by the Sarbanes-Oxley Act of 2002, and the "real-time" demands of users described above, will intensify the pressure on the auditing profession to develop standards to provide real-time assurance to users of financial data regarding its completeness, accuracy and relevance as well as the effectiveness of the design and operation of the company's internal controls.

Interim reporting is not required under US GAAP, although quarterly reports of publicly traded companies is mandated under SEC rules. The information required in those interim reports is substantially less than is mandated under GAAP for annual sets of financial statements, but the extent of informational content in interim financial statements is an evolving matter. For example, FAS 132(R), which replaced FAS 132 in late 2003, does require expanded disclosures about pension and other benefit plan costs and associated information in interim financial reports of both publicly held and nonpublic companies. (See Chapter 16 for details.)

Although much of the discussion that follows relates to quarterly reporting, the rules and concepts are equally applicable to interim reports covering monthly or other interim periods.

Sources of GAAP				
APB	*FAS*	*FIN*	*FTB*	*EITF*
28	3, 16, 69, 95, 109, 128, 130, 131, 148	18	79-9	86-13, 98-9, D-70

DEFINITIONS OF TERMS

Discrete view. An approach to measuring interim period income by viewing each interim period separately without regard to the annual period to which it relates.

Estimated annual effective tax rate. The average annual tax rate which reflects the application of graduated income tax rates to estimates of annual earnings, adjusted for the effects of available tax credits.

Integral view. An approach to measuring interim period income by viewing each interim period as an integral part of the annual period. Expenses are recognized in proportion to revenues earned through the use of special accruals and deferrals.

Interim reporting. Financial reporting for a period of less than a year, (e.g., a month or quarter).

Last-twelve-months reports. Financial reporting for the twelve-month period which ends on a given interim date.

Liquidation of LIFO inventories. Occurs when quarterly unit sales exceed purchases and costs associated with one or more previous year's LIFO layers are released into cost of goods sold.

Seasonality. The normal, expected occurrence of a major portion of revenues or costs in one or two interim periods.

Year-to-date reports. Financial reporting for the period which begins on the first day of the current fiscal year and ends on a given interim date during the year.

CONCEPTS, RULES, AND EXAMPLES

Revenues

As explained elsewhere in this book, revenue recognition practices have received a great deal of attention in recent years, largely because of aggressive reporting (including financial reporting fraud) that came to light in a number of restatements of previously issued financial statements and in SEC enforcement actions and private litigation actions. However, the underlying principles established by GAAP have not been altered and have remained essentially unchanged for many decades, notwithstanding the promulgation of certain interpretive literature (such as the SEC's Staff Accounting Bulletin 101). Revenues are recognized as earned during an interim period using the same principles followed in annual reports. This rule applies to both product sales and service revenues. For example, product sales cutoff procedures are applied at the end of each interim period in the same manner that they are applied at year-end, and revenue from long-term construction contracts is recognized at interim dates using the same method used at year-end.

Product Costs and Direct Costs

Product costs (and costs directly associated with service revenues) are treated in interim reports in the same manner as in annual reports (i.e., notwithstanding nominal adherence to the integral view of interim reporting, GAAP mandates the discrete approach for revenue recognition). However, APB 28 provides for four integral view exceptions, described below.

1. The gross profit method may be used to estimate cost of goods sold and ending inventory for interim periods.
2. When inventory consists of LIFO layers and a portion of the base period layer is liquidated at an interim date, but it is expected that this will be replaced by year-end, the anticipated cost of replacing the liquidated inventory is included in cost of sales of the interim period.
3. An inventory market decline reasonably expected to be restored by year-end (i.e., a decline deemed to be **temporary** in nature) need not be recognized in the interim period. The Emerging Issues Task Force (Issue 86-13) reached a consensus that situations not requiring a write-down are generally limited to seasonal price fluctuations. If an inventory loss from a market decline that is recognized in one period is followed by a market price recovery, the reversal is recognized as a gain in the subsequent interim period. Recognition of this gain in the later interim period is limited to the extent of loss previously recognized. This is in marked contrast to lower of cost or market write-downs in annual financial statements, which cannot later be restored.
4. Firms using standard cost accounting systems ordinarily report purchase price, wage rate, and usage or efficiency variances in the same manner as used at year-end. Planned purchase price and volume variances are deferred if expected to be absorbed by year-end.

The first exception above eliminates the need for a physical inventory count at the interim date. The other three exceptions attempt to synchronize the quarterly statements with the annual report. For example, consider the LIFO liquidation exception. Without this exception, interim cost of goods sold could include low earlier year or base-period costs, while annual cost of goods sold would include only current year costs.

Several additional issues are encountered when using LIFO for interim reporting.

1. What is the best approach to estimate interim LIFO cost of sales?
2. As noted above, when an interim liquidation occurs that is expected to be replaced by year-end, cost of sales includes the expected cost of replacement. How is this adjustment treated on the interim balance sheet?
3. How is an interim liquidation that is **not** expected to be replaced by year-end recorded?

These problems are not addressed in APB 28. The only literature related to these problems is the AICPA Task Force Issues Paper, *Identification and Discussion of Certain Financial Accounting and Reporting Issues Concerning LIFO Inventories.* (See Appendix B of Chapter 7.)

The Issues Paper describes two acceptable approaches to measuring the interim LIFO cost of sales. The first approach makes specific quarterly computations of the LIFO effect based on year-to-date amounts. This is accomplished by reviewing quarterly price level changes and inventory levels. The second approach projects the expected **annual** LIFO effect and then allocates that projection to the quarters. The allocation can be made equally to each quarter or can be made in relation to certain operating criteria per quarter.

The Issues Paper also describes two acceptable approaches to treating the interim liquidation replacement on the balance sheet. The first approach is to record the adjustment for the effect on pretax income of the replacement as a deferred credit in the current liabilities section. The second approach is to record the adjustment as a credit to an inventory valuation allowance.

When an interim LIFO liquidation occurs that is not expected to be reinstated by year-end, the effect of the liquidation is recognized in the period in which it occurs to the extent that it can be reasonably determined. A company using dollar-value LIFO may allocate the expected effect of the liquidation to the quarters affected.

It should be noted that LIFO costing is almost entirely tax-driven, since few actual situations exist where the physical flow of goods follows a last-in, first-out pattern. Were it not for the LIFO conformity rule under the Internal Revenue Code, GAAP might well prohibit LIFO for financial reporting purposes entirely. Recently, international accounting standards have been revised to bar LIFO costing; it will be interesting to see how, given the imperative toward convergence, US GAAP addresses this issue.

Other Costs and Expenses

The integral view is more clearly evident in how GAAP treats costs incurred in interim periods. Most other costs and expenses are recognized in interim periods as incurred. However, an expenditure that **clearly benefits** more than one interim period (e.g., annual repairs or property taxes) is allocated among the periods benefited. The allocation is based on estimates of time expired, benefit received, or activity related to the specific periods. Allocation procedures are to be consistent with those used at year-end reporting dates. However, if a cost incurred during an interim period cannot be readily associated with other interim periods, it is not arbitrarily assigned to those periods. Application of these interim reporting expense principles is illustrated in the examples below.

1. Costs expensed at year-end dates that benefit two or more interim periods (e.g., annual major repairs) are assigned to interim periods through the use of deferrals or accruals.
2. Quantity discounts given customers based on annual sales volume are allocated to interim periods on the basis of sales to customers during the interim period relative to estimated annual sales.
3. Property taxes (and like costs) are deferred or accrued at a year-end date to reflect a full year's charge to operations. Charges to interim periods follow similar procedures.
4. Advertising costs may be deferred to subsequent interim periods within the same fiscal year if such costs clearly benefit the later interim periods. Advertising costs may be accrued and charged to interim periods preceding the time the service is received if there is an advertising program clearly implicit in the sales arrangement. See Chapter 9 for a discussion of the specialized accounting for direct-response advertising prescribed by SOP 93-7. Those rules apply to both interim and annual reporting periods.

Costs and expenses subject to year-end adjustment, such as bad debts expense and discretionary bonuses, are assigned to interim periods in a reasonable and consistent manner to the extent they can be reasonably estimated.

Income Taxes

At each interim date, the reporting entity is required to make its best **estimate of the effective tax rate** expected for the full fiscal year. This estimate reflects expected federal and state tax rates, tax credits, and the effects of applying other tax planning techniques. However, changes in tax legislation are reflected in interim periods only after the enactment date of the legislation. This process is necessary to avoid distortions that would result if early interim periods reflected the entire effect of lower tax brackets, while later periods suffered from having all income taxed at higher bracket amounts. Since income taxes apply to annual income, not to interim periods on stand-alone bases, an integral approach is clearly warranted.

The accounting for income taxes in interim periods is discussed extensively in Appendix A to Chapter 15.

Discontinued Operations and Extraordinary Items

Extraordinary items and the effects of the disposal of a component of the entity (as defined in CON 144) are reported separately in the interim period in which they occur. The same treatment is given to other unusual or infrequently occurring events. No attempt is made to allocate these items over the entire fiscal year.

Materiality is evaluated by relating the item to the expected annual results of operations. Thus, an item to be reported in an early interim period may be judged material but later, when estimated results for the full fiscal year are known with greater precision, be found immaterial; the opposite pattern may also occur, with a presumed immaterial item being later found material to full-year results of operations. Either of such eventualities is inherent in the interim reporting process and would not be deemed an error in need of correction.

Accounting Changes

Retroactive changes in accounting principle are handled on the same basis as in annual reports. Previously issued interim financial statements are retroactively restated.

When a cumulative effect type change occurs in the first quarter, the cumulative effect is included in the first quarter's net income. However, if the cumulative effect change occurs in later quarters, it is treated as if it occurred in the first quarter (to conform with the annual treatment). Therefore, previous quarters' financial statements are restated to reflect the change, and the cumulative effect as of the beginning of the year is included in the first quarter's net income.

The treatment of accounting changes in interim reports is covered extensively in the Appendix to Chapter 20.

Earnings Per Share

The same procedures used at year-end are used for earnings per share computations and disclosures in interim reports. Note that annual earnings per share generally will not equal the sum of the interim earnings per share amounts, due to such factors as stock issuances during the year and market price changes.

Contingencies

In general, contingencies at an interim date are accrued or disclosed in the same manner required for annual reports. The materiality of the contingency is evaluated in relation to the expected annual results.

Certain adjustments related to prior interim periods, such as a settlement of litigation or an income tax dispute, are accorded special treatment in interim reports. If the item is material, directly related to prior interim periods of the current fiscal year, and become reasonably estimable in the current interim period, it is reported as follows:

1. The portion directly related to the current interim period is included in that period's income.
2. Prior interim periods are restated to reflect the portions directly related to those periods.
3. The portion directly related to **prior years** is recognized in the restated first quarter income of the current year.

Seasonality

The operations of many businesses are subject to material seasonal variations. Such businesses are to disclose the seasonality of their activities to avoid the possibility of misleading interim reports. APB 28 also recommends that such businesses supplement their disclosures with information for twelve-month periods ending at the interim date of the current and preceding year.

Interim Reporting Considerations for Publicly Traded Companies

Quarterly reporting. Condensed (summarized) interim financial statements are required to be filed with the SEC on a quarterly basis on Form 10-Q (Regulation S-X, Rule 10-01) or Form 10-QSB. The minimum captions and disclosures required to be included in these financial statements are summarized in the Disclosure Checklist in Appendix A. Although such financial statements are informational tools used by investors, creditors, and analysts, they are not presented in sufficient detail to constitute a fair presentation of the company's financial position and results of operations in accordance with GAAP.

With the issuance of FAS 148 in December 2002, new interim disclosures are now required regarding stock-based employee compensation if the employer elected to use the APB 25 intrinsic value method in any period presented.

Fourth quarter adjustments. When the fourth quarter results are not reported separately, the annual financial statements of publicly traded companies are to include a footnote disclosing the effects on the fourth quarter of accounting changes made during the quarter; disposals of components of the entity; extraordinary, unusual, or infrequently occurring items; and the aggregate effect of year-end adjustments having a material effect on the quarter's results.

Accelerated reporting requirements. In order to provide stakeholders with relevant, actionable information on a more timely basis, the SEC requires certain events that occur between regular quarterly reporting deadlines to be reported on its Form 8-K in accordance with an accelerated timetable as set forth below.

Form 8-K Item number	*Event requiring disclosure*	*Filing deadline*
1	Changes in control of the registrant	Within 15 calendar days after occurrence
2	Acquisition or disposition of material amounts of assets (other than in the ordinary course of business)	Within 15 calendar days after occurrence
3	Bankruptcy or receivership	Within 15 calendar days after occurrence
4	Changes in auditor	Within 5 business days after occurrence
6	Resignations of directors	Within 5 business days after occurrence
8	Change in fiscal year	Within 15 calendar days after the date that the registrant decides to change its fiscal year
10	Code of ethics amendments or waivers granted	Within 5 business days after occurrence

EMERGING ISSUES TASK FORCE ISSUES SUMMARIES

86-13 Recognition of Inventory Market Declines at Interim Reporting Dates

A consensus was reached that, in accordance with APB 28, inventory is to be written down to the lower of cost or market unless substantial evidence is available that the market value will recover before the inventory is sold, or when LIFO is used, that the inventory level will be restored by year-end. Task Force members noted that generally a write-down is required unless the decline is due to seasonal price fluctuations.

98-9 Accounting for Contingent Rent in Interim Financial Periods

A consensus was reached that lessors are not to recognize contingent rental income until the target that causes the contingent rental income is reached.

A consensus was also reached that lessees are to recognize contingent rental expense in the period before the end of the fiscal year when the achievement of the target that triggers the contingent rental expense becomes probable. If the assessment of probable target achievement changes during the year, previously recognized rental expense is reversed.

20 SEGMENT REPORTING

PERSPECTIVE AND ISSUES

Segment reporting, the disclosure of information about different components of an enterprise's operations as well as information related to the enterprise's products and services, its geographic areas, and its major customers, is a relatively recent development in the history of financial reporting. It was necessitated by the growing popularity of conglomerates (i.e., entities comprising disparate operations or diverse products and services—for which the presentation of only aggregated financial information would not provide users with sufficient insights into management decision making, past performance, and future prospects.

The primary benefit of segment reporting is the release of "hidden data" from consolidated financial information. Different segments may possess different levels of profitability, risk, and growth. This important information is merged in the consolidated amounts. Assessing future cash flows and their associated risks can be aided by segment data. For example, knowledge of the level of enterprise operations in a growing or declining product line can help in the prediction of cash flow, while knowledge of the scope of enterprise operations in an unstable geographic area can help in the assessment of risk. In general, information about the nature and relative size of an enterprise's various businesses is considered useful.

Still, several arguments have historically been offered against segment reporting. These are as follows:

1. Comparison of segment data between companies is misleading due to the wide variety of measurement techniques in use.
2. Lack of user knowledge could render segment information meaningless or misleading.
3. Disclosure of such information to competitors, labor unions, etc. could harm the enterprise.
4. Such disclosure may discourage management from taking reasonable business risks to avoid reporting unsatisfactory segment data.
5. The investor invests in the entire company and has no right to expect segment information.

6. Accounting classification and allocation problems may be inherent in segment reporting.
7. Information overload—Financial reports have become too detailed and complex for the average user.

Despite the concerns listed above, segment reporting is an important tool in analyzing companies that are diversified in terms of the types of businesses in which they engage or the geographic locations in which they operate. In addition, over the years, financial analysts have consistently requested that financial statement data be more disaggregated. Academic research has also demonstrated the value of disaggregated information for economic decision making purposes.

FAS 131, *Disclosures about Segments of an Enterprise and Related Information*, currently governs the way publicly held businesses are required to report disaggregated information in financial reports to stockholders, including interim reports. The statement defines operating segments as distinct revenue-producing components of the enterprise about which separate financial information is produced internally, and whose operating results are regularly reviewed by the enterprise.

The approach used in FAS 131 is a "management approach," meaning it is based on the way management organizes segments internally to make operating decisions and assess performance. This differs significantly from the original standard mandating segment disclosures, FAS 14. The management approach, in general, provides that external financial reporting will closely conform to internal reporting, thus giving financial statement users the ability to view the reporting entity's segments in the same manner as internal decision makers.

Financial information can be segmented in several ways: by types of products or services, by geography, by legal entity, or by type of customer. FAS 131 requires that each reportable segment report its profit or loss, certain specific revenue and expense items, and its assets, among other items. The entity is required to reconcile segment information with its consolidated general-purpose financial statements.

In addition, FAS 131 requires that all public enterprises report information about revenues for each product and service, about countries in which the enterprise earns revenues and holds assets, and about major customers, even if this information is not used by the enterprise in making operating decisions.

The statement does not restrict segment reporting to purely financial information. It also requires a description of the company's rationale or methods employed in determining the composition of the segments. This description includes the products or services produced by the segment, differences in measurement practices between a segment and the consolidated entity, and differences in the segment's measurement practices between periods.

The current US standard, FAS 131, closely resembles the revised international standard on segment reporting, IAS 14, which was adopted several years earlier. Thus, as US and international standards converge over the next several years, there will be little or no need to readdress segment requirements under either regime.

Sources of GAAP		
FAS	*FTB*	*EITF*
131	79-4, 79-5	D-70

DEFINITIONS OF TERMS

Assets test. One of the three 10% tests; used to determine whether operating segments are separately reportable.

Chief operating decision maker. A person whose general function (not specific title) is to allocate resources to, and assess the performance of, the segments of an enterprise.

Common costs. Operating expenses incurred by the enterprise for the benefit of more than one segment.

Corporate assets. Assets maintained for general corporate purposes and not used in the operations of any segment.

Expenditures for segment assets. Additions to a segment's long-lived assets; generally, property, plant, and equipment.

Financial report. Includes any aggregation of information that includes one or more complete sets of financial statements, such as an annual report to stockholders or a filing with the Securities and Exchange Commission.

Foreign operations. Operations located outside of the enterprise's home country that generate either unaffiliated or intraenterprise revenues.

General corporate expenses. Expenses incurred for the benefit of the corporation as a whole, which cannot be reasonably allocated to any segment.

Geographic area. An individual country (domestic or foreign).

Intersegment sales. Transfers of products or services, similar to those sold to unaffiliated customers, between operating segments.

Major customer. A customer responsible for at least 10% of an enterprise's revenues.

Management approach. The method chosen by FASB to determine the information to be reported; it is based on the way that management organizes the segments internally for making operating decisions and assessing performance.

Nonpublic enterprise. An enterprise other than one (1) whose debt or equity securities trade in a public market on a foreign or domestic stock exchange, or in the over-the-counter market (including securities quoted only locally or regionally) or (2) that is required to file financial statements with the US Securities and Exchange Commission. An enterprise is no longer considered a nonpublic enterprise when its financial statements are issued in preparation for the sale of any class of securities in a public market. Nonpublic enterprises include certain mutual associations, cooperatives, nonbusiness organizations, and partnerships that often make their financial statements available to a broad class, such as insurance policyholders, depositors, members, contributors, or partners.

Operating profit and loss test. One of the three 10% tests; used to determine whether operating segments are separately reportable.

Operating segment. A component of an enterprise that earns revenues and incurs expenses, about which separate financial information is available that is evaluated regularly by the chief operating decision maker in deciding how to allocate resources and in assessing performance.

Profit center. Those components of an enterprise that sell primarily to outside markets and for which information about revenue and profitability is accumulated. They are the smallest units of activity for which revenue and expense information is accumulated for internal planning and control purposes.

Reportable segments. Segments considered to be significant to an enterprise's operations; a segment that has passed one of three 10% tests or has been identified as being reportable through other criteria (e.g., aggregation, etc.).

Revenues test. One of three 10% tests; used to determine whether operating segments and major customers are reportable.

Segment assets. Those tangible and intangible assets directly owned or used by a segment, including any allocated portion of assets used jointly by more than one segment.

Segment operating profit or loss. All of a segment's revenue minus its operating expenses, including any allocated revenues or expenses (e.g., common costs).

Segment reporting. Disclosure of information about different components of an enterprise's operations as well as information related to the enterprise's products and services, its geographic areas, and its major customers.

Segment revenue. Revenue from sales to unaffiliated customers and from intersegment sales or transfers.

75% test. A test used to determine whether the reportable segments of an enterprise represent a sufficient portion of the enterprise's total operations.

Transfer pricing. The pricing of products or services between segments or geographic locations.

CONCEPTS, RULES, AND EXAMPLES

Applicability of FAS 131

FAS 131 applies to public business enterprises. The statement does not apply to not-for-profit organizations or to **nonpublic enterprises** who are, nevertheless, encouraged to voluntarily provide the segment disclosures described in FAS 131.

Operating Segments

In FAS 131, an **operating segment** is defined as

> *A component of an enterprise engaged in business activity for which it may earn revenues and incur expenses, about which separate financial information is available that is evaluated regularly by the* ***chief operating decision makers*** *in deciding how to allocate resources and in assessing performance.*

This general definition leaves it up to management's judgment to determine operating segment classifications. However, FASB believes meaningful segment information will be provided in external **financial reports** because the externally reported segment information must conform with the segment information that is used internally. FASB provides standards to assist enterprises in determining which operating segments are reportable segments.

Reportable Segments

A segment is considered to be a reportable segment if it is significant to the enterprise as a whole because it satisfies **one** of the three quantitative **10% tests** described below.

Revenues test. Segment revenue (unaffiliated and intersegment) is at least 10% of the combined revenue (unaffiliated and intersegment) of all operating segments.

Operating profit and loss test. Segment operating profit (loss) is computed as revenues minus operating expenses. Both revenues and operating expenses consist of unaffiliated and intersegment components. The absolute amount of segment operating profit or loss is at least 10% of the **greater,** in absolute amount, of

1. Combined operating **profits** of all operating segments reporting a profit.
2. Combined operating **losses** of all operating segments reporting a loss.

Assets test. Segment assets are at least 10% of the combined assets of all operating segments. **Segment assets** are those assets used exclusively by the segment and any allocated portion of assets shared by two or more segments. Assets held for general corporate purposes are not assigned to segments.

Interperiod comparability must be considered in conjunction with the results of the 10% tests. If a segment fails to meet the tests, but has satisfied the tests in the past and is expected to in the future, it is considered reportable in the current year for the sake of comparability. Similarly, if a segment which rarely passes the tests does so in the current year as the result of an unusual event, that segment may be excluded to preserve comparability.

After the 10% tests are completed, a **75% test** must be performed. The combined **unaffiliated** revenue of all **reportable** segments must be at least 75% of the combined unaffiliated revenue of all operating segments. If the 75% test is not satisfied, additional segments must be designated as reportable until the test is satisfied. The purpose of this test is to ensure that reportable segments account for a substantial portion of the entity's operations.

The following example illustrates the three 10% tests and the 75% test.

Operating segment	*Unaffiliated revenue*	*Intersegment revenue*	*Total revenue*	*Operating profit*	*Operating (loss)*	*Assets*
A	$ 90	$ 12	$ 102	$11	$ --	$ 70
B	120	--	120	10	--	50
C	110	20	130	--	(40)	90
D	200	--	200	--	--	140
E	140	300	440	--	(100)	230
F	380	--	380	60	--	260
G	144	--	144	8	--	30
Total	$1,184	$332	$1,516	$89	$(140)	$870

NOTE: Because the $140 total operating losses exceed the $89 total operating profits, the $140 is used for the 10% test.

Summary of Test Results

x = Passed test – Reportable segment

Operating segment	*Revenues (10% of $1,516 = $152)*	*Operating loss (10% of $140 = $14)*	*Assets (10% of $870 = $87)*	*75% of unaffiliated revenues test*
A				
B				
C		x	x	$110
D	x		x	200
E	x	x	x	140
F	x	x	x	380
G				
				830
			75% of $1,184	888
			Revenue shortfall	$ (58)

Note that the aggregate revenues of the reportable segments that passed the 10% tests are $58 short of providing the required coverage of 75% of unaffiliated revenues. Consequently, an additional operating segment (A, B, or G) will need to be added to the reportable segments in order to obtain sufficient coverage.

Certain other factors must be considered when identifying reportable segments. An enterprise may consider aggregating two or more operating segments if they have similar economic characteristics and if the segments are similar in all of the following areas:

1. The nature of the products and services
2. The nature of the production processes
3. The type of customer for their products and services
4. The methods used to distribute their products or provide their services
5. The nature of the regulatory environment

This aggregation can occur prior to performing the 10% tests if the enterprise desires.

Additionally, the enterprise may combine information on operating segments that do not meet any of the 10% tests to produce a reportable segment, but only if the segments meet a majority of the aggregation criteria discussed above. Note that information about operating segments that do not meet any of the 10% thresholds may still be disclosed separately. By utilizing the aggregation criteria and quantitative thresholds (10% tests) for determining reportable segments, the statement uses a modified **management approach**.

The number of reportable segments should not be so great as to decrease the usefulness of segment reporting. As a rule of thumb, FASB suggests that if the number of reportable segments exceeds ten, segment information may become too detailed. In this situation, the most closely related operating segments should be combined into broader reportable segments.

Refer to the diagram in the Appendix to Chapter 2. It provides an example of the different components of an enterprise used for various accounting and reporting purposes.

Accounting Issues

Since segment revenue as defined by FAS 131 includes **intersegment sales, transfer pricing** becomes an issue. Rather than establishing a basis for setting transfer prices, FASB requires companies to use the same transfer prices for segment reporting purposes as are used internally. Since most segments are organizational **profit centers,** internal transfer prices would generally reflect market prices, but even if this is not the case, these same transfer prices must be used for segment disclosures.

Another issue in determining operating profit or loss is the allocation of **common costs**. Common costs are operating expenses incurred by the enterprise for the benefit of more than one operating segment. Again, segment reporting is required to conform to internal management reporting. Accordingly, these costs are only allocated to a segment for external reporting purposes if they are included in the measure of the segment's profit or loss that is used internally by the chief operating decision maker.

Difficulties can arise in distinguishing common costs from **general corporate expenses**. General corporate expenses are not operating expenses from the point of view of any operating segment; they are incurred for the benefit of the corporation as a whole and cannot be reasonably allocated to any operating segment. Common costs, on the other hand, benefit two or more segments and can be allocated to those segments in a manner determined by management to support internal decision making by the reporting entity.

Similarly, only those assets that are included internally in the measure of the segment's assets used to make operating decisions are reported as assets of the segment in external financial reports. If management allocates amounts to segment profit or assets internally and those amounts are used by the chief operating decision maker, then those amounts are to be allocated on a reasonable basis and disclosed.

Segment Disclosures

FAS 131 requires several disclosures regarding the enterprise's reportable segments. They include

1. **General information**—An explanation of how management identified the enterprise's reportable segments, including whether operating segments have been aggregated, is to be presented. Additionally, a description of the types of products and services from which each reportable segment derives its revenues should be provided.
2. **Certain information about reported segment profit and loss, segment assets and the basis of measurement**—This will include certain revenue and expense items included in segment profit and loss, as well as certain amounts related to the determination of segment assets. Also, the basis of measurement for these items must be disclosed.

3. **Reconciliations**—The enterprise must reconcile the segment amounts disclosed to the corresponding consolidated entity amounts.
4. **Interim period information**—Although the interim disclosures are not as extensive as in the annual financial report, certain segment disclosures are required in interim financial reports.

See the Appendix for an illustrative example of the disclosures required for segment reporting. Additionally, FAS 131 provides an illustrative example.

Restatement of Previously Reported Segment Information

Segment reporting is required on a comparative basis when the associated financial statements are comparative. Therefore, the information must be restated to preserve comparability whenever the enterprise has changed the structure of its internal organization in a manner that causes a change to its reportable segments. The enterprise must explicitly disclose that it has restated the segment information of earlier periods.

Entity-Wide Disclosures

In addition to segment data, FAS 131 mandates that certain entity-level disclosures be made. The entity-wide disclosures are required for all reporting entities subject to FAS 131, even those that have only a single reportable segment.

Products and services. Revenue from external customers for each product and service or each group of similar products and services is to be reported by the enterprise unless impracticable. If deemed to be impracticable, that fact is to be disclosed. If the company's reportable segments have been organized around products and services, then this disclosure will generally not be required.

Geographic areas. An enterprise separately discloses revenues from external customers and long-lived assets attributable to its domestic operations and **foreign operations**. If the company's reportable segments have been organized around geographic areas, then these disclosures will generally not be required.

An enterprise's domestic operations are those operations located in the enterprise's home country that generate either unaffiliated or intra-enterprise revenues. The enterprise's foreign operations are similar operations located outside of the enterprise's home country.

If the enterprise functions in two or more foreign **geographic areas,** to the extent revenues or assets of an individual foreign geographic area are material, then these amounts are separately disclosed. In addition, the enterprise's basis for attributing revenue to different geographic areas is disclosed. A geographic area is defined as an individual country. If providing this information is impracticable, that fact is to be disclosed.

Major customers. If an enterprise earns 10% or more of its revenue on sales to a single external customer, that fact and the amount of revenue from each such customer must be disclosed. Also, the segment making these sales must be disclosed. This disclosure provides information on concentrations of risk.

A group of customers under common control, such as subsidiaries of a common parent, is regarded as a single customer. Similarly the various agencies of a government are considered to be a single customer. An insuring entity (such as Blue Cross) is not considered to be the customer unless that entity (rather than the patient) controls the decision as to the doctor, type of service, etc.

EMERGING ISSUES TASK FORCE ISSUES SUMMARIES

Topic D-70 Questions Related to the Implementation of FASB Statement 131

FASB staff addressed the following inquiries regarding the implementation of FAS 131:

1. Depreciation and amortization expense is required to be disclosed for each reportable segment even if the chief operating decision maker uses earnings before income taxes, depreciation, and amortization (EBITDA) to evaluate segment performance and receives reports that include each segment's depreciation and amortization separately from EBITDA.
2. Sometimes, in practice, the chief operating decision maker uses different measures of performance to evaluate different segments. The example is given that some segments may be evaluated based on operating income and others based on net income. In applying the 10% of operating profit test, a consistent method is to be applied to all segments in making the determination of which are reportable segments. FASB Staff pointed out, however, that the disclosures are still required to include the actual measure of profit or loss that the chief operating decision maker uses to evaluate the performance of each reportable segment.

FASB TECHNICAL BULLETINS

79-4 Segment Reporting of Puerto Rican Operations

Puerto Rican operations of US enterprises are not considered to be foreign operations subject to the disclosure requirements of FAS 131. However, voluntarily providing the additional disclosures is permitted.

APPENDIX

COMPREHENSIVE ILLUSTRATION

The following illustration is provided for a hypothetical company, Resources Unlimited. The illustration provides segment disclosures by legal entity.

NOTE: FAS 131 provides illustrative segment disclosures by product line.

Description of the types of products and services from which each reportable segment derives its revenues

Resources Unlimited has four reportable segments: Wholesale Corporation, Retail Corporation, Library Corporation, and Software Corporation. Wholesale Corporation buys and resells used elementary and college textbooks. Retail Corporation operates 200 college book stores and a related e-commerce website selling both new and used college textbooks, trade books, sports apparel, and other sundries. Library Corporation sells library books primarily to elementary school libraries. Software Corporation develops and sells library systems application software.

Measurement of segment profit or loss and segment assets

The accounting policies of the segments are the same as those described in the summary of significant accounting policies except the first-in-first-out (FIFO) method of inventory valuation is used for segment reporting. In addition, Resources Unlimited allocates interest expense to each segment based on the segment's average borrowings from the corporate office. However, the related debt is not allocated to the segments and remains on the corporate balance sheet. Resources Unlimited evaluates performance based on profit or loss before income taxes not including nonrecurring gains and losses.

Resources Unlimited accounts for intersegment sales and transfers as if the sales or transfers were transacted with third parties (i.e., at current market prices).

Factors management used to identify the enterprise's reportable segments

Resources Unlimited's business is conducted through four separate legal entities that are wholly owned subsidiaries. At the company's inception, each entity was founded and managed by a different Resources Unlimited stockholder/family member. Each corporation is still managed separately, as each business has a distinct customer base and requires different strategic and marketing efforts.

Information about profit and loss and assets

The amounts in the illustration are assumed to be the amounts in reports used by the chief operating decision maker. Resources Unlimited allocates interest expense to the segments, however, income taxes and other unusual items are not allocated.

(Table in thousands)

	Wholesale Corporation	*Retail Corporation*	*Library Corporation*	*Software Corporation*	*Totals*
Revenues from external customers	$197,500	$263,000	$182,300	$102,200	$745,000
Intersegment revenues	23,000	--	--	--	23,000
Interest revenue	250	150	--	--	400
Interest expense	1,570	2,150	1,390	2,700	7,810
Depreciation and amortization	8,600	13,100	7,180	6,070	34,950
Segment profit	12,100	13,500	9,900	5,100	40,600
Segment assets	121,200	153,350	100,600	85,000	460,150
Expenditures for segment assets	7,200	12,700	5,600	6,700	32,200

Reconciliations

An illustration of reconciliations for revenues, profit and loss, assets, and other significant items is shown below. In general, this illustration assumes that there are no unreported operating segments, but there is a corporate headquarters, thus most reconciling items relate to corporate revenues and expenses.

As discussed previously, the company recognizes and measures inventory based on FIFO valuation for segment reporting. The consolidated financial statements are assumed not to include discontinued operations or the cumulative effect of a change in accounting principle.

	($000 omitted)
Revenue	
Total revenues for reportable segments	$768,000
Elimination of intersegment revenue	(23,000)
Total consolidated revenue	$745,000
Profit and loss	
Total profit for reportable segments	$40,600
Elimination of intersegment profits	(6,100)
Unallocated amounts relating to corporate operations:	
Interest revenue	500
Interest expense	(800)
Depreciation and amortization	(1,900)
Unrealized gain on trading securities	1,865
Income before income taxes and extraordinary items	$34,165
Assets	
Total assets for reportable segments	$460,150
Corporate short-term investments, land and building	25,100
Adjustment for LIFO reserve in consolidation	(9,200)
	$476,050

Other significant items

	Segment totals	Adjustments	Consolidated totals
Expenditures for segment assets	$32,200	800	$33,000

The reconciling adjustment is the amount of expenditures incurred for additions to the corporate headquarters building, which is not included in the segment information.

Products and services

Used textbooks	$296,125
New textbooks	72,150
Trade books	45,700
Sports apparel	41,325
Sundries	5,200
Library books	182,300
Library software	102,200
Total consolidated revenue	$745,000

Geographic information

	Revenues*	Long-lived assets
United States	$687,400	$253,200
Foreign countries	57,600	18,800
Total	$745,000	$272,000

* *Revenues are attributed to countries as follows: For Wholesale Corporation and Library Corporation, the country in which the customer takes delivery. For Retail Corporation the country in which the retail store is located or, for internet sales, the country to which the merchandise is delivered. For Software Corporation, the country where the host server on which the software is installed is located.*

Major customers

An illustration of the required disclosures is not provided in this example as Resources Unlimited has no major customers, as defined in FAS 131.

21 ACCOUNTING CHANGES AND CORRECTION OF ERRORS

PERSPECTIVE AND ISSUES

Under US GAAP, management is granted the flexibility of choosing from an array of alternative methods to account for the same economic transactions. Examples of this abound throughout this publication in such diverse areas as the different cost-flow assumptions used to account for inventory and cost of sales, different methods of depreciating long-lived assets, and different methods of identifying operating segments. The professional literature (in the areas of accounting principles, auditing standards, quality control standards, and professional ethics) is emphatic that, in choosing from the various alternatives, management is to choose principles and apply them in a manner that results in financial statements that are representationally faithful to economic substance over form and fully transparent to the user.

Changes can occur due to changes in the assumptions and estimates underlying the application of accounting principles and methods of applying them, changes in the acceptable principles by a standards-setting authority, or other types of changes.

The accounting for and disclosure of changes in accounting for given transactions are issues that have confronted the accounting profession for many years. The problem has been particularly sensitive because of the impact that alternative ways of accounting for specific transactions, and of disclosing the effects of such changes, often has on financial statement analysis, and thus on investment and other decisions. Financial analysis presumes the consistency and comparability of financial statements across periods and among entities within industry groupings. Any type of accounting change creates an inconsistency, and since some change is inevitable the challenge is to present the effects in a manner that is most readily comprehended by users of financial statements, who may make various adjustments of their own to make the information comparable for analysis purposes.

This concern is exacerbated by the fact that there has been, in the late 1900s and early 2000s, a growing crisis of confidence about the accuracy of financial reports and the credibility of parties associated with preparing and auditing them. The number and magnitude of restatements of previously issued financial statements, with reportedly as many as 10% of all publicly traded companies having at least one such restatement over a recent four-year period, has raised disturbing questions about management manipulation and the possible complicity, or at least negligence, of external auditors. The enactment of the Sarbanes-Oxley Act of 2002 and the restructuring of oversight of the auditing profession are two consequences of the series of unfortunate developments, and the move to "converge" US GAAP and international accounting standards is a further indicator of the premium now being placed on accurate, transparent financial reporting.

When contemplating a potential change in accounting principles, a primary focus of management should be to consider its effect on financial statement comparability. APB 20 was issued to standardize the reporting of the effects of various classes of accounting changes, so that this information would be reported and disclosed in a manner such that the understandability of financial statements would be enhanced and analysis of the reporting entity's financial position and results of operations would be facilitated.

In APB 20 the Board defined an accounting change as being a change in

1. Accounting principle
2. Accounting estimate
3. Reporting entity

While the correction of an error in previously issued financial statements (which is often referred to as a "restatement") is not considered an accounting change, per se, this subject is also dealt with by APB 20.

The Board concluded that in the preparation of financial statements there is an underlying presumption that an accounting principle, once adopted, should not be changed in accounting for events and transactions of a similar type. This consistent use of accounting principles was believed to enhance the utility of financial statements. The presumption that an enterprise should not change an accounting principle may be overcome only if management justifies the use of an alternative acceptable accounting principle on the basis that it is preferable.

APB 20 contains no definition of preferability or criteria by which to make such assessments. Because there is no universally agreed-upon set of objectives for external financial reporting, what is preferable to one industry or company is not necessarily considered preferable to another. This leads to some of the same consistency problems in reporting that existed prior to the issuance of APB 20.

SAS 69 (discussed in Chapter 1) requires that an entity adopt the accounting principles set forth in pronouncements with effective dates after March 15, 1992. An entity initially applying an accounting principle after that date (including those making an accounting change) must follow the applicable GAAP hierarchy set forth in SAS 69. An entity following an established accounting principle that was effective on or before March 15, 1992, need not change its accounting until a new pronouncement is issued.

According to FAS 111, an entity making a change in accounting principle to conform to the recommendations of a statement of position, a practice bulletin, or an EITF consensus is to record and report the change as specified in the pronouncement. In the event the pronouncement is silent regarding these matters, the entity is to report the change in accounting principle according to the rules outlined in this chapter. However, EITF consensuses are usually applied prospectively to transactions occurring after the consensus has been reached, unless otherwise stated.

In late 2003, FASB proposed a revision to the reporting of voluntary changes in accounting principle. This proposal would essentially conform US GAAP practice to that under international accounting standards (IFRS), and was made as part of the joint FASB-IASB effort to achieve convergence of these two major sets of standards. If adopted, this would replace APB 20 and would instead require retrospective application of a newly adopted accounting policy for most changes in accounting principle, including changes in accounting principle required by issuance of new pronouncements. FASB would, however, retain the right to require different transition provisions for changes in accounting principle mandated by the issuance of new pronouncements when it deems such differences to be appropriate. The FASB proposal would also require the reporting of a change in depreciation, amortization, or depletion method as a change in an accounting estimate rather than a change in principle, as is currently required under APB 20.

IMPORTANT NOTE: The discussion in this chapter, apart from that identified as being based on the FASB proposal, is derived from and consistent with the requirements under APB 20. If the FASB proposal is, as has been indicated, adopted for years beginning after December 15, 2004, then accounting for changes in accounting principles will be altered as indicated in the discussion of the Exposure Draft, and will no longer be in conformity with APB 20.

In February 2003, the FASB staff began issuing FASB Staff Positions (abbreviated in this publication as FSP and discussed more fully in Chapter 1) to provide guidance on the application of its authoritative literature. Unless otherwise specified, FSP will be effective for new transactions or arrangements entered into after the beginning of the first fiscal quarter following the date of final posting of the FSP to the FASB Web site (http://www.FASB.org). Absent specific guidance contained in a FSP, the enterprise may either apply it prospectively or may apply it to prior transactions as the cumulative effect of a change in accounting principle.

Sources of GAAP		
APB	*FAS*	*FIN*
20, 28	3, 16, 111	1, 20

DEFINITIONS OF TERMS

Accounting change. In the context of APB 20, an accounting change is one of three types of modifications that affect a reporting entity's accounting principles and practices, or its application of them. The three types of accounting changes are: (1) a change in accounting principle from one generally accepted accounting principle to another alternative that is considered preferable, (2) a change in an accounting estimate, and (3) a change in the reporting entity. Although, technically, corrections of errors in prior periods' financial statements (commonly referred to as "restatements") are not considered accounting changes, their treatment is also governed by APB 20.

Accounting principle. A methodology used to measure and report the monetary effects of economic events in financial statements. Acceptable accounting principles are either prescribed by a recognized standard-setting body in an authoritative pronouncement or, in the absence of a relevant pronouncement, are predominantly followed by entities that engage in transactions of a similar nature or operate in a particular industry or profession. In the context of APB 20, accounting principles encompass both accounting practices and the methods of applying them.

Change in accounting estimate. A revision of an accounting measurement based on the occurrence of new events, additional experience, subsequent developments, better insight, and improved judgment. Refining previously made estimates is an inherent part of the accounting process.

Change in accounting estimate effected by a change in accounting principle. A change in accounting estimate that is inseparable from the effect of a related change in accounting principle (for example, a change in depreciation method).

Change in accounting principle. A change from one generally accepted accounting principle to another generally accepted accounting principle, including the methods of applying the principles. This does not include selection and adoption of an accounting principle to account for types of events occurring for the first time in the operations of a given reporting entity.

Change in reporting entity. A special type of change in accounting principle that results in financial statements that, in effect, are those of a different reporting entity. Financial statements are prepared for an entity that is different from the one reported on in previous financial statements.

Comparability. The quality of information that enables users to identify similarities in and differences between two sets of economic circumstances. Normally, comparability is a quantitative assessment of a common characteristic.

Consistency. Conformity from period to period with unchanging policies and procedures. Enhances the utility of financial statements to users by facilitating analysis and understanding of comparative accounting data.

Cumulative effect. The difference between the retained earnings balance at the beginning of the year in which a change is reported and the beginning retained earnings balance that would have been reported if the new principle had been applied retroactively in all prior periods that would have been affected.

Error. Mathematical mistakes, mistakes in applying accounting principles, oversight or misuse of available facts, and use of unacceptable GAAP.

Pro forma. Disclosure, in order to enhance comparability, of the effects of applying an accounting principle to a particular period or periods in which it has not been in effect, as if it had been effect.

In recent years, the concept of pro forma disclosure has been used in a different context. Many publicly held companies, in particular, have issued quarterly and annual "earnings releases" to the press that attempt to recast or interpret its GAAP-basis earnings on a "pro forma basis." These pro forma numbers are purportedly designed to provide investors, creditors, and analysts with added insight into the company's future earnings and cash flow prospects by removing from the GAAP-basis amounts the effects of transactions that are unusual or nonrecurring (which are sometimes referred to as "special items"). Although the stated intent may be laudable, this practice has arguably contributed to the erosion in confidence in the credibility of management and in the financial reporting process itself. This is because there is no uniformity (comparability) in how companies measure and report "pro forma" earnings, there is no auditor association with these numbers, and a company is not constrained to follow the same methodology for tallying pro forma earnings from period to period. In fact, studies reveal that pro forma earnings are much more likely to be higher than GAAP earnings than lower.

The SEC paid close attention to the abuses associated with this practice and in its Accounting and Auditing Enforcement Release 1499, issued early in 2002, announced for the first time that it had issued a cease and desist order against a registrant that had produced an earnings release that "was materially misleading because it created the false and misleading impression that the Company had exceeded earnings expectations primarily through operational improvements, when in fact it had not."

Effective March 28, 2003, the SEC adopted Regulation G and related final rules as required by the Sarbanes-Oxley Act of 2002, governing the disclosure or release by registrants of non-GAAP financial information. Under Regulation G, the presentation of non-GAAP information by registrants must include a reconciliation of the non-GAAP information to the most directly comparable GAAP financial measure.

Restatement of financial reports. The recasting of a previously determined and published balance sheet or operating statement and its republication where there has been a substantial change in accounting principles or policies or a correction of a prior period error.

This term is not defined in authoritative accounting literature but rather is used in practice by financial statement issuers.

CONCEPTS, RULES, AND EXAMPLES

APB 20 describes three methods to reflect accounting changes and the type of change for which each is to be used. These are

1. Retroactive
2. Current
3. Prospective

Retroactive treatment requires an adjustment to all current and prior period financial statements for the effect of the accounting change. Prior period financial statements presented currently for comparative purpose are restated on a basis consistent with the newly adopted principle.

Current treatment requires reporting the cumulative effect of the accounting change in the current year's income statement as a special item. Prior period financial statements are **not** restated.

Prospective treatment of accounting changes requires **no** restatement of prior period financial statements and **no** computing or reporting of the accounting change's cumulative effect in the current period's income statement. Only current and/or future periods' financial statement data will reflect the effects of the accounting change.

Each of the types of accounting changes and the proper treatment prescribed for them is discussed in detail in the following sections.

Change in Accounting Principle

When management contemplates a change in accounting principle, APB 20 mandates that it consider whether the new principle is "preferable" to the principle that it is intended to replace. If the change is made, the disclosures accompanying the financial statements of the period of change are to include management's justification for the change. In accordance with FIN 1, this preferability assessment must be made from the perspective of financial reporting, and not from an income tax perspective; thus, favorable tax consequences do not justify a change in financial reporting practices.

According to APB 20, the term "accounting principle" includes the accounting principles and practices used by an enterprise as well as its methods of applying them. FIN 1 elaborated on this by stating that a change in the components used to cost a firm's inventory is a change in accounting principle.

APB 20 provides that changes in accounting principles are to be accounted for currently using the cumulative effect method. However, there are a few highly specific exceptions to this general rule set forth by the standard. One of these occurs when an authoritative standard-setting body issues a new standard. The accounting for the change resulting from the adoption of the standard will be prescribed by transition provisions included in the new pronouncement. Each new FAS has its own transition rules. Absent an exception to the general rule, however, APB 20 requires that the cumulative effect method be used for most changes in accounting principles, and that no restatement to be made to prior periods' financial statements.

The **cumulative effect** method is applied using the following four steps:

Step 1 — Previously issued financial statements are not restated.

Step 2 — The cumulative effect of changing to the new accounting principle on retained earnings at the beginning of the period in which the change occurs is a separately stated caption on the face of the income statement and is included in computing net income of the period of the change.

Step 3 — The effect of adopting the new principle on income before extraordinary items and net income, including per share amounts of the period of change, is disclosed in the notes to the financial statements.

Step 4 — Income before extraordinary items and net income computed on a pro forma basis (defined below) are shown on the face of the income statements for all periods presented as if the newly adopted principle had been applied during all periods affected. The nature of and justification for the change is disclosed in the notes to the financial statements of the period in which the change is made.

Under the provisions of APB 20, **income for the period of the change is to be computed using the newly adopted principle** while all other periods are to be presented as they originally appeared (step 1). **Restatement will occur only in the disclosures and the pro forma calculations.** Note, however, that under the FASB proposal which is expected to be adopted before year-end 2004, most changes in accounting principle will be accounted for under the retroactive method, and all prior periods presented will have to be restated (unless impracticable to do so), in contrast to the approach mandated for the past thirty-three years. (See the discussion later in this chapter for a detailed look at the FASB's proposal.)

The cumulative effect of a change in accounting principle is to appear as a single amount on the income statement between extraordinary items and net income (step 2). The amount shown is the difference between

1. The amount of retained earnings at the beginning of the period, and
2. The amount of retained earnings that would have been reported at that date if the new accounting principle had been applied retroactively to all prior periods affected.

The cumulative effect is generally determined by

1. Calculating income before income taxes applying both the new principle and the old principle for all prior periods affected.
2. Computing the difference between the two incomes for each prior period.
3. Adjusting these differences for the income tax effects.
4. Totaling the (net of income tax) differences for each prior period.

This total represents the cumulative effect adjustment at the beginning of the current period. The cumulative effect will either be an addition to or a subtraction from current income depending on how the change to the new principle affects income. Generally, only the direct effects of the change and the related income tax effect are included in the cumulative effect calculation (i.e., if the company changes its method of computing depreciation, only the effects of the change in depreciation expense, net of income tax, are considered to be direct effects). Indirect effects, such as the effect on a profit sharing contribution or bonus payments that would have occurred as a result of the change in net income, are not included in the cumulative effect computation unless these are to be actually recorded (e.g., where the liability recorded for the profit-sharing expense is to be adjusted, or a recovery is to be obtained from the employees who have already been provided with bonuses based on the now revised results of operations).

Step 3 requires that the effects of the change on income before extraordinary items and net income be disclosed for the year of the change. This is the difference between applying the old accounting principle and the new principle on an after-tax basis in the year of the change. The amounts are disclosed for both the total effect and the per share effect (for public companies). In addition, the nature of and justification for the change must be disclosed, clearly indicating why the newly adopted principle is preferable.

The computation of income on a pro forma basis must be made for each period presented accompanying the current year's financial statements. The objective is to facilitate comparability by presenting income before extraordinary items and net income for each of those prior periods as if the new principle had been applied. This is achieved by adjusting each period's income before extraordinary items as previously reported (i.e., applying the old accounting principle). The adjustment is made by adding or subtracting the difference in income, net of income tax, for each period to income before extraordinary items as previously reported. The difference, net of income tax, is the change in net income that would have occurred had the new principle been applied instead of the old principle. This results in presenting pro forma income before extraordinary items that reflects the application of the new principle. Pro forma net income is then calculated as normally from the adjusted income before extraordinary items. The per share amounts required are based upon the pro forma income before extraordinary items and net income amounts.

The pro forma calculation required by step 4 differs from that of the cumulative effect. It is to include both the direct effects of the change and the "nondiscretionary" adjustments of items **based** on income before income taxes or net income. Examples of nondiscretionary items would be profit sharing expense, incentive compensation, or certain royalties. These expenses are potentially based on formulas tied to a specified percentage of net income. The related income tax effects are recognized for **both** the direct and nondiscretionary adjustments. The pro forma calculation is to be shown on the face of the financial statements for income before extraordinary items and net income. The earnings per share amounts (both basic and diluted as defined in FAS 128 and discussed in Chapter 18) for both are also computed and shown for each period presented in the financial statements of public companies. According to FAS 128, if space is not available on the face of the financial statements, the pro forma information may be disclosed prominently in the notes to the financial statements.

The following example illustrates the computations and disclosures necessary when applying the cumulative effect method. This particular example is adapted from the one that is included in Appendix A of APB 20.

Example of cumulative effect

Isenstein, Inc. decides in 2005 to adopt the straight-line method of depreciation for plant equipment. The straight-line method will be used for all new acquisitions as well as for previously acquired plant equipment for which depreciation had been provided using an accelerated method.

The following assumptions are being made:

1. The direct effect of the change is limited to the change in accumulated depreciation.
2. The income tax rate is a flat 40% for all years.
3. The executive incentive bonus is the only nondiscretionary item affected by the change. It is 10% of pretax accounting income.
4. There are 1,000,000 shares of common stock outstanding throughout the entire period affected by the change.
5. An additional 100,000 shares would be issued if all the outstanding bonds were converted to common stock. Annual interest on this bond obligation is $25,000 (net of income tax).
6. For 2004 and 2005 the income before extraordinary item is given as $1,100,000 and $1,200,000 respectively. There is an extraordinary item in each year amounting to $100,000 for 2004 and ($35,000) for 2005. The extraordinary items are included in the example to illustrate the proper positioning of the cumulative effect adjustment on the income statement.

	Increase (decrease) in net income			
Year	*Excess of accelerated depreciation over straight-line depreciation*	*Direct effects of change, net of tax*	*Nondiscretionary item, net of tax*	*Adjustment to obtain pro forma amounts*
Prior to 2001	$ 20,000	$ 12,000	$ (1,200)	$ 10,800
2001	80,000	48,000	(4,800)	43,200
2002	70,000	42,000	(4,200)	37,800
2003	50,000	30,000	(3,000)	27,000
2004	30,000	18,000	(1,800)	16,200
Total at beg. of 2005	$250,000	$150,000	$(15,000)	$135,000

The following narrative provides assistance in grasping the computational aspects of the information given above. The "excess of accelerated depreciation over straight-line depreciation" is given in this example. It is generally determined by recomputing the depreciation under the new method and obtaining the difference between the two methods. The "direct effects of change, net of tax" represents the effect of the actual change (i.e., depreciation) upon income before extraordinary items adjusted for the income tax effects. For example, in the years prior to 2001 the change in depreciation methods (from accelerated **to** straight-line) resulted in a $20,000 reduction in depreciation expense (or an increase in income). The net of tax number is $12,000 because the $20,000 increase in income is reduced by an $8,000 (40% x $20,000) increase in income tax expense.

The "nondiscretionary item, net of tax" represents the income statement items affected indirectly as a result of the change. In this case, it was given that the executive incentive bonus equal to 10% of pretax accounting income was the only "nondiscretionary item" affected. Thus, in years prior to 2001, when pretax accounting income increased by $20,000, the bonus expense would have been $2,000 higher ($20,000 x 10%). APB 20 indicates that this also be computed net of income tax, and because the expense would have increased by $2,000, income taxes would have decreased by $800 ($2,000 x 40%). The net of income tax increase in expense is $1,200. The **pro forma** amounts are to include both the direct and indirect effects of the change. The computation for years prior to 2001 in this example is as follows:

	Increase (decrease) in net income
Decrease in depreciation expense	$20,000
Increase in income taxes attributable to reduction in depreciation expense	(8,000)
Decrease in depreciation expense, net of income tax effect	12,000
Increase in compensation expense	(2,000)
Decrease in income taxes attributable to increase in compensation expense	800
Increase in compensation expense, net of income tax effect	(1,200)
Net effect of change in prior period's depreciation	$10,800

The pro forma amounts computed in the example are needed for disclosure purposes so that 2004 income can be shown on a comparative basis with 2005 net income (i.e., adding the 2004 income before the change. The pro forma increase or decrease will result in 2004 net income that reflects the same accounting principles as 2005 net income).

Below is the proper method of presentation and disclosure required by APB 20 for this example.

On the Face of the Income Statement

	2005	*2004*
Income before extraordinary item and cumulative effect of a change in accounting principle	$1,200,000	$1,100,000
Extraordinary item (description), net of income tax	(35,000)	100,000
Cumulative effect on prior years (to December 31, 2004) of changing to a different depreciation method, net of income tax	150,000	--
Net income	$1,315,000	$1,200,000
Per share amounts:		
Earnings per common share—assuming no dilution:		
Income before extraordinary item and cumulative effect of a change in accounting principle	$1.20	$1.10
Extraordinary item	(0.04)	0.10
Cumulative effect on prior years (to December 31, 2004) of changing to a different depreciation method	0.15	--
Net income	$1.31	$1.20
Earnings per common share—assuming dilution:		
Income before extraordinary item and cumulative effect of a change in accounting principle	$1.11	$1.02
Extraordinary item	(0.03)	0.09
Cumulative effect on prior years (to December 31, 2004) of changing to a different depreciation method	0.14	--
Net income	$1.22	$1.11
Pro forma amounts assuming the new depreciation method is applied retroactively:		
Income before extraordinary item and cumulative effect of a change in accounting principle	$1,200,000	$1,116,200
Earnings per common share—assuming no dilution	$1.20	$1.12
Earnings per common share—assuming dilution	$1.11	$1.04
Net income	$1,165,000	$1,216,200
Earnings per common share—assuming no dilution	$1.17	$1.22
Earnings per common share—assuming dilution	$1.08	$1.13

In the Notes to the Financial Statements

Note A: Change in Depreciation Method for Plant Equipment

During 2005 the company decided to change its method of computing depreciation on plant equipment from sum-of-the-years' digits (SYD) to the straight-line method. The company made the change because the straight-line method better matches revenues and cost amortization and, therefore, is a preferable accounting principle. The new method has been applied retroactively to equipment acquisitions of prior years. The effect of the change in 2005 was to increase income before extraordinary items and net income by approximately $10,000 (or $.01 per share). The adjustment of $150,000 (net of $100,000 in income taxes) included in 2005 income is the cumulative effect of applying the new method retroactively. The pro forma amounts shown on the income statement have been adjusted for the effect of the retroactive application of the new depreciation method, the change in incentive compensation expense which would have been incurred had the new method been used, and the related income taxes for both.

If the company elected to disclose the pro forma amounts in notes to the financial statements and not on the face of the income statement, the following disclosure would have been included as part of Note A.

The following pro forma amounts show the effect of the retroactive application of the change from the SYD to the straight-line method of depreciation.

	Actual	Pro forma
2005		
Income before extraordinary items	$1,200,000	$1,200,000
Basic earnings per share*	$1.20	$1.20
Diluted earnings per share*	$1.11	$1.11
Net income	$1,315,000	$1,165,000
Basic earnings per share	$1.31	$1.17
Diluted earnings per share	$1.22	$1.08

* *FAS 128 uses these captions but allows for alternatives such as those above.*

	Actual	Pro forma
2004		
Income before extraordinary items	$1,100,000	$1,116,200
Basic earnings per share	$1.10	$1.12
Diluted earnings per share	$1.02	$1.04
Net income	$1,200,000	$1,216,200
Basic earnings per share	$1.20	$1.22
Diluted earnings per share	$1.11	$1.13

Notice how in the above example the four steps provided in APB 20 are followed.

Step 1 — No restatement takes place on the face of the income statements. The 2004 results provided for comparative purposes are the same as those originally reported.

Step 2 — The cumulative effect of the change is included on the face of the income statement as a single amount. The $150,000 shown in 2005 represents the total direct effect net of income tax for all years prior to 2005. The effect of the change in 2005 is included in depreciation expense which is part of the computation of net income for 2005.

Step 3 — The required disclosure of the 2005 effects of the change, both in total and the per share amounts, is usually done in the notes to the financial statements. This is assumed to be $10,000 in the example above or $.01 per share.

Step 4 — The pro forma amounts are used to make the results from the two years comparable. 2004 income before extraordinary items is increased by $16,200 to $1,116,200. This $16,200 is the amount found in the original table across from 2004. Notice also how 2005 net income no longer contains a cumulative effect adjustment. This is because 2005 and 2004 earnings, under the pro forma computations, are derived using the same accounting principles.

As was noted earlier, there are five specific situations set forth in APB 20 for which a change in accounting principle is to be accounted for retroactively in the financial statements.

1. A change from LIFO to another inventory method
2. A change in the method of accounting for long-term contracts
3. A change to or from the full cost method of accounting for exploration costs in the extractive industries
4. A change made by a company first issuing financial statements for the purpose of obtaining additional equity capital, effecting a business combination, or registering securities
5. A change mandated by an authoritative pronouncement (this case is not specified by APB 20, and standard setters have generally required that the effects of adopting a new standard be recognized currently). FIN 20 has also indicated that an AICPA SOP may mandate the accounting treatment given the change to adopt its provisions.

The process of restating the financial statements in these situations was favored because it did not require that the cumulative effect of the change be included in net income of the period of change. Rather, each of the years presented is adjusted to reflect the new accounting principle. The cumulative effect is calculated in the same manner shown earlier for accounting changes receiving current treatment. **However, the cumulative effect on all periods prior to the earliest period presented is treated as an adjustment to beginning retained earnings of that period.** The net income of each period presented is recomputed applying the new principle. Thus, the adjustment to beginning retained earnings includes all income effects prior to each period presented, and the recomputed net income includes the effect of the new principle on income for each period presented.

Together these two adjustments restate the retained earnings ending balance for each period presented to the amount it would have been had the new principle always been consistently applied. This restatement process is followed for all periods presented. Also, the nature of and justification for the change must be disclosed in the year that the change is made. In addition, the effect of the change on income before extraordinary items, net income, and the related per share amounts is disclosed for all periods presented. Subsequent financial statements do not need to repeat the disclosures.

The restatement need only reflect the direct effects of the change in accounting principle. An exception to this general rule arises if the direct effect results in a change in a nondiscretionary item that will actually be recorded by the company. For example, assume that profit-sharing expense is based on net income. If the company changes its method of accounting for long-term construction contracts, that change results in an increase or decrease in income in each of the prior years. This increase or decrease in income, had it been known during those earlier periods, would have changed the amount of the profit-sharing expense required during the applicable years. Reported profit-sharing expense for the earlier years would only be recognized for the purpose of the restatement if an underpayment is now to be paid (or if an excessive payment is to be recovered). If the profit-sharing agreement does not require an adjustment to the actual contribution, the increase in profit-sharing expense would not be recognized in the restated financial statements.

The following illustration is an adaptation of Appendix B in APB 20 and illustrates the proper restatement in a situation where the company changes its method of accounting for long-term construction contracts. As mentioned above, this is one of the five situations for which APB 20 requires retroactive treatment.

Example of retroactive treatment

During 2005 Newburger Company decided to adopt the percentage-of-completion method of accounting for all of its long-term construction contracts. The company had used the completed contract method in previous years and maintained records that were adequate to retroactively apply the percentage-of-completion method.

The following assumptions are made for this example:

1. A constant tax rate of 40%.
2. 1,000,000 common shares outstanding in all periods affected by the change.
3. An additional 100,000 shares would be issued if all of the outstanding bonds were converted. The annual interest on this bond obligation is $15,000 (net of tax).

	Pretax accounting income		*Increase (decrease) in income*	
Year	*Percentage-of-completion method*	*Completed-contract method*	*Direct*	*Net of tax effect*
Prior to 2001	$1,800,000	$1,300,000	$500,000	$300,000
2001	900,000	800,000	100,000	60,000
2002	700,000	1,000,000	(300,000)	(180,000)
2003	800,000	600,000	200,000	120,000
Total at beg. of 2004	4,200,000	3,700,000	500,000	300,000
2004	1,000,000	1,100,000	(100,000)	(60,000)
Total at beg. of 2005	5,200,000	4,800,000	400,000	240,000
2005	1,100,000	900,000	200,000	120,000
Total	$6,300,000	$5,700,000	$600,000	$360,000

Following is the proper method of presenting and disclosing this type of change as prescribed by APB 20.

On the Face of the Income Statement

	2005	*Restated see Note A 2004*
Income before extraordinary item*	$ 660,000	$ 600,000
Extraordinary item (description), net of tax	--	(80,000)
Net income	$ 660,000	$ 520,000
Per share amounts:		
Basic earnings per common share:		
Income before extraordinary item	$.66	$.60
Extraordinary item	--	(.08)
Net income	$.66	$.52
Diluted earnings per common share:		
Income before extraordinary item	$.61	$.56
Extraordinary item	--	(.07)
Net income	$.61	$.49

**Income before extraordinary item is computed as follows:*

	2005	*Restated 2004*
Pretax accounting income	*$1,100,000*	*$1,000,000*
Income taxes computed at 40%	*(440,000)*	*(400,000)*
Income before extraordinary item	*$ 660,000*	*$ 600,000*

On the Statement of Retained Earnings

	2005	*Restated see Note A 2004*
Balance at beginning of year, as previously reported		$17,330,000
Add adjustment for the cumulative effect on prior years of retroactively applying the new method of accounting for long-term contracts (Note A)		300,000**
Balance at beginning of year, as restated	$18,150,000	$17,630,000
Net income	660,000	520,000
Balance at end of year	$18,810,000	$18,150,000

***This is the resultant amount of the change less the income tax effect through 2003.*

In the Notes to the Financial Statements

Note A: Change in Method of Accounting for Long-term Construction Contracts

In 2005 the company changed its method of accounting for long-term construction contracts from the completed contract method to the percentage-of-completion method. The change was made because management believes that the new method results in a more accurate recognition of revenue and a better matching of revenue and costs. The financial statements of prior periods have been restated to apply the new method retroactively. The effect of the accounting change on income of 2005 and on income previously reported for 2004 is

	Increase (decrease)	
	2005	2004
Effect on:		
Income before extraordinary item and net income	$120,000	$(60,000)
Basic earnings per common share	.12	(.06)
Diluted earnings per common share	.11	(.05)

The balance of beginning retained earnings at January 1, 2004, has been adjusted for the effect (net of income taxes) of retroactively applying the new method of accounting to years prior to 2004.

Note that the income statement does not highlight the change. This lack of disclosure has been the major argument surrounding the use of this method. While both periods reflect the change in income resulting from the change, the average user of the financial statements may not refer to the notes in order to understand the change.

The only change shown in the financial statements is the cumulative effect adjustment that is part of the Statement of Retained Earnings. This amount is determined by totaling the effect of the change for all periods prior to the earliest period presented in the financial statements and is reflected as an adjustment to the beginning balance of retained earnings.

The notes to the financial statements must disclose the nature of and reason for the change. In addition, the effect of the change on income before extraordinary items and net income (including the related per share amounts for public companies) is disclosed for all of the years presented. In this case, the change for 2005 and 2004 is to increase (decrease) net income by $120,000 and ($60,000), respectively.

Cumulative effect not determinable. The Board also realized that there would be certain circumstances in which the pro forma amounts or the cumulative effect amount would not be available. If the pro forma amounts cannot be determined or reasonably estimated for the individual prior periods, the cumulative effect is shown on the income statement and the reason for not showing the pro forma amounts is disclosed in the notes to the financial statements. In an instance where the cumulative effect cannot be determined, disclosure will be limited to showing the effect of the change on the results of operations for the period of the change (including public company per share data) and to explaining the reason for omitting accounting for the cumulative effect and disclosure of pro forma results. The Board specified the change from the FIFO to LIFO method of inventory pricing as one circumstance under which it would be impossible to determine the cumulative effect.

Example of change from FIFO to LIFO

During 2005 Warady Inc. decided to change the method used for pricing its inventories from FIFO to LIFO. The inventory values are as listed below using both FIFO and LIFO methods. Sales for the year were $15,000,000 and the company's total purchases were $11,000,000. Other expenses were $1,200,000 for the year. The company had 1,000,000 shares of common stock outstanding throughout the year.

Inventory values

	FIFO	LIFO	Difference
12/31/04 Base year	$ 2,000,000	$2,000,000	$ --
12/31/05	4,000,000	1,800,000	2,200,000
Variation	$(2,000,000)	$ 200,000	$(2,200,000)

The computations for 2005 would be as follows:

Net income	*FIFO*	*LIFO*	*Difference*
Sales	$15,000,000	$15,000,000	$ --
Cost of goods sold			
Beginning inventory	2,000,000	2,000,000	--
Purchases	11,000,000	11,000,000	--
Goods available for sale	13,000,000	13,000,000	--
Ending inventory	4,000,000	1,800,000	2,200,000
	9,000,000	11,200,000	(2,200,000)
Gross profit	6,000,000	3,800,000	2,200,000
Other expenses	1,200,000	1,200,000	--
Net income	$ 4,800,000	$ 2,600,000	$2,200,000

The following footnote would be an example of the required disclosure in this circumstance:

Note A: Change in Method of Accounting for Inventories

During 2005, the company changed its method of accounting for all of its inventories from first-in, first-out (FIFO) to last-in, first-out (LIFO). The change was made because management believes that the LIFO method provides a better matching of costs and revenues. In addition, the adoption of LIFO conforms the company's inventory pricing policy to the one that is predominant in the industry. The change and its effect on net earnings ($000 omitted except for per share) and earnings per share for 2005 are as follows:

	Net earnings	*Earnings per share*
Net earnings before the change	$4,800	$4.80
Reduction of earnings by the change	2,200	2.20
Net earnings	$2,600	$2.60

There is no cumulative effect of the change on prior years because beginning inventory on January 1, 2005, at LIFO is the same as that which was reported on a FIFO basis at December 31, 2004. As a result of this change, the current period's financial statements are not comparable with those of any prior periods.

The FIFO cost of inventories valued at LIFO exceeds the carrying amount by $2,200,000 at December 31, 2005.

Change in amortization method. Another special case in accounting for a change in principle takes place when a company chooses to change the systematic pattern of depreciating the costs of long-lived assets to expense. When a company adopts a new method of depreciation for newly acquired identifiable long-lived assets and uses that method for all new assets of the same class without changing the method used previously for existing assets of the same class, there is no adjustment required to the financial statements since the change is being adopted prospectively (i.e., in the current and future periods). In these special cases, a description of the nature of the method changed and the effect on net income, and income before extraordinary items (and related per share amounts for public companies) is disclosed in the period of the change. Should the new method be adopted for all assets, both old and new, then the change in accounting principle would require the cumulative effect adjustment previously illustrated.

Reclassifications

Occasionally, a company will choose to change the way it applies an accounting principle that results in a change in the way that a particular financial statement caption is displayed or the individual accounts that comprise a caption. These reclassifications may occur for a variety of reasons that include

1. In management's judgment, the revised methodology more accurately reflects the economics of a type or class of transaction.
2. An amount that was immaterial in previous periods and combined with another number has become material and warrants presentation as a separate line item.

3. Due to changes in the business or the manner in which the financial statements are used to make decisions, management deems a different form of presentation to be more useful or informative.

In order to maintain comparability of financial statements when such changes are made, the financial statements of all periods presented must be reclassified to conform to the new presentation.

Such reclassifications, which usually affect only the statement of income, do not affect reported net income or retained earnings for any period since they result in simply recasting amounts that were previously reported. Normally a reclassification will result in an increase in one or more reported numbers with a corresponding decrease in one or more other numbers. In addition, these changes reflect changes in the application of accounting principles either for which there are multiple alternative treatments, or for which GAAP is silent and thus management has discretion in presentation.

Reclassifications are not explicitly dealt with in GAAP but nevertheless occur in practice. The following examples are adapted from actual notes that appeared in the summary of significant accounting policies of publicly held companies:

Example 1

Effective January 1, 2005, the company removed the impact of intellectual property income, gains and losses on sales and other than temporary declines in market value of certain investments, realized gains and losses on certain real estate activity, and foreign currency transaction gains and losses from the caption, "Selling, General and Administrative Expenses" on the Consolidated Statement of Income. Custom development income was also removed from the "Research, Development, and Engineering" caption on the Consolidated Statement of Income. Intellectual property and custom development income are now recorded in a separate caption in the Consolidated Statement of Income. The other items listed above are now recorded as part of "Other Income and Expense." Results of prior periods have been reclassified to conform to the current year presentation.

Example 2

Effective January 1, 2005, management has elected to reclassify certain expenses in its consolidated statements of income. Costs of the order entry function and certain accounting and information technology services have been reclassified from cost of sales to selling, general, and administrative expense. Costs related to order fulfillment have been reclassified from selling, general, and administrative expense to cost of sales. These reclassifications resulted in a decrease to cost of sales and an increase to selling, general, and administrative expense of $31.8 million, and $36.2 million for the years ended December 31, 2004 and 2003, respectively.

Change in Accounting Estimate

The preparation of financial statements requires frequent use of estimates for such items as asset service lives, salvage values, lease residuals, asset impairments, collectibility of accounts receivable, warranty costs, pension costs, etc. Future conditions and events that affect these estimates cannot be estimated with certainty. Therefore, changes in estimates will be inevitable as new information and more experience is obtained. APB 20 requires that changes in estimates be handled currently and prospectively. "The effect of the change in accounting estimate is accounted for in (1) the period of change if the change affects that period only or (2) the period of change and future periods if the change affects both." For example, on January 1, 2005, a machine purchased for $10,000 was originally estimated to have a ten-year life and no salvage value. On January 1, 2010 (five years later), the asset is expected to last another ten years. As a result, both the current period and the subsequent periods are affected by the change. Annual depreciation expense over the remaining life would be computed as follows:

$$\frac{\text{Book value of asset} - \text{Salvage value}}{\text{Remaining useful life}} = \frac{\$5{,}000 - 0}{10 \text{ yrs}} = \$500/\text{yr.}$$

A permanent impairment affecting the cost recovery of an asset, as described by FAS 144, is not a change in accounting estimate. However, an impairment is treated as an operating expense of the period in which it is recognized, in effect as additional depreciation. (See the discussion in Chapter 9.)

The APB concluded that a change in accounting estimate that is effected by a change in accounting principle be reported as a change in accounting estimate. For example, a company may change from deferring and amortizing a cost to recording it as an expense when incurred because the future benefits of the cost have become doubtful. In this instance, the company is changing its accounting principle (from deferral to immediate recognition) because of its change in the estimate of the future value of a particular cost. The rationale is that the effect of the change in accounting principle is inseparable from the effect of the change in estimate. Because the two are indistinguishable, changes of this type are to be considered changes in estimates according to APB 20. However, the change must be clearly indistinguishable to be combined. The ability to compute each element independently would preclude combining them as a single change. Also, under generally accepted auditing standards such a change is deemed a change in accounting principle for purposes of applying the consistency standard and thus, the auditor's report would be required to include an "emphasis paragraph" highlighting the change.

Note that under the proposed replacement for APB 20 (see Appendix to this chapter), all changes in depreciation method will henceforth be considered as changes in accounting estimates. The rationale is identical to that described in the preceding paragraph, but under APB 20 this change was handled as a change in accounting principle, not a change in estimate.

Change in Reporting Entity

An accounting change which results in financial statements that are, in effect, the statements of a different reporting entity is reported by restating the financial statements of all prior periods presented in order to show financial information for the new reporting entity for all periods. The following qualify as changes in reporting entity:

1. Consolidated or combined statements in place of individual statements
2. Change in the group of subsidiaries for which consolidated statements are prepared
3. Change in the companies included in combined statements

Correction of an Error

APB 20 and FAS 16 govern the accounting for error corrections. APB 20 identifies examples of errors and indicates that they are to be treated as prior period adjustments. FAS 16 reiterates this treatment for accounting errors and provides guidance for the disclosure of prior period adjustments.

APB 20 defines errors as resulting from mathematical mistakes, mistakes in the application of accounting principles, or the oversight or misuse of facts known to the accountant at the time the financial statements were prepared. APB 20 also states that a change from an unacceptable (or incorrect) accounting principle to a correct principle **is** considered a correction of an error, not a change in accounting principle. Such a change should not be confused with the preferability determination discussed earlier that involves two or more acceptable principles, while an error correction pertains to the recognition that a previously used method was not an acceptable method at the time it was employed.

The essential distinction between a change in estimate and the correction of an error depends upon the availability of information. An estimate requires correction because by its nature it is based upon incomplete information. Later data will either confirm or contradict the estimate and any contradiction will require revision of the estimate. An error misuses existing information available at the time and is discovered at a later date. However, this discovery is not as a result of additional information or subsequent developments.

While errors occur that affect both current and future periods, APB 20 emphasizes the reporting of the correction of an error occurring in previously issued financial statements. Errors affecting both current and future periods do not require disclosure as they are presumed to have been discovered and corrected prior to the issuance of the financial statements.

The required disclosure regarding the correction of an error is set forth by APB 20 and includes the nature of the error and the effect of its correction on income before extraordinary items, and net income (and the related per share amounts for public companies) in the financial statements of the period in which the error was discovered and corrected. This disclosure does not need to be repeated in subsequent periods. According to APB 20, the correction of an error in the financial statements of a prior period discovered subsequent to their issuance is reported as a prior period adjusted in the financial statements of the subsequent period. In some cases, however, this situation necessitates the recall or withdrawal of the previously issued financial statements and their revision and reissuance.

The major criterion for determining whether or not to report the correction of an error is the materiality of the correction. According to APB 20, there are many factors to be considered in determining the materiality of the error correction. Materiality should be considered for each correction individually, as well as for all corrections in total. If the correction is determined to have a material effect on income before extraordinary items, net income, or the trend of earnings, it is disclosed in accordance with the requirements set forth in the preceding paragraph.

Thus, a prior period adjustment is presented in the financial statements as follows:

Retained earnings, 1/1/05, as previously reported	xxx
Correction of error (description) in prior period(s) (net of $___ income taxes)	xxx
Adjusted balance of retained earnings at 1/1/05	xxx
Net income	xxx
Retained earnings, 12/31/05	xxx

In comparative statements, prior period adjustments are also shown as adjustments to the beginning balances in the retained earnings statements. The amount of the adjustment to be made to the earliest statement being reported on is measured as the cumulative effect of the error on periods prior to the earliest period presented.

Example of prior period adjustment

Assume that Truesdell Company had overstated its depreciation expense by $50,000 in 2003 and $40,000 in 2004, both due to mathematical mistakes. The errors that affected both the financial statements and the income tax return in 2003 and 2004 are found in 2005.

Truesdell's statements of retained earnings for 2005 and 2004 prior to any adjustments to correct these errors were presented as follows:

	2005	2004
Retained earnings 1/1	$305,000	$250,000
Net income	90,000	80,000
	395,000	330,000
Dividends	45,000	25,000
Retained earnings, 12/31	$350,000	$305,000

The following prior period adjustment is required in 2005 to correct the financial statements (assuming a 40% flat income tax rate and ignoring the accrual of tax penalties and interest that would be due when amending the prior years' income tax returns):

Accumulated depreciation	90,000	
Income taxes payable		36,000
Retained earnings		54,000

Assuming that we are presenting two-year comparative statements, the comparative statement of retained earnings would appear as follows (all figures other than corrections are assumed):

	2005	*2004 Restated*
Retained earnings, 1/1 (as previously reported)		$250,000
Adjustments (See Note 1)		30,000
Restated as of 1/1	$359,000	$280,000
Net income	90,000	104,000
	$449,000	$384,000
Dividends	45,000	25,000
Retained earnings, 12/31	$404,000	$359,000

Note 1: The balance of retained earnings at the beginning of 2004 has been restated from the balance previously reported to reflect an adjustment of $30,000 ($50,000 net of $20,000 income tax effect) for an overstatement of depreciation expense in 2003. In addition, 2004 depreciation, as originally reported, was overstated by an additional $24,000 ($40,000 net of $16,000 income tax effect). Consequently, net income for 2004 has been restated to reflect this $24,000 increase. The aggregate effect of the correction of both errors results in an increase of $54,000 ($90,000 net of $36,000 income tax effect) to ending retained earnings at December 31, 2004.

Summary of Accounting for Accounting Changes and Error Correction

(See the following page.)

SUMMARY OF ACCOUNTING FOR ACCOUNTING CHANGES AND ERROR CORRECTION

	Reporting in financial statements						Accounting entries	
	Footnote disclosures				Statement disclosures			
			Effect on income before x-items, NI, EPS					
	Nature of item	Justification*	Current yr. only	All periods presented	Retroactive treatment; previous financial statements restated	Cumulative effect treatment: pro formas shown for all years	Direct dr./cr. to retained earnings	Cumulative effect
Accounting Changes								
In Principle								
General—change in principle or method of application from one acceptable GAAP to another. (Change from unacceptable GAAP is correction of error.)	x	x	x			x		x
Special • LIFO to another method • Change in method of accounting for long-term construction contracts. • Change to or from "full cost" method of accounting in the extractive industries.	x	x		x	x		x	
Special Exemptions for closely held corporation when it changes principles before its initial public offering.	x	x			x		x	
FASB Mandated Example asset retirement obligations	x		x			x		x
In Estimate** Natural occurrences because judgment is used in preparation of statements. New events, more experience, and additional information affect earlier good-faith esitmates.	x***		x***					
In Reporting Entity*** Includes consolidated or combined statements in place of individual statements, change in group of subsidiaries for which consolidated statements are prepared, and change in companies included in combined statements.	x	x		x	x			
Reclassifications Changes in the method of displaying or aggregating amounts in the statement of income. No effect on net income.	x							
Error Correction Mathematical mistakes, mistakes in applying principles, oversight or misuse of available facts, change from unacceptable to acceptable GAAP.	x			x	x		x	

* *Should clearly explain why the newly adopted accounting principle is preferable.*
** *Change in estimate effected by a change in principle is accounted for as a change in estimate.*
*** *For **material** changes affecting more than just the current year.*

NOTE: Guidance provided above is based on APB 20; the expected replacement of APB 20 by the proposed FASB statement, anticipated to occur before year-end 2004, is not reflected in this table. Readers are directed to the Appendix to this chapter for information on those anticipated changes.

APPENDIX A

ACCOUNTING CHANGES IN INTERIM PERIODS

The relevant GAAP governing the treatment of accounting changes in interim periods is contained in APB 20, 28, and FAS 3 (which provides clarification and examples). Of particular concern in FAS 3 is the treatment to be accorded cumulative-effect-type accounting changes (including a change to LIFO for which the cumulative effect cannot be determined) and accounting changes made in the fourth quarter by publicly traded companies.

The treatment of a cumulative effect change in an interim period depends upon the quarter in which the change is made. If the cumulative-effect-type accounting change is made in the first quarter, then the cumulative effect on the beginning balance of retained earnings is included in the net income of the first quarter. Again, the income for the first quarter of the current period is computed using the newly adopted method, and the cumulative effect of the change is shown on the income statement after extraordinary items and before net income. In accordance with APB 20, the comparative periods are not restated.

If the cumulative-effect-type accounting change is made in a period other than the first quarter, then no cumulative effect of the accounting change is included in the net income of the period. Rather, the prechange interim periods of the year in which the change is made are restated to reflect the newly adopted accounting principle. The cumulative effect on the beginning balance of retained earnings is then shown in the first interim period of the year in which the change is made. This method of presentation is used in any year-to-date or other financial statements that include the first interim period.

FAS 3 requires that the following disclosures be made regarding a cumulative-effect-type accounting change in an interim period in addition to the treatment described above for the actual amount of the cumulative effect (related per share amounts are required for public companies):

1. In the financial statements for the period in which the change is made, the nature of and justification for the change
2. Disclosure of the effect of the change on income from continuing operations, and net income, for the interim period in which the change is made.
3. If the change is made in other than the first interim period, the effect of the change on income from continuing operations, and net income for each prechange interim period, and the restated amounts of income from continuing operations, and net income for each prechange interim period.
4. In the period in which the change is made, the pro forma amounts for income from continuing operations, and net income for
    a. The interim period in which the change is made
    b. Any interim periods of prior years for which financial information is presented

    If no prior fiscal year information is presented, then disclosure is made, in the period of the change, of the actual and pro forma amounts of income from continuing operations, and net income for the interim period of the immediately preceding fiscal year that corresponds to the interim period in which the change is made. The pro forma amounts are to be calculated in accordance with APB 20 (discussed earlier).
5. The same disclosures described in 1. and 2. above are made regarding any year-to-date or last-twelve-months financial statements that include the period of the change.
6. For a postchange interim period (same fiscal year), the effect of the change on income from continuing operations, and net income for the postchange period

As noted above, a change to the LIFO method of pricing inventories generally results in a situation where the cumulative effect is not determinable. If such a change occurs in the first interim period, then the same disclosures described above for the cumulative-effect-type accounting change are required, with the exception of the pro forma amounts. If the change is made in a period other than the first interim period, the disclosures include those mentioned above **and** restatement of the financial information presented for prechange interim periods of that year reflecting the adoption of the new accounting principle.

The following examples illustrate the foregoing principles relative to a cumulative-effect-type accounting change made in both the first interim period and other than the first interim period. The same facts and assumptions are used for both examples.

Example of accounting change in first interim period

In 2005, Elsie Enterprises decided to adopt the straight-line method of depreciation for plant equipment. The new method will be used for both new acquisitions and previously acquired plant equipment. In prior periods, the company had used an accelerated method of computing depreciation on plant equipment. The following assumptions are made:

1. The effects of the change are limited to the direct effect on depreciation and the indirect effect on incentive compensation, as well as the related income tax effects.
2. Incentive compensation is 10% of pretax accounting income.
3. There is a constant flat income tax rate of 50%.
4. There were 1,000,000 shares of common stock issued and outstanding throughout the periods covered, with no potential for dilution.
5. The company presents comparative interim statements.
6. Assume that the following information is given for years 2004 and 2005:

Period	*Net income on the basis of old accounting principle (accelerated depreciation)*	*Direct effect of change to straight-line depreciation*	*Direct effect less income taxes*	*Net effect after incentive compensation and related income taxes*
Prior to first qtr. 2004		$ 20,000	$ 10,000	$ 9,000
First quarter 2004	$1,000,000	30,000	15,000	13,500
Second quarter 2004	1,200,000	70,000	35,000	31,500
Third quarter 2004	1,100,000	50,000	25,000	22,500
First nine months, 2004	3,300,000	150,000	75,000	67,500
Fourth quarter 2004	1,100,000	80,000	40,000	36,000
Total at beg. of 2005	$4,400,000	$250,000	$125,000	$112,500
First quarter 2005	$1,059,500*	$ 90,000	$ 45,000	$ 40,500*
Second quarter 2005	1,255,000	100,000	50,000	45,000
Third quarter 2005	1,150,500	110,000	55,000	49,500
First nine months, 2005	3,465,000	300,000	150,000	135,000
Fourth quarter 2005	1,146,000	120,000	60,000	54,000
	$4,611,000	$420,000	$210,000	$189,000

* *The net income for 2005 has been broken down into income based on the old accounting principle and the effect of the change. This is done for illustrative purposes. These numbers are unrealistic in the sense that the 2005 net income would be computed based on the new principle (e.g., the first quarter net income is $1,100,000, which is $1,059,500 + 40,500).*

The first example applies the FAS 3 criteria applicable to a change made in the first quarter. In interim reporting the same principles are followed that apply to annual financial reporting. The cumulative effect is considered to be a change in the beginning balance of retained earnings and, therefore, effective at the beginning of the year. To include the cumulative effect in any interim period other than the first, or year-to-date including the first, would be misleading. In this case we are dealing with the first period, and the $125,000, representing the direct effects net of tax, is presented on the face of the income statement. As with annual reporting, the pro forma amounts reflecting the direct and indirect effects of the change are also presented. In this case the 2005 number already reflects the change, and from the given information we can see that the total effect on the first quarter of 2004 was to increase net income by $13,500.

The notes, as required, state the nature of and justification for the change. Also included in the notes are the total cumulative effect, the effect on the earnings of the first quarter of the year in which the change is made (this disclosure makes allowable a comparison between statements), and the nature of the pro forma amounts. Essentially, if the change is made in the first quarter, the reporting and disclosure requirements are very similar to those in annual financial statements.

The following quarterly financial statements and note illustrate these principles:

	Three months ended March 31,	
	2005	*2004*
Income before cumulative effect of a change in accounting principle	$1,100,000	$1,000,000
Cumulative effect on prior years (to December 31, 2004) of changing to a different depreciation method (Note A)	125,000	--
Net income	$1,225,000	$1,000,000
Amounts per common share:		
Income before cumulative effect of a change in accounting principle	$1.10	$1.00
Cumulative effect on prior years (to December 31, 2004) of changing to a different depreciation method (Note A)	0.13	--
Net income	$1.23	$1.00
Pro forma amounts assuming the new depreciation method is applied retroactively (Note A):		
Net income	$1,100,000	$1,013,500
Net income per common share	$1.10	$1.01

Note A: Change in Depreciation Method for Plant Equipment

During the first quarter of 2005, the company decided to change the method of computing depreciation on plant assets from the accelerated method used in previous periods to the straight-line method. The change was made to better match the depreciated cost of the asset to the revenue produced by it. The retroactive application of the new method resulted in a cumulative effect of $125,000 (net of $125,000 in income taxes) that is included in the income for the first quarter of 2005. The effect of the change on the first quarter of 2005 was to increase income before cumulative effect of a change in accounting principle by $40,500 ($.04 per share) and net income by $165,500* ($.17 per share). The pro forma amounts reflect the effect of retroactive application on depreciation, the change in incentive compensation expense that would have occurred in 2004 had the new method been in effect, and the related income taxes.

* *The sum of the first quarter effect of $40,500 and the cumulative effect of $125,000.*

Example of accounting change in other than first interim period

In this case, the change is made in the third quarter of the year and the company is presenting comparative financial information for both the current quarter and year-to-date. The cumulative effect is not presented in the period of the change because it relates to the beginning of the year. Thus, in the illustration below the three months ended September 30 do not include an amount for the cumulative effect; however, the nine-month statements do. The presentation of the three-month statements reflects the effect of the accounting change for 2005 and does not reflect this change for 2004. The 2004 statement is the same as it was presented in the prior year. The pro forma amounts and the disclosure in the notes provide the information necessary to make these two interim periods comparable.

The nine-month statement for 2005 reflects the effect of the change for the entire nine-month period. Thus, the results of the six-month period for 2005 added to the three-month results would not equal the amounts shown in the nine-month statement. This is because the prior statement for the six-month period would not have reflected the new principle that the three-month and nine-month figures do. Again, the 2004 numbers are presented as they were in the previous year. The remainder of the example is really no different from the disclosure required for any other accounting change, with one exception. The exception is that the effect of the change on the preceding interim periods must also be disclosed. Note that the cumulative effect is included in the first period. The total of the three individual quarters now equal the total income shown in the nine-month statement.

	Three months ended September 30,		*Nine months ended September 30,*	
	2005	*2004*	*2005*	*2004*
Income before cumulative effect of a change in accounting principle	$1,200,000*	$1,100,000	$3,600,000**	$3,300,000
Cumulative effect on prior years (to December 31, 2004) of changing to a different depreciation method (Note A)	--	--	125,000	--
Net income	$1,200,000	$1,100,000	$3,725,000	$3,300,000
Amounts per common share:				
Income before cumulative effect of a change in accounting principle	$1.20	$1.10	$3.60	$3.30
Cumulative effect on prior years (to December 31, 2004) of changing to a different depreciation method (Note A)	--	--	0.13	--
Net income	$1.20	$1.10	$3.73	$3.30
Pro forma amounts assuming the new depreciation method is applied retroactively (Note A):				
Net income	$1,200,000	$1,122,500	$3,600,000	$3,367,500
Net income per common share	$1.20	$1.12	$3.60	$3.37

* *Computed as the $1,150,500 net income based on the old accounting principle plus the $49,500 net effect of the change after incentive compensation and related income taxes.*

** *Computed as the $3,465,000 net income based on the old accounting principle plus the $135,000 net effect of the change after incentive compensation and related income taxes.*

Note A: Change in Depreciation Method for Plant and Equipment

During the third quarter of 2005, the company decided to change the method of computing depreciation on plant assets from the accelerated method used in previous periods to the straight-line method. The change was made to better match the depreciated cost of the asset to the revenue produced by it. The retroactive application of the new method resulted in a cumulative effect of $125,000 (net of $125,000 in income taxes) that is included in the income for the nine months ended September 30, 2005. The effect of the change on the three months ended September 30, 2005, was to increase net income by $49,500 ($.05 per share); the effect of the change on the nine months ended September 30, 2005, was to increase income before cumulative effect of a change in accounting principle by $135,000 ($.14 per share) and net income by $260,000 ($.26 per share).*** The pro forma amounts reflect the effect of retroactive application on depreciation, the change in incentive compensation expense that would have occurred in 2004 had the new method been in effect, and the related income taxes.

*** *The sum of the $125,000 cumulative effect and the $135,000 nine months' effect.*

The effect of the change on the first and second quarters of 2005 is as follows:

	Three months ended	
	March 31, 2005	*June 30, 2005*
Net income as originally reported	$1,059,500	$1,255,000
Effect of change in depreciation method	40,500	45,000
Income before cumulative effect of a change in accounting principle	1,100,000	1,300,000
Cumulative effect on prior years (to December 31, 2004) of changing to a different depreciation method	125,000	--
Net income as restated	$1,225,000	$1,300,000
Per share amounts:		
Net income as originally reported	$1.06	$1.26
Effect of change in depreciation method	0.04	0.04
Income before cumulative effect of a change in accounting principle	1.10	1.30
Cumulative effect on prior years (to December 31, 2004) of changing to a different depreciation method	0.13	--
Net income as restated	$1.23	$1.30

APPENDIX B

EXPOSURE DRAFT OUTSTANDING: REPORTING ACCOUNTING CHANGES

As a part of the FASB's efforts to achieve convergence between US GAAP and international accounting standards (IFRS) as promulgated by the International Accounting Standards Board, in late 2003 an Exposure Draft was released that will, if adopted, replace APB 20 and significantly alter the reporting of the effects of changes in accounting principles. It will also change the manner in which changes in depreciation and amortization methods are reported, effectively removing these from the category of changes in accounting principle and redefining these as being instead changes in estimate. It is expected that the replacement for APB 20 will be approved and issued in 2004, to become effective for fiscal years beginning after December 15, 2004. If adopted as anticipated, much of the guidance in this chapter will be rendered obsolete; accordingly, this Appendix presents many of the illustrative materials **as they will be under the anticipated replacement standard**. Readers are cautioned that many proposed changes are enacted and become effective later than first planned, and also that final standards often differ markedly from Exposure Drafts.

Changes in Accounting Principle

As explained in the body of the chapter, under APB 20 the cumulative effect method was generally prescribed for reporting the effect of changes in accounting principle, although a number of discrete exceptions were also set forth. The strength of the cumulative effect method was that it obviated the need to redetermine income statement amounts for prior periods. The weakness was that comparisons made by financial statement users would be distorted by having current period data prepared in conformity with one accounting principle and the earlier, nominally comparable period data prepared using a different accounting principle.

While individual users and financial statement preparers could debate the trade-off between ease of preparation and loss of interperiod comparability, with the current urge to achieve convergence between US GAAP and IFRS another factor entered into the debate: the disparate methods prescribed under these two systems of accounting standards made comparisons across entities inherently difficult, when one entity was reporting in conformity with US standards and the other in accordance with IFRS. A number of extant standards are now being reexamined to ascertain whether the US GAAP approach or the IFRS approach is conceptually sounder; the intention is to revise the weaker standard to closely model after the stronger one.

In the specific case of reporting on the effects of accounting changes, FASB has concluded that the IFRS approach is the stronger, conceptually, and accordingly has proposed to replace APB 20 with a standard which largely follows that under IFRS (namely, IAS 8). There are two major implications of this change if adopted. First, the cumulative effect method will be largely dispensed with, in favor of restatement of prior periods results of operations determined consistent with the newly adopted accounting principle. And second, changes in depreciation (or amortization) methods will henceforth be treated as changes in estimate, and thus the effects will be reported prospectively only.

Proposed method of reporting change in principle. The proposed replacement for APB 20 would require retrospective application for changes in accounting principle, unless it is **impracticable** to determine either the cumulative effect or the period-specific effects of the change. When it is found to be impracticable to determine the period-specific effects of an accounting change on one or more individual prior periods presented, the new standard would require that the new accounting policy be applied to the balances of assets and liabilities as of the beginning of the earliest period for which retrospective application is practicable and that a corresponding adjustment be made to the opening balance of retained earnings (or other appropriate balance sheet caption) for that period. In other words, the cumulative effect method would be used to adjust beginning retained earnings of the earliest period for which restatement can be effected. When it is impracticable for an entity to determine the cumulative effect of applying a change in accounting principle to all prior periods, then the new accounting principle would be applied as if the change were made prospectively from the earliest date practicable.

Impracticability. According to the draft standard, as of mid-2004, it would be deemed impracticable to apply the effects of a change in accounting principle retrospectively, if **any** of the following conditions could be shown to exist:

a. The effects of retrospective application are not determinable.
b. Retrospective application would require making assumptions about management's intent in a prior period.
c. Retrospective application requires significant estimates as of a prior period, and it is not possible to objectively determine whether information used to develop those estimates would have been available at the time the affected transactions or events would have been recognized in the financial statements or whether information arose subsequently.

Justification for change in principle. The requirement under APB 20 would be carried forward under the new standard. Thus, to change from one acceptable accounting principle to another, it would be necessary to be able to assert that the new principle is preferable under the circumstances. This follows from the traditional presumption, when preparing financial statements, that an accounting principle once adopted should not be changed in accounting for events and transactions of a similar type. This in turn is grounded in the reasonable belief that consistent use of accounting principles from one accounting period to another enhances the usefulness of financial statements by facilitating analysis and understanding of comparative accounting data. Given this belief, a change in accounting principle may be supported only when the entity justifies the use of an alternative acceptable accounting principle on the basis that it is preferable.

The issuance of a new pronouncement by a designated standard-setting body, which either creates a new accounting treatment, interprets an existing principle, or expresses a preference for an existing accounting alternative is considered sufficient support for making a change in accounting principle, assuming that the established US GAAP hierarchy is followed (as set forth in SAS 69—see discussion in Chapter 1). Justification for all other changes rests with the entity proposing the change.

Disclosures accompanying changes in principle. For all changes in accounting principle, the draft standard would require disclosure of the nature of the change. Justification for a change in accounting principle will have to be disclosed in the financial statements of the period in which the change is made, and the justification for the change will have to clearly explain why the newly adopted accounting principle is preferable.

When a change in accounting principle has an effect on the current period or any prior period presented, or may have an effect in subsequent periods, the reporting entity is required to disclose (1) the effect of the change on each financial statement line item and any per share amounts affected for the current period and all prior periods presented; (2) the amount of any adjustment relating to periods prior to those presented; and (3) a statement that comparative information has been retrospectively adjusted or else that retrospective application is impracticable because one of the conditions cited above exists. If retrospective application is impracticable, the reporting entity is to disclose the reasons therefor, and a description of the alternative method used to report the change.

Furthermore, when a reporting entity makes a change in an estimate that affects several future periods (e.g., a change in service lives of depreciable assets), the proposed standard continues the APB 20 requirement that it disclose the effect on income before extraordinary items, net income, and related per share amounts of the current period. Disclosure of the effects on those income statement amounts is not necessary for estimates made each period in the ordinary course of accounting for items such as uncollectible accounts receivable or inventory obsolescence, but disclosure is required if the effect of a change in the estimate is material.

Changes in Accounting Estimate

Changes in accounting estimates are clearly distinguishable from changes in principle. As defined in the FASB's proposal, changes in estimate involve the adjustment of the carrying amount of an asset or liability that is the necessary consequence of the assessment, in conjunction with the periodic presentation of financial statements, of the present status and expected future benefits and obligations associated with assets and liabilities. Changes in accounting estimates result from new information or subsequent developments and, accordingly, from better insight or improved judgment.

Under APB 20, changes in estimates are to be accounted for prospectively, and the draft replacement for this standard would continue this treatment. Common examples of changes in estimate are the provisions (reserves) for uncollectible receivables and inventory obsolescence, the expected service lives and salvage values of depreciable assets, and accruals for warranty obligations. Since financial statements are the end product of numerous estimates, it has long been held that restatement of previously issued financial statements to reflect changes in estimate (not, it must be stressed, corrections of errors) would be unwarranted and confusing, and create many situations in which financial statements once issued could be endlessly revised in subsequent periods.

Changes in Accounting Estimate Effected by Change in Principle

The proposed replacement for APB 20 does make a new and important exception for changes in methods of depreciation or amortization. Previously, a change in accounting method (e.g., from straight-line to declining balance) would be accounted for as a change in principle, as described in the body of this chapter. The accumulated depreciation (amortization) as of the beginning of the period in which the change in method was being made, computed under the new method of accounting, would be compared to the actual accumulated depreciation (amortization) as of that date, and a cumulative effect adjustment would be recorded to bring the balance up or down to the new, desired level.

However, under the proposed replacement standard, changes in depreciation and amortization methods would henceforth be defined as **changes in accounting estimate effected by change in principle**. Simply put, it has been determined that the inherent vicissitudes of the cost allocation process, by which the cost of plant and other long-lived assets and intangibles is spread over the period of use, are such that a change in method is merely another avenue by which the allocations over time can be manipulated. Since the underlying principle is that changes in estimate are accounted for prospectively, and given that distinction between changes in method and changes in the estimated remaining useful lives of the assets are but two expressions of this allocation process, FASB has decided to ban the former cumulative effect method of reporting changes in depreciation method. Henceforth, change in method and change in estimated remaining useful economic life will be handled in the same manner.

Other Matters Addressed in FASB Proposal

In addition to continuing prior guidance regarding the reporting changes in accounting estimates, the proposed FASB statement would bring forward the guidance currently contained in APB 20 for reporting (1) the correction of an error in previously issued financial statements, and (2) a change in the reporting entity. It would also carry forward the guidance in APB 20 on justification for a change in accounting principle. Finally, the proposal, if adopted, would carry forward the guidance contained in FAS 3, *Reporting Accounting Changes in Interim Financial Statements*. By addressing each of the topics, however, the new standard will bring together in one standard all these related requirements, thereby eliminating the current separate guidance in FAS 3.

22 FOREIGN CURRENCY

PERSPECTIVE AND ISSUES

Since World War II, international activity by US corporations has increased significantly. Not only are transactions consummated with independent foreign entities, but also with foreign subsidiaries of US parents. In addition, foreign companies have purchased such venerable US companies as Chrysler Corporation, Amoco Corporation, and Universal Studios.

To facilitate the proper analysis of foreign operations by financial statement users, transactions and financial statements denominated in foreign currencies must be expressed in a common currency (i.e., US dollars). The generally accepted accounting principles governing the translation of foreign currency financial statements and foreign currency transactions into US dollars are found primarily in FAS 52. Additional guidance in this area is provided by FIN 37. These principles apply to the translation of

1. Foreign currency transactions (e.g., exports, imports, and loans) that are denominated in other than a company's functional currency
2. Foreign currency financial statements of branches, divisions, subsidiaries, and other investees which are incorporated in the financial statements of a US company by combination, consolidation, or the equity method

The objectives of translation are to provide

1. Information relative to the expected economic effects of rate changes on an enterprise's cash flows and equity
2. Information in consolidated statements relative to the financial results and relationships of each individual foreign consolidated entity as reflected by the functional currency of each reporting entity

Companies use hedging strategies to attempt to manage their risk and minimize their exposure to fluctuations in the exchange rates of foreign currencies. Hedge accounting under FAS 133 is covered at the end of this chapter.

Sources of GAAP		
FAS	*FIN*	*EITF*
52, 133	37	92-4, 92-8, 93-9, 01-5 D-12, D-16, D-55, D-56, D-71

DEFINITIONS OF TERMS

Conversion. The exchange of one currency for another.

Current exchange rate. The rate at which one unit of a currency can be exchanged for (converted into) another currency. For purposes of translation of financial statements in accordance with FAS 52, the current exchange rate is the rate at the end of the period covered by the financial statements or at the dates of recognition in those statements with respect to revenues, expenses, gains, and losses.

Discount or premium on a forward contract. The foreign currency amount of the contract multiplied by the difference between the contracted forward rate and the spot rate at the date of inception of the contract.

Foreign currency. A currency other than the functional currency of the entity being referred to (for example, the dollar could be a foreign currency for a foreign entity). Composites of currencies, such as the Special Drawing Rights on the International Monetary Fund (SDR), used to set prices or denominate amounts of loans, etc., have the characteristics of foreign currency for purposes of applying FAS 52.

Foreign currency statements. Financial statements that employ as the unit of measure a functional currency that is not the reporting currency of the enterprise.

Foreign currency transactions. Transactions whose terms are denominated in a currency other than the entity's functional currency. Foreign currency transactions arise when an enterprise (1) buys or sells goods or services on credit whose prices are denominated in foreign currency, (2) borrows or lends funds and the amounts payable or receivable are denominated in foreign currency, (3) is a party to an unperformed forward exchange contract, or (4) for other reasons, acquires or disposes of assets or incurs or settles liabilities denominated in foreign currency.

Foreign currency translation. The process of expressing in the enterprise's reporting currency amounts that are denominated or measured in a different currency.

Forward exchange contract. An agreement to exchange at a specified future date currencies of different countries at a specified rate (forward rate).

Functional currency. The currency of the primary economic environment in which the entity operates; normally, that is the currency of the environment in which an entity primarily generates and expends cash.

Local currency. The currency of a particular country being referred to.

Monetary items. Cash, claims to receive a fixed amount of cash, and obligations to pay a fixed amount of cash.

Nonmonetary items. All balance sheet items other than cash, claims to cash, and cash obligations.

Remeasurement. If an entity's accounting records are not kept in its functional currency, remeasurement into the functional currency is required. Monetary balances are translated by using the current exchange rate, and nonmonetary balances are translated by using historical exchange rates.

Reporting currency. The currency in which an enterprise prepares its financial statements.

Reporting enterprise. An entity or group of entities whose financial statements are being referred to. For the purposes of this discussion, those financial statements reflect

(1) the financial statements of one or more foreign operations by combination, consolidation, or equity method accounting; (2) foreign currency transactions; or (3) both.

Spot rate. The exchange rate for immediate delivery of currencies exchanged.

Transaction date. The date on which a transaction (for example, a sale or purchase of merchandise or services) is recognized in accounting records in conformity with generally accepted accounting principles. A long-term commitment may have more than one transaction date (for example, the due date of each progress payment under a construction contract is an anticipated transaction date).

Transaction gain or loss. Transaction gains or losses result from a change in exchange rates between the functional currency and the currency in which a foreign currency transaction is denominated. They represent an increase or decrease in (1) the actual functional currency cash flows realized upon settlement of foreign currency transactions and (2) the expected functional currency cash flows on unsettled foreign currency transactions.

Translation adjustments. Translation adjustments result from the process of translating financial statements from the entity's functional currency into the reporting currency.

CONCEPTS, RULES, AND EXAMPLES

Translation of Foreign Currency Financial Statements

Selection of the functional currency. Before the financial statements of a foreign branch, division, or subsidiary are translated into US dollars, the management of the US company must make a decision as to which currency is the **functional currency** of the foreign entity. Once chosen, the functional currency cannot be changed unless economic facts and circumstances have clearly changed. Additionally, previously issued financial statements are not restated for any changes in the functional currency. The functional currency decision is crucial because different translation methods are applied which may have a material effect on the US company's financial statements.

The Financial Accounting Standards Board defines functional currency but does not list definitive criteria that, if satisfied, would result in the selection of an entity's functional currency. Rather, realizing that such criteria would be difficult to develop, the Board instead listed various factors that were intended to give management guidance in making the functional currency decision. These factors include

1. Cash flows (Do the foreign entity's cash flows directly affect the parent's cash flows and are they immediately available for remittance to the parent?)
2. Sales prices (Are the foreign entity's sales prices responsive to exchange rate changes and to international competition?)
3. Sales markets (Is the foreign entity's sales market the parent's country or are sales denominated in the parent's currency?)
4. Expenses (Are the foreign entity's expenses incurred primarily in the parent's country?)
5. Financing (Is the foreign entity's financing primarily from the parent or is it denominated in the parent's currency?)
6. Intercompany transactions (Is there a high volume of intercompany transactions between the parent and the foreign entity?)

If the answers to the questions above are predominantly yes, the functional currency is the **reporting currency** of the parent company (i.e., the US dollar). If the answers are predominantly no, the functional currency would most likely be the **local currency** of the foreign entity, although it is possible for a foreign currency other than the local currency to be the functional currency.

Translation methods. The Board chose the following two methods to translate a company's foreign company's financial statements into US dollars. The primary distinction between the methods is the classification of assets and liabilities (and their corresponding income statement amounts) that are translated at either the current or historical exchange rate.

The first method is known as the **current rate method** and is the approach mandated by FAS 52 when the functional currency is the **foreign currency**. All assets and liabilities are translated at the current rate. The stockholders' equity accounts are translated at the appropriate historical rate. And those revenues and expenses that occur evenly over the year may be translated at the weighted-average rate for the year. The basis of this method is the "net investment concept" wherein the foreign entity is viewed as a separate entity in which the parent invested, rather than being considered part of the parent's operations. The Board's reasoning was that users can benefit most when the information provided about the foreign entity retains the relationships and results created in the environment (economic, legal, and political) in which the entity operates.

The rationale for this approach is that foreign-denominated debt is used to purchase assets that create foreign-denominated revenues. These revenue-producing assets act as a hedge against changes in the settlement amount of the debt due to changes in the exchange rate. The excess (net) assets will, however, be affected by this foreign exchange risk, and this effect is recognized by the parent.

The second method is the **remeasurement method,** which is sometimes referred to as the **monetary/nonmonetary method**. This is the approach required by FAS 52 when the foreign entity's accounting records are not maintained in the functional currency (e.g., when the US dollar is designated as the functional currency for a Brazilian subsidiary). This method translates monetary assets (cash and other assets and liabilities that will be settled in cash) at the current rate. Nonmonetary assets, liabilities, and stockholders' equity are translated at the appropriate historical rate. The appropriate historical rate would be the exchange rate at the date the transaction in the nonmonetary account originated. Also, the income statement amounts related to nonmonetary assets and liabilities, such as cost of goods sold (inventory), depreciation (property, plant, and equipment), and goodwill amortization (goodwill), are translated at the same rate as used for the related balance sheet translation. Other revenues and expenses occurring evenly over the year may be translated at the weighted-average exchange rate for the period.

If the foreign entity's local currency is the functional currency, FAS 52 requires the current rate method when translating the foreign entity's financial statements. If, on the other hand, the US dollar is the functional currency, FAS 52 requires the remeasurement method when translating the foreign entity's financial statements. Both of these methods will be illustrated below. All amounts in the following two illustrations, other than exchange rates, are in thousands, but the trailing zeros have been dropped in order to focus on the concepts.

Application of the Current Rate Method

Assume that a US company has a 100% owned subsidiary in Italy that commenced operations in 2004. The subsidiary's operations consist of leasing space in an office building. This building, which cost 500 euros, was financed primarily by Italian banks. All revenues and cash expenses are received and paid in euros. The subsidiary also maintains its accounting records in euros. As a result, management of the US company has decided that the euro is the functional currency of the subsidiary.

The subsidiary's balance sheet at December 31, 2004, and its combined statement of income and retained earnings for the year ended December 31, 2004, are presented below in euros.

Italian Company
Balance Sheet
At December 31, 2004

Assets		*Liabilities and Stockholders' Equity*	
Cash	€ 50	Accounts payable	€ 30
Accounts receivable	20	Unearned rent	10
Land	100	Mortgage payable	400
Building	500	Common stock	40
Accumulated depreciation	(10)	Additional paid-in capital	160
		Retained earnings	20
Total assets	€660	Total liabilities and Stockholders' equity	€660

Italian Company
Statement of Income and Retained Earnings
For the Year Ended December 31, 2004

Revenues	€200
Expenses (including depreciation of €10)	170
Net income	30
Retained earnings, January 1, 2004	--
Less dividends declared	(10)
Retained earnings, December 31, 2004	€ 20

Various exchange rates for 2004 are as follows:

€1 = $1.05 at the beginning of 2004 (when the common stock was issued and the land and building were financed through the mortgage)
€1 = $1.09 weighted-average for 2004
€1 = $1.12 at the date the dividends were declared and paid and the unearned rent was received
€1 = $1.18 at the end of 2004

Since the euro is the functional currency, the Italian Company's financial statements must be translated into US dollars by the **current rate method**. This translation process is illustrated below.

Italian Company
Balance Sheet Translation
(The euro is the functional currency)
At December 31, 2004

Assets	Euros	Exchange rate	US dollars
Cash	€ 50	1.18	$ 59.00
Accounts receivable, net	20	1.18	23.60
Land	100	1.18	118.00
Building, net	490	1.18	578.20
Total assets	€660		$778.80
Liabilities and Stockholders' Equity			
Accounts payable	€ 30	1.18	$ 35.40
Unearned rent	10	1.18	11.80
Mortgage payable	400	1.18	472.00
Common stock	40	1.05	42.00
Additional paid-in capital	160	1.05	168.00
Retained earnings	20	See income statement	21.50
Translation adjustments	--	See computation below	28.10
Total liabilities and stockholders' equity	€660		$778.80

Italian Company
Statement of Income and Retained Earnings
Statement Translation
(The euro is the functional currency)
For the Year Ended December 31, 2004

	Euros	Exchange rate	US dollars
Revenues	€200	1.09	$218.00
Expenses (including depreciation of €10 [$10.90])	170	1.09	185.30
Net income	30	1.09	32.70
Retained earnings, January 1	--	--	--
Less dividends declared	(10)	1.12	(11.20)
Retained earnings, December 31	€ 20		$ 21.50

Italian Company
Statement of Cash Flows
Statement Translation
(The euro is the functional currency)
For the Year Ended December 31, 2004

	Euros	Exchange rate	US dollars
Operating activities			
Net income	€ 30	1.09	$ 32.70
Adjustments to reconcile net income to net cash provided by operating activities			
Depreciation	10	1.09	10.90
Increase in accounts receivable	(20)	1.09	(21.80)
Increase in accounts payable	30	1.09	32.70
Increase in unearned rent	10	1.12	10.90
Net cash provided by operating activities	60		32.70
Investing activities			
Purchase of land	(100)	1.05	(105.00)
Purchase of building	(500)	1.05	(525.00)
Net cash used by investing activities	(600)		(630.00)
Financing activities			
Proceeds from issuance of common	200	1.05	210.00
Proceeds from mortgage payable	400	1.05	420.00
Dividends paid	(10)	1.12	(11.20)
Net cash provided by financing activities	590		618.80
Effect of exchange rate changes on cash	N/A		37.50
Increase in cash and equivalents	50		59.00
Cash at beginning of year	0		0
Cash at end of year	€ 50	1.18	$ 59.00

Note the following points concerning the current rate method:

1. All **assets and liabilities** are translated using the **current exchange rate** at the balance sheet date (€1 = $1.18). All revenues and expenses are translated at the rates in effect when these items are recognized during the period. Due to practical considerations, however, weighted-average rates can be used to translate revenues and expenses (€1 = $1.09).
2. **Stockholders' equity** accounts are translated by using historical exchange rates. Common stock was issued at the beginning of 2004 when the exchange rate was €1 = $1.05. The translated balance of retained earnings is the result of the weighted-average rate applied to revenues and expenses and the specific rate in effect when the dividends were declared (€1 = $1.12).
3. **Translation adjustments** result from translating all assets and liabilities at the current rate, while stockholders' equity is translated by using historical and weighted-average rates. The adjustments have no direct effect on cash flows. Also, the

translation adjustment is due to the net investment rather than the subsidiary's operations. For these reasons, the cumulative translation adjustments balance is reported as a component of accumulated other comprehensive income (AOCI) in the stockholders' equity section of the US parent company's consolidated balance sheet. This balance essentially equates the total debits of the subsidiary (now expressed in US dollars) with the total credits (also in dollars). It also may be determined directly, as shown next, to verify the translation process.

4. The translation adjustments credit of $28.10 is calculated as follows for the differences between the exchange rate of $1.18 at the end of the year and the applicable exchange rates used to translate changes in net assets:

Net assets at inception (Land and building of $600 – Portion financed by mortgage of $400)	200 ($1.18 – $1.05)	=	$26.00 credit
Net income	30 ($1.18 – $1.09)	=	2.70 credit
Dividends declared	10 ($1.18 – $1.12)	=	0.60 debit
Translation adjustment			$28.10 credit

5. The translation adjustments balance that appears as a component of AOCI in the stockholders' equity section is cumulative in nature. Consequently, the change in this balance during the year is disclosed as a component of other comprehensive income (OCI) for the period. In the illustration, this balance went from zero to $10.30 at the end of 2004. The financial statement presentation of other comprehensive income is covered in Chapter 3. In addition, assume the following occurred during 2005:

Italian Company
Balance Sheet
At December 31

	2005	2004	Increase/(Decrease)
Assets			
Cash	€ 100	€ 50	€50
Accounts receivable, net	--	20	(20)
Land	150	100	50
Building, net	480	490	(10)
Total assets	€ 730	€660	€70
Liabilities and Stockholders' Equity			
Accounts payable	€ 50	30	€20
Unearned rent	0	10	(10)
Mortgage payable	450	400	50
Common stock	40	40	0
Additional paid-in capital	160	160	0
Retained earnings	30	20	10
Total liabilities and stockholders' equity	€730	€660	€70

Italian Company
Statement of Income and Retained Earnings
For the Year Ended December 31, 2005

Revenues	€220
Operating expenses (including depreciation exp. of 10)	170
Net income	50
Retained earnings, Jan. 1, 2005	20
Less: Dividends declared	(40)
Retained earnings, Dec. 31, 2005	€ 30

Exchange rates were

€1 = $1.18 at the beginning of 2005
€1 = $1.22 weighted-average for 2005
€1 = $1.30 at the end of 2005
€1 = $1.28 when dividends were declared in 2005 and additional land bought by incurring mortgage

The translation process for 2005 is illustrated below.

Italian Company
Balance Sheet Translation
(The euro is the functional currency)
At December 31, 2005

	Euro	Exchange rate	US dollars
Assets			
Cash	€100	1.30	$ 130.00
Land	150	1.30	195.00
Building	480	1.30	624.00
Total assets	€730		$949.00
Liabilities and Stockholders' Equity			
Accounts payable	€50	1.30	$ 65.00
Mortgage payable	450	1.30	585.00
Common stock	40	1.05	42.00
Additional paid-in capital	160	1.05	168.00
Retained earnings	30	See income statement	31.30
Translation adjustments	--	See computation below	57.70
Total liabilities and stockholders' equity	€730		$949.00

Italian Company
Statement of Income and Retained Earnings
Statement Translation
(The euro is the functional currency)
For the Year Ended December 31, 2005

	Euros	Exchange rate	US dollars
Revenues	€220	1.22	$268.40
Expenses (including depreciation of €10 [$12.50]))	170	1.22	207.40
Net income	50	1.22	61.00
Retained earnings, 1/1/05	20	--	21.50
Less: Dividends declared	(40)	1.28	(51.20)
Retained earnings, 12/31/05	€ 30		$ 31.30

Italian Company
Statement of Cash Flows
Statement Translation
(The euro is the functional currency)
For the Year Ended December 31, 2005

	Euros	Exchange rate	US dollars
Operating activities			
Net income	€ 50	1.22	$61.00
Adjustments to reconcile net income to net cash provided by operating activities			
Depreciation	10	1.22	21.20
Decrease in accounts receivable	20	1.22	24.40
Increase in accounts payable	20	1.22	24.40
Decrease in unearned rent	(10)	1.22	(12.20)
Net cash provided by operating activities	90		109.80
Investing activities			
Purchase of land	(50)	1.28	(64.00)
Net cash used by investing activities	(50)		(64.00)
Financing activities			
Mortgage payable	50	1.28	64.00
Dividends	(40)	1.28	(51.20)
Net cash provided by financing activities	10		12.80
Effect of exchange rate changes on cash	N/A		12.40
Increase in cash and equivalents	50		71.00
Cash at beginning of year	50		59.00
Cash at end of year	€100	1.30	$130.00

Using the analysis presented before, the **change** in the translation adjustment attributable to 2005 is computed as follows:

Net assets at January 1, 2005	€220	($1.30 – $1.18)	=	$ 26.40	credit
Net income for 2005	€ 50	($1.30 – $1.22)	=	4.00	credit
Dividends for 2005	€ 40	($1.30 – $1.28)	=	.80	debit
Total				$29.60	credit

The balance in the cumulative translation adjustment component of accumulated other comprehensive income (AOCI) at the end of 2005 is $57.70. ($28.10 from 2004 and $29.60 from 2005.)

6. The use of the equity method by the US parent company in accounting for the subsidiary would result in the following journal entries (in $000s), based upon the information presented above:

	2004		2005	
Original investment				
Investment in Italian subsidiary	210*		--	
Cash		210		--

* *€40 of common stock + 160 of additional paid-in capital = 200 translated at €1.05 = $210.*

	2004		2005	
Earnings pickup				
Investment in Italian subsidiary	32.70		61	
Equity in subsidiary income		32.70		61
Dividends received				
Cash	11.20		51.20	
Investment in Italian subsidiary		11.20		51.20
Translation adjustments				
Investment in Italian subsidiary	28.10		29.60	
OCI—Translation adjustments		28.10		29.60

Note that in applying the equity method to record this activity in the US parent company's accounting records, the parent's stockholders' equity should be the same whether or not the Italian subsidiary is consolidated. Since the subsidiary does not report the translation adjustments on its financial statements, care should be exercised so that it is not forgotten in the application of the equity method.

7. If the US company disposes of its investment in the Italian subsidiary, the cumulative translation adjustments balance becomes part of the gain or loss that results from the transaction and is eliminated. For example, assume that on January 2, 2006, the US company sells its entire investment for €300. The exchange rate at this date is €1 = $1.30. The balance in the investment account at December 31, 2005, is $299 as a result of the entries made previously.

	Investment in Italian Subsidiary	
1/1/04	10.00	
	32.70	11.20
	28.10	
1/1/05 balance	259.60	
	61.00	
	29.60	51.20
12/31/05 balance	299.00	

The following entries would be made by the US parent company to reflect the sale of the investment:

Cash (€300 x $1.30 conversion rate)	390.00	
Investment in Italian subsidiary		299.00
Gain from sale of subsidiary		91.00
AOCI—Translation adjustments	57.70	
Gain from sale of subsidiary		57.70

If the US company had sold a portion of its investment in the Italian subsidiary, only a pro rata portion of the accumulated translation adjustments balance would have become part of the gain or loss from the transaction. To illustrate, if 80% of the Italian subsidiary was sold for €250 on January 2, 2006, the following journal entries would be made:

Cash (€250 x $1.30 exchange rate)	325.00	
Investment in Italian subsidiary (80% x $299)		239.20
Gain from sale of subsidiary		85.80
AOCI—Translation adjustments (80% x $57.70)	46.16	
Gain from sale of subsidiary		46.16

Application of the Remeasurement Method

In the previous situation, the euro was the functional currency because the Italian subsidiary's cash flows were primarily in euros. Assume, however, that the financing of the land and building was in US dollars instead of euros and that the mortgage payable is denominated in US dollars (i.e., it must be repaid in US dollars). Although the rents collected and the majority of the cash flows for expenses are in euros, management has decided that, due to the manner of financing, the US dollar is the functional currency. The accounting records, however, are maintained in euros.

The remeasurement of the Italian financial statements is accomplished by use of the **remeasurement method** (also known as the monetary/nonmonetary method). This method is illustrated below using the same information that was presented before for the Italian subsidiary.

Italian Company
Balance Sheet (Remeasurement)
(The US dollar is the functional currency)
At December 31, 2004

	Euros	*Exchange rate*	*US dollars*
Assets			
Cash	€ 50	1.18	$ 59.00
Accounts receivable, net	20	1.18	23.60
Land	100	1.05	105.00
Building, net	490	1.05	514.50
Total assets	€660		$702.10
Liabilities and Stockholders' Equity			
Accounts payable	€ 30	1.18	$ 35.40
Unearned rent	10	1.12	11.20
Mortgage payable	400	1.18	472.00
Common stock	40	1.05	42.00
Additional paid-in capital	160	1.05	168.00
Retained earnings	20	(See income statement)	(26.50)
Total liabilities and stockholders' equity	€660		$702.10

Italian Company
Statement of Income and Retained Earnings (Remeasurement)
(The US dollar is the functional currency)
For the Year Ended December 31, 2004

	Euros	*Exchange rate*	*US dollars*
Revenues	€ 200	1.09	$218.00
Expenses (not including depreciation)	(160)	1.09	174.40
Depreciation expense	(10)	1.05	(10.50)
Remeasurement loss	--	See analysis below	(48.40)
Net income (loss)	30	--	(15.30)
Retained earnings, January 1	--	--	--
Less dividends declared	(10)	1.12	(11.20)
Retained earnings, December 31	€ 20		$(26.50)

Italian Company
Remeasurement Loss
(The US dollar is the functional currency)
For the Year Ended December 31, 2004

	Euros			US dollars	
	Debit	Credit	Exchange rate	Debit	Credit
Cash	€ 50		1.18	$59.00	
Accounts receivable, net	20		1.18	23.60	
Land	100		1.05	105.00	
Building, net	490		1.05	514.50	
Accounts payable		€ 30	1.18		$ 35.40
Unearned rent		10	1.12		11.20
Mortgage payable		400	1.18		472.00
Common stock		40	1.05		42.00
Additional paid-in capital		160	1.05		168.00
Retained earnings		--	--		--
Dividends declared	10		1.12	11.20	
Revenues		200	1.09		218.00
Operating expenses	160		1.09	174.40	
Depreciation expenses	10		1.05	10.50	
Totals	€840	€840		$898.20	$946.60
Remeasurement loss				48.40	
Totals				$946.60	$946.60

Italian Company
Statement of Cash Flows (Remeasurement)
(The US dollar is the functional currency)
For the Year Ended December 31, 2004

	Euros	Exchange rate	US dollars
Operating activities			
Net income (loss)	€30	See income statement	$ (15.30)
Adjustments to reconcile net income to net cash provided by operating activities			
Remeasurement loss	--	See income statement	8.40
Depreciation	10	1.05	10.50
Increase in accounts receivable	(20)	1.09	(21.80)
Increase in accounts payable	30	1.09	32.70
Increase in unearned rent	10	1.12	11.20
Net cash provided by operating activities	60		25.70
Investing activities			
Purchase of land	(100)	1.05	(105.00)
Purchase of building	(500)	1.05	(525.00)
Net cash used by investing activities	(600)		(630.00)
Financing activities			
Proceeds from issuance of common	200	1.05	210.00
Proceeds from mortgage payable	400	1.05	420.00
Dividends paid	(10)	1.12	(11.20)
Net cash provided by financing activities	590		618.80
Effect of exchange rate changes on cash	N/A		44.50
Increase in cash and equivalents	50		59.00
Cash at beginning of year	0		0
Cash at end of year	€50	1.18	$59.00

Note the following points concerning the remeasurement method:

1. **Assets and liabilities** which have historical cost balances (nonmonetary assets and liabilities) are remeasured by using historical exchange rates (i.e., the rates in effect when the transactions occurred). Monetary assets and monetary liabilities, cash and those items that will be settled in cash, are remeasured by using the current exchange rate at the balance sheet date. In 2005, the unearned rent from year-end

2004 of €10 would be remeasured at the rate of €1 = $1.12. The unearned rent at the end of 2004 is not considered a monetary liability. Therefore, the $1.12 historical exchange rate is used for all applicable future years. See the appendix at the end of this chapter for a listing of accounts that are remeasured using historical exchange rates.

2. **Revenues and expenses** that occur frequently during a period are remeasured, for practical purposes, by using the weighted-average exchange rate for the period. Revenues and expenses that represent allocations of historical balances (e.g., depreciation, cost of goods sold, and amortization of intangibles) are remeasured using historical exchange rates. Note that this is a different treatment as compared to the current rate method.
3. If the functional currency is the US dollar rather than the local foreign currency, the amounts of specific line items presented in the reconciliation of net income to net cash flow from operating activities will be different for nonmonetary items (e.g., depreciation).
4. The calculation of the remeasurement gain (loss), in a purely mechanical sense, is the amount needed to make the dollar debits equal the dollar credits in the Italian company's trial balance.
5. The remeasurement loss of $48.40 is reported on the US parent company's consolidated income statement because the US dollar is the functional currency. When the reporting currency is the functional currency, as it is in this example, it is assumed that all of the foreign entity's transactions occurred in US dollars (even if this was not the case). Accordingly, remeasurement gains and losses are taken immediately to the income statement in the year in which they occur as they can be expected to have direct cash flow effects on the parent company. They are not deferred as a translation adjustments component of AOCI as they were when the functional currency was the euro (applying the current rate method).
6. The use of the equity method of accounting for the subsidiary would result in the following entries by the US parent company during 2004:

	Debit	Credit
Original investment		
Investment in Italian subsidiary	210.00	
Cash		210.00
Earnings (loss) pickup		
Equity in subsidiary loss	15.30	
Investment in Italian subsidiary		15.30
Dividends received		
Cash	11.20	
Investment in Italian subsidiary		11.20

Note that remeasurement gains and losses are included in the subsidiary's net income (net loss) as determined in US dollars before the earnings (loss) pickup is made by the US company.

7. In highly inflationary economies, those in which cumulative inflation is greater than 100% over a three-year period, the FASB requires that the functional currency be the reporting currency, that is, the US dollar. The remeasurement method must be used in this situation even though the factors indicate the local currency is the functional currency. The Board made this decision in order to prevent the evaporation of the foreign entity's fixed assets, a result that would occur if the local currency was the functional currency.

Summary of Current Rate and Remeasurement Methods

1. Before **foreign currency financial statements** can be translated into US dollars, management of the US parent company must select the functional currency for the foreign entity whose financial statements will be incorporated into theirs by consolidation, combination, or the equity method. As the examples illustrated, this decision is important because it may have a material effect upon the financial statements of the US company.
2. If the functional currency is the local currency of the foreign entity, the current rate method is used to translate foreign currency financial statements into US dollars. All assets and liabilities are translated by using the current exchange rate at the balance sheet date. This method insures that all financial relationships remain the same in both local currency and US dollars. Owners' equity is translated using historical rates, while revenues (gains) and expenses (losses) are translated at the rates in existence during the period when the transactions occurred. A weighted-average rate can be used for items occurring frequently throughout the period. The translation adjustments (debit or credit) which result from the application of these rules are reported in other comprehensive income and then accumulated and reported as a separate component of stockholders' equity of the US company's consolidated balance sheet (or parent-only balance sheet if consolidation is not deemed appropriate).
3. If the functional currency is the parent company's reporting currency (the US dollar), the foreign currency financial statements are remeasured in US dollars. All foreign currency balances are restated in US dollars using both historical and current exchange rates. Foreign currency balances which reflect prices from past transactions are remeasured using historical rates, while foreign currency balances which reflect prices from current transactions are remeasured using the current exchange rate. Remeasurement gains/losses that result from the remeasurement process applied to foreign subsidiaries that are consolidated are reported on the US parent company's consolidated income statement.

The above summary can be arranged in tabular form as shown below.

Functional currency	*Functional currency determinants*	*Translation method*	*Reporting and display*
Local currency of foreign company	a. Operations not integrated with parent's operations b. Buying and selling activities primarily in local currency c. Cash flows not immediately available for remittance to parent d. Financing denominated in local currency	Current rate (all assets/ liabilities translated using current exchange rate; revenues/expenses use weighted-average rate; equity accounts use historical rates)	Accumulated translation adjustments are reported in equity section of the US parent company's consolidated balance sheet as part of accumulated other comprehensive income (AOCI). Changes in accumulated translation adjustments reported as a component of other comprehensive income (OCI). Effect of exchange rates on cash included in reconciliation of beginning and ending cash balances on statement of cash flows.

Functional currency	*Functional currency determinants*	*Translation method*	*Reporting and display*
US dollar	a. Operations integrated with parent's operations b. Buying and selling activities primarily in the US and/or US dollars c. Cash flows immediately available for remittance to parent d. Financing denominated in US dollars	Remeasurement (monetary assets/liabilities use current exchange rate; historical cost balances use historical rates; revenues/expenses use weighted-average rates and historical rates, the latter for allocations like depreciation expenses).	Remeasurement gain/ loss is reported on the US company's consolidated income statement. Remeasurement gain/loss shown as a reconciliation item between net income and cash flows from operations in the statement of cash flows. Effect of exchange rates on cash included in reconciliation of beginning and ending cash balances on statement of cash flows.

Foreign Operations in the US

With the world economy as interconnected as it is, entities in the US are sometimes the subsidiaries of parent companies domiciled elsewhere in the world. The financial statements of the US company may be presented separately in the US or may be combined as part of the financial statements in the foreign country.

In general, financial statements of US companies are prepared in accordance with US generally accepted accounting principles. However, adjustments may be necessary to conform these financial statements to the accounting principles of the foreign country of the parent company where they will be combined or consolidated.

Translation of Foreign Currency Transactions

According to FAS 52, a **foreign currency transaction** is a transaction " ... denominated in a currency other than the entity's functional currency." Denominated means that the amount to be received or paid is fixed in terms of the number of units of a particular foreign currency regardless of changes in the exchange rate. From the viewpoint of a US company, a foreign currency transaction results when it imports or exports goods or services to or from a foreign entity or makes a loan involving a foreign entity and agrees to settle the transaction in currency other than the US dollar (the functional currency of the US company). In these situations, the US company has "crossed currencies" and directly assumes the risk of fluctuating exchange rates of the foreign currency in which the transaction is denominated. This risk may lead to recognition of foreign exchange **transaction gains or losses** in the income statement of the US company. Note that transaction gains or losses can result only when the foreign transactions are denominated in a foreign currency. When a US company imports or exports goods or services and the transaction is to be settled in US dollars, the US company is not exposed to a foreign exchange gain or loss because it bears no risk due to exchange rate fluctuations.

The following example illustrates the terminology and procedures applicable to the translation of foreign currency transactions. Assume that US Company, an exporter, sells merchandise to a customer in Italy on December 1, 2004, for €10,000. Receipt is due on January 31, 2005, and US Company prepares financial statements on December 31, 2005. At the transaction date (December 1, 2004), the spot rate for immediate exchange of foreign currencies indicates that €1 is equivalent to $1.30. To find the US dollar equivalent of this transaction, the foreign currency amount, €10,000, is multiplied by $1.30 to get $13,000. At December 1, 2004, the foreign currency transaction is recorded by US Company in the following manner:

Accounts receivable—Italy (€)	13,000	
Sales		13,000

The accounts receivable and sales are measured in US dollars at the **transaction date** using the spot rate at the time of the transaction. While the accounts receivable is measured and reported in US dollars, the receivable is denominated or fixed in euros. This characteristic may result in foreign exchange transaction gains or losses if the spot rate for the euro changes between the transaction date and the date the transaction is settled (January 31, 2005).

If financial statements are prepared between the transaction date and the settlement date, all receivables and liabilities denominated in a currency other than the functional currency (the US dollar) must be restated to reflect the spot rates in effect at the balance sheet date. Assume that on December 31, 2004, the spot rate for euros is €1 = $1.32. This means that the €10,000 are now worth $13,200 and that the accounts receivable denominated in euros has increased by $200. The following adjustment is recorded on December 31, 2004:

Accounts receivable—Italy (€)	200	
Foreign currency transaction gain		200

Note that the $13,000 credit to sales recorded on the transaction date is not affected by subsequent changes in the spot rate. This treatment exemplifies the two-transaction viewpoint adopted by the FASB. In other words, making the sale is the result of an operating decision, while bearing the risk of fluctuating spot rates is the result of a financing decision. Therefore, the amount determined as sales revenue at the transaction date is not altered because of a financing decision to wait until January 31, 2005, for payment of the account. The risk of a foreign exchange transaction loss can be avoided either by demanding immediate payment on December 1, 2004, or by entering into a **forward exchange contract** to hedge the exposed asset (accounts receivable). The fact that, in the example, US Company did not take either action is reflected by requiring the recognition of foreign currency transaction gains or losses in its income statement (reported as financial or nonoperating items) in the period during which the exchange rates changed. This treatment has been criticized, however, because earnings will fluctuate because of changes in exchange rates and not because of changes in the economic activities of the enterprise.

On the settlement date (January 31, 2005), assume the **spot rate** is €1 = $1.31. The receipt of €10,000 and their conversion into US dollars is recorded as follows:

Foreign currency (€)	13,100	
Foreign currency transaction loss	100	
Accounts receivable—Italy (€)		13,200
Cash	13,100	
Foreign currency (€)		13,100

The net effect of this foreign currency transaction was to receive $13,100 in settlement from a sale that was originally measured (and recognized) at $13,000. This realized net foreign currency transaction gain of $100 is reported on two income statements—a $200 gain in 2004 and a $100 loss in 2005. The reporting of the gain or loss in two income statements causes a temporary difference between pretax accounting income and taxable income. This results because the 2004 unrealized transaction gain of $200 is not taxable until 2005, the year the transaction was completed or settled. Accordingly, deferred income tax accounting is required for unrealized foreign currency transaction gains or losses.

Intercompany Transactions and Elimination of Intercompany Profits

Gains or losses from intercompany transactions are reported on the US company's consolidated income statement unless settlement of the transaction is not planned or anticipated in the foreseeable future. In that case, which is atypical, gains and losses arising from intercompany transactions are reflected in the accumulated translations adjustments component of accumulated other comprehensive income in stockholders' equity of the US entity. In the typical situation (i.e., gains and losses reported on the US entity's income statement) gains and losses result whether the functional currency is the US dollar or the foreign entity's local currency. When the US dollar is the functional currency, foreign currency transaction gains and losses result because of one of the two situations below.

1. The intercompany foreign currency transaction is denominated in US dollars. In this case, the foreign subsidiary has a payable or receivable denominated in US dollars. This may result in a foreign currency transaction gain or loss that would appear on the foreign subsidiary's income statement. This gain or loss would be translated into US dollars and would appear on the US entity's consolidated income statement.
2. The intercompany foreign currency transaction is denominated in the foreign subsidiary's local currency. In this situation, the US entity has a payable or receivable denominated in a foreign currency. Such a situation may result in a foreign currency transaction gain or loss that is reported on the US parent entity's income statement.

The above two cases can be easily altered to reflect what happens when the foreign entity's local currency is the functional currency. The gain or loss from each of these scenarios would be reflected on the other entity's financial statements first (i.e., the subsidiary's rather than the parent's and vice versa).

The elimination of intercompany profits due to sales and other transfers between related entities is based upon exchange rates in effect when the sale or transfer occurred. Reasonable approximations and averages are allowed to be used if intercompany transactions occur frequently during the year.

Foreign Currency Hedges

Foreign currency denominated assets/liabilities that arise in the normal course of business are often hedged with offsetting forward exchange contracts. This process, in effect, creates a natural hedge. Normal accounting rules (i.e., FAS 52) apply, and the FASB decided not to change this accounting treatment in the implementation of FAS 133. The application of hedge accounting is generally more restrictive under FAS 133 than it was under FAS 52. FAS 133 specifies hedge accounting related to four foreign currency hedges discussed below. (See Chapter 6 for a complete discussion of derivatives and hedging.)

1. **Unrecognized firm commitment.** Either a derivative instrument or a nonderivative financial instrument (such as a receivable in a foreign currency) can be designated as a hedge of an unrecognized firm commitment attributable to changes in foreign currency exchange rates. If the requirements for a fair value hedge are met, then this hedging arrangement can be accounted for as a **fair value hedge**.
2. **Available-for-sale securities.** Prior to FAS 133, a firm commitment to purchase a trading security and several transactions related to held-to-maturity securities were permitted to use hedging accounting under certain conditions. FAS 133 has eliminated the use of hedge accounting for both trading and held-to-maturity securities (in many cases hedge accounting was not required anyway) and limited the use of hedge accounting to transactions for securities designated as available-for-sale. Derivative instruments can be used to hedge debt or equity available-for-sale securities. However, equity securities must meet two additional criteria.

a. They cannot be traded on an exchange denominated in the investor's functional currency.
b. Dividends must be denominated in the same foreign currency as is expected to be received on the sale of the security.

If the above criteria are met, hedging instruments related to available-for-sale securities can be accounted for as **fair value hedges**.

3. **Foreign currency denominated forecasted transactions.** This is an expansion in FAS 133 for the permitted use of hedge accounting. Only derivative instruments can be designated as hedges of foreign currency denominated forecasted transactions. A forecasted export sale with the price denominated in a foreign currency might qualify for this type of hedge treatment. Forecasted transactions are distinguished from firm commitments (discussed in 1. above) because the timing of the cash flows remains uncertain. This additional complexity results in hedging instruments related to foreign currency denominated forecasted transactions being accounted for as cash flow hedges (rather than fair value hedges). Hedge accounting is permissible for transactions between unrelated parties, and under special circumstances (not discussed here) for intercompany transactions.
4. **Net investments in foreign operations.** The accounting for net investments in foreign operations has not changed from the FAS 52 rules, except that the hedging instrument has to meet the new "effectiveness" criterion. The change in the fair value of the hedging derivative is recorded as other comprehensive income which increases or decreases accumulated other comprehensive income in the equity section of the balance sheet.

Measuring hedge effectiveness. While any entity may utilize hedging strategies, under the provisions of FAS 133 the transaction must meet a number of important conditions in order to qualify for **hedge accounting**. Among these conditions (discussed in greater detail in Chapter 6) are the establishment, at inception, of criteria for measuring hedge effectiveness and ineffectiveness. Periodically, each hedge must be evaluated for effectiveness, using the pre-established criteria, and the gains or losses associated with hedge ineffectiveness must be reported currently in earnings, and not deferred. In the instance of foreign currency hedges, FAS 133 states that reporting entities must exclude from their assessments of effectiveness the portions of the fair value of forward contracts attributable to spot-forward differences (i.e., differences between the spot exchange rate and the forward exchange rate).

In practice, this means that reporting entities engaging in foreign currency hedging will recognize changes in the above-described portion of the derivative's fair value in earnings, in the same manner that changes representing hedge ineffectiveness are reported, but these are not considered to represent ineffectiveness. These entities must estimate the cash flows on the forecasted transactions based on the current spot exchange rate, appropriately discounted for time value. Effectiveness is then assessed by comparing the changes in fair values of the forward contracts attributable to changes in the dollar spot price of the pertinent foreign currency to the changes in the present values of the forecasted cash flows based on the current spot exchange rate(s).

Example

On October 1, 2004, Braveheart Co. (a US company) orders from its European supplier, Gemutlicheit GmbH, a machine that is to be delivered and paid for on March 31, 2005. The price, denominated in euros, is €4,000,000. Although Braveheart will not make the purchase until the planned delivery date, it has immediately entered into a firm commitment to make this purchase and to pay €4,000,000 upon delivery. This creates a euro liability exposure to foreign exchange risk; thus, if the euro appreciates over the intervening six months, the dollar cost of the equipment will increase.

To reduce or eliminate this uncertainty, Braveheart desires to lock in the purchase cost in euros by entering into a six-month forward contract to purchase euros on the date when the purchase order is issued to and accepted by Gemutlicheit. The spot rate on October 1, 2004, is $0.95 per euro and the forward rate for March 31, 2005 settlement is $0.96 per euro. Braveheart enters into a forward contract on October 1, 2004, with the First Intergalactic Bank to pay US $3,840,000 in exchange for the receipt of €4,000,000 on March 31, 2004, which can then be used to pay Gemutlicheit. No premium is received nor paid at the inception of this forward contract.

The transaction is a firm commitment consistent with the requirements of FAS 133, and fair value hedge accounting is used in accounting for the forward contract.

Assume the relevant time value of money is measured at ½% per month (a nominal 6% annual rate). The spot rate for euros at December 31, 2004, is .97, and at March 31, 2005, it is 1.01. The forward rate as of December 31 for March 31 settlement is .99.

Entries to reflect the foregoing scenario are as follows:

Date	Entry	Debit	Credit
10/1/04	*No entries, since neither the forward contract nor the firm commitment have value on this date*		
12/31/04	Forward currency contract	118,218	
	Gain on forward contract		118,218
	To record present value (at ½% monthly rate) of change in value of forward contract [= change in forward rate (.99 – .96) x €4,000,000 = $120,000 to be received in three months, discounted at 6% per annum]		
	Loss on firm purchase commitment	78,812	
	Firm commitment obligation		78,812
	To record present value (at ½% monthly rate) of change in amount of firm commitment [= change in spot rate (.97 – .95) x €4,000,000 = $80,000 to be paid in three months, discounted at 6% per annum]		
	Gain on forward contract	118,218	
	Loss on firm purchase commitment		78,812
	P&L summary (then to retained earnings)		39,406
	To close the gain and loss accounts to net income and thus to retained earnings		
3/31/05	Forward currency contract	81,782	
	Gain on forward contract		81,782
	To record change in value of forward contract {[= (1.01 – .96) x €4,000,000 = $200,000] – gain previously recognized ($118,218)}		
	Loss on firm commitment	161,188	
	Firm commitment obligation		161,188
	To record change in amount of firm commitment {[= (1.01 – .95) x €4,000,000] less loss previously recognized ($78,812)}		
	Firm commitment obligation	240,000	
	Machinery and equipment	3,800,000	
	Cash		4,040,000
	To record purchase of machinery based on spot exchange rate as of date of contractual commitment (.95) and close out the firm commitment obligation (representing effect of change in spot rate during commitment period)		
	Cash	200,000	
	Forward contract		200,000
	To record collection of cash on net settlement of forward contract [= (1.01 – .96) x €4,000,000]		
	Gain on forward contract	81,782	
	P&L summary (then to retained earnings)	79,406	
	Loss on firm purchase commitment		161,188
	To close the gain and loss accounts to net income and thus to retained earnings		

Observe that in the foregoing example the gain on the forward contract did not precisely offset the loss incurred from the firm commitment. Since a hedge of an unrecognized foreign currency denominated firm commitment is accounted for as a fair value hedge, with gains and losses on hedging positions and on the hedged item both being recorded in current earnings, it may appear that the matter of hedge effectiveness is of academic interest only. However, according to FAS 133, even if both components (that is, the net gain or loss representing hedge ineffectiveness, and the amount charged to earnings which was excluded from the measurement of ineffectiveness) are reported in current period earnings, the distinction between them is still of importance.

With respect to fair value hedges of firm purchase commitments denominated in a foreign currency, FAS 133 directs that "the change in value of the contract related to the changes in the differences between the spot price and the forward or futures price would be excluded from the assessment of hedge effectiveness." As applied to the foregoing example, therefore, the net credit to income in 2004 ($39,406) can be further analyzed into two constituent elements: the amount arising from the change in the difference between the spot price and the forward price, and the amount resulting from hedge ineffectiveness.

The former item, not attributed to ineffectiveness, arose because the spread between spot and forward price at hedge inception, (.96 – .95 =) .01, grew to (.99 – .97 =) .02 by December 31, for an impact amounting to (.02 – .01 =) .01 x €4,000,000 = $40,000, which, reduced to present value terms, equaled $39,406. The remainder of the net credit to earnings in December 2004, ($118,218 – 39,406 =) $78,812, relates to the spread between the spot and forward rates on December 31 and is identifiable with hedge ineffectiveness.

Forward Exchange Contracts

It was stated previously that foreign currency transaction gains and losses on assets and liabilities that are denominated in a currency other than the functional currency can be hedged if a US company enters into a forward exchange contract. The following example shows how a forward exchange contract can be used as a hedge, first against a firm commitment and then, following delivery date, as a hedge against a recognized liability.

FAS 133 states a general rule for estimating the fair value of forward exchange rates is to use the changes in the forward exchange rates, and discount those estimated future cash flows to a present-value basis. An entity will need to consider the time value of money if significant in the circumstances for these contracts. The following example does not apply discounting of the future cash flows from the forward contracts in order to focus on the relationships between the forward contract and the foreign currency denominated payable.

Example

Durango, Inc. enters into a firm commitment with Dempsey Ing., Inc. of Germany, on October 1, 2004, to purchase a computerized robotic system for €6,000,000. The system will be delivered on March 1, 2005, with payment due sixty days after delivery (April 30, 2005). Durango, Inc. decides to hedge this foreign currency firm commitment and enters into a forward exchange contract on the firm commitment date to receive €6,000,000 on the payment date. The applicable exchange rates are shown in the table below.

Date	Spot rates	Forward rates for April 30, 2004
October 1, 2004	€1 = $1.15	€1 = $ 1.17
December 31, 2004	€1 = $1.18	€1 = $1.189
March 1, 2005	€1 = $1.18	€1 = $1.185
April 30, 2005	€1 = $1.20	

The example on the following pages separately presents both the forward contract receivable and the dollars payable liability in order to show all aspects of the forward contract. For financial reporting purposes, most companies present just the net fair value of the forward contract that would be the difference between the current value of the forward contract receivable and the dollars payable liability. Note that the foreign currency hedges in the il-

Forward contract entries

(1) 10/1/04 (forward rate for 4/30/04 €1 = $1.17)

	Dr.	Cr.
Forward contract receivable	7,020,000	
Dollars payable		7,020,000

This entry recognizes the existence of the forward exchange contract using the gross method. Under the net method, this entry would not appear at all, since the fair value of the forward contract is zero when the contract is initiated. The amount is calculated using the 10/1/04 forward rate for 4/30/05 (€6,000,000 x $1.17 = $7,020,000).

Net fair value of the forward contract = $0

Note that the net fair value of the forward exchange contact on 10/1/04 is zero because there is an exact amount offset of the forward contract receivable of $7,020,000 with the dollars payable liability of $7,020,000. Many companies present only the net fair value of the forward contract on their balance sheets, and therefore, they would have no net amount reported for the forward contract at its inception.

(2) 12/31/04 (forward rate for 4/30/05 €1 = $1.189)

	Dr.	Cr.
Forward contract receivable	114,000	
Gain on hedge activity		114,000

The dollar values for this entry reflect, among other things, the change in the forward rate from 10/1/04 to 12/31/04. However, the actual amount recorded as gain or loss (gain in this case) is determined by all market factors.

Net increase in fair value of the forward contract = (1.189 – 1.17 = .019 x €6,000,000 = $114,000).

The increase in the net fair value of the forward exchange contract on 12/31/04 is $114,000 for the difference between the $7,134,000 ($7,020,000 plus $114,000) in the forward contract receivable and the $7,020,000 for the dollars payable liability. Many companies present only the net fair value on their balance sheet, in this case as an asset. And, this $114,000 is the amount that would be discounted to present value, if interest is significant, to recognize the time value of the future cash flow from the forward contract.

(4) 3/1/05 (forward rate for 4/30/05 €1 = $1.185)

	Dr.	Cr.
Loss on hedge activity	24,000	
Forward contract receivable		24,000

Hedge against firm commitment entries

(3) 12/31/04

	Dr.	Cr.
Loss on hedge activity	114,000	
Firm commitment		114,000

The dollar values for this entry are identical to those in entry (2), reflecting the fact that the hedge is highly effective (100%) and also the fact that the market recognizes the same factors in this transaction as for entry (2). This entry reflects the first use of the firm commitment account, a temporary liability account pending the receipt of the asset against which the firm commitment has been hedged.

(5) 3/1/05

	Dr.	Cr.
Firm commitment	24,000	
Gain on hedge activity		24,000

These entries again will be driven by market factors, and they are calculated the same way as entries (2) and (3) above. Note that the decline in the forward rate from 12/31/04 to 3/1/05 resulted in a loss against the forward contract receivable and a gain against the firm commitment [1.185 – 1.189 = (.004) x €6,000,000 = ($24,000)].

Forward contract entries

Net fair value of the forward contract = $90,000
The net fair value of the forward exchange contract on 3/1/05 is $90,000 for the difference between the $7,110,000 ($7,134,000 minus $24,000) in the forward contract receivable and the $7,020,000 for the dollars payable liability. Another way of computing the net fair value is to determine the change in the forward contract rate from the initial date of the contract, 10/1/04, which is $1.185 – $1.17 = $.015 x €6,000,000 = $90,000. Also note that the amount in the firm commitment temporary liability account is equal to the net fair value of the forward contract on the date the equipment is received.

(7) 4/30/05 (spot rate €1 = $1.20)

	Debit	Credit
Forward contract receivable	90,000	
Gain on forward contract		90,000

The gain or loss (gain in this case) on the forward contract is calculated using the change in the forward to the spot rate from 3/1/05 to 4/30/05 [€6,000,000 x ($1.20 – $1.185) = $90,000]

Net fair value of the forward contract = $180,000

The net fair value of the forward exchange contract on 4/30/05 is $180,000 for the difference between the $7,200,000 ($7,110,000 plus $90,000) in the forward contract receivable and the $7,020,000 for the dollars payable liability. The net fair value of the forward contract at its terminal date of 4/30/05 is based on the difference between the contract forward rate of €1 = $1.17 and the spot rate on 4/30/05 of €1 = $1.20. The forward contract receivable has reached its maturity and the contract is completed on this date at the forward rate of €1 = $1.17 as contracted on 10/1/04. If the entity recognizes an interest factor in the forward contract over the life of the contract, then interest is recognized at this time on the forward contract, but no separate accrual of interest is required for the accounts payable in euros.

(9) 4/30/05

	Debit	Credit
Dollars payable	7,020,000	
Cash		7,020,000
Foreign currency units (€)	7,200,000	
Forward contract receivable		7,200,000

This entry reflects the settlement of the forward contract at the 10/1/04 contracted forward rate (€6,000,000 x $1.17 = $7,020,000) and the receipt of foreign currency units valued at the spot rate (€6,000,000 x $1.20 = $7,200,000).

Hedge against a recognized liability entries

(6) 3/1/05 (spot rate €1 = $1.18)

	Debit	Credit
Equipment	6,990,000	
Firm commitment	90,000	
Accounts payable (€)		7,080,000

This entry records the receipt of the equipment, the elimination of the temporary liability account (firm commitment), and the recognition of the payable, calculated using the spot rate on the date of receipt (€6,000,000 x $1.18 = $7,080,000).

(8) 4/30/05

	Debit	Credit
Transaction loss	120,000	
Accounts payable (€)		120,000

The transaction loss related to the accounts payable reflects only the change in the spot rates and ignores the accrual of interest. [€6,000,000 x ($1.20 – $1.18) = $120,000]

(10) 4/30/05

	Debit	Credit
Accounts payable (€)	7,200,000	
Foreign currency units (€)		7,200,000

This entry reflects the use of the foreign currency units to retire the account payable.

lustration are **not** perfectly effective. However, for this example, the degree of ineffectiveness is not deemed to be sufficient to trigger income statement recognition per FAS 133. (Hedge effectiveness is discussed in Chapter 6.)

The transactions that reflect the forward exchange contract, the firm commitment and the acquisition of the asset and retirement of the related liability appear below. The net fair value of the forward contract is shown below each set of entries for the forward exchange contract.

In the case of using a forward exchange contract to speculate in a specific foreign currency, the general rule to estimate the fair value of the forward contract is to use the forward exchange rate for the remainder of the term of the forward contract.

EMERGING ISSUES TASK FORCE ISSUES SUMMARIES

92-4 Accounting for a Change in Functional Currency When an Economy Ceases to Be Considered Highly Inflationary

When a foreign subsidiary's economy is no longer considered highly inflationary, the entity converts the reporting currency values into the local currency at the exchange rates on the date of change on which these values become the new functional currency accounting bases for nonmonetary assets and liabilities.

92-8 Accounting for the Income Tax Effects under FASB Statement 109 of a Change in Functional Currency When an Economy Ceases to Be Considered Highly Inflationary

The Task Force reached a consensus that, deferred taxes on the temporary differences that arise as a result of a change in the functional currency are treated as an adjustment to the cumulative translation adjustments portion of stockholders' equity (accumulated other comprehensive income).

93-9 Application of FASB Statement 109 in Foreign Financial Statements Restated for Price-Level-Adjusted Financial Statements

Accounting Principles Board Statement 3 (the portion not rescinded by SOP 93-3) states that price-level-adjusted financial statements are preferred for foreign currency financial statements of entities operating in highly inflationary economies when they are intended for readers in the United States. The result is that the tax bases of the assets and liabilities in these financial statements are often restated for inflation. This statement provides guidance on the asset-and-liability approach of FAS 109 as it relates to these financial statements. A consensus was reached on the following issues: (1) how temporary differences are to be computed under FAS 109 and (2) how deferred income tax expense or benefit for the year is to be determined. With regard to the first issue, temporary differences are computed as the difference between the indexed income tax basis amount and the related price-level restated amount of the asset or liability. The consensus reached on the second issue is that the deferred income tax expense or benefit is the difference between the deferred income tax assets and liabilities reported at the end of the current year and those reported at the end of the prior year. The deferred income tax assets and liabilities of the prior year are recalculated in units of the current year-end purchasing power.

01-05 Application of FASB Statement 52 to an Investment Being Evaluated for Impairment That Will Be Disposed Of

Under FAS 52, accumulated foreign currency translation adjustments are reclassified to net income only when realized upon sale or upon complete or substantially complete liquidation of the investment in the foreign entity. This issue addresses whether a reporting entity is to include the translation adjustments in the carrying amount of the investment in assessing impairment of an investment in a foreign entity that is held for disposal if the planned disposal will cause some or all of the translation adjustments to be reclassified to net income. The consensuses were that an entity that has committed to a plan that will cause the translation adjustments for an equity method investment or consolidated investment in a foreign entity to be reclassified to earnings is to include the translation adjustments as part of the carrying amount of the investment when evaluating that investment for impairment. An entity would also include the portion of the translation adjustments that represents a gain or loss from an effective hedge of the net investment in a foreign operation as part of the carrying amount of the investment when making this evaluation.

APPENDIX

ACCOUNTS TO BE REMEASURED USING HISTORICAL EXCHANGE RATES

1. Marketable securities carried at cost (equity securities and debt securities not intended to be held until maturity).
2. Inventories carried at cost
3. Prepaid expenses such as insurance, advertising, and rent
4. Property, plant, and equipment
5. Accumulated depreciation on property, plant, and equipment
6. Patents, trademarks, licenses, and formulas
7. Goodwill
8. Other intangible assets
9. Deferred charges and credits, except policy acquisition costs for life insurance companies
10. Deferred income
11. Common stock
12. Preferred stock carried at issuance price
13. Revenues and expenses related to nonmonetary items
    a. Cost of goods sold
    b. Depreciation of property, plant, and equipment
    c. Amortization of intangible items such as goodwill, patents, licenses, etc.
    d. Amortization of deferred charges or credits, except policy acquisition costs for life insurance companies

Source: FAS 52.

23 PERSONAL FINANCIAL STATEMENTS

PERSPECTIVE AND ISSUES

AICPA Statement of Position (SOP) 82-1, *Personal Financial Statements,* addresses the preparation and presentation of personal financial statements, or, more specifically, financial statements of individuals or groups of related individuals (i.e., families). Personal financial statements are generally prepared to organize and plan an individual's financial affairs on a more formal basis. Specific purposes that might require the preparation of personal financial statements include the obtaining of credit, income tax planning, retirement planning, gift and estate planning, or the public disclosure of financial affairs. The aforementioned purposes allow the users of personal financial statements to determine whether to grant credit, in assessing the financial activities of individuals, in assessing the financial affairs of public officials and candidates for public office, and for similar purposes. Estimated current values of assets and liabilities are used in the preparation of personal financial statements as this information has more value than historical cost data to the users of such statements.

Sources of GAAP
SOP
82-1

DEFINITIONS OF TERMS

Estimated current value of an asset. The amount for which an item could be exchanged between a buyer and a seller, each of whom is well informed and willing, and neither of whom is compelled to buy or sell.

Estimated current amount of liabilities. Payables and other liabilities should be presented at the discounted amounts of cash to be paid. The discount rate should be the rate implicit in the transaction in which the debt was incurred. If, however, the debtor is able to discharge the debt currently at a lower amount, the debt should be presented at the lower amount.

Net worth. The difference between total assets and total liabilities, after deducting estimated income taxes on the differences between the estimated current values of assets and the estimated current amounts of liabilities and their tax bases.

CONCEPTS, RULES, AND EXAMPLES

Personal financial statements may be prepared for an individual, husband, wife, or family. An individual may elect to have a personal financial statement prepared for himself/herself without including his/her spouse. If property is held in joint tenancy, as community property, or through a similar joint ownership arrangement, the individual's ownership interest may not be evident. If such is the case, the individual may require the advice of an attorney to determine, under state law, what interest in the property should be included among the individual's assets.

Personal financial statements consist of

1. **Statement of financial condition**—The only required financial statement, the statement of financial condition presents the estimated current values of assets, the estimated current amounts of liabilities, estimated income taxes on the differences between the estimated current values of assets and liabilities and respective tax bases, and net worth at a specified date.
2. **Statement of changes in net worth**—An optional statement, this statement presents the primary sources of increases and decreases in net worth.
3. **Comparative financial statements**—Optional statements, the inclusion of a comparison of the current period's financial statements with one or more previous period's financial statements is often desired.

The accrual basis, rather than the cash basis of accounting, should be used in preparing personal financial statements. The presentation of personal financial statements does not require the classification of assets and liabilities as current and noncurrent. Instead, assets and liabilities are presented in order of liquidity and maturity.

In personal financial statements, **assets** should be presented at their **estimated current value**. This is an amount at which the item could be exchanged assuming both parties are well informed, neither party is compelled to buy or sell, and material disposal costs are deducted to arrive at current values. A specialist may have to be consulted in the determination of the current value of certain types of assets (e.g., works of art, jewelry, restricted securities, investments in closely held businesses, and real estate). **Liabilities** should be presented at the lesser of the discounted amount of cash to be paid or the current cash settlement amount. The use of recent transactions involving similar types of assets and liabilities, in similar circumstances, constitutes a satisfactory means of determining the estimated current value of an asset and the **estimated current amount of a liability**. If recent information cannot be obtained, other methods can be used (e.g., capitalization of past or prospective earnings, the use of liquidation values, the adjustment of historical cost based on changes in a specific price index, the use of appraisals, and the use of the discounted amounts of projected cash receipts and payments). The methods used should be followed consistently from period to period unless the facts and circumstances dictate a change to different methods. Income taxes payable should include unpaid income taxes for completed tax years and the estimated amount for the elapsed portion of the current tax year. Additionally, personal financial statements should include the estimated income tax on the difference between the current value (amount) of assets (liabilities) and their respective tax bases as if they had been realized or liquidated. The table below summarizes the methods of determining "estimated current values" for assets and "estimated current amounts" for liabilities.

Assets and liabilities	*Discounted cash flow*	*Market price*	*Appraised value*	*Other*
• Receivables	x			
• Marketable securities		x		If traded on valuation day: closing price. If not traded: valuation must fall in range (bid and asked price)
• Options—securities		x		Difference between exercise price and current value of asset; if material, discount the difference

Assets and liabilities	*Discounted cash flow*	*Market price*	*Appraised value*	*Other*
• Options—other assets*				
• Investment in life insurance				Cash value less outstanding loans
• Investment in closely held business	x		x	Liquidation value, multiple of earnings, reproduction value, adjustment of book value or cost
• Real estate	x		x	Sales of similar property
• Intangible assets	x			Net proceeds from current sale or discounted cash flows from asset; otherwise, may use cost of asset
• Future interests (nonforfeitable rights)**	x			
• Payables and other liabilities	x			Discharge amount if lower than discounted amount
• Noncancelable commitments***	x			
• Income taxes payable				Unpaid income tax for completed tax years and estimated income tax for elapsed portion of current tax year to date of financial statements
• Estimated income tax on difference between current values of assets and current amounts of liabilities and their respective tax bases				Computed as if current value of assets and liabilities had been respectively realized or liquidated considering applicable tax laws and regulations, recapture provisions and carryovers.
• Uncertain obligations*				Not covered by SOP 82-1; follow FAS 5

* *Taken from: "Personal Financial Statements," Michael D. Kinsman and Bruce Samuelson,* ***Journal of Accounting****, September 1987, pp. 138-148.*

** *Rights have all of the following attributes: (1) are for fixed or determinable amounts; (2) are not contingent on holder's life expectancy or occurrence of a particular event (e.g., disability/death), and (3) do not require future performance of service by holder.*

*** *Commitments have all of the following attributes: (1) are for fixed or determinable amounts; (2) are not contingent on others' life expectancies or occurrence of a particular event (e.g., disability/death); and (3) do not require future performance of service by others.*

Business interests that comprise a large portion of a person's total assets should be shown separately from other investments. An investment in a separate entity that is marketable as a going concern (e.g., closely held corporation) should be presented as one amount. If the investment is a limited business activity, not conducted in a separate business entity, separate asset and liability amounts should be shown (e.g., investment in real estate and related mortgage; of course, only the person's beneficial interest in the investment is included in his/her personal financial statements).

The CPA must decide whether to valuate the net investment him/herself or to defer valuation to a specialist. Because of the risk of litigation and the liability coverage limitations on valuation functions, many CPAs prefer using a specialist. If the CPA does the valuation, s/he must ensure that s/he has attained a sufficient level of competence to perform the engagement. The possible valuation methods available are discounted cash flow, appraised value, liquidation value, multiple of earnings, reproduction value, adjustment of book value (e.g., equity method), or cost.

The following disclosures are typically made in either the body of the financial statements or in the accompanying notes. (This list is not all-inclusive.) Source: SOP 90-1.

1. A clear indication of the individuals covered by the financial statements
2. That assets are presented at their estimated current values and liabilities are presented at their estimated current amounts

3. The methods used in determining the estimated current values of major assets and the estimated current amounts of major liabilities or major categories of assets and liabilities, and changes in methods from one period to the next
4. If assets held jointly by the person and by others are included in the statements, the nature of the joint ownership
5. If the person's investment portfolio is material in relation to his or her other assets and is concentrated in one or a few companies or industries, the names of the companies or industries and the estimated current values of the securities
6. If the person has a material investment in a closely held business, the person's ownership percentage as well as the name, nature of, and summarized financial information for the business
7. Description of intangible assets and their estimated useful lives
8. The face amount of life insurance the individual owns
9. Certain nonforfeitable rights, such as pensions based on life expectancy
10. The methods and assumptions used to calculate the estimated income taxes on the differences between the estimated current values of assets and the estimated current amounts of liabilities and their tax bases as well as a statement that the provision will probably differ from the amounts eventually paid as the timing and method of disposal as well as changes in the tax laws and regulations will affect the actual taxes to be paid
11. Unused operating loss and capital loss carryforwards and any other unused deductions or credits
12. The differences between the estimated current values of major assets and the estimated current amounts of major liabilities or categories of assets and liabilities and their tax bases
13. Maturities, interest rates, collateral, and other pertinent details relating to receivables and debt
14. Certain noncancellable commitments such as operating leases

APPENDIX

HYPOTHETICAL SET OF PERSONAL FINANCIAL STATEMENTS

Marcus and Kelly Imrich
Statements of Financial Condition
December 31, 2005 and 2004

	2005	2004
Assets		
Cash	$ 381,437	$ 207,621
Securities		
Marketable (Note 2)	128,787	260,485
Tax-exempt bonds (Note 3)	1,890,222	986,278
Certificate of deposit	20,000	10,000
Loans receivable (Note 4)	262,877	362,877
Partnership and venture interests (Note 5)	935,000	938,000
Real estate interests (Note 6)	890,000	2,500,000
David Corporation (Note 7)	2,750,687	2,600,277
Cash surrender value of life insurance (Note 8)	388,000	265,000
Personal residences (Note 9)	2,387,229	2,380,229
Deferred losses from partnerships	68,570	60,830
Vested interest in David Corporation benefit plan	545,960	530,960
Personal jewelry and furnishings (Note 10)	513,000	6,700
Total assets	$11,161,769	$11,109,257
Liabilities		
Mortgage payable (Note 11)	$ 254,000	$ 267,000
Security deposits—rentals	--	5,700
Income taxes payable—current year balance	9,800	10,680
Total liabilities	263,800	283,380
Estimated income taxes on difference between estimated current values of assets and estimated current amounts of liabilities and their tax bases (Note 12)	555,400	731,000
Net Worth	10,342,569	10,094,877
Total liabilities and net worth	$11,161,769	$11,109,257

Marcus and Kelly Imrich
Statement of Changes in Net Worth
For the Years Ended December 31, 2005 and 2004

	Year ended December 31, 2005	2004
Realized increases in net worth		
Salary and bonus	$ 200,000	$ 175,000
Dividends and interest income	184,260	85,000
Distribution from limited partnerships	280,000	260,000
Gain on sales of marketable securities	58,240	142,800
	722,500	662,800
Realized decreases in net worth		
Income taxes	180,000	140,000
Interest expense	25,000	26,000
Real estate taxes	21,000	18,000
Personal expenditures	242,536	400,000
	468,536	584,000
Net realized increase in net worth	253,964	78,800
Unrealized increases in net worth		
Marketable securities (net of realized gains on securities sold)	37,460	30,270
Benefit plan—David Corporation	15,000	14,000
Personal jewelry and furnishings	20,000	18,000
	72,460	62,270

	Year ended December 31, 2005	2004
Unrealized decreases in net worth		
Estimated income taxes on the difference between the estimated current values of assets and the estimated current amounts of liabilities and their tax bases	78,732	64,118
Net unrealized decrease in net worth	(6,272)	(1,848)
Net increase in net worth	247,692	76,952
Net worth at the beginning of year	10,094,877	10,017,925
Net worth at the end of year	$10,342,569	$10,094,877

Marcus and Kelly Imrich
Notes to Financial Statements

Note 1: The accompanying financial statements include the assets and liabilities of Marcus and Kelly Imrich. Assets are stated at their estimated current values, and liabilities at their estimated current amounts.

Note 2: The estimated current values of marketable securities are either (1) their quoted closing prices or (2) for securities not traded on the financial statement date, amounts that fall within the range of quoted bid and asked prices.

Marketable securities consist of the following:

	December 31, 2005		December 31, 2004	
Stocks	*Number of shares*	*Estimated current values*	*Number of shares*	*Estimated current values*
Susan Schultz, Inc.			1,000	$122,000
Ripley Robotics Corp.	500	$ 51,927	1,000	120,485
L.A.W. Corporation	300	20,700	100	5,000
Jay & Kelly Corp.	300	20,700	200	5,000
J.A.Z. Corporation	200	35,460	200	8,000
		$128,787		$260,485

Note 3: The interest income from state and municipal bonds is not subject to federal income taxes but is, except in certain cases, subject to state income tax.

Note 4: The loan receivable from Carol Parker, Inc. matures January 2012 and bears interest at the prime rate.

Note 5: Partnership and venture interests consist of the following:

	Percent owned	*Cost*	*Estimated current value 12/31/2005*	*Estimated current value 12/31/2004*
East Third Partnership	50.0%	$ 50,000	100,000	100,000
631 Lucinda Venture	20.0	10,000	35,000	38,000
27 Wright Partnership	22.5	10,000	40,000	50,000
Eannarino Partnership	10.0	40,000	60,000	50,000
Sweeney Venture	30.0	100,000	600,000	600,000
Kelly Parker Group	20.0	20,000	100,000	100,000
707 Lucinda Venture	50.0	(11,000)	--	--
			$935,000	$938,000

Note 6: Mr. and Mrs. Imrich own a one-half interest in an apartment building in DeKalb, Illinois. The estimated fair market value was determined by Mr. and Mrs. Imrich. Their basis in the apartment building was $1,000,000 for both 2005 and 2004.

Note 7: Kelly Imrich owns 75% of the common stock of the David Corporation. A condensed statement of assets, liabilities, and stockholders' equity (income tax basis) of David Corporation as of December 31, 2005 and 2004 is summarized below.

	2005	2004
Current assets	$2,975,000	$3,147,000
Investments	200,000	200,000
Property and equipment (net)	145,000	165,000
Loans receivable	110,000	120,000
Total assets	$3,430,000	$3,632,000
Current liabilities	$2,030,000	$2,157,000
Other liabilities	450,000	400,000
Total liabilities	2,480,000	2,557,000
Stockholders' equity	950,000	1,075,000
Total liabilities and stockholders' equity	$3,430,000	$3,632,000

Note 8: At December 31, 2005 and 2004, Marcus Imrich owned a $1,000,000 whole life insurance policy.

Note 9: The estimated current values of the personal residences are their purchase prices plus their cost of improvements. Both residences were purchased in 2003.

Note 10: The estimated current values of personal effects and jewelry are the appraised values of those assets, determined by an independent appraiser for insurance purposes.

Note 11: The mortgage (collateralized by the residence) is payable in monthly installments of $1,083 a month, including interest at 10% a year through 2021.

Note 12: The estimated current amounts of liabilities at December 31, 2005, and December 31, 2004, equaled their tax bases. Estimated income taxes have been provided on the excess of the estimated current values of assets over their tax bases as if the estimated current values of the assets had been realized on the statement date, using applicable tax laws and regulations. The provision will probably differ from the amounts of income taxes that eventually might be paid because those amounts are determined by the timing and the method of disposal or realization and the tax laws and regulations in effect at the time of disposal or realization.

The estimated current values of assets exceeded their tax bases by $1,850,000 at December 31, 2005, and by $1,770,300 at December 31, 2004. The excess of estimated current values of major assets over their tax bases are

	December 31,	
	2005	*2004*
Investment in David Corporation	$1,400,000	$1,350,000
Vested interest in benefit plan	350,000	300,000
Investment in marketable securities	100,000	120,300

24 SPECIALIZED INDUSTRY GAAP

BANKING AND THRIFT

PERSPECTIVE AND ISSUES

In early 2004 the AICPA issued the long-awaited new AAG, *Depository and Lending Institutions: Banks and Savings Institutions, Credit Unions, Finance Companies and Mortgage Companies.* This replaces former guides for each of these industries and reflects the new, unified set of requirements for all such institutions. Among other things, this Guide incorporates requirements set forth by FAS 150, FIN 46(R), FTB 01-1, and various FSP and EITFs.

While at one time regulator-imposed rules (regulatory accounting principles, or RAP) were mandated for official filings and were also often utilized for general purpose financial reporting, this is no longer true. Today, financial reporting by banks and thrifts must comply with GAAP, although some specialized industry guidance does exist within that body of standards. In general, certain unique characteristics of financial services entities do demand that certain accounting and financial reporting matters require more elaboration and interpretation than do these same principles when applied to less specialized entities. These more complex areas are summarized below.

The thrift and (to a lesser degree) banking industries endured difficult times in the 1980s and early 1990s, largely due to very difficult interest rate environments, and a record number of banks and thrifts failed. The insolvencies of the thrift insurance fund (FSLIC) and, to a lesser extent, of that for the banks (FDIC), seemed possible, and extraordinary steps were taken by regulators to avert such an event. Mergers were encouraged, and in some cases insolvent institutions (i.e., those for which liabilities exceeded assets, when both were marked-to-market values) were acquired by healthier banks or thrifts. In some instances, acquisitions were motivated by an unorthodox accounting treatment, whereby the net deficit was accounted for as "supervisory goodwill," to be amortized over an agreed-upon period (typically, fifteen to twenty-five years), with the net unamortized goodwill being considered a "valid asset" for purposes of computing regulatory capital (rather than being deducted, as would otherwise have been the case).

While the accounting profession objected to this treatment (since this supervisory goodwill failed to meet the usual definition of goodwill as being related to excess future earnings potential), it ultimately was forced to acquiesce but did impose certain requirements in FAS 72, which imposed certain special accounting for supervisory goodwill. FAS 72 has recently been amended (and largely eliminated) by FAS 147, discussed in this section. (Supervisory goodwill, as an acceptable asset for banks and thrifts, was eliminated by controversial legislation in 1989 and 1991, which spawned a wave of litigation against the Federal government which continues to the present time.)

Under current GAAP (FAS 142), any goodwill remaining is no longer amortized, but is to be tested for impairment annually, and more often under defined circumstances (see general discussions in Chapters 9 and 11).

Banks and savings institutions are exempted from the need to present certain cash flow information by FAS 104. Specifically, gross amounts for such high-volume transaction categories as deposits and withdrawals need not be disclosed. They are not exempt from presenting cash flow statements, however.

Lenders often incur a sizable number of costs directly related to the origination or purchase of loans and normally receive different nonrefundable fees at the inception of the loans. Historically, disparate accounting procedures were applied in the accounting for these costs and fees. FAS 91, *Accounting for Nonrefundable Fees and Costs Associated with Originating or Acquiring Loans and Initial Direct Costs of Leases,* eliminated this diversity. This standard enumerated various categories of costs and fees and set forth the required accounting for each of them. Most fees previously recognized at inception of the loan are now deferred and amortized, via the effective yield method, over the term of the arrangement.

FAS 114 imposed a more rational set of requirements for accounting for impaired loans than did its predecessor standard, FAS 15. While previously many actual impairments escaped accounting recognition, GAAP now requires loss recognition whenever loans are restructured, unless these involve only an extended payment schedule with full contractual rates of interest being applied to the new due dates. Apart from loan restructurings, however, the issue of when to provide loss reserves, and how these are to be determined, continues to receive a good deal of attention from accounting standard setters and regulatory authorities. The banking regulators and the SEC have indicated that heightened scrutiny is to be applied to loan loss provisions, and interpretative guidance has been offered on the interplay between FAS 5 and 114.

The AICPA has produced two Statements of Position that heavily impact accounting by banks. The first of these, SOP 01-6, *Accounting for Certain Entities (Including Entities with Trade Receivables) That Lend to or Finance the Activities of Others,* reconciles and conforms the accounting and financial reporting provisions of AICPA AAG applicable to banks and saving institutions, credit unions, and finance companies. It provides revised accounting guidance for sales of loan servicing rights and makes other recommendations, although it does not establish new GAAP. The provisions for this SOP are discussed in detail in this chapter.

The AICPA issued SOP 03-3, *Accounting for Certain Loans and Debt Securities Acquired in a Transfer,* to address the accounting for the differences between contractual and expected future cash flows of acquired loans when these differences are attributable, at least in part, to credit quality. Under this standard, when loans are acquired with evidence of deterioration in credit quality since origination, the acquirer must estimate the cash flows expected to be collected on the loan; this is to be done both at the purchase date and periodically over the lives of the loans. Cash flows expected to be collected in excess of the purchase price will be recognized as yield, while contractual cash flows in excess of expected cash flows will not be so recognized, since to do so would probably cause later recognition of bad debts. This SOP is also addressed in detail later in this section.

Sources of GAAP

APB	*FAS*	*FIN*	*FTB*	*EITF*	*SOP*	*AAG*
23	72, 91, 104, 109, 114, 115, 118, 134, 140, 147, 150	9, 46(R)	85-1, 87-3, 01-1	84-4, 84-9, 84-19, 84-20, 84-21, 84-22, 84-31, 85-7, 85-8, 85-13, 85-18, 85-20, 85-24, 85-26, 85-31, 85-41, 85-42, 85-44, 86-21, 86-31, 86-38, 87-22, 87-34, 88-17, 88-19, 88-20, 88-25, 89-3, 89-19, 90-18, 90-21, 92-5, 93-1, D-2, D-4, D-21, D-34, D-35, D-47, D-49, D-54, D-57, D-67, D-74, D-78, D-80	01-6, 02-1	*Depository and Lending Institutions: Banks and Savings Institutions, Credit Unions, Finance Companies and Mortgage Companies*

DEFINITIONS OF TERMS

Accretable yield. In the context of loans acquired in transfers, the cash flows expected to be collected in excess of the initial investment.

Carrying amount. The face amount of the interest-bearing asset plus (or minus) the unamortized premium (or discount).

Commitment fees. Fees charged for entering into an agreement that obligates the enterprise to make or acquire a loan or to satisfy an obligation of the other party under a specified condition. For purposes of this Statement, the term **commitment fees** includes fees for letters of credit and obligations to purchase a loan or group of loans and pass-through certificates.

General reserve. Used in the context of the special meaning this term has in regulatory pronouncements and in the US Internal Revenue Code.

Incremental direct costs. Costs to originate a loan that (1) result directly from and are essential to the lending transaction and (2) would not have been incurred by the lender had that lending transaction not occurred.

Long-term interest-bearing assets. For purposes of this section, these are interest-bearing assets with a remaining term to maturity of more than one year.

Net-spread method. Under this method, the acquisition of a savings and loan association is viewed as the acquisition of a leveraged whole rather than the acquisition of the separate assets and liabilities of the association.

Nonaccretable difference. In the context of loans acquired in a transfer, the excess of contractual cash flows over the amount of expected cash flows.

Origination fees. Fees charged to the borrower in connection with the process of originating, refinancing, or restructuring a loan. This term includes, but is not limited to, points, management, arrangement, placement, application, underwriting, and other fees pursuant to a lending or leasing transaction and also includes syndication and participation fees to the extent they are associated with the portion of the loan retained by the lender.

Pretax accounting income. Represents income or loss for a period, exclusive of related income tax expense, determined in conformity with generally accepted accounting principles.

Reserve for bad debts. Term is used in the context of the special meaning this term has in regulatory pronouncements and in the US Internal Revenue Code.

Separate-valuation method. Under this method, each of the identifiable assets and liabilities (assumed) of the acquired savings and loan association is accounted for in the consolidated financial statements at an amount based on fair value at the date of acquisition, either individually or by types of assets and types of liabilities.

Taxable income. Represents pretax accounting income (1) adjusted for reversal of provisions of estimated losses on loans and property acquired in settlement of loans, gains or losses on the sales of such property, and adjusted for permanent differences and (2) after giving effect to the bad debt deduction allowable by the US Internal Revenue Code assuming the applicable tax return were to be prepared based on such adjusted pretax accounting income.

CONCEPTS, RULES, AND EXAMPLES

Justifying a Change in Accounting Principle

The following sources are preferred for banking and thrift industries that must justify a change in accounting principle:

1. AAG, *Depository and Lending Institutions: Banks and Savings Institutions, Credit Unions, Finance Companies and Mortgage Companies* (2004)
2. Statement of Position 83-1, *Reporting by Banks of Investment Securities Gains or Losses*
3. Statement of Position 01-6, *Accounting for Certain Entities (Including Entities with Trade Receivables) That Lend to or Finance the Activities of Others*
4. Statement of Position 03-3, *Accounting for Certain Loan and Debt Securities Acquired in a Transfer*

Acquisition of a Banking or Thrift Institution

The following discussion applies not only to the acquisition of a savings and loan association, but also to acquisition of savings and loan holding companies, commercial banks, mutual savings banks, credit unions, and other depository institutions with assets and liabilities of the same type.

Purchase method. In accounting for the acquisition of a banking and thrift institution, the fair value of the assets and liabilities acquired must be determined using the **separate-valuation method**. Under this method, each of the identifiable assets and liabilities acquired are accounted for individually, or by type, at its fair value at the date of acquisition. The total amount is reported in the consolidated financial statements.

Note that use of the **net-spread method** is **not** considered appropriate for this type of business combination. The net-spread method, which views acquisition of the institution as a leveraged whole, does not appropriately recognize the fair value of individual, or types of, assets and liabilities.

Liabilities acquired are accounted for at their present value at the date of acquisition. The present value of savings deposits due on demand equals the face amount plus interest accrued or accruable at the acquisition date. The present value of other liabilities assumed is calculated by using interest rates for similar liabilities in effect at the date of acquisition.

While in earlier years some bank and thrift mergers were accounted for as poolings, the promulgation of new accounting standards in mid-2001 meant that all mergers will henceforth be accounted for as purchases. Goodwill is no longer subject to amortization, but must be tested for impairment at least annually. (See Chapters 9 and 11.)

Identified intangible assets. The purchase price of a banking or thrift institution may include intangible benefits from the purchase, such as the capacity of acquired assets to generate new business. Intangible assets that can be separately identified at a determinable fair value are to be assigned a portion of the total purchase price and are amortized over their estimated lives. Any portion of the purchase price that cannot be identified with specific tangible and intangible assets (less liabilities assumed) is assigned to goodwill. Under GAAP prior to the promulgation of FAS 142, goodwill was to be amortized; under current standards, amortization is to cease, with impairment testing, at least annually, being substituted.

Unidentifiable intangible asset. An unidentifiable intangible asset arises when the fair value of liabilities assumed exceeds the fair value of tangible and identified intangible assets acquired. This asset is amortized over a period no greater than the estimated remaining life of any **long-term interest-bearing assets** acquired. Amortization is applied to the **carrying amount** of the interest-bearing assets expected to be outstanding at the beginning of each subsequent period. If, however, the assets acquired do **not** include a significant portion of long-term interest-bearing assets, the unidentifiable intangible asset is amortized over a period not exceeding the estimated average remaining life of the existing customer base acquired. Amortization in any case shall not exceed forty years.

In the sale or liquidation of a large segment, or separable group, of the operating assets of an acquired banking or thrift institution, the portion of the unidentifiable intangible asset identified with that segment, or separable group, shall be included in the cost of the assets sold. If the sale or liquidation of a large portion of the interest-bearing assets significantly reduces the benefits of the unidentifiable intangible asset, any reduction shall be recognized as a charge to income.

Regulatory-assisted combinations. While in the current environment such transactions have been exceedingly rare, bank regulatory authorities may grant financial assistance to encourage a bank acquisition. Generally, this is done when a failing bank is sold to a solvent one and the amount of any such direct assistance is less than the cost would have been incurred honoring the deposit insurance commitment, net of recoveries on assets held by the failing bank. Under GAAP, the assistance should be accounted for as part of the combination if receipt of the assistance is probable and the amount to be received is reasonably estimable. Otherwise, assistance should be reported as a reduction of the unidentifiable asset (goodwill), with any excess over that amount being reported in income. If the grantee is required to repay all or a portion of the assistance, a liability would be recognized, together with a charge against income. Assistance received must be disclosed in the financial statements.

Of primarily historical interest now is another form of "assistance" that had been offered by regulatory authorities during the "thrift crisis" of the mid-1980s (which also affected some banks). This was the right to treat the excess of acquired liabilities over acquired assets as an asset (called "supervisory goodwill"), which was permitted for purposes of computing regulatory capital. During that era, the objective was to avoid having the large numbers of thrift and bank failures deplete the insurance funds (FSLIC and FDIC). Later this was seen as having created other problems, and laws passed in 1989 and 1991 effectively eliminated this accounting treatment, which in turn contributed to another wave of institutional failure when formerly technically solvent banks were judged insolvent.

Many of the institutions which failed or were forced to shrink operations due to the change in federal policy sued for breach of contract. Some of these cases are yet untried (or are being appealed) as of 2004, and those that have been concluded have yielded mixed results. In some cases the government will be required to make some restitution to the savings institutions. EITF Topic D-78, *Accounting for Supervisory Goodwill Litigation Awards or Settlements,* states that any settlements received should be accounted for not as governmental financial assistance (as that is described in FAS 72), but rather in the same manner as other litigation awards would normally be reported. These are not to be deemed extraordinary gains, but rather are to be included in operating income, with adequate disclosure made to avoid the drawing of misleading inferences regarding possible recurrence. Unsettled claims should be accounted for as only contingent gains (i.e., these should be disclosed, if material, but may not be accrued until and unless realized).

Elimination of special accounting for goodwill associated with bank and thrift mergers. The thrift, and later, banking crises of the 1980s gave rise to a number of unusual and often unwise practices. One of these was the invention of "supervisory goodwill," which sometimes was used as an inducement to relatively stronger institutions to acquire those that were, on a mark-to-market (i.e., fair value) basis, already insolvent. The net liabilities assumed, in such instances, was recognized as the intangible asset goodwill, although this would not have generally qualified as such under existing GAAP, since it often did not imply excess future earnings potential, the usual working definition for goodwill. However, thrift and banking regulators permitted the combined institutions to present this asset on their balance sheets, subject to amortization over agreed-upon periods, and to treat the unamortized balance as a qualified asset for capital computation purposes (whereas goodwill was otherwise to be deducted from equity for this calculation).

The accounting profession had objected to the recognition of supervisory goodwill for GAAP-basis reporting purposes, but ultimately had to acquiesce, if reluctantly. In FAS 72, certain parameters were established for the amortization periods to be applied to such supervisory goodwill (referred to as an "unidentifiable intangible asset" in that standard). Thus, the intangible was to be amortized over a period no longer than the estimated remaining life of interest-bearing assets (loans and investments) acquired, which would typically be shorter than the agreed-to terms under the various acquisition agreements then being encouraged by the regulators. FAS 72 was an attempt to mitigate, but not eliminate, the distortions caused by the regulatory recognition of supervisory goodwill.

Beginning in 1989 this situation changed, first with the passage of the Financial Institutions Reform, Recovery and Enforcement Act, and then later with the (1991) FDIC Improvement Act. Supervisory goodwill was eliminated from regulatory filings, and although this did not require that such goodwill be deleted from GAAP-basis financial statements, this was largely the consequential effect. More recently, accounting for purchase business combinations has been revised by FAS 141, and the accounting for goodwill has been materially altered by FAS 142.

In light of the foregoing, FASB promulgated FAS 147, in recognition of the fact that special accounting for goodwill of financial institutions is no longer needed. The requirements of FAS 141 deal with the assignment of purchase price to the various acquired assets and assumed obligations, and FAS 142 specifies the accounting for goodwill. FAS 147 also specifies that acquisitions of branches are to be accounted for as business combinations, if a branch meets the definition of a business, with the possibility of recognizing goodwill in such a transaction. If the branch does not meet the definition of a business, the transaction is to be accounted for as merely the acquisition of assets, and goodwill cannot be recognized. (The definition of a business is set forth in EITF 98-3.)

The guidance in FAS 147 does not apply to combinations of mutual associations, which remain governed by previous literature, including FAS 72. It stipulates that the guidance of FAS 144 must be applied to the long-term customer relationship intangibles often recognized in acquisitions of financial institutions—including depositor-relationship intangibles, borrower-relationship intangibles, and credit cardholder intangibles. The impairment testing of servicing assets, another commonly encountered bank or thrift intangible, is set forth by FAS 140, rather than by FAS 144.

Under FAS 147's transition provisions, intangibles recognized previously continue to be accounted for under FAS 72 if they arose in transactions **other than** business combinations. However, for those that arose in business combinations, the remaining unamortized balances are to be transferred to goodwill unless they can be identified as other specific intangibles (e.g., customer relationships). Amounts reclassified to goodwill are to be prospectively accounted for in accordance with FAS 142 (i.e., no longer subject to amortization, but tested at least annually for impairment). The standard provides guidance on transitional testing for impairment of goodwill, as well as for certain acquired long-term customer relationship intangibles to be held and used.

Bad-Debt Reserves

Both stock and mutual savings and loan associations are required by regulatory authorities to place a portion of their earnings into a **general reserve** as protection for depositors. Savings and loan associations are allowed by the IRS to maintain a **bad-debt reserve** and to deduct any additions to their reserve in determining taxable income. Since this method differs from the method for determining bad debt expense, **pretax accounting income** and **taxable income** will differ.

Accounting by Creditors for Impairment of a Loan

A persistent practice problem has been in the proper determination of loan loss provisions. Since such reserves are necessarily matters of judgment, the possibility of manipulation (by either understatement or overstatement) in order to manage reported earnings or otherwise bias perceptions about the thrift's or bank's performance has always existed. In more recent years, this has received greater attention, first by the issuance of a detailed standard on accounting for impaired loans (FAS 114), and later by several FASB, SEC and banking regulatory authority policy announcements.

Under FAS 114, loans are deemed impaired when it is probable that a creditor will be unable to collect all amounts contractually due, including both principal and interest. This determination is made by applying normal loan review procedures. Once impairment has been identified, the creditor institution must compute the present value of all the estimated future cash flows, using the loan's effective interest rate as the discount factor. The effective rate is defined as the loan's contractual rate as adjusted for any deferred loan fees, premiums, or discounts. It is this effective rate, and not the market rate at the time of determination of impairment, which must be used to compute the loss provision.

If the computed present value of the expected future cash flows is less than the carrying amount of the loan, an impairment will be recognized and recorded in a valuation allowance. Significant changes in the amount and/or timing of future estimated cash flows require that the creditor recalculate the amount of the loan's impairment. Adjustments, subject to the LCM criteria, will be reflected through changes in the valuation allowance.

In the event of a formal loan restructuring through a troubled debt restructuring, the loan is remeasured at the fair market value at the date of the restructuring. This treatment differs from an impairment because it is assumed that a new, formally restructured loan reflects current market conditions; therefore, no impairment is deemed to exist.

The standard, as amended, provides that impairment losses be recognized as bad debts when measured; however, no guidance is provided on the recognition and measurement of amounts later recovered.

Recently, new attention has been given to the relationship between FAS 5 and 114 as definitive guidance for the provision of loss reserves. In several articles and a recent EITF Topic (D-80, *Application of FASB Statements No. 5 and No. 114 to a Loan Portfolio*), the FASB has indicated that loss provisions must be based only on **probable** losses which have occurred as of the balance sheet date, even if the individual loan which may have been impaired cannot be identified. Predictions of likely future losses to be incurred, even if such predictions have been historically highly accurate, cannot be used to anticipate losses that have not yet occurred. The SEC and banking regulatory agencies have lately expressed great interest in this matter (principally, it is assumed, due to a concern with the possibility of earnings management), and have essentially promised to enforce this informal FASB guidance as if it were part of the promulgated standards. Among other things, all loss provisions must be supported by appropriate documentation.

In fact, there is no conflict between FAS 5 (in force since 1975) and FAS 114 (effective 1995): losses are to be provided when it is probable that the asset has been impaired and the amount is subject to reasonable estimation. FAS 114 is more specific than FAS 5 in that it requires certain methods of measurement for loans that are individually considered impaired, but it does not fundamentally change the recognition criteria for loan losses. FAS 114 provides guidance on measurement and disclosure for loans that are identified for evaluation and that are individually deemed to be impaired (because it is probable that the creditor will be unable to collect all the contractual interest and principal payments as scheduled in the loan agreement). It also includes all loans that are restructured in a troubled debt restructuring involving a modification of terms, except for those loans that are excluded from the scope of the standard.

In determining the existence and extent of impairment, "environmental" factors such as existing industry, geographical, economic, and political factors, should be given consideration. Obviously, the distinction between existing environmental factors and forecasts of changes in these factors over the near-term horizon is a subtle one, but it is one which must be maintained, since the latter cannot be used to justify current period loan loss provisions. For example, even if the consensus economic forecast is for a recession (which normally results in greater loan losses being experienced as current debtors face financial difficulties) if that downturn is not being experienced at the balance sheet date, loss reserves cannot be boosted to anticipate loan quality deterioration that has not yet occurred.

FASB has noted that some loans that are specifically identified for evaluation may be individually impaired, while other loans that are not impaired individually pursuant to FAS 114 may have specific characteristics that indicate that there would be probable loss in a group of loans with those characteristics. Loans in the first category must be accounted for under FAS 114, and loans in the second category should be accounted for under FAS 5. Under FAS 5, a loss is accrued if characteristics of a loan indicate that it is probable that a group of similar loans includes some losses even though the loss could not be identified with a specific loan. Characteristics or risk factors must be specifically identified to support an accrual for losses that have been incurred but that have not yet reached the point where it is probable that amounts will not be collected on a specific individual loan. A creditor should not ignore factors and information obtained in the evaluation of the loan's collectibility.

For example, if an individual loan specifically identified for evaluation is fully collateralized with risk-free assets, then consideration of that loan as sharing characteristics with a group of uncollateralized loans is inappropriate. Under FAS 5, a loss is recognized if characteristics of a loan indicate that it is probable that a group of similar loans includes some losses even though the loss could not be identified to a specific loan. However, a loss would be recognized only if it is probable that the loss has been incurred at the date of the financial statements and the amount of loss can be reasonably estimated.

If a creditor concludes that an individual loan specifically identified for evaluation is impaired, an allowance in addition to one measured under FAS 114 may **not** be established. That is, the FAS 114 allowance should be the sole measure of impairment for that loan. This is equally true if the measurement of impairment under FAS 114 results in no allowance. For example, a creditor might conclude that a given collateral-dependent loan is impaired, because it is probable that the creditor will be unable to collect all the contractual interest and principal payments as scheduled in the loan agreement. The creditor might, however, measure the impairment using the fair value of the collateral, which could result in no allowance if the fair value of the collateral is greater than the recorded investment in the loan. Further consideration of the need for a loss reserve by applying FAS 5 to these facts would not be legitimate.

Particularly objectionable is the practice of increasing (or not decreasing) the allowance for loan losses in "good" economic times to provide for losses expected to occur in the future. This income smoothing technique is invalid under all circumstances, and cannot be rationalized by citing the historical cyclicality of the economy and the reasonable likelihood that higher losses will follow periods having lower loss experience. Reporting entities can anticipate that these practices will be closely scrutinized by the SEC and other regulatory authorities.

Nonrefundable Loan Fees and Costs

Loan origination fees. These fees should be **deferred** and recognized over the life of the loan as an adjustment of interest income. If there are any related direct loan origination costs, the **origination fees** and origination costs should be **netted,** and only the net amount should be deferred and amortized via the interest method. Origination costs include those **incremental costs** such as credit checks and security arrangements, among others, pertaining to a specific loan.

The only exception to the foregoing rule would be in the instance of certain loans that also qualify as debt instruments under FAS 115. For those carried in the "trading securities" portfolio, related loan origination fees should be charged to expense when incurred; the requirement that these be carried at fair value would make adding these costs to the asset carrying amounts a useless exercise.

Example 1

Debtor Corp. wishes to take out a loan with Klein Bank for the purchase of new machinery. The fair market value of the machinery is $614,457. The loan is for ten years, designed to give Klein an implicit return of 10% on the loan. The annual payment is calculated as follows:

$$\text{Annual payment} = \frac{\$614{,}457}{PV_{10,}10\%} = \frac{614{,}457}{6.14457} = \$100{,}000$$

Unearned interest on the loan would be $385,543 [(10 x $100,000) – $614,457].

Klein also is to receive a "nonrefundable origination fee" of $50,000. Klein incurred $20,000 of direct origination costs (for credit checks, etc.). Thus, Klein has **net** nonrefundable origination fees of $30,000. The new net investment in the loan is calculated below.

Gross investment in loan (10 x $100,000)	$1,000,000
Less: Unamortized net nonrefundable origination fees	(30,000)
	970,000
Less: Unearned interest income (from above)	385,543
Net investment in loan	$ 584,457

The new net investment in the loan can be used to find the new implicit interest rate.

$$\frac{100{,}000}{(1+i)^1} + \frac{100{,}000}{(1+i)^2} + \ldots + \frac{100{,}000}{(1+i)^{10}} = \$584{,}457$$

where i = implicit rate

Thus, the implicit interest rate is 11.002%. The amortization table for the first three years is set up as follows:

(a) Loan payments	*(b)* Reduction in unearned interest	*(c)* Interest revenue (PV x implicit rate of 11.002%)	*(d)* Reduction in net orig. fees (c-b)	*(e)* Reduction in PV of net invest (a-c)	*(f)* PV of net loan investment
					$584,457
$100,000	$61,446*	$64,302	$2,856	$35,689	548,759
100,000	57,590**	60,374	2,784	39,626	509,133
100,000	53,349***	56,015	2,666	43,985	465,148

* *($614,457 x 10%) = $61,446*
** *[$614,457 – ($100,000 – $61,446)] x 10% = $57,590*
*** *[$575,900 – ($100,000 – $57,590)] x 10% = $53,349*

Commitment fees and costs. Often fees are received in advance in exchange for a **commitment** to originate or purchase a loan. These fees should be deferred and recognized upon exercise of the commitment as an adjustment of interest income over the life of the loan, as in Example 1 for origination costs and fees. If a commitment expires unexercised, the fees should be recognized as income upon expiration.

As with loan origination fees and costs, if **both** commitment fees are received and commitment costs are incurred relating to a commitment to originate or purchase a loan, the **net** amount of fees or costs should be deferred and recognized over the life of the loan.

If there is a **remote** possibility of exercise, the commitment fees may be recognized on a straight-line basis over the commitment period as "service fee income." If there is a subsequent exercise, the unamortized fees at the date of exercise shall be recognized over the life of the loan as an adjustment of interest income, as in Example 1.

In certain cases, commitment fees are determined retroactively as a percentage of available lines of credit. If the commitment fee percentage is nominal in relation to the stated rate on the related borrowing, with the borrowing earning the market rate of interest, the fees shall be recognized in income as of the determination date.

Example 2

Glass Corp. has a $2 million, 10% line of credit outstanding with Ritter Bank. Ritter charges its annual commitment fee as 0.1% of any available balance as of the end of the prior period. Ritter will report $2,000 ($2 million x 0.1%) as service fee income in its current income statement.

Fees and costs in refinancing or restructurings. (Assume this is not a troubled-debt restructuring.) When the terms of a refinanced/restructured loan are as favorable to the lender as the terms for loans to customers with similar risks who are not in a restructuring, the refinanced loan is treated as a **new** loan, and all prior fees of the old loan are recognized in interest income when the new loan is made.

When the above situation is not satisfied, the fees or costs from the old loan become part of the net investment in the new loan.

Example 3

Jeffrey Bank refinanced a loan receivable to $1,000,000, at 10% interest, with annual interest receipts for ten years. Jeffrey's "normal" loan in its portfolio to debtors with similar risks is for $500,000 at 9% interest for five years. Jeffrey had loan origination fees from the original loan of $20,000. These fees are recognized in income **immediately** because the terms of the restructuring are as favorable to Jeffrey as a loan to another debtor with similar risks.

Example 4

Assume the same facts as in Example 3 except that the refinanced terms are $500,000 principal, 7% interest for three years. Since the terms of the restructuring are **not** as favorable to Jeffrey as a loan to another debtor with similar risks, the $20,000 origination fees become part of the new investment in the loan and recognized in interest income over the life of the new loan, as in Example 1.

Purchase of a loan or group of loans. Fees paid or fees received when purchasing a loan or group of loans should normally be considered part of the initial investment; to be recognized in income over the lives of the loans. However, if the loans qualify as debt securities under FAS 115 and are held in the lender's "trading securities" portfolio, these fees should be reported in income when paid or received, and not added to the cost of the loans.

Special arrangements. Often lenders provide demand loans (loans with no scheduled payment terms). In this case, any net fees or costs should be recognized on a straight-line basis over a period determined by mutual agreement of the parties, usually over the estimated length of the loan.

Under a revolving line of credit, any net fees or costs are recognized in income on a straight-line basis over the period that the line of credit is active. If the line of credit is terminated due to the borrower's full payment, any unamortized net fees or costs are recognized in income.

Example 5

Green Bank received $50,000 as a nonrefundable origination fee on a $2 million demand loan. Green's loan dictates that any fees are to be amortized over a period of ten years. Therefore, $5,000 ($50,000 x 1/10) of origination fees will be recognized as an addition to interest income each year for the next ten years.

Financial statement presentation. The unamortized balance of origination, commitment, and other fees/costs that are recognized as an adjustment of interest income shall be reported on the balance sheet as part of the loan balance to which they relate. Except for any special cases as noted in the above paragraphs, the amount of net fees/costs recognized each period as an adjustment will be reported in the income statement as part of interest income.

Accounting for Loans Acquired by Transfer

Banks commonly acquire loans originated by other financial intermediaries. In some cases, these are impaired when acquired; that is, due to changes in the borrowers' credit risks, the expected cash flows from the purchased loans may not equal the contractual cash flows. (Note that the differences in expected cash flows versus contractual cash flows arising from changes in interest rates during the interval from loan inception to loan acquisition is a separate issue; the resulting discount or premium would be amortized by the effective yield method over the expected term of the loan.)

AcSEC issued SOP 03-3, *Accounting for Certain Loans and Debt Securities Acquired in a Transfer,* to address the accounting for the differences between contractual and expected future cash flows of acquired loans when these differences are attributable, at least in part, to credit quality. This SOP amended certain provisions of Practice Bulletin 6.

Under the provisions of SOP 03-3, purchased loans are to be displayed at the initial investment amount on the balance sheet. The amount of any discount is not to be displayed in the balance sheet nor should the acquirer carry over an allowance for loan losses established by the seller. This prohibition applies equally to stand-alone purchases of loans and to those which occur as part of purchase business combinations. Expanded disclosure requirements have also been established.

When loans are acquired with evidence of deterioration in credit quality since origination, the acquirer will be required to estimate the cash flows expected to be collected on the loan. This exercise is to be done both at the purchase date and again periodically over the lives of the loans. Cash flows in excess of the initial investment (purchase price) expected to be collected should be recognized as yield; this is referred to as "accretable yield." On the other hand, contractual cash flows in excess of expected cash flows (the nonaccretable difference) should **not** be recognized as yield. (Accretion of this amount would necessitate, in most instances, later recognition of bad debt expense, and thus would distort multiple periods' results of operations.)

Changing expectations of future cash flows are to be handled differently, depending on whether these are decreases or increases. If, subsequent to acquisition, there are decreases in the probable cash flows, impairments are to be recognized. In other words, such a development cannot be handled prospectively as a yield adjustment over the remaining lives of the loans.

By contrast, probable increases in subsequent cash flows expected to be collected should be recognized prospectively as a yield adjustment. In cases where a new, higher yield on a loan is established (due to a probable increase in cash flows to be collected), that yield should be used as the effective interest rate in any later test for impairment.

If loans are refinanced or restructured after acquisition, these cannot be accounted for as new loans, unless these are troubled debt restructurings, addressed by FAS 15, 114, and 115).

Under the provisions of the SOP, acquired loans are not to be aggregated for purposes of determining evidence of postorigination credit deterioration. Rather, each loan, even if purchased in a pool, must be individually evaluated. However, subsequent pooling or aggregation of smaller-balance homogeneous loans is allowed for purposes of recognition, measurement, and disclosure. To be accounted for in the aggregate, loans must have a common credit risk (such as past due status or credit score) and have a common predominant risk characteristic (such as type of loan or date of origination). Furthermore, aggregation is limited to loans purchased in the same fiscal quarter.

The SOP does not provide general guidance as to the recognition of income, because that guidance does not exist for originated loans. However, income recognition will still be prohibited on loans for which an investor expects to substantially improve the collateral for resale or expects to use the collateral in operations.

Variable loans with index rate decreases, contractual cash flow decreases, and expected cash flow decreases should be evaluated based on the change in expected cash flows attributable to the decrease in index rates. Those changes should be recognized prospectively, rather than as impairments. The decrease in expected cash flows due to index rate decreases must be ascertained, and those changes are to be evaluated against the loan's contractual payments receivable, which must be calculated based on the index rate as it changes over the life of the loan.

Conforming Practice by all Financial Institutions

SOP 01-6, *Accounting for Certain Entities (Including Entities with Trade Receivables) That Lend to or Finance the Activities of Others,* became effective for fiscal years beginning after December 15, 2001. This standard reconciled and conformed the accounting and financial reporting provisions of the former AICPA AAG applicable to banks and saving institutions, credit unions, and finance companies. It furthermore added mortgage companies and corporate credit unions to the scope of coverage. The standard applies, additionally, to all entities which finance other entities, even via normal trade credit arrangements, and thus directs the accounting to be employed by manufacturers, retailers, wholesalers, and other business enterprises. The provisions of SOP 01-6 have been incorporated into the new AAG, *Depository and Lending Institutions: Banks and Savings Institutions, Credit Unions, Finance Companies and Mortgage Companies.*

SOP 01-6 provides revised accounting guidance for sales of loan servicing rights, in order to comply with the revenue recognition model set forth in EITF Issue 95-5, *Determination of What Risks and Rewards, if Any, Can Be Retained and Whether Any Unresolved Contingencies May Exist in a Sale of Mortgage Loan Servicing Rights.* It also adopts the basis allocation approach set forth in FAS 140. It made it clear that all entities which lend to or finance the activities of others are subject to the accounting guidance found in the Guide, *Audits of Finance Companies,* including insurance companies to the extent they engage in lending activities, notwithstanding that the finance companies Guide explicitly excluded such enterprises from its scope.

The SOP eliminated differences in accounting and disclosure established by the respective Guides and carried forward accounting guidance for transactions determined to be unique to certain financial institutions. It did not create new accounting guidance (i.e., new GAAP is not established). The formerly separate Guides have now been superseded by the new Guide, *Depository and Lending Institutions.*

SOP 01-6 requires that, to the extent management has the intent and the ability to hold them for the foreseeable future or until maturity or payoff, loans should be reported on the balance sheet at outstanding principal adjusted for any charge-offs, the allowance for loan losses, any deferred fees or costs on originated loans, and any unamortized premiums or discounts on purchased loans. Nonmortgage loans held for sale should be reported at the lower of cost or fair value. When a decision is made to sell loans not previously held for sale, those loans should be reclassified as held-for-sale and carried at the lower of cost or fair value.

With regard to credit losses, these are to be deducted from the allowance. Loan balances should be charged off in the periods in which the loans are deemed uncollectible. Recoveries of amounts previously charged off should be recorded when received. Credit losses on off-balance-sheet instruments should be reported separately from valuation accounts for recognized instruments.

Under SOP 01-6, standby commitments to purchase loans are reported in one of two ways, depending on whether the settlement date is within a reasonable time and whether the entity has the intent and ability to accept delivery without selling assets. If both conditions are met, the entity should record the loans purchased at cost, net of the standby commitment fee received, on the settlement date If one or both conditions are not met, or if the entity does not have the intent and ability to take delivery without selling assets, the standby commitment fee (which is essentially a written put option premium) should be reported as a liability. Thereafter, the liability should be reported at the greater of the initial standby commitment fee or the fair value of the written put option, with the unrealized gains or losses included in current operations.

A transfer of servicing rights should only be accounted for as a sale if the transfer qualifies as a sale under EITF 95-5, *Determination of What Risks and Rewards, If Any, Can Be Retained and Whether Any Unresolved Contingencies May Exist in a Sale of Mortgage Loan Servicing Rights,* **and** if (1) the seller has written approval from the investor (if required), (2) the buyer is a currently approved seller/servicer, (3) if a seller-financed sale, the nonrefundable down payment is large enough to demonstrate the buyer's commitment to complete the transaction, and (4) the transferor receives adequate compensation for any temporary servicing it performs. Sales of servicing rights previously sold should be recognized in income consistent with this provision and FAS 140.

The SOP also addresses a number of other issues. Thus, Federal Home Loan Bank and Federal Reserve Bank stock is to be classified as a restricted investment security, carried at cost, and evaluated for impairment. Also, any delinquency fees are to be recognized in income when chargeable, assuming collectibility is reasonably assured. Prepayment fees are not recognized in income until the loans or trade receivables are prepaid, except as set forth by FAS 91. Finally, accrual of interest income should not be affected by the possibility that rebates may be calculated using a method different than the interest method, except as set forth in FAS 91.

With regard to financial statement disclosures, the SOP requires that the summary of significant accounting policies state the basis of accounting for loans, trade receivables, and lease financings; the method used to determine the lower of cost or market of nonmortgage loans held for sale, the classification and method of accounting for interest-only strips, loans, and other receivables or retained interests in securitizations; and the method for recognizing interest income on loan and trade receivables, including the method of amortizing net deferred fees or costs. The accounting policies note should also describe the criteria for placing loans on nonaccrual status, for charging off uncollectible loans and trade receivables, and for determining past due or delinquency status.

The financial statement notes should include a description of the accounting policies and methodology used to estimate the allowance for loan losses, and any liability for off-balance-sheet credit losses, as well as the related charges for loan, trade receivable, or other credit losses. Aggregate gains or losses on sales of loans or trade receivables should be presented separately in the financial statements or disclosed in the notes thereto. Major categories of loans or trade receivables should be presented separately either in the balance sheet or the notes, as should the allowance for credit losses, the allowance for doubtful accounts, and any unearned income. Receivables held for sale should be separately reported.

The SOP also requires that foreclosed and repossessed assets be reported separately on the balance sheet or disclosed in the notes. The recorded investment in loans and trade receivables on nonaccrual status should be disclosed, as should the amount of loans and trade receivables past due ninety days or more and still accruing.

The amount of securities deposited with state regulatory authorities (if required) should be disclosed. The carrying amount of loans, trade receivables, securities, and financial instruments that serve as collateral for borrowings should also be disclosed.

One requirement set by the new standard effectively resurrects a disclosure which had been specified under FAS 105 but which was dropped when FAS 105 was effectively superseded by FAS 133. The earlier standard required disclosure of the extent, nature, terms, and credit risk of financial instruments not limited to derivatives with off-balance-sheet credit risk. FAS 133's disclosure requirements for financial instruments with off-balance-sheet credit risk are limited to derivative instruments as defined in that standard. However, certain instruments commonly used by lending institutions, including off-balance-sheet loan commitments, financial guarantees, and letters of credit, are not included within the definition of derivatives. AcSEC concluded that the disclosure requirements for off-balance-sheet financial instruments, previously addressed in FAS 105, should still be applied to entities within the scope of SOP 01-6.

Previously, GAAP for banks and savings institutions did not require disclosure of capital requirements for branches of foreign banks, because those branches do not have capital. However, branches are subject to requirements to maintain certain levels of capital-equivalent deposits and may be required to maintain other specified reserves. Since failure to comply with those requirements potentially has an adverse impact on the reporting entity, disclosures about the balance requirements and a branch's compliance are required under SOP 01-6. Similarly, capital requirements for trust operations are unpublished, are subject to variations of interpretation as between regulatory agencies, and may not be uniformly applied to the trust operations of all institutions. Nonetheless, to the extent that an institution has been advised of an expectation that certain trust-related capital levels be maintained, its compliance with those expectations should be disclosed.

Cash Flow Statement

Banks, savings institutions, and credit unions are **not** required to report gross cash receipts and payments for the following:

1. Deposits placed with other financial institutions
2. Withdrawals of deposits
3. Time deposits accepted
4. Repayments of deposits
5. Loans made to customers
6. Principal collections of loans

If an enterprise is part of a consolidated enterprise, net cash receipts and payments of the enterprise should be reported separate from the gross cash receipts and payments of the consolidated enterprise.

EMERGING ISSUES TASK FORCE ISSUES SUMMARIES

84-4 Acquisition, Development, and Construction Loans

The Task Force discussed the treatment of ADC loans as loans, investments, or interests in a joint venture and the accounting for a partial sale of the arrangement. These issues were resolved by the issuance of the AICPA Notice to Practitioners, ADC Arrangements, which covers ADC arrangements in which the lender expects to participate in residual profit and gives guidance on accounting and reporting concerns.

84-9 Deposit Float of Banks

The Task Force agreed that to allow banks to delay recording assets and liabilities for checks deposited until collection is made from the drawee bank would constitute an accounting change. However, a consensus was reached that the change would be difficult to justify because this approach is conceptually flawed.

84-19 Mortgage Loan Payment Modifications

The Task Force discussed agreements in which the lender allows the borrower to make larger payments for some period (at least twelve payments) and is then relieved of his remaining obligation. A consensus was reached that the loss related to the forgiven portion should be accrued over the period of the larger payments.

84-20 GNMA Dollar Rolls

A consensus was reached on the treatment of only one of the four types of GNMA rolls. The Task Force agreed that forward commitment dollar rolls should be marked to market. The remaining issues were resolved by SOP 85-2, which was subsequently amended by SOP 90-3.

84-21 Sale of a Loan with a Partial Participation Retained

In some instances, an enterprise may sell a loan but retain a share in the interest income as well as servicing rights. The Task Force debated whether the present value of the future interest inflows should be recognized immediately or over the life of the loan and agreed that the accounting treatment specified in the AICPA AAG, *Savings and Loan Associations*, should be followed.

84-22 Prior Years' Earnings Per Share Following a Savings and Loan Association Conversion and Pooling

The Task Force agreed that when a mutual savings and loan association converts to stock ownership and pools with another S&L, its EPS should be excluded from the restated combined EPS for years before the date of conversion. The method of presentation must be disclosed.

84-31 Equity Certificates of Deposit

The Task Force concluded that contingent interest expense resulting from equity certificates of deposit is recognized concurrently with gains relating to the assets upon which the equity is given.

85-7 Federal Home Loan Mortgage Corporation Stock

The Task Force debated the proper accounting for the new class of nonvoting, participating preferred stock issued on December 6, 1984, to members of the Federal Home Loan Banking System. A consensus was not reached, although the majority opinion was that the stock is a nonmonetary asset that should be accounted for at fair value in accordance with APB 29. The issue was subsequently resolved by FTB 85-1, which concurred with the Task Force and further stated that the resulting income is extraordinary.

85-8 Amortization of Thrift Intangibles

When a banking or thrift institution is acquired, the excess of the fair value of liabilities over the fair value of assets should be amortized to expense in accordance with

FAS 72. Any other goodwill resulting from the combination should be amortized according to APB 17.

85-13 Sale of Mortgage Service Rights on Mortgages Owned by Others

The Task Force agreed that a gain should be recognized upon the sale of mortgage service rights that include participation in the future interest stream of the loans.

85-18 Earnings Per Share Effect of Equity Commitment Notes

The Task Force concluded that neither equity commitment notes nor equity contract notes should be included in earnings per share computations.

85-20 Recognition of Fees for Guaranteeing a Loan

A consensus was reached that a guarantor should recognize loan guarantee fees as revenue over the term of the guarantee. Any direct costs related to the guarantee must be recognized in the same manner. If material, footnote disclosure is required, and the probability of loss should be continually assessed.

85-24 Distribution Fees by Distributors of Mutual Funds That Do Not Have a Front-End Sales Charge

The Task Force concluded that the currently used cost deferral method should be maintained. Under this method, fees expected to be received over some future period should be recognized upon receipt. Deferred incremental direct costs are amortized while indirect costs are expensed as incurred.

85-26 Measurement of Servicing Fees under FASB Statement 65 When a Loan Is Sold with Servicing Retained

The Task Force debated whether mortgage bankers should consider servicing fee rates set by secondary market makers (GNMA, FHLMC, FNMA) to be the minimum for a normal servicing fee rate. A consensus was not reached, but the issue was subsequently resolved by FTB 87-3, which states that these rates should be considered normal for transactions with those agencies.

85-31 Comptroller of the Currency's Rule on Deferred Tax Debits

The Task Force reached a consensus that the Comptroller's Banking Circular 202, which limits the net deferred tax debits allowable on a bank's statement of condition, applies only for regulatory purposes and does not affect GAAP financial statements.

85-41 Accounting for Savings and Loan Associations under FSLIC Management Consignment Program

When a troubled thrift is closed under the Management Consignment Program (MCP), its assets (tangible and identifiable intangible) and liabilities are transferred at fair value to a newly chartered federal mutual association. FV constitutes the new cost basis, which should not be adjusted to market on a continuing basis but instead maintained according to GAAP. Any excess of liabilities over assets is recorded as deficit equity. The proper accounting is the same for both stock and mutual institutions, and the transfer does not constitute a business combination.

85-42 Amortization of Goodwill Resulting from Recording Time Savings Deposits at Fair Values

When a financial institution is acquired by purchase, the excess of the fair value of liabilities over the fair value of assets (FAS 72 goodwill) should be amortized over a period up to the remaining life of the long-term interest-bearing assets acquired. Any other goodwill resulting from the combination should be amortized according to APB 17.

85-44 Differences between Loan Loss Allowances for GAAP and RAP

The Task Force reached a consensus that loan loss allowances recorded by S&Ls may differ under regulatory accounting principles (RAP) and GAAP. However, auditors must make certain that any differences are justifiable.

86-21 Application of the AICPA Notice to Practitioners Regarding Acquisition, Development, and Construction Arrangements to Acquisition of an Operating Property

The Task Force concluded that AICPA Notice to Practitioners, *ADC Arrangements*, which deals with real estate ADC arrangements of financial institutions, should also be considered in relation to ADC arrangements transacted by non-financial institutions, shared appreciation mortgages, and loans on operating real estate. The Task Force also reached consensus that paragraphs 3-5 of that Notice should be consulted in determining the nature of expected residual profit on the arrangement.

86-31 Reporting the Tax Implications of a Pooling of a Bank and a Savings and Loan Association

A consensus was reached regarding the tax effects of a required reduction in bad-debt reserves (for tax purposes) in a merger of a savings and loan association and a banking, insurance, or other financial institution. The tax effects should be accounted for as an expense in the current period's combined financial statements of the merged entity.

The Task Force also reached a consensus that after the bad-debt reserves are adjusted for the merger transaction, deferred taxes should be recorded for the difference between bad-debt reserves for tax and financial purposes.

86-38 Implications of Mortgage Prepayments on Amortization of Servicing Rights

An excess service fee receivable (resulting from a higher than normal servicing fee) must be written down to the present value of the remaining future excess service fee revenue discounted with the same factor used to calculate the original receivable.

87-22 Prepayment to the Secondary Reserve of the FSLIC

The secondary reserve of the FSLIC was eliminated as of December 31, 1986, although member institutions were not notified until May 1987. The Task Force agreed that this represents a subsequent event and that the related amounts should be written off as a loss against 1987 operating income.

87-34 Sale of Mortgage Servicing Rights with a Subservicing Agreement

The Task Force discussed events in which a mortgage loan servicer (transferor) transfers the servicing rights and related risks to an unaffiliated enterprise (transferee), which then makes a subservicing agreement whereby the transferor services the loans for a fixed fee. A consensus was reached that income recognition should be deferred and that treatment as a sale or a financing depends on the circumstances surrounding the transaction. However, this consensus does not apply to temporary subservicing agreements. In addition, a loss should be recognized currently if loan prepayments may result in future servicing losses.

88-17 Accounting for Fees and Costs Associated with Loan Syndications and Loan Participations

The Task Force agreed that there are no material differences between loan syndications and some loan participations and thus both should receive the same accounting treatment. In addition, a transaction structured legally as a participation which actually constitutes an in-substance syndication should be accounted for as a syndication. A transaction structured legally as a syndication must also meet certain criteria to be accounted for as such by the lead syndicator.

88-19 FSLIC-Assisted Acquisitions of Thrifts

The Task Force reached a consensus on several issues, which are listed below.

1. In a tax-sharing agreement, the Thrift acts as a conduit for tax benefits accruing to the FSLIC and records only its net benefit in accordance with GAAP.
2. In applying FAS 72, assets covered by yield maintenance assistance are considered interest-bearing, even if they are not.
3. When allocating the purchase price, the stated interest rate is considered the market rate and is used to determine the fair value of the acquired assets.
4. The basis of an asset covered by yield maintenance assistance is carried over to any new covered asset to which it is converted.
5. Contingency losses related to the acquisition are recorded net of reimbursements under indemnification provisions of the assistance agreement.
6. If the assistance includes a note receivable from the FSLIC and the sale of equity securities to the FSLIC, the note should be offset against that equity.
7. If issue 6 applies, then the Thrift should net divided payments made to the FSLIC against cash received from the FSLIC as interest on the note. This net amount is recorded as regulatory assistance.

FAS 109 and SEC Staff Accounting Bulletin provide additional guidance.

88-20 Difference between Initial Investment and Principal Amount of Loans in a Purchased Credit Card Portfolio

The Task Force agreed that the excess of the purchase price of a credit card portfolio including cardholder relationships over the amounts due should be allocated between the credit card loans acquired and the cardholder relationships acquired. The premium related to cardholder relationships is an identifiable intangible asset and is amortized over the period of benefit. The premium related to the loans is amortized over the life of the loans.

88-25 Ongoing Accounting and Reporting for a Newly Created Liquidating Bank

The Task Force concluded that the assets and liabilities of liquidating banks should be reported at fair value as of the date of the financial statements, with subsequent increases and decreases in fair value included in the results of each period. The initial valuation method should be used to determine fair value each period. SEC Staff Accounting Bulletin 82 provides additional guidance.

89-3 Balance Sheet Presentation of Savings Accounts in Financial Statements of Credit Unions

The Task Force agreed that the savings accounts deposited in a credit union must be unequivocally listed as a liability if the financial statements of the credit union are to comply with the AICPA Credit Union Guide. The statement of financial condition must present savings accounts either as the first item in the liabilities and equity section or as a separate subtotal before total liabilities.

89-19 Accounting for a Change in Goodwill Amortization for Business Combinations Initiated prior to the Effective Date of FASB Statement 72

A consensus was reached that an enterprise can adopt the provisions of FAS 72 to account for goodwill obtained in a purchase-type business combination occurring prior to the effective date of the statement. As the adoption of FAS 72 results in a change in accounting principle, it should be recorded as a cumulative effect adjustment.

The Task Force noted that this consensus applies specifically to FAS 72 and should not be applied to other situations.

Additionally, the consensus on this issue does not prevent an enterprise from applying the special exemption for an initial public distribution.

90-18 Effect of a "Removal of Accounts" Provision on the Accounting for a Credit Card Securitization

The Task Force concluded that credit card securitizations with "removal of accounts" provisions should be recognized as sales transactions under FAS 77 as long as the removal meets any specified terms, doesn't reduce the interests of the investor in the pool, and doesn't reduce the seller's percentage interest below a contractually specified level.

90-21 Balance Sheet Treatment of a Sale of Mortgage Servicing Rights with a Subservicing Agreement

The Task Force agreed that such transactions (discussed in Issue 87-34) should be accounted for as a sale if substantially all the risks and rewards of ownership have been transferred to the buyer. If substantially all the risks and rewards have **not** been transferred, then the transaction must be accounted for as a financing.

92-5 Amortization Period for Net Deferred Credit Card Origination Fees

A consensus was reached that credit card origination costs that qualify for deferral in accordance with FAS 91 should be netted against the credit card fee charged, if any, and the net amount should be amortized on a straight-line basis over the term of the credit card or one year, depending on the significance of the fee.

Additionally, for both purchased and originated credit cards, the accounting policies, the net amount capitalized, and the amortization period should be disclosed.

93-1 Accounting for Individual Credit Card Acquisitions

A consensus was reached that credit card accounts acquired individually should be accounted for as originations under FAS 91 and EITF Issue 92-5.

FASB TECHNICAL BULLETINS

87-3 Accounting for Mortgage Servicing Fees and Rights

Normal servicing fee rates for mortgage loans are those set by federally sponsored secondary market makers (GNMA, FHLMC, FNMA). For transactions with those agencies or for mortgage loans sold to private sector investors where the seller retains servicing rights, normal servicing rates should be considered. In the latter case, a stated servicing fee rate that differs from the normal rate requires adjustment to the sales price to yield the normal rate. In either case, a loss should be accrued if expected servicing costs exceed anticipated fees based on the stated servicing fee rate. If the servicer refinances a mortgage loan and actual prepayments differ from any anticipated prepayments, then the servicing asset must be adjusted.

01-1 Effective Date for Certain Financial Institutions of Certain Provisions of Statement 140 Related to the Isolation of Transferred Assets

This technical bulletin granted financial institutions extended mandatory implementation dates for several provisions of FAS 140, which superseded FAS 125. These pertain exclusively to isolation criteria under FAS 140 (which determine whether transfers are to be accounted for as sales or as secured borrowings). (FAS 140 is addressed in Chapters 5 and 6.) The phase-in for certain very limited provisions of FAS 140 is delayed to 2006 for qualifying financial institutions.

BROADCASTING

PERSPECTIVE AND ISSUES

FAS 63 sets forth accounting and reporting standards for the broadcasting industry. A broadcaster is an enterprise or an affiliated group of enterprises that transmits radio or television program material. Broadcasters acquire program exhibition rights through license agreements. A typical license agreement for program material (e.g., features, specials, series, or cartoons) covers several programs (a package) and grants a television station, group of stations, network, pay television, or cable television system (licensee) the right to broadcast either a specified number or an unlimited number of showings over a maximum period of time (license period) for a specified fee. Ordinarily, the fee is paid in installments over a period generally shorter than the license period. The agreement usually contains a separate license for each program in the package. The license expires at the earlier of the last telecast allowed or the end of the license period. The licensee pays the required fee whether or not the rights are exercised. If the licensee does not exercise the contractual rights, the rights revert to the licensor with no refund to the licensee.

Sources of GAAP
FAS
63

DEFINITIONS OF TERMS

Barter. The exchange of unsold advertising time for products or services.

Broadcaster. An enterprise or an affiliated group of enterprises that transmits radio or television program material.

Daypart. An aggregation of programs broadcast during a particular time of day (e.g., daytime, evening, late night) or programs of a similar type (e.g., sports, news, children's shows).

License agreement for program material. A typical license agreement for program material (e.g., features, specials, series, or cartoons) covers several programs (a package) and grants a television station, group of stations, network, pay television, or cable television system (licensee) the right to broadcast either a specified number or an unlimited number of showings over a maximum period of time (license period) for a specified fee.

Network affiliation agreement. A broadcaster may be affiliated with a network under a network affiliation agreement. Under the agreement the station receives compensation for the network programming that it carries based on a formula designed to compensate the station for advertising sold on a network basis and included in the network programming.

CONCEPTS, RULES, AND EXAMPLES

Accounting for License Agreements

A broadcaster accounts for a license agreement for program material as a purchase of rights. Thus, an asset and a liability are recorded for the program rights purchased and the liability incurred when the license period begins and the broadcaster has met the following requirements:

1. Knows or can reasonably determine the cost of each program
2. Has accepted the program material according to the license agreement
3. Has access to the program for the first telecast (unless an agreement with another licensee prevents the telecast)

The asset is capitalized and the liability reported at either the gross amount of the liability for program rights or, alternatively, at the present value of the liability calculated using an imputed rate of interest. In the latter case, the difference between the gross and net amounts is reported as interest. Under either method, the capitalized costs are allocated to each program within a package based on the relative value of each program to the broadcaster.

The asset is separated into current and noncurrent portions based on expected time of program usage. The liability is likewise segregated according to the payment maturities.

Amortizing Capitalized Costs

The capitalized costs are amortized to expense as the program rights are used; generally based on the estimated number of program telecasts. However, licenses granting the right to unlimited broadcasts of programs such as cartoons are amortized over the license period, since the number of telecasts may be indeterminable.

Feature programs and program series require specific treatment. Feature programs are amortized program-by-program, unless amortization as a package produces approximately the same result. Syndicated programs are amortized as a series. If the broadcaster considers the first showing to be more valuable than reruns, the series is amortized using an accelerated method. If each showing is equally valuable, straight-line amortization is used.

Example of accounting for program license agreements

On July 31, 2005, Lakie Media Company executed a license agreement for three movies, which it plans to televise on its local television station. The agreement allows the broadcast of each movie twice during the license period. Lakie is a calendar year-end company. The appropriate rate for imputing interest is 12%. Additional facts and assumptions are as follows:

	License Period			*First telecast*		*Second telecast*	
Film	*From*	*To*	*Film availability date*	*Date*	*% of Total revenue*	*Date*	*% of Total revenue*
A	10/1/05	9/30/07	9/1/05	3/1/06	60%	6/1/07	40%
B	10/1/05	9/30/07	9/1/05	5/1/06	70%	7/1/07	30%
C	11/1/05	8/31/07	10/1/05	6/1/06	75%	8/1/07	25%

Payment terms and discounted present value data are as follows (Films A and B were acquired as a package):

	Payment		*Discount period**	
Film(s)	*Date*	*Amount*	*From*	*To*
A & B	7/31/05	$1,000		
	12/31/05	6,000	10/1/05	12/31/05
	12/31/06	6,000	10/1/05	12/31/06
		13,000		
C	12/31/06	3,750	11/1/05	12/31/06
		$16,750		

* *Discounted from the first day of the license period to the date of payment.*

Based on management's estimates of expected advertising revenues, Film A represents 70% and Film B 30% of the total package A and B.

Present value approach. When each film's license period begins, an asset and a liability are recorded at the present value of the liability. Since the first three payments apply to the package of films A and B, the $12,027 combined present value (see the amortization schedule below) must be allocated to these films according to the 70%/30% assumption stated above.

Film	*Asset and liability recognized*	
A	$ 8,419	($12,027 x 70%)
B	3,608	($12,027 x 30%)
	12,027	
C	3,283	
	$15,310	

In this case, all costs are capitalized in 2005 because all of the films' licensing periods begin in that year (assuming the three conditions are met).

The amount capitalized as an asset is amortized according to the percentage of revenues to be earned each year from each film. Interest is accrued on the unpaid balance of the liability for each film. Note that for films A and B, the unpaid balance at December 31, 2005, is $11,027 ($12,027 – the $1,000 downpayment).

Amortization Schedules—Annual Compounding

Description	*Date*	*Payment*	*Interest at 12%*	*Principal*	*Balance*
Films A and B					
Down payment	7/31/05	$ 1,000.00	--	$ 1,000.00	--
Discounted obligation	10/1/05				$11,027.23
Payment	12/31/05	6,000.00	$ 329.91	5,670.09	5,357.14
Payment	12/31/06	6,000.00	642.86	5,357.14	--
		13,000.00	972.77	12,027.23	
Film C					
Original obligation	11/1/05				3,283.44
Accrued interest	12/31/06	--	64.77	(64.77)	3,348.21
Payment	12/31/06	3,750.00	401.79	3,348.21	--
		3,750.00	466.56	3,283.44	
		$16,750.00	$1,439.33	$15,310.67	

	2005	*2006*	*2007*	*Total*
Amortization of film rights				
Film A				
$12,027 x 70% = $8,419 x 60%		$ 5,051		
$12,027 x 70% = $8,419 x 40%			$3,368	$ 8,419
Film B				
$12,027 x 30% = $3,608 x 70%		2,526		
$12,027 x 30% = $3,608 x 30%			1,082	3,608
				12,027

	2005	*2006*	*2007*	*Total*
Film C				
$3,283 x 75%		2,462		
$3,283 x 25%			821	3,283
Total amortization of film rights		$10,039	$5,271	15,310
Interest expense per amortization schedule				
Films A and B	$330	$ 643		973
Film C	65	402		467
	$395	$ 1,045		1,440
				$16,750

Gross method. Costs are capitalized at the gross amount of the liability.

Film	*Asset and liability recognized*	
A	$ 9,100	($13,000 x 70%)
B	3,900	($13,000 x 30%)
C	3,750	
	$16,750	

Again, since the license period for all the films begins in 2005, the assets and liabilities are recognized in that year.

Under the gross approach, no interest is accrued on the unpaid liability. Thus the only expense recognized is the amortization of the program cost.

	Year of expense recognition				*Total*
Film	*2006*		*2007*		
A	$5,460	(1)	$3,640	(4)	$ 9,100
B	2,730	(2)	1,170	(5)	3,900
C	2,813	(3)	937	(6)	3,750
	$11,003		$5,747		$16,750

(1) $9,100 x 60% (4) $9,100 x 40%
(2) $3,900 x 70% (5) $3,900 x 30%
(3) $3,750 x 75% (6) $3,750 x 25%

Accounting for Network Affiliation Agreements

A broadcaster may be affiliated with a network under a network affiliation agreement. Under the agreement, the station receives compensation for the network programming that it carries based on a formula designed to compensate the station for advertising sold on a network-wide basis and included in the network programming. Program costs, a major expense of television stations, are generally lower for a network affiliate than for an independent station because an affiliate does not incur program costs for network programs.

Upon termination of a network affiliation agreement, immediate replacement, or an agreement to replace the affiliation, the broadcaster will recognize a loss measured by the unamortized cost of the previous affiliation less the fair value of the new affiliation. No gain is recognized if the fair value exceeds the unamortized cost. If the terminated affiliation is not replaced, its unamortized cost is charged to expense.

Accounting for Barter Transactions

Broadcasters may exchange unsold advertising time for products or services. The broadcaster benefits (providing the exchange does not interfere with its cash sales) by exchanging otherwise unsold time for such things as programs, fixed assets, merchandise, other media advertising privileges, travel and hotel arrangements, entertainment, and other services or products. Such transactions are reported at the fair value of the services or products (except when advertising time is exchanged for programs).

Barter revenue is recognized as the commercials are broadcast. The products or services received in exchange are reported when received or used. A liability results if products or services are received before the commercial is aired, and a receivable results if the commercial is aired first.

Reporting and Disclosure

The capitalized cost of program rights is reported in the balance sheet at the lower of unamortized cost or net realizable value. Net realizable value is estimated on a package, series, program-by-program, or daypart basis. Daypart is an aggregation of programs broadcast during a particular time of day (e.g., daytime, evening, late night) or programs of a similar type (e.g., sports, news, children's shows). Broadcasters generally sell access to viewing audiences to advertisers on a daypart basis. If the broadcaster expects the usefulness of a program to diminish, the program may have to be written down from unamortized cost to estimated net realizable value. This establishes a new cost basis for the program. The write-down is not permitted to be restored in future periods.

Network affiliation agreements are reported in the balance sheet as intangible assets.

CABLE TELEVISION

PERSPECTIVE AND ISSUES

FAS 51 sets forth accounting and reporting standards for the cable television industry. These standards apply to cable television systems in the prematurity period. During the prematurity period, the cable television system is partially under construction and partially in service. The prematurity period begins with the first earned subscriber revenue. Its end will vary with the system's circumstances but will be determined based on plans for completion of the first major construction period or achievement of a specified predetermined subscriber level at which no additional investment will be required for other than cable television plant. The length of the prematurity period varies with the franchise development and construction plans. Except in the smallest systems, programming is usually delivered to portions of the system, and some revenues are obtained before construction of the entire system is complete. Thus, virtually every cable television system experiences a prematurity period during which it is receiving some revenue while continuing to incur substantial costs related to the establishment of the total system.

Sources of GAAP
FAS
34, 51, 142, 144

DEFINITIONS OF TERMS

Cable television plant. The cable television plant refers to the equipment required to render service to subscribers including:

Head-end. This includes the equipment used to receive signals of distant television or radio stations, whether directly from the transmitter or from a microwave relay system. It also includes the studio facilities required for operator-originated programming, if any.

Cable. This consists of cable and amplifiers (which maintain the quality of the signal) covering the subscriber area, either on utility poles or underground.

Drops. These consist of the hardware that provides access to the main cable, the short length of cable that brings the signal from the main cable to the subscriber's television set, and other associated hardware, which may include a trap to block particular channels.

Converters and descramblers. These devices are attached to the subscriber's television sets when more than twelve channels are provided or when special services are provided, such as "pay cable" or two-way communication.

Direct selling costs. Direct selling costs include commissions, the portion of a salesperson's compensation other than commissions for obtaining new subscribers, local advertising targeted for acquisition of new subscribers, and costs of processing documents related to new subscribers acquired. Direct selling costs do not include supervisory and administrative expenses or indirect expenses, such as rent and other facilities costs.

Subscriber-related costs. Costs incurred to obtain and retain subscribers including costs of billing and collection, bad debts, and mailings; repairs and maintenance of taps and connections; franchise fees related to revenues or number of subscribers; general and administrative system costs, such as salary of the system manager and office rent; programming costs for additional channels used in the marketing effort or costs related to revenues from, or number of subscribers to, per channel or per program service; and direct selling costs.

CONCEPTS, RULES, AND EXAMPLES

Accounting during the Prematurity Period

Before the first subscriber revenue is earned by the cable company, the beginning and end of the prematurity period must be established by management. This period generally will not exceed two years. Once the prematurity period has been established, it may not be changed except in extraordinary circumstances.

Separate accounting is required for any portion[1] of a cable television system that is in the prematurity period and that is distinct from the rest of the system. This distinction is made if the portion is characterized by a majority of the following differences:

- Accountability (e.g., separate forecasts, budgets, etc.)
- Investment decisions (e.g., separate ROI, breakeven, etc.)
- Geographical (e.g., separate franchise area)
- Mechanical (e.g., separate equipment)
- Timing (e.g., separate inception of construction or marketing)

If the portion meets these requirements, it will be charged costs of the entire system only if these costs are directly traceable to that portion. Separate projections are also developed for that portion.

During the prematurity period, costs incurred for the plant are capitalized as usual. General and administrative expenses and subscriber-related costs are considered period costs. Subscriber-related costs are costs incurred to obtain and retain subscribers to the cable television system.

System costs that will benefit the cable system upon completion (e.g., programming costs), and that will remain fairly constant despite changes in the number of subscribers, are separated into amounts benefiting current operations (which are expensed currently) and amounts allocable to future operations (which are capitalized). The amount to be currently expensed is determined by multiplying the total monthly system costs by a fraction calculated each month during the prematurity period as follows:

---

[1] *The word "segment" has been used by some television enterprises. However, since FAS 131 uses segment in a different context, the FASB uses the word "portion" instead of "segment" to refer to the part of a cable television system that is still in the prematurity period.*

$$\text{Current portion of system costs benefiting future periods} = \frac{\begin{array}{l}\text{Greatest of}\\ \text{a) Average \# of subscribers expected that month as estimated at beginning of prematurity period,}\\ \text{b) Average \# of subscribers assuming straight-line progress towards estimated \# of subscribers at end of prematurity period, or}\\ \text{c) Average \# of actual subscribers}\end{array}}{\text{Total \# of subscribers expected at end of prematurity period}}$$

During the prematurity period, interest cost is capitalized using an interest capitalization rate as described in FAS 34. The amount of interest cost to be capitalized is determined as follows:

$$\text{Interest cost capitalized} = \text{Interest capitalization rate} \times \text{Average amount of qualifying assets during the period}$$

FAS 34 defines qualifying assets. The amount of capitalized interest cost may not exceed actual interest cost for the period.

Depreciation and amortization during the prematurity period are determined as follows:

$$\text{Depreciation and amortization expense} = \text{Monthly depreciation and amortization, of total capitalized costs expected on completion of the prematurity period (using depreciation method to be used at completion of prematurity period)} \times \text{Fraction used to determine monthly system costs to be expensed currently}$$

Amortization

Amortizable life for portions built at different times. Costs that have been capitalized for a portion of a cable television system that is in the prematurity period and that are clearly distinguishable on the basis of differences in timing between construction of that portion and the rest of the system are amortized over the same depreciation period used by the main cable plant.

Installation revenues and costs. A cable television system recognizes initial hookup revenue to the extent of the direct selling costs associated with that revenue. Any excess over the direct selling costs is deferred and amortized to income over the average period that subscribers are expected to be connected to the system.

Initial installation costs are capitalized and depreciated over a period that does not exceed the period used to depreciate the cable plant. After the initial installation, any costs incurred to disconnect or reconnect subscribers are charged to expense as incurred.

Franchise application costs. A cable television franchise is a right granted by a municipality to provide service to its residents. The treatment of franchise application costs depends upon whether or not the application is successful. If successful, the application costs are capitalized and amortized as intangible assets over the life of the franchise agreement. If unsuccessful or abandoned, all application costs are charged to expense.

Impairment. Capitalized plant and amortizable intangible assets are subject to the impairment provisions outlined in FAS 144 (discussed in detail in Chapter 9). Any of the system's intangible assets deemed to have an indefinite life are tested for impairment at least annually under the provisions of FAS 142. A separate evaluation is made for portions of the cable television system that are in their prematurity period. If total capitalized costs reach the maximum recoverable amount, capitalization continues. However, the provision to record an impairment loss to reduce capitalized costs to recoverable value is increased.

COMPUTER SOFTWARE DEVELOPERS

PERSPECTIVE AND ISSUES

As technology has come to play a more important role in businesses, increasing levels of activity have been devoted to the development of computer software. This involves a number of undertakings.

- Software licensed, purchased, or leased from others for internal use
- Software obtained from others for resale in the normal course of business (either on a stand-alone basis or as part of a larger product)
- Software developed internally for sale to others
- Software developed internally for the developer's own use

Software can be licensed, purchased, or leased and can reside on the user's hardware or be "hosted" by an application service provider (ASP) and leased to the user for remote use over the Internet. A growing set of accounting standards deal with some, but not all, of these issues.

The accounting for the cost of software developed internally for sale (or lease, etc.) to others is addressed by FAS 86; it provides that costs incurred prior to the point at which technological feasibility has been demonstrated are to be expensed as research and development costs, but specified costs incurred subsequently are capitalized, and later amortized or expensed (e.g., as cost of sales) as appropriate.

The cost of software acquired from others for resale in the normal course of business is not separately addressed by GAAP, but would be handled as are any other inventory costs. The usual inventory costing methods (LIFO, FIFO, etc.) and financial reporting concerns (lower of cost or market, etc.) are applicable to such situations.

SOP 98-1 addresses accounting for the costs of software acquired from others, or developed internally, for internal use. Internal-use software and the related rules regarding costs of developing websites are discussed in connection with the discussion of intangible assets in Chapter 9. This standard establishes the conditions that must be met before internal use software costs are capitalized. To qualify for capitalization, costs must have been incurred **subsequent** to the completion of the conceptual formulation, design and testing of possible project alternatives (including the process of vendor selection for purchased software). In addition, management at the appropriate level of authority must have authorized funding for the development project and conclude that it is probable that the project will be completed and the software will be used to perform the intended functions. This prerequisite is roughly analogous to the "technological feasibility" threshold prescribed by FAS 86 for software to be sold or leased to customers. Costs that are eventually capitalized under SOP 98-1 will be amortized over the period of expected economic benefit, as is the case with all other long-lived assets used in the business.

The increasingly central role of technology has received the attention of accounting standard setters in another arena as well. For enterprises that sell computer software and associated goods and services (program upgrades, maintenance agreements, etc.), complicated issues of revenue recognition arise. AcSEC has responded by issuing a series of Statements of Position to provide guidance regarding the recognition of revenue on software sales including multiple-element arrangements that can include the cost of the software bundled with elements of training, upgrades, and postcontract customer support (PCS).

Due to the complexity of the issues involved in software revenue recognition, this topic is given a rather detailed exposition in the following pages.

Sources of GAAP		
FAS	*EITF*	*SOP*
2, 86	96-6, 97-13, 00-3, 03-5	97-2, 98-4, 98-9

DEFINITIONS OF TERMS

Coding. Generating detailed instructions in a computer language to carry out the requirements described in the detail program design. The coding of a computer software product may begin prior to, concurrent with, or subsequent to the completion of the detail program design.

Customer support. Services performed by an enterprise to assist customers in their use of software products. Those services include any installation assistance, training classes, telephone question and answer services, newsletters, on-site visits, and software or data modifications.

Detail program design. The specifications of a computer software product that take product functions, features, and technical requirements to their most detailed, logical form and enables coding of the product.

Maintenance. Activities undertaken after the product is available for general release to customers to correct errors (commonly referred to as "bugs") or keep the product updated with current information. Those activities include routine changes and additions.

Product design. A logical representation of all product functions in sufficient detail to serve as product specifications.

Product enhancement. Improvements to an existing product that are intended to extend the life or improve significantly the marketability of the original product. Enhancements normally require their own product design and may require a redesign of all or part of the existing product.

Product masters. A completed version, ready for copying, of the computer software product, the documentation, and the training materials that are to be sold, leased, or otherwise marketed.

Testing. Performing the steps necessary to determine whether the coded computer software product meets function, feature, and technical performance requirements set forth in the product design.

Working model. An operative version of the computer software product that is completed in the same software language as the product to be ultimately marketed, performs all the major functions planned for the product, and is ready for initial customer testing (usually referred to as **"beta testing"**).

CONCEPTS, RULES, AND EXAMPLES

Costs of Software Developed Internally for Sale or Lease

A separate set of accounting issues arise in connection with the costs of computer software developed internally for lease or sale to others. The principal issue relates to the point in the development process at which development efforts are no longer characterized as research and development (R&D). The costs of R&D activities are required to be expensed currently as discussed in Chapter 9. The determination of this milestone has important accounting significance because specified costs incurred subsequent to the completion of R&D may be deferred (i.e., inventoried) and later reclassified as cost of sales as the finished products are sold or leased.

FAS 86 established the concept of **technological feasibility** to demarcate the point at which it is proper to begin to defer costs. According to this standard, all costs of development are considered research and development costs until technological feasibility has been established. This point is reached when all the necessary planning, designing, **coding,** and testing activities have been completed, to the extent these activities are necessary to establish that the product in question can meet its design specifications. Design specifications, in turn, may include such product aspects as functions, features, and technical performance requirements.

If the process of creating the software involves a **detail program design,** evidence of having achieved technological feasibility includes having performed these steps

1. The product design (the logical representation of the product) and detailed program design have been completed. This step includes having demonstrated that the necessary skills, hardware, and software technologies are accessible to the entity for completion of product development.
2. The detailed program design has been documented and traced to product specifications, thus demonstrating completeness and consistency.
3. The detailed program design has been reviewed for any high-risk elements, such as unproven functions or product innovations, and any such high-risk elements have been resolved through coding and testing.

If the software development effort does **not** involve creation of a detailed program design, then the following steps would require completion to demonstrate technological feasibility:

1. A product design and working model of the software have been completed.
2. The completeness of the working model and its consistency with the product design have been confirmed by testing.

If all the foregoing steps in either of the above listings have been completed as applicable, then technological feasibility has been demonstrated, and qualifying costs of producing **product masters** incurred thereafter are capitalized as production costs. Such costs include additional coding and testing activities that occur after the establishment of technological feasibility. The costs of producing product masters include not only the master copy of the software itself but also related user documentation and training materials. In the nonauthoritative opinion of the FASB Staff, capitalized production costs may include allocated indirect costs (e.g., occupancy costs related to programmers). This practice is inconsistent, however, with GAAP for software developed for internal use which prohibits such allocations (see Chapter 9).

Capitalization of software costs ceases, however, once the product is available for general release to customers of the entity. Period costs, such as maintenance and ongoing **customer support** efforts, are expensed as incurred.

The capitalized production costs must be amortized, beginning when the product is first available for general release to customers. Amortization is computed on a product-by-product basis, which means that costs related to development of earlier products cannot be "rolled forward" into the costs of newer products, thereby delaying expense recognition. Periodic amortization must be the greater of (1) an amount determined with reference to total estimated revenues to be generated by the product, or (2) an amount computed on a straight-line basis with reference to the product's expected life cycle.

Example of amortization of capitalized computer software development costs

Assume total costs of $30,000 have been capitalized at the point product sales begin. Management estimates that the product will eventually generate revenues of $5,100,000 over a period of four years. For the current period (½ of a year), revenues of $600,000 have been earned. Capitalized costs of $3,750 must be amortized, which is the greater of the pro rata amount based on estimated total revenues to be derived from product sales [($600,000 ÷ $5,100,000) x $30,000 = $3,529] or the amount determined on a straight-line basis ($30,000 ÷ 4 x ½ = $3,750).

Other costs, such as product duplication, training material publication, and packaging, are capitalized as inventory on a unit-specific basis and expensed as cost of sales when product sales revenues are recognized.

Capitalized production costs are subject to annual evaluation for net realizable value; if impairment adjustments are recognized, the written-down amount becomes the new cost basis for further amortization purposes, as well as for comparison to net realizable value in the following period.

Capitalized inventory costs are subject to the same lower of cost or market evaluation as is required for inventories of tangible goods (see Chapter 7).

Software Revenue Recognition

The basic principles underlying SOP 97-2 are set forth in the following paragraphs.

Licensing vs. sales. AcSEC was concerned that transfers of rights to software by licenses rather than by outright sales (a technique widely employed to provide vendors with legal recourse when others engage in unauthorized duplication of their products) were being accounted for differently. It concluded that any legal distinction between a license and a sale should not cause revenue recognition to differ.

Product may not equate with delivery of software. AcSEC observed that arrangements to deliver software, whether alone or in conjunction with other products, often include services. Services to be provided in such contexts commonly involve significant production, modification, or customization of the software. AcSEC therefore concluded that in such circumstances physical delivery of the software might not constitute the **delivery** of the final product contracted for, absent those alterations. This resulted in the new requirement that such arrangements be accounted for as construction-type or production-type contracts in conformity with ARB 45 and SOP 81-1. However, if the services do not entail significant production, modification, or customization of the software, the services are accounted for as a separate element.

Delivery is the key threshold issue for revenue recognition. This is consistent with the principles set forth in CON 5, *Recognition and Measurement in Financial Statements of Business Enterprises*, which states that

> *An entity's revenue-earning activities involve delivering or producing goods, rendering services, or other activities that constitute its ongoing major or central operations, and revenues are considered to have been earned when the entity has substantially accomplished what it must do to be entitled to the benefits represented by the revenues. . . [t]he two conditions (being realized or realizable and being earned) are usually met by the time the product or merchandise is delivered. . . to customers, and revenues. . . are commonly recognized at time of sale (usually meaning delivery).*

Revenue must be allocated to all elements of the sales arrangement, with recognition dependent upon meeting the criteria on an element-by-element basis. Under prior GAAP, the accounting for vendor obligations remaining after delivery of software was dependent upon whether or not the obligation was deemed to be significant. Under SOP 97-2, however, all obligations are accounted for and revenue is allocated to each element of the arrangement, based on vendor-specific objective evidence (VSOE) of the fair values of the elements. Revenue associated with a particular element is not recognized until the revenue-recognition conditions established by the SOP are met, as the earnings process related to that element will not be considered complete until that time.

Fair values for revenue allocation purposes must be vendor-specific. When there are multiple elements of an arrangement, revenue is generally recognized on an element-by-element basis as individual elements are delivered. Revenue is allocated to the various elements in proportion to their relative fair values. Under SOP 97-2, this allocation process requires that VSOE of fair value be employed, regardless of any separate prices stated in the contract for each element, since prices stated in a contract may not represent fair value and, accordingly, might result in an unreasonable allocation of revenue. AcSEC concluded that this approach is consistent with the accounting for commingled revenue as set forth in the current standard on accounting for franchise fee revenue. The use of surrogate prices, such as those published by competitors or industry averages, was rejected because of the wide differences in products and services offered by vendors. Separate transaction prices for the individual elements comprising the arrangement, if they are also being sold on that basis, would be the best such evidence, although under some circumstances (such as when prices in the arrangement are based on multiple users rather than the single user pricing of the element on a stand-alone basis) even that information could conceivably be invalid for revenue allocation purposes. Relative sales prices of the elements included in the arrangement are to be used whenever possible.

The earnings process is not complete if fees are subject to forfeiture. Even when elements have been delivered, if fees allocated to those elements are subject to forfeiture, refund, or other concession if the vendor does not fulfill its delivery responsibilities relative to other elements of the arrangement, those fees are not treated as having been earned. The potential concessions are an indication that the customer would not have licensed the delivered elements without also licensing the undelivered elements. For that reason, there must be persuasive evidence that fees allocated to delivered elements are not subject to forfeiture, refund, or other concessions before revenue recognition can be justified. Thus, for example, in determining the persuasiveness of the evidence, the vendor's history of making concessions that were not required by the provisions of an arrangement is more persuasive than are terms included in the arrangement that indicate that no concessions are required.

Operational Rules Established by SOP 97-2

1. If an arrangement to deliver software or a software system, either alone or together with other products or services, requires significant production, modification, or customization of software, the entire arrangement is accounted for in conformity with ARB 45, *Long-Term Construction-Type Contracts*, and SOP 81-1, *Accounting for Performance of Construction-Type and Certain Production-Type Contracts*.
2. If the arrangement does not require significant production, modification, or customization of software, revenue is recognized when **all** of the following criteria are met:
    a. Persuasive evidence of an arrangement exists;
    b. Delivery has occurred;
    c. The vendor's fee is fixed or determinable; and
    d. Collectibility is probable.
3. For software arrangements that provide licenses for multiple software deliverables (multiple elements), some of which may be deliverable only on a when-and-if-available basis, these deliverables are considered in determining whether an arrangement includes multiple elements. The requirements with respect to arrangements that consist of multiple elements are applied to all additional products and services specified in the arrangement, including those described as being deliverable only on a when-and-if-available basis.

4. For arrangements having multiple elements, the fee is allocated to the various elements based on VSOE of fair value, regardless of any separate prices stated for each element within the contract. VSOE of fair value is limited to the following:
   a. The price charged when the same element is sold separately; or
   b. For an element not yet being sold separately, the price established by management, if it is probable that the price, once established, will not change before the separate introduction of the element into the marketplace.

   The revenue allocated to undelivered elements cannot later be adjusted. However, as is traditional under GAAP, if it becomes probable that the amount allocated to an undelivered element of the arrangement will result in a loss on that element, the loss must be immediately recognized. When a vendor's pricing is based on multiple factors such as the number of products and the number of users, the amount allocated to the same elements when sold separately must consider all the relevant factors of the vendor's pricing structure.

   SOP 98-9 amended the guidance of SOP 97-2 with regard to multiple-element arrangements not accounted for as long-term construction contracts when (1) there is VSOE of the fair values of all **undelivered** elements, (2) VSOE does not exist for one or more of the delivered elements, and (3) all other revenue recognition criteria have been satisfied. In such cases, the newly defined "residual" method of allocation of selling price is to be utilized. This results in deferral of the aggregate fair value of the undelivered elements of the arrangement (to be recognized later as delivery occurs), with the excess of the total arrangement fee over the deferred portion being recognized in connection with the delivered components. This change was made to accommodate the situation whereby software is commonly sold with one "free" year of support, where additional years of support are also marketed at fixed prices; in this case, the fair value of the "free" support is deferred (and amortized over the year), while the software itself is assigned a revenue amount which is the difference between the package price and the known price of one year's support.
5. If a discount is offered in a multiple-element arrangement, a proportionate amount of the discount is applied to each element included in the arrangement, based on each element's fair value without regard to the discount. However, no portion of the discount is allocated to any upgrade rights.
6. If sufficient VSOE does not exist for the allocation of revenue to the various elements of the arrangement, all revenue from the arrangement is deferred until the earlier of the point at which (1) such sufficient VSOE does exist, or (2) all elements of the arrangement have been delivered. The exceptions to this guidance, provided in SOP 97-2, are as follows:
   a. If the only undelivered element is postcontract customer support (PCS), the entire fee is recognized ratably over the contractual PCS period, or when the PCS rights are implicit in the arrangement, over the period that PCS is expected to be provided to the customer.
   b. If the only undelivered element is services that do not involve significant production, modification, or customization of the software (e.g., training or installation), the entire fee is recognized over the period during which the services are expected to be performed.
   c. If the arrangement is in substance a subscription, the entire fee is recognized ratably over the term of the arrangement, if stated, otherwise over the estimated economic life of the products included in the arrangement.

d. If the fee is based on the number of copies delivered, how the arrangement is accounted for depends on whether the total fee is fixed, and on whether the buyer can alter the composition of the copies to be received, as follows:

(1) If the arrangement provides customers with the right to reproduce or obtain copies of two or more software products at a specified price per copy (**not** per product) up to the total amount of the fixed fee, an allocation of the fee to the individual products generally cannot be made, because the total revenue allocable to each software product is unknown at inception and depends on subsequent choices to be made by the customer and, sometimes, on future vendor development activity. Nevertheless, certain arrangements that include products that are not deliverable at inception impose a maximum number of copies of the undeliverable product(s) to which the customer is entitled. In such arrangements, a portion of the arrangement fee is allocated to the undeliverable product(s). This allocation is made assuming that the customer will elect to receive the maximum number of copies of the undeliverable product(s).

(2) In arrangements in which no allocation can be made until the first copy or product master of each product covered by the arrangement has been delivered to the customer, and assuming the four conditions set forth above are met, revenue is recognized as copies of delivered products are either (a) reproduced by the customer, or (b) furnished to the customer if the vendor is duplicating the software. Once the vendor has delivered the product master or the first copy of all products covered by the arrangement, any previously unrecognized licensing fees are recognized, since only duplication of the software is required to satisfy the vendor's delivery requirement and such duplication is incidental to the arrangement. Consequently, the delivery criterion is deemed to have been met upon delivery to the customer of the product master or first copy. When the arrangement terminates, the vendor recognizes any licensing fees not previously recognized. Revenue is not recognized fully until at least one of the following conditions is met: either (a) delivery is complete for all products covered by the arrangement, or (b) the aggregate revenue attributable to all copies of the software products delivered is equal to the fixed fee, provided that the vendor is not obligated to deliver additional software products under the arrangement.

(3) The revenue allocated to the delivered products is recognized when the product master or first copy is delivered. If, during the term of the arrangement, the customer reproduces or receives enough copies of these delivered products so that revenue allocable to the delivered products exceeds the revenue previously recognized, the additional revenue is recognized as the copies are reproduced or delivered. The revenue allocated to the undeliverable product(s) is reduced by a corresponding amount.

7. The portion of the fee allocated to a contract element is recognized when the four revenue recognition criteria are met with respect to the element. In applying those criteria, the delivery of an element is considered not to have occurred if there are undelivered elements that are essential to the functionality of the delivered element, because functionality of the delivered element is considered to be impaired.
8. No portion of the fee can be deemed to be collectible if the portion of the fee allocable to delivered elements is subject to forfeiture, refund, or other concession if

any of the undelivered elements are not delivered. If management represents that it will not provide refunds or concessions that are not required under the provisions of the arrangement, this assertion must be supported by reference to all available evidence. This evidence may include the following:

a. Acknowledgment in the arrangement regarding products not currently available or not to be delivered currently;
b. Separate prices stipulated in the arrangement for each deliverable element;
c. Default and damage provisions as defined in the arrangement;
d. Enforceable payment obligations and due dates for the delivered elements that are not dependent on the delivery of future deliverable elements, coupled with the intent of the vendor to enforce rights of payment;
e. Installation and use of the delivered software; and
f. Support services, such as telephone support, related to the delivered software being provided currently by the vendor.

EMERGING ISSUES TASK FORCE ISSUES SUMMARIES

96-6 Accounting for the Film and Software Costs Associated with Developing Entertainment and Educational Software Products

Both software developers and motion picture companies engage in development of software products that combine entertainment (e.g., including well-known cartoon characters and film storylines in the software) and education. The term "edutainment" has been coined to refer to these hybrid products. Diversity in accounting practice had arisen whereby different companies engaged in edutainment development were using different combinations of GAAP to account for the same activities.

The SEC staff announced that

1. Edutainment products developed for sale or lease, or that are otherwise marketed are to be accounted for under FAS 86.
2. Costs subject to FAS 86 accounting include film costs incurred in the development of the product that would otherwise be accounted for under FAS 53 (subsequently superseded and replaced by SOP 00-2, *Accounting by Producers and Distributors of Films,* discussed later in this chapter).
3. Exploitation costs (marketing, advertising, publicity, promotion, and other distribution expenses) are to be expensed as incurred unless they qualify for capitalization as direct response advertising under SOP 93-7, *Reporting on Advertising Costs.*

The EITF did not reach a consensus on this issue as a result of the SEC announcement which it tacitly appears to agree with.

97-13 Accounting for Costs Incurred in Connection with a Consulting Contract or an Internal Project That Combines Business Process Reengineering and Information Technology Transformation

A consensus was reached that all expenditures incurred for business process reengineering activities (either by insiders or outsiders) are to be expensed immediately. Guidance also applies when business process reengineering activities are part of development or implementation of internal-use software. Finally, the accounting for internal-use software development and acquisition of property, plant, and equipment are not affected by this consensus.

Another consensus was reached that in cases where a third party is engaged for a business process reengineering project, the entire consulting contract price is to be allocated to each activity on the basis of the relative fair values of the separate components.

00-3 Application of AICPA SOP 97-2, *Software Revenue Recognition*, to Arrangements That Include the Right to Use Software Stored on Another Entity's Hardware

Some software users do not actually receive and load applications software on their computers, but instead merely access and use it via the Internet, on the vendor's or a third party's server, on an as-needed basis. (Commonly, the applications are "hosted" by companies known as application service providers, or ASPs.) In such arrangements, the customer is paying for two elements—the right to use the software and the storage of the software (and sometimes, the customer's proprietary data) on the provider's hardware.

When a vendor provides hosting, several revenue recognition issues may arise. First, the relationship between the customer and the ASP may be structured in the form of a service agreement providing Internet access to the specified site, without a corresponding software license. In such instances, the application of SOP 97-2 to the arrangement was unclear. Second, when the transaction is structured as a software license with a service element, evaluation of how the arrangement meets the delivery requirement of SOP 97-2 was unclear.

In its consensus on this issue, the EITF found that SOP 97-2 only applies if the customer has the right to take possession of the software at any time during the hosting period, without significant penalty, and install the software on its own hardware or contract with another service provider to host it. Most, if not all, ASP arrangements would not provide this option to the customer and therefore SOP 97-2 would not apply. The EITF notes that hosting arrangements might involve multiple elements to be accounted for in a possible variety of ways.

For those few hosting arrangements meeting the foregoing criteria, and thus subject to SOP 97-2, software delivery is deemed to have occurred when the customer first has the option to take possession. The criteria of SOP 97-2 must be met in order for the ASP to recognize revenue allocable to the software element; revenue relating to the hosting element is recognized as that service is provided.

03-5 Applicability of AICPA Statement of Position of 97-2, *Software Revenue Recognition*, to Non-Software Deliverables in an Arrangement Containing More-Than-Incidental Software

SOP 97-2, *Software Revenue Recognition*, provides authoritative guidance regarding the amounts and timing of revenue recognition in transactions involving the sale or license of computer software. Such transactions are often structured to bundle other software-related "elements" with the software such as future upgrades, postcontract customer support (PCS), training, customization, or other services. Those bundled arrangements are referred to as multiple-element arrangements (MEA).

In this issue, the EITF considered whether revenue recognition for *nonsoftware elements* of an MEA are within the scope of the SOP.

The EITF reached a consensus that in an MEA that includes software that is "more than incidental" to the arrangement, SOP 97-2 applies to the software-related elements enumerated above as well as any nonsoftware element for which the software element is essential to its functionality.

EMPLOYEE BENEFIT PLANS, INCLUDING PENSION FUNDS

PERSPECTIVE AND ISSUES

Employee benefit plans have become increasingly important and diverse. Using assets that are segregated from the plan sponsor, they provide benefits to employees and former employees in accordance with a plan agreement. The provisions of the plan agreement deal with such matters as eligibility, entitlement to benefits, funding, plan amendments, operation and administration, allocation of responsibilities among the fiduciaries, and fiduciaries' ability to delegate duties. A few examples of employee benefit plans are pension plans, profit-sharing plans, stock bonus plans, 401(k) plans, 403(b) plans, disability plans, health care plans, life insurance plans, unemployment benefit plans, tuition assistance plans, dependent care plans, and cafeteria/flexible benefit plans. For accounting and reporting purposes, the plans are divided into three major types: defined benefit pension plans, defined contribution pension plans, and health and welfare benefit plans.

Employee benefit plans that are sponsored by and provide benefits to the employees of state and local governmental entities[2] are outside of the scope of this publication. Readers instead should refer to the Wiley publication, *GAAP for Governments*.

All authoritative pronouncements in the GAAP hierarchy apply to employee benefit plans unless the pronouncement specifically excludes them from its scope. Certain authoritative pronouncements apply specifically to employee benefit plans. Because those pronouncements are particularly relevant to the transactions of employee benefit plans, they are discussed in this chapter.

FAS 35, *Accounting and Reporting by Defined Benefit Pension Plans*, is the principal standard involving the accounting and reporting of employee benefit plans. Although FAS 35's provisions apply only to defined benefit pension plans, the AICPA AAG, *Audits of Employee Benefit Plans,* requires defined contribution plans and employee health and welfare benefit plans to apply specialized accounting principles and practices that are similar to those prescribed by FAS 35. FAS 35 applies only to ongoing plans, not to plans that are terminated or expected to be terminated. The Statement describes the objectives of plan financial statements and the necessary components of a complete set of plan financial statements.

FAS 102, *Statement of Cash Flows—Exemption of Certain Enterprises and Classification of Cash Flows from Certain Securities Acquired for Resale*, exempts defined benefit pension plans and certain other employee benefit plans from FAS 95's requirement to present a statement of cash flows.

FAS 110, *Reporting by Defined Benefit Pension Plans of Investment Contracts,* requires defined benefit pension plans to report all investment contracts, including guaranteed investment contracts issued by insurance companies, at fair value. Only contracts that incorporate mortality or morbidity risk (insurance contracts) may be reported at contract value.

The Audit Guide (AAG) mentioned above is the primary AICPA pronouncement that sets standards for employee benefit plans. In addition to providing accounting and reporting guidance for the plans, it provides summaries of statutory rules and regulations applicable to employee benefit plans and illustrative financial statements.

SOP 92-6, *Accounting and Reporting by Health and Welfare Benefit Plans,* establishes standards for health and welfare benefit plans. It divides the diverse universe of plans into

---

[2] *See Chapter 1, Researching GAAP Problems, for a definition of "governmental entity."*

two major types: defined benefit health and welfare plans and defined contribution health and welfare plans. It requires defined benefit health and welfare plans to use certain provisions of FAS 106, *Employer's Accounting for Postretirement Benefits other than Pensions,* to measure benefit obligations. In addition, SOP 92-6 applies many of the measurement and disclosure provisions of FAS 35 to health and welfare plans.

SOP 94-4, *Reporting of Investment Contracts Held by Health and Welfare Benefit Plans and Defined Contribution Pension Plans,* requires defined contribution plans and health and welfare benefit plans to report insurance and investment contracts in a manner similar to the requirements of FAS 110.

SOP 99-2, *Accounting for and Reporting of Postretirement Medical Benefit 401(h) Features of Defined Benefit Pension Plans,* specifies the accounting for and disclosure of 401(h) features of defined benefit pension plans that offer medical benefits to retirees in addition to the normal retirement benefits.

SOP 99-3, *Accounting for and Reporting of Certain Defined Contribution Plan Investments and Other Disclosure Matters,* amends the AAG and SOP 94-4 to simplify the required disclosures about investments. It also supersedes Practice Bulletin 12, which required information about net assets and significant components of the changes in net assets for each investment fund option of a defined contribution pension plan.

SOP 01-2, *Amendment to Audit Guide and SOP 92-6, with Respect to Benefit Obligations,* amends the AAG and SOP 92-6 to modify the presentation requirements for information about benefit obligations, to clarify the measurement date for benefit obligations, to establish standards for postemployment benefit plans, and to add three new disclosures.

This section presents a highly summarized discussion of accounting and reporting standards by employee benefit plans. Readers who desire a more in-depth discussion should refer to the Wiley publication, *GAAP for Employee Benefit Plans.*

This chapter does not describe an employer's requirements for reporting information about employee benefit plans. That information is described in Chapter 16.

Sources of GAAP

FAS	AAG	SOP
35, 102, 110	*Audits of Employee Benefit Plans*	92-6, 94-4, 99-2, 99-3, 01-2

DEFINITIONS OF TERMS

Accumulated plan benefits or **benefit obligations.** Benefits that are attributable to services rendered by employees before the date at which the actuarial present value of the plan obligation is computed.

Defined benefit pension plan. A plan that promises stated or otherwise determinable pension benefits to participants based on factors such as compensation, years of service, and age.

Defined contribution pension plan. A plan in which benefits are based on amounts contributed, investment experience, and allocated forfeitures, net of administrative expenses. Each participant's benefits are computed based on his or her individual account.

Health and welfare benefit plan. Plans that provide benefits such as medical, dental, visual, or other health care, insurance, disability, vacation, education, or dependent care.

Net assets. The residual interest in the assets of an employee benefit plan that remains after deducting its liabilities. The liabilities of a plan do not include its accumulated plan benefits (defined benefit pension plans) or its benefit obligation (defined benefit health and welfare plans).

Plan sponsor. The company, association, employee group, or other group of representatives that established or maintains the plan.

CONCEPTS, RULES, AND EXAMPLES

In addition to varying by basic type (defined benefit pension plan, defined contribution pension plan, and health and welfare benefit plan), employee benefit plans vary by operating and administrative characteristics. Plans can be established by one employer or a group of controlled corporations, in that case they are referred to as single employer plans. Alternatively, they can include the employees of many employers who are related in some way, often by all being parties to a collective-bargaining agreement. Those plans are referred to as multiemployer plans. A plan can be either contributory or noncontributory. A contributory plan requires both the employer and the participants to fund (contribute to) the cost of the future benefits. In a noncontributory plan, the participants do not fund any part of the cost of the future benefits. Insured plans are funded through insurance contracts. Self-funded plans are funded through contributions and investment return. Split-funded plans are funded by a combination of insurance contracts, contributions, and investment return.

Complete Set of Financial Statements

The primary objective of a plan's financial statements is to provide the information necessary to assess the plan's ability to pay benefits when due. Thus, financial statements are to include information about the plan's resources, the results of transactions and events that changed the plan's resources, the stewardship of management over the plan's resources, and any other facts necessary to understand the information provided.

A complete set of financial statements includes a statement of net assets available for benefits as of the end of the plan year (balance sheet equivalent), a statement of changes in net assets available for benefits for the plan year ended (income statement equivalent), and notes to the financial statements. In addition, defined benefit plans must include information about the actuarial present value of accumulated benefits and changes in the accumulated benefits. That information can appear either as additional financial statements or in the notes to financial statements.

FAS 102 exempted defined benefit pension plans from the requirement that a statement of cash flows be provided. Other employee benefit plans were also exempted if they report similar to defined benefit pension plans, including FAS 35's requirement to report plan investments at fair value. Although not required, presentation of a statement of cash flows is encouraged if it would provide useful information about the plan's ability to pay future liabilities, as would be the case if the plan either holds illiquid investments or purchases investments using borrowed funds.

FAS 130, *Reporting Comprehensive Income,* requires that changes in equity other than transactions with owners be reported in financial statements in the period in which they are recognized. The statement of changes in net assets available for benefits is a comprehensive income statement because all changes in net assets available for benefits are reflected in that statement. Thus, although it did not specifically exempt employee benefit plans from its provisions, FAS 130 did not change the reporting for employee benefit plans.

Statement of Net Assets Available for Benefits

Most investments of the plan are reported at fair value. If there is an active market, quoted market prices are used. If market quotations are not available, investments are valued "in good faith" by the plan's trustees and administrator. The selling price of similar investments or discounted cash flows can be useful in estimating fair value. The use of an independent expert may be necessary for the valuation of certain investments. Investment contracts with an insurance company, bank, or other financial institution are reported at fair value. Only insurance contracts—contracts that incorporate mortality or morbidity risk (defined benefit pension plans) or that are fully benefit-responsive (defined contribution plans and health and welfare plans)—may be reported at contract value, and then only if the plan reports at contract value in its annual report filed with government agencies. The financial statements are to identify plan investments by type of investment and indicate how fair value was determined. It is not necessary to disclose the original cost of investments in the basic financial statements. Plans are to disclose in the notes to the financial statements any investments representing 5% or more of the net assets available for benefits as of the end of the year.

Contributions receivable include those due as of the reporting date from participants, employers, withdrawing employers of a multiemployer plan, and other sources (such as a state or federal government in the case of a grant or subsidy). Receivables arise from formal commitments of an employer, legal requirements, or contractual requirements. The receivables are to be reduced by an allowance for uncollectible amounts if warranted.

Long-lived assets (such as buildings, equipment, furniture and fixtures, and leasehold improvements) that are used in the plan's operations are presented at cost less accumulated depreciation or amortization.

Statement of Changes in Net Assets Available for Benefits

The statement of changes in net assets available for benefits is a comprehensive income statement that includes all recognized transactions and events that change the net assets available for benefits. At a minimum, the statement is to include separate amounts for

1. Contributions from
    a. Employer(s)—separating cash from noncash contributions
    b. Participants, including those transmitted by the plan sponsor
    c. Other identified sources
2. Net appreciation or depreciation (realized and unrealized amounts may be combined) in fair value for each significant class of investment, presented by
    a. Investments measured by quoted market prices
    b. Investments measured by some other means
3. Investment income (not including appreciation or depreciation in fair value)
4. Payments to plan participants for benefits, excluding amounts paid by insurance contracts that are not included in plan assets
5. Payments to insurance companies to purchase contracts that are excluded from plan assets
6. Administrative expenses
7. Other changes, if necessary, with appropriate description(s)

Transactions with Related Parties (FAS 57)

Transactions between a plan sponsor and its employee benefit plans are subject to the disclosure requirements of FAS 57, *Related-Party Disclosures*. The required disclosures include

1. The nature of the relationship
2. A description of the transactions for each of the periods in which a statement of changes in net assets available for benefits is presented

3. The dollar amounts of transactions for each of the period in which a statement of changes in net assets available for benefits is presented
4. The effects of any change from the prior period in the method of establishing terms of the transaction
5. The amounts due from related parties at the date of each statement of net assets available for benefits

The disclosures are not permitted to represent that transactions were made at arm's length unless such representations can be substantiated.

Risks and Uncertainties

Employee benefit plans must disclose the information required by SOP 94-6, *Disclosures of Certain Significant Risks and Uncertainties.* Risks that are unique to employee benefit plans include

1. A significant industry downturn that could cause employees to retire early in order to avoid being laid off, especially if the plan's participants are concentrated within a particular industry or with a single employer
2. Likelihood that an employer will significantly increase pension or health and welfare benefits in order to avoid a union walkout
3. A planned downsizing that is expected to offer early retirement to employees
4. Investments in the stock of the employer

Defined Benefit Pension Plans

In addition to the statement of net assets available for benefits and the statement of changes in net assets available for benefits, defined benefit pension plans must provide information about the actuarial present value of accumulated plan benefits and changes in the actuarial present value of accumulated plan benefits. The information can be included as separate financial statements or as schedules in the notes to the financial statements.

Accumulated plan benefits include the present value of future benefits to retired or terminated employees or their beneficiaries, to beneficiaries of deceased employees, and to present employees or their beneficiaries. Whenever possible, plan provisions are to govern the measurement of accumulated plan benefits. If the benefits earned in each year are not determinable from the plan's provisions, a formula for measurement is provided in FAS 35. When calculating accumulated plan benefits, an ongoing plan is to be assumed, analogous to the going concern assumption used in preparing GAAP financial statements of other types of entities. Thus, interest rates used for discounting expected future payments are based on rates of return on investments for the benefit deferral period, and employee turnover and employee mortality are considered.

At a minimum, the information provided in the financial statements for accumulated plan benefits is to include

1. Vested benefits of participants currently collecting benefits
2. Other vested benefits
3. Nonvested benefits
4. Accumulated contributions of active employees in contributory plans, if applicable

Either a reconciliation or a narrative description is to identify significant factors affecting the accumulated plan benefits from the beginning of the year to the end. The information is to include

1. Effects of plan amendments
2. Changes in the nature of the plan, such as a merger or a spin-off

3. Changes in actuarial assumptions
4. Benefits accumulated during the year
5. Benefits paid during the year
6. Interest component (from amortizing the discount)
7. Other changes

The last four items can be combined into a single "other changes" category.

Defined Contribution Pension Plans

The three general types of defined contribution plans are profit-sharing plans, money purchase pension plans, and stock bonus plans. A profit-sharing plan is a plan that is neither a pension plan, as defined in the Internal Revenue Code, nor a stock bonus plan. Employer contributions to a profit-sharing plan are either discretionary or based on a fixed formula. Although the plan is called a profit-sharing plan, the contributions need not be made from the profits of the plan sponsor. A money purchase plan is a pension plan that bases employer contributions on a fixed formula that is unrelated to profits. A stock bonus plan is a plan that makes its distributions to participants in the stock of the employer unless the participant chooses otherwise. Within these three categories of plans are more specialized plans, such as 401(k) plans, 403(b) plans, savings plans, employee stock ownership plans, target benefit plans, and Keogh plans.

The three primary differences between defined contribution plans and defined benefit plans are

1. Employer contributions are determined at the discretion of the employer or according to a contractual formula, rather than being actuarially determined.
2. Individual accounts are maintained for each plan participant, rather than a single account in which all participants partake.
3. Benefits are determined based on the amount accumulated in a participant's account at the time he or she retires or withdraws from the plan, rather than being defined in the plan agreement. If vested, the account's value is either paid to the participant or used to purchase an annuity for the participant.

The liabilities of a defined contribution plan include accounts payable, amounts owed for securities purchases, and borrowings. The liabilities are not to include amounts that have not been paid to withdrawing participants. Those amounts are included in net assets available for benefits (representing the participants' equity in the plan net assets) and disclosed in the notes to the financial statements. Because those amounts are liabilities for regulatory purposes, a note to reconcile the financial statements to the Form 5500 may be necessary to comply with the Employee Retirement Income Security Act of 1974 (ERISA), as amended.

Employee Health and Welfare Plans

Defined benefit health and welfare plans stipulate a determinable benefit amount, which may take the form of a payment directly to the participant or a payment to a third party (such as a service provider or an insurance company) on the participant's behalf. Factors such as length of employment, age, and salary level determine the level of benefits to be provided. The contributions from the employer may be determined actuarially, by actual claims paid, or by a formula established by the plan sponsor. Regardless of the manner in which the plan is funded, the plan is a defined benefit health and welfare plan if its purpose is to provide a defined benefit.

Like defined benefit pension plans, defined benefit health and welfare plans must include information in their financial statements about the actuarial present value of benefit obligations earned by having performed past service. A benefit obligation exists if all of the following conditions are met:

1. The participants' rights to receive benefits are attributable to services already rendered.
2. The participants' benefits vest or accumulate.
3. Payment of benefits is probable.
4. The amount can be reasonably estimated.

If conditions 1. and 2. are not met, the obligation exists if the event that gives rise to the liability has already occurred and the amount can be reasonably estimated. The benefit obligations are reported as of the end of the plan year and include the actuarial present value of

1. Claims payable currently to active or retired participants
2. Claims of active participants that were incurred but have not yet been reported (IBNR)
3. Insurance premiums due
4. Accumulated eligibility credits and postemployment benefits, net of amounts currently payable
5. Postretirement benefits for retired participants and their beneficiaries, other plan participants who are eligible to receive benefits, and active participants who are not yet eligible to receive benefits.

Benefit obligations of defined benefit health and welfare plans, similar to accumulated plan benefits of defined benefit pension plans, do not appear as liabilities on the statement of net assets available for benefits. Instead, they are presented either as a separate financial statement, on the face of another financial statement, such as the statement of net assets available for benefits, or in the notes to the financial statements. Regardless of the location selected, the information about benefit obligations is required to be presented in its entirety in the same location.

A reconciliation, presented as a separate statement, on the face of another financial statement, or in the notes to the financial statements, is to identify significant factors changing the benefit obligation from the beginning of the year to the end. The changes are classified into at least three categories: (1) amounts currently payable, which includes claims payable, claims IBNR, and premiums due insurance companies, (2) accumulated eligibility credits and postemployment benefits, net of amounts currently payable, and (3) postretirement benefit obligations. The information for each category is to include

1. Effects of plan amendments
2. Changes in the nature of the plan, such as a merger or a spin-off
3. Changes in actuarial assumptions
4. Benefits accumulated during the year
5. Benefits paid during the year
6. Interest component (from amortizing the discount)
7. Other changes

The last four items can be combined into a single "other changes" line.

Defined contribution health and welfare plans, like other defined contribution plans, maintain an account for each participant that determines the amount of benefits that the participant will eventually receive. The terms of a defined contribution health and welfare plan agreement determine the contribution that will be made by the employer or participant into each account. Defined contribution health and welfare plans do not report information about benefit obligations because a plan's obligation is limited to the amounts accumulated in the participants' accounts.

Government Regulations

Pursuant to the requirements of ERISA, the federal government oversees the operating and reporting practices of employee benefit plans. ERISA establishes minimum standards for participation, vesting, and funding. It defines the responsibilities of plan fiduciaries and standards for their conduct. It requires plans to annually report summarized plan information to plan participants.

The Department of Labor (DOL) and the Internal Revenue Service (IRS) are authorized to issue regulations establishing reporting and disclosure requirements for employee benefit plans that are subject to ERISA. Each year, plans are required to report certain information to the DOL, the IRS, and the Pension Benefit Guaranty Corporation (if applicable). For many plans, the information is reported using Form 5500, which includes financial statements prepared in conformity with GAAP and additional supplementary financial schedules.

Various provisions of the Internal Revenue Code apply to employee benefit plans. If an employee benefit plan qualifies under Section 401(a) of the Code, certain favorable tax treatments apply. For example, if a plan is qualified, the plan sponsor receives current deductions for contributions to the plan, and the plan participants do not pay income taxes on those contributions or the accumulated earnings on them until benefits are distributed to them. In addition, plan participants may receive favorable tax treatment on the distributions. Qualified plans are exempt from income taxes, except for taxes on unrelated business income. Nonqualified plans, which generally provide benefits selectively only to a few key employees, are not entitled to those favorable treatments.

Terminating Plans

If a decision has been made to terminate a plan, the plan is a terminating plan, even if another plan will replace the terminated plan. A terminating plan may continue to operate for as long as necessary to pay accrued benefits. Prominent disclosure of the relevant circumstances is necessary in all financial statements issued by the plan after the decision to terminate is made. Financial statements of a terminating plan are prepared on the liquidation basis of accounting for plan years ending after the termination decision. For plan assets, the change to the liquidation basis may have little or no effect, since many assets are already reported at current market value. However, the liquidation basis for accumulated plan benefits (defined benefit pension plans) and benefit obligations (defined benefit health and welfare plans) may differ from the actuarial present value of benefits for an ongoing plan. For example, certain or all benefits may become vested upon plan termination.

STATEMENTS OF POSITION

92-6 Accounting and Reporting by Health and Welfare Plans

SOP 92-6 divides health and welfare plans into two major types: defined benefit health and welfare plans and defined contribution health and welfare plans. The SOP requires many of the measurement and disclosure provisions of FAS 35 to be used in reporting health and welfare plans. For example, it requires defined benefit health and welfare plans to provide information about benefit obligations, including postretirement benefit obligations. It also requires defined benefit health and welfare plans to use certain provisions of FAS 106, *Employer's Accounting for Postretirement Benefits other than Pensions,* to measure benefit obligations.

SOP 92-6 also provides guidance for recognizing claims incurred but not reported (IBNR) and accumulated eligibility credits. For self-funded plans, the cost of IBNR includes the present value of the estimated cost of settling the claims, even if the costs will be incurred after the financial statement date. For insured plans, the cost of IBNR that will be paid by an insurance company is to be excluded from the benefit obligations of the plan. The calculation of the obligation for accumulated eligibility credits is required to consider mortality rates and the expected employee turnover.

94-4 Reporting of Investment Contracts Held by Health and Welfare Benefit Plans and Defined Contribution Pension Plans

SOP 94-4 requires health and welfare benefit plans and defined contribution pension plans to report investment contracts with fully benefit-responsive features at contract value. Other investment contracts are reported at fair value. Benefit responsiveness is the extent to which the terms of the investment contract permit and require withdrawals by the participant. To be fully benefit-responsive, a contact must provide participants access to their account at contract value for all transactions permitted by the plan, without limitations other than administrative provisions designed to control the costs of the plan. Insurance contracts, as defined by FAS 60, *Accounting and Reporting by Insurance Enterprises,* must be presented using the same valuation method (either fair value or contract value) as used in the annual report filed by the plan with certain governmental agencies pursuant to ERISA. Plans not subject to ERISA present insurance contracts as if the plans were subject to the reporting requirements of ERISA.

99-2 Accounting for and Reporting of Postretirement Medical Benefit 401(h) Features of Defined Benefit Pension Plans

This statement specifies the accounting for and disclosure of 401(h) features of defined benefit pension plans. Defined benefit pension plans are required to record the aggregate amount of net assets held in a 401(h) account related to health and welfare obligations as both assets and liabilities on the face of the statement of net assets available for pension benefits. They are required to disclose the fact that the 401(h) account assets are available only to pay retirees' health benefits. The financial statements of the related health and welfare benefit plan must include the 401(h) account assets used to fund health benefits and the changes in those assets. The health and welfare benefit plans must disclose in the notes to its financial statements that retiree health benefits are funded through a 401(h) account of the defined benefit pension plan.

99-3 Accounting for and Reporting of Certain Defined Contribution Plan Investments and Other Disclosure Matters

SOP 99-3 amends the Audit Guide and SOP 94-4 to simplify the required disclosures about investments. For defined contribution plans, it removes the requirement to provide information about participant-directed investment programs in a separate fund (column) of the financial statements. It also supersedes Practice Bulletin 12, *Reporting Separate Investment Fund Option Information of Defined Contribution Pension Plans.* Instead, it requires defined contribution plans that provide both participant-directed and non-participant-directed programs to disclose information about the net assets available for benefits and changes in those net assets for the nonparticipant programs. The information must be provided in sufficient detail to identify the types of investments and the changes in them. If any investment has a value equal to 5% or more of the net assets available for benefits and is also non-participant-directed, that fact must be disclosed in the financial statements. In addition, SOP 99-3 amends SOP 94-4 to remove the requirements to provide necessary disclosures for benefit-responsive investment contracts "by investment option."

01-2 Accounting and Reporting by Health and Welfare Benefit Plans

SOP 01-2 amends the Audit Guide and SOP 92-6 to modify the presentation requirements for information about benefit obligations, to clarify the measurement date for benefit obligations, to establish standards for postemployment benefit plans, and to add three new disclosures. It permits information about benefit obligations and changes in benefit obligations to be presented in notes to the financial statements. It clarifies that the measurement date of benefit obligation information is as of the fiscal year-end; however, that requirement does not preclude the plan from using the most recent obligation valuation and rolling it forward to account for subsequent events, such as employee service, benefit payments, and changes in the discount rate. SOP 01-2 requires postemployment benefit plan obligations to be recognized using criteria similar to those used in FAS 106, *Employer's Accounting for Postretirement Benefits other than Pensions*. The SOP requires that a plan disclose (1) the weighted-average assumed discount rate used to measure the plan's obligation for postemployment benefits, (2) investments representing 5% or more of the net assets available for benefits as of the end of the plan year, and (3) the portion of a plan's estimated cost of providing postretirement benefits that is funded by retiree contributions.

FINANCE COMPANIES

PERSPECTIVE AND ISSUES

The new AAG, *Depository and Lending Institutions: Banks and Savings Institutions, Credit Unions, Finance Companies and Mortgage Companies*, which for the first time unifies guidance for all types of financial institutions, was issued in early 2004. Previously, GAAP for the finance industry was largely to be found in *Audits of Finance Companies* (AAG, 1999) and SOP 92-3, *Accounting for Foreclosed Assets.*

Finance companies provide lending and financing services to consumers (consumer financing) and to business enterprises (commercial financing). Some financing companies engage solely in consumer or commercial financing activities; others engage in both types.

Manufacturers, retailers, wholesalers and other business enterprises may provide financing to encourage customers to buy their products or services. Such financing is known as captive financing activity and may be provided by those companies or affiliated companies. Although most companies originally financed only their own products and services, many have expanded their financing activities to include a wide variety of products and services sold by unaffiliated businesses.

Consumer financing activities include direct consumer loans, retail sales contracts, and insurance services.

Commercial financing enterprises often provide a wide range of services, including factoring arrangements, revolving loans, installment and term loans, floor plan loans, and lease financing.

SOP 01-6, *Accounting by Certain Entities (Including Entities with Trade Receivables) That Lend to or Finance the Activities of Others*, became effective for fiscal years beginning after December 15, 2001. This SOP conformed the accounting by various institutions such as banks, thrifts, credit unions, finance companies, corporate credit unions, and mortgage companies. It also is applicable to the financing activities of manufacturers, retailers, wholesalers, and other business enterprises.

SOP 01-6 eliminated differences in accounting and disclosure established by the respective financial institution Guides, but carries forward accounting guidance for transactions determined to be unique to certain financial institutions. It did not create new accounting guidance.

The new AAG, *Depository and Lending Institutions,* has the following features:

- Mortgage companies and corporate credit unions are explicitly included in the scope of the combined Guide.
- Regulatory capital disclosures are required for mortgage companies, credit unions, banks, and thrifts.
- Credit unions report amounts placed in their deposit insurance fund as an asset if such amounts are fully refundable, due to unique legal and operational aspects of the credit union share insurance fund. Banks and thrifts expense payments to their deposit insurance fund as incurred. Both practices have been preserved because of differences in how the funds operate.
- Finance companies record purchases and sales of securities on the settlement date, whereas banks, thrifts, and credit unions follow trade date accounting. Under the SOP, finance companies follow trade date accounting.
- FAS 114, *Accounting by Creditors for Impairment of a Loan,* and 118, *Accounting by Creditors for Impairment of a Loan—Income Recognition and Disclosures,* address loan impairment measurement and disclosure requirements, but they do not specify how to recognize income on impaired loans. The Guide for finance companies gives specific guidance on the recognition of interest income on impaired loans. Under the SOP, such guidance for finance companies will be eliminated.
- Certain disclosures for credit unions will be eliminated. These disclosures include, for example, additional information about repurchase agreements, servicing assets, and deposit liabilities.

Sources of GAAP

FAS	*FIN*	*SOP*	*EITF*	*AAG*
91, 124, 127, 140	41, 42	92-3, 96-1, 01-6, 02-1	95-22	*Depository and Lending Institutions: Banks and Savings Institutions, Credit Unions, Finance Companies and Mortgage Companies*

DEFINITIONS OF TERMS

Accounts receivable loan. A loan collateralized by the accounts receivable of the borrower.

Dealer reserves. Finance company liabilities for dealers' shares of finance charges on retail contracts purchased from dealers.

Direct consumer loan. A two-party transaction in which the finance company lends funds directly to the borrower; such a loan may or may not be collateralized.

Discount. Amount deducted from the face value in advance as a charge for the loan or a deduction for interest at the time of the loan or any charge for credit that is precomputed and included in the face of the instrument.

Discount loan. A loan that is written with the interest or finance charges included in the face amount of the note. Discount loans are also called **precompute** or **add-on loans**.

Effective interest rate. The implicit rate of interest based on the amount advanced and the amount and timing of the specified repayments over the period of the contract.

Factor. A company that engages primarily in factoring.

Factoring. Purchase, usually without recourse, of individual accounts receivable arising in the client's ordinary course of business. Under a factoring agreement, the finance company also provides credit checking, collection, and recordkeeping services.

Floor plan checking. Physical inspection of dealer's inventories that are collateral for advances to the dealer to be repaid from the proceeds from sale of specific items. Sometimes referred to as floor plan auditing.

Floor planning. Financing of dealers' inventories, particularly automobiles and other consumer goods, sometimes referred to as **wholesaling**. The dealers are obliged to repay the supplier or manufacturer from proceeds of sale of specific items, or after an elapsed period even though inventory is not sold.

Interest-bearing loan. A loan that is written at the principal amount advanced to the borrower and bearing interest computed monthly on the unpaid balance.

Interest method. A method of computing income under which interest income on a fixed-rate obligation is accrued over the life of the loan based on a constant rate (percent) of interest applied to the outstanding loan balance. As a result, the amount of income recognized at a given time is directly proportional to the outstanding loan balance. Also called the **actuarial method**.

Inventory loan. A loan collateralized by inventory of the borrower.

Nonrefundable fee. Any charge made in connection with a loan that does not have to be refunded to the borrower when the loan is prepaid.

Origination fee. An amount charged by finance companies for originating, refinancing, or restructuring a loan. The amount may be intended to cover costs such as underwriting, loan application processing, and reviewing legal title to property involved.

Overadvance (in factoring). An amount advanced to a client in excess of the amount of uncollected receivables purchased by the factor.

Points. Amounts, generally expressed as a percent of the loan, charged for granting loans, that primarily are adjustments of yield but also may be intended to cover costs such as underwriting, loan application processing, and reviewing title to collateral.

CONCEPTS, RULES, AND EXAMPLES

Finance Receivables

Finance receivables include both interest-bearing and discount loans. The face amount of an interest-bearing or simple interest loan is equal to the amount of cash loaned; unearned interest is not computed. Conversely, for discount loans the amount of cash loaned is less than the face value of the loan. This difference represents unearned interest income to the borrower, and as such, is recognized by the lender over the life of the loan.

Allowance for Loan Losses

A finance company should maintain an allowance for loan losses that is adequate to cover estimated losses. The allowance for loan losses decreases the carrying amount of loans receivable to net realizable value. FAS 5 and 114 provide guidance for the recognition of estimated losses from the uncollectibility of receivables. FAS 5 requires that an allowance for loan losses be established when it is probable that a loan has been impaired and the amount can be reasonably estimated. FAS 114 requires that impairment of a loan be based on the present value of expected future cash flows discounted at the loan's effective interest rate or at the loan's market price or at the fair value of the collateral of the loan if applicable.

Interest Income and Nonrefundable Loan Fees

The interest method should be used to account for interest income in accordance with FAS 91, *Accounting for Nonrefundable Fees and Costs Associated with Originating or Acquiring Loans and Initial Direct Costs of Leases*. Under this method, often called the actuarial method, interest on installment loans is computed and accrued over the lives of the loans to arrive at constant interest rates throughout the loans' lives. Use of this method produces loans that are carried at amounts equal to future receipts discounted at original implicit interest rates. The accounting for nonrefundable loan fees is also covered in FAS 91. (See the treatment of this area under the section on Banking and Thrift.)

Accounting for Loans Acquired by Transfer

Finance companies may acquire loans originated by other financial intermediaries. In some cases, these will have been impaired at the date they are acquired, due to changes in the borrowers' credit risks occurring subsequent to origination. AcSEC's long-running project to develop guidance on this matter culminated in the issuance of SOP 03-3, *Accounting for Certain Loans and Debt Securities Acquired in a Transfer*. The statement addresses the accounting for the differences between contractual and expected future cash flows of acquired loans when these differences are attributable, at least in part, to credit quality.

SOP 03-3 is discussed under the Banking and Thrift sections of this chapter.

Other Items

Factoring commissions. The amount a finance company charges as a factoring commission is dependent on such variables as sales volume, number of invoices issued, collection activities, and patterns of returns and chargebacks. Finance companies should recognize factoring commissions over the periods in which services are rendered. A finance company is considered as rendering services from the time a customer's credit is approved until the customer's account is settled.

Advances and overadvances to factoring clients. Finance companies generally do not treat advances to clients as receivables. Instead, advances are applied against amounts owed to clients from the purchase of the client's receivables. Finance companies generally limit advances to percentages of the unpaid amounts of factored receivables. Overadvances, which are amounts in excess of outstanding receivables purchased, should be recorded as loans receivable.

Repossessed assets acquired in liquidation of receivables. Finance companies may repossess goods or other property that collateralize loans when they foreclose on uncollectible loans. Repossessed assets are typically sold as soon as possible to minimize losses from defaulted loans. Certain types of collateral, such as automobiles, may be readily salable in wholesale or other markets. Repossessions of such collateral are fairly common. Repossessions on commercial loans can result in significant losses because of the bargain prices associated with reselling inventories, plant, property, and equipment.

Terms of recourse arrangements include the following:

1. Full recourse—The dealer is required to pay off the uncollected receivable balance to the finance company at the date of repossession.
2. Partial or limited recourse—The dealer is liable for repossession losses up to an agreed amount.
3. Nonrecourse—Loss is borne entirely by the finance company.

Dealer reserves and holdbacks. Finance companies account for dealer reserves and holdbacks as liabilities. Dealer reserve accounts are credited for the dealers' share of the finance charges. Dealer reserve accounts may be charged as the result of customers paying off contracts early, losses on full or partial recourse contracts, and from payments to dealers in excess of minimum requirements.

Sales of receivables. A finance company may decide to sell a portfolio of receivables to another finance company or financial institution. FAS 140, *Accounting for Transfers and Servicing of Financial Assets and Extinguishment of Liabilities*, controls whether such transactions should be accounted for as sales of receivables or as loans collateralized by receivables. Generally, a transfer is treated as a sale if the transferor surrenders control of the receivables. The provisions of FAS 140 are addressed in Chapters 5 and 6.

GOVERNMENT CONTRACTORS

PERSPECTIVE AND ISSUES

ARB 43 governs the accounting and income recognition issues concerning cost-plus-fixed-fee and fixed-price supply contracts. The fees under government cost-plus-fixed-fee contracts are recognized as income on the basis of partial performance if there is reasonable assurance of realization. Fees are also accrued as they become billable unless this accrual is not reasonably related to the proportionate performance of total work to be performed.

This pronouncement also covers renegotiation (refunds of excessive profits) and contracts terminated for the convenience of the government.

Sources of GAAP
ARB
43 (Chapter 11)

DEFINITIONS OF TERMS

Contractors. In the context of this discussion, contractors are enterprises that sell products or services to the US government pursuant to a formal contract. The relationship to the government can be direct (a prime contract between the enterprise and the government) or indirect (a subcontract between the enterprise and a prime contractor).

Contract. A legal agreement obligating a contractor (referred to as the "general contractor" or "prime contractor") to provide products or services to the US government. The term also refers to subcontracts obligating subcontractors to indirectly perform in a similar manner under the supervision and control of the prime contractor.

Cost-plus-fixed-fee contracts. An agreement that provides for contractors to receive a specified fixed fee and to be reimbursed for their allowable costs. Because title passes to the government and the contractor obtains an unconditional right to partial payment prior to delivery, delivery of the finished product is not necessarily evidence of performance.

Disposal credits. Deductions from the termination claim receivable for approved retention or sale of inventory previously included in the claim.

No-cost settlements. Settlements in which the contractor waives the right to make a claim. No sale is recorded and applicable costs retain their usual classification

Service contracts. Contracts in which the contractor acts only as an agent.

Supply contracts. Contract in which the contractor's services extend beyond that of an agent. Contracts include services such as the use of the contractor's own facilities and the contractor assumes responsibility to creditors for material and services, and to employees for salaries.

Subcontractor's claims. Claims made in conjunction with a terminated contract resulting from costs incurred under the terminated contract that did not result in the transfer of billable materials or services to the contractor before termination.

CONCEPTS, RULES, AND EXAMPLES

Cost-plus-fixed-fee contracts (CPFFC) are used for the manufacture and delivery of products, the construction of plants and other facilities, and for management and other services. The amount of the flat-fee payment is usually determined by the ratio of the actual expenditures to the total estimated expenditures. CPFFC may be cancelled and terminated by the government. If this occurs, the **contractor** is entitled to reimbursement for expenditures and an appropriate portion of the fixed fee.

Normally, profits are recognized when the right to full payment is unconditional. However, revenues can be accrued and profits recognized for partial performance when total profit can be reasonably estimated and realization is reasonably assured. The fees are usually accrued as they become billable. Because risk is minimal and there is no credit problem, billable amounts are indicative of realization. The contractor's fee is considered earned when it is billable and when the related costs are incurred or paid. Accrual based on billable amounts is an application of the percentage-of-completion method, rather than a deviation from the accrual method. The fee is considered billable when approved by the government. An alternative date is used when a determination is made that estimated and final costs are significantly different. Accrual of the fee upon delivery or based on percentage of completion is more appropriate when excess costs are substantial.

For **supply contracts,** reimbursable costs and fees are included in sales. For **service contracts,** only fees are included in sales. Unbilled amounts are included in the balance sheet as a receivable but are to be captioned and presented separately from billed receivables. Advances in CPFFC are generally intended to assist the contractor in financing its costs. Thus, in general, advances are treated as liabilities and are not offset against contract receivables. Advances are permitted to be offset against **contract** receivables only when there is an expectation that the advances will be applied against those specific charges. Any such offsets require disclosure in the financial statements.

Renegotiation

Renegotiation typically addresses a refund to the government of "excessive" profits. In reality, it is more of an adjustment of the selling price. The financial statements are to disclose situations when a substantial portion of a contractor's business consists of contracts that are subject to renegotiation. When a reasonable estimate of renegotiation refunds can be made, a provision is shown as a deduction from revenue in the income statement and as a current liability on the balance sheet. Deferred income taxes are adjusted accordingly. When a reasonable estimate cannot be made, disclosure is required along with the reasons for the inability to make an estimate. Footnote disclosure is also required regarding material uncertainties and their significance, and regarding the basis for determining the renegotiation provision.

Terminated Defense Contracts

These contracts are contracts terminated for the convenience of the government. Profits accrue as of the effective date of termination and are included in financial statements after the termination. Disclosure is made of all material facts and circumstances. Termination claims are recorded as a single amount even if they consist of several different types of cost reimbursements. Material termination claims are to be captioned separately from other receivables and such claims receivable directly from the government are to be presented separately from related claims against other contractors. Claims receivable are classified as current assets unless there is an indication of extended delay, such as a serious disagreement indicative of probable litigation. Pretermination contract advances are shown as a deduction from claims receivable and adequately explained. Termination loans are classified as current liabilities and cross-referenced to the related claims receivable.

Material termination claims are separately captioned in the revenues section of the contractor's statement of income. When inventory is reacquired by the contractor after including it in a termination claim, it is recorded as a purchase. The credit is applied against the termination claim receivable.

INSURANCE

PERSPECTIVE AND ISSUES

The two major types of insurance companies are life and property and casualty. Each category is further subdivided into stock companies and mutual associations. Due to the regulated nature of the insurance industry, financial reporting may be in conformity to **statutory accounting principles (SAP)** or GAAP. Furthermore, publicly held companies subject to SEC accounting rules will account for certain transactions and events in other manners dictated by those requirements. While accounting principles under GAAP are broadly applicable to all types of insurance companies (including those dealing in such specialized products as mortgage insurance, title insurance, and reinsurance), the nature of the estimation process (such as for claims liabilities) differs substantially depending upon the character of the risks assumed.

The main contrasts between SAP and GAAP arise from the more conservative nature of SAP, which is a reflection of the insurance regulatory agencies' concern with protection of the policyholders' interests, and hence with the liquidity and solvency of the insurance companies. Accordingly, under SAP certain costs, such as policy acquisition expenses, are written off as incurred; certain nonliquid assets, such as property and furniture, are not recognized; and claims liabilities are very conservatively estimated. In contrast to this essentially short-term perspective, financial statements prepared on the GAAP basis are more concerned with the value of the companies' investments and net worth on a going concern basis.

The primary source of insurance industry GAAP is FAS 60. Although mutual insurance companies and certain other organizations had initially not been required to apply this standard, FAS 120 later extended its requirements to these enterprises. Insurance contracts are categorized as short duration (which includes most property and liability insurance) or long duration (which includes most life, mortgage, and title insurance). Nominal insurance contracts that are effectively investment contracts, however, are not accounted for as insurance. The AAG, *Audits of Property and Liability Insurance Companies*, was issued in June 1998.

Current industry-specific guidance can be found in the AICPA's AAG, *Life and Health Insurance Entities*, which was revised in 2001. This Guide discusses those aspects of accounting and auditing unique to life and health insurance entities, and contains significant discussions of statutory accounting practices (SAP), which comprise laws, regulations, and administrative rulings adopted by various states that govern the operations and reporting requirements of life insurance entities. It does not reflect SAP under the National Association of Insurance Commissioners (NAIC) codification project, but AcSEC subsequently issued SOP 01-5, *Amendments to Specific AICPA Pronouncements for Changes Related to the NAIC Codification,* which requires insurance enterprises to disclose, at the date of each balance sheet presented, beginning with financial statements for fiscal years ending on or after December 15, 2001, a description of the prescribed or permitted statutory accounting practice and the related monetary effect on statutory surplus of using an accounting practice that differs from either state-prescribed statutory accounting practices or NAIC statutory accounting practices. Retroactive application of these provisions is not permitted.

AcSEC issued SOP 03-1, *Accounting and Reporting by Insurance Enterprises for Certain Non-Traditional Long-Duration Contracts and for Separate Accounts,* which addresses the classification and valuation of liabilities, as well as disclosures for nontraditional annuity and life insurance contracts issued by insurance enterprises. Several of the conclusions reached on these topics are discussed later in this section.

Sources of GAAP

FAS	FIN	SOP	EITF	AAG
5, 60, 91, 97, 109, 113, 114, 115, 120, 124	40	92-5, 94-5, 95-1, 97-3, 98-7, 00-3, 01-5	92-9, 93-6, 93-14, 99-4	*Audits of Property and Liability Insurance Companies, Life and Health Insurance Entities*

CONCEPTS, RULES, AND EXAMPLES

Premium Income

Premium income is recognized differently for short and long duration contracts. For short duration contracts, premium income is recognized over the contract term in proportion to the amount of insurance provided. In the case of long duration contracts, revenue is accrued as the premiums become due from policyholders, except for contracts that provide benefits over a term longer than the premium payment term (such as twenty-year life policies), in which case income is recognized over the longer period during which benefits may be provided.

Claim Cost Recognition

Costs of benefits are recognized when insured events such as property damage occur. Estimated costs are accrued for as claims incurred but not yet reported. For long duration contracts, the present values of estimated future benefits are accrued, net of the present values of future net premiums to be collected. Accrual of these benefit obligations generally involves actuarial determinations. Accountants may be dependent on the services of specialists in such cases, as they are in computing costs related to defined benefit pension plans. Recognition of other expenses is governed by the matching concept. For example, costs that vary with acquisition activity are capitalized and amortized over the period during which premium income is earned. Catastrophic losses (as from natural disasters such as hurricanes) are accrued under the guidelines of FAS 5: when impairment of the asset or incurring of a liability is probable and the amount is reasonably estimable.

Investments

The other major concern of GAAP for insurance enterprises relates to the presentation of investments held. FAS 115 established the accounting requirements for investments in debt and marketable equity securities. Briefly, those investments must be categorized as being either held-for-trading, available-for-sale, or held-to-maturity. Investments falling within the first two categories should be reported at fair value, with value changes affecting the trading securities portfolio being reflected in income, while changes in the available-for-sale portfolio are reported in a separate equity account. Securities to be held to maturity are accounted for at amortized historical cost, absent a permanent decline in value. Equity securities that do not meet the definition of "marketable" are also to be reported at fair value, with gains or losses reported in stockholders' equity.

Deferred Income Taxes

GAAP requires that deferred income taxes be provided for temporary differences. An exception was previously provided under the "indefinite reversal criterion," for stock life insurance companies only, for differences designated as policyholders' surplus. However, FAS 109 provides that, for such differences arising after 1992, deferred taxes must be provided, consistent with thc accounting prescribed for all other temporary differences. Furthermore, if changed circumstances suggest that pre-1993 differences are in fact differences that are likely to reverse, deferred taxes are to be provided, with the provision reflected in current period tax expense.

Other Matters

Reinsurance. Another specialized topic area pertinent to insurance companies is that of reinsurance. After a lengthy period of development and discussion, a new standard, FAS 113, was promulgated. This standard, which amends FAS 60, eliminates the former practice of reporting assets and liabilities net of the effects of reinsurance. It requires that reinsurance receivables, including amounts related to claims incurred but not reported, be reported as assets, consistent with the manner in which liabilities relating to the underlying reinsured contracts are accounted for. The standard also establishes criteria for recognition as reinsurance, and sets forth detailed accounting for long and short duration contracts, as well as new disclosure requirements. The Board also ended another long-standing controversy by releasing FIN 40, which clarifies that GAAP applies essentially equally to mutual insurance companies as it does to stock companies, unless explicit exceptions were established. Regulatory reporting can no longer, therefore, be deemed to be in accordance with GAAP.

Loss reserves. The AICPA has also been actively reviewing insurance company accounting practices and auditing issues. SOP 92-4 addressed matters relating to estimation of loss reserves, and a number of auditing concerns relating to reserves, reinsurance, loss adjustment expenses, and other topics. SOP 92-5 concerns accounting for foreign property and liability reinsurance, and concludes that except for special circumstances, only the periodic method is acceptable in accounting for foreign reinsurance premiums. SOP 94-5 requires disclosures where permission was received from the National Association of Insurance Commissioners to use different accounting practices. SOP 95-1 covers capitalization and amortization costs and several other matters for mutual life insurance companies. FAS 120 requires that the provision of this SOP be applied to assessment enterprises, fraternal benefit societies, and stock life insurance companies.

Guaranty funds. SOP 97-3 addresses matters pertaining to guaranty funds and certain other insurance-related assessments. Existing practice has been quite diverse, but SOP 97-3 essentially applies the criteria of FAS 5, *Accounting for Contingencies*, to these matters, with the exception that practice can be substantially conformed. The key elements of this standard are discussed in the following paragraphs.

Under the standard, guaranty fund and similar assessments would be recognized when (1) it has been imposed or is deemed probable of being imposed, (2) the event obligating an entity to pay the assessment has occurred, and (3) the amount of the assessment can be reasonably estimated. All three conditions would have to be fulfilled before a liability could be accrued. Discounting to present value will be permitted. The SOP offers specific guidance regarding the ability to reasonably estimate the liability for assessments.

Guaranty funds are essentially state-mandated insurance funds used to settle claims against insolvent insurers and, typically, all licensed insurers are assessed premiums based on the volume of defined lines of business they conduct in the given state. A variety of methods have been applied in determining the amounts of guaranty fund assessments (e.g., retrospectively, based on premiums written over the past two years; or prospectively, based on business written over the next several years following an insolvency of a failed insurer), with the result that entities upon which assessments are being levied have been inclined to use different methods of recognizing the cost and related obligation. In general, to warrant accrual under SOP 97-3, an insolvency of another insurer would have to have occurred, since the presumption would be that the assessments would become probable (the threshold criterion) when there has been a formal determination of another entity's insolvency. An example of an exception would be when the state uses prospective premium-based guaranty fund assessments; if the reporting entity **cannot** avoid the obligation by ceasing to write policies, the obligating event would be the determination of insolvency, but if it **could** avoid the assessment, the obligating event is the writing of premiums **after** the insolvency.

Surplus notes. AICPA Practice Bulletin 15, *Accounting by the Issuer of Surplus Notes*, affects accounting by certain insurance companies that issue a security known as surplus notes. It requires that these instruments be accounted for as debt and included in the liabilities caption of the balance sheet. Furthermore, interest must be accrued over the term of the notes, whether or not payment of interest and/or principal has been approved by an insurance company. However, disclosure is required as to the status of the request for approval.

A project to produce an industry accounting guide for insurance agents and brokers, was dropped after several years of development, when the intended beneficiaries could not agree on a number of key matters.

Deposit accounting. In 1998 the AICPA completed its project on deposit accounting. Prior to the issuance of SOP 98-7, guidance on how to apply the deposit method has not been available in the professional literature.

The new standard applies to entities entering into short duration insurance and reinsurance contracts that do **not** transfer insurance risk, or multiple year contracts that either do not transfer insurance risk or for which insurance risk transfer is not determinable. Insurance risk is comprised of timing risk and underwriting risk, and one or both of these may not be transferred to the insurer (assuming entity in the case of reinsurance) under certain circumstances. For example, many workers' compensation policies provide for "experience adjustments" which have the effect of keeping the underwriting risk with the insured, rather than transferring it to the insurer; in such instances, deposit accounting would be prescribed.

Under the provisions of SOP 98-7, for contracts that transfer only significant timing risk, or that transfer neither significant timing nor underwriting risk, a deposit asset (from the insured's or ceding entity's perspective, respectively, for insurance and reinsurance arrangements) or liability (from the insurer's or assuming entity's perspective, respectively, for insurance and reinsurance arrangements) should be recognized at inception. The deposit asset or liability should be remeasured at subsequent financial reporting dates by calculating the effective yield on the deposit to reflect actual payments to date and expected future payments. Yield is to be determined as set forth in FAS 91, using the estimated amounts and timings of cash flows. The deposit is to be adjusted to that which would have existed at the balance sheet date had the new effective yield been applied since inception of the contract; thus, expense or income for a period will be determined by first calculating the necessary amount in the related balance sheet account.

For contracts that transfer only significant underwriting risk, a deposit asset or liability is also established at inception. However, subsequent remeasurement of the deposit does not occur until such time as a loss is incurred that will be reimbursed under the contract; instead, the deposit is reported at its amortized amount. Once the loss occurs, the deposit should be remeasured by the present value of expected future cash flows arising from the contract, plus the remaining unexpired portion of the coverage. Changes in the deposit arising from the present value measure are to be reported in the insured's income statement as an offset against the loss to be reimbursed; in the insurer's income statement, the adjustment should be reported as an incurred loss. The reduction due to amortization of the deposit is reported as an adjustment to incurred losses by the insurer. The discount rate used to compute the present value is to be the rate on government obligations with similar cash flow characteristics, adjusted for differences in default risk, which is based on the insurer's credit rating. Rates are determined at the loss date(s) and not revised later, absent further losses.

For insurance contracts with indeterminate risk, the procedures set forth in SOP 92-5 (the open-year method) should be applied. This involves balance sheet segregation of amounts that have not been adjusted due to lack of sufficient loss or other data. When sufficient information becomes available, the deposit asset or liability is adjusted, which is to be reported as an accounting change per APB 20.

The AICPA has been contemplating issuing either an SOP or an industry AAG on mass tort exposure of insurance enterprises. This would include guidance on accounting issues that arise in connection with such mass tort exposures as asbestos and environmental claims and address how the various components of such liabilities are to be measured. Further, it would deal with application of present value concepts to mass tort liabilities and consider the methods used to estimate these obligations. Disclosure requirements would also be established.

An SOP is being developed to deal with the growing matter of **nontraditional long duration insurance contracts**. The SOP will address the classification and valuation of liabilities as well as disclosures for nontraditional annuity and life insurance contracts issued by insurance enterprises. Among the tentative conclusions are

1. Sales inducements that are earned by the customer immediately, such as "day-one bonuses," should be expensed immediately, whereas sales inducements that are earned over a period of time, such as persistency bonuses or enhanced yields, should be expensed over time;
2. Separate accounts should be recorded in the financial statements of the insurance enterprise that owns them, and should be reported as single line items on the respective sides of the balance sheet (one-line presentation) if all of the following criteria are met:
    a. Assets reside in a legally recognized separate account
    b. The separate account is bankruptcy remote from the insurance enterprise
    c. The policyholder directs allocation of investments
    d. All investment performance (net of contract fees) is passed through to the policyholder (including contracts with minimum guarantees, but excluding contracts with caps or ceilings)
3. The guaranteed portion of separate accounts with minimum guarantees should be recorded as a liability in the general account, consistent with the bifurcation approach for embedded derivatives in FAS 133, *Accounting for Derivative Instruments and Hedging Activities.* Seed money and other insurance company funds invested in separate accounts should be classified and valued as any other general account asset.

Demutualizations. SOP 00-3, *Accounting by Insurance Enterprises for Demutualizations and Formations of Mutual Insurance Holding Companies and for Certain Long Duration Participating Contracts,* addressed the increasingly common phenomenon of **demutualizations** (whereby formerly mutually owned insurers issue stock), as well as the formation of insurance holding companies (MIHC). A key concern is the accounting for the "closed block" of assets and liabilities, and of earnings allocable to the closed block. This pertains to mechanisms designed to protect the adjustable policy features and dividend expectations of **participating** life insurance policyholders from the competing interests of stockholders. Typically, the plan of demutualization describes how the closed block will operate. The closed block assets and cash returns on those assets will not inure to the stockholders of the demutualized company; instead, all cash flows from these assets will be used to benefit the closed block policyholders. The insurance enterprise remains obligated to provide for minimum guarantees under the participating policy, and it is consequently possible under certain circumstances that additional "stockholder" funds will have to be used to meet the contractual benefits of the closed block policyholders. The assets designated to the closed block are subject to the same liabilities, with the same priority in the case of insolvency or in liquidation, as assets outside the closed block. In many situations, commissions and other expenses (including management expenses) of operating and administering the closed block will not be charged to the closed block. Unless the state insurance department consents to an earlier termination, the closed block will continue in effect until the date on which none of the policies in the closed block remains in force.

Alternatives to the closed block have arisen in practice encompassing, for a number of types of contracts, various mechanisms believed by the insurance enterprise and state insurance regulators to be appropriate in the specific circumstances. Closed block alternative mechanisms have been used in lieu of closed blocks for certain participating life contracts to commit to the insurance regulator that the insurance company will continue to follow its established dividend practices. Closed block alternative mechanisms also have been used to protect nonguaranteed elements of participating and nonparticipating insurance contracts such as interest credits on deferred annuities and adjustable premiums on adjustable premium term business. In some instances, the methodology and limitations defined in the agreements with the state insurance regulators have considered only specific profit components, such as mortality experience on a block of term insurance or investment spreads on a block of annuities, and in other instances have considered virtually all components of product profitability. Where there is a limitation on the profits that may inure to the stockholders, there generally is a formal agreement between the insurance company and the insurance regulators that defines (1) the contracts covered by the limitation, (2) the profit limitation calculation, and (3) the timing and manner (for example, as policy dividends, reduced premiums, or additional benefits) in which amounts that may not be distributed to stockholders are to be distributed to policyholders.

Some of the more important conclusions reached by AcSEC were as follows:

1. The classification of expenses related to a demutualization and the formation of an MIHC should be considered other than extraordinary expense.
2. Closed block assets and liabilities from the closed block should be included with the corresponding financial statement items of the insurance enterprise.
3. AcSEC has concluded that SOP 95-1, *Accounting for Certain Insurance Activities of Mutual Life Insurance Enterprises*, should continue to be applied after conversion to a stock company. However, provisions of FAS 60, *Accounting and Reporting by Insurance Enterprises*, relating to dividends on participating contracts should apply to such contracts sold before the date of demutualization or date of formation of the MIHC.

4. The maximum future contribution of the closed block to the earnings of the company is typically the excess of the GAAP liabilities over the GAAP assets at the date of demutualization. Under FAS 60, a dividend liability should be established for current earnings that will be paid to policyholders through future benefits. From a shareholder perspective, excess earnings of the closed block that will never inure to the shareholders should be set up as a liability. AcSEC decided upon establishment of a dividend liability for excess earnings due to policyholders that cannot inure to shareholders.
5. For a "distribution-form" demutualization, an insurance enterprise should reclassify all of its retained earnings as of the date of demutualization to capital stock and additional paid-in capital accounts. A "subscription-form" demutualization should not, in and of itself, result in reclassification of retained earnings. AcSEC concluded that the equity accounts of the MIHC at the date of formation should be determined using the principles for transactions of companies under common control with the amount of retained earnings of the demutualized insurance enterprise, before reclassification to the capital accounts, being reported as retained earnings of the MIHC.

Nontraditional Long-Duration Contracts

AcSEC's extended project on nontraditional long-duration contracts came to fruition with the issuance of SOP 03-1, *Accounting and Reporting by Insurance Enterprises for Certain Nontraditional Long-Duration Contracts and for Separate Accounts.* This addresses the classification and valuation of liabilities as well as disclosures for nontraditional annuity and life insurance contracts issued by insurance enterprises. The requirements under this standard are set forth in the following paragraphs.

The portion of separate account assets representing contract holder funds are to be measured at fair value and reported in the insurance enterprise's financial statements as a summary total, with an equivalent summary total for related liabilities, if the separate account arrangement meets all the specified criteria. If the arrangement does not meet the criteria, assets representing contract holder funds should be accounted for as general account assets, and any related liability should be accounted for as a general account liability.

Assets underlying an insurance enterprise's proportionate interest in a separate account do not represent contract holder funds, and thus are not to be separately reported and valued. If a separate account arrangement meets the criteria in SOP 03-1 and (a) the terms of the contract allow the contract holder to invest in additional units in the separate account or (b) the insurance enterprise is marketing contracts that permit funds to be invested in the separate account, the assets underlying the insurance enterprise's proportionate interest in the separate account should be accounted for in a manner consistent with similar assets held by the general account that the insurance enterprise may be required to sell.

If the enterprise's proportionate interest in the separate account is less than 20% of the separate account, and all of the underlying investments of the separate account meet the definition of securities under FAS 115 or FAS 60, or the definition of cash and cash equivalents, the enterprise may report its portion of the separate account value as an investment in equity securities classified as trading under FAS 115.

Assets transferred from the general account to a separate account should be recognized at fair value to the extent of third-party contract holders' proportionate interest in the separate account if the separate account arrangement meets the criteria set forth in the SOP. Any gain related to the third-party contract holder's proportionate interest should be recognized immediately in earnings of the general account of the insurance enterprise, if the risks and rewards of ownership have been transferred to contract holders using the fair value of the asset at the date of the contract holder's assumption of risks and rewards. A guarantee of the asset's value or minimum rate of return or a commitment to repurchase the asset would indicate that the risks of ownership have not been transferred, and no gain can be recognized. If the separate account arrangement does not meet the criteria in the SOP, the transfer generally should have no financial reporting effect (that is, general account classification and carrying amounts should be retained). In certain situations loss recognition may be appropriate.

The basis for determining the balance that accrues to the contract holder for a long-duration insurance or investment contract that is subject to FAS 97 is the accrued account balance. The accrued account balance equals

1. Deposit(s) net of withdrawals;
2. Plus amounts credited pursuant to the contract;
3. Less fees and charges assessed;
4. Plus additional interest (for example, persistency bonus); and
5. Other adjustments, such as appreciation or depreciation recognized under this SOP, to the extent not already credited.

For contracts that have features that may result in more than one potential account balance, the accrued account balance should be the highest contractually determinable balance that will be available in cash or its equivalent at contractual maturity or the reset date, without reduction for future fees and charges. The accrued account balance should not reflect any surrender adjustments (for example, market value annuity adjustments, surrender charges, or credits). For contracts in which amounts credited as interest to the contract holder are reset periodically, the accrued balance should be based on the highest crediting rate guaranteed or declared through the reset date.

For a contract not accounted for under FAS 133 that provides a return based on the total return of a contractually referenced pool of assets either through crediting rates or termination adjustments, the accrued account balance should be based on the fair value of the referenced pool of assets (or applicable index value) at the balance sheet date, even if the related assets are not recognized at fair value.

To determine the accounting under FAS 97 for a contract that contains death or other insurance benefit features, the enterprise should first determine whether the contract is an investment or universal-life-type contract. If the mortality or morbidity risks are other than nominal and the fees assessed or insurance benefits are not fixed and guaranteed, the contract should be classified as a FAS 97 universal-life-type contract. A rebuttable presumption is that a contract has significant mortality risk where the additional insurance benefit would vary significantly in response to capital markets volatility. The determination of significance should be made at contract inception, other than at transition, and should be based on a comparison of the present value of expected excess payments (that is, insurance benefit amounts and related incremental claim adjustment expenses in excess of the account balance) to be made under insurance benefit features to the present value of all amounts expected to be assessed against the contract holder (revenue).

For contracts classified as insurance contracts that have amounts assessed against contract holders each period for the insurance benefit feature that are assessed in a manner that is expected to result in profits in earlier years and subsequent losses from that insurance benefit function, a liability should be established in addition to the account balance to recognize the portion of such assessments that compensates the insurance enterprise for benefits to be provided in future periods in accordance with the guidance in the SOP.

If a reinsurer assumes the insurance benefit feature, it should assess the significance of mortality and morbidity risk within the reinsurance contract according to the guidance in

SOP 03-1, regardless of whether there is an account balance. The reinsurer should determine the classification of the reinsurance contract as an investment contract or as an insurance contract at the inception of the reinsurance contract. For reinsurance contracts, the mortality or morbidity risk could be deemed other than nominal even if the original issuer did not determine mortality or morbidity to be other than nominal. Similarly, the issuer of a contract that provides only an insurance benefit feature that wraps a noninsurance contract, for example, a guaranteed minimum death benefit related to a mutual fund balance, should evaluate its contract in the same manner. A reinsurer or issuer of the insurance benefit features of a contract should calculate a liability for the portion of premiums collected each period that represents compensation to the insurance enterprise for benefits that are assessed in a manner that is expected to result in current profits and future losses from the insurance benefit function. That liability should be calculated using the methodology described in SOP 03-1.

Contracts may provide for potential benefits in addition to the account balance that are payable only upon annuitization, such as annuity purchase guarantees, guaranteed minimum income benefit (GMIB), and two-tier annuities. Insurance enterprises should determine whether such contract features should be accounted for under the provisions of FAS 133. If the contract feature is not accounted for under the provisions of FAS 133, an additional liability for the contract feature should be established if the present value of expected annuitization payments at the expected annuitization date exceeds the expected account balance at the expected annuitization date in accordance with the guidance in SOP 03-1.

Sales inducements provided to the contract holder, whether for investment or universal-life-type contracts, should be recognized as part of the liability for policy benefits over the period for which the contract must remain in force for the contract holder to qualify for the inducement or at the crediting date, if earlier, in accordance with the SOP. No adjustments should be made to reduce the liability related to the sales inducements for anticipated surrender charges, persistency, or early withdrawal contractual features.

Sales inducements that are recognized as part of the liability under SOP 03-1, that are explicitly identified in the contract at inception, and that meet the criteria specified in the SOP should be deferred and amortized using the same methodology and assumptions used to amortize capitalized acquisition costs.

The financial statements of an insurance enterprise should disclose information about the following:

1. Separate account assets and liabilities; the nature, extent, and timing of minimum guarantees related to variable contracts; and the amount of gains and losses recognized on assets transferred to separate accounts.
2. An insurance enterprise's accounting policy for sales inducements, including the nature of the costs capitalized and the method of amortizing those costs; the amount of costs capitalized and amortized for each of the periods presented; and the unamortized balance as of each balance sheet date presented.
3. The nature of the liabilities and methods and assumptions used in estimating any contract benefits recognized in excess of the account balance pursuant to the SOP.

EMERGING ISSUES TASK FORCE ISSUES SUMMARIES

92-9 Accounting for the Present Value of Future Profits Resulting from the Acquisition of a Life Insurance Company

The Task Force noted that industry practice is to amortize the present value of future profits (PVP) using an interest method with accrual of interest added to the unamortized balance. In the past, there has been some diversity in the application of this method in practice, and so the EITF has worked to standardize this practice. The first consensus reached was that the interest rate used to amortize PVP should be the liability or contract rate. The second consensus was that changes in estimates of future gross profits on FAS 97 contracts should be accounted for as a catch-up adjustment. And finally, PVP and any related liability should be subject to the premium deficiency test required in FAS 60 and 97.

93-6 Accounting for Multiple-Year Retrospectively-Rated Contracts by Ceding and Assuming Enterprises

A number of issues involving retrospective rating provisions contained in reinsurance contracts were resolved in this set of consensuses. These address criteria for the recognition and amounts of assets and liabilities by the assuming and ceding enterprises, respectively, and accounting for changes in coverage during the reinsurance period. A number of conditions were identified, satisfaction of which are necessary for a contract to be treated as reinsurance, and in their absence such contracts are to be accounted for by the deposit method.

93-14 Accounting for Multiple-Year Retrospectively-Rated Insurance Contracts by Insurance Enterprises and Other Enterprises

This EITF addresses how enterprises other than insurance companies should account for contracts with insurance companies covering various types of risks such as product and environmental liability risks. This EITF also addresses "pooled risk" contracts and reinsurance contracts entered into by a captive insurer. A consensus was reached that in order for a contract to be considered insurance it must indemnify the insured party as this would result in a transfer of risk. If no transfer of risk exists (FAS 5), then the contract is not considered insurance, and the balance of the premium less any amount to be retained by the insurer should be accounted for as a deposit. Other consensuses follow those reached in EITF 93-6.

99-4 Accounting for Stock Received from the Demutualization of a Mutual Insurance Company

This offers guidance on the accounting for those formerly mutual insurance companies that have undergone demutualization transactions and converted to stock enterprises. In order to effect a demutualization, a company may be required to issue consideration, often in the form of stock, to existing participating policyholders in exchange for their current membership interests. The receipt of such stock has no direct effect on the policyholders' contractual interests of their insurance policies (for example, it does not alter the cash surrender value of their life insurance policies). However, the governance of the mutual insurance company and, in particular, the participating policyholders' interest in that governance are modified. The EITF's consensus was that stock received from a demutualization should be accounted for at fair value with a gain recognized in income from continuing operations.

STATEMENTS OF POSITION

92-5 Accounting for Foreign Property and Liability Reinsurance

This addressed the lack of uniformity of practices among foreign reinsurers, and in particular how US insurers were to account for property and liability reinsurance assumed from foreign companies.

94-5 Disclosures of Certain Matters in the Financial Statements of Insurance Enterprises

This SOP supplements the disclosure requirements in other FASB and SEC pronouncements. Required disclosures are set forth for insurance enterprises that have received permission by the insurance department in their domiciliary states to use accounting practices other than those prescribed by state laws, regulations, and rules and by the National Association of Insurance Commissioners (NAIC). This statement also defines liability for unpaid claims and claims adjustment expenses and lists the related disclosures required.

95-1 Accounting for Certain Insurance Activities of Mutual Life Insurance Enterprises

Provides guidance on applying FAS 60, 97, and 113 in accounting for mutual life insurance contracts. Capitalization and amortization of acquisition costs is discussed. Premiums are to be reported as revenue when due from policyholders. Death and surrender benefits are reported as expenses, and annual dividends are reported separately as expenses. The calculation of estimated gross margin and liability for future policy benefits is described.

97-3 Accounting by Insurance and Other Entities for Insurance-Related Assessments

In order to address the diversity in practice of accounting for assessments made by government agencies against insurance activities such as workers' compensation second injury funds, this SOP imposed accrual accounting requirements and set forth the conditions that must be met before a liability may be recognized.

98-7 Deposit Accounting: Accounting for Insurance and Reinsurance Contracts That Do Not Transfer Insurance Risk

This provides guidance on how to account for insurance and reinsurance contracts that do not have the effect of transferring insurance risk. It applies to all entities and all types of insurance or reinsurance contracts, other than long duration life and health insurance contracts. The method prescribed by this SOP is "deposit accounting."

00-3 Accounting by Insurance Enterprises for Demutualizations and Formations of Mutual Insurance Holding Companies and for Certain Long Duration Participating Contracts

This SOP provides necessary guidance to the proper accounting for demutualization transactions and also for the formation of mutual insurance holding companies. It also provides guidance to stock insurers that choose to apply SOP 95-1 to account for participating policies within the scope of that SOP.

01-5 Amendments to Specific AICPA Pronouncements for Changes Related to the NAIC Codification

This specifically amended SOP 94-5 to require disclosure of the entity's prescribed or permitted statutory accounting practice and the related monetary effect on statutory surplus of using accounting methods that differ from either the state-prescribed statutory practices, or the NAIC statutory practices.

INVESTMENT COMPANIES

PERSPECTIVE AND ISSUES

An investment company pools shareholders' funds to provide shareholders with professional investment management. Investment companies' activities include selling capital shares to the public, investing the proceeds in securities, and distributing net income and net realized gains to its shareholders.

The AAG, *Audits of Investment Companies,* was completely revised in 2000. It discusses those aspects of accounting and auditing unique to investment companies, and will provide new guidance on accounting for offering costs, amortization of premium or discount on bonds, liabilities for excess expense plans, reporting complex capital structures, payments by affiliates, and financial statement presentation and disclosures for investment companies and nonpublic investment partnerships.

To address FASB concerns regarding the scope of the Guide, AcSEC has undertaken a project to address whether more specific attributes of an investment company can be identified to determine if an entity is within the scope of the Guide. Until this project is finalized, an entity should consistently follow its current accounting policies for determining whether the provisions of the Guide apply to investees of the entity or to subsidiaries that are controlled by the entity. Tentative conclusions of this project are summarized below. An Exposure Draft was issued in late 2002, but as of mid-2004 a final SOP has yet to be produced.

Sources of GAAP	
FAS	*SOP*
102, 126	93-1, 93-2, 93-4, 95-2, 95-3, 01-1

DEFINITIONS OF TERMS

Closed-end fund. An investment company having a fixed number of shares outstanding, which it does not stand ready to redeem. Its shares are traded similarly to those of other public corporations.

Closed-up fund. An open-ended investment company that no longer offers its shares for sale to the general public but still stands ready to redeem its outstanding shares.

Equalization. An accounting method used to prevent a dilution of the continuing shareholders' per share equity in undistributed net investment income caused by the continuous sales and redemptions of capital shares.

Ex-dividend or ex-distribution. Synonym for **shares being traded without dividend or without capital gains distribution**. The buyer of a stock selling ex-dividend does not acquire a right to receive a previously declared but not-yet-paid dividend. Dividends are payable on a fixed date to shareholders recorded on the stock transfer books of the disbursing company as of a previous date of record. For example, a dividend may be declared as payable to holders of record on the books of the disbursing company on a given Friday. Because five business days are allowed for delivery of the security in regular-way transactions on a stock exchange or over-the-counter, the exchange or the National Association of Securities Dealers (NASD) declares the stock ex-dividend as of the opening of the market on the preceding Monday or on one business day earlier for each intervening nontrading day. Therefore, anyone buying the stock on and after Monday is not entitled to the dividend. In the case of nontraded shares of mutual funds, the ex-dividend date is the same as the record date.

Open-end investment company. A mutual fund that is ready to redeem its shares at any time and that usually offers its shares for sale to the public continuously.

CONCEPTS, RULES, AND EXAMPLES

Several types of investment companies exist: management investment companies, unit investment trusts, collectible trust funds, investment partnerships, certain separate accounts of life insurance companies, and offshore funds. Management investment companies include open-end funds (mutual funds), closed-end funds, special purpose funds, venture capital investment companies, small business investment companies, and business development companies.

All of the investment companies mentioned have the following characteristics:

1. Investment activity—Investing in assets, usually in securities of other entities, for current income, appreciation, or both.
2. Unit ownership—Ownership in the investment company is represented by stock or other units of ownership, to which proportionate shares of net assets can be attributed.
3. Pooling of funds—The funds of the investment company owners are pooled together to take advantage of professional investment management.
4. Reporting entity—The investment company is the primary reporting entity.

Accounting Policies

The accounting policies for an investment company result from the company's role as a vehicle through which investors can invest as a group. These policies are largely governed by the SEC, Small Business Administration, and specific provisions of the Internal Revenue Code relating to investment companies.

Investment companies report all investment securities at market value, or if quoted market values are not available, at fair values as determined by management. Along with other industry groups for which specialized GAAP already existed, calling for presentation of all investments at market value (a group that includes broker-dealers and defined benefit pension plans), investment companies were exempted from the provisions of FAS 115.

Security purchases and sales are generally recorded at the trade date; therefore, the effects of all securities trades entered into by the investment company to the date of the financial statements are included in the financial report.

Investment companies record dividend income on the ex-dividend date, not on the later record or payable date. The rationale for this treatment is that the market price of market securities may be affected by the exclusion of the declared dividend. Additionally, investment companies record a liability for dividends payable on the ex-dividend date because mutual fund shares are purchased and redeemed at prices equal to or based on net asset value. If investors purchase shares between the declaration and ex-dividend dates they are entitled to receive dividends; however, investors purchasing shares after the ex-dividend date are not entitled to receive dividends.

Open-end investment companies often employ the practice of equalization. This theory states that the net asset value of each share of capital stock sold comprises the par value of the stock, undistributed income, and paid-in capital and other surplus. When shares are sold or repurchased, the investment company calculates the amount of undistributed income available for distribution to its shareholders. Based on the number of shares outstanding, the investment company determines the per share amount; this amount is credited to an equalization account when shares are sold. Conversely, the equalization account is charged when shares are repurchased.

Accounting for High-Yield Debt Securities

The accounting by creditors for investments in "step interest" and "PIK" debt securities, if these qualify as "high-yield" securities, is addressed by the Guide. Step interest bonds are generally unsecured debentures that pay no interest for a specified period after issuance, then pay a stipulated rate for a period, then a higher rate for another period, etc., until maturity. Thus, they combine some of the characteristics of zero-coupon bonds with some features of current interest bonds. PIK (payment in kind) bonds pay some or all interest in the form of other debt instruments ("baby" or "bunny" bonds), which in turn may also pay interest in the form of baby bonds. All babies mature at the due date of the parent bond.

The Guide, as amended, requires that the effective interest method should be used for step interest bonds; to the extent that interest income is not expected to be realized, a reserve against the income should be established. A previously employed technique, the bifurcation method, is no longer acceptable. For PIK bonds, the effective interest method is also required; the market value method, which was widely used in the past, can no longer be employed.

Exemptions from the Requirement to Provide a Statement of Cash Flows

The following conditions must be met for an investment company to be exempted from providing a statement of cash flows:

1. Substantially all of the entity's investments were highly liquid.
2. The entity's investments are carried at market value.
3. The entity had little or no debt, based on average debt outstanding during the period, in relation to average total assets.
4. The entity provides a statement of changes in net assets.

Taxes

Investment companies that distribute all taxable income and taxable realized gains qualifying under Subchapter M of the Internal Revenue Code are not required to record a provision for federal income taxes. If the investment company does not distribute all taxable income and taxable realized gains, a liability should be recorded at the end of the last day of the taxable year. The rationale for recording on the last day of the year is that only shareholders of record at that date are entitled to credit for taxes paid.

Commodity Pools

The AICPA issued SOP 01-1, *Amendment to Scope of Statement of Position 95-2, "Financial Reporting by Nonpublic Investment Partnerships," to Include Commodity Pools,* to deal with the failure to address accounting for commodity pools in other professional literature. It stipulates that investment partnerships which are commodity pools subject to regulation by the CFTC are subject to the guidance of SOP 95-2. Thus, notwithstanding the rapid turnover common among such pools, the financial statements must include a schedule of investments.

In adopting this requirement, AcSEC rejected arguments that disclosure of investments would result in competitive harm or provide adversaries with the knowledge to enter into positions that might harm the reporting entity, such as by creating a "short squeeze." It determined that the information needs of the investors in these partnerships would be paramount to concerns over competitive risks that could be exacerbated by such disclosures.

Clarification of the Scope of the Investment Companies Guide

AcSEC, in responding to concerns raised by FASB, has undertaken a project to clarify the scope of the investment companies AAG issued in 2000. This will take the form of a SOP, issuance of which has been long delayed. Some of the tentative conclusions reached to date are

- For purposes of the separate financial statements of an entity, the Guide would be applicable to entities that are regulated as investment companies and other entities whose primary business activity involves investing for current income, capital appreciation, or both. The SOP would identify conditions that should be evaluated to determine whether the entity's primary business activity is investment activity, including whether investees function as separate autonomous businesses. Entities that meet the conditions would be required to apply the provisions of the Guide in presenting their financial statements. Entities not meeting those conditions would be prohibited from applying the provisions of the Guide.
- The SOP would also set forth conditions to be evaluated in determining whether the specialized industry accounting principles of the Guide applied by a subsidiary (or equity method investee) should be retained in the financial statements of the parent company (or an investor that applies the equity method of accounting to its investments in the entity). Those conditions are intended to evaluate relationships between the parent company or equity method investor and investees that may indicate that investees are not separate autonomous businesses from the parent company or equity method investor. If those conditions are not met, the specialized industry accounting principles of the Guide would not be retained in the financial statements of the parent company or equity method investor. In that case, the financial information of the investment company would be adjusted to reflect the accounting principles that would apply to the entity assuming it did not qualify as an investment company within the scope of the Guide.

STATEMENTS OF POSITION

93-1 Financial Accounting and Reporting for High-Yield Debt Securities by Investment Companies

The Division concluded that for PIK and step bonds, (1) the effective-interest method should be used to determine interest income; (2) a reserve against income should be established for interest income not expected to be realized; (3) the cost plus any discount should not exceed undiscounted future cash collections; (4) SEC yield-formula calculations must be made; and (5) all high-yield and restricted debt securities whose values were estimated should be indicated in the portfolio. For defaulted debt securities, any interest receivable written off that had been recognized as income constitutes a reduction of income. Write-offs of purchased interest increase the cost basis and represent an unrealized loss until the security is sold. "Capital infusions" are accounted for as an addition to the cost basis, while related "workout expenditures" are recorded as unrealized losses. Any ongoing expenditures to protect the value of the investment are recorded as operating expenses. Auditors should consider additional pricing valuation audit procedures.

93-2 Determination, Disclosure, and Financial Statement Presentation of Income, Capital Gain, and Return of Capital Distributions by Investment Companies

This statement was developed to clarify the reporting of shareholder distributions that exceed the tax-basis current and accumulated earnings and profits in GAAP financial statements. The statement recommends that the caption "tax return of capital" be used to report such distributions.

93-4 Foreign Currency Accounting and Financial Statement Presentation for Investment Companies

Transactions denominated in a foreign currency must originally be measured in that currency. Reporting exchange rate gains and losses separately from any gain/loss on the investment due to changes in market price is allowable but not required.

95-2 Financial Reporting by Nonpublic Investment Partnerships

This statement pertains to investment partnerships that are exempt from SEC registration under the Investment Company Act of 1940. Specifically, the statement requires that the financial statements include a condensed schedule of securities that categorizes investments by type, country or geographic region, and industry; discloses pertinent information concerning investments comprising greater than 5% of net assets; and aggregates any securities holdings less than the 5% of net assets threshold. The statement of operations for nonpublic investment companies shall be presented in conformity with requirements for public investment companies per the *Audit Guide* so as to reflect their comparable operations. The financial statements shall also present management fees and disclose their computation.

95-3 Accounting for Certain Distribution Costs of Investment Companies

This statement requires investment companies with enhanced 12b-1 plans or board-contingent plans for which the board has committed to pay costs to recognize a liability and the related expense, for the amount of excess costs. This liability should be discounted at an appropriate current rate if the amount and timing of cash flows are reliably determinable and if distribution costs are not subject to a reasonable interest charge. Excess costs are recorded as a liability as the fund has assumed an obligation to pay the 12b-1 fee after the termination of the plan to the extent that the distributor has excess costs.

01-1 Amendment to Scope of Statement of Position 95-2, *Financial Reporting by Nonpublic Investment Partnerships,* to Include Commodity Pools

This extends the disclosure requirements under SOP 95-2 to commodity pools regulated by the CFTC.

MORTGAGE BANKING

PERSPECTIVE AND ISSUES

Mortgage banking comprises two activities.

1. The origination or purchase of mortgage loans and subsequent sale to **permanent investors,** and
2. Long-term **servicing** of the mortgage loan.

To the extent that mortgage banking activities discussed in this section may be undertaken by subsidiaries or divisions of commercial banks or savings institutions, the same accounting and reporting standards apply. Normal, nonmortgage lending of those enterprises, however, is accounted for in accordance with the lender's normal accounting policies for such activities.

Mortgage loans held for sale are valued at the lower of cost or market. Mortgage-backed securities are reported under FAS 115 as held-to-maturity, trading, or available-for-sale, depending on the entity's intent and ability to hold the securities.

Loan origination fees and related direct costs for loans held for sale are capitalized as part of the related loan and amortized, using the effective yield method. However, fees and costs associated with **commitments** to originate, sell, or purchase loans are treated as part of the commitment, which is a derivative accounted for under FAS 133.

Loan origination fees and costs for loans held for investment are deferred and recognized as an adjustment to the yield.

SOP 01-6, *Accounting by Certain Entities (Including Entities with Trade Receivables) That Lend to or Finance the Activities of Others,* provides uniform and consistent guidance for the accounting and reporting practices for similar transactions by various types of depository and lending institutions, and has now been incorporated in a unified AAG released in 2004. The SOP includes in its scope, corporate credit unions and mortgage companies and, in fact, affects disclosure practices for any entity that extends credit to customers. (See the summary under the Banking and Thrift Institutions section of this chapter for a discussion of the general disclosure requirements for all enterprises. These general requirements also apply, when applicable, to mortgage banking enterprises and are not repeated in this section.) In addition, the SOP prescribes required disclosures for mortgage banking enterprises regarding their regulatory capital and net worth requirements.

Sources of GAAP

FAS	FTB	SOP	AAG
65, 91, 115, 133, 134, 140, 149	87-3	01-6	*Depository and Lending Institutions: Banks and Savings Institutions, Credit Unions, Finance Companies and Mortgage Companies.*

DEFINITIONS OF TERMS

Affiliated enterprise. An enterprise that directly or indirectly controls, is controlled by, or is under common control with another enterprise; also, a party with which the enterprise may deal if one party has the ability to exercise significant influence over the other's operating and financial policies.

Current (normal) servicing fee rate. A servicing fee rate that is representative of servicing fee rates most commonly used in comparable servicing agreements covering similar types of mortgage loans.

Federal Home Loan Mortgage Corporation (FHLMC). Often referred to as "Freddie Mac," FHLMC is a private corporation authorized by Congress to assist in the development and maintenance of a secondary market in conventional residential mortgages. FHLMC purchases and sells mortgages principally through mortgage participation certificates (PC) representing an undivided interest in a group of conventional mortgages. FHLMC guarantees the timely payment of interest and the collection of principal on the PC.

Federal National Mortgage Association (FNMA). Often referred to as "Fannie Mae," FNMA is an investor-owned corporation established by Congress to support the secondary mortgage loan market by purchasing mortgage loans when other investor funds are limited and selling mortgage loans when other investor funds are available.

Gap commitment. A commitment to provide interim financing while the borrower is in the process of satisfying provisions of a permanent loan agreement, such as obtaining a designated occupancy level on an apartment project. The interim loan ordinarily finances the difference between the floor loan (the portion of a mortgage loan commitment that is less than the full amount of the commitment) and the maximum permanent loan.

Government National Mortgage Association (GNMA). Often referred to as "Ginnie Mae," GNMA is a US governmental agency that guarantees certain types of securities (mortgage-backed securities) and provides funds for and administers certain types of low-income housing assistance programs.

Internal reserve method. A method for making payments to investors for collections of principal and interest on mortgage loans by issuers of GNMA securities. An issuer electing the internal reserve method is required to deposit in a custodial account an amount equal to one month's interest on the mortgage loans that collateralize the GNMA security issued.

Mortgage-backed securities. Securities issued by a governmental agency or corporation (e.g., GNMA or FHLMC) or by private issuers (e.g., FNMA, banks, and mortgage banking enterprises). Mortgage-backed securities generally are referred to as **mortgage participation certificates** or **pass-through certificates** (PC). A PC represents an undivided interest in a pool of specific mortgage loans. Periodic payments on GNMA PC are backed by the US government. Periodic payments on FHLMC and FNMA PC are guaranteed by those corporations and are not backed by the US government.

Mortgage banking enterprise. An enterprise that is engaged primarily in originating, marketing, and servicing real estate mortgage loans for other than its own account. Mortgage banking enterprises, as local representatives of institutional lenders, act as correspondents between lenders and borrowers.

Permanent investor. An enterprise that invests in mortgage loans for its own account, for example, an insurance enterprise, commercial or mutual savings bank, savings and loan association, pension plan, real estate investment trust, or FNMA.

Securitization. The transformation of a pool of financial assets (e.g., mortgages) into securities (asset-backed securities).

Servicing. Mortgage loan servicing includes collecting monthly mortgagor payments, forwarding payments and related accounting reports to investors, collecting escrow deposits for the payment of mortgagor property taxes and insurance, and paying the taxes and insurance from the escrow funds when due.

Standby commitment. A commitment to lend money with the understanding that the loan probably will not be made unless permanent financing cannot be obtained from another source. Standby commitments ordinarily are used to enable the borrower to obtain construction financing on the assumption that permanent financing will be available on more favorable terms when construction is completed. Standby commitments normally provide for an interest rate substantially above the market rate in effect when the commitment is issued.

CONCEPTS, RULES, AND EXAMPLES

Mortgage Banking Activities

A mortgage banking enterprise (MBE) acts as an intermediary between borrowers (mortgagors) and lenders (mortgagees). MBE activities include purchasing and originating mortgage loans for sale to **permanent investors** and performing **servicing** activities during the period that the loans are outstanding. The mortgage loans offered for sale to permanent investors may be originated by the MBE (in-house originations); purchased from realtors, brokers, or investors; or converted from short-term, interim credit facilities to permanent financing. The common technique used by the MBE to market and sell the loans is referred to as **securitization** because the mortgage loans receivable are pooled and converted to mortgage-backed securities and sold in that form.

MBE customarily retain the rights to service the loans that they sell to permanent investors in exchange for a servicing fee. The servicing fee, normally a percentage of the mortgage's outstanding principal balance, compensates the MBE for processing of mortgagor payments of principal, interest and escrow deposits, disbursing funds from the escrow accounts to pay property taxes and insurance on behalf of the mortgagor, and remitting net proceeds to the permanent investor along with relevant accounting reports.

Mortgage loans. The MBE is required to classify mortgage loans that it holds as either (1) held-for-sale, or (2) held for long-term investment.

Loans held-for-sale. Mortgage loans held for sale are reported at the lower of cost or market as of the balance sheet date. Any excess of cost over market is accounted for as a valuation allowance, changes in which are to be included in income in the period of change.

Determination of cost basis. The following matters must be considered with respect to the cost basis used for the purposes of the lower of cost or market value determination:

1. If a mortgage loan has been identified as a hedged item in a fair value hedge under FAS 133, the cost basis used reflects adjustments to the loan's carrying amount for changes in the loan's fair value attributable to the risk being hedged.
2. Purchase discounts on mortgage loans reduce the cost basis and are not amortized as interest revenue during the period that the loans are held for sale.
3. Capitalized costs attributable to the acquisition of mortgage servicing rights associated with the purchase or origination of mortgage loans are excluded from the cost basis of the mortgage loans.

Determination of market value. The market value of mortgage loans held for sale is determined by type of loan; at a minimum, separate determinations are made for residential and commercial loans. Either an aggregate or individual loan basis may be used in determining the lower of cost or market for each type of loan. Market values for loans subject to investor purchase commitments (committed loans) and loans held for speculative purposes (uncommitted loans) must be determined separately as follows:

1. For **committed** loans, market value is defined as fair value.
2. For **uncommitted** loans, market value is based on quotations from the market in which the MBE normally operates, considering
   a. Market prices and yields sought by the MBE's normal market outlets,
   b. Quoted Government National Mortgage Association (GNMA) security prices or other public market quotations of rates for long-term mortgage loans, and
   c. Federal Home Loan Mortgage Corporation (FHLMC) and Federal National Mortgage Association (FNMA) current delivery prices.

Loans held for long-term investment. Mortgage loans may be transferred from the held-for-sale classification to the held-for-long-term investment classification only if the MBE has both the intent and ability to hold the loan for the foreseeable future or until maturity. The transfer to the long-term investment classification is recorded at the lower of cost or market value on the date of transfer. Any difference between the loan's adjusted carrying amount and its outstanding principal balance (e.g., purchase discounts as discussed above) is recognized as a yield adjustment using the interest method.

If recoverability of the carrying amount of a mortgage loan held for long-term investment is doubtful and the impairment is judged to be other than temporary, the loan's carrying amount is reduced by the amount of the impairment to the amount expected to be collected with the related charge recognized as a loss. The adjusted carrying value becomes the loan's new cost basis and any eventual gain on recovery may only be recognized upon the loan's sale, maturity, or other disposition.

Mortgage-backed securities. The securitization of mortgage loans held-for-sale is accounted for as a sale of the mortgage loans and purchase of mortgage-backed securities.

Classification and valuation. After the securitization of a held-for-sale mortgage loan, any mortgage-backed securities retained by the MBE are classified as (1) trading, (2) available-for-sale, or (3) held-to-maturity under the provisions of FAS 115, as amended by FAS 134. As is the case with the MBE's mortgage loans held for investment, the MBE must have both the intent and ability to hold the mortgage-backed securities for the foreseeable future or until maturity in order to classify them as held-to-maturity. If the MBE had committed to sell the securities before or during the securitization process, the securities are required to be classified under the trading category. Mortgage-backed securities held by a not-for-profit organization are stated at fair value under FAS 124.

The fair value of **uncommitted** mortgage-backed securities collateralized by the MBE's own loans is ordinarily based on the market value of the securities. If the trust holding the loans may be readily terminated and the loans sold directly, fair value of the securities is based on the market value of either the loans or the securities, depending on the entity's intentions. Fair value for other uncommitted mortgage-backed securities is based on published yield data.

Repurchase agreements. Mortgage loans or mortgage-backed securities held for sale may be temporarily transferred by an MBE to another financial institution under a formal or informal agreement which serves as a means of financing these assets. Such agreements are accounted for as collateralized financing arrangements; the loans and securities transferred under the agreements are still reported by the MBE as held for sale.

A formal repurchase agreement specifies that the MBE retains control over future economic benefits and also the risk of loss relating to the loans or securities transferred. These assets are subsequently reacquired from the financial institution upon the sale of the assets by the mortgage banking enterprise to permanent investors.

An informal repurchase agreement exists when no formal agreement has been executed but loans or securities are transferred by an MBE that does all of the following:

1. Is the sole marketer of the assets
2. Retains any interest spread on the assets
3. Retains risk of loss in market value
4. Reacquires uncollectible loans
5. Regularly reacquires most or all of the assets and sells them to permanent investors

When mortgage loans held for sale are transferred under a repurchase arrangement, they continue to be reported by the transferor as loans held for sale. Mortgage-backed securities sold under agreements to repurchase are reported as trading securities as defined in FAS 115.

Servicing Mortgage Loans

Rights to service mortgage loans for others are recognized as separate assets by an MBE. If the enterprise acquires such rights through purchase or origination of mortgage loans and retains them upon sale or securitization, the total cost of the mortgage loans must be allocated between the rights and the loans (without the rights) based on their relative fair values. If it is impossible to determine the fair value of the mortgage servicing rights apart from the mortgage, the MBE/transferor records the mortgage servicing rights at zero value (FAS 140). Otherwise, mortgage servicing rights are capitalized at their fair value and recognized as a net asset if the benefits of servicing the mortgage are expected to be more than adequate compensation to the servicer for performing the duties. If the benefits of servicing the mortgage are not expected to adequately compensate the servicer, the servicer recognizes a liability. The asset Mortgage Servicing Contract Rights is initially measured at its fair value. Subsequent impairment is recognized as follows:

1. The mortgage servicing assets are stratified based on predominant risk characteristics.
2. Impairment is recognized through a valuation allowance for an individual stratum. The amount of impairment equals the carrying amount for a particular stratum minus its fair value.
3. The valuation allowance is adjusted to reflect changes in the measurement of impairment after the initial measurement of impairment.

Servicing fees. Servicing fees are usually based on a percentage of the outstanding principal balance of the mortgage loan. When a mortgage loan is sold with servicing rights retained, the sales price must be adjusted if the stated rate is materially different from the **current (normal) servicing fee rate** so that the gain or loss on the sale can be determined. The adjustment is

Adjustment	=	Actual Sales Price	–	Estimated sales price obtainable if normal servicing fee rate had been used

This adjustment allows for recognition of normal servicing fees in subsequent years.

The adjustment and any recognized gain or loss are determined as of the sale date. If estimated normal servicing fees are less than total expected servicing costs, then this loss is accrued on the sale date as well.

Sales to Affiliated Enterprises

When mortgage loans or mortgage-backed securities are sold to an **affiliated enterprise,** the carrying amount of the assets must be adjusted to lower of cost or market as of the date that management decides that the sale will occur. This date is evidenced by formal approval by a representative of the affiliated enterprise (purchaser), issuance of a purchase commitment, and acceptance of the purchase commitment by the seller. Any adjustment is charged to income.

If a group of (or all) mortgage loans are originated specifically for an affiliate, then the originator is an agent of the affiliated enterprise. In this case, the loans are transferred at the originator's cost of acquisition. This treatment does not apply to "right of first refusal" or similar contracts in which the originator retains all risks of ownership.

Issuance of GNMA Securities

An issuer of **GNMA** securities who elects the **internal reserve method** must pay one month's interest cost to a trustee. This cost is capitalized (at no greater than the present value of net future servicing income) and amortized.

Loan and Commitment Fees and Costs

Mortgage bankers may pay or receive loan and commitment fees as compensation for various loan administration services. These fees and costs are accounted for as described in the following paragraphs.

Loan origination fees received. Loan origination fees and related direct costs are deferred and amortized, using the effective yield method. Fees and costs associated with **commitments** to originate, sell, or purchase loans, however, must be considered part of the commitments, which are deemed to be derivatives under FAS 133. FAS 149 amended FAS 133 to remove the accounting for such fees and costs from the guidance of FAS 91, effective for transactions originated or modified after June 30, 2003. Previously, these fees were capitalized and FAS 149 indicates that these previous transactions are not to be re-characterized. If the loan is held for investment, loan origination fees and costs are recognized as an adjustment of yield using the effective interest method.

Services rendered. Fees for specific services rendered by third parties as part of a loan origination (e.g., appraisal fees) are recognized when the services are performed.

Commitment fees paid to investors on loans held for sale. Residential or commercial loan commitment fees paid to permanent investors are recognized as expense when the loans are sold or when it is determined that the commitment will not be used. Since residential loan commitment fees typically cover groups of loans, the amount of fees recognized as revenue or expense relating to an individual transaction is calculated as

$$\text{Revenue or expense recognized on individual transaction} = \text{Total residential loan commitment fee} \times \frac{\text{Amount of individual loan}}{\text{Total commitment amount}}$$

Loan placement fees (fees for arranging a commitment directly between investor and borrower) are recognized as revenue once all significant services have been performed by the MBE. In some cases, an MBE secures a commitment from a permanent investor before or at the same time a commitment is made to a borrower and the latter commitment requires

1. Simultaneous assignment to the investor, and
2. Simultaneous transfer to the borrower of amounts paid by the investor.

The fees related to such transactions are also accounted for as loan placement fees.

Expired commitments or early repayment of loans. At the time that a loan commitment expires unused or is repaid before repayment is due, any related fees that had been deferred are recognized as revenue or expense.

Reporting

An MBE must, on its balance sheet, distinguish between mortgage loans and mortgage-backed securities that are held for sale and those that are held for long-term investment. The notes to the financial statements are to disclose whether the MBE used the aggregate method or the individual-loan method to determine the lower of cost or market.

SOP 01-6, *Accounting by Certain Entities (Including Entities with Trade Receivables) That Lend to or Finance the Activities of Others,* contains specific capital disclosure requirements including, at a minimum

1. A description of the minimum net worth requirements related to
   a. Secondary market investors, and
   b. State-imposed regulatory mandates.
2. The actual or possible material effects of noncompliance with those requirements.
3. Whether the entity is in compliance with the regulatory capital requirements including, as of the date of each balance sheet presented, the following measures:
   a. The amount of the entity's required and actual net worth
   b. Factors that may significantly affect adequacy of net worth such as potentially volatile components of capital, qualitative factors, or regulatory mandates.
4. If the entity is not in compliance with capital adequacy requirements as of the most recent balance sheet date, the possible material effects of that condition on amounts and disclosures in the financial statements.

5. Loan servicers with net worth requirements imposed by more than one source are to disclose the new worth requirements of
   a. Significant servicing covenants with secondary market investors with commonly defined servicing requirements.
   b. Any other secondary market investor where violation of the net worth requirement would have an adverse effect on the business, and
   c. The most restrictive third-party agreement if not already included in the above disclosures.

The SOP points out that noncompliance with minimum net worth requirements may trigger substantial doubt about the entity's ability to continue as a going concern.

MOTION PICTURES

PERSPECTIVE AND ISSUES

The production, sale, licensing, and distribution of motion pictures (and television series) are fraught with uncertainties. The industry is speculative in nature with studios routinely investing multimillion dollar sums in the hope that the production will achieve critical acclaim and that moviegoers will flock to the box office, purchase licensed merchandise tied to the film and its characters, and purchase and rent videos and DVDs. Due to the uncertainties involved in estimating the revenues that will be earned and costs that will be incurred over a film's life, an acceptable estimation methodology is required to achieve proper matching of costs and revenues and accurately reflect the results of the film's financial performance. This methodology is provided in SOP 00-2, *Accounting by Producers or Distributors of Films*.

Sources of GAAP	
SOP	*EITF*
00-2	87-10, 96-6

DEFINITIONS OF TERMS

Cross-collateralized. A contractual arrangement granting distribution rights to multiple films, territories and/or markets to a licensee. In this type of arrangement, the exploitation results of the entire package are aggregated by the licensee in determining amounts payable to the licensor.

Distributor. The owner or holder of the rights to distribute films. Excluded from this definition, for the purposes of applying SOP 00-2, are entities that function solely as broadcasters, retailers (such as video stores), or movie theaters.

Exploitation costs. All direct costs incurred in connection with the film's distribution. Examples include marketing, advertising, publicity, promotion, and other distribution expenses.

Film costs. Film costs include all direct negative costs incurred in the physical production of a film, including allocations of production overhead and interest capitalized in accordance with FAS 34. Examples of direct negative costs include costs of story and scenario; compensation of cast members, extras, directors, producers, and miscellaneous staff; costs of set construction and operations, wardrobe and accessories; costs of sound synchronization; rental facilities on location; and postproduction costs such as music, special effects, and editing.

Film prints. The materials containing the completed audio and video elements of a film which are distributed to a theater to exhibit the film to its customers.

Firm commitment. An agreement with a third party that is binding on both parties. The agreement specifies all significant terms, including items to be exchanged, consideration, and timing of the transaction. The agreement includes a disincentive for nonperformance that is sufficiently large to ensure the expected performance. With respect to an episodic television series, a firm commitment for future production includes only episodes to be delivered within one year from the date of the estimate of ultimate revenue.

Market. A distribution channel located within a certain geographic territory for a certain type of media, exhibition, or related product. Examples include theatrical exhibition, home video (laser disc, videotape, DVD), pay television, free television, and the licensing of film-related merchandise.

Nonrefundable minimum guarantee. Amount to be paid by a customer in a variable fee arrangement that guarantees an entity a minimum fee on that arrangement. This amount applies to payments paid at inception, as well as to legally binding commitments to pay amounts over the license period.

Overall deal. An arrangement whereby an entity compensates a creative individual (e.g. producer, actor, or director) for the exclusive or preferential use of that party's creative services.

Participation costs. Frequently, persons involved in the production of a film are compensated, in part or in full, with an interest (referred to as a "participation") in the financial results of the film. Determination of the amount of compensation payable to the participant is usually based on formulas (participations) and by contingent amounts due under provisions of collective bargaining agreements (residuals). The recipients of this compensation are referred to as participants and the costs are referred to as participation costs. Participations may be paid to creative talent (e.g. actors or writers), or to entities from whom distribution rights are licensed.

Producer. An individual or enterprise that is responsible for all aspects of a film. Although the producer's role may vary, his or her responsibilities include administration of such aspects of the project as initial concept, script, budgeting, shooting, postproduction, and release.

Revenue. Amounts earned by an entity from its direct distribution, exploitation, or licensing of a film, before deduction for any of the entity's direct costs of distribution. In markets and territories where the entity's fully or jointly owned films are distributed by third-party distributors, revenue is the net amount payable to the entity by the distributor. Revenue is reduced by appropriate allowances, estimated returns, price concessions, or similar adjustments, as applicable.

Sale. The transfer of control of the master copy of a film and all of the associated rights that accompany it.

Set for production. A film qualifies as being set for production when all of the following conditions have been met: (1) management with relevant authority authorizes (implicitly or explicitly) and commits to funding the film's production; (2) active preproduction has begun; and (3) the start of principal photography is expected to begin within six months.

Territory. A geographic area in which a film is exploited, usually a country. In some cases, however, a territory may be contractually defined as countries with a common language.

CONCEPTS, RULES, AND EXAMPLES

SOP 00-2, *Accounting by Producers or Distributors of Films,* provides the authoritative guidance with respect to accounting for arrangements to sell, license, or exhibit films. The term "film" is generic and includes intellectual property produced on traditional celluloid film as well as videotape, digital, or other video-recording formats. The content or format of films includes (1) feature films, (2) television series, (3) television specials, and (4) similar products (including animated films and television programming). The guidance in the SOP applies to producers and distributors who own or hold rights to distribute or **exploit** films. The SOP **does not** apply to the following specialized industries or applications that have their own specialized GAAP:

1. The recording industry (FAS 50)
2. Cable television (FAS 51)
3. Broadcasters (FAS 63)
4. Computer software to be sold, leased, or otherwise marketed (FAS 86)
5. Software revenue recognition (SOP 97-2)
6. Entertainment and educational software products (EITF 96-6)

There are many varieties of contractual sales or licensing arrangements governing the rights or group of rights to a single or multiple films. The film's producer (referred to in the SOP and in this discussion as "the entity") may license it to distributors, theaters, exhibitors, or other licensees (referred to in the SOP and in this discussion as "customers") on an exclusive or nonexclusive basis in a particular market or territory. The terms of the license may be for a fixed (or flat) fee or the fee may be variable based on a percentage of the customer's revenue. If the arrangement is variable, it may include a nonrefundable minimum guarantee payable either in advance or over the licensing period.

Revenue Recognition

An entity recognizes revenue from a sale or licensing arrangement only when **all** of the following conditions are met:

1. Persuasive evidence exists of a sale or licensing arrangement with a customer.
2. The film is complete and, in accordance with the terms of the arrangement, has been delivered or is available for immediate and unconditional delivery.
3. The license period for the arrangement has started and the customer can begin exploitation, exhibition, or sale.
4. The arrangement fee is fixed or determinable.
5. Collection of the arrangement fee is reasonably assured.

If any of the above conditions has not been met, the entity defers recognizing revenue until all of the conditions are met. If the entity recognizes a receivable on its balance sheet for advances under an arrangement for which all of the above conditions have not been met, a liability for deferred revenue of the same amount is to be recognized until such time as all of the conditions have been met.

Persuasive evidence of an arrangement. This condition is met solely by documentary evidence that sets forth, at a minimum, the following terms: (1) the license period, (2) the film or films covered by the agreement, (3) a description of the rights transferred, and (4) the consideration to be exchanged. If the agreement is ambiguous regarding the parties' rights and obligations, or if there is significant doubt as to the ability of either party to perform under the agreement, revenue is not recognized. Acceptable documentary evidence must be verifiable (e.g., a contract, a purchase order, or an online authorization).

Delivery. The delivery condition may be satisfied by an arrangement providing the customer with immediate and unconditional access to a film print held by the entity. The customer may also receive a **lab access letter** that authorizes it to order a film laboratory to make the film immediately and unconditionally available for its use. Under these conditions, the delivery condition is satisfied if the film is complete and available for immediate delivery.

Some licensing arrangements require the entity to make **significant changes** to the film after it becomes initially available. Significant changes are changes that are additive to the film and that result from the entity creating additional content after the film becomes initially available. The changes can consist of the reshooting of selected scenes or adding additional special effects. When such changes are required to be made to the film, the arrangement does not meet the delivery condition. The costs incurred for these significant changes are added to **film costs** and subsequently recorded as expense when the related revenue is recognized.

Changes that are not considered to be significant changes include insertion or addition of preexisting film footage, addition of dubbing or subtitles to existing footage, removal of offensive language, reformatting to fit a broadcaster's screen dimensions, or adjustments to allow for the insertion of television commercials. Such insignificant changes do not alter the film's qualification to meet the delivery condition. The expected costs of these insignificant changes are accrued and charged directly to expense by the entity at the time that revenue recognition commences even if they have not yet been incurred.

Commencement of exploitation. Some arrangements impose on the customer a release date or **"street date"** before which the film may not be exhibited or sold. Such a date defines the commencement date of the exploitation rights. The entity does not begin to recognize revenue on the arrangement until this restriction has expired.

Fixed or determinable arrangement fee. When there is a **flat fee** that covers a **single film,** the amount of the fee is, of course, considered fixed and determinable and the entity recognizes the entire license fee as revenue when all of the conditions set forth above have been satisfied.

If the flat fee applies to **multiple films,** some of which have not been produced or completed, the entity allocates the fee to each individual film by market or territory based on relative fair values of the rights to exploit each film under the licensing arrangement. The entity bases the allocations to a film or films not yet produced or completed on the amounts that would be refundable if the entity did not ultimately complete and deliver the films to the customer. The entity allocates the remaining flat fee to completed films based on the relative fair values of the exploitation rights to those films under the arrangement. These allocations may not be adjusted subsequently even if better information becomes available. After making the allocations described above, the entity recognizes revenue for each film when all of the above conditions are met with respect to that film by market and territory. If the entity is not able to determine relative fair values for the exploitation rights, then the fee is not fixed or determinable and the entity may not recognize revenue until such a determination can be made and it meets all five of the conditions.

An entity's arrangement fees may be **variable** based on a percentage of the customer's revenue from exploitation of the film. When all five conditions have been met, the entity commences revenue recognition as the customer exploits or exhibits the film.

Certain variable fee arrangements include a **nonrefundable minimum guarantee** whereby the customer guarantees to pay the entity a nonrefundable minimum amount that is applied against the variable fees on a film or group of films that are not **cross-collateralized**. In applying the revenue recognition conditions, the amount of the nonrefundable minimum guarantee is considered to be fixed and determinable and is recognized as revenue when all of the other conditions have been met. If the nonrefundable minimum guarantee is applied against variable fees from a group of films on a cross-collateralized basis, the amount of the minimum guarantee attributable to each individual film cannot be objectively determined. In this situation, the entity recognizes revenue as described in the preceding paragraph (i.e., when all five of the conditions have been met as the customer exhibits or exploits each film). Under this scenario, if there is a remaining portion of the nonrefundable minimum guarantee that is unearned at the end of the license period, the entity recognizes the remaining guarantee as revenue by allocating it to the individual films based on their relative performance under the arrangement.

Returns and price concessions can affect whether the arrangement fee meets the condition of being fixed and determinable. The factors to consider include the provisions of the arrangement between the entity and its customer and the entity's policies and past actions related to granting concessions or accepting product returns. If the arrangement includes a right-of-return provision or if its past practices allow for such rights, the entity must meet all of the conditions in FAS 48, in order for it to recognize revenue. Among those conditions is a requirement that the entity be able to reasonably estimate the amount of future returns. FAS 48 is discussed in detail in Chapter 8.

Barter revenue. If an entity licenses programming to television stations in exchange for a specified amount of advertising time on those stations, the exchange is accounted for as a nonmonetary exchange in accordance with APB 29 as interpreted by EITF 93-11. See the discussion of nonmonetary transactions in Chapter 9.

Modifications of arrangements. If, during the term of a licensing arrangement, the entity and its customer agree to **extend an existing arrangement** for which all of the revenue recognition conditions have been met, the accounting follows the same rules cited above for flat-fee arrangements, variable fee arrangements, and variable fee arrangements with minimum guarantees.

For modifications that are not extensions of an existing arrangement, the modification is accounted for as a new arrangement and a termination of the former arrangement. At the time the former arrangement is terminated, the entity accrues and expenses all costs associated with the arrangement or reverses previously reported revenue to reflect refunds and concessions that result from the new arrangement. In addition, the entity adjusts accumulated film cost amortization and accrued participation costs attributable to the excess revenue. The new arrangement fee is accounted for by applying the provisions of the SOP.

Example

Eva Enterprises produced a film that did not meet revenue expectations. The film was originally projected to gross $9,500,000 and to date has only earned $2,300,000.

The original arrangement called for a fixed fee of $150,000. Eva had previously met all five criteria for recognizing the $150,000 fixed fee as revenue. To placate its customers, Eva negotiated a new arrangement that reduced the original fixed fee from $150,000 to $80,000 and substituted a variable component based on 1% of the customers' revenues from exploiting the film. The effects of the new arrangement on Eva's revenue are computed as follows:

Revenue recognizable under new arrangement	
Fixed fee	$ 80,000
Variable fee earned to date (1% of $2,300,000)	23,000
	103,000
Original fixed fee recognized as revenue	150,000
Reduction in revenue due to new arrangement	$(47,000)

In addition to the adjustment above, Eva also must adjust its previously recorded accumulated amortization of film costs and accrued participation costs attributable to the excess revenue previously recorded. Prospectively, the new arrangement is accounted for in accordance with the provisions of the SOP.

Product licensing. Any revenue from licensing arrangements to market film-related products is deferred until the release date of the film.

Present value. Revenue that an entity recognizes in connection with licensing arrangements is recorded at the present value of the license fee computed in accordance with APB 21 as of the date that the entity first recognizes the revenue.

Costs and Expenses—Components

Costs associated with the production and bringing to market of a film can be categorized as one of the following:

1. Film costs
2. Participation costs
3. Exploitation costs
4. Manufacturing costs

Film costs. **Film costs** are presented separately on the entity's balance sheet. They consist of direct negative costs, production overhead, and production period interest capitalized in accordance with FAS 34. **Direct negative costs** include costs to acquire the rights to intellectual property (e.g., film rights to books or stage plays, or original screenplays); the cost of adaptation or development of the property; compensation of the cast, directors, producers, extras, and other staff members; costs of set construction and operations, wardrobe and accessories; costs of sound synchronization; on-location rental facilities; and postproduction costs such as music, special effects, and editing. **Production overhead** includes allocation of costs of individuals or departments with exclusive or significant responsibility for the production of films. However, production overhead does not include general and administrative expenses, the costs of certain **overall deals,** or charges for losses on properties sold or abandoned. If the entity presents a classified balance sheet, unamortized film costs are presented as a noncurrent asset. The amortization of film costs is explained later in this section.

Participation costs. Participation costs are contingent compensation paid to creative talent such as actors or writers, or to entities from whom the distribution rights are licensed, such as the publisher of a novel on which a screenplay is based (these recipients are referred to as participants). The costs are computed (accrued) based on contractual formulas (participations) and by contingent amounts due under provisions of collectively bargained union agreements (residuals). The accrual of these costs is discussed later in this section.

Exploitation costs. Exploitation costs are the direct costs associated with the film's distribution. The advertising cost component of exploitation costs is accounted for in accordance with SOP 93-7 which is discussed in Chapter 9. All other exploitation costs, including marketing costs, publicity, promotion, and other distribution expenses, are expensed as incurred.

Manufacturing costs. The cost of making theatrical **film prints** is charged to expense over the period benefited. The cost of manufacturing and/or duplication of products to be held for sale such as videocassettes and digital video discs is charged to expense on a unit-specific basis when the related product revenue is recognized. Unsold inventories are to be evaluated at each balance sheet date, for net realizable value and obsolescence.

Costs and Expenses—Amortization of Film Costs and Accrual of Participation Costs

Amortization of capitalized film costs and accrual (expensing) of participation costs commences when the film is released and the entity begins to recognize revenue from the film. The method used to compute the amortization of film costs and the accrual of participation costs is called the **individual-film-forecast-computation method**. This method amortizes film costs using the following formula:

$$\frac{\text{Current period actual revenue}}{\text{Estimated remaining unrecognized ultimate revenue as of the beginning of the fiscal year}} \times \text{Unamortized film costs at the beginning of the fiscal year} = \text{Film cost amortization for the fiscal year}$$

Similarly, participation costs are accrued and expensed using the following formula:

$$\frac{\text{Current period actual revenue}}{\text{Estimated remaining unrecognized ultimate revenue as of the beginning of the fiscal year}} \times \text{Unaccrued ultimate participation costs at the beginning of the fiscal year} = \text{Amount of participation costs to be accrued (expensed) for the fiscal year}$$

Irrespective of the above calculation, participation costs are subject to special rules. The liability is only accrued if it is probable that there will be a sacrifice of assets to settle the entity's obligation under the participation agreement. In addition, at each balance sheet date, accrued participation costs must at least equal the amounts that the entity is obligated to pay at that date.

Using this formulaic approach, if the actual results from the exploitation of the film are realized as originally estimated, the entity would earn a constant rate of profit over the ultimate period for each film before considering exploitation costs, manufacturing costs and other period costs.

It is, of course, likely that the actual results will vary from the estimates and that the estimates will require review and refinement. At each reporting date, the entity reviews and revises estimates of ultimate revenue and ultimate participation costs to reflect the most current information available to it. As a result of this review, the denominator is revised to include only the remaining ultimate revenue at the beginning of the fiscal year of change. In this way, these changes in estimate are accounted for prospectively as of the beginning of the fiscal year of the change. The numerator is unaffected by the change since it is based on actual results. The entity uses this revised denominator in the fraction applied to the net unamortized film costs and to the film's unaccrued ultimate participation costs. The difference between expenses determined using the new estimates and any amounts previously recorded as expense during that fiscal year are charged (or credited) to the income statement in the period (e.g., quarter) during which the estimates are revised.

Ultimate revenue. In general, ultimate revenue to be included in the denominator of the fraction includes estimates of revenue to be recognized by the entity from the exploitation, exhibition, and sale of a film in all markets and territories. There are, however, certain limitations that apply to the determination of ultimate revenue.

1. The period over which ultimate revenue for a film may be estimated is limited to ten years following the date of the film's initial release.
2. For previously released films acquired as part of a film library, the period over which ultimate revenue may be estimated is limited to twenty years from the date of acquisition of the library. A film must have been initially released at least three years prior to the acquisition date of the film library in order to be categorized as part of the library for the purposes of applying this limitation.
3. Ultimate revenue includes estimates of revenue for a market or territory only if persuasive evidence exists that the revenue will be earned, or if an entity can demonstrate a history of earning revenue in that market or territory. Ultimate revenue includes estimates of revenue from newly developing territories only if an existing arrangement provides persuasive evidence that the entity will realize the revenue.
4. Ultimate revenue includes estimates of revenue from licensing arrangements with third parties to market film-related products only if there is persuasive evidence that the revenue from that arrangement will be earned for that particular film (e.g., a signed contract to receive a nonrefundable minimum guarantee or nonrefundable

advance) or if the entity can demonstrate a history of earning revenue from that form of arrangement.

5. Ultimate revenue includes estimates of the portion of the wholesale or retail revenue from an entity's sale of peripheral items (such as toys and apparel) attributable to the exploitation of themes, characters, or other contents related to a particular film only if the entity can demonstrate a history of earning revenues from that form of exploitation in similar kinds of films. Under this limitation, the amount of revenue to be included in ultimate revenue is an estimate of the amount that would be earned by the entity if rights for such a form of exploitation had been granted under licensing arrangements with third parties. Thus, the entity's estimate of ultimate revenue does not include the entire gross wholesale or retail revenue from the sale of peripheral items, but rather, the amount that it would realize in net license fees from the sales.
6. Ultimate revenue excludes estimates of revenue from unproven or undeveloped technologies.
7. Ultimate revenue excludes estimates of wholesale promotion or advertising reimbursements to be received from third parties. These reimbursements are accounted for as an offset against exploitation costs.
8. Ultimate revenue excludes estimates of amounts related to the sale of film rights for periods after those identified in 1. and 2. above.

With respect to episodic television series, the following rules apply:

1. The period over which ultimate revenue for an episodic television series may be estimated is limited to ten years from the date of delivery of the first episode or, if the series is still in production, five years from the date of delivery of the most recent episode, if later.
2. Ultimate revenue includes estimates of secondary market revenue (revenue from syndication of the series to markets other than the initial market) for produced episodes only if the entity can demonstrate through its experience or industry norms that the number of episodes already produced, plus those for which a firm commitment exists and the entity expects to deliver, can be licensed successfully in the secondary market.
3. Ultimate revenue excludes estimates of amounts related to the sale of rights for periods after those identified in 1. above.

Ultimate revenue is a gross undiscounted amount and does not include amounts representing projections of future inflation. The portion of ultimate revenue that is expected to be received in a foreign currency is valued at current spot rates.

Ultimate participation costs. The estimate of unaccrued ultimate participation costs to be used in the individual-film-forecast-computation method is made using assumptions consistent with the entity's estimates of film costs, exploitation costs, and ultimate revenue subject to the limitations set forth above. If, at any balance sheet date, the recognized participation costs liability exceeds the estimated unpaid ultimate participation costs for an individual film, the excess liability is first applied to reduce unamortized film costs with any remaining excess credited to income. If the entity continues to incur participation costs after the film costs have been fully amortized, the participation costs are accrued and expensed as the related revenues are recognized.

Example of individual film forecast computation method

Paula Pictures incurred film costs and earned revenues from its motion picture, Arachno-Man, as follows:

	Year 1	*Year 2*
1. Film cost, including capitalized interest (FC)	$15,000	
2. End-of-year estimate of ultimate revenue (UR)	36,000	$30,000
3. Remaining ultimate revenue at beginning of year* (RUR)	--	11,000
4. Actual earned revenues for the year (ER)	19,000	5,000
5. End-of-year estimate of ultimate participation costs (UPC)	3,600	3,000
6. Actual participation costs for the year (APC)	1,600	500

* *Revised estimate of ultimate revenue less actual revenue earned from date of release through the beginning of the year.*

The individual film forecast computation method is applied as follows:

Year 1

Film cost amortization:

$$\frac{\$19{,}000 \text{ ER}}{\$36{,}000 \text{ UR}} \times \$15{,}000 \text{ FC} = \$7{,}917 \text{ Film cost amortization}$$

Accrual of participation costs:

$$\frac{\$19{,}000 \text{ ER}}{\$36{,}000 \text{ UR}} \times \$3{,}600 \text{ UPC} = \$1{,}900 \text{ Accrued participation costs}$$

Year 2

Film cost amortization:

$$\frac{\$5{,}000 \text{ ER}}{\$11{,}000 \text{ RUR*}} \times \$7{,}083\text{** Unamortized film costs} = \$3{,}220 \text{ Film cost amortization}$$

* *Computed as Year 2 revised estimate of ultimate revenue of $30,000 less actual revenue recognized in prior year of $19,000.*

** *Computed as film cost of $15,000 less prior amortization expense recognized of $7,917.*

Accrual of participation costs:

$$\frac{\$5{,}000 \text{ ER}}{\$11{,}000 \text{ RUR}} \times \$1{,}100 \text{ Remaining ultimate participation costs***} = \$500$$

*** *Computed as Year 2 revised estimate for ultimate participation costs of $3,000 less the prior year accrued amount of $1,900.*

Valuation of Unamortized Film Costs

Consistent with the rules for recognizing impairment of long-lived assets in FAS 144, the SOP sets forth examples of events or changes in circumstances that indicate that the entity must assess whether the fair value of the film (whether it has been completed or is still in production) is less than the carrying amount of its unamortized film costs.

1. An adverse change in the expected performance of the film prior to its release
2. Actual costs substantially in excess of budgeted costs
3. Substantial delays in completion or release schedules
4. Changes in release plans, such as a reduction in the initial release pattern
5. Insufficient funding or resources to complete the film and to market it effectively
6. Actual performance subsequent to release fails to meet prerelease expectations

Upon making the comparison between the film's fair value and its unamortized costs, any excess of the unamortized costs over the fair value is to be written off as an operating expense on the income statement. Amounts written off may not be subsequently restored.

The fair value of a film is often estimated using a traditional discounted cash flow model. The limits regarding the number of years of revenue to include in the determination of ultimate revenue do not apply to the estimation of future cash flows associated with the film for the purpose of determining the film's fair value. Factors to be considered by management in estimating future cash inflows for a film include

1. The film's performance in prior markets, if previously released
2. The public's perception (the popularity and market appeal) of the film's story, cast, director, or producer
3. Historical results of similar films
4. Historical results of the cast, director, or producer on prior films
5. The running time of the film

In addition to estimating the film's cash inflows, management must estimate future costs to complete the film (if any), future exploitation and participation costs, and other necessary cash outflows necessary to achieve the estimated cash inflows.

When using the traditional discounted cash flow method to estimate fair value, the estimates of future cash inflows and outflows represent management's best estimates of the most likely cash flows. The discount rate used is adjusted to consider the level of risk inherent in investing in a project of this nature.

When using the expected cash flow approach to estimate fair value (which is preferred and encouraged by FAS 144), all possible relevant future cash inflows and outflows are probability-weighted by period and the estimated average for each period used. In employing this method, the discount rate is risk-adjusted as described above only if the probable expected cash flows have not already been risk-adjusted. Guidance for applying these two estimation techniques is contained in CON 7 and illustrated in Chapter 9.

Subsequent events. When evidence of the possible need for a write-down of unamortized film costs arises after the date of the balance sheet but before the entity issues its financial statements, a rebuttable presumption exists that the conditions leading to the write-off existed at the balance sheet date. When this situation arises, whether the film was released before or after the balance sheet date, the entity uses this subsequent evidence to compute the adjustment necessary to record a change in estimate in its financial statements. If management is able to demonstrate that the conditions leading to the write-down did not exist at the balance sheet date, the presumption can be overcome, and the recognition of the effects of the change in estimate can be postponed until the subsequent period. However, full disclosure of the circumstances and amounts is required in the current financial statements.

EMERGING ISSUES TASK FORCE ISSUES SUMMARIES

87-10 Revenue Recognition by Television "Barter" Syndicators

A consensus was reached that revenue from the sale of advertising time acquired from a barter is recognized when the criteria of SOP 00-2 are met and either a noncancelable contract is signed by both parties or the advertising has been aired.

NOT-FOR-PROFIT ORGANIZATIONS

PERSPECTIVE AND ISSUES

Not-for-profit organizations have several characteristics that distinguish them from business enterprises. First, and perhaps foremost, not-for-profit organizations exist to provide goods and services without the objective of generating a profit. Rather than obtaining resources by conducting exchange transactions at a profit or from capital infusions from owners, a not-for-profit organization obtains most resources from others that share its desire to serve a chosen mission—an educational, scientific, charitable, or religious goal. Although not-for-profit organizations can be "owned" or controlled by another, the ownership interest is unlike that of business enterprises because the "owner" cannot remove resources from the entity for personal use or gain; the resources must be used for a mission-related purpose. Examples of not-for-profit organizations are: churches and religious organizations, colleges and universities, healthcare organizations, libraries, museums, performing arts organizations, civic or fraternal organizations, federated fund-raising organizations, professional and trade associations, social clubs, research organizations, cemeteries, arboretums, and zoos.

Specifically excluded from the list of not-for-profit organizations are organizations that exist to provide dividends, lower costs, or other economic benefits directly and proportionately to their members, participants, or owners, such as mutual insurance companies, credit unions, farm or utility cooperatives, and employee benefit plans. Further, some not-for-profit organizations are governmental[3] and are required to follow the standards of the Governmental Accounting Standards Board (GASB). Governmental organizations are outside of the scope of this publication. Readers instead should refer to the Wiley publication, *GAAP for Governments.*

All authoritative pronouncements in the GAAP hierarchy, including EITF consensuses, apply to not-for-profit organizations unless the pronouncement specifically excludes not-for-profit organizations from its scope. Certain authoritative pronouncements apply specifically to not-for-profit organizations. Because those pronouncements are particularly relevant to the transactions of not-for-profit organizations they are discussed in this chapter.

FAS 93, *Recognition of Depreciation by Not-for-Profit Organizations,* issued in 1987, was the first standard issued by the FASB that applied specifically to not-for-profit organizations. It requires not-for-profit organizations to depreciate their long-lived assets and to disclose balances for the major classes of assets, depreciation for the period, accumulated depreciation, and the organization's policy for computing depreciation.

FAS 116, *Accounting for Contributions Received and Contributions Made,* establishes standards for recognition and display of contributions received and contributions made. It requires all contributions received and made to be measured at fair value and recognized in the period the gift is made. It applies to any contribution of assets, including contributions of cash, securities, supplies, long-lived assets, use of facilities or utilities, services, intangible assets, or unconditional promises to give those items in the future.

FAS 117, *Financial Statements of Not-for-Profit Organizations,* establishes standards for the general-purpose financial statements issued by not-for-profit organizations. It defines a complete set of financial statements for most organizations as a statement of financial position, a statement of activities, a statement of cash flows, and accompanying notes. It requires an organization's net assets and its revenues, expenses, gains, and losses to be classified based on the existence or absence of restrictions imposed by donors.

FAS 124, *Accounting for Certain Investments Held by Not-for-Profit Organizations,* establishes standards for investments held by not-for-profit organizations. It requires equity securities with readily determinable fair values and debt securities to be reported at fair value with the resulting holding gains and losses reported in the statement of activities. It also establishes standards for reporting investment return, including losses on donor-restricted endowment funds.

FAS 136, *Transfers of Assets to a Not-for-Profit Organization or Charitable Trust That Raises or Holds Contributions for Others,* establishes standards for transfers of assets to a not-for-profit organization or a charitable trust that raises or holds contributions for others. Although it primarily affects federated fund-raising organizations, community foundations, and institutionally related foundations, all organizations are subject to its standards because they can be the beneficiaries of the contributions raised by those organizations.

---

[3] *See Chapter 1, Researching GAAP Problems, for a definition of "governmental entity."*

The FASB is currently working on a project that will establish standards for accounting and reporting of mergers, acquisitions, and other combinations in which a not-for-profit organization is the acquiring entity. (In order to expedite the finalization of FAS 141 and 142, combinations of mutual enterprises and not-for-profit organizations were excluded from those standards.) FASB expects to issue Exposure Drafts of new standards governing each of these in the second quarter of 2004 with final statements projected to be issued in the second quarter of 2005.

Combinations in which the acquiring entity is a not-for-profit organization, unlike combinations in which the acquiring entity is a business enterprise, cannot be assumed to be an exchange of commensurate value. Acquired not-for-profit organizations lack owners who are focused on receiving a return on and return of their investment. Moreover, the parent or governing body of an acquired organization may place its mission effectiveness ahead of achieving maximum price when negotiating a combination agreement. Thus, when two not-for-profit organizations combine, it will be necessary to determine if there was an exchange of commensurate value (in which case, standards similar to FAS 141 would be applied) or if there is a contribution inherent in the transaction that would be reported in accordance with FAS 116.

If there is a contribution inherent in the transaction, it would be measured as the excess of the net fair values of the identifiable assets acquired and the liabilities assumed over the fair value of the consideration exchanged. If the acquired entity is a business enterprise, the contribution inherent in a combination would be measured as the excess of the fair value of the acquired business enterprise over the cost of that business enterprise. The primary difference is that no goodwill would be recognized in most contributions of not-for-profit organizations, although it would be in the contributions of business entities.

In the rare cases in which the sum of the fair values of the liabilities assumed exceeds the sum of the fair values of the identifiable assets acquired, the acquiring organization would initially recognize that excess as an unidentifiable intangible asset (goodwill). The proposed standards are discussed in greater detail in Chapter 11.

As part of the combinations project, the FASB is also considering whether not-for-profit organizations should apply FAS 142's impairment standards to the goodwill received in a combination. The FASB decided that if the acquired entity is a business enterprise that will continue to be operated as a business enterprise, FAS 142 would apply. However, if the acquired entity is another not-for-profit organization or is a business enterprise that will be converted to a not-for-profit organization, a two-path method of accounting for goodwill subsequent to acquisition would apply, as follows:

- Reporting units primarily supported by fees or other charges to third parties for goods and services would test goodwill for impairment using the FAS 142 method.
- Reporting units not primarily supported by fees or other charges to third parties would test goodwill for impairment using a trigger-based approach that writes off goodwill in its entirety if certain triggering events occur. At the date of acquisition, the acquiring organization would identify the reasons goodwill arose in the transaction and determine triggering events related to those reasons that would indicate that goodwill is significantly impaired. The FASB intends to include examples to help acquiring organizations identify appropriate triggering events.

Two AICPA AAG provide standards for not-for-profit organizations. *Health Care Organizations* applies to providers of health care services, including hospitals, nursing homes, medical clinics, continuing care retirement communities, health maintenance organizations, home health agencies, and rehabilitation facilities. *Not-for-Profit Organizations* applies to all other nongovernmental not-for-profit organizations. Both Guides discuss the aspects of financial statement preparation and audit particularly relevant to the organizations within their scope. In addition, each provides a helpful listing of all category A GAAP pronouncements and their applicability to not-for-profit organizations.

SOP 94-3, *Reporting of Related Entities by Not-for-Profit Organizations,* establishes standards for consolidation by not-for-profit organizations of investments in for-profit entities and other not-for-profit organizations. It also describes the disclosures required when related entities are not consolidated because the relationship does not meet the criteria of control and economic benefit.

SOP 98-2, *Accounting for Costs of Not-for-Profit Organizations and State and Local Governmental Entities That Include Fund-Raising,* establishes standards for the functional classification of expenses incurred in activities that combine program or management and general components with fund-raising. It requires that all costs of the combined activity be classified as fund-raising expenses unless three criteria—purpose, audience, and content—are met.

SOP 02-2, *Accounting for Derivative Instruments and Hedging Activities by Not-for-Profit Health Care Organizations, and Clarification of the Performance Indicator,* clarifies that the performance indicator required to be reported in the financial statements of a not-for-profit health care organization is analogous to income from continuing operations of a business (for-profit) enterprise.

This chapter contains a highly summarized discussion of accounting and reporting standards for not-for-profit organizations. Readers who desire a more in-depth discussion should refer to the Wiley publication, *Not-for-Profit GAAP.*

Sources of GAAP		
FAS	*AAG*	*SOP*
93, 116, 117, 124, 136	*Not-for-Profit Organizations, Health Care Organizations*	94-3, 98-2, 02-2

DEFINITION OF TERMS

Agent. An entity that acts for and on behalf of another. For example, a not-for-profit organization acts as an agent for and on behalf of a donor if it receives resources from the donor and agrees to transfer the resources or the return generated by investing those resources to another entity named by the donor. Similarly, a not-for-profit organization acts for and on behalf of a beneficiary if it agrees to solicit contributions in the name of the beneficiary and distribute any contributions thereby received to the beneficiary.

Collections. Works of art, historical treasures, or similar assets that meet the following three criteria: (1) they are held for public exhibition, education, or research in service to the public rather than for financial gain; (2) they are protected, kept unencumbered, cared for, and preserved; and (3) they are subject to a policy that requires that the organization use the proceeds from the sale of an item to acquire another item for the collection.

Contribution. A voluntary and unconditional transfer of assets to an entity (the donee) from another entity that does not expect to receive equivalent value in exchange and does not act as an owner (the donor). A contribution can also take the form of a settlement or cancellation of the donee's liabilities.

Donor-imposed restriction. A donor stipulation that specifies a use for contributed resources that is narrower than the limitations that result from the nature of the organization, the environment in which it operates, and the purposes specified in its articles of incorporation, bylaws, or similar documents. A restriction may be temporary or permanent. A **temporary restriction** is a restriction that will expire (be satisfied) either by an action of the organization (such as spending the resources for the purpose described by the donor) or by the passage of time. A **permanent restriction** never expires. Instead, it requires that the contributed resources be maintained permanently, although it allows the organization to spend the income or to use the other economic benefits generated by those resources.

Donor-imposed condition. A donor stipulation that specifies a future and uncertain event whose occurrence (or failure to occur) gives the donor the right of return of resources it has transferred or releases the donor from the obligation to transfer assets in the future. For example, "I will contribute one dollar for each dollar raised during the month of July in excess of $10,000," includes a donor-imposed condition. If only $9,000 is raised, the donor has no obligation to transfer assets.

Endowment fund. A fund of cash, securities, or other assets held to provide income for the support of a not-for-profit organization. A **donor-restricted endowment fund** is a fund established by a donor that specifies that the gift must be invested permanently to generate support (a permanent endowment fund) or invested for a specified period of time (a term endowment fund). A **quasi endowment fund** is a fund established by an organization's governing board to provide income for a long, but usually unspecified, period of time. A quasi endowment fund may be created from unrestricted resources or from resources that are for a restricted purpose but not required by the donor to be invested.

Intermediary. An organization that acts as a facilitator for the transfer of resources between two or more other parties. An intermediary generally does not take possession of the assets transferred.

Net assets. The residual interest in the assets of a not-for-profit organization that remains after deducting its liabilities. Net assets are divided into three categories—permanently restricted, temporarily restricted, and unrestricted—based on the nature and existence (or absence) of donor-imposed restrictions. **Permanently restricted net assets** are the portion of net assets that result from contributions and other inflows of resources that are subject to permanent donor-imposed restrictions. Permanently restricted net assets are not permitted to be expended or used up. **Temporarily restricted net assets** are the portion of net assets that result from contributions and other inflows of resources that are subject to temporary donor-imposed restrictions. They are permitted to be expended or used up as long as their use is consistent with the limitations imposed by the donor. **Unrestricted net assets** are the portion of net assets that are neither permanently nor temporarily restricted by donors. The use of unrestricted net assets is subject only to the limitations imposed by the nature of the organization, its articles of incorporation or bylaws, and the environment in which it operates.

Promise to give. A written or oral agreement to contribute resources to another entity at a future date. A promise to give can be either conditional or unconditional. The obligation of the donor who makes a **conditional promise to give** is dependant on the occurrence (or failure to occur) of a donor-imposed condition. An **unconditional promise to give** depends only on the passage of time or demand by the donee for payment of the promised assets.

Trustee. An entity that holds and manages assets for the benefit of a specified beneficiary in accordance with a charitable trust agreement.

Voluntary health and welfare organization. An organization formed for the purpose of attempting to prevent or solve health and welfare problems of society, and in many cases, of particular individuals.

CONCEPTS, RULES, AND EXAMPLES

Complete Set of Financial Statements

Financial statements are intended to help donors, creditors, and others who provide resources to a not-for-profit organization assess the services provided by the not-for-profit organization and its ability to continue to provide those services. The statements should also help them assess whether management has properly discharged its stewardship responsibilities and whether it has performed satisfactorily in its other management duties.

FAS 117, *Financial Statements of Not-for-Profit Organizations,* requires all not-for-profit organizations to present a statement of financial position, a statement of activities, a statement of cash flows, and notes to the financial statements any time it purports to present a complete set of financial statements. In addition, voluntary health and welfare organizations are required to present a statement of functional expenses as an additional basic financial statement. In most ways, the content and format of those financial statements are similar to the financial statements prepared by business enterprises.

However, three major differences between not-for-profit organizations and business enterprises cause differences in the content and format of financial statements of not-for-profit organizations. First, there is no profit motive in the nonprofit sector, and thus no single indicator of performance comparable to a business enterprise's net income or bottom line. In fact, the best indicators of the performance of a not-for-profit organization are generally not measurable in dollar amounts but rather in the reader's qualitative judgment about the effectiveness of the organization in achieving its mission. Nevertheless, dollars are the language of financial reporting. Information to help assess performance is provided in financial statements (1) by reporting revenues and expenses gross rather than net and (2) by classifying expenses based on the mission-related programs and supporting activities they sustain, rather than by their natural classifications (salaries, utilities, depreciation, etc.).

Second, because the bottom line of a not-for-profit organization's statement of activities is not a performance measure, but simply a change in net assets for the reporting period, there is no need for not-for-profit organizations to distinguish between components of comprehensive income as business enterprises do. All revenues, expenses, gains, and losses are reported in a single statement rather than being divided between an income statement and a statement of other comprehensive income.

Third, not-for-profit organizations receive contributions, a type of transaction that is without counterpart in business enterprises. Those contributions often are subject to donor-imposed restrictions which can affect the types and levels of service that a not-for-profit organization can offer. Because donor-imposed restrictions are prevalent, recurring, and, in some cases, permanent, financial reporting by not-for-profit organizations needs to reflect the nature and extent of donor-imposed restrictions and changes in them that occur during the reporting period.

Net Assets and Changes in Net Assets

The nature and extent of donor-imposed restrictions are reported in the statement of financial position by distinguishing between the portions of net assets that are permanently restricted, temporarily restricted, and unrestricted. Separate line items on the face of that statement or details in the notes to the financial statements are used to meet the requirement to disclose the amounts for different types of permanent and temporary restrictions.

Changes in donor-imposed restrictions are reported in the statement of activities. The organization's revenues, expenses, gains, and losses for the period are classified into the three classes of net assets so that the statement of activities reports amounts for the change in permanently restricted net assets, the change in temporarily restricted net assets, and the change in unrestricted net assets, as well as the change in net assets in total. Transactions and events that do not change the net assets of the organization as a whole, but only their classification, are reported separately as reclassifications. Reclassifications are events that simultaneously increase one class of net assets and decrease another. For example, unrestricted net assets increase and temporarily restricted net assets decrease when the purchase of a long-lived asset fulfills a donor-imposed restriction to acquire long-lived assets with the gift (sometimes referred to as a release of restrictions).

Not-for-profit organizations often use fund accounting as a tool for tracking compliance with donor-imposed restrictions and internal designations. Fund accounting is a system of recording resources whose use is limited either by donors, granting agencies, governing boards, law, or legal covenants. A separate fund (a self-balancing group of accounts composed of assets, liabilities, and net assets) is maintained for each purpose limitation. For external reporting, a fund may be classified entirely in one net asset class or it may need to be allocated among two or three classes. (For an example of the allocations necessary to restate a fund balance to net asset classes, see the discussion of endowment funds in "Investments" in this section.)

Reporting Revenues

Revenues are reported in the statement of activities as increases in unrestricted net assets unless the use of the resources received is subject to a donor-imposed restriction. Thus, contribution revenues increase unrestricted net assets, temporarily restricted net assets, or permanently restricted net assets, depending on the existence and nature of donors' restrictions. Revenues from most exchange transactions (such as sales of goods or services) are classified as unrestricted.

Revenues from exchange transactions only increase restricted net asset classes if a preexisting donor-imposed restriction limits the use of the resources received. For example, if a donor contributes a car to the local library and requires that the proceeds from the sale of the car be used to purchase children's books, the proceeds from the sale of the car (an exchange transaction) increase temporarily restricted net assets. Investment income and gains (which are also exchange transactions) increase unrestricted net assets unless a donor required that the gift be invested and the investment return used for a restricted purpose. For example, assume a donor contributes securities worth $85,000 to a zoo, requires that all dividends and gains be retained and reinvested until the accumulated value is $100,000, and states that the $100,000 must be maintained as a permanent endowment fund, the income of which is to be used for the purchase of animals. In the early years of the endowment, before the accumulated value reaches $100,000, investment income and gains increase permanently restricted net assets. Investment income and gains earned after the accumulated value of the fund reaches $100,000 increase temporarily restricted net assets with the restriction expiring upon use of those funds to purchase animals.

FAS 116, *Accounting for Contributions Received and Contributions Made*, requires contributions to be recognized as revenue at the time of the gift and measured at the fair value of the contributed assets regardless of the form of the assets contributed. Donor-imposed restrictions do not change the timing of recognition of a contribution. Donor-imposed restrictions, or the absence of them, affect only a contribution's classification as an increase in permanently restricted net assets, temporarily restricted net assets, or unrestricted net assets. Donor-imposed conditions, however, affect the timing of recognition. Because a contribution is an unconditional transfer, a transfer of assets subject to donor-imposed conditions is not a contribution yet, although it may become one at a future date. Conditional transfers are not recognized as contribution revenues until the conditions are substantially met. Thus, the distinction between donor-imposed restrictions and donor-imposed conditions is very important to the timing of recognition. If a donor's stipulations do not clearly state whether a gift depends on meeting a stated stipulation and the ambiguity cannot be resolved by communicating with the donor or by examining the circumstances surrounding the gift, a transfer is presumed to be conditional.

Unconditional promises to give cash or other assets are recognized in financial statements when the promise is made and received, provided that there is sufficient evidence in the form of verifiable documentation (written, audio, or video). If payments of the promises are due in future periods, the promise has an implied time restriction that expires on the date the payment is due. Thus, unless circumstances surrounding the receipt of the promise indicate that the donor intended the gift to support the current period's activities, unconditional promises increase temporarily restricted net assets. The present value of estimated future cash flows is used to measure unconditional promises to give, although short-term promises (due in less than one year) may be reported at net realizable value. Conditional promises are not recognized as revenue until the conditions are substantially met; however, they are required to be disclosed in notes to the financial statements.

In a manner similar to recognizing promises to give, a beneficiary recognizes contributions held on its behalf by an agent, trustee, or intermediary. For example, if the assets held by the agent were transferred subject to a condition that is not yet met, the beneficiary does not recognize its potential rights to the assets held by the agent. If a beneficiary has an unconditional right to receive cash flows from a charitable trust or other pool of assets, the beneficiary recognizes its rights when the beneficial interest is created and measures the rights using the present value of the estimated expected cash flows. However, if the beneficiary and the agent, trustee, or intermediary are financially interrelated organizations, the beneficiary reports its rights to the assets held using a method similar to the equity method of accounting for investments. (For further discussion, see "Transfers received as an agent, trustee, or intermediary" in this section.)

The value of volunteer services received by the organization is recognized in certain circumstances. Contributed services that create or improve a nonfinancial asset (such as building a shed or replacing a roof) are recognized as revenue as contributions either by valuing the hours of service received or by measuring the change in the fair value of the nonfinancial asset created or improved. Other contributed services are recognized only if they meet all three of the following criteria: (1) they require specialized skills, (2) they are provided by persons possessing those skills, and (3) they would typically need to be purchased if not provided by donation. If volunteer services neither meet those three criteria nor create or improve nonfinancial assets, they cannot be recognized in the organization's financial statements. However, organizations are required to describe the programs or activities for which contributed services are used, the nature and extent of services received for the period (regardless of whether those services are recognized), and disclose the amount recognized as revenues.

An organization that maintains works of art, historical treasures, and similar assets in collections, as defined, does not recognize gifts of items that are added to its collections unless it also capitalizes its collections. However, gifts that are not added to collections or items given to organizations that do not maintain collections in accordance with the definition are recognized as revenues and measured at the fair value of the assets received.

Reporting Expenses

Expenses are recognized in the statement of activities as decreases in unrestricted net assets. Financing an expense with donor-restricted resources does not make the expense restricted; instead, it releases the restriction on the restricted resources, causing a reclassification to be reported in the statement of activities.

Expenses must be reported by functional classifications either on the face of the statement of activities or in the notes to the financial statements. The functional classifications describe the major classes of program services and supporting activities of an organization. Program services are the mission-related activities of the organization that result in goods and services being distributed to clients, customers, or members. They are the activities that are the major purpose of and the major output of the organization. For example, a not-for-profit organization with the mission of enhancing the lives of the community's senior citizens might have senior center, home visits, transportation services, and home maintenance as its program expense classifications. Supporting activities are all activities of a not-for-profit organization other than program services. Fund raising expenses and management and general are two common supporting activity classifications.

FAS 117 encourages, but does not require, most not-for-profit organizations to provide an analysis of expenses by natural classification. Information about expenses by natural classifications (salaries, benefits, rent, depreciation, and so forth) can help readers of the financial statements understand the mix of fixed and discretionary costs incurred by the organization. Only voluntary health and welfare organizations are required to report information about expenses by both functional and natural classification. Those organizations must provide that information in a matrix format in a statement of functional expenses.

FAS 93, *Recognition of Depreciation by Not-for-Profit Organizations,* requires the depreciation of land, buildings, and equipment used by not-for-profit organizations. An exception to that requirement is provided for certain works of art, historical treasures, and similar assets. If a not-for-profit organization can demonstrate both (1) that an asset individually has cultural, historical, or aesthetic value worth maintaining in perpetuity and (2) that the organization has the ability to protect and preserve that value essentially undiminished and is doing so, depreciation need not be recognized. Depreciation expense is a natural expense classification that must be allocated to programs and supporting activities in reporting expenses by functional classification.

Transfers Received as an Agent, Trustee, or Intermediary

FAS 136, *Transfers of Assets to a Not-for-Profit Organization or Charitable Trust That Raises or Holds Contributions for Others,* establishes standards for transactions in which a donor makes a contribution by using an agent, trustee, or intermediary. (Agents, trustees, and intermediaries are referred to as recipient organizations.) The donor transfers assets to the recipient organization. The recipient organization accepts the assets from the donor and agrees to use the assets on behalf of or transfer the assets, their investment return, or both to another entity—the beneficiary—named by the donor. FAS 136 also establishes standards for transactions that take place in a similar manner but are not contributions because the transactions are revocable, repayable, or reciprocal. FAS 136 does not set standards for recipient organizations that are trustees.

In general, a recipient organization reports a liability if it accepts assets from a donor and agrees to use those assets on behalf of or transfer those assets to another organization or individual specified by the donor. When it subsequently spends the assets on behalf of the beneficiary or transfers the assets, their return, or both to the beneficiary, the nonprofit organization reduces the liability it recorded earlier. If the assets received from the donor are donated materials, supplies, or other nonfinancial assets, the recipient organization may choose either to (1) report the receipt of the assets as liability to the beneficiary concurrent with recognition of the assets received or (2) not to report the transaction at all. The choice is an accounting policy that must be applied consistently from period to period and disclosed in the notes to the financial statements.

If the donor explicitly grants the recipient organization variance power, the recipient organization, rather than the beneficiary, recognizes contribution revenue. Variance power is the unilateral power to direct the transferred assets to an entity other than the specified beneficiary. Unilateral power means that the recipient organization does not have to contact the donor, the beneficiary, or any other interested party in order to substitute a different beneficiary. Variance power must be granted by the instrument transferring the assets.

If the recipient organization and the specified beneficiary are financially interrelated organizations, the recipient organization reports contribution revenue and the specified beneficiary recognizes its interest in the net assets of the recipient organization using a method similar to the equity method of accounting for investments in common stock. Organizations are financially interrelated if the relationship between them has both of the following characteristics: (1) one organization has the ability to influence the operating and financial decisions of the other and (2) one organization has an ongoing economic interest in the net assets of the other. The ability to influence the operating and financial decisions of the other can be demonstrated in several ways: (1) the organizations are affiliates as defined in FAS 57, *Related-Party Disclosures*, (2) one organization has considerable representation on the governing board of the other, (3) the charter or bylaws of one organization limit its activities to those that are beneficial to the other, or (4) an agreement between the organizations allows one organization to actively participate in the policymaking processes of the other. An ongoing economic interest in the net assets of another is a residual right to the other organization's net assets that results from an ongoing relationship. A common example of financially interrelated organizations is a foundation that exists to raise, hold, and invest assets for a specific beneficiary that it supports.

In addition to establishing standards for contributions transferred to beneficiaries via agents, trustees, and intermediaries, FAS 136 sets standards for transfers that take place in a similar manner but are not contributions because the terms of the transfer or the relationships between the parties make the transfer revocable, repayable, or reciprocal. Transfers are recognized by the recipient organization as liabilities if one or more of the following situations are present: (1) the transfer is subject to the transferor's right to redirect the transferred assets to another beneficiary, (2) the transfer is accompanied by the transferor's conditional promise to give, (3) the transferor controls the recipient organization and specifies an unaffiliated beneficiary, or (4) the transferor specifies itself or its affiliate as the beneficiary of a transfer that is not an equity transaction. An equity transaction is a transfer that has all of the following terms: (1) the transferor specifies itself or its affiliate as beneficiary, (2) the transferor and the recipient organization are financially interrelated organizations, and (3) neither the transferor nor its affiliate expects payment of the transferred assets (although payment of investment return is allowable). Equity transactions are reported by the recipient organization as a separate line item in the statement of activities.

Investments and Endowment Funds

FAS 124, *Accounting for Certain Investments Held by Not-for-Profit Organizations,* requires investments in equity securities with readily determinable fair values and all debt securities to be reported at fair value. Although the standard applies to the same securities that FAS 115 covers for business enterprises, accounting for the resulting gains and losses is different than specified by that standard. Gains and losses (both realized and unrealized) are reported in a not-for-profit organization's statement of activities.

The AAG establishes standards for reporting other investments. The appropriate standards to apply depend on whether the not-for-profit organization is a college or university, a voluntary health and welfare organization, a health care organization, or another type of not-for-profit organization. Most organizations have the option of reporting their other investments at either cost or at the lower of cost or market.

Many of the investments held by not-for-profit organizations are held as the investments of endowment funds. Endowment funds generally are established by gifts from donors who desire to provide support for the organization permanently (a permanently restricted endowment fund) or for a specified period of time (a term endowment fund). In addition, a governing board may determine that certain resources be invested and that only the return generated be spent by the organization. These board-designated amounts are referred to as quasi endowment funds or funds functioning as endowment. The net assets of an endowment fund are classified in accordance with the restrictions placed on the resources by donors, if any. Because a donor can place different restrictions on each source of the net assets (original gift, investment gains and losses, and investment income), each source must be examined separately to achieve the proper classification.

Each source is unrestricted unless its use is temporarily or permanently restricted by the donor or by a law that extends the donor's restriction to the source. Thus, the net assets of an endowment fund created by the governing board from a large unrestricted bequest (or from unrestricted net assets) are classified as unrestricted because no donor was involved in the transaction of creating the endowment fund and all amounts transferred to that fund are free of donor-imposed restrictions.

In contrast, assume that a donor contributes $50,000 to a museum and stipulates that the gift be invested in perpetuity and the investment income be used to purchase works of art. The donor further stipulates that any gains on the investment be added to the original gift and invested in perpetuity. The donor's original gift ($50,000) increases permanently restricted net assets because of the stipulation that the gift be invested in perpetuity. The income earned by the investment of the gift increases temporarily restricted net assets. When works of art are purchased, the restriction on net assets resulting from the income is fulfilled and the net assets are reclassified to unrestricted net assets. The realized and unrealized gains from investment of the gift increase permanently restricted net assets because the donor required that those gains also be reinvested in perpetuity.

In most cases, the classification of the original gift and the investment income is straightforward because donors explicitly state the time and purpose restrictions on them. Classification of gains and losses on the investments is not as clearly determinable unless the donor explicitly states how gains are to be used and whether losses must be restored immediately from other sources, from future gains on the investments, or not at all. However, donors are often silent in their agreements about those matters.

In the absence of explicit donor restrictions, the law in most states provides some direction about the restrictions on investment gains of donor-restricted endowment funds. The Uniform Management of Institutional Funds Act (UMIFA) extends certain donor restrictions to the net appreciation (accumulated net gains) of donor-restricted endowment funds. In states that have adopted UMIFA, net appreciation is expendable unless the donor states otherwise. UMIFA provides that the net appreciation can be spent for the uses and purposes for which the endowment fund was established. Thus, unless the donor specifies otherwise, gains increase unrestricted net assets if the endowment's income is not restricted by the donor, and gains increase temporarily restricted net assets if the endowment's income is temporarily restricted by the donor. Assume in the earlier example of the $50,000 gift to the museum that the donor was silent about the use of gains earned by investing the original gift. In a state that has adopted UMIFA, the accumulated gains on the endowment fund would be restricted to the purchase of artwork because the law requires that the donor's restriction be extended to those gains. The restrictions on those temporarily restricted net assets expire when the museum purchases works of art even if the money to purchase the work of art is not withdrawn from the fund. Thus, this single endowment fund can be composed of permanently restricted net assets (the original $50,000 gift), temporarily restricted net assets (the gains on which restrictions have not yet been met), and unrestricted net assets (the gains on which restrictions have been met).

FAS 124 requires that losses on the investments of an endowment fund reduce temporarily restricted net assets to the extent that temporary restrictions on net appreciation have not yet been met before the loss occurs. The remainder of the loss, if any, reduces unrestricted net assets. If the losses reduce the value of the fund below the level required by the donor or by law, future gains that restore the value to the required level are classified as unrestricted net assets.

Expanding on the previous example, assume that several years after the fund was established, the assets of the fund have increased in value to $65,000. Assume also that the classification of the net assets in the fund is: $50,000 permanently restricted (the original gift), $10,000 temporarily restricted (accumulated gains on which the restrictions have not been met), and $5,000 unrestricted (gains on which the restriction was met by purchasing a work of art with unrestricted funds in years after the inception of the fund). A market correction causes the value of the investments to fall to $58,000. The $7,000 loss decreases temporarily restricted net assets from $10,000 to $3,000. Assume that a further market correction reduces the value of the investments another $9,000 from $58,000 to $49,000. The $9,000 loss reduces temporarily restricted net assets by $3,000 (the amount remaining after the $7,000 loss decreased the original $10,000) and reduces unrestricted net assets by $6,000. After recording the loss, the classification of the $49,000 value of the endowment fund would be: $50,000 permanently restricted (the original gift) and ($1,000) deficit in unrestricted net assets. A not-for-profit organization is required to disclose the amount by which the value of the endowment fund is less than the level required by the donor.

Continuing the example, assume that the next year the value of the investments increases from $49,000 to $53,000. The $4,000 gain increases unrestricted net assets by $1,000 (the restoration of the deficit) and increases temporarily restricted net assets by $3,000. After the gain, the net assets of the endowment fund are $50,000 permanently restricted (the original gift) and $3,000 temporarily restricted for the purchase of works of art.

Collections

Not-for-profit organizations are allowed an exception to the normal requirement to capitalize purchases of property, plant, and equipment. If a not-for-profit organization maintains collections of works of art, historical treasures, or similar assets in the manner defined in FAS 116, it can choose whether it will capitalize and report those collections in its statement of financial position. To qualify for the exception, an organization must (1) hold the items for public exhibition, education, or research in service to the public rather than for financial gain, (2) protect the items, keep them unencumbered, care for them, and preserve them, and (3) use the proceeds from the sale of any items to acquire other items for the collection. If an organization meets those criteria, it can choose one of the following policies: (1) capitalize its collections, (2) capitalize only collection items acquired after the adoption of FAS 116, or (3) not capitalize any collections. An organization cannot selectively choose to capitalize only certain collections.

If an organization does not capitalize its collections, transactions involving collection items must be reported separately on the face of its statement of activities. Similarly, if an organization chose to capitalize its collections prospectively when it adopted FAS 116, it would separately report transactions involving collection items not previously capitalized. Descriptions of the collections, including information about stewardship policies and items deaccessed (removed from the collection), must be included in notes to the financial statements by organizations that do not capitalize their collections or that capitalize them prospectively.

Capitalization is required of works of art, historical treasures, and similar assets that are not collection items, even if those items are held by organizations that regularly maintain collections. Thus, if a museum does not capitalize its collections and it is given a work of art that it does not to add to its collection (perhaps because it duplicates other collection items), the museum would recognize that contribution and report the asset in its statement of financial position as a work of art held for sale.

Split-Interest Agreements

A split-interest agreement is an arrangement in which a donor transfers assets to a not-for-profit organization or to a charitable trust and requires the benefits of ownership of those assets be split among two or more beneficiaries. Charitable gift annuities, annuity trusts, charitable remainder unitrusts, charitable lead trusts, and pooled (or life) income funds are examples of split-interest agreements. The AAG provides standards for reporting the initial gifts that create these funds and the annual adjustments necessary to report them properly. Accounting for split-interest gifts is a complex area; the following discussion is highly summarized and overly simplified.

Not-for-profit organizations are required to report their interests in irrevocable split-interest agreements. If another party, such as a bank, holds the assets, a not-for-profit organization recognizes its interest as a contribution and measures its interest at fair value, usually based on the present value of the cash flows to be received. If the not-for-profit organization holds the assets and is also a beneficiary of the agreement, it reports the fair value of the assets received from the donor as its assets and reports the actuarially computed present value of the payments to be made to other beneficiaries as its liability. The difference between the two amounts is the contribution received by the not-for-profit organization. Each year thereafter, the liability to the beneficiaries is recomputed based on revaluations of the amounts to be paid, the expected lives of the beneficiaries, and other relevant actuarial assumptions.

The net assets resulting from most split-interest agreements are classified as temporarily restricted because they are subject to time restrictions and often purpose restrictions. The net assets are time-restricted either because the distributions are not yet due (when amounts are held by a third party) or because the contribution amount cannot be used by the not-for-profit organization until the death of the beneficiary or some other future specified date. However, the net assets are classified as permanently restricted if the donor has permanently restricted the organization's use of the assets. (For example, the donor requires that the not-for-profit organization use the remaining assets to create a permanent endowment fund at the end of the agreement.) Similarly, if upon the establishment of the agreement the organization can immediately spend the contribution portion without restriction, as is the case for some gift annuities, the net assets would be classified as unrestricted.

Revocable split-interest agreements are not recorded unless the not-for-profit organization holds the assets. Assets received by a not-for-profit organization that acts as trustee under a revocable agreement are recognized as refundable advances at their fair value.

STATEMENTS OF POSITION

94-3 Reporting of Related Entities

SOP 94-3 provides guidance on reporting investments in majority-owned for-profit subsidiaries, investments in common stock in which the not-for-profit organization owns a 50% or less voting interest, and certain relationships with other not-for-profit organizations.

If a not-for-profit organization has a controlling financial interest in a for-profit organization (generally a majority voting interest), it follows the standards in ARB 51, *Consolidated Financial Statements,* as amended by FAS 94, C*onsolidation of All Majority Owned Subsidiaries.* Not-for-profit organizations as defined in FAS 117 are specifically exempted from following the consolidations provisions of FIN 46(R), *Consolidation of Variable Interest Entities.* FIN 46(R) does, however, include an anti-abuse provision that provides that the scope exemption does not apply if the not-for-profit organization is being used by a business enterprise in a manner similar to a variable interest entity in order to circumvent FIN 46(R). Variable interest entities are discussed at length in Chapters 11 and 14.

If a not-for-profit organization has significant influence over the operating and financial policies of the investee (generally owns 20% or more but less than 50% of the voting stock), it either follows the standards in APB 18, *The Equity Method of Accounting for Investments in Common Stock,* or, if permitted by the AAG, reports the investment at fair value.

Different combinations of control and economic interest determine the appropriate accounting for relationships with other not-for-profit organizations, as shown in the following table. Control is defined for purposes of this SOP as the direct or indirect ability to determine the direction of management and policies through ownership, contract, or otherwise. Economic interest is defined for the purposes of this SOP as an interest in another entity that exists if (1) the other entity holds or utilizes significant resources that must be used for the purposes of the reporting organization, either directly or indirectly by producing income or providing services or (2) the reporting organization is responsible for the liabilities of the other entity.

Control?	Economic interest?	Standards
Yes, via ownership of a majority voting interest	Yes	Consolidate.
Yes, via ownership of a majority voting interest	No	Consolidate.
Yes, via majority voting interest in the board of the other entity, as a majority owner	Yes	Consolidate.
Yes, via majority voting interest in the board of the other entity, as a majority owner	No	Consolidation is prohibited, and disclosure required.
Yes, via a contract or an affiliation agreement	Yes	Consolidation is permitted, but not required.
Yes, via a contract or an affiliation agreement	No	Consolidation is prohibited, and disclosure required.
No	Yes	Consolidation is prohibited, and disclosure required.
No	No	Consolidation is prohibited. No disclosure required.

In all cases, consolidation is prohibited if control is likely to be temporary or does not rest with the majority owner. If consolidation is prohibited but consolidated financial statements were presented in accordance with SOP 78-10, *Accounting Principles and Re-*

porting Practices for Certain Nonprofit Organizations (otherwise superseded), organizations may continue to consolidate the other organizations.

Certain disclosures are necessary if consolidated statements are not presented. If consolidated statements are not presented when consolidation is permitted, but not required, the not-for-profit organization must disclose the identity of the other organization, the nature of the relationship, and summarized financial data in addition to the information required by FAS 57, *Related-Party Disclosures*. If consolidation is prohibited, the not-for-profit organization must disclose the information required by FAS 57.

98-2 Accounting for Costs of Activities of Not-for-Profit Organizations and State and Local Governmental Entities That Include Fund-Raising

Many not-for-profit organizations solicit contributions as part of activities that also serve their program or management and general functions. For example, an organization that has a mission of reducing the incidence of cancer might conduct a direct mail campaign and include in an envelope a listing of lifestyle changes that will lessen the risks of cancer and a request for contributions. When a fund-raising activity is conducted in conjunction with an activity that serves a program or other support purpose, the activity is referred to as a joint activity. Users of the financial statements of not-for-profit organizations are particularly interested in the extent to which the organization is able to minimize its fund-raising and management and general costs. Because neither of these types of costs directly benefit the beneficiaries of the organization's programs, successful organizations attempt to minimize them as a percent of the organization's support and revenue. Since the effectiveness of the management of a not-for-profit organization is often judged on operating metrics of this nature, there is a natural incentive to maximize the portion of the costs of these joint activities that is characterized as program expenses.

SOP 98-2 establishes standards for reporting the costs of joint activities. It begins with the presumption that the costs of a joint activity are reportable as fund-raising expenses. To overcome that presumption, three criteria must be met: purpose, audience, and content. If all three of the criteria are met, the costs of a joint activity are to be charged as follows:

- Costs identifiable with a particular function are charged to that function.
- Joint costs are allocated between fund-raising and the appropriate program or management and general function.

Joint costs are the costs of conducting joint activities that are not directly identifiable with a particular component of the activity. Joint costs might include the costs of salaries, professional fees, paper, printing, postage, event advertising, telephones, broadcast airtime, and facility rentals.

Determining whether all three criteria are met is complicated because the purpose and audience criteria have additional tests within them. The purpose test includes a call to action test, a compensation or fees test, a similar scale and same medium test, and an other evidence test. The audience criteria includes a prior donor test, an ability and likelihood to contribute test, and a need to use or reasonable potential for use test. Failure of one of the additional tests often causes the activity to fail the criterion.

If any of the three criteria is not met, all costs of the joint activity must be reported as fund-raising expense. "All costs" includes the costs that would have been considered program or management and general if they had been incurred in a different activity. There is an exception to the rule that all costs are charged to fund-raising expense if one or more of the criteria is not met. The costs of goods or services provided in an exchange transaction (sometimes referred to as a quid pro quo contribution) that is part of the joint activity are charged to cost of goods sold rather than fund-raising expense. For example, the costs of direct donor benefits, such as the value of items sold at a fund-raising auction or meals served at a fund-raising dinner, are not charged to fund-raising expenses.

SOP 98-2 requires that the method used to allocate the joint costs be rational and systematic and that it result in a reasonable allocation of costs. The method selected is to be applied consistently given similar facts and circumstances. No particular method of allocation is required by the SOP, but three allocation methods are illustrated: the physical units method, the relative direct cost method, and the stand-alone joint-cost-allocation method.

Organizations that allocate joint costs are required to disclose the types of activities in which joint costs have been incurred, a statement that the costs have been allocated, and the total amount of joint costs allocated, and the portion of joint costs allocated to each functional expense category. The SOP also encourages disclosure of the amount of joint costs for each type of joint activity.

02-2 Accounting for Derivative Instruments and Hedging Activities by Not-for-Profit Health Care Organizations, and Clarification of the Performance Indicator

The AAG requires that a not-for-profit health care organization include within its statement of activities an intermediate subtotal called a performance indicator. This SOP clarifies that the performance indicator is analogous to income from continuing operations of a business (for-profit) enterprise, and thus would exclude items that are required to be reported in or reclassified from other comprehensive income, extraordinary items, the effect of discontinued operations, the cumulative effect of accounting changes, transactions with owners acting in that capacity, and equity transfers from entities that control the reporting entity, are controlled by the reporting entity, or are under common control with the reporting entity. The performance indicator also excludes restricted contributions, contributions of and reclassification related to gifts of long-lived assets, unrealized gains and losses on investments not restricted by donors or law (except for investments classified as trading), and investment returns restricted by donors.

Health care organizations are required to apply the provisions of FAS 133, *Accounting for Derivative Instruments and Hedging Activities,* in the same manner as business enterprises, including the provisions pertaining to cash flow hedge accounting. The gain or loss items that affect a business enterprise's income from continuing operations similarly affect the not-for-profit health care organization's performance indicator, and the gain or loss items that are excluded from a business enterprise's income from continuing operations (such as items reported in other comprehensive income) are to be excluded from the performance indicator.

Not-for-profit heath care organizations are to provide disclosures similar to those required by paragraphs 45 and 47 of FAS 133. When applying paragraph 47, they are to disclose the activity affecting the amount of accumulated derivative gains or losses that have been excluded from the performance indicator (because they do not report accumulated other comprehensive income).

OIL AND GAS PRODUCERS

PERSPECTIVE AND ISSUES

Oil and gas producing activities are those activities that involve the acquisition of mineral interests in properties, exploration, development, and production of crude oil, including condensate and natural gas liquids, and natural gas. Specialized GAAP does not address refining, marketing, or transportation issues. The successful efforts method of accounting adheres to a traditional historical cost basis. Property acquisition costs, whether the property is proved or unproved, are capitalized as incurred. For other costs incurred under this method, a direct relationship between the costs incurred and specific reserves discovered is required before costs are permitted to be capitalized. Under the successful efforts method, costs that cannot be directly related to the discovery of specific oil and gas reserves are expensed immediately as incurred, analogous to research and development.

The use of the successful efforts method is preferred, but not required by GAAP. An oil and gas producing company is permitted to use, as an alternative to the successful efforts method, a prescribed form of the full cost method permitted by the SEC. All enterprises are required to disclose the method used for accounting for costs incurred and the method of disposition used for capitalized costs. The SEC requires additional disclosures for publicly traded companies.

For an enterprise that uses the full cost method of accounting, assets being depreciated, depleted, or amortized are considered to be in use in the earning activities of the enterprise and, consequently, do not qualify for interest capitalization. However, assets employed in ongoing exploration or development activities but that are not yet engaged in earning activities and not presently being depreciated, depleted or amortized, are subject to interest capitalization.

Exploratory wells or tests that are in progress at the end of the period present unique accounting issues. If, subsequent to the end of the period, but before the financial statements are issued, a well or test is found to be unsuccessful, the incurred costs, less salvage value, are expensed. Retroactively restated financial statements are not permitted.

Sources of GAAP	
FAS	*FIN*
19, 25, 69, 144	33, 36

CONCEPTS, RULES, AND EXAMPLES

The following is a discussion of the recommended treatment of oil and gas activities as per FAS 19. (Note that this treatment is recommended, but not required.)

The costs of the special types of assets used in oil and gas producing activities are capitalized when incurred. Some examples include

1. Mineral interests in properties
   a. Unproved—Properties with no proved reserves
   b. Proved—Properties with proved reserves
2. Wells and related equipment and facilities
3. Support equipment and facilities
4. Uncompleted wells, equipment, and facilities

These costs are amortized as reserves are produced and, along with lifting (production) costs, are classified as costs of production. Periodically, unproved properties are evaluated for impairment. If impaired, a loss is recognized.

Acquisition costs incurred to obtain oil and gas properties through purchase, lease, etc., are capitalized.

Geological and geophysical costs, unproved properties' carrying costs, and the costs of dry hole and bottom hole contributions are expensed. Drilling costs are capitalized until a determination has been made as to the success of the well. If successful, these costs are transferred to uncompleted wells, related equipment, and facilities. The cost of drilling, less residual value, is charged to expense if proved reserves are not found.

Development costs are incurred in order to

1. Get access to and prepare well locations
2. Drill and equip development wells
3. Set up production facilities
4. Provide better recovery systems

These costs are capitalized as uncompleted equipment and facilities until drilling or construction is completed.

The cost of support equipment is capitalized and depreciated. This depreciation, along with other operating costs, is allocated to exploration, development, or production costs, as appropriate.

Production involves different costs ranging from lifting to field storage. These costs, together with depreciation, depletion, and amortization of capitalized acquisition, exploration, and development costs, are part of the cost of the oil and gas produced.

Unproved properties are reclassified to proved properties upon discovery of proved reserves. When proved reserves are found, the costs capitalized as uncompleted wells, equipment, and facilities are reclassified as completed wells, equipment, and facilities. Capitalized costs are amortized or depleted by the unit of production method. Estimated residual values must be considered when determining amortization and depreciation rates.

Any information that becomes available between the end of the period and the date when the financial statements are issued is to be considered in the evaluation of conditions existing at the balance sheet date. With respect to the costs of a company's wells, related equipment, facilities, and the costs of related proved properties, the provisions for impairment as outlined in FAS 144 are applicable.

RECORDING AND MUSIC

PERSPECTIVE AND ISSUES

FAS 50 sets forth accounting and reporting standards for the recording and music industry. In this industry, business is transacted through license agreements, contractual arrangements entered into by an owner (licensor) of a music master or copyright. License agreements are modifications of the compulsory provisions of the copyright law. The licensor grants the licensee the right to sell or distribute recordings or sheet music for a fixed fee paid to the licensor or for a fee based on sales. This section presents the proper accounting by both the licensor and the licensee for license agreements in the recording and music industry.

The industry is currently attempting to adapt its business models for copyright protection, product distribution, and artist compensation to new electronic distribution channels. The new business models that inevitably evolve may require additional accounting guidance.

Sources of GAAP
FAS
50

DEFINITIONS OF TERMS

Advance royalty. An amount paid to music publishers, producers, songwriters, or other artists in advance of their earning royalties from recording or sheet music sales. These amounts are based on contractual terms and are generally nonrefundable.

License agreements. Contractual arrangements entered into by an owner (licensor) of a master or music copyright and a licensee that grant the licensee the right to sell or distribute recordings or sheet music for a fixed fee paid to the licensor or for a fee based on sales.

Minimum guarantee. An amount paid in advance by a licensee to a licensor for the right to sell or distribute recordings or sheet music.

Recording (or record) master. The master tape resulting from the performance of the artist. It is used to produce tapes for use in making cartridges, cassettes, and compact discs.

Royalties. Amounts paid to producers, songwriters, or other artists for their participation in making recordings and to sheet music publishers for their copyright interest in music.

CONCEPTS, RULES, AND EXAMPLES

Accounting by Licensors

Revenues. A license agreement is considered an outright sale when the licensor has

1. Signed a noncancelable contract
2. Agreed to accept a specified fee
3. Transferred the music rights to the licensee, who is able to use them
4. Fulfilled all significant duties owed the licensee

When all of these conditions are met, the earnings process is complete and revenue is recognized if there is reasonable assurance that the license fee is fully collectible.

In some cases the licensee pays a minimum guarantee, which is an amount paid in advance to a licensor for the right to sell or distribute recordings or sheet music. A minimum guarantee is first recorded by the licensor as a liability and then amortized to income as the license fee is earned. If the amount of the fee that is earned is indeterminable, then straight-line recognition of revenue from the guarantee is required over the license period.

Example

A licensor receives a $10,000 minimum guarantee under a five-year license agreement. The entry to record the receipt of cash is

Cash	10,000	
Liability under license agreement		10,000

The licensor recognizes revenue from the guarantee on a straight-line basis. At the end of each year of the license period, the licensor records the following entry:

Liability under license agreement	2,000	
License fees earned (revenue)		2,000

A licensor may charge fees for such items as free recordings beyond a certain number given away by a recording club. The amount of such fees is not determinable when the license agreement is made. Therefore, the licensor can recognize revenue only when the amount can be reasonably estimated or when the license agreement expires.

Cost of artist compensation. Royalties are paid to producers, songwriters, or other artists for their participation in making recordings and to music publishers for their copyright interest in music. Amounts for artists are determined by the terms of personal service contracts negotiated between the artists and media companies and usually are determined based upon a percentage of sales activity and license fee income, adjusted for estimated sales returns. Publishing royalties are generally based on copyright or other applicable laws. Royalties are recorded as a period expense of the licensor.

Advance royalties are amounts paid to music publishers, producers, songwriters, or other artists in advance of their earning royalties. Such royalties are based on contractual terms and are generally nonrefundable. Advance royalties are recorded as assets if the licensor expects that the artist's recording will be successful enough to provide for full recovery of the advance from future royalties due the artist. As royalties are subsequently earned by the artist, the capitalized advance is charged to expense. The advance must be apportioned between current and noncurrent assets according to how soon each portion is expected to be charged to expense. If it later appears that the advance will not be fully recovered from subsequent royalties earned by the artist, then the unrecoverable portion is charged to expense in the period in which the loss becomes apparent.

Cost to produce masters. A master is the media that contains the recording of the artist's performance. The costs of producing a master include (1) the cost of the musical talent (musicians, vocal background, and arrangements); (2) the cost of the technical talent for engineering, directing, and mixing; (3) costs for the use of the equipment to record and produce the master; and (4) studio facility charges. Under the standard type of artist contract, the media company bears a portion of the costs and recovers a portion of the cost from the artist out of designated royalties earned. However, either party may contractually agree to bear all or most of the cost.

The portion of the cost that is paid by the media company is recorded as an asset if the company expects that sales of the artist's recording will be successful enough to provide for full recovery of the accumulated costs. If this is not the case, then these costs are expensed. Any amount capitalized is amortized over the useful life of the recording in a manner that relates the costs to estimated net revenue to be realized. Costs to produce masters that are recoverable from the artist's royalties are treated as advanced royalties by the media company.

Accounting by Licensees

When a licensee pays a minimum guarantee in advance, the guarantee is recorded as an asset and then amortized to expense according to the terms specified in the license agreement. If it later appears that the minimum guarantee is not fully recoverable through use of the rights received under the agreement, then the unrecoverable portion is charged to expense.

Fees for which the amount is indeterminable before the agreement expires are sometimes stipulated in the license agreement. An example is a fee charged to a recording club for free recordings beyond a certain number given away. The licensee must estimate the amount of such fees and accrue them on a license-by-license basis.

REGULATED OPERATIONS

PERSPECTIVE AND ISSUES

Although various businesses are subject to regulatory oversight to greater or lesser degrees, as used in GAAP the term **regulated operations** refers primarily to public utilities, whose ability to set selling prices for the goods or services they offer is constrained by government actions. Generally, the regulatory process has been designed to permit such enterprises to recover the costs they incur, plus a reasonable rate of return to stockholders. However, given the political process of rate-setting by regulatory authorities, and the fact that costs such as those for plant construction escalated greatly during the past decade or so, the ability to recover all costs through rate increases has become less certain. For this and other reasons, specialized GAAP has been promulgated.

Sources of GAAP		
FAS	*FTB*	*EITF*
71, 90, 92, 98, 101, 143, 144	87-2	92-7, 92-12, 93-4, 97-4

CONCEPTS, RULES, AND EXAMPLES

These accounting principles apply to regulated enterprises only if they continue to meet certain criteria, which relate to the intended ability to recover all costs through the rate-setting process. When and if these conditions are no longer met, due to deregulation or a shift to rate-setting which is not based on cost recovery, then application of the specialized GAAP is to terminate.

Asset Recognition

If certain costs are not recognized for current rate-setting purposes, but it is probable that the costs will be recovered through future revenue, then these costs can be capitalized even though a nonregulated enterprise would be required to expense these costs currently. Deferred costs can include an imputed cost of equity capital, if so accounted for rate-setting purposes, even though this would not normally be permitted under GAAP. Thus, the regulatory process can result in the accounting recognition of an asset that would not otherwise be recognized by a commercial enterprise. If at any time it becomes apparent that the incurred cost will not be recovered through generation of future revenue, that cost is to be charged to expense. If a regulator subsequently excludes specific costs from allowable costs, the carrying value of the asset recognized is to be reduced to the extent of the excluded costs. Should the regulator allow recovery of these previously excluded costs or any additional costs, a new asset is to be recognized and classified as if these costs had been initially included in allowable costs.

Imposition of Liabilities

In other situations, the regulatory process can result in the accounting recognition of a liability. This usually occurs when regulators mandate that refunds be paid to customers, which must be accrued when probable and reasonably estimable, per FAS 5, *Accounting for Contingencies*. Furthermore, regulatory rates may be set at a higher level, in order to recover costs expected to be incurred in the future, subject to the caveat that such amounts will be refunded to customers if it later becomes apparent that actual costs incurred were less than expected. In such cases, the incremental rate increase related to recovery of future costs must be accounted for as a liability (unearned revenue), until the condition specified is satisfied. Finally, regulators may stipulate that a gain realized by the utility will be returned to customers over a specified future period; this will be accounted for by accrual of a liability rather than by recognition of the gain for accounting purposes.

Phase-in Plans

Special rules apply to phase-in plans, as defined in FAS 92, *Regulated Enterprises—Accounting for Phase-in Plans*. If a phase-in plan was ordered by regulators for a plant that had been substantially constructed before 1988, then all allowable costs which are deferred for regulatory purposes, subject to the phase-in plan, are also deferred for financial reporting purposes. However, imputed cost of capital permitted by regulators (in effect, interest on the deferred costs) cannot be capitalized for financial reporting. Specific criteria must be met in order to utilize phase-in accounting, and the method cannot be employed for plants not constructed until after 1987.

Abandonment

Accounting for abandonments is also stipulated for regulated enterprises. If an abandonment occurs or becomes probable, any costs which are probable of not being recovered are required to be written off as a loss. Furthermore, if the return on the investment that will be recoverable will not be equal to the normal rate of return, then an additional loss accrual must be recognized currently. This loss is measured by the difference between the projected future revenues, discounted at the enterprise's incremental borrowing rate, and the remaining costs to be recovered. The amount of loss to be recognized obviously depends on the enterprise's estimate of time to elapse until rate increases are effective, and the length of time over which the increases will remain in effect. These estimates may change over time, and the effect of revisions in the estimate will be reflected in earnings in the periods the new estimates are made.

The carrying value of the costs of an abandoned plant is increased during the period from the abandonment until recovery occurs through rate increases as promised by the regulatory authorities. If full return of investment is anticipated, the cost of abandoned assets is accreted at the rate (the enterprise's overall cost of capital) permitted for rate-setting purposes. If partial or no return on investment is expected, the asset value is accreted at the same rate that was used to compute the loss accrual, which is the enterprise's incremental borrowing rate. During the recovery period, the costs of the abandoned plant are amortized. If full return on investment is expected, this amortization is to be computed on the same basis as is permitted for rate-setting purposes. If partial or no return is expected, amortization is recognized in amounts that provide a constant rate of return on the unamortized balance of the investment in the costs of the abandoned plant.

Deferred Income Taxes

Deferred taxes must be provided consistent with FAS 109. There are no exemptions or special provisions for income tax accounting for regulated enterprises. Assets or liabilities related to future rate increases or decreases are temporary differences within the meaning of FAS 109.

Accounting for Liabilities Related to Asset Retirement Obligations

Historically, and particularly since the advent of nuclear energy generation, public utilities have faced the problem of accounting for costs which are expected to be incurred attendant upon the retirement from service of the generating facilities. Environmental and other laws and regulations typically mean that very substantial costs have to be borne, in order to dispose of waste, restore the land (not merely the power generating facility site, but, in the case of coal-fired plants, restoration of the strip mining locations) and ameliorate other problems. In 1994 FASB began to consider whether the projected costs of decommissioning nuclear power plants should be accrued or otherwise recognized as expense over the period of use of the plant. Ultimately, the project was expanded to address all asset retirement obligations, and a standard, FAS 143, *Asset Retirement Obligations,* was finally issued in 2001.

Chapter 9 presents a detailed examination of FAS 143, and that discussion is not duplicated here. In brief, however, this pronouncement establishes standards for measuring the future cost to retire an asset and recognizing it in the financial statements as a liability and correspondingly, as part of the depreciable cost of the asset. FAS 143 applies to legal obligations associated with the retirement of tangible long-lived assets that result from their acquisition, construction, development and/or normal operation. It does not apply to situations where moral suasion is to be applied to encourage cleanup efforts, even if the reporting entity has a history of making such voluntary gestures. However, the principle of "promissory estoppel" does create legal obligations even absent contractual or statutory requirements, in some cases.

If costs, such as those related to nuclear decommissioning, are legal obligations, the present value of the future expenditures is recognized as an added cost of the asset, and as a liability, at acquisition. Further cost accretion is required due to the passage of time. Depreciation charges are based on the recorded cost of the asset, including the estimated future retirement costs. Changes in estimates, which are inevitable, are handled differently if increases versus decreases, as described in Chapter 9.

Accounting for Asset Impairments

While not unique to regulated industries (public utilities, in particular), the issue of asset impairment will often be dealt with in these operations, due to the large investment in very long-lived fixed assets and the potential impact of changes in technology over time. FAS 144 addresses this issue. Briefly, under defined conditions, assets must be reviewed to determine whether their carrying value will be fully recovered from future cash flows from using and disposing of them. If the future estimate of cash flows over the asset's (or group of assets') remaining estimated useful life, undiscounted, is less than the carrying value, the asset is considered impaired, and the carrying value is reduced to the fair value of the asset with the impairment loss being charged to expense in the current period. Typically, a projected cash flows approach is used in estimating value, although in some instances a more direct approach, relying on market prices, might be usable. FAS 144 is discussed in detail in Chapter 9.

Accounting for Deregulation and "Stranded Costs"

In recent years the utilities industries have been undergoing vast changes in the regulatory environment. The wholesale electricity markets were essentially deregulated in 1996, and the apparent governmental intent is to fully deregulate public utilities within the next several years. This will have significant effects on the financial reporting of many of the entities operating in these industries, since under GAAP many had recognized regulatory assets and regulatory liabilities which will no longer be recognizable once full deregulation occurs. Also, certain costs may no longer be recoverable in a deregulated environment, transforming certain assets into "stranded costs."

A consensus in EITF 97-4 has addressed the matter of deregulation. When deregulation legislation has been enacted affecting all or a portion of the entity's operations, it is to cease applying FAS 71 to the affected operations. In cases in which the effects of deregulation are imposed by means of a rate order, such an order would have to be sufficiently detailed so that the entity would be able to determine how it will be affected. Regulatory assets would not, however, be immediately written off; instead, an evaluation of regulatory cash flows would be conducted to determine whether an impairment had occurred and to determine whether the portion of the business from which the regulatory cash flows are derived is still subject to FAS 71. Only if the asset is impaired (applying FAS 144 criteria) or if FAS 71 is no longer applicable would the asset be written off before being recovered. Similarly, regulatory liabilities would not be reclassified into income until the obligation is eliminated by the regulatory authority.

A related concern is whether the new regulatory assets or liabilities must be given recognition to reflect expenses and obligations that will arise from the portion of the business being deregulated. The same "source of cash flow" type of analysis noted above is to be applied to make these determinations. Thus, a cost or obligation is recognized as a regulatory asset or liability, respectively, once it is expensed or incurred after FAS 101 is applied to that portion of the operations, if it has been designated for recovery or settlement, respectively, via regulated cash flows.

EMERGING ISSUES TASK FORCE ISSUES SUMMARIES

91-6 Revenue Recognition of Long-Term Power Sales Contracts

A consensus was reached that Nonutility Generators (NUG) are to recognize the lesser of (1) the amount billable under the contract or (2) a formula-based pricing arrangement, as revenue. The formula-based pricing arrangement is determined by the kilowatt-hours (kwhs) made available during the period multiplied by the estimated average revenue per kwh over the term of the contract for the fixed or scheduled price period of the contract. Revenue is not to be recognized utilizing the formula-based pricing arrangement if its only purpose is to establish liquidating damages. Additionally, a receivable arises when the amounts billed are less than the amount computed pursuant to the formula-based pricing arrangement and if the contract requires a payment, probable of recovery, to the NUG at the end of the contract term.

92-7 Accounting for Rate-Regulated Utilities for the Effects of Certain Alternative Revenue Programs

A consensus was reached regarding the treatment of additional revenues of rate-regulated utility companies that are to be billed in the future under alternative revenue programs. The EITF abstract identifies two types of alternative revenue programs, defined as Type A and Type B. The revenues from alternative revenue programs are to be recognized when the events permitting billing of the revenues have occurred and three specific criteria that are discussed in the abstract are met.

The Task Force also notes that rate-regulated utilities recognizing revenues from an alternative revenue program that do not meet the conditions of this consensus must amend the plan or change the program to meet the conditions.

92-12 Accounting for OPEB Costs by Rate-Regulated Enterprises

If the regulator includes other postemployment benefits, (OPEB), costs in rates on a pay-as-you-go basis, the regulatory asset relating to the cost under FAS 106 is not to be recognized. The Task Force also reached a consensus that the regulatory asset for a rate-regulated enterprise is to recognize the difference between FAS 106 costs and the OPEB costs if future revenue will at least offset the deferred cost and meet four specific criteria. The four specific criteria are discussed in detail in the EITF Consensus.

93-4 Accounting for Regulatory Assets

The Task Force reached a consensus that a rate-regulated enterprise that fails to initially meet the asset recognition criteria can recognize a regulatory asset for other postemployment benefits costs in a future period when applicable criteria are met. This consensus applies also to all regulatory assets recognized pursuant to FAS 71 criteria.

Additionally, the Task Force noted that the carrying amount of the regulatory asset to be recognized is to be reduced by any impairment that may have occurred.

96-17 Revenue Recognition under Long-Term Power Sales Contracts That Contain Both Fixed and Variable Pricing Terms

This pronouncement extends the consensus of EITF 91-6. Fixed price arrangements are to be handled in accordance with EITF 91-6. Variable price arrangements in which the rate is at least equal to expected costs are to recognize revenue as billed, in accordance with the provisions of the contract for that variable price period. A long-term power sales contract is to be reviewed periodically to determine whether it is a loss contract, in which case the loss is to be recognized immediately. Finally, the Task Force observed that any premium related to a contractual rate in excess of the current market rate is to be amortized over the remaining portion of the contract for long-term power sales contracts acquired in a purchase business combination.

TITLE PLANT

PERSPECTIVE AND ISSUES

FAS 61, *Accounting for Title Plant,* presents accounting and reporting standards for costs relating to the construction and operation of title plants. A title plant comprises a record of all transactions or conditions that affect titles to land located in a specified area. The length of time spanned by a title plant depends upon regulatory requirements and the time frame required to gather sufficient information to efficiently issue title insurance. Updating occurs frequently as documentation of the current status of a title is added to the title plant.

This pronouncement applies to enterprises such as title insurance companies, title abstract companies, and title agents that use a title plant in their operations. The standard provides that costs directly incurred to construct a title plant are to be capitalized when the entity can use the title plant to do title searches and that such capitalized costs are not normally depreciated. The statement also requires that the costs of maintaining a title plant and of doing title searches be expensed as incurred.

Sources of GAAP
FAS
61, 144

DEFINITIONS OF TERMS

Title plant. Consists of (1) indexed and catalogued information for a period concerning the ownership of, and encumbrances on, parcels of land in a particular geographic area; (2) information relating to persons having an interest in real estate; (3) maps and plats; (4) copies of prior title insurance contracts and reports; and (5) other documents and records. In summary, a title plant constitutes a historical record of all matters affecting title to parcels of land in a particular geographic area.

CONCEPTS, RULES, AND EXAMPLES

Acquisition Costs

The cost of constructing a title plant includes the cost of obtaining, organizing, and summarizing historical information pertaining to a particular tract of land. Costs incurred to assemble a title plant are to be capitalized until the record is usable for conducting title searches. Costs incurred to construct a backplant (a title plant that predates the time span of an existing title plant) must also be capitalized. However, an enterprise may capitalize only those costs that are directly related to and traceable to the activities performed in constructing the title plant or backplant.

The purchase of a title plant or backplant, or an undivided interest therein (the right to its joint use) is recorded at cost as of the date acquired. If the title plant is acquired separately, it is recorded at the fair value of consideration given.

Capitalized title plant costs are not amortized or depreciated unless an impairment in the carrying amount of the title plant occurs. The following events or changes in circumstances can indicate that the carrying amount may not be recoverable. An impairment may be indicated by the following circumstances (not intended to be an exhaustive list):

1. Changing legal or statutory requirements
2. Economic factors, such as changing demand
3. Loss of competitive advantage
4. Failure to maintain an up-to-date title plant
5. Circumstances that indicate obsolescence, such as abandonment of title plant

The provisions of FAS 144 apply to any such impairment. See Chapter 9 for a complete discussion of this topic.

Operating Costs

Costs of title plant maintenance and of conducting title searches are required to be expensed currently. A title plant is maintained through frequent, often daily, updating which involves adding reports on the current status of specific real estate titles and documentation of security or other ownership interests in such land. A title search entails a search for all information or documentation pertaining to a particular parcel of land. This information is found in the most recently issued title report.

Once a title plant is operational, costs may be incurred to convert the record from one storage and retrieval system to another or to modify the current storage and retrieval system. These costs may **not** be capitalized as title plant. However, they may be separately capitalized and amortized using a systematic and rational method.

Reporting Title Plant Sales

The sale of a title plant is to be reported separately. The amount to be reported is determined by the circumstances surrounding the sale as follows:

Terms of sale	*Amount reported*
Sale of title plant and waiver of all rights to future use	Amount received less adjusted cost of title plant
Sale of undivided ownership interest (rights to future joint use)	Amount received less pro rata portion of adjusted cost of title plant
Sales of copies of title plant or the right to use it	Amount received

Note that in the last instance the amount reported is simply the amount received. In this case, no cost is allocated to the item sold unless the title plant's value drops below its adjusted cost as a result of the sale.

APPENDIX A

DISCLOSURE CHECKLIST

The disclosure checklist presented below provides a quick reference to those disclosures that are common to the financial statements of most business enterprises. Selected references to items required by the SEC, for public companies only, are also incorporated.

DISCLOSURE CHECKLIST INDEX

GENERAL

A. Basis of Reporting

1. Name of entity for which statements are being presented (if d/b/a different name than legal name, indicate both). ____
2. Titles of statements should be appropriate (certain titles denote and should be reserved for GAAP financial statements; other titles denote other comprehensive basis of accounting [OCBOA] financial statements). ____
3. Dates and periods covered should be clearly stated. ____
4. If comparative statements are presented, repeat footnotes from prior years to extent appropriate. ____
5. Differences between "economic" entity and legal entity being presented should be noted (e.g., consolidated or not? subsidiaries included and excluded, combined statements?, etc.) Disclose summarized financial information for previously unconsolidated subsidiaries. ____
6. For SEC reporting—identify new accounting principles not yet adopted and expected impact of adoption. ____

B. Accounting Policies

1. Description of business unless otherwise apparent from statements themselves. ____
2. Identify and describe significant accounting principles followed and methods of applying them that materially affect statements; disclosures should include principles and methods that involve
   a. Selection from acceptable alternatives. ____
   b. Principles and methods peculiar to the company's industry. ____
   c. Unusual or innovative applications of generally accepted accounting principles. ____
   d. Principles of consolidation or combination. ____

3. If there have been any material changes in classifications made to previously issued financial statements, these should be noted. _____

C. Accounting Changes

1. Nature and justification of change in accounting principle. _____
   a. The effect of the new principle on income before extraordinary items and on net income of the period of change. _____
   b. The cumulative effect of change on beginning retained earnings as a separate item. _____
   c. Unless specifically not required by a standard, disclose pro forma effects of retroactive application for both income before extraordinary items and net income; report pro forma amounts in both current and future reports for all periods presented that are prior to the change and that would have been affected; if income statement is presented for current period only, actual and pro forma amounts for immediately preceding period (also respective per share data). _____
   d. If the change does not involve a cumulative effect adjustment (e.g., when changing depreciation lives only for new acquisitions), describe change in method and its effect on income before extraordinary items and net income (also related per share amounts for the period of the change). _____
   e. If required pro forma amounts cannot be computed or reasonably estimated for individual prior periods although the cumulative effect on retained earnings at beginning of period can be determined, explain reason for not showing pro forma amounts by period. _____
   f. When the effect on opening retained earnings cannot be computed, (e.g., a change from FIFO to LIFO) report the effect of change on results of operations for the period of change; explain reason for omitting accounting of cumulative effect and disclosure of pro forma amounts for prior years. _____
   g. If reinstatement of prior period reports is required under standard: state nature of and justification for change in accounting principle in period of change; report the effect on income before extraordinary items and net income for all prior presented (also per share amounts thereof); and disclose differences between opening balances of shareholders' equity accounts and balances previously reported. _____
2. For change in reporting entity, nature of change and reason for it; also, effect of change on income before extraordinary items and net income for all periods presented (also per share amounts). _____
3. For a change in accounting estimate, if the change affects several future periods (e.g., for change in useful lives of fixed assets), disclose the effect on income before extraordinary items and net income of current period (and related per share amounts). _____
4. For the correction of an error, disclose the nature of the error in previously issued statements and the effect of its correction on income before extraordinary items and net income (only in period of discovery and correction), with per share equivalents. _____

D. Related Parties

1. Nature of relationship and amounts due to or from related parties with significant terms and manner of settlement. _____
2. For each income statement presented, a description of and dollar amounts of transaction, including those to which no or nominal amounts are assigned, as well as guarantees or other terms which are needed for understanding of financial statement impact, and description of any change in terms. _____
3. Economic dependency (e.g., major customer, supplier, franchisor, franchisee, distributor, general agent, borrower, or lender) should be described and amount of transactions disclosed. _____

4. Nature and extent of related-party leases. _____
5. The nature of control relationship, even absent any transactions, of companies under common ownership or management control, if such could lead to operating results or financial position significantly different than what would have resulted if entities were autonomous. _____
6. Amount of investments in related parties. _____

E. Contingencies and Commitments

1. When accruals are not made because probable loss could not be estimated, describe the nature of the contingency. _____
2. Report the upper limit of range of estimates for cases in which lower limit is accrued because no best estimate exists. _____
3. The nature of reasonably possible losses and either the estimated amount of the loss or a statement that no estimate is possible. _____
4. Describe unasserted claims for which it is both probable that a claim will be asserted, and reasonably possible that an unfavorable outcome will result. _____
5. Report events occurring after balance sheet date that may give rise to a loss contingency, either via a footnote or by means of a pro forma presentation. _____
6. Gain contingencies may be disclosed (but not accrued), if described such that the likelihood of realization is not overstated. _____
7. Disclose about guarantees, including guarantees of the indebtedness of others
    a. The nature of the guarantee, including the approximate term, how the guarantee arose, and the events or circumstances that would require the guarantor to perform under the guarantee. _____
    b. The maximum potential amount of the future payments (undiscounted) that the entity would be required to make, or if the guarantee provides no limitation on future payments, that fact. _____
    c. The reasons why the maximum future payments cannot be estimated, if the entity is unable to estimate that amount. _____
    d. The current carrying amount of the liability. _____
    e. The nature of any recourse provisions that would enable the entity to recover from third parties any amounts paid under the guarantee, and the extent to which the proceeds are expected to cover the amount in (b) above. _____
    f. A description of any assets (collateral) that can be liquidated to recover amounts paid under the guarantee, and the extent to which the proceeds from liquidation are expected to cover the amount in (b) above. _____
8. Disclose material commitments and purchase obligations. _____
9. Describe any pending renegotiation of government contracts. _____
10. Pending litigation in which the entity is involved should be described, with gross potential losses and potential recovery (e.g., from insurance) separately identified. _____
11. Tax contingencies or disputes to which the entity is a party should be noted. _____
12. Unused letters of credit. _____
13. Environmental risks and liabilities should be described. _____
14. Accounts or notes receivable sold with recourse; other guarantees to repurchase receivables. _____
15. Unusual purchase or sales commitments. _____
16. Compensated absences or postemployment benefits that cannot be reasonably estimated but that otherwise meet criteria for accrual should be described. _____

F. Risks and Uncertainties

1. Nature of operations including description of major products, services, principal markets served, locations, and relative importance of operations in various businesses and basis for determination of relative importance (e.g., sales volume, profits, etc.). _____

2. Explanation that the preparation of financial statements requires the use of management's estimates. _____
3. Significant estimates used in the determination of the carrying amounts of assets or liabilities or in the disclosure of gain or loss contingencies when, based on information known to management prior to issuance of the financial statements it is at least reasonably possible that the effect on the financial statements of a condition, situation, or set of circumstances existing at the balance sheet date for which an estimate has been made will change in the near term due to one or more future confirming events and the effect of the change would be material to the financial statements. (If the estimate involves a loss contingency covered by FAS 5, include an estimate of the possible loss or range of loss, or state such estimate cannot be made.) _____
4. Vulnerability due to concentrations in the volume of business with a particular customer, supplier, or lender; revenue from particular products or services; available sources of supply of materials, labor, or other inputs; and market or geographic area. (For concentrations of labor subject to collective bargaining agreements, disclose both the percentage of the labor force covered by a collective bargaining agreement and the percentage of the labor force covered by a collective bargaining agreement that will expire within one year. For concentrations of operations located outside of the entity's home country, disclose the carrying amounts of net assets and the geographic areas in which they are located.) _____

G. Nonmonetary Transactions

1. Nature of transaction. _____
2. Gain or loss and basis of accounting for assets transferred. _____
3. For advertising barter transactions
   a. Amount of revenue and expense recognized from advertising barter transactions. _____
   b. Volume and type of advertising surrendered and received (e.g., number of equivalent pages, broadcast minutes) that was not recognized in the income statement because the fair value was not determinable. _____

H. Subsequent Events, if Material

1. Adjust financial statements for conditions existing at balance sheet date. _____
2. Disclose for conditions subsequent to balance sheet (consider pro forma presentation); examples are: for sale of a bond or capital stock issue, purchase or sale of a business, settlement of litigation when event giving rise to claim occurred subsequent to balance sheet date, loss of plant or inventories as a result of fire or flood, losses on receivables resulting from conditions (such as a customer's major casualty) arising subsequent to balance sheet date, significant net realized and unrealized marketable equity security gains and losses after the date of the financial statements, substantial loans to insiders or affiliates, significant long-term investments, substantial dividends not in the ordinary course of business, loss contingencies arising after the date of the financial statements, or significant foreign currency rate changes after the balance sheet date and their effects on unsettled balances pertaining to foreign currency transactions. _____

I. Rights and Privileges of Various Equity Securities Outstanding

1. Show each class separately and any changes during the period. _____
2. Par value, assigned or stated value should be disclosed. _____
3. Liquidation preferences are to be stated. _____
4. Participations (for preferred classes) are to be disclosed. _____
5. Call, conversion, and exercise data are to be noted. _____
6. Redeemable preferred stock should be described. _____

J. Variable Interest Entities (VIE)

Notes to the preparer:

(1) Disclosures required by FAS 140 regarding a VIE are to be included in the same note to the financial statements as the information required by this section.

(2) Information regarding VIE may be aggregated for similar entities if separate reporting would not provide the user with additional material information.

1. Disclosures to be made by the primary beneficiary (unless that party also holds a majority voting interest)
   a. The nature, purpose, size, and activities of the VIE. _____
   b. The carrying amount and classification of consolidated assets that are collateral for the VIE's obligations. _____
   c. Any lack of recourse by creditors (or beneficial interest holders) of a consolidated VIE to the general credit of the primary beneficiary. _____
2. Disclosures to be made by an enterprise that holds a significant variable interest in a VIE but is *not* the primary beneficiary
   a. The nature of its involvement with the VIE and when that involvement began. _____
   b. The nature, purpose, size, and activities of the VIE. _____
   c. The enterprise's maximum exposure to loss as a result of its involvement with the VIE. _____
3. An enterprise that does not apply FIN 46(R) to one or more VIE or potential VIE because after exhaustive efforts it is unable to obtain the necessary information is to make the following disclosures:
   a. The number of entities to which FIN 46(R) is not being applied and the reason why the information required to apply FIN 46(R) is not available. _____
   b. The nature, purpose, size (if the information is available), and activities of the VIE or potential VIE and the nature of the enterprise's involvement with those entities. _____
   c. The enterprise's maximum exposure to loss as a result of its involvement with the entity or entities. _____
   d. The amount of income, expense, purchases, sales, or other measure of activity between the reporting enterprise and the entity (entities) for all periods presented. (If not practicable to present the prior period information in the first set of financial statements to which this requirement applies, that prior period information may be omitted.) _____
4. In financial statements initially issued after December 31, 2003, and prior to the effective date of FIN 46(R), if it is reasonably possible that an enterprise will initially consolidate or disclose information about a VIE when FIN 46(R) becomes effective, the reporting enterprise is required to disclose the following information:
   a. The nature, purpose, size, and activities of the VIE. _____
   b. The enterprise's maximum exposure to loss as a result of its involvement with the VIE. _____

K. Other Disclosures

1. Asset valuation allowances. _____
2. Pledged and encumbered assets. _____
3. Current and noncurrent classifications, if so utilized. _____
4. For derivatives, the hedging or trading objectives and policy. _____

BALANCE SHEET

A. Cash and Cash Equivalents

1. Segregate and classify the amount of restricted cash according to the nature of the restriction. _____
2. Compensating balances disclosed as to their nature and amount (if use of cash on balance sheet is not restricted, separate presentation on balance sheet is not required). _____
3. Overdrafts are to be presented as a current liability. _____
4. If uninsured balances are material, concentration of credit risk must be disclosed. _____
5. For SEC, foreign bank balances are to be distinguished. _____

B. Receivables

1. Separately report each major category of loans and trade receivables. _____
2. Separately report receivables involving officers, employees, and other related parties and disclose amount and nature of transactions. _____
3. The allowance for doubtful accounts or loan losses and the current period provision. _____
4. Any unearned income, unamortized premiums or discounts, and any net unamortized deferred fees and costs related to loans or trade receivables. _____
5. The recorded investment in loans (and trade receivables, if applicable) on nonaccrual status, as of each balance sheet presented. _____
6. The recorded investment in loans (and trade receivables, if applicable) on accrual status that are past due ninety days or more, as of each balance sheet presented. _____
7. The carrying amount of financial instruments that serve as collateral for borrowings. _____
8. The amount of receivables held for sale. _____
9. The amount and nature of receivables sold without recourse. _____
10. The amount of foreclosed or repossessed assets, which can be included in the other assets category if the notes to thc financial statements disclose the amount. _____
11. Credit balances reclassified as a current liability. _____
12. Concentrations of risk. _____
13. Transfers of receivables with recourse. _____
14. For impaired loans, disclose
    a. For each balance sheet
        (1) Investment in impaired loans. _____
        (2) Amount of allowance for credit losses. _____
        (3) Policy of income recognition for interest. _____
    b. For each income statement, disclose the average investment in impaired loans, interest income recognized and activity in the allowance for credit losses account. _____
15. For noninterest-bearing notes or inappropriate stated interest rates, disclose the discount or premium, the effective rate of interest and face amount, amortization for the period, and issue costs. _____
16. All other nontrade receivables (e.g., tax refunds, contract claims, etc.) are separately presented. _____
17. The basis for accounting for trade receivables, loans receivable, and lease financings, including those held for sale. _____
18. The method for recognizing interest income on loan and trade receivables, including related fees and costs, and the method of amortizing net deferred fees or costs. _____
19. The accounting policies and methodology used to estimate the allowance for doubtful accounts and/or loan losses, including the factors that influenced management's judgment (such as existing economic conditions and historical losses). _____

20. The accounting policies and methodology used to estimate any liability for off-balance-sheet credit losses, including the factors that influenced management's judgment. ____
21. The policy for placing loans (and trade receivables, if applicable) on nonaccrual status. ____
22. The policy for recording payments received on loans (and trade receivables, if applicable) that are in nonaccrual status. ____
23. The policy for resuming interest accruals on loans that are in nonaccrual status. ____
24. The policy for charging off uncollectible trade receivables and loans. ____
25. Whether past due or delinquency status is based on how recently payments have been made or on contractual terms. ____
26. Whether aggregate or individual asset basis is used in determining the lower of cost or fair value of nonmortgage loans held for sale. ____
27. The aggregate amount of gains or losses on sales of loans or trade receivables (including the amounts of adjustments to record receivables held for sale at the lower of cost or fair value) separately presented in the financial statements or disclosed in the notes. ____
28. The classification and method of accounting for receivables that can be contractually prepaid or otherwise settled in a way that the entity would not recover substantially all of its recorded investment. ____
29. For certain loans or debt securities acquired in a transfer (per SOP 03-3), the following disclosures are required:

    a. How prepayments on loans receivable are accounted for ____
    b. For loans acquired through purchase, including in a business combination, separately for loans accounted for as debt securities and for those not accounted for as debt securities

        (1) The outstanding balance (undiscounted cash flows owed) ____
        (2) The carrying amount at the beginning of the period ____
        (3) The carrying amount at the end of the period ____
        (4) A reconciliation of the amount of accretable yield at the beginning of the period to the amount of accretable yield at the end of the period ____
        (5) For loans acquired in the current period

            (a) The contractually required payments receivable ____
            (b) The cash flows expected to be collected ____
            (c) The fair value at acquisition ____
            (d) The carrying amount of any acquired loans in nonaccrual status ____

        (6) The carrying amount of all loans in a nonaccrual status ____
        (7) For loans not accounted for as debt securities

            (a) The amount of any expense recognized for impairment ____
            (b) The amount of any reduction in a valuation allowance for losses that results from an increase in cash flows previously expected to be collected ____
            (c) The amount of the allowance for uncollectible loans at the beginning of the period ____
            (d) The amount of the allowance for uncollectible loans at the end of the period ____

C. Marketable Securities

For all classifications (trading, available-for-sale, or held-to-maturity), disclose the following information:

1. Fair value. ____
2. Gross unrealized gains. ____
3. Gross unrealized losses. ____

4. Amortized cost for each major security type. _____
5. Maturity date for those debt instruments held to maturity. _____
6. For each period for which the results of operations are presented, disclose
   a. Proceeds from sales of available-for-sale securities and gross realized gains and gross realized losses on those sales. _____
   b. Basis on which cost was determined in computing realized gain or loss. _____
   c. Gross gains and gross losses included in earnings from transfers of securities from available-for-sale category into trading category. _____
   d. Change in net realized holding gain or loss on available-for-sale securities that has been included in separate component of shareholders' equity during the period. _____
   e. Change in net unrealized holding gain or loss on trading securities that has been included in earnings during the period. _____
7. For any sales/transfers from held to maturity classification, disclose
   a. Cost of security. _____
   b. Realized or unrealized gain or loss. _____
   c. Circumstances leading to decision to sell or transfer the security. _____
8. For SEC reporting—Substantial post-balance-sheet market decline. _____

D. Inventories

1. Basis of valuation (cost, lower of cost or market, etc.). _____
2. Cost flow assumption (FIFO, LIFO, etc.). _____
3. Classification (materials, work in process, etc.), with amounts of inventory in each. _____
4. Inventory accounting principles peculiar to a particular industry. _____
5. Pledging of inventories in borrowing agreements. _____
6. Product financing arrangements. _____
7. Accrued net losses on firm purchase commitments. _____
8. Liquidation of LIFO inventories and effects on income. _____
9. Lower of cost or market "losses," if material. _____

E. Investments—Equity Method

1. Name of each investee and the percentage of ownership of common stock. _____
2. Accounting policies with respect to each of the investments. _____
3. Difference between the carrying amount for each investment and its underlying equity in the investee's net assets and the accounting treatment of the difference between these amounts. _____
4. For those investments which have a quoted market price, the aggregate value of each investment. _____
5. If investments in investees are considered to have a material effect on the investor's financial position and operating results, summarized data for the investor's assets, liabilities, and results of operations. _____
6. If potential conversion of convertible securities and exercise of options and warrants would have material effects on the investor's percentage of the investee. _____

F. Other Investments

For equity and debt securities

1. Classification as a held-to-maturity or an available-for-sale investment. _____
2. Basis of accounting. _____
3. Any valuation accounts in stockholders' equity which reflect unrealized gains and losses and any income statement effects. _____

G. Property, Plant, and Equipment

1. Classes of assets, including separate identification of
   a. Assets held and used. _____

   b. Assets held for sale. _____
   c. Assets under construction and not in service. _____
   d. Idle assets. _____
2. The bases of valuation. _____
3. The methods of computing depreciation. _____
4. The amount of accumulated depreciation either by classes of assets or in total. _____
5. A description of and the amount of any assets pledged as collateral. _____
6. Capitalized interest cost
   a. The total amount of interest cost incurred during the period. _____
   b. The amount which has been capitalized. _____
7. Estimated costs to complete, for major construction. _____
8. Capitalized preproduction costs related to long-term supply agreements. Aggregate amount of assets recognized
   a. Pursuant to agreements providing for contractual reimbursement of preproduction design and development costs. _____
   b. Molds, dies, and other tools that the supplier owns. _____
   c. Molds, dies, and other tools that the supplier does not own. _____
9. Asset retirement obligations (ARO)
   a. General description of ARO and the related long-lived assets. _____
   b. Description of how the fair value of the liability for ARO was determined. _____
   c. Funding policy, if any, for ARO. _____
   d. Fair value of assets, if any, that are legally restricted to satisfy the liability. _____
   e. Reconciliation of the beginning and ending aggregate carrying amount of the liability separately showing the changes resulting from
      (1) Additional liability incurred during the current period. _____
      (2) Settlements of the liability during the current period. _____
      (3) Accretion expense. _____
      (4) Revisions in expected cash flows. _____
      (5) Explanation of any significant changes in ARO not otherwise apparent. _____
10. Impairment, asset disposals, exit activities, and discontinued operations (including lessee's early termination of leases and early termination of other executory contracts)
   a. If an impairment loss is recognized for assets classified as held and used
      (1) Description of impaired assets (asset groups) and situation surrounding impairment. _____
      (2) Amount of impairment loss and method of determining fair value. _____
      (3) If impairment losses are not reported separately or parenthetically, the caption that includes the losses. _____
      (4) The business segment affected, if applicable. _____
   b. For assets (or disposal groups) sold or classified as held-for-sale during the period
      (1) Facts and circumstances leading to the expected disposal _____
      (2) Expected manner and timing of the disposal _____
      (3) Gain or loss recognized for initial or subsequent write-downs to fair value less cost to sell and the income statement caption in which included, if not separately stated. _____
      (4) Amounts of revenue and pretax profit or loss reported as discontinued operations, if applicable. _____
      (5) For public companies, the segment in which the long-lived asset or disposal group is reported _____
      (6) For exit activities, the disclosures are listed in Income Statement (O). _____

c. Reclassifications

(1) If assets were reclassified from held-for-sale to held-and-used during the period

(a) Facts and circumstances leading to the decision. _____

(b) Effect on the results of operations for the period in which the decision was made and any prior periods presented. _____

(2) If assets held and used meet the criteria for reclassification to held-for-sale after the date of the balance sheet but before issuance of the financial statements

(a) The carrying amount of the major assets and liabilities included as part of the disposal group. _____

(b) The facts and circumstances leading to the expected disposal. _____

(c) The expected manner and timing of the disposal. _____

H. Intangibles

1. For each major class of intangible asset

a. Gross carrying amount. _____

b. Accumulated amortization. _____

c. Amortization expense for all periods presented. _____

d. Aggregate amortization expenses for each of the five succeeding fiscal years as of the date of the latest balance sheet presented. _____

e. Method of amortization. _____

f. A description of any intangible asset not being amortized, the total carrying amount as of the date of each balance sheet presented and the method used to estimate its fair value. _____

g. With respect to goodwill

(1) Changes in the carrying amount during the period including goodwill acquired, impairment loss recognized, portion included in the gain or loss on disposal of all or a portion of a reporting unit and, for entities reporting segment information, that information for each segment and any significant changes in the allocation of goodwill by segment. _____

h. For each goodwill impairment loss recognized during any periods presented

(1) Description of the facts and circumstances leading to the impairment. _____

(2) Description of the reporting unit for which the impairment loss is recognized, the adjusted carrying amount of goodwill of that reporting unit, and the amount of the impairment loss. _____

(3) If a recognized impairment loss is an estimate pending finalization, that fact and the reasons it has not been finalized and, in subsequent periods, the nature and amount of any significant adjustments made to the initial estimate of the impairment loss. _____

(4) For entities required to report segment information, the segment to which the impaired goodwill relates. _____

(5) In a period in which negative goodwill is recognized as an extraordinary gain, the information required for such gains (See "Income Statement—D. Extraordinary Gains" in this Appendix). _____

2. In the year of acquisition, the following information as of acquisition date

a. For each class of intangible asset

(1) A description of the assets and their recorded amounts. _____

(2) Key assumptions and methodologies used to value them. _____

(3) Description of amortization method and, if not straight-line, the reasons. _____

(4) Weighted-average amortization period. _____

(5) Any residual value assumed in determining the amount to be amortized (if significant in relation to the carrying amount of the intangible asset class). _____

b. A description and the carrying amount of any significant intangible asset presumed to have either a useful economic life greater than twenty years or an indefinite life, the useful life assigned, and the factors supporting that life. _____

c. With respect to goodwill

(1) The amount of acquired goodwill. _____

(2) The amount of acquired goodwill related to each segment (for entities required to report segment information). _____

(3) The amount of acquired goodwill that is deductible for income tax purposes. _____

3. R&D expenditures

a. The total research and development costs charged to expense for each period for which an income statement is presented. _____

b. For contractual agreements

(1) The terms of significant agreements under the R&D arrangements as of the date of each balance sheet presented. _____

(2) The amount of compensation earned and costs incurred under contract for each period for which an income statement is presented. _____

4. Deferred charges and other assets

a. Charges, segregated by type. _____

b. Carrying value of capitalized computer software. _____

5. Computer software

a. Capitalized value. _____

b. Amortization. _____

c. Write-downs to realizable value. _____

6. Capitalized direct-response advertising _____

7. For obligations to service financial assets

a. Amounts of servicing assets/liabilities recognized and amortized. _____

b. Fair value of items (methods and assumptions). _____

c. Risk and amounts of impairment. _____

I. Accounting for Transfers and Servicing of Financial Assets

1. For all servicing assets and liabilities

a. The amounts recognized and amortized during the period. _____

b. Fair value of such recognized items including methods and assumptions. _____

c. Risk characteristics of assets used to measure impairment. _____

d. Activity in the valuation allowance for impairment. _____

2. For securitizations accounted for as a sale

a. Accounting policies for initially and subsequently measuring retained interests, including how fair value was determined. _____

b. A description of the entity's continuing involvement with the transferred assets. _____

c. The gain or loss from the securitizations. _____

d. The key assumptions used in measuring the fair value of retained interests, both initially and subsequently. _____

e. A sensitivity analysis or stress test showing the hypothetical effect on the fair value of retained interests for two or more variations from the expected level for each key assumption used in measuring the fair value of retained interests. _____

f. Cash flows between the securitization SPE and the entity. _____

3. For securitized assets that the entity continues to service
   a. The total principal amount outstanding of the securitized assets and any other financial assets that the entity manages with them, the portion that has been derecognized, and the portion that continues to be recognized for each category reported on the balance sheet. _____
   b. Delinquencies at the end of the period. _____
   c. Credit losses, net of recoveries, during the period. _____
4. Other disclosures
   a. Security required for repurchase agreements or security lending transactions. _____
   b. Fair value of assets transferred, or description and reasons why fair value cannot be measured. _____
   c. Any assets pledged as collateral that are not separately reported on the face of the balance sheet. _____
   d. Fair value of any assets accepted as collateral, and the amount that has been sold or repledged. _____

J. Current Liabilities

1. For accounts payable, disclose amounts that are
   a. Trade. _____
   b. Nontrade. _____
   c. Related parties (affiliates; investees for which the equity method is used; employee trusts; principal owners; management, immediate families of owners and management; or any party capable of significantly influencing a transaction). _____
2. Callable obligations:
   For long-term obligations which have become callable due to a violation of the debt agreement, report
   a. A description of covenants violated. _____
   b. In unclassified balance sheet, include surrounding circumstances with disclosure of long-term debt maturities. _____
   c. Obligation that will be classified as noncurrent because it is probable that a violation of debt agreement will be cured within a grace period or a waiver has been obtained. _____
3. Income taxes payable
   a. Current portion. _____
   b. Deferred portion. _____
4. Notes payable
   a. Description of note. _____
   b. Classified by type
      (1) Trade creditors. _____
      (2) Bank. _____
      (3) Factors or other financial institutions. _____
      (4) Holders of commercial paper. _____
      (5) Related parties (see Accounts Payable, 1.c.). _____
      (6) Employees, underwriters, and promoters (other than related parties). _____
   c. Describe assets used as security. _____
   d. Interest rate. _____
   e. Aggregate maturities and maturities for next five years. _____

5. Product warranties

   a. The nature of the product warranty, including how the warranty arose and the events or circumstances in which the entity must perform under the warranty. _____
   b. The entity's accounting policy and methodology used in determining its liability. _____
   c. A reconciliation of the beginning and ending liability balances showing separately the changes during the period attributable to warranties issued, claims paid or otherwise settled, and any adjustments to the liability. _____
   d. The nature and extent of any recourse provisions or available collateral that would enable the entity to recover the amounts paid under the warranties. _____
   e. The disclosures required by FAS 57 if the warranties are made to benefit related parties. _____

6. Other current liabilities

   a. Accruals. _____
   b. Advances or deposits. _____
   c. Current portions of long-term liabilities. _____
   d. Compensated absences. _____
   e. Liabilities not recorded because amounts could not be estimated. _____
   f. Short-term debt expected to be refinanced

      (1) Terms of new obligation incurred or expected to be incurred. _____
      (2) Terms of equity securities issued or expected to be issued. _____

   g. Bank overdrafts. _____
   h. Special termination benefits. _____
   i. Credit balances in accounts receivable. _____
   j. Terms, interest rates, collateral, and other significant information about the underlying obligation. _____

K. Deferred Tax Assets and Liabilities

1. Classify as current if related to asset or liability that is current or will result in net taxable or deductible amounts next year. Otherwise classify as noncurrent. _____
2. Total of deferred tax liabilities. _____
3. Total of deferred tax assets. _____
4. Report the valuation allowance for deferred tax assets, allocated pro rata between current and noncurrent deferred tax assets, and changes in allowance during the year. _____
5. Deferred tax liabilities and assets attributable to different taxpaying components or to different tax jurisdictions should not be offset. _____
6. The approximate tax effect of each type of temporary difference and carryforward that gives rise to a significant portion of deferred tax liabilities and assets. For non-SEC reporting, disclose the types of temporary differences and carryforwards but may omit disclosure of the tax effects of each type. _____
7. The amounts and expected timing of reversals of deductible temporary differences. _____
8. Any portion of the valuation allowance for deferred tax assets for which subsequently recognized tax benefits will be allocated to reduce goodwill or other noncurrent intangible assets of an acquired entity or directly to contributed capital. _____
9. The amounts and expiration dates of operating loss and tax credit carryforwards for tax purposes. _____

L. Long-Term Debt and Debt Extinguishment

1. Notes and bonds

   a. The aggregate amount of debt shown as a long-term liability on the face of the financial statements net of the current portion due within one year and any discount or premium. _____

b. The detail relating to each debt issue, including

(1) Nature of the liabilities. _____
(2) Maturity dates. _____
(3) Interest rates (effective and stated). _____
(4) Call provisions. _____
(5) Conversion privileges. _____
(6) Restrictive covenants (i.e., sinking fund requirements, restrictions on retained earnings, etc.). _____
(7) Assets pledged as collateral (these assets are shown in the asset section of the balance sheet). _____
(8) Amounts due to related parties including officers, directors, and employees, and terms of settlement. _____
(9) Disclosure of notes or bonds issued subsequent to the balance sheet date. _____
(10) Amounts of unused letters of credit. _____

c. The current portion of the long-term debt is shown as a current liability unless other than current assets will be used to satisfy the obligation. _____

d. Long-term debt is classified as current if the debtor is in violation of a debt covenant at the balance sheet date which

(1) Makes the obligation callable within one year, or _____
(2) Will make the obligation callable within one year if the violation is not cured within a specified grace period. _____

e. The debt referred to in d. above need not be reclassified if either of the following conditions are met:

(1) The creditor has waived or has subsequently lost the right to demand repayment for one year (or, if longer, the operating cycle) from the balance sheet date, or _____
(2) It is probable (likely) that the violation will be cured by the debtor within the grace period stated in the terms of the debt agreement, thus preventing the obligation from being called. _____

2. For the extinguishment of debt the following information provided either on the face of the financial statements or in the notes:

a. A description of the extinguishment transaction, including the sources of the funds used, if practicable. _____
b. The income tax effect of the transaction. _____
c. The amount and the per share amount of the aggregate gain or loss, net of tax. _____
d. For debt considered to be extinguished by an in-substance defeasance, a general description of the transaction and the amount of debt that is considered extinguished at the end of the period so long as that debt remains outstanding. _____
e. A description of the restrictions on assets set aside solely for satisfying scheduled payments on a specific debt obligation. _____

3. Troubled debt restructurings

a. Disclosures by the debtor

(1) A description of the changes in terms and/or major features of the settlement. _____
(2) The aggregate gain on restructuring and the related tax effect. _____
(3) The aggregate net gain or loss on the transfer of assets recognized during the period. _____
(4) The per share amount of the aggregate gain or loss, net of tax. _____

b. Disclosures by the creditor

(1) For the outstanding restructured receivables, the aggregate recorded investment. _____
(2) The amount of commitments to lend additional funds to debtors owing receivables whose terms have been modified by restructurings. _____
(3) The recorded investment amount for which impairment has been recognized, including the total allowance for credit losses related to those impaired loans, and recorded investments not requiring an allowance. _____
(4) The activity in the allowance for credit losses account, including the balance in the allowance for credit losses account at the beginning and end of each period, additions charged to operations, direct write-downs charged against the allowance, and recoveries of amounts previously charged off. _____
(5) The creditor's interest income recognition policy on impaired loans, including how cash receipts are recorded. _____
(6) For each period of operation, the amount of interest income related to impaired loans, the average investment impaired and if practical, the amount of interest income using a cash-basis method. _____

4. Unconditional purchase obligations are to be disclosed, if all the following criteria are met:

   a. It is noncancelable, or cancelable only

      (1) Upon the occurrence of some remote contingency. _____
      (2) With the permission of the other party. _____
      (3) If a replacement agreement is signed between the same parties. _____
      (4) Upon payment of a penalty in an amount such that continuation of the agreement appears reasonably assured. _____

   b. It is negotiated as part of a supplier's product financing arrangement for the facilities that will provide the contracted goods or services or for costs related to those goods or services (e.g., carrying costs for contracted goods); and _____
   c. It has a remaining term in excess of one year. _____
   d. If the obligation fulfills the foregoing criteria and is recorded on the balance sheet, the following disclosures are required:

      (1) Aggregate amount of payments to be made. _____
      (2) Aggregate amount of maturities and sinking fund requirements for all long-term borrowings. _____

   e. If the obligation is not recorded on the balance sheet, then the following footnote disclosures are required:

      (1) The nature and term of the obligation(s). _____
      (2) The total amount of the fixed or determinable portion of the obligation(s) at the balance sheet date in the aggregate and for each of the next five years, if determinable. _____
      (3) The nature of any variable components of the obligation(s). _____
      (4) The amounts purchased under the obligation(s) (as in take-or-pay or through-put contracts) for each period for which an income statement is presented. _____

5. For contingently convertible debt securities, disclose the qualitative and quantitative terms that users need to understand the potential impact of conversion, including: events or changes in circumstances that would cause the contingency to be met and features necessary to understand the conversion rights, the conversion price and number of shares, events or changes that could adjust or change any features of the securities, and the manner of settlement upon conversion.

M. Financial Instruments and Derivatives

1. The method and significant assumptions used to estimate fair value. _____
2. If not practicable to estimate fair value, disclose pertinent information such as carrying amount, effective interest rate, and maturity and the reason why it is not practicable. _____
3. Disclose all significant concentrations of credit risk arising from all financial instruments (except financial instruments of a pension plan and certain other financial instrument identified in FAS 107), whether from an individual counterparty or groups of counterparties, including:
    a. Information about the (shared) activity, region, or economic characteristic that identifies the concentration. _____
    b. The maximum amount of loss due to credit risk that, based on the gross fair value of the financial instrument, the entity would incur if parties to the financial instruments that make up the concentration failed completely to perform according to the terms of the contracts and the collateral or other security, if any, for the amount due proved to be of no value to the entity. _____
    c. The company's policy of requiring collateral or other security to support financial instruments subject to credit risk, information about the entity's access to that collateral or other security, and the nature and a brief description of the collateral or other security supporting those financial instruments. _____
    d. The company's policy of entering into master netting arrangements to mitigate the credit risk of financial instruments, information about the arrangements for which the entity is a party, and a brief description of the terms of those arrangements, including the extent to which they would reduce the entity's maximum amount of loss due to credit risk. _____
4. For companies that hold or issue derivative instruments that are not hedging instruments, disclose
    a. The purpose of the derivative activity. _____
    b. The objectives for holding or issuing those instruments within a context needed to understand those objectives. _____
    c. The strategies for achieving those objectives. _____
5. For companies that hold or issue derivative instruments that are designated and qualify as hedging instruments, disclose the following:
    a. The objectives for holding or issuing those instruments within a context needed to understand those objectives. _____
    b. The strategies for achieving those objectives. _____
    c. The entity's risk management policy for each of the types of hedges, including a description of the items or transactions for which risks are hedged. _____
6. For fair value hedges, disclose for derivative instruments, as well as nonderivative instruments that may give rise to foreign currency transaction gains or losses, that have been designated and have qualified as fair value hedging instruments and for the related hedged items
    a. The net gain or loss recognized in earnings during the reporting period representing
        (1) The amount of the hedges' ineffectiveness _____
        (2) The component of the derivative instruments' gain or loss, if any, excluded from the assessment of hedge effectiveness, and a description of where the net gain or loss is reported in the statement of income or other statement of financial performance. _____
    b. The amount of net gain or loss recognized in earnings when a hedged firm commitment no longer qualifies as a fair value hedge. _____

7. For cash flow hedges, disclose for derivative instruments that have been designated and have qualified as cash flow hedging instruments and for the related hedged transactions
   a. The net gain or loss recognized in earnings during the reporting period representing
      (1) The amount of the hedges' ineffectiveness. _____
      (2) The component of the derivative instruments' gain or loss, if any, excluded from the assessment of hedge effectiveness, and a description of where the net gain or loss is reported in the statement of income or other statement of financial performance. _____
   b. A description of the transactions or other events that will result in the reclassification into earnings of gains and losses that are reported in accumulated other comprehensive income, and the estimated net amount of the existing gains or losses at the reporting date that is expected to be reclassified into earnings within the next twelve months. _____
   c. The maximum length of time over which the entity is hedging its exposure to the variability in future cash flows for forecasted transaction excluding those forecasted transactions related to the payment of variable interest on existing financial instruments. _____
   d. The amount of gains and losses reclassified into earnings as a result of the discontinuance of cash flow hedges because it is probable that the original forecasted transactions will not occur. _____
8. For hedges of the net investment in a foreign operation, disclose, for derivative instruments, as well as nonderivative instruments that may give rise to foreign currency transaction gains or losses under FAS 52, that have been designated and have qualified as hedging instruments for hedges of the foreign currency exposure of a net investment in a foreign operation, the net amount of gains or losses included in the cumulative translation adjustment during the reporting period. _____
9. On the face of the balance sheet, in a statement of changes in equity or in the footnote, the following:
   a. The beginning and ending derivative gain or loss. _____
   b. The related change associated with the current period hedging transactions. _____
   c. The net amount of any reclassification into earnings. _____
   d. In the year of initial adoption of FAS 133 only, the amount of gains and losses reported in accumulated other comprehensive income and associated with the transition adjustment that are now being reclassified into earnings during the next twelve months following the date of initial application. _____
10. Except for those financial instruments specifically exempted under FAS 107, as amended by FAS 133, disclose (except for small, nonpublic entities as set forth in FAS 133):
    a. The fair value of financial instruments and related carrying amount for which it is practicable to estimate that value. _____
    b. The methods and significant assumptions used to estimate fair value of financial instruments. _____
11. If not practicable to estimate the fair value of a financial instrument or classes of financial instruments, provide
    a. Information pertinent to estimating fair value of that financial instrument or class of financial instruments, such as carrying amount, effective interest rate, and maturity date. _____
    b. The methods and significant assumption used to estimate fair value of financial instruments. _____

12. For forward sales contracts, forward purchase contracts, purchased put options, and purchased call options that are indexed to, and potentially settled in, a company's own stock, disclose the gains and losses that are included in earnings. _____
13. Disclose any gains or losses on written put options that require net cash settlement or give the counterparty a choice of net cash settlement or settlement in the company's stock. _____
14. Disclose the accounting policy for the premium paid (time value) to acquire an option that is classified as held-to-maturity or available-for-sale. _____

N. Pensions and Other Postretirement Benefits

1. Defined benefit plans

 a. Schedule reconciling beginning and ending balances of the benefit obligation, separately showing if applicable (not required for nonpublic entities)

  (1) Service cost. _____
  (2) Interest cost. _____
  (3) Contributions by plan participants. _____
  (4) Actuarial gains and losses. _____
  (5) Changes in foreign currency exchange rates. _____
  (6) Benefits paid. _____
  (7) Plan amendments. _____
  (8) Business combinations. _____
  (9) Divestitures. _____
  (10) Curtailments. _____
  (11) Settlements. _____
  (12) Special termination benefits. _____

 b. Schedule reconciling beginning and ending balances of the fair value of plan assets, separately showing if applicable (not required for nonpublic entities)

  (1) Actual return. _____
  (2) Changes in foreign currency exchange rates. _____
  (3) Employer contributions. _____
  (4) Employee or retiree contributions. _____
  (5) Benefits paid. _____
  (6) Business combinations. _____
  (7) Divestitures. _____
  (8) Curtailments. _____
  (9) Settlements. _____

 c. Information on the funded status, amounts unrecognized in the balance sheet, and amounts recognized in the balance sheet including, as applicable (not required for nonpublic entities)

  (1) Unamortized prior service cost amount. _____
  (2) Unrecognized net gain (loss) amount (those not yet reflected in market-related value should also be included). _____
  (3) Unamortized net obligation or net asset amount still remaining from that recorded at FAS 87 and FAS 106 date of initial application. _____
  (4) Accrued liabilities or prepaid assets, intangible asset and accumulated other comprehensive income (as a result of recording an additional minimum liability). _____

 d. Net periodic benefit cost recognized, separately showing (not required for nonpublic entities)

  (1) Service cost. _____
  (2) Interest cost. _____
  (3) Expected return on plan assets. _____

(4) Amortization of unrecognized transition asset or obligation. _____
(5) Recognized gains or losses. _____
(6) Recognized prior service costs. _____
(7) Recognized settlement or curtailment gain or loss. _____

e. Amount in other comprehensive income for the period due to a change in the additional minimum pension liability. _____

f. Assumed weighted-average rates for

(1) Discount rate. _____
(2) Expected long-term rate on plan assets. _____
(3) Compensation rate increase (if applicable for pay-related plans). _____

g. Information about plan assets

(1) For each major category of plan assets, such as equities, debt instruments, and real estate, disclosure is required of the percentage of the fair value of total plan assets held as of the measurement date used for each balance sheet presented. _____
(2) A narrative description of investment policies and strategies employed, addressing target allocations for major asset classes, presented on a weighted-average basis as of the measurement date, as well as other factors that are pertinent to an understanding, such as information about investment goals, risk management practices, and permitted and prohibited investments. _____
(3) A narrative explanation of the basis upon which the expected long-term return on assets has been ascertained. _____

h. For defined benefit plans, the accumulated benefit obligation must be disclosed (in addition to the projected benefit obligation) _____

i. The benefits expected to be paid in each of the next five fiscal years plus the aggregate of the five years thereafter, developed using the same assumptions that are used to measure the employer's benefit obligation, and including benefits that will be attributable to estimated future employee service. _____

j. The amount of contributions expected to be paid into the plan during the next fiscal year; the aggregate of the amounts required by funding regulations or laws, discretionary amounts, and noncash contributions may be reported. _____

k. The measurement dates used to determine pension and other postretirement benefit measurements, for at least the plans making up a majority of plan assets and obligations. _____

l. Health care cost trend rate(s)

(1) Used to measure expected costs of benefits covered by the plan (gross eligible charges). _____
(2) Direction and pattern of change together with

(a) The ultimate trend rate(s). _____
(b) The time when that rate is expected to be achieved. _____

m. The effect of both a 1% increase and a 1% decrease in the assumed health care cost trend rates on

(1) Service and interest cost components aggregated. _____
(2) Health care APBO (based on the substantive plan and while holding all other assumptions constant). _____

n. Other, if applicable

(1) Employer and related parties

(a) Amounts and types of securities included in plan assets. _____

(b) Approximate amount of annual benefits covered by annuity contracts issued by the above. _____
(c) Any significant transactions with the plan. _____

(2) Alternative amortization methods used. _____
(3) Existence and nature of substantive commitments. _____
(4) Termination benefits recognized

(a) Nature of event. _____
(b) Cost. _____

o. If not otherwise apparent, an explanation of matters of significance in regard to changes in

(1) Benefit obligation. _____
(2) Plan assets. _____

2. Two or more defined benefit plans (pension, postretirement, or both)

a. Should provide most useful information

(1) May be aggregated for pension and may be aggregated for postretirement plans.

(a) If combined, plans where the accumulated benefit obligations are in excess of plan assets should show

1] Aggregate benefit obligation. _____
2] Aggregate fair value of assets. _____

(b) If combined, pension plans with APBO in excess of plan assets should show

1] Aggregate pension benefit obligation. _____
2] Aggregate pension fair value of assets. _____

(2) May be disaggregated in groups. _____

b. Amounts recognized in the balance sheet separately

(1) Prepaid benefit costs. _____
(2) Accrued benefit liabilities. _____

c. US pension and OPEB plans and outside US plans may be combined unless benefit obligations outside the US are significant relative to the total and those plans use significantly different assumptions. _____

3. Defined contribution plans

a. Amount of cost separate from defined benefit plans

(1) Pension. _____
(2) Other postretirement. _____

b. Description of nature and effect of significant changes affecting comparability. _____

4. Multiemployer plans

a. Total amount of contributions without disaggregation. _____
b. Description of nature and effect of significant changes affecting comparability. _____
c. In case of withdrawal, FAS 5 applies. _____

5. Nonpublic entities may elect the following in lieu of required disclosures:

a. Benefit obligation, fair value of assets, funded status. _____
b. Employer contributions, participant contributions, benefits paid. _____

c. Amounts recognized in balance sheet

   (1) Prepaid assets. _____
   (2) Accrued liabilities. _____
   (3) Intangible assets. _____
   (4) Accumulated other comprehensive income. _____

d. Net periodic benefit cost

   (1) Recognized in net income. _____
   (2) Recognized in other comprehensive income. _____

e. Assumed weighted-average rates for

   (1) Discount rate. _____
   (2) Expected long-term rate on plan assets. _____
   (3) Compensation rate increase (if applicable for pay-related plans). _____

f. Health care cost trend rate is

   (1) Used to measure expected costs of benefits covered by the plan (gross eligible charges). _____
   (2) Direction and pattern of change together with

      (a) The ultimate trend rate(s). _____
      (b) The time when that rate is expected to be achieved. _____

g. Employer and related parties (if applicable)

   (1) Amounts and types of securities included in plan assets. _____
   (2) Approximate amount of annual benefits covered by annuity contracts issued by the above. _____
   (3) Any significant transactions with the plan. _____

h. If applicable, significant nonroutine events, such as amendments, curtailments, settlements, combinations, and divestitures. _____

O. Leases—Lessees

1. For capital leases, disclose

   a. The gross amount of assets recorded under capital leases presented by major classes according to function or nature. _____
   b. Future minimum lease payments in the aggregate and for each of the next five fiscal years with separate deductions made for executory costs (including any profit thereon) included in the minimum lease payments, and the amount of imputed interest needed to reduce the net minimum lease payments to present value. _____
   c. Total of minimum sublease rentals to be received in the future under noncancelable subleases. _____
   d. Total contingent rentals actually incurred for each period for which an income statement is presented. _____
   e. Depreciation on capital leases should be separately disclosed. _____

2. For sale-leaseback transactions, disclose

   a. In addition to requirements of FAS 13 and 66, financials of seller-lessee shall describe terms of sale-leaseback transaction, including future commitments, obligations, provisions, or circumstances requiring or resulting in seller-lessee's involvement. _____
   b. Where seller-lessee has accounted for transaction by deposit method or as a financing

      (1) The obligation for future minimum lease payments as of the date of the latest balance sheet presented in the aggregate and for each of the five succeeding fiscal years. _____

(2) The total of minimum sublease rentals, if any, to be received in the future under noncancelable subleases in the aggregate and for each of the five succeeding fiscal years. _____

3. For operating leases having a remaining noncancelable term in excess of one year, disclose
   a. Future minimum lease payments in the aggregate and for each of the next five fiscal years. _____
   b. Total of minimum rentals that will be received under noncancelable subleases. _____
4. For all operating leases
   a. Present rental expense disclosing separately the amount for minimum rentals, contingent rentals, and sublease rentals. _____
   b. Rental payments for leases with terms of a month or less that were not renewed may be excluded. _____
5. General description required of lessee's leasing arrangements including, but not limited to
   a. Basis of computing contingent rental payments. _____
   b. Existence and terms of renewal or purchase options and escalation clauses. _____
   c. Restrictions imposed by leasing agreements such as on dividends, additional debt, and further leasing arrangements. _____

P. Leases—Lessors

1. For sales-type and direct financing leases, disclose
   a. Components of the net investment in leases including the following:
      (1) Future minimum lease payments to be received with separate deductions for amount representing executory costs (including any profit thereon), and the accumulated allowance for uncollectible lease payments. _____
      (2) Unguaranteed residual values accruing to benefit of lessor. _____
      (3) For direct financing leases only, initial direct costs. _____
      (4) Unearned interest revenue. _____
   b. Future minimum lease payments to be received for each of the next five fiscal years. _____
   c. Total contingent rentals included in income for each period for which an income statement is presented. _____
2. For operating leases, disclose
   a. The cost and carrying amount (if different) of property leased or held for leasing, segregated by major classes of property according to function or nature, and the total amount of accumulated depreciation. _____
   b. Minimum rentals on noncancelable leases in the aggregate and for each of the next five fiscal years. _____
   c. Total contingent rentals included in income for each period for which an income statement is presented. _____
3. A general description of the lessor's leasing arrangements. _____
4. For an investment in leveraged leases recorded net of the nonrecourse debt, the net of the balances of following accounts shall represent the initial and continuing investment in leveraged leases:
   a. Rentals receivable, net of portion of rental applicable to principal and interest on nonrecourse debt. _____
   b. A receivable for amount of investment tax credit to be realized on transaction. _____
   c. Estimated residual value of leased asset. _____

d. Unearned and deferred income consisting of

(1) Estimated pretax income (or loss), after deducting initial direct costs, remaining to be allocated to income over the lease term. _____

(2) Investment tax credit remaining to be allocated to income over lease term. _____

e. For leverage leases, for each income statement presented, disclose

(1) Pretax income from leveraged leases. _____

(2) Tax effect of that pretax income. _____

(3) Amount of investment tax credit recognized as income. _____

Q. Equity-Like Instruments Classified as Liabilities

1. Issuers of financial instruments within the scope of FAS 150 must disclose

a. The nature and terms of the financial instruments. _____

b. The rights and obligations embodied therein. _____

c. Information about settlement alternatives, if any, in the contract. _____

d. The entity that controls the settlement alternatives. _____

2. For all outstanding financial instruments and for each settlement alternative, issuers disclose

a. The amount that would be paid, or the number and fair value of shares that would be issued, determined under the conditions specified in the contract, if the settlement were to occur at the reporting date. _____

b. How changes in the fair value of the issuer's equity shares would affect those settlement amounts. _____

c. The maximum amount that the issuer could be required to pay to redeem the instrument by physical settlement, if applicable. _____

d. The maximum number of shares that could be required to be issued, if applicable. _____

e. That a contract does not limit the amount that the issuer could be required to pay or the number of shares that the issuer could be required to issue, if applicable. _____

f. For a forward contract or an option indexed to the issuer's equity shares, the forward price or option strike price, the number of issuer's shares to which the contract is indexed, and the settlement date or dates of the contract, as applicable. _____

3. For entities having no equity instruments outstanding but having financial instruments in the form of shares, all of which are mandatorily redeemable financial instruments required to be classified as liabilities, disclose the components of the liability that would otherwise be related to shareholders' interest and other comprehensive income (if any) subject to the redemption feature. _____

R. Stockholders' Equity

1. The following should be disclosed:

a. The sources of capital supplied to the firm. _____

b. The legal restrictions on the distribution of invested capital. _____

c. The legal, contractual, managerial, and financial restrictions on the distribution of dividends to stockholders. _____

d. The priorities of the classes of stockholders in a partial or final liquidation. _____

2. Capital stock and additional paid-in capital

a. For each class of stock, disclose

(1) Par, stated, or assigned value. _____

(2) Number of shares authorized, issued, and outstanding. _____

(3) Number of shares held in treasury. _____

(4) Conversion terms of preferred, if applicable, including call prices, rates, and dates. Additionally, the amount of redemption requirements for all issues of stock that are redeemable at fixed or determinable prices on fixed or determinable dates must be disclosed for each of the five years following the date of the latest balance sheet presented. _____
(5) Changes in the number of shares authorized, issued, and outstanding during the year and changes in the equity accounts. _____
(6) Liquidation values, if different than par, in the aggregate for preferred. _____
(7) For preferred classes of stock, any dividend preferences, special privileges, etc. _____
(8) Any unusual voting rights. _____

b. The amount of cumulative dividends in arrears, per share and in aggregate. _____
c. Aggregate securities issuable under rights or warrants, as well as their prices, and exercise and expiration dates. _____
d. Any discount on capital stock. _____
e. The amount of subscribed shares not yet issued. _____
f. Deferred compensation expense offset against the paid-in capital account, "Stock options outstanding." _____
g. Stock dividends distributable in total or at par or stated value with the excess included in additional paid-in capital. Also acceptable is deferment of their recording until issuance. However, disclosure is necessary in the notes. _____
h. The amount of capital stock issued in business combinations (purchase or pooling) or agreements to issue additional shares at a later date. _____
i. Transactions affecting equity subsequent to the date of the financial statements (recapitalization, sales of stock, etc.). _____
j. Additional paid-in capital, listed by source, along with any changes during the period. _____
k. Any changes in the capital accounts of partners or sole proprietors. _____

3. Retained earnings

a. Appropriation and segregation of retained earnings, as well as their nature, cause, and amount. Changes in these accounts should be disclosed. _____
b. Nature and dollar amounts of restrictions on retained earnings (treasury stock, lease covenants, etc.). _____
c. Date retained earnings for ten years following quasi reorganization. _____
d. Increase/decrease results from combination by pooling of interests (revenues, expenses, extraordinary items, and net income). _____
e. Prior period adjustments, net of tax and in gross. For correction of an error, in the period discovered, disclose

(1) Nature of the error on previous statements. _____
(2) Effect of correction on income before extraordinary items, net income, and related per share amounts. _____

4. Dividends

a. Dividends in aggregate and per share as well as the nature and extent of any restrictions on retained earnings limiting availability of dividends. _____
b. The amount of dividends in arrears, per share and in aggregate. _____
c. Dividends declared after balance sheet date, prior to opinion date, unless a long-established history of regular payment dates exists and the dividend is not abnormal in amount. _____
d. For stock dividends and stock splits, disclosure of the amounts capitalized, per share and in total. Historical presentations of earnings per share should be restated in an equivalent number of shares so the figures are presented on a comparable basis. _____

5. Treasury stock
   a. If treasury stock is accounted for by the cost method, present total cost of treasury stock as a deduction from total stockholders' equity. Disclose number of shares held in treasury. _____
   b. If treasury stock is accounted for by the par value method, present par value of treasury stock as a deduction from par value of issued shares of same class. Any related additional paid-in capital from treasury stock is netted with corresponding additional paid-in capital without separate disclosure. Disclose number of shares held in treasury. _____
   c. If treasury stock is accounted for by the constructive retirement method, disclose number of shares held in treasury. _____
6. Compensatory stock plans
   a. Plan description, including general terms of awards such as vesting requirements, maximum term of options granted, and the number of shares authorized for grants of options or other equity instruments. _____
   b. For each year for which an income statement is provided, state
      (1) Number and weighted-average exercise prices of the following options: those outstanding at the beginning and at the end of the year; those exercisable at the end of the year; and those granted, exercised, forfeited, or expired during the year. _____
      (2) Weighted-average grant-date fair value of options granted during the year and additional required disclosures if exercise prices of some options differ from the market price of the stock on the grant date. _____
      (3) Number and weighted-average grant-date fair value of equity instruments other than options, such as shares of nonvested stock, granted during the year. _____
      (4) Description of method and significant assumptions used during the year to estimate the fair value of options. _____
      (5) Total compensation cost recognized for stock-based employee compensation awards. _____
      (6) Terms of significant modifications of outstanding awards. _____
   c. For options outstanding at the latest balance sheet date, the range of exercise prices and the weighted-average remaining contractual life. _____
7. Employee stock ownership plans (ESOP)
   a. Description of the plan, including basis for determining contributions, groups covered, nature and effect of matters affecting comparability of information across periods. _____
   b. The basis for releasing shares by leveraged and pension reversion ESOP. _____
   c. Accounting policies pertinent to ESOP transactions. _____
   d. Compensation cost recognized during the period. _____
   e. Numbers of shares allocated, committed to be released, and held in suspense by the ESOP. _____
   f. Fair value amount of unearned compensation at year-end. _____
   g. Nature of any repurchase obligations and aggregate fair value thereof. _____
8. For SEC only, disclose
   a. Dividend payout restrictions. _____
   b. Stock subscriptions. _____
   c. Redemption requirements on redeemable stock. _____
   d. Separate classification for redeemable preferred stock. _____

INCOME STATEMENT

A. Basic Disclosures

1. Revenues and related costs with the following categories separately stated, if applicable
   a. Product sales net of discounts, returns, and allowances. _____
   b. Rental revenues. _____
   c. Service revenues including billings for out-of-pocket costs. _____
   d. Other revenue. _____
2. Income or loss before extraordinary items. _____
3. Extraordinary items. _____
4. Income taxes. _____
5. Discontinued segments. _____
6. Depreciation. _____
7. Interest expense. _____
8. Gain or loss from extinguishment of debt. _____
9. Foreign currency realized gains and losses. _____
10. Marketable securities gains and losses. _____
11. Research and development expenses. _____
12. S Corporation election—No income tax effect. _____

B. Marketable Securities

1. Proceeds from sales of available-for-sale securities and the gross realized gains and gross realized losses on those sales. _____
2. Basis on which cost was determined in computing realized gain or loss. _____
3. The gross gains and gross losses included in earnings from transfers of securities from the available-for-sale category into the trading category. _____
4. The change in net unrealized holding gain or loss on available-for-sale securities that has been included in other comprehensive income during the period. _____
5. The change in net unrealized holding gain or loss on trading securities that has been included in earnings during the period. _____

C. Income Taxes

1. State if entity is not subject to income taxes because income is taxed directly to owners. State the net difference between tax and book bases of assets and liabilities. _____
2. State amounts allocated to
   a. Current tax expense or benefit. _____
   b. Deferred tax expense or benefit (exclusive of the effects of other components listed below). _____
   c. Investment tax or other credits. _____
   d. Government grants (to the extent recognized as a reduction of income tax expense). _____
   e. The benefits of operating loss carryforwards. _____
   f. Tax expense that results from allocating certain tax benefits either directly to contributed capital or to reduce goodwill or other noncurrent intangible assets of an acquired entity. _____
   g. Adjustments of a deferred tax liability or asset for enacted changes in tax laws or rates or a change in the tax status of the enterprise. _____
   h. Adjustments of the beginning-of-the-year balance of a valuation allowance because of a change in circumstances that causes a change in judgment about the realizability of the related deferred tax asset in future years. _____

3. Amounts allocated to
    a. Continuing operations. _____
    b. Discontinued operations. _____
    c. Extraordinary items. _____
    d. Cumulative effect of accounting changes. _____
    e. Prior period adjustments. _____
    f. Gains and losses included in comprehensive income but excluded from net income. _____
    g. Capital transactions. _____
4. Reconcile statutory tax rates to actual rates for significant items (nonpublic enterprises need only disclose the nature of significant reconciling items). _____
5. Amounts and expiration dates for operating loss and tax credit carryforward for financial reporting. _____
6. If consolidated return filed, separately issued financial statements should state
    a. Amount of current and deferred tax expense for each income statement. _____
    b. Tax-related balances due to or from affiliates for each balance sheet. _____
    c. The method of allocating consolidated amounts of current and deferred tax expense and effects of any change in that methodology. _____
7. Cumulative effect of change (similar to change in accounting principle) for earliest restated financial statements. _____
8. When a deferred tax liability is not recognized because of the exceptions to comprehensive recognition of deferred taxes, the following information shall be disclosed:
    a. A description of the types of temporary differences for which a deferred tax liability has not been recognized and the types of events that would cause those temporary differences to become taxable. _____
    b. The cumulative amount of each type of temporary difference. _____
    c. The amount of the unrecognized deferred tax liability for temporary differences related to investments in foreign subsidiaries and foreign corporate joint ventures that are essentially permanent in duration if determination of that liability is practicable or a statement that determination is not practicable. _____
    d. The amount of the deferred tax liability for temporary differences other than those in c. above (i.e., undistributed domestic earnings, the bad-debt reserve for tax purposes of a US savings and loan association or other qualified thrift lender, the policyholders' surplus of a life insurance enterprise, and the statutory reserve funds of a US steamship enterprise) that is not recognized. _____

D. Extraordinary Items

1. Segregated and shown net of tax. _____
2. Adequate explanations of nature of extraordinary item(s). _____
3. Infrequent or unusual items shown separately although not extraordinary; not shown net of tax. _____
4. For adjustment of amounts reported in prior period that do not qualify as prior period adjustments, classify separately in same manner as original item, with year of origin, nature and amount. _____

E. Interim Financial Information

1. Provide the minimum captions and disclosures required when publicly traded entities report summarized interim financial information. These required disclosures are

a. Sales or gross revenues, provision for income taxes, extraordinary items, cumulative effect of a change in principle, and net income. _____
b. Basic and diluted earnings per share. _____
c. Seasonal revenues, costs, and expenses. _____
d. Significant changes in income tax estimates. _____
e. Discontinued operations and extraordinary, unusual, or infrequently occurring items. _____
f. Contingencies. _____
g. Effect of changes in accounting principles or estimates. _____
h. Significant changes in financial position. _____

2. When summarized financial information is reported on a regular quarterly basis, the above captions and disclosures are presented for the current year and the current year-to-date (or preceding twelve months), with comparable data for the preceding year. _____

F. Segment Data

1. General information on segments including:

a. Factors used to identify the enterprise's reportable segments, including the basis of organization (e.g., whether management has chosen to organize the enterprise around differences in products and services, geographic areas, regulatory environments, or a combination of factors and whether operating segments have been aggregated). _____
b. Types of products and services from which each reportable segment derives its revenues. _____

2. The following about each reportable segment if the specified amounts are included in the measure of segment profit or loss reviewed by the chief operating decision maker:

a. Revenues from external customers. _____
b. Revenues from transactions with other operating segments of the same enterprise. _____
c. Interest revenue. _____
d. Interest expense. _____
e. Depreciation, depletion, and amortization expense. _____
f. Unusual items. _____
g. Equity in the net income of investees accounted for by the equity method. _____
h. Income tax expense or benefit. _____
i. Extraordinary items. _____

3. Disclose the following about each reportable segment if the specific amounts are included in the determination of segment assets reviewed by the chief operating decision maker:

a. The amount of investment in equity method investees. _____
b. Total expenditures for additions to long-lived assets other than financial instruments, long-term customer relationships of a financial institution, mortgage and other servicing rights, deferred policy acquisition costs, and deferred tax assets. _____

4. An explanation should be provided of the measurements of segment profit or loss and segment assets for each reportable segment; at a minimum, these shall include the following:

a. The basis of accounting for any transactions between reportable segments. _____
b. The nature of any differences between the measurements of the reportable segments' profits or losses and the company's consolidated income before income taxes, extraordinary items, discontinued operations, and the cumulative

effect of changes in accounting principles (if not apparent from the reconciliations); for example, accounting policies and policies for allocation of centrally incurred costs that are necessary for an understanding of the reported segment information. _____

c. The nature of any differences between the measurements of the reportable segments' assets and the company's consolidated assets (if not apparent from the reconciliations); for example, accounting policies and policies for allocation of jointly used assets that are necessary for an understanding of the reported segment information. _____

d. The nature of any changes from prior periods in the measurement methods used to determine reported segment profit or loss and the effect, if any, of those changes on the measure of segment profit or loss. _____

e. The nature and effect of any asymmetrical allocations to segments; for example, an enterprise might allocate depreciation expense to a segment without allocating the related depreciable assets to that segment. _____

5. Reconciliations of the totals of segment revenues, reported profit or loss, assets, and other significant items to corresponding company amounts, as follows:

   a. The total of the reportable segments' revenues to the enterprise's consolidated revenues. _____

   b. The total of the reportable segments' measures of profit or loss to the company's consolidated income before income taxes, extraordinary items, discontinued operations, and the cumulative effect of changes in accounting principles. _____

   c. The total of the reportable segments' assets to the company's consolidated assets. _____

   d. The total of the reportable segments' amounts for every other significant item of information disclosed to the corresponding consolidated amount. _____

6. Company-wide disclosures (required for all companies subject to FAS 131 including those companies that have a single reportable segment)

   a. Revenues from external customers for each product and service or each group of similar products and services unless it is impracticable to do so. (The amounts of revenues reported shall be based on the financial information used to produce the enterprise's general-purpose financial statements. If providing the information is impracticable, that fact shall be disclosed.) _____

   b. Revenues from external customers

      (1) Attributed to the enterprise's country of domicile. _____

      (2) Attributed to all foreign countries in total from which the enterprise derives revenues unless it is impracticable to do so. (If revenues from external customers attributed to an individual foreign country are material, those revenues shall be disclosed separately. Also disclose the basis for attributing revenues from external customers to individual countries.) _____

   c. Long-lived assets other than financial instruments, long-term customer relationships of a financial institution, mortgage and other servicing rights, deferred policy acquisition costs, and deferred tax assets

      (1) Located in the enterprise's country of domicile. _____

      (2) Located in all foreign countries in total in which the enterprise holds assets unless it is impractical to do so. (If assets in an individual foreign country are material, those assets shall be disclosed separately.) _____

   d. If providing the geographic information is impracticable, that fact shall be disclosed. _____

7. Major customers

   If revenues from transaction with a single external customer amount to ten percent or more of an enterprise's revenues, disclose that fact, the total amount of revenues from each such customer, and the identity of the segment or segments reporting the revenues. _____

8. Earnings before income tax disclosures

   Depreciation and amortization expense for each reportable segment, when the chief operating decision maker evaluates the performance of its segments based on earnings before interest, taxes, depreciation, and amortization. _____

G. Development Stage Enterprises

1. The financial statements should be identified as those of a development stage company and should include a description of the nature of the development stage activities. _____
2. The financial statements for the first fiscal year in which the company is no longer considered to be in the development stage should disclose that in prior years it had been in the development stage. If financial statements for prior years are presented for comparative purposes, the cumulative amounts and other additional disclosures required below need not be shown. _____
3. On the balance sheet, any cumulative net losses should be reported with a descriptive caption such as "deficit accumulated during the development stage" in the stockholders' equity section. _____
4. Report the cumulative amounts of revenue and expenses since inception. _____
5. Report the cumulative amounts of sources and uses of cash since inception. _____
6. Present in the statement of stockholders' equity all transactions since inception. _____
7. Disclose the date of each stock issuance in the statement of changes in stockholders' equity. _____
8. Disclose the basis for stock issued for other than cash. _____

H. Long-Term Construction Contracts

1. The method of recognizing income (percentage-of-completion or completed-contract). _____
2. If the percentage-of-completion method is used, the method of computing percentage of completion (e.g., cost-to-cost, efforts-expended). _____
3. If the completed-contract method is used, the justification for its use should be indicated. _____
4. Length of the operating cycle; if greater than one year, the range of contract durations should be disclosed. _____
5. The basis of recording inventory. _____
6. The effect of changes in estimates. _____
7. The accounting for deferred costs. _____
8. The accounting for general and administrative expenses. _____
9. Criteria for determining substantial completion (e.g., compliance with specifications, acceptance by customer). _____
10. Information on revenues and costs arising from claims. _____

I. Research and Development

1. Expenditures. _____
2. R&D arrangements.
   a. Terms including royalties, purchase provisions, license agreements and funding. _____
   b. Amounts earned and costs incurred each period for which an income statement is presented. _____

J. Sales Where Collection Is Uncertain

1. Method and justification of accounting for installment basis sales. _____
2. Yearly gross profit rates. _____
3. Contractual terms such as interest and repossession provisions. _____
4. Average length of installment contracts. _____

K. Revenue Recognition

1. Basis for recognizing revenue and cost of sales for each material type of transaction. _____
2. If the company is a party to multiple-deliverable arrangements (MDA)
   a. The nature of the company's MDA. _____
   b. The company's accounting policies regarding recognition of revenue on MDA including provisions relative to performance, cancellation, termination, or refund. _____
   c. Whether deliverables are separable into units of accounting. _____
   d. The method of accounting for each element. _____
   e. The method used to determine each element and value it. _____
3. When a right of return exits
   a. Description of return privilege granted to customers. _____
   b. Length of time covered by the return privilege. _____
   c. Estimated amount of returns. _____
   d. Material changes in estimates of returns. _____

L. Other Reporting

1. Financing arrangements—Real estate and product financing. _____
2. Real estate sales. _____
3. Futures contracts. _____
4. Service sales transaction.
   a. The revenue recognition method used and its justification. _____
   b. Information concerning unearned revenues. _____
   c. Information concerning deferred costs. _____
   d. Periods over which services are to be performed. _____

M. Foreign Currency

1. Aggregate transaction gain or loss that is included in the entity's net income. _____
2. Analysis of changes in accumulated translation adjustments which are reported as other comprehensive income. At a minimum, the disclosures should include
   a. Beginning and ending amounts of the translation adjustments account. _____
   b. Aggregate adjustment for the period resulting from translation adjustments, and gains and losses from certain hedges and intercompany balances. _____
   c. Amount of income taxes for the period allocated to translation adjustments. _____
   d. Amounts transferred from the translation adjustments account and included in determining net income as a result of the (partial) sale or liquidation of the foreign operation. _____
3. Significant rate changes subsequent to the date of the financial statements including effects on unsettled foreign currency transactions. Rate changes subsequent to the balance sheet date are not incorporated into the financial statements for the period just ended. _____

N. Business Combinations under Purchase Accounting

1. Name and brief description of the acquired enterprise and the percentage of voting shares acquired. _____

2. The period for which the results of operations of the acquired enterprise are included in the income statement of the acquiring enterprise. _____
3. The cost of the acquired enterprise and, if applicable, the number of shares of stock issued or issuable, the value assigned to those shares, and the basis for determining that value. _____
4. Contingent payments, options, or commitments specified in the acquisition agreement and the accounting treatment that will be followed should any such contingency occur. _____
5. A condensed balance sheet disclosing the following for each major asset and liability caption of the acquired enterprise:
   a. The book values as reflected in the acquired enterprise's financial records at the date of acquisition before fair value adjustments. _____
   b. The fair values assigned at the date of acquisition. _____
6. For any purchase price allocation that has not been finalized, that fact and the reasons therefore and, in subsequent periods, the nature and amount of any material adjustments made to the initial allocation of the purchase price. _____
7. The amounts of
   a. Acquired goodwill. _____
   b. Acquired goodwill related to each segment (for entities that are required to report segment information in accordance with Statement 131). _____
   c. Acquired goodwill that is deductible for income tax purposes. _____
8. For individually immaterial business combinations which have been completed, if those combinations are material in the aggregate, disclose the following information
   a. The number of enterprises acquired and a brief description of those enterprises. _____
   b. The aggregate cost of the acquired enterprises, the number of shares of stock issued or issuable, and the value assigned to those shares. _____
   c. The aggregate amount of any contingent payments, options, or commitments and the accounting treatment that will be followed should any such contingency occur (if potentially significant in relation to the aggregate cost of the acquired enterprises). _____
   d. The amounts of
      (1) Acquired goodwill. _____
      (2) Acquired goodwill related to each segment (for entities that are required to report segment information in accordance with Statement 131). _____
      (3) Acquired goodwill that is deductible for income tax purposes. _____
9. For any material business combination completed after the balance sheet date but before the financial statements are issued, the information identified in items 1-7 above (unless not practicable). _____

O. Costs to Exit or Dispose of an Activity

1. In the period in which an exit or disposal activity is initiated and any subsequent period until the activity is completed, describe the exit or disposal activity, including the facts and circumstances leading to the expected activity and the expected completion date. _____
2. For each major type of cost associated with the exit or disposal activity (for example, onetime termination benefits, contract termination costs, and other associated costs), disclose
   a. The total amount expected to be incurred in connection with the activity. _____
   b. The amount incurred in the period. _____
   c. The cumulative amount incurred to date. _____

d. A reconciliation of the beginning and ending liability balances showing separately the changes during the period attributable to costs incurred and charged to expense, costs paid or otherwise settled, and any adjustments to the liability with an explanation of the reason(s) therefor. _____
e. The line item(s) in the statement of activities in which the costs are aggregated. _____

3. For each reportable segment, the total amount of costs expected to be incurred in connection with the activity, the amount incurred in the period, and the cumulative amount incurred to date, net of any adjustments to the liability with an explanation of the reason(s) therefor. _____
4. If a liability for a cost associated with the exit or disposal activity is not recognized because its fair value cannot be reasonably estimated, disclose that fact and the reasons therefor. _____

P. Earnings Per Share

1. For each income statement presented
   a. Reconciliation of the numerators and the denominators of the basic and diluted per share computations for income from continuing operations. _____
   b. Effect that has been given to preferred dividends in arriving at income available to common stockholders in computing basic EPS. _____
   c. Securities (including those issuable pursuant to contingent stock agreements) that could potentially dilute basic EPS in the future that were not included in the computation of diluted EPS because to do so would have been antidilutive for the period(s) presented. _____
2. Earnings per share amounts for income from continuing operations and net income, shown on the face of income statement for all periods presented. _____
3. If applicable, per share amounts for discontinued operations, extraordinary items, and cumulative effect of an accounting change, presented either on face of income statement or in notes to financial statements. _____
4. For latest income statement, provide a description of any transaction that occurs after end of the period but before issuance of financial statements that would have changed materially the number of common shares or potential common shares outstanding at end of period if transaction had occurred before end of period. _____
5. Amounts should be restated when stock dividends, splits, or reverses occur after close of period but before statements are issued with appropriate disclosure. _____
6. When operations of a prior period have been restated, earnings per share data also should be restated; the effect of the restatement, expressed in per share terms, should be disclosed in year of restatement. _____
7. Disclose EPS for income from continuing operations when there are discontinued operations of a segment of a business. _____

STATEMENT OF CASH FLOWS

A. Basis

1. Definition of cash and cash equivalents adopted. _____
2. Summarize noncash investing and financing activities _____

B. Format

1. Reconcile net income to net cash flow. _____
2. If direct method used, display major categories of gross cash receipts and cash payments. _____
   a. Cash receipts
      (1) Cash receipts from sale of goods or services. _____
      (2) Interest and dividends received. _____

(3) Other operating cash receipts. _____

b. Cash payments

(1) Payments to employees and other suppliers of goods or services. _____
(2) Income taxes paid. _____
(3) Interest paid. _____
(4) Other operating cash payments. _____

c. Reconcile net income or loss to net cash flow from operating activities. _____

3. If indirect method used

a. Present reconciliation of net income or loss to cash flow from operating activities, separately reporting all major items, either within the statement or in a separate schedule. _____
b. Disclose both interest and income taxes paid in a schedule following the statement or in the notes. _____

4. Report cash flows from purchases and sales or maturities of trading securities under operating activities. _____
5. Report cash flows from investing activities:

a. Report separately cash inflows and outflows. _____
b. Report gross for each security classification in the statement of cash flows, the cash flows from purchases, sales and maturities of available-for-sale securities, and separately for held-to-maturity securities. _____

6. Report cash flows from financing activities

a. Report separately cash inflows and outflows. _____
b. Effect of exchange rate changes on cash balances held in foreign currencies shown separately on statement of cash flows. _____
c. Cash payments for debt issue costs. _____

STATEMENT OF COMPREHENSIVE INCOME

A. Format Options

1. Continuation of income statement (preferred by FASB). _____
2. Separate statement starting with net income. _____
3. Part of statement of stockholders' equity. _____

B. Disclosures

1. Total amount for comprehensive income. _____
2. Amounts of other comprehensive income by type. _____
3. Reclassification adjustment(s) for items included in net income also included in other comprehensive income in this period or prior period _____

a. Face of financial statement in which comprehensive income reported. _____
b. Notes to financial statements. _____
c. Gross display on face of financial statement or net display on face of financial statement and gross display in notes to financial statements except for minimum pension liability which does not have reclassification adjustments. _____

4. Cumulative amounts of other comprehensive income by type

a. Face of balance sheet. _____
b. Statement of changes in stockholders' equity. _____
c. Notes to financial statements. _____

SPECIALIZED INDUSTRY GAAP

A. Banking and Savings Institutions

(See the AICPA Audit and Accounting Guide, *Banks and Savings Institutions*.)

B. Broadcasting Industry

1. License agreements for program material not reported due to failure to meet the specified conditions. _____

C. Computer Software Costs and Revenues

1. Amount of research and development costs charged to expense during the period. _____
2. Amount of capitalized computer software costs amortized to expense during the period. _____
3. Unamortized computer software costs at the end of the period. _____
4. Amount of capitalized computer software costs written down to net realizable value. _____

D. Franchisor Accounting

1. Nature of all significant commitments resulting from franchise agreements. _____
2. Description of services not yet substantially performed. _____
3. If collectibility is uncertain
   a. Use of installment or cost recovery method. _____
   b. Sales price of franchises including deferral of both costs and revenue. _____
   c. Amounts originally deferred but later recognized due to resolution of uncertainty. _____
4. Initial franchise fees segregated from other franchise fee revenue and contribution to net income of such initial fees. _____
5. Saturation point of locations or other expectation of decline in future initial franchise fee revenue. _____
6. Segregation of franchisor owned outlet revenues and expenses from other activities. _____
7. Other
   a. Franchises sold or purchased or operated. _____
   b. Franchisor owned outlets. _____
   c. Significant changes in the outlets during the period. _____

E. Government Contracts

1. Contracts subject to renegotiation for which reasonable estimates are not determinable include
   a. Reasons for inability to estimate. _____
   b. Material uncertainties and significance thereof. _____
   c. Basis for measuring renegotiation provision. _____
2. For terminated defense contracts
   a. Material facts and circumstances. _____
   b. Disclose termination claims separately. _____
   c. Report as sales separately. _____
3. Each federal, state, or local governmental unit
   a. Treated as a single customer. _____

F. Insurance Industry Transactions

1. Liabilities for claims and claim adjustment expenses.
   a. Basis for estimating liabilities. _____

b. For short-term contracts carried at present value
   (1) Carrying amount. _____
   (2) Discount rate used. _____
   (3) Claim adjustment expenses. _____
   (4) Consideration of anticipated investment income in determining if a premium deficiency exists. _____

2. Future policy benefits owed.
   a. Methods and assumptions. _____
   b. Average rate of expected investment yields. _____

3. Capitalized acquisition costs
   a. Nature. _____
   b. Method of amortization. _____
   c. Amount amortized during the period. _____

4. Reinsurance transactions
   a. Nature, purpose, and effect of ceded transactions. _____
   b. Methods of income recognition on reinsurance contracts. _____
   c. Short-term contracts—Premiums from direct business, reinsurance assumed and ceded. _____
   d. Long-term contracts—Premiums and amounts assessed against policyholders, reinsurance assumed and ceded, premiums and amounts earned. _____
   e. Concentration of credit risk on reinsurance receivables and premiums. _____

5. Participating insurance
   a. Relative percentage. _____
   b. Method of accounting for dividends. _____
   c. Amount of dividends. _____
   d. Additional income allocated to participating policyholders. _____

6. Statutory accounting practices
   a. Statutory capital and surplus
      (1) Actual amount. _____
      (2) Amount required by statute (if significant compared to actual). _____
   b. Statutory restrictions of the payment of dividends
      (1) Nature. _____
      (2) Amount of retained earnings restricted. _____

7. Income tax disclosures. _____

G. Mortgage Banking Activities

1. Method used to determine lower of cost or market value—aggregate vs. individual loan basis. _____
2. Servicing rights capitalized during the period
   a. Amount. _____
   b. Method of amortization. _____
   c. Amount of amortization for the period. _____
3. Fair value of capitalized servicing rights, including methods and assumptions used and explanation of reasons if not practical to estimate. _____
4. Risk characteristics for stratifying servicing rights in measuring impairment. _____
5. Changes in servicing rights valuation allowance. _____

H. Motion Picture Industry

1. The portion of the costs of completed films expected to be amortized during the upcoming operating cycle. _____
2. The components of film costs separately for theatrical films and direct-to-television product including
   a. Released. _____
   b. Completed and not released. _____
   c. In production. _____
   d. In development or preproduction. _____
3. The percentage of unamortized film costs for released films, excluding acquired film libraries, expected to be amortized within three years from the balance sheet date. If that percentage is less than 80%, additional information should be provided including the period required to reach an amortization level of 80%. _____
4. For acquired film libraries
   a. The amount of remaining unamortized costs. _____
   b. The method of amortization. _____
   c. The remaining amortization period. _____
5. The amount of accrued participation liabilities expected to be paid during the upcoming operating cycle. _____
6. The method of accounting for revenue, film costs, and exploitation costs. _____
7. The effect on income before extraordinary items, net income, and related per share amounts of the current fiscal period for a change in estimate that affects several future periods. _____

I. Oil and Gas Producing Activities

FAS 69 requires publicly traded enterprises to disclose the following oil and gas producing data as supplementary (not part of the financial statements) information:

1. Proved oil and gas reserves. _____
2. Capitalized costs. _____
3. Acquisition, exploration, and development costs. _____
4. Results of operations. _____
5. Standardized measure of discounted future cash flows relating to proved reserves. _____

J. Employee Benefit Plans

1. The plan's accounting policies should disclose a description of methods and assumptions
   a. Used to determine fair value. _____
   b. Used to determine the actuarial present value of the accumulated benefit obligation (APVAPB). _____
   c. Changed during the current period. _____
2. The financial statements should disclose the following:
   a. Plan descriptions—Including vesting and benefit provisions. _____
   b. Significant plan amendment descriptions—Indicate if APVAPB does not include the effects of the amendments. _____
   c. Priority order of participants' claims to assets. _____
   d. Benefits guaranteed by Pension Benefit Guaranty Corp. _____
   e. Funding policy and any period changes. In addition, the following should make the disclosure indicated:
      (1) Contributory plan—Method of determining contributions. _____
      (2) ERISA—Whether minimum funding requirements were met. _____

f. Disclosure of a minimum funding waiver or a request for one from the IRS is required. _____
g. Policy concerning insurance companies and the purchase of contracts that are excluded from plan assets. Disclosure should be made of the amount of dividend income related to excluded contracts. _____
h. Income status of the plan. _____
i. Investments that are 5% or more of plan assets should be identified. _____
j. Significant real estate or other transactions between the plan and the sponsor, the employer, or the employee organization. _____
k. Infrequent or unusual events that occur between the benefit information date and the issuance of statements that would aid in the determination of the plan's ability to pay benefits. _____

(See also: AICPA Audit and Accounting Guide, ***Audits of Employee Benefit Plans.****)*

K. Recording and Music Industry

1. Licensors

a. Commitments to pay advance royalties in the future. _____
b. Future royalty guarantees. _____
c. Cost of record masters borne by the record company and capitalized as assets (disclose separately). _____

L. Regulated Operations

1. Refunds

a. Effect on net income, when recognized in period(s) different than related revenue

(1) Not recognized as an extraordinary item. _____

2. Discontinuation of specialized accounting

a. Reasons for discontinuation. _____
b. Portion of operations to which the discontinuation applies. _____
c. Net adjustment reported as an extraordinary item. _____

APPENDIX B

INTERNATIONAL VS. US ACCOUNTING STANDARDS

The International Accounting Standards Committee was founded in 1973 by representatives of professional bodies in Australia, Canada, France, Germany, Japan, Mexico, the Netherlands, the United Kingdom, Ireland, and the United States, and grew to include representatives from ninety-one countries. From 1973—by coincidence, the birth date of the current US standard setter, the FASB—until December 2000, the IASC's members had included all the professional accountancy bodies that are members of the International Federation of Accountants (IFAC). As of January 2000, these comprised 143 member bodies in 104 countries, representing over two million accountants.

From its formation, the IASC engaged in a standard-setting program that is now on the cusp of truly worldwide recognition. Prior to the transition to the new IASB (discussed below), the IASC had issued forty-one international accounting standards (IAS), of which, after a series of revisions, thirty-four remain in force. Also issued to date have been a number of Exposure Drafts (at least one of which preceded the final issuance of each standard). A number of Interpretations of these standards have also been issued by the former Standing Interpretations Committee (SIC).

For many years the IASC labored in relative obscurity, being viewed as of importance mainly to less developed nations lacking standard-setting capabilities, and as something of a "debating society" which over time had the potential to reduce, but not eliminate, differences among the major national financial reporting standards. The goal was said to be to *harmonize* standards. A major impediment was (and remains) a lack of enforcement authority, unlike national bodies, which have the support of national auditing standard setters and securities regulatory bodies, which attempt to impose discipline on the preparer and auditor communities.

The IASC began to gain a higher profile in the mid-1990s, when it undertook several major standards improvement programs, resulting in substantially reducing available alternative methods of recording identical economic transactions or events. The first of these, the *Comparability/ Improvements Project*, culminated with the promulgation of ten revised standards that took effect in 1995. Even more importantly, IASC embarked on its *Comprehensive Core Set of Standards* program that year, motivated by a historic agreement with the International Organization of Securities Commissions (IOSCO), which committed IASC to revisions of the standards that IOSCO deemed essential for its consideration of possible endorsement of the IAS for purposes of cross-border securities registrations. IASC completed these changes and promulgation of the required new standards occurred at year-end 1998, with about eleven standards being revised or newly issued, setting forth important new rules dealing with financial instruments and hedging activities, which remain controversial today.

The completion of the core set of standards was a major achievement. IASC expected that, having performed its part of the bargain, IOSCO would likewise deliver on its explicit and implicit commitments—namely, full and unqualified support for cross-border registrations using IAS standards. When endorsement came after several years' delay, however, it contained only a mixed message. To an extent, this was a consequence of the rivalry between the IASC and the FASB, which opposed endorsement and had apparently harbored its own hopes of becoming the de facto world-wide standard setter.

The US SEC, the most important member of IOSCO, permitted it to ratify the core set of standards, but also required the endorsement to provide that so-called "supplemental treatments" could be imposed by national securities regulators. (IOSCO cannot mandate acceptability of IAS-based financial reporting, it can only recommend this to the sovereign regulators charged with protecting investors in their respective jurisdictions.)

These supplemental treatments prescribed are as follows:

- **Reconciliation**—Requiring reconciliation of certain items to show the effect of applying a different accounting method, in contrast with the method applied under IASC standards;

- **Disclosure**—Requiring additional disclosures, either in the presentation of the financial statements or in the footnotes; and
- **Interpretation**—Specifying use of a particular alternative provided in an IASC standard, or a particular interpretation in cases where the IASC standard is unclear or silent.

Scores of such reconciling items, expanded disclosures, and interpretive matters have been identified, although it is not expected that any jurisdiction would mandate all or even most of these. (See *Wiley IAS* for a comprehensive listing of these various items.) As of mid-2004 the SEC had not relaxed its requirements for foreign registrants filing financial statements prepared under IFRS, and thus the longstanding Form 20-F reconciliation of earnings and net worth to US GAAP remains a necessity.

Meanwhile, largely as a consequence of widely reported financial reporting frauds and audit failures of the late 1990s and early 2000s, there has been a spirited debate over whether US GAAP-style rules-based accounting standards (i.e., with copious, detailed guidance on how implementation is to be effected) or IASB-style principles-based standards (setting forth only general guidance, leaving interpretation to the judgment of preparers and auditors) would be more effective in restraining financial reporting fraud. This debate was based on the misguided perception (largely promoted by IASB advocates) that the two sets of standards really are located at diametrically opposed positions on a continuum, which they are not. In fact, all valid standards are based on conceptual foundations and all standards, including IFRS, include some implementation guidance. This debate seems fated to fade away without any resolution.

Many nominal differences currently exist between the IFRS and US GAAP, but a listing of truly substantive discrepancies is much shorter. FASB published (first in 1996, then in revised form in 1999) a study setting forth over 250 of these apparent differences, motivated partly by its desire to forestall SEC acceptance, without reconciliation, of financial statements of foreign filers prepared in conformity with IAS. A closer look, however, reveals that

1. The number of meaningful differences was then and remains much lower, and
2. In many instances where substantive differences do exist (e.g., permitting revaluations of long-lived assets to current value amount), the related disclosure requirements are extensive enough to minimize the risk that users could be misled.

In fact, with regard to some of the cited differences, it is arguable (e.g., in the case of accounting for certain financial instruments under IAS 39 vs. under SFAS 133) that the IFRS approach is in fact superior to that under corresponding US standards.

The aforementioned flurry of financial reporting frauds brought home, as never before, the importance of expediting the "convergence" of the major sets of financial reporting standards. Convergence is seen as being politically feasible, whereas wholesale abandonment of one set of standards (whether US GAAP or IFRS), while more efficient, would not be palatable. In late 2002 the IASB and the FASB issued a memorandum of understanding (the "Norwalk Agreement") pledging their best efforts to (1) make their existing financial reporting standards fully compatible as soon as is practicable, and (2) to coordinate their future work programs to ensure that once achieved, compatibility is maintained.

Following this declaration, the two boards began a "short-term convergence" project to remove as many impediments to convergence as possible (although new ones have managed to arise: witness IASB's recent amendment of IAS 2 to ban LIFO accounting for inventories, which FASB would be loathe to do unless the IRS' conformity rule is dropped), with a commitment to undertake longer-term projects for any remaining incompatibilities as of January 1, 2005. Among the areas targeted by this project are: accounting for disposal of non-current assets and presentation of discontinued operations; costs associated with exit or disposal activities; accounting for government grants; inclusion of costs of idle capacity and spoilage in inventory costs; presentation of accounting policy and estimate changes and corrections of errors; depreciation on assets held for disposal or otherwise idled; interperiod tax allocation methodology; accounting for long-term construction contracts; reporting under hyperinflationary conditions; and joint venture accounting (use of the proportionate consolidation method). Exposure Drafts of any resulting proposed changes have not, as of early 2004, been published.

On the FASB side, a number of convergence activities are under way also, mostly addressing rather detailed technical issues that separate US GAAP from IFRS. At least one proposed change—requiring fair value accounting for nonmonetary exchanges of productive assets now recorded as book value swaps—is a clear admission of the superiority of the IASB's position on the issue. On some matters, FASB has decided to maintain divergent positions, based on its perception that its current rules are superior to those adopted by IASB. On the whole, however, convergence appears to be a process which both boards are committed to, so that over time (some believe five to ten years might be a reasonable expectation) virtually all differences may disappear, leaving two sets of standards a formality to satisfy nationalistic imperatives. Still, some major hurdles (e.g., optional use of revalued amounts under IFRS for plant assets, prohibited under US GAAP) will have to be overcome for this to ultimately transpire.

IASB has directed its staff to develop proposals that would serve to eliminate differences from FASB standards in the areas of property, plant, and equipment; investments in real estate; and joint venture accounting. Other projects which would similarly help achieve convergence involve purchase method accounting, accounting for income taxes (deferred taxes), for restructuring costs (contingencies), and for research and development costs. The four new IFRS standards published in 2004 (IFRS 2 through 5) have also, in effect, reflected convergence efforts.

The FASB, as noted above, has tackled a number of convergence projects and has, as of mid-2004, several proposals outstanding. It plans to revise the accounting for nonmonetary exchanges to comply with IFRS (by recognizing gain or loss on such exchanges, even if not the culmination of the normal earnings process); to conform to IFRS on retrospective accounting for voluntary changes in accounting principles; and to adopt the IFRS position on expensing rather than capitalizing certain inventory costs (idle capacity and spoilage).

Developments favorable to wider use of IFRS. Several significant events have occurred over the past several years, the effect of which has been to improve the standing of IFRS and to raise the probability that full acceptance of IFRS-based financial reporting by international capital markets will ultimately be achieved. First, the European Commission's (EC) Single Market Commissioner announced in 1995 that the European Union had abandoned its previously expressed goal of developing unique European standards of accounting. This gave a clear boost to the IASB's efforts, by removing the specter of yet another layer of national and supranational accounting standards. Then, in 2000, the EU published *EU Financial Reporting Strategy: The Way Forward*, which stated that companies within the EU seeking listings on EU stock market would no longer have the free choice of preparing their consolidated financial statements in accordance with either their own national accounting standards or US GAAP. Instead, these entities will be required to employ only IFRS, beginning in 2005 (and, due to the comparative financial statement requirements, the 2004 financials will also have to be prepared in conformity with IFRS). This proclamation of support for the IASB standards was regarded by most as a major breakthrough for the IASB. While as of mid-2004 there remain certain matters yet to be resolved (all of which pertain to accounting for certain financial instruments), the Europe 2005 initiative is on track for full implementation as planned.

With about 7,000 publicly held European companies set to begin reporting under IFRS, these standards will soon gain much wider recognition. Many of the European companies have US-based subsidiaries or investees, or enter into joint ventures with US-based enterprises, and there is bound to be growing interest in, or need to, communicate financial information in a manner dictated by the European parent entity or joint venture partner.

Some of the most highly technical standards under IFRS (and, generally too, under US GAAP), are those addressing financial instruments, impairment of assets, business combinations, segment reporting, income taxes, earnings per share, and interim financial reporting. These are difficult because of the underlying subject matter (e.g., interim reporting can be viewed as integral to the full fiscal year of which they are a constituent part, or alternatively as stand-alone periods to be reported upon).

Other standards under IFRS (and, to an extent, under US GAAP) suffer from poor or confusing writing in the standards themselves. For example, the IFRS dealing with related-party disclosures, provisions and contingencies, and investments in associates all suffer from this flaw. The related-party disclosure standard (IAS 24) contains an essentially circular definition of "close members of the family," defined as: "those that may be expected to influence, or be influenced by, that person in their dealings with the enterprise." The standard on provisions, contingent liabilities, and contingent assets (IAS 37) uses terms such as "probable outflow of resources" and "prejudicial to interest," which resist mechanical definition. The standard on accounting for investments in associates (IAS 28) prescribes the use of the "equity method" when there is "significant influence," which is evidenced by, for example, "participation in policy making processes" and "material transactions between the investor and investee."

Finally, under IFRS (but much less so under US GAAP) some standards offer radically different alternative methods of accounting which remain equally acceptable for financial reporting purposes. The standard on property, plant, and equipment allows either the use of historical cost or of "revaluation"—and there is substantial diversity in terms of frequency of updating values among enterprises which elect the revaluation option. (US GAAP prohibits revaluation.) As to borrowing costs associated with self-constructed assets, IFRS permits either immediate expensing or capitalization (only the latter is permitted in the US). Cash flow statements can use either the direct or indirect methods of presenting operating cash flows (the same choice is offered under US GAAP), and also gives the choice, regarding the presentation of interest and dividend income, of including this in operating or investing cash flows (no choice given in the US). Finally, investment property may be accounted for under the fair value or the cost model (again, no choice offered under US GAAP).

Thus, in reporting under IFRS, the concern must be not merely for the existing (but rapidly diminishing) differences between US GAAP and IFRS, per se, but also about the *methods elected* by the parent entity to report under IFRS. Of lesser concern, but still important, under IFRS there are often *optional* disclosure recommendations, in addition to the mandatory ones (under US GAAP, all disclosure requirements should be deemed mandatory). Finally, both US GAAP and IFRS are dynamic sets of standards, subject to refinement, revision, and supersession. Neither offers a fixed reference point over more than a short time horizon.

Wiley IAS discusses all existing IFRS requirements in great detail, but given the great and growing interest in these matters, the following table sets forth a comparison between US GAAP and IFRS as it exists in mid-2004. The comparisons have been organized consistent with the chapters in this book.

GAAP 2005 chapter	*Topic*	*US GAAP treatment*	*IFRS treatment*
1	General guidance	No comprehensive guide to statement presentation is offered; however, basic financial statements are the same under both sets of standards; GAAP departures, when necessary, are audit reporting issue	Comprehensive guidance on presentation of financial statements provided; minimum line items identified for all financial statements; fair presentation goal may necessitate IFRS departures
		FASB's Conceptual Framework is similar to IASB's Framework for the Preparation and Presentation of Financial statements	FASB's Conceptual Framework is similar to IASB's Framework for the Preparation and Presentation of Financial Statements; latter is less detailed.
		Comparative financials urged, but not required; greater specificity as to location of disclosures in body of statements or in notes	Comparative financials are required, including footnote data; disclosure can often be optionally in financials or in notes
		Formal GAAP hierarchy defined	No hierarchy established beyond IAS
2	Balance Sheet	Limited guidance on offsetting of assets and liabilities; classified balance sheet not required, but definition of current/noncurrent differs from IFRS somewhat	Specific guidance on offsetting of assets and liabilities; classified balance sheet not mandatory, some difference from GAAP definitions of current/noncurrent
		Some differences from IFRS re: exclusion of long-term debt being refinanced, etc.	Some differences re: exclusion of long-term debt from current liabilities, etc.
3	Statements of Income and Comprehensive Income	Estimated operating results of a discontinuing operation are included in the measurement for the expected gain or loss on disposal; timing of segregation of discontinuing operations from continuing operations may differ from that under IFRS	Actual operating results of a discontinuing operation are reported as incurred; timing of recognition of gain or loss in discontinuance and income or loss from activities of the discontinuing operation may differ from US GAAP
		Restructuring costs recognized when there is little discretion to avoid costs; most costs recognized when later incurred	Restructuring costs recognized when announced or commenced, which is earlier than under US GAAP
			Separate statement of changes in equity required
		Display of total comprehensive income is mandatory, but various modes of presentation are allowed	Display of total comprehensive income is optional, but current project may result in closer approximation of US GAAP method
		Extraordinary item classification still permitted	Extraordinary item classification now banned

GAAP 2005 chapter	*Topic*	*US GAAP treatment*	*IFRS treatment*
4	Statement of Cash Flows	Interest paid and dividends received must be classified as operating cash flows, and dividends paid must be classified as financing cash flows	Choice allowed in classifying 1. Dividends and interest paid or received as operating cash flows, or 2. Interest or dividends paid as financing cash flows and interest or dividends received as investing cash flows
		Overdrafts cannot be included in cash (show as financing source of cash)	Overdrafts can be included in cash under defined conditions
5	Cash, Receivables and Prepaid Expenses	No specific guidance offered under US GAAP or IFRS	No specific guidance offered under either set of standards
6	Short-Term Investments and Financial Instruments	Stricter definition of "sales" resulting in more recognition of secured borrowing transactions	Slightly looser definition of "sales" of financial assets
		Basis adjustment arising from firm commitments and forecasted transactions not in initial measurement of hedged item; hedging gains and losses on cash flow hedges recorded in other comprehensive income when they occur, reclass to income with hedged item	Hedging gains and losses from cash flow hedges of firm commitments and of forecasted transactions can be included as part of the initial measurement of the cost basis of the related hedged item (basis adjustment)
		Hedging for part of term of hedged item not permitted	Hedging for part of term of hedged item permitted if effectiveness can be shown
		Hedging effectiveness can be assumed in limited circumstances (using "shortcut method")	Hedging effectiveness must be demonstrable
			New option to designate any financial asset or liability for measurement at fair value with changes in current income
		"Macrohedging" not permitted	"Macrohedging" is permitted
7	Inventory	Recognition in interim periods of inventory losses from market declines that reasonably can be expected to be restored in the fiscal year not required	Recognition in interim periods of inventory losses from market declines that reasonably can be expected to be restored in the fiscal year is required; guidance in the areas of disclosure and accounting for inventories of service providers offered
		Allowable methods include FIFO, average cost, and LIFO	LIFO costing now banned

GAAP 2005 chapter	*Topic*	*US GAAP treatment*	*IFRS treatment*
7	Inventory	Fewer restrictions on cost elements which can be added to inventory under IFRS	Certain costs (idle capacity, spoilage) cannot be added to overhead charge in inventory cost
		Lower of cost or market adjustments cannot be reversed later	Lower of cost or market adjustments must be reversed later under defined conditions
8	Special Revenue Recognition Areas—Contract Accounting	Use of completed contract method under certain circumstances is required; revenue-cost and gross-profit approaches to percentage-of-completion both allowed	If percentage cannot be reliably estimated, use of cost recovery method required; "revenue-cost" approach to percentage of completion mandatory
	Special Revenue Recognition Areas—General Guidance	No standard on revenue recognition in general, but SEC requirements offer guidance	Specific guidance on revenue recognition principles for selected industries
9	Long-Lived Assets (Tangible)	Change in depreciation method treated as cumulative effect item, but IFRS method may be adopted; mandatory capitalization of construction period interest costs	Change in method accounted for prospectively; optional expensing or capitalization of construction period interest
		Major overhauls generally expensed	Major overhauls added to asset cost
		Impairment suggested when book value exceeds gross expected future cash flows; second step to measure impairment uses discounted present value of cash flows	Impairment suggested when book value exceeds greater of value in use (discounted cash flows) or fair value less cost to sell
		Impairments cannot be reversed	Impairments reversed under defined conditions
		Cost basis required	Alternatively can use cost basis or revaluation to fair value
			IFRS has been brought into closer conformity with US GAAP as to component depreciation, accrual of asset retirement obligations
		Like-kind exchanges of productive assets generally accounted for at book value, but current proposal would adopt IFRS approach	Like-kind exchanges are now measured at fair value, with gain or loss recognized

GAAP 2005 chapter	*Topic*	*US GAAP treatment*	*IFRS treatment*
9	Long-Lived Assets (Intangible)	Research and development costs are all expensed, related cash flows in "operating"; goodwill not amortized, but tested for impairment; trigger for impairment recognition excess over fair value; cost basis required for intangibles	Research costs expensed, but development capitalized and amortized with cash flows shown as "investing"; goodwill amortized; revaluation of intangibles permitted
		Measurement of goodwill impairment uses special method, requires first comparing fair value of cash generating unit to book value including goodwill, then comparing implied goodwill, then comparing implied goodwill to carrying value	Measurement of goodwill impairment similar to other long lived assets, requires only single step computation
		No reversals of impairments	Impairments can be reversed, under defined conditions, except for goodwill
		Revaluations never permitted	Revaluation of intangibles permitted under limited circumstances
10	Investments	Classification as trading, available-for-sale, or held-to-maturity limited to securities; equity method required for investee accounting	Classification as trading, available-for-sale, or held-to-maturity applies to all types of financial assets, not just to securities; choice of equity, cost, fair value methods for some investees
		If held-to-maturity securities are sold, use of this category is thereafter prohibited	If held-to-maturity securities are sold, use of this category is prohibited for next two years
		Equity method of accounting similar under US GAAP and IFRS	
		Joint ventures generally accounted for by equity method, but some exceptions permit proportional consolidation method	Joint ventures accounted for by equity method or proportional consolidation
		No need to conform investor and investee accounting policies	Need to conform investor and investee accounting policies
		Passive investments in nontraded equities can be valued only at cost	Passive investments in nontraded equities can be valued at fair value or cost
		Investment property must be accounted for by cost (and depreciation) method	Investment property can be accounted for by cost (and depreciation) method, or by fair value method with changes taken to income

GAAP 2005 chapter	*Topic*	*US GAAP treatment*	*IFRS treatment*
11	Business Combinations and Consolidated Financial Statements	Poolings now prohibited; consolidation rules effectively based on majority ownership criterion, but special consolidation requirements apply to Variable Interest Entities (VIE); closing date generally used for recognizing acquisitions (purchases)	Poolings (unitings) permitted under narrow set of conditions, but project to eliminate on agenda; consolidation rules based on control criterion; control date used for recognizing acquisitions (purchases)
		Consolidation of majority owned subsidiaries required unless control is not exercised by parent	Consolidation required unless control is not exercised by parent, or unless control is temporary (to lapse within twelve months)
		No promulgated rules governing "parent company only" financial statements, but use of equity method would be acceptable	In "parent company only" financials, the investment in subsidiaries, equity investees, and joint ventures may be presented at cost or under rules for investments in securities, but not equity method
		Qualifying SPE escape consolidation	Consolidate controlled SPE
		Not necessary to conform parent and subsidiary accounting policies	Need to conform parent and subsidiary accounting policies
		Minority interest in consolidated subsidiary can be presented in liabilities, in equity, or in special category	Minority interest included in equity
		Purchased in-process R&D expensed	Purchased in-process R&D capitalized
		Subsequent expenditures on acquired in-process R&D expensed	Subsequent expenditures on acquired in-process R&D generally capitalized
		Negative goodwill credited against nonfinancial assets acquired, with excess as gain	Negative goodwill credited to gain immediately
12	Current Liabilities and Contingencies	Different recognition threshold for timing of recognition of liabilities associated with a restructuring than under IFRS	A variety of recognition criteria for different items that may enter into the measurement of a provision are identified, missing under US GAAP
		Short-term debt refinanced before statement issuance date can often be shown as noncurrent	Short-term debt refinanced before balance sheet date can be shown as noncurrent
13	Long-Term Debt	Convertible debt classified as liability	Convertible debt assigned to both debt and equity based on relative fair values
		Noncurrent presentation of defaulted debt if waiver granted before statement issuance date	Noncurrent presentation of defaulted debt if waiver granted before balance sheet date only

GAAP 2005 chapter	*Topic*	*US GAAP treatment*	*IFRS treatment*
14	Leases	Similar to IFRS, but with more guidance on specialized topics; deferral of profit on sale-leasebacks	Very similar to US GAAP; profit recognition on sale-leasebacks permitted if fair value priced
		Separate accounting for land and building in combined lease depends on terms and materiality of land	Separation of land and building components of lease is now mandatory
		Third-party guarantees cannot be included in minimum lease payments to determine whether capital lease criteria are met	Third-party guarantees must be included in minimum lease payments to determine whether capital lease criteria are met
		Present value of lease payments computed using incremental borrowing rate	Present value of lease payments computed using implicit rate
		Output contracts are leases	Output contracts are not leases
15	Income Taxes	Prohibits recognition of effects of temporary differences related to 1. Foreign currency nonmonetary assets when the reporting currency is the functional currency, and 2. Intercompany transfers of inventory or other assets remaining within the company	Recognize effects of rate changes when "substantively enacted" which may precede US GAAP recognition
		Deferred tax assets and liabilities are current or noncurrent based on related asset or liability	Deferred tax assets and liabilities are noncurrent
		Post-business-combination recognition of deferred tax asset eliminates goodwill, then other intangible assets, with any excess taken to income	Post-business-combination recognition of deferred tax asset eliminates goodwill with any excess taken to income
16	Pensions	Expense recognition for certain types of equity compensation benefits; opposed to mandatory stock compensation expensing; prior service cost to be amortized over the expected service life of existing employees; contributions to multiemployer plans expenses	Expense for equity compensation benefits not recognized, but current agenda item; prior service cost related to retirees and active vested employees to be expensed; benefit obligation for multiemployer recognized

GAAP 2005 chapter	*Topic*	*US GAAP treatment*	*IFRS treatment*
16	Pensions	Recognition of a minimum liability on the balance sheet to at least the unfunded accumulated pension benefit obligation	No minimum liability to be reported in the balance sheet
		No limitation on recognition of pension assets	Limitation on recognition of pension assets
		Curtailment gains recognized when employees terminate or plan suspension is adopted	Curtailment gains or losses recognized when announced; computed differently than US GAAP
		Anticipating changes in the law that would affect variables such as state medical or social security benefits expressly prohibited	Anticipate changes in future postemployment benefits based on its expectations in the law
17	Stockholders' Equity	Mandatorily redeemable preferred shown as "mezzanine" with dividends deducted to derive income available for common shareholders	Mandatorily redeemable preferred shown as liability with dividends deducted as expense
		Current proposal to eliminate intrinsic value method for stock-based compensation, require fair value recognition in current expense similar to IFRS	Mandatory income statement recognition of effect of stock-based compensation measured at fair value
		Tax benefits related to share-based payment credited to equity	Tax benefits related to share-based payments credited to equity only if in excess of compensation expense
18	Earnings Per Share	Very similar to IFRS, but with more detailed guidance on calculations	Similar to US GAAP. Calculation of year-to-date EPS (versus previously reported interim date) varies from US GAAP
19	Interim Reporting	Some timing differences in recognition of interim revenues and expenses vs. IFRS	Some timing differences in recognition of interim revenues and expenses vs. US GAAP
		Basic principle is that interim period is integral to full year, but actual requirements depart from this in many instances	Basic principle is that interim period is discrete period, but actual requirements depart from this in many instances
20	Segment Reporting	"Management approach" provides flexibility in defining segments; segment results using internal managerial approach OK, even if these differ from financial statements	Specific requirements governing the format and content of a reportable segment; segment results using same accounting policies as financial statements
		Disclosures based on primary classification, with some additional items (major customers, etc.)	Both primary and secondary classifications have disclosure implications

GAAP 2005 chapter	*Topic*	*US GAAP treatment*	*IFRS treatment*
21	Accounting Changes and Corrections of Errors	Correction of errors must be prior period/opening retained earnings adjustment; cumulative-effect method for changes in accounting principle, although restatement of prior periods is required for certain changes	Choice permitted re: correction of "fundamental" errors; either prior period/opening retained earnings, or else current income effect; changes in principle can be restatement, cumulative effect, or prospectively; no guidance on changes in entities Retrospective restatement for correction of errors now mandatory
		Effect of voluntary changes in principles reported as cumulative effect in year of change in most cases, but US GAAP may adopt IRFS approach	Voluntary changes in principles require restatement of prior years financials, if practicable
22	Foreign Currency	Exchange losses to be expensed in all instances	Exchange losses on a liability for the recent acquisition of an asset invoiced in a foreign currency either as 1. Charge to expense, or 2. Add to the cost of the asset when the related liability cannot be settled and there is no practical means to hedge
		Current exchange rate use to translate all balance sheet items, including goodwill and fair value adjustments	Either current exchange rate or historical exchange rate permitted in translating goodwill and fair value adjustments to assets and liabilities arising from purchase accounting for acquisition of foreign entity if foreign currency is functional currency Goodwill and fair value adjustments are deemed part of acquired assets/liabilities and translated at current rate
23	Personal Financial Statements	Current value reporting required	No published guidance
24	Specialized Industry GAAP	No primary guidance for government grants, agriculture	Guidance provided for government grants, agriculture, reporting by banks, reporting of insurance contracts
		Specialized guidance on inventories related to the motion picture, software, and agricultural industries, and others, found in "secondary" GAAP sources such as AICPA Guides, SOP, etc.	No such guidance offered; there is no "secondary" source for GAAP guidance

A

O

P

U